A STANDARD SWAHILI-ENGLISH DICTIONARY

(FOUNDED ON
MADAN'S SWAHILI-ENGLISH DICTIONARY)

By the former

INTER-TERRITORIAL LANGUAGE COMMITTEE
FOR THE EAST AFRICAN DEPENDENCIES

under the direction of

THE LATE FREDERICK JOHNSON

Nairobi
OXFORD UNIVERSITY PRESS
Dar es Salaam

Oxford University Press

OXFORD GLASGOW
NEW YORK TORONTO MELBOURNE AUCKLAND
PETALING JAYA SINGAPORE HONG KONG TOKYO
DELHI BOMBAY CALCUTTA MADRAS KARACHI
NAIROBI DAR ES SALAAM CAPE TOWN

and associates in

BERLIN IBADAN

Published with the authority of the Inter-territorial Language (Swahili) Committee to the East African Dependencies.

B. J. RATCLIFFE,
Secretary, I.L.C.

Reprinted in Kenya by permission of Oxford University Press, Walton Street, Oxford OX2 6DP

FIRST EDITION 1939
Reprinted 1942, 1945, 1948, 1951, 1955, 1959, 1963, 1964, 1967, 1969, 1970 (twice), 1971 (twice), 1973, 1974, 1975, 1976, 1977 (twice) 1978, 1979, 1981, 1982, 1984, 1985, 1986, 1987 (twice), 1989 (twice)

Published by Oxford University Press, Eastern Africa, P.O. Box 72532, Science House, Monrovia Street, Nairobi and printed by Acme Press (Kenya) Limited, Factory Street, P.O. Box 40497 Nairobi, Kenya.

FOREWORD

By THE BISHOP OF ZANZIBAR

of the Universities' Mission to Central Africa

THE publication of a Standard Dictionary is always a landmark in the history of a language.

The Universities' Mission to Central Africa has been allowed to have an important share in the discovery and elucidation of the Swahili language, and in this connexion the names of Steere and Madan can never be forgotten. They were not merely pioneers but scholars, and this fact has given a lasting permanence to their labours.

Since the days of these two men, however, time has brought many changes together with increased knowledge, and an inspection of this new work will quickly prove how necessary was the present revision and how profitable it is bound to be. It is a matter of good fortune that the revision of these two dictionaries was placed in the capable hands of the late Frederick Johnson, formerly Secretary of the Inter-territorial Language (Swahili) Committee, which has done so much to standardize the language and to preserve its orthography from confusion.

It is surely the duty of every one living in a new country to gain as far as possible an adequate and correct knowledge of its language, and this duty belongs not merely to Government officials and members of Missions who are obliged to pass examinations in order to qualify for their work, but also to all who are engaged in commerce, agriculture, and other pursuits, for without such knowledge there can be no mutual understanding which is both necessary for our own success, as well as for the uplift of the people of the country, in which we should all claim to have a share.

This conspectus of the Swahili language will therefore help us all to find that the language is more worthy of our serious study than perhaps we had previously considered.

✠ THOMAS ZANZIBAR

May 1939

PREFACE

THIS dictionary is founded on Madan's Swahili-English dictionary, but in many ways it can be said to be a new work. Madan's dictionary was compiled in 1903 and dealt with the dialect of Swahili commonly spoken in Zanzibar City, but it has proved to be invaluable also on the mainland. However, since 1903, the progress of Mission work, education, civilization and commerce in East Africa have made Swahili of even greater importance than it was in Madan's time; hence the need for a more comprehensive vocabulary on the mainland as well as in Zanzibar.

The need for a revision of Madan's works, or for new Swahili dictionaries, was first seriously suggested at an Education Conference held at Dar-es-Salaam, Tanganyika Territory, in 1925, in connexion with which a Committee sat to consider and make recommendations for the standardization of the Swahili language as a step in creating a literature for the East African Dependencies; but it was not until the Inter-Territorial Language (Swahili) Committee for the East African Dependencies was formed in 1930, that details were discussed, and the real work was not begun until the middle of 1933.

The Committee's original intention was that the work of revision should be divided among as many Swahili scholars as possible, and invitations to co-operate were sent to those considered capable of doing the work, but it was found that most of them were already over-burdened in their own spheres of work, shortage of staff being a chronic condition in East Africa. Therefore, the Secretary of the Inter-Territorial Language Committee was entrusted with carrying out the work on the lines suggested by the Committee.

Full use has been made of the existing Swahili dictionaries, especially those of Krapf and Madan, but many words not included in previous dictionaries will be found in this new work, and definitions have been revised where necessary. Meanings and usages of words may have become restricted, extended, or modified in other ways since they were first recorded, for it must be remembered that the Great War, together with the progress in Mission work, education, civilization and commerce already mentioned, have profoundly influenced the natives of East Africa, and therefore Swahili their *lingua franca.*

The arrangement of this dictionary differs from Madan's. Nouns, adjectives, &c., derived from verbs, will as a general rule be found under the appropriate verb, a reference to the verb being given with the word when it appears in alphabetical order. This arrangement has the advantage of firmly establishing the connexion between derivatives and their verbs—not always apparent otherwise—and in many cases a wider meaning can be associated with derivatives when they are linked up with their verbs.

As in Madan's dictionary, words thought to be of non-Bantu origin are marked, but the principle is to give the original words where possible. These words have been traced by independent search through the dictionaries of languages most likely to have had an influence on the vocabulary of Swahili. In the majority of cases the Swahili forms of the words so closely resemble the originals that there appears to be no doubt about their derivation, but there are cases where the connexion is not so apparent—perhaps the full meanings of the originals are not given in the dictionaries consulted, or perhaps the meanings have become restricted or altered in transition from the original language to Swahili. In such cases possible original words have been suggested.

It will be understood that some of the words given as Persian, Hindi, Turkish or Arabic may be common to two or more of those languages or may have been borrowed through Hindi. Here may be a suitable place to remark on the lack of influence exercised on the Swahili vocabulary by both Portuguese and German. There are a few words which can be traced to Portuguese; but none worth recording, except 'Mdachi' from 'Deutsche', can be attributed to German. The Egyptian dialect of Arabic appears to have had a distinct influence on the Swahili vocabulary as well as the classical Arabic of the Zanzibar Arabs. This influence may have arrived via the Nile, and a study of its extent would be of deep interest.

A number of words previously thought to be of non-Bantu origin have now been established as Bantu, while some not hitherto marked as of non-Bantu origin have been traced to outside sources. Some words have been included, which, if analysed from the phonetic point of view, are strictly not Swahili. These, however, are in more or less common use and have been borrowed by Swahili in their present form from neighbouring Bantu languages, just as it borrowed words from non-Bantu sources—the readiness with which words can be adapted to Swahili being one of the factors to which it owes its usefulness and popularity. A few words adapted from English, but not in common use, have been included because, in the absence of suitable Swahili words, they were recommended by the Inter-Territorial Language Committee for use in text-books and school lessons.

In a work of this nature it is not possible to mention by name all who have helped, but the following have been of especial assistance, and the Committee wish to express gratitude to them: the Rev. Canon Broomfield and the Rev. Canon Hellier, both of the Universities' Mission to Central Africa and Readers of the Inter-Territorial Language Committee; the Rev. Canon Dale, formerly of the Universities' Mission to Central Africa; the Rev. B. J. Ratcliffe, Reader[1] of the Inter-Territorial Language Committee for Kenya Colony; the Rev. K. Roehl of the Berlin Lutheran Mission; the Rev. Dr. Reusch of the Leipzig Mission; the Rev. F. Gleiss of the Bethel Mission; Mr. W. Hendry, Director of Education, Zanzibar; Messrs. G. B. Johnson, L. W. Hollingsworth, and L. A. Buchanan of the Education Department, Zanzibar; the late Alice Werner, Professor of Swahili and Bantu Languages, School of Oriental Studies, London; Messrs. C. Seymour-Hall and G. H. Shelswell-White of Zanzibar; Mr. J. H. Vaughan of Zanzibar who supplied useful information regarding the names of birds; Messrs. P. J. Greenway, Botanist, East African Agricultural Research Station, J. F. P. Soper of the Agricultural Department, Zanzibar, and E. G. Staples of the Agricultural Department, Uganda, who supplied much useful information regarding trees, shrubs and plants; and finally the clerks of the Inter-Territorial Language Committee, Mr. R. K. Watts, Mr. P. Mzaba, and Seyyid Majid Khalid Barghash.

F. JOHNSON.

9 May, 1939.

[1] Later, Secretary to the Committee.

ABBREVIATIONS

EASILY recognized abbreviations are used for the common grammatical names of parts of speech and their varieties—conjugation, moods, tenses, &c.

The principal forms of the verb-stem are distinguished as *Cs.* Causative, *Cv.* Conversive (formerly called Reversive), *Deriv.* Derived, *Dir.* Direct, *Dur.* Durative, *Inf.* Infinitive, *Inten.* Intensive, *Pot.* Potential, *Prep.* Prepositional (formerly called Applied), *Rd.* Reduplicated, *Rf.* Reflexive, *Rp.* Reciprocal, *St.* Stative (formerly called Neuter), *Stc.* Static, *Ten.* Tenacious. Note: *D.* is prefixed before an abbreviation to indicate that the form is doubled, e.g. *D.Prep.* means double prepositional form, or prepositional form of a prepositional form.

Ps. denotes Passive, *Act.* Active, *Pos.* Positive, *Neg.* Negative, *Trans.* Transitive, *Intrans.* Intransitive.

Pfx. Prefix includes (for convenience) infix, suffix, and affix—the same formative element being often medial or final as well as initial.

The chief languages referred to are: *Ar.* Arabic, *Hind.* Hindi, *Pers.* Persian, *Turk.* Turkish, *Eng.* English, *Port.* Portuguese.

The following may also be noted:

a. = adjective.
adv. = adverb.
amplic. = amplicative.
comp. = compound.
conj. = conjunction.
conjug. = conjugation.
cf. = compare.
conn. = connect, connected.
contr. = contrast, contrary in meaning.
dem. = demonstrative.
dim. = diminutive.
dist. = distinguish, distinct in meaning.
esp. = especially.
fig. = figurative, in a figurative sense.
follg. = a word or article immediately following.
imp. = imperative.
int. = interjection.
interrog. = interrogative.
lit. = literally, in a literal sense.
loc. = locative.
n. = noun.
obs. = observe.
opp. = opposed to, of opposite meaning.
perh. = perhaps.
pers. = personal, person.
prec. = a word or article immediately preceding.
prep. = preposition.
prob. = probably.
pron. = pronoun.
pronom. = pronominal.
prov. = proverb.
rel. = relative.
syn. = synonymous, in a wide sense, illustrative of the general, or of a special, meaning of a word.
transp. = transposition.
usu. = usual, usually.
v. = verb.

A SWAHILI-ENGLISH DICTIONARY

(Words marked * appear not to be of *Bantu* origin).

A

A represents the sound of *a* in 'far', or of *a* in 'pat' when short.

A! A-aa! A-h! Aha! A-haa! int. of wonder, pleasure, pain, acquiescence, dissent, &c., according to the mode of expression, intonation, and the length of the vowel.

Aali,* a. good, superior, first rate. *Kitu hiki ni aali,* this thing is very good, only used of things, and then seldom. (Cf. *bora, teule.* Ar. اعال.)

Aasi,* v. See **Asi.**

Abadan,* adv. used only with negatives, never, e.g. *sitakuja kwako abadan,* I shall never come to your place. (Cf. *kamwe.*) **Abadi,** adv. ever, always, constantly, *kazi yake ni kuiba abadi,* he is always stealing. (Cf. *daima, sikuzote, kila mara, milele.* Ar. ابد.)

Abd.* See under **Abudu.**

Abedari,* n. a large block or pulley, used in dhows. (Cf. *henza, kapi, gofia, roda, korodani.* ? corruption of Port. *aberdanas,* small ropes to make firm the lines of the shrouds.)

Abedari!* int. See **Habedari.**

Abiri,* v. pass over, cross over, i.e. a river, lake, sea, but also used for travel as a passenger by any kind of conveyance, e.g. ship, railway, motor-car, aeroplane, &c. Prep. **Abiria,** Cs. **Abirisha,** put across, ferry over, convey as a passenger, &c. **Abiria,** n. a passenger. *Meli ya abiria,* a passenger steamer. *Gari la abiria,* a passenger train, as opp. to *gari la bidhaa* (or *mizigo*), a goods train. *Motakaa ya abiria,* a taxi. (Cf. *vuka, safiri.* Ar. عبر.)

Abudu,* v. serve, worship, adore, used only of religious worship and service. *Abudu Mungu,* serve or worship God. *Abudu sanamu,* worship idols. Prep. **Abudia,** give worship to, worship in (for, on account of, &c.). *Njia ya kumwabudia Mungu,* the way, manner, &c., of worshipping God. Cs. **Abudisha,** cause to worship, teach how to worship, &c. **Abd,** n. servant, slave, but only used in such names as Abdallah, Abdulrahamani, &c. **Ibada,** n. (1) worship, divine service; (2) regular service, habit, characteristics, e.g. *amefanya mabaya kuwa ibada yake,* he always does evil. **Maabadi,** n. a place of worship. **Maabudu,** n. (1) worship; (2) object of worship. **Mwabudu,** n. *wa-* a worshipper. (Cf. *abadi, tumika, sujudu, dini,* and *tabia, kazi, mazoea.* Ar. عبد.)

Abunuwas,* n. the name in stories of Arabic origin, of the character who invariably comes off best owing to his shrewdness like the *sungura* (hare) in stories of African origin.

Acha, v. the main idea is, ceasing or breaking off connexion with something, and may be rendered in many ways, with many shades of meaning, e.g. (1) leave, leave off, leave behind, let go, let pass, let be, go (part, depart) from, e.g. *acha kufanya upuzi,* leave off doing foolish things. *Sikuachi,* I will not let you go. *Tuliacha vitu vingi,* we left behind many things. (2) abandon, neglect, desert, e.g. *kuku amewaacha watoto wake,* the hen has deserted (or neglected) her chicks. (3) acquit, release, pardon, e.g. *alikamata mwizi akamwacha,* he caught a thief and then released him, let him go. *Acha mtumwa huru,* let a slave go free (set him at liberty). (4) allow, permit, give leave, e.g. *watu wengine huwaacha watoto wao wafanye wapendavyo,* some people allow their children to do as they please. (5) separate from, divorce, e.g. *amemwacha mkewe*, he has separated from (divorced) his wife. *Ametuacha mkono*, he has died, i.e. he has gone from (our) hand. The Imp. *Acha!* is used in many ways colloquially: *Acha!* Stop! Let go! Leave off! As an expletive, e.g. *acha* (or, *waache*) *wachuuzi wachume faida nyingi!* trust the shopkeepers for profiteering! *Acha ngoma zivume!* just let the drums boom, i.e. did not they make a tremendous noise! Ps. **Achwa.** Prep. **Achia,** leave to (for &c.), bequeath, e.g. *kuachia mtoto mali*, to bequeath property to a child. D. Prep. **Achilia,** pardon, forgive, pass over. *Mungu amemwachilia makosa yake*, God has pardoned his offences. St. **Achika.** St. of Prep. and Pot. **Achilika,** be excusable, &c. *Makosa haya yanaachilika*, these offences (or, errors) are excusable, forgivable. Cs. **Achisha,** cause to leave, e.g. *achisha mtoto kunyonya*, wean a child. *Ulimwachisha mkewe*, you caused him to leave (divorce) his wife. Rp. **Achana,** leave each other, part, diverge, be different, be inconsistent. *Wameachana*, they have left each other, i.e. divorced. *Njia zinaachana*, the roads (means, methods) diverge. *Maneno yameachana*, the statements do not agree, cannot be reconciled. *Achana na*, part from. (Cf. *saza, bakiza, toka, tupa.*)

Achali,* n. chutney, pickles, slices of mango mixed with chillies, vinegar or lime or lemon juice, and pepper. (Cf. *kachumbari.* Hind. and Pers. اچار.)

Achama, v. open the mouth wide, gape.

Achana, v., Achilia, v. See under **Acha.**

Ada,* n. (1) custom, manner, habit, wont; (2) customary present, commission or fee given on certain occasions, or for assistance in certain customs, rites, &c., e.g. fee of doctor, teacher, workman, those assisting at a wedding, &c. These fees or gifts have also other names descriptive of the services rendered. Some are: *haka, hongera, pukusa, upatu, singizi, kiinuamgongo, fichuo, karo,* &c., &c. Prov. *Ada ya mja hunena, mwungwana ni kitendo*, a slave usually only talks, a freeman acts. (Cf. *desturi, mila, tabia, mazoea.* Ar. عادة.)

Adabu,* n. good manners, politeness, proper behaviour, courtesy, civility, etiquette. The remark *huna adabu*, you have no manners, is much stronger than the expression in English, and is tantamount to 'you are a guttersnipe'. *Fanya adabu*, behave with courtesy, &c. *Tia adabu*, make polite, teach good manners, which may include chastisement to that end. **Adibu,** a. decorous, good mannered, civil, polite. **Adibu, v.** also Cs. **Adibisha,** teach manners to. St. **Adibika. Taadabu,** v. same as *adibu.* (Dist. *adhabu* and cf. *malezi, heshima, makini, taratibu.* Ar. ادب.)

Adamu,* n. Adam. **Mwanadamu,** n. (*wanadamu*) a human being, member of the human race, either male or female. **Binadamu,** n. a man. **Uanadamu,** n. also **Ubinadamu,** n. human nature, humanity. (Cf. *mtu, mlimwengu, mwana.* Ar. ادم.)

Adawa,* n. See **Daawa, Uadui,** and **Adui.**

Aden,* n. (1) the garden of Eden; (2) Aden, the port. (Ar. عدن.)

Adesi,* n. lentils. (Cf. *dengu.* Ar. عدسة.)

Adha,* n. trouble, discomfort. Rarely used. See **Udhia** under **Udhi, v.** (Ar. اذى.)

Adhabu,* n. (1) punishment, chastisement, correction; (2) torment, persecution. *Tia adhabu*, punish, also sentence (a prisoner). **Adhibu,** v. also Cs. **Adhibisha, v.** (1) punish, chastise; (2) give trouble (to), torment, persecute, plague. St. **Adhibika.** (Dist. *adabu*, and cf. *sumbua, udhi, tesa.* Ar. عذب.)

Adhama,* n. greatness, grandeur, glory, majesty, exaltation. **Adhimu,** a. great, exalted, &c. *Leo nimeona mambo adhimu,* to-day I have seen something important (great, exalted, &c.). **Adhimu,** v. and Cs. **Adhimisha,** celebrate, honour, glorify, exalt, magnify, e.g. *adhimisha sikukuu,* celebrate a festival. Prep. **Adhimia. Taadhima,** n. honour, respect, &c., also like *adhama.* **Taadhimika,** v. appear pleasing, pleasant to the eyes, be glorious, be majestic. (Cf. *utukufu, ukuu, sifa, tukuza, shangilia.* Ar. عظم.)

Adhana,* n. the call of the muezzin, the Muhammadan call to prayer. **Adhini,** v. call to public prayers, of the muezzin according to Muhammadan ritual. Prep. **Adhinia,** (1) call to (on behalf of, at, &c.); (2) *kumwadhinia mtoto,* the custom of making the usual call to prayer in a newly-born child's presence to bear witness that he is a Muhammadan. **Mwadhini,** n. *wa-* a muezzin. (Ar. اذن.)

Adhibisha,* v., **Adhibu,** v. See under **Adhabu.**

Adhimu,* a. and v. See under **Adhama.**

Adhini,* v. See under **Adhana.**

Adhiri,* v. put to shame, lower, debase, bring into disrepute, &c. (Cf. *tweza, hizi.* Ar. عذر loathe, be disgruntled with.)

Adhuhuri,* n. noon, between noon and 2 p.m., one of the Muhammadan hours of prayer. (Cf. *alasiri, alfajiri, magharibi.* Ar. الظهر.)

Adi,* v. accompany a person part of his way, as a polite attention, for the more usual *sindikiza.* (Cf. *aga.* Ar. ودع take leave of.)

Adia,* n. a present. (Cf. *zawadi, tunzo, hedaya.* Ar. عطية.)

Adia,* v. See **Wadia.**

Adibisha,* v., **Adibu,** v. See under **Adabu.**

Adili,* n. *ma-* (often used in the plur. *Maadili*) good, righteous conduct, life, &c., impartiality in dealing with people. **Adili,** a. right, righteous, just, impartial. **Adili,** v. be impartial, just, righteous, &c. Cs. **Adilisha,** teach righteous conduct to, give moral training to. **-adilifu,** a. upright, honourable, moral, righteous, impartial. (Cf. *-ema, -nyofu, haki.* Ar. عدل.)

Adimika,* v. be unobtainable, be very scarce. *Chakula kimeadimika,* food is unobtainable, there is great scarcity of food. **Adimu,** a. rare, scarce, unobtainable. (Cf. *ghali, shida, kosekana, haba, -chache.* Ar. عدم.)

Adinasi,* n. See **Wadinasi** under **Wadi,** n. (A).

Adua,* v. make an offering to the spirits, or prepare a charm against the effects of the evil eye, or of harm which may be caused by a person envying, or casting covetous eyes on, or praising one's property. (Cf. *zindua, zingua, zindika, kaga.* Ar. عدو averting.)

Adui,* n. (— and *ma-*) enemy, foe, opponent. **Uadui,** n. enmity, hostility. (Cf. *mtesi, mshindani, chuki, hasimu.* Ar. عدو.)

Afa,* n. *ma-* (often used in the form *maafa*), (1) disaster, damage, calamity, ill luck, terror, horror, injury; (2) a person or thing causing misfortune, calamity, &c. *Fulani ni afa huleta maafa,* so and so is an ill-omened person, he usually brings bad luck, calamity, &c. (Cf. *kitisho, kioja, hofu, ogofya, kisirani, mdhana.* Ar. آفة.)

Afadhali,* adv. See under **Fadhili.**

Afendi,* n. sir, master. As a rule used only by soldiers and police. (Turk. افندى.)

Afia,* n. See **Afya.**

Afikana,* v. See under **Afiki.**

Afiki,* v. agree with, accord with, correspond to, be same as, fit. Seldom used except in following forms: Rp. **Afikiana** (sometimes *afikana*), agree together, come to an agreement, make a contract, pact, bargain; come to an understanding, be reconciled. Cs. **Afikianisha**, conciliate, pacify, bring to terms, reconcile. **Afikiano,** n. *ma-* usu. in the plur. *maafikiano,* and sometimes *maafikano,* (1) agreement, contract, pact, settlement; (2) mutual understanding (respect, esteem). **Mwafaka,** n. *mi-* agreement, bargain, pact, conspiracy, plot. (Cf. *patana, lingana, fanana, maagano, mapatano.* Ar. وفق.)

Afisi,* n. an office. **Afisa,** n. *ma-* an officer. (Eng.)

Afiuni,* n. See **Afyuni.**

Afkani,* a. used only in the expression, *akili afkani,* deficient in intelligence. (Ar. افق.)

Afriti,* n. (1) an evil genius; (2) an evilly disposed, wicked malevolent person. (Cf. *baa, pepo, mwovu.* Ar. عفريت.)

Afu,* n. blossoms of the wild jasmine *mwafu,* used for perfume. **Mwafu,** n. *mi-* the wild jasmine tree. (? Ar. افا scent.)

Afu,* v. also **Afua,** v. save, deliver, pardon, preserve, cure. **Afu,** n. (— and *ma-*) also **Afua,** n. (— and *ma-*) often used in the forms *maafu* and *maafua,* deliverance from calamity, ill luck, disaster, &c.; preservation. *Afua ni mbili, kufa na kupona,* deliverance is of two kinds, dying or getting better. (Cf. *ponya, okoa, samehe.* Ar. عفا.)

Afya,* n. good health, sound condition. Often used with a qualifying adj. *Sina afya siku hizi,* I am not in good health nowadays. *Afya njema (mbaya),* good (bad) health. *Bora afya,* health is the chief thing. *Bora afya kuliko mali,* health is better than riches. Also in the expression *buheri wa afya* health and strength. (Cf. *siha, uzima, hali.* Ar. عافية.)

Afya, v. a very rarely used Cs. form of *apa,* which see.

Afyuni,* n. opium. (Cf. *kasumba, majuni, paru.* Ar. افيون.)

Aga, v. (A) take leave of, say goodbye to. *Aga (agana) buriani,* say a last farewell, i.e. when people are not sure of meeting again. Fig. of the sunset, *jua liagapo miti,* when the sun takes leave of the trees. Prep. **Agia,** take leave of (for, on behalf of, &c.). *Niagie baba yangu,* say good-bye to my father for me. Rp. **Agana,** take leave of each other, exchange farewells. **Agano,** n. *ma-* leave-taking, farewell, but seldom used in this sense, see under *Aga,* v. (B) following. **Mwago,** n. *mi-* act (manner, &c.) of saying good-bye, of leave-taking.

Aga, v. (B), agree with, promise to, engage, usually in the Rp. **Agana,** make mutual agreement, come to terms, conclude a bargain, make a pact. Cs. **Aganisha,** reconcile, bring to terms. Prep. **Agia,** (1) make a promise, but usually with the sense given under *Aga,* v. (A), make a promise would usually be *ahidi*; (2) befit, agree with, become. *Mambo hayo hayakumwagia,* those matters did not befit him. Cs. **Agiza,** order, commission, direct, give instructions. *Fanya kama nilivyokuagiza,* do as I directed you. Prep. **Agizia,** order on behalf of, commission for, &c., *Nimemwagizia kasha langu,* I have sent him to fetch my box. *Niagizie saa,* order a watch (or a clock) for me. **Agano,** n. *ma-* (often used in the plur.), agreement, promise, contract, pact, mutual understanding.

Agano Jipya, the New Testament. *Agano la Kale*, the Old Testament. **Agizo**, n. *ma-* (often used in the plur.), instruction, injunction, direction, command, order, request. **Kiaga**, n. *vi-* a promise, agreement. **Mwago**, n. *mi-* a present given by a man to his first wife when she has agreed that he should take a second wife, also of presents given on reconciliation between people. (Cf. *patana*, *afiki*, *ahidi*, *usia*, *mkataba*.)

Agano, n. *ma-* See under **Aga**, v. (A) and (B).

Aghalabu,* adv. also **Aghlabu**, usually, more often, chiefly, as a rule, mainly, e.g. *maji huchotwa kwa ndoo, aghalabu na ng'ombe*, water is drawn by means of buckets, but usually by oxen. (Ar. اغلب).

Agia, v. See under **Aga**, v. (A) and (B).

Agizo, n. *ma-*. See under **Aga**, v. (B).

Agosti,* n. the word adopted for August, the month. (Eng.).

Agua, v. (A), predict, prophesy, divine, presage, interpret dreams, omens, &c. Prep. **Agulia**, foretell to (for, about, &c.), explain a dream to, &c., *Bao la kuagulia*, a divining board. Ps. **Aguliwa**. **Aguzi**, n. *ma-* usually in the plur. predictions, prophesies, interpretations of dreams, omens, &c. **Mwaguzi**, n. *wa-* a diviner, one who interprets dreams, &c. **Uaguzi**, n. interpretation of dreams, prediction, prophecy, the calling (method, fee, &c.) of a diviner. (Cf. *bashiri*, *fasiri*, and *bao*, *ramli*, *feli*.)

Agua, v. (B), treat medically, supply medicine, attend a sick person, but esp. perform certain rites to remove a spell, or witchcraft or cure an illness thought to be caused by spirits (*pepo*). Prep. **Agulia**. Ps. **Aguliwa**. Cs. **Aguza**. **Aguzi**, n. *ma-* usu. in the plur. medical treatment, medicines, appliances and things required for sick nursing, but usu. things required for removing a spell, witchcraft, &c. **Mwaguzi**, n. *wa-* one who attends a sick person, a nurse, also the person who performs the rites to remove a spell, &c. **Uaguzi**, n. sick nursing, the calling (method, fee, &c.) of a nurse, or one who performs the rites to remove a spell. (Cf. *punga*, *ugua*, *ganga*, and prec.)

A-h! Aha! Ahaa! See under **A!**

Ahadi,* n. promise, covenant, agreement, engagement. *Toa* (*funga*, *-pa*) *ahadi*, make a promise. *Vunja ahadi*, break a promise. *Timiza* (*fikisha*, *shika*, *tekeleza*) *ahadi*, keep (fulfil, &c.) a promise. Prov. *Ahadi ni deni*, a promise is a debt. **Ahidi**, v. promise, engage, contract, &c. Prep. **Ahidia**. Ps. **Ahidiwa**. Rp. **Ahidiana**, promise each other, make a mutual agreement. Sometimes heard as *wahadi*. (Cf. *patana*, *kubali*, *afiki*, *mkataba*. Ar. عهد.)

Ahali,* n. (1) a wife. *Ahali zangu*, my wives. (2) family, relations, folk, kindred, kinsman. Used comprehensively, and sometimes in contrast with near relations. *Wazazi na ndugu na ahali*, parents, brothers, and relations. *Ndugu na ahali*, brothers and (other) relations. (Cf. *akraba*, *jamaa*, *ukoo*, *ufungu*, *utani*, *ndugu*. Ar. اهل.)

Ahasante.* See **Asante**.

Ahera,* n. the next world, future life, i.e. after death, paradise, also Hades. (Cf. *kuzimu*, *peponi*, *jehanum*.) **Aheri**, n. the end, the last stage, finish. *Toka awali hata aheri*, from first to last, from beginning to end. (Cf. *mwisho*, *kikomo*. Ar. آخر.)

Ahi,* n. brother. Sometimes used for friend. Also **Yahe**, (1) with the same meaning, and (2) the common herd. *Sisi akina yahe*, we the common herd, the rabble, the ordinary people. (Cf. *ndugu*, *rafiki*, and *watu*. Ar. اخ.)

Ahidi,* v. See under **Ahadi**.

Ahiri,* v. stand over, be behindhand, be put off (deferred, postponed, adjourned), tarry, remain behind. Ps. **Ahiriwa.** Cs. **Ahirisha,** postpone, delay, adjourn, defer, cause to wait. *Arusi imeahirishwa,* the wedding has been postponed. **Taahari,** v. be late, delay, tarry. **Taahira,** n. delay. (Cf. *aheri, usiri, ngoja, kawia, limatia, weka.* Ar. اخر.)

Ahlaki,* n. See **Halaiki.**

Ahlmashauri,* n. See **Halmashauri** under **Shauri.**

Ahsante.* See **Asante.**

Ahueni,* n. better condition regarding health, e.g. *leo amepata ahueni,* to-day he is better in health. Sometimes heard as *hueni.* (Cf. *ashekali, nafuu, jambo.* Ar. اهون.)

Aibika,* v. See under **Aibu.**

Aibu,* n. disgrace, shame, scandal, dishonour, reproach. **Aibika,** v. St. be put to shame, dishonoured, disgraced. Cs. **Aibisha,** disgrace, dishonour, shame. (Cf. *fedheha, haya, tweza, hizi.* Ar. عيب.)

Aidha,* conj. further, moreover, next, then. (Cf. *kadhalika, thama, tena, basi, kisha.*) Often with *wa,* i.e. *wa aidha,* and moreover, and so. (Ar. ايضا.)

Aika, v. sometimes heard for *yeyuka,* which see.

Aili,* v. blame. Cs. **Ailisha,** used in the same way as *aili.* **Uaili,** n. blame, guilt. (Cf. *laumu.* Ar. عال.)

Aina,* n. kind, class, genus, family, species, sort, sample. **Aini,** v. classify, specify, define, point out, distinguish, show. Ps. **Ainiwa.** Cs. **Ainisha,** like *aini,* distinguish, choose, &c. St. **Ainika.** (Cf. *onyesha, eleza, dhihirisha, chagua,* and *jinsi, namna.* Ar. عين.)

Ajabu,* v. wonder, be astonished, feel surprise. Prep. **Ajabia.** St. **Ajabika.** Cs. **Ajabisha,** but this form is seldom used, the usual form being **Staajabu** (and sometimes *taajabu*) be greatly astonished, surprised, filled with wonder. Prep. **Staajabia.** St. **Staajabika.** Cs. **Staajabisha. Ajabu,** n. (—and *ma-*) (1) wonder, amazement, astonishment, admiration; (2) a wonder, anything startling or wonderful. *Ona ajabu,* feel wonder, be astonished. **Ajabu, Ajib,** and **Ajibu,** adv and a. wonderfully, extraordinarily, surprisingly. *Kubwa ajabu,* marvellously great. Often used to strengthen *sana,* and *mno. Nyingi mno ajabu,* exceedingly many; as a. wonderful, surprising, extraordinary, marvellous. **Staajabu,** n. *ma-* (also sometimes *taajabu,* n. *ma-*) wonder, a wonder, same as *ajabu.* (Cf. *shangaza, toshewa, maka,* and *mwujiza, shani.* Ar. عجب.)

Ajali,* n. accident, fate, chance, destiny, doom, appointed end, death. *Leo imetimia ajali yako,* to-day your hour is come. *Ajali haina kinga wala kafara,* there is no prevention or sacrifice of avail against fate. *Kupatikana na ajali,* meet one's fate, die. (Cf. *bahati, nasibu, sudi, kifo, tukio.* Ar. الاجل.)

Ajara,* n. See under **Ajiri.**

Ajazi,* v. be weak, feeble, slack, late, remiss. St. **Ajizika,** used in the same way as *ajazi.* **Ajizi,** n. and a. slackness, remissness, lateness. *Mtu huyu ana ajizi,* this person is slack, remiss, slow. *Chakula hiki hutia ajizi maungoni,* this food makes the body slack and weak; as a. feeble, remiss, slack. **Uajizi,** n. delay, remissness. (Cf. *legea, choka, nyong'onyea,* and *ulegevu, uchovu, dhaifu, utepetevu, uzembe, usiri.* Ar. عجز.)

Ajemi,* n. for *uajemi,* which see.

Ajib, Ajibu,* a. and adv. See under **Ajabu.**

Ajihi,* v. visit a person living at a distance. (Cf. *zuru, wajihi,* Ar. واجه.)

Ajili,* n. cause, reason, sake. *Kwa ajili ya,* because of, for the sake of, on account of, by reason of. *Alikufa* *kwa ajili yetu*, he died for our sakes. (Cf. *sababu, maana, hoja, kisa.* Ar. اجل.)

Ajiri,* v. hire, engage for wages. Ps. **Ajiriwa.** Cs. **Ajirisha**, get for hire, let on hire, employ for wages. **Ajara**, n., **Ijara**, n. but more usu. **Ujira**, hire, wages. (Cf. *tuma, utumishi, mshahara, panga, kodi.* Ar. اجر.)

Ajizi,* n. See under **Ajazi.**

Ajuza,* n. a very old woman (an old man is *shaibu*). (Cf. *kizee, mzee, mkongwe.* Ar. عجوز.)

Aka! int. expression of astonishment, annoyance, impatience, denial, &c.

Aka, v. build, using stone, bricks, and mortar, work as a mason, as opposed to *jenga*, which is used of building with poles, sticks, and mud, as natives do their houses. Prep. **Akia.** Ps. **Akwa.** Cs. **Akisha** (and seldom, **Asha**), have mason's work done, cause to build, order to be built. **Mwashi,** n. *wa-* a mason, a builder in stone and mortar. **Uashi,** n. the craft of a mason, masonry, building in stone, also pay of a mason. (Contr. *jenga, unda.*)

Akali,* n. and a. a few of, some. *Akali ya vitu, vitu akali*, a few things. *Nipe akali ya misumari*, give me a few nails. (Cf. *haba, -chache, baadhi*, but as a rule a few of, and some, are not rendered in Swahili, e.g. a few nails is *misumari*, i.e. *nipe misumari*, give me some nails. Ar. اقل.)

Akania,* v. lead by means of a bridle. **Akania,** n. a bit and bridle. (Cf. *hatamu, lijamu.* ? Ar. اكنان guard.)

Akarabu,* n. the hand of a watch or clock, but usu. *mkono* or *mshale.* (Ar. عقرب.)

Akari,* n. intoxicating liquor. (Cf. *ulevi.* Ar. عقار.)

-ake, the invariable part of the Poss. Pron. 3 Pers. Sing., his, hers, her, its, of him (her, it). The Poss. Pron. always follows the noun of thing possessed, and changes its initials according to the class of noun it follows—see Grammars. Additional emphasis and precision is given by adding *yeye, mwenyewe*, or both, e.g. *Kiti chake*, his chair. *Kiti chake mwenyewe*, his own chair. *Kiti chake yeye mwenyewe*, his very own chair.

Akia, v. (1) swallow, gulp down; (2) throw food into the mouth; (3) gorge. (Cf. *bwakia, meza, la, gugumia.*)

Akiba,* n. store, reserve, stock, what is laid by for the future. *Weka akiba kwa siku za dhiki*, put aside, store up, for a time of scarcity or need. Prov. *Akiba haiozi*, a reserve never goes bad, i.e. always comes in useful. (Ar. عقب that which follows, rest, remainder, &c.)

Akida,* n. *ma-* formerly a leader, commander, esp. of soldiers, but in Tanganyika Territory only known as an Arab or Native—not necessarily of the tribe, put in charge of an area, i.e. a kind of political agent largely employed under the German régime, now replaced by native authorities. In some places an *akida* is simply an office messenger, or retainer of a native chief. (Ar. عقد.)

Akidi,* v. (1) suffice (for), be enough (for); (2) finish. (Cf. *tosha*, and *maliza.* Ar. عقد conclude, end, result, ratify.)

Akifia,* v. entrust with, i.e. property, money, &c. Ps. **Akifiwa.** Cs. **Akifisha.** (Ar. وقف, endow.)

Akifisha,* v. See **Wakifisha** under **Wakifu.**

Akifu,* v. See **Wakifu.**

Akika,* n. (1) a feast made at the first hair-cutting of a child, i.e. when it is 8 days old, or perhaps held later. A goat is killed and the bones are buried whole. These are said by some to change into a camel at the last day and take the person to *ahera.* (2) a funeral feast for a child.

Akiki, n. (1) *soma akiki,* read the burial service for a child; (2) the goat slain at the feast of the first hair-cutting, see above. (Cf. *muhanga, kafara.* Ar. عقيق.)

Akiki,* n. (1) see under **Akika**; (2) a kind of red stone, cornelian, used for putting in rings, ear-rings, &c. (Ar. عقيق.)

Akili,* n. (1) mind, intellect, understanding, reason, sense, intelligence, consciousness; (2) ability, cleverness, judgement, discretion; (3) a trick, ruse, clever plan, happy thought. *Fanya akili,* use the brains, exercise intelligence, devise a plot, think of a ruse, discover a way out. *Katika akili sangu,* according to my view, so far as I understand. *Fuata akili yako,* follow your judgement. Prov. *Akili mali,* wits (are) wealth. *Hana akili,* he has no sense, he is a fool. (Cf. *busara, ufahamu, utambuzi, ujuzi, moyo, welekevu, also hila, werevu.* Ar. عقل.)

Akina,* n. also **Kina,** and sometimes **Wakina,** family, race, lineage, house, blood, connexion, folk, &c. Used as a kind of generalized plural: *Akina* (or *kina,* or *wakina*) *sisi,* we, such as we are, people like us; or it may simply mean a person himself, e.g. *Akina fulani,* may mean (1) So-and-so himself; (2) So-and-so and his family, followers, tribe, acquaintances, &c.; (3) So-and-so's family, followers, tribe, &c. *Akina bibi,* the women-folk. *Akina bwana,* the men-folk. As a rule it is used as a title of respect, but it may be used with a contemptuous or scornful sense: *Oh! akina fulani!* Oh, the So-and-so's! i.e. with a derogatory sense of—they are nobodies, they do not count. (Ar. plur. of قن, a slave, son of slaves born in the house, and so followers, hence its use sometimes in a derogatory sense.)

-ako, the invariable part of Poss. Pron. 2 Pers. Sing., your, yours, of you. (See under **-ake,** for the use of *wewe* and *mwenyewe* for emphasis.)

Akrab Magharibi,* Arab. South-West. (Cf. *kusi* and *magharibi.*)

Akrab Matlai,* Arab. South-East. (Cf. *kusi* and *matlai.*)

Akraba,* n. kinsman, relation, used of near relationship only. *Akraba za kuumeni (kukeni),* near relations on the father's (mother's) side. (Cf. *karibu, ahali, jamaa, utani, ukoo, ufungu, ndugu.* Ar. اقرب.)

Akram,* n. also **el akram,** honoured, respected. Only used in the complimentary introduction of letters written in Arabic style. Ar. اكرام.)

-akwe. See **-ake.**

Ala!* int. expression of annoyance, impatience, &c. (Ar. الا Ho! Have a care! &c.)

Ala,* n. (1) (—*ma-* and *nyala*), sheath, scabbard, case of knife, sword, &c. (Cf. *uo.* Perh. from Ar. حلى adornment of sword.) (2) sing. and plur. any sort of instrument, apparatus, tool, utensil, machine, e.g. *tumepata kila ala ya muziki,* we have every kind of musical instrument. (Ar. آلة tool, instrument, &c.)

Alaala!* int. immediately. See **Halahala.**

Alafu,* n. See **Elfu.**

Alama,* n. sign, mark, token, trace, indication, vestige. *Tia alama,* put a mark on, mark. *Hakuna hata alama,* there is not even a sign (trace, vestige, &c.). (Cf. *ishara, dalili.* Ar. علامة.)

Alamsiki,* Good-bye—used on any occasion. (Ar. abbreviation of الله لمسك.)

Alamu,* n. flag, banner, signal of warning, danger, &c. (Ar. علم.)

Alasiri,* n. (1) afternoon; (2) one of the regular Muhammadan times of prayer, from 3.30 p.m. to 4.30 p.m. (Cf. *alfajiri, adhuhuri, magharibi.* Ar. العصر.)

Alau.* See under **Walau.**

Aleik, Aleikum.* See under **Salamu.**

Alfabeti,* n. the alphabet. (Eng.).

Alfafa,* n. the dressing put on the wound after circumcision to prevent it being knocked. (Ar. لفافة bandage.)

Alfajiri,* n. (1) dawn, daybreak; (2) one of the regular Muhammadan times of prayer, about 4 a.m. (Cf. *alasiri, adhuhuri, magharibi.* Ar. فجر.)

Alfu,* n. See **Elfu.**

Alhamdulillahi!* int. Praise be to God. An expression commonly used on hearing good news, of recovery from illness, delivery from danger, difficulty, &c., also on hearing of a death. (Ar. الحمد لله. Cf. *hamdu* and *Allah.*)

Alhamisi,* n. Thursday, lit. the fifth (day). The names of the days of the week are: *Jumamosi,* the 1st day (Saturday); *Jumapili,* the 2nd day (Sunday); *Jumatatu,* the 3rd day (Monday); *Jumanne,* the 4th day (Tuesday); *Jumatano,* the 5th day (Wednesday); *Alhamisi,* lit. the 5th day (Thursday); *Ijumaa,* the day of assembly, the Muhammadan Lord's day (Friday). Thus in name, there are two 5th days—Thursday is the 5th day according to the old oriental reckoning which regards the Sabbath as the last day and Sunday as the first day of the week. Wednesday is the 5th day from, but not including Friday, which is the Muhammadan equivalent of Sunday. In some places Sunday, i.e. *Jumapili,* is referred to among Christians as *Siku ya Bwana,* the Lord's day. (Ar. الخميس.)

Alia, v. make a mark on the body as by a blow with a stick, &c. St. **Alika,** make a sharp, short crack, snap, click, report. Cs. **Alisha,** cause to give a sharp crack, snap, &c. e.g. as when a person pulls or depresses the joints of his fingers and makes them crack, an action common with many natives. Used also of the crackling of roasted grains of Indian corn (*bisi*), and such noises. *Alisha mtambo wa bunduki,* make the trigger of a gun click, cock the trigger. **Walio,** n. (*ma-* and *nyalio*) a mark, as on the body made by a stick, &c. **Mwaliko,** n. *mi-* a crackling sound, click, snap, clap. **Mwalishi,** n. *wa-* one who makes a crackling noise, &c. (Cf. *piga, liza, data, tatarika,* also *mbarika* from the same root. Dist. the following.)

Alika, v. (1) invite, call, summon, give injunctions to, challenge; (2) treat a sick person, confine to the house for medical treatment, also used of a young girl confined so that she shall not be seen by strangers. *Alika vita,* summon to battle. *Alika karamuni,* invite to a feast. Ps. **Alikwa,** (1) be invited, summoned; (2) be kept indoors for medical treatment, &c. Cs. **Alisha,** also **Alisa,** used in the same way as *alika* (2). **Jaliko,** n. *ma-* same as *mwaliko.* **Mwaliko,** n. *mi-* an invitation, summons, call. **Mwalishi,** n. *wa-* one who calls, invites, e.g. to a wedding, feast, &c. (Cf. *karibisha, tawa.*)

Aliki,* v. hang, hang up, suspend, attach. (Cf. *tundika, tungika, angika.* Ar. علق.)

Alisa, v. See **Alisha** under **Alika.**

Allah,* n. God. Seldom used except in Arabic expressions and formulas, such as: *Allah akbar,* God is great. *La illahi ila Allah,* there is no God but God, the first clause of Muhammadan creed, which is sung over and over again by the funeral procession on its way to the grave. *Alhamdu lilahi,* praise be to God. *Inshallah,* if it pleases God. *Bismillahi,* in the name of God. *Allah bilkheri*, God prosper you. *Wallahi*, by God. (Cf. *Rabi, Mola, Mungu*. Ar. الله.)

Almari,* n. a chest of drawers. A single drawer of the chest or of a table is *saraka*, also *mtoto*, which see. (Hind. الماري or Port. *armario*.)

Almaria,* n. embroidery. (Cf. *nakshi, darizi*. Port. *alamar*.)

Almasi,* n. (1) a diamond; (2) a common personal male name. (Ar. الماس.)

Ama,* conj. either . . . or. *Ama hii ama hii*, either this or that. *Wa ama*, yet, and further. *Ama si-vyo?* Or is it not so? Do you not admit it? (Cf. *au*, and neg. *wala*. Ar. ام or, and اما Is it not?)

Ama!* int. (1) expression of annoyance, impatience, &c., like *ala*, and *ati*, also (2) used in asking a question. *Ama! huna habari ya mambo yaliyo-tokea jana?* I say, have not you heard of what took place yesterday? *Ama! yeye ni mjinga tu*, Oh! he is only a fool. (Ar. عما truly, indeed, &c.)

Amali,* n. (1) an act, action, thing done; (2) business, occupation, practice. *Amali yake ni kuchuuza*, his business is that of trading. *Mtu wa amali*, an energetic, practical, busy man. (3) a kind of charm. (Cf. *hirizi*.) **Amili,** v. (1) manage, make, work, effect, bring about; (2) sometimes used in the sense of taking part in an evil, base action or venture. **Mwamali,** n. treatment, action, &c. (Cf. *tendo, kazi, uchumi, shughuli, utendaji*. Ar. عمل.)

Amana,* n. trust, security, a thing entrusted to any one, a pledge, a deposit. *Ameweka amana kwangu*, he has deposited something in trust with me. *Weka amana*, make a deposit, give a security. **Amani,** n. peace, security, safety, confidence, *Wakati wa amani*, a time of peace, security, quietness. *Amani iwe kwenu*, peace be with you. **Amania,** v. confide in, trust with confidence. **Amin,** and **Amina,** Amen, so be it. **Amini,** v. believe, trust, have faith in, put confidence in. *Namwamini Mungu*, I believe in God, i.e. I trust and have faith in Him. *Nilimwa-mini na fedha zangu*, I entrusted him with my money. Prep. **Aminia.** St. **Aminika,** be worthy of trust. *Mtu huyu haaminiki*, this person is not to be trusted. Cs. **Aminisha,** (1) cause to believe, inspire with faith (confidence, trust); (2) entrust to, entrust with, commit to the care of; (3) Inten. have trust (about), feel confidence. *Hawakuaminisha kuenda mbele*, they did not venture to go forward. **Amini,** n. fidelity, trustworthiness, faithfulness, honesty, integrity. **Amini, -amini, -ami-nifu,** a. faithful, honest, trustworthy. **Imani,** n. (1) faith, trust, confidence, honesty, uprightness, &c. *Upanga wa imani*, a kind of double-handed sword; (2) religious faith, belief, object of belief, creed. *Imani kwa Mungu*, faith towards God. *Imani ya Mitume*, the Apostles' creed. **Mwamana,** n. *wa-* a trustful person. *Asiye mwamana haaminiwi*, he who does not trust others, himself cannot be trusted. **Mwamini,** n. *wa-*, **Mwaminifu,** n. *wa-* a trusting, believing, trustworthy person. **Uamini, Uaminifu,** n. honesty, straightforwardness, trustworthiness, &c. (Cf. *tumaini, sadiki, tege-mea, shahada*. Ar. أمن.)

Amara,* n. (1) urgent affairs, pressing business; (2) aid, assistance, i.e. in the inquiry on taking leave of a person. *Haja amara?* Is there anything I can do for you? (Ar. امر.)

Amari,* n. the cable of an anchor. (Prob. through Port. *amarra*, cable.)

Amba, v. (A), slander, abuse, speak against. Ps. **Ambwa.** Note: this sense is confined to the Direct and

Ps. form only. The Prep. and other Der. forms have an entirely different sense, see below. **Amba** is used with the relative prefix added in the sense of a simple relative pronoun 'who, which'—followed by finite verb, for instance, with a perfect tense which cannot take a relative infix, e.g. things which are broken, *vitu ambavyo vimevunjika,* as dist. from *vitu vilivyovunjika,* things which were broken. They who have gone, *wao ambao wamekwenda,* &c. It is often followed by '*kwamba*' the infinitive, (*ku-amba*), e.g. *watu ambao kwamba wa tayari,* people who are ready; also by *kwa* with the relative particle affixed, to denote 'by whom or which', e.g. *njia ambazo kwazo tunaweza kufika,* roads by which we are able to arrive. *Maneno ambayo kwayo aliwadanganya,* words by which he deceived them. **Amba,** but as a rule the infinitive **Kwamba** is used as a conjunction with or without *ya* (*ya kwamba*), 'saying'. This form has varied meanings which are translatable according to the context defining the particular sense of 'saying' intended, e.g. (i) (stating) that, so to say, e.g. *akasema kwamba* (or *ya kwamba*) *ndivyo,* and he said that it was so; (ii) often preceded by *kama* (supposing) if, as if, supposing, e.g. *alisema* (*kama*) *kwamba ana hakika,* he spoke as if he were sure; (iii) (objecting) though, e.g. *si kama kwamba yeye ni mfalme,* it is not as though he were the king; (iv) whether or whether—*kwamba ni ya moto au kwamba ni ya baridi,* whether it be hot or whether it be cold. Sometimes it is heard in the expression *kwambaje?* How is it? *Kwambaje kwako?* How are you? Prep. **Ambia,** tell, say to, inform (by word of mouth)—always with an object infix. In indirect narration it is often followed by *kama, ya kuwa, kuwa, ya kwamba,* that, also sometimes in direct narration. *Alimwambia kuwa* (*ya kuwa, kwamba, ya kwamba*), *walisema hayo,* he told him that they said those (words). *Alimwambia* (*kuwa,* &c.): *Walisema hayo,* he told him: They said those (words). Ps. **Ambiwa,** be told. D. Prep. **Ambilia,** speak much to, or against. St. and Pot. **Ambilika,** be approachable for speech, &c., be affable. *Mtu wa kuambilika,* an affable, approachable person. *Mtu huyu haambiliki,* this person cannot bear being spoken to, he is hard-hearted, not approachable (on behalf of others), also he cannot be told anything, i.e. he cannot keep a secret, he would let it out. Rp. of Prep. **Ambiana.** Rf. **Jigamba** (the g representing an initial consonant dropped before the stem *amba,* cf. *jambo,* which also comes from this verb), boast, brag, vaunt oneself. **Kigambo,** n. *vi-* an affair, matter, case. **Mgambo,** n. *mi-* a public proclamation. *Mbiu ya mgambo,* formerly a buffalo horn blown to call people together to hear a proclamation or announcement. **Mwambaji,** n. *wa-,* **Mwambi,** n. *wa-,* a slanderer, backbiter, grumbler. (Cf. *sema, nena, jambo.*)

Amba, v. (B), adhere, be in contact, &c. The Dir. form is not in use, probably owing to the possible confusion with *amba* (cf. prec.) and *wamba,* which see. Ten. **Ambata,** stick to, adhere to, be in contact with, cleave to, be attached to, cling, clasp. *Ulimi wangu uliambata kaakaani,* my tongue cleaved to the roof of my mouth. Prep. **Ambatia.** St. and Pot. **Ambatika.** Cs. **Ambatisha,** cause to cling to, &c. Rp. **Ambatana,** cling together, cleave together, &c. *Rafiki huambatana,* friends stick together. *Karatasi zote zimeambatana,* all the papers are stuck together. St. of Dir. **Ambika,** be brought into contact, hold together, be stuck together. Cs. **Ambisha,** and **Ambisa,** cause to adhere, bring into contact, as of things glued, cemented, &c. *Ambisha mashua*, put a boat alongside another, e.g. of bringing a small boat alongside a big one which cannot reach the shore. Cv. **Ambua**, remove, take off, separate something adhering, e.g. *ambua ngozi* (*gamba*, &c.), remove the skin (bark, &c.). Prep. **Ambulia**, (1) remove for (with, &c.); (2) fig. get, e.g. *umeambulia faida gani?* What profit did you pull off? Ps. **Ambuliwa.** St. **Ambuka.** *Ngozi imeambuka*, the skin has peeled off (as after an illness, or cast by a snake, &c.). Cs. **Ambukiza**, cause to be peeled off (removed, cast) and hence infect with disease, carry infection, contagion, be infectious, contagious, peeling of the skin being the result of some diseases. *Ugonjwa wa kuambukiza*, an infectious (contagious) disease. **Ambo**, n. *ma-* gum, glue, any substance which sticks or causes coherence. **Ambukizo**, n. *ma-* (1) a peeling off, that which causes a peeling or stripping off, and so (2) infection, that which causes infection. **Chamba**, n. *vya-* (1) anything which sticks or adheres; (2) the cornea of the eye; (3) bark of a tree. **Gamba**, n. *ma-* (*g* represents an initial consonant dropped before the stem, *amba*), scale of a fish, outer covering, bark of a tree, &c., also sometimes of any small detached part of an outer skin of an animal, e.g. of a tortoise, &c. **Uambukizo**, n. infection, infectiousness. **Wambiso**, n. (for *u-ambiso*), adherence, condition of being fastened together, holding together, attachment, clasping.

Amba-, rel. See under **Amba**, v. (A).

Ambaa, v. Dur. of **Amba** (cf. *paka*, *pakaa*; *tanda*, *tandaa*), restricted in meaning: pass near to without actual contact, without touching, affecting, recognizing, hurting, &c. *Naomba maovu yakuambae*, I pray that evil may not touch you. *Tuliambaa pwani pwani*, we hugged the shore. *Waliambaa hatari*, they escaped danger (though it was very near them). *Nilimwambaa*, I passed him by (without seeing, recognizing, saluting, &c.). Cs. **Ambaza**, cause to pass near but without actual contact, i.e. of a vessel hugging the shore, of evil, of skirting a table, wall, &c. **Mwambao**, n. *mi-* (1) the coast-line, shore, edge of sea (cf. *pwani*). *Safari ya mwambao*, a coasting voyage. (2) an act of passing near to, skirting, coasting, hugging the shore, &c. **Mmwambao**, n. *wa-*, one who dwells on the coastal belt. (Cf. *amba*, v. (B), *tambaa*, and dist. *amba*, v. (A) and *wamba*.)

Ambari,* n. ambergris. Sometimes used to burn together with *ubani* (cf. *ubani*, *fukiza*); also eaten to improve one's figure, make one stouter, more virile, &c. *Ambari ya maji kupwa na maji kujaa*, ambergris (eaten at) low tide and high tide, i.e. it is thought by some that to have the desired affect, the ambergris should be eaten by a person while he is actually standing in the sea. If eaten at high tide, while standing in much water, the result is stoutness, if at low tide, in shallow water, the result is slimming. (Ar. عنبر.)

Ambata, v. See under **Amba**, v. (B).

Ambia, v. See under **Amba**, v. (A).

Ambika, v. (1) see under **Amba**, v. (B); (2) build or set a fish-trap, i.e. a fence of reeds, thin sticks, wire netting, &c., in shallow water; (3) bait a fishing-line.

Ambisha, v., **Ambo**, n. *ma-*, **Ambua**, v., **Ambukiza**, v., **Ambukizo**, n. *ma-*. See under **Amba**, v. (B).

Amdelahane,* n. a kind of soft silky material.

Amerikani,* n. (1) a kind of unbleached calico—others are *gamti*, *japani*, *membei*; (2) America; (3) an American.

Ami,* n. uncle, father's brother.

Sometimes **Amu**, esp. in **Binamu**, a cousin, son of father's brother. (Cf. *bin*. Ar. عم.)

Amia,* v. protect a plantation or garden from birds and animals by keeping watch and making noises to frighten them away. **Mwamizi**, n. *wa-* one who protects a plantation from birds, &c. (Cf. *linda*. From the same root as *hami* and *himaya*.)

Amili,* v. See under **Amali**.

Amin, Amina, Amini, v., **Amini**, a. **-amini**, a. **-aminifu,*** a. See under **Amana**.

Amiri,* n. See under **Amri**.

Amiri,* v. begin a thing, e.g. *amiri shamba*, begin a new garden. *Amiri mji*, begin a new village. (Cf. *maliki*, *anza*. Ar. عمر.)

Amka, v. awake, rouse oneself, regain life (consciousness, strength, &c.). Prep. **Amkia**, (1) wake up at (in, for, &c.); (2) pay a morning visit to, make an early call, visit formally (the recognized custom of dependants to patrons, children to parents, and subordinates to superiors); (3) greet, accost, salute, address, pay respects to; (4) fig. of early dawn, i.e. *Jumamosi usiku kuamkia Jumapili*, late on Saturday night, as Sunday is dawning. Cs. **Amsha**, awaken, rouse up (from sleep lethargy, &c.). *Amsha tamaa*, rouse desire, lust. *Amsha kinywa*, take breakfast. **Kiamshakinywa**, n. *vi-*, **Chamshakinywa**, n. *vy-* breakfast, something taken to break the night's fast. **Maamkio**, n. plur., and **Maamkizi**, n. plur. visits, greetings, salutations, paying of respects. Note: **Amkua**, v. is used in the same way as *amkia* in some places, esp. Mombasa. (Cf. *ondoka*, *zinduka*, *chamka*, *fufua*.)

Amkua, v. See under **Amka**.

Amri,* n. (1) a command, order, direction; (2) authority, rule, government. *Toa amri*, issue an order. *Shika* (*fuata*) *amri*, obey (execute, carry out) an order. *Tangua amri*, rescind an order. *Huna amri juu yangu*, you have no authority over me. *Amri ya Mungu*, the will of God, providence, chance—an expression commonly used to account for anything which has happened, frequently the result of one's own carelessness, neglect, ignorance, &c. *Sina amri katika mambo haya*, I have no say (authority, jurisdiction, responsibility, orders, &c.) in these matters. *Nani mwenye amri hapa?* Who is the responsible head here? **Amiri**, n. a commander, leader, officer, esp. of soldiers. **Amuru**, v. command, order, direct, commission, exercise authority. *Aliniamuru niende*, he ordered me to go. The Deriv. forms are made from a stem *amri*, hence Prep. **Amria**, give orders about (for, at, &c.). Ps. **Amriwa**, *Ameamriwa asifanye neno*, he has been ordered not to do anything. Cs. **Amrisha**, give strict orders, have orders issued, but esp. cause to be ordered, drilled, hence, command, drill, take a parade of soldiers, &c. (Ar. امر.)

Amu,* n. See under **Ami**.

Amua, v. (1) stop a quarrel, end a dispute, interfere and stop persons quarrelling; (2) judge, be umpire, arbitrate. Prep. **Amulia**, arbitrate between. *Tuamulie shauri hili*, decide this case for us. Ps. **Amuliwa**, have a case settled by arbitration. **Maamuzi**, n. plur. arbitration, judgement, verdict. **Mwamua**, n. *wa-*, **Mwamuzi**, n. *wa-* a mediator, arbitrator, umpire, judge. (Cf. *patanisha*, *suluhisha*, *hukumu*.)

Amuru,* v. See under **Amri**.

Amwa, v. suck. Cs. **Amwisha**, suckle. (Cf. *nyonya*.)

Ana, verb-form he (she) has.

-anana, a. soft, thin, gentle. *Upepo mwanana*, a gentle breeze, *maji maanana*, gentle, still, slowly running clear water. *Mtu mwanana*, a gentle, kindly person. (Cf. *-ororo*, *laini*, *-pole*.

Anasa,* n. (1) pleasure, enjoyment, luxury; (2) often used in the sense of over-luxuriousness, self-indulgence, sensuality. *Nyumba ya anasa,* a well-ordered house (luxurious, with every convenience, &c.). *Kaa kwa anasa,* live a comfortable (or self-indulgent) life. **Anisi,** v. please, cheer, give pleasure to, indulge, gratify desires of. **Anisi,** a. pleasing, luxurious, &c. **Taanasa,** v. seek pleasure, live luxuriously, also as n. same as *anasa*, n. **Taanisi,** v. same as *anisi*, v. (Cf. *raha, furaha, ridhisha, pendeza.* Ar. انس.)

Andaa, v. prepare, put in order, arrange, esp. of preparing food, cakes, &c. Prep. **Andalia,** prepare for (with, in, &c.). *Aliniandalia chakula,* he prepared food for me. *Tuliandalia vita* (*matata, kazi,* &c.), we prepared for war (trouble, work, &c.). Stc. **Andama,** follow in order, accompany, follow up, be next in order, succeed in order. *Mwezi umeandama,* the new moon has followed on, has begun. Prep. **Andamia,** follow after (for, with, &c.). Cs. **Andamiza.** Rp. **Andamana,** follow one another in order, go in procession, e.g. *andamana na,* associate with, follow about, be companion to. *Yeye si mtu wa kuandamana naye,* he is not a fit person to associate with. **Andamano,** n. *ma-* (often used in the plur.) a following in order, of people, events, &c., a train, procession, retinue, &c. **Andamizi,** n. *ma-* usu. in the plur., see below. **-andamo,** a. following, succeeding. *Mwezi mwandamo,* the new moon, i.e. the moon following on. **Andao,** n. *ma-* preparations, arrangements. *Andao la maiti,* arrangements of a corpse for burial, funeral arrangements. **Andazi,** n. *ma-* usu. in the plur. confectionery, pastry, &c., various kinds are: *bumunda, ladu, kitumbua, mkate wa kumimina,* (*wa kuchapa, wa sinia, wa tambi, wa mofa,* &c.). **Maandalio,** n. plur. preparations, esp. of food, cooking and serving a meal. **Maandamano,** n. plur., **Maandamizi,** n. plur. a following in order, procession, train, &c. **Mwandaliaji,** n. *wa-* one who arranges, sets in order, hence a servant who sets table, &c. **Mwandamano,** n. *mi-* a following in order, procession, retinue, &c. **Mwandamizi,** n. wa- (1) a follower, attendant; (2) a successor, one who follows next. **Mwandamo,** n. *mi-* act, time, manner, &c., of following, a coming after, &c. *Mwandamo wa mwezi,* the beginning of a month. **Mwandani,** n. *wa-* companion, friend, associate. **Mwandao,** n. *mi-* same as *andao*, n. **Mwandazi,** n. *wa-* (1) a pastry cook, confectioner; (2) a servant who prepares the table or plates, &c., for a meal. **Uandamo,** n., **Uandamizi,** n. a following, a procession. (Cf. *panga, ratibu, tengeneza, fuata,* and *andika,* following, which is apparently derived from the same stem, *anda,* not now in use.)

Andika, v. (cf. prec. which is apparently from the same stem) (1) set in order, lay out, arrange, like *andaa,* which see. *Andika meza,* set a table. (2) write, e.g. *andika barua* (*hati, kitabu, tangazo,* &c.), write a letter (document, book, notice, &c.); (3) register, enrol, enter in a book, &c. *Andika watu wa kazi* (*askari, wapagazi,* &c.), enrol workmen (soldiers, porters, &c.); (4) draw. *Andika picha* (*mstari*), draw a picture (line). Ps. **Andikwa,** be written, enrolled, registered, arranged, &c. *Limeandikwa,* kismet, said of something which cannot be avoided, it is fated. Rp. and Pot. **Andikana,** (1) be possible to be written down; (2) used of workmen, porters, &c., engaging themselves together, i.e. at the same time; (3) write down each other, as of a headman, recruiting from his own tribe, friends. Cs. **Andikanya,** arrange in piles, one on the other

Prep. **Andikia,** lay a table for a meal, wait at table, write to (for, with, &c.), *Nilimwandikia barua,* I wrote a letter to (or for) him. St. and Pot. **Andikika.** Rp. of Prep. **Andikiana,** write to (or for) each other, correspond with each other. Cs. **Andikisha,** (1) cause to write, dictate; (2) cause a meal to be laid, cause to be set in order, &c. Ps. of Prep. **Andikiwa,** be written or arranged for (to, &c.), *Nimeandikiwa barua,* I have had a letter written to (or for) me. **Andiko,** n. *ma-* usu. in the plur. (1) something written, a book, document, letter, &c. *Maandiko Matakatifu,* the Holy Scriptures. (2) a setting in order, putting ready. **Maandiko,** n. plur. place, time, manner of writing, putting in order, preparation, esp. of serving meals. **Maandishi,** n. plur. like *maandiko,* but esp. the style of arranging or writing. *Maandishi yake ni mabaya,* his style of writing is bad. **Mwandikaji,** n. *wa-*, **Mwandiki,** n. *wa-* (1) one who arranges, serves, waits at table, a waiter; (2) a writer, copyist, amanuensis, clerk. **Mwandiko,** n. *mi-* (1) act or style of writing; (2) what is written, but this is generally *maandiko*; (3) arrangements. *Mwandiko wa chapa,* print script. *Mwandiko wa michoro,* cursive writing. **Mwandishi,** n. *wa-*, same as *mwandikaji,* but sometimes bears an intensive meaning, e.g. a good writer, an expert clerk.

Anga, n. (1) light, brightness, lustre (but this is usu. *mwanga* or *mwangaza,* see below); (2) upper air, sky, bright expanse of the atmosphere; (3) fig. enlightenment, illumination, inspiration. *Ndege wa anga,* birds of the air. *Anga la jua,* sunshine. **Angaa,** v. (1) shine, be bright; (2) fix the eyes upon an object. Prep. **Angalia,** (1) pay attention (to), look at, observe, notice; (2) be careful, beware (of), take care. *Angalia!* (Imp.) Behold! Observe! Take care! Take special note! Ps. **Angaliwa,** Cs. **Angaza,** (1) be light, give light, shine. *Mwezi huangaza dunia usiku,* the moon shines on the world at night. (2) Inten. look intently (at), fix attention (on). Sometimes with *macho,* e.g. *angaza macho,* fix the eyes on. (3) remain awake and keep watch at night. *Niliangaza usiku kucha,* I kept awake the whole night. (4) fig. enlighten, throw light on, instruct. Prep. of Cs. **Angazia,** e.g. *Mbona umeniangazia macho?* Why are you looking at me so intently? **-anga,** a. clear, shining. *Maji maanga,* clear, transparent water, but usu. *-angavu.* **-angalifu,** a. careful, observant, attentive. **-angavu,** a. (1) bright, shining, luminous, radiant, polished, &c.; (2) transparent, clear, as of water, &c.; (3) fig. enlightened, clever, quick-witted. **Kianga,** n. *vi-* a burst of light or sunshine, ray of light, reflected brightness, interval of brightness or fine weather. **Kiangaza macho,** n. *vi-* a present given for finding something which was lost, lit. an eye-brightener (cf. *utotole*). **Kiangazi,** n. the season, i.e. when the sun is strongest between the rainy seasons. **Mwanga,** n. *mi-* (1) a light, shining, that which gives light. *Mwanga wa jua (taa, moto,* &c.), the light of the sun (lamp, fire, &c.). (2) *wa-* a clever, enlightened, bright-witted person. **Mwangalizi,** n. *wa-* (1) a careful, observant person; (2) caretaker, guardian. **Mwangavu,** n. *wa-* a clever, enlightened, intellectual, bright-witted person. **Mwangaza,** n. *mi-* (1) light, brightness, clearness, &c. *Mwangaza wa taa,* the light of a lamp. (2) a hole admitting light, an aperture, small window, loophole; (3) fig. enlightment; (4) publicity, making known, showing, advertising, &c. *Jambo hili li katika mwangaza,* this matter is open to all, public property. (5) way of escape, ruse, bright idea, &c., *Nilikuwa* *katika shida nikapata mwangaza,* I was in difficulty and I discovered a way out. **Mwangazi,** n. *wa-* a clever, informed person, one who informs others, one capable of throwing light on a matter or with a flair for finding ways out of difficulties, &c. **Uangalifu,** n. carefulness, attention. **Uangalizi,** n. *ma-* often used in the plur. *maangalizi,* charge, notice, observation. **Uangavu,** n. (and sometimes *wangavu*), brightness, lustre, glow, transparency, &c., and fig. intelligence. **Ulanga,** n. mica. (Cf. *ng'aa, ng'ariza.*)

Anga, v. (1) be suspended, float in the air—rarely used with this meaning; (2) bewitch, use witchcraft, probably because of the power of levitation ascribed to a type of wizards and witches. They are said to be able to pass through the air, and also cause corpses to leave their graves, and people leave their beds when asleep and float in the air from their houses. Stc. **Angama,** be suspended, be in mid-air, hang. *Aliangama mtini,* he was caught and remained suspended in the tree, i.e. in mid-air. St. and Pot. **Angika,** hang up, hang, suspend, esp. against a wall, on a peg, hook, or branch. Cv. **Angua,** (1) let fall, drop, take down, throw down. *Angua nazi* (*embe,* &c.), throw down coco-nuts (mangoes, &c.). (2) Fig. pass into a state of, fall into, as of laughing, weeping, &c. *Wote waliangua kicheko,* they all burst out laughing. *Waliangua kilio,* they burst out crying. Ps. **Anguliwa,** be knocked down, be taken down from suspended position. St. **Anguka,** (1) fall down, fall, drop, have a downward tendency, direction; (2) fig. be ruined, meet with disaster; (3) befall, happen. Prep. **Angukia,** (1) fall down into (on, before, &c.); (2) come upon, fall in with. *Walimwangukia miguu,* they fell at his feet, i.e. submitted to him. *Kuangukiwa na msiba,* to be overtaken by a misfortune. Cs. **Angusha,** (1) fell, throw down violently; (2) bring to ruin, overthrow, send as a blow. *Mungu alimwangushia mabaya,* God sent down misfortunes upon him. **Angamo,** n. *ma-* condition of being in suspense, of being hung up, suspended. **Anguko,** n. *ma-* often used in the plur. *maanguko,* (1) a fall, drop, downward movement, &c.; (2) ruin; (3) something fallen, a ruin. *Maanguko ya maji,* a waterfall. **Chango,** n. *vya-* a peg, rail, hook, anything on which to suspend something. **Kiango,** n. *vi-* a small frame or bracket hung against a wall to carry a lamp, &c., lamp-stand, lamp-holder, &c. **Mwanga,** n. *wa-* a wizard, sorcerer (see *uanga,* below). **Mwango,** n. *mi* (1) amplic. of *kiango*; (2) also sometimes heard for *mlango,* which see. **Mwangushi,** n. *wa-*, **Mwanguzi,** n. *wa-* one who throws down, overthrows, or causes to fall (destroy, ruin, &c.). *Mwangushi wa nazi,* one who picks coco-nuts as a livelihood (but this is usu. *mkwezi*). **Uanga,** n. the cult of a society of night masqueraders called *waanga* (sing. *mwanga*) believed by some to be magicians and cannibals, who cause the death of their relations or enemies by witchcraft. After the victim has been buried they disinter the body at night by striking the grave with a magic wand, which causes it to open. After the corpse has been removed it closes again. A feast is then made of the corpse. According to another version of the superstition, the corpse is spirited away before it is placed in the grave wrappings and a dummy substituted. (Cf. *mchawi, mlozi, poromoka, tundika.*)

-anga, a., **Angaa,** v. See under **Anga,** n.

Angaika, v. See **Hangaika.**

Angalia, v., **-angalifu,** a. See under **Anga,** n.

Angama, v. See under **Anga, v.**

Angamia, v. be destroyed, be utterly vanquished, perish. *Watu wengi waliangamia vitani,* many people perished in the war. Cs. **Angamiza,** (1) destroy, vanquish, utterly defeat; (2) also used of property, ruin, waste. **Mwangamizi,** n. *wa-* a destroyer, one who ruins either life or property. **Maangamizi,** n. plur. that which causes ruin, misfortune, &c. **Maangamizo,** n. plur. accident, calamity, destruction, death. **Uangamizi,** n. *ma-* often used in the plur. (1) that which causes ruin, &c.; (2) ruin, destruction, collapse.

Angamo, n. *ma-*. See under **Anga, v.**

Angao, adv. and conj. sometimes **Angalao,** even though, even if, although, e.g. *nipatie tumbako, angao ni kidogo,* get me some tobacco, even though it be only a small quantity. (Cf. *hata, kama, ingawa.*)

-angavu, a., **Angaza, v.** See under **Anga,** n.

Angika, v. See under **Anga, v.**

-angu, a. the invariable part of Poss. Pron. 1 Pers. Sing., my, mine, of me.

Angua, v. (1) see under **Anga, v.**; (2) hatch, *angua mayai,* hatch out eggs. Ps. **Anguliwa.** *Yai moja limeanguliwa,* one egg has been hatched out.

Anguka, v., **Anguko,** n. *ma-*, **Angusha,** v. See under **Anga, v.**

Ania,* v. (1) intend, resolve, desire, have in mind; (2) speak on behalf of, defend, argue for. (Cf. *tetea, gombania, kusudi, azimu,* and *nuia.* Ar. نوى.)

Anika, v. set out to dry or air, expose to sun or air. *Anika nguo (mablanketi, mchele,* &c.), set out clothing (blankets, rice, &c.) in the sun or air. Ps. **Anikwa.** Prep. **Anikia.** Cs. **Anikisha.** Cv. **Anua,** take out of the sun, air, rain, &c. Prep. **Anulia.** Ps. **Anuliwa.** St. **Anuka,** be taken out of the sun, rain, air, &c. but more usually used of the weather clearing up, e.g. *kumeanuka sasa,* it has now stopped raining, it is fine again, the clouds have cleared away. (Cf. *tanda* and derivatives.)

Anisi,* v. and a. See under **Anasa;** and dist. *hanithi.*

Anjili,* n. See **Injili.**

Ankra,* n. invoice, account, bill of sale, reckoning, used in commerce. (Cf. *orodha, hesabu.* Hind. انك.)

Anna,* n. one-sixteenth of a rupee, the coinage of India. Value 4 pice, or 12 pies, i.e. one penny. (Hind. انا.)

Anua, v. See under **Anika.**

Anwani,* n. address of a letter. *Andika anwani ya barua,* write the address of a letter. (Ar. عنوان.)

Anza, v. begin, commence, start, be at the beginning, be the first. *Anza mwanzoni,* begin at the beginning. *Anza kazi,* begin work. *Anza kusema,* begin to speak. Inf. **Kwanza** (for *ku-anza*), adv. and *ya kwanza,* first, firstly, in the first place, to begin with. *-a kwanza,* first. *Mtu wa kwanza,* the first man. *Ngoja kwanza,* wait a little, just a moment. Ps. **Anzwa.** St. **Anzika.** Prep. **Anzia,** begin at (in, for, with, &c.). Cs. **Anzisha,** cause to begin, set in motion, set on foot, institute, start, &c. Cs. of D. Prep. **Anzilisha, Anziliza,** sometimes used as Inten. of special earnestness, effort or occasion. Ps. of Cs. **Anzishwa,** be started, be set in motion, be set on foot, &c. **Chanzo,** n. *vya-* (1) the beginning of something, a start, a first step, source, origin; (2) a first principle, ground, reason. **Mwanzo,** n. *mi-* act, time, method of beginning, start, commencement, first stage, source, origin, primary principle. *Kitabu cha Mwanzo,* the book of Genesis. *Mwanzo mpaka mwisho,* from the first to the last, from beginning to end. *Mwanzoni,* in the beginning, at the first, at first. (Cf. *tangulia, takadamu, zindika, asili.*)

Anzali,* n. an abject, despised person. (Cf. *mnyonge*. Ar. نذل.)

Anzwani,* n. Johanna Island, one of the Comoro group. (? a locative from Pers. انجو an island.)

-ao, a. the invariable part of Poss. Pron. 3 Pers. Plur., their, theirs.

Apa, v. take an oath, swear a formal oath. *Apa Kurani*, swear by the Koran. *Apa yamini*, swear by the right hand (a solemn oath, sworn with the right hand on the Koran). Prep. **Apia,** swear to (about, with, in, &c.). Cs. **Apisha,** and rarely **Afya,** cause to swear, put on oath, administer an oath to, adjure. Cs. (2) **Apiza,** usually has an Inten. meaning, swear at, curse. Rp. **Apizana,** curse each other. Cv. **Apua,** retract an oath, rarely used except in the phrase, *kuapa na kuapua*, vowing and then retracting. Rp. of Prep. **Apiana,** take an oath together, join in swearing. **Apizo,** n. *ma-* a curse, imprecation, often used in the plur. **Kiapo,** n. *vi-* (1) an oath, a trial by oath or by ordeal. *Fanya* (*apa, kula*) *kiapo*, take an oath. *Lisha* (*apisha*) *kiapo*, administer an oath. *Kula kiapo*, submit to an ordeal. (2) a charm, used as a protection against theft in plantations, &c. Various kinds of ordeals are: *kiapo cha moto, cha mkate, cha sindano, cha mibano* or *mawano, cha mchele, cha kibao, cha mwavi, cha kago*. **Mwapaji,** n. *wa-* one who swears on oath. **Mwapishi,** n. *wa-* one who administers an oath. **Mwapizi,** n. *wa-* one given to cursing. **Uapo,** n. (*nyapo*), a swearing, an oath, usu. in the sense of an oath imposed upon oneself.

Aprili,* n. April. (Eng.)

Apua, v. See under **Apa.**

Arabu,* n. used in *Bara Arabu*, Arabia, also **Uarabu.**

Arabuni,* n. a deposit paid on an article in advance as a guarantee. Ar. عربون.)

Araka,* n. arrack, used of any intoxicating liquor. (Ar. عرق, distilled spirits.)

Ardhi,* n. soil, ground, earth, dry land as opposed to sea. (Cf. *udongo, nchi*. Ar. ارض.)

Ari,* n. disgrace, shame, reproach, dishonour, a thing to make one blush, but usu. effort, trouble, exertion, &c., expended to avoid shame or disgrace, to keep one's reputation, not to be thought lazy, incompetent, mean, lacking in hospitality, &c. *Kazi ilikuwa kama kwamba itanishinda, lakini nilifanya ari*, it seemed as though the work would prove too much for me, but I made a special effort (so as not to be shamed by being thought incompetent, or lacking in strength, &c.). Often used of eagerness to return hospitality equal to that received, or play a return game (i.e. football, &c.). (Cf. *ghera*. Ar. عار.)

Aria,* n. part, section, party, following—rarely heard. (Prob. a corruption of *raia*, which see.)

Aridhia,* v. explain, inform, set before, e.g. *aliniaridhia maneno*, he placed the matter before me. Ps. **Aridhiwa.** St. **Aridhika.** (Cf. *arifu, eleza*. Ar. عرض.)

Arifu,* v. inform, tell, but esp. by letter. Ps. **Arifiwa.** Prep. **Arifia. Arifu,** a. well-informed, ingenious, knowing. **Maarifa,** n. (1) knowledge, intelligence, information, news; (2) a plan, means of getting over a difficulty, &c. *Tulikuwa karibu kushindwa, tukafanya maarifa*, we were just about beaten, but we made a suitable plan, and found a way out of the difficulty. **Maarufu,** a. well-known, known, celebrated, famous, well-informed. **Taarifa,** n. **Taarifu,** n. a report, either written or spoken. (Ar. عرف.)

Aroba,* n. and a. four, for the common *nne*. Chiefly used in conjunction with some other Arabic numeral, e.g. **Arobatashara,** fourteen. **Arobaishirini** (for *aroba-u-ishirini*) twenty-four. **Aroba mia,** four hundred. **Aroba elfu,** four thousand. **Arobaini,** forty, *-a arobaini*, &c. fortieth, &c. *Arobaini* is also used of the period of forty days after a woman has given birth, during which period she is considered to be unclean. She usually remains in the house and does not perform her customary household duties until she has been purified. (Cf. *eua, takasa*. Ar. اربعة.)

Arobaini,* n. and a., **Arobaishirini,** n. and a., **Arobatashara,** n. and a. See under **Aroba.**

Arusi,* n. (1) nuptials, wedding, both of the ceremony and the feast; (2) the bride and bridegroom are also referred to as *arusi*, but they are also called *bibi arusi*, the bride, and *bwana arusi*, the bridegroom. *Arusi imejibu*, see under **Kisarawanda.** (Cf. *nikahi, ndoa*. Ar. عرس.)

Asa,* v. forbid, warn. (Ar. اصاء admonishing, counselling.)

Asaa,* conj. if, e.g. *asaa Mungu akinijalia*, if God grants me—rarely used. (Cf. *kama, ikiwa, iwapo*. Ar. عس.)

Asali,* n. honey, syrup. *Asali ya nyuki*, bees' honey. *Asali ya miwa*, syrup from the sugar-canes, treacle, molasses. *Asali ya tembo*, made by boiling palm wine. (Cf. *uki*, for bees' honey. Ar. عسل.)

Asante,* used as an expression of thanks, gratitude, approval, &c. Thank you. Frequently the Bantu words *vyema, vema*, and *vizuri* are used with this sense. (Ar. احسنت.)

Asha, v. See under **Aka,** v.

Ashakum,* a word used before mentioning something not usually mentioned, e.g. vulgar, or shameful, to ask pardon for doing so. Pardon me for what I am about to say. (Ar. حاشاكم without offence to you.)

Ashara,* n. and a. ten, rarely used except in the Arabic numerals, *edashara*, eleven; *thenashara*, twelve; *thelatashara*, thirteen, &c. (Ar. عشرة.)

Ashekali,* a. better (of health, after sickness), fit, improved in health. *Pata ashekali*, get better. *Najiona ashekali leo*, I feel (myself) better to-day. (Cf. *ahueni, sijambo, hujambo*, Ar. اشكل.)

Asherati,* n. dissipation, profligacy, debauchery, but usually adultery, fornication. *-a asherati*, dissipated, immoral, &c. **Mwasherati,** n. *wa-* an immoral person, profligate, adulterer, fornicator, &c. **Uasherati,** n. the character, deeds, life, &c., of a profligate, adulterer, immoral person. (Cf. *ufasiki, ufisadi, uzini, upotevu, upotovu*. Ar. اشراة iniquity.)

Asherini,* n. and a. See **Ishirini.**

Ashiki,* v. have a passion for (usually in the sexual sense), be enamoured of, be in love with. **Ashiki,** n. strong desire, affection, wish, fondness, longing, usu. of sexual desire. (Cf. *mahaba, mapenzi, tamaa, uchu, huba*. Ar. عشق.)

Ashiria,* v. signal to, make a sign to (with, for, &c.), indicate by signs (to). Ps. **Ashiriwa. Ishara,** n. (1) a sign, signal, omen, indication, warning, hint; (2) token; (3) a wonder, remarkable thing, fact, &c. *Kufanya (toa) ishara*, like *ashiria*, make a signal. **Taashira,** n. same as *ishara*. (Cf. *onya, konyeza, dalili*. Ar. اشار.)

Asi,* v. (1) disobey, fail to carry out instructions; (2) fail to carry out duties or obligations; (3) rebel (against), mutiny. Ps. **Asiwa.** Prep. **Asia,** rebel against (at, on account of, &c.). Cs. **Asisha,** cause to rebel, incite to rebel, abet in disobedience, &c. **Maasi**, n. disobedience, rebellion, mutiny, revolt, desertion, rebelliousness. **Maasum**, and **Mwasi**, n. *wa-* a rebel, disobedient person. **Uasi**, n. same as *maasi* above. (Cf. *halifu*. Ar. عاص.)

Asili,* n. (1) beginning, origin, source, ancestry, family. *Watu wa asili*, aborigines. *Hana asili wala fasili*, he is a nobody, he has neither good family nor standing. (2) nature, inborn temperament. *Yeye asili yake ni mpumbavu*, he is a born fool. (3) essence, fundamental principle, ground, reason. *Asili yake nini hata umefanya hivi?* What was the reason for your doing that? (4) *asili ya sehemu*, a denominator in arithmetic. **Asili**, adv. originally, by nature, in old time. *Sikufanya jambo hilo asili*, I absolutely did not do that, i.e. it is against my nature to do such an action. **Asilia**, a. original, genuine. (Cf. *mwanzo, chanzo*. Ar. اصل.)

Askafu,* n. *ma-*. See **Askofu.**

Askari,* n. soldier, guard, armed attendant. *Askari polisi* (or, *polisi, ma-*), a policeman. *Andika* (*tia, changa*) *askari*, enrol soldiers. *Amrisha askari*, drill soldiers. **Uaskari**, n. profession, pay, &c., of a soldier. (Cf. *rugaruga*. Ar. عسكري.)

Askofu,* n. *ma-* a bishop. (Ar. اسقف.)

Astahili,* n. See under **Stahili.**

Aste,* adv. slowly—chiefly used by workers on cranes, winches, &c. (Hind. آهستے.)

Asuahi,* a. See under **Sahihi.**

Asubuhi,* n. morning. *Asubuhi na mapema*, early in the morning. *Tangu asubuhi hata jioni*, from morning until evening. adv. in the morning. (Ar. صبح with article prefixed. Cf. *sabalkheri, alasiri, alfajiri, adhuhuri, kucha*.)

Asusa,* n. food of any description eaten when drinking beer, spirits, &c., but usu. well-cooked meat. (? Ar. from حسس, put meat on the coals.)

Atamia, v. also **Tamia**, and perh. **Otamia**); (1) sit on eggs, brood (of a hen); (2) bring up, rear, educate, sometimes heard as *latamia*. Cs. **Atamisha**, put eggs under a hen, get a hen to sit on eggs. Ps. **Atamiwa.** (? Prep. of Stc. of *ota*, v. (C)).

Ateri,* n. artery, adopted for use in text-books and school lessons. (Eng.)

Athari,* n. (1) mark, spot; (2) deficiency, blemish; (3) a wound, sore, hurt. **Athiri**, v. hurt, blemish, mar, destroy. (Cf. *haribu, alama, jeraha*. Ar. اثر.)

Ati! also **Eti!** a common int. or expletive expressing surprise, or calling attention. Generally can be translated by 'I say!', as it is from the verb *ti*, say, found in many Bantu languages. *Ati wewe!* I say you! *Niache ati!* leave me alone, I say! *Ati! husema watu ni wapumbavu*, I say! they say that men are fools.

Atibu,* v. blame, reproach, find fault with. Ps. **Atibiwa.** St. **Atibika.** (Cf. *laumu, suta, karipia, aili*. Ar. عتب.)

Atika, v. replant, i.e. take from a nursery and plant out, of young coco-nut-trees, clove-trees, seedlings, &c. (Cf. *pandikiza* under *panda*, v.)

Atikali,* v. understand, estimate, know. (Cf. *fahamu, jua, kisi*. Ar. تعقل.)

Atilika,* v. be injured, deformed, &c., as the result of an accident, illness, &c. (St. from Ar. عطل.)

Atlasi,* n. *nguo ya atlasi*, satin. (Ar. اطلس.)

Atua, v. split, crack, e.g. of splitting logs for firewood, &c. St. **Atuka**, be split. *Nchi imeatuka kwa joto la jua*, the ground is cracked by the heat of the sun (as it does sometimes in the hot dry season). **Mwatuko,**

n. *mi-* a split, as in the earth. (Cf. *chanja, pasua, tema.*)

Au,* conj. or. *Au kwenda au kukaa,* either to go or to remain. (Cf. *ama,* and neg. *wala.* Ar. او.)

Aua, v. (1) survey, view, examine, trace, track out. *Aua shamba,* survey an estate, mark out boundaries of a plantation, &c. *Aua nyayo,* follow up tracks of men or animals. (2) sometimes heard for *eua,* which see. Ps. **Auliwa.** St. **Auka.** *Shamba lote limeauka,* the whole estate has been inspected. Prep. **Aulia,** e.g. *vipande vya kuaulia,* surveying instruments, pegs for marking out a plantation, &c. Cs. **Ausha,** or **Auza,** cause (employ, send) to survey, show about, show the sights of. (Cf. *kagua, angalia, tazamia,* and dist. *eua.*)

Audhubillahi!* int. used as an expletive or int. of impatience, surprise, &c. God preserve us! Botheration! Would you believe it! What next! (Ar. عوذ بالله.)

Auka, v. develop, reach the stage of bearing fruit—seldom heard.

Aula,* a. better, superior, more deserving, fitting. *Kitu hiki ni aula kuliko kile,* this thing is better than that. *Biashara siku hizi ni aula kuliko zamani,* trade is now better than formerly. *Jambo hili ni aula. . . ,* this matter is more important, or better than. . . . Often used in the expression *Si aula,* it is not important, it is nothing. (Ar. اولى.)

Aula,* i.e. *au la,* or not, or otherwise.

Auni,* v. assist, aid, help. **Auni,** n. also **Muawana,** n. aid, help. (Cf. *saidia, msaada, ujima.* Ar. عاون.)

Aunsi,* n. an ounce. (Eng. Cf. *wakia.*)

Auradi,* n. See **Uradi.**

Aushi,* n. and a. See under **Ishi.**

Avya, v. waste, destroy, e.g. *avya fedha* (*mali*) waste money (property). *Avya mimba,* abort, procure abortion. (Cf. *haribu, poteza.*)

Awadha,* v. also **Awaza,** allot, arrange, dispose—seldom heard. The noun **Mwawadhi.** Also **Mwawazi** is a title of God, the Disposer of events. (Cf. *gawa, panga, tengeneza.* Ar. وزع.)

Awali,* n. beginning, start, first place. **Awali,** a. first, and adv. (1) firstly, at first; (2) just, nearly, almost. *Awali ya nchi,* border or boundary of a country, i.e. where it begins, not the whole boundary. *Awali ni awali, awali mbovu hapana,* a beginning is a beginning, there is no beginning which is bad. *Tangu awali hata aheri,* from beginning to end, from start to finish. *Awali Mungu!* lit. the beginning is God, Here goes! Here's for luck! a workman's rejoinder to the overseer's call of *Kazi!* Work! (Cf. *asili, mwanzo, kwanza.* Ar. اول.)

Awaza,* v. See **Awadha.**

Awini,* v. See **Auni.**

Aya,* n. a short section or division of a book, esp. of the Koran, a paragraph. (Cf. *juzuu.* Ar. آية.)

Ayala,* n. a hart. (Ar. ايل.)

Ayami,* a. *Siku ayami,* many days —seldom used. (Ar. يوم a day.)

Ayari,* n. (1) a knave, rogue, impostor, impudent cheat. (Ar. عيار.) (2) a rope for hoisting a sail, which passes through the pulley at the top of a mast.

Azali,* a. eternal, without beginning. (Ar. ازل.)

Azima,* n. a charm, talisman. **Azimu,** v. prepare a charm. (Cf. *hirizi, kago,* &c., and dist. follg. Ar. عزم.)

Azima, v. borrow or lend. Prep. **Azimia,** borrow for, lend to, &c. **Azimo,** n. *ma-* often used in the plur. anything borrowed, a loan, a debt. **Mwazimo,** n. *mi-* a loan, act of lending or borrowing.

Azimia, v. See under **Azima, v.** and **Azimu, v.**

Azimio,* n. *ma-*. See under **Azimu, v.**

Azimo, n. *ma-*. See under **Azima, v.**

Azimu,* v. (1) See **Azima,** n.; (2) resolve, intend, purpose, decide on, propose. Prep. **Azimia,** used in the same way as *azimu*. **Azima,** n. *ma-*, **Azimio,** n. *ma-* often used in the plur. intention, resolve, purpose, scheme, plans, programme (of work, &c.). (Cf. *kusudia, nuia, nia*. Ar. عزم.)

Aziri,* v. slander, disparage, bring into disrepute. **Izara,** n. disgrace, the result of being disparaged, or being accused. (Cf. *singizia, chongea, masingizio*. Ar. عزر.)

Azizi,* n. a rarity, curiosity, costly thing, treasure. **Azizi,** a. precious, rare, valuable, and of persons, excellent, highborn. (Cf. *tunu, ajabu, thamani, bora*. Ar. عزيز.)

Azur,* n. perjury—rarely heard. See **Zuri,** n. (Ar. زور.)

B

B represents the same sound as in English. In some words *b* is not distinguished from *p* by some natives, probably partly the result of Swahili being written in Arabic script, as Arabic has no *p*, and *b* is usually employed both for the letter *b* and *p*. Therefore words not found under *b* may be looked for under *p*.

Baa,* n. *ma-* (1) evil, disaster, calamity, anything which brings bad luck or disaster; (2) an ill-omened person, one who causes disaster, brings bad luck. (Cf. *shari, msiba, -korofi, kisirani, balaa*. Ar. بلاء calamity.)

Baada,* adv. after, afterwards, only used of time or of sequence of events. **Baada ya,** prep. (1) after, in succession to, &c. *Baada ya salamu nakuarifu*, after greetings I inform you—a common beginning to letters. (2) with *yake*, or its abbreviation *-ye*, as an enclitic, *baadaye*, thereafter, afterwards, then, next. *Nenda baadaye*, go afterwards. **Baidi,** v. be apart, be separate. Cs. **Baidisha,** e.g. *kujibaidisha*, put oneself apart from, avoid. (Cf. *halafu, kisha, ndipo, tenga, epa*. Ar. بعد.)

Baadhi,* n. some, a portion, a section—of something mentioned previously or understood, or a particular portion of a whole or large number. *Baadhi ya watu*, some of the people. Some, unless indicating a particular portion, as a rule is not translated, e.g. *watu wanacheza mpira*, (some) people are playing football. *Baadhi ya watu* (or, *watu wengine*) *wanacheza mpira*, some of the people are playing football (others are not). *Watu wamegawanyika baadhi mbili*, the people are divided into two parties. (Ar. بعض.)

Baathi,* v. also **Buathi,** raise up, seldom heard, and only in the phrase *Siku ya kubaathiwa*, the day of the general resurrection. (Cf. *amka, fufua, kiyama.* Ar. بعث.)

Bab,* n. See **Babu,** n. (C).

Baba, n. (1) father; (2) uncle on the father's side; (3) ancestor; (4) patron, protector, guardian. *Baba mzazi,* is used of actual paternity when necessary to distinguish. Paternal uncles are distinguished as *mkubwa,* if older, and *mdogo,* if younger, than the father. Maternal uncle is *mjomba. Baba wa kambo,* step-father. *Baba wa kupanga,* father by adoption. *Baba ya watoto,* or *babewana,* an owl, considered to be a bird of ill omen, which causes convulsions in a newly born child should it settle on the roof of the house in which the child is lying. (Cf. *babu,* (B).) **Ubaba,** n. the characteristics, condition of a father, paternity, fatherhood.

Baba, v. bind tightly. (Cf. *kaza, funga, kaba.*)

Babaika, v. be confused in one's speech as with fear, in prevaricating; talk meaningless nonsense, as a sick person in delirium, &c. Cs. **Babaisha.** Rp. of Cs. **Babaishana,** confuse each other in speech. **Babaiko,** n. *ma-* foolish, meaningless talk, confused statements. Cf. *gugumiza, bwata, payuka.*)

Babaje, n. a species of large sea slug, bêche-de-mer, also called *kojojo, kojozi,* and *jongoo la pwani.*

Babaka, v. (1) argue, contend (cf. *bisha, kaidi*); (2) see **Babuka** under **Babua.**

Babata, v. tap, strike lightly, as a worker in metal beating metal to make it thin. St. **Babatika.** Cs. **Babatisha.**

Babewatoto, n. also **Babewana,** an owl thought to cause a child to have convulsions should it settle on the roof of a house in which a young child is lying. (Cf. *babu* (B.).)

Babu, n. (A) (1) grandfather; (2) male ancestor.

Babu, n. (B) convulsions of a child, thought to be caused by a cormorant (*mnandi*), or an owl (*babewana,* or *babewatoto*), settling on the roof of the house in which it is lying. Some coast people place a crab on a stick on the roof—this is supposed to prevent the bird from settling there.

Babu,* n. (C) kind, sort, class, used in commerce. *Kitambaa cha babu kuu,* is thicker or twice the width of the usual sort, i.e. *cha babu ndogo.* (Cf. *namna, aina.* Ar. بابة.)

Babua, v. strip off or bruise the skin, as with fire, hot water, or an illness. St. **Babuka,** be disfigured, as by the skin stripping off, or by a skin disease, &c. Prep. **Babulia.** Ps. **Babuliwa.** (Cf. *ambua.*)

Badala,* n. (A) (1) a substitute, thing given in exchange; (2) a person filling the place of another, substitute. *Badala ya,* in place of, instead of. **Badili,** v. change, become changed, exchange (whether by giving or taking interchange), esp. of exchange of goods, i.e. barter. *Badili mali,* barter goods. *Badili fedha,* change money, whether for other coin or for its equivalent. *Badili zamu,* change guard, take an appointed spell of work, &c. *Badili nguo,* change clothes, put on other clothes. Also used in arithmetic for conversion of *£. s. d.,* and for reduction in sums. Ps. **Badiliwa,** be changed, altered. St. and Pot. **Badilika,** change, be changed, be capable of change, be fit for exchange, be liable to change, &c. Prep. **Badilia.** Cs. **Badilisha,** (1) cause to change or be changed; (2) get changed, e.g. *nitabadilisha vitabu hivi,* I shall change these books, i.e. I shall get others for them. Rp. of Cs. **Badilishana,** change with each other, barter—of several people wrangling over a barter, also **Badiliana,** in the same sense. Rd. **Badilibadili,** of frequent, rapid, or vexatious changes. **Badili,** n. *ma-*

(1) change, exchange, alteration, successive change, repetition; (2) same as *badala*, above. **-badilifu,** a. (1) changing, changeable, liable to change; (2) of character, whimsical, shifty, unstable. **Badiliko,** n. *ma-* change of circumstances (condition, customs, &c.). **Ubadili,** n. also **Ubadilifu,** n. change, changeableness, exchange, interchange. (Cf. *geua, pindua.* بدل.)

Badala,* n. (B) the name given to a sect or community of Indians who work in dhows, or get a livelihood by fishing or keeping cattle and goats. (Hind.?)

Badani,* n. the front or back piece of a *kanzu*, sometimes called *kimo*. (Cf. *kanzu.* Ar. بدن body, trunk.)

Badhiri,* v. squander money, waste money or goods. **-badhiri,** and **-badhirifu,** extravagant, prodigal, wasteful. **Budhara,** n. wastefulness in using money, &c. **Mbadhirifu,** n. *wa-* an extravagant person, waster of money or property. **Ubadhiri,** n. and **Ubadhirifu,** n. extravagance, prodigality. (Cf. *upotevu.* Ar. بذر.)

Badili,* v., **-badilifu,** a., **Badiliko,** n. *ma-*, **Badilisha,** v. See under **Badala,** n. (A).

Badiri,* n. applied to various celestial phenomena and omens. (Ar. بدر full moon.)

Bado,* adv. (1) not yet. Frequently used with the *-ja-* not yet tense, e.g. *Hajafanya bado*, he has not yet done it. *Hajafa bado*, he has not yet died. Also with the Infinitive, *shauri hili bado kukatwa*, this matter has not yet been settled, is still undecided; (2) still, e.g. *yumo nyumbani bado*, he is still in the house. *Huyu ni mtoto bado*, he is still a child. *Amelala bado*, he is still asleep. *Watu tisa wamesalia bado*, nine people still remain. *Bado kidogo*, still a little, i.e. soon, presently, not yet, after a while. (Ar. بعد not yet.)

Bafe, n. a kind of venomous snake, a puff-adder.

Bafta,* n. a kind of thin bleached calico, used for lining garments. Different kinds are: *themanini, dondo* (with a lot of dressing in it), *maradufu* (heavy), &c. (Ar. بفتة or Pers. بافته.)

Bagala,* n. a kind of sailing vessel with a large square stern, high poop, and long prow, used in trade with India. Sometimes double masted. (Pers. بغل stem of a ship.)

Baghairi.* See under **Ghairi.**

Baghala,* n. a mule. (Cf. *nyumbu.* Ar. بغل.)

Baghami,* n. a fool. (Cf. *mpumbavu, mjinga.* Ar. بقامة weak of intellect, or بجم simpleton, stupid.)

Bagua, v. separate, put apart, divide off. *Bagua ng'ombe*, used of each man separating his own cattle from the common herd. St. **Baguka,** (1) be separated; (2) be at variance, quarrel. Ps. **Baguliwa.** Rp. **Baguana.** Rp. of St. **Bagukana,** i.e. quarrel among each other, be divided into separate parties or factions. (Cf. *tenga, farakana.*)

Bahameli,* n. velvet. See **Mahameli.**

Bahari,* n. (1) sea, ocean; (2) fig. of what is very extensive, vast, immeasurable. *Elimu ni bahari*, learning is a sea, i.e. a vast subject. *Bahari ya Sham*, the Red Sea. **Baharia,** n. *ma-* a sailor, member of ship's crew—also often applied to a boat-boy. (Ar. بحر.)

Bahasa,* a. cheap. (Cf. *rahisi.* Ar. بخس.)

Bahasha,* n. (— and of size, *ma-*) (1) an envelope; (2) satchel, bag, packet, valise, bundle, roll of blankets, clothes, &c. *Bahasha ya nguo*, a bundle or roll of clothes. (Cf. *furushi, peta.* Turk. بقچه bundle.)

Bahashika,* v. be deceived, be nonplussed, not know what to do. (Cf. *duwaa, pumbaa, fadhaika*. St. from Ar. بخس injure, wrong.)

Bahati,* n. luck—either good or bad—fortune, chance. *Kwa bahati*, by good luck. *Bahati njema (mbaya)*, good (bad) luck. *Asiye na bahati habahatishi*, one who is not fortunate, does not trust to luck. **Bahatisha,** v. trust to luck, guess, speculate, make a venture. Prep. **Bahatishia.** Ps. **Bahatishwa.** (Cf. *kisia, nasibu, sudi*. Pers. بخت.)

Bahili,* n. and a. a miser, parsimonious person; as a. miserly, parsimonious, grasping. Prov. *Mali ya bahili huliwa na wadudu*, a miser's possessions are usually eaten by insects. **Ubahili,** n. miserliness, niggardliness. (Cf. *ukabidhi, choyo, unyimivu, nyiminyimi*. Ar. بخل.)

Baidi,* v. See under **Baada.**

Baina,* n. usu. **Bayana,** clearness, clear knowledge, certainty, clear evidence, explanation. **Baina ya,** prep. between, among. *Ugomvi ulitokea baina ya watu*, a dispute arose among the people. *Baina ya Mombasa na Unguja*, between Mombasa and Zanzibar (cf. *katikati*). **Baini,** v. (1) see clearly, know for certain, distinguish, recognize; (2) make clear, prove, show. St. **Bainika,** be clear, be manifest, be plainly shown. Pot. **Bainikana,** be evident to all, be notorious. Cs. **Bainisha,** make very plain, make clear, demonstrate. Ps. of Cs. **Bainishwa.** **-bainifu,** a. clear, plain, evident, notorious, &c. **Bayana,** n. same as *baina*, above. **Mbayana,** n. *wa-* a well-known or notorious person. **Ubaini, Ubainifu, Ubayana,** n. clearness, demonstrability, notoriety, demonstration, evidence, explanation. (Cf. *dhahiri, wazi, maarufu, julikana, tambulikana*. Ar. بين.)

Baisikeli,* n. a bicycle. The spokes are *tindi, njukuti*, or *henzarani*; the hub, *kinu* or *kikombe*; the mudguards, *bango, ma-*; the ball-bearings, *gololi*; the chain, *mnyororo*; handlebars, *usukani*; outer cover of tire, *mpira wa nje*; inner tube, *mpira wa ndani*; frame, *farasi*. (Eng. bicycle.)

Bajia,* n. a small cake of ground beans and pepper. (Hind. بهجيا.)

Bajuni, n. *ma-* a native of the coast north of Mombasa.

Baka,* n. *ma-* mark on the body, birth-mark, scar, ringworm; also used of marks on animals, i.e. of colour. (Cf. *paku, bato, doa*. Ar. بقع.)

Baki,* v. remain, be left over, stay behind. *Wao walikwenda, mimi nilibaki*, they went, I remained behind. Prep. **Bakia,** remain over to (for, in, &c.). Cs. **Bakisha,** and **Bakiza,** leave behind, cause to remain. Prep. of Cs. **Bakizia,** *nibakizie kidogo*, leave a little for me. **Baki,** n. *ma-* (1) that which remains over, remainder, residue; (2) in arithmetic, that which remains after subtraction, difference, balance in accounting. *Mtu baki*, a neutral person, i.e. in a quarrel, argument, guild, club, &c. (Cf. *saa, sazo*. Ar. بقي.)

Bakora,* n. (1) a walking-stick, formerly one with a crooked handle made of *mkwaju* or *mtobwe*; (2) a stroke with a stick, *alipigwa bakora kumi*, he received ten strokes with a stick; (3) a gift given by a father to a master when placing his son with him to learn a trade. (Cf. *ufito, kigongo, kibarango, rungu, mkongojo, mpweke, kipiki, fimbo*. Ar. بقارى a cudgel.)

Bakshishi,* n. gratuity, gift, dole, tip. (Pers. بخشيش.)

Bakua, v. sometimes heard for *bakwia*, which see.

Bakuli,* n. (— and of size, *ma-*) a basin, any large deep dish. (Ar. باقول.)

Bakwia, v. take away by force, rob. (Cf. *bakua, bekua, pokonya, kwepua.*)

Balaa,* n. trouble, difficulty, damage, grief, calamity, a plague, pest. *Mwaka huu una balaa ya panya,* there is a plague of rats this year. *Mtoto huyu balaa sana,* this child is very troublesome, naughty. (Cf. *baa.* Ar. بلا.)

Balamwezi, n. See **Mbalamwezi.**

Balanga,* n. See **Mbalanga.**

Balari,* n. a kind of chisel. (? Pers. فولاد steel.)

Balasi,* n. *ma-* (1) a large jar with a narrow neck, usu. used for storing water (cf. *kasiki, nzio, gudulia.* Ar. بلاصي); (2) see **Barasi.**

Balehe,* v. (1) come to (sexual) maturity, become of marriageable age, reach the age of puberty; (2) of plants and trees, &c., reach the stage of bearing fruit. **Balehe,** n. *ma-*, **Mbalehe,** *wa-* a boy or girl who has reached puberty. **Ubalehe,** n. puberty, marriageable age, adult state. (Cf. *komaa, pevuka, -pevu, utu uzima.* Ar. بلغ.)

Bali,* conj. but, on the contrary, used of contrast. (Cf. *lakini, ila.* Ar. بل.)

Bali,* n. an ear-ring. (Cf. *kipuli.* Hind. بالي.)

Balozi,* n. *ma-* a consul, political agent; in some places a District Commissioner, Administrator. **Ubalozi,** n. status, work, position, salary, &c., of a consul. (Turk.? through Ar. باليوس.)

Balungi,* n. *ma-* (1) the fruit of the *mbalungi,* pomelo, shaddock, citrus decumana; (2) grapefruit. (Pers. بالنگو citron.)

Bamba, n. (A) counsel, case, affair—not often heard, *shauri* is the usual word. Prov. *Bamba na waume ni bamba; hakuna bamba la mume,* counsel of a number of men is counsel; there is no counsel of one man (alone).

Bamba, n. (B) *ma-* (1) a flat thin piece of anything, such as metal, cardboard, millboard, corrugated iron, plate or sheet of metal, &c. *Bamba la ng'amba,* shell of a tortoise. *Bamba la chuma,* hoop-iron. (2) in some places, used to denote a tin, such as is used for petrol, kerosene, &c., elsewhere called *debe*; and also for corrugated iron, elsewhere called *bati.* **Mbamba,** n. *mi-* sometimes used for a shovel, dustpan, or similar utensil. **Bambo,** n. *ma-* (1) an iron instrument grooved and pointed, used for drawing samples of rice, &c., from a sack; (2) a long strip of plaited grass (leaves of the *mwaa*) used for making coarse mats, baskets, &c., and for cording native bedsteads. **Ubamba,** n. (*bamba*) same as *bamba,* n. **Ubambo,** n. *ma-* same as *bambo,* n. (Cf. *ukambaa,* also *-embamba, bati, debe.*)

Bamba, v. arrest, catch, hold. Ps. **Bambwa.** (1) be arrested. *Tumebambwa na polisi,* we have been arrested by the police. (2) show fight, be firm in demanding one's rights. Cv. **Bambua,** strip off, peel off. St. **Bambuka,** be stripped or peeled off. (Cf. *ambua.*)

Bambika, v. steep in water. (Cf. *chovya, loweka.*)

Bambo, n. *ma-.* See under **Bamba,** n. (B.)

Bambua, v. See under **Bamba, v.**

Bamia,* n. *ma-* Okra, lady's fingers, the fruit of the *mbamia, Hibiscus esculentus*; when unripe the pods are used as a vegetable. (Cf. *binda.* Pers. and Ar. باميا.)

Bamvua, n. spring tide. (Cf. *maji makuu.*)

Bana, v. (1) press, squeeze, pinch, hold as in a vice or tweezers, &c.; (2) also in Intrans. sense, stick fast, jam. St. **Banika,** (1) be fixed—usu. of meat, fish, &c., fixed between two sticks for roasting at a fire; (2) also Trans. set to roast at a fire. Prep. **Bania,** press to (with, in, &c.),

jibania nguo, gird up one's clothes as for work, a journey, &c. Ps. **Banwa.** Cs. **Banza,** (1) *jibanza ukutani,* squeeze oneself up against a wall, as for allowing a person to pass; (2) *jibanza,* fig. skulk, lurk, hide oneself. Rp. **Banana.** Cv. **Banua,** loosen, unfasten, slacken pressure, &c. **Bano,** n. *ma-* (1) anything used for applying pressure, or for holding in position by pressure, a carpenter's cramp, &c.; (2) act or condition of being pressed, cramped, &c. **Banzi,** n. *ma-* a spit, for roasting fish or meat on. **Kibano,** n. *vi-* small forceps, split stick, see *kibanzi,* follg. **Kibanzi,** n. *vi-* a splinter, chip. *Kibanzi cha ukuni,* a splinter of firewood. *Vibanzi vya shoka,* chips made when cutting with an axe. **Mbano,** n. *mi-* (1) act of applying pressure, of squeezing, &c.; (2) any instrument for grasping, holding, applying pressure, forceps, hand vice, stick split at the end, &c. (Cf. *kaza, songa, mentari, gandamiza.*)

Banada,* n. also **Banaderi,** the coastal ports north of Mombasa, esp. Barawa, Marka, Mogadishu. (Cf. *bandari.*)

Banagiri,* n., **Banajili,** n. See **Bangili.**

Banda, n. *ma-* a large shed (usu. without walls), a workshop, &c. *Banda la farasi,* a stable. *Banda la motakaa,* a garage. **Kibanda,** n. *vi-* a small hut, shed, workshop, a hovel.

Bandama, n. the spleen. (Cf. *wengu.*)

Bandari,* n. a harbour, roadstead, port. (Pers. بندر a port.)

Bandera,* n. See **Bendera.**

Bandi, n. *ma-* stitching, a row of stitches, a stitch, esp. of the coarser kinds of sewing. *Fanya (piga, shona) bandi,* baste, tack, run (in sewing). *Piga bandi, halafu kupiga jongo nene,* run and fell a seam. (Cf. *shikizo, ponta, shulu,* and *shona.* Prob. from same root as *bandika.*)

Bandia,* n. a doll. *Mtoto wa bandia,* a doll, sometimes made from a cucumber (*tango*) and plaited grass or cloth, &c. (Cf. *mwanasesere.* ? from Ar. بنات the plural of *bint,* girls.)

Bandika, v. (St. of Dir. form **Banda,** not now in use), (1) put on, stick on, fasten on, apply, attach, esp. of causing something to adhere to a surface. *Bandika tikiti ya posta,* stick a postage stamp on. *Bandika dawa,* apply medicine, plaster. *Amejibandika mzigo,* he has loaded himself with a load. (2) fig. be attached to a person, follow him about, &c. *Amejibandika kwa fulani,* he has attached himself to so-and-so, i.e. never leaves him. Ps. **Bandikwa.** Prep. **Bandikia.** Cs. **Bandikisha,** and **Bandikiza,** like *bandika,* also in an Inten. sense, i.e. put on something extra, add something to a load, &c. Cv. of Dir. form, **Bandua,** take off, detach, remove, strip off, peel off, relieve of. St. **Banduka.** *Magome ya mti yamebanduka,* the bark has stripped off the tree. *Mkia wa nyani haumbanduki nyani,* the ape's tail never becomes detached from an ape, i.e. an ape's habits never change. Rp. and Pot. of Cv. **Bandukana,** i.e. *Fulani na fulani hawabandukani,* So-and-so and so-and-so never leave each other (are great friends). Prep. **Bandulia.** Ps. **Banduliwa. Mbandiko,** n. *mi-* (1) the act of putting or sticking something on, an application; (2) anything stuck on, i.e. a plaster, &c. **Mbanduko,** n. *mi-* a taking off, removing, a stripping off (of a plaster, &c.).

Bandu, n. descriptive of the noise made when cutting with an axe.

Bandua, v., **Banduka,** v. See under **Bandika.**

Banduru,* n. bilge, place in ship's hold from which water is baled out, ship's well. (Cf. *ngama.* ? Pers. بن bottom, and دور remote.)

Bange, n. a kind of fish, not considered good eating by most Europeans.

Bangi,* n. bhang, the leaf of *mbangi*, i.e. Indian hemp (*Cannabis sativa*) often chewed or smoked, and used in various sweet preparations, a strong intoxicant. (Cf. *mbangi, paru, boza, majuni, afyuni*. Pers. بنگ.)

Bangili,* n. a bangle, armlet, bracelet. (Cf. *kikuku*. Hind. بنگری.)

Bango, n. *ma-* mudguard of a cycle or motor-car, &c.

Banguzi, n. *ma-* a large ulcer or sore. (Cf. *donda*.)

Bania, v., **Banika,** v. See under **Bana.**

Banja, v. crack, break, e.g. a nut, &c. Ps. **Banjwa.** Prep. **Banjia.** St. and Pot. **Banjika. Mbanjo,** n. *mi-* a breaking, cracking.

Bano, n. *ma-*, **Banua,** v. See under **Bana.**

Banyani,* n. *ma-* a Banyan, an Indian who is a follower of Brahma, i.e. neither a Christian nor a Muhammadan—they are usually small retail tradesmen, or craftsmen, such as carpenters, tinsmiths, barbers, &c. (Hind. بنیا.)

Banza, v., **Banzi,** n. *ma-*. See under **Bana.**

Bao, n. *ma-* (1) a large board usually of a special kind or for a special purpose, e.g. a bench or table; and also (2) a playing-board, for chess, draughts, cards, but most commonly for the game *bao*, or *bao la mtaji*, like a chess-board with 64 (sometimes 32) holes for squares, and seeds or pebbles for counters. *Cheza bao*, play the *bao* game. Hence *bao* is also used of (3) a game generally, or victory in a game, e.g. a goal at football. *Tuliwafunga* (or *tuliwatia*) *mabao sita*, we scored six goals. (4) a diviner's board, esp. *bao la mchanga*, a board covered with sand, also called *ramli* (which see), and *kibunzi*. *Piga bao*, or *tazamia bao*, consult a divining board, take the omens. **Ubao,** n. (*mbao*) (1) a board, plank, cut timber; (2) a teacher's blackboard. *Pasua mbao*, saw planks. **Kibao,** n. *vi-* (1) a small board, shelf, &c.; (2) a slate, such as is used in school; (3) a card for winding thread or wool on, *uzi wa kibao*, a card of thread. **Kimbaombao,** n. (1) *vi-* used as a nickname for a tall thin person; (2) a chameleon, also called *kigeugeu, kinyonga, lumbwi*. (? Port. *pao*, or perh. from *pao*. See under **Paa,** v. (A).)

Bapa, n. *ma-* used of a broad, flat, or slightly rounded surface, e.g. *bapa la upanga*, the flat blade of a sword, the flat as opp. to the sharp edge (*makali*). *Bapa la uso*, broad forehead or broad cheek (face). *Bapa la kisu*, knife blade. **Ubapa,** n. (*bapa*) (1) same as *bapa*; (2) flatness.

Bara,* n. (1) land in general, as opp. to sea; (2) the hinterland when referred to by coast-dwelling natives, the mainland generally when referred to by island-dwelling people, i.e. those living in Zanzibar. *Pwani na bara*, the coast and the hinterland. (3) a country, large tract of land, e.g. *Bara Arabu*, Arabia; *Bara Hindi*, India. **Barabara,** n. a highway, a broad road, as dist. from a forest path, or narrow road. (Ar. بر.)

Baraba,* a. and adv. also **Barabara,** just as it should be, quite right, exact, proper, without a flaw. *Fanya kazi barabara*, do work well, correctly, just as it should be done. *Fedha hii ni barabara*, this is the exact amount of money. *Saa sita barabara*, exactly at noon. (Pers. برابر.)

Barabara,* n. (1) see under **Bara,** n.; (2) a. and adv. see under **Baraba.**

Baradhuli,* n. a simpleton, dupe, dull-witted person. **Ubaradhuli,** n. foolishness, simpleness, being easily duped. *Ujinga wa kuuza si ubaradhuli wa kununua*, being foolish in selling is better than being duped in buying. (Cf. *mjinga, mpumbavu, mzuzu*. Ar. برزل.)

Barafu,* n. ice. (Pers. برف.)

Baragumu,* n. (— and of size, *ma-*) a horn used as a musical instrument or for giving signals, war horn, blown through a hole near the small end. (Cf. *paanda, gunda, pembe, siwa.* Ar. بوزي a horn, and كون news, war.)

Baraji,* n. a rope attached to the after end of the yard-arm in a native vessel, halyard. (Cf. *hamarawi, foromali.* ? Ar. برج support.)

Baraka,* n. also sometimes *mbaraka, mi-* (1) a blessing, generally; (2) prosperity, progress, advantage, plenty of food, abundant harvest, &c.; (3) a favour, a gift. (Cf. *heri, pendeleo, neema.*) **Bariki,** v. bless, favour, prosper (used of God and also of calling down a blessing on). Prep. **Barikia,** give a blessing to (for, with, &c.), also used of a salesman or auctioneer accepting a final bid, with the significance that his blessing goes with the goods. Used as a noun in the following expression. *Mungu bariki,* God the blesser, a common expression when saved from danger or difficulty, &c. **Mabruki,** n. a common personal male name. **Tabaruki,** and **Tabaruku,** v. (1) begin prayers (in a meeting); (2) join together in prayer or meet together for conversation. (Ar. بارك.)

Barakinya,* n. a brig, schooner—seldom heard. (Port. *barquinha.*)

Barakoa,* n. a kind of mask or veil covering the face down to the mouth, all but the eyes. Formerly worn in public by Muhammadan women, generally of the upper class, now rarely worn. As a rule the *buibui* is worn. (Ar. برقع.)

Barangeni,* n. a kind of dhow of two colours or with a white stripe. (From dual of Pers. برنگ of two colours.

Barare, n. See **Parare.**

Barasi,* n. (1) see **Balasi**; (2) black or light coloured patches on the hands or feet, said to be caused by leprosy or yaws. (Ar. برص leprosy.)

Baraste,* n. a properly made road, i.e. one which has been ballasted and rolled—heard only in Zanzibar. (? Eng. ballast.)

Barawai,* n. See **Mbayuwayu.**

Barawaji,* n. a cloth not much used now, like a silk shawl, worn round the waist. (Cf. *deuli*? Ar. بارع exceedingly beautiful, and وجاح veil, covering.)

Baraza,* n. place of public audience or reception, a verandah, a stone seat in the entrance hall, or against the wall outside a house, or a raised platform with stone seats and sometimes roofed over in front of the house, for receiving visitors, holding an audience, transacting business, for gossiping in, &c. Up-country, frequently a large shed in which the headman of a village holds his meetings, or built for the Administrative Officer for meetings. Hence also (1) a meeting, reception, public audience, court of law, council; (2) members of the council, cabinet, committee, elders of the tribe, &c. **Barizi,** v. (1) hold a reception, give an audience, summon a council, receive guests, sit in state; (2) attend an audience, go to a council (meeting, reception, &c.); (3) sit out of doors, sit together in a garden, &c. Rp. **Bariziana,** take counsel together. (Ar. برز appear, issue. Cf. also Pers. بارجا a royal court.)

Barazahi,* n. paradise, the period from death to the resurrection. (Cf. *kuzimu.* Ar. برزخ.)

Bari,* v. put aside, avoid, as a rule only used in the Rf. form, *jibari,* avoid, separate oneself from. (Cf. *epuka.* Ar. بر deprive.)

Baridi,* n. (1) cold, chill, dampness; (2) wind, air, draught (but *upepo* is better); (3) coolness, refreshment, relief (from heat, exhaustion), comfort; (4) fig. coolness of manner, dullness, lack of interest, repelling aspect of tone (also used of sexual coldness). It may imply both pleasant and unpleasant sensations. *Baridi nyingi*, great cold, much wind. *Maji ya baridi*, cold water as opp. to *maji ya moto*, hot water, or fresh water, as opp. to *maji ya chumvi*, salt (sea) water. (5) mildness, *maneno ya baridi*, gentle words. *Tumbako baridi*, mild tobacco. (6) *ugonjwa wa baridi*, ague, fever. **Baridisha**, v. sometimes heard, but usu. *burudisha*, see below. **Buruda**, n. prayers for the sick and dying, Muhammadan 'Visitation of the Sick'. **Burudai**, n. same as *buruda*. **Burudi**, v. be (get) cool, be cold, but usu. the St. **Burudika**, be cooled, refreshed, relieved, comforted. Ps. **Burudiwa.** Prep. **Burudia.** Cs. **Burudisha**, cool, refresh. Ps. of Cs. **Burudishwa**, be cooled, refreshed, comforted, eased. **Baridi yabis**, n. rheumatism. **Maburudisho**, n., **Maburudi**, n. recreation, refreshment, relief. **Tabaradi**, v., **Tabaridi**, v., and **Tabarudu**, v. same as *burudisha*, see above. **Ubaridi**, n. (1) coldness, coolness; (2) gentleness; (3) comfort, convalescence; (4) lack of interest, indifference. **Uburudisho**, n. coolness, refreshment, recreation, relief. (Cf. *poa, fariji, upepo*. Ar. برد.)

Bariki,* v. See under **Baraka.**

Bariyo,* n. food left over till morning from the last evening's meal. (Cf. *mwiku*, and *bari*. Ar. ? البارح yesterday.)

Barizi,* v. See under **Baraza.**

Barua,* n. a letter, but also used generally of a written form such as a testimonial, permit, &c. **Kibarua**, n. *vi-* and adv. dim. of *barua*, but chiefly a casual labourer who works for daily wages or on a monthly basis, from the card (*kipande, vi-*) with spaces for marking each day's work. *Kazi ya kibarua*, casual labour, paid by the day (or month), but the latter is usu. *kazi ya kipande*. As adv. *kufanya kibarua*, work as a casual labourer, do casual labour. (Cf. *cheti, hati*. Ar. بروة.)

Barubaru,* n. a strong vigorous youth. (Cf. *beberu*. Ar. بيع prime of youth.)

Baruti,* n. gunpowder. (Turk. باروت.)

Basbasi,* n. mace, the inner husk of the nutmeg. (Ar. بسباسة.)

Basha,* n. the king in a suit of playing cards, also called *mzungu wa nne* (because it scores 4). (Pers. باشا.)

Bashiri,* v. (1) foretell, predict; (2) announce, bring tidings, report news of something which has taken place but is not yet known to the person being told, esp. of good news. A common expression is *Bashiri heri!* May the news be good! Prep. **Bashiria.** Ps. **Bashiriwa. Mbashiri**, n. (1) *wa-* one who foretells, a prophet; (2) a bringer of news. **Ubashiri**, n. (1) prediction; (2) announcement, proclamation. (Cf. *tabiri, agua, hubiri, tangaza*. Ar. بشر.)

Basi, also **Bas*** (1) conj. very commonly used as a connective in narration, often heading each succeeding paragraph in a story, 'well, and so, accordingly, and then, &c.'; (2) int. generally expressing contentment or resignation, 'It is enough, very well, that will do'; but also it is often an order or decision, 'Stop that! That is all! No more! Have done with it!' It is one of the commonest and most expressive interjections in Swahili, and capable of conveying very different shades of meaning, according to the tone of voice and expression, from the highest gratification to the extreme of mortification and disgust, in many ways similar to the

English 'Well!' A whole series of distinct ideas may be conveyed by it, e.g. at the close of a bargain a dialogue may be heard carried on with it alone. *Basi?* (interrogatively and doubtfully), Is that really all that you can give me, your lowest terms? *Basi*, (with decision) Those are my final terms. *Basi*, (with reluctant resignation) Well, I suppose I must accept it, or (with disdain or disgust) Well, I would not dream of accepting it at that figure, or (with satisfaction), Very well, that will suit me, &c. *Basi!* (final consent) Be it so! Done! Agreed! &c. Sometimes it is used as a noun. *Ndiyo basi?* Is that the end (final, finish)? *Ndiyo basi*, it is the end, &c. (Pers. or Ar. بس.)

Bastola,* n. a pistol. (? the same word through Ar.)

Basua,* n. confusion of mind, weakness of intellect. (Ar. بصا stupid.)

Bata, n. *ma-* the name applied to many species of duck, also to the Pigmy goose. *Bata Bukini*, a Madagascar duck. *Bata mzinga*, a turkey. (Cf. *salili*. A widespread word for duck in Bantu, see also Ar. بطة.)

Bata, v. also Rd. **Batabata**, walk flat footed, waddle; walk as a child does when it is just learning to walk. Cv. **Batua**, used with the same meaning. **-batabata**, a. level, flat. **Batobato**, n. *ma-* an open flat place where dancing takes place.

Batela,* n. a small boat. (Port. *batel*, or Hind. بتيلا.)

Bati,* n. *ma-* (1) tin, block tin, sheet tin, galvanized iron. *Ezeka kwa mabati*, roof with sheets of corrugated iron. *Tia bati*, tin, i.e. cover a copper vessel with tin. (2) a method of plaiting women's hair, e.g. *amesuka bati leo*. (Ar. بيض to tin, or Hind. پتي thin sheet of metal.)

Batili,* v. (1) annul, cancel, make worthless or ineffective, hence (2) defy, treat as though cancelled or ineffective, and so transgress. St **Batilika**. Cs. **Batilisha**. Ps. **Batiliwa**. **Batili**, a., and **Batilifu**, a. (1) worthless, invalid, ineffective; (2) tending to, or with the characteristics of annulling, &c. *Hoja batili*, a futile argument. *Nikahi hii batili*, this marriage is null and void. (3) untrue, false. **Ubatili**, n. nullity, emptiness, vanity, futility, uselessness, falseness. (Cf. *tangua, futa, ondoa, vunja*. Ar. بطل.)

Batini,* n. the belly, only used, and that rarely, in a fig. manner of the innermost thoughts or intentions. (Cf. *nafsi, dhamira*. Ar. بطن.)

Batiza,* v. baptize. **Ubatizo**, n. baptism. (Eng.)

Batli,* n. a ship's log-book. (Ar. باطلى.)

Bato, n. *ma-* ringworm on the head.

Batobato, n. *ma-* (1) marking, coloured spots or stripes, of an animal or insect; (2) see under **Bata**, v. **Kibatobato**, n. *vi-* dim. of *batobato*. (Cf. *paku, doa, baku*.)

Batua, v. See under **Bata**, v.

Bau, n. *ma-*. See **Bao**.

Baura,* n. anchor of European pattern and make, with two flukes (*makombe*). Also called *nanga ya baura*. (Cf. *nanga*. ? Eng. bower.)

Bavu, n. *ma-* (1) see under **Ubavu**; (2) force, strength, e.g. *chukua kitu kwa bavu*, rob, take by force. **Bavuni**, adv. loc. alongside, at the side. **Kibavu**, or **Kibavubavu**, adv. sideways.

Bawa, n. *ma-* (1) the wing of a bird or insect; (2) anything resembling or which does the work of a wing, i.e. *bawa la eropleni*, the wing of an aeroplane. **Kibawa**, n. *vi-* dim. **Ubawa**, n. (*mbawa*), (1) a wing; (2) sometimes used of a wing feather.

Bawaba,* n. a hinge. (Cf. *pata*. ? from same root as follg.)

Bawabu,* n. *ma-* door-keeper, house-porter, turnkey. **Ubawabu**, n. office (work, pay, &c.) of a door-keeper, &c. (Cf. *mngoje mlango.* Ar. بواب.)

Bawasiri,* n. piles, haemorrhoids. (Cf. *kikundu, futuri, mjiko.* Ar. بواسير.)

-baya, a. bad, in the widest sense, i.e. possessing the quality of not being acceptable, whether materially, morally, intellectually, or aesthetically, i.e. a quality which is offensive (in whatever degree or way) to feeling, conscience, reason, or taste. It may therefore be rendered in a great number of ways in English, e.g. painful, unpleasant, inconvenient, defective, ugly, erroneous, wrong, wicked, &c. **Baya,** n. *ma-* (but usu. in the plur.), badness, wicked acts, &c. **Ubaya,** n. badness, wickedness in an abstract sense, i.e. of character quality, corruptness, ugliness, &c. (Cf. *-ovu, duni.*)

Bayana,* n. See under **Baina.**

Bazazi,* n. *ma-*, **Mbazazi,** n. *wa-* trader, shopkeeper, but usually of one who pushes himself forward by advertising or using trickery or devices for getting people's custom, hence a person who uses sharp practice, cheat, sharper, &c. **Ubazazi,** n. sharp practice in trading, cheating, &c. (Cf. *laghai, mdanganyifu.* Ar. بزاز.)

Beba, v. carry as native women do their children in a cloth on the back or hip or as porter does a load. Prep. **Bebea.** Cs. **Bebesha,** (1) place a load on the back, &c.; (2) fig. steal, purloin. Ps. **Bebwa.**

Beberu,* n. *ma-* (1) a he-goat; (2) fig. a strong man. (Cf. *barubaru.* Hind. بربري.)

Bedani,* n. also **Behedani,** n. a kind of sticky substance used by women for dressing their hair, also the seeds from which it is prepared. (Prob. Pers. بهدانه of the best seed, from به good, elegant, and دانه berry, seed.)

Bedari.* See **Abedari.**

Bedawi.* See **Bedui.**

Bedeni,* n. *ma-* a kind of Arabian sailing vessel, with cut-water and mast perpendicular, sharp stern, and high rudder-head. (Ar. بطن small boat.)

Bedui,* n. *ma-* a Bedouin, wanderer, nomad, outcast. (Ar. بداوة.)

Bee! int. also **Ebbe!** for *lebeka!* which see.

Bega, n. *ma-* shoulder—of man or animal. *Chukua mzigo begani* (*kwa bega, juu ya bega*), carry a load on the shoulder. (Cf. *fuzi, mtulinga.*)

Behedani,* n. See **Bedani.**

Behewa,* n. *ma-* (1) inner court surrounded by buildings and open to the air, as in some of the large stone houses at the coast and in Zanzibar; (2) a compartment (or carriage) of a train. *Behewa la bidhaa* (*abiria*), a baggage (passenger) compartment. (3) a go-down for storing goods, a large shed, &c. (Ar. بهو.)

Bei,* n. value, price, cost. *Kupiga bei,* to make a bargain, discuss price. *Bei hiari,* mortgage with option of realizing by sale. *Bei rehani,* or, *rehani bei,* mortgage with right to amount of debt only; pawn, pledge. *Bei gani?* What price? *Vitu hivi havina bei,* these things are valueless. (Cf. *kiasi, kima, thamani.* Ar. بيع.)

Beina,* adv. sometimes heard for *baina,* which see.

Beit al Mal.* Treasury. (Ar. بيت المال.)

Beja, v. scorn, treat scornfully or disdainfully, be negligent over, fail to observe or act properly, treat lightly. In some places heard as *beza* (Cf. *beza, bera, dharau, sinzilia.*)

Bekua, v. (1) keep off, ward off, parry, strike aside, divert, receive and return a ball (blow, &c.), defend oneself, counteract. *Bekua mainzi,* keep off flies. *Bekua mchele katika pishi,* knock off the overflowing rice in a full measure. (2) take away by force, plunder (cf. *kwepua, pokonya*); (3) scorn, treat contemptuously (cf. *dharau, beza*). Ps. **Bekuliwa.** St. **Bekulika.** Prep. **Bekulia.** Rp. **Bekuana.** (Cf. *kinga, epa, linda.*)

Belenga, v. strut, walk proudly, show off.

Belghamu,* n. phlegm. (Cf. *kohozi.* Ar. بلغم.)

Beluwa,* n. trouble, confusion, much difficulty. (Cf. *udhia, ghasia, balaa.* Hind. and Pers. بلوا.)

Bemba, v. (1) inquire into a person's affairs secretly, or slyly, without the person's knowledge; (2) wheedle, cajole, fawn on, coax; (3) solicit prostitution, seduce. St. and Pot. **Bembeka.** Cs. of St. and Pot. **Bembekeza.** Cs. **Bembeleza,** usu. with Inten. force, (1) coax very much, &c.; (2) soothe, quieten, as a mother to a child. *Amenibembeleza nimfanyizie kazi,* he has coaxed me into making a job for him. *Mama amembembeleza mtoto,* the mother has soothed (quietened) the child. *Bembeleza macho,* put on a coaxing expression, but usu. of covert signs between men and women. Rp. **Bembelezana.** **Bembe,** n. *ma-* pastry, confectionery, sweetmeats, esp. of a lover's presents or dainty dishes sent to a man as a sign of affection or regard, esp. at the end of the fast of Ramadhan. **-bembe,** a. enticing, coquettish. **Mbembe,** n. *wa-*, **Mbembelezi,** n. *wa-*, **Mbembezi,** n. *wa-* (1) a coaxing, insinuating, smooth-tongued, persuasive person; (2) procurer, or person given to seduction of women. **Ubembe,** n. also **Umbembelezi,** n. (1) coaxing, wheedling, allurement; (2) prostitution. *Kuuliza ubembe,* to ask about something pretending to know nothing about it while knowing all about it.

Bembejea, v. curry favour with, beg from.

Bendera,* n. (1) a flag (cf. *beramu*); (2) *kitambaa cha bendera* is sometimes applied to red cotton cloth, because the Zanzibar flag is red. *Tweka bendera,* hoist a flag. *Shusha* (*tua*) *bendera,* lower a flag. *Mimi bendera, hufuata upepo* I am like a flag, I follow the wind, i.e. I've no choice of my own. (Ar. بندرة or Port. *bandeira.*)

Benibeni,* adv. askew, awry, e.g. *mambo yao yamekwenda benibeni,* their affairs have gone awry. (Cf. *upogoupogo, upande.* Ar. بين بين in between, i.e. neither this nor that, cf. *baina.*)

Benua, v. also **Binua,** cause to project, stick out, bulge, protrude, put forward, expose to view. *Benua kidari* (or, *kifua*), stick the chest out. *Kujibenua,* to stretch oneself. Ps. **Benuliwa.** St. **Benuka,** bulge, stick out, be convex. **Mbenuko,** n. *mi-* a protruberance, a curve, roundness, plumpness. **Mbinu,** n. like *mbenuko. Mbinu ya mkono* (*ya mguu*), a double-jointed arm (or leg), i.e. so that when stretched out with the palm uppermost the elbow-joint curves upwards (or in the case of the leg, when straightened, the knee-joint sticks out at the back), considered to be well shaped.

Bera, v. scorn, treat lightly, with contempt. (Cf. *beja, beza, dharau.*)

Beramu,* n. a flag. (Cf. *bendera.* Port. *beirame,* kind of cotton cloth.)

Berenge,* n. *ma-*. See **Kiberenge.**

Bereu,* n. grease mixed with lime, used for caulking native vessels. (Cf. *deheni.* Port. *breu,* ship pitch and tar.)

Besera,* n. the poles, rods, or framework of a bedstead on which the mosquito net is hung. *Kitanda cha besera,* bedstead fitted with a frame or poles for a mosquito net. (Hind. بسیرا.)

Betabeta, v. twist and turn, curve about, as of a road. (Cf. *peta, pinda.*

Beti,* n. *ma-* (1) a small pouch,

cartridge pouch (prob. Eng. belt); (2) plur. of *ubeti*, which see.

Beua, v. scorn, treat in disdainful manner, disregard, and of things, discard. Prep. **Beulia.** Ps. **Beuliwa.** (Cf. *dharau, beza.*)

Beza, v. scorn, treat lightly, disdain, &c. (Cf. *bera, dharau.*) **Bezo,** n. *ma*- scornful words or actions. **Mbezi,** n. *wa*- a scornful, proud, supercilious person. (Cf. *fidhuli.*)

Bi,* prep. by, with, in, &c. Used in a few phrases, e.g. *bi nafsi yangu* (*yako, yake*, &c.), by myself (yourself, himself, &c.), also in a few words, *bilashi, bismilahi*, &c. (Ar. ب.)

Bi, abbreviation of *bibi*, which see.

Bia,* n. (A) co-operation, partnership, association in business, pleasure, &c. *Changa bia*, take equal shares in paying expenses. *Gawa bia*, share out equally. *Safiri bia*, travel together, each paying his own expenses. *Kula bia*, feed together, each one bringing his own food, or each one paying towards the cost. *Nunua bia*, purchase jointly. (Cf. *kikoa, shirika*. Prob. from Ar. بيع buying and selling, bartering being of mutual benefit.)

Bia, n. (B) *ma*- an earthenware vessel, basin, &c., for serving up food or for straining coco-nut juice into. **Kibia,** n. *vi*- dim.

Biabia, v. be diligent, active, do work with a will, &c. (Cf. *bangaika, jitihadi.*)

Biashara,* n. trade, commerce, buying and selling. *Fanya biashara*, trade. *Mfanya biashara*, a trader, merchant. (Cf. *uchuuzi*. Ar. باع to sell; شرى to buy.)

Bibi,* n. (— and *ma*-) a term of respectful reference and address to women, now fallen into evil days in some places because of its use to refer to concubines of Europeans. (1) in general, lady, madam, miss, &c.; (2) mistress of a household; (3) grandmother; (4) often used by a man when referring to his wife, *bibi yangu*, syn. with *mke wangu*, my wife. When there are several ladies in a household, they are distinguished as *bibi mkubwa* (or *bimkuu*), the mistress, and *bibi mdogo*, of the others. Sometimes the phrase *Kina* or (*akina*) *bibi*, the lady folk, the ladies, is used with courteous vagueness of one or more of the ladies. Often shortened to *Bi*, i.e. *Bi Mariamu, Bi mkubwa*, &c. (5) the queen in a pack of playing cards, also called *Mzungu wa mbili*. **Kibibi,** n. *vi*- (1) dim. of *bibi*, young mistress, young lady, &c.; (2) the name sometimes given for a peacock or peahen, also called *tausi*; (3) numbness, cramp, i.e. of the foot, &c., going to sleep. (Pers. بی بی.)

Bibidia, v. thrust out and turn down the lower lip as a sign of derision or contempt.

Biblia,* n. the Bible, but usu. *Agano la Kale*, Old Testament, and *Agano Jipya*, New Testament. (Cf. *msahafu.*)

Bibo,* n. *ma*- cashew apple, fruit of the *mbibo*, also called *kanju*; its seeds are called *korosho*. (Port. *bibo.*)

-bichi, a. (1) unripe, young, immature —also used of persons; (2) raw, fresh, newly gathered, e.g. of eggs, grass, meat, vegetables, &c.; (3) damp, as of earth, clay, clothes, &c.; (4) uncooked, as of meat, and food generally. **Ubichi,** n. unripeness, rawness, moistness, immaturity, greenness.

Bidhaa,* n. trade goods, merchandise. (Ar. بضاعة.)

Bidi,* v. put pressure on, make obligatory on, compel, oblige, esp. of moral pressure, duty, honour, privilege. Used as an impersonal verb. *Ilianibidi kuleta mashahidi*, I was bound to produce witnesses. *Ikabidi*, and it became necessary, there was an obligation. *Iliambidi kufanya* *neno*, he was compelled (obliged) to do something. *Imenibidi*, I feel bound to.... Ps. **Bidiwa**, be under an obligation to. Prep. **Bidia**. Cs. **Bidisha**, and Inten. Rf. *jibidisha*, take special pains. **Bidii**, n. effort, energy, exertion, exercise (of strength, or will), moral force, willingness to work. *Fanya bidii*, work hard, take pains, show energy (interest, earnestness). *Mtu wa bidii*, a man of energy, willing worker. (Cf. *pasa, lazima, shurutisha, utendaji, jitihadi*. Ar. بدا do first before anything else.)

Bihi,* v. repudiate, forego, forgive, i.e. of a debt, obligation, &c. (Cf. *burai, kanusha*. Ar. اباح to allow.)

Bikari,* n. pair of compasses, compass for drawing. (Ar. بيكار.)

Bikira,* n. *ma-* (1) a virgin (cf. *mwanamwali*); (2) also used for referring to the beginning of anything, e.g. *shamba bikira*, a new plantation, i.e. just newly begun. **Bikiri**, v. deprive of virginity, deflower. Ps. **Bikiriwa**. **Ubikira**, n. virginity, the condition of being a virgin. (Cf. *kizinda, tomoa*. Ar. بكر.)

Bila,* prep. without, not having, except by, apart from. Sometimes wrongly followed by *ya*. *Siwezi kukaa bila mke*, I cannot remain without a wife. *Bila udhuru*, without excuse. *Gari bila magurudumu*, a cart without wheels. *Mali bila daftari hupotea bila habari*, possessions without an account book are lost without knowledge. (Cf. *pasipo, pasina*.) **Bilashi**, adv. without (getting) anything, for nothing, in vain, gratis, gratuitously. (Cf. *bure*). (Ar. بلا and بلاش.)

Biladia,* n. anything belonging to or appertaining to a town, e.g. *nyimbo za biladia*, the songs sung in a town. *Sheria za biladia*, laws relating to a township. (Ar. بلدي.)

Bilahi!* (*Billahi!*) int. By God! (Ar. بالله.)

Bilashi,* adv. See under **Bila**.

Bilauri,* n. (1) glass, crystal; (2) a tumbler, wineglass, &c. (Cf. *kioo, kikombe*. Ar. بلور.)

Bildi,* n. (1) a plummet, sounding lead; (2) the weight of a clock. (Cf. *timazi, chubwi*. Ar. بلد.)

Bilimbi,* n. fruit of the cucumber tree *mbilimbi*, used in native chutneys. (Cf. Port. *bilimbinos, bilimbi, Malus indica*.)

Bilingani,* n. *ma-* a dark purple vegetable, fruit of the egg plant, bringal, aubergine, sometimes called 'mad apple'. **Mbilingani**, n. *mi-* the egg plant. (Ar. باذنجان.)

Bilisi,* n. and v. See **Ibilisi**.

Biliwili, n. a kind of fish, not considered to be good eating by Europeans.

Bilula,* n. a tap, turncock. (? Ar. بلال who waters.)

Bima,* n. (1) insurance against loss, accidents, &c., indemnity. *Lipa* (*toa*) *bima*, pay (effect) insurance of goods in commerce. *Fanya masharti ya bima*, draw up a deed of insurance. (2) lottery, raffle. *Cheza bima*, hold a raffle or lottery (also called *bahati nasibu*). (Cf. *fidia*. Hind. بيما.)

Bimbashi,* n. *ma-* a native non-commissioned officer. (Turk.)

Bimbiriza, v. flare up, as the flames of a fire. Rp. **Bimbirizana**, quarrel, shove each other about in quarrelling, incite each other to quarrel.

Bin,* n. son (of) (Ar. for common *mwana*). **Binadamu**, n. member of the human race, human being, man. Hence *kibinadamu*, of a human kind, human, natural to man. **Ubinadamu**, n. human nature, humanity. (Cf. *Adamu*). **Binamu**, n. a cousin, i.e. son of paternal uncle. (Cf. *amu*.) (Ar. ابن.)

Binamu,* n. See under **Bin**, or **Ami**.

Binda,* n. *ma-* okra, lady's fingers, an Indian vegetable, *Hibiscus esculentus*, also called *bamia*. **Mbinda,** n. *mi-* the plant on which *binda* grows. (Hind. بهندي.)

Bindo, n. *ma-* but more usu. in the dim. **Kibindo,** n. *vi-* a fold of the loin-cloth, used as a pocket for carrying things in. *Kinga bindo*, hold out a fold of the loin-cloth to receive something. Prov. *Hamadi ni iliyo bindoni, silaha ni iliyo mkononi*, that which you have in your pocket is your safeguard (or security), that which you have in your hand is your weapon (i.e. whatever it may be). From the use of *Hamadi!* as an interj. when saved from stumbling, falling, &c., prob. from the Ar. عمد prop up, support. (Cf. *pinda, upindo, winda, ubinda.*)

Bingirika, v. roll as of a stone down a hill, &c. (Cf. *fingirika.*)

Bingwa, n. *ma-* a capable, clever workman. **-bingwa,** a. clever, expert at work, &c. **Ubingwa,** n. cleverness, proficiency, expertness at work, &c. (Cf. *stadi, fundi, hodari.*)

Bini,* v. forge, counterfeit. **Mbini,** n. *wa-* forger. **Ubini,** n. act (method, &c.) of forging, forgery. (Ar. بن.)

Binti,* n. *ma-* a daughter, young lady. When followed by the father's name without preposition, forms the usual designation of all women. *Binti Ali*, the daughter of Ali, i.e. Miss Ali. The names of two kinds of cassava are *binti Athmani*, and *binti Ali*. The name of a kind of bird, *binti Chuma*, Kersten's Weaver Finch, *Ploceus bicolor*, also called *kinanda*. (Ar. بنت.)

Binua, v. See **Benua.**

Binya, v. nip, pinch. (Cf. *finya.*)

Biri,* n. tobacco leaf rolled up for smoking as used by some Indians. (Hind. بيرا.)

Biriani,* n. same as *birinzi*, which see.

Birigiji,* n. and a. a kind of cloth of a light brownish yellow colour, also its colour. (Corruption of Belgique.)

Birika,* n. *ma-* (1) a large metal vessel for holding water, water-jug, a kettle; (2) cistern, tank, bath—of masonry. (Ar. بركة and ابريق.)

Biringa, v., **Biringana,** v., **Biringika,** v. variants of *viringa, viringana, viringika.*

Birinzi,* n. a particular dish of cooked food—meat, rice, pepper, &c.—a kind of *pilau*. (Pers. برنج rice.)

Bisari, n. an annual 1 to 2 ft. tall used as a pot herb, *Anethum graveolens.*

Bisbis, n. See **Bisibisi.**

Bisha, v. (1) strike, knock, beat, hit against. The word used for knocking at a door, *bisha mlango*, also for shouting to ask leave to enter a house, room, &c., *bisha hodi* (also *piga hodi*). (2) oppose, resist, argue or quarrel with; (3) sometimes used of joke, jest; (4) (of a ship) beat, tack. *Bisha chombo*, work a ship to windward. Ps. **Bishwa.** Prep. **Bishia.** Rp. **Bishana,** joke together, argue with each other, wrangle. **-bishi,** a. (1) captious, argumentative, contradictory, obstinate; (2) good-humoured, joking, jesting. **Bisho,** n. (1) a knock, call at the door; (2) a blow; (3) working to windward, beating, tacking. *Upepo wa bisho* (*mbisho*) head wind. *Piga mbisho*, beat to windward. **Mabishano,** n. plur. (1) contention, argument, dispute, quarrel; (2) opposition, contradiction; (3) jesting, foolish repartee. **Mbishi,** n. *wa-* an obstinate, argumentative person. **Mbisho,** n. *mi-* like *bisho*. **Ubishi,** n. (*mbishi* and *ma-*), (1) opposition, contrariness, strife, argumentativeness; (2) joking, a joke, jest, fun, *Ubishi mwingi huvuta mateto*, joking carried too far leads to quarrelling, (Cf. *piga, gonga, ugomvi, shindana.*

upuzi, mzaha. ? Ar. بش of a cheerful open countenance.

Bishaushi,* n. sergeant, formerly used by the Germans in Tanganyika Territory for native soldiers. (Cf. *ombasha, shaushi, soli.* ? Turk. باشاويش.)

-bishi, a., **Bisho,** n. See under **Bisha.**

Bisi, n. parched or toasted Indian corn or millet, pop-corn. *Mahindi au mtama uliokaangwa.* Sometimes called *mbisi.* (? from the Ar. cry بس, i.e. prepare to eat the dish بسيسة, i.e. flour or meal, &c., roasted in butter.)

Bisibisi,* n. a screwdriver. (Hind. or perhaps from Eng. bracepiece.)

Bismillahi.* In the name of God. (Ar. بسم الله.)

Bitana,* n. any thin material used for lining a garment. (Ar. بطانة.)

-bivu, a. ripe of fruit. *Matunda mabivu,* ripe fruit. **Ubivu,** n. ripeness, of fruit. (Cf. *iva,* v.)

Biwi, n. *ma-* heap of plantation or garden rubbish, sweepings, refuse, leaves, &c.

Bizari,* n. small seed such as pepper, turmeric, cardamom, coriander, caraway, &c., used in making curries, hence sometimes curry powder. (Ar. بزر.)

Bizimu,* n. a buckle, brooch, clasp or fastener. (Ar. ابزيم.)

Blanketi,* n. *ma-* a blanket. (Eng.)

Boba, v. bind—seldom used.

Bobari,* n. a gouge, rounded chisel, also called *ngabu.*

Boboka, v. used of words coming out with a rush, blurt out words, &c. Ps. **Bobokwa,** e.g. *Mtu yule alibobokwa na maneno mengi,* words simply burst from that man.

Bodoa, v. used only in Rf. *jibodoa,* praise oneself, boast, vaunt oneself.

Bofu, n. *ma-* amplic. of **Kibofu,** n. *vi-* the usual word used for the urinary bladder. Note: a football bladder is *mpira (wa ndani).*

Bofulo, n. *mkate wa bofulo,* bread of European kind and make.

Bofya, v. See under **Bopa.**

Boga, n. *ma-* pumpkin, gourd; the plant is called *mboga.* Dist. from *mboga* used as sing. and plur. generally for all kinds of vegetables, and sometimes for any kind of relish whether it be meat, fish, or vegetable.

Bogoa, v. sometimes heard for *pogoa.*

Bohari,* n. (— and *ma-*) storehouse, warehouse, large shop, magazine, go-down, &c. (Cf. *ghala, duka.* Hind. بكهار.)

Bohora,* n. *ma-* a member of one of the two chief sects or divisions of Muhammadan Indians, the other being the Khoja.

Boi,* n. *ma-* house servant, personal attendant, domestic, native waiter or attendant, office boy, &c. **Uboi,** n. the work, position, &c., of a native house servant, &c. (Cf. *mtumishi.* Eng. boy.)

Boji,* n. (1) a kind of intoxicating liquor. (Cf. *pombe, boza.* Ar. بوزي beer.) (2) gruel. (Cf. *uji.*)

Bokoa, v. (1) penetrate with force; (2) obtain a plentiful harvest, or obtain anything plentifully.

Bokoboko, n. (1) a particular dish of cooked food, wheat-flour, meat, ghee, all mixed together; (2) used to describe anything soft or jelly-like; (3) a kind of banana which is very soft when cooked, also called *makojozi,* or *ngazija*; (4) a kind of sugar-cane with a soft outer part.

Bokoka, v. come off, as the handle of a knife, the flesh off a bone or the body, &c.

Boma,* n. *ma-* any kind of raised structure for defensive or protective purposes (1) earthwork, outer wall, rampart, mound, pallisade, stockade, fence, and hence (2) fort, redoubt, castle; (3) throughout Tanganyika Territory, used of the Government offices, esp. administrative office; (4) the skeleton of a native's house, i.e. without the roof, and the bare poles of the walls unmudded. (Cf. *ngome, jenga,* and *bomoa*. Pers. برم garrison, place where one can dwell in safety.)

Bomba,* n. *ma-* (1) a pump. *Bomba la kuvutia maji,* a pump for drawing water. (2) a chimney of a house or steamer; (3) any kind of large pipe; (4) a syringe such as is used for giving injections, an enema, &c. *Daktari alimpiga bomba* (or, *sindano*), the doctor gave him an injection (enema). (Port. *bomba.*)

Bombo,* a. (1) *Suruali bombo,* the name given to a kind of very wide short trousers worn by some natives, particularly young Nyasa men; (2) in some places the name given to influenza. See **Bombom** (2). (Cf. *kaputula.*)

Bombom,* n. (1) a bomb (cf. *kombora*); (2) the name given in some places for influenza, pneumonia, and chest complaints which are often fatal. See **Bombo** (2).

Bombwe, n. *ma-* cut figure, carved or worked pattern, carving, sculpture, the lines round the cover of a book, pattern in weaving baskets, &c. *Kata mabombwe,* carve figures (patterns). **Kibombwe,** n. *vi-* dim. (Cf. the more usual *choro, nakshi.*)

Bomoa, v. break down, break through, fell, as of a wall, fence, house, &c. Ps. **Bomolewa.** St. **Bomoka,** fall down, collapse, &c. Prep. **Bomolea,** e.g. *mtaimbo wa kubomolea,* a crowbar to break down a wall with, &c. Cs. **Bomosha. Bomoko,** n. *ma-* often used in the plur. (1) act of demolishing, &c.; (2) ruins, anything broken down and in ruins, the ruins of a house, &c. **Mbomoshi,** n. *wa-* one who throws down (demolishes, destroys, ruins, &c.), a destroyer, revolutionist. (Cf. *boma,* also *pomoa, poromoa.*)

Bomu, n. *ma-* (1) a particular sort of dance, not often practised now; (2) the sound of a large deep-sounding drum, boom; (3) *bomu la gogo,* a long drum with a deep, booming sound.

Bonde, n. *ma-* valley, hollow between hills, low-lying country. **Kibonde,** n. *vi-* dim.

Bonge, n. *ma-* a lump of anything, of earth, thread or twine rolled up, &c. (Cf. *donge, tonge.*)

Bongo, n. *ma-* sometimes heard for *ubongo,* which see.

Bong'oa, v. stoop, bend down so that the buttocks stick out. This word is seldom used except in rather vulgar joking between people of equal age, i.e. not by children to adults and vice versa. Prep. **Bong'olea,** same as *bong'oa,* but more vulgar, in fact its use seems to be confined to bending down for a particular purpose, i.e. sodomy. St. **Bong'oka.** (Cf. *fuama, fulama,* which is used of ordinary bending, but also like *bong'oa,* and *bong'olea,* and *inama* which is the safest word to use.)

Bonyea, v. be dented with pressure or by being knocked, i.e. as of fruit or anything soft being pressed with the fingers, or of a tin, &c., being knocked and dented. St. **Bonyeka.** Cs. **Bonyeza,** press in, make an impression on, dent, examine by feeling and pressing. Ps. **Bonyezwa.** (Cf. *tomasa* which is used of feeling or touching, and *bopa*).

Bopa, v. (1) be soft to the touch, feel soft, as of ripe fruit, an abscess, &c.; (2) feel anything soft, as ripe fruit, &c.; (3) sink in, become hollow (concave), dented, i.e. hollow cheeks, &c. Cs. **Bofya. Bopo,** n. *ma-* (1) soft place, mud hole, pit, esp. where water stands; (2) an impression made by pressing; (3) the act of pressing in. (Cf. *bonyea, tomasa.*)

Bora,* a. of special quality (importance, or value), fine, high class, first-rate, excellent, good, noble, &c.,

often used with implied comparison, 'better, the better, best'. *Bora afya,* there is nothing like good health. *Nguo bora,* very excellent cloth (or, clothes). **Ubora,** n. excellence, fine quality. (Cf. *afadhali,* and *-ema, -zuri.* Ar. بر be superior.)

Bori,* n. (1) clay bowl of a hookah pipe (*buruma*) (cf. *toza, kiko.* Pers. بوری a tube); (2) *ma-* in some places, the fruit of the *mkunazi,* elsewhere *kunazi.*

Boriti,* n. (and of size *ma-*) (1) thick poles of the mangrove (cf. *mkoko, mkandaa*), used to support concrete ceilings and roofs of certain kinds of houses; hence (2) a beam, large piece of timber or steel, a girder, &c. (? Port. *barrote,* beam, joist.)

Borohoa,* n. a native dish, cooked peas or beans, pounded into a paste of thick broth and flavoured. (? Pers. بورا dish of minced meat and spices.)

Boromoka, v., **Boromoko,** n. *ma-*. See **Poromoka** and **Poromoko.**

Boronga, v. make a mess, muddle, fuss, bungle, mix. *Boronga kazi,* do a job badly (in muddling, unworkmanlike way). **Borongo,** n. *ma-* a muddle, mess, bungle. *Kazi ya borongo,* a badly done job. Often Rd. *borongoborongo.* (Cf. *haribu, fuja, vuruga.*)

Boshori,* n. a Balaclava helmet. (? Ar. بشر human skin—because of its tight fittting.)

-bovu, a. (1) bad, chiefly of physical condition, i.e. rotten, unsound, unhealthy, spoilt, decomposed, putrid. Hence, also (2) worthless, unfit for use or service. *Mtu mbovu,* an unhealthy, weak, unreliable person. (Cf. the more comprehensive word *-baya,* and *-ovu,* which indicates usually bad moral condition.) **Ubovu,** n. rottenness, unsoundness, corruption, badness, weakness, putrefaction.

Boya,* n. *ma-* a buoy. (Port. *boia.*)

Boza,* n. an intoxicating liquor. (Pers. بوزه.)

Bozi,* n. *ma-* a fool, simpleton, a dull useless person. **Bozibozi,** a. idle, dull, stupid, incapable. **Ubozi,** n. idleness, dullness, stupidity, foolishness. (? From prec.)

Bua, n. *ma-* stalk, stem, of the larger grasses, e.g. of *mtama,* millet; or *muhindi,* maize. Used for house walls, fencing, and firing. **Ubua,** n. (*mbua*) (1) stalk, stem of the smaller kind of grain-bearing grasses, i.e. of *mpunga,* rice; *mawele,* bullrush millet; (2) the substance or material of a stalk, stem, &c.

Buabua, v. hew or cut a little, i.e. slice pieces from the top. (Cf. *lenga.*)

Buathi,* v. See **Baathi.**

Buba, n. yaws.

Bubu, n. *ma-* a dumb person. *Tui bubu,* see under *tui.* **Ububu,** n. dumbness. Sometimes heard as *bubwi.*

Bubujika, v. bubble out, burst forth in a flood. *Bubujika machozi,* burst into a flood of tears. *Bubujika maneno,* come out with a torrent of words. **Bubujiko,** n. *ma-* a spring of water, a bursting forth, a bubbling up, &c. (Cf. *foka, jiajia.*)

Buburusha, v. push, shove, **Ps. Buburushwa.** Rp. **Buburushana,** e.g. *watu walikuwa wakibuburushana,* the people were pushing and shoving each other, wrestling.

Bubuta, v. beat, strike. (Cf. *piga, buta.*)

Bubwi, n. See **Bubu.**

Buchari,* n. a large knife. (Cf. *jisu, sime, shembea.* Hind. بوچهری.)

Budaa, v. become lumpy, as of porridge not sufficiently cooked, &c.

Budhara,* n. See under **Badhiri.**

Budi,* n. escape, way out, alternative, means of avoiding. Generally used with negative parts of *kuwa na,* to have, e.g. *hakuna budi* necessarily, undoubtedly, it must be so. *Sina budi,* I must, I cannot avoid it.

Rarely used with an affirmative. *Ana budi gani asione haya?* How can he avoid feeling ashamed? *Basi! mimi nina budi ya kulia?* What! Can I help crying, i.e. have I any any way out of crying? Also used impersonally. *Haina budi kuniambia habari yako,* there is no escape from telling me about yourself. *Bila budi,* inevitable, surely. (Ar. بد escape.)

Bufuu, n. *ma-* an empty shell. *Bufuu la kichwa,* a skull. *Bufuu la nazi,* an empty coco-nut shell. Also *bupu, bupuru, fuu, fuvu.*

Buga, v. (1) seek for, esp. of going about cadging food, sponge (cf. *doea, doya, rondea*); (2) glean in a field.

Buge, n. *ma-* a person with a finger or toe missing.

Bughudha,* n. abhorrence, hatred, ill feeling, slander. **Bughudhi,** v., **Bughudhu,** v. (1) abhor, hate; (2) revile; (3) speak evil of one in his absence. (Ar. بغض.)

Bugi, n. said to be a kind of preparation used by thieves, &c. It is supposed to make the people in a house fall into a deep sleep, and to cause the doors of the house to open.

Bugia, v. throw a little of something into the mouth, as natives do sometimes, i.e. tobacco, groundnuts, &c., and chew them. **Mbuge,** n. *wa-* a person who is always throwing pieces of food, &c., into his mouth; one who is always chewing. **Ubuge,** n. greed, gluttony, the habit of continually chewing something. (Cf. *bwakia, bwia.*)

Bugu, n. *ma-* a thick kind of withy, used as a cord or rope in building, &c.

Buguika, v. burst out, but cf. *bubujika* which is more usual.

Buheri,* used in the phrase *Buheri wa afya,* on a person's recovery from an illness, with health and strength. (Cf. *heri.*)

Buhumu, n. *ma-* lungs. (Cf. *pafu, yavuyavu.*)

Buhuri,* n. a vapour bath for illness, fumigation, &c., made by burning incense or by boiling medicine, roots, &c., in water and making a vapour for that purpose. (Cf. *fukiza, ubani, udi.* Ar. بخور incense; بخار vapour, steam.)

Bui, n. (A) a children's game like hide-and-seek, in which the seeker is blindfolded. (Cf. *kizuizui.*)

Bui, n. (B) a large spider, tarantula, &c. **Buibui,** n. (1) spider, *utando wa buibui,* a spider's web; (2) a black garment worn by some women when they go out of doors, covering them from head to foot.

Bujua, v. squeeze out, e.g. the stone from fruit, &c. (Cf. *pujua.*)

Buki, n. (1) Madagascar. Often used in the loc. form *Bukini*; (2) a kidney (cf. *figo, nso*). **-buki,** a. of Madagascar. **Mbuki,** n. *wa-* a Malagasy. *Bata la bukini,* a goose.

Buku, n. *ma-* a very large long-tailed rat. (Cf. *ndezi.*)

Bukua, v. hunt out a secret, discover and reveal scandal, &c. Prep. **Bukulia.** St. **Bukuka. Mbukulia,** n. *wa-* one who gets hold of and tells secrets, scandal, &c., a gossip, scandalmonger, telltale. **Mbukuzi,** n. *wa-* same as *mbukulia.* **Ubukuzi,** n. (1) scandal; (2) tale-telling, scandalmongering. (Cf. *dakua, mdakuzi.*)

Bulangeti,* n. *ma-*. See **Blanketi.**

Buldani,* n. district. (Cf. *mtaa, tarafa, wilaya, jimbo.* Ar. بلدان.)

Buli,* n. *ma-* a teapot. Sometimes *buli ya kahawa,* is used for a coffee-pot, but the usual word is *mdila* or *dele.* (Port. *bule.*)

Bulibuli,* a. *kofia ya bulibuli,* a white, embroidered skull-cap, also called *kofia ya kazi.* (Ar. بلبل nightingale, prob. a trade-mark.)

Bulule,* n. sometimes used for *bilula,* which see.

Buluu,* n. the colour blue. (Eng. blue.)

Bumba, n. *ma-* lump, packet, small

parcel, &c. *Bumba la udongo*, a clod of earth. *Bumba la tumbako*, a plug or packet of tobacco. *Bumba la nyuki*, a cluster of bees, when swarming. **Kibumba**, n. *vi-* dim. Sometimes heard as *pumba*.

Bumbi, n. Upland cress, *Barbarea vulgaris*.

Bumbuaza, v. confuse, discomfort, astonish, astound, nonplus. **Bumbuazi**, n. utter perplexity, helpless amazement, confusion of the senses. *Shikwa na bumbuazi*, be dumbfounded, lose one's senses. (Perh. from the same root as *pumbaa*. Cf. *shangaza, duwaza, tunduwaa.*)

Bumbura,* n. a kind of dried fish, Bombay duck. (Hind. بونبل.)

Bumburuka, v. be frightened away with great haste, be startled, as of game, birds, &c. Cs. **Bumburusha**, startle, start up, frighten away, scare. (Cf. *kurupuka.*)

Bumbwi, n. rice-flour mixed with sugar, scraped coco-nut, and a little water or coco-nut juice (*tui*), and eaten without being cooked—usually by children. Also called *bwimbwi* and *kigodo*.

Bumia,* n. beam forming sternpost of native vessel, fastened to the keel (*mkuku*), and carrying the rudder-post (*fashini*). (? Pers. بن stern of ship.)

Bumunda, n. *ma-* a kind of dumpling or fritter (*andazi*) made of flour and banana.

Bunda,* n. *ma-* a parcel, bale. (Cf. *furushi*. Eng. bundle.)

Bundi, n. Wood owl, *Strix Woodfordii*.

Bunduki,* n. gun, rifle, musket. *Piga bunduki*, fire a gun. *Elekeza* (or, *lenga*) *bunduki*, point (aim) a gun. *Bunduki ya jiwe*, or *ya gumegume*, or *ya gobori*, a flintlock gun. *Bunduki ya mrao*, a matchlock gun. *Bunduki ya kushindiliwa*, or *ya fataki*, a muzzle-loading gun. *Bunduki ya kuvunja*, or *ya kukunja*, a sporting (hinged) gun (rifle). *Bunduki ya viasi*, or *korofindo*, a breech-loading rifle. *Bunduki ya midomo miwili* (or *mitutu miwili*, or *kasiba mbili*), a double-barrelled gun. Common trade guns are sometimes called *bunduki ya kindoro*, or *ya makoa*. (Ar. also Hind. and Pers. بندوق.)

Bunga, a. *Mtu bunga*, a fool, one lacking in sense. (Cf. *mjinga, mpumbavu, punguani.*)

Bungala,* n. Bengal. Used to describe kinds of rice, bananas, and sugar-cane.

Bungo, n. *ma-* the fruit, rather like a medlar, of a creeping plant, the sap of which is like indiarubber.

Bungu, n. (1) a large stinging fly (hornet?) which bores large holes in timber; (2) a small biting fly, also a borer; (3) a kind of caterpillar. **Bungua**, v. bore holes in grain, timber, &c., used of boring flies and insects. St. **Bunguka**, be destroyed by borers, of timber, grain, &c. The timber and grain become powder, i.e. *hubunguka*.

Bunguu, n. a large earthenware dish for serving up food. **Kibunguu**, n. *vi-* dim. (Cf. *bia*, n. (B).)

Buni,* n. coffee berry, fruit of the *mbuni*. *Buni ya kahawa*, coffee bean. (Ar. بنّ.)

Buni,* v. (1) construct, contrive, compose, invent, make for the first time; (2) fabricate, make up (what is false), imagine, write fiction, &c. *Buni kitabu*, write a book. *Buni kitu kisicholambulikana*, invent an unfathomable contrivance. *Maneno haya ya kubuniwa*, these are purely imaginary (or invented) statements. *Alibuni neno asilotumwa*, he invented a message he was not charged with. **Mbuni**, n. *wa-* inventor, author, originator, deviser. (Cf. *zua, tunga, vumbua*. Ar. بنى.)

Bunju, n. a poisonous fish of the Diodon (globe-fish) kind.

Bunta,* n. a pontoon, landing-stage. (? Eng. pontoon.)

Bunzi, n. *ma-* (1) a large stinging fly which builds a clay nest; (2) sometimes heard for *gunzi*, a maize cob.

Bupu, n. *ma-*, also **Bupuru,** *ma-*, an empty shell, i.e. of a coco-nut, also *bupu* (*bupuru*) *la kichwa*, the skull.

Buraa,* n. (A) a kind of Muscat cloth. (Cf. *kitambi*. From name of place where it is made.)

Buraa,* n. (B) forgiveness of obligation, debt, offence. **Burai,** v. forgive, exculpate, exonerate, give up or renounce a claim, let off payment. *Mwanamke aliburai mahari yake*, the woman gave up her claim to dowry. Ps. **Buraiwa.** Prep. **Buraia.** Cs. **Buraisha.** (Cf. *bihi*, *samehe*. Ar. برّأ.)

Buraha,* n. rest, ease, comfort. **Burahi,** v. rest, take one's ease, make oneself comfortable. (Cf. *pumzika*, *raha*. Ar. بره.)

Burai,* v. See under **Buraa.**

Burangeni,* n. See **Barangeni.**

Burashi,* n. a brush, hair-brush, paint-brush, &c. (Eng. brush.)

Bure,* adv. (1) gratis, gratuitously, for nothing, without payment; (2) uselessly, vainly, in vain, for no good cause or result, idly, fruitlessly. *Kazi bure*, labour for nothing, i.e. wasted or unpaid. *Kutukana watu bure*, abuse people without cause. *Maneno ya bure*, idle (frivolous, foolish) words. (Hind. برا worthless, useless, or Ar. برع bestow of free will.)

Buri,* n. a small elephant tusk, when just beginning to grow. (Ar. بوري a horn.)

Buriani,* n. last words, farewells, leave-takings, esp. of people going on a journey. *Kuwapa rafiki buriani*, to give friends a farewell (send-off). *Kutakana* (*agana*) *buriani*, exchange farewell greetings, i.e. beg for mutual forgiveness. (Ar. بران, see *buraa*.)

Buruda, n., **Burudai,** n., **Burudi,** v., **Burudika,** v., **Burudisha,** v., **Burudisho,*** n. *ma-*. See under **Baridi.**

Buruga, v. (1) stir up, mix together, e.g. in preparing food; (2) put into confusion, disorder, muddle; (3) stir up the soil, prepare a bed for planting, by hoeing and removing weeds, &c., *buruga udongo*. Ps. **Burugwa.** Prep. **Burugia.** St. **Burugika.** Cs. of Rp. **Buruganya,** stir up together, mix together. **Mburugo,** n. *mi-* a stirring up, a mixing, a muddling, disorder, mess. (Cf. *vuruga*.)

Buruhani,* n. power with God, i.e. used of holy people, &c., who, whatever they pray for, have their prayers answered. *Ana buruhani*, he is specially gifted with power with God. (Ar. برهان, proof, evidence.)

Buruji,* n. (1) battlement, indented parapet of a house, fort, &c.; (2) in some places used of the gaps left in the bottom of a fence built in shallow water, behind which are placed fish-traps (Ar. بروج); (3) a bugle, a bugler. (? Eng. bugle.)

Buruma,* n. a hookah, a water pipe, i.e. the smoke passes through a bowl filled with water. (Cf. *kiko*. ? Ar. برم stone vessel for cooking, kettle.)

Burunga, v. make balls of earth or clay. (Cf. *viringa*.)

Burura, v. pull, haul, drag along on the ground. **Maburuzo,** n., **Mbururo,** n. *mi-* also **Mbuuzo,** n. *mi-* (1) a pulling, hauling, dragging; (2) track or marks made by pulling something along the ground, or by something dragging itself along, i.e. *mbururo* (or *mbuuzo*) *wa nyoka*, the marks or track of a snake. (Cf. follg. and *kokota*, *vuta*.)

Buruta, v. same as *burura*, which see.

Busara,* n. (1) good sense, practical wisdom, prudence, sagacity, skill, &c.; (2) plan, device, stratagem. *Leta busara*, employ a device. **Taba-**

suri, n. same as *busara*—seldom heard. (Cf. *akili, werevu*. Ar. بصر.)

Busati,* n. a kind of matting made at Muscat, also used of any matting made of the stalks or grass of wheat, rice, &c. (Ar. بسط.)

Busha,* n. also **Fusha**, (1) gunwad, tow (for cleaning a gun or cannon); (2) elephantiasis of the scrotum. (Cf. *mshipa*. Port. *bucha*.)

Bushashi,* n. a kind of thin muslin, also tissue paper, but usu. *shashi* is used. (Ar. شاش.)

Bushuti,* n. a long cloak worn by some men, decorated with gold threadwork, esp. at the chest and back. (Cf. *joho* which is similar, but has long sleeves. Ar. ? بساط covering.)

Bustani,* n. a garden. (Ar. or Pers. بستان.)

Busu,* v. kiss. *Busiana mikono*, kiss each other's hands. **Busu**, n. *ma-* a kiss. (Cf. *nonea*. Pers. بوس.)

Busuri,* v. observe, be careful, take care. (Cf. *angalia* and *busara*. Ar. بصر.)

Buta, v. beat. (Cf. *bubuta, piga*.)

Butaa,* n. astonishment. (Cf. *ushangao*. (Ar. بهتة astonishment.)

Butu, a. blunt. *Kisu butu*, a blunt knife. **Butua**, v. cut off the end, make blunt. **Ubutu**, n. bluntness, i.e. of a tool or cutting instrument, &c. (Cf. *kibubutu*. ? Port. *boto*, blunt.)

Buu! int. make less noise! Be quiet!

Buu, n. *ma-* maggot, grub, larva. *Buu la nyuki*, a bee grub. *Buu wambe*, an insect which causes a rash. (Cf. *jana, funza*.)

Buyu, n. *ma-* calabash, fruit of the *mbuyu*. The pith and small kernels are called **Ubuyu**, and are edible. The husk **Kibuyu**, n. *vi-* is used for making vessels for drinking out of, and also for carrying water in.

Buza,* n. intoxicating liquor prepared with honey. Nubian beer. (Ar. بوظة.)

Buzi, n. *ma-* amplic. of **Mbuzi**, which see.

Bwabwaja, blether, talk nonsense. (Cf. *babaika, payuka, bwata*.)

Bwaga, v. throw off, throw down, relieve oneself of (as to, with). *Bwaga mzigo*, tip a load off one's shoulders, throw it on the ground. *Bwaga moyo*, rest the mind, throw off melancholy, be cheered. *Bwaga wimbo*, give a lead in singing. *Bwaga matukano*, let off a volley of abuse. *Bwaga manza*, cause contention, litigation, &c. *Jibwagia moyo*, relieve one's mind. Cs. **Bwagaza**. *Jibwagaza*, throw oneself down, sprawl on the ground. **Mbwago**, n. *mi-* a fall down, slump.

Bwakia, v. throw into the mouth, i.e. pieces of food, nuts, tobacco, &c. (Cf. *bugia, bwia*.)

Bwakua, v. take by force, snatch away. Prep. **Bwakulia**. Ps. **Bwakuliwa**. (Cf. *pokonya, nyang'anya, bekua*.)

Bwana, n. (— and *ma-*) used (1) in reference, 'master, owner, possessor' of slaves, house, plantation or other property, and generally 'great man, dignitary, worthy, personage'; (2) in address, 'master, Mr., Sir', often *bwana mkubwa*, to show respect, and contr. *bwana mdogo*, of the next in rank, or inferior. *Bwana* is also often used by women when referring to their husbands. (3) *bwana* is also used frequently in a loose general sort of way when addressing womenfolk, and also by womenfolk when speaking to other women. Hence one may hear two women speaking together: *Ndiyo bwana, nilikwenda huko bwana, nikaona mambo ya ajabu bwana*. Yes sir, I went there sir, and I saw wonderful things. And of a man speaking to a woman, *Ee bwana, usifanye upuzi huo bwana*. I say sir, don't be so foolish sir.

Kibwana, n. *vi-* dim. of *bwana*, see under **Jana**, n. (A). **Ubwana**, n. (1) mastership, qualities (rights, powers) of a master; (2) an overbearing, domineering, tyrannical, masterful character.

Bwata, v. speak nonsense, go on speaking just for the sake of speaking. (Cf. *payuka, babaika.*)

Bwawa, n. *ma-* marsh, boggy ground, such as round a lake, &c.

Bweha, n. also sometimes *mbweha*, n. a fox, jackal.

Bweka, n. cry, bark (as a dog). (Cf. *lia, gumia.*)

Bwende, n. *ma-* an old piece of cloth worn round the loins when working in the fields, &c. (Cf. *demu.*)

Bweni, n. the sleeping quarters of young unmarried boys (or girls). Frequently huts are built in villages for the accommodation of the young unmarried boys, and separate ones for the young unmarried girls. (Cf. *gane.*)

Bwenzi, n. a large tuft of hair left on the top of the head when shaving it. (Cf. *sunzu, kishungi, denge.*)

***Bweta**, n. small box, such as a desk, work-box, cash-box, jewel-case, &c. **Kibweta**, n. *vi-* dim. (Port. *bueta.*)

Bwia, v. throw into the mouth, as of pieces of food, nuts, tobacco, &c. (Cf. *bugia, bwakia*).

Bwimbwi, n. rice-flour mixed with sugar and scraped coco-nut or coconut juice (*tui*) eaten uncooked, usu. by children. Also called *bumbwi* and *kigodo.*

CH

Ch represents the sound of *ch* in church. In the Mombasa dialect of Swahili, *t* is often heard where *ch* is used in the Zanzibar and Standard Swahili, as in *tupa* for *chupa*; *utungu* for *uchungu*; *nti* for *nchi*; *tukua* for *chukua*, &c. Sometimes *ch* and *t* are used indiscriminately, even in the Zanzibar and Standard Swahili (cf. *kutwa* and *kucha*). *Ch* is difficult to distinguish from *j* in the pronunciation of some natives, therefore words not found under *ch* may be looked for under *J*. Note: In many Bantu languages this sound is represented by *c* alone.

Cha, prep. form of *-a*, meaning of—see Grammars.

Cha, v. (A), fear, be afraid of, reverence, be in awe of, most frequently used (esp. in Zanzibar) of reverent fear of God. *Kumcha Mungu*, to fear God. Note: (1) the St. form **Cheka** is usu. quite a different word (cf. *cheka*, laugh); (2) the other derived forms of this verb must be distinguished from identical forms made from other stems. Ps. not in use, but sometimes the Ps. of Prep. **Chewa** is used instead, i.e. *jina lako lichewe*, may your name be feared (revered). Prep. **Chea**. D.Prep. **Chelea**, fear for, be apprehensive about (because of, through, &c.). *Nachelea kuchelewa*, I am apprehensive about being late. *Nachelea jambo hili, kuenda* *litakuwa baya*, I fear on account of this matter, perhaps it will be bad. Cs. **Chesha.** Rp. **Chana. Cheleo,** n. *ma-* sometimes used in the plur. (1) awe, reverence, fear; (2) object of fear, reverence, awe, &c. **Kicho,** n. *vi-* (1) fear, awe, reverence; (2) that which causes or inspires fear, awe, reverence. **Mcha,** n. *wa-*, **Mchaji,** n. *wa-* one who fears, but generally used with *Mungu*, or *Mungu* understood. *Mcha* (*mchaji*) *Mungu*, a God-fearing, upright person. **Mchea,** n. *wa-*, **Mcheaji,** n. *wa-* one who fears for, &c. *Mchea mwana kulia, hulia yeye*, he who fears for his child's crying, will cry himself. **Mchelea,** n. *wa-*, **Mcheleaji,** n. *wa-* a nervous, apprehensive person. *Mchelea bahari si msafiri*, one who is nervous about the sea is no traveller. **Uchaji,** n. fear, respect, reverence, awe, &c., esp. of God. (Cf. *hofu, ogopa, tisha.*)

Cha, v. (B), dawn, change to dawn, be morning. *Kunakucha*, it is dawning. *Kumekucha*, dawn has come. *Hakujakucha*, it is not yet dawn. The infinitive, *kucha*, is regularly used as a noun, dawn, morning. Also commonly with or without *usiku*, of the whole period of darkness ending with dawn. *Usiku kucha*, all night long. *Hakulala kucha*, he had no sleep all night. Prep. **Chea.** D.Prep. **Chelea,** be belated, i.e. overtaken by sunrise. *Jua limenichea*, the sun rose while I was still in bed (asleep), I was surprised, overtaken by sunrise. No Ps. in use. Ps. of Prep. **Chewa,** be overtaken by dawn, hence a form of respectful morning greeting is *Kuchewa?* or *Habari za kucha?* How does the dawn find you? Are you well this morning? To which the reply is *Kuchewa*, I am well this morning. The Ps. of the D. Prep. **Chelewa,** with meaning similar to *chewa*, has developed a special meaning, and is used generally of, be late, be too late, remain an unusual or unexpected time. *Sikukawia wala sikuchelewa*, I did not delay nor was I late. *Ukuni huu umechelewa moto sana*, this piece of wood has kept hot a very long time. *Maji yamechelewa kisimani*, water still remains in the well. Cs. of D. Prep. **Cheleza,** cause to remain till morning (i.e. all night), and so cause to remain an unusual time, keep (preserve, leave) for a purpose. *Wakamcheleza mtoto shimoni*, they let the child remain in the pit (for safety, &c.). *Nimekuchelezea wali hata alfajiri*, I have left some rice for you (to eat) in the morning, i.e. saved from the evening meal. Also used in an Inten. sense, to remain a long time at night without getting sleep. Another Cs. form, **Chelewesha,** is used as the Cs. of the general meaning of *chelewa*, and so cause to be late, delay, put obstructions in the way. (Note: what is prob. the Cv. form *chua* appears to have become *chwa*. This form, together with its derivatives, is shown separately for convenience of reference.) **Cheleo,** n. *ma-* delay. **Chelezo,** n. *ma-* something causing delay. **Chelewa,** n. usu. used of the condition of a man the morning after an orgy of drinking. **Kichea,** n. brightness, dawn, also of becoming bright after cloudiness. **Macheo,** n. plur. dawn, sunrise, also where the sun rises, i.e. the east. **Uchao,** n., **Uche,** n. early morning, when the sun begins to rise. **Ucheachea,** n. also **Uteatea,** dawn, brightness after cloudiness, &c. *Kwanza anga ilikuwa na utusitusi, sasa ina ucheachea*, at first it was dull (dark, cloudy), now it is bright. (Contr. *utusitusi.*) (Cf. *mchana, alfajiri, asubuhi, mapambazuko, weupe, panda, chomoza.*)

Chaa, n. (1) a kind of fish considered to be good eating by Europeans; (2) a group of people cultivating together; (3) a stable or enclosure for cattle—locally Mombasa.

Chacha, v. (1) ferment, as dough, native beer, &c.; (2) froth, foam, form a scum; (3) turn sour, go bad, spoil, as stale food, &c.; (4) fig. be sour in temper, cross, irritated. Ps. **Chachwa.** Prep. **Chachia.** St. **Chachika.** Cs. **Chachisha,** (1) make sour, sharp, acid; (2) provoke, exasperate. Cv. **Chachua,** cause fermentation. St. **Chachuka,** (1) turn sour, ferment; (2) foam, froth. *Wali umechachuka leo*, the rice has gone sour to-day. *Bahari imechachuka*, the sea is frothy (yeasty, churning). **Chachu,** n. anything producing fermentation, yeast, leaven, such as *pombe*, &c. **Uchachu,** n. sourness, as of fermentation.

Chachaga, v. wash—used only of washing clothes by rubbing in the hands and dabbing on a board or stone, as of delicate fabrics. Prep. **Chachagia.** Ps. **Chachagwa.** (Cf. *fua, chanyata.*)

Chachari, n. *ma-* (1) usu. in the plur., restlessness or awkwardness caused by nervousness or excessive excitement; (2) resistance, trouble, e.g. caused by a person arrested attempting to escape from his captor; (3) mischievousness, departure from orderliness, e.g. as of a dancer leaving the other dancers and dancing by himself, showing off.

Chachatika, v. (1) tingle (of the blood, nerves); (2) sizzle (of fat boiling).

Chachawa, v. (1) jump about with pleasure or excitement, e.g. as children do when pleased or excited; (2) take up one's work (habit, routine, &c.), with renewed vigour after a period of laxity, laziness, satiety, &c. (Cf. *chaga, charuka.*)

Chachawiza, v. interrupt or drown anybody's speaking by making a noise or confusion. **Chachawizo,** n. *ma-* noise, confusion, interruption. (Cf. *hinikiza, dakiza, ghasia, ukelele, fujo.*)

-chache, a. few in number, small (little) in quantity, not much, not many, slight, deficient; (2) rare, not easily got, scarce, (and so) of value. *Siku chache*, a few days. *Watu wachache*, not many people. *Akili zake chache*, or *mchache wa akili*, he is deficient in sense. **Uchache,** n. (1) fewness, scarcity, want, slightness; (2) rarity, being scarce, (and so) of value. *Uchache wa moyo*, lack of spirit, feebleness of character. (Cf. *haba, ghali, adimika, uchechefu.*)

Chachia, v. involve in difficulties, hamper, perplex, press on, be too much for one. Ps. **Chachiwa.** (Perh. the same as **Tatia,** which see, under **Tata,** v.).

Chachu, n., **Chachua**, v., **Chachuka**, v. See under **Chacha.**

Chadi, n., v. and adv. often heard for **Jadi.**

Chafi, n. a kind of broad black fish, sometimes called *tasi.*

-chafu, a. dirty, filthy, unclean, impure, obscene. *Nguo chafu*, dirty clothes. *Maneno machafu*, obscene language. **Chafua,** v. (1) make dirty, soil, spoil; (2) make in a mess, disorder, disarrange, disturb; (3) of the sea, make rough. Cs. (seldom used) **Chafusha.** St. **Chafuka,** be dirty, in a mess, disarranged, &c. *Bahari ilichafuka sana*, the sea was very rough. *Mambo yamechafuka*, affairs are in confusion. *Alichafuka moyo* (or *tumbo*) his stomach was upset, he was sick. Prep. **Chafulia.** *Amenichafulia nguo*, he has dirtied my clothes. Ps. **Chafuliwa. Chafuko,** n. *ma-*, often used in the plur., disorder, muddle, mess, chaos, disorganization, unsettlement, confusion. **Mchafuko,** n. *mi-* same as *chafuko*. **Mchafuzi,** n. *wa-* one who causes disorder, muddle, &c. **Uchafu,** n. uncleanness, filthiness, dirt, &c. **Uchafuko,** n. same as *chafuko*. (Cf. *taka, najisi, vuruga, fuja, ghasia.*)

Chafu, n. *ma-*. See **Shavu.**

Chafua, v., **Chafuko**, n. *ma-*. See under **-chafu.**

Chafuo, n. a poisonous kind of fly, tsetse. (Cf. *mbung'o, mbungu.*)

Chafya, n. a sneeze. *Piga* (*enda*) *chafya*, sneeze. If a sick man sneezes, it is said to be a sign of his getting better. If a child sneezes, his mother or father says *Kua* (grow), or *Kua kama mgomba, mnazi unakawilia*, grow up like a banana plant, a coconut-tree takes a long time, or *Kulia juu, chini kuna moto*, grow upwards, it is hot below. Muhammadans sometimes say, *Alhamdulillahi*, Praise be to God.

Chaga, v. (1) take up one's work (a habit, routine, &c.) with renewed vigour after a period of laxness (cf. *charuka, chachawa*); (2) begin a habit, work, action, &c. *Simba amechaga kukamata watu siku hizi*, a lion has begun to catch people lately. (3) be prevalent, e.g. *homa imechaga*, fever is prevalent (cf. *charuka*); (4) be disturbed, stirred up. Cs. **Chagiza,** has a special Inten. meaning: (1) insist, be insistent, pester, importune (for money, &c.), dun. *Fulani amenichagiza nimlipe fedha yake*, So-and-so has dunned me to pay him his money. (2) press with argument, be insistent in conversation, and so, be garrulous.

Chagina, n. and a. bold, brave person. (Cf. *hodari, shujaa, shupavu.*)

Chagiza, v. See under **Chaga.**

Chago, n. (1) part of a bedstead on which the head rests, also called **Mchago** and **Uchago**; (2) a kind of crab.

Chagua, v. (1) choose, select, pick out, make a choice; (2) of biased or partial selection, garble, give a false colour to, be unfair. Prov. *Mchagua jembe si mkulima*, a man who is fastidious about his hoe is not a husbandman. Ps. **Chaguliwa.** Prep. **Chagulia.** St. **Chagulika.** Cs. **Chaguza,** offer choice to, give an order (leave, right) to choose. Rp. **Chaguana.** The Rd. form *chaguachagua*, is used of dainty, critical selection. **-chaguzi,** a. given to choosing, dainty, critical, &c. **Mchaguzi,** n. *wa-* one who chooses, discriminates, but usu. one who is fastidious, pernickety. **Uchaguo,** n. **Uchaguzi,** n. a choosing, choice, discrimination, daintiness, fastidiousness, habit of criticism. (Cf. *teua, pembua.*)

Chai,* n. tea. (Hind. Pers., &c. چای)

Chaka, n. *ma-* (1) clump of trees, dense part of a forest; (2) the hot season, i.e. December to February, but usu. called *msimu* and *kaskazi.* (Cf. *mwaka.*) **Kichaka,** n. *vi-* dim. of (1).

Chakaa, v. get old, become worn, wear out, be used up (worn, faded), be past work—of things and persons. *Nguo zimechakaa*, the clothes are worn out. Prep. **Chakalia.** Cs. **Chakaza,** use up, wear out. **-chakavu,** a. worn out, old. (Cf. *fifia, dhoofika, -kuukuu.*)

Chakaazi, n. a leafless, much-branched succulent tree up to 30 ft. tall with inconspicuous small yellow flowers, used medicinally, as a fish poison and as a protective hedge on account of its very caustic latex which on entering the eyes causes temporary blindness, *Euphorbia tirucalle.*

Chakacha, v. (1) rustle, as of grass when one goes through the forest, &c.; (2) pound, break small, as seeds in a mortar. *Chakacha menoni*, crunch with teeth. Ps. **Chakachwa.** St. and Pot. **Chakachika,** be pounded, be poundable. Prep. **Chakachia.** Cs. **Chakachisha.** (Cf. *twanga, ponda, seta, vunja*). **Chakachachakacha,** n. a rustling sound, i.e. as of dry grass or leaves, or silk dress, &c. **Mchakacho,** n. *mi-* (1) a crushing, a pounding; (2) a crackling, rustling, crunching sound, e.g. of feet on dry grass, leaves, &c. **Uchakacho,** n. a rustling sound, crackling, &c., of dry leaves, clothes, &c. (Cf. *chakarisha.*)

Chakari, adv. much, very, in a high

degree. *Kunywa chakari*, to drink very much, or be very drunk.

Chakarisha, v. (1) stir up, rouse, startle, as of an animal in a forest; (2) make a rustling noise as when passing through dry grass, &c. (Cf. *chakacha*.)

-chakavu, a. See under **Chakaa**.

Chake, form of *-ake*, his, hers, her, its, of him (her, it).

Chaki,* n. chalk, whiting, putty powder. (Eng. chalk.)

Chako, form of *-ako*, your, yours, of you.

Chakogea, n. *vy-*. See under **Oga**, v.

Chakula, n. *vy-*. See under **La**, v.

Chakura, v. (1) often Rd., scrape with the feet as a fowl, or a horse with its hoofs; (2) fig. spy upon, search diligently. **Mchakuro**, n. *mi-* (1) a scratching; (2) the sound of scratching or scraping; (3) a diligent search, or spying into. (Cf. *chakacha. chakarisha, para, papura, pekua, chokoa*.)

Chale, n. cut, gash, incision such as those made as tribal marks, for ornamental tattooing, or for medical purposes, &c. *Chale zetu za kuchanjiana hazijapona*, our gashes for making blood friendship have not yet healed. *Mganga alimchanja chale thelathini*, the doctor made thirty incisions, e.g. to reduce inflammation. **Chale cha pwani**, n. a sea urchin, said to be very poisonous should it pierce the skin. (Cf. *tojo, chanja, toja, kata, nembo*.)

Chali, adv. on the back, i.e. of a recumbent, supine position. *Lala chali*, lie on the back. Also **Chalichali**. (Cf. *kitani, kwa tani, kwa chani, kingalingali, mgongoni, kimgongogongo*.

Chama, n. *vy-* club, guild, society, association. *Wanachama*, members of a club. (Cf. *kikao, kikoa*.)

Chamba, n. See under **Amba**, v. (B).

Chamba, v. wash oneself after calls of nature. (Cf. *kokona* for other ways of cleansing oneself after such calls.)

Chambi, n. also **Chamvi**, a movement in certain dances. One of the dancers leaves the circle or row and goes into the centre of the dancers, then one of the other sex comes out also and they meet in the centre and dance a while, after which they return once more to their places in the circle or row. The action is called *Kupeana chambi* (or *chamvi*). (Cf. *chobea* which is used of the same movement, but the couple go through the movements usu. associated with coition, i.e. *kuchezesha viuno*.)

Chambo, n. *vy-* (1) bait for catching animals, fish, &c. *Chambo cha kuvulia samaki*, fish bait. *Chambo cha kutegea ndege*, bait for trapping birds. *Tia chambo katika ndoana*, bait a hook. (2) also used fig. of anything used to entice a person. Prov. *Mtego bila chambo haunasi*, a trap without bait catches nothing.

Chambua, v. also **Chamvua**, (1) clean, dress pick over, esp. of appropriate preparation of various products for use, cooking, marketing, e.g. *chambua samaki*, prepare a fish by removing the skin and bones. *Chambua pamba*, clean cotton by removing the seeds, dirt, and leaves. *Chambua nyama*, remove meat from a bone and cut it into small pieces. (2) tease, of rope, cloth, fibre, &c.; (3) generally clean up, give a finish to, improve appearance, &c., by teasing, &c.; (4) fig. criticize, cross-examine, expose the faults of, show up a person, abuse a person by mentioning all his faults, i.e. 'pull him to pieces'. Prep. **Chambulia**. Ps. **Chambuliwa**. **Tamvua**, n. *ma-* and **Utamvua**, n. (for *t* and *ch*, see note on *ch*) anything picked or teased out, hence a fringe, lappet, &c. (Cf. *ambua*, Cv. of *amba*, v. (B).)

Chamburo, n. a kind of pliers used by jewellers and craftsmen who make silver chains, &c. (Cf. *chambua*.)

Chamchela, n. (1) a whirlwind; (2) a spirit supposed to cause a whirlwind, and propitiated as such with offerings. (Cf. *kinyamkela.*)

Chamka, v. (1) recur, i.e. of recurring sickness, or headache, &c.; (2) spread, as of a sore. **Chamko,** n. recurrence, i.e. of fever, sickness, &c. (Cf. *amka.*)

Chamkano, n. *ma-* (1) a separating, faction, division; (2) section of a crowd dispersing.

Chamko, n. See under **Chamka.**

Chamshakinywa, n. See under **Amka.**

Chamvi, n. same as *chambi,* which see.

Chamvua, v. same as *chambua,* which see.

Chana, n. a bunchlet cluster, on the great fruit stem (*mkungu*) produced by the banana plant (*mgomba*), the single fruit being *dole,* and the fruit generally *ndizi.*

Chana, v. slit, separate, part, comb. *Chana miyaa,* slit leaves for plaiting, so *chana makuti,* of coco-nut fronds. *Chana nywele,* comb hair. Prep. **Chania.** St. **Chanika,** be in rags, be threadbare, torn to ribbons, combed out, &c. Ps. **Chanwa.** Cv. **Chanua,** (1) tease, comb out; (2) put out leaves (of plants generally). Prep. **Chanulia.** Ps. **Chanuliwa.** St. **Chanuka. Chane,** n. a slip of leaf, made by slitting it up finely or coarsely, for use in plaiting mats, cords, &c. **Chanuo,** n. a large comb, often of wood, with long coarse teeth. **Kichane,** n. *vi-* a small splinter, something split off, or teased off. **Kichanio,** n. *vi-* a comb, anything used for teasing or combing. **Kitana,** n. *vi-* (for *kichana*), a small comb. (Cf. Pers. شانه a comb.)

Chanda, n. *vy-* a finger, a toe, seldom used except in the vicinity of Mombasa, the usu. word is *kidole.*

Chandalua,* n. (— and *vy-*) mosquito net, sometimes also applied to awnings, canopy, covering of any material used for protection against sun, rain, insects, &c. (Hind. چندوا)

Chando, n. a certain kind of dance in which the partners meet in the centre of the ring, and after dancing a while return to their places. This is called *kupeana chambi.* (Cf. *chambi, tarazia.*)

Chane, n. See under **Chana, v.**

Changa, v. (A), (1) collect together, for any special purpose; (2) put together, mix, shuffle (as of cards). *Changa fedha,* collect money by way of voluntary contributions. *Changa askari,* muster soldiers, levy a force. *Changa mali kulipa deni,* collect money for payment of a debt. *Kula kwa kuchanga,* hold a club, or subscription feast, each person contributing. (Cf. *kula bia.*) St. **Changika.** Prep. **Changia,** e.g. *mali ya kuchangiwa,* money collected to give for a special (or charitable) purpose. Cs. **Changisha** and **Changiza.** Rp. of Cs. **Changizana,** join in getting contributions, put subscriptions together. Rp. **Changana,** of people joining together for a special purpose, e.g. as of volunteers for war, &c. Cs. of Rp. **Changanya,** (1) collect together, mix, form into one mass; (2) make in a mess, muddle, confuse. *Changanya tembo na maji,* mix palm-wine and water. *Changanya mashamba,* put plantations together, i.e. make them into one. *Changanya maneno,* confuse words, i.e. of two languages. Ps. **Changanywa.** St. **Changanyika,** be mixed together, be confused. Cs. **Changanyisha,** and **-iza,** (1) mix, adulterate; (2) cause confusion in, perplex. Stc. **Changamana** (also sometimes **Tangamana**), be in a mixed up condition, often with *na* (1) be mixed up with; (2) mix with people, join together in society, &c.; (3) be adjoining (border[illegible]g on, next to). *Shamba limech[illegible]gamana na pwani,* the estate adjoins the shore. Cv. **Changua,** take to pieces disconnect, take or put apart anything collected together—used of dismembering and cutting up animals for food. *Changua misitu,* cut down trees in a forest, i.e. to make a plantation. Cv. of Rp. **Changanua,** separate what is mixed, resolve into constituent parts, analyse, simplify what is compound. **Chango,** n. (1) contribution, subscription, esp. of money or food for a common object; (2) levy, muster. *Chango ya watu,* a muster of people. **Changamano,** n. *ma-* (*tangamano*), state of being mixed together, of being one, hence, concord, agreement. **Changanyiko,** n. *ma-* same as *mchanganyiko,* see under. **Changanyo,** n. *ma-* same as *mchanganyo,* see below. **Kichanganyiko,** n. *vi-* a factor in arithmetic. *Hesabu za vichanganyiko,* practice sums. **Mchanganyiko,** n. *mi-* a mixture. **Mchanganyo,** n. *mi-* a mixing up. **Mchango,** n. *mi-* collecting, getting together, joining in undertaking, contribution, e.g. *mchango wa askari,* mustering of soldiers. *Mchango wa mali,* raising funds from different sources. **Uchango,** n. collection of subscriptions, &c.

Changa, v. (B), (1) chop up, cut up, as of firewood into small pieces, or meat and bone together; (2) hurt, ache, as of feeling pain in the bones.

-changa, a. young, immature, undeveloped, unripe, in an early stage of growth or experience, both of animal and plant life. *Mtoto mchanga,* a young child. *Kitoto kichanga,* a very young child. *Embe changa,* half-grown mangoes. *Mahindi machanga,* maize not fully developed. *Askari mchanga,* a raw recruit. **Uchanga,** n. immaturity, unripeness, early stage of development, babyhood, littleness. (Cf. *-bichi.*)

Changamana, v., **Changamano,** n. *ma-*. See under **Changa,** v. (A).

-changamfu, a. agreeable, enlivening, good-humoured, cheerful. **Changamka,** v. become cheerful, look bright and happy, be in good spirits, be in a buoyant mood. *Amechangamka,* he has recovered his spirits, he is happy. Used of the sun coming out bright after cloud or rain. Also of scenery, *nchi inachangamka,* the view has become bright, clear to the eye. Prep. **Changamkia.** Cs. **Changamsha,** cheer up, revive the spirits, gladden, exhilarate. Ps. **Changamshwa.** Cv. **Changamua,** make cheerful—rarely used. **Changamko,** n. *ma-* entertainment, amusement, pastime, play, anything that raises the spirits, also **Kichangamko,** n. *vi-*. (Cf. *amka, furahi, chekelea, mchezo, mazungumzo.*)

Changanua, v., **Changanya,** v., **Changanyika,** v., **Changanyiko,** n. *ma-*, **Changanyo,** n. *ma-*. See under **Changa,** v. (A).

Changarawe, n. grit, small stones, fine gravel, bits of stone in sand or rice. Not so fine as *mchanga,* sand; finer than *kokoto,* small stones.

Chango, n. (1) see under *changa,* v. (A); (2) (— and *ma-*) smaller intestines, plur. of *uchango*; (3) round intestinal worms; (4) *chango la uzazi,* the umbilical cord. **Uchango,** n. same as *chango,* (2), (3), and (4). (Cf. *uchengelele, tegu, matumbo.*)

Chango, n. *vy-*. See under **Anga,** v.

Changu, n. (1) a kind of fish, very good eating. There are several kinds, *changu chole, changu kawaa,* &c.; (2) form of *-angu,* my, mine.

Changua, v. See under **Changa,** v. (A).

Chani, adv. also **Tani,** on the back, in a recumbent, supine position, same as *chali,* which see.

Chani, n. or **Chanui,** n. a sea-porcupine.

Chanikiwiti, a. green, grass green (from *ki-(j)ani* and *kiwiti* for *kibichi,* i.e. fresh grass (leaves), and so of light green colour).

Chanja, n. used of many objects made of wicker-work, interwoven twigs, osiers, wattles, e.g. a screen, a kind of hurdle, a crib for holding animals' food, a kind of sieve or strainer, a frame for smoking meat on over a fire, but principally a shelf or stand for storing grain in a house. *Chanja ya chuma*, a grid-iron. *Chanja ya kuanikia nyama moshini*, a frame for drying meat on in the smoke. *Ingia nyumbani hata mvunguni hata juu ya chanja*, go inside the house and look even under the bed and even on the store-shelf.

Chanja, v. (1) cut into, make cut a (incision, gash) in. *Chanja uchale*, make an incision (with knife, razor, lancet). *Chanja mti*, make cuts in a tree (whether to obtain sap or remove bark). (2) cut up, split in pieces, make by cutting up. *Chanja kuni*, split logs for firewood. (3) vaccinate. *Chanja ndui*, vaccinate against small-pox. Note: often used in a Ps. sense, *nimechanja ndui*, I have been vaccinated against small-pox. Ps. **Chanjwa.** Prep. **Chanjia.** Rp. **Chanjana.** Rp. of Prep. **Chanjiana**, make incisions in each other, i.e. in making blood-friendships. **Chanjo**, n. a gash, cut, incision, vaccination. *Piga chanjo la mti*, make a cut in a tree. **Mchanjo**, n. *mi-* a cutting, lopping, &c. (Cf. *chenga, pasua, tema, kata, toja*.)

Chanjari, adv. See **Sanjari.**

Chanjo, n. See under **Chanja, v.**

Chano, n. *vya-* flat round wooden platter with a low rim, sometimes with a stand in one piece, forming a low table. Used as (1) plate for serving up food; (2) a board for carrying mortar, &c.; (3) a wash table. *Chano cha shetani* (*cha pepo*), a dish or tray containing articles of food, sweet things, trifles, as an offering to the spirit in exorcism, or for the person who is being exorcized to eat.

Chanua, v., **Chanuo**, n. See under **Chana, v.**

Chanyata, v. (1) slice up (of bananas, cassava, and various kinds of food); (2) wash clothes gently, as of delicate fabrics, or give them a hasty washing. **Mchanyato**, n. *mi-* (1) a dish of bananas, cassava, &c., boiled and pounded; (2) a hasty or gentle washing of cloth.

Chanyatia, n. a kind of fish found in mangrove swamps.

Chanzi, n. sometimes heard for *ganzi*, which see.

Chanzo, n. *vy-*. See under **Anza.**

Chao, n. (1) a roller used for putting under a boat when it is being launched; (2) form of *-ao*, their, theirs.

Chapa, a. much, in great quantity, e.g. *alitoka damu chapa*, he bled profusely.

Chapa, v. beat, hit, strike—for the more common *piga*. *Nitakuchapa*, I will beat you. *Chapa miguu*, stamp on the ground, tramp, walk heavily. Cv. **Chapua**, (1) give a blow (to), strike (with). *Chapua miguu*, stamp, tramp, walk quickly. (2) speed up, beat harder, of a drum, or any action. Cs. of Prep. with more Inten. sense, **Chapuliza**, used in the same way as *chapua*. St. **Chapuka**, put force into, speed up. *Chapuka upesi*, step out, hurry up. **Chapa**, n. (1) stroke, blow, but esp. (2) of the result of a blow, stamp, mark, and hence used of various objects stencil, printer's type, trade mark, brand. *Alimpiga chapa kila mtu mkononi*, he branded each man on the arm. *Pipa limeandikwa* (or *pigwa*) *chapa*, the cask has a mark on it. *Piga chapa kitabu*, print a book. (Cf. Hind. چهاپ a seal, printing, &c.). **Chapuchapu**, adv. and int. Quick! Make haste! Hurry up! **Chapuo**, n. a small kind of drum, **Mchapo**, n. *mi-* (1) a stroke with a stick, whip, &c.; (2) a whip, something to strike with.

Chapeo,* n. hat (of European kind), helmet—rarely used. (Cf. *kofia*, Port. *chapeo*.)

Chapua, v., **Chapuchapu,** adv., **Chapuka,** v. See under **Chapa,** v.

Chapukia, v. be savoury, pleasant, of food. **Chapwa,** a. unpleasant to the taste, nasty, insipid.

Chapuliza, v., **Chapuo,** n. See under **Chapa,** v.

Chapwa, a. See under **Chapukia.**

Charakisha, v. a variant of *chakarisha,* which see.

Charaza, v. (1) play, dance, play on an instrument; (2) do anything without pause or with vigour or skill. *Kumcharaza mtu fimbo,* to beat a person with a stick, without pause, vigorously, &c. *Kucharaza cherehani,* work a sewing-machine with skill. *Charaza baisikeli,* ride skilfully on a cycle. Ps. **Charazwa.** St. **Charazika.**

Charo, n. *vy-* a company of travellers, a caravan, for the common *msafara* or *safari.*

Charuka, v. (1) take up one's work (habit, routine, &c.) with renewed vigour after a period of laxness or abstinence. *Fulani amecharukwa na kichaa,* So-and-so has been attacked again by madness (cf. *chachawa*). (2) begin a habit, work, action, &c. *Simba amecharuka kukamata watu,* the lion has commenced (or begun again) to catch people. (Cf. *chaga.*)

Chata, v. make a sizzling sound, e.g. as of termites, &c., when disturbed.

Chatu, n. a python.

Chavu, n. *ma-*. See **Shavu.**

Chawa, n. a louse. Prov. *Kidole kimoja hakivunji chawa,* a single finger does not kill a louse.

Chaza, n. an oyster. Sometimes heard as *shaza.* (? Pers. شس (صدف) an oyster.)

Chazi, n. a liane, *Cissus rotundifolia.*

Chazo, n. a sucker-fish.

Chea, v. see under **Cha,** v. (A) and (B).

Checha, v. (1) slice, such as slicing cassava, &c. (cf. *lenga*); (2) contradict, forbid (cf. *gomba, kataza*); (3) dig up the earth in a plantation (cf. *lima*). **Cheche,** n. (1) a slice or small piece of anything, such as cassava, which has been sliced, &c.; (2) a spark. *cheche ya moto,* a spark of fire.

Cheche, n. (1) see under **Checha,** v.; (2) a small black and white animal, rather like a mongoose, said to be able to emit a very disagreeable odour, so strong that if it enters a beehive, all the bees die. It is said that if its skin is burned in a village, it causes all the people to quarrel among themselves. Also called *nyegere*; a kind of skunk?

Chechea, v. walk carefully, as with a limp, &c. Prep. of Stc. **Chechemea,** be lame, walk carefully or with a limp. Cs. **Chechesha,** also **Checheza,** (1) help to walk by holding the arm, used of helping a sick man or a child just beginning to walk; (2) cause to use carefully, e.g. *nina mafuta ya kunichecheza mpaka mwisho wa mwezi,* I have oil, but if it is to last me to the end of the month, I must use it very carefully.

Chechele, n. (1) a small insect—like a caterpillar—if one steps on it, it is said to make one forget one's destination, or lose one's wits; (2) forgetfulness, e.g. *kuchukuliwa na chechele,* to be seized with forgetfulness.

Chechemea, v., **Chechesha,** v. See under **Chechea.**

Chechevu, n. hiccup, also called *kwikwi.*

Checheza, v. See under **Chechea.**

Chefuka, v. cause a feeling of sickness, or nausea. *Moyo unanichefuka,* I feel sick. **Kichefuchefu,** n. nausea, a sick feeling. (Cf. *kigagazi.*)

Chega, v. shave off, cut the hair. (Cf. *nyoa.*)

Chegama, v. (1) same as *egama,* which see; (2) be washed up by the sea, e.g. *ndoo hii imechegama,* this bucket has been washed up by the sea. (3) also used of a beachcomber. *Fulani huchegama pwani,* So-and-so relies on the beach, i.e. is a beachcomber. (2) and (3) rarely used. (Cf. *egama, tegemea.*)

Chege, a. (1) moist, watery. *Muhogo huu ni chege,* this cassava is watery (or, *muhogo mchege*), i.e. when boiled it is not floury (cf. *chepechepe, chelema*). (2) stupid, foolish, inane. (Cf. *bozi, -jinga, -pumbavu, baridi.*)

Chege, n. *ma-* also **Tege,** *ma-* bow-leg, bandy-leg. *Ana machege,* or *ana chege la miguu,* he is bandy-legged.

Chego, n. *ma-*. See **Gego.**

Cheka, v. (1) laugh, smile, grin; (2) laugh at, mock, ridicule. *Tulimcheka sana,* we laughed at him heartily. Ps. **Chekwa.** St. **Chekeka.** Prep. **Chekea.** D. Prep. **Chekelea,** smile, smile at, Ps. **Chekelewa.** Cs. **Chekesha,** cause to laugh, amuse, excite, ridicule (amazement). **Cheko,** n. a laugh, laughter. *Piga cheko kubwa,* utter roars of laughter. Often used with the verb *angua,* e.g. *walu wote waliangua cheko,* the whole company burst out laughing. **-cheshi,** a. amusing, entertaining, laughable. **Kicheko,** n. *vi-* a laugh, a smile, giggle, grin. **Mchekeshaji,** n. *wa-* an amusing, droll person, a wag, a clown, a merry smiling person. **Mchekeshi,** n. *wa-*, **Mcheshi,** n. *wa-* one who causes people to smile, like *mchekeshaji.* **Mcheko,** n. *mi-* act (manner, circumstances) of laughing, laughter, &c. **Ucheshi,** n. good temper, laughter, humour, wit.

Chekea mwezi, n. Water-dikkop or Stone-curlew, *Burhinus vermiculatus.*

Chekecha, v. (1) sift, i.e. shake about in a sieve; (2) retrench. **Chekecheke,** n. (1) a sieve; (2) retrenchment. **Mchekecho,** n. *mi-* a sifting.

Chekechea, n. Fire-crowned Bishop-bird, *Euplectes hordacea.*

Chekecheke, n. See under **Chekecha.**

Chekehukwa, n. name of a bird, Dotterel.

Cheko, n. See under **Cheka.**

Chekwa, adv. also **Chekwachekwa,** in large quantities. *Vitu vimejaa chekwa uwanjani,* the open space is simply crowded with things. *Nyota zimeenea chekwa uwinguni,* the sky is full of stars. (Cf. *wingi, pomoni, jaa.*)

Chelea, v. See under **Cha,** v. (A) and (B).

Cheleko, n. and int. a word used to express joy at a wedding or when a girl begins menstruation. In some places the girl is carried pick-a-back, while the women sing or shout *Mwanangu amevunja ungo, cheleko chanduma* (*cha-ni-uma*), lit. my daughter has reached puberty, and child-bearing hurts me, i.e. the joy felt at the girl having grown up is so great that it hurts the mother. *Cheleko* is derived from a verb *eleka* or *weleka,* which in some Bantu languages means bear children. (Cf. *mbeleko.*)

Chelema, a. watery (used of cassava, vegetables, &c., which are watery, not floury, when cooked). (Cf. *chege.*) **Mchelema,** n. watery cassava or potatoes, &c., which do not turn floury when cooked.

Cheleo, n., **Chelewa,** v. See under **Cha,** v. (A) and (B).

Chelewa, n. (1) see under **Cha,** v. (B); (2) a kind of rattle used in dances, made by putting either stones or seeds into a tin; (3) the vein in a leaf.

Cheleza, v. (1) see under **Cha,** v. (B); (2) unload cargo from a ship. *Meli iko bandarini inacheleza,* the boat is in the harbour unloading cargo.

Chelezo, n. *vy-* (1) see under **Cha,** v. (A) and (B); (2) under **Elea,** v. (A).

Chembe, n. (1) a grain, a minute separate part of a thing, a single small thing, e.g. grain of sand (*mchanga*), of corn (*nafaka*), &c. *Chembe chembe,* in grains, grain by grain, granular. Also sometimes used with a negative to express complete absence, e.g. *hana akili hata chembe,* he has no sense, not even a grain. *Hakubakiza kitu hata chembe,* he left nothing, not even a grain. (2) the head of an arrow, spear-head, &c., perh. from *ki-(j)embe*; (3) (pl. *vyembe*) *chembe cha moyo*, pit of the stomach, i.e. depression between cartilage of false ribs.

Chembeu, n. a kind of blunt chisel used for caulking. (Cf. *kalafati*.)

Chemchemi, n. a spring of water. (Cf. *chemka*.)

Chemka, v. bubble up, and so of hot water when it begins to bubble, boil. Cs. **Chemsha**, cause to boil, boil. Prep. **Chemshia**. Ps. **Chemshwa**. **Chemko**, n. boiling, bubbling. (Cf. *tokosa*, *pika* which are used for cooking by boiling.)

Chemua, v. sneeze. (Cf. *chafya*.)

Chenene, n. a kind of large cricket that makes a screeching noise at night; it burrows into the ground. (Cf. *nyenze*, *nyenje*.)

Cheneo, n. *vy-*. See under **Enea**.

Cheneta, v. (1) prepare unripe maize ready for cooking; (2) itch, irritate, smart. (Cf. *chonyota*.)

Chenezo, n. See under **Eneo**.

Chenga, n. (1) a kind of fish; (2) see under **Chenga**, v.

Chenga, v. cut, lop, e.g. heads of millet, stalks of ripe grain, brushwood for firing or fencing, &c. Ps. **Chengwa**. Prep. **Chengea**. **Chenga**, adv. used of evading by trickery, e.g. *kupiga chenga*, dodge, avoid, evade. *Nilimwona anakuja nikampiga chenga*, I saw him coming and I dodged him (evaded him without his seeing me). Also used of dribbling in football, i.e. *kupiga chenga*. **Chenga**, n. small piece, grain, i.e. of rice, maize, &c., when beaten in a mortar before it is flour. **Chengachenga**, small bits, chips, snippings, also adj. composed of grains, granular. *Unga wa chengachenga*, flour which contains small pieces, i.e. has not been thoroughly pounded or ground to flour. **Mchengo**, n. *mi-* cutting, esp. of wood, trees, bushes, stalks, &c.

Chengo, n. *vy-* (1) house, a man's dwelling or village; (2) a place where a caravan rests, camp. *Mtu akifika chengo cha mtu, humtegemea*, if a person goes to a person's house (place, &c.) he becomes dependent on him. Cf. An Englishman's home is his castle. (Cf. *maskani*, *kitende*.)

Chenu, form of *-enu*, your, yours, of you.

Chenza, n. *ma-* a large kind of Mandarin orange, fruit of the *mchenza*. Some are red or blood oranges. The best are called *chenza za Kiajemi*, i.e. Persian, and a small kind *kangaja*.

Cheo, n. *vy-* (1) measure, measurement, dimensions, size. *Toa cheo*, fix the size. *Cheo cha kuanzia kitako cha kikapu*, measurement for beginning the bottom of a basket—and so settling the size. *Kupita cheo*, beyond measure, excessively (cf. *kiasi*, *kadiri*, *kimo*, *ukubwa*). (2) rank, degree, station, status (cf. *daraja*, *hali*); (3) a rod of iron, brass, or ivory used as a wand by a medicine man when exorcizing spirits. The person being exorcized (*mteja*) holds one end of the rod, and the exorcist the other end. This is said to put the exorcist in communication with the spirit. It is also used by diviners when searching for lost articles. (4) a board used for plaiting *ukili*; (5) a stake used for removing the husks of coco-nuts (cf. *kifuo*). Prob. from the same root as *elea*, v. (B).

Chepe, n. *ma-* an inconsiderate, ill-bred, mannerless person. **Chepe**, adv. swaggering, in an ill-bred, inconsiderate manner.

Chepechepe, a. wet, soaked, soppy, moist. **Uchepechepe**, n. moisture, wetness. (Cf. *maji maji*, *rutuba*, *lowa*, *loweka*.)

Cherehani,* n. used generally of small foreign machines, but esp. sewing-machines. *Cherehani ya kushonea*, a sewing-machine. *Kazi ya cherehani*, machine sewing. **Cherehe**, n. a grindstone. (Pers. چرخ a wheel,

&c., anything revolving, and خان belonging to the house.)

-cheshi, a. See under **Cheka.**

Chete, n. the day on which a market is held, also the place in which it is held. Used chiefly in the north, i.e. Tanga to Mombasa. (Cf. *soko*; *gulio*.)

Chetezo, n. *vy-* a vessel, often of earthenware, in which to burn incense or sweet-smelling aromatic substances, a censer. (Cf. *kifukizo, ubani, uvumba, manukato*.)

Cheti,* n. (— and *vy-*) note, ticket, passport, certificate, 'chit', &c. (Cf. *hati, barua*. Hind. چٹی).

Chetu, form of *-etu*, our, ours, of us.

Cheu, n. a returning of food to the mouth from the stomach. **Cheua,** v. (1) ruminate, chew the cud (of ruminant animals); also (2) used of food returning to the mouth from the stomach, i.e. *mtoto amecheua maziwa*, the child has returned the milk from his stomach to his mouth. Cf. **Cheusha,** cause eructation. St. **Cheuka,** return to the mouth from the stomach.

Chewa, n. a large kind of fish with a very broad head and large mouth, giant rock-cod. *Fulani ana kinywa kama chewa*, So-and-so has a mouth like a *chewa*, of one with a very large mouth, or who opens his mouth very wide when he yawns or when eating his food, or in astonishment.

Chewa, v. See under **Cha,** v. (A) and (B).

Cheza, v. (1) play, sport, play a game, make a move in a game; (2) idle, waste time, not be in earnest, trifle; (3) act, work, move, esp. of the easy motion of a machine running well, or a hinge, bolt, wheel, watch, &c.; (4) drill, be drilled (as soldiers); (5) be loose, not fixed, as a small peg in a large hole. Ps. **Chezwa.** Prep. **Chezea,** play with (in, for, &c.), make sport of, mock. *Kitu cha kuchezea watoto*, a toy, something for children to play with. St. **Chezeka.** Cs. **Chezesha.** Inten. play about with. *Chezesha unyago*, put into the initiation rites, see *unyago*. *Chezesha farasi*, make a horse prance. Rd. **Chezacheza,** trifle, be loose, &c. **Chezo,** n. *ma-* sport, game, play, pastime. **Mcheza,** n. *wa-*, **Mchezaji,** n. *wa-*, and **Mchezi,** n. *wa-* one who plays, a gay sportive person, a player, an actor. *Mchezaji* is used of one who plays habitually, or is a skilled player. **Mchezo,** n. *mi-* (1) a game, pastime, amusement, sport; (2) a mockery, &c. *Usikifanye mchezo*, don't make a mock of it. *Mambo haya si mchezo*, these matters are not to be taken lightly, or made a mock of. (Cf. *masihara, mzaha, laabu*.)

Chicha, n. (1) the white nutty part inside a ripe coco-nut, when it has been scraped or grated out with a *mbuzi*, and the oil (*tui*) strained out by passing water through it, or merely squeezing it, in which case the oil is called *tui bubu*. It is generally considered refuse, used for cleaning the hands with, and thrown to the fowls. (2) the residuum or lees of other oil-producing seeds and also of native beer (*pombe, tembo*); (3) the secretion inside the prepuce of an uncircumcised person. (Cf. *tui, kasimele*.)

Chichiri, n. a bribe. (Cf. *rushwa, hongo*.)

Chigi, n. name of a small yellow bird.

Chika, n. Abyssinian Dock, a perennial herb with stems up to 12 ft. tall.

Chikicha, v. sometimes *tikita*, cut with a sawing motion, as with something blunt. (Cf. *kichichi*.)

Chikichi, n. the fruit of the *mchikichi*, the palm-oil tree. The nuts (*chikichi*) are crushed for oil, which is called *mawese*. **Kichikichi,** n. *vi-* the small nut or kernel contained in the *chikichi* fruit.

Chiku, n. See **Chiriku.**

Chikwaya dume, n. *Dichapetalum mossambicense*. **Chikwaya jike,** n. *Dichapetalum macrocarpum*.

Chimba, v. (1) dig, make (get) by digging—of excavation, not as *lima*, of cultivation. *Chimba shimo*, dig a pit, sink a shaft (mine), make a hole. *Chimba kaburi*, dig a grave. *Chimba njugu*, dig up ground-nuts. *Chimba udongo*, dig out earth, soil. (2) fig. harm, cause trouble or misfortune to, esp. parents, see *chimvi* below. Prep. **Chimbia**. Cs. **Chimbisha**. St. **Chimbika**. Cv. **Chimbua**, similar in use to *chimba*, dig out, dig up, get by digging, &c. St. **Chimbuka**, used esp. of the sun or moon, 'appear, begin to shine, rise', i.e. come up from the earth, become visible, &c. Used whether from horizon or from clouds. Also Cs. and Inten. **Chimbuza**, in the same sense, force its way out, make its appearance. **Chimbo**, n. *ma-* digging, place dug, pit, mine. **Chimbuko**, n. *ma-* (1) same as *chimbo*; (2) a first start, a beginning, source. **Chimvi**, n. *ma-* also **Mchimbi**, n. *wa-*, **Mchimvi**, n. *wa-*, **Mtimbi**, n. *wa-*, **Mtimvi**, n. *wa-*, and **Timvi**, n. *ma-* (1) a person considered of ill omen, unlucky, a menace to family or neighbours, e.g. a child born with front teeth or other peculiarities, a child at whose birth the mother dies, &c. *Huyu ni chimvi amemchimba mama yake*, he is an unlucky child, he has dug (a grave for?) his mother. (2) also said of owls, (and *chimvi* and *timvi*, certain actions of dogs, fowls, animals), which are supposed to bring ill luck; (3) a witch, but only one who makes charms, &c., by roots, parts of corpses he digs up or causes to rise from the grave—not used of those who charm or influence without visible agency. (Cf. *mwanga* and *uanga*.) **Uchimvi**, n. bad luck, see *chimvi*, above. (Cf. *kigego, kisirani, kitimbi, chira*.)

China, v. be too late, remain beyond the usual time, fail to materialize, fail to get what was expected, &c., be disappointed, &c., *samaki imechina*, the fish has remained (in the shop) too long, it is now bad. *Mwali huyu amechina*, this girl has remained single too long, i.e. of a girl who is very late in getting a husband. *Mti huu umechina*, this tree has failed, i.e. the other trees of the same kind are now bearing fruit, but this one is late. *Mtu huyu alitumaini kupata kitu, lakini amechina*, this person expected to get something, but he has been disappointed, i.e. failed to get it. (Cf. *selelea, doda, dolola*.)

Chingirisha, v. pour off liquid gently so as to leave the sediment behind. (Cf. *gida*.)

Chini, n. (1) loc. of *nchi*, on the ground, the bottom part; (2) a euphemism for the genital organs. **Chini**, adv. (1) down, below, under, at the bottom, on the ground, downstairs, underground, &c.; (2) in a lower place, on foot, at a lower part; (3) in a low (inferior, subject, humble) state (rank, condition, &c.). Often *kwa chini*, in the same senses. *-a chini* forms an adjective bearing any of the above meanings. *Yuko chini*, he is downstairs, or underneath, or at the bottom. *Lala chini*, lie on the ground. *Wengine huenda chini, wengine juu ya farasi*, some go on foot, some ride on horses. *Njia ya chini*, a subterranean passage. *Chini ya himaya ya Waingereza*, under the protection (Government) of the English. *Chini kwa chini*, absolutely at the bottom, also underneath or at the bottom the whole distance or time, &c.; also, secretly.

Chinja, v. (Mombasa, *tinda*) (1) slaughter, cut the throat of, kill—esp. of killing animals for food; (2) cut level the rim of a clay vessel in making it. **Chinjo**, n. *ma-* (sometimes used in the plur.) act (place, operation) of slaughtering, slaughter-house—also sometimes massacre, battlefield. **Chinjoni**, n. *ma-* abattoir. **Chinyango**, n. a piece of meat forming a native butcher's perquisite.

Kichinja (kitinda) mimba, n. *vi-* the last child a woman bears. **Kichinjo,** n. *vi-* same as *mchinjo.* **Machinjioni,** n. plur. the sharp, cutting edge of a knife (also called *makali*), the back of the knife being called *mafutuni.* **Mchinjaji,** n. *wa-* a butcher, a slaughterer. **Mchinjo,** n. *mi-* act (place, manner, &c.) of slaying, slaughter, butchery, massacre.

Chinusi, n. a kind of spirit, supposed to live in the water and drag people down and drown them, swimmer's cramp; dist. *chunusi.*

Chinyango, n. See under **Chinja.**

Chiocho, n. same as *joko,* under **Oka.**

Chipua, v. sprout, shoot up—of any plant showing signs of life. St. **Chipuka,** used like *chipua.* Prep. **Chipukia.** Cs. **Chipukisha,** and **Chipuza,** often used as Inten. sprout vigorously. **Chipukizi,** n. *ma-*, **Chipuko,** n. *ma-* shoot, young plant. **Kichipukizi,** n. *vi-* dim. **Uchipuko,** n. (*chipuko*), shoot, sprout, blade—of growing plant.

Chira, v. sometimes *chura, kumchira mtoto ni kumvunja,* i.e. the meaning of *kumchira* a child is to harm it—if either of the parents break the customary restrictions or taboos placed on them after a child is born, the child is supposed to suffer. For instance, if they have intercourse within the prohibited period after the birth of the child, it is supposed to cause the child to become ill with a kind of rickets (?) called *nyongea* or *chirwa.* **Chirwa,** n. a kind of illness, rickets (?), result of *kuchira.*

Chiriku, n. also **Chiku** (1) name of a bird, Finches—*Fringillidae*; (2) a garrulous person, a chatterer.

Chiririka, v. also **Tiririka,** flow, trickle, run off, glide—as water, or snake, &c. Prep. **Chiririkia.** Ps. **Chiririkiwa. -chirizi,** a. trickling. *Machozi machirizi,* trickling tears. **Mchirizi,** n. *mi-* anything for collecting or draining away water, a gutter, a channel, a stick or leaflet or blade of grass for leading rain-water from the trunk of a tree to a pail, &c. Also, the eaves of a house from which rain drips or trickles. **Mchiriziko,** n. *mi-* a trickling, or gliding, as of a snake or water, &c.

Chirwa, n. See under **Chira.**

Cho, a rel. particle agreeing with *Ki-* class nouns used independently only in such phrases as *cho chote,* any whatsoever.

Choa, n. ringworm.

Chobea, v. usu. in the Rp. **Chobeana,** of certain dances where one of each sex leave the circle or row of dancers, meet opposite each other in the centre, and after going through the motions usually connected with coition (*chezesha kiuno*), return to their places. (Cf. *chambi.*)

Chocha, v. (1) poke, prod, stir up, e.g. an animal in a hole, &c. Prep. **Chochea,** poke at, stir up, as a fire or lamp. *Chochea utambi wa taa kwa kijiti,* poke at the wick of a lamp with a bit of stick. (2) fig. stir up trouble, incite, excite, provoke, cause irritation or sensation, &c. Ps. **Chochewa.** D. Prep. **Chochelea.** Ps. **Chochelewa.** St. **Chocheleka.** Cs. and Inten. **Chocheleza,** provoke, irritate, excite, rouse passion, &c. *Alimchochelezea maneno ya fitina,* he stirred up discord against him. **Kichocheo,** n. *vi-* (1) act (method or instrument) of stirring up, e.g. a poker, making up a fire, stoking; (2) also fig. provocation, taunt, provocative speech, &c. **Kichocho,** n. *vi-* (1) sensation, anything which rouses or tends to rouse excitement, stimulus, &c.; but usu. (2) bilharzia, a disease generally called *kisonono cha damu,* because it causes blood in the urine. **Mchocheo,** n. *mi-*, **Mchocho,** n. *mi-* a poking up, a rousing, stimulation, incitement. (Cf. *chochota, chokoa, choka, choma.*)

Chochoro, n. *ma-* but usu. *kichochoro, vi-* alley, passage, esp. of narrow passages between houses in a native town, also **Mchochoro, n.** *mi-* and **Uchochoro.**

Chochota, v. feel raw, smart, irritate, e.g. like a sore which has had iodine or similar medicine applied. **Mchochota,** n. *mi-* an itching or irritating place on the body. (Cf. *chonyota.* Prob. a Ten. form of Cv. of *chocha,* v.)

Chogoe, n. same as *kingoe,* see under **Ngoeka.**

Choka, v. (1) become tired, get weary, be fatigued (worn out, overdone), be in need of a change. *Nimechoka,* I am tired. With noun of things, *choka safari* (*jua, kazi,* &c.), be tired of travelling (weary with the heat, worn out by work). *Choka na mtu,* be weary of a person's company or actions. (2) lose strength, good properties, of inanimate things, e.g. *shamba limechoka,* or *udongo umechoka,* the plantation (earth) is deficient in productive power, the earth is used up. Prep. **Chokea.** Cs. **Chokeza, Chokesha,** but usu. **Chosha,** weary, fatigue, make tired, &c. Ps. **Choshwa.** Rp. of Cs. **Choshana,** weary each other. Rp. **Chokana,** e.g. all be weary together. **-choshi,** a. tiresome, tiring. **-chovu,** a. (1) weary, tired, fatigued, worn out, bored, exhausted; (2) tiresome, tiring, wearying, boring. **Mchoshi,** n. *wa-* a wearying tiresome person, a bore. **Mchovu,** n. *wa-* (1) a person who soon becomes tired, weary, &c.; (2) a bore, tiresome person. **Uchovu,** n. *ma-* (1) weariness, fatigue; (2) producing weariness, tediousness, dullness. (Cf. *chakaa, fifia.*)

Chokaa, n. (1) lime, got by burning coral rag (*matumbawe*), &c.; (2) white plaster. *Paka nyumba chokaa,* whitewash a house. (3) mortar, i.e. a mixture of lime with sand and red earth. Lime is also used for chewing with tobacco. *Umeleta tambuu haina chokaa,* you have brought betel leaves (but) it has no lime. (Cf. *tambuu,* and *uraibu.*)

Chokea, n. stye (in the eye). Said by some to be the result of having spoken slightingly or badly of one's father-in-law or mother-in-law. The cure in which case is to rub the stye with a cloth which has been worn by the one disparaged.

Chokesha, v., Chokeza, v. See under **Choka.**

Choki, n. a liane with yellowish white flowers and woody fruits containing seeds covered with fawn-coloured silky hairs, *Strophanthus Kombe*; an arrow poison is obtained from the seeds.

Chokoa, v. also **Chokocha, Chokochoa,** and **Chokora, v.** pick at, poke, esp. of working at a hard substance with a pointed instrument, knife, or finger, e.g. clear out a hole, take up weeds, a shell-fish from a hole in a rock, &c. *Chokoa meno,* clean the teeth with a toothpick. *Chokoa pweza,* poke out a cuttle-fish from the rocks. Cs. **Chokoza,** tease, bully, annoy, vex. Prep. **Chokolea.** Ps. **Chokolewa.** Ps. of Cs. **Chokozwa.** Prep. **Chokozea.** Rp. **Chokozana,** tease each other, bully each other, vex each other. **Chokochoko, n.** discord, trouble, annoyance, quarrelling, &c. **Chokora,** n. *ma-* a kitchen boy, one who does odd jobs. **-chokozi,** a. annoying, vexing, troublesome, tending to cause strife or annoyance, &c. **Mchokocho,** n. *mi-* (1) act of poking with a stick, &c.; (2) aggravation, strife, annoyance, &c. **Mchokoo, n.** *mi-* a pointed stick used for digging or for spearing fish, &c. **Mchokozi,** n. *wa-* (1) an annoying, aggravating person; (2) an inquisitive person, one who is always poking into affairs. *Huyu mchokozi ajua pweza alipo,* this fellow is a sly dog, he knows what is what (lit. he knows where the cuttle-fish is). **Uchokozi,** n. teasing, annoyance, quarrelsomeness. (Cf. *chocha, chochota.*)

Chole, n. (1) see under **Changu, n.**; (2) a kind of bird.

Choma, v. (A) (1) pierce, stab, prick, thrust (something into); (2) hurt the feelings (of), provoke, give pain to, excite; (3) pain, hurt. *Choma mtu kisu*, stab a man with a knife. *Maneno yake yanichoma*, his words hurt me. *Kidole kinachoma*, the finger hurts. Ps. **Chomwa.** St. **Chomeka**, i.e. (1) be pierced (hurt, angry, &c.); and also Trans. (2) e.g. *chomeka mkuki*, stick a spear in the ground. *Chomeka kisu kiunoni*, stick a knife into waist band (girdle). Prep. **Chomekea**, used in Trans. sense, stick into, but esp. of new pieces of thatch into an old roof. Cs. **Chomekeza**, Inten., stuff, stick in using force, &c. Prep. **Chomea.** *Chomea majani mfukoni*, stuff grass into a bag. D. Prep. **Chomelea**, i.e. stick pieces into, e.g. of sticks for a boundary, pieces of new thatch into a roof, &c. Rp. **Chomana.** Cv. **Chomoa**, (1) draw out, take out, expose, bring to light. *Chomoa mkuki*, draw out a spear from anything. *Chomoa kisu*, draw (unsheath) a knife. *Chomoa mwiba*, extract a thorn. (2) frequently used of borrowing, e.g. *nimemchomoa shilingi mbili*, I have borrowed two shillings from him. Prep. **Chomolea**, (1) draw out for (with, at, &c.); (2) frequently in the sense of stealing, e.g. *nimemchomolea shilingi mbili*, I have stolen two shillings from him. Cf. *chomoa*, (2). Cs. **Chomoza**, make a way out, come out, appear, stick out, esp. of the sun rising or appearing from behind a cloud. *Jua linachomoza*, the sun bursts forth. *Maua yanachomoza*, the flowers are beginning to appear. *Rasi inachomoza*, the cape juts out (comes into sight). **Chomeo**, n. *ma-* (1) anything used for pricking or piercing, i.e. a sharp-pointed stick, &c.; (2) the hole or smart left after extracting a thorn or anything similar; (3) backbiting, anything causing annoyance or hurt. **Chomo**, n. *ma-* stab, prick, &c. **Kichomi**, n. *vi-* (1) a stabbing pain, pricking sensation; (2) pleurisy, from the stabbing pain in the side accompanying it. **Kichomo**, n. *vi-* act (process, method, instrument, &c.) of stabbing. **Mchomo**, n. *mi-* irritation, smart, pricking, stabbing. **Uchomozi**, n. coming out, bursting out (of the sun). (Cf. *penyeza, tomea, tomesha*, and *choma*, v. (B).)

Choma, v. (B), (1) apply fire to, set on fire, burn, brand, cauterize; (2) also intrans. burn, scorch. *Jua linachoma*, the sun is very hot, it burns, it scorches. *Choma moto*, apply fire. *Choma nyumba moto* (or *kwa moto*), set a house on fire. Ps. **Chomwa.** St. **Chomeka**, be burnt. Prep. **Chomea.** Rp. **Chomana. Chomeo**, n. *ma-* anything used for cooking, baking, &c., e.g. a gridiron, furnace. **Chomo**, n. *ma-* (1) a burn; (2) burnt stuff, dross, slag. *Chomo la chuma*, iron slag, refuse of smelting furnace. **Kichomo**, n. *vi-* act (process, method, &c.) of burning, used of cautery. **Mchomo**, n. *mi-* (1) process, act, &c., of burning; (2) cooking. (Cf. *ungunza, teketeza*, and *choma*, v. (A).)

Chombo, n. *vy-* (1) implement, instrument, utensil, tool, piece of furniture, movable, of any kind or description. *Vyombo* includes all personal belongings, chattels, household apparatus, baggage. *Chombo cha kufanyia kazi*, an instrument to work with. *Vyombo vya seremala*, carpenter's tools. *Weka vyombo vyangu nyumbani*, place my things in the house (cf. *samani, zana, ala, kifaa*). (2) a cooking-pot being the most universal and necessary utensil, *chombo*, by itself commonly refers to a vessel for containing something, 'pot, pan, jug, jar, cup' (cf. *chungu, kibia, sufuria*); (3) a native sailing-vessel, a dhow. In this sense it includes a number of varieties, e.g. *jahazi, merikebu, mtepe, betela, bedeni, gangi*, in fact any kind of sailing-vessel. *Panda* (*ingia*) *chomboni*, go on board (embark in) a vessel. *Shuka* (*telemka*) *chomboni*, land, go ashore, disembark. Prov. *Chombo hakiendi ila kwa nyenzo*, a vessel does not go without something sending it along, i.e. requires work.

Chomeka, v., **Chomeo**, n. *ma-*, and **Chomo**, n. *ma-*. See under **Choma**, v. (A) and (B).

Chomoa, v. See under **Choma**, v. (A).

Chomoza, v. See under **Choma**, v. (A) and (B).

Chondo, n. (1) a kind of large native xylophone (cf. *marimba* which is a small one); (2) a drum beaten to spread the news of a death or to call a meeting of people.

Chonga, v. cut to shape, shape with a cutting instrument, whence a variety of meanings according to the instrument used and shape produced, 'hack, chip, bevel, dress, square, point, smooth, carve, &c.' *Chonga mti*, trim (dress, square) a tree ready for cutting into planks. *Chonga boriti*, trim (square) a pole (for a rafter). *Chonga kijiti*, cut a stick to a point. *Chonga kalamu*, sharpen a pencil. *Chonga mtumbwi*, cut out a canoe. Also *chonga maneno*, invent (add to, modify) a story. *Chonga sanamu*, cut out figures. *Chonga mawe*, dress stones. Ps. **Chongwa.** St. **Chongeka**, be shaped, pointed, usu. *chongoka*, see below. Prep. **Chongea**, (1) cut with (for, in, &c.); (2) cut a little of the flower stalk of the coco-nut tree so that the palm-wine may flow freely, but also common in (3) fig. sense, tell tales about, inform against, betray, complain of, accuse (esp. unkindly, or falsely), slander, discredit, and still more emphatically, D. Prep. **Chongelea**, and Inten. **Chongeleza**, *Alinichongea kwa maneno mabaya kwa jumbe*, he discredited me with evil words to the chief. *Mtu huchongewa na ulimi wake*, a man is betrayed by his own tongue. Cs. **Chongesha.** Rp. of Prep. **Chongeana.** Cv. **Chongoa**, (1) cut to shape, round off, cut to an angle (point), bring to a point, sharpen. *Chongoa kikaango*, round off a cooking-pan (in the making of it). St. **Chongoka**, (1) be sharp pointed, jagged, e.g. of craggy, precipitous rocks; (2) stick out, as anything rounded, pointed, jagged, &c., as a cape into the sea, the nose, &c. *Mlima umechongoka sana*, the mountain has a very pointed summit. **Chonge**, n. a canine (pointed) tooth, cuspid, but also anything brought to a point, or pointed, the result of the action of the verb *chonga*. *Chonge za meno*, teeth filed to a point. **Chongelezo**, n. *ma-* what is told to a person's discredit or disadvantage—tales, unkind gossip, scandal, &c. **Chongo**, n. same as *mchongo*, follg. **Mchongo**, n. *mi-* a cutting, act of cutting, making a cut—with an axe knife, &c. *Mchongo wa kalamu*, sharpening a pencil. **Mchongezi**, n. *wa-*, **Mchongelezi**, n. *wa-* a slanderer, a bearer of false tales, a betrayer, &c. **Uchongezi**, n., **Uchongezo**, n., and **Uchongelezi**, n. slander, betrayal, &c.

Chongera, v. See **Chongea** under **Chonga.**

Chongo, n. (A) see under **Chonga**; (B) the condition of being bereft of one eye. *Mwenye chongo*, a one-eyed person. *Ana chongo*, he has lost an eye. **Uchongo**, n. (1) being one-eyed; (2) discharge from a weak or diseased eye. (Cf. *utongo*.)

Chongoa, v. See under **Chonga.**

Chongoe, n. *vy-* a large kind of fish.

Chongoka, v. See under **Chonga.**

Chonjo, n. incitement to quarrel. *Kutia chonjo*, to incite to quarrel or fight. **Chonjomoa**, v. incite, stir up. (Cf. *ushawishi*, *fitina*, *shonga*, perh. a Der. of *chonga*.)

Chonyota, v. feel raw, smart, i.e. like a sore which has had iodine applied, &c. (Cf. *chochota*.)

Choo, n. *vy-* privy, water-closet, cess-pit. *Enda chooni* (or, *choo*), go to the lavatory or water-closet. Used (1) of the action of the bowels. *Pata choo* have a motion. *Funga choo*, be constipated. *Choo safi*, free action of the bowels. (2) *choo kikubwa*, is used of solid excreta, *choo kidogo*, of urine. Other terms used for going to the closet are *enda haja*, *enda msalani*, and of micturition, *kojoa*, *tabawali*.

Chooko, n. See **Choroko**.

Chopa, v. (1) take out a handful of anything; (2) trade in a small way, hawk goods about the country. Cv. **Chopoa**, (1) pull out from a bundle, e.g. a stick from a bundle of sticks, &c.; (2) pull out anything which has stuck; (3) snatch from the hand, take away suddenly, seize by surprise, pluck away, filch. St. **Chopoka**, slip from the grasp, be filched away, escape, extricate oneself, e.g. from a snare, &c. *Sungura alichopoka mkononi mwa simba*, the hare slipped from the paws of the lion. *Kikombe kilichopoka mkononi*, the cup slipped from the hand. Prep. **Chopolea.** Ps. **Chopolewa. Chopa**, n. *ma-* a handful of what can be gathered and held in the fingers, as sticks, ropes, bits of wood, &c. **Kichopa**, n. *vi-* a small bundle, &c. **Mchopozi**, n. *wa-* a snatcher, filcher. (Cf. *nyakua*, *vura*, and *bunda*, *furushi*, *kirobota*.)

Chopi, adv. *enda chopi*, be lame on one side, walk lamely.

Chopoa, v. See under **Chopa**.

Chora, v. carve, engrave, make marks as with a tool, pencil, &c. **Chorachora**, v. scribble, write in a crabbed, illegible hand. **Choro**, n. *ma-* marks made with a tool, engraving, scratch, scrawl, bad writing, hieroglyphics. **Kichoro**, n. *vi-* dim. of *choro*, but also small, illegible writing. **Mchorachora**, n. *wa-* a scrawler, scribbler, bad writer. **Mchoro**, n. *mi-* carving, engraving, making a scratch or scrawl. **Mchorochoro**, n. *mi-* scribbling, scrawling, scratching of tools, &c.

Choroa, n. a name for the fringe-eared Oryx.

Choroko, n. also **Chooko**, green gram, a small dark-green pea, often mixed with rice and other grain for food. The plant is called *mchoroko*.

Chosha, v., **-choshi**, a. See under **Choka**.

Chosho, n. for *ki-osho*. See under **Osha**.

Chota, v. take up a little of, take a pinch of, take up by bits (pieces). *Chota maji*, take up water a little at a time, i.e. in a small cup or vessel. *Chota kuni*, take a little firewood. Ps. **Chotwa.** St. and Pot. **Choteka.** Prep. **Chotea.** *Kazi yake kumchotea maji mwalimu*, his duty is to supply the teacher with water. Cs. **Chotesha** and **Choteza. Choto**, n. *ma-* a small part (piece, bit, quantity, amount, a scrap, a pinch). **Mchoto**, n. *mi-* the act of taking a small piece, quantity, &c., also like *choto*.

Chotara, n. a half-breed person. (? Ar. شطر half.)

Chote, form of *-ote*, all.

Choto, n. *ma-*. See under **Chota.**

-chovu, a. See under **Choka.**

Chovya, v. put (into), plunge (into), dip (into). *Chovya kidole katika mchuzi*, dip the finger in gravy. *Chovya nguo katika maji*, plunge the clothes in water. Ps. **Chovywa.** Prep. **Chovyea.** St. and Pot. **Chovyeka. Chovyo**, n. *ma-* a dip, what is got by a dip. **Mchovya**, n. *wa-* one who dips into things, e.g. Prov. *Mchovya asali hachovyi mara moja*, he who dips his finger in honey, does not do it (only) once. **Mchovyo**, n. *mi-* a dipping, plunging into liquid—and so used of tempering metals, process of plating or coating.

Choyo, n. See under **Moyo.**

Chozi, n. (1) name applied generally to sunbirds, *Nectariniidae*, also *kisozi*; (2) *ma-* a tear, tear-drop; (3)

anything resembling a tear, drop, gum on trees, &c. *Toka (lia) machozi*, shed tears. *Bubujika machozi*, burst into a flood of tears. *Machozi yalimchuruzika usoni*, tears trickled down his face.

Chua, v. apply friction, hence (1) file, rub as with a file, rub so as to remove the husk, e.g. of rice, &c.; (2) massage, chafe; (3) fig. deceive with fine words; (4) fig. of quarrelling, &c., jar, rub, make discord, cause friction. Note: the Rf. *jichua* is used of masturbation. (Cf. *singa, pura, punyeto*.) Prep. **Chulia**. *Jiwe la kuchulia*, a grindstone. Ps. **Chuliwa**. St. **Chulika**, *chulika mafuta*, have oil rubbed in. Rp. **Chuana**, rub each other, rub against each other, and fig. quarrel with each other. Cs. **Chusha**, jar on, rub the wrong way, annoy, irritate. *Tabia za Fulani zimenichusha*, the mannerisms of So-and-so have annoyed me, they jarred on me. **Chua**, n. and **Chuya**, n. grains of rice, &c., or refuse of grain which cannot be pounded in a mortar. (Cf. *chubua, chuna*.)

Chub! int. (the *ch* being mainly heard) expressing contempt, or impatience, or, Make less noise! Be quiet!

Chubua, v. take the skin off, abrade, bruise badly. *Kiatu changu kimenichubua mguu*, my shoe has rubbed the skin off my foot. Ps. **Chubuliwa**, Prep. **Chubulia**, *alimkanyaga mtoto akamchubulia ngozi*, he trod on the child and rubbed the skin off. St. **Chubuka**. *Mgongo wangu umechubuka*, my back is raw, chafed, bruised. **Chubuko**, n. *ma-* a bruise, abrasion, raw place. (Cf. *chua, chuna*.)

Chubwi, n. a plummet, a sinker—attached to fishing-line. (Cf. *bildi, timazi*.)

Chuchia, v. move to and fro, shake, hence (1) used of calling the spirits into the head in the exorcism of spirits, i.e. *kuchuchia pepo ni kumwita au kumchuchia kichwani*, the meaning of *kuchuchia* a spirit, is to call it or cause it to mount to the head. This is done by the exorcist placing his hand on the patient's head and moving it gently to and fro. (2) *kumchuchia mtoto*, to put a child to sleep by rocking it or moving it to and fro. **Chuchio**, n. *ma-* the act of calling a spirit in exorcism. (Cf. *tikisa, punga*, v. (A) and (B).)

Chuchu,* n. the nipples of the breast, *chuchu za maziwa*. (Hind. چوچی.)

Chuchumaa, v. squat on the haunches. Cs. **Chuchumaza**. (Cf. *chutama*.)

Chuchumia, v. reach up (to), stretch up to, as by rising on tiptoe, or of an animal on its hind legs. *Mbuzi anachuchumia*, the goat is standing on its hind legs.

Chuchunge, n. a sword-fish. (Cf. *mchumbururu*.)

Chudi, n. and v. sometimes heard for *jadi*.

Chugachuga, v. be in a state of uneasiness because of being unprepared, e.g. on hearing that a visitor or enemy is coming. **Machugachuga**, n. plur. uneasiness, confusion of mind, doubt.

Chuguu, n. an ant-heap. **Kichuguu**, n. *vi-* dim. Also called *kisuguu, vi-*.

Chui, n. a leopard.

Chuja, v. (1) filter, strain, i.e. by passing water through, as of through a *kifumbu* when straining coco-nut juice (*tui*); (2) strain out, remove by filtering or straining; (3) cleanse, purify. *Chuja maji yenye taka*, filter dirty water. *Chuja nazi kwa kifumbu kupata tui*, strain (grated) coco-nut in a bag to get the milky extract. *Mungu achuje taka za mioyo yetu*, may God take away the impurities of our hearts. (4) fig. choose out, separate. *Jumbe amewachuja waliotoa kodi*, the chief has separated those who have paid tax. Ps. **Chujwa**. Prep. **Chujia**. St. **Chujika**. Cv. **Chujua**, used chiefly with the sense of spoil with water by washing, or dilution. *Amechujua uji wangu*, *una maji*, he has spoilt my gruel, it is watery. Ps. **Chujuliwa.** Prep. **Chujulia.** St. **Chujuka,** e.g. (1) *nguo hizi zimechujuka,* these clothes are spoilt (in colour) by washing. *Rangi hii haichujuki*, this colour does not wash out, it is a fast colour. (2) fig. be no longer pleasing, e.g. *jambo hilo limekwisha nichujuka,* that thing no longer pleases me. **Chujio,** n. a filter, strainer. **Chujo,** n. (— and *ma-*) (1) what is got by straining or filtering. *Chujo ya asali,* molasses, treacle. (2) a strainer, filter.

Chuki, n. ill humour, bad temper, dislike, resentment, also sulkiness, which, however, is usu. *kimwa* or *nuna. Mtu wa chuki* (or *wa chuki-chuki*), one who is quick-tempered, easily put out, ready to take offence, given to sulkiness. *Ana chuki,* he is offended, he is sulky. *Ona chuki,* be in a bad temper. *Tia chuki,* offend, vex, make angry. **Chukia,** v. hate, abhor, have ill feeling towards (e.g. anger, resentment, disgust, loathing, aversion), dislike. Ps. **Chukiwa,** be hated, disgusted, &c. Cs. **Chukiza,** cause to dislike, offend, put out, disgust. *Jichukiza,* (1) grow angry of oneself, be angry gratuitously, pretend to be angry; (2) cause others to hate one, by one's actions, &c. Ps. **Chukizwa.** Rp. **Chukiana,** hate one another. Cs. of Rp. **Chukizana,** provoke each other. **Chukio,** n. *ma-* usu. in the plur. feeling of hatred, offence, sulkiness, abhorrence. **Chukizo,** n. *ma-* usu. in the plur. objects of hate, things which cause offence or abhorrence, &c.

Chuku, n. (1) a cupping horn. *Piga chuku,* cup with a cupping horn (cf. *umika, ndumiko*); (2) exaggeration. *Piga chuku,* make a false impression, exaggerate, tell an incredible story, draw the long-bow, sometimes conveyed by the expression, *tia chumvi,* lit. add salt. *Maneno haya si chuku,* those statements are not exaggerations.

Chukua, v. (1) carry, bear (a load), take on one's back (shoulders or head, or in one's hands), e.g. as a caravan porter (*mpagazi*) or town porter (*mchukuzi, hamali*). *Chukua mzigo,* carry a load. (2) take, conduct, convey, lead. *Chukua mtoto huyu kwa baba yake,* take this child to his father (cf. *peleka,* in this sense). (3) take away, carry off, remove, transport. *Chukua taka,* remove a mess (cf. *ondoa*). (4) also of the feelings, carry away, transport, overwhelm (of joy, sorrow, &c.); (5) bear up under (passively), i.e. endure, put up with, take peaceably, be resigned to (cf. *vumilia, stahimili, shukuru*); (6) bear the weight (responsibility) of, support, maintain, sustain. *Anawachukua wazee wake,* he is supporting his parents (cf. *kimu, ponya, ruzuku, saidia*). (7) take (in capacity), contain, hold, have capacity for (of a vessel, measure, &c.), and fig. include, involve, allow of. *Chombo hiki kinachukua pishi tatu,* this vessel holds three pishi (cf. *weka*). (8) take up, use, require. *Safari ile ilichukua siku nyingi,* that journey occupied many days. *Zawadi hizi zitachukua nguo nyingi,* these presents will require a lot of cloth. *Chukua* has many applications, e.g. *neno hili lachukua mambo mengi,* this word includes many things, i.e. has many meanings. *Chukua mimba,* be pregnant. *Nguo hizi zinakuchukua,* these clothes suit you well. Ps. **Chukuliwa.** Prep. **Chukulia,** carry to (for, from, &c.), feel for (towards, about, &c.). *Nikuchukulie,* let me carry it for you. St. and Pot. **Chukulika.** *Inachukulika,* (1) it is not too heavy to be carried; (2) it is endurable. Rp. **Chukuana,** e.g. give mutual support, agree together, be relevant. *Mambo haya yanachukuana,* these affairs are relevant, they hang together, are bound up in each other. Rp. of Prep. **Chukuliana,** be compatible agree, tolerate each other's company, bear with one another. Cs. **Chukuza**, employ a person to carry, lay a burden on, &c. Rp. of Cs. **Chukuzana**, (1) carry in turns. *Watu wanachukuzana mzigo*, the people are carrying the load in turns. (2) accompany each other (cf. *fuatana*), but in this sense it usually implies that each one is compelling or obliging the other to go with him, e.g. *shauri liliwashinda wakachukuzana mbele ya bwana*, the case could not be settled by them and so they obliged each other to go before the master. **Mchukuzi**, n. *wa-* a bearer, carrier, porter. **Uchukuzi**, n. getting carried, conveyance, cost of carriage, porterage.

Chuma, n. *vy-* (1) iron, a piece of iron. *Chuma cha pua* (or *pua* alone), steel. *Chuma cha suezi*, best quality iron, steel. *Mabamba ya chuma*, iron of a flat kind, hoop iron, iron plate, sheets of iron, &c. (cf. *bamba*). *Pao* (or *fito*) *za chuma*, iron rods, bar iron. *Chuma cha noti*, a tuning-fork. (2) also used fig. of persons: *Mtu huyu ni chuma*, this man is dependable, strong, a mainstay, &c., but also in the sense of difficult, miserly, hard-hearted, &c.

Chuma, v. (1) pluck, gather—of fruit, flowers, &c.; (2) make a profit, esp. in trade or business, gain in trade, prosper, be well paid. *Watu huenda kuchuma bara*, people go to make money up country. Ps. **Chumwa**. Prep. **Chumia**. Ps. of Prep. **Chumiwa**. St. **Chumika**. Cs. **Chumisha**. **Chumo**, n. *ma-* (1) plucking, gathering, of fruit, flowers, &c.; (2) profit, gain, source of gain, employment. **Chumi**, n. cowrie-shells used as counters in playing games. **Uchumi**, n. also **Uchumo**, n. (1) way of earning profits, trade, business, occupation; (2) profits, earnings, salary. (Cf. *vuna, faida*.)

Chumba, n. *vy-* room, chamber, apartment, i.e. part of a *nyumba*. *Nyumba hii ina vyumba vingi*, this house has many rooms. *Chumba cha kulala*, bedroom, dormitory. *Chumba cha kulia*, a dining-room, refectory. **Jumba**, n. *ma-* (1) a large house, mansion, palace; (2) the shaft, handle, housing of a plane, drill, &c. **Kijumba**, n. *vi-* dim. of *jumba*. **Kinyumba**, n. *vi-* and adv. condition of an unmarried woman, living with a man as his wife (cf. *hawara*). Also *-a kinyumba*, things concerning the household, or house, not to be spoken of outside. **Nyumba**, n. (— and of size *ma-*) (1) a house—properly of a native house, made of poles, sticks, wattles, earth, grass, &c., and called *nyumba ya miti, ya udongo, ya makuti, ya majani*, &c., but extended also to a house of any kind, as of masonry, *nyumba ya mawe*, or of corrugated iron, *nyumba ya mabati*, &c.—also sometimes of structures made by animals, birds' nests, lairs, burrows—more commonly called *tundu, kitundu*; and fig. of objects resembling a house, e.g. *nyumba ya randa*, the stock of a plane. (2) household—but this is more commonly *watu wa nyumbani* or simply *nyumbani*, as in the polite inquiry, *Hujambo* (or, *u hali gani*) *nyumbani?* How are your family? Prov. *Nyumba kuu haina nafasi*, a great house has little room. *Nyumba ya udongo haihimili kishindo*, a house of mud cannot stand a shock. **Mchumba**, n. *wa-* one who seeks or is sought in marriage, suitor, lover, sweetheart, fiance. **Uchumba**, n. relation of lovers, of lover and sweetheart, wooing, being wooed, lover's gift. In some places the lover supplies his bride with clothes during the period of courting, *nguo za uchumba*. **Unyumba**, n. relation of husband and wife, *kuvunja unyumba*, to divorce or separate husband and wife. (Cf. *umba*, and for words connected with house-building, &c., see *jenga, aka, kandika* (materials), *mti, udongo, kombamoyo, ufito, kamba, nguzo, mwamba, bati, jiwe, chokaa*, *tofali* (roof and roofing), *paa, kipaa, pao, kuti, jani, nyasi, ezeka.*)

Chumi, n., **Chumo**, n. See under **Chuma**, v.

Chumvi, n. (1) salt; (2) saltness, pungency (of flavour or quality). *Maji ya chumvi*, salt water, brine, sea water, contr. *maji ya baridi, maji ya mvua, maji matamu*, fresh water. *Chumvi ya haluli*, sulphate of magnesia, Epsom salts. *Maneno yake chumvi*, his remarks were pungent. had a flavour. (3) *chumvi* is also used in a colloquial or idiomatic way (*a*) *tia chumvi*, put salt in, but also in the sense of exaggerate, like *piga chuku*, see under *chuku*. (*b*) *kula chumvi nyingi*, of long life, e.g. *Fulani amekula chumvi nyingi*, So-and-so has lived long. (Cf. *munyu, chunyu.*)

Chuna, v. skin, flay, take the whole skin off. Also sometimes used of stripping bark off a tree. *Chuna kamba*, get (strips of bark for) rope. Ps. **Chunwa**. St. **Chunika**. Cv. **Chunua**, scrape skin off, skin, same as *chuna*. *Alichunua uso wake*, he scraped the skin off his face. Ps. **Chunuliwa**. St. **Chunuka**. See also **Chunuka**, v. **Chuno**, n. usu. in the plur. *machuno*, process of skinning, flaying an animal. **Mchuni**, n. *wa-* also **Mchunaji**, n. *wa-* one who flays animals. (Cf. *chubua, ambua, chua.*)

Chunga, v. (A) (1) tend, take care of, act as guardian to, but esp. of animals, i.e. act as keeper or herdman of sheep, cattle, goats, &c., feed, take to pasture, graze, &c.; (2) help a sick man on the road. **Machunga**, n. plur. also in loc. **Machungani**, pasturage, pastures, feeding places for animals. (Cf. *malisho*). **Mchunga**, n. *wa-* a guardian, one who has care of animals, e.g. shepherd, herdsman, groom, &c.—with or without a preposition. *Mchunga (wa) ng'ombe*, a cowherd. **Mchungaji**, n. *wa-* same as *mchunga*, but the *-ji* suffix denotes a professional or habitual occupation, shepherd, &c. (Cf. *tunza, angalia, hifadhi, linda.*)

Chunga, v. (B) (1) sift, separate fine from coarse particles, e.g. of flour for cooking, or lime for plaster, &c., by shaking and tossing in a flat basket (cf. *chekecha, pepeta*, and *tunga*, n.); (2) in fig. sense, tremble for fear. Cv. **Chungua**, also Cs. and Inten. **Chunguza**, (1) look carefully (anxiously, thoroughly) into; (2) spy into private affairs or matters which are hidden. D. Prep. **Chungulia**, look at (down upon, into), esp. of furtive or critical and thorough examination, i.e. peep at, pry into. cast a glance at, inspect closely. Ps. **Chunguliwa**. D. D. Prep. **Chungulilia**, *ufa wa kuchungulilia*, a peephole. **Mchunguzi**, n. *wa-* (1) a critical person, one given to prying; (2) one who delves into things, a seeker of knowledge, &c. **Uchunguzi**, n. prying, criticism, curiosity, inquisitiveness. (Cf. *dadisi, pekua, doea.*)

-chungu, a. (1) bitter, acrid, sour, sharp in taste, acid; (2) disagreeable, unpleasant, painful; (3) angry, dour. *Dawa chungu*, bitter medicine. **Uchungu**, n. (1) sharp pain, smart, bitterness, bitter taste; (2) fig. resentment, anger, offended feeling, grudge; *-a uchungu*. (Cf. *-kali.*)

Chungu, n. (A) *vy-* the commonest kind of cooking-pot—usually a round, rather shallow vessel of baked earthenware, red or black in colour, of various sizes, and with a lid of the same material. *Chungu meko* (cooking-pot and cooking-stones) is an expression used like 'from hand to mouth', also *kazi ya kijungu jiko*, work which brings in sufficient for the pot only, of hand-to-mouth existence. **Jungu**, n. *ma-* used for the larger sizes of cooking-pots. **Kichungu**, n. *vi-* dim. of *chungu*. **Mkungu**, n. *mi-* an earthenware dish used for cooking, and also its lid. *Mkungu wa tanu*, the lid of a cooking-pot. **Ungu**,

n. (*nyungu*), same as *chungu*. (Cf. for other household utensils, *bakuli, bunguu, bia, chano, hero, waya, fua, kombe, kaango, mtungi, sufuria, chombo.*)

Chungu, n. (B) (— and of size *ma-*) a heap, a quantity, a pile, a mass. *Chunguchungu*, in heaps, piles, quantities. *Vitu vilikuwapo chunguchungu*, there were heaps (or piles) of things there.

Chungu, n. (C), an ant, of a common small kind, and so used more generically than other names of species. (Cf. *mchwa, siafu, maji moto, sisimizi.*)

Chungua, v., **Chungulia**, v., **Chungulilia**, v., **Chunguza**, v. See under **Chunga**, v. (B).

Chungwa, n. *ma-* the common sweet orange, fruit of the *mchungwa*. (Cf. for other varieties: *chenza, danzi, limau, kangaja, ndimu, balungi, furungu.*)

Chunjua, n. a small hard protuberance on the skin, a wart. (Cf. *sugu.*)

Chuno, n. *ma-*, **Chunua**, v. See under **Chuna**.

Chunuka, v. set the heart on, be enamoured of, but more usu. *tunuka*, which see. **Chunusi**, n. pimple, acne, it is thought by some that if a young man or woman has acne, it is a sign that one of the other sex is enamoured of him or her. (Cf. *kipele, kijiwe*, and dist. *chinusi.*)

Chunyu, n. incrustation of salt, deposit from salt water. *Ardhi hii ina chunyu*, this earth contains salt. *Nimeoga maji ya chumvi, mwili wangu una chunyu*, I have bathed in sea water (and now) my body is covered with salt. (Cf. *munyu, chumvi, nyunyu.*)

Chuo, n. *vy-* (1) book; (2) school, *mwana chuoni*, or *vyuoni*, a boy (scholar), one who attends school, also an educated, learned man, a scholar, a man of books. *Enda chuoni*, go to school. *Tiwa chuoni*, be sent to school. **Uo**, n. (*vyuo*), cover, case, scabbard, sheath. *Uo wa kisu*, sheath of a knife. *Uo wa kitabu*, cover, binding of a book, hence *chuo*, above (but usu. *jalada* is used for a binding). (Cf. also *nguo*, from the same root.)

Chupa, n. (— and of size *ma-*) (1) a bottle. *Chupa ya kutilia marashi*, a bottle for putting scent in. *Chupa ya divai*, a bottle of wine. Also (2) the womb, e.g. *kuvunja chupa*, of the first stages of childbirth.

Chupa, v. jump down from above, or from branch to branch in a tree, &c. Prep. **Chupia**, move quickly, rush, dash, gallop. Cs. **Chupisha**.

Chura, n. *vy-* a frog.

Chura, v. See **Chira**.

-churo, a. unlucky, of ill omen. *Mtoto mchuro*, a child who is considered unlucky, who brings bad luck to the household, tribe, or community. **Uchuro**, n. ill luck, ill omen. (Cf. *chimvi, kisirani, mkosa, baa.*)

Churua, n. See **Surua**.

Churupuka, v. slip from the hand, from the grasp, escape, from a trap, &c. (Cf. *chopoka.*)

Churura, v. also **Churuza**, v. trickle, glide, run down, as of a tear, trickle of water through a leak, &c. St. **Chururika** and **Churuzika**, (1) trickle, run off, be drained away, as water from a roof, blood from a wound, rain from a tree, &c. (cf. *tiririka*); (2) fig. of animals and humans becoming thin and emaciated through illness, e.g. *mnyama huyu amechuruzika, hata akichinjwa simli, afadhali mwache afe ujusi*, that animal is so thin and emaciated that even if it is killed I will not eat it, better leave it to die a natural death. (Cf. *nyorora, konda.*) **Chururu**, n. an excessive leaking of water, as of a very bad roof. (Cf. *tiririka*, and dist. *chuuza.*)

Chusa, n. *vy-* a harpoon used for spearing large fish, such as *papa, nguru, chewa*.

Chusha, v. See under **Chua**.

Chutama, v. squat on the haunches. (Cf. *chuchumaa.*)

Chuuza, v. (A) also **Chuza**, sometimes heard for *churuza*.

Chuuza, v. (B) keep a small shop, do a retail business, hawk goods about, be a pedlar. **Mchuuzi**, n. *wa-* a small trader, shopman, retail dealer, pedlar, stall-keeper (sometimes heard as *churuza* and *mchuruzi*). **Uchuuzi**, n. occupation, income, &c., of a retail shopkeeper.

Chwa, v. (prob. Cv. form of *cha*, v. (B), *chua* having become contracted to *chwa*, cf. *nywa* from *nya*, also *twa* from *tua* and note on *ch* and *t*, under *ch*; also *shua*), set (of the sun), end (of daylight). *Kumekuchwa*, it is past sunset, the sun has set. *Mchana utakuchwa*, the day will come to an end. Like *kucha*, its Dir. form, *kuchwa*, is used as a noun, but for the whole preceding period of the day. *Kuchwa* (and *kutwa*), a whole day. (Note: *kutwa* is heard more frequently than *kuchwa* when used in this sense.) Often used in combination with the Infinitive of the Dir. form *kucha*. *Kuchwa* (or *kutwa*) *kucha*, all day and all night. *Kucha hata kuchwa* (or *kutwa*), from morning till evening, i.e. sunrise till sunset. *Nimeshinda leo kutwa* (or *kuchwa*), I have remained all day to-day. *Shilingi kutwa*, a shilling a day. *Mshahara wa kutwa*, a day's wages. *Mchana kutwa*, all day. *Kesho kutwa*, the day after to-morrow, i.e. when to-morrow's sun has set. Prep. **Chwea**, e.g. *jua limekuchwea njiani, lala hapa*, the sun has set before your journey is over (lit. has set on, or for, you), sleep here. Ps. of Prep. **Chwewa**, and Ps. of D. Prep. **Chwelewa**, be overtaken by sunset or darkness. *Tulichwewa* (or *tulichwelewa*) *na jua*, we were overtaken by darkness. **Machwa**, n. plur. (also **Machweo**, n. plur.) sunset, where the sun sets, i.e. the west. (Cf. *jioni, usiku, magharibi*, also *tua, chua, shua*.)

D

D represents the same sound as in English, but in some words is not clearly distinguished from *t*. Thus words not found under *D* may be looked for under *T*. In Mombasa dialect *d* sometimes represents the *j* of Standard Swahili.

Daa, n. a kind of worm dug up on the muddy part of the shore, much used by fishermen as bait.

Daawa,* n. legal process, civil suit, litigation, legal claim, dispute. **Dai**, v. and rarely *daha*, v. (1) summons, prosecute, sue at law, accuse, charge; (2) claim in court, demand as a right, claim. *Nakudai*, I sue you, I claim from you. The Rf. *jidai* frequently implies claiming falsely or without justice. *Alijidai usultani*, he claimed a sultanship without a right to it. Ps. **Daiwa**. Prep. **Daia**, claim on behalf of (in reference to, for, from, &c.), act as solicitor for. Rp. **Daiana**, of counter-claims, cross-suits.

Dai, n. *ma-* (sometimes used in the plur.), legal process, suit, claim, for the more usual *daawa.* **Mdai,** n. *wa-* a claimant, plaintiff, prosecutor, creditor. **Mdaiwa,** n. *wa-* one being sued, debtor, defendant in a case. **Mdaawa,** n. *wa-* same as *mdai*; also **Mdaawa,** n. *mi-* same as *dai,* n. (Ar. دعوى.)

Daba,* n. *ma-* (1) sometimes used for *debe,* which see; (2) a fool, simpleton (cf. *mpumbavu, mjinga.* Ar. دعب); (3) a small metal box, e.g. a cigarette case. (Hind. دبا.)

Dabwadabwa, a. soft, flabby, saturated with water, oil, &c. Also *debwedebwe. Wali wa dabwadabwa,* soft, watery, boiled rice.

-dachi,* a. commonly used for 'German'. **Mdachi,** n. *wa-* a German. **Kidachi,** the German language, characteristics, &c. **Udachi,** n. Germany, also *Ulaya Udachi.* (Cf. *Jeremani.* Ger. *deutsch.*)

Dada, n. (— and *ma-*) (1) sister, esp. elder sister; (2) a term of endearment, respect, or familiarity among women.

Dadisi,* v. (1) pry, be inquisitive, be curious (about); (2) ask unnecessary questions. Ps. **Dadisiwa.** St. **Dadisika.** **Mdadisi,** n. *wa-* a curious, inquisitive, prying person. **Udadisi,** n. *ma-* curiosity, inquisitiveness, &c. (? Ar. دس spy out.)

Dadu,* n. game, esp. of dice. (Port. *dado.*)

Dafi,* a tambourine. (Ar. دف.)

Dafina,* n. (1) hidden treasure, treasure trove; (2) an unexpected present; (3) treasure. (Ar. دفينة.)

Daftari,* n. an account book, ledger, catalogue, list, register. (Ar. دفتر.)

Dafu, n. *ma-* a coco-nut in the stage when it is full of milk, further described as (1) *bupu la dafu, punje ya dafu, dafu la kukomba, dafu la kulamba,* i.e. when just beginning to form a soft layer of nutty substance in the shell, which can be licked or easily scraped off, and (2) *tonga la dafu,* when the nutty substance has become thick and tough. *Maji ya dafu,* coco-nut milk. *Dafu* is also commonly used for the milk itself. (Cf. *nazi* and *ulambilambi.*)

Dafurao,* adv. face to face. *Kupiga, kupigana,* or *kugongana dafurao,* to strike, collide head on. (Ar. دفر push back.)

Dagaa,* n. very small fish, fish in an early stage, like whitebait, a favourite dish with natives. *Tanda dagaa,* catch *dagaa* by means of a large sheet of calico, as the native women do. (? Ar. دقة a minute thing, &c.)

Daghadagha,* v. (1) taunt, state in an uncertain manner; (2) be uncertain. Also as n. confusion of mind. (Ar. دغدغ.)

Dagla,* n. a kind of long coat ornamented with gold braid or thread. (Hind. دگلا.)

Daha,* v. See under **Daawa.**

Dahari,* adv. always, constantly, perpetually. Also n. time, age. (Cf. *daima, muda.* Ar. دهر.)

Dahili,* v. associate with a person, and be familiar with all his affairs, i.e. know all his 'ins and outs'. **Dahili,** n. *ma-* (often in plur.) questions, inquiries. **Mdahalo,** n. *mi-* a debate, discussion. (Ar. دخل.)

Dai,* v. See under **Daawa.**

Daima,* adv. perpetually, permanently, constantly, continually, always. *Namwona daima akipita,* I see him constantly passing. **-a daima,** a. continual, permanent, lasting. **Dawamu,** adv. same as *daima,* sometimes used to give emphasis, *daima dawamu,* absolutely always. **Dumu,** v. remain, continue, endure, last, abide. *Dumu daima,* last for ever. **Dum daima,** adv. intensive of *daima* and *dawamu.* Prep. **Dumia.**

Dumia kazi, remain at, persevere in work. Also, remain with, attend on—of service. Cs. **Dumisha.** (Cf. *hudumu, endelea, sikuzote.* Ar. دوم.)

Daka, v. (1) catch, snatch, seize, get hold of—with a sudden, quick movement, e.g. catch a ball thrown in the air, pounce on a thief, appropriate greedily; (2) *daka maneno*, make a smart response (quick repartee, sharp reply). Ps. **Dakwa.** Prep. **Dakia**, jump or pass or step over, as of a log, pool of water, muddy place, leap from branch to branch of a tree, jump on to a vehicle when in motion. Cs. **Dakiza**, object to, rebut, contradict, interrupt speech, 'cut in' on a conversation. Cv. **Dakua**, let out secrets, gossip at random, talk indiscreetly. Prep. of Cs. **Dakuliza**, contradict, protest against, object to, rebut. **Daka**, n. *ma-* recess, receptacle, niche in a wall, cupboard. *Daka la mlango*, a recess above a door. **Dakizo**, n. *ma-* contradiction, rebutment, objection, demurrer. **Kidaka**, n. *vi-* (1) dim. of *daka*; (2) that which catches; *kidaka tonge*, the uvula, i.e. that which catches the ball of food (*tonge*) placed in the mouth. **Mdakizi**, n. *wa-* eavesdropper, gossip-monger. **Mdako**, n. *mi-* a children's game in which they throw up and catch pebbles, &c. **Mdaku**, n. *wa-* tale-bearer, slanderer, &c., same as *mdakizi*. **Mdakulizi**, n. *wa-* one who contradicts, one given to objecting, &c. **Udaku**, n. (1) objection, demurrer, protest; (2) news got hold of secretly, gossip, rumour. **Udakuzi**, n. habit of getting hold of stories, telling tales, &c. (Prob. not Bantu. See Ar. دك, blow, collision, shock, &c., and Pers. دق contradiction, opposition, &c.)

Dakawa,* n. a towing-line, tow-rope, i.e. *kamba ya kufungashia*. (Prob. a corruption of Ar. قطر tow by transp.)

Dakika,* n. a minute, the 60th part of an hour, but often used as any small division of time. *Kwa dakika moja*, in a twinkling, at once. (Ar. دقيقة.)

Dakizo, n. *ma-*. See under **Daka.**

Daktari,* n. *ma-* a doctor of medicine, sub-assistant surgeon, &c., as opposed to *mganga*, a native medicine-man. **Udaktari**, n. the art of medicine, the work (fee, &c.) of a doctor. (Cf. *tabibu*. Eng. doctor.)

Daku,* n. the last food taken before dawn during the fast of Ramadhan. (Prob. from Ar. دق announce, &c., from the custom of notifying people by beating a drum or in other ways so that they may not miss the meal.)

Dakua, v., **Dakuliza**, v. See under **Daka.**

Dalali,* n. an auctioneer, broker. **Udalali**, n. the profession, fee, &c., of an auctioneer or broker. Salesman's fee or commission. (Cf. *nadi, lilamu.* Ar. دلال.)

Dalasini,* n. cinnamon, from the tree *mdalasini*. (Pers. دارصينى, a Chinese tree.)

Dalia,* n. a yellow mixture or powder, used by women for personal adornment, sometimes called *uzuri*. It is also used in preparing a body for burial. (Ar. طلاء salve, &c., what is smeared upon.)

Dalili,* n. sign, token, mark, trace, indication, evidence, signal. *Dalili ya mvua ni mawingu*, the sign of rain is clouds. *Dalili ya mguu*, footprint. Frequently used with a negative, *hakuna hata dalili*, there is not even a sign, vestige, &c. (Ar. دليل.)

Dalji,* adv. *kuenda dalji*, to walk gracefully, or when used of a horse, amble, go at an even pace, neither quickly nor slowly. (Ar. داج walking slowly.)

Dalki,* adv. sometimes heard for *telki*.

Dama,* n. a game played on a board like chess, draughts, a kind of *bao*, which see. (Port. *dama*.)

Dambwa, n. *ma-* a secret place where the arrangements for the circumcision rites are made.

Damisi,* a. a light-hearted, jolly fellow. **Udamisi,** n. joviality, fun. (Cf. *mcheshi, mkunjufu, mbishi*. ? Ar. دعموس a court favourite who has access everywhere.)

Damka, v. never used except in the Rf. in the expression *kujidamka*, get up very early in the morning. (Cf. *lawa*.)

Damu,* n. blood. *Nyama na damu*, flesh and blood. *Anatoka damu*, he is bleeding. Also of the menses, *ingia damuni*, menstruate. (Cf. *hedhi*.) *Watu wenye damu moja*, relatives; an expression also used of husband and wife who have many children. (Ar. دم.)

Dandalo, n. a kind of dance. (Cf. *ngoma*.)

Danga, n. white yam, *Dioscorea alata*.

Danga, v. take up little by little, get a little at a time, scoop up carefully (of water in a pit), i.e. *danga maji*. (Cf. *chota*.)

Dang'a, n. beestings, the first milk of animals after giving birth.

Danganya, v. elude, delude, deceive, defraud, cheat, beguile, impose on, belie. Ps. **Danganywa.** St. **Danganyika.** Prep. **Danganyia.** Cs. **Danganyisha. -danganyifu,** a. deceptive, delusive, cheating. **Danganyo,** n. *ma-* a trick, imposture, deception, cheating. **Mdanganyi,** n. *wa-*, **Mdanganyifu,** n. *wa-* a cheat, deceiver, &c. **Udanganyifu,** n. *ma-* craftiness, cunning, deceitfulness, imposture. (Cf. *punja, hadaa, kalamkia, kopa, ghilibu*.)

Danguro,* n. *ma-* house of ill fame, bawdy-house, brothel. **Danguroni,** loc. used of the quarter of a town where the brothels are situated. (? Corruption of Port. *dançador*, a dancer.)

Danzi, n. *ma-* a bitter orange, fruit of the **Mdanzi,** n. *mi-*.

Dapa, n. sometimes heard for *tapa*, n. which see.

Dara,* v. to seize, catch, touch, arrest. (Cf. *shika, kamata, gusa*. Pers. در.)

Daraba,* n. the arrangement used as a lavatory in a dhow or native vessel. (Ar. ? دربا need, necessity, cf. *haja* (4).)

Darabi,* n. *ma-* a rose apple, fruit of the *mdarabi*, sometimes also called *pera* (guava) *la Kizungu*. (? Pers. دار tree, and آب splendour, &c.)

Daraja,* n. *ma-* (1) step, set of steps, stairs, staircase, bridge; (2) (—) degree, rank, dignity, social station. *Alishuka katika daraja*, he descended the staircase. *Daraja kubwa (bora)*, high rank. (Cf. *ngazi, ulalo*, and for rank, *cheo*. Ar. درجة.)

Daraka,* n. *ma-* (often used in the plur.), an arrangement, appointment, obligation, liability, duty, undertaking. *Madaraka ya nyumbani*, household arrangements. *Chukua madaraka*, take on responsibilities. *Kazi yenye madaraka mengi*, a work with many responsibilities. *Madaraka bila kiasi*, unlimited liabilities. *Madaraka ya kiasi*, limited liabilities. **Diriki,** v. in general, have power (will, time, opportunity, &c., for), and so (1) be able, be in time (for), reach, succeed, attain, manage, arrange; (2) venture, undertake, guarantee, incur responsibility (for). *Nilitaka kuenda, sikudiriki*, I wanted to go, but I could not manage it. *Sijadiriki kuisha kusema*, before I could finish speaking. **Tadaraki,** v., **Tadariki,** v. same as *diriki*. (Cf. *wajibu, faulu, weza, wahi, tengenezo*. Ar. درك.)

Darasa,* n. *ma-* (1) class, meeting, for reading or study. *Madarasa*, school, academy; (2) a class-room; (3) teaching, instruction. **Durusi,** v.

study a book, meet in class, attend school, teach a class. (Cf. *mafundisho, elimu, chuo, soma.* Ar. درس.)

Dar-es-Salaam,* n. capital of Tanganyika Territory. (Ar. دارالسلام.)

Dari,* n. upper floor, upper story, ceiling, roof, esp. of a flat roof. (Cf. *sakafu, orofa.* Pers. دار.)

Darii,* n. See **Deraya.**

Darizi,* v. weave a border (to), make an embroidered edging (on)—of a silk braid-like border to a turban, wrists and front of *kanzu,* &c. **Darizi,** n. embroidery. (Ar. درز.)

Darubini,* n. telescope, microscope, or similar optical instrument. (Pers. دوربين.)

Darumeti,* n. inside woodwork of native vessel, joists carrying the deck, cross-beams, &c. (Ar. ? دعامة support, prop.)

Dasi,* n. (1) rope sewn into the edge of a sail for strength, and distinguished as *dasi ya bara,* on the upper (yard) side, *dasi ya chini,* on the lower, *dasi ya goshini,* and *ya demani,* on the lower and broader ends; (2) thread used in making sails; (3) a sickness of donkeys. (Pers. دسه a weaver's clue of thread; and ? دعش a disease.)

Dasili,* n. a powder made of the dried and pounded leaves of a tree *mkunazi* (the Chinese date or Jube-jube-tree), used as a detergent for a kind of skin disease. Also called *ghasili.* (Ar. غسيل lotion.)

Dasturi,* n. bowsprit, also called *mlingoti wa maji.* (Dist. *desturi.* ? Pers. دستور a large log laid across a ship as ballast.)

Data, v. crackle, make a noise such as twigs breaking. (Cf. *alika.*)

Dau,* n. (1) a large native-built boat, both ends sharp and projecting, and usually with a square matting sail, but without outriggers. Prov. *Dau la mnyonge haliendi joshi, likienda joshi ni Mungu kupenda,* The boat of a poor man does not go straight ahead, but if it does, it is because God wills it. (2) the pool in playing the card game *kamari.* (Ar. داو.)

Daulati,* n. for the more usual *dola,* the ruling power, government. (Cf. *dola, serikali.* Ar. دولة.)

Dawa,* n. (— and rarely *ma-*) medicine, medicament, anything supplied by a doctor, including 'charm, talisman, &c.' used by native medicine men. *Dawa ya kuhara* (or *ya kuharisha*), a purgative, aperient. *Dawa ya kutapisha,* an emetic. *Dawa ya kunywa,* medicine for internal use. *Dawa ya kutia* (*kupaka, kubandika, kujisugua*), medicine for external use. *Dawa ya miti-shamba,* herbal medicine, made from leaves, bark, roots, or trees. *Madawa ya uwongo-uwongo,* quack medicines. *Dawa ya sindano,* injections of medicine. (Ar. دواء.)

Dawaa,* v. See **Duwaa.**

Dawamu,* adv. and v. See **Daima.**

Dawati,* n. writing-desk, writing-case. Dim. **Kidawati, n. *vi-*.** (Ar. دواة.)

Dazani,* n. a dozen. (Eng.)

Debe,* n. *ma-* tin can, commonly of 4 gallons, such as those in which petrol and kerosene is imported and sold. Often used for drawing water. (Hind. دبا.)

Debwani,* n. (1) a kind of loin-cloth; (2) also a turban cloth—an Indian cloth, mostly of silk, with red or brown stripes, and worn on the head as a turban. (? Pers. ديبا brocade.)

Debwedebwe, a. See **Dabwadabwa.**

Dede, adv. *kusimama dede,* to stand uncertainly as a child just beginning to walk stands when not held.

Defa,* n. time, occasion, i.e. *alipiga defa mbili,* he struck twice. (Ar. دفع.)

ege, n. (1) infantile convulsions,

fits (cf. *kifafa*); (2) a kind of moth; (3) a large bird (cf. *ndege*); (4) a look of envy, which is said to cause misfortune, e.g. to stare at a person eating something, and the something drops on the ground, *amemtia dege*.

Dege la watoto, n. a fern. *Pteris longifolia*.

Deheni,* n. a water-proofing mixture of lime and fat, used on the bottoms of native vessels. **Deheni**, v. apply *deheni*. (Ar. دهن.)

Deka, v. (1) give oneself airs, live in style, play the grandee; (2) show conceit, be arrogant, be unpleasant. Cs. **Dekeza**, coax, spoil, i.e. of a child by letting it have its own way too much or by coaxing or petting it. (Cf. *endekeza, tundua*.) Rf. *jideka*, of a woman's gait and bearing. (Cf. *takabari, jivuna, jiona*.)

Dekua, v. bring down with one shot, e.g. a bird with a stone, fruit from off a tree with a stick, &c. **Udekuaji**, n. expertness in shooting or knocking down at first shot, as a bird or fruit with a stick or stone, &c.

Dele,* n. a coffee-pot made of brass or other metal. (Ar. دلو.)

Dema, n. also **Ndema**, a kind of fish-trap of open wickerwork. (Cf. *mgono, mtego*.)

Demani,* n. (1) sheet (rope) of mainsail of a native sailing-vessel. Hence (2) lee side (in navigation), also called *upande wa demani* (*wa demanini*), *upande wa chini*. Contr. *joshi, joshini*. (3) season of the year from end of August to beginning of November, when the south monsoon slackens and gradually dies away—spring time in Zanzibar and coast opposite. Also sometimes of the whole season of the south monsoon, from April to October. (Contr. *musimu*, and see *mwaka*. Pers. دامن.)

Demu, n. *ma-* dim. **Kidemu**, *vi-* an old piece of cloth or rag worn round the loins or a woman's breasts, i.e. as when working in a field, &c.

Denge, n. (A) a mode of wearing the hair, a patch on the top of the head only. **Dengua**, v. (1) (or *kata denge*), shave the head from side to side across the front; (2) wear a cap right on the front of the forehead.

Denge, n. (B) (1) *denge wa mbuzi*, a male goat; (2) a goat pen built on poles, raised off the ground.

Dengu,* n. lentils imported from India, and usually mixed with grain, &c., for food. (Cf. *adesi, choroko, mbaazi, kunde*. Pers. دانگو.)

Dengua, v. (1) see under *denge*, n. (A); (2) remove with one blow, *alimdengua kichwa*, he took off his head with one blow. (Cf. *dekua*.)

Deni,* n. (— and *ma-*) a debt, loan, money obligation. *Fanya* (*jipasha*) *deni*, get into debt, borrow. *Lipa deni*, discharge a debt, repay a loan. **Maduyuni**, n. and **Mdeni**, n. *wa-* a debtor, a person in debt. (Cf. *azima, kopa, wia, wiwa*. Ar. دين.)

Deraya,* n. armour, coat of mail, cuirass, sometimes *durui, darii, dirii*. (Ar. درع.)

Desemba,* n. December. (Eng.)

Deski,* n. *ma-* a school desk. (Eng.)

Deste,* n. *ma-* a vessel in which to store *halua*, Turkish delight. (Ar. دست.)

Desturi,* n. custom, usage, regular practice, routine, precedent. (Cf. *kawaida, ada, mila, madhehebu*. Ar. and Pers. دستور.)

Detepwani, n. the name of a small bird, the pied kingfisher, also called *mtilili, kisharifu*.

Deua, v. (1) take off, as a pot from the fire (cf. *epua*); (2) turn, esp. turn the head in a scornful or proud manner, treat with scorn. (Cf. *geua, dharau*.)

Deuli,* n. (1) a waistband of silk, cloth, shawl, or scarf worn round the waist on top of a *jambia*, which see; (2) a pall, cloth for covering a bier. (Cf. *subaya*. Ar. ديل.)

Devu, n. *ma-*. See **Udevu.**

Dhabihu,* n. a sacrifice, a thing offered or animal killed for an offering to God, or spirits (*mizimu*)—both act and object. **Dhabihu,** v. sacrifice, offer a sacrifice (cf. *tambika*). **Madhabahu,** n. (1) place of sacrifice; (2) an abattoir, public slaughter-house. **Madhabuha,** n. a thing sacrificed, victim, offering in a sacrifice. (Cf. *tambiko, kafara, mhanga.* Ar. ذبائح and ذبح.)

Dhahabu,* n. gold. (Cf. *madini.* Ar. ذهب.)

Dhahi,* v. sacrifice an animal—rarely used. (Ar. ضحى.)

Dhahiri,* a. evident, plain, clear. **Dhahiri,** v. also **Dhihiri,** but usu. in the Cs. **Dhihirisha,** make clear, show, explain. Ps. **Dhihirishwa,** (1) be exposed for sale, shown; (2) make clear, explained. St. **Dhihirika.** Ps. **Dhihiriwa. -dhihirifu,** a. clear, evident, plain, like *dhahiri.* **Udhahiri,** n. and **Udhihirifu,** n. (1) making clear or evident, manifestation, demonstration; (2) clearness, plainness. (Cf. *wazi, baini.* Ar. ظهر.)

Dhaifu,* a. (1) weak, feeble, infirm, powerless; (2) of a poor quality, deficient, insignificant, mean, base, despicable, e.g. *kijumba cha udongo dhaifu,* a mud hovel is not stable. *Kila kitendo dhaifu kiko kwake,* he is an example of every kind of baseness. **Dhoofika,** v. also sometimes *dhoofu,* become weak (infirm, feeble), lose strength (force). Cs. **Dhoofisha. Udhaifu,** n. weakness, debility, insignificance, &c. (Ar. ضعيف.)

Dhakari,* n. penis. (Cf. *mboo, uume, jengelele.* Ar. ذكر.)

Dhalili,* a. low, humbled, humiliated, poor, abject, wretched, contemptible, meek, submissive, obsequious. (Ar. ذليل.)

Dhalimu,* a. unjust, oppressive, tyrannical, fraudulent, violent. Sometimes as v. be unjust, &c., but commonly **Dhulumu,** v. treat unjustly, defraud, oppress. Ps. **Dhulumiwa. Dhulumu,** n. *ma-* injustice, fraud, oppression, violence. **Mdhalimu,** n. *wa-* also **Dhalimu,** n. *ma-* tyrant, an unjust person, an oppressor, &c. **Udhalimu,** n. injustice, tyranny, wrong, oppression, iniquity. (Ar. ظلم.)

Dhamana,* n. surety, guarantee, warrant, certificate, bail. *Weka dhamana,* find bail, give surety. *Komboa dhamana,* surrender to bail. **Dhamini,** v. guarantee, become surety, be sponsor, give bail, go bail. *Amemdhamini rafiki yake,* he has gone bail for his friend. *Tumemdhamini kuwa tutamlipa,* we have certified him that we will pay him. **Dhamini,** n. and **Mdhamini,** n. *wa-* a surety, trustee, one who goes bail for another, a hostage, guarantor, sponsor. **Udhamini,** n. like *dhamana.* (Ar. ضمن.)

Dhambi,* n. (— and rarely *ma-*) crime, religious offence, sin, i.e. offence of the worst class (worse than *hatia* and *kosa*), but from the Muhammadan point of view, i.e. formal and utilitarian rather than moral. (Ar. ذنب.)

Dhamini, v. and n. See under **Dhamana.**

Dhamira,* n. and **Dhamiri,** n. real intention, secret thought, mind, resolution, inner consciousness, conscience. *Ni dhamira yake kufanya vita,* his real intention is to make war. Also as v. think of, intend, e.g. *alimsamehe yale aliyodhamiria,* he forgave him the thought of his heart. (Cf. *dhana, ania, kusudi, wazo, moyo, mradi, maarubu, madhumuni.* Ar. ضمير.)

Dhana,* n. thought, idea, notion, suspicion. **Dhani,** v. think, be of opinion, fancy, suppose, suspect. Prep. **Dhania,** think of (about, in favour of, against, &c.), suspect, e.g. *amedhaniwa mwivi*, he is suspected of being a thief. **Udhani**, n. also **Udhanifu**, n. guessing, chancing. (Cf. *fikiri, waza, shuku, tuhumu*. Ar. ظن.)

Dhara,* n. often in plur. *madhara*, hurt, harm, violence. **Dhuru**, v. hurt, damage, cause loss or injury to, harm. *Haidhuru*, a common expression meaning, 'it does not matter, it is all the same, never mind' (cf. *mamoja*). Ps. **Dhuriwa.** St. **Dhurika.** (Ar. ضر.)

Dharau,* v. scorn, slight, despise, treat with contempt, insult. Ps. **Dharauliwa.** St. **Dharaulika. Dharau**, n. scorn, contempt, insult. (Cf. *tweza, hizi, tusha, fidhulia, beza*. Ar. ? اضرع.)

Dharuba,* n. (1) stroke, blow, rush—blow of an axe, sudden calamity, &c.; (2) rarely, in arithmetic, multiplication. (Dist. *dhoruba*. Ar. ضرب.)

Dharura,* n. sudden unexpected happenings, commotion. (Ar. ضرورة.)

Dhati,* n. (1) purpose, intention, resolve, free will. *Amefanya haya kwa dhati ya moyo*, he has done this of his own free will. (2) essence, innermost self. (Ar. ذات.)

Dhiaka,* n. See **Zaka**, n. (B).

Dhibiti,* v. guard, protect against, manage. Cs. **Dhibitisha.** Note: these words are seldom used, probably because of their similarity in sound to those made from *thabiti*, which see. **Madhubuti**, a. precise, accurate, trustworthy, honest, reliable, strong, firm, durable, resolute, solid. (Ar. ضبط.)

Dhihaka,* n. mockery, ridicule, scorn. **Dhihaki**, v. ridicule, mock, deride, make fun of, laugh at, e.g. *kunidhihaki, kunifanya* (*kunifanyizia*) *dhihaka*, to mock me. Ps. **Dhihakiwa.** (Ar. ضحك.)

Dhihiri,* v., **-dhihirifu**, a., **Dhihirisha**, v. See under **Dhahiri.**

Dhii,* v. (1) waste away, pine, be spoiled, be consumed; (2) be hard driven, be ruined, be distressed. Ps. **Dhiiwa.** St. **Dhiika.** Cs. **Dhiisha**, *Mungu anamdhiisha*, God is sending him ruin. (Cf. *konda, nyorora, dhoofu*. Ar. ضاع.)

Dhiki,* v. press hard on, put in difficulties, reduce to straits, distress. Ps. **Dhikiwa.** St. **Dhikika**, for which **Dhiki** is also used, i.e. be hard-pressed, be in difficulties, e.g. *kama umedhikika na neno uniambie*, if you are in any difficulty, tell me. **Dhiki**, n. (1) narrowness, want of space, confinement; (2) being pressed, annoyance, distress, &c. **Udhiki**, n. (1) want of room, narrowness, tightness; (2) distress, annoyance, poor circumstances. (Ar. ضيق.)

Dhikiri,* n. (1) mention the name of God; (2) to take part in the ritual called *dhikiri*, which might be described as a meeting, or sort of dance, in which the people meet in order to mention the name of God, it is accompanied by the repeated *Allah hai*, God, the living One. (Sometimes heard as *zikri*. Ar. ذكر.)

Dhila,* n. also **Dhili**, mean condition, abasement, low state. **Dhili**, v. abase, humble, bring low, set at nought. Prep. **Dhilia.** Ps. **Dhiliwa.** St. **Dhilika. Dhili**, a. low, mean, despicable. **-dhilifu**, a. poor, mean, insignificant. **Udhalifu**, n. **Udhilifu**, n. *ma-* abjectness, wretchedness, poverty, abasement, humiliation, bringing low, degradation. *Madhilifu*, troubles, disasters, adversities. (Ar. ذل.)

Dhiraa,* n. a cubit—measure of length, from elbow to finger-tip. *Dhiraa kamili*, or to the knuckle, *dhiraa konde*—about 18 inches, half a yard (*wari*). Commonly called *mkono*. (Ar. ذراع.)

Dhoofika,* v., **Dhoofu,** v. See under **Dhaifu.**

Dhoruba,* n. a hurricane, storm of wind and rain, tempest. (Cf. *tufani, kimbunga,* dist. *dharuba.* Ar. ضربه.)

Dhuha,* n. (1) the period between sunrise and noon; (2) the Muhammadan prayer of that period. (Ar. ضحى.)

Dhuku,* v. taste, try the taste of, but commonly *onja* is used. (Cf. *tamu, ladha.* Ar. ذوق.)

Dhukuru,* v. (1) remember, think, consider; (2) same as *dhikiri,* which see. (Ar. ذكر.)

Dhulu,* v. come to light, be discovered—seldom used. (Ar. دلّ point out, show.)

Dhulumu,* v. and n. See **Dhalimu.**

Dhumna,* n. dominoes, game of dice. (Cf. *dadu.* Ar. ضاما.)

Dhuria,* n. descendants, e.g. *dhuria zake,* his children. (Cf. *mtoto, mwana.* Ar. ذريه.)

Dhuru,* v. See under **Dhara.**

Dia,* n. money paid for a life, fine for murder, ransom. (Cf. *fidia, fidi.* Ar. دية.)

Dibaji,* n. (1) good style in writing; also used of the string of complimentary titles in Arab letter writing; (2) preamble, an introduction to a book or speech, approach in a lesson. **Udibaji,** n. (1) adornment, artistic form, style; (2) mere form as opposed to substance, and so delusion, outward show, deceit. (Ar. ديباجة.)

Didima and **Didimia,** v. sink down, go to the bottom, penetrate. St. **Didimika.** Prep. of St. **Didimikia,** bore into, e.g. of a tool. Cs. **Didimisha,** cause to sink down, force down (into, &c.). *Didimisha nguo mkobani,* stuff clothes into a wallet. (Cf. *tota, zama, shindilia.*)

Difu,* n. *ma-* (1) the fibre binding the young leaves of the coco-nut round the growing stem, sometimes used for straining and for kindling a fire (also called *kilifu, vi-* sometimes); (2) a piece of the bone of a camel or ox used by some school children as a pen or pencil. (Ar. ليف fibres, esp. of palm tree.)

Digali,* n. the stem of a hookah tobacco pipe. (Cf. *kiko.* Ar. زغل to suck.)

Dike,* adv. exactly, just so, in the same way—also *tike.* (Ar. دقة.)

Diko,* n. *ma-* a landing-place. (Ar. دك level sand.)

Dila,* n. a vessel, tin, &c., for bailing out a boat. (Ar. دلو.)

Diladila, a. See **Tilatila** under **Tia.**

Dimba, n. *ma-* (1) the place or camp in which the initiates are kept in the circumcision rites (cf. *jando, ukumbi, unyago*); (2) a plantation which has been left and then returned to. (Cf. *konde.*)

Dimbwi, n. *ma-* pool, puddle, e.g. left on the shore at low water. Dim. **Kidimbwi,** *vi-.*

Dinari,* n. gold coin—found only in stories of Arabic origin. (Ar. دينار from Lat. *denarius.*)

Dinda, v. (1) stand firm, be firm or taut, as of a rope, &c. (cf. *kaza, kita*); (2) be contrary, contradict, oppose (cf. *bisha, kaidi, pinga*); (3) of a person, have an erection of the penis; of the penis, be erect. (Cf. *simika, disa.*)

Dindi, n. *ma-.* See **Lindi.**

Dindia, v. sink down, go to the bottom, penetrate. (Cf. *didimia.*)

Dini,* n. religion, creed, worship. (Ar. دين.)

Dira,* n. a mariner's compass. (Ar. دائرة.)

Dira,* v. cut or shave the hair. (? Ar. طرّ sharpen, see form طرّ be long, of hair.)

Diradira,* v. See under **Duara.**

Dirii,* n. See **Deraya.**

Diriki,* v. See under **Daraka.**

Dirisha,* n. *ma-* window. (Cf. *mwangaza.* Pers. دريچه.)

Disa, v. of the penis, be erect (obscene). (Cf. *dinda, simika.*)

Divai,* n. wine in general. (Cf. *mvinyo*, used mainly of spirits. French *du vin.*)

Diwani,* n. *ma-* (1) councillor, public functionary, magnate; (2) the court or council chamber of a king, &c.; (3) a book of poetry. (Ar. ديوان.)

Doa, n. *ma-* spot, blotch, mark, stain. *Doa la mafuta*, a grease spot. *Madoadoa*, used as an adj. spotted, variegated, of different colours, speckled. (Cf. *raka, baka.*)

Dobi,* a. heavily laden, *chombo hiki ki dobi*, this vessel is heavily laden. (? Ar. دأب driving violently forward.)

Dobi,* n. *ma-* one who washes clothes as a trade—usually a man. **Udobi**, n. occupation (work, fee, &c.) of a laundryman. (Hind. دهوبى.)

Doda, v. (1) remain so long as to turn bad, as of perishable goods in a shop (cf. *china, selelea*); (2) drip (cf. *tona, dolola, dondoka*); (3) try to get something and fail, be very long in attaining one's desire.

Dodi, n. *ma-* (1) fine wire, whether brass or iron; (2) a bracelet of fine wire, hair, or thread. **Udodi**, n. (*dodi*) same as *dodi.*

Dodo, n. *ma-* (1) a young woman's breast before it has fallen; (2) a very large kind of mango is called *embe dodo.*

Dodoki,* n. *ma-* the fruit of a loofah. When young it is used as a vegetable and for making curries. One type is also retted and used in the same way as a sponge. The plant is *mdodoki.*

Dodosa, v. (1) drawl, hesitate in speech or reading; (2) cross question. (Cf. *kokoteza, dadisi.* ? Ar. تدس from دس.)

Doea,* v. (1) spy, reconnoitre, pry into other people's affairs; (2) frequent people's houses at meal-time in the hope of being invited to food. Also Rd. **Doeadoea. Mdoea**, n. *wa-* (1) a spy, one who spies into people's affairs; (2) a sponge, one who frequents people's houses at meal-times in the hope of being invited to food. (Cf. *doya, doria, rondea, peleleza, dukiza, dusa.* Ar. دور.)

-dogo, a. little (in condition, quality, or quantity), small, slight, unimportant, young. *Mtoto mdogo*, a small child. *Ndugu mdogo*, a younger brother. *Baba mdogo*, father's younger brother, uncle. *Mtu mdogo*, a small (or poor) man. **Kidogo**, adv. a little, rather, not very, not much, in small amount. Used as a. to denote 'small in quantity'. *Watu kidogo*, a few people. But *watu wadogo*, small (poor, inferior) people. *Maji kidogo*, a little water. With negat. '(not) at all, (not) in the least, (none) whatever'; esp. with *hata*. *Sikupi hata kidogo*, I will not give you a single bit, I will not think of giving you any. Sometimes redupl. for emphasis, *vitanda vidogo vidogo*, or *vidogodogo*, very small bedsteads. **Udogo**, n. littleness, smallness, insignificance.

Dohani,* n. (1) smoke (cf. *moshi*, Ar. دخان); (2) a chimney. (Ar. داخنة); (3) a tall narrow basket used for carrying fruit, &c., to market (prob. so called because of its shape).

Dokeza, v. (1) give a hint of, suggest, tell something which is secret, inform in confidence; (2) apply a small quantity, such as medicine, liquid, &c. Cv. **Dokoa**, break off a little portion, if of animals, with the teeth, if of humans, with the hand (cf. *mega*)—also like *dokeza*. Prep. **Dokolea**, share with, i.e. of news, information, &c. **Kidokezi**, n. *vi-*, **Kidoko**, n. *vi-* (1) a click, smack. *Piga kidoko*, give a click with the tongue, smack the lips. (2) a hint, a sign, secret suggestion; (3) a kind of fish.

Dola,* n. Government, authorities, for the common *Serikali*. (Cf. *daulati, himaya.* Ar. دول.)

Dole, n. *ma-* amplic. of *kidole.*

Dolola, v. (1) drip saliva, slaver, as a child, or an old person in sleep, &c. (cf. *udende, udelele, mate, dovuo*); (2) try to get something and fail, be very long in attaining one's desire; (3) of things in a shop—remain a long time without getting a price. (Cf. *doda, china, selelea.*)

Domo, n. *ma-*. See under **Mdomo.**

Dona, v. peck, pick at, pick up bit by bit as a bird does its food. *Ndege hudona mchele,* the birds pick up rice. Prep. **Donea,** used of a bird caressing another with its beak. Cs. **Donesha.** Rp. **Donana,** *kuku wanadonana,* the fowls are pecking each other. Cv. **Donoa,** (1) peck at (with beak or fangs), e.g. of fowls and snakes, also of fish nibbling at bait. *Nyoka alimdonoa juu ya utosi,* the snake struck him on the crown of his head. (2) fig. kiss. **Mdono,** n. *mi-* a bite, in fishing. (Cf. *dondoa, pekua, busu, nonea.*)

Donda, n. *ma-* large sore, ulcer. *Donda ndugu,* spreading, confluent ulcer. Dim. **Kidonda,** *vi-*. **Dondoa,** v. form sores. (Cf. *jeraha, banguzi.*)

Dondo, n. *ma-* (1) large tiger cowrie-shell, used by tailors for smoothing down seams to a good surface. (Cf. *kauri.*) Hence perh. (2) dressing for cloth, starch, chalk, &c., used to give a good surface and appearance to inferior material. *Nguo ya dondo,* glossy calico, with much dressing in it. (3) a kind of crab, not eaten, *kaa dondo.*

Dondoa, v. (1) pick up bit by bit, pick up grain by grain as fowls do (cf. *dona*); (2) let fall bit by bit, drop, cause to drip; (3) see under *donda*; (4) make selections (from), compile knowledge (by). St. **Dondoka,** drip, fall bit by bit. **Dondo,** n. *ma-* selections, notes, extracts, quotations, choice bits, e.g. in an anthology.

Dondoo, n. *ma-* (1) see **Dondoro;** (2) see under **Dondoa.**

Dondoro, n. (1) the steinbuck, also called *dondoo*; (2) a kind of hornet or stinging fly.

Donge, n. *ma-* small rounded mass, clot, ball, lump. *Donge la uzi,* a ball of thread. *Damu inafanya madonge,* the blood is forming clots. (Cf. *tonge, ma-* which is generally used of balls of food, such as are made with the fingers before putting it into the mouth.) Dim. **Kidonge,** n. *vi-* a small rounded mass, a pill, tablet, &c.

Dongoa, n. *ma-* lump, mass. (Cf. prec.)

Donoa, v. See under **Dona.**

Dopa,* n. *ma-* a sail-maker's palm, for coarse sewing. (? Ar. طبة strip of leather.)

Doria,* n. (1) white muslin (Hind. دريائي); (2) the advance guard of an army, an outpost, spy, patrol. (Ar. دورية.)

Dosari,* n. blemish, defect, kink, &c. (Cf. *waa, ila, hitilafu.* Ar. دثر dirt, dregs, &c.)

Doti,* n. a piece of cloth suited for, and worn as, a loin-cloth, *shuka,* i.e. about 2 yards of full width, or 4 yards of narrow material. (Hind. دهوتي.)

Dovuo, n. saliva which drips from some people in their sleep. (Cf. *udelele, dolola, mate, ute.*)

Doya,* v. (1) also *doyadoya,* spy, reconnoitre, go as a spy, sometimes heard as *doea*; (2) sponge, i.e. go to people's houses at meal-times in the hope of being invited to food. **Mdoya,** n. *wa-* (1) a spy, one who spies in other people's affairs; (2) a sponge, one who frequents people's houses in the hope of being invited to food. (Cf. *doea, doria, rondea, peleleza, dukiza, dusa.* Ar. دور.)

Dua,* n. (1) a prayer, special supplication, request made in prayer. *Omba dua,* offer a prayer, make a request to God. (2) a curse, a spell, i.e.

amepigwa dua, he has been bewitched. (Cf. *omba, sala*. Ar. دعاء.)

Duala,* v. sometimes heard for *duwaa*, v. which see.

Duara,* n. used of (1) a wheel, circle, flat round object, and (2) any machine of which the principal feature is a wheel, e.g. a crane (which is now generally *winchi* or *slingi*), windlass, capstan, &c. (cf. *gurudumu, mviringo*). **Diradira,** v. use evasive statements, beat about the bush. **Duru,** v. surround, be round, go round, put round (cf. *zunguka*). **Duru,** n. turn in a round of drinks, &c., e.g. when people drink native palm-wine, they drink by turn, one after another; the distributor is called *mshika duru*. *Duru yangu*, my turn to drink. (Ar. دور.)

Duazi,* n. *ma-* or **Duwazi.** See under **Duwaa.**

Duba,* v. be partly full. (Cf. *shinda*. Ar. دوب.)

Dubu,* n. a bear. (Ar. دب.)

Dubwana,* n. *ma-* a person of extraordinary size, a giant, a colossus. Also used as adj. **-dubwana,** of anything gigantic—animal, tree, or other object. (? Hind. دبوانا cause to sink or drown.)

Dude,* n. *ma-* the vaguest and most general term for referring to any object of which one does not know the name, a thing, a what-do-you-call-it, an object. *Dude gani hili?* What in the world is this object? Dim. **Kidude,** *vi-* (prob. from the same root as follg.).

Dudu,* n. *ma-* of size, large insect. **Kidudu,** *vi-* is the dim. **Kijidudu,** n. *vi-* a minute animal, hence germ, microbe, &c. **Mdudu,** *wa-* the most general term for insect, including ants, flies, grubs, worms, and all small creeping and flying creatures. Also used of various diseases caused by, or attributed by the natives to, parasites and other insects on the body, e.g. *mdudu wa kidoleni* (or *mdudu upande*) a whitlow. (Ar. دود.)

Duduka, v. be disfigured (by illness or disease). *Duduka uso*, have the face pitted, marked as by small-pox, &c. Ps. **Dudukwa,** *Nimedudukwa na pele*, I am disfigured by an eruption (cf. *umbua*). Prep. of Stc. **Dudumia,** make a hole, perforate by force. St. **Dudumika.** Cs. **Dudumiza.** Rp. **Dudumikana,** get each other into confusion. Cs. of St. **Dudumikiza,** press in tightly (cf. *didimia*). **Dudumizi,** n. *ma-* the white-browed coucal, also called *tipitipi, shundi*, and *gude*. **Duduvule,** n. *ma-* a stinging insect which bores in wood. **Kidudusi,** n. *vi-* a spot, pimple, or similar blemish. (Cf. *kipele, kijiwe, dutu, chunusi*.)

-dufu,* a. and n. *ma-* dull, insipid, tasteless, flat, uninteresting, good for nothing—of persons and things. *Tumbako dufu*, or *dufu la tumbako*, mild, flavourless tobacco. *Mtu dufu*, or *dufu la mtu*, a stupid, inane, dull person. **Udufu,** n. (1) poorness of quality, esp. *udufu wa ardhi*, barrenness of land; (2) foolishness, insipidity. (? From same Ar. root as *dhaifu*.)

Dugi, a. blunt, *kisu dugi*, a blunt knife, *kalamu dugi*, a blunt pencil (cf. *butu*). **Dugika,** v. be blunt.

Duguda, v. shake. Cs. **Dugudisha.** (Cf. *tikisa, tukuta*.)

Duhushi,* v. look for, spy into, search out. (Cf. *tafuta, peleleza*. Ar. دحش.)

Duka,* n. *ma-* shop, stall. *Tembea madukani*, walk in the bazaar. *Weka duka*, open a shop. *Vunja duka*, close a shop, give up business. (Ar. دكان, the final *-an* being treated as a locative and dropped, or دك a small shop.)

Dukiza, v. or **Dukisa,** intrude oneself, listen secretly, try to overhear. *Jidukiza*, play the eavesdropper, push in or intrude where not wanted (offensively). **Dukizi**, n. *ma-* eavesdropping, scandal-mongering. **Mdukizi**, n. *wa-* eavesdropper, gossip-monger, slanderer. **Mdukuo**, n. *mi-* a tap, push, poke, thrust—given with stick, finger, or open hand, e.g. *mtie mdukuo wa shavu*, poke him in the cheek. (Prob. a variant of *dakiza*, see under **Daka**.)

Dukuduku,* n. confusion of mind, perplexity, disquiet, &c., the result of anger, bitterness, grudge, &c. (Cf. *daghadagha, wasiwasi, dungudungu*.)

Dum,* adv. See under **Daima**.

Duma, n. a cheetah.

Dumaa, v. (1) fail of full development; be stunted in growth, of trees, people, and animals; be smaller than the usual species (cf. *via*); (2) fig. used of a person lacking intelligence.

Dume, n. *ma-*. See under **Ume**.

Dumiliza, v. make blood friendship by mutual incisions, i.e. *kuchanjiana uchale*.

Dumu,* n. *ma-*, **Mdumu**, n. *mi-* can, pot, jug, mug, esp. of metal.

Dumu,* v. See under **Daima**.

Dunda, v. knock against with force. **Mdundo**, n. *mi-* (1) used of a rolling, rumbling sound as of a drum; (2) a kind of drum. (Cf. *gonga, ngurumo*, and Hind. دنك a kettle-drum.)

Dundiza, v. See **Dunduiza**.

Dundu, n. *ma-* (1) dried gourd of large pumpkin used for carrying and storing water and other liquids; (2) a bale; (3) the scavenger beetle.

Dunduiza, v. begin to ripen, of fruit. (Cf. *tundiza*.)

Dunduliza, v. place aside, save up, place in reserve. (Cf. *akiba, weka, limbika*.)

Dundumio, n. the larynx, Adam's apple. (Cf. *kikoromeo*.)

Dunga, v. pierce, bore, esp. used of boring the ears for the insertion of ornaments. **Kidungadunga**, n. *vi-* a boring insect, weevil. (Cf. *toboa, toga*.)

Dunge, n. *ma-* a cashew apple in green, unripe stage—fruit of the *mbibo*.

Dungu, n. *ma-* a stage or platform, raised from the ground and often roofed over, for a watchman guarding crops on a plantation. (Cf. *kilindo, kilingo*.)

Dungudungu,* n. *ma-* (1) used to describe anything of unusual shape or quality, 'a wonder, marvel, curiosity' (cf. *ajabu, kioja*); (2) a bad person, a deformed person; (3) anything badly made; (4) confusion of mind because of bitterness of spirit, &c. (cf. *daghadagha, dukuduku, wasiwasi*.)

Dungumaro, n. (1) a kind of evil spirit; (2) a drum used in expelling such a spirit. (Cf. *pepo, punga, mteja*.)

Duni,* a. inferior, low, mean, abject, worthless. *Mtu duni*, a nobody, an insignificant person. *Hali duni*, an abject condition. (Cf. *dhaifu, -nyonge, hafifu, -dogo*. Ar. دون.)

Dunia,* n. the world, universe, earth (as a whole). *Fariki dunia*, depart from the world, die. *Mtu wa dunia*, a worldly man. *Mambo ya dunia*, or simply *dunia*, the way of the world, worldly affairs, the spirit of the age. (Cf. *ulimwengu*. Ar. دنيا.)

Dunzi, n. See **Mdunzidunzi**.

Dupa, v. (1) step over, as of a log, &c. (cf. *kiuka*); (2) press forward, press upon, rest heavily on. (Cf. *lemea*.)

Dura,* n. a parrot. (Cf. *kasuku*. Ar. درة.)

Duru,* v. and n. See under **Duara**.

Durui,* n. See **Deraya**.

Durusi,* v. See under **Darasa**.

Dusa,* v. also the Prep. **Dusia**, used in the same sense, sponge, get one's food and living by sponging on others. (Cf. *duzi, doea, doya, rondea*. Ar. دس spy out.)

Dusumali,* n. a coloured handkerchief or scarf worn by some women on the head as a kind of turban. (Cf. *utaji*. Pers. دستمال.)

Duta, v. (1) rebound, return, reverberate, i.e. of a ball bouncing, an echo; (2) hit, strike before rebounding, bounce.

Dutu, n. *ma-* (1) shape, appearance, substance, constitution (cf. *sura, umbo, mandhari, kitu*); (2) wart, spot, pimple, or similar blemish (cf. *kipele, sugu, kidudusi, kijiwe.*)

Duwaa,* v. be dumbfounded, nonplussed, be still, silent, motionless, e.g. of one amazed, deceived, fascinated, deep in thought. **Duwazi,** n. *ma-* also **Duazi,** one struck dumb with amazement, fascinated, nonplussed. (Cf. *dawaa, tunduwaa, shangaa, pumbaa.* Ar. دوار giddiness.)

Duzi,* n. *ma-* (1) eavesdropper, talebearer, gossip-monger, slanderer (cf. *dusa, mdukizi, mpelelezi*); (2) a semi-wild male cat. (Cf. *paka shume* or *nunda.* Ar. دس spy out.)

E

E represents the sound of *ai* in 'fail', or of *e* in 'pet', when short.

Ebee.* See under **Labeka.**

Ebo! int. of surprise, contempt—only used to children and inferiors.

Ebu!* int. also **Hebu!** Well then! Come then! An expression drawing attention, sometimes used like 'I say' but frequently used in expostulation or reproof. (Ar. هب.)

Eda,* n. time of customary ceremonial mourning, or seclusion from company of a woman after a death or divorce. *Alikaa eda akavaa kaniki miezi minne,* she remained in seclusion and wore mourning four months, i.e. *kuweka eda.* (Cf. *tanga.* Ar. عدة.)

Edaha,* n. a sacrifice or offering made for some special object. (Cf. *sadaka, tambika, adua.* Ar. وادع conciliate.)

Edashara,* n. and a. eleven. *-a edashara,* eleventh. (Cf. *kumi na moja.* Ar. حد عشر.)

Edeni,* n. used sometimes for *aden,* which see.

Ee! int. O—in invocation or assent. *Ee Mungu,* O God. *Ee bwana,* O sir. *Ee walla, Ee waa,* O yes! All right! Certainly, sir!

Efendi,* n. See **Afendi.**

Egama, v. (Stc. form of *ega,* not now in use), be in a leaning, resting, or reclining position, i.e. propped on elbow or supported. Rf. **Jiegama,** place oneself in a resting position, recline, prop oneself (in position). Prep. **Egamia,** rest on, lean on, recline on. *Ameegamia ukutani,* he is leaning against a wall. Cs. **Egamisha,** cause to lean, prop, support. Prep. **Egemea,** (1) lean on, rest on, be supported by; (2) trust to, rely upon. Ps. **Egemewa,** be leaned upon, be a support (to), be trusted (by). Cs. **Egemesha, Egemeza,** (1) prop up; (2) confirm, help to establish, give support to, find ground for. Cs. **Egesha,** cause to rest, bring into close contact, make secure, &c. *Egesha chombo pwani,* bring a vessel to land, moor, make fast. *Egesha mashua ngazini,* secure a boat to the gangway of a ship. Ps. **Egeshwa.** Rp. **Egeshana,** bring together, come into contact, e.g. moor two vessels alongside. **Egemeo,** n. *ma-* prop (e.g. handrail or bulustrade of staircase), support, ground of belief or action. **Mwega,** n. *mi-* a prop (cf.

nguzo, mwao). **Mwegamo, n.** *wa-* the person who holds a dead body while it is being washed. (Cf. *tegemea, chegama*.)

Ehee! int. of assent.

Ehuka, v. See under **Mwehu.**

-ekevu, a. See under **Elea, v.** (B).

Ekua, v. break, break up, break down, cause to give way, undermine. *Ekua dari*, break through a concrete ceiling. *Maji yameekua ngazi*, the water has broken down the steps (by undermining them). *Mwizi ameekua mlango*, the thief has broken down the door. St. **Ekuka,** be broken, e.g. *boriti ya dari imeekuka*, a rafter of the ceiling has given way. (Perh. for *wekua*, Cv. of *weka*. Cf. *tekua*.)

-ekundu, a. red, of all shades and varieties, scarlet, purple, pink, &c. Of European complexion, 'fair, fresh, ruddy', of native 'light coloured, reddish yellow', esp. of Arabs. (*-ekundu, -eupe*, white, and *-eusi*, black, are the only simple adjs. of colour in Swahili, others are supplied by reference to typical objects.) **Wekundu,** n. redness.

Elafu, n. and a. See **Elfu.**

Elea, v. (A) (1) float, be afloat, swim, (of things) be on the surface. *Chombo kinaelea*, the vessel is floating. Hence (2) fig. a floating feeling in the stomach, nausea, of uncomfortable, nervous, sick feeling. Cs. **Eleza,** cause to float, but usu. with different meanings, see under **Elea, v.** (B). **Chelezo, n.** *vy-* a buoy, life-buoy, anchor-buoy, a float for showing where a fisherman's lines are, or where an anchor is. **Maelezi, n.** plur. floating, being afloat, anchorage, roadstead, moderately deep water. (Cf. *ogelea*.)

Elea, v. (B) be clear, be intelligible. *Maneno yake yamenielea*, his statement is intelligible to me, I understand what he says. Ps. **Elewa.** *Sielewi maana*, I do not see the meaning. Cs. **Eleza,** explain, make clear. *Nitakueleza habari*, I will explain the matter to you. Prep **Elezea,** like *eleza*, but often to explain for, on behalf of another. Cs. of Prep. **Eleleza,** (1) explain thoroughly, i.e. explain how a piece of work has to be done, &c.; (2) follow a pattern, imitate work, follow instructions given regarding work, &c. St. **Eleka,** not in use. Prep. of St. **Elekea,** (1) point to, be directed towards, incline to, tend to, be opposite, face, correspond to, agree with; (2) be rightly directed, be satisfactory, turn out well, succeed. *Anaelekea kuenda*, he is inclined to go. *Maneno haya yanaelekea*, these words seem as though they are true. Cs. **Elekeza,** point, direct, show the way to. *Seremala huwaelekeza wanafunzi wake*, the carpenter gives directions to his apprentices. *Elekeza chombo*, steer a ship. *Elekeza bunduki*, aim a gun. *Elekeza kidole*, point a finger. *Elekeza njia*, show the road. *Elekeza nia*, direct the attention. Rp. of Cs. **Elekezana,** come to an agreement, of people among themselves. Rp. **Elekeana,** be directed towards each other, or to a common point, be facing one another, be opposite (contradictory), agree, correspond. Obs. also **Elekana,** Rp. of *eleka*, correspond. Cs. **Elekanya,** pile up one on another. **-elekevu,** a. sometimes shortened to *-lekevu*, and *-ekevu*, handy, easy to instruct, apt, having a capacity for, or a knack of. **Elezo,** n. *ma-* usu. in plur. explanation, description, comment. *Maelezo ya somo*, presentation of a lesson. **Kielekezo, n.** *vi-* a sign, hint. **Kielelezo,** n. *vi-* same as *kielezo*, but more particular and inten. in meaning. **Kielezo, n.** *vi-* act (process, manner, means) of showing or explaining, explanation, pattern, model, illustration, comment (cf. *mfano, namna, jinsi*). **Maelekeo, n.** inclination, tendency. **Mwelewa,** n. *wa-* one who understands, who is intelligent, takes a thing in. **Mwelezo, n.** *mi-*

explanation, sign, indication, exposition, programme. **Uelekeo**, n. direction (of a place). **Uelekevu**, n. attention, understanding, capability of understanding. (Cf. *onyesha*.)

Eleka, v. carry astride on the hip—as native women do their children, secured by the arm or a cloth. **Mbeleko**, n. also **Mbeko, Ubeleko**, a piece of calico used by women for carrying a child on the back or hip while at work or walking. Such a cloth is a usual wedding present, made to the bride's mother. *Ondoa* (*vunja*) *mbeleko*, put to shame. **Mweleka**, n. *mi-* (1) a leather sling used for carrying a gun; (2) *kupigana* (*kushindana*) *mieleka*, fight (contest) by wrestling. (Cf. *beba*.)

Elekanya, v., **Elekea**, v., **-elekevu**, a., **Elekeza**, v. See under **Elea**, v. (B).

Elektrisiti,* n. electricity. (Eng. Cf. *umeme*, *stimu*.)

Eleleza, v. See under **Elea**, v. (B).

Elemea, v. (1) go anywhere with a rush and noise; (2) surrender, submit to, place one's trust in. (Cf. *angukia*, *tegemea*.) See also **Lemea**, v. which is sometimes used in the same sense.

Eleza, v. See under **Elea**, v. (A) and (B).

Elfeen,* n. and a. two thousand. (Ar. see follg.)

Elfu,* n. *ma-* and a. a thousand. Rd. **elfu elfu**, of an enormous number, myriads. *-a elfu*, thousandth. (Cf. *laki*, *halaiki*, *lukuki*. Ar. الف.)

Elimisha,* v. see under **Elimu**.

Elimu, n. knowledge, learning, wisdom, science, education, doctrine, teaching. *Elimu ndio mwanga uongozao*, knowledge is the guiding light. **Elimisha**,* v. Cs. impart knowledge to, instruct, teach, educate. Ps. **Elimishwa**. **Taalamu**, v. know, be learned in, be educated. **-taalamu**, a. educated, scholarly, well-informed. **Mtaalamu**, n. *wa-* an educated, learned, well-informed person, a scholar, a sage. (Cf. *fundisha*, and *jifunza*, under *funda*, v. (C); also *maalum* from same root. Ar. علم and تعلم.)

-ema, a. good—including goodness of all kinds and degrees, whatever commends itself to feeling, taste, reason, or conscience, and translatable in a corresponding variety of ways, 'pleasant, beautiful, sensible, right'. *Mungu ni mwema*, God is good. *Chakula chema*, nice food. *Kazi njema*, sound workmanship. *Uso mwema*, a handsome face. *Dawa njema lakini si njema*, the medicine is effective but nasty. **Vyema, vema**, adv. well, rightly, nicely, properly, &c. A common rejoinder of assent is *vyema! vema!* and *njema!* Very well! Certainly! Good! (Cf. *inshallah*, *eewallah*, *taibu*.) *Sema vyema* (or *vema*), speak clearly. *Tengeneza vyema* (or *vema*), arrange carefully. **Mema**, n. plur. good (acts, affairs, &c.). *Mema na maovu ndio ulimwengu*, the world is a mixture of good and bad. Prov. *Njema haziozi*, good (deeds) never go bad. **Wema**, n. goodness, excellence (of any kind). (Cf. *-zuri*, *-zima*, and contr. *-baya*, *-ovu*, *-bovu*.)

-embamba, a. (1) narrow, thin, slim, pinched, confined; (2) fine, delicate, minute (in texture, fabric, grain). *Mtu mwembamba*, a thin spare man. *Mlango mwembamba*, a narrow entrance. *Mchanga mwembamba*, fine sand. *Uji mwembamba*, thin, watery gruel. *Hewa nyembamba*, penetrating thin air. *Nguo nyembamba*, fine, thin cloth, gauze. **Wembamba**, n. narrowness, thinness, slenderness, fineness, delicacy (of fabric, texture, grain, &c.). (Cf. *bamba*, and contr. *-pana*, *-nene*.)

Embe,* n. (— and of size *ma-*), mango, the fruit of the *mwembe*, *mi-*. Different kinds are called: *dodo*, *boribo*, *sindano*, *bungala*, *mawazo*, *koko, embe maji, kihoranzi*, &c. (Hind. انب.)

Embwe, n. a kind of gum or glue. *Embwe ya mbuyu*, a sticky paste made from the fruit of the baobab-tree (*mbuyu*).

Enda, v. go—including a wide range of meanings under the general idea of motion, such as (1) go, move forward, proceed, progress; (2) begin to go, start off; (3) go away, depart, withdraw; (4) go on, keep on, continue; (5) move, have motion, be in motion, act, work, operate; (6) make its way, occur, have a use, be possible. **Enda**, go away, is commonly followed by a pronom. adj. with pfx. *z*, as if with *njia* in the plur. understood. *Nakwenda* or *naenda zangu*, I am going away. *Nenda* (more usual than *enda* in the Imp.) *zako*, go away, also *zake, zetu, zenu, zao*. The Rf. form *jienda* is used of automatic, easy, or perpetual motion, e.g. *mashua inajienda*, the boat goes of itself. Rd. form *endaenda*, denotes continued motion, 'go on and on'. *Enda* is used in some phrases idiomatically without the idea of movement, e.g. *enda chafya*, sneeze; *enda mwayo*, yawn; *enda wazimu*, be mad, act as a madman. *Enda* is also used in a semi-auxiliary with future meaning and often followed by an Infinitive Mood without the Infinitive sign *ku-*. *Maji yaenda letwa*, water is going to be brought, but usu. including the idea of some one going for it. *Watu walikwenda kuitwa*, the people were sent for. *Mwivi aenda hukumiwa*, the thief is going to be tried. *Enda tembea*, go for a walk. *Enda kwa miguu*, go on foot. *Enda kwa farasi*, ride on a horse. *Enda kwa gari*, drive in a car. *Kwenda joshi*, i.e. *chombo kinakwenda joshi*, the boat is going straight ahead. *Chombo kinakwenda mrama*, the vessel is rolling. *Kwenda shoti*, trot, e.g. *farasi wake alikwenda shoti*, his horse went at a trot. *Kwenda pecha*, stagger, reel, e.g. *mlevi kuenda pecha*, a drunken man staggers. Prep. **Endea**, go to (for, by, in, &c.), *Endea kuni*, go for (to fetch) firewood. This form should be used with caution with an objective prefix. *Nilimwendea*, I went to her, but also with her, i.e. had sexual intercourse with her. Rf. *jiendea*, go voluntarily, walk for pleasure, amuse oneself, stroll about. St. and Pot. **Endeka**, admit of going upon, be passable, be practicable, e.g. of a road. *Njia hii haiendeki*, this road is impassable. *Hakuendeki*, of the weather or circumstances generally, 'travelling is out of the question'. Cs. of St. **Endekeza**, (1) make able to go, and so 'adapt, fit, put in order, put to rights'; (2) also used of spoiling anybody, esp. a child by too lenient treatment, coaxing, petting, &c. D. Prep. **Endelea**, Inten. in meaning: (1) move on, progress, advance, increase, often further defined by *mbele*, forward. *Endelea nyuma*, go back, recede, decrease, &c.; (2) continue indefinitely, have no end. The Cs. of this form **Endeleza**, cause to go on, prolong, keep working at, make progress with, is also used of spelling, i.e. making the letters or words go on. *Endeleza neno hili*, spell this word. Cs. **Enza**, but usu. **Endesha**, cause to go, set in motion, permit to go, assist to go, send, dispatch, pay passage of, show the way to, accompany, &c. *Endesha mtoto*, teach the child to walk. *Endesha kazi*, push on a job. *Tumbo la kuendesha*, diarrhoea. Rp. **Endana**, e.g. *magurudumu yake yanaendana vizuri*, its wheels all work together beautifully, e.g. of the works of a watch. *Note*: In the simple tenses **Enenda** is often used, but not usually in any derived forms. *Wakaenenda*, and they went. *Tumbo la kuenenda*, diarrhoea. The Imp. as a rule is *nenda* or *enenda*, with plur. *nendeni* or *enendeni*. **-endapo**, a verb-form used with pers. pfx., and sometimes *endapo* only for all persons, as a conj. 'in case of, if, when it happens that', e.g. *nendapo nikifa au kuugua*, suppose I died or was taken ill (from *-enda* with the generalized meaning 'happen, take place', and *-po*, i.e. the general relative form of *enda*). **Endeleo**, n. *ma-* usually in plur. form, going on, progress, advance, success. **Enenzi**, n. *ma-* (from *enenda*) esp. in the plur. form, going, walking, pace, gait, way of going on, behaviour. *Maenenzi ya polepole* (*ya haraka, ya upesi*), slow (hasty, quick) going. **Huenda** (*enda* with pfx. *hu-* of customary or repeated action) used as adv., it happens sometimes, at times, and so 'possibly, it may be, there is a chance, &c.' (cf. *labda, yamkini*). **Kiendeleo**, n. *vi-* make a forward movement, progress, process, but usually *endeleo, ma-*. **Mwenda**, n. *wa-* verbal of *enda*, one who goes. *Huyu ni mwenda pekee*, this man is a solitary person. *Mwenda wazimu*, a madman. *Mwenda nguu*, a despairing person. **Mwendeleo**, n. *mi-* progress, advance, movement. **Mwendelezi**, n. *wa-* one who causes to go on, one who carries on or forward, and so in various senses of *endeleza*, e.g. (1) a persistent, persevering, progressive person; (2) one who copies, one who spells words. **Mwendeshaji**, n. *wa-*, **Mwendeshi**, n. *wa-* with the same meaning as (1) of *mwendelezi*, one who causes to go, a driver, &c. **Mwendo**, n. *mi-* (1) a going, moving, motion, proceeding, progress; (2) way (manner, style) of going, gait, behaviour, course, &c. *Vunja mwendo*, prevent progress. *Mwendo wa jua*, the sun's course, orbit. *Mwendo wa pigo*, rhythm (in music). *Piga mwendo*, beat time. **Mwenendo**, n. *mi-* (1) going on, moving, &c., like *mwendo*, but often (2) fig. proceedings, behaviour, conduct, manner of life, &c. **Mwenenzi**, n. *wa-* (1) one who goes, a traveller; (2) one who causes to go, hence, powerful, mighty. **Mwenzi**, n. (*wenzi*) from a Cs. form of *enda*, i.e. *enza*, cause to go, accompany, share the actions of, hence (1) a friend, companion, associate, acquaintance; (2) of things as well as persons, fellow, counterpart, match, double, something resembling or corresponding to another, e.g. *hakuna msiba usio na mwenziwe*, misfortune never comes alone. (Cf. *rafiki, sahibu.*) Note: the abstract nouns of the foregoing can be made by prefixing U- in place of the class prefixes, *Uendeleo* (*wendeleo*), *Uendelezi* (*wendelezo*), *Uendo* (*wendo*), &c. **Wenzo**, n. (*nyenzo*) a lever, roller, e.g. *mti huu hauendi ila kwa nyenzo*, this piece of wood cannot be moved without the help of rollers.

Enea, v. abound, become abundant, be spread out (abroad, over), be extended over (among, in), be diffused in, permeate, cover the whole extent of, become generally known (among, to, in), be distributed (to), be coextensive (with). *Mungu aenea dunia yote*, God is omnipresent, He pervades the whole world. *Maji yameenea nchi yote*, the water has inundated the whole country. *Aliwagawanyia watu vikombe, vikaenea*, he divided the cups among the people, and they were sufficient. *Sahani zitaenea*, the plates will do, there is sufficient for the needs. Cs. **Eneza**, (1) spread, extend, cause to cover, distribute; and hence (2) measure one thing with another, take measure of, judge, compare, cause to fit. *Walienezana*, they compared themselves. *Alieneza mtoto wake*, he took his son's measurement. *Mungu amemwenezea kila mtu riziki yake*, God has put the means of living in every man's hands. *Eneza habari*, publish news, advertise, spread abroad information. Rf. *jieneza*. *Alijieneza mwili mzima silaha*, he armed himself from head to foot. Cs. **Enza** (as from *ena*), also *enenza*, (1) examine, inspect, consider; (2) measure, take the measure of, compare by measurement. **Cheneo**, n. *vy*- (*ki-eneo*) extending, extent, area. **Chenezo**, n. *vy*- (*ki-enezo*) a measure, measuring-rod or line. Anything used for measuring with (stick, strip of cloth, tape-measure, &c.). **Eneo**, n. *ma*- extent, spread, range, reach, province, covering, power, extent covered or affected, sphere of influence. *Eneo la Mungu*, omnipresence of God. **Enezi**, n. *ma*- spreading out, extension, distribution. **Kieneo**, n. *vy*- same as *cheneo* above, i.e. area, extent, &c. **Mwenea**, n. *wa*- one who spreads out (pervades, extends) esp. as title of God, as omnipresent, i.e. *Mwenea pote*. **Mweneza**, n. *wa*-, **Mwenezi**, n. *wa*- one who allots (distributes, gives out), esp. as a title of God, the Giver of good to all. (Cf. *jaa*, *tosha*.)

Enenda, v. See under **Enda**.

Enenza, v. See under **Enea**.

Enenzi, n. See under **Enda**.

Eneo, n. *ma*-, **Eneza**, v., **Enezi**, n. *ma*-. See under **Enea**.

Enga, v. (1) split up, slice up—used of preparing cassava (*muhogo*), &c., for cooking (cf. *lenga*); (2) coddle, pet—of treating a child with over-carefulness, sometimes Rd. *engaenga mtoto*, spoil a child by petting (cf. *endekeza*, under *enda*); (3) look at. (Cf. *tazama*.)

Engaenga, v. (1) see (2) of *enga*, above; (2) be on the verge of tears, near to crying.

Engua, v. skim, take scum off, remove froth, &c., as of fermenting liquor, or in cookery.

Enhee! also **Ehee!** int. yes! well! &c.

-enu, a. pronom. of 2 Pers. Plur., your, yours, of you.

-enye, a. having, possessing, with, in a state or condition of. Always followed by a noun or equivalent, defining the object, state, condition, &c., referred to. Largely used to supply the lack of adjectives in Swahili, admitting as it does of combination with (1) Nouns, e.g. *-enye mali*, wealthy, *-enye mawe*, stony, *-enye uzuri*, beautiful, *-enye kuwa*, self-existent, *-enye enzi*, all-powerful, *-enye watu wengi*, populous, *-enye tumbo*, corpulent, *-enye mimba*, pregnant; (2) Verb-forms: *-enye kutawala*, ruling, reigning, *-enye kwenda*, capable of movement, &c. *Penye*, *kwenye*, and *mwenye* are also commonly used for defining time, place, and circumstances. *Penye mwitu*, in a forest. Prov. *Penye urembo ndipo penye urimbo* (*ulimbo*), where there is beauty, there also is a trap (i.e. birdlime). *Kwenye Ijumaa*, on Friday. *Mwenye hapo*, when he is absent, in his absence (cf. *-enyewe*, following). **Mwenye**, n. (*wenye*) (also *mwene* (*wene*) in some dialects) one who possesses, an owner, an independent person. Also sometimes used as a complimentary title, like sir, and in proper names, *Mwenyehija*, *Mwenyeamani*, &c. (but then it is frequently pronounced *mwenyi*, and *mwinyi*). *Mwenye* (*mwinyi*) *mkuu*, a chief. **Mwenyeji**, n. (*wenyeji*) the regular possessor (*-enye* and the formative *-ji*), hence (1) master of a house, householder, owner, occupant, citizen, inhabitant of a town, native (of a place); (2) host, in relation to guests (*wageni*).

-enyewe, a. used to express identity, distinctness, and (of persons) personality. *Mtu mwenyewe*, the man himself, the very person, the particular individual. *Kasha lenyewe*, the actual box. *Vitu vyenyewe*, the very things. Often with the personal pronouns, *mimi mwenyewe*, *wewe mwenyewe*, &c., I myself, you yourself. Sometimes with *nafsi* added, *nipo mwenyewe nafsi yangu*, here I am my own proper, particular self. *Sitaki mwenyewe*, I utterly refuse, I will not have it—a strong emphatic refusal. Also with *-ji* in reflexive verbs, e.g.

alijiumiza mwenyewe, he hurt himself. *Mali ya mwenyewe,* the property of the owner, i.e. of some one else, not mine nor yours. **Mwenyewe,** n. (*wenyewe*), owner, sometimes used as *mwenyeji* or *mwenye,* e.g. *yule simba ndiye mwenyewe* (perh. for *mwenye wake*) *asali,* that lion is owner of the honey.

Enyi! int. of 2 Pers. Plur., You there! I say you! (for *ee ninyi!*) (Cf. *ewe* for *ee wewe.*)

Enzi,* n. power, might, dominion, rule. *Mwenye enzi,* as a title of God, Almighty God. Also sometimes *Mwenyezi. Kiti cha enzi,* chair of state, throne. **Enzi,** v. share greatness with, place a person in a position of honour and respect. (Ar. عز might, honour.)

Epa, v. get out of the way, avoid being hit by, swerve from, flinch, shirk, e.g. of avoiding a missile, a blow, or any danger of the sort. *Epa jiwe,* avoid the stone. Ps. **Epwa.** St. **Epeka.** Prep. **Epea.** *Epea* is also used for another point of view, viz. fail to hit, not be in the line of, miss a mark, i.e. of throwing a missile, &c. *Bunduki yaepea,* the gun misses, does not shoot straight. But St. and Pot. **Epeka,** be avoided, be avoidable, *Inaepeka,* it is avoidable, you can get out of it. Cs. **Epesha.** Rp. **Epana.** Cv. **Epua,** put out of the way, move away, take off, remove. *Epua* (but frequently in this sense *ipua* is used) *chungu motoni,* take the pot off the fire. St. **Epuka,** like *epa,* avoid, get out of the way of, abstain from, withdraw from, keep from. *Ananiepuka,* he avoids me, keeps out of my way—also *anaepukana nami.* Ps. **Epukwa,** be avoided. Prep. **Epukia.** Cs. of St. **Epukisha.** Rp. **Epukana,** be estranged, disunited, discordant, keep out of each other's way—less pointed and deliberate than *epushana.* Prep. **Epulia,** e.g. *chuma cha kuepulia sufuria,* an iron handle for lifting off a cooking-pot. Cs. of Prep. **Epuliza,** cause to remove, allow to take away. Cs. **Epusha,** Inten. reject, put away, avoid, keep at a distance. *Nimeepushwa,* I am kept from, forbidden to do (take, &c.). Rp. of Cs. **Epushana,** e.g. of people refusing to recognize each other in passing, avoiding each other.

-epesi, a. (1) quick, agile, swift, active, nimble, willing, energetic; (2) overquick, hasty, rash, impatient, fiery, quick-tempered; (3) light (in weight or importance, &c.), easily moved, light in texture, fine, thin, delicate, insignificant, of no weight or consequence. **Upesi,** adv. quickly, lightly, e.g. *njoo upesi,* come at once, *kimbia upesi,* run away quickly. Also **Upesi,** n. and **Wepesi,** n. speed, quickness, velocity, easiness, agility, lightness in movement—but *wepesi* commonly of lightness in weight. (Cf. *rahisi,* and as adv. *hima, mara, sasa hivi,* and contr. *-zito.*)

Epua, v., **Epuka,** v. See under **Epa.**

-erevu, a. shrewd, clever, cunning, resourceful, crafty—not often a term of praise, but not always in disparagement. **Erevuka,** v. become shrewd, be clever in a cunning way have worldly wisdom, have the eyes open. Cs. **Erevusha,** make wise, teach cunning or prudence to, open the eyes of, initiate in the ways of the world. **Werevu,** n. cunning, cleverness, shrewdness, worldly wisdom, but usually of a sly, dishonest cunning.

Eropleni,* n. an aeroplane. (Eng.)

Esha,* n. also **Isha,** the latest Muhammadan hour of prayer. Used for the period from 6.30 p.m. to 8.30 p.m. (Ar. عشية.)

Eti! int. See **Ati!**

-etu, invariable part of poss. pron. 1 Pers. Plur., our, ours, of us.

Eua, v. (1) make white, whiten, clean, cleanse, purify, but only used in a ceremonial sense, purification after defilement of childbirth, &c., by the usual Muhammadan rites, or a sprinkling as a charm against disease; (2) remove a spell or witchcraft, remove a taboo or forbidden article of diet. Prep. **Eulia.** Ps. of Prep. **Euliwa,** be purified, cleansed, &c. *Mwanamke ameeuliwa ujusi,* the woman has been purified of her uncleanness. **-eupe,** a. (1) white, of any shade or kind, light-coloured, bright, clear, transparent; (2) clean, clear of all obstruction, open, unoccupied; (3) pure, righteous. *Watu weupe,* white people, Europeans, but it is also used of light-coloured Arabs, Indians, &c. *Moyo mweupe,* a pure, honourable, upright, character. *Nchi haina mwitu, nyeupe,* the country is open and treeless. **Kweu,** n. sometimes for the usual *kweupe,* clearness, dawn, light. *Mbele kweu na nyuma kweu,* brightness before and behind. Also used when a person is too late for something, e.g. *kweu sasa,* there is nothing now, you are too late, all is over. **Kweupe,** n. for *ku-eupe,* brightness, whiteness, clearness, dawn, light, clear space, fine weather. *Ni kweupe,* it is dawn, it is fine weather (cf. *kucha,* and contr. *giza, usiku*). **Peupe,** n. an open place, clearing in a forest, square in a town, unoccupied ground. **Weu,** n. (*nyeu*) clearing, open space for planting, place free from trees, forest glade. **Weuo,** n. making white, purifying, cleaning. **Weupe,** n. (1) whiteness, white or grey colour, a light tint in general; (2) light as opp. to shade or darkness, brightness, and esp. of the dawn, morning light; (3) cleanness; (4) fig. purity, innocence, integrity, guilelessness. (Cf. *safisha, takasa, tohara, edaha, adua.*)

-eusi, a. black (of any shade or kind), dark coloured, gloomy, dim, dusky, dark, including dark shades of blue, green, red, &c., colours being grouped according to relative lightness and darkness. *Watu weusi,* natives of Africa (in general), i.e. non-Europeans. **Peusi,** n. a dark place. **Weusi,** n. (1) blackness, black or dark colour, a dark tint in general (e.g. of blue, green, red); (2) absence of light, darkness, gloom, obscurity (not used of dirt as such, or in fig. (moral) sense, like *weupe*).

Ewaa!* int., **Eewaa!** int. commonly used in assent by inferiors or slaves, 'Yes, Sir.' Also of approval, 'Just so, that is right.' (Ar. *ee wallah,* Yes by God! Cf. *inshallah, wallahi,* &c.)

Ewe! int. for *ee wewe!* You there! I say, you!—in calling attention or in remonstrance. (Cf. *enyi.*)

Ewedeka, v. See **Weweseka.**

Ezeka, v. (1) thatch, cover with thatch, i.e. usually with grass, reeds, or coco-nut leaves, *makuti. Ezeka paa,* cover a roof with thatch. *Ezeka nyumba,* thatch a house. (2) fig. beat, e.g. *atakuezeka kigongo,* he shall lay a stick on you, i.e. beat you. *Atakuezeka makofi,* he shall box your ears. *Waliezekana makofi,* they boxed each other's ears. Ps. **Ezekwa.** Prep. **Ezekea,** of men or material, *sina mtu wa* (*mali ya*) *kuniezekea,* I have no one (no means) to do my thatching. Cv. **Ezua,** take thatch off, strip a roof, uncover the rafters—as is done when a fire is spreading in a native town or village. **Ezeko,** n. *ma-* (1) thatching, grass, leaves, material for thatching; (2) method, &c., of thatching. **Mwezekaji,** n. *wa-* a thatcher. **Mwezeko,** n. *mi-* act (method, fee, &c.) of thatching.

Ezi,* n. might, power. *Mwenyezi Mungu* (for *mwenye ezi*), God Almighty. (Ar. عزّ might.)

Ezua, v. See under **Ezeka.**

F

F represents the same sound as in English. *F* and *v* are not clearly distinguishable in some words, as in the adjectival termination *-fu* or *-vu*, e.g. in *-kamilifu*, *-vumilivu*, and in words like *fukiza* (*vukiza*), &c., though a difference of meaning is often involved. This confusion may have arisen owing to the fact that in writing Swahili in Arabic characters *f* had to stand also for *v*, as the Arabic alphabet contains no *v*, and this may have had an influence on the pronunciation. Hence words not found under *f* may be looked for under *v*.

Fa, v. (1) die, perish, cease to live (be, act, work, feel); (2) lose strength, decay, fade, be benumbed; (3) come to an end. *Kufa*, or *kufa kwa*, *maradhi* (*njaa*, *maji*, *baridi*, &c.), to die by pestilence (famine, drowning, cold, &c.). *Njia imekufa*, the path is disused. *Saa imekufa*, the watch (or clock) has stopped. *Mkono umekufa ganzi*, the arm is benumbed, is asleep, has cramp. *Desturi inakufa*, the custom (usage) is dying, is disappearing. Prov. *Heri kufa macho kuliko moyo*, better be blind than despairing. Prep. **Fia**, esp. in local sense, *fia bara* (*bahari*), die up country (at sea). *Kufa jua* and *kufia jua* are used of sunstroke. Esp. common in the Ps. **Fiwa**, have a death in one's family, or among one's friends. *Alifiwa na mtoto*, he lost his child. *Tumefiwa nyumbani*, one of our relations has died. *Nakimbia pafiwapo*, *nakimbilia paliwapo*, I run from a place of bereavement, I run to a place of feasting. D. Prep. **Filia**, die for, on behalf of, also Inten. perish, *afilie mbali*, may he perish utterly. Cs. **Fisha**, cause to die, put to death. *Jifisha*, destroy oneself, syn. *jiua*. **Kifa**, n. *vi-* dying. *Kifa uwongo*, the sensitive plant—lit. the death shammer. **Kifo**, n. *vi-* act (circumstances, place, manner, &c.) of dying, death. *Hawakuona kifo chake alikofia*, they did not see where his death took place. **Kifu**, n. *vi-* a dead thing, and adv. as if dead. **Mafa**, n. plur. (1) place of burial, cemetery (cf. *makaburini*); (2) a man who inherits the wife or wives, children, and property of a deceased brother is said to take *mafa*, i.e. *ametwaa mafa ya ndugu yake*. **Mafu**, n. death, dead thing, rarely used except of *maji mafu*, neap tide. **Mfisha**, n. *wa-*, **Mfishaji**, n. *wa-* (1) one who kills, a slaughterer; (2) one who brings death, a title of God. **Mfiwa**, n. *wa-* a bereaved person, an orphan. **Mfu**, n. *wa-* a dead person. **Ufu**, n. state of being dead, death, deadness, numbness.

Faa, v. be of use, be of avail, be good of its kind, help, be enough, do (i.e. suffice). *Dawa aliyopewa ilimfaa*, the medicine he was given suited him, did him good. Frequently used with the impersonal pfx. *i-*, e.g. *itafaa*, it will do. *Haifai*, it is of no use, nonsense, rubbish. *Maneno yasiyofaa*, improper language. Prep. **Falia.** Rp. **Faana**, give mutual assistance, be of use to each other, &c. **Fana**

is sometimes used in the same way as *faa* (for similar forms, see *poa, pona*; *pua, puna*; *sonoa, sonona*, &c. Rp. **Fanana**, do for each other, and so be like, be similar, resemble—with *na* of object compared. *Amefanana na mbuzi*, he is like a goat. **Fanya**, Cs. of *fana*, given separately for convenience of reference. Cs. **Fananisha**, make like, liken, compare. **Kifaa**, n. *vi-* a useful thing, a thing for use, personal belongings, household necessaries, utensil, &c. *Vifaa vya chuoni*, school furniture, apparatus, &c. *Vifaa vya kuandikia*, things requisite for writing, writing materials. **Kifani**, n. *vi-* but usu. **Kifano**, n. *vi-* that which does, i.e. a similar thing, that which matches, a fellow, a parallel, a match, an equal. *Kitu hiki hakina kifani*, this thing is unequalled, it is unique. **Mafaa**, n. plur. use, utility, profit, advantage, e.g. *ng'ombe hawa hawana mafaa*, these oxen are no good. **Mfano**, n. *mi-* something which is of use, i.e. as a substitute, likeness, resemblance, similitude, emblem, sample, pattern, parable. *Mfano wa maneno*, an allegory, parable. *Kwa mfano wa*, or only *mfano wa*, like. **Ufananaji**, n. likeness, similarity, resemblance. **Ufanani**, n. same as *ufananaji*, n. (Cf. *fanya*.)

Fadhaa,* n. dismay, confusion, perplexity, trouble, disquiet, bustle, agitation. *Shikwa na fadhaa*, be thrown into confusion. **Fadhaika**, v. be troubled, disturbed, confused, &c. Cs. **Fadhaisha**. (Cf. *duwaa, pumbaa, shangaa*. Ar. فضح.)

Fadhili,* v. do a kindness (to), confer a favour (on), put under an obligation, esp. as the act of a superior. Ps. **Fadhiliwa**. St. **Fadhilika**, receive a favour. Cs. **Fadhilisha**, put under an obligation. **Afadhali**, adv. rather, better of more than one course, &c., preferably. *Afadhali uende*, you had better go. *Kwetu sisi ni afadhali* (conditions, &c.) are better with us at our place. *Ni afadhali kuishi kuliko kufa*, it is better to live than to die. **Fadhili**, n. favour, kindness, benefit, privilege. *Nimekula fadhili yao*, I have experienced kindness from them, I am under an obligation to them. *Hana* (or *hajui*) *fadhili*, he has no sense of gratitude. Prov. *Fadhili ya punda ni mashuzi*, the gratitude of a donkey is a breaking of wind, i.e. that's all the return you get for kindness to a donkey, or that is its way of showing gratitude. *Fadhili ya nyuki ni moto*, all the thanks a bee gets is fire, i.e. referring to smoking them out of their hives to get their honey. **Mfadhili**, n. *wa-* a benefactor. **Tafadhali**, v. please, do a kindness to, be good to. Esp. in Imp. as a form of polite request—be so kind as to, if you please, and so of making a polite request, e.g. *akamtafadhali bwana mkubwa ampige adui yake*, and he begged the master to smite his enemy. Sometimes a Cs. **Tafadhalisha** is heard as an Inten. or Cs. **Ufadhili**, n. kindness, privilege, obligation. (Ar. فضل.)

Fafanisha, v. liken, compare, explain (i.e. use comparison and illustration), make clear. *Nikifafanishe na nini?* What shall I liken it to? *Fafanisha maneno*, explain a statement, make a clear statement. Cv. **Fafanua**, v. (1) explain; (2) recognize, understand, see clearly. St. **Fafanuka**, be clear, be known, be intelligible. Cs. **Fafanusha**, same as *fafanisha*. Prep. **Fafanulia**, make clear to. **Ufafanuzi**, n. *ma-* explanation, revelation, interpretation. (Cf. *linganisha, fananisha, eleza*.)

Fagia, v. sweep (with brush, broom, besom). Ps. **Fagiwa**. Prep. **Fagilia**, sweep at, sweep away (for, with, in, &c.). *Pamefagiliwa vizuri*, the place is well swept. **Fagio**, n. *ma-* (1) a large brush, broom, besom—

for sweeping floors, &c.; (2) a woody herb up to 4 ft. tall with yellow flowers, used as a broom, *Sida carpinifolia*. Also **Ufagio** (*fagio*) for smaller sorts, i.e. a bundle of leaf-strips or twigs tied together and used for rough sweeping, e.g. footpaths, floors, &c.

Fahali,* n. *ma-* bull. Prov. *Mafahali wawili hawakai zizi moja*, two bulls cannot live in the same farmyard. Used also descriptively of men, of special manliness, vigour, courage, &c. (Ar. فحل.)

-fahamivu,* a. See under **Fahamu.**

Fahamu,* v. (1) know, perceive, comprehend, understand; (2) remember, recall to mind, bear in mind; (3) be conscious, have one's senses. Often in Imp. as a kind of expletive. *Fahamu!* take notice! observe! Lo and behold! I tell you! Ps. **Fahamiwa.** St. **Fahamika,** Prep. **Fahamia.** Cs. **Fahamisha,** cause to know, inform, instruct, remind, put in mind. **Fahamivu,** a. intelligent, acute, with quick comprehension, having a good memory. **Fahamu,** n. also **Ufahamu** (*fahamu*), (1) recollection, memory; (2) intelligence, sense, consciousness, recognition, comprehension. *Alipotewa na fahamu*, he lost consciousness. **Ufahamivu,** n. understanding, perspicacity. (Cf. *tambua, jua, akili, busara.* Ar. فهم.)

Faharasa,* n. the table of contents of a book, index. (Ar. فهرس.)

Fahari,* n. (1) grandeur, glory, pomp, sublimity, magnificence; (2) display, show, ostentation; (3) pride in the sense of feeling pride because of, e.g. *aliona fahari juu ya mtoto wake*, he was proud of his son. *Jumbe amekaa kwa fahari*, the chief lives in grandeur. *Piga fahari*, play the grandee, make a vulgar show of wealth. **Fahari,** v. but more freq. *faharisha* or *fanya fahari*, make a display, show off. (Cf. *utukufu, ukuu, sherehe.* Ar. فخر.)

Fahirisi,* n. See **Faharasa.**

Faida,* n. profit, gain, advantage, interest. *Faida ya gawio*, a dividend. **Faidi,** v. get profit (from), derive benefit (from, by), turn to good account, prosper, frequently used of getting pleasure at an entertainment, feast, &c. *Leo nimefaidi*, to-day I have prospered (got gain), &c., also, I have received pleasant things, food, drink, entertainment, &c. Prep. **Faidia.** *Mambo yamemfaidia*, things have been to his advantage, he has profited. (Cf. *chuma, nafuu, chumo, pato.* Ar. فائدة.)

Faiti,* v. delay, detain. St. **Faitika,** be delayed, be kept back, be hindered (from going, &c.). Sometimes heard as *fawiti*. (Cf. *ahiri, chelewesha, weka.* Ar. فوت.)

Faja,* n. a stable (not well known). (Cf. *zizi.* ? Ar. فج.)

Fajaa,* n. and adv. sudden death, suddenly, unawares. (Ar. فجاة.)

Fakaika,* adv. See **Fakefu** under **Fauka.**

Fakefu,* adv. See under **Fauka.**

Fakiri,* n. also **Fukara,** a poor person, beggar, often followed by *hohehahe*. **Fukarika,** v. become poor. **Ufukara,** n. utter destitution, beggary, poverty. (Cf. *maskini,* Ar. فقر.)

Falaki,* n. astronomy, astrology, esp. in the phrase *piga falaki*, i.e. (1) take the omens, by observing the stars or in other ways, cast a horoscope; (2) fig. take time to consider. (Cf. *piga bao, ramli, ndege, unajimu.* Ar. فلك.)

Falaula!* int. Oh, that! Were it not for so-and-so. (Cf. *laiti.* Ar. فلاولا.)

Fali,* n. (1) an omen, either good or bad; (2) luck, chance, fate, either good or bad. *Usinitie fali mbaya*, do not bring bad luck to me. *Maneno* *yako naomba yanipatie fali njema,* I pray that your words bring me good luck. (Cf. *bahati, sudi.* Ar. فال.)

Falka,* n. the hold of a ship. (Ar. ? فلك a ship.)

Faluda,* n. gruel made of milk and maize flour. (Ar. فالوذ.)

Fana, v., **Fanana,** v., **Fananisha,** v. See under **Faa.**

Fanaka,* n. prosperity, success, benefit, favour, comfort. **Fanikia,** v. turn out well for, succeed. Ps. **Fanikiwa,** have (a thing) turn out well, succeed, prosper. **Ufanisi,** n. prosperity, success, comfort, beneficence. (Ar. فنق.)

Fani,* a. worthy, fitting, prosperous. (Ar. فنع.)

Fanidi,* v. select by comparing. *Jifanidi,* compare onself with others, and think oneself better, &c. (Ar. فند.)

Fanikia,* v. See under **Fanaka.**

Fanusi,* n. lantern, lamp. (Cf. *taa.* Ar. فانوس.)

Fanya, v. (Cs. of *fana,* derived from *faa,* but shown separately because of its common use like a direct form. For similar forms, cf. *poa, pona, ponya; pua, puna, punya.*) Cause to do, cause to be useful or of avail, hence make. One of the commonest verbs in Swahili, always implying some result, purpose, or object beyond mere act, for which *tenda* is used. Its many applications may be distinguished as—(1) make, make to be, produce, manufacture, fashion. *Fanya kasha (njia, shamba),* make a box (road, plantation). *Fanya mali,* amass wealth. *Fanya shauri,* make a plan, consider (cf. *umba,* and *huluku* of actual creation). (2) do, work at, engage in (of the operation rather than the result). *Fanya kazi,* work, labour. *Fanya biashara,* carry on trade. *Fanya shughuli,* attend to business. *Nifanyeni?* (for *nifanye nini?*) What steps am I to take? What am I to do? *Fanya vyo vyote,* act recklessly, at random. (3) bring about a result, cause, compel. *Fanya aende,* take steps to make him go, make him go. (This sense is usually expressed by the Cs. form of verbs or by another word of definite compulsion, e.g. *lazimu, shurutisha, juzu.*) (4) bring into play, allow to happen, give spontaneous vent to, esp. of the feelings, 'feel, show'. *Fanya furaha,* rejoice. *Fanya hofu (hasira),* be afraid (angry). *Fanya fahari,* give oneself airs, play the grandee. (5) make in imagination, suppose, regard as. *Ulifanya mimi mgonjwa,* you thought (made out) that I was ill (when I was not). *Jifanya,* make oneself, pretend to be, disguise oneself as. *Usifanye mzaha,* do not suppose it is a joke, do not make fun or mock at it. Ps. **Fanywa.** St. and Pot. **Fanyika,** e.g. be done, be able to be done, be practicable. Prep. **Fanyikia,** be done for (for the benefit of, &c.), turn out well for; and also 'be favourable to, favour, give prosperity to'. *Nimefanyikiwa,* I have prospered, things have gone well with me. (Cf. *fanikiwa* under *faa.*) Prep. **Fanyia,** do for (with, at, &c.). Cs. **Fanyiza** also **Fanza,** cause to make, cause a making of, cause to be made, repair, put in order, mend, have (a thing) done (by giving orders, personal attention, &c.), provide, get ready. *Nifanzie nyumba hii,* have this house put in order for me. *Nitafanyiza,* I will have it done (see to it). *Fanza chakula,* get a meal ready. Sometimes Inten., e.g. *wakamfanza kila namna,* they did all sorts of things to him (of ill-natured treatment). Rp. **Fanyana,** of mutual concerted action, co-operation, e.g. with *kazi,* work; *shauri,* deliberation; *biashara,* trade. **Mfanya,** n. *wa-* followed by a noun, a doer, maker, one who practises, also **Mfanyi,** *wa-*, e.g. *mfanyi biashara,* a trader, a merchant. *Mfanyi matata,* a troublesome person. (Cf. *tenda, tengeneza.*)

Fara,* n. brim, brim-full. *Pishi ya fara,* a full *pishi* (see *pishi*), about 6 lb. weight. *Fara ya pishi,* is also used for 12 *pishi,* i.e. *fara,* a dozen. Adv. *fara* or *farafara,* e.g. *Kutia fara,* to fill a measure and wipe off the top so that the contents are level with the brim. *Kujaa farafara,* to be quite full to the brim. **Fori,** adv., also **Fulifuli,** adv. in large quantities, abundantly. (? Ar. Cf. *fura.*)

Faradhi,* n. also sometimes **Faridha,** (1) a matter of necessity, obligation, prescribed duty, esp. of religion. *Kula ni faradhi ya kila mtu,* everybody must eat (cf. *lazima, sharti*); (2) place of resort, haunt, usual abode. *Mahali ulapo chakula ndipo penye faradhi yako,* where you take your meals, that is your abode. (Ar. فرض.)

Faragha,* n. privacy, seclusion, leisure, retirement, secrecy. *Fulani hana faragha,* So-and-so cannot keep a secret. *Mpeleke faraghani umwambie,* take him aside and tell him. Adv. *faragha,* secretly, privately. (Cf. *siri, upweke.* Ar. فرغ.)

Faragua,* v. show off, vaunt oneself, as a man with a case before a court when he realizes that he has a good chance of winning his case. (Prob. derived from prec.)

Faraja,* n. comfort, relief, cessation of pain, ease, consolation. *Pata faraja,* be relieved. **Fariji,** v. comfort, console, relieve, ease, bless. Ps. **Farijiwa.** St. and Pot. **Farijika,** e.g. *hafarijiki kabisa,* she is quite inconsolable. Prep. **Farijia. Mfariji,** n. *wa-* one who comforts, a comforter, a consoler. (Cf. *burudisha, tuliza.* Ar. فرج.)

Faraka,* n. (1) a comb-like instrument for keeping threads apart, part of a weaver's loom; (2) a division, sect. Rp. **Farakana,** v. become parted, be estranged, be separated. **Farakano,** n. *ma-* a dividing off, separation, a sect. *Mafarakano ya dini fulani,* the sects of a certain religion. **Fariki,** v. (1) depart (from), part company (with), but esp. (2) die, decease. *Amefariki dunia,* he has departed this life (lit. from the world). Prep. **Farikia.** Ps. **Farikiwa,** e.g. *amefarikiwa na mumewe,* she has lost her husband (by death or desertion). Cs. **Farikisha. Mfariki,** n. *mi-* (1) same as *faraka*; (2) *wa-* one who separates himself from his home, &c. **Mfaruku,** n. *wa-* a bereaved person. (Cf. *ondoka, tenga, chamkana, fa.* Ar. فرق to divide, فارق die, abandon.)

Faranga,* n. *ma-*, also Dim. **Kifaranga,** *vi-* young bird, nestling, and esp. chick, chicken. (Cf. *kinda, mtoto.* Port. *frangão.*)

-faransa,* a. French. *Mfaransa, wa-* a Frenchman. *Kifaransa,* the French language, of the French kind. *Ufaransa* or *Ulaya Faransa,* France. (Ar. فرانس.)

Farasi,* n. (1) horse. *Enda kwa farasi,* ride, go on horseback. (Contr. *enda kwa miguu.*) *Panda farasi,* mount a horse. *Mpanda farasi,* a horseman, trooper (in cavalry). *Shuka juu ya farasi,* dismount. *Mpanda farasi wawili, hupasuka msamba,* one who mounts two horses, splits in two. (2) in joinery, crossbar, tie-beam; (3) a trestle, esp. on which wood is placed to be sawn, a bicycle frame or similar contrivance. (Ar. فرس.)

Faridha,* n. See under **Faradhi.**

Fariji,* v. See under **Faraja.**

Fariki,* v. See under **Faraka.**

Farisha,* n., **Farishi,** n. See **Firashi.**

Farisi,* a. expert, capable. **Ufarisi,** n. expertness, capability. (Ar. فراسة.)

Faru, n. sometimes heard for *kifaru.*

Faruma,* n. a block on which to put caps after washing to prevent them from shrinking or losing their shape. (Port. *forma,* a last, block, &c.)

Farumi,* n. ballast in a ship. (? Ar. فرم; cf. افرم to fill.)

Fasaha,* a. also **Fasihi,** correct, pure, elegant, lucid (in taste or style), esp. of speech or writings. **Ufasaha,** n. and **Ufasihi,** elegance, aesthetic taste, purity of style, correct form, esp. in speaking and literature. (Ar. فصاحة.)

Fashini,* n. (1) a block of wood fastened to the stern-post (*bumia*) in a native-built vessel, and carrying the rudder; (2) the part in front of a dhow in which the ribs are attached. (Cf. *omo.* Prob. from Pers. پا opposite to, from the other side, and سينة prow or stem of ship.)

Fasihi,* a. See under **Fasaha.**

Fasiki,* n. an immoral, profligate, dissolute, vicious person. **Ufasiki,** n. vice, viciousness, debauchery, fornication, adultery, &c. (Cf. *ufisadi, upotevu, uasherati, uzinzi.* Ar. فاسق.)

Fasili,* n. sprout, shoot. *Hana asili wala fasili,* he has neither root nor offshoot, i.e. family or connexions, position or prospects. (Ar. فصل.)

Fasili,* v. cut out a garment. (Ar. فصل.)

Fasiri,* v. explain, interpret, translate. Ps. **Fasiriwa.** Prep. **Fasiria.** Cs. **Fasirisha. Tafsiri,** v. explain, interpret, expound, make intelligible, translate. Prep. **Tafsiria. Tafsiri,** n. *ma-* an explanation, translation. **Mfasiri,** n. *wa-* an expounder, interpreter, translater. (Ar. فسر.)

Fataki,* n. gun cap. Also used of crackers, and other small fireworks. (? Ar. فتق cleave, rip, split, see also فشك cartridge.)

Fatiha,* n. prelude, but usu. the first chapter of the Koran, read at weddings, funerals, visiting graves (*zuru*), &c. (Ar. الفاتحة.)

Fatiisha,* v. be inquisitive, search, pry into. (Cf. *dadisi, pekua, doea, peleleza.* Ar. فتش.)

Fauka,* adv. also **Foko,** more, used in the phrase *fauka ya,* more than, but the usu. expression is *zaidi ya.* See *zaidi.* **Fakaika,** adv. also **Fakefu,** adv. much more, much less, not to speak of. (Cf. *sembuse, licha.* Ar. فاق exceed, and فوق above, beyond.)

Faulu,* v. (1) succeed, obtain one's wish; (2) of a vessel, get round (a point), get past, weather. (Cf. *feli.* Ar. فعول effective, efficacious.)

Fauwa,* also **Fahuwa,** sometimes used in the sense of, it does not matter, it is all the same, e.g. *akija asije, fauwa,* whether he comes or not, it is all the same to me. (Cf. *haidhuru, mamoja.* Ar. فهو indeed, but it is so.)

Fawiti,* v. See **Faiti.**

Februari,* n. February. (Eng.)

Fedha,* n. (1) silver; (2) money, coin, cash—in general. *Ana fedha nyingi,* he is very wealthy. *Fedha ilivunja nguu, milima ikalala,* money broke the summit of the hills and they became level, i.e. money is all powerful. *Fedha tayari, fedha taslimu, fedha mkononi,* ready money. (Cf. *sarafu, pesa, nakudi.* Ar. فضّة).

Fedhaluka,* n. *marijani ya fedhaluka,* the true red coral. *Ushanga wa fedhaluka,* a shiny semi-transparent kind of bead. (Cf. *marijani,* coral, and Ar. فيض beauty, &c., and لك kind of red colour.)

Fedheha,* n. disgrace, a disgraceful thing, shame, scandal. **Fedhehi,** v. disgrace, bring shame on, dishonour, put to shame. Ps. **Fedhehewa.** St. **Fedheheka.** Cs. **Fedhehesha.** (Cf. *aibu, haya, soni, tahayarisha, tweza.* Ar. فضح.)

Fefe, n. a perennial grass up to 6 ft. tall usu. found on black cotton soils, sometimes used as a thatch, *Hyparrhenia rufa*.

Felefele,* n. an inferior kind of millet. (? Ar. فلفل pepper, i.e. likening the inferior grain to pepper.)

Feleji,* n. steel of a good quality. *Upanga wa feleji*, a long straight double-edged sword. (Pers. فولاد best steel.)

Feleti,* v. (1) let go, discharge, release, procure release of, esp. of discharging an obligation or debt for some one; (2) run away, abscond. (Cf. *samehe, burai, toroka*. Ar. فلت release, and افلت escape.)

Feli,* v. (1) come across a person doing a shameful action, or in a situation which causes him to feel shame, e.g. discover somebody in the act of adultery, come across a person naked, &c.; (2) do harm to one. **Feli**, n. (1) act, deed, way of acting; (2) misdeed. *Ndiyo feli ya yule mtoto*, that is what the boy did, the way he went on. Often used in the sense of a bad action, *umrudi aache feli yake*, reprove him that he may leave off his (bad) ways. *Feli billahi*, act of God, is often used with much the same meaning as I don't know, God knows, in answer to a question. (Cf. *fira, fila*. Ar. فعل act, deed, misdeed.)

Fenesi,* n. *ma-* the jak-fruit, fruit of the *mfenesi*. *Fenesi la kizungu*, is used of both durian and bread-fruit. See *mfenesi*. (Hind. پهنس.)

Ferdausi,* n. Paradise. (Pers. فردوس.)

Fereji,* n. *ma-* a large ditch, channel. Usu. *mfereji*. (Ar. فرج.)

Feruzi,* n. turquoise, also a proper male name, like *Almasi*. (Ar. فيروز.)

Feta,* v. See **Fetwa**.

Fethaluka,* n. See **Fedhaluka**.

Fetwa,* v. give a legal decision, judge a point of (Muhammadan) law, give judgement. **Fetwa**, n. a legal decision. (Cf. *hukumu, kata*. Ar. فتوى.)

Feuli,* n. the hold of a ship. (? Ar. فلا open space.)

Fi,* prep. on, with, &c., in such phrases as *saba fi saba*, seven by seven, seven times seven; but usu. expressed by *saba mara saba*. (Ar. في.)

Fia, v. See under **Fa**.

Ficha, v. hide (from), conceal (from), disguise, take shelter (from), give shelter (to), cover. With double obj. *amenificha habari*, he has concealed the news from me. *Alimficha kofia*, he hid his cap from him. Ps. **Fichwa**, (1) be hidden from (something); (2) be kept from seeing (knowing, hearing something). St. and Pot. **Fichika**. Prep. **Fichia**. *Alimfichia kofia*, he hid his cap for him (at his request), or for him, i.e. to his loss or sorrow, like the Dir. *ficha*. Cs. **Fichisha**. Rp. **Fichana**, conceal (or hide) from each other. Stc. **Fichama**, be in the state of being hidden. Rp. **Fichamana**, be in the state of being hidden away all together (or by common consent). Rf. *jificha*, e.g. *kujificha mvua*, take shelter from rain. Cv. **Fichua**, (1) uncover, take from concealment; (2) give the present *fichuo*, which see. **Ficho**, n. *ma-* usually in the plur. hiding-place, concealment, disguise. **Fichuo**, n. *ma-* a taking from concealment, but usually in the sense of a gift given by the bridegroom to the bride on seeing her face for the first time after the marriage ceremony, or to a girl on reaching puberty when she comes from being concealed, or a boy when he comes out of the circumcision school. **Kificho**, n. *vi-* act (process, manner, place, &c.) of hiding, place of concealment, a stealthy (underhand) manner. *Kwa kificho*, in a secret way. *Mambo ya kifichoficho*, intriguings, underhand ways. **Mfichaji**, n. *wa-*, **Mfichifichi**, n. *wa-* (1) one who habitually conceals, a very reserved or retiring person; (2) a secretive, sly person.

Fidhuli,* a., and **-fidhuli**, arrogant, insulting, officious, self-asserting. **Fidhulika**, v. be arrogant, bluster, use insulting language, swagger, be insolent. **Mfidhuli**, n. *wa-*, also **Fidhuli** *ma-* and **Fudhali**, n. *ma-* an insolent, rude, overbearing, insulting person. **Ufidhuli**, n. insolence, arrogance, contemptuous temper, outrage, wanton insults. (Cf. *kiburi*. Ar. فضول.)

Fidi,* v. ransom, pay ransom for, deliver by payment. *Mali yake imemfidi katika kifungo*, his wealth got him out of prison. Ps. **Fidiwa.** Prep. **Fidia.** *Amemfidia baba yake kwa shilingi elfu*, he has redeemed his father by paying a thousand shillings. **Fidia**, n. ransom, fine, money paid as composition or reparation. *Huyu si fidia ya gidamu ya kiatu cha baba yangu*, he is not worth my father's shoe-lace. **Kifidio**, n. *vi-* same as *fidia*, n., also **Ufidio. Ufidiwa**, n. salvation, being ransomed, being released from restraint. (Cf. *dia, komboa*. Ar. فدي.)

Fidla,* n. a fiddle, violin. (Eng.)

Fidua, v. also **Fudua**, uncover anything which is covered, turn inside out, &c., but in many places used only of exposing the glans, also of the first washing after circumcision. (Cf. *fudifudi*.)

Fifia, v. be dying away, fade, pine, dribble away, disappear, e.g. of a flower, an ink spot, a scar, colour, &c. Ps. **Fifiwa.** Prep. **Fifilia**, disappear completely, &c., e.g. *rangi yake imefifilia mbali*, its colour has completely faded away. Cs. **Fifiliza**, (1) cause to fade away, wipe out, filch, e.g. of cheating in order to filch away money; (2) fig. pretend not to hear an order or something that you do not wish to hear, pretend to forget something or misunderstand. **Ufifi** and **Ufifilizi**, n. pretence of forgetting or not hearing, or not understanding.

Figa, n. *ma-* esp. in the plur., i.e. three stones or lumps of ant-hill earth used for supporting a cooking-pot over a fire, also called *mafya*. (See *jifya*.)

Figau, n. a cooking arrangement used in dhows, &c.

Figili,* n. a kind of radish, both root and leaves are used as vegetables. The plant is called *mfigili, mi-*. (Ar. فجل.)

Figo, n. kidney, also called *nso, buku*.

Fii,* n. discord, quarrelling, evil intention, trouble. *Usifanye* (or *usitie*) *fii*, do not cause trouble or discord. (Cf. *fitina*. ? Ar. فاعي angry.)

Fiili,* n. an action, same as *feli*, which see.

Fika, v. arrive (at), reach, get to, come (to). *Fika Unguja*, arrive at Zanzibar. *Fika mji* or *mjini*, arrive at town. *Fika kwake*, reach his home. Prep. **Fikia.** *Barua yako imenifikia*, your letter has reached me. Ps. **Fikiwa.** St. Pot. **Fikika**, be accessible, be approachable, be hospitable. D. Prep. **Fikilia.** *Nimefikiliwa na wageni*, I have had an arrival of guests, I am engaged with guests. Cs. of Prep. **Fikiliza** and **Fikilisha**, cause to arrive, bring about, hence carry out (a promise, engagement). *Fikiliza mabaya*, bring evil (on). *Fikiliza ahadi*, perform a promise. Cs. **Fikisha**, (1) cause to reach; (2) enable to reach, e.g. *chakula hiki kitanifikisha kwetu*, this food will take me home. *Nitamfikisha mbele njiani*, I will conduct him some way on the road. Prep. of Cs. **Fikishia**, e.g. *alimfikishia mbele mzigo*, he carried his load ahead for him. Prep. of Cs. of Prep. **Fikilishia**, e.g. *fikilishia matukano*, abuse. Rp. of Cs. **Fikizana**, bring together. Rp.

Fikana, arrive together. Rp. of Prep. **Fikiana**, meet together, arrive at the same place. Rp. of D. Prep. **Fikiliana**, come to the same place, end, &c., e.g. *maneno haya yanafikiliana*, these statements converge on the same point, come to the same thing, coincide. **Kifiko**, n. *vi-* act (time, manner, place, circumstances, &c.) of arriving, point arrived at, stage of a journey, destination. **Mfiko**, n. *mi-* arrival, reach, range. *Mfiko wa risasi*, range of a bullet (gunshot, rifle). (Cf. *ja, pata, wasili.*)

Fikicha, v. crumble in the fingers, rub to pieces, e.g. of lumps of flour, clods of earth, and husking grain by rubbing. Also used of rubbing the eyes. *Usijifikiche macho*, do not rub your eyes. Ps. **Fikichwa**. St. **Fikichika**, be capable of rubbing to pieces, be friable. Prep. **Fikichia**.

Fikinya, v. crumble. (Cf. *fikicha.*)

Fikira,* n. sometimes **Fikara**, thought, thoughtfulness, meditation, consideration, reflection. *Ana fikira zake*, he is thoughtful. *Yuko katika fikira zake*, he is buried in thought, in a brown study. **Fikiri**, v. think (about), ponder (over), meditate (upon), consider, reflect (about). Ps. **Fikiriwa**. St. and Pot. **Fikirika**. Prep. **Fikiria**. Cs. **Fikirisha**, cause to think, make thoughtful, sober. **Tafakari**, v. same as *fikiri*. (Cf. *waza, ona*. Ar. فكر.)

Fila,* n. See **Lila**.

Filifili,* n. a carpenter's square.

Filimbi, n. a kind of flute, a whistle, fife. (Cf. *kipenga, mluzi.*)

Filisi,* v. (1) sell up a person's goods for debt, declare bankrupt, distrain on goods of, make bankrupt, ruin; (2) make the highest bid at an auction sale; (3) win all a person's money at cards, &c. Ps. **Filisiwa**. St. **Filisika**—of persons or goods. Prep. **Filisia**. Cs. **Filisisha**. **Mfilisi**, n. *wa-* (1) one who forces another into ruin, bankruptcy, &c., a distrainer, defrauder, embezzler; (2) one who makes the highest bid at an auction sale. **Mfilisika**, n. *wa-* a bankrupt, a ruined person. **Ufilisi**, n. bankruptcy, selling up a person's goods for debt. (Cf. *futa, komba*. Ar. فلس.)

Fimbi, n. the crowned hornbill, *Lophoceros melanoleucos*. Also called *kwembe*.

Fimbo, n. a stick, esp. a light stick carried in the hand, a walking-stick, a switch. *Piga fimbo*, beat with a stick.

Finga, v. protect by charm, as a field against thieves, or house against burglars. Cs. **Fingiza**, prevent, forbid. **Fingo**, n. *ma-* a charm to prevent thieves from entering a house, &c. (Cf. *kaga, hirizi.*)

Finginyika, v. (1) wriggle, writhe, like a snake after it has been killed, also (2) move the buttocks in circular motion when walking or dancing. (Also heard as *vinginyika.*)

Fingirika, v. (also occurs as *bingirika* and *vingirika*) go by rolling (by turning round or over and over), roll round, be rolled along, as a log—not as a stationary revolving wheel. Cs. **Fingirisha**, push along, roll over and over, roll (something) along.

Fingiza, v. **Fingo**, n. *ma-*. See under **Finga**.

Finika, v. *Kimvita* for *funika*, which see.

Finya, v. (1) pinch, pinch up, nip, press with the fingers or nails; (2) make (or be) narrow (pinched, contracted), and hence (3) scowl. *Finya jicho*, half-close the eye. *Finya uso*, scowl. *Kiatu kinanifinya*, the boot pinches me. Rd. **Finyafinya**, used of pinching up, or crumbling small, as food for children. Dur. **Finyaa**, shrink, shrivel, become thin and emaciated, as of an old person's skin and body (cf. *sinyaa*). Rp. **Finyana**, (1) be pinched together, be wrinkled, be creased, be folded; (2) be narrowed, contracted, cramped, confined. *Uso wake umefinyana*, his face is frowning, wrinkled. *Mlango umefinyana*, the door is narrow. *Adui sharti afinyane*, the enemy must certainly shrivel up. **Finyo**, n. *ma-* crease, fold, narrow place, narrowness. *Mafinyo ya uso*, wrinkles on the face, whether as a frown or a grimace. *Njia ya finyo*, a narrow road. **Mfinyo**, n. *mi-* a nip or pinch, as with the fingers. (Cf. *minya, kama, kunja, -embamba, nywea.*)

Finyanga, v. knead clay, with hands or feet as potters do, and hence 'do potter's work, make vessels of clay'. **Mfinyanzi**, n. *wa-* a worker in clay, a potter. *Mfinyanzi hulia gae*, a potter eats off a potsherd, i.e. cannot afford to use his own wares. (Cf. the cobbler's wife goes barefoot.) **Ufinyanzi**, n. art (trade, work, wages, &c.) of a potter. (Prob. from same root as prec.)

Finyo, n. *ma-*. See **Finya.**

Fira, n. the spitting cobra, a large grey snake.

Fira,* v. commit sodomy, either with male or female. Ps. **Firwa.** Rp. **Firana. Mfiraji**, n. *wa-* one addicted to sodomy. (Cf. *lawiti*. Ar. فعل see form, فاعل a paederast.)

Firaka,* n. penis. (Ar. فرقم.)

Firari,* n. (1) penis; (2) passive agent in sodomy. (Cf. *dhakari, mboo, uume*. ? From same root as *fira*, v.)

Firashi,* n. a bed coverlet, quilt. (Cf. *furushi*. Ar. فراش.)

Firidi,* v. smell nice, pleasant. (Cf. *nukia*. Ar. فريد unique.)

Firigisi,* n. gizzard. (Prob. a comp. Ar. فرا foremost, middle, &c., and cf. غص be full to choking, or كيس bag, pouch, &c.)

Fisadi,* n. *ma-*, also **Mfisadi**, n. *wa-* a corrupter, esp. a corrupter of women, seducer, immoral person. **Fisidi**, v. destroy, abuse, use in a wrong way, corrupt, seduce, esp. of corrupting women. **Ufisadi**, n. vice, viciousness, corruption. Also in sense of slander, stir up strife, &c. (Cf. *fitina*.) *Aliwafanyia ufisadi hata akawagombanisha*, he occasioned a quarrel between them by his slander. (Cf. *mpotovu, mlongozi, asherati, fasiki*. Ar. فسد.)

Fisha, v. Cs. of *fa*.

Fisi, n. the common kind of hyena. (Cf. *kingugwa, simba marara*.)

Fisidi,* v. See under **Fisadi.**

Fitina,* n. (1) discord, variance, antagonism, quarrelling, misunderstanding, mischief. *Fanya* (*tia*) *fitina*, cause discord, slander, be cause of discord. (2) tumult, insurrection; (3) a source of discord, an agitator, a firebrand, but used of a person, it is generally **Mfitini**, *wa-*. **Fitini**, v. cause discord among, make mischief, &c. Ps. **Fitiniwa.** St. **Fitinika.** Prep. **Fitinia.** Cs. **Fitinisha.** Rp. **Fitiniana. Ufitina**, n. same as *fitina*. (Cf. *ugomvi, uasi*. Ar. فتنة.)

Fitiri,* n. (1) alms given at the end of Ramadhan, the Muhammadan month of fasting; (2) an offering of grain. (Ar. فطر.)

Fito, n. plur. of *ufito*, which see.

-fiwa, a. Ps. form of *fa*, which see.

Fiwi, n. the lima bean, fruit of the *mfiwi, mi-*, which see.

Flotile,* n. See **Furutile.**

Fofofo, adv. completely, absolutely, but only used with *kufa*, to die, and *kulala*, to lie down or sleep. *Amekufa* (*amelala*) *fofofo*, he is absolutely dead (fast asleep).

Foka, v. (1) spurt out, boil over, come out with a rush, as water from a spring, from a hole in a boat, or of a vessel boiling over. *Chungu kinafoka*, the cooking-pot is boiling over. Also (2) fig. blurt out a rush of words as in anger, excitement, &c. Prep. **Fokea**, spurt out of (on to, &c.),

i.e. as a river overflowing and covering the neighbouring fields, &c. (Cf. *bubujika, chemka, fura.*)

Foko,* a. See **Fauka.**

Fola,* n. a gift given by a person when he holds a baby for the first time. (Ar. فول favourable omen.)

Fondogoa, n. the smell of mouldy or fermenting flour.

Fora, v. beat, get the better of, succeed, used in games of cards, &c., and work. **Fora, n.** *kutia fora,* to win in a game, or succeed in an undertaking, i.e. a particular task of work. (Cf. *shinda, pita, fuzu,* and *faulu.* (Ar. فرع surpass.)

Fori, adv. See under **Fara.**

Forodha,* n. custom house. The locative form *forodhani* is commonly used at the coast for the place where goods are unladen from ships, &c., and for the Customs House. (Ar. فرضة.)

Foromali,* n. yard (of a ship), i.e. the spar that carries the sail. It is controlled by braces fore, *baraji,* and aft, *hamrawi,* and hoisted by the *henza,* which see. (Prob. a comp. Ar. فرا upper, &c., and مدّ stretch, extent, or ملا what fills a space, smooth stuff, tent, &c.)

Foronya,* n. a pillow-case. (Port. *fronha.*)

Forosadi,* n. also **Forsadi,** mulberry, fruit of the *mforosadi, mi-,* which see. (Ar. فرصاد.)

Forota,* v. snore in one's sleep. (Cf. *koroma.* Prob. a corruption of *korota,* which see.)

Forsadi,* n. See **Forosadi.**

Frasila,* n. a measure of weight, about 35 lb. (? Ar. فار and سلّه, i.e. a full basket, or perh. corruption of Eng. parcel, the commercial term.)

Fua, n. (A) (1) a kind of small root from which a red dye is made for dyeing the leaf strips which are made into mats, &c.; (2) see under **Fua, v.**

Fua, n. *ma-* (B) (1) see under **Fua, v.;** (2) in the plur. *mafua,* chest, chest complaint (see **Kifua** and **Kamasi**).

Fua, v. beat, strike, hammer, but usually limited to certain operations, viz. (1) of smith's work, work at (a metal), make (of metal). *Fua chuma (shaba, fedha),* work in iron (brass, silver), follow the trade of blacksmith (silversmith, &c.). *Fua kisu (jembe, shoka),* make a knife-blade (hoe, axe-head). (2) of laundry work, wash clothes in the native way, dashing them on a stone or board; (3) of husking coco-nuts by dashing them on a pointed stake. Ps. **Fuliwa.** St. and Pot. **Fulika.** *Madini hii haifuliki,* this metal is unworkable. Prep. **Fulia,** e.g. work metal for (with, at, &c.), wash for. Cs. **Fulisha,** and **Fuliza,** e.g. (1) set to work as smith or washerman, employ, have work done by them. Also (2) of the artisan procuring work. *Fulisha nguo,* get clothes for washing, i.e. take in washing. Also Inten. keep on at, hammer at, cause to hammer or keep on, continue doing—in a general sense, quicken, hasten. *Fuliza mwendo,* go speedily. Cs. of D. Prep. **Fuliliza,** also **Fululiza,** and Prep. **Fulilizia,** keep on doing without pause. Ps. form (2) **Fuawa,** be beaten, hammered, e.g. of a vessel aground, and exposed to the full force of the waves. **Fua,** n. (— or *ma-* of size), a round wooden tray with raised rim used for washing clothes on, a shallow wooden bowl for hand washing, &c. **Fuawe,** n. anvil, i.e. something to be hammered upon. **Fuo,** n. place where clothes are washed. **Kifuo,** n. *vi-* pointed stake fixed in the ground used for ripping the husks off coco-nuts. **Mfua,** n. *wa-* one who beats, esp. of one who works in metal with hammer, &c., a smith, governing a noun following, e.g. *mfua chuma (dhahabu, fedha,* &c.), a blacksmith (goldsmith, silversmith, &c.). *Mfua nguo,* one who washes clothes, a washerman, but usually called *dobi*. **Mfua,** n. *mi-*, **Mfuo,** n. *mi-* (1) a beating, hammering, &c. *Mfuo wa mawimbi,* the beating of the waves on the shore. (2) the beach, i.e. where the waves beat; (3) (also **Mvua** and **Mvuo**) bellows, such as are used by a worker in metal, blacksmith, &c. *Fukuta* (or *vukuta*) *mifua* (*mifuo*), work bellows. **Mfulizo,** n. *mi-* causing to go on, giving an energetic impetus, a pull, tug, haul, thrust, shove, &c., a going on and on, a regular progression, series, succession. *Siku tano mfulizo,* five consecutive days. *Mfulizo wa masomo,* a course of lessons. **Mfululizo,** n. *mi-* like *mfulizo,* but Inten. *Mfululizo wa milima,* a range of mountains. **Ufuaji,** n. the act (manner, occupation, charge) of beating, washing clothes, &c. (Cf. *piga, babata.*)

Fuadi,* n. heart. (Cf. *moyo.* Ar. فؤاد.)

Fuama, v. also **Fulama** and **Furama,** lie or bend down with the head on the arms, stomach downwards, but not touching the ground, and the buttocks raised. Sometimes used in an obscene sense. Cs. **Fuamiza,** or **Fuamisha,** turn over into the position indicated in *fuama.* (Cf. *bong'oa.*)

Fuasa, v. See under **Fuata.**

Fuata, v. (1) follow, come next to, succeed, come behind, pursue; (2) imitate, copy, accompany (in music), do like, be like; (3) obey, keep to, abide by, be follower (adherent) of. *Fuata maji yaendako,* swim with the stream. *Bendera yafuata upepo,* the flag follows the wind. *Nitafuata wimbo kwa zomari,* I will follow the tune with the flageolet. Often *fuata nyuma,* follow behind. *Fuata sheria,* keep the law. *Fuata Muhammadi,* be a Muhammadan. Ps. **Fuatwa.** Prep. **Fuatia,** follow after, more with the idea of catching up with. Cs. **Fuatisha,** often Inten. copy carefully, make a copy of. Another Cs. form, **Fuasa** (cf. *pasa* from *pata, nasa* from *nata,* &c.), (1) copy, imitate, follow a pattern; (2) cause to follow, i.e. tow. Rp. **Fuatana,** (1) accompany, follow in a crowd; (2) ensue, be the result of, e.g. *ugonjwa hufuatana na upotevu wa maisha,* sickness follows together with (or after, or as the result of) a life of profligacy. **Fuatano,** n. *ma-* a following, succession, esp. in plur., e.g. *mafuatano ya sauti,* a tune, melody. **Kifuasi,** n. *vi-* something following, an even number. (Cf. *shufwa.*) **Mfuasi,** n. *wa-* (1) a follower, adherent, retainer, disciple; (2) a pursuer, tracker. **Ufuasi,** n. (*fuasi* and *ma-*) (1) following, accompanying, e.g. of musical accompaniment; (2) discipleship, &c., act or condition of following, imitation. (Cf. *andama.*)

Fuawa, v., **Fuawe,** n. See under **Fua,** v.

Fudhali,* n. *ma-*. See under **Fidhuli.**

Fudifudi, adv. also **Fulifuli,** on the face, face downwards. *Lala fudifudi,* or *kifudifudi,* lie on the face. *Walipouona utukufu wake walianguka fudifudi,* when they saw his glory, they fell on their faces. **Fudikiza,** v. turn upside down (inside out, face downwards), turn over, e.g. of cards in playing. *Ngalawa ilifudikizwa na mawimbi lakini haikuzama kwa sababu ya mirengu yake,* the canoe was turned over by the waves, but it did not sink because of its outriggers. **Kifudifudi,** adv. like *fudifudi,* also **Kifulifuli.** (Cf. *fidua, fudua, pindua.*)

Fudua, v. See **Fidua.**

Fufua, v. cause to revive, bring to life again, resuscitate, restore, revive. *Fufua maiti,* bring a dead man to life. *Fufua mgonjwa,* give strength to an invalid. *Fufua deni,* bring up a forgotten debt. *Fufua desturi* (*sheria, chama*), revive a custom (law, association or guild). St. **Fufuka.** Prep. **Fufulia.** Cs. **Fufusha.** **Mfufuaji,** n. *wa-*, **Mfufuzi,** n. *wa-*, one who raises from the dead, restorer of life, strength, &c. **Ufufuo,** n. resurrection, raising from death to life, restoring, renewing, restarting. **Ufufuko,** n. a being raised from death to life, &c. (Cf. *amka, baatha, kiyama.*)

Fufutende, a. lukewarm, tepid. (Cf. *vuguvugu.*)

Fuga, v. (1) keep in confinement, rear, breed (of tame animals, stock, poultry, &c.); (2) tame, domesticate, break in (of wild animals). *Fuga ng'ombe* (*mbuzi, kuku, njiwa, watumwa*), keep (rear, breed) cattle (goats, fowls, pigeons, slaves). Ps. **Fugwa.** St. and Pot. **Fugika,** be tamed or tameable, e.g. *farasi huyu hafugiki,* this horse cannot be tamed or broken in. Prep. **Fugia.** Cs. **Fugisha,** e.g. of professional horse-breaking. **Fugo,** n. *ma-* breeding, rearing, domestication, &c., of animals (also formerly used of slaves). **Mfuga,** n. *wa-*, **Mfugaji,** n. *wa-* a trainer, breeder of animals, &c. **Mfugo,** n. *mi-* (1) taming, breeding, rearing of birds or animals; (2) a tame domesticated animal or bird, hence, *mifugo,* flocks and herds. *Nina mifugo mingi,* I have many kinds of animals. (3) in some places, one of a litter given as payment to the person who has attended to the breeding.

Fuja, v. (1) bungle, stir up, destroy (as of work, &c.), make a mess of, disarrange; (2) use in a wrong way, as of wasting money, food, &c. *Fuja mali* (*chakula, nguo,* &c.), squander money (food, clothing, &c.). Ps. **Fujwa.** Prep. **Fujia.** St. **Fujika.** **Fujo,** n. *ma-* disorder, mess, bungle, disturbance, uproar, tumult. *Nyumba ya fujo,* a disorderly, much frequented house. *Kazi ya fujo,* work badly finished. *Fujo la mali* (*chakula,* &c.), wasting of property (food, &c.). **Fujofujo,** n. an utter mess. **Mfujaji,** n. *wa-* a waster, disorderly person, bungler, &c.

Fuka, n. (1) a thin kind of porridge (of rice-flour, with sugar, honey, spice, &c.) served to guests at an entertainment or festival; (2) a thin kind of gruel flavoured with much pepper and cardamom, given to women after giving birth, said to clean the stomach.

Fuka, v. (frequently heard as *vuka*) give out smoke or fumes, smoke, turn to smoke or vapour—with or without *moshi,* evaporate, be vaporized. *Nyumba yao haifuki moshi,* no smoke rises from their house. Prep. **Fukia.** Cs. **Fukiza,** and sometimes **Fukisha,** cause to give out smoke, turn to vapour, make fumes with smoke (i.e. apply smoke to), fumigate, cense, burn incense, e.g. *fukiza maiti* (*nyumba*), fumigate a corpse (a house) with incense. *Fukiza udi,* burn aloe wood—for fumigation. Also used of giving a vapour bath for illnesses, &c. **Fukuta** (from Cv. form *fukua,* not used in this sense) (also sometimes *vukuta*), throb as of a sore, or smart, as when medicine is applied, &c. **Fukizo,** n. *ma-* (1) vapour, fumes, steam, smoke; (2) anything burnt or used for fumigation or vapour baths, incense, &c. **Fukuto,** n. *ma-* (1) sweat, a drop of sweat, condensed vapour, heat of the body; (2) throbbing, smarting. **Fusho,** n. something used for fumigation, something to be burnt, as a charm, or sanitary medicine. **Kifukizo,** n. *vi-* act of burning incense, fumigation, substance used in fumigation or vapour baths. **Kifuku,** n. the hot rainy season, when the air is very humid and causes people to perspire. **Mfukuto,** n. *mi-* like *fukuta.* **Ufukizo,** n. *ma-* producing or causing smoke, burning of aromatics, fumigants, &c., fumigation. Plur. is used of the things so used. **Ufukuto,** n. *ma-* exhalation (produced by heat), vapour, steam, smell of perspiration, fug.

Fukara, n., **Fukarika,*** v. See under **Fakiri.**

Fukia, v. (from a Dir. form *fuka*, prob. disused because of *fuka*, v. give out smoke, &c.), fill in (a hole, grave, &c.), dig in, cover in. *Fukia kaburi*, fill up a grave. Ps. **Fukiwa.** St. **Fukika.** Prep. **Fukilia.** St. and Pot. **Fukilika**, be filled in, be capable of being filled in, e.g. *tundu linafukilika kwa udongo*, the hole can be filled in with earth. Cs. **Fukiza.** Rp. **Fukiana.** Cv. **Fukua**, dig out, dig up, esp. of something which has been dug in, make a hole. *Fisi alifukua maiti*, a hyena dug up a corpse. *Fukua muhogo* (*njugu*, *mizizi*), dig up cassava (ground-nuts, roots). Ps. **Fukuliwa.** St. **Fukuka**, be dug out, be hollowed, be concave. Prep. **Fukulia.** Cs. **Fukulisha.** Rp. **Fukuana.** **Fukuo**, n. *ma-* the action of digging out, excavation. **Fuko**, n. *ma-* (1) a hole dug out, excavation; (2) a mole. **Mfukuaji**, n. *wa-*, **Mfukuzi**, n. *wa-* digger, miner, pitman. (Cf. *chimba*.)

Fukiza, v., **Fukizo**, n. *ma-*. See under **Fuka.**

Fuko, n. *ma-* (1) see under **Fukia**, v.; (2) amplic. of *mfuko*.

Fukombe, n. See **Furukombe.**

Fukua, v., **Fukuo**, n. *ma-*. See under **Fukia.**

Fukuta, v., **Fukuto**, n. *ma-*. See under **Fuka.**

Fukuza, v. (1) force out, drive out, esp. in hunting or war, and hence both (2) drive off, chase away, banish, and (3) go in pursuit of, hunt, try to catch. *Mbwa wakawafukuza nguruwe*, the hounds chased the pigs. Prep. **Fukuzia**, usually with the idea of chasing with the intention of catching, or with Inten. meaning. *Wamefukuzia mbali adui*, they have chased the enemy quite away. *Tuliwafukuzia wezi*, we ran after the thieves (in order to catch them). Ps. **Fukuzwa.** Cs. **Fukuzisha.** Rp. **Fukuzana**, of children chasing one another, but also used of one or more persons chasing another or more, e.g. *askari na wezi walifukuzana*, lit. the soldiers and the thieves ran after each other, but meaning that the soldiers ran after the thieves. **Fukuzano**, n. *ma-* usually in the plur. a general driving out, i.e. persecution, &c. **Mfukuzi**, n. *wa-* one who drives away, a persecutor. (Cf. *kimbiza*, *winda*, *fuata*. Prob. Cs. of *fukua*, see under **Fukia**, with extended meaning.)

Fulama, v. See **Fuama.**

Fulana,* n. an undervest, sweater. (Eng. flannel?)

Fulani,* n. such a one, a certain one, so-and-so, such and such (things), alluding indefinitely to persons or things for reference only. *Fulani amesema*, somebody has said. *Nataka bidhaa fulani*, I want such and such goods. (Ar. فلان a certain person. فلاني such and such.)

Fulifuli, adv. See **Fudifudi**, and under **Fara.**

Fuliza, v., **Fululiza**, v. See under **Fua.**

Fulusi,* n. (1) a kind of fish like *nguru*; (2) money, cash, a general term. (Ar. فلوس small coin.)

Fuma, v. (A) weave, knit, crochet, and also of connecting together, forming a fabric, by sewing, &c. Ps. **Fumwa.** St. **Fumika.** Prep. **Fumia.** Cs. **Fumisha.** Rp. **Fumana.** Cv. **Fumua**, undo (what is woven, matted, sewn, connected together), and so (1) unravel, unpick, take to pieces, unstitch, &c.; (2) reveal, disclose, make clear, explain. *Fumua uzi*, unstitch. *Fumua nywele*, let down the hair. *Fumua nguo*, rip (pull in pieces) calico, &c. *Fumua moto*, pull a fire to pieces, take sticks out of a fire. *Fumua makuti*, take out (decayed) thatch. *Fumua mali*, squander money, be prodigal. Also in Intrans. sense, *mtama unafumua*, the millet is coming into ear. *Maua yanafumua*, the flowers are coming out. Ps. **Fumuliwa.** Prep. **Fumulia.** St. **Fumuka.** *Nguo imefumuka*, the dress has become unsewn, undone. *Mashua imefumuka*, the boat has opened at the seams. Rp. **Fumukana**, e.g. of people separating after a meeting, 'disperse'. **Fumukano**, n. *ma-* separation, breaking up, dispersal, e.g. of people after a meeting. **Mfuma**, n. *wa-*, **Mfumaji**, n. *wa-*, **Mfumi**, n. *wa-* one who weaves, a weaver. *Mfuma nguo*, a weaver of cloth. *Kitanda cha mfumi*, a weaver's loom. *Mfumaji wa hariri*, a silk weaver. **Mfumo**, n. *mi-* (1) art (act, process, &c.) of weaving; (2) texture, fabric. **Mfumua**, n. *wa-*, **Mfumuaji**, n. *wa-* an undoer, a pryer, e.g. *mfumua maneno nje*, of a spy or tale-bearer. (Cf. *shona, fumba.*)

Fuma, v. (B) strike or pierce with a sharp instrument, i.e. a spear, &c. **Fume**, n. *ma-* wounded (by a spear). **Fumo**, n. a spear. (Cf. *choma, tupa.*)

Fumania, v. come on suddenly, take in the act, intrude in the house of, surprise, frequently in the sense of discovering or coming on somebody in the act of doing wrong, i.e. in the act of adultery, &c. Ps. **Fumaniwa.** St. **Fumanika.** Cs. **Fumaniza.** **Fumanizi**, n. (1) the act of discovering somebody doing a wrongful or shameful act; (2) food being eaten when a person calls unexpectedly. (Cf. *fuma*, v. (A), *gundua.*)

Fumatiti, n. a kind of nightjar. (Cf. *babewana, bundi.*)

Fumba, v. (1) shut, close, by bringing things, or parts, together. *Fumba macho*, close the eyes. *Fumba kinywa*, shut the mouth. *Fumba mkono*, clasp the hand. *Fumba miguu*, close the legs together. (2) mystify, make a mystery about, disguise, use in an obscure way. *Fumba maneno*, use unintelligible language. *Fumbo humfumba mjinga*, a parable mystifies a simpleton. Rf. *jifumba*, shut oneself up (in meditation, study, &c.). Ps. **Fumbwa.** St. **Fumbika**, be closed up, e.g. *maua yanafumbika*, the flowers are closing. Prep. **Fumbia**, shut up in (for, by, &c.), talk darkly about, &c. Cs. **Fumbisha.** Rp. **Fumbana**, close together, e.g. *hata macho yake yakafumbana*, till his eyes closed. Stc. **Fumbama**, be in state of being mystified, and so lose one's senses, be dazed, light headed, e.g. *huyu amefumbama akili yake*, this man is not in his right mind. Ten. **Fumbata**, cause to come together or in contact, hence, enclose (with hands, arms, or legs), grasp, clutch, encompass. *Siwezi kuufumbata mti huu kwa mikono yangu*, I cannot get my arms round this tree. *Amefumbata fedha mkononi*, he has grasped the money in his hand. Ps. **Fumbatwa.** St. and Pot. **Fumbatika**, be grasped, also be graspable, e.g. *konzi ya maji haifumbatiki*, water cannot be grasped in the fist. Prep. **Fumbatia.** Cs. **Fumbatisha.** Cv. **Fumbua**, unclose, open, lay open, reveal, disclose by separating things or parts which were close together, e.g. *fumbua mkono*, open the closed hand, and so of eyes, mouth, legs, &c. *Fumbua maana*, unfold the meaning. *Fumbua majani*, make openings in high grass, for air or planting. Ps. **Fumbuliwa.** St. **Fumbuka.** Prep. **Fumbulia.** Cs. **Fumbulisha.** Rp. **Fumbuana.** **Fumba**, n. *ma-* (1) a matting bag used as a sleeping-bag or for burying corpses, a mat doubled lengthwise and the ends sewn up; (2) lump, clod, *Fumba la unga*, a lump in flour. *Fumba la mtama*, caked millet. (3) the pad under the foot of an animal in which the claws are hidden, e.g. of a cat, dog, lion, leopard, &c. **Fumbo**, n. *ma-* anything puzzling, hidden, mysterious, and so 'puzzle, problem, dark saying, hint, proverb, parable, riddle'. *Sema kwa mafumbo*, speak in an unintelligible, difficult way. *Maneno ya fumbo* and *fumbo la* *maneno*, mysterious language. **Kifumba**, n. *vi-* dim. of *fumba*. **Kifumbu**, n. *vi-* a small round basket or bag used for squeezing coco-nut in, and straining out the juice (*tui*), a strainer. **Mfumba**, n. *wa-*, **Mfumbaji**, n. *wa-* a person who mystifies, &c. **Mfumbua**, n. *wa-*, **Mfumbuaji**, n. *wa-* a person who explains, clears up mysteries, &c.

Fumbi, n. *ma-* a stream. (Cf. *kijito*.)

Fumbo, n. *ma-*, **Fumbua**, v. See under **Fumba**.

Fume, n. *ma-*. See under **Fuma**, v. (B).

Fumo, n. (1) see under **Fuma**, v. (B); (2) *ma-* also **Mfumo**, n. *wa-* an old title for a chief.

Fumua, v., **Fumukano**, n. *ma-*. See under **Fuma**, v. (A).

Funda, n. *ma-*. See under **Funda**, v. (B).

Funda, v. (A) pound, bruise, triturate, pulverize, e.g. rice, pepper, ginger, &c., in a mortar (*kinu*), also 'pound up together, mix with other ingredients', e.g. *funda unga*, mix the meal. Ps. **Fundwa**. St. **Fundika**, &c. **Funde**, n. *ma-* that which has been pounded, &c. *Ugali wa funde*, porridge made of green maize.

Funda, v. (B) and **Fundira**. *Funda maji*, fill the mouth with water, i.e. till the cheeks are distended. **Funda**, n. *ma-* a large mouthful of liquid or solid, distending the cheeks. *Funda la shavu*, a large mouthful. *Piga mafunda*, take large mouthfuls, gulps, draughts, either to be swallowed, or for rinsing the mouth out after a meal and to be ejected. (Cf. *sukutua*.)

Funda, v. (C) instruct, but esp. of household and tribal instruction as distinct from instruction given in school. Cs. **Fundisha**, and **Funza**, Inten. teach, instruct, educate—the work of a *fundi*. Ps. **Fundishwa**, **Funzwa**. Prep. **Fundishia**, e.g. *vitu vya kufundishia*, aid to teaching, school accessories. Rp. **Fundishana**. Rf. *jifundisha*, learn, but usu. *jifunza*. *Jifunza kwa moyo*, learn by heart. **Fundi**, n. *ma-* a person skilled in any art, craft, or profession, and so able to instruct others in it, a skilled workman, one who has learnt his trade, a trained artisan or craftsman, e.g. mason, carpenter, tailor, smith, washerman, &c.—*mwalimu* being commonly used of the higher professions, esp. of teaching. **Fundisho**, n. *ma-*, **Funzo**, n. *ma-*, teaching, what is taught, instruction, doctrine. **Mfundishi**, n. *wa-*, **Mfunza**, *wa-*, **Mfunzaji**, *wa-*, **Mfunzi**, *wa-*, a teacher. **Mkufunzi**, n. *wa-*, a more usual form of **Mkurufunzi**, n. *wa-* an apprentice who has finished his time, a skilled apprentice. **Mwanafunzi**, n. *wa-* a pupil, one who is being taught. **Uanafunzi**, n. apprenticeship, period, &c., of being under instruction.

Funda, v. (D) (Dir. form not now in use.) St. **Fundika**, make a knot, tie up, usu. *piga fundo*. Cv. **Fundua**, (1) undo a knot, untie, unfasten, and (2) fig. explain a difficulty, get over a crisis. *Fundua chupa*, uncork a bottle, but this is generally *zibua*, also used of plants budding. Ps. **Funduliwa**. Cs. **Fundusha**, and **Funduza**. **Kifundo**, n. *vi-* (1) a knot. *Piga kifundo cha nguo*, tie a knot in one's clothes, tie up in one's clothes. (2) protuberance, joint—as resembling a knot. *Kifundo cha mguu*, the ankle. *Kifundo cha mkono*, the wrist. *Mwili wa kifundokifundo*, i.e. with small knot-like swellings on the body. **Fundo**, n. *ma-* (1) knot, anything resembling a knot; (2) fig. a difficulty, grudge, esp. (3) ill feeling, resentment. *Fundo la mti* (*muwa*), a knot in wood or tree (sugar-cane). *Fundo la uzi*, knot in thread. *Fundo la nguo*, clothes tied in a knot. *Fundo la utepe*, a rosette. *Fundo la chombo*, cross-beam in a dhow (cf. *mwashiri*). *Fundo la ushanga* consists of ten strings (*kete*) of beads. *Fundo la moyo*, ill feeling, resentment, grudge.

Also (4) a purse, usually consisting of a knotted piece of the waist cloth. *Siku ya mashaka, fundo,* for the day of adversity, a purse. *Fundo la mguu,* the ankle, also *kifundo. Piga fundo,* tie a knot. *Maji yalinipiga fundo,* the water choked me. **Mfundo,** n. *mi-* like *fundo.*

Funde, n. *ma-*. See under **Funda,** v. (A).

Fundi, n. *ma-*. See under **Funda,** v. (C).

Fundika, v. (1) see under **Funda,** v. (A) and (D); (2) prepare a woman's hair ready for plaiting. (Cf. *suka.*)

Fundira, v. See under **Funda,** v. (B).

Fundisha, v., **Fundisho,** n. *ma-*. See under **Funda,** v. (C).

Fundo, n. (1) see under **Funda,** v. (A); (2) see under **Funda,** v. (D); (3) a crossbeam which fixes the mast to the false keel in a sailing vessel.

Fundua, v. See under **Funda,** v. (D).

Funga, v. (1) fasten, make fast, tie, bind, secure. *Funga mzigo,* tie up a load, finish packing. *Funga mlango,* shut, close (fasten) the door (cf. *shindika* or *vugaza mlango*). *Funga barua,* seal up a letter. *Funga choo,* constipate, be constipated. *Funga kamba* (or *na kamba*), fasten with a cord. *Funga hesabu,* liquidate, i.e. a company, &c. (2) shut in, enclose, imprison, put in fetters. *Funga gerezani* (*minyororoni, kifungoni*) put in prison (in chains under arrest). (3) overcome (in a game or contest), win, checkmate, put in difficulties, convict. *Tuliwafunga mabao sita,* we won six games against them. *Neno lake lilimfunga mwenyewe,* his own statement convicted him. (4) decide upon, embark on, begin, take decisive steps towards. *Funga biashara,* conclude a bargain. *Funga vita,* begin operations in war. *Funga shauri,* resolve on a plan. *Funga safari,* set out on a journey. (5) *Funga* is also used as Intrans. in various senses, e.g. fast. *Leo sisi tunafunga,* to-day we are fasting. *Ramadhani ni mwezi wa kufunga,* Ramadhan is the month of fasting. *Mvua inafunga,* it is a settled rain. Rf. *jifunga,* as above, esp. (1) devote oneself, engage onself, give special attention. *Jifunga kusoma,* apply oneself to study (*kwa kazi,* to work, *na adui,* with an opponent, in strife). (2) get oneself into a fix, contradict oneself, hamper oneself. *Amejifunga kwa ulimi wake,* he is convicted by his own tongue. (3) *jifunga,* avoid child-bearing. Ps. **Fungwa.** St. and Pot. **Fungika,** (1) be closed; (2) be closeable, e.g. *mlango haufungiki,* the door cannot be closed. Prep. **Fungia,** fasten with (to, by, &c.), e.g. *alimfungia na farasi kwa kamba,* he fastened the horse to him by a cord. *Nimefungiwa nyumbani,* I am locked out of the house. *Fungiwa deni,* be imprisoned for debt. Cs. **Fungisha,** cause to fasten, cause to be fastened, and Inten. bind tight, confine close. *Nitamfungisha,* I will have him put in prison. *Mvua inakufungisha ndani,* the rain keeps you indoors. *Fungisha (mji) njia,* blockade a town (road). Also **Fungasa,** and **Fungasha,** cause to be fastened, but usually of one boat towing another. Rp. **Fungana,** (1) fasten together, or with *na,* fasten to; (2) be fastened together, e.g. of clouds, forest, 'be dense, be thick'. Cs. of Rp. **Funganya,** of a work of common interest and co-operation. *Funganya mizigo,* join in a general packing of loads. Cs. (2) of Rp. **Funganisha,** e.g. *jahazi na jiwe,* make fast a vessel to a rock. Stc. **Fungama,** be in a fixed, tight, dense, &c., condition. Rp. **Fungamana,** e.g. of interlacing branches, &c. *Mwitu umefungamana,* the forest is thick and impenetrable. *Hapa pamefungamana miiba,* here is a dense mass of thorns. Cv. **Fungua,** (1) unfasten, undo, untie, unbind, let loose, release, set free, open, &c. *Fungua* *mlango*, unfasten a door (cf. *shindua*). *Fungua mkono*, open the hand (like *fumbua*), give a gift. Rf. *jifungua*, (1) give birth to a child, be confined; (2) cease fasting. *Nipe kidogo nifungue kinywa*, give me a morsel to break my fast. St. and Pot. **Funguka.** Prep. **Fungulia**, unfasten for (with, by, &c.), e.g. *nifungulie mzigo huu*, relieve me of this load, or unfasten this load for me. *Fungulia ng'ombe*, turn out the cattle to graze. Cs. **Funguza**, force (induce, allow, &c.) to open, cause to undo, &c. *Akawafunguza wale watu*, and he had those people set free. Also 'give a meal to' after fasting. *Alitufunguza*, he caused us to break our fast. Rp. **Funguana. Fungo**, n. (1) fast, period of fasting; (2) a medicine made from the roots of the *ndago*, supposed to make a child's teeth firm. **Funguo**, n. plur. of *ufunguo*, also of breaking of a fast, but usually *mfunguo*. **Kifungo**, n. *vi-* a fastening, act (process, method, &c.) of fastening, something which fastens. Hence a wide variety of meanings, defined by the context, or by another word, e.g. (1) button, stud, brooch, buckle, clasp, chain, cord, or other contrivance for fastening; (2) prison, place of confinement, whether chain (*minyororo*), fetters (*pingu*), stocks, (*mkatale*), enclosure, or cell. *Peleka kifungoni*, send to prison. (3) fig. bond, charter, that which binds (seals, cements, &c.), e.g. Muhammad is called *kifungo cha dini*, i.e. the force which holds religion together, the corner-stone of the faith. *Kifungo* may also mean (4) a puzzle, a poser, a dilemma; (5) an act of fasting; (6) bondage, slavery. **Kifungua**, n. *vi-* an opener, an unfastener. A verbal noun governing the word following, e.g. *kifungua kopo*, a tin opener. *Kifungua mlango*, a present for opening a door. *Kifungua kinywa*, breakfast. *Kifungua mimba*, a first-born child. **Kifunguo**, n. *vi-* dim. of *ufunguo*, a small key. Also of a private key, a thief's key, skeleton key. **Mafungia, n.** plur. a fastening, locking up, e.g. *mafungia ng'ombe*, the time when the cattle return from grazing, when they are fastened in the enclosure. **Mafungulia, n.** plur. unfastening, esp. *mafungulia ng'ombe*, as a mark of time, grazing time, about 8–9 a.m. when the dew has gone and the sun is not too hot. **Mfunga, n.** *wa-* one who fastens, fasts, &c. *Mfunga hesabu*, a liquidator. **Mfungizo**, n. *mi-* a fastening up, an investment, blockade, siege. **Mfungo**, n. *mi-* (1) a fastening, shutting, closing, tying, &c., and (2) esp. fasting—used both of such fasts as the month of Ramadhan and of the carnival immediately preceding it. **Mfungua**, n. *wa-* one who opens, unfastens, &c. **Mfunguo**, n. *mi-* unfastening, untying, loosing, releasing, &c., used to describe the nine months following the month of fasting, Ramadhan, viz. *mfunguo mosi, pili, tatu*, &c.—the remaining being called by the Arabic names *Rajabu, Shabani*, and *Ramadhani*. **Mfungwa**, n. *wa-* one who is fastened, a prisoner, convict, &c. **Ufunguo**, n. (*funguo*) (1) act (means, mode, &c.) of opening, commencement, exordium; (2) a key—the commonest use, e.g. *kila mlango na ufunguo wake*, every door has a key (means of opening); (3) *tia ufunguo*, used of winding up a watch or clock.

Funga nyumba, n. a much-branched shrub up to 10 ft. tall, with scattered spines and small dense spikes of pink and yellow flowers and clusters of twisted pods, used medicinally and as an antidote to snake-bite, *Dichrostachys glomerata*.

Fungate, n. honeymoon—period of seven days after marriage, during which food is supplied by relations. (*Fungate* = seven in some Bantu languages.)

Fungo, n. (1) see under **Funga, v.**;

(2) a kind of speckled civet cat—smaller than *ngawa*.

Fungu, n. (A) *ma-* (1) portion, piece, share, lot. *Fungu la nyama,* a portion of meat. *Fungu zima,* a large share. (2) heap, pile, and esp. of sandbanks, shoals, reefs, &c., in the sea. *Chombo kimepanda funguni,* the vessel has run on a sandbank. Also of a pile of stones over a grave. (3) a verse of prose, bar of music, &c. *Vunja fungu,* used of customary visit to a grave after forty days, with a valedictory offering, the Muhammadan belief being that, until forty days have expired, the soul remains in the body, after which it departs. **Fungule,** n. (i.e. *fungu lake*) the fee or payment of a *mganga*. **Kifungu,** n. *vi-* dim. (Cf. *sehemu, kipande, gawa.*)

Fungu, n. (B) cockscomb. An annual herb up to 4 ft. tall with dense spikes of green, yellow, or crimson flowers. The stems and leaves are used as a vegetable. *Celosia argentea* and *C. cristata.*

Fungua, v. See under **Funga.**

Fungule, n. See under **Fungu.**

Funguo, n. See under **Funga.**

Funika, v. (1) cover, cover up, put a covering on; (2) fig. conceal, disguise. *Funika chungu,* put a lid on a cooking-pot. *Funika kitabu,* close a book. *Funika maneno,* speak obscurely. *Jifunika mkeka,* cover oneself with a mat. Ps. **Funikwa.** St. and Pot. **Funikika,** be covered up, concealed, &c., e.g. *jua limefunikika na mawingu,* the sun is concealed by clouds. Prep. **Funikia.** Cs. **Funikiza,** and **Funikisha,** cause to cover, cause to be covered. *Maji yamefunikisha nchi,* water has covered (flooded) the country. Cv. **Funua,** (1) uncover, unfold, lay open, undo; (2) disclose, reveal, explain, show. *Funua chungu,* take the lid off a cooking-pot. *Funua chuo,* open a book. *Funua mabawa,* spread the wings. Ps. **Funuliwa.** St. **Funuka,** be uncovered, be opened out, e.g. *maua yanafunuka,* the flowers are opening, coming out. *Mwitu unafunuka,* the forest is getting more open, is passable. Prep. **Funulia,** open, reveal, uncover (for, with, to, &c.). *Akamfunulia maana,* and he explained to him the meaning. **Funiko,** n. *ma-* amplic. of *kifuniko,* n. *vi-* anything which covers (1) top, lid, cover, case, &c.; (2) fig. concealment, hiding. **Kifunuo,** n. *vi-* unfolding, uncovering, revealing, &c., that which unfolds, reveals, &c. **Mfuniko,** n. *mi-* (1) an act of covering over, or of being covered over; (2) a lid, cover, anything that covers, like *kifuniko.* **Ufunuo,** n. like *kifunuo.* (Cf. *eleza, fichua, fungua.*)

Funo, n. the common duiker. (Cf. *kiduku.*)

Funua, v. See under **Funika.**

Fununu,* n. a rumour, something which is not known for certain, or only partly known. (Ar. فنون.)

Funutu, n. also **Tunutu,** a grasshopper, also used of young locusts. (Cf. *panzi, parare, nzige, maige.*)

Funza, n. *ma-* grub, maggot, worm, also jigger, but see **Tekenya.**

Funza, v. See under **Funda,** v. (C).

Funzo, n. *ma-*. See under **Funda,** v. (C).

Fuo, n. *ma-* (1) see under **Fua,** v.; (2) scum, froth, foam. (Cf. *povu.*)

Fupa, n. *ma-* amplic. of *mfupa.*

-fupi, a. (1) short, low (in stature, length, or height); (2) brief, concise, abridged. **Fupika,** v. be shortened, be lessened (in height, length, stature), be abbreviated, &c. Cs. **Fupisha,** and **Fupiza,** make short, abbreviate, abridge, summarize. **Kifupi,** adv. and n. of a short, abbreviated kind, in a brief way, a short piece. **Ufupi,** n. shortness, brevity. **Ufupisho,** n. *ma-* shortening, contraction, summary, abbreviation, précis, abridgement. *Mafupisho ya masomo ya kila siku,* daily lesson notes (in teaching). *Mafupisho*, summary, synopsis.

Fura, v. (1) rise up, effervesce, swell, be puffed. *Mimba ya mtama imefura*, the bud of the millet swells—as it ripens, and finally bursts. (2) fig. swell with anger, rage, indignation, *alifura kwa hasira*, he swelled with rage, boiled over with rage, &c. St. **Furika**, swell up, run over, boil over, overflow (over), make an inundation. Cs. **Furisha**, cause an overflow, inundate. **Furiko**, n. *ma-* usually in the plur. overflowing, flood, inundation. **Furufuru**, n. (1) confusion, perplexity, disorder; (2) a cloud. **Ufurufuru**, n. anger, ire. (Cf. *fara, gharikisha, jaa, enea, chemka, bubujika, foka*. ? Ar. فور boil, or Bantu *-pula*, swell up, boil up, *u* is a closed vowel which causes *p* to become *f* in Swahili.)

Furaha,* n. joy, pleasure, happiness, bliss, delight, gladness, mirth, merriment. *Fanya* (*ona*) *furaha*, be happy. *Pokea kwa furaha*, welcome, also adv. gladly, with joy. **Furahi**, v. rejoice, be glad, feel pleasure, be happy, be pleased, enjoy oneself. Ps. **Furahiwa**, be pleased (with), be made happy (by), be rejoiced (at). *Tulifurahiwa sana na barua yako*, we were delighted with your letter. Prep. **Furahia**, rejoice at (in, for, &c.). Cs. **Furahisha**, gladden, cheer, rejoice, delight. *Ametufurahisha leo*, he has caused us to be happy today. **-furahifu**, joyous, cheering, pleasant. (Cf. *changamsha, kunjua, pendeza*. Ar. فرح.)

Furama, v. See **Fuama**.

Furika, v., **Furiko**, n. *ma-*. See under **Fura**.

Furkani,* n. a name of the Koran. (Cf. *Kurani*. Ar. الفرقان.)

Furufuru, n. See under **Fura**.

Furukombe, n. also **Fukombe**, African sea eagle, *Cuncuma vocifer*.

Furukuta, v. (1) move about restlessly, toss about on a bed, as when ill, excited, unable to sleep, &c.; (2) throb, or of any restless movement. (Cf. *fukuta, pwita*.)

Furungu,* n. *ma-* (1) shaddock, fruit of the *mfurungu, mi-* (from same root as *balungi*); (2) anklet (usually of silver). (Pers. برنجن anklet.)

Furusha, v. rout an enemy, drive away birds with stones, startle game, &c.

Furushi,* n. *ma-* bundle, packet, package. Dim. **Kifurushi**, n. *vi-*. (From same root as *firashi*, Ar. فرش.)

Furutile,* n. also **Flotile**, a workshop, dockyard. (? German *Flotille*.)

Fusa, v. (A) (1) beat, make soft by gentle beating, e.g. *atakufusa hata ulainike*, he will beat you until you are tender, e.g. until you have no strength left; (2) attack. *Ugonjwa ulimfusa*, sickness attacked him. Prep. **Fusia**, lay down a bed of small stones and rubbish for a concrete floor or roof, or fill in foundations. **Fusi**, n. *ma-*, also **Kifusi**, n. *vi-* the mud of the walls, &c., of a house which has been demolished. **Ufusio**, n. a sprinkling of small stones on a freshly laid concrete floor, beaten in to bring it to a smooth surface. (Dist. *ufusio* under *fusa*, v. (B).)

Fusa,* v. (B) escape of wind, like out of a burst ball or tyre, also of breaking wind without noise. **Ufusio**, n. an escape of wind, breaking of wind without noise. (Dist. *ufusio* under *fusa*, v. (A). Ar. فسا).

Fusahi,* v. annul, sometimes used in the sense of make poor. *Mungu amemfusahi*, God has made him poor, i.e. separated from him. (Ar. فسخ.)

Fusha, n. *ma-* a gun wad. (Cf. *busha*.)

Fusho, n. See under **Fuka**.

Fusi, n. *ma-*, **Fusia**, v. See under **Fusa**, v. (A).

Fususi,* n. a gem, a precious stone. (Ar. فصوص.)

Futa, v. (A) (1) wipe, wipe out (away, off), clean up; (2) remove, obliterate, abolish, cause to be forgotten. *Futa vumbi nguoni*, wipe dust off clothes. *Futa kamasi*, wipe the nose. *Mungu anifute dhambi zangu*, may God wipe away my sins. *Tulicheza kamari nikamfuta kabisa*, we played *kamari* and I 'cleaned him out', won all his money. Ps. **Futwa.** St. Pot. **Futika**, e.g. *hii yafutika, hii haifutiki*, this is able to be wiped out (obliterated, forgiven), this is not. Prep. **Futia**, wipe with (for, &c.), e.g. *kitambaa cha kufutia*, a cloth to wipe with, a duster, a towel. Cs. **Futisha**, set to wipe, wipe hard. Rp. **Futana. Mfuto**, n. *mi-* (1) a wiping, sweeping, clearing off, erasing, abolition, absolution; (2) used to denote a common, plain, rough, inferior article of any kind, e.g. *mlango wa mfuto*, a plain door, without carving or ornamentation. *Mkeka wa mfuto*, a plain, cheap mat. (Cf. *pangusa, sugua, batili, ondoa, samehe, komba.*)

Futa, v. (B) unsheathe. *Alifuta upanga (sime, kisu)*, he unsheathed a sword (large knife, knife). Note: this may be *vuta*, which see, but when unsheathing is meant, it is usu. pronounced as *futa*. (Cf. *chomoa.*)

Futahi,* n. good luck. **Futahi**, v. escape from danger, bad luck, &c. Cs. **Futusha**, save, succour, cause to thrive. (Ar. فتح.)

Futari,* n. first meal in the evening after a day's fast, usu. rice gruel (*uji*). **Futuru**, v. take the first meal after a day's fast. Prep. **Futuria.** Cs. **Futurisha**, provide with a first meal after a fast. (Ar. فطر.)

Futi, n. (A) *ma-* the knee. *Maji ya mafuti*, water up to the knees.

Futi,* n. (B) a foot (measure), also a foot rule, tape measure. (Eng.)

Futika, v. St. of a form *futa*, envelope, fold in, not now in use in Swahili—used in a Trans. sense—put in the pocket, stick in the waistcloth, tuck in the girdle—as a native does his knife, money, or any small article such as a plug of tobacco, &c. Ps. **Futikwa.** Prep. **Futikia.** Cs. **Futikisha.** Cv. **Futua**, (1) open out, undo a bundle (or girdle), take out of a bundle, pocket, &c., pluck out; (2) fig. bring to light, make known, expose. *Futua manyoya ya kuku (ndevu)*, pluck off the feathers of a fowl (hairs of a beard). *Futua kibofu cha ng'ombe*, take out the bladder of an ox. Rf. *jifutua*, make a show of oneself, boast, brag. Prep. **Futulia**, provoke. Ps. **Futuliwa.** St. and Pot. **Futuka.** (1) be brought to light, be brought out; (2) be provoked, be annoyed at somebody's remarks, be angry; (3) go quickly and suddenly; (4) stick out, as something in one's pocket, &c. *Kitovu chake kimefutuka*, his navel sticks out (referring to hernia of the umbilical cord). (5) come out, i.e. as of feathers of a fowl or bird when it is moulting, also of fur or hair. Prep. **Futukia**, be in a passion with. Cs. **Futusha.** (Cf. *choma, tia.*)

Futuri,* n. (1) a short span, as a measure, from the tip of the thumb to the tip of the forefinger—as distinct from *shibiri*, a full span from thumb to little finger; (2) haemorrhoids. (Cf. *morita*, and *bawasiri, kikundu*. Ar. فتر.)

Futuru,* v. See under **Futari** and **Futika.**

Futusha, v. See under **Futahi.**

Fuu, n. (A) a small black berry, the edible fruit of the *mfuu.*

Fuu, n. (B) *ma-* also **Fuvu**, empty shell, husk. **Kifuu**, n. *vi-* (1) an empty shell—see *fuvu*; (2) a cuttle-fish bone, i.e. *kifuu cha ngisi.* **Ufuu**, n. the inner shell of the coco-nut.

Fuuza, v. sometimes heard for *fuliza* and *fululiza*, see under **Fua.**

Fuvu, n. *ma-* also **Fuu**, empty shell, husk. *Fuvu la kichwa*, the skull. *Fuvu la nazi*, shell of a coco-nut, but usu. *kifuu*. *Fuvu la yai*, egg-shell, but usu. *kaka*.

Fuwaa, v. be stunted in growth, shrivel, shrink up. (Cf. *via, sinyaa, nywea*.)

Fuzi, n. *ma-* the shoulder, i.e. the tip as distinct from *bega*. (Dist. *vuzi*.)

Fuzu,* v. succeed, win, as in a competition, game, or examination. (Cf. *shinda, faulu, weza, pita*. Ar. فوز.)

Fyanda, v. crush, bruise, hurt, &c., as of a stone or something similar falling on one's finger, foot, &c. (Cf. *ponda, seta, vyoga*.)

Fyata, v. (1) put (or hold) between the legs. *Fyata nguo* (*mikono*), tuck the loin-cloth (hands) between the legs. *Fyata mkia*, put the tail between the legs. (2) fig. hold the tongue, *fyata ulimi wako*, keep your tongue between your teeth, i.e. control your tongue. Cs. of Cv. of Dir. **Fyusa**, set a trap to catch animals. Cv. **Fyatua**, let go suddenly anything which has been gripped, let off (of something which is holding a spring, a trap, &c.). St. and Pot. **Fyatuka**. *Bunduki imefyatuka*, the spring of the gun has sprung, it has gone off suddenly. Prep. **Fyatulia**. Cs. **Fyatusha**. Cs. of Div. **Fyatiza**, used of beating with a switch which bends round the body. **Fyatuko**, n. *ma-* and **Mfyatuko**, n. *mi-* a letting go of something gripped, releasing a spring, trap, &c. **Mfyuso**, n. *mi-* a kind of trap.

Fyeka, v. cut down trees and undergrowth ready for making a plantation or garden, clear away weeds and undergrowth. *Fyeka mwitu*, make a clearing in a forest. Ps. **Fyekwa**. Prep. **Fyekea**. Cs. **Fyekesha**. Cv. **Fyekua**, same as *fyeka*. **Fyeko**, n. *ma-* esp. in the plur. clearing operations, things cleared away, also the place cleared. **Mfyeka**, n. *wa-* one who clears forest or cuts grass.

Fyeruka, v. become angry. *Roho imemfyeruka*, he has become angry.

Fyoa, v. (1) cut. *Fyoa masuke ya mtama*, cut ears of millet. (2) of using cutting or abusive language, reply insolently. Cs. (1) and Inten. (of *fyona*, not in use) **Fyonya**, make chirping sound with lips, expressive of contempt or disgust. Cs. (2) **Fyonza**, suck, suck at, suck out. *Fyonza ziwa la mama*, suck the mother's breast (but generally *nyonya*). *Mbu hufyonza damu ya watu*, mosquitoes suck the blood of people. Cs. (3) (of *fyoa*) **Fyoza**, treat scornfully, make a mock of. **-fyozi**, a. abusive, scornful. **Mfyozaji**, n. *wa-*, **Mfyozi**, n. *wa-* an abusive, scornful, insolent person. **Ufyozi**, n. (1) a sound like chirping, a sign of contempt or scorn; (2) contempt, scorn. (For form cf. *poa, pona, ponya, poza*.)

Fyuka, v., **Fyusa**, v. See under **Fyata**.

G

G, represents the same sound as in English 'go'. Obs. *ng'*, now written ŋ in many Bantu languages, represents the velar nasal pronounced as the *ng* in 'sing'; *gh* represents the Arabic *Ghain* in the few words in which it is commonly retained as a deep guttural, but it is frequently heard as harsh *h*, or omitted altogether. *G* is sometimes difficult to distinguish from *k* in the pronunciation of some natives, therefore words not found under *g* may be looked for under *k*.

Gaagaa, v. also **Garagara, Galagala,** (1) roll from side to side, turn restlessly as a man in pain, or in delirium, or as an animal wallowing on the ground, or a ship in a swell; (2) fig. be lazy, listless, indifferent, have nothing to do, loll. Cs. **Gaagaza. Mgaagaa,** n. *wa-* an idler, restless person, 'beachcomber', 'rolling stone'. Prov. *Mgaagaa na upwa hali wali mtupu,* he that haunts the shore does not eat plain rice, i.e. he always picks up something. **Mgaagaa paka,** n. *mi-* the name of a tree, *Fida cordifolia,* the fibre of which is used for brooms; it is said that if a cat (*paka*) sees this tree it rolls about on the ground and cannot get up again! (Cf. *furukuta, geuka, pinduka.*)

Gadi,* n. *ma-* (A) prop, shore, e.g. to keep a vessel upright, when stranded, or a tree inclined to fall. *Tia magadi,* shore up. **Gudi,** n. a dock for ships, also a place where they are propped up for repairing. (Cf. *jahabu.* Ar. قاعدة pedestal.)

Gadi,* n. *ma-* (B) a sentry-go, period on guard of soldier or policeman. (Eng. guard.)

Gadimu,* v. prop, shore up. Ps. **Gadimiwa.** St. **Gadimika.** Prep. **Gadimia,** prop up with (for, to, on, &c.). Cs. **Gadimisha.** (Cf. *tegemeza, imarisha,* and *gidamu.* Ar. قدم front part, hence prop.)

Gae, n. *ma-* a large potsherd, a large broken piece of metal, glass, earthenware, &c. **Kigae,** n. *vi-* dim.

Gafi,* a. See **Ghafi.**

Gaga, n. *ma-* amplic. of **Kigaga,** *vi-* dry hard scale, scurf, scab, &c., crust as on water, tartar on the teeth, and similar incrustations. **Ugaga,** n., **Ugwagwa,** n. same as *gaga.*

Gagamiza, v. (1) penetrate with force; (2) roll or press together. (Cf. *bokoa, penya, gandamiza.*)

Gaidi,* n. *ma-* a robber, plunderer, thief. (Cf. *mwizi, mnyang'anyi.* Ar. كيد.)

Galagala, v. See **Gaagaa.**

Galawa, n. See **Ngalawa.**

Gale, n. See **Ugale.**

Galili, n. shell of a tortoise, crab, or turtle. (Cf. *gamba.*)

Galme,* n. (1) *mlingoti wa galme,* small second mast aft in a large dhow, mizzen mast, carrying its own sail; (2) a kind of small sail in a dhow. (Ar. قلب middle of anything.)

Gamba, v. and n. See under **Amba,** v. (B).

Gambusi, n. (1) a kind of musical instrument like a banjo or mandolin; (2) a kind of fish.

Gamti,* n. (1) a kind of unbleached calico; (2) a kind of rice

Gana, n. See **Kana.**

Ganda, n. See **Ng'anda.**

Ganda, v. (1) coagulate, become hard, set (of glue, blood, jelly, &c.); become frozen, get thick (of milk, liquid, &c.). *Maziwa yameganda,* the milk is curdled. *Mito imeganda kwa baridi,* the rivers are frozen with the cold. (2) stick to, cleave to, embrace closely, clasp. *Alimganda shingoni,* he clasped him round the neck. Ps. **Gandwa.** St. **Gandika.** Prep. **Gandia.** Cs. **Gandisha.** Stc. **Gandama,** be in a condition of sticking together, be stuck, be hard, be frozen, be curdled, be coagulated. *Asali imegandama na bakuli,* the honey is sticking to the basin. Ps.

Gandamwa, have something sticking to, e.g. *niligandamwa na kupe,* I had ticks sticking to me. St. and Pot. **Gandamika.** Prep. **Gandamia,** stick to, adhere, cling to, be true to. *Gandamia rafiki,* hold fast (be true, faithful) to a friend. Cs. **Gandamiza,** press heavy on, cause to stick together or to become compact, e.g. *gandamiza mtu chini,* pin a man to the ground. Also Inten., e.g. *gandamiza ulimwengu,* cling to, take to one's heart, the world. Rp. of Stc. **Gandamana,** be in a condition of sticking fast together, of being very hard, set, firm, &c. *Maji yamegandamana,* the water is frozen hard. Cv. **Gandua,** (1) unfasten, pull away, separate something adhering closely; (2) fig. rescue from danger, save in a crisis, get out of a scrape. Ps. **Ganduliwa.** St. **Ganduka.** Prep. **Gandulia.** **Ganda,** n. *ma-* husk, rind, shell, outer covering of trees, plants, fruits, &c. *Ganda la yai,* egg-shell. *Ganda la chungwa,* orange peel. *Ganda la mkate,* crust of bread. *Maganda ya mahindi,* the sheath enclosing the cob of maize. **Gandalo,** n. *ma-* cleft stick or tree used as a kind of stocks (*mkatale*) for imprisoning mad people. **Gando,** n. *ma-* claw of a lobster (*kamba*) and crab (*kaa*), Prov. *Kaa akiinua gando mambo yamekatika,* when the crab raises his claw, there is an end of the matter. **Mganda,** n. *mi-* a bundle, a sheaf, e.g. of rice or other crop. **Mgandisho,** n. *mi-* anything that causes coagulation, &c. **Mgando,** n. *mi-* anything coagulated or stuck together, e.g. *mgando wa chuma,* iron smelted and run out to cool, pig iron (cf. *mkuo*). *Piga chuma mgando,* make wrought iron. **Ugandamano,** n. coagulation. **Ugandisho,** n. the property of causing coagulation, &c. **Ugando,** n. like *mgando.*

Gane, n. sleeping-quarters of the young unmarried boys or girls of a village. (Cf. *bweni.*)

Ganga, v. bind up, fasten together, splice, mend (what is injured or broken). Hence esp. of doctor's work generally, 'apply remedy, cure, heal'. *Ganga mguu,* put a leg in splints. *Ganga jeraha,* bandage a wound. *Ganga tumbo,* attend to the stomach. Ps. **Gangwa.** St. **Gangika.** Prep. **Gangia.** Cs. **Gangisha.** Rp. **Gangana.** Cv. **Gangua,** v. (1) same as *ganga,* v.; (2) save, get out of a difficulty, set free from a charm, &c. (Cf. *agua, topoa opoa.*) **Gango,** n. *ma-* appliance for holding together what is separate or severed, cramp, brace, splint, splice, joining, patch. Dim. **Kigango,** n. *vi-*. **Mganga,** n. *wa-* a native doctor, medicine man. **Mgango,** n. *mi-* (1) a binding up, splicing, mending; (2) time (method, means, &c.) of curing, giving medical attention. **Mganguzi,** n. *wa-* same as *mganga.* **Uganga,** n., **Uganguzi,** (1) art (profession, fee) of a native doctor, doctoring, healing, surgical and medical aid—including use of charms, &c.; (2) medicine, charm, e.g. *pika* (*fanya, weka*) *uganga,* concoct (make, place in position) native medicine. (Cf. *uguza, tibu.*)

Gange, n. *ma-* a kind of limestone or soft chalk rock.

Gangi, n. a kind of dhow. (Ar. كنجة.)

Gango, n. *ma-*. See under **Ganga.**

Gangua, v. See under **Ganga.**

Gani, a. (1) Interrog. of what sort, what kind of, why? what?—never used without a noun preceding. *Kitu gani?* What is it? *Sababu gani?* Why? *Jinsi gani?* How? *Wakati gani?* When? *Mahali gani?* Where? *Habari gani?* What is the news? How are you? *Mtu gani?* always suggests primarily 'a man of what tribe (place, or country)'. *Tutaeleza sababu gani hufanya hivi,* we shall explain the reason why it does this. (2) a. rel. 'what', e.g. *tutawaonyesha tu watu wa namna gani,* we shall show them what kind of men we are.

Ganja, n. *ma-* but more usually **Kiganja**, n. *vi-* the palm of the hand. (Cf. *kitanga.*)

Ganjo, n. *ma-* (1) a deserted village or town; (2) fig. ruin, desolation. (Cf. *mahame* under *hama.*)

Ganzaganza, v. (1) hesitate; (2) speak in a hesitating lazy manner; (3) be clumsy; (4) prevaricate. (Cf. *sita, kokoteza, goteza.*)

Ganzi, n. deadness, numbness, often used with the verb *fa*, die. *Mguu umekufa ganzi*, my foot is asleep (benumbed). Often of the teeth, *tia* (*fanya*) *ganzi la meno*, set the teeth on edge. *Meno yangu yafanya ganzi*, my teeth are set on edge.

Gao, n. *ma-* (1) the palm of the hand, a handful, with the hand open, e.g. *nipatie gao moja la unga*, get a handful of flour for me; (2) a very large shield—an ordinary one is **Ngao**, a smaller one is **Kigao**, *vi-*.

Garagara, v. See **Gaagaa.**

Gari,* n. *ma-* any vehicle on wheels, cart, wagon, carriage, barrow, perambulator, bicycle, but the latter is now generally *baisikeli*. *Gari la moshi*, locomotive, sometimes called *mashine* or *mtambo*. *Gari la gurudumu moja*, a wheelbarrow. (Hind. گاڑی.)

Gati,* n. landing-pier or stage. *Meli imefunga gatini*, the ship is tied up alongside the landing-stage. (Hind. گھات.)

Gaugau, n. also **Geugeu**, a kind of flat fish or sole.

Gawa, n. a nightjar, also called *kiruka njia.*

Gawa, v. divide up, distribute, deal out, place in parts (pieces, portions, shares). *Gawa chakula*, divide out food. *Gawa karata*, deal (playing) cards. Ps. **Gawiwa.** St. **Gawika.** Prep. **Gawia**, share with, give a portion to, often used of giving a portion for nothing, as a gift, e.g. *nigawie tumbako*, give me some of your tobacco. Cs. **Gawisha.** Rp. **Gawana**, e.g. *utakachopata tutagawana sawasawa mimi na wewe*, whatever you get, you and I shall share alike. Cs. of Rp. **Gawanya**, used in the same way as *gawa*, but prop. of mutual arrangement or equal rights, whereas *gawa* is rather the act of an official, superior, or benefactor, e.g. *tugawanye; gawa wewe*, let us have a division; do you act as divider. Ps. **Gawanya.** St. and Pot. **Gawanyika**, be divided, be divisible. Rp. and Pot. **Gawanyikana.** Cs. **Gawanyisha. Gawio**, n. *ma-* division, apportionment, sharing. **Kigawanye**, n. *vi-* dividend in arithmetic. *Kigawanye kilicho kidogo*, the lowest common measure, L.C.M. **Kigawanyo**, n. *vi-* divisor, in arithmetic. *Kigawanyo kilicho kikubwa*, highest common factor, H.C.F. **Kigawe**, n. *vi-* like *kigawanye*. **Kigawo**, n. *vi-* like *kigawanyo*. **Mgawanya**, n. *wa-*, **Mgawanyi**, n. *wa-* a divider, a distributor. **Mgawo**, n. *mi-* a dividing, division, distribution, partition. **Mgawanyo**, n. *mi-* like *mgawo*.

Gayagaya, n. *ma-* a kind of mat used for lolling on, resting or lounging on during the daytime. (Cf. *mkeka, jamvi, msala.*)

Gazeti,* n. *ma-* a newspaper, journal. (Eng.)

Gea, v. (1) throw; (2) leave behind, abandon. (Cf. *tupa.*)

Gego, n. *ma-* a molar tooth.

Geli, n. (1) a child's game, like tip-cat; (2) a large knife.

Gema, v. gash or make an incision in a tree to get its sap, esp. of getting palm wine from the coco-nut tree. *Gema tembo, gema mnazi*, of cutting the growing flower-stem of the coco-nut tree, from which the sap flows into a calabash fastened to it. Also used of getting india-rubber by making an incision in the bark of the tree, *gema mpira*. A special knife is used (*kotama*). Prov. *Mgema akisifiwa tembo kulitia maji*, if the palm-wine tapper is praised because of his palm wine he dilutes it with water. Ps. **Gemwa.** Prep. **Gemea.** Cs. **Gemesha,** employ (allow, undertake, contract) to tap coco-nut trees. **Mgema,** n. *wa-*, **Mgemi,** n. *wa-* one who taps coco-nut trees to get the palm wine. **Mgemo,** n. *mi-* the work (fee, method, time, &c.) of tapping trees. **Ugema,** n. like *mgemo.*

Genge, n. *ma-* cliff, precipice, escarpment, ravine.

-geni, a. strange, foreign, novel, outlandish, extraordinary, queer, curious. *Jambo geni,* a strange occurrence. *Maneno ya kigeni,* a foreign language. **Mgeni,** n. *wa-* (1) a stranger, new-comer, foreigner; (2) a guest. **Ugeni,** n. (1) state or condition of a stranger or foreigner, newness, strangeness; (2) state of being a guest; (3) a foreign region or country, foreign parts—in this respect it may mean merely the country of a different tribe. *Safiri ugenini,* travel abroad, in foreign countries, in the country of another tribe.

Gereza,* n. prison, fort used as a prison, barracks. *Tia (weka, funga, peleka) gerezani,* put in prison. *Toa (fungua, ondoa) gerezani,* let out of prison. (Cf. *kifungo.* Port. *igreja.*)

Geua, v. (1) change, make different, alter, but the Cs. *geuza* is generally used in this sense; (2) fig. treat with scorn, contempt, thrust aside, of persons, e.g. *usinigeue,* don't treat me as though I were nobody. Ps. **Geuliwa.** St. and Pot. **Geuka,** (1) be changed, be changeable, be alterable, alter; (2) change position, turn oneself, turn round; (3) change in appearance, be transformed, be disguised. *Aligeuka akamwona,* he turned round and saw him. *Amegeuka mwingine,* he has become another person. Prep. of St. **Geukia,** turn to (from, for, &c.). Prep. **Geulia.** Cs. **Geuza,** cause to change, alter, pervert, turn round, &c. **-geugeu,** a. changeable, fickle, wayward. *Mambo ya kigeugeu,* constant changes. **Geuzi,** n. *ma-* usually in plur. that which causes change, alteration, shifting, turn, transformation. **-geuzi,** a. changeable, fickle, unsettled, always changing. **-geuzo,** *ma-* change, alteration, &c., i.e. of the affect not the cause. **Kigeugeu,** n. *vi-* a. and adv. (1) changeable, fickle, whimsical, unstable, wayward thing or person, of a changeable kind, in an uncertain fluctuating way, hence (2) a chameleon. (Cf. *lumbwi, kinyonga.*) **Ugeuzi,** n. (*geuzi, mageuzi*), changing, changeableness, change, variation, turning round. (Cf. *badili.*)

Geza,* v. try on, i.e. of clothing. **Kigezo,** n. *vi-* (1) a pattern for making clothes from; (2) a measuring line or wand. (Pers. گز a rod for measuring.)

Ghadhabu,* n. rage, fury, passion, anger, exasperation, used with such verbs as *fanya, ona, ingia,* also *ingiwa (na), shikwa (na), patwa (na).* **Ghadhibika,** v. be furious, be enraged, be in a passion. Cs. **Ghadhibisha,** exasperate, enrage, provoke. Prep. **Ghadhibikia,** be vexed with (for, &c.). (Cf. *hasira, uchungu, kasirani, kasirika.* Ar. غضب be angry.)

Ghafala,* n. See **Ghafula** and **Mghafala** under **Ghafilika.**

Ghafi,* n. the gross weight of anything, but usu. in the sense of getting short weight, i.e. the packing being weighed together with its contents. **Ghafi,** a. also **Ghafighafi,** of inferior quality, trifling, insignificant, valueless. (Cf. *hafifu, duni.* ? Ar. خف be of little importance.)

Ghafilika,* v. (1) be thoughtless neglectful, inattentive, imprudent, and hence (2) be taken unawares. Prep. **Ghafilikia.** Cs. **Ghafilisha,** (1) distract, come on suddenly, take unawares; (2) neglect, fail to attend to. *Ghafilisha kazi,* forget to do work, do it in a careless inattentive manner. **Ghafula,** n. suddenness, sudden occurrence. Often used as adv. and also *kwa ghafula,* suddenly, unexpectedly. **Mghafala,** n. *mi-* (1) carelessness, inattention, forgetfulness, thoughtlessness, &c.; (2) *wa-* a simpleton, a heedless, inattentive person. **Taghafali,** v. (1) be taken unawares, be surprised, be off one's guard; (2) be unmindful (of), omit to notice; (3) take by surprise, make a sudden attack (or demand) on. Ps. **Taghafaliwa.** St. **Taghafalika,** e.g. be taken by surprise. Cs. **Taghafalisha.** (Cf. *-zembe.* Ar. غفل.)

Ghaibu,* n. a thing not obtainable because it is distant, absence. *Kusoma kwa ghaibu,* to recite from memory. **Ghibu,** v. be lost. (Cf. *potea.*) **Ughaibu,** n. a distant place, condition of being unobtainable, absent. (Ar. غيب.)

Ghaidhi,* n. (1) anger; (2) determination, resolution, exertion. (Cf. *hasira, jadi, ghadhabu.* Ar. غيظ.)

Ghairi,* v. change one's mind, alter plan, annul, do something unexpected, sudden, or surprising. Sometimes as a n. a sudden change, surprise, disappointment. *Tia ghairi,* cause to change one's mind, disappoint, surprise. Also with *ya* as a prep. *ghairi ya,* without, except, apart from, without regard to. **Baghairi** and **Minghairi,** prep. without, except, other than, same as *ghairi ya.* (Ar. غير.)

Ghala,* n. store-room, store-house, magazine, godown. *Weka vyakula ghalani,* put away food in the store. (Cf. *uchaga, bohari.* Pers. غوله granary.)

Ghalati,* n. a lie, fault, mistake. (Cf. *uwongo, kosa.* Ar. غلط.)

Ghali,* a. (1) scarce, rare, hard to get; (2) dear, expensive, costly. *Chakula ni ghali siku hizi,* food is dear these days. *Fedha ni ghali,* money is scarce. *Sitaki ghali, nataka rahisi,* I do not want an expensive one, I want a cheap one. **Ghalika,** v. (1) be rare, occur infrequently; (2) be dear, be costly, rise in price. Cs. **Ghalisha,** raise the price of, make scarce, rare, make valuable, &c. (Cf. *haba, adimika.* Ar. غال.)

Ghalibu,* v. See **Ghilibu,** and adv. see **Aghalabu.**

Ghalika,* v., **Ghalisha,** v. See **Ghali.**

Ghamu,* n. grief, sorrow, distress. *Tia ghamu,* grieve. *Fanya (ingiwa na) ghamu,* be grieved. (Cf. *sikitiko, majonzi, huzuni,* and dist. **hamu.** Ar. غم.)

Ghani,* v. sing. **Ghani,** n. *ma-* a song. (Cf. *imba.* Ar. غنى.)

Ghanima,* n. good luck, prosperity. (Cf. *bahati, sitawi, neema.* Ar. غنم obtain.)

Gharadhi,* n. aim, object, intention —seldom used. (Cf. *kusudi, nia.* Ar. غرض.)

Gharama,* n. expense, outlay, payment. *Fanya (toa) gharama,* lay out money, incur expense. **Gharimia,** v.Prep. spend money, or incur expense for. St. **Gharimika.** Cs. **Gharimisha.** (Ar. غرم.)

Gharighari,* adv. (seldom used), *gharighari ya mauti,* near to death. (Ar. غرغرة death rattle.)

Gharika,* n. flood, deluge, inundation. **Ghariki,** v. be covered with water, be flooded, sink into water. Cs. **Gharikisha,** (1) cause a flood (over), make a flood (in), inundate. *Maji yamegharikisha nchi,* water has flooded the country. Also (2) fig. overwhelm (of words, actions, misfortunes, &c.). **Gharikisho,** n. *ma-* a flood, inundation. (Cf. *furika.* Ar. غرق.)

Gharimia,* v. See under **Gharama.**

Ghashi,* n. deceit, guile. (Cf. *ghoshi.*)

Ghasi,* v. make confusion, confuse, complicate, bustle. **Ghasia,** n. confusion, complication, bustle, hurry, medley, crowding, and used of various things involving these ideas, and of annoyances generally, e.g. *ghasia nyingi leo,* a lot of troubles to-day; *pana ghasia mjini,* there is a disturbance in the town, a street crowd or riot. (Cf. *chafuko, fujo, zahama.* Ar. غص.)

Ghasili,* n. See **Dasili.**

Ghera,* n. jealousy, zeal, but usu. the effort made to avoid disgrace, dishonour, shame, at failing to return hospitality, &c. (Cf. *ari, wivu.* Ar. غار.)

Ghibu,* v. See under **Ghaibu.**

Ghilibu,* v. get the better of, beat, often used in the sense of getting the better of by cheating or by sharp practice. **Mghalaba,** n. competition, rivalry. *Bei ni mghalaba,* commerce is competition. (Cf. *shinda, pita.* Ar. غلب.)

Ghofira,* n. pardon, forgiveness of sins, absolution—used only of God. *Ghofira ya dhambi,* pardon of sins. **Ghofiri,** v. forgive, pardon, absolve. Ps. **Ghofiriwa.** St. **Ghofirika.** Prep. **Ghofiria,** grant forgiveness to. *Mungu amemghofiria dhambi zake,* God has absolved him from his sins. Cs. **Ghofirisha.** (Cf. *samehe, achilia, fungulia, ondolea, futa* (A). Ar. غفر.)

Ghorofa,* n. but usu. *orofa,* n. upper story, upper room. (Ar. غرفة.)

Ghoshi,* v. also **Ghushi,** adulterate, falsify, debase. *Ameghushi buni kwa kuzichanganya na kunde,* he has adulterated the coffee beans by mixing them with *kunde* (a common sort of bean). Ps. **Ghushiwa,** be adulterated, e.g. *kitu kilichoghushiwa,* an adulterated article. **Ughoshi,** n. also **Ughushi,** adulteration, mixing. (Cf. *haribu, changanya, saliti.* Ar. غش deceive, falsify.)

Ghuba,* n. a bay, an inlet of the sea (Cf. *hori.* Ar. غب low ground on which water lies.)

Ghubari,* n. a cloud of rain or dust. (Cf. *wingu, ukungu.* Ar. غبرة.)

Ghulamu,* n. (1) a youth (male), a young man; (2) the knave in a suit of playing cards, also called *Mzungu wa tatu.* (Cf. *kijana, mwanamume, mvulana.* Ar. غلام.)

Ghumia,* v. (1) faint, lose consciousness; (2) be astounded, dumbfounded, overwhelmed, taken a-back. Ps. **Ghumiwa,** in the same sense. Cs. **Ghumisha.** (Cf. *zimia, zirai,* and *tunduwaa, shangaa, duwaa, pumbaa.* Ar. غمي.)

Ghuri,* v. cheat, beguile, deceive. St. **Ghurika,** also **Ghururika,** be proud, vain, puffed up, because of wealth, or of anything transient, which may pass and leave one in an humble estate. **Ghururi,** n. arrogance, self-conceit, infatuation, vanity, folly, blindness, but all with the meaning of because of transient things. (Cf. *danganya, batili.* Ar. غر.)

Ghurubu,* n. the setting of the sun, sunset, usu. *magharibi,* which see. (Ar. غرب.)

Ghururi,* n., **Ghururika,** v. See under **Ghuri.**

Ghushi,* v. See **Ghoshi.**

Ghusubu,* v. compel, coerce, take away by force, violate. (Cf. *nyang'anya, pokonya, iba, shawishi.* Ar. غصب.)

Gida, v. pour liquid gently out of a vessel in order to leave the sediment. (Cf. *chingirisha.*)

Gidamu,* n. (1) small leather thong in a sandal, passing between the toes from sole to cross-piece, and holding it on the foot; (2) the bow of a dhow. (Cf. *omo.* ? Ar. قدم.)

Giligilani,* n. coriander seed, used

in curry powder, the plant is *mgili-gilani*. (Ar. جلجلان.)

Gimbi, n. millet beer. (Cf. *pombe*.)

Ginsi,* n. See **Jinsi**.

Gisi,* v. sometimes heard for *kisi*, which see.

Giza, n. (— and *ma*-) sometimes heard as *kiza*, (1) darkness, gloom, blackness (of night, not of colour). *Tia giza*, darken. *Giza la* (and sometimes *ya*) *usiku*, the darkness of night. *Macho yake yaona* (or *yameingia*) *giza*, his eyes are dim; also (2) fig. ignorance, uncivilized state, &c. (Cf. *weusi*.)

Goboa, v. (1) break off with the hand, as a cob (*kibunzi* or *gunzi*) of maize; (2) clean cotton, cloves, &c., by picking off the stalks; (3) extract (but see *kongoa, ng'oa*); (4) strip off, as of bark of a tree (but see *ambua*). Ps. **Gobolewa**. Prep. **Gobolea**. St. and Pot. **Goboka**. (Cf. *konyoa, chambua, pujua*.)

Gobori,* n. a muzzle-loading gun. (Cf. *bunduki*. Prob. a corruption of carbine. See **Korobai**.)

Godoro,* n. *ma*- a mattress. (Hind. گُدڑی.)

Goe, n. See under **Ngoeka**.

Gofia,* n. pulley, such as is attached to the rope (*henza*) which hoists the sail in a native sailing vessel. (Cf. *kapi, roda, korodani, abedari*. ? form of *kofia*.)

Gofu, n. *ma*- ruin (of house, &c.). *Gofu la mtu*, a thin emaciated person. *Gofu la nyumba*, a ruined house. **-gofu**, a. emaciated, broken down, in ruins. **Gofua**, v. emaciate, wear out the strength of, reduce to a skeleton (or to ruins). Also Cs. **Gofusha**, in the same sense. *Maradhi yamemgofusha*, illness has broken him down. (Cf. *konda, nyorora, churuzika, goigoi*.)

Gogadima, n. a shrub with recurved spines, *Capparis corymbosa*.

Gogo, n. *ma*- (1) log, trunk of a tree when felled, e.g. *gogo la mnazi*, of a coco-nut tree. **Kigogo**, n. *vi*- dim. and adv. *lala kigogo*, sleep (lie) like a log, i.e. motionless, in a dead sleep.

Gogota, v. knock at, tap, hammer at. Also **Gota**, v. and **Gotagota** with the same meaning, the latter, however, is used of continuous tapping or drumming. Ps. **Gogotwa** (**Gotwa**). Cs. **Gogoteza** (**Goteza**) cause to knock, e.g. *goteza maneno*, of ill-pronounced speech, the opposite of fluent speaking. *Gotagota maneno*, of jumbling words of different dialects together. Rp. **Gotana**, like *gongana*, e.g. *vyombo vinagotana*, the vessels are knocking together. **Gogota**, n. woodpecker, also called *kigogota* and *gongonola*. (Cf. *piga, gonga, dunda*.)

Goigoi, n. and a. a lazy, idle, weak person, and as a. lazy, idle, weak, useless. (Cf. *-vivu, dhaifu, duni*.)

Goka, v. retch. (Cf. *kokomoka, tapika*.)

Goko, n. *ma*- the shin-bone. (Cf. *muundi*.)

Gole,* n. *ma*- (1) phlegm, expectorated matter, also mucus of the nose; (2) expectoration or saliva of a whale; (3) the crop of a bird; (4) a pellet of opium (*afyuni*) prepared for smoking. (Cf. *kamasi, belghamu, umio*. Pers. گلو gullet, throat, and Hind. گولی pellet.)

Golegole, n. sometimes *goligoli*, **Goregore**, the Tanganyika kakelaar, *Phoeniculus purpureus*.

Gololi,* n. *ma*- a marble (for playing with), round ball of glass such as are used as stoppers in some kinds of bottles of soda water, &c., ball-bearings of cycles, motor-cars, &c. (Pers. غلوله marble, pellet.)

Goma, n. amplic. of *ngoma*.

Goma, v. refuse, be firm in demanding one's right, show fight, *watu wamegoma hawataki kufanya kazi*, the people have struck, they won't work (i.e. until their affairs are settled to their satisfaction).

Gomba, n. *ma-* fibre of the banana plant, *mgomba*, which see.

Gomba, v. (1) contradict, forbid, gainsay; (2) argue (with), quarrel (with), wrangle. *Anagomba na mkewe*, he is squabbling with his wife. Prep. **Gombea**, argue (for, against, at, &c.), press a claim. *Gombea ngazi*, quarrel over the gangway. *Gombea cheo*, stand up for one's rank (position, status). *Alitukanwa kwa sababu alikugombea*, he was abused because he stood up for you. Cs. **Gombeza** (followed by Neg. Subjunctive) (1) strictly forbid; (2) make quarrel, make a quarrel, scold. *Tumegombezwa tusiende*, we are forbidden to go. St. of Cs. **Gombezeka**, be blameworthy, deserve scolding. Rp. **Gombana**, quarrel with each other, squabble. **-gomvi**, a. quarrelsome, contentious. **Magombezi**, n. plur. opposition, prohibitions, that which causes a quarrel. **Magombezo**, n. plur. quarrellings. **Mgomba**, n. *wa-* like *mgomvi*, but governing a noun following. **Mgombezi**, n. *wa-* one who continually forbids others. **Mgomvi**, n. *wa-* a quarrelsome person, brawler. **Ugomvi**, n. (*gomvi, magomvi*) quarrelsomeness, contentiousness, bad temper, wrangling, a quarrel. (Cf. *bisha, zoza, kataza, tela, nenea*.)

Gomba kanzu, n. a perennial mat grass growing in sand near the sea shore, good fodder, *Stenotaphrum demidiatum*.

Gombeza, v. See under **Gomba**, v.

Gombo, n. *ma-* leaf (sheet) of a book, but usu. *ukurasa*.

Gome, n. *ma-* the hard external covering of trees and some animals, bark, shell. *Ambua magome*, strip off the bark. Used of shell of crustaceans—lobster, &c., also of mollusca, and as a colloquial word for a rupee in Zanzibar.

-gomvi, a. See under **Gomba**, v.

Gona, v. lie down, sleep, but usu. *lala* is used; the following derivatives are, however, in common use. Cs. **Gonya**, cause to sleep, but only used of pacifying spirits of the dead, e.g. *gonya koma*, appease spirits of ancestors (cf. *tambika*). **Kigono**, n. *vi-* a camping-place, place slept in on a journey. **Mgoni**, n. *wa-* an adulterer (cf. *mzinzi, mwasherati*). **Ngono**, n. plur. (Note: sing. rarely used), (1) sexual intercourse; (2) sleeping-turn, a wife's turn or time for sleeping with her husband; (3) sleeping time, night. **Nyono**, the breathing of a person when asleep. **Ugoni**, n. (1) a fine imposed for adultery; (2) an act of adultery; (3) act of surprising one committing adultery. **Ugono**, n. (*ngono*) same as *ngono* above.

Gonasokola, n. a herb or shrub, *Acalypha* sp. Also called *mtata*.

Gonda, n. a kind of lizard, also called *mjusi Islamu*. (Cf. *mjusi*.)

Gondi, n. *ma-* claw of a crab, or lobster, &c. (Cf. *gando*.)

Gonga, v. beat, strike, knock. *Gonga mlango*, knock at a door. Ps. **Gongwa**. Prep. **Gongea**. Rp. of Prep. **Gongeana**, e.g. *kugongeana bilauri*, to strike glasses together in drinking healths. Cs. **Gongeza**. Rp. **Gongana**, knock against each other, collide, e.g. *vyombo vinagongana*, the vessels are colliding. Prep. of Stc. of Cv. **Gongomea**, hammer, give blows to, drive with blows, as rivets, nails, pegs, stakes, &c., and so 'nail up'. Ps. **Gongomewa**, be fastened, nailed up. **Gongo**, n. *ma-* amplic. of *kigongo, vi-* a thick, heavy stick, cudgel, club, bludgeon. (Cf. *piga, bisha*.)

Gongo, n. *ma-* (1) see under **Gonga**; (2) see under **Mgongo**.

Gongomea, v. (1) see under **Gonga**, (2) put heated metal on the ground to cool.

Gongonola, n. the woodpecker, also called *gogota* and *kigogota*.

Gong'otoa, v. hatch out eggs. (Cf. *angua*.)

-gonjwa, a. sick, ill, unwell, indisposed. **Mgonjwa**, n. *wa-* a sick person, an invalid, used of any bodily ailment, serious or slight. (Cf. *mwele.*)

Gonjweza, v. cause to be ill, make ill or sick. *Jigonjweza*, pretend to be sick, sham sickness, behave as if sick. **Ugonjwa**, n. *ma-* sickness, illness, disease, ill health. *Shikwa* (*patwa na, patikana na, ingia*) *ugonjwa*, get ill. *Tia* (*fanya, leta*) *ugonjwa*, cause sickness. *Ondoa* (*ponya*) *ugonjwa*, cure sickness. *Toka ugonjwani, poa ugonjwa*, recover from sickness. (Cf. *maradhi, uele.*)

Gonya, v. See under **Gona.**

Goregore, n. See **Golegole.**

Gorong'ondo, n. *ma-* the leg of an ox or any kind of animal.

Gorong'ondwa, n. a kind of lizard.

Gorong'ondwa, v. go zigzag, go crooked. (Cf. *pogo* under *pogoa*, and *mshazari.*)

Gota, v. see also **Gogota**, knock, tap, rap, strike. *Gota mlango*, tap at a door. Rd. **Gotagota**, of drumming on an instrument. **Mgoto**, n. *mi-* (1) act of beating, knocking together, blows, strokes, clashing, sudden meeting, conflict, and (2) commonly of the sound of such beating, e.g. *mgoto wa makasia*, the beat of oars—both act and sound; *mgoto wa maji*, the sound of meeting or falling water.

Goti, n. *ma-* knee. *Piga magoti*, kneel down. *Pia ya goti*, knee-cap.

Govi, n. *ma-*, also **Ngovi**, the prepuce. An uncircumcised person is referred to as *mwenye ngovi* (*govi*). (Cf. *zunga.*)

Goya, n. See under **Ngoeka.**

Guba,* n. See **Kikuba.**

Gubeti,* n. prow of a native vessel; head, figure-head, often projecting far in front, and ornamented with carving, &c., described as *kikono cha omo*, as being like a hand held out from the bow. (Cf. *omo, -hanamu*. Ar. كبد middle, principal part, see *shetri*, poop, stern, which also simply means part of a thing.)

Gubi, n. *ma-* leaf-stalk of coco-nut tree (*mnazi*).

Gubigubi, a. See under **Gubika.**

Gubika, v. cover over. Ps. **Gubikwa.** Cs. **Gubisha.** Cv. **Gubua**, uncover. **Gubigubi**, a. covered from head to foot, as with a garment. *Amejifunika gubigubi*, he has covered himself from head to foot. **Magubiko**, n. plur. (1) formerly a present given by caravans to a chief for permission to rest in his country; (2) secret matters.

Gubiti,* n. a stick of boiled sugar, a sweetmeat liked very much by children. (Pers. كبيته kind of sweetmeat.)

Gubu,* n. annoyance, trouble, vexation. *Mtu mwenye gubu*, one who will not let a matter rest, one who nags, one who annoys by harping on a subject. (Ar. غب recurrence.)

Gubua, v., **Gubigubi**, a. See under **Gubika.**

Gude, n. (1) the white-browed coucal, also called *dudumizi, shundi*, and *tipitipi*; (2) a tool used for boring, an awl.

Gudi,* n. *ma-*. See under **Gadi**, n. (A).

Gudulia,* n. pitcher, porous water-jar, water-cooler of earthenware, with a bottle-like neck. (Ar. قدرة narrow bottle, pot.)

Gugu, n. *ma-* weed, undergrowth, wild plant of no value. *Gugu mwitu*, a plant resembling corn tare. *Lala maguguni*, sleep in the bush; used also as indeclin. adj. (like *mwitu*), wild, uncultivated, from the jungle. **Kigugu**, n. *vi-* also adv. (1) a small weed or wild plant; (2) like a weed, like weeds, in a wild uncultivated way, e.g. *nyumba hizi zimejengwa kigugu*, these houses are built like weeds—all huddled together. *Panda kigugu*, plant too close together.

Gugumia, v. (1) drink to the dregs; (2) swallow with a gurgling sound, gulp; (3) stutter, falter in speaking. Cs. and Inten. **Gugumiza**, (1) gulp,

gulp down, swallow with a gurgling sound, or with difficulty, splutter in the water—as a swimmer in rough water or man out of his depth; (2) also of defective utterance. *Mgonjwa amegugumiza maji*, the sick man has swallowed some water with an effort. *Agugumiza maneno*, he talks in a jerky, spluttering way. **Kigugumizi**, n. *vi-* and adv. stammering, stuttering, speaking in jerks or gulps, &c., described as *kigugumizi cha maneno*, or *maneno ya kigugumizi*. (Cf. *goteza, kokoteza.*)

Gugumu, n. an unpleasant odour of the human body; that of the perspiration of some people's armpits is called *kikwapa* and *kutuzi*.

Gugumua, n. a reed grass up to 12 ft. tall, with somewhat spiny leaf-tips and heads of white or buff flowers, growing in swamps and on the margins of lakes and rivers. The stems are used for hut building, fences, matting, and general wicker-work and arrow shafts, *Phragmites communis*.

Guguna, v. (1) gnaw, bite at, chew; (2) carp at, annoy, molest. Ps. **Gugunwa**. St. and Pot. **Gugunika**. Prep. **Gugunia**. Cv. **Gugunua**, make a contemptuous sound, annoy. (Cf. *fyonya, ng'ong'a.*)

Gugurusha, v. also heard as **Gurugusha**, (1) of movement, producing a rustling or scraping sound, as of a rat, rustle about, shuffle along, rattle about; (2) twirl round like a grind-stone; (3) drag, haul along on the ground. (Cf. *chakarisha, zunguka, burura, buruta, furukuta.*)

Guguta, n. cob of maize with the grains removed. **Kiguguta**, n. *vi-* dim. (Cf. *gunzi, kigunzi.*)

Guia, v. (1) seize, catch, hold. *Guia mnyama*, catch an animal in a trap; also (2) fig. overtake, as of darkness. *Niliguiwa na giza*, I was overtaken by darkness. Ps. **Guiwa**. Cs. **Guiza**. (Cf. *shika, kamata, nasa, tega*, all of which are more common.)

Gulabi,* n. *ma-* litchee, fruit of the *mgulabi*.

Gulegule, n. a kind of fish like a porpoise.

Gulio, n. *ma-* a market, a place for buying and selling things, but *soko* is more common at the coast. **Kigulio**, n. *vi-* same as *gulio*.

Guma, v. also Prep. **Gumia** with the same meaning, growl, bark as of a dog when startled. **Gumio**, n. *ma-* also **Mgumio**, n. *mi-* a bark (of a dog). (Cf. *bweka.*)

Gumba, a. solitary, alone, sterile. *Kidole gumba*, the thumb. *Mtu gumba* (also *mgumba*, n. *wa-*), a childless sterile man, and therefore solitary, alone.

Gumbizi, n. dizziness, vertigo. (Cf. *kizunguzungu, kisulisuli.*)

Gumbu, n. a kind of musical instrument made out of a calabash.

Gumegume, n. *bunduki ya gumegume*, a flint-gun.

Gumia, v., **Gumio**, n. *ma-*. See under **Guma**.

-gumu, a. (1) hard, tough, firm, solid, strong. (Contr. *-ororo, laini, dhaifu.*) (2) hard to deal with, difficult, laborious, puzzling. (Contr. *rahisi, -epesi.*) (3) brave, resolute, courageous, obstinate, self-willed, fixed, unyielding; (4) inexorable, hard-hearted. (Contr. *-ema, -pole, -a huruma.*) **Ugumu**, n. hardness, obstinacy, difficulty, &c. **Vigumu**, in an adv. sense, *ni vigumu kusadiki mambo hayo*, it is difficult to believe those things. (Cf. *-shupavu, -zito.*)

Guna, v. (1) grunt, grumble, murmur; (2) express disapproval, indignation, contempt, 'protest, complain, sneer at'. **Guno**, n. *ma-* grunt, grumble—sound expressive of indignation or contempt. **Mguno**, n. *mi-* a grumbling, grunting, murmuring, complaining, discontent. (Cf. *nung'unika, nuna.*)

Gunda, n. *ma-* a horn used for blowing. Dim. **Kigunda**, *vi-*. (Cf. *pembe, baragumu, siwa.*)

Gundi,* n. gum paste (for sticking things), rubber solution, &c. (Hind. گوند.)

Gundua, v. come upon unexpectedly, take by surprise, catch unawares, startle, start (a wild animal from its lair), &c. Ps. **Gunduliwa.** St. and Pot. **Gunduka.** Prep. **Gundulia,** steal upon, approach secretly, stalk. (Cf. *nyemelea*). Cs. **Gundulisha.** Rp. **Gunduana.** (Cf. *shtusha, shtuka, fumania, nyemelea, vumbua.*)

Gunga, v. (1) treat medically, give medical attention; (2) refrain from eating certain foods for health reasons, keep a taboo; (3) warn; (4) overcome a temptation; (5) coax. **Mgunga,** n. *wa-* a person who is undergoing medical treatment and in consequence of which is refraining from certain foods, &c. (Cf. *ganga, zia* (4), *mwiko, mziro.*)

Gungu, n. *ma-* an old term for a mode of dancing, a figure in a dance, e.g. *gungu la kukwaa,* the stumbling figure; *gungu la kufunda,* the pounding figure. Seldom heard now.

Guni,* n. *ma-* (1) a matting bag used for packing dates (Hind. گون); (2) a carpenter's spokeshave (? confusion between Hind. گنيا a mason's or carpenter's square); (3) blank verse as opp. to rhymed poetry, *Mashairi yenye vina* (Ar. غنى song). **Kiguni,** n. *vi-* dim. of (1).

Gunia,* n. *ma-* a coarse bag or sack chiefly used for packing rice and grain, also the material from which it is made, sackcloth. (Hind. گون.)

Guno, n. *ma-.* See under **Guna.**

Gunzi, n. *ma-* cob of maize after the grain has been removed. Dim. **Kigunzi,** *vi-.* (Cf. *guguta.*)

Gura, v. move one's dwelling to another place. (Cf. *hama.*)

Guru,* n. (1) *sukari guru,* a coarse unrefined kind of sugar made from the cane, and sold in dark-coloured lumps; (2) sometimes heard for *nguru,* which see. (Hind. گر.)

Gurudumu,* n. *ma-* a wheel. (Pers. گردون.)

Guruguru, n. *ma-* (1) a large kind of burrowing lizard; (2) a kind of sole which is very good eating.

Gurugusha, v. (1) variant of *gugurusha,* which see; (2) bungle, make a mess of work, spoil work.

Gururu,* n. thick milk. (Ar. غرر (plur.) anything white, the best of a thing.)

Guruta, v. smooth with a press, put through the rollers of a mangling machine, mangle—of clothes and linen generally. *Guruta nguo hizi vizuri,* mangle these clothes properly. Ps. **Gurutwa.** St. and Pot. **Gurutika.** Prep. **Gurutia.** Cs. **Gurutisha.** **Guruto,** n. *ma-* a mangle, press. **Mguruto,** n. *mi-* the act of mangling, pressing, &c.

Gusa, v. touch, finger, handle with the fingers. Ps. **Guswa.** St. and Pot. **Gusika.** Prep. **Gusia.** Rp. **Gusana.** **Mguso,** n. *mi-* a touch. (Cf. *tomasa, papasa, bonyeza.*)

Guta, v. (1) bawl, shout, cry out; (2) push, gore, as of an ox. Prep. **Gutia.** Cs. **Gutisha.** (Cf. *lia, piga kelele.*)

Gutu, n. *ma-* stump, remainder. *Gutu la mkono,* stump of a mutilated arm. (Cf. *kikono.*) *Gutu la mnazi,* trunk of a coco-nut-tree with the crown broken off. **-gutu,** a. blunt. **Kigutu,** n. *vi-* dim. (Cf. *butu.*)

Gutua, v. (1) take away suddenly, do anything suddenly; (2) startle, frighten, surprise; (3) set a dislocated limb. Cs. **Gutusha.** St. **Gutuka.**

Guu, n. *ma-* amplic. of *mguu.*

Guzi, n. *ma-, guzi la mnazi,* the dead dry midriff of coco-nut-tree, collected and used for firewood.

Gwa, v. fall down—seldom heard. (Cf. *anguka.*)

Gwafua, v. (1) show the teeth and snarl, attack with teeth bared, as of a dog or wild animal; (2) seize and bite at suddenly.

Gwanda, n. *ma-* a garment like a smock or short *kanzu* reaching to the knees, made of calico, sometimes worn by men.

Gwaraza, v. grind, make a grinding sound, e.g. *gwaraza meno*, grind the teeth. (Cf. *saga*.)

Gwaride,* n. *ma-* drill, parade. *Kucheza gwaride*, to drill. (Ar. عرض parade, review.)

Gwaru, n. the cluster bean, pods used for curries, fruit of the *mgwaru*.

Gwasi, n. a warthog. (Cf. *mbango*.)

Gwaya, v. tremble (for fear, cold, &c.). (Cf. *tetemeka*.)

Gwia, v. See **Guia**.

Gwiji, n. and a. brave, expert, smart, clever (person), generally used of *waganga*, i.e. medicine men.

H

H represents the same sound as in English. It stands for both forms of the Arabic *h* in words of Arabic origin, and also for the Arabic *kh*, which is usually softened to *h* in pronunciation. *Kh* is still sometimes retained, however, in the spelling of proper names containing that sound, i.e. *Khalifa, Khalfani*, &c.

Haba,* a. (1) little (in quantity), few; (2) rare, scarce; (3) not enough, deficient, too little, short (in amount). *Chakula haba*, not enough food. *Siku haba*, a few days, insufficient time; used as a n., 'a little' of anything (cf. *kidogo*). Prov. *Haba na haba hujaza kibaba*, little and little fills the measure. **Uhaba**, n. (1) fewness, scantiness, rarity; (2) being too few. (Cf. *-chache, kidogo, kitambo, punje*. Ar. حب grain, seed.)

Haba,* n. See under **Hebu**, v.

Hababi,* n. master, my Lord, sir. (Cf. *bwana, maulana*. Ar. حبيب.)

Habali,* a. irresponsible, irascible, hot-tempered—seldom used. (Ar. خبل.)

Habari,* n. (1) news, report, message, information; (2) events, matters, proceedings, things. Common in salutations, of persons meeting, e.g. *Habari?* or *Habari gani?* How are you? How are you getting on? Or *Habari za siku nyingi?* How have you been this long time past? *Niambie habari zako*, Tell me your news. *Kwa habari ya jambo lile*, as to that matter. *Habari zangu zilizonipata*, things that happened to me. *Jinsi gani kutufanya habari ile?* What did you treat us like that for? **Hubiri**, v. give information (to, about), inform, bring news (to, about), announce, report, relate. *Hubiri Injili*, preach the Gospel. Ps. **Hubiriwa**. Prep. **Hubiria**. Cs. **Hubirisha**. **Hubiri**, n. *ma-* (1) message, &c., like *habari*; (2) a sermon. **Mhubiri**, n. *wa-* a preacher, one who announces or brings news. (Cf. *arifu, simulia, eleza, tangaza, jambo.* Ar. خبر.)

Habedari!* int. Look out! Make way! Take care! Protect yourself against! *Habedari! njia uendako ni hatari,* Have a care! the road you are going in is dangerous. (Cf. *hadhari, simile, angalia.* Pers. خبردار.)

Habeshi,* n. *ma-*, also **Mhabeshi**, *wa-* an Abyssinian. (Ar. حبشي.)

Habithi,* n. (1) a cruel, corrupt, malicious, evil person; (2) cruelty, wickedness, corruption. (Cf. *fasiki, fisadi, katili, -baya, -ovu.* Ar. خبث.)

Hadaa,* v. cheat, deceive, outwit. Ps. **Hadaiwa**. St. and Pot. **Hadaika**, be deceived. **Hadaa**, n. deception, cunning, trickery, &c. (Cf. *danganya, punja, kalamkia,* also *hila ujanja, werevu.* Ar. خدع.)

Hadhara,* adv. in front of, in the presence of, before. *Alinipiga hadhara ya watu,* he struck me in public, before people. **Hudhuria**, v. Prep. be present (at), attend a meeting, form an audience. *Enyi watu mliohudhuria*—the opening words of a speech, address to an audience, All you who are present, equivalent to *enyi watu mliopo hapa* (cf. *-wapo*). Cs. **Hudhurisha**. **Hudhurio**, n. *ma-* an attendance, e.g. at school, &c. **Hadhiri**, v. also Cs. **Hadhirisha**, make public, show before people. (Ar. حضر.)

Hadhari,* v. exercise care, be cautious, act with prudence, be on guard (against), avoid. *Hadhari kwa adui,* be on guard against (be on the lookout for) the enemy. *Jihadhari!* a common cry of warning, Mind yourself! Look out! Take care!—like *simile* and *habedari*. **Hadhari**, n. caution, care, prudence. Common in such phrases as *kuwa na hadhari,* to be on one's guard; *kutia hadhari,* to put on one's guard, to caution. Also *fanya hadhari.* **Tahadhari**, v. same as *hadhari. Tahadhari kabla ya katari,* be on guard against danger. (Cf. *angalia, jilinda, kuwa macho.* Ar. حذر.)

Hadhi,* n. comfortable circumstances, position of respect, honour, circumstances befitting, such as is due to a wife or husband in her or his own house, &c. (Cf. *heshima, staha, cheo.* Ar. حظ.)

Hadhiri,* v. See under **Hadhara**.

Hadi,* (1) prep. until, up to, as far as, as much as—implying a point, object, degree, or condition in view. *Toka hapa hadi huko,* from here to there. *Tangu asubuhi hadi jioni,* from morning to evening. (2) conj. (*a*) connective, so, then, next, *hadi asubuhi,* so in the morning. *Hadi siku moja,* one day; (*b*) subordinative, so as to, *Nitafanya akili gani hadi tugawe sawasawa?* What plan shall I devise so that we may divide equally? (3) adv. *Hadi nitampiga,* I will even beat him, I will go so far as to beat him. (Used practically in the same way as *hata, mpaka.* Ar. حد limit, boundary.)

Hadimu,* n. *ma-*, also **Mhadimu**, n. *wa-* servant, attendant, slave (also *Mhadimu, wa-*, one of the original inhabitants of Zanzibar, now living mostly in the east and south of the island). **Hudumu**, v. serve, wait (on), attend (on). Ps. **Hudumiwa**. St. **Hudumika**. Prep. **Hudumia**, serve, be in attendance upon, serve (at, with, &c.). Cs. **Hudumisha**. **Huduma**, also **Hudumu**, n. service, attendance, &c. (Cf. *tumika, ngoja.* Ar. خدم.)

Hadithi,* n. story, tale, account, report, history, legend, fiction. *Ni hadithi tu,* it is only a story, mere fiction. **Hadithi**, v. but generally Prep. **Hadithia**, narrate (to, about, in, &c.), tell stories, describe, recount, report (to, about, in, &c.). Ps. **Hadithiwa**, be told, e.g. *tumehadithiwa*, we have been told. (Cf. *ngano, simulia, kisa, hekaya*. Ar. حدث.)

Hafifu,* a. trifling, insignificant, poor in quality, valueless, frivolous. Sometimes a v. is made **Hafifisha**, reduce to insignificance, make light of, &c. **Tahafifu**, a. same as *hafifu*. **Uhafifu**, n. commonness, poor quality, worthlessness, insignificance. (Cf. *dhaifu, ghafi, duni, -nyonge*. Ar. خفف.)

Hai,* a. alive, living, having life, animate. **Hui**, v. become alive, revive, rise from the dead, both of animal and plant life. Ps. **Huiwa**. St. **Huika**, be given life, e.g. *amehuiwa na Mungu, naye amehuika*, he has been restored to life by God, and has revived. Cs. **Huisha**, restore to life, revive, save, keep alive. *Hui* is also used in this act. sense. **Uhai**, n. life, the condition of being alive. (Cf. *-zima, ishi, fufua*. Ar. حي.)

Haiba,* n. beauty of countenance, appearance, but esp. of character. (Cf. *uzuri, wema*. Ar. هيبة).

Haidhuru,* neg. of impersonal form of *dhuru*, v. which see, meaning it does not matter, never mind, do not bother, it is all the same.

Haini,* n. traitor, betrayer, deceiver, renegade. **Haini**, v. betray, deceive. **Uhaini**, n. betrayal, perfidy, treachery. (Cf. *saliti, toa, danganya*. Ar. خون deceive, &c.)

Haitasa, a neg. impersonal form of *tasa*, v. meaning not yet be; rarely used except in Mombasa. *Sitasa kwenda*, I have not yet gone. *Saa haitasa*, the time is not yet finished.

Haja,* n. (1) need, want, appeal for aid, request; (2) reason, cause, ground, excuse, claim, right; (3) what is needed, necessaries, belongings, engagements; (4) calls of nature. *Toa haja kwa, taka haja kwa*, make a request to, request something of. *Sina haja nayo*, I have no need of it. *Haina haja kugombana*, there is no reason for quarrelling. *Kwenda haja*, to go to the lavatory. *Shikwa na haja*, feel the need of going to the lavatory. **Hoja**, n. also **Huja**, (1) want, need, necessity; (2) what is urgent or pressing, business, concern; (3) urgent request, argument, logical demonstration. *Kwa hoja ya*, on account of. *Hakuna hoja*, there is no objection. *Jambo hili lina hoja nyingi*, this is a very troublesome affair. *Hoja* preceded by *si* is often used with the meaning of not only, e.g. *si hoja ya hiki tu ila kile pia*, not only this, but also that as well. **Hoji**, v. and **Huji**, cross-question, examine, ply with arguments. Sometimes Rd. *hojihoji*. *Alimhojihoji hata akasema neno alilo nalo*, he kept on asking until he said what he knew. Prep. **Hojia**. Ps. **Hojiwa**. Rp. **Hojiana**. **Uhaji**, n. necessity, need, being in want. (Cf. *taka, hitaji, dadisi, tafuta*. Ar. حوج want, need, and حجة proof argument, pretext, &c.)

Hajambo, verb-form—Neg. Pfx. of 3 Pers. Sing. combined with *jambo*, thing, affair, matter—he is not (affected by) anything, there is nothing the matter with him. See **Jambo**. Note: this form, and that with the 2 Pers. Sing. *hujambo*, are often used as nouns meaning better in health, improvement in health, &c. *Alikuwa mgonjwa, leo amepata hajambo (hujambo)*, he was ill, but to-day he is better.

Haji,* n. pilgrimage to Mecca. **Hiji**, v. or *enda haji*, go as a pilgrim to Mecca. See **Uhaji**, n. (A). (Ar. حج.)

Hajiri,* v. remove (from), leave, emigrate, move house. **Mhajiri**, n. *wa-* one who moves from his home and settles elsewhere. (Cf. *hama*. Ar. هاجر.)

Hajivale, n. the African Harrier-hawk, *Gymnogenys typicus*. (Cf. *shakevale*.)

Haka,* n. payment for privilege, e.g. *kushika haka*, make pay an entrance fee to an association, club, guild, or pay footing, as a stranger intruding, impose a fine for breach of rules of a club, &c. (? Ar. حيق consequence of a wicked action falling back on the perpetrator.)

Hakali,* n. used in the same way as *haka*, prec. (? Ar. عقل intelligence.)

Hakamu,* n. used in the same way as *haka* and *hakali*, prec. (Ar. حكم cf. *hukumu*.)

Haki,* n. (1) justice, right, lawfulness. *Mtu wa haki*, a just man. *Hukumu haki*, or *kwa haki*, judge justly. *Shika* (or *fanya*) *haki*, be just, deal justly. A common expletive is *Mtume wa haki* the prophet (i.e. Muhammad) of righteousness, &c. (2) in general, absolute justice, righteousness. *Mungu ni mwenye haki*, God is the Righteous One; (3) in particular, a claim, right, privilege, a just share. *Nipe haki yangu*, give me my wages, my dues. *Nakuuliza kwa haki*, I have a right to ask you. **Stahika**, v. be worthy, respected. **Stahiki**, v. be fitting (proper, suitable, becoming), be obligatory on, be a duty, be worthy (deserving) of. **-stahiki**, a. deserving, honourable, respected. **Ustahiki**, n. esteem, honour, worthiness. (Cf. *heshima*, *wajibu*, *juzu*, *stahi*. (Ar. حق and استحق.)

Hakika,* n. certainty, reality, genuineness, fact, essential, truth. *Mambo haya ni hakika*, these are facts. *Hakika yako*, truth as to you, you certainly, e.g. *hakika yako umekosa*, you are certainly wrong. *Sina hakika nalo*, I am not sure about it. As adv. truly, certainly, really. **Hakiki**, v. make sure about, ascertain, investigate, prove, know for certain. Ps. **Hakikiwa**. St. and Pot. **Hakikika**, e.g. *haihakikiki*, certainty is unattainable. Prep. **Hakikia**, inquire into (about, for, at). Cs. **Hakikisha**, cause to investigate, and Inten. make a strict inquiry, have a matter gone into. (Cf. *yakini*, *kweli*, *halisi*. Ar. حقيقة.)

Hakimu,* n. *ma-*. See under **Hukumu**.

Hakiri,* v. treat with contempt, despise, abase. Cs. **Hakirisha**, e.g. as Inten. vilify, scorn. (Cf. *dharau*, *tweza*. Ar. حقر.)

Hakuna, verb-form, often used as simple negative, no, not so, it is not. (Cf. *hamna*, *hapana*, *la*, *siyo*.)

Halafa,* n. (1) an oath. (Cf. *kiapo*. Ar. حلف.) (2) See under **Halifu**.

Halafu,* adv. after a bit, afterwards, presently, not yet. Also commonly *halafu yake*, afterwards. Always of time. (Cf. *baada*, *baadaye*, *bado kidogo*, *hatima*, *nyuma*.) **Halifu**, v. leave behind, esp. at death, i.e. bequeath. (Cf. *acha*, *rithisha*. From the same root as *halifu* and *hitilafu*. Ar. خلف.)

Halahala!* int. immediately! at once! (Cf. *upesi*, *sasa hivi*. Ar. حالا immediately.)

Halaiki,* n. much (of), many, abundance, collection, crowd. *Halaiki ya watu*, a crowd of people, many people. (Cf. *wingi*, *kundi*, *umati*, *kaumu*. Ar. خلائق or علق troop, herd, &c.)

Halali,* a. lawful, permissible, allowed, rightful, optional, available, ceremonially clean. *Mke wa halali yake*, his lawful wedded wife. *Halali kwenda*, you may go if you like. Also as a n., *halali yako*, it is right for you, you may. *Ni halali yako kula nyama hii*, it is right (lawful, e.g. according to your religion) to eat this meat. *Kichwa changu ni halali yako*, my head is at your mercy. Cs. **Halalisha**, make lawful, legalize, declare right, free from legal or ceremonial objections or disabilities. Ps. **Halalishwa.** (Cf. *haki*, and contr. *haramu.* Ar. حلل.)

Halasa,* n. (1) profit in trade; (2) rarely met with—sailor's wages. **Halisi,** v. get profit in trade. (Cf. *chuma, faida.* Ar. خلص.)

Hali,* n. state, condition, circumstances, case. A common form of address is *Hali gani?* or *U hali gani?* How are you? (Cf. *habari, jambo, salamu.*) *Sina hali,* I am in poor circumstances. *Kwa kila hali,* in any case. *Hali moja na,* on same side as, of same views as, the same as, &c. Often used in the sense of 'seeing that'. *Mbona ulifanya hivyo hali ulijua imegombezwa?* Why did you do that seeing that you knew (being in the condition of, being cognizant of the fact that), it is forbidden. Also as 'meanwhile'. *Alikwenda hali analia,* she went crying (in the meanwhile, i.e. as she was going). Sometimes **Uhali,** n. is used for *hali.* (Ar. حال.)

Halifu,* v. (A) oppose, contradict, contravene, rebel (against), disobey. *Halifu mfalme,* or *kwa mfalme,* rebel against the king. *Halifu sheria,* transgress the law. Cs. **Halifisha,** incite to disobedience, &c. **Halafa,** n. opposition, difference. **Halifu,** a. rebellious, disobedient, headstrong. **Hilafu,** n. same as *halafa.* **Uhalifu,** n. (*halifu* and *ma-*) disobedience, transgression, breaking rules, rebellion, naughtiness. (Cf. *asi, kaidi, pinga, bisha, teta.* From the same root as *halafu* and *hitilafu.* Ar. خالف.)

Halifu,* v. (B) bequeath. See under **Halafu.**

Halili,* n. beloved person. (Ar. خليل.)

Halimtumwa, n. a kind of sweet potato. (Cf. *kiazi.*)

Halisi,* a. real, genuine, true, exact, precise, accurate. *Mwungwana halisi,* a true, genuine gentleman. Also adv. exactly, perfectly, really, just, just so. (Cf. *hasa, sawasawa, kweli.* Ar. خالص.)

Halisi,* v. See under **Halasa.**

Halkumu,* n. jugular vein. (Ar. حلقوم.)

Halmashauri,* n. See under **Shauri.**

Halua,* n. a common sweetmeat made of flour, eggs, sugar, ghee, &c. Turkish delight. (Ar. حلوى.)

Halula,* n. an abscess, boil, or swelling in the throat, inflammation of the throat, swelling of the glands of the throat, esp. those just underneath the jaw, quinsy. (Cf. *hijabu, mlezi.* Ar. خلل disorder.)

Haluli,* n. a purgative medicine. *Chumvi ya haluli,* sulphate of magnesia, Epsom salts. (Cf. *sanamaki.* Ar. خلل looseness.)

Halzeti,* olive oil, sometimes *mafuta ya halzeti.* (Ar. زيتونة olive, زيت oil.)

Hama, v. change habitation, emigrate, flit, remove (from). *Hama nyumba* (*mji, nchi*), move from a house (town, country). Prep. **Hamia,** move to. Cs. **Hamisha,** e.g. cause to remove, eject, banish, transport, move from a place (of persons or objects). **-hamaji,** a. wandering, nomad, migratory, homeless. **Hamiji,** n. *wa-* (1) wandering, unsettled, homeless person, a nomad, pilgrim, tramp, vagrant; (2) one who constantly moves things about. **Hame,** n. *ma-* also **Kihame,** n. a deserted place, an abandoned village or town. **Uhamaji,** n. migration, i.e. of customary migration such as of birds, &c. (Cf. *hujuru, hajiri.*)

Hamadi!* int. used frequently when a person stumbles. Cf. the Prov. under *bindo.* (Ar. ? عمد prop up, support.)

Hamaki,* v. be seized with sudden temper, become suddenly vexed. **Hamaki,** n. sudden anger, violent sudden burst of temper. (Ar. حنق.)

Hamali,* n. *ma-* (1) porter, carrier, coolie, but only in coast towns such as Zanzibar, Mombasa, &c. (Cf. *mchukuzi, mpagazi.*) (2) freight, used in such terms as *gari la hamali*, a cart used for carrying loads, drawn by men, a hamali cart. **Himila,** n. (1) load, burden, for the common *mzigo*; (2) pregnancy (cf. *mimba*). *Mke wangu ana himila, amechukua mimba*, my wife is with child, she has conceived. **Himili,** v. (1) bear, support; (2) bear, endure, accept, be equal to; (3) be pregnant. (Cf. the common *chukua.*) Ps. **Himiliwa. Mhimili,** n. *mi-* that which carries (bears, supports a beam, post, prop, bearing). **Mhimili,** n. *wa-* a patient enduring person. **Stahimili,** v. endure, support, persevere, put up with, be patient. **-stahimilivu,** a. patient, persevering, long-suffering. Prov. *Mstahimilivu hula kibivu*, a patient man eats ripe (fruit). **Ustahimili,** n., **Ustahimilivu,** n. patience, perseverance, endurance. (Cf. *vumilia, saburi.* Ar. حمل.)

Hamamu,* n. a public bath, bathing establishment. (Cf. *hodhi.* Ar. حمام.)

Hamanika, v. be confused, busy with affairs, trouble, anxious, excited. (Cf. *hangaika.* ? St. form from Ar. همه be perplexed.)

Hamaya,* n. See **Himaya.**

Hamdu,* n. See under **Himidi.**

Hame, n. *ma-*. See under **Hama.**

Hami,* v. protect, defend. (Cf. *himaya, linda, hifadhi* and *amia* which is prob. from the same root. Ar. حمى.)

Hamira,* n. leaven, yeast, made by mixing flour and water and leaving them to turn sour. (Cf. *chachu.* Ar. خمير.)

Hamisha, v., **-hamishi** a. See under **Hama.**

Hamna, verb-form: there is not inside, there is not, no—same as *hakuna, hapana*, but with *m* of reference to interior.

Hamrawi,* n. rope attached to lower or forward end of the yard in a native vessel, to steady it and assist in shifting, when tacking. (Cf. *henza.* ? corruption of Ar. مرارى hempen rope.)

Hamsa,* n. and a. five. Rarely used alone, for the common Bantu *tano. Hamsa mia*, five hundred. **Hamsini,** n. and a. fifty. *-a hamsini*, fiftieth. **Hamstashara,** n. and a. fifteen. *-a hamstashara*, fifteenth. **Hamsauishirini,** n. and a. twenty-five. *-a hamsauishirini*, twenty-fifth, for the commoner *ishirini na tano.* (Ar. خمسه.)

Hamu,* n. longing, yearning, anxiety, love, desire for something (either good or bad). *Kuwa na* (or *kuona*) *hamu*, desire, long for, yearn after. (Cf. *shauku, uchu, ashiki*, and dist. *ghamu.* Ar. هم.)

Hamumi,* n. a kind of tobacco for smoking. (Cf. *tumbako.* ? Ar. حومان kind of plant.)

Hanamu,* n. and a. (1) oblique, aslant, sideways. *Kata hanamu*, cut obliquely. (2) *Hanamu ya chombo*, the cutwater of a vessel. *Hanamu ya ubao*, the sloping edge, bevel, &c., of a board. (Cf. *mshazari, kombo.* Ar. حنو bend, crook.)

Handaki,* n. *ma-* ditch, trench, channel (artificial). (Cf. *shimo, mfereji.* Ar. خندق.)

Hando,* n. *ma-* a copper vessel, similar to the earthenware *mtungi*, with narrow circular opening at the top, used chiefly by Indians for carrying and storing water. (Hind. هاندي.)

Hangaika, v. sometimes heard as *angaika*, be confused, busy with affairs, troubled, excited, anxious. Cs. **Hangaisha,** confuse, trouble, make anxious. St. **Hangaika. Hangaiko,** n. *ma-* anxiety, ado, worry (over affairs, much work, things going wrong, things coming unexpectedly, &c.). (Cf. *hamanika, shughulika, wasiwasi.*)

Hani,* v. mourn (with), pay a visit of condolence (to), join in a formal mourning. (Cf. *matanga.* Ar. هناء.)

Hanithi,* n. and a. (1) a sexual pervert; (2) impotent man (sexually); (3) a catamite; (4) a sodomite. As a. perverted (sexually), filthy, shameful (all with reference to sexual perversion). (Ar. خنث.)

Hanjari,* n. a scimitar, for the common *jambia.* (Ar. خنجر.)

Hanziri,* n. a pig, for the common *nguruwe.* (Ar. خنزير.)

Hanzua,* n. a kind of sword dance. (Ar. prob. from same root as prec.)

Hao, pron. of ref. 3 Pers. Plur. those referred to, those there.

Hapa, a. pron. of place, this place. *Hapa pazuri,* this is a nice place. *Toka hapa mpaka mjini,* from here to the town. *Njoo hapa,* come here. Sometimes *papa hapa,* just here, on this very spot. **Hapo,** a. pron. of reference. Used of place, time, and also more generally of circumstances. *Toka hapo!* get out of that! go along! *Hapo kale,* in the days of old, once upon a time, often at the beginning of stories. *Tangu hapo, tokea hapo,* from long ago, ever so long, also from now onwards, after now. *Hapo,* in that case, under the circumstances. *Akikataa, hapo mpige,* if he refuses, then (under those circumstances, &c.) beat him. *Hapo mbali,* that was a different case. Also *papo hapo,* just there, at that very place (time, crisis).

Hapana, verb-form, there is not there, there is none, no—same as *hakuna, hamna,* but with *pa,* agreeing with place. Commonly used as a simple negation, like *hakuna, la, siyo. Hapana (hakuna) mvua leo,* there is no rain to-day.

Hapo, verb-form, also **Hayupo,** (1) he (she) is not there; (2) see under **Hapa.**

Hara,* n. district of town, seldom used except with locative. *Harani,* the villages, district, &c., used by pedlars, hawkers going about travelling or bartering in the villages. (Ar. حارة quarter of city.)

Hara,* v. have looseness of the bowels, have diarrhoea. *Hara damu,* have dysentery, pass blood with the stools. *Dawa ya kuhara* (also with Cs. *kuharisha*), an aperient, a laxative, a purge. Cs. **Harisha,** cause to have looseness of the bowels, e.g. *Chakula hiki chaniharisha,* this food gives me diarrhoea. **Harisho,** n. (1) diarrhoea; (2) powerful purge. (Cf. *endesha* under *enda.* Ar. خر.)

Harabu,* n. (— and *ma-*) a destructive person, a spoiler, a ruffian, a vandal. **-harabu,** a. destructive, violent. **Haribu,** v. injure, destroy, spoil, damage, ruin, demoralize. *Haribu kazi,* spoil work. *Haribu safari,* break up an expedition. *Haribu nchi,* devastate a country. *Haribu mimba,* cause miscarriage. *Haribu moyo,* pervert, corrupt. Ps. **Haribiwa.** Prep. **Haribia.** St. and Pot. **Haribika.** Prep. **Haribikia,** be ruined, in respect of, suffer loss of. Ps. **Haribikiwa,** be the victim of violence, be robbed of everything, be utterly ruined. Cs. **Haribisha,** inflict ruin on. Rp. and Pot. **Haribikana,** be liable to destruction. **-haribifu,** a. destructive, wasteful, prodigal, doing harm, spoiling. *Mharibifu wa mali,* a spendthrift. **Mharabu,** n. *wa-* a destructive person, a destroyer, a vandal (like *harabu*). **Uharabu,** n. destructiveness, vandalism. **Uharibifu,** n. destruction, spoiling, corruption, mortality, waste. (Cf. *poteza, vunja, angamiza, potoa,* and derivatives. Ar. خرب.)

Haradali,* n. mustard, but *mastadi*

(Eng. mustard) is generally used. (Ar. خردل.)

Haragi,* *ma-*. See **Haragwe.**

Haragwe,* n. *ma-* a bean. The plant is *mharagwe*. (Pers. خرقی kind of grain.)

Haraja,* n. expense, outlay (of money), expenditure. **Hariji,** (v. spend money, incur expense. Prep. **Harijia,** spend money on, incur outlay for, make provision for, be liberal to. Ps. **Harijiwa.** (Cf. *gharimia*, which is more usual. Ar. خرج.)

Haraka,* n. haste, hurry, bustle, excitement. *Fanya haraka*, make haste. *Enda kwa haraka*, go (or be) in a hurry. Prov. *Haraka haraka haina baraka*, hurry, hurry, has no blessing. Also adv., in a hurry, hastily, flurriedly. Sometimes as a v. make haste, hurry. Cs. **Harakisha** and **Harikisha,** cause haste (bustle, excitement), and Inten. bewilder, flurry, &c. **Taharaki,** v., **Taharuki,** v. be in a hurry, be bustled, be excited—from any strong emotion. Prep. **Taharukia.** Cs. **Taharukisha.** (Cf. *hima, hangaika, chafuka, hamanika, fadhaika*. Ar. حراك motion.)

Haram,* n. the Pyramids, also **Ihramu.** (Ar. هرم.)

Haramia,* n. *ma-* an outlaw, pirate, brigand, highway robber. **Haramu,** a. forbidden, unlawful, prohibited, i.e. by Muhammadan law or custom. *Mwana wa haramu*, an illegitimate child, a bastard. Used as a term of abuse. Prov. *Funika kawa mwana haramu apite*, Cover up (with the *kawa*) that the bastard (here is meant a bad smell caused by somebody breaking wind) may pass. **Harimu,** v. make illegal, declare unlawful, forbid, ban, interdict, excommunicate. Ps. **Harimiwa.** Prep. **Harimia,** forbid to, declare wrong for, &c. Cs. **Harimisha,** often Inten., and so instead of the Dir. *harimu*, declare illegal, according to Muhammadan law and custom. *Harimisha mtu kitu*, interdict some one from something. *Tumeharimishwa vileo*, we are forbidden intoxicants. **Harimu,** n. *ma-* person or thing forbidden. *Maharimu*, persons within the prohibited degrees of consanguinity and so forbidden to each other. **Uharamia,** n. brigandage, piracy, outlawry. (Cf. *gombeza, kataza, rufuku*. Ar. حرم.)

Harara,* n. heat, warmth, (1) of the body, high temperature, inflammation, prickly heat, rash produced by heat. *Ameshikwa na harara*, he is hot, feverish. (2) fervency, hot temper, rashness, precipitancy. *Harara ya moyo, moyo wa harara, moyo harara*, a passionate disposition, quick temper. **Hari,** n. (1) fervour; (2) heat in general, and esp. perspiration, sweat. *Hari ya jua*, the heat of the sun. *Mwili wangu una hari*, my body is hot. *Toka hari*, perspire. *Hari sanitona*, sweat drops off me. **Uharara,** n. (1) warmth, heat; (2) fervour, impetuosity, hastiness of temper. (Cf. *moto, joto, jasho, hamaki*. Ar. حر be hot, and حرارة heat.)

Haria.* See **Heria.**

-haribifu,* a., **Haribika,** v., **Haribu,** v. See under **Harabu.**

Hariji,* v. See under **Haraja.**

Harimisha,* v., **Harimu,** v. See under **Haramia.**

Hariri,* n. silk. (Ar. حرير.)

Harisha,* v., **Harisho,** n. See under **Hara,** v.

Harufu,* n. scent, smell, odour, of any kind, good or bad. (Cf. *nuka, vunda*. Ar. حرافة.)

Hasa,* adv. See under **Husu.**

Hasama,* n. See **Hasimu.**

Hasanati,* n. See **Hisani.**

Hasara,* n. loss, damage, injury. *Pata hasara*, lose. *Tia hasara*. cause loss to. *Lipa hasara*, pay damages, repay, make amends. *Faida na hasara*, profit and loss. **Hasiri**, v. injure, damage, hurt, inflict loss on. Ps. **Hasiriwa**. Prep. **Hasiria**. Cs. **Hasirisha**. (Cf. *dhuru, haribu, poteza*. Ar. خسارة.)

Hasha!* int. certainly not! by no means! impossible! God forbid!—a very emphatic negative. (Cf. *la, siyo, hapana, hakuna*. Ar. حاشا.)

Hashakum.* See **Ashakum**.

Hasho,* n. *ma-* a piece of wood used as a patch, let in or fixed on, to close a hole, &c. Dim. **Kihasho**, n. *vi-*. (Ar. حشو stuffing, wad.)

Hasi,* v. castrate, geld. Ps. **Hasiwa**. **Mhasi**, n. *wa-* (1) a castrated man or animal, a eunuch, but more usually for animals, *maksai* or *mahsai*, and for men, *towashi*; (2) one who gelds or castrates. **Uhasi**, n. castration, being a eunuch. (Cf. *hasua, maksai*. Ar. خصى.)

Hasidi,* v. envy, grudge, be jealous of. Also **Husudu**, from which the derivatives are usually made. Ps. **Husudiwa**. Prep. **Husudia**. **Hasidi**, n. *ma-* a jealous person, enemy, spiteful person. **Husuda**, envy, jealousy, spitefulness, enmity. **Uhasidi**, n., and **Uhusuda**, n. envy, spite, malignity. (Cf. *wivu, ghera*. Ar. حسد.)

Hasimu,* n. *ma-*, also **Hasama**, antagonist, rival, adversary, opponent, esp. a person with whom you have quarrelled and are not now on speaking terms. (Cf. *adui, mtesi*.) **Hasimu**, v., also **Husumu**, v. strive, contend, avoid because of a quarrel or ill feeling, break off friendship because of quarrel, be sulky. (Cf. *nunia*.) **Uhasama**, enmity, violence, sulkiness. (Ar. خاصم.)

Hasira,* n. anger, wrath, passion. *Kuwa na hasira*, to be angry. *Kutia hasira*, to enrage. Used with many verbs, e.g. *fanya, ona, piga, shikwa na, ingia, ingiwa na, patwa na*, &c. (Cf. *kasirisha, ghadhabu, uchungu, chuki*, and dist. *hasiri*. Ar. حصر oppression of heart.)

Hasiri,* v. See under **Hasara**.

Hasua,* n. the testicles. (Cf. *pumbu, korodani, makende*. Ar. خصية.)

Hata,* (1) prep. until, up to, as far as, as much as—implying a point, object, degree, or condition in view. *Toka hapa hata huko*, from here to there. *Tangu asubuhi hata jioni*, from morning to evening. *Simpi hata moja*, I will not give him as much as one (even one). Often with *kidogo*, after a negative, i.e. not in the least, not even a little, not at all. Also without *kidogo*, but in the same sense. *Habari hii si kweli hata*, this report is not true at all. Sometimes even with negative only implied, e.g. *Amekwenda? Hata!* Has he gone? Not he! (2) conj. (*a*) connective, so, then, next, often merely transitional and not requiring translation. *Hata asubuhi*, so in the morning. *Hata siku moja*, one day, once upon a time. (*b*) subordinative, so as to, even if, though. *Nitafanya akili gani hata tugawe sawasawa?* What plan shall I devise, so that we may divide equally? *Hata akija na mkuki usikubali*, even if he comes with a spear, do not consent. (3) adv. *Hata nitampiga*, I will go as far as to beat him. *Bahati yako hata nimekuja*, thanks to your good luck, I have even come, I am positively here. Note: as *hata* means 'until' and 'even', care must be taken, as it may cause ambiguity. *Siji hata Jumapili*, I will not come *until* Sunday, or I will not come *even* on Sunday. This ambiguity can be avoided by using *mpaka* for 'until'. *Siji mpaka Jumapili*, I will not come until Sunday. (Cf. *mpaka, hadi, ingawa*. Ar. حتى.)

Hatamu,* n. bridle, i.e. the mouth strap to guide or fasten an animal with. The bit is *lijamu*. (Cf. *akania*. Ar. خطم.)

Hatari,* n. danger, peril, risk, jeopardy. **Hatirisha,** v. Cs. put in danger, endanger, risk, imperil. Rf. *jihatirisha*, risk oneself, i.e. *jitia hatarini*. (Cf. *ponza*. Ar. خاطر.)

Hati,* n. written note, memorandum, document, certificate, writing esp. of an official, legal, or formal kind. *Kuandika hati*, to write a document, also write, i.e. used of a writing lesson. *Hati ya mkono*, handwriting. (Cf. *barua, waraka, cheti, mwandiko, maandiko*. Ar. خط.)

Hatia,* n. (1) fault, transgression, crime, sin; (2) guilt, blame, culpability. *Tia hatiani*, find fault with, accuse, find guilty. *Tiwa hatiani*, be convicted (of). *Kuwa na hatia na (mtu)*, may mean either to have done a wrong to, or to have a charge against. (Cf. *kosa, dhambi, lawama*. Ar. خطئ.)

Hatibu,* n. *ma-* a preacher. **Hutuba,** n. a reading of the Koran, a sermon, address, homily. **Hutubu,** v. read the Koran publicly, preach, give an address. Prep. **Hutubia.** (Cf. *hubiri*. Ar. خطب.)

Hatiki,* v. trouble, annoy—seldom used. (Cf. *sumbua, udhi*. Ar. هتك.)

Hatima,* n. end, conclusion. Often used with the enclitic *-ye*. **Hatimaye,** adv. finally, at last, in the end, and sometimes as prep. after, e.g. *hatima kufa kwake*, after his death. **Hitima,** n. a Muhammadan service, or office, in conclusion of some event, i.e. a reading of certain portions of the Koran, esp. (1) a funeral service; (2) service at a house-warming; (3) a feast given at such a ceremony, e.g. *siku ya tatu hufanya hitima, yaani hupika wali*, after three days of mourning a feast is made, i.e. rice is cooked. *Kusoma hitima kaburini*, to read passages at the grave. **Hitimu,** v. end, come to an end, be completed. Most common in the special sense 'finish education, complete a course of reading or instruction, end an apprenticeship, become a qualified teacher or workman'. *Mtoto huyu amehitimu*, this child has finished his schooling, usually referring to the teaching given in the Koranic schools. Prep. **Hitimia.** Cs. **Hitimisha.** (Cf. *isha, maliza, timiza, kamilisha*. Ar. ختم.)

Hatinafsi, n. and **Hayatinafsi,*** n. used of a person taking an action without consulting anybody because he thinks they may try to persuade him not to do it; going one's own way without asking advice. (Ar. هاة manner, way, fashion, &c., and *nafsi*, which see.)

Hatirisha,* v. See under **Hatari.**

Hatua,* n. (1) step, pace in walking. *Pima kwa hatua*, measure by paces. *Hatua mbili mbele*, two paces forward. *Ni hatua*, it is some distance away, used in indicating that some place is rather far away. (2) fig. progress, also of the stages in progress, in working a sum, &c.; (3) opportunity, time. *Nitakuja nipatapo hatua*, I shall come when I get an opportunity. (Ar. خطوة.)

Haula.* See **Lahaula.**

Hawa,* n. (1) longing, strong inclination, passionate desire, lust, passion (cf. *shauku, huba, mapenzi, ashiki, tamaa, roho, maelekeo, uchu*); (2) sometimes heard for *hewa*, which see; (3) Eve, the first woman, sometimes *Ewa*. (Ar. هوى passionate desire, حواء Eve.)

Hawa, pron. these, plur. of *huyu*.

Hawaa,* n. See **Hawara.**

Hawafu,* n. sometimes heard for *hofu*.

Hawala,* n. money order, cheque, draft, of exchange. (Cf. *hundi, hati*)

Hawili, v. change, transfer. (Ar. حوالة.)

Hawara,* n. a paramour. (Ar. عهر or خور whore.)

Hawili,* v. See under **Hawala.**

Haya!* int. used to call to action or effort, Come on! Now then! Work away! Step out! Make haste! &c. (Ar. هي.)

Haya,* n. (1) shame, modesty, bashfulness, shamefacedness; (2) cause of shame, disgrace; (3) humility, respect, reverence. *Tia haya*, make ashamed. *Fanya* (*ona*) *haya*, feel shame, be shy. *Hana haya*, he is a shameless (impudent, brazen) person. **Tahayari,** n. same as *haya*. **Tahayari,** v. become ashamed, be abashed, be shy, be humilitated. Also St. **Tahayarika,** in the same sense. Cs. **Tahayarisha,** make ashamed, &c. **Tahayuri,** n. shame, confusion, disgrace. (Cf. *soni, sibu, hizi, fedheha*. Ar. حياء.)

Haya, pron. these, plur. of *hili*.

Hayati,* n. departed, deceased. *Hayati mfalme*, the deceased king. (Cf. *marehemu*. Ar. حياتى pertaining to lifetime, cf. *hai*.)

Hayati nafsi,* usu. abbreviated to *hatinafsi*, which see.

Hayawani,* n. (1) brute, beast; (2) a person just like an animal, i.e. shameless, stupid, brute, idiot. **Uhayawani,** n. the condition, state, characteristics, &c., of a brute, beast, &c. (Cf. *mnyama*. Ar. حيوان.)

Hayo, prep. of reference, those referred to, those yonder, those.

Hayuko, verb-form, he (she) is not there.

Hazama,* n. a nose ornament, nose ring or pendant. (Cf. *kishaufu, kikero*. Ar. حزام.)

Hazamu,* n. *ma-* girdle, commonly in the plur. (Cf. *mshipi, ukanda, masombo*. Ar. حزام.)

Hazina,* n. treasure deposit of money, exchequer, privy purse. (Cf. *dafina, mali, akiba*. Ar. خزينة.)

Heba,* n. *ma-*. See **Haiba.**

Hebu! int. See **Ebu!**

Hebu,* v. like, be pleased with, take a fancy to. **Haba,** n., **Mahaba,** n., **Huba,** n., and **Mahuba,** n. love, friendship. **Muhebi,** n. beloved, friend, dear, also as a. affectionate—used only as a rule in letter writing after the Arabic fashion. **Stahabu,** v. (1) like, prefer, be pleased (with); (2) deserve, e.g. *kwa uhalifu wake astahabu adhabu*, for his disobedience he deserves punishment, but *stahili* is generally used in this sense. *Nastahabu kwenda kuliko kukaa*, I would rather go than remain. (Cf. *penda, afadhali*. Ar. حب and استحب.)

Hedaya,* n. (sometimes heard as *hidaya*), gift, present, usually of something rare, costly, or wonderful. *Kitu cha hedaya*, a costly gift. (Cf. *zawadi, tuzo*. Ar. هدية.)

Hedhi,* n. menses, menstruation (also *mwezi* or *damu*). *Kuwa na hedhi*, to menstruate (also *kuingia mwezini*, or *damuni* and simply *kutumia*). (Ar. حيض.)

Hekaheka,* n. confusion, much noise; also shouts of encouragement, such as in games. (Cf. *heko*.)

Hekalu,* n. *ma-* a temple, the temple at Jerusalem. (Cf. *msikiti, kanisa*. Ar. هيكل.)

Hekaya,* n. (1) story, anecdote; (2) remarkable incident. (Cf. *hadithi, kisa, ngano, habari, kioja*. Ar. حكاية.)

Hekemua, v. stretch oneself as on waking up or getting up from a cramped position.

Hekima,* n., **Hekimiza,** v. See under **Hukumu.**

Heko!* int. Hurrah! Well done! (Cf. *hekaheka*.)

Hela!* int. used in the same way as *ebu!* and *simile!* Well then! Come then! Make way! (Ar. هلا Well then! Come! &c.)

Hema,* n. a tent. *Piga hema,* pitch a tent. *Ng'oa hema,* strike a tent. (Ar. خيمة.)

Hema, v. pant, gasp for breath, breathe with difficulty or heavily, be exhausted. Ps. **Hemewa,** be fully occupied, exhausted with work. (Cf. *tweta, choka, lemewa.*)

Hemera, v. go to buy food in the plantations on the outskirts of a town.

Henezi, adv. slowly. (Cf. *pole, taratibu.*)

Henza,* n. halyard—the thick rope by which the heavy yard and sail of a native vessel is hoisted. It passes over a sheave at the masthead, and carries a double or treble pulley (*gofia*) connected with another (*abedari*) on deck by a smaller rope (*jirari*), giving the necessary purchase. (Cf. *tanga.* ? corruption of Ar. حندريس halyard.)

Henzarani,* n. (sometimes *henzerani*), a cane. (Ar. خيزران.)

Heri,* n. happiness, blessedness, good fortune, good luck, success, advantage. *Heri yako ni yetu,* your happiness is ours. *Mtu wa heri,* a fortunate (happy, enviable) man. *Kujaliwa heri,* to be granted good fortune. *Kufunuliwa heri,* to make a lucky guess, hit on a happy idea. *Kumtakia mtu heri,* to wish one well, bless one. Common in the formula of leave-taking. *Kwa heri,* good-bye, or *Kwa heri ya kuonana,* good-bye till we meet again. Also *Heri,* it is well, it is best (like *afadhali*), e.g. *heri uende,* you had better go. *Heri adui mwerevu kama rafiki mpumbavu,* rather a sly enemy than a foolish friend. **Uheri,** n. condition of being blessed, &c. (Cf. *sabalkheri, masalkheri, bahati, nafuu, neema.* Ar. خير.)

Heria,* (1) a nautical expression. Let go the sheet; (2) used by winch and crane workers, for lower! (Port. *arrier.*)

Hero, n. a small wooden dish, sometimes on legs, used for serving food on. **Kihero,** n. *vi-* dim.

Heroe, n. flamingo (Pemba).

Herufi,* n. a letter of the alphabet, a written character. *Herufi za Kiarabu,* Arabic writing, characters. (Ar. حرف.)

Hesabu,* v. (1) count, calculate, reckon up; (2) consider. Ps. **Hesabiwa.** St. and Pot. **Hesabika,** be counted, be countable, e.g. *hazihesabiki,* they cannot be counted, in the sense that they are too many, also, that they are worthless. Prep. **Hesabia,** (1) reckon with (to the credit of, against, &c.); (2) consider as, i.e. *alihesabiwa mjinga,* he was considered to be a fool. **Hesabu,** n. (1) reckoning, calculation, enumeration; (2) a bill, an account (of money, measure, value); (3) the art of counting, numeration, arithmetic, a sum, i.e. an arithmetical example. *Kitabu cha hesabu,* an account book, like *daftari,* also an arithmetic text-book. *Toa hesabu,* give an account. *Andika katika hesabu,* put down to an account. *Fanya hesabu,* reckon up, calculate, work a sum. *Taka hesabu,* demand an account. *Hesabu za kichwani,* mental arithmetic. *Hesabu za vichanganyiko,* practice sums. (Ar. حسب.)

Heshima,* n. (1) honour, dignity, position, rank; (2) respect, reverence, modesty, courtesy. *Hana heshima,* he has no dignity, also he is disrespectful. *Wekea (wekeana) heshima,* treat (each other) with honour. *Heshima ni kitu cha bure,* politeness costs nothing. **Heshimu,** v. honour, pay respect to, treat with courtesy. **Mahashumu,** n. and a. an honoured, respected person; as a. honourable, respected. **Muhashamu,** a. a complimentary title in the Arabic style of beginning a letter, honoured.

(Cf. *tukuza, jali, stahi, utukufu, daraja, cheo, adabu, haya.* Ar. حشمة.)

Hesi,* n. a screw. Also *msumari wa hesi.* (Cf. *parafujo, msumari, skrubu.*)

Hewa,* n. air, atmosphere. *Punga hewa,* go for a change of air. (Ar. هواء.)

Hiana,* a. See under **Hini.**

Hiari,* n. choice, option. *Hiari yako,* just as you like. *Kazi ya hiari,* voluntary labour. **Hiari,** v. choose, prefer. **Hitari,** v. like *hiari,* choose, select, prefer. Ps. **Hitariwa.** Cs. **Hitarisha,** i.e. cause to choose, give choice (to). **Hitiari,** n. like *hiari,* n. choice, selection, preference. *Hitiari yako,* as you like it (i.e. *upendavyo*). *Nadhari na hitiari ni kwako,* the decision and choice lie with you. (Cf. *chagua, penda.* Ar. خيار.)

Hiba,* n. (1) gift, present, keepsake, souvenir, given as a sign of affection, hence also (2) bequest, legacy. (Cf. *zawadi, tuzo.* Ar. هبة.)

Hicho, a. of reference, that referred to before, that yonder.

Hidaya,* n. See **Hedaya.**

Hidi,* v. convert, lead aright. (Cf. *ongoa.* Ar. هدى.)

Hidima,* adv. with expedition, diligently, quickly. (Prob. from same root as *hadimu,* i.e. like a slave.)

Hifadhi,* v. preserve, keep, protect, save. *Mungu amhifadhi,* may God keep him. Ps. **Hifadhiwa.** St. **Hifadhika.** Prep. **Hifadhia. Hifadhi,** n. guard, careful watch. (Cf. *linda, tunza, ponya, okoa, opoa.* Ar. حفظ.)

Hii, a. dem. this.

Hijabu,* n. (1) neuralgia; (2) swollen glands in the neck. (Cf. *mlezi.* Ar. حاجب eyebrow, i.e. where pain is felt.)

Hiji,* v. make the pilgrimage to Mecca. See **Haji.**

Hiki, a. dem. this.

Hila,* n. cunning device, trick, craft, stratagem, deceit. *Fanya hila,* use cunning, try to circumvent. *Mtu wa hila,* a wily, sly man. (Cf. *hadaa, danganya, werevu, ujanja.* Ar. حيلة.)

Hilafu,* n. See under **Halifu.**

Hilali,* n. a crescent. (Ar. هلال.)

Hili, a. dem. this. **Hilo,** of reference to a thing already mentioned, that.

Hiliki,* n. also **Iliki,** cardamom. (Hind. الاچى.)

Hiliki,* v. be lost, destroyed, be ruined, perish. (Cf. *angamia, potea.* Ar. هلك.)

Hima,* adv. quick, quickly, hastily, in a hurry. *Fanya hima,* make haste. *Twende hima,* let us go quickly. *Hima! hima!* quick! quick! **Hima,** n. energy, urgency, importance. **Himiza,** v. hasten, hurry, cause to be done (to go) quickly. *Himiza watu kazi,* make men work quickly. *Himiza chakula,* hurry on a meal. **Himu,** v. same as *himiza.* **Muhimu,** a. important, special, significant, urgent, particular, also as n. an important matter. (Cf. *upesi, haraka, mbio, harakisha, kimbiza, endesha.* Ar. همة.)

Himaya,* n. protection, guardianship. *Chini ya himaya ya Kiingereza* (or *Uingereza*), under the protection of the British (Government). (Cf. *ulinzi, tunza* also *amia* and *hami* from the same Ar. root. Ar. حماية.)

Himdu,* n. See under **Himidi.**

Himidi,* v. thank, praise, extol, magnify, esp. of praise to God. Ps. **Himidiwa. Hamdu,** n., **Himdu,** n., and **Himidi,** n. praise. *Al hamdu lilahi,* praise be to God, a common expression on hearing good or bad news, on being delivered from danger, difficulty, &c. (Cf. *sifu, sifa.* Ar. حمد.)

Himila, n., **Himili,*** v. See under **Hamali.**

Himiza, v., **Himu,*** v. See under **Hima.**

Hina,* n. henna, prepared from the

plant *mhina, mi-*, a very favourite red dye. The plant is also called *mhanuni*. (Ar. حناء.)

Hindi,* n. *ma-* a single grain of maize, a seed of the plant *muhindi*. *Mahindi*, is used collectively of maize. *Unga wa mahindi*, flour made from maize. *Ugali wa mahindi*, *ugali* (which see), made from maize flour.

Hini,* v. (1) refuse to give (to), withhold (from), keep back (from). *Amenihini fedha yangu*, he has kept back my money. *Jihini*, deny oneself, e.g. *jihini chakula*, deny oneself food. (2) make little of, scorn. Cs. **Hinisha.** *Jihinisha*, practise self-denial, treat things (food, &c.) as though you thought little of them. **Hiana,** n. a mean spirited person, one who prevents others from using what is useless to him, 'dog in the manger'. **Uhiana,** n. meanness of spirit. (Ar. خن.)

Hinikiza, v. out-talk a person by making a noise, interrupt some one speaking. (Cf. *dakiza, chachawiza*. ? Cs. of Ar. خنق strangle, choke.)

Hirimia,* v. purpose, decide, intend. (Cf. *kusudia, azimia, nia*. Ar. هرمان mind, intellect.)

Hirimu,* n. (1) age period of life, and esp. of youth, from 10 to 25; (2) one of the same age, a contemporary. *Vijana vya hirimu moja*, young people of the same age. (Cf. *umri, marika, ujana*. ? Ar. حريم companion, friend.)

Hirizi,* n. charm, amulet, i.e. *uganga wa kuvaa mwilini*, medicine to wear on the person. Often a small leather case containing a sentence from the Koran, but also pieces of prepared skin, root, &c. (Cf. *kinga, kago, azima, dawa, talasimu*. Ar. حرز.)

Hisa,* n. (1) part, portion, share; (2) in arithmetic, quotient. (Cf. *fungu, sehemu*. Ar. حصة.)

Hisabu,* v. and n. See **Hesabu.**

Hisani,* n. kindness, favour, goodness. *Kwa hisani yako*, by your kindness. *Alinifanyia hisani nyingi*, he granted me many favours. **Mhisani,** n. *wa-* one who does good works for others, a benefactor. (Cf. *fadhili, wema*. Ar. احسان.)

Hisi,* v. feel, recognize, perceive, sense. (Cf. *fahamu, ona, tambua*. Ar. حس.)

Hitaji,* v. need, require, be in need, lack, want, feel want of, desire. Often impersonal, e.g. *yahitaji mashahidi wawe watu waaminifu*, it is necessary that witnesses should be trustworthy. Ps. **Hitajiwa.** St. **Hitajika.** Prep. **Hitajia,** like *hitaji, ahitajia kupigwa*, he needs to be beaten. Rp. **Hitajiana. Hitaji,** n. *ma-* usually in the plur. things required, necessities, wants, petitions, exigency. **Mhitaji,** n. *wa-* (1) a person who wants (needs something), applicant, candidate, petitioner; (2) one who is needy, in want, poor. **Uhitaji,** n. (*hitaji* and *ma-*) (1) want, need, requirement, desire; (2) indigence, necessitous condition. (Cf. *haja, taka*. Ar. احتاج.)

Hitari, v., **Hitiari,*** n. See under **Hiari.**

Hitilafu,* n. (1) difference, discord; (2) defect, blemish. *Shauri lao moja wala hapana hitilafu*, their intention is the same and there is no difference. *Aliona hitilafu kidogo*, he noticed a small variation. **Hitilafu,** v. be different, make a difference. Rp. **Hitilafiana,** be different, distinct from each other. (Cf. *tofauti, mbalimbali, achana*. From the same root as *halafu* and *halifu*. Ar. اختلف.)

Hitima, n., **Hitimu,*** v. See under **Hatima.**

Hivi, a. dem. these. Also commonly as adv. thus, in this manner, accordingly, so. *Sasa hivi* (also *hivi sasa*), at this very moment, immediately, on the spot. *Leo hivi*, this very day.

Hivyo, a. dem. of reference, those (already referred to). Also adv. in that very manner, in the manner already described, so. Often *vivyo hivyo,* just so, exactly so, and so on, describing a course of events, &c., which went on, or which are going on, in the same manner.

Hiyana,* n. See **Hiana** under **Hini.**

Hiyo, a. dem. of reference, that (those) already mentioned or referred to.

Hizaya,* n. curse, disgrace; seldom used. *Mwana hizaya,* son of a curse, a cursed, disgraced person. **Hizi,** v. disgrace, put to shame, dishonour, insult, inflict punishment. *Mtoto amemhizi baba yake,* the child has disgraced his father. **Stihizai,** v. same as *hizi,* v. but rarely heard. (Cf. *aibisha, fedhehesha, tahayarisha, tweza.* Ar. خزى.)

Hizi, a. dem. these. *Siku hizi,* lately, nowadays. Also *zizi hizi,* just these, these very. **Hizo,** as the form of reference, those already mentioned or referred to before.

Hobe!* int. Go! Clear off! (Cf. *nenda, ondoka.* Ar. هب depart, pace along briskly.)

Hobelahobela,* adv. anyhow, without arrangement, without skill, &c. In a disorderly fashion, e.g. of many people trying to carry a load without a previous understanding, i.e. each person going his own gait. (Ar. خلطة what is done in a hurry and badly.)

Hodari,* a. (1) strong, firm, stable, solid; (2) active, energetic, brave, earnest, strong-willed. Used of strength generally in substance, construction, character, &c., but usually of persons. *Mtu hodari wa kazi (wa vita, wa maneno),* an effective, able mechanic (soldier, orator). **Uhodari,** n. courage, stability. (Cf. *thabiti, -a nguvu, -gumu, -shupavu, jasiri.* Ar. عدر to be bold.)

Hodhi,* n. a bath, large vessel for holding water, boiler, tank, either of cement or metal. (Cf. *birika.* Ar. حوض.)

Hodhi,* v. and n. See **Hozi.**

Hodi,* n. used as a polite inquiry before entering a house or room, 'May I come in?' and, unless an answer is given—usually the same word or *karibu,* come in—good manners forbid entry. (Prob. a word introduced by Arabs from Muscat meaning 'safety, well-being', and so equivalent to *wokovu, salama.* Hence as an interrogative, Is all well? all well? and the answer, 'all well', by the same word—or by *karibu,* which see.)

Hofia,* v. See under **Hofu.**

Hofu,* n. (1) fear, apprehension, awe; (2) cause of fear, danger. *Kuwa na hofu,* to be afraid. *Fanya (ona, ingia, ingiwa na, patwa na, shikwa na) hofu,* be frightened, be seized with fear **Hofu,** v. feel fear, be afraid of. Ps. **Hofiwa.** St. **Hofika.** Prep. **Hofia,** fear for (about, in, &c.). Cs. **Hofisha,** terrify, frighten. (Cf. *afa, mwafa, ogopa, oga, kitisho, cha uchaji, kicho* Ar. خوف.)

Hogo, n. *ma-.* See **Muhogo.**

Hohehahe,* n. a solitary, destitute, outcast person or state. Cf. such phrases as *maskini (fukara) hohehahe,* utterly poor and destitute. *Ni hohehahe tu,* he is quite forlorn. (Pers. see *hoi.*)

Hoho, n. *pilipili hoho,* red pepper as dist. from *pilipili manga,* black pepper. *Mkate wa hoho,* a cake flavoured with pepper.

Hoi,* a. helpless, in a bad state, e.g *alikuwa hoi kwa ugonjwa (ulevi),* he was helpless on account of sickness (drunkenness). (Pers. هاى هاى cries of distress or bewilderment.)

Hoihoi,* n. noise, clamour. *Hoihoi ya arusi,* noise, clamour, rejoicings at a wedding. (Pers. هاى هاوى noisy mirth, festivity, &c.)

Hoja, n., **Hoji,*** v. See under **Haja.**

Homa,* n. fever, any sickness with a

high temperature. *Shikwa na homa,* have an attack of fever. *Homa ya vipindi,* intermittent fever. *Homa ya papasi,* Spirillum tick fever. *Homa ya malaria,* malaria fever. (Ar. حمى.)

Hondo, n. the crowned hornbill, also called *kwembe* and *hondohondo.*

Honga, v. make a payment, to secure an end, hence, bribe, pay toll, pay one's way, pay a footing, frequently in a bad sense. *Kumhonga mwanamke,* seduce a woman with a bribe. Prep. **Hongera, Hongea,** and **Hongela,** pay for, secure an end, advance a stage, get past a crisis, be acquitted, get cleared of a charge. Thus of a woman after childbirth, *leo nimehongera,* I was delivered today. Succeed in any private or secret undertaking, ceremony, &c., e.g. bathe for the first time after circumcision, i.e. get over the danger. Also, *arusi amehongera,* the bridegroom has consummated the marriage. Cs. **Hongeza,** (1) cause to pay toll, blackmail; (2) cause (help, allow) to advance a stage, or to secure an end, e.g. procure acquittal. Also of congratulations after some event or crisis, e.g. after a journey, childbirth, &c. *Mtu akisafiri akirudi watu huja kumhongeza,* when a man returns from a journey, people come to congratulate him. *Akamhongeza binti yake kuzaa,* he congratulated his daughter on her delivery. **Hongo,** n. (1) toll, tribute, blackmail—used of customary presents given to native chiefs for leave to pass through their country; (2) money paid to seduce a woman, &c. **Hongera,** n. congratulations; also a present given at the time of congratulating. (Cf. *rushwa, mlungula, chichiri, upenyezi, salimu, pukusa, pongeza, bakshishi, tongoza.*

Honi,* n. motor horn, syren. (Eng. horn.)

Horji,* n. a padded quilt for putting on the top of a donkey's saddle. (Ar. خرج.)

Hori,* n. (1) creek, inlet, gulf, arm of the sea. (Cf. *ghuba.* Ar. خور.) (2) *ma-* a kind of canoe, with raised stem and stern; (3) a drinking or food trough for animals. (Pers. آخور stall for horses.)

Hospitali,* n. a hospital, dispensary. (Eng.)

Hota, v. used of treating a woman with medicine so that she can bear children. **Hoto,** n. the medicine used in *kuhota.*

Hoteli,* n. an hotel, restaurant, coffee shop. (Cf. *mkahawa.* Eng.)

Hoto, n. See under **Hota.**

Hotuba,* n. See under **Hatibu.**

Hoza, n. medicine prepared for children who are teething.

Hozahoza, v. remove doubt or difficulty.

Hozi,* v. get, possess, have. **Hozi,** n. possession, but in some places restricted to waste land bordering on a plantation and claimed by the owner of the plantation. (Ar. حوز.)

Hua, n. Lesser Red-eyed Dove (*Streptopelia semitorquata*). (Cf. *pugi, ninga, njiwa, tetere,* other kinds of doves.)

Huba,* n. See under **Hebu,** v.

Hubiri,* v. and n. *ma-.* See under **Habari.**

Hudhud,* n. Hoopoe. (Ar. هد هد.)

Hudhuria, v., **Hudhurio,*** n. *ma-.* See under **Hadhara.**

Hudhurungi,* n. a yellowish-brown, or light-brown cotton cloth used for making *kanzu,* also its colour. (Ar. اضريج a yellow garment.)

Huduma, n., **Hudumu,*** n. and v. See under **Hadimu.**

Huenda. See under **Enda.**

Hueni,* n. See **Ahueni.**

Hui, v., **Huisha,*** v. See under **Hai.**

Huja, n., **Huji,*** v. See under **Haja.**

Hujambo, verb-form, Are you well? You are well. The commonest form of salutation. Frequently *jambo* alone is used. *Hujambo* is also often used as a noun (also *hajambo*), better health, improvement in health, &c. *Leo amepata hujambo* (or *hajambo*), to-day he has got an improvement in his health, is better. See **Jambo.**

Hujuru,* v. See **Hajiri.**

Huko, adv. dem. of general reference, in that case referred to, with those circumstances in view, in connexion with that environment, but commonly of place and time, 'from (to, at, in, &c.) that place (or time), there, thither, thence, then', &c. *Huko na huko*, hither and thither, here and there. *Huko uendako*, where you are going to, your destination. *Huko utokako*, where you come from, your starting-point. *Huko nyuma*, (1) meanwhile; (2) yonder in the rear. *Huko huko*, just yonder, just there, under those precise circumstances. *Huko* is also used to suggest the world beyond, the other world, the world of spirits. **Huku,** a. dem. (1) this. *Huku* followed by the *ki-* tense or present, is frequently used in the sense of while, meanwhile, of an action performed simultaneously with another. *Alikwenda huku analia*, he went crying (as he went). *Aliwapiga huku akiwakaripia*, he beat them while scolding them. (2) adv. usually of place, here, near, in this place, but also of environment generally. *Huku kuzuri*, it is pleasant here (in our present circumstances). *Huku na huku*, this way and that, hither and thither. *Kuku huku*, just here.

Hukumu,* v. give an official (or authoritative) pronouncement (on), give judgement in a civil or criminal case, decide, pass sentence (on), exercise authority (over), be ruler. *Alimhukumu auawe*, he ordered him to be put to death, he passed sentence of death upon him. So of other verdicts, *apigwe, afungwe, alipe, auzwe*, &c., or *kupigwa*, &c. Ps. **Hukumiwa.** Prep. **Hukumia,** give judgement, &c., on (for, at, &c.). Cs. **Hukumiza** and **Hukumisha. Hakimu,** n. *ma-* judge, ruler, chief. **Hekima,** n. wisdom, knowledge, judgement. (Cf. *elimu, busara, akili, maarifa.*) **Hekimiza,** v. cause to know, give instruction to, inform, direct. *Amehekimiza tukutunze*, he has directed us to take care of you. Ps. **Hekimizwa. Hukumu,** n. judgement, (1) (in general), jurisdiction, authority, supreme power; (2) legal process, trial; (3) sentence, verdict, decision, order, either in a civil or criminal case; (4) also used of state and time. *Hukumu ya saa kumi*, about the tenth hour. *Mwenye hukumu*, the supreme ruler, sovereign. *Peleka hukumuni*, send for trial. *Anasikia hukumu yako*, he obeys your order. *Hukumu ya kufa*, capital sentence. (Cf. *kata, amua, tawala, amuru.*) **Mahakma,** n. place of judgement. (Ar. حكم.)

Hulka,* n. state, natural condition, constitution, characteristics. **Huluku,** v. create, but used only of the creation of the world by God. **Mahluki,** n., **Mahluku,** n. a human being. (Cf. *umba, tabia, maumbile, sifa.* Ar. خلق.)

Hulu,* v. stop doing an action, leave off. *Hahulu kuja hapa*, he won't leave off coming here. (Cf. *acha, koma.* Ar. خلى.)

Huluku,* v. See under **Hulka**

Humo, adv. dem. of reference to an interior, in that place (referred to), inside, yonder, in there. *Humo mwetu*, in our house yonder. *Mumo humo*, just in there, in that very place. **Humu,** (1) adj. dem. this; (2) adv. dem. in this place, inside here. *Mumu humu*, just in here, in this very place.

Humusi,* n. a fifth part. (Ar. خمس.)

Hundi,* n. draft, cheque, money order, bill of exchange. (Cf. *hawala.* Hind. هنڈي.)

Huni,* v. (1) wander about for no good purpose, disobey, be a vagabond; (2) leave one's own side, party, &c., and go to the other, rebel, turn traitor; (3) leave off going (coming, &c.), stop. **Mhuni**, n. *wa-* (1) vagabond, profligate, wastrel, gadabout; (2) a traitor; (3) a lawless person, outcast. **Uhuni**, n. vagabondage, lawlessness, condition of having no fixed abode. (Cf. *asi, hulu.* Ar. خون be unfaithful.)

Huntha,* n. a hermaphrodite. (Ar. not generally known, from same root as *hanithi.* خنثى.)

Huo, a. dem. of reference, that there, that yonder, referred to before.

Huri, n. *ma-*, **Huria**, n. *ma-*, **Huru,*** n. *ma-* a freeman, a person who is not a slave, free born or emancipated. *Acha* (*weka, andikia*) *huru*, set free, emancipate. **Huru**, a. free, emancipated, &c. **Huria**, n. freedom, i.e. in the sense of being able to do what one wishes. **Uhuru**, n. freedom from slavery, liberty, emancipation. (Cf. *mwungwana.* Ar. حر.)

Huruma,* n. (1) sympathy, consideration, fellow feeling, kindliness; (2) mercy, pity, compassion. *Mwenye huruma*, compassionate, sympathetic, kind. *Kuwa na huruma*, to be kind, merciful, &c. *Fanya* (*ona, ingia, ingiwa na*) *huruma*, have kindly feeling. **Hurumia**, v. Prep. pity, have pity (compassion, sympathy) for, have mercy on. (Cf. *rehema*, of which perhaps *huruma* is a form, by a common transposition of Ar. consonants, or Pers. خرمى pleasure, joy, &c.)

Hurunzi,* n. See **Kurunzi**.

Husika,* v. See under **Husu**.

Huss!* int. make less noise! be quiet! silence! (Ar. هس.)

Husu,* v. (1) give a share (to), assign as a person's share (right, due, privilege, &c.). Esp. in the Prep. **Husia**, e.g. *alimhusia kadiri yake*, he assigned him his proper share. (2) be assigned as share, be closely (specially, exclusively) concerned with, be the privilege (right, monopoly, peculiar property, quality) of, belong to, be limited to, refer only to, concern, be specially connected with, be confined to. *Ada yetu iliyotuhusu*, the fee which is our special privilege. *Maneno yasiyomhusu*, statements which do not apply to him. *Ndugu yake amhusuye*, his nearest relative. *Neno lihusulo bwana zao*, a peculiar privilege of their masters. Often used in the St. **Husika**, in this sense. *Ni mhalifu kwa neno lililohusika*, he is rebellious as regards a special duty. *Neno hili lahusika na watu hawa tu*, this word applies only to these persons. Rp. **Husiana**, be relevant, be connected, concern each other. **Hasa**, adv. expressly, exactly, wholly, completely, very much. **Hususa**, adv. and a. same as *hasa*, and as a. particular, special, exact. **Mahsusi**, a. particular, special, exact. **Uhusiano**, n. relevancy. (Cf. *gawia, halisi, barabara, kabisa, sana.* Ar. خص and خصوصا.)

Husuda, n., **Husudu,*** v. See under **Hasidi**.

Husuma, n., **Husumu,*** v. See under **Hasimu**.

Husuni,* n. fortress, fort, castle. (Cf. *ngome, gereza, boma.* Ar. حصن.)

Husuru,* v. reduce to straits, oppress, besiege. Ps. **Husuriwa**. St. **Husurika**. (Cf. *onea, zunguka, mazingiwa.* Ar. حصر.)

Hususa,* adv. and a. See under **Husu**.

Hutuba, n., **Hutubu,*** v. See under **Hatibu**.

Hututi,* a. See under **Mahututi**.

Huu, a. dem. this, sometimes redupl. *huu huu*, this very one, this same.

Huwa, verb-form, it is (was, will be) customary, i.e. *hu-* of customary action, and *-wa*, v. be. Commonly used as adv. (1) regularly, commonly, e.g. *kila siku huwa wanakwenda,* every day as a rule they go; (2) perhaps, it may be, possibly, sometimes. (Cf. *labda, huenda.*)

Huyo, a. dem. of reference, that there, that yonder, that already referred to. **Huyo! Huyo!** There he is! That is he! in a hue and cry after a thief, or chase after animals. **Huyu,** a. dem. this.

Huzuni,* n. grief, sorrow, distress, mourning, calamity, disaster. *-enye huzuni,* sorrowful, depressed, downcast. So *-a huzuni. Kuwa na huzuni,* to be sad, to be sorrowful. *Fanya (ona, ingia, shikwa na) huzuni,* feel sorrow, be distressed, &c. Prep. **Huzunia,** grieve at (for, about, in, &c.). Ps. **Huzuniwa,** (not in use) be grieved, be caused grief. St. **Huzunika.** Cs. **Huzunisha.** (Cf. *hamu, majonzi msiba, matanga, maombolezo, sikitika, lilia.* Ar. حزن.)

I

I represents the sound of *ee* in 'feel', and of *i* in 'pit', when short.

Iba, v. steal, thieve, embezzle, kidnap, purloin, filch, &c. (*kwiba* is sometimes used as the stem of the verb in some tenses). *Iba arusi* anticipate marriage. Ps. **Ibwa,** be stolen. St. and Pot. **Ibika,** be stolen, be capable of being stolen. Prep. **Ibia,** steal from, rob, e.g. *amemwibia mali yake,* he has stolen his property from him. Ps. **Ibiwa,** be stolen from, lose by theft. *Tumeibiwa,* we have been robbed. Rp. **Ibiana,** steal from each other. Rp. **Ibana,** steal each other, used of man and woman having unlawful intercourse. Cs. **Ibisha,** cause to steal, incite to theft. **Jivi,** n. *ma-*, **Jizi,** n. *ma-* a notorious, habitual thief. **Kijivi,** n. and adv. a thievish person, thief, brigand; and as adv. in a thievish (sneaking, underhand) way. **Mwibaji,** n. *wa-*, **Mwivi,** n. (*wevi*), **Mwizi,** n. (*wezi*), a thief, robber, kidnapper, swindler. **Wizi,** n. (*u-izi*), thieving, robbery, theft. (Cf. *nyang'anya.*)

Ibada,* n. See under **Abudu.**

Ibilisi,* n. the Devil, Satan. **Bilisi,** v. tempt to do wrong, persuade to do wrong. **Ubilisi,** n. temptation, persuasion to do evil, devilry, madness. (Cf. *shawishi, shetani.* Ar. ابليس.)

Ibra,* n. See **Ibura.**

Ibura,* n. (1) something wonderful, a miracle, a very rare occurrence, &c.; (2) spot, patch of colour, mark, stain, speck, blot. (Cf. *ajabu, kioja, mwujiza, waa.* Ar. عبرة anything wonderful, and عبر destroy, ruin.)

Idadi,* n. reckoning, counting, number from the point of view of magnitude, computation. *Bila idadi,* without number, numberless. (Cf. *hesabu, namba.* Ar. عدد.)

Idara,* n. in Zanzibar, a Department. (Ar. ادارة).

Idhini,* n. sanction, permission, authorization, leave. *Alitaka idhini ya baba yake,* he begged for his father's consent. *Alitoa idhini,* he gave consent. **Idhini, v.** sanction, allow, authorize, assent to. Ps. **Idhiniwa.** St. **Idhinika.** Prep. **Idhinia.** Cs. **Idhinisha.** (Cf. *ruhusa, kubali, ridhia.* Ar. اذن.)

Idi,* n. (1) Muhammadan festival. *Idi el fitr,* or *Idi ndogo,* the festival at the end of the fast of Ramadhan. *Idi el haji* or *Idi kubwa,* the festival in commemoration of Muhammad's journey to Mecca. (2) a common male personal name. Ar. عيد.)

Idili,* n. effort, enthusiasm, perseverance. (Cf. *juhudi.* Perhaps from the same root as *adili,* or Ar. ظل continuing, not ceasing to do.)

Ifya, v. (1) be vexed with a person; be overcome by a difficulty, circumstances; (2) torment a person until he becomes vexed. (Cf. *chukiza, kasiri.*)

Iga, v. (1) imitate, copy, but commonly (2) in the sense, ape, mock, counterfeit, mimic, caricature. *Iga maneno ya Kiswahili,* try to talk Swahili. *Iga kwa maneno,* imitate the speech (of). *Hodari wa kuiga,* a clever mimic. Ps. **Igwa.** St. and Pot. **Igika.** Prep. **Igia.** Cs. **Igiza,** frequently used in the same sense as *iga,* also Inten. of copying with effort, copy closely. **Igizo,** n. *ma-* act of imitating. *Matendo ya maigizo,* dramatization. **Mwiga, n.** *wa-*, **Mwigaji,** n. *wa-* one who imitates (or copies), but commonly, a mocker, mimic, caricaturist. **Mwigo,** n. *mi-* (1) imitation, copying; (2) mimicry, mockery, counterfeit, forgery, caricature. **Uigaji,** n. imitating, copying, &c. (Cf. *fuata, dhihaka, mzaha.*)

Ihramu,* n. (1) the clothes worn by Muhammadans when doing the pilgrimage (Ar. احرام); (2) the pyramids, also *haram.* (Ar. اهرام.)

Ihsani,* n. See **Hisani.**

Ihtiari,* n. See **Hitiari** under **Hiari.**

Ihtilafu,* n. See **Hitilafu.**

Ijabu,* n. See **Hijabu.**

Ijapo, Ijapokuwa. See under **Ja.**

Ijara,* n. See under **Ajiri.**

Ijumaa,* n. Friday. **Ijumaa Kuu,** Good Friday. (Ar. الجمعة.)

Ika, v. place, put. (Cf. *weka, ikiza.*)

Ikirahi,* n. See under **Karaha.**

Ikiwa, verb-form, if it be, often used as a conj. if, supposing, &c.

Ikiza, v. Cs. lay across, set in position (from side to side), spread over. *Ikiza nyumba boriti,* place in position the beams in a house to carry a concrete roof, &c. Also used in cookery, *ikiza sukari,* spread with sugar. Ps. **Ikizwa.** *Nyumba imeikizwa dari,* the house has had a ceiling put on. (Cf. *laza, tanda.*)

Iko, verb-form, it is (they are) there. Pfx. with locative *-ko.* **Ikoje,** interrog. How is it? How does it go? What is it like? (colloquial).

Ikrahi,* n. See **Karaha.**

Iktisadi,* n. economy, thrift. (Cf. *wekevu.* Ar. اقتصاد.)

Ikweta,* n. the equator, the word adopted for use in text-books and school lessons. (Eng.) (Cf. *Istiwai.*)

Ila,* conj. except, unless, but. *Hana ila mke mmoja,* he has but one wife. *Wote walikwenda ila yeye,* they all went except him. (Cf. *isipokuwa.* Ar. الا.)

Ila,* n. defect, blemish, drawback, disgrace, stain, blot. *Mtu mzuri, lakini ana ila,* a good man, but he has faults. (Cf. *hitilafu, walakini, waa, tofauti.* Ar. علة.)

Ilakini.* See **Lakini.**

Ilani,* n. a notice, proclamation. (Cf. *tangazo.* Ar. اعلان an advertisement.)

Ili,* conj. in order that, that. Used with Subj. and Infin. e.g. *amekwenda mjini ili kununua* (or *anunue* or *akanunue*) *chakula,* he has gone to the village to buy food. (Ar. على.)

Iliki,* n. also **Hiliki,** cultivated

cardamom, used in making curries, *Elettaria cardamomum.* (Hind. الاچى.)

Ilmu,* n. See **Elimu** under **Elimisha.**

Ima, v. a. and adv. See **Wima.**

Imamu,* n. a leader, i.e. the minister of a Muhammadan mosque, who conducts the prayers. (Ar. امام.)

Imani,* n. See under **Amini.**

Imara,* n. and a. firmness, compactness, hardness, strength, stability, solidity—material and moral. *Ukuta huu hauna imara,* this wall has no strength. *Mtu wa imara,* a resolute, brave, strong-willed man. As a. firm, strong, hard, unbreakable, solid, courageous, brave. **Imarika,** v. be strong, be firm, be solid, be established firmly. Cs. **Imarisha,** establish, make firm, strong, solid, &c. (Ar. عمار.)

Imba, v. sing, sing of. Ps. **Imbwa.** St. **Imbika.** Prep. **Imbia.** Cs. **Imbisha,** cause to sing, instruct in singing, strike up a song. **Mwimba,** n. *wa-,* **Mwimbaji,** n. *wa-* a singer, songster, chorister. **Mwimbishi,** n. *wa-* one who teaches, or leads singing, a singing master, a conductor. **Wimbaji,** n. singing as a practice, profession, manner of singing. **Wimbo,** n. for *u-imbo,* (*nyimbo*), a song, hymn, singing.

Imla,* n. dictation. (Ar. املاء.)

Ina,* a. certainly, truly. (Cf. *kweli, hakika.* Ar. ان.)

Ina, v. Direct form not now in use in Swahili, but the following derivatives are: Stc. **Inama,** stoop, bend down, bow, slope, let down, decline, sink, depress. Used Trans. and Intrans. *Ukuta huu umeinama,* this wall has sunk, or slopes downwards. *Inama kichwa,* bow the head. *Mji wote umejiinama,* the whole city is depressed. Prep. **Inamia,** bow to, incline towards, be directed to, depend on. *Nyumba hii imeniinamia,* this house depends on me. Cs. of Stc. **Inamisha,** cause to bend down, depress, &c. St. **Inika,** (1) give a downward direction to, lay over on one side, give a cant (tilt, downward bend or turn) to, let hang down, turn down at the edge, &c.; (2) fig. humble, bring low, depress. *Inika chombo,* careen a vessel (for repairs). *Usiuinike mzigo,* do not let your load cant over to one side. *Inika kichwa, jiinika,* hang down the head (in grief or shame). Also *jiinika,* (1) make a bow, bow oneself gracefully; (2) lie on one's side. *Inika mti,* bend down a tree (to get the fruit). *Nani awezaye kumwinika mfalme?* Who can humiliate a king? Ps. **Inikwa.** Prep. **Inikia.** Cs. **Inikisha** and **Inikiza,** (1) e.g. *mwalimu ameinikiza watu kwa kusali,* the minister taught the congregation to bow down at prayers; (2) bribe. Cv. **Inua,** (1) set up, raise up, build up, pile up, lift up, raise, hoist; (2) fig. inspirit, cheer, restore, cure, set up. *Inua mzigo,* raise a load. (Cf. *twika.*) *Inua mtoto,* lift up a child. *Inua macho,* raise the eyes. (Cf. *vua macho.*) *Inua mgonjwa,* restore an invalid. Ps. **Inuliwa.** St. and Pot. **Inuka,** (1) be raised, e.g. *nchi yote imeinuka,* the whole country is elevated, is a table-land; (2) stand up; (3) fig. advance in position or condition. Prep. **Inukia,** (1) get better of sickness; (2) begin to prosper. Prep. of Cv. **Inulia.** Cs. **Inuliza,** *inuliza mzigo,* help a man up with his load. **Jinamizi,** n. *ma-* from Cs. form *inamiza,* (1) bending (oneself) down, bowing down, e.g. *mahali pa jinamizi,* a place where you must bend down; (2) fig. humility, self-humiliation; (3) nightmare. *Jinamizi limenilemea,* I am oppressed by a nightmare. **Kiinamizi,** n. *vi-* (1) bending, stooping down as for work; (2) a reward for exertion, e.g. the portion of meat received by a slaughterer as his fee. **Kiinikizo,** n.

vi- (1) a heavy load; (2) a bribe. **Kiinua,** n. *vi-* that which raises up, e.g. *kiinua mgongo,* a back raiser, i.e. gratuity to one who has been bending over work. **Mwinamishi,** n. *wa-* (1) one who causes to bend (stoop); (2) one who submits to another. **Mwinamo,** n. *mi-* a stooping, a bending down, declivity, a slope. **Mwinuko,** n. *mi-* a raising up, a hill, an elevation. **Ujinamizi,** n. like *jinamizi.*

Inadi,* n. same as *inda,* which see, but also provocation, perversity, obstinacy, &c. (Ar. عناد.)

Inama, v. See under **Ina.**

Inchi,* n. an inch. (Eng. Cf. *futi, yadi, maili.*)

Inda,* n. meanness of spirit, wilfulness. *Fulani ana inda,* So-and-so is a dog-in-the-manger, he prevents others from enjoying what is useless to him, &c.; spite. (Ar. عناد.)

Inde, n. Guinea grass. A perennial tussock grass up to 5 ft. tall, sometimes used for thatching, and the inflorescences made into hand brooms, *Panicum maximum.*

Ingawa, also **Ingawaje,** verb-form, though it be, often used as a conj. though, even though.

Ingereza.* See **Uingereza** under **Mwingereza.**

-ingi, a. many, much, large (in quantity), plentiful, abundant. **Wingi,** n. much (of), plenty, abundance, a quantity, a great deal. *Wingi wa samaki,* an abundance of fishes.

Ingia, v. (1) go in (to), come in (to), enter, get in, fall in; (2) share in, take part in, engage in; (3) penetrate, pass into (a condition, state, &c.); (4) be imported. *Ingia nyumbani* (or *nyumba,* or *katika nyumba*), go into a house. Note: this is the term used for a man taking a wife to his home. *Ingia chomboni,* go on board a vessel, embark (also *panda chomboni*). *Ingia safarini,* join an expedition, or start on a journey. *Ingia baridi,* become cold. *Ingia kutu,* get rusty. Esp. common of the feelings, e.g. *ingia hofu,* be affected by fear, feel fear, be alarmed, and so with *kiburi, furaha, hasira, huzuni,* &c. The Ps. **Ingiwa** is common in the same sense, *ingiwa na,* or *ingiwa.* St. and Pot. **Ingika.** Prep. **Ingilia,** esp. of entry with a purpose, e.g. go in for, pry into, &c. *Alimwingilia mwanamke,* he went in to see the woman—hence live with, cohabit. Cs. **Ingiliza,** e.g. *ingiliza kazini,* introduce to work, instal in office. Cs. of simple form **Ingiza,** usu. inten. of causing, allowing, procuring entry. *Vitu viingizwavyo,* imports. **Ingisha,** of special effort or force in entry. Cs. of Rp. **Ingizana.** Rp. **Ingiana. Mwingilizi,** n. *wa-* (1) one who introduces, &c., but usu. (2) a man who inherits his brother's widow, according to the custom of some tribes. **Mwingizaji,** n. *wa-*, **Mwingizi,** n. *wa-* one who introduces a custom, &c., one who imports. (Cf. *penya, enda* (*-ja*) *ndani.*)

-ingine, a. other, another, different, some, a second. *-ingine . . . -ingine,* some . . . some, some . . . others. *-ingine -ingine,* of different kinds, assorted, miscellaneous, of all sorts. As a rule 'some' is not translated unless a part of the whole under consideration is indicated, i.e. some people were playing, *watu walikuwa wakicheza,* but, some were playing (others were not), *wengine walikuwa wakicheza.* **Vingine,** as adv. variously, in another way. *Vingine, vingine,* in different ways (degrees, classes, sorts), in all sorts of ways. **Vinginevyo,** in some other way, in any other way, and so with relative affixed to other forms, e.g. *mtu mwingineo,* some other person, any one else. (Cf. *baadhi.*)

Ini, n. *ma-* the liver. Sometimes fig. of inmost seat of feelings, like *moyo,* e.g. *maneno yale yalimkata ini,* those words cut him to the heart. (Cf. *kiini* from the same root.)

Inika, v. See under **Ina, v.**

Injili,* n. the New Testament. (Ar. انجيل.)

Inkishafi,* n. the Revelations—name of a poem. (From same root as *Kashifu.*)

Insha,* n. an essay, composition. (Ar. انشا.)

Inshallah, adv. Used as the commonest and most trivial form of assent, 'Oh yes, Certainly, Of course'. (Cf. *vyema, naam, ndiyo.* Ar. ان شاء الله please God.)

Inua, v., **Inuka,** v., and **Inukia.** See under **Ina,** v.

Inzi, n. (— and *ma-*) a fly—in general, the common house-fly.

Ipi, a. interrog. which? what? See **-pi.** Also generally, *kama ipi?* of what sort? how?

Ipua, v. take off the fire (a cooking-pot, &c.). (Cf. *epua, ondoa, telekua.*)

Irabu,* n. a vowel sign in writing Arabic. (Cf. *voweli, vokali.* Ar. اعراب.)

Isa,* n. a proper name. Also the name for Jesus Christ known to Muhammadans—often with the addition *bin Mariamu.* (Ar. عيسى.)

Isha,* n. The Muhammadan prayers after sunset, during the period from about 6.30 p.m. to 8.30 p.m. (Ar. عشية.)

Isha, v. end, come to an end, bring to an end, make an end of, finish, close, complete. (The infinitive form *kwisha* is frequently used after some tense pfxs. of the indic. esp. *na, ta, me,* and after the relative in a verb-form, e.g. *amekwisha, alipokwisha.* (For similar use of the infinitive cf. *ita, iba, oga.*) *Maneno yamekwisha,* the debate has come to an end. *Akala akaisha akaenda zake,* he ate and finished, and went away. *Alipigana nao akawaisha,* he fought with them and killed them. *Kwisha kazi,* to finish a job. *Isha* is constantly used as a semi-auxiliary of time, expressing completion more emphatically than the tense pfx. *-me-.* Thus used it is commonly followed by the stem only of the principal verb, without the infinitive pfx. *ku-.* *Amekwisha fanya,* he has already done it. *Alipokwisha kuja,* when he had actually arrived. *-a kwisha,* last, extreme, worst. Ps. **Ishwa.** St. and Pot. **Ishika.** Prep. **Ishia,** e.g. *mke wangu ameniishia mali,* my wife has used up my property. *Chakula kimetuishia,* lit. food is finished for us, we have no food left, our food is finished. *Nimeishiwa na chakula,* my food has come to an end. *Ngoja nikuishie maneno,* wait till I finish my message to you. D. Prep. and Inten. **Ishilia,** marking completion for some special purpose or of a particular kind. *Wakaishilia mwezi,* they waited for the month to come to an end. So of *mwaka, kazi, maneno,* when there is a particular object in view. Cs. **Ishiza** (seldom heard). Cs. of D. Prep. **Ishiliza,** bring to an end, end. **Kisha,** adv. afterwards, then, moreover, in fine. *Yeye ni mwizi kisha ni mwongo,* he is a thief, moreover he is a liar. *Tulikula, kisha tuliondoka,* we ate and afterwards (then) left. **Mwisho,** n. *mi-* (time, place, manner, means) of ending, bringing to an end, end, result, conclusion, final step, extreme limit, consummation, annihilation, death. Often as adv. finally, lastly. *-a mwisho,* final, last, extreme. (Cf. *koma, upeo, mpaka, maliza.*)

Ishara,* n. See under **Ashiria.**

Ishi,* v. last, endure, continue, live, remain. *Aishi milele,* may he live for ever. *Mti huu hauishi sana,* this wood does not last long. **Aushi,** n. and a. life, wear, durability, permanence, long lasting. *Vyombo vya aushi,* things (ornaments, tools, utensils, &c.) which last a long time. *Sijala kitu hiki aushi yangu,* I have never eaten this (sort of) thing in my whole life. **Maisha,** n. (1) continuance, duration, permanence; (2) life (in respect of length and duration), period of living, mode of life. E.g. *mti huu una maisha sana*, this wood is very durable. *Maisha maovu*, evil living. *Maisha mengi*, long life. Also as an adv. *maisha na milele*, for life and for ever, i.e. for ever and ever. *Utufunge maisha yetu*, imprison us for life. *Mpaka maisha*, till life ends, the whole life long. *Maisha nyingi*, many lives, i.e. life periods, cf. *maisha mengi*, above. *Maisha* is life in respect of length and content; *umri*, time of life, age; *uzima*, life as manifest in the living condition, state of living; *roho*, the life-principle, soul, spirit. **Maishilio**, n. what one lives by, i.e. work, occupation, business, &c. (Cf. *endelea*, *dumu*, *kaa*. Ar. عاش.)

Isilahi,* n. See **Masilahi** under **Suluhu**.

Isimu,* n. also **Ismu**, (1) name; (2) a person himself, or thing itself. *Ismu ya mtu*, each person. (Cf. *jina*. Ar. اسم).

Isipokuwa, verb-form, as conj. except, unless.

Islamu,* n. See under **Silimu**.

Israfil,* the angel of death, also **Izraili**. (Ar. اسرافيل).

Istiska,* n. (1) a Muhammadan prayer for rain; (2) dropsy. (Ar. استسقى and استسقا.)

Istiwai,* n. Arab, equator, but usu. *Ikweta* is used from English. Ar. خط الاستواء.)

Ita, v. call, call to, summon, invite, name (for use of *kwita*, &c., in some forms, see notes on *isha*). *Amekwenda kumwita*, he has gone to call him, but note the idiom in which the Ps. **Itwa** is used. *Amekwenda kuitwa*, some one has gone to call him. *Unakwitwa* (or *unaitwa*), you are summoned, somebody wants you. St. and Pot. **Itika**, be called, obey a summons, answer to a call, respond, acknowledge a salute, reply. *Aliitwa, akaitika*, he was called and replied. *Nyote mwaitika Vuga*, you all accept the supremacy of Vuga. *Itika radhi*, give a favourable reply, assent. Prep. of St. **Itikia**, answer for, reply to, correspond to, and in music accompany, follow the lead of, chime in, and fig. correspond to, harmonize with, suit, agree with. Cs. **Itikiza**, cause to reply, teach harmony to, also Inten. assent to, give a reply. Rp. of Cs. **Itikizana**, reply to each other, all shout together in response, acclaim, correspond, harmonize, sing (play) in harmony. Prep. **Itia**, call to, summon for (by, in, &c.). *Akataaye kuitwa, hukataa aitiwalo*, he who rejects a call, rejects what he is called for. Cs. **Itisha**, send somebody to call, cause to be called, order. Rp. **Itana**. **Itiko**, n. *ma-* a reply. **Itikio**, n. *ma-* a reply to, refrain, chorus, an acceptance, consent. **Kiitikio**, n. *vi-*, **Kiitiko**, n. *vi-* response, musical refrain. **Mwita**, n. *wa-*, **Mwitaji**, n. *wa-* a caller, one who calls. **Mwito**, n. *mi-* (1) act (time, manner, &c.) of calling, a summons, an invitation, a call; (2) fig. vocation. **Wito**, n. vocation, calling. (Cf. *alika*, *taja*.)

Itakadi,* v. believe. **Itikadi**, n. (1) faith, belief in a religion or tradition or customs handed down from father to son; (2) perseverance, effort. (Cf. *amani*, *dini*, *madhehebu*, and *bidii*, *jitahidi*, *juhudi*. Ar. اعتقاد.)

Itibari,* n. trust, faith, regard, respect, esteem, respectability. *Hakuna itibari siku hizi, wenye maduka hawakubali kutukopesha*, there is no faith nowadays, the shopkeepers won't give us credit. (Cf. *amani*, *tumaini*, *stahi*. Ar. اعتبار.)

Itifaki,* n. agreement, concord, harmony. (Ar. اتفاق.)

Itika, v. See under **Ita**.

Itikadi,* n. See under **Itakadi**.

Itikio, n. *ma*, **Itiko**, n. *ma-*. See under **Ita**.

Ituri,* n. perfume. (Cf. *manukato, marashi.* Ar. عطر.)

Iva, v. (1) become ripe, get ripe, mature, become cooked (done, fit to eat), come to a head; (2) fig. come to a point, be ready for action (or execution), be fully prepared. *Embe zinaiva,* the mangoes are ripening. *Nyama imeiva,* the meat is cooked. *Jipu limeiva,* the boil has come to a head. *Mambo yameiva,* all things are prepared. Prep. **Ivia.** Cs. **Ivisha.** (Cf. *-bivu, -pevu,* and *tayari.*)

Iwapo, verb-form, when (where, it is when (where)) they are. Used as a conj. when, if, in case, supposing, even if, although. *Iwapo una akili, ungoje,* if you have sense, wait.

Iza,* v. reject, dislike, refuse. (Cf. *chukia, kanusha, zia.* ? Ar. عواذ abhorrence.)

Izara,* n. disgrace, shame. (Cf. *aibu, haya, fedheha.* Ar. عزر.)

Izraili,* n. the angel of death, also **Israfil.** (Ar. عزرائيل.)

J

J represents (1) in words of Arabic origin the same sound as *j* in 'jar'; (2) in words of Bantu origin the sound is often more like *dy,* e.g. the word *juu* is pronounced more like 'dew' than 'Jew'. *J* is difficult to distinguish from *ch* in the pronunciation of some natives, therefore words not found under *j* may be looked for under *ch.*

Ja, v. (1) come; (2) of events, happen, turn out, result. As in other monosyllabic verb-stems, the Infin. form *kuja* is used to form some tenses, and *yu* is sometimes used as the 3 Pers. Sing. in the Pres. Indic. i.e. *yuaja,* for *aja.* The Imperative in this verb is irregular, viz. *njoo, njoni,* for 2 Pers. Sing. and Plur. *Alikuja nyumbani,* he came to the house. *Naja kwako na barua hii,* I approach you with this letter. *Umekuja kushtakiwa* (or *shtakiwa*), some one has come to accuse you. *Atakuja kuuawa,* he will come to be killed, i.e. one of these days he will be killed. Prep. **Jia,** come to (for, about, at, in, &c.). *Maneno tuliyojia kwako ni haya,* that is the errand on which we came to you. *Siku uliyojia,* the day on which you came. *Mgeni amenijia leo,* a visitor has come to me to-day. The Ps. is used by itself of receiving visits, e.g. *nimejiwa,* I have a visitor, I have a friend with me. St. and Pot. **Jika,** be approachable, be accessible. *Mji huu haujiki,* this town cannot be arrived at. Rd. **Jiajia,** (1) of repeated or troublesome visits, *Wananijiajia tu,* they keep on coming and bothering me; (2) spurt out, come out in spurts or rushes. (Cf. *bubujika, foka.*) Rf. *jijia,* e.g. *nikawa kujijia zangu hata chini,* and I just fell (came) anyhow (helplessly) to the bottom. D. Prep. **Jilia,** with usual derivatives, come to (at, for, &c.) with a special purpose, in a special way. Cs. not in use. *Ja* (like *isha* and *toa*) is occasionally used as a semi-auxiliary followed by a verb in its stem form, e.g. *amekuja twaa*, he has come to taking, he actually takes (or has taken). *Atakuja ua watu*, he will come to killing people, one day he will commit a murder. And it regularly furnishes the formative element *ja* in three forms of the Swahili verb system, viz. (*a*) in the Deferred tense, with a Negative Prefix preceding, e.g. *hajaja*, he has not yet come, and (*b*) in its Subjunctive form, e.g. *asijelala*, without his yet lying down, before he lies down. Obs. also *ja* for *je* sometimes in the latter case, e.g. *asijalala* for *asijelala*, *asijawa* for *asijekuwa*. Sometimes *ja* is heard without a negative preceding, e.g. *ujaonapi?* where have you yet seen? Also there is a semi-auxiliary use of *-sija*, *-sije*, e.g. *wasije kudhurika*, lest they come to be hurt. *Asije mtu mwingine akatudhuru*, lest another man chance to come and hurt us. (*c*) In the 'tense of Possible Condition', i.e. with the relative *-po* of time, place, or condition, e.g. *nijapolala, siwezi kugeuka*, even if I lie down, I cannot turn over. *Wajapokuja*, even if they come. *Wajapo hawaji*, though they do not come. Verb-forms **Ijapo, Ijapokuwa**, and **Japo** are used simply as conjunctions, even if, supposing that, although. **Jilio**, n. *ma-* coming, approach, advent, usu. in plural. **Jio**, n. *ma-* coming, approach, seldom used except in the locative, *jioni*, evening. *Jio la usiku*, approach of night, evening. **Jioni**, loc. form of *jio*, used as n. or adv. evening, in the evening. *Jioni hivi* (or *hii*, or *leo*), this evening. **Kajia**, n., **Kijia**, n. *vi-* dim. of *njia*, little path, track, &c. **Kijio**, n. *vi-* the evening meal, the last food eaten at night. **Mja**, n. *wa-* one who comes, and so (1) a new-comer, foreigner—also *mja na maji*, or *mja maji*, one from over the seas; (2) a slave, seldom used except in the prov. *Ada ya mja hunena, mwungwana ni kitendo*, a slave talks, but a free man acts, and in **Mjakazi**, n. *wa-* a female slave. **Kijakazi**, n. *vi-* a young slave-girl, dim. of *mjakazi*. (Note: *-kazi* is feminine termination in some Bantu languages.) **Mjio**, n. *mi-* coming, arrival. **Njia**, n. method of approach, hence, (1) path, road, way, track; (2) way (or means) of proceeding, method, means; (3) progress, effect, influence. *Njia kuu*, highway. *Njia panda*, a parting of roads, cross-ways. *Njia ya kukata*, a short cut. *Njia ya reli*, a railway track. *Maneno yenye njia* forcible (effective, practical) suggestions. *Njia mbili zilimshinda mzee fisi, alipasuka msamba*, two roads were too much for old man hyena, he split in two. **Ujia**, n. (*njia, majia*), a passage, narrow path—used (rarely) to mark a difference from the common general term *njia*, which is its plural form. **Ujio**, n. (*majio*) act (manner, time, &c.) of coming, approaching. **Ujaji**, n. coming, rarely used. (Cf. *fika, wasili*.)

Jaa, n. (A) rubbish heap, dunghill, place where dust and refuse are thrown. (Cf. *jalala*.)

Jaa,* n. (B) the north, i.e. point of the compass—rarely heard. (Cf. *kaskazi, kibla*. ? Ar. جاء approaching, i.e. going north to Arabia.)

Jaa, v. (1) become full (of); (2) fill up a given space, be plentiful, abound, swarm. Used of any vessel or space, and of its contents. *Mtungi umejaa maji*, the pitcher is full of water. *Maji yamejaa mtungini*, the water fills the pitcher. *Nchi imejaa miti*, the country abounds in trees. *Nzige walijaa kote kote*, locusts swarmed everywhere. *Maji ya kujaa* (*ya kupwa*), high (low) tide. Ps. **Jawa**, be filled, be full, like Act. but esp. of what are not natural, suitable, usual contents. *Jawa na hofu* (*wazimu, kiburi*), be filled with fear (frenzy, conceit). Prep. **Jalia**, be full up to,

Jalia hata juu (not usual). Cs. **Jaza,** (1) make full, fill (the ordinary process); (2) also sometimes used of: wind up a watch or clock, *jaza saa.* (Cf. *ufunguo.*) Rp. of Cs. used as Inten. **Jazana,** be absolutely full, be crowded, be jostling together. Rp. of Prep. **Jaziana,** fill for each other. Cs. **Jaliza,** indicates a step further, a more complete (or additional) filling. **Jazi,** n. *ma-* increase, addition. **Jazo,** n. *ma-* like *jazi.* **Ujalivu,** n. fullness, being full, satiety. **Ujazi,** n. fullness, abundance, plentiful supply. (Dist. Cs. form *jaza,* v. from Ar.)

Jaahiri,* a. See **Jahili.**

Jabali,* n. *ma-* (1) a rock, rocky hill or mountain or cliff; (2) rock (as a substance), stone; (3) raised line of needlework across the back in a native dress, *kanzu.* (Cf. *mwamba, mlima, jiwe, genge.* Ar. جبل rocky hill, &c., also ridge or hump, e.g. of a camel.)

Jabari,* n. (1) Supreme Ruler, Muhammadan title of God; (2) a brave, fearless, proud person; (3) a violent person; (4) same as *jabali.* (Ar. جبّار.)

Jadi,* n. (A) an ancestor, descent, origin, pedigree, genealogy, lineage. *Sina jadi naye,* he is no relation of mine. (Cf. *nasaba, asili, ukoo, mlango, kabila.* Ar. جد.)

Jadi,* n. (B), also **Majadi,** exertion, seriousness, strong desire, longing, yearning, diligence. **Jadi,** v. desire strongly, be insistent in demanding. **Jadi,** adv. very much, excessive, seriously. (Ar. جد.)

Jadili,* v. cross question, ask, inquire, argue. Rp. **Jadiliana,** argue together, reason with each other. **Jadiliano,** n. *ma-* argument, debate, contention. (Cf. *hoji, dadisi, bishana, semezana, shindana.* Ar. جادل.)

Jaha,* n. honour, glory, prosperity. *Mtu aliyeshushiwa jaha,* a person who has been granted good fortune. *Kilango cha jaha,* the gate of Paradise. (Cf. *utukufu, ukuu, usitawi, heshima.* Ar. جاه.)

Jahabu,* v. shore up a vessel in order to caulk or repair it. **Jahabu,** n. *ma-* the place where vessels are shored up in order to be caulked or repaired. (Cf. *gudi.* Ar. جراب empty ship.)

Jahanum,* n. Gehenna, Hell. (Cf. *Jahim.* Ar. جهنم.)

Jahazi,* n. (— and *ma-*) ship, dhow, vessel of any description. (Cf. *chombo, merikebu, meli.* Ar. جهاز.)

Jahili,* a. (1) merciless, cruel; (2) foolish, ignorant. **Ujahili,** n., **Ujuhula,** n. mercilessness, cruelty; (2) foolishness, ignorance. (Cf. *katili, -jinga, -pumbavu.* Ar. جهول and جهل.)

Jahim,* n. Hell. (Cf. *Jahanum.* Ar. جحيم.)

Jaja, n. (1) a perennial herb with small yellow, blue, mauve, or lilac flowers, *Aneilema aequinoctiale*; (2) a perennial herb with small blue flowers, *Commelina imberbis.*

Jaji,* n. *ma-* a judge. **Ujaji,** n. work (position, pay, &c.) of a judge. (Cf. *hakimu, kadhi, mwamuzi.* Eng. judge.)

Jalada,* n. cover of a book, binding. **Jalidi,** v. (1) bind a book; (2) whip, scourge, but see **Mjeledi.** (Ar. جلد scourge, جلد bind a book.)

Jalala, n. dust heap, rubbish heap. (Cf. *jaa,* n. (A).)

Jalali,* n. the Glorious One, a Muhammadan title of God. (Ar. جلال.)

Jali,* v. give honour to, heed, respect, reverence. (Cf. *stahi, heshimu, sikiliza, tii.* Ar. اجل honour.)

Jalia,* v. (1) see under **Jaa, v.**; (2) grant (to), give power (opportunity) to, enable, be gracious (to), esp. of God's favour and help. *Mungu akinijalia,* if God enables me, God willing.

Ps. **Jaliwa.** *Nitakwenda nikijaliwa,* I will go if I can (if I am allowed), if all is well, God willing. **Majaliwa,** n. plur. (1) what is granted, aid, help, favour, talent, grace of God. *Majaliwa si mamoja,* all talents are not alike. (2) a common personal male name. (Prep. of Ar. جعل make, do, effect, &c.)

Jalidi,* n. black frost. (Ar. جليد.)

Jalidi,* v. See under **Jalada.**

Jaliko, n. *ma-* a variant of *mwaliko.* See under **Alika.**

Jaluba,* n. small ornamental box of metal used for chewing-mixture, *uraibu,* &c. **Kijaluba,** n. *vi-* dim. (Ar. جراب.)

Jamaa,* n. a number of persons gathered or collected together, family, society, company, assembly, gathering, meeting. *Mtu wa jamaa,* member of family, kinsman. *Enyi jamaa mliohudhuria hapa* (on addressing an audience), my friends here present. Also of a single person, one of a family, friend. *Huyu ni jamaa,* this person is a connexion (friend) of mine. **Jamii,** v. (A) collect together, but commonly Cs. **Jaamisha,** in the same sense. Care should be exercised in using *jamii,* see the meaning given under *jamii,* v. (B). **Jaamati,** n. a mosque, place of meeting. **Jamia,** n., **Jamii,** n. a collection of objects, group, company, number, mass, body, total, sum. *Jamii ya watoto,* a lot of children. *Jamii ya mali,* the whole sum of money. *Jamia ya makadhi,* bench of judges. *Jamia ya watu,* the mass of men, most people, the public. *Jamia ya maneno,* the words taken together, the whole sentence, context. Also as adv. in a mass, collectively, as a whole, all together. *Wote jamii,* all the lot, the whole lot. **Jumuiya,** n. like *jamia* and *jamii,* a society, association, confraternity, community. **Ujamaa,** n., **Ujamii,** n. relationship, kin, brotherhood. (Cf. *ndugu, mkutano, mkusanyiko, jumla.* Ar. جمع.)

Jamala,* n. courtesy, good manners, elegance, beauty, grace, gracious (kind, obliging) behaviour, affability. *Jamala yako haikupotei,* you will not lose by your kindness. **Tajamala,** n. a favour. **Tajamali,** v. do a favour to. (Cf. *adabu, madaha, fadhili.* Ar. جمل.)

Jamanda,* n. *ma-* a round basket of plaited grass, usually with a cover. **Kijamanda,** n. *vi-* (1) dim.; (2) a small basket-work blinker, or cover, for fastening over the eyes of a camel while at work. (Cf. *kikapu, kidoto, lindo.* ? A corruption of Pers. جامدان clothes box, basket, &c.)

Jamba, v. break wind with noise. (Cf. *shuta, shuzi, fusa.*)

Jambazi,* n. *ma-* a rogue, cunning cheat, charlatan. (Pers. جنباظ.)

Jambeni,* n. a cross-cut saw used by two men. (Ar. جنبين on either side.)

Jambia,* n. also **Jamvia,** a curved broad-bladed dagger, worn in the belt by some Arabs, often highly ornamented. (Pers. جنبيه.)

Jambo, n. (*mambo*), (1) matter, affair, circumstances, business, thing (never of a concrete kind, which is *kitu*); (2) matter of importance, difficulty, trouble. *Jambo hili gumu,* this matter is difficult. *Amenitenda kila jambo la wema,* he has treated me with every possible kindness. *Mambo ya serikali,* official (public) affairs. *Ulimwengu una mambo,* the world is full of troubles. *Jambo* is the commonest form of greeting for all classes, 'How do you do?' and also the commonest form of reply, 'I am quite well'. *Jambo* thus used represents in the greeting *Hu jambo* (or strictly *huna jambo,* though this is never heard), and *hujambo* is the more correct and respectful form, spoken interrogatively, i.e. You have nothing the matter with you? Nothing the matter? You are well? Similarly in the reply, *jambo* is for the more correct *sijambo*, i.e. *sina jambo*, I have nothing the matter, I am quite well. *Jambo* with the Negat. Pfx. of the Pres. Tense is used as a verb, with the special sense of being well or improving in health or general condition, both of persons and things, e.g. *sijambo*, I am well, I am better, matters are improving with me. *Nchi yote sasa haijambo*, the whole country is now in a better state. *Haijambo*, it (the weather) is finer. Cf. the corresponding use of the Negat. Pres. of *weza*, i.e. *siwezi*, *huwezi*, &c., I am ill. **Hajambo** also **Hujambo,** like *hawezi*, is sometimes used like a noun, e.g. *nikapata hajambo* (or *hujambo*), I got a better state (of health). *Tukawa sote hatujambo*, and we all were in a better state of health. **Mambo, n.** plur., when used independently, often means affairs of importance, difficulties, problems, hardships, e.g. *ulimwengu una mambo*, the world is full of difficulties. *Mambo mengi*, like *visa vingi*, complications, puzzles, perplexities. So used as an int. i.e. wonderful! very awkward! a poser! (From *amba*, v. (A). Cf. *neno*, word, matter, thing. Contr. *kitu*, a concrete thing, substance, and dist. *mambo*, plur. of *wambo* (*uambo*), the word frequently used for 'tent pegs'.)

Jamdani,* n. white brocade. (Cf. *zari*. Pers. جام دانی kind of embroidered cloth.)

Jamhuri,* n. (1) a meeting; (2) a republic. (Ar. جمهوريه a republic, جمهور multitude.)

Jamia,* n. See under **Jamaa.**

Jamii,* v. (1) see under **Jamaa, n.**; (2) copulate (also to have an emission of semen, whether in coition or any other way). (Ar. جامع.)

Jamvi,* n. *ma-* a piece of floor matting, of the common coarse kind made of plaited strips of leaf, used in houses, mosques, shops, &c., and esp. on verandahs for guests to sit on. (Cf. *mkeka*, *msala*. Prob. from Ar. جناب a title of honour and hence a place for guests to sit, see Ar. تكريم honour, also cushion of honour. See also Ar. جنب guest, &c., and Persian هم جنب sitting together, friend.)

Jamvia,* n. See **Jambia.**

Jana, n. *ma-* (A) (1) a fine large child, e.g. *jana dume*, a very fine boy (cf. *mwana* below); (2) a large youth, but this is usu. *kijana*, see below; (3) grub, larva, young (of an insect). *Majana ya nyuki*, bees in the grub stage. (Cf. *buu*.) **Kijana,** n. *vi-* dim. of *mwana* (see below), meaning generally a young person, male or female, but also with special meanings, as youthfulness is viewed in reference to (1) age, (2) relationship, (3) physical development, (4) social position. (1) As to age, the *kijana* has ceased to be an *mtoto mchanga*, and is not yet *mtu mzima*, though still an *mtoto*. *Mtoto apatapo miaka saba, amekuwa kijana mwenye akili*, when a child reaches seven years of age, he is a *kijana*, and is possessed with sense. *Amekuwa kijana, aweza kusema*, he is a *kijana*, he can speak (for himself). *Wewe kijana, sisi watu wazima*, you are a *kijana*, we are adults. (2) As to relationship, *kijana* means merely son or daughter. (3) As to physical development, *kijana* means any one in full vigour and capable of bearing arms, i.e. from boyhood till past the prime of life, as contr. with *mtoto* on one side, and *mzee* on the other, and practically synonymous with *mzima*. (4) As to social relations, *kijana* means a dependant, servant, slave. It is also used of the 'master of the house' with reference to his own property. (Cf. use of *mwana* for 'mistress of the house', i.e. perhaps heir of the house and so rightful owner.) **Mwana**, n. (*wana* and *waana*), (1) specifically, child, son, daughter, dependant—of relationship as such, without reference to age. (Cf. *mtoto*, which often connotes age.) *Huyu ni mwanangu*, this is my child. *Alioa akazaa mwana*, he married and begot a child. *Mwana (wa) Adamu*, usu. *mwanadamu*, *wa-* a child (or descendant) of Adam, a human being, one of the human race. *Mwanamwali*, a maid, a virgin. (2) in general, without reference to relationship, a person, one of a class. e.g. *mwanamume* (*mwanamke*), a man (woman). *Mwana maji*, a sailor. *Mwanafunzi*, an apprentice, pupil, learner. *Mwana sheria*, a lawyer. *Mwana vyuoni*, a scholar. *Wanakuwa wana wazima*, they are becoming grown up people (adults). *Mwana* has also various special senses, e.g. (*a*) lady of the house, mistress—and in addressing such a one, madam—like *bibi*, *bibi mkubwa*. Younger ladies of the house are called *wa akina* (or *kina*, or *akina*) *mwana*, or *mamwana*. (*b*) used in polite reference or address to one's own mother—madam. (*c*) a recess in a grave, closed by the *kiunza*, is called *mwana ndani*. (Cf. use of *mtoto*, of appendages of various kinds). **Uana**, n. childhood, period (condition, characteristics, &c.) of being a child, also in *uanaume*, *uanamke*, *uanafunzi*. **Ujana**, n. (1) youthfulness, youth, age of *kijana*; (2) smartness, spruceness. *Yule mzee anafanya mambo ya ujana*, that old man makes a fine show (i.e. just like a youth). (Cf. *msichana*, *mvulana*, *mtwana*, *bwana*.)

Jana, n. (B) and adv. yesterday, day before the present, period preceding the present. *Siku ya jana*, yesterday. *Mwaka wa jana* or *mwaka jana*, last year. (Cf. *juzi*, *leo*, *kesho*.)

Janaa,* n. also **Janaha**, shame, disgrace. (Cf. *aibu*, *haya*, *fedheha*. Ar. جناح.)

Janaba,* n. pollution, defilement, used of ceremonial uncleanness according to Muhammadan rules, caused by coition. (Cf. *unajisi*, *ujusi*, *uchafu*. Ar. جنابة.)

Janaha,* n. See **Janaa**.

Jando, n. *ma-* the initiation or circumcision rites. *Kutia mtoto jandoni*, to place a boy in the circumcision school. (Cf. *unyago*, *ukumbi*.)

Janga, v. grumble, blame, accuse. (Cf. *shtaki*, *nung'unika*). **Janga**, n. *ma-* difficulty, trouble, annoyance, danger, calamity. (Cf. *shida*, *matata*, *taabu*, *hatari*, *balaa*.)

Jangwa, n. *ma-* desert, wilderness, waste, barren ground, bare (desolate) country. (Cf. *nyika*, *pori*, *pululu*, *wangwa*.)

Jani, n. *ma-* leaf, blade of grass. *Majani*, leaves, grass, herbage of any kind. **Kijani**, n. *vi-* dim. also adv. like grass, hence, *kijani kibichi*, or *majani mabichi*, green, as a colour, the colour of fresh grass. *Majani mabivu*, dark green. (Bantu, but cf. Ar. جن be covered with vegetation.)

Janibu,* n. locality, place, side, flank. (Cf. *mahali*, *upande*. Ar. جنب.)

-janja, a. sly, smart, clever in a cunning way, deceitful. **Janja**, n. *ma-* amplic. of *mjanja*, below, i.e. a very clever rogue. **Janjuzi**, n. used in the phrase, *janja na janjuzi*, a very clever rogue, and a cleverer one still, i.e. when a rogue meets his match and is outwitted. **Mjanja**, n. *wa-* cheat, impostor, knave, rogue, sharper. **Ujanja**, n. craftiness, cunning, roguery, deceit, fraud. (Cf. *-erevu*, *hila*, *udanganyifu*.)

Januari,* n. January. (Eng.)

Japo, conj. also **Ijapo** but usu. **Ijapokuwa**, even if, although—see under **Ja**, v. (Cf. *iwapo*, *kwamba*.)

Jarabati,* a. See under **Jaribu**.

Jarari,* n. halyard, a rope running

through a pulley (*abedari*) on deck, and another (*gofia*) attached to the thicker rope (*henza*), by which the mainyard and sail of a native vessel are hoisted. (Cf. *tanga* and *kamba*. Ar. جرار.)

Jaribosi,* n. *ma-* coloured tinfoil or paper used for decorating the rolls of paper worn by some women in holes (*mapete*) bored in their ears, tinfoil, silver paper. (? Ar. جربز cheat, i.e. of sham jewellery.)

Jaribu,* v. (1) experience, make trial of, test, prove—only incidentally with any idea of trying, in the sense of 'do one's best', 'make an earnest endeavour' (for which see *jitahidi, kaza, fanya, bidii, shika*); (2) in moral sense, test, tempt. *Alijaribu kuutikisa mti*, he tried to shake the tree. *Jaribu safari*, attempt a journey. *Jaribu upanga*, test a sword. Ps. **Jaribiwa.** St. and Pot. **Jaribika,** be liable (open) to test (or temptation). Prep. **Jaribia,** make an attempt on, have a try at (for, with, in, &c.) Cs. **Jaribisha. Jaribio,** n. *ma-*, **Jaribu,** n. *ma-* that which tries (tests, proves the nature or mettle), a trial, trouble, difficulty, temptation. **Jarabati,** a. and **Mjarabati,** a. tried, tested, proved, e.g. *dawa jarabati*, a tested remedy. (Cf. *onja, angalia, tazamia, pima, kadiri*. Ar. جرب.)

Jarife,* n. *ma-* drag-net, seine—of European make. (Cf. *juya, kimia, wavu*. Ar. جرف.)

Jasho,* n. (1) sweat, perspiration; (2) high temperature, sultriness, heat—causing perspiration. *Hakulaliki nyumbani kwa jasho*, it is impossible to sleep indoors because of the heat. *Fanya* (*toka*) *jasho*, perspire, sweat. (Cf. *hari, moto, mvuke, fukuto*. Ar. جاش.)

Jasi,* n. (1) a kind of soft friable stone rubbed on the fingers when plaiting mats, also sometimes on the face and skin to make it soft, like face-powder (Ar. جص); (2) *ma-* ornament worn in the lobe of the ear, often a round silver plate. (Cf. *kipuli, kipini, jaribosi*, for ear ornaments. (Ar. جزء piece, morsel, cf. Eng. trinket.)

Jasiri,* v. be bold, audacious, dare, venture, risk, make a brave (foolhardy, venturesome) effort. *Alijasiri njia peke yake*, he risked travelling alone. Ps. **Jasiriwa.** St. and Pot. **Jasirika.** Prep. **Jasiria,** venture on, make a try at. **Jasiri,** a. brave, venturesome, audacious, dauntless, foolhardy. **Mjasiri,** n. *wa-* brave, fearless, foolhardy, audacious, venturesome person. **Ujasiri,** n. foolhardiness, audacity, venturesomeness, bravery, &c. (Cf. *thubutu, shujaa, jahili, -shupavu, -gumu*. Ar. جسر.)

Jasisi,* v. pry into, spy upon, explore carefully. **Jasusi,** n. *ma-* also **Mjasusi,** n. *wa-* a spy, betrayer, sly person, inquisitive, prying person, private detective, plain-clothed policeman. **Ujasusi,** n. inquisitiveness, prying, betrayal. (Cf. *mpelelezi, mdoya, haini, saliti*. Ar. جاسوس.)

Jawa, v. See under **Jaa,** v.

Jawabu,* n. *ma-* (1) answer, reply, in arithmetic, the answer to a sum; (2) affair, matter, concern (cf. *jambo*). *Jawabu liwe lote* (or *na liwe jawabu lo lote*), be the matter what it may. *Amefanya jawabu kuu*, he has done a great thing. *Jawabu la kesho huandaa leo*, the business of tomorrow one gets ready to-day. **Jibu,** v. answer, reply, respond, retort. Ps. **Jibiwa,** be answered, receive an answer, &c. St. and Pot. **Jibika,** be answerable, admit of an answer, &c. Rp. of St., and Pot. **Jibikana,** in same sense as *jibika*. Prep. **Jibia.** Cs. **Jibiza** and **Jibisha.** *Alimjibisha majibu*, he compelled him to reply, or he caused an answer to be given to him (the other person). Rp. of

Cs. **Jibizana,** e.g. of a class conducted by method of question and answer. **Jibio,** n. *ma-* sometimes used for *jibu*. **Jibu,** n. *ma-* (usu. in the plur.) answer, reply, retort, response. *Leta majibu*, bring an answer. *Pa* (*toa*) *jibu*, give an answer. **Majibizano,** n. plur. teaching by questions and answer, catechetical instructions. (Ar. جواب.)

Jaza, v. (A). See under **Jaa, v.**

Jaza,* v. (B) and **Jazi,** v. reward, make a present to, grant a favour to, give maintenance (to), supply (to), requite, punish. *Mungu amemjazi mengi*, God has been bountiful to him. Prep. **Jazia. Jaza,** n. *ma-* and **Jazi,** n. *ma-* (1) see under **Jaa, v.**; (2) a gift, reward, favour, recompense; (3) authority given by teachers, &c., **to** read before others, i.e. like a blessing given before the act. **Jazua,** n. also **Jezwa** and **Jizya,** (1) a present, reward, &c.; (2) the present given by the bridegroom to his bride if he finds her to be a virgin. **Ujazi,** n. bountifulness. (Dist. from *jaza* Cs. of *jaa*, **v.** and its derivatives. Ar. جازى.)

Jazi, n. *ma-* (1) see under **Jaa, v.**; (2) see under **Jaza, v.** (B).

Jazo, n. *ma-*. See under **Jaa, v.**

Jazua,* n. See under **Jaza, v.** (B).

Je, interrog. particle. How? Well? What now? Answer me! Tell me! &c. *Je, bwana, hujambo?* Well, sir, how are you? *Je, ni halali?* Tell me, is it lawful? Often used to introduce a question which otherwise might be taken as a statement, e.g. *Amejibuje?* How did he answer? What is his reply? *Kumekuwaje huko?* How do matters go there? What happened? *Nifanyeje?* How am I to act? What shall I do? Also often colloquially affixed to verb-forms made from locatives with prefixes of class. *Ikoje? Kukoje? Vikoje?* &c. How is it? How are they? How are things? What are they (or what is it) like? (Cf. *nini, jinsi gani?*)

Jebu,* n. *ma-* an ornament worn by some women, braid passing over the head and hanging under the chin, often from the veil. (Hind. جهبا a pendant.)

Jedhamu,* n. usu. *jethamu*.

Jedwali,* n. a table, i.e. timetable, table of imports, exports, &c. (Cf. *orodha*. Ar. جدول.)

Jefule,* n. violence, roughness, tyranny, brutal behaviour. (Cf. *jeuri, udhalimu, ukorofi*. ? Ar. جفاء oppressing, &c., or جفل put to flight, &c.)

Jemadari,* n. *ma-* commanding officer (of soldiers), a general. (Cf. *amiri, afisa*. Hind. and Pers. جمعدار.)

Jembe, n. *ma-* hoe, of native make, the common instrument of cultivation—a flat pear-shaped piece of hammered iron with a spike (*msuka*) passing through, and fixing it to, a short stout wooden handle (*mpini* or *kipini*). Also used with description for any kind of cultivating tool. *Jembe la Ulaya* (or *kizungu*), a spade, but also sometimes used for a plough. *Piga jembe*, weed or use a hoe. **Chembe,** n. *vy-* the tip of an arrow, arrow-head. **Kijembe,** n. *vi-* dim. (1) small cutting instrument, penknife, lancet (cf. *kijisu*); (2) fig. of cutting, sarcastic, ironical language, i.e. *maneno ya kijembe, sema kijembe. Kupiga vijembe*, give a person information or advice by talking as though about another person. **Kiembe,** n. *vi-* see **Chembe,** above. **Kiwembe,** n. *vi-* a small razor, a knife (*kisu*), dim. of **Wembe, n.** (*nyembe*) a razor.

Jenabu,* n. a title of respect, used only in letters written after the Arabic fashion. (Ar. جناب).

Jeneza,* n. a bier, i.e. *kitanda cha kuchukulia maiti kaburini*, a bedstead for carrying a corpse to burial. It has handles and a frame to support a covering (cf. *subaya*), or an ordinary bedstead is used turned upside down. (Cf. *machela, susu, tusi*. Ar. جنازة.)

Jenga, v. construct, build—a house in the native way, of poles, sticks, and grass, &c., but also extended to building in general. (Cf. *aka*, v. which is the correct word for building in stone, and *unda*, v. which is correct for building a ship, or with wood.) Ps. **Jengwa.** St. and Pot. **Jengeka.** Prep. **Jengea,** build for (with, in addition to, at, &c.). Cs. **Jengesha,** cause to build, have built, order to be built. Cv. **Jengua,** take a building to pieces, demolish, pull down. (Cf. more usual *bomoa, vunja*.) **Jengo,** n. *ma-* (often used in the plur.) a building, a building operation, material for building, a house, shed, enclosure. *Toa jengo*, design, draw, make a plan of a building. *Jengo la mawe na chokaa*, a structure of stones and mortar. *Majengo*, building materials. **Jenzi,** n. *ma-* usually used in the plur. building, mode of building. *Ndiyo majenzi yao*, that is the way they build. **Mjengo,** n. *mi-* (1) act (process, style, method) of building, architecture, also (2) thing built, erection, structure, e.g. encampment, hut, &c. **Mjenzi,** n. *wa-* a builder, esp. in native style, i.e. of wooden structure. (Cf. *mwashi*, of stone work). Prov. *Kwenye miti hakuna wajenzi*, where there are trees, there are no builders—things go by contraries. **Ujenzi,** n. *ma-* (often used in the plur.) building operations, construction, designing, architecture. *Majenzi*, buildings—also **Majengo.** (Cf. *aka, unda*.)

Jeraha,* n. *ma-* a wound, sore, ulcer. **Kijeraha,** n. *vi-* dim. *Tia jeraha*, wound. *Pata jeraha*, be wounded. **Jeruhi,** v. wound. Ps. **Jeruhiwa,** be wounded. **Majeruhi,** n. (both Sing. and Plur.) a wounded person, wounded persons, and as a. wounded. (Cf. *kidonda, choma, umiza*. Ar. جرح.)

Jeremani,* n. *ma-* a German, but usu. *mdachi*.

Jeruhi,* v. See under **Jeraha.**

Jeshi,* n. *ma-* a great company, assemblage, host, troop, army. *Jeshi la askari*, an army—usually larger than *kikosi* or *kundi*. *Fanya* (*changa, kusanya*), *jeshi*, muster (levy, enrol), an army. (Cf. *kundi, kikosi*. Ar. جيش.)

Jeta,* n. a lazy person who does not bestir himself to get things he wants, but asks others to fetch them, though the things may be quite near to him. (Prob. from Hind. جات name of an Indian tribe, from the habit that the small Indian shopkeeper has of squatting in his shop at ease, and asking his customers to reach him things not immediately within his own reach.)

Jetea, v. also **Nyetea,** rely on, trust to, be confident in, be puffed up by. *Jetea ulimwengu*, rest the hopes on this world, of a worldly person (*mlimwengu*). Rf. *jijetea*, be self-confident, be self-reliant, be arrogant. *Mwanamke huyu anajetea ujana wake*, this woman relies on her youth, as her stock-in-trade. (Cf. *tegemea, egemea, tumainia, jivunia*.)

Jethamu,* n. elephantiasis, leprosy. (Cf. *ukoma, matana*. Ar. جذام.)

Jeuri,* n. violence, outrage, brutality, assault, injustice, oppression. *Mwenye jeuri*, a tyrant, oppressor, ruffian. *Fanya* (*piga, toa*) *jeuri*, act in a violent (brutal, outrageous) way. But note: *Nitatoa jeuri yake*, means, I shall put an end to (or frustrate) his brutality, &c. As a. violent, tyrannical, &c. **Ujeuri,** n. violence, tyranny, &c., but *jeuri* is generally used. (Cf. *udhalimu, ukatili*. Ar. جور.)

Jezwa,* n. See **Jazua** under **Jaza,** v. (B).

Ji (before vowels often *j-*), a prefix used as 1. formative only (*a*) initial, before stems of (i) nouns of *Ma* class 5 when they would be otherwise monosyllabic in the Singular, e.g. *jiwe* (plur. *mawe*, not *majiwe*); *jicho* (plur. *macho*, not *majicho*); *jino* (plur. *meno*, for *ma-ino*, indicating an *i* in the root); *jiko* (plur. *meko*, for *maiko*). Note: sometimes the *-ji-* is retained in the plurals, see below for its significance. (ii) Declinable adjectives when the root is monosyllabic or begins with a vowel, to mark agreement with the Sing. of the *ma-* class, e.g. *jipya, jingi, jike, jekundu*, &c. (*b*) Medial, between *ki-* diminutive and the stem of nouns, in both sing. and plur., esp. when confusion might otherwise arise with a different word, e.g. *kijitu*, dim. of *mtu* (not *kitu*, a thing); *kijiti*, dim. of *mti* (not *kiti*, a seat); *kijiko* (not *kiko*, a pipe); *kijiwe* (not *kiwe*); *kijibwa* (not *kibwa*). It also occurs in dim. of *neno*, *kijineno* for *kineno*. (iii) Terminal, attached to nouns directly formed from a verb, and commonly conveying the notion of habitual, customary, general action, e.g. from *iga*, imitate, *mwiga*, one who imitates, and *mwigaji*, a regular imitator, caricaturist. From *omba*, beg, *mwomba*, one who begs, *mwombaji*, a professional beggar. (Cf. *ulaji*, as customary manner of eating, or usual food, and obs. such words as *kinywaji*, that which is drunk, in contr. with *kinywa*, where *ji* is mainly distinctive. This *ji* is from the termination *-ga*, found in many dialects, the *a* changing to *i* to form the noun of agent, and then effecting the *g* (cf. for similar changes, *gomba, mgomvi*; *pika, mpishi*; *jenga, mjenzi*, &c.), hence *chunga*, herd, *chungaga*, herd habitually, &c., the noun from the former is *mchunga*, from the latter *mchungaji*; *omba*, beg, *ombaga*, beg habitually, &c., the noun from the former *mwomba*, from the latter *mwombaji*). 2. Amplicative, i.e. denoting relative largeness before any suitable monosyllabic noun, and some disyllables, e.g. *jitu, jibwa, jisu, jiguu, jumba* (*ji-umba*, cf. *nyumba*), *jombo* (*ji-ombo*, cf. *chombo*), *jivuli, jinywa*. (Contr. *ki*, as corresponding diminutive prefix.) 3. Reflexive, in verbs (often strengthened by a *nafsi* following) and verbal nouns (e.g. *jisifu, majisifu, jivuna, majivuno*, &c.), and either (*a*) simple, *jiua*, commit suicide, *jificha*, hide oneself, *jihadhari*, guard oneself, *jiweka vema*, behave onself, or (*b*) with a range of meaning both wide and delicately shaded, mostly centring on such ideas as independence, wilfulness, interested action, personal aims, and objects, or gain, carelessness, indifference, random, or chance action, &c., and capable of conveying alike a gross insult, or a subtle innuendo. A few examples are: *jienda*, of easy, automatic, perpetual motion. *Jiendea*, take a walk (for pleasure), run amuck (like a madman). *Jijia*, come on one's own concerns (independently), jog along. *Jikohoza*, give a significant cough. *Jigonjweza*, feign sickness, sham. *Jiona*, be conceited. *Jikalia*, lead a life of ease and idleness. *Jipitia*, go about one's own devices. *Kizee ajipitie impendezavyo*, the old lady can go about her business as she likes. *Ji-* being a prefix of such common use and wide application, words not found under *ji-* may be looked for under the letter following *ji-*.

Jia, v., Jiajia, v. See under **Ja, v.**

Jibini,* n. cheese. (Ar. جبن.)

Jibiwi, n. *ma-* amplic. of *biwi*.

Jibu,* v. and n. *ma-*. See under **Jawabu.**

Jibwa, n. *ma-* a very large dog. (Cf. *mbwa*.)

Jicho, n. (*macho*) (1) eye. *Fumba jicho*, close the eye. *Fumbua jicho*, open the eye. Note: the expression *kufumba na kufumbua* is frequently used without *eye*, in the sense, 'in a twinkling of the eye', 'in a moment', 'there and then'. *Finya jicho*, half-close the eye. *Angaza*, or *kaza jicho*, look fixedly, rivet the eye. *Tupa jicho*, cast a glance. *Ng'ariza jicho*, glare, stare. *Pepesa jicho*, wink. *Rembua macho*, turn up the eyes, show the whites of the eyes. *Vua macho*, look up. *Jicho* and the plur. *macho*—as the organs of sight are used in idiom, i.e. *kufa jicho*, in the sense of die to the eye, i.e. be no longer pleasing, e.g. *nguo hizi zimekwisha kufa jicho*, these clothes are no longer pleasing to the eye. Also in the same sense with *toka*. *Mtoto huyu ametoka machoni*, this child no longer pleases. Also *kuwa na jicho la kutazama*, and the Negative *kutokuwa na jicho la kutazama*, the former of being proud to see, the latter to be ashamed to see, or feeling shame on account of the person doing a mean act, e.g. *nilipofanya hivyo nilikuwa sina jicho la kutazama watu*, when I did that, I was ashamed to look at people. *Ukifanya hivyo sitakuwa na jicho la kutazama watu*, if you do that, I shall be ashamed to look at people. *Macho* is often used of wakefulness, or being awake, and fig. of vigilance, as n., a., and adv. *Ana macho*, or *yu macho*, he is awake. *Kaa macho*, remain awake, keep watch at night (cf. *kesha*). *Walikuwa macho*, they were awake, i.e. on the alert. (2) spring, place where water bubbles from the ground. *Jicho la maji*, a spring of water (cf. *chemchemi*); (3) bud of a flower, when just opening (cf. *tumba*, *chipukizi*). For conditions of the eye, see *upogo*, *upofu*, *chongo*, *chokea*, *makengeza*, *chamba cha jicho*. *Jicho* is also used of envy, evil eye, &c. *Kumwonea mtu jicho*, look at a person with an envious eye, evil eye, jealousy, with bitterness, grudge, &c. **Kijicho**, n. *vi-* dim. of *jicho* (1) sly (sidelong, envious, malignant, evil) glance; (2) envy, malice, ill will. *Fanya kijicho*, be envious, be jealous. *Ana kijicho rohoni*, he feels envious, he is jealous. *Hana kijicho nawe*, he bears you no malice. (Cf. *husuda*, *wivu*.) **Kimacho**, adv. wide awake, in a wakeful condition, alert, on the watch. *Lala* (*kaa*) *kimacho*, lie (remain) awake.

Jidai,* v. See under **Dai**.

Jifunza, v. Rf. of Cs. of *funda*, v. (C), learn, i.e. teach oneself. *Jifunza kwa moyo*, learn by heart.

Jifya, n. (*mafya*), cooking-stone—one of three used to support a cooking-pot over the fire. (Cf. *figa*, *jiko*.)

Jigamba, v. Rf. of *gamba*, v. (see under **Amba**, v. (A)), vaunt oneself, boast, brag, show off. Prep. **Jigambia**. Other forms are rare. (Cf. *jisifu*, *jivuna*, *jiona*.)

Jiinika, Rf. of *inika*, which see under **Ina**, (1) make a bow; (2) lie on one's side.

Jika, v. (1) bear down, strain as a woman in labour at child-birth, a fowl laying an egg, or a person going to stool; (2) St. of *ja*, v.

Jike, n. *ma-*. See under **-ke**.

Jiko, n. (*meko*), fire-place, hearth, kitchen. Often in the loc. form, *jikoni*, the kitchen. *Mtoto wa jikoni*, a kitchen boy. *Mkaa jikoni*, a stay-at-home. The plur. *meko* is used most commonly for the three stones which support a cooking-pot over a fire (cf. *jifya*, *figa*). *Fulani hajapata jiko*, So-and-so has not yet got a cooking place, i.e. he has not yet married. *Kazi ya kijungu jiko*, work which brings in sufficient for the pot only, i.e. of a hand-to-mouth existence.

Jilawa, v. (Rf. of *lawa* not now in use), get up very early in the morning. (Cf. *mapema*, *jidamka*.)

Jilio, n. *ma-*. See under **Ja**, v.

Jilisi,* v. sit down. **Majilisi**, n. a reception room, place for conversation. (Cf. *sebule*, *baraza*. Ar. جلس.)

Jiliwa,* n. also **Jiriwa**, a vice, for

holding things firm. (Corruption of Ar. عور handle, haft, &c.)

Jimbi, n. *ma-* (1) a male fowl, a cock. *Jimbi lawika*, the cock crows (cf. *jogoo, pora*). (2) a root of the *myugwa*, the taro plant. The roots are edible, and the leaves (*mayugwa*) are like spinach when cooked, *Colocasia antiquorum*; (3) bracken, *Pteridium aquilinum*.

Jimbo, n. *ma-* (1) inhabited country, district, province (cf. *wilaya, mtaa, mudiria*); (2) a medicine made from a kind of leaves, used for bathing newly-born children, also to give to the mother just after child-birth as a purge.

Jina, n. *ma-* name, i.e. proper name. *Jina lako nani?* What is your name? *Jina la kupanga*, nickname (borrowed name). *Tia (-pa) jina*, give a name. *Jina lake linaitwaje?* what is its name? (Cf. *taja*.)

Jinai,* n. and a. crime, criminal. *Kesi ya jinai*, a criminal case. (Ar. جناية.)

Jinaki.* See under **Nakawa**.

Jinamizi, n. *ma-*. See under **Ina, v.**

-jinga, a. ignorant, stupid. **Kijinga**, a. and adv. ignorant, in a foolish way, stupidly. **Mjinga**, n. *wa-* simpleton, ignoramus, dupe, and esp. of innocent ignorance, inexperience, and so a new-comer, raw recruit, tenderfoot. **Ujinga**, n. rawness (of a new-comer), ignorance, simplicity, folly. *Ujinga wa mtu ni werevu wake*, a man's simplicity is (often) his shrewdness. (Cf. *-pumbavu, baradhuli*.)

Jingi, n. *ma-* one of the two upright posts of a native frame for rope-making, supporting a cross board (*bao la jingi*).

Jingizi, n. also **Zingizi**, the present given to, or a feast made for, the old women who helped at a birth.

Jini,* n. *ma-* a fairy, a spirit, genie—supernatural and capricious, but not always malignant, like *shetani*. **Ujini**, n. (1) the home of the genii, spirits, demons; (2) wickedness, devilry. (Cf. *pepo, zimwi*. Ar. جن.)

Jino, n. (*meno*) (1) tooth; (2) various objects resembling a tooth as projecting, gripping, catching, e.g. cog (of a wheel), ward (of a lock), strand (of a rope), plug (of tobacco), battlement (on a wall—but this is generally *buruji*), &c. *Kamba ya meno matatu*, a rope of three strands. *Jino zima la tumbako*, a whole plug of tobacco, not a cutting. *Ota jino*, cut a tooth—of a child. *Ng'oa jino*, extract a tooth. *Naumwa jino*, or *jino laniuma*, I have toothache. *Jino la nyuma*, back tooth, molar. *Toa meno*, show the teeth. *Tafuna kwa meno*, gnaw, nibble, chew with the teeth. *Nunuza meno*, help a child to teethe by rubbing its gums. *-a meno meno*, battlemented, jagged, serrated. **Kimenomeno**, n. and adv. a disease of the mouth, pyorrhoea; saw-like, having teeth. (Cf. *chonge, gego, pembe, kibogoyo*.)

Jinsi,* n. sort, kind, quality, class, way, method, procedure. Also conj. how, as; frequently used with the relative of manner *-vyo-*, e.g. *niambie jinsi ilivyofanyizwa*, tell me how it was made. *Siwezi kueleza jinsi ninavyompenda*, I cannot explain how much I love him. *Ilitukia jinsi alivyosema*, it turned out just as he said. (Cf. *namna*, which is more concrete in meaning, kind, pattern, &c. Ar. جنس.)

Jinywa, n. *ma-* amplic. of *kinywa*. See under **Nywa**.

Jio, n. *ma-*. See under **Ja, v.**

Jiografia,* n. the word adopted for geography in text-books and school lessons. (Eng.)

Jioni, n. loc. form of *jio*, used as a n. and adv. evening, in the evening. See under **Ja, v.**

Jipu, n. *ma-* boil, abscess. *Jipu limeiva*, the boil has come to a head.

Jipu limetumbuka, the boil has burst. *Jipu litatoka usaha,* the boil will discharge matter. (Cf. *hijabu, mlezi, halula.*)

Jipweteka, v. Rf. of *pweteka,* not in use now, throw oneself down in a sitting position, sometimes *jipweteka pwata.*

Jipya, a. form of *-pya.*

Jira, n. cumin seed, *Cuminum Cyminum.*

Jirani,* n. (— and *ma-*) (1) neighbour, one living near; (2) anything near, adjacent, adjoining, on the boundary. *Nyumba yangu ni jirani ya nyumba yake,* my house is next to his. *Shamba jirani,* adjacent plantation. *Tunakaa jirani,* we live next to each other. Prov. *Heri jirani karibu kuliko ndugu mbali,* a near neighbour is better than a far off relation. **Ujirani,** n. (1) having neighbours, neighbours, neighbourliness, e.g. *ujirani ni fedha katika kasha,* having neighbours is (like having) money in a safe; (2) neighbourhood, neighbouring district. (Ar. جيران.)

Jiri,* v. (1) come to pass, take place, take effect. *Haikujiri neno,* it does not affect you; (2) pass, of time and things, e.g. *maji haya yanajiri,* this water is passing. *Mambo yamejiri,* the matters have passed. Cs. **Jirisha,** e.g. *mfalme alijirisha sheria,* the king gave effect to the laws, enforced the law. (Cf. *tukia, tokea, -ja, -wa, pita, enda.* Ar. جرى flow, اجرى carry out, execute.)

Jiriwa,* n. See **Jiliwa.**

Jisifu, v. Rf. of *sifu.* **Jisifu,** n. *ma-.* See under **Sifa,** n.

Jisu, n. *ma-* amplic. of *kisu.*

Jitahidi,* v. also **Jitihadi,** make an effort, exert oneself, try hard, strain at. Cs. **Jitahidisha,** in Inten. sense, make a great effort. **Jitihada,** n. also **Jitihadi,** n. effort, endeavour, exertion. *Jitihadi haiondoi amri ya Mungu,* human effort is powerless against God's will. **Juhudi,** n. effort, exertion, strain, ardour, zeal, painful stress, agony. *Ana juhudi ya kazi,* he is a zealous worker. *Fanya juhudi,* take great pains. *Juhudi si pato,* trying is not the same as succeeding. **Ujitahidi,** n. energy, exertion, effort, perseverance, &c. (Cf. *bidii, kaza, shika, nia.* Ar. جهد, exertion, effort, اجتهد strive after.)

Jitanibu,* v. (1) move from one place to another; (2) show off, vaunt oneself. (Cf. *hama, takabari.* Ar. اجتنب.)

Jiti, n. *ma-* amplic. of *mti.*

Jitimai,* n. grief, sorrow, affliction. (Cf. *majonzi, huzuni.* Ar. اغتم grieve.)

Jito, n. *ma-* amplic. of *mto.*

Jitu, n. *ma-* amplic. of *mtu.*

Jituka, v. be startled. (Cf. *shtuka,* prob. from same root.)

Jivi, n. *ma-* (1) amplic. of *mwivi,* see under **Iba;** (2) wild hog. (Cf. *ngiri, mbango.*)

Jivu, n. *ma-* often in the plur. *majivu,* ashes of burnt material. a. *jivujivu,* or *kijivu,* or *rangi ya majivu,* ash colour, grey, ash-like.

Jivuli, n. *ma-* amplic. of *kivuli.*

Jiwa, v. See under **Ja,** v.

Jiwe, n. (*mawe*), or to indicate large size. **Jiwe,** *ma-* a stone, a large stone, a piece of stone, stone (as material). *Nyumba ya mawe,* a stone house. *Jiwe la thamani,* a precious stone (cf. *kito*). *Mawe!* is used as a contemptuous expletive, Rubbish! Nonsense! Humbug! I don't believe you! *Jiwe la kusagia,* a millstone. *Jiwe la manga,* a kind of whetstone (cf. *kinoo*). *Piga* or *pigia mawe,* throw stones at, stone. *Mtupo wa jiwe,* a stone's throw. *Jiwe* is also used for a weight of a pair of scales or balances. **Kijiwe,** n. *vi-* dim. and adv. (1) a small stone, like a stone; (2) a small pimple or spot on the face, acne. **Kawe,** n., **Kiwe,** n. *vi-* a very small stone, dim. of *jiwe.*

Kikawe, n. *vi-*, a very tiny stone. **Mbwe**, n. a small stone, pebble; sometimes white ones are used for decorating the graves of Muhammadans, the *Mwalimu* saying *La ilahi illa llahu* over them before they are placed on the grave, i.e. *kuhalilia*. (For other kinds of stones, cf. *jasi, mwamba, jabali, kokoto, changarawe, mchanga*.)

Jizi, n. *ma-*. See under **Iba**.

Jizla,* n. a measure of weight, about 10 *frasila*, or 60 *pishi*, i.e. about 350–60 lb. (Ar. جزل a basket.)

Jizya,* n. See under **Jaza**, v. (B).

Jodari,* n. a kind of dried fish, like dried shark.

Jogoo, n. *ma-* a male fowl, a cock. *Jogoo lawika*, the cock crows. *Jogoo la kwanza*, first cockcrow, about 2 a.m. *Jogoo la pili*, second cockcrow, just before dawn, 4 a.m. *Majogoo ndiyo saa ya shamba*, the cock is indeed the clock in the country. Prov. *Likiwika lisiwike, kutakucha*, whether (the cock) crows or not, dawn will come. (Cf. *jimbi, pora, kuku*.)

Johari,* n. (1) a jewel, a gem, a precious stone, e.g. *zumaradi, yakuti, almasi, feruzi, lulu*; (2) nature, essence, i.e. *johari za mtu ni mbili, akili na haya*, the most precious qualities of a man are these two, intelligence and modesty. (Cf. *kito*. Ar. جوهر jewel, essence, nature.)

Joho,* n. (— and *ma-*) (1) woollen cloth; (2) a long loose coat or cloak, open in front, and often richly embroidered, worn by some Arabs and well-to-do people. (Cf. *kanzu, nguo, bushuti, mfuria*. Ar. جوخ.)

Joka, n. *ma-* amplic. of *nyoka*.

Joko, n. See under **Oka**.

Jombo, n. *ma-* amplic. of *chombo*.

Jongea, v. move (pass) on, make a move, move, either of approaching or going away. *Jongea uvulini*, move into shade. *Jongea huku, nipishe mimi*, move aside and let me pass. Prep. **Jongelea**, move to, approach, go up to or away from. &c. *Alinijongelea mpaka nilipo*, he came close up to where I was. Cs. **Jongeza**. (Cf. *enda, pita, sogea*.)

Jongo, n. *ma-*. See under **Mgongo**.

Jongomeo, n. the next world. (Cf. *ahera, kuzimu*.)

Jongoo, n. *ma-* (1) a millipede. *Jongoo panda*, a large kind of millipede. Prov. *Mtupa jongoo hutupa na mti wake*, he who throws away a millipede, throws away the stick it is on as well; (2) a euphemism for a sexually impotent man, cf. *jongoo halipandi mtungi*, a cryptic saying referring to a man's impotence; (3) *jongoo la pwani*, bêche-de-mer, a large sea-slug, also called *babaje, kojojo*, and *kojozi*.

Jora,* n. a length of calico, calico in the piece (about 30 yards). (Cf. *taka*, n. Hind. جور.)

Jore, n. (1) a bird, the broad-billed Roller (*Eurystomus afer*); (2) sometimes heard for *jeuri*.

Joshi,* n. windward or weather side, in navigation; also called *upande wa juu*, upper side. Contr. *demani*, lee side. *Upande wa joshini*, weather side, windward. *Pindua chombo kwa joshini*, tack about, 'bout ship. *Enda joshi*, sail near the wind, used of a dhow, going straight ahead. *Joshi la tanga*, the lower, forward part of the sail in a native vessel; also one of the ropes of the front sail of a sailing vessel. *Enda joshi mbili tatu*, is used of loading up a dhow. *Kalia joshi*, (1) be to windward of, and so, (2) have an advantage over, have the best position as to. *Huyu anakukalia joshi*, this man has the better position, menaces your safety. (3) amplic. of *moshi*. (Ar. جوش middle course, &c.)

Josho, n. See under **Osha**.

Joto, n. See under **Ota**, v. (C).

Joya, n. a white spongy substance sometimes found filling the shell of a coco-nut, instead of being deposited as the usual lining of nutty hard substance on the inside—also the nut thus filled. *Joya la nazi*, either the substance or the nut. *Kama joya*, spongy, porous, full of holes. Prov. *Nyumba yangu ni joya, atakaye huingia*, my house is like a spongy coco-nut, any one who likes goes into it. (Cf. *nazi*.)

Jozi,* n. (1) a pair, brace, couple—of anything. *Jozi ya viatu*, a pair of shoes; (2) a whole pack of cards, one is *karata*, see under **Karata**; (3) a nut, kernel. (Ar. جوز.)

Jua, n. *ma-* (1) the sun, sunshine, fine weather; (2) time of day (as judged by the position of the sun). *Jua kali* (*jingi*), hot sun, hot weather. *Jua kichwani* (*vichwani*), time of sun over-head, noonday. *Jua kucha* (*kupanda, kutoka, kuchomoza*), sunrise. *Jua kuchwa* (*kutwa, kutua, kushuka*), sunset. *Jua linaaga miti*, the sun is taking farewell of the trees, i.e. is setting. *Macho* or *macheo ya jua*, sunrise, the Orient, the East. *Machweo ya jua*, sunset, the West. *Jua limekuwa alasiri* (*adhuhuri, magharibi*), the time of the day is afternoon (noon, evening, &c.). *Katika jua saa moja*, at 7 a.m. The time is often shown by stretching the arm at the angle the sun will be when the time wished to be indicated is reached, and saying *Jua hivi*, the sun thus.

Jua, v. know, know about, understand, be acquainted with. *Najua jambo hili* (*mtu huyu*), I know this affair (this person). *Sijui maneno ya Kiingereza*, I do not know the English language. *Najua kufua chuma*, I know smith's work. *Namjua aliko*, I know where he is. Ps. **Juliwa**. St. and Pot. **Julika**, and **Julikana**, be known, be knowable, be intelligible. Cs. **Julisha** (rarely **Juza**), cause to know, make known, inform. Also **Juvya**, and **Juvisha** (sometimes meaning 'make impertinent, provoke to or teach impertinence'). Rp. **Juana**, know each other, *nimewajuanisha*, I have introduced them to each other. Note: The root of this verb is *juwa* (*w* being the bilabial fricative, and the *l* in the derivatives has been introduced by false analogy with other verbs ending in *ua*, which were formerly *ula*. This explains the causative form *-juvya*, and also the adjective *-juvi*, and noun, *mjuvi* and *mjuzi*.) **Kijuvi**, n. and adv. an impertinent child, a bit of impertinence, a saucy remark, and impertinently, &c. **Mjuvi**, n. *wa-* a saucy, impudent, inquisitive, prying, intruding person. **Mjuzi**, n. *wa-* one who knows, a well-informed, large minded, sagacious, wise person. *Mwenyezi Mungu ni msikivu na mjuzi wa kila neno*, Almighty God hears and knows everything. **Ujuvi**, n. impudence, impertinence, sauciness, precocity, knowingness. **Ujuzi**, n. possession of knowledge, wisdom, sagacity, practical experience. (Cf. *fahamu, tambua*.)

-juba,* a. fearless, brave. (Cf. *hodari*. Ar. جبّ overcome, vanquish, &c.)

Juba,* n. (— and *ma-*) (1) a kind of coat, open in front, with collar and wide sleeves of cloth (or unlike the *joho*) of calico and linen. (Cf. *joho, kanzu, nguo*. Ar. جبة.) (2) a mortising chisel. (Cf. *patasi, chembeu*. ? Ar. جب cut off.)

Juburu,* v. compel, force, sometimes used in the sense of encourage. (Ar. جبر. Cf. *jabari*.)

Jugumu,* v. speak scornfully, disparagingly of. (Cf. *sema* with objec. pfx. *kumsema mtu*. Ar. جخّم arrogant, insolent.)

Juha,* n. *ma-* an idiot, simpleton, ignoramus. (Cf. *mjinga, mpumbavu, baradhuli*. Ar. جحّ.)

Juhudi,* n. See under **Jitahidi**.

Juju,* n. *ma-* Gog and Magog. Some

Muhammadans say that *Juju, Majuju* shall come on the last day of the world and eat up the houses and stones. (Ar. ماجوج Magog, ياجوج Gog.)

Jukumu,* n. (1) trader's risk, payment for taking risk, insurance. *Lipa jukumu,* insure (goods, in trading). *Chukua jukumu,* take the risk, guarantee. (2) responsibility, e.g. *kujichukulia jukumu,* to place oneself in a responsible position or in danger. **Jukumu,** v. take responsibility. (Hind. جوکهم risk, danger.)

Jukwaa,* n. *ma-* also **Jukwari,** scaffolding, staging, stage, scaffold. (Cf. *ulingo, dungu.*)

Julai,* n. July. (Eng.)

Juma,* n. *ma-* a week. *Juma moja,* one week. *Juma zima,* a whole week. The days of the week are **Jumamosi,** Saturday; **Jumapili,** Sunday; **Jumatatu,** Monday; **Jumanne,** Tuesday; **Jumatano,** Wednesday; **Alhamisi,** Thursday; **Ijumaa,** Friday. **Ijumaa,** is the Muhammadan Holy day, equivalent to the Christian Sunday, it is the day of assembly. Cf. *jamaa, jamii. Msikiti wa jumaa,* the mosque of the congregation. *Juma* is a very common personal male name. (Ar. جمعة.)

Jumba, n. *ma-*. See under **Chumba.**

Jumbe, n. *ma-* chief, headman. (Cf. *diwani, mwinyi, mkuu, mudiri.*)

Jumla,* n. (1) the sum, total, a lot, all together; (2) also adv. wholesale, in lots. **Jumlisha,** v. Cs. add up, sum up, put all together, in arithm. addition, to add up, tot up. Ps. **Jumlishwa.** (Cf. *jumuiya.* Ar. جمل.)

Jumu,* n. also **Nujumu,** fortune, luck. (Cf. *bahati, sudi, nasibu.* Ar. نجم star, prediction, appointed time), *jumuiya.* See under **Jamaa.**

Jumuiya, n. See under **Jamaa.**

Jungu, n. *ma-*. See under **Chungu.**

Juni,* n. June. (Eng.)

Jura, n. *ma-* (1) an idiot, simpleton, ignoramus. (Cf. *mjinga, mpumbavu, baradhuli,* from same root as *juha*). (2) a large frog, amplic. of *chura.*

Jurawa, n. Grey-headed Sparrow. (Cf. *shorewanda.*)

Juta,* v. regret, feel the loss of, miss, be sorry for, feel remorse for. *Najuta maovu niliyofanya,* I regret the evil that I have done. *Ukifanya hivi utajuta,* If you do that, you will regret it. St. and Pot. **Jutika.** Prep. **Jutia.** Cs. **Jutisha.** Rp. of Prep. **Jutiana,** join in regretting. **Juto,** n. *ma-* usually in plur. (1) regret, remorse, sorrow for what is past. *Fanya* (*ona, ingiwa na,* &c.) *majuto,* feel remorse. *Shikwa* (*patwa*) *na majuto,* have a fit of remorse. *Walijuta sana majuto makuu,* they very bitterly regretted it. Prov. *Majuto ni mjukuu, mwishowe huja kinyume,* regret is (like) a grandchild, its end turns out to be contrary (to what was expected). (Cf. *toba, sikitika.* Rf. form from Ar. عتّ blame, rebuke.)

Juto, n. *ma-* (1) see under **Juta;** (2) sometimes heard for *jito,* amplic. of *mto.*

Juu, adv. and (with *ya*) prep. (1) of position—above, high up, over, on, upon, up (to) above, from above, upstairs, on the top (of). *Juu ya nyumba,* on the top of the house. *Aliyeko juu mngojee chini,* wait below for he who is above. *Panda juu,* go upstairs. *Shuka juu ya farasi,* dismount from a horse. Also of rank, dignity, &c. *Aliye juu ni juu,* i.e. a great man is out of reach. *Juu, iliyo juu, palipo juu, juu yake,* are used of 'the top' of a thing. *Hapa ndipo juu,* here is indeed the top, the highest point. (2) Resting on, dependent on, obligatory on, morally binding on, the business of, the duty of, &c. *Juu yako,* you are responsible, it depends on you. *Juu ya mfalme kutawala,* it is the king's business to rule. *Nguo* *na nyumba ni juu yako, chakula ni juu yangu,* clothing and house is your affair, but I am responsible for the food. (3) over and above, in addition to, beside. *Juu ya mambo haya,* besides all this. *Mpe shilingi juu ya mshahara wake,* give him a shilling in addition to his wages. (4) about, concerning, as to, in respect of, with regard to. *Mtoto hufanya adabu juu ya mwalimu wake,* a pupil treats his teacher with all respect. *Fanya shauri juu ya safari yako,* make plans for your journey. *Alisema mengi juu yake,* he talked a great deal about him. (5) against, in opposition to, to the prejudice (harm, loss) of. *Huna nguvu juu yangu,* you have no power against (over) me. *Walileta vita juu ya adui,* they made war upon (against) the enemy. (6) in an excited, perplexed, alarmed state or condition (of mind and feeling). *Moyo wake u juujuu, ana moyo wa juu juu,* he is excited, has taken offence, is angry, has lost his head, &c. The Rd. form *juujuu* is also often used with different shades of meaning, e.g. (1) high up, very high, exalted. *Tazama kijuujuu,* take a bird's-eye, synoptic, general view. (2) proud, arrogant, supercilious; (3) superficial, foolish, shallow, excited, perplexed, &c. *Waliulizwa ya juujuu,* they were asked the usual (civil) questions. *Mambo ya juujuu,* indifferent matters, gossip, topic of the hour, superficial affairs. *Tulisemezana juujuu,* we had a chat together. **Kijuujuu,** n. and adv. superficial, insignificant, foolish. *Kuchukuliwa kijuujuu,* to be carried away unknowingly. (Contr. *chini.*)

Juvisha, v., **Juvya,** v. Cs. See under **Jua,** v.

Juya,* n. *ma-* a seine, drag-net, made of native materials. (Cf. *jarifa, wavu, kimia.* Ar. ? جر drag, draw.)

Juza, v. Cs. See under **Jua,** v.

Juzi, n. *ma-* the day before yesterday. Prov. *Juzi na jana si kama ya leo,* the day before yesterday and yesterday are not the same as to-day, i.e. don't judge by what happened on previous occasions. *Mwaka juzi* or *mwaka wa juzi,* the year before last. Also indefinitely, *juzi,* or *juzi juzi,* a few days ago, lately. *Juzi hivi,* the other day. *Tangu majuzi yale,* some time ago. *Mtu wa juzi,* a new-comer, a young person. *Kushinda juzi,* three days ago. (Cf. *jana, kesho.*)

Juzu,* v. be permissible, be allowable, be suitable, be fitting for, be right for, be duty of. *Nguo hizi hazimjuzu,* these clothes do not suit him, are not proper for him. *Neno hili lajuzu nami,* this matter is right for me, is my duty. Prep. **Juzia,** be right for, be allowed to, be obligatory for. *Mwanamke huyu anijuzia kumwoa,* it is right for me to marry this woman. So *imenijuzia kumwoa.* Also n. and a., of what is allowable, within one's duty, and so (often) morally binding, obligatory. (Cf. *pasa, wajibu, faa.* Ar. جاز.)

Juzuu,* n. division, section, chapter of a book, esp. of the Koran. *Anasoma juzuu ya thelathini,* he is reading the thirtieth chapter. (Cf. *sura, kitabu, chuo.* Ar. جزء.)

K

K represents the same sound as in English. For the sound of the Arabic *kh* see remarks on *kh*. *K* is sometimes difficult to distinguish from *g* in the pronunciation of some natives, therefore words not found under *k* may be looked for under *g*.

Ka is a diminutive prefix of nouns and adjectives, more emphatic than *ki-*, but is rarely used in Swahili though found in many other Bantu dialects, e.g. *katoto*, a tiny child; *kajiwe*, a very small stone; *kagongo kafupi*, a very short little club; *paka kadogo*, a very small kitten. *Kadogo* is used sometimes like *kidogo*, as adv., in a very small degree, infinitesimally, to a very small amount.

-ka-. For the significance of *-ka-* as a tense prefix, see Grammars.

Kaa, n. *ma-* (1) a piece of charcoal, also extended to mean 'a lump of coal'. *Makaa*, charcoal, coal, embers. Mineral coal is sometimes distinguished as *makaa ya mawe*, stone coal. *Makaa ya moto*, live embers. *Makaa zimwe* (*ya zimwe*, *mazimwe*), slaked embers, cinders, dead (burnt out) coal. *Makaa moshi* (*ya moshi*), soot (cf. *masizi*). *Choma makaa*, make charcoal. (2) (—) a crab, the most generic term, including many varieties, e.g. *kaa makoko* (*ya pwani*), *chago*, *ngadu*, *mwanamizi*, *change*, *kururu*, &c.; (3) *ma-* frond, *kaa la mtende*, a frond of a date-tree; (4) *ma-* also **Kaala**, n. *ma-* and **Kaakaa**, n. *ma-* the palate.

Kaa, v. (1) stay, stop, rest, remain, wait; (2) sit, sit down, take a seat; (3) dwell, live (in), inhabit, reside (at); (4) continue, last, endure. *Unakaa wapi? Nakaa shamba* (*mjini*), Where do you live? I live in the country (town). *Kaa kitako*, sit on the haunches, squat, sit down. *Nimekaa*, I am seated—often a polite rejoinder (whether seated or not) to the invitation *karibu*, come in. *Nguo hii imekaa sana*, this cloth has lasted a long time, has worn well. *Nchi hii inakaa watu*, this country is inhabited, i.e. *imekaliwa na watu*. Ps. **Kaliwa** (rarely *kawa*). St. and Pot. **Kalika**, and Pot. **Kalikana**, be habitable, &c. *Siku hizi nyumba hazikaliki kwa ajili ya jasho*, at present it is not possible to remain indoors because of the heat. Prep. **Kalia**, wait for (with, in, by, &c.). *Alimkalia nabii Musa njiani*, he waited for the prophet Moses in the road. *Kumkalia mtu matanga*, to join in the mourning for a person. *Imemkalia tamu*, it has remained agreeable to him. *Akakalia nywele zake*, and she waited for her hair, e.g. she let it go untrimmed. *Wakakaliana karibu*, and settled near each other. Note: the Rf. *jikalia* usually means, remain idle, wait idly, live a life of ease, self-indulgence, &c. Cs. **Kalisha**, and perhaps *kaza*, which see. **Kikao**, n. *vi-* act (place, time, style, form) of sitting, dwelling, &c. Hence various meanings, e.g. (1) sitting, seat, dwelling-place, habitat (cf. *maskani*); (2) stay, duration of residence, season of residence; (3) posture, position, office, dignity (cf. *mahali*, *cheo*, *daraja*); (4) style of living, social standing, place in society, conduct (cf. *maisha*, *mwenendo*); (5) society, club, mess, set, (cf. *chama*, *kikoa*, *jamaa*), e.g. *kikao chake Unguja*, he lives in Zanzibar. *Kikao cha mizinga*, where cannon are kept, battery. *Katika kikao chao walichokaa*, in their company, at their meeting. *Sipendi kikao chake*, I do not like the way he goes on. **Makazi**, n. plur. dwelling, mode of living, dwelling-place, residence, environment. **Mkaa**, n. *wa-* one who sits, remains, lives, &c., an inhabitant, a resident, an occupant. **Mkaaji**, n. *wa-*, **Mkazi**, n. *wa-* an inhabitant, regular occupant, a stay-at-home, not a traveller. *Ukiwa mkazi, jenga*, if you are come to stay, build a house. **Mkalio**, n. *mi-* a customary wedding fee, one of several given to the bride's attendants, lit. sitting by—like *kiosha miguu*, *kipa mkono*, *kifungua mlango*, &c. **Ukaaji**, n. mode of living, &c., like *makazi* and *ukazi*. **Ukao**, n. (*kao* and *makao*) act (place, manner, &c.) of remaining (staying, residing), way of living, posture. **Ukazi,** n. act of residing (staying, remaining), right to reside, payment for lodging, mode of living, &c. (Cf. *keti, shinda, ngoja, ishi, dumu,* and *kaza,* prob. a Cs. form.)

Kaaba,* n. the Kaaba, at Mecca. (Ar. كعبة.)

Kaaka, n. *ma-*, **Kaakaa,** n. *ma-*. See **Kaa,** n. (4).

Kaanga, v. (often heard as *kanga*) fry, braise, cook with fat, i.e. *oka kwa samli* (or *kwa mafuta*). *Kaanga nyama,* cook meat with fat. *Kaanga moto,* heat, warm. *Mayai ya kukaanga,* poached (fried) eggs. *Kaanga ngoma,* warm a drum at a fire to tighten the skin. Hence, *ngoma ya kukaanga,* fig. for delay, i.e. a pause in a dance. **Kaango,** n. (— and *ma-*) a cooking-pot, of earthenware, properly for cooking with fat, a frying-pan. **Kikaango,** n. *vi-* dim. of *kaango.* **Ukaango,** n. (*kaango*), (1) frying, cooking with fat; (2) a very large cooking-pot. Cs. **Kanza** (and sometimes **Kaanza**), heat up, warm up food, warm oneself at a fire, esp. *kukanza mikono* (or *miguu*), to warm the hands (or feet). **Kanzo,** n. *ma-* (*kaanzo*), a heating or warming up. **Kikanza,** n. *vi-* (1) a warming up; (2) something which warms. (For endings in *-ga* and *-za* with similar meanings cf. *kinga, kinza*; *pinga, pinza.*)

Kaba,* v. press tight, squeeze. *Kaba roho,* seize by the throat, throttle, choke. *Walimkaba roho hata akazimia,* they throttled him till he became unconscious. (Cf. *bana, songa, kaza, saki, shika, kamata.* Ar. ? غب, see form تغبب seize a sheep by the throat.)

Kaba,* n. lining of the *kanzu* on neck and shoulders. (Ar. قبة.)

Kabaila,* n. *ma-* an important man, a man of high birth. **Ukabaila,** n. importance, high position, prominence. (Cf. *mwungwana, mkuu.* Ar. قابلة capable, worthy.)

Kabari,* n. (— and *ma-*) a wedge (of wood or iron), e.g. to split logs with. (Ar. خابور.)

Kabati,* n. *ma-* a cupboard, meat-safe, sideboard, safe, &c., anything similar to a cupboard. (Eng. cupboard.)

Kabibu,* a. narrow. (Cf. *-embamba.* Ar. ضيق.)

Kabidhi,* v. (1) take in the hand, receive, hold, lay hands on, seize, keep. Also (2) with Cs. meaning, cause to hold in the hand, put in the hand (of), deliver (to), give (to), *Amemkabidhi mwenye deni,* (1) he has seized the debtor, also (2) he has given (it) to the debtor. *Kabidhi mali,* hoard, economize. *Ulikabidhi thamani,* you received the value. *Unakabidhi watoto mali yao,* you are handing over to the children their property. *Niliwakabidhi fedha wale warithi,* I gave the money to those inheritors. Ps. **Kabidhiwa.** Prep. **Kabidhia.** Cs. **Kabidhisha,** cause to receive, hand over (to), deliver (to). Note: the Dir. form is used frequently with a Cs. meaning. **Kabidhi,** n. charge, care, guardianship, e.g. *mali imo katika kabidhi yangu,* the property is in my charge. **Kabidhi,** a. economical, grasping, close-fisted, miserly. (Cf. *choyo, bahili.*) **Mkabidhi,** n. *wa-* verbal of *kabidhi,* one who holds, keeps, &c., and so (1) a trustee, one who holds property or money; (2) a miser, an economizer, a thrifty person. **Stakabadhi,** v. receive, &c., same as *kabidhi.* **Stakabadhi,** n. (1) a receipt, acknowledgement, quittance (of money paid, &c.); (2) earnest money, pledge (of a bargain made). **Takabadhi,** v. receive, &c., like *kabidhi* (1). Ps. **Takabadhiwa.** Prep. **Takabadhia.** Cs. **Takaba-**

dhisha, cause to receive, give in charge of, entrust with. **Ukabidhi**, n. economy, close-fistedness, hoarding. (Cf. *pokea, pa; hozi*. Ar. قبض.)

Kabila,* n. *ma-* tribe, clan—a smaller division than *taifa* and larger than *ufungu, jamaa*. (Ar. قبيلة.)

Kabili,* v. (1) be in front, be opposite. face (towards), front, point to, correspond to, be directed towards, be exposed to; (2) incline towards, tend to, be inclined to, be likely to, have a propensity for—rarely used in this sense; (3) confront, brave, defy, oppose, be contradictory to. *Nilimkabili uso kwa uso*, I met him face to face. *Mahali palipokabili upepo*, a place exposed to the wind. *Ulimwengu unakabili mvua*, the weather portends rain. *Hatuwezi kuikabili bahari ile*, we cannot steer for (navigate, face) that sea. *Walizikabili risasi zetu*, they boldly faced our bullets. Ps. **Kabiliwa.** Prep. **Kabilia.** Rp. **Kabiliana**, be opposite, face each other, confront each other, have a mutual attraction, correspond. Cs. **Kabilisha**, e.g. *nitakukabilisha na bwana*, I will confront you with (present you to) the master. *Kabilisha mtu*, send a man in a given direction. *Kabilisha barua*, dispatch a letter, forward a letter to its destination. *Kabilisha moyo*, set the heart on, resolve. **Kabili**, a. brave, straightforward. **Kabla**, conj. and (with *ya*) prep. before, almost exclusively of time, previously, antecedently, in advance of. Followed by a verb in the negative, usu. the *ja* tense and often with *bado* or else a relative. *Kabla hajaja bado*, before he arrived (or arrives). *Kabla haijatiwa nanga*, before casting the anchor. *Kabla atakapokuja* (*ajapo*), before he shall come (comes). *Kabla ya kuja*, before arrival. *Kabla ya siku chache*, before long, or a few days before. **Mkabala**, adv. mostly in prep. phrase, *mkabala wa*, in front of, facing, opposite, corresponding to, fronting. Also, in front, future, (Cf. *tokea, simamia, wa mbele ya. kutana, lingana na, mbele*. Ar. قابل.)

Kabisa,* adv. utterly, altogether, quite, wholly, exactly. *Njema kabisa*, as good as can be. *Sitaki kabisa*, I absolutely refuse. (Cf. *kamwe, hasa, halisi*. ? Ar. كبس press, &c.)

Kabla,* conj. and prep. See under **Kabili.**

Kabuli,* n. (1) see under **Kubali;** (2) an Indian dish of rice, curry, &c. (Cf. *pilau*. Hind. قبولى.)

Kaburi,* n. *ma-* grave, tomb, sepulchre, place of burial. *Makaburi*, or *makaburini*, a cemetery. *Chungulia kaburini*, have one foot in the grave, said of a person who has been at death's door. (Cf. *mava*, and for to bury, *zika*. Ar. قبر.)

Kabwiri, n. a very small kind of fish.

Kachumbari,* n. pickles, chutney. (Hind. كچومر.)

Kadamnasi,* adv. See under **Kadamu.**

Kadamu,* n. *ma-* also **Mkadamu**, n. *wa-* foreman—used of the third in authority of the men superintending work on an estate, the headman being *msimamizi*, the second *nokoa*. Also adv. before, but usu. *mbele* is used. **Kadamnasi**, adv. in public, before people. *Alinisema maneno mabaya kadamnasi ya watu*, he said evil things about me in public. (Cf. *mbele, hadhara*.) **Kadimisha**, v. Cs. cause to go before, send in advance. **Takadamu**, v. go before, go forward, precede, proceed, be in advance of, lead the way. **Kidamu**, v. sometimes used like *takadamu*. **Kidamu**, n. the front part of a vessel, bow, but usu. *omo* or *gubeti*. (Cf. *tangulia*. Ar. قدم and تقدم.)

Kadhabu,* n. See under **Kadhibisha.**

Kadhalika,* adv. in like manner,

likewise, similarly, in the same. *Yeye mpumbavu na wewe kadhalika*, he is a fool, and so are you. (Cf. *aidha, thama, vile vile, vivyo hivyo, pia.* Ar. كذلك.)

Kadha wa kadha,* a. and adv. (1) thus and thus, and so on, et cetera, many other such, many more; (2) an uncertain number, a few, rather a lot, &c. *Watu kadha wa kadha*, rather a lot of people. (Cf. *vivi hivi, vivyo hivyo.* Ar. كذا, كذا.)

Kadhi,* n. *ma-* judge—i.e. the one who is appointed to deal with questions of Muhammadan law. (Cf. *hakimu, mwamuzi.* Ar. قاضي.)

Kadhia,* n. affairs, things which happen. (Cf. *mambo.* Ar. قضية.)

Kadhibisha,* v. refute, deny, give the lie to. **Kadhabu,** n. seldom used, a liar. (Cf. *mwongo.* Ar. كذب.)

Kadi,* n. an invitation. (Eng. card.)

Kadimisha,* v. See under **Kadamu.**

Kadiri,* v. (1) estimate, reckon, calculate, fix the value of, put a limit on; (2) form an opinion on, consider, weigh, judge. *Kadiri mali*, make a valuation of property. *Nakadiri maneno haya ni kweli*, I judge that this statement is true. Ps. **Kadiriwa.** St. and Pot. **Kadirika,** e.g. be limited, be measureable, be moderate (in amount, behaviour, &c.), be finite. *Kufa ni faradhi ya iliyokadirika*, death is a necessary condition of what is finite. *Anatakabari mno, hakadiriki*, he shows great arrogance, he has no moderation. *Maneno yasiyokadirika*, unmeasured (or unintelligible) language. Prep. **Kadiria.** Cs. **Kadirisha,** e.g. put a limit to, restrain, cause a valuation (estimate) to be made, &c. **Kadiri,** n. (1) amount, measure, extent, capacity, value, rank; (2) moderation, self-control, temperance. *Kadiri ya watu kumi wamekuja*, as many as ten people have come. *Kadiri gani?* What amount? How much? *Kaa mahali pa kadiri yako*, remain in a place suited to your condition. **Kadiri,** adv. conj. and (with *ya*) prep. in various senses, (1) about, nearly, up to; (2) as much as, as long as, as often as, whilst, when, as; (3) moderately, on an average, in a certain degree, e.g. *kadiri utakapofanyiwa maovu uniite*, whenever you are badly treated, call me. *Kadiri ya kukaa kitako*, just when he was sitting down. Common also with the relative of manner, *-vyo-*, e.g. *kadiri awezavyo*, as far as he can, to the best of his ability. *Kadiri alivyokupenda, ndivyo utakavyompenda*, you shall like him just as much as he liked you. **-kadirifu,** a. (1) calculating, given to estimating, &c.; (2) considerate, careful, moderate, temperate, &c. **Ukadirifu,** n. (1) estimation, valuation, assessment; (2) moderation, temperance. (Cf. *jinsi, kiasi, pima, kisi, thamini.* Ar. قدر.)

Kadogo, a invar. dim. of *-dogo*, and more emphatic than *kidogo*, exceedingly small, minute, infinitesimal, tiny. Also adv. in a very small degree. (Cf. *-dogo.*)

Kafara,* n. *ma-* an offering, a charm, a sacrifice made to avert evil. *Toa kafara*, make an offering, sacrifice. *Chinja kafara*, kill (an animal) as an offering. (Ar. كفر.)

Kafi, n. *ma-* paddle, small steering oar. *Piga kafi*, use a paddle, paddle. (Cf. *kasia.*)

Kafila,* n. a caravan. (Rarely heard, for common *msafara* and *safari.* Ar. قافلة.)

Kafini,* v. cover up, wrap (i.e. of a corpse in a shroud). *Mtu aliyekufa hukafiniwa kwa sanda*, a dead man is wrapped up in a shroud. (Rarely heard, for common *funika, vika.* Ar. كفن.)

Kafiri,* n. *ma-* one who is not of the Muhammadan religion, an infidel, an unbeliever, an atheist, a pagan, an apostate. **Kufuru**, v. (1) treat with mockery or contempt, revile, curse, and esp. (2) with reference to religion, become an unbeliever, apostatize, blaspheme, commit sacrilege, renounce God. Ps. **Kafuriwa**. St. **Kafurika**. Prep. **Kafuria**. Cs. **Kafurisha**, make (consider, treat as, force to be, urge to be, &c.) an unbeliever, cause to blaspheme. **Makufuru**, n. infidelity, sacrilege, blasphemy. **Ukafiri**, n. blasphemy, apostasy, sacrilege, &c. (Ar. كفر.)

Kafua, v. thresh grain, beat off husks. (Cf. *pura*.)

Kafuri,* n. camphor. (Ar. كافور.)

Kaga, v. protect by charm, put a charm on (in, near, &c.), e.g. *kaga shamba* (*mwili, kaburi*), protect by charm a plantation (person, grave). **Kago**, n. *ma-* (and *mago*) a charm (for protection or preservation). *Kago la fisi*, charm against a hyena. **Ukago**, n. protection, preservation, by charm. (Cf. *kafara, dawa, hirizi, talasimu*.)

Kagua, v. inspect, survey, examine. *Kagua shamba*, inspect a plantation. *Kagua askari*, inspect, hold a parade of troops. *Kagua shule* (*skuli, chuo*), inspect a school, hold an examination. *Kagua hesabu*, audit accounts. Ps. **Kaguliwa**. St. **Kagulika**. Prep. **Kagulia**. **Mkaguo**, n. *mi-* inspection, visitation, review. **Mkaguzi**, n. *wa-* an inspector, examiner, reviewer. **Ukaguzi**, n. (1) inspection, examination, survey; (2) inspecting, reviewing, &c.

Kahaba,* n. *ma-* also **Mkahaba**, n. *wa-*, prostitute, male or female. **Ukahaba**, n. (1) prostitution, fornication; (2) manner, fee, &c., of prostitution. (Cf. *malaya, danguro, mkware*. Ar. قحبة.)

Kahafi,* n. the top centre piece of a white skull-cap such as are worn by some natives, the other part is called *mshazari*. (Cf. *kofia*. Ar. اقحاف.)

Kaharabu,* n. amber. (Pers. كاهربا.)

Kahawa,* n. coffee, i.e. the beverage, the berry being *buni*, or *buni ya kahawa*, and the plant *mbuni*. **Kahawia**, a. like coffee, coffee-colour. **Mkahawa**, n. *mi-* coffee-house, restaurant, café. **Mgahawa**, n. *mi-* is also heard. (Ar. قهوة.)

Kahini,* n. *ma-*, usu. *kuhani*, n. *ma-* (1) the word used in the Bible for a priest under the Jewish dispensation (*kasisi* is used of a Christian priest); (2) soothsayer, a person who predicts by use of a divining board (*ramli*), also used sometimes for (3) deceiver, swindler. (Cf. *kasisi, tabiri, agua*. Ar. كهن divine, foretell, كاهن soothsayer, priest.)

Kai,* v. give in, surrender. (Cf. *angukia miguuni, shika miguu*. ? Ar. كعا be timid.)

Kaida,* n. (1) the second month after Ramadhan; (2) see **Kawaida**. (Ar. ذو القعدة.)

Kaidi,* v. be obstinate, be headstrong, rebel, refuse to obey, contradict. Cs. **Kaidisha**, e.g. incite to disobedience. **-kaidi**, a. obstinate, refractory, disobedient, rebellious, &c. **Mkaidi**, n. *wa-* an obstinate, argumentative person. **Ukaidi**, n. obstinacy, disobedience, &c. (Cf. *bisha, pinga, kataa*. Ar. كيد.)

Kaimia, v. force oneself to do anything, do although the doing involves difficulties, hardships, &c. (Cf. *kalifu*. Ar. اقام persevere (in).)

Kaimu,* n. *ma-* (A) superintendent, guardian, manager, agent, vicegerent, viceroy. *Bwana atakuwa kaimu wa shughuli ile*, the chief will undertake that business. **Makamu**, n. and a. (1) substitute, deputy, manager; (2) *mtu wa makamu*, a middle-aged person, neither a youth nor an old man; (3) state of things. **Ukaimu**, n. office (status, work,

&c.) of a manager, agent, vice-regent, vice-royalty. (Cf. *wakili*, *waziri*, *naibu*. Ar. قام take one's place, قيم agent, manager.)

Kaimu,* n. *ma-* (B) one who exorcizes spirits. **Ukaimu**, n. act, fee, &c., of one who exorcizes spirits. (Cf. *mganga*. ? Ar. كمم overcome, or كيميا alchemy.)

Kajayeye, n. a kind of cassava. (Cf. *muhogo*.)

Kajekaje, n. small cords used to fasten the sail to the yard, in a native vessel.

Kajia, n. dim. of *njia*. See under **Ja**, v.

Kaka, n. *ma-* (1) elder brother, often used playfully or colloquially, cf. *dada*; (2) an empty shell, e.g. of an egg, or the rind of a fruit, e.g. of an orange (but *ganda* is more usual for fruit); (3) a disease affecting the hand, a whitlow, *mdudu wa kidoleni*; (4) a leech (cf. *ruba*). (Bantu *-kaka*, elder relative, cf. also Pers. كاكا elder brother.)

Kakaka, n. a kind of vegetable.

Kakakaka, adv. in a hurry, in a rush (press, bustle). **Kikaka**, n. *vi-* hastiness, bustle, hurry, in a hurry. *Mbona wafanya kikaka?* Why are you in such a hurry?

Kakakuona, n. an animal like an armadillo—some natives believe that if its scales are burned wild animals will not come near.

-kakamavu, a., **Kakamia**, v., **-kakamizi**, a. See under **Kakamka**.

Kakamka, v. make a muscular effort, strain—as in lifting a load, breaking stone, or in travail. **Kakamia**, v. strain after, make a sudden or violent effort to do, or to get, something, be stubborn. Cv. **Kakamua**, is used in the same way. Rf. *jikakamua*, strain oneself to do some difficult task. **-kakamavu**, a. sly, cunning, intelligent in a sly way (cf. *-erevu*). **-kakamizi**, a. stubborn, relentless. **Mkakamavu**, n. *wa-* a shrewd, sly, clever, impudent person.

Kakara,* n. struggling, wrestling, e.g. *walikuwa katika kakara*, they were struggling and wrestling together. (Cf. *kukuru*, *kikiri*, with the same meaning. Ar. كرك confusion.)

Kakasi, n. also **Ukakasi**, bitter dry, as of the teeth after eating something astringent, like an unripe banana, &c. (Cf. *ukamvu*, *ugege*.)

Kakata, v. feel pain, ache, as of a pain in the stomach, &c. (Cf. *kata*, *keketa*.)

Kakatua, v. break anything hard, esp. with the teeth. St. and Pot. **Kakatuka**.

Kakawana, v. be strong, athletic, well knit, muscular, also n. *ma-* a strong well-built man.

Kaki,* n. a thin hard-baked biscuit or cake (Pers. كعك, كك); (2) khaki drill, which is much used for making shorts, trousers, and coats, &c. Pers. khākī خاكى dust-coloured.

Kakindu, n. a slender erect herb with white flowers semi-parasitic on the roots of grasses, *Striga pubiflora*.

Kala,* n. (1) a collar (Eng.); (2) a kind of wild cat. (Cf. *kalakonje*.)

Kalab,* n. See under **Kelb**.

Kalafati,* v. caulk (the seams of a wooden vessel)—the tool used being *chembeu*. Ps. **Kalafatiwa**. **Kalafati**, n. caulking material, usually cotton and grease. (Ar. قلفط.)

Kalakonje, n. a kind of wild cat. (Cf. *kala*.)

Kalala, n. *ma-* also **Karara**, (1) the tough leathery sheath of coco-nut flower-stem; (2) honeycomb.

Kalambezi, n. the horse mackerel.

Kalamka, v. also **Karamka**, be quick witted, be wide awake, be sharp (intelligent, on the alert), have one's eyes open. Prep. **Kalamkia** (usually) be too sharp for, outwit, deceive, cheat. Ps. of Prep. **Kalamkiwa**, be deceived, taken in, &c.

Kalamzi, a. sly, crafty, cunning, sharp, &c. (Cf. *danganya, punja, hadaa, -erevu, -janja.*)

Kalamu,* n. pen or pencil. *Chonga kalamu,* point a pencil. *Kalamu ya wino,* a pen. (Ar. قلم.)

Kalamzi, a. See under **Kalamka.**

Kalasha,* n. tusk of ivory, smaller than *buri.* (Cf. *pembe, buri.* Ar. قلاش small, short.)

Kalasia,* n. small brass vessel with narrow neck. (Cf. *hando.* Hind. كلسا.)

Kale, n. old times, antiquity, the past, former ages. *Watu wa kale,* old times, past ages. *Hapo kale,* once upon a time, long ago. *Kikale,* of the old style, old-fashioned, antiquated. *-a kale,* old, ancient. *Kale na kale,* for ever and ever, everlastingly. *-a kikale,* antiquated. (Cf. *zamani.*) **Mkale,** n. *wa-* an ancient, esp. the founder of a clan or family.

Kalenda,* n. a calendar. (Cf. *takwimu.* Eng.)

-kali, a. (1) sharp, having a sharp edge, cutting, e.g. *kisu kikali,* a sharp knife; (2) sharp to the taste, acid, sour, bitter, e.g. *siki kali,* sour vinegar (opp. to *laini, tamu,* and cf. *chungu*); (3) sharp in temper, severe, stern, cross, cruel, fierce, e.g. *ng'ombe mkali,* a fierce ox (opp. to *-pole, -a huruma*); (4) keen, intense, vehement, brave, *jua kali, tembo kali,* scorching sun, strong palm wine. *Watu wakali,* warlike, savage people (opp. to *-legevu, -vivu*). **Karipa,** v. but usu. in its Prep. **Karipia,** use harsh language to, reprimand, scold, chide. Ps. **Karipiwa. Karipio,** n. *ma-* scolding, reprimand. (Note: the *l* has become *r*; for the *-pa* termination, see note under *pa.*) (Cf. *laumu, kemea, shutumu.*) **Makali,** n. the sharp part, edge, point, of a thing, e.g. *makali ya upanga,* the edge of a sword (also called *machinjioni*), as opp. to *butu,* blunt (also called *mafutu*). The flat is called *bapa.* **Ukali,** n. *ma-* (1) a sharp, acid taste; (2) sharpness, keenness, edge; (3) strong character, firmness, resolution, spirit, bravery; (4) cruelty, severity, tyranny, fury. (Cf. *-chungu, katili, -shupavu.*)

Kalia, v., **Kalika,** v. See under **Kaa,** v.

Kalibu,* n. (1) a mould, e.g. for bullets; (2) a mould for casting concrete, such as for drain-pipes, sections for wells, &c.; (3) a heating pot or furnace. (Cf. *subu, ita, joko, tanuu.* Ar. قالب.)

Kalifu,* v. discomfort, cause annoyance to, impose a difficult matter upon one, trouble, i.e. *usijikalifu kwenda,* don't force yourself to go, i.e. don't trouble yourself. **Takalifu,** v. take pains over work, &c. **Takalifu,** n. discomfort, annoyance, trouble, worry. **Ukalifu,** n. (1) intensity, severity, keenness, e.g. *ukalifu wa jua,* scorching heat of the sun; (2) a forcing oneself to do something against one's will. **Utakalifu,** n. weariness, discomfort, as of one tired, yet forcing himself to do something. (Cf. *sumbua, shughulika, bidii, lemea.* Ar. كلف and تكلف.)

Kalima,* n. word. **Mkalimani,** n. *wa-* interpreter, i.e. in a professional sense, one who is employed to translate into and from another tongue. **Mkalimu,** n. *wa-* a teacher, sometimes used for the common *mwalimu.* (Cf. *nena.* Ar. كلم.)

Kalua,* n. *ma-* the name given to a sect of Indian fishermen, also, in some places, to boat-boys. (? Hind.)

Kama,* conj. (1) as a particle of comparison in general (*a*) as, such as, like, as if, as though, e.g. *yeye ni kama mimi,* he is like me. *Ruka kama ndege,* fly like a bird. *Mtu mfupi kama wewe,* a short man like you. *Kama hivi* (*vile*), as thus, like this, in this way, for instance. With a noun, often supplies a lacking adjective, e.g. *kama maji*, like water, i.e. liquid, fluid, watery, also fluent, easy. *Kama majani*, green. With *nini*, forms an expletive or adv. of emphasis, e.g. *kubwa kama nini*, wonderfully great, so great that it is impossible to say what it is like. *Zuri kama nini*, inexpressibly beautiful. With a verb, *kama* is commonly followed by the relative of manner *-vyo-*, e.g. *kama upendavyo*, as you please. *Kama ulivyosema*, as you said. (Note: *kama umesema* means if you have said.) (*b*) like, as it were. almost, about, nearly, of vague comparison, e.g. of numbers, *askari kama mia*, about a hundred soldiers. *Nyingi kama si nyingi*, a moderate number. *Anapenda kama hapendi*, he half-likes it. (*c*) in the definite comparison of two or more objects, 'as compared with' rather than, and not (cf. *kuliko*), e.g. *afadhali kuweka mali kama kuitumia yote*, it is better to save money than to use it all up. *Yeye mkubwa kama wewe*, he is bigger than you, he is big compared with you. *Heri kupotea nikafa kama kuwa hai*, better I should be lost and die than live. *Bora dhahabu kama fedha*, gold is more valuable than silver. (2) as a subordinate particle (*a*) that —of reported speech, &c. *Nasema kama ndivyo*, I say that it is so. *Nimesikia kama hajui*, I hear that he does not know. *Aliamuru kama aende*, he ordered that he should go. *Alisema kama, Nikienda nitajuta*, He said, If I go I shall regret. (Cf. similar use of *kuwa, ya kwamba, kwamba*.) (*b*) If, supposing that, though, i.e. conditional, e.g. *kama una homa nenda kwa daktari*, if you have fever, go to the doctor. *Kama hutaki, basi*, if you do not like (it) that's the end of the matter. Also often with Pres. Partic., *kama ukipenda*, if you like. *Kama fedha ikipatikana, nitalipa*, if the money is forthcoming I will pay. Also with the Contingent Tenses, both affirmative and negative, *kama ningemwambia angefanya*, should I tell him he would do it. *Kama nisingaliangalia ningalitumbukia*, if I had not taken care, I would have fallen in. (*c*) Whether, if, e.g. *sijui kama yuko*, I do not know whether he is there. *Alimwuliza kama ndivyo*, he asked him whether it was so. (*d*) followed by *kwamba*, as though. *Alifanya kama kwamba anataka kunipiga*, he made as though he were going to beat me. *Usisimame kama kwamba umechoka*, do not stand as though you were tired. In this use, one often hears *kana* instead of *kama*. (For comparative use cf. *sawa na, mfano wa, methali ya, kuliko*. For conditional use cf. *ikiwa, endapo*, and the use of *-ki-, -sipo-, -nge-*, and *-ngali-* in verbs. Ar. كما.)

Kama, v. squeeze, but esp. of milking, e.g. *kama ng'ombe maziwa*, milk a cow, or simply, *kama*. Ps. **Kamwa.** St. and Pot. **Kamika.** Prep. **Kamia,** (1) to squeeze out for, &c., but usu. (2) threaten, dun, be insistent in demanding anything; wring money, &c., out of a person. Ps. **Kamiwa.** Rp. **Kamiana.** Cs. **Kamisha,** e.g. *kamisha ng'ombe za watu*, act as milkman, undertake milking. Cv. **Kamua**, similar in meaning to *kama*, squeeze, wring, compress, squeeze out, e.g. *kamua nguo*, wring wet clothes. *Kamua chungwa*, squeeze the juice out of an orange. *Kamua jipu*, squeeze out an abscess. *Kamua mafuta*, extract oil by pressure. Ps. **Kamuliwa.** St. and Pot. **Kamulika.** Prep. **Kamulia,** e.g. *akamkamulia ndimu mwilini*, and he squeezed lime-juice over his body. Cs. **Kamulisha.** **Kamio,** n. *ma-* a threat, insistent demand, &c. **Ukamio,** n. menacing, threatening, squeezing out, reproaches, evil intention. (Cf. *songa, kaba, ogofya, tisha, shikiliza, chagiza*.)

Kamani,* n. the mainspring of a watch or clock. (Pers. كمان.)

Kamari,* n. any game of chance played for money stakes, esp. a game of cards. *Kucheza kamari*, to play a game of chance for a money stake. (Ar. قمر.)

Kamasi, n. *ma-* (often used in the plur.) mucus from the nose, catarrh. *Siwezi kamasi*, I have a cold in my head (cf. *mafua, kifua*). *Futa makamasi*, wipe the nose. *Penga kamasi* (or simply *penga*), blow the nose. *Vuta makamasi*, sniffle.

Kamata, v. (prob. Ten. of *kama*, cf. *-ta* ending in *ambata, fumbata, nata*, &c.), take forcible hold of, catch hold of, seize with the hands (arms, claws, a trap, &c.), grasp, clasp, make a prisoner of, arrest, usually of something or some one going quickly or trying to escape. *Chui alikamata kuku*, a leopard caught a fowl. Ps. **Kamatwa**. St. and Pot. **Kamatika**, e.g. *maji hayakamatiki*, water cannot be caught hold of. Prep. **Kamatia**, e.g. seize with, grasp at, get a partial hold of, &c. Cs. **Kamatisha**, also Intens. hold fast. Rp. **Kamatana**, grapple, e.g. in wrestling. (Implies some effort, difficulty to overcome.) **Kamata**, n. sometimes heard for influenza, pneumonia, and cerebro-spinal meningitis. (Cf. *shika, guia, nasa*.)

Kamba,* n. (A) cord, rope—the most generic term, properly of the native kind, but made of twisted coco-nut fibre (*makumbi*). Hence, *kamba ya kumbi, kamba ya nazi*, to distinguish it from *kamba ya Ulaya*, European, hempen rope, and *kamba ya miwaa*, rope of plaited leaf strips. *Piga* (*funga*) *kamba*, tie with a rope, cord, but also like *songa kamba, suka* (*sokota, pota*) *kamba*, make a rope by twisting or plaiting. **Ukambaa**, n. (*kambaa*) cord of plaited leaf-strips, like *shupatu*, e.g. *ukuukuu wa kamba si upya wa ukambaa*, in a rope old fibre is better than new leaf strips. The ropes of a native sailing-vessel have various names, all of non-Bantu origin, e.g. *amari, baraji, hamrawi, dasi, henza, jarari, demani, joshi, dakawa, mjiari*, or *ujari*. Various materials for binding or fastening the poles and rafters in native building are *ubugu, ugomba, ung'ong'o, ununu, ukindu*, and *miwaa*. (Cf. also *ugwe, katani, kitani*. ? Ar. كنبار.)

Kamba, n. (B) *ma-*, *kamba ya nyuki* (or *asali*), honeycomb.

Kamba, n. (C) lobster, crayfish, prawn, shrimp, sometimes distinguished as *kamba ya pwani*, and *kamba ya bahari*. **Mkamba**, n. *mi-* a larger species of sea crab. (Cf. *kaa, uduvi*.)

Kambare, n. freshwater catfish, with broad flat head and fleshy feelers, barbel.

Kambi,* n. *ma-* encampment, camp. *Kupiga kambi*, to pitch camp. *Kuvunja kambi*, to break camp. (Eng. camp? Cf. *boma, kituo*.)

Kambo, n. *baba* (*mama*) *wa kambo*, step-father (-mother). *Mtoto wa kambo*, step-child. **Kikambo**, n. and adv. the relation of step parent and child; and as adv. as a step-father (-mother) would do.

Kambuka, v. dry up, wither. (Cf. *kauka, nyauka*.)

Kambusi, n. See **Gambusi**.

Kame, a. barren, desert, waste, uncultivated. **Ukame**, n. desolation, with ref. to wilderness, desert, &c. (Cf. *nyika, jangwa, pori*.)

Kamia, v. See under **Kama, v.**

Kamili,* v. complete, finish, make perfect, also be complete, be finished. But these meanings are usually taken by the Cs. and St. or Ps. forms. Ps. **Kamiliwa**. St. **Kamilika**. Cs. **Kamilisha**, bring to perfection, complete, end, &c. **Kamili**, a. complete, perfect, whole, entire, unimpaired. **-kamilifu**, a. same as *kamili*. **Takamali**, v. be complete. **Ukamili**, n. also **Ukamilifu**, completeness, perfection, consummation. (Cf. *maliza, timiza, timiliza, isha.* Ar. كامل.)

Kamio, n. See under **Kama**, v.

Kamna,* n. *cheza kamna*, play the game of *bao*. *Kumtia mtu kamna*, beat a person at cards. (? Ar. كمن ambush.)

Kampani,* n. sometimes *kumpuni*. (1) a commercial house, a trading association, a company; (2) a company of soldiers. (Eng. company.)

Kamsa,* n. an alarm of fire, of escape of a prisoner, &c. (Ar. كبسة surprise assault, &c.)

Kamua, v. See under **Kama**, v.

Kamusi,* n. a lexicon, a dictionary. (Ar. قاموس.)

Kamwe, adv. always with a negative preceding, (not) at all, (not) once, (not) in the least, (not) ever (i.e. never, by no means). *Si kitu kamwe*, it is nothing at all. *Sitaki kamwe*, I will have nothing to do with it. (Prob. adv. made from *mwe*, a Bantu root for one, cf. *ka-dogo*; for pfx. *ka-*.) Hence *sitaki kamwe*, I do not want it, not even once. (Cf. *kabisa, halisi, hata kidogo*.)

Kana,* conj. sometimes used in the same way as *kama*, conj. (Ar. كان.)

Kana,* n. rudder, handle, tiller, i.e. *mkono wa usukani*. (Port. *canna* or Hind. كان.)

Kana, v. deny, negative, say 'no', disown, refuse, e.g. *kwanza mwizi alikana, sasa amekiri*, at first the thief denied, now he acknowledges. *Baba alimkana mtoto*, the father disowned the child. Ps. **Kanwa**. St. and Pot. **Kanika**, and Pot. **Kanikana**, e.g. *haikanikani*, it is undeniable. Prep. **Kania**, refuse to, deny to (about, for, on the part of, by, at, &c.). Cs. **Kanya**, forbid, rebuke. *Kanya mtoto wako asifanye tena*, rebuke or forbid your child to do it again. Also **Kanisha** (rarely) and usu. **Kanusha** (from Cv. *kanua*, not now in use), make to disown, deny, gainsay, often Inten. deny emphatically, e.g. refute, *ameyakanusha mafundisho yake*, he has absolutely refuted his teaching. **Kano**, n. see *mkano* below. **Kanyo**, n. *ma-* see *mkanyo* below. **Mkana**, n. *wa-* one who denies, repudiates, &c. *Mkana Mungu*, an atheist. **Mkano**, n. *mi-* a denial, refusal, repudiation, &c. **Mkanya**, n. *wa-* one who forbids or rebukes. **Mkanyo**, n. *mi-* prohibition, rebuke, repudiation. (Cf. *kataa, kataza*.)

Kanadili,* n. *ma-* a projection from quarter or stern of native vessel, used as a closet (*choo*)—also quarter gallery. (Ar. ? كندل copper vessel used for water, i.e. for use after defecation.)

Kanchiri,* n. a cloth worn by some women just below the breasts to support them. (Cf. *sidiria*. Ar. قشر kind of garment.)

Kanda, n. (— and *ma-*) (1) a bag of native (plaited) matting—often used for grain, broader at the bottom than at the mouth; (2) plur. of *ukanda*, which see; (3) a foul, shameless, ribald person (cf. *hanithi*. ? Pers. كنده.) **Kikanda**, n. *vi-* dim. of (1) and (2) above.

Kanda, v. knead with the hands, press and work with the fingers, massage, shampoo. *Kanda unga*, knead flour (dough). *Kanda udongo*, knead clay—as a potter. *Kanda mwili*, massage the body, to give relief in pain or weariness, or merely as a luxury. Prep. **Kandia**. Cs. **Kandisha**. St. and Pot. **Kandika**, chiefly used in an Act. sense of the operation of covering the wooden framework of a native hut with clay which has been kneaded, to form the walls. *Kandika nyumba udongo* (or *kwa udongo*), plaster a house with prepared clay. Ps. **Kandikwa**. **Kandiko**, n. *ma-* material for native plastering, i.e. earth or clay which has been kneaded. **Mkando, n.** *mi-* the act of kneading, massaging, &c.

Kandanda, n. a football match, or game.

Kandarinya,* **n.** a kettle, tea kettle, seldom, if ever, used now. (Cf. *birika, buli.* Port. *caldeirinha.*)

Kande, n. (1) stores, supplies, provision for a journey, usually whole maize or millet grains cooked; (2) a particular dish of food cooked for New Year's day (*Nairuzi*), in which seven kinds of grain are included.

Kandika, v., Kandiko, n. *ma-*. See under **Kanda, v.**

Kandili,* n. *ma-* lantern. (Cf. *fanusi, taa.* Ar. قنديل.)

Kando, n. side, edge, margin, brink (esp. of river or sea), bank, coast. *Kando ya mto,* the margin of the river. Used commonly as adv. and (with *ya*) prep., on one side, aside, by the side, on the verge or edge, e.g. also *kandokando. Weka kando* (or *kandokando*) *ya,* put by the side of. *Kando zote,* on all sides. *Alikwenda kandokando,* he went by the side, i.e. following along the brink. **Ukando,** n. (*kando*), with the same meaning as *kando.* (Cf. *ukingo, upande.*)

Kang'a, v. See **Kanganya.**

Kanga, n. (1) piece of cloth worn by women, the common town garment. One piece is worn tucked in just above the breasts reaching down to the ankle, another worn over both shoulders or over one shoulder, or over the head. They are of various colours and patterns. In some places they are called *leso* and *shiti.* (2) the common speckled guinea-fowl (Helmet Guinea-fowl, *Numida mitrata*)—the crested species is called *kororo*; (3) *kanga la mnazi,* the fruit stem or stalk bearing the nuts on a coco-nut tree, when stripped of the nuts, the bare stalk, dry stem. (The same when growing and with the nuts on is called *utawi,* cf. *mnazi.*)

Kangaga, n. *ma-* (1) tall coarse reeds or grasses which grow round lakes or marshes, flags (i.e. the plant), *Scleria* sp.; (2) a fern with fronds up to 5 ft. tall growing in dense clumps in salt marshes on the coast, *Acrostichum aureum.*

Kangaja, n. *ma-* (1) small mandarin orange, fruit of the *mkangaja,* n. *mi-* (cf. *mchenza*); (2) a kind of fish with a disagreeable smell; (3) a tussock herb with stems up to 3 ft. tall, *Cyperus distans*; (4) also applied to *Scleria* sp.

Kanganya, v. also sometimes *kang'a,* puzzle, intrigue, surprise, startle, e.g. *inanikanganya katika roho yangu,* it puzzles me, it intrigues me. (Cf. *tatiza.*)

Kangara, n. beer made from the husks of maize, fermented with sprouts of bull-rush millet (*ulezi, wimbi*) and sweetened with sugar or honey. (Cf. *pombe, gimbi.*)

Kang'ata, v. feel great pain or ache as if in the bones. **Kang'ata,** n. ache or pain as if in the bones. (Cf. *kakata, pekecha.*)

Kani,* n. anger, strength, energy, insistence, e.g. *ameshika kani twende tu,* he has resolved that we go, i.e. he is so insistent that we must go. (Ar. قاسي be hard, violent.)

Kaniki,* **n.** a dark blue calico or cotton, worn by some women in the same way as *kanga,* which see. It is frequently used as a mourning dress, and also when a woman is menstruating as an intimation to her husband that she is not to be approached.

Kanisa,* n. *ma-* church. (Cf. *msikiti, hekalu.* Ar. كنيسة.)

Kanja, n. *ma-* the leaf of the coconut palm when the fronds are plaited together, *makuti ya viungo.*

Kanji, n. starch. (Cf. *wanga.*)

Kanju,* n. *ma-* fruit of the cashew tree. **Mkanju, n.** *mi-*. In some places called *mbibo.* (Hind. كاجو.)

Kano, n. *ma-* (1) large sinew or tendon (of animals); (2) a denial, &c., see under **Kana**, v.; (3) anything very small. **Mkano**, n. *mi-* also **Ukano**, (1) a sinew, tendon; (2) a denial, &c., see under **Kana**, v.

Kantara,* n. a bridge, rarely heard. (Cf. *daraja*, *ulalo*. Ar. قنطرة.)

Kanu, n. an animal like a wild cat or weasel; a great pest, as it steals fowls.

Kanuni,* n. that which is regular (necessary, indispensable), a fundamental rule, a necessary condition, general law governing treatment of a subject, a canon. (Cf. *faradhi*, *sharti*, *kawaida*, *hakika*, *yakini*. Ar. قانون.)

Kanusha, v. See under **Kana**, v.

Kanwa, n. *ma-*. See under **Nywa**.

Kanya, v. See under **Kana**, v.

Kanyaga, v. (1) tread on, put foot on, tread under foot; (2) fig. used of beating soundly, *Fulani amemkanyaga sana*, So-and-so has given him a sound beating. (Cf. *vyoga*.)

Kanyo, n. *ma-*. See under **Kana**, v.

Kanza, v. See under **Kaanga**, v.

Kanzi,* n. treasure, hoard, esp. of anything valuable which has been hidden in a place dug in the earth. (Cf. *akiba*, *hazina*, *dafina*. Ar. كنز.)

Kanzo, n. See under **Kaanga**.

Kanzu,* n. formerly the usual outer garment of men, but now rapidly being superseded by European or semi-European dress. It is a long-sleeved calico gown, described by some of the earlier visitors to East Africa as a 'bed-gown', reaching from the neck to the ankles, usually plain white or yellowish brown (*hudhurungi*), with or without lines of silk stitchwork, red or white, on the neck, wrists, and front, fastened with a small button or tassel at the throat. Worn over a loin-cloth, often with a light doublet, or under a coloured sleeveless open waistcoat (*kisibau*), or a cloth cloak (*joho*). Worn also by some women, but then shorter, of coloured and varied materials, and with red binding. *Kanzu* are distinguished as *ya kufuta*, plain, common, *ya tiki*, with white cotton stitching at the neck, *ya kazi*, with ornamental stitching, and according to material, *ya bafta ya hudhurungi*, &c. (Cf. for parts, &c., *badani*, *taharizi*, *sijafu*, *kikwapa*, *jabali*, *mhalbori*, *kaba*, *tiki*, *mrera*, *kiboko*, *kinara*, *darizi*, *mjusi*, &c., and for tailoring, *shona*, *mshoni*. Ar. قميص shirt, &c.)

Kao, n. *ma-*. See under **Kaa**, v.

Kapa, adv. *kwenda kapa*, go away conquered, used esp. in games of cards.

Kapa, n. a sort of coat without sleeves. (Cf. *kwapa*.)

Kapani,* n. a kind of scales or balances. (Pers. كپان.)

Kapatula, n. See **Kaputula**.

Kapela, n. *ma-* or **Kapera**, an unmarried man.

Kapi, n. (— and *ma-*) (1) a pulley—consisting of a sheave (*roda*) enclosed in a block (*makupa*) (for various sorts see *gofia*, *abedari*); (2) chaff, husks, *kapi za mpunga* (*za mahindi*), the husks of rice (of maize).

Kapilari,* n. a capillary, the word adopted for use in text-books and school lessons. (Eng.)

Kapile, n. cooked food of any description, sold in the market.

Kapu, n. *ma-*. See under **Kikapu**.

Kapungu, n. (1) an eagle; (2) a kind of shark.

Kaputa, n. a kind of dance used in exorcism of spirits.

Kaputula, n. (1) shorts, i.e. trousers reaching to just above the knee; (2) influenza. (Prob. from Nyanja verb, *kubutula*, cut off, introduced during the Great War when shorts became known in this part of East Africa, and used for influenza because it appeared simultaneously with the shorts!) (Cf. *butua*, cut off the end, make blunt; and *butu*, blunt.)

Kara, n. *ma-* (1) a splinter, spark, small piece; (2) a pause made in reading the Koran when another person takes up the reading. (? Ar. قر rest.)

Karabai,* n. a pressure lamp, either for petrol or kerosene, also used of an acetylene lamp. (Ar. كهربائي electric.)

Karadha,* n. money on loan, advance, credit, but without interest being charged. **Karidhi**, v. (1) lend money, esp. make an advance for commercial purposes, accommodate with money or goods, but without charging interest; (2) also Cs. borrow, get an advance. Ps. **Karidhiwa.** (Cf. commoner, *kopa, kopesha, azima.* Ar. قرض.)

Karafuu,* n. cloves, the flower bud of the *mkarafuu*, n. *mi-*, the most valuable and abundant article of commerce in Zanzibar and Pemba, except coco-nuts. (Ar. قرنفل.)

Karaha,* n. aversion, disgust, abhorrence. **Kirihi**, v. (1) loathe, abhor, hate, abominate, feel aversion (disgust, dislike, &c.); (2) give offence, provoke, insult, disgust, treat disrespectfully, &c. Ps. **Kirihiwa.** St. **Kirihika.** Cs. **Kirihisha**, e.g. offend, aggravate, exasperate. **Kirahi**, n. (sometimes heard as *ikirahi* or *ikrahi*), being offended, disgust, causing offence, provocation, insult, words or actions which cause offence, disgust, abhorrence, insult, &c. **Makuruhi**, a. offensive, in bad taste, wrong, abhorrent. (Cf. *chukia, kasirisha.* Ar. كره.)

Karakana,* n. workshop, manufactory. (Cf. *kiwanda.* Pers. كارخانه.)

Karakoni,* n. See **Korokoni.**

Karama,* n. (1) an honour, privilege, valuable possession, gracious act, generous behaviour; (2) gracious gift, talent, accomplishment, esp. a gift of God in answer to prayer. **Karamu**, n. a feast, banquet, festive entertainment. **Karimu**, a. liberal, openhanded, generous. **Mkarimu**, n. *wa-* a hospitable, kind, generous person. **Kirimu**, v. treat hospitably, entertain, feast, give a present (to). *Tumkirimu mgeni*, let us entertain the guest. *Amemkirimu ng'ombe*, he has made him a present of an ox. Ps. **Kirimiwa.** St. **Kirimika.** Prep. **Kirimia**, e.g. make a present to, be generous to. **Takaramu**, n. and **Takarimu**, n. same as *karama.* **Takarimu**, v. same as *karimu.* **Ukarimu**, n. generosity, liberality, hospitality, open-handedness. (Cf. *kipawa, kipaji.* Ar. كريم.)

Karamka, v. See **Kalamka.**

Karamu,* n. See under **Karama.**

Karanga, n. (1) the pea-nut, groundnut when roasted, but also used commonly for it when raw. See **Njugu.** (2) *karanga mwitu*, a perennial prostrate herb with white or pale mauve flowers and jointed pods, *Desmodium adscendens.*

Karani,* n. *ma-* clerk, secretary, amanuensis, supercargo, &c. (Cf. *katibu, mwandishi.* ? Ar. from قرا to read, or Pers. كاران factor, agent.)

Karara, n. *ma-*. See **Kalala.**

Karasa, n. a small animal which steals fowls.

Karasia,* n. See **Kalasia.**

Karata,* n. card, playing-card. A pack of playing-cards is called *jozi*, the pips are *ng'anda* or *ganda.* Ace is *ree* or *rei*; seven of any suit is *seti* or *jike*; spades, *shupaza*; hearts, *kopa*; clubs, *pao*; diamonds, *uru.* King is *Mzungu wa nne* or *basha.* Queen, *Mzungu wa pili* or *bibi*, and Jack, *Mzungu wa tatu, ghulamu*, or *jaji* (judge). Various card games are: *Wahed u sitini, chanis* (Eng. chance), *turufu mapiku.* To shuffle, *kupiga* or *kuchanganya.* To deal, *kugawa.* To cut, *kukata.* (Port. *carta.*)

Karatasi,* n. paper, a piece of paper. (Ar. قرطاس.)

Karela,* n. an annual or short-lived perennial climbing herb with pale yellow flowers and small spiny cucumber-like fruits which are eaten when young, *Momordica charantia*. (Hind. کریلا.)

Karibia,* v. Prep. of **Karibu**, which is never used as a verb excepting in the invitation to come in, join a party, &c., usually in reply to the request, *hodi*, which see: (1) come near (to), go near (to), approach, move close to, enter; (2) approximate, be near. Ps. **Karibiwa**. Cs. **Karibisha**, bring near, move close, invite as a guest, welcome, entertain. *Karibisha chakula* (*kiti*), invite to a meal (offer a seat to). *Tulikaribishwa vizuri*, we were hospitably treated, we were entertained in a splendid manner. Rp. **Karibiana**. **Karibu**, n. near relation, kinsman. *Watu hawa karibu zangu*, these people are relations of mine. Also *mtu wa karibu*, a relation. Adv. and (with *ya* and *na*) prep., (1) of space, near, close to; (2) of time, presently, shortly, lately, recently; (3) in general, nearly, almost, about. *Hivi karibu* (or *karibuni*), just lately. *Alikuja karibu*, he came near, or, he arrived recently, but the latter would usually be *alikuja karibuni hivi*. (Cf. *sogea, alika, pata, ndugu*. Ar. قرب.)

Karidhi,* v. See under **Karadha**.

Karimu,* a. See under **Karama**.

Karini,* n. also **Karne** and **Karni**, a century. (Ar. قرن.)

Karipa, v., **Karipio**, n. *ma-*. See under **-kali**.

Kariri,* v. repeat, say over and over again, recite, rehearse. Ps. **Kaririwa**. St. **Karirika**. Prep. **Kariria**, say over to (for, at, &c.). Cs. **Karirisha**. **Kikariri**, n. and adv. repetition, repeated action, saying over and over again, repeatedly. (Ar. كرر.)

Karne, n., **Karni**,* n. See **Karini**.

Karo,* n. fee, honorarium, a present, such as a pupil may give to his teacher. (Ar. كرا wages, salary.)

Kasa, n. a sea-turtle. (Cf. *ng'amba, kobe*. ? From Pers. کاسه پشت.)

Kasa,* adv. less, less by, short by, usu. in connexion with *robo, thumuni*, or similar words, e.g. *rupia mbili kasa* (or *kasoro*) *thumuni*, two rupees less four annas. *Saa sita kasa robo*, a quarter to twelve, lit. six hours less a quarter. **Kasoro**, adv. used in the same way as *kasa*; also as a noun, defect, blemish. *Ni kizuri, lakini kina kasoro*, it is good, but not altogether so, i.e. it has a defect, blemish, &c. (Cf. *pungua*. Ar. قص and قصر.)

Kasabu,* n. gold cloth, cloth with gold thread embroidery, &c. (Ar. قصب.)

Kasama,* n. (1) the joining of the bow of a sailing vessel (? Ar. قسم divide); (2) an oath (Ar. قسم); (3) see under **Kasimu**.

Kasha,* n. *ma-* box, chest, cupboard, packing case. *Kasha la fedha*, (1) a silver box; (2) a money box, safe. (Cf. *sanduku*. Port. *caixa*.)

Kashabi,* v. press sugar cane to make sugar—rarely used. (Cf. *shindika*. Pers. کسب sediment produced by pressing.)

Kashabu,* n. (1) a wooden rod which draws the threads of the web apart in native weaving (Ar. خشبة a piece of wood); (2) a kind of coloured bead, often of silver or gold, hollow, and of very thin glass. (Cf. *siniguse*. Ar. قصبة anything hollow made of gold or silver.)

Kashata,* n. a kind of confectionery, boiled sugar with grated coco-nut, coco-nut cream. (Ar. قشطة.)

Kashida,* n. a kind of shawl, worn

by Muhammadan teachers and that type of person. (Pers. كشيد kind of needlework.)

Kashifa,* n. slander, libel, false statements, information about a person which should be kept secret, which is liable to put him to shame, &c. **Kashifu,** v. slander, libel, make false statements about a person, or reveal secrets about him which are liable to shame him, &c. Ps. **Kashifiwa.** Prep. **Kashifia,** search out a person's secrets and tell others about them, spy upon in order to see actions done in privacy, &c., and then reveal them with the intent to cause shame. *Amemkashifia nyumba yake,* he spied upon him in the privacy of his house. **Ukashifu,** n. slander, disparagement. (Cf. *aibisha chongea, singizia.* Ar. كشف.)

Kasi,* adv. of intensity, used with verbs, much, very much, very, with energy (vehemence, violence, &c.), e.g. *enda kasi,* go with force, go quickly. *Mto unapita kasi,* the river runs quickly, has a strong current. **Kasi,** n. (1) *tia* (*piga*) *kasi,* apply force, tighten. *Sokota kwa kasi,* twist forcibly; (2) the twist in string, thread, fishing-line, &c., *tia kasi mshipi,* twist a fishing-line. **Kasikasi,** a. twisted, contorted, e.g. *uso wake una kasikasi,* his face is twisted, e.g. with anger, displeasure, &c. (Cf. *kaza, kunja, sokota.* Ar. قاس.)

Kasia, n. *ma-* (1) an oar. *Piga* (*vuta*) *kasia,* row. (Cf. *kafi.*) (2) a name for the Oribi.

Kasiba,* n. barrel (of a gun). *Mdomo kama kasiba,* small round mouth—a point of beauty. (Cf. *mwanzi, mdomo, mtutu.* Ar. قصبة.)

Kasida, n., **Kasidi,*** n. See **Kusudi.**

Kasiki,* n. (— and *ma-*) a large earthen jar (for water, ghee, &c.). (? Port. *casco,* barrel, or Eng. cask.)

Kasimile,* n. coco-nut cream, the thick oily juice squeezed from the grated nut by a strainer, before any water is mixed with it, i.e. *maji ya nazi yaliyokamuliwa mbele katika kifumbu,* also called *tui la kasimile,* or *tui halisi.* The same nut when mixed with water and strained again, produces *tui la kupopolea,* a white milky fluid. (Cf. *tui.* ? From Ar. كشفة cream of milk, and ميل taste.)

Kasimu,* v. divide (for the common *gawa, gawanya*). **Kasama,** n. and **Mkasama,** (1) a division, part, portion; (2) in mathematics, division. (Cf. *gawa.* Ar. قسم.)

Kasirani,* n. anger, bitterness of heart, vexation. **Kasiri,** v. but the Cs. form **Kasirisha** is usually used, e.g. cause to be angry, vex, provoke, enrage, exasperate. Ps. **Kasiriwa.** St. **Kasirika,** be angry, be vexed. Prep. of St. **Kasirikia,** be angry with. Prep. **Kasiria.** (Cf. *hasira, ghadhabu, uchungu,* and dist. *kisirani.* Ar. قصر cast down one's looks.)

Kasiri,* n. end. *Alasiri kasiri,* late afternoon. 5 p.m., i.e. *mwisho alasiri.* (Seldom heard. Cf. *hatima, mwisho.* Ar. قصر.)

Kasisi,* n. *ma-* a priest. Cf. *padre.* Ar. قسيس minister.)

Kaskazi,* n. (1) northerly wind, north monsoon. *Kaskazi inavuma,* the north wind is blowing. (Cf. *kusi* south wind, and *upepo.*) (2) season of the north monsoon, i.e. December to March, the hottest part of the year at the coast round about Dar es Salaam and Mombasa, also called *musimu,* and sometimes *chaka*; (3) northerly direction, the north. Also called *kibula, kibla.* Locative, **Kaskazini,** in the north, northwards. (Cf. *shemali,* and *jaa.* Prob. very ancient and from the same source as Ar. قيظ heat. Cf. قائظ قيظ intensely hot summer weather. As one goes north from Zanzibar and the coast opposite the heat increases, and the hot winds come from the north.)

Kasoro,* adv. and n. See under **Kasa.**

Kastabini,* n. a thimble, also heard as *kustabani* and *subana.* (Ar. كستبان.)

Kasuku, n. a parrot. (Cf. *dura.*)

Kasumba,* n. opium. (Cf. *afiuni.*)

Kaswende, n. syphilis. (Cf. *sekeneko, tego.*)

Kata, n. (1) a ladle, dipper, scoop, used for drinking, or dipping water from a hole—usually a coco-nut shell, with one end cut off, and fixed to the end of a stick (cf. *upawa,* ? Ar. قدح a drinking cup); (2) a round pad, usually of leaves, grass, or a folded strip of cloth, placed on the head when carrying a load, water-jar, &c.; (3) a charm; (4) a taboo. (Cf. *hirizi, mwiko, kago,* &c.)

Kata,* v. (1) cut, cut off, cut away, cut short, cut up, or in pieces; (2) fig. divide, reduce, bring to an end, decide, frustrate. The noun following may define the thing cut, the nature of the cutting, the effect produced, or the instrument used. *Kata miti,* cut down trees. *Kata maji,* go up stream. *Kata njia,* take a short cut. *Kata kisu* (or *kwa kisu*), cut with a knife. *Kata nguo,* cut cloth, often in the sense 'buy a piece of cloth, order a new dress or suit'. *Kata nakshi,* carve (in wood or stone). *Kata fedha* (or *mshahara*), reduce (or withhold) a sum due (or a part of wages, i.e. as a fine, &c.). Note: *kata mshahara,* is also sometimes used of getting an advance of wages. *Kata maneno* (*shauri, kesi*), conclude, decide a case. *Kata hukumu,* decide a suit, give sentence, pronounce judgement. *Kata tamaa,* bring hopes to an end, despair, despond, be desperate. *Kata kiu,* quench thirst. *Kata hamu,* satisfy sexual appetite. (3) cancel, in fraction sums; (4) *kata notisi,* take out a summons. Ps. **Katwa,** implying an agent, as present or prominent in the mind. St. and Pot. **Katika,** in which the fact rather than the agency is in view, e.g. *hukumu imekatwa,* the judge has decided the case. *Hukumu imekatika,* a verdict has been given. *Kusi imekatika,* the south wind is coming to an end. Prep. of St. **Katikia,** be cut off, &c., at (for, in, &c.), e.g. *muhogo ulikatikia humo,* the cassava broke off where it stood. *Ugwe hukatikia pembamba,* cord breaks at the thinnest part. Pot. **Katikana,** be capable of being cut, &c., be possibly cut. Prep. **Katia,** cut at (into, off, from, a part of, &c.), e.g. *katia hesabu,* cut off from, chop at, make a cut in (not cut down). *Katia njia,* cut into (strike on) a road. *Ni kiasi changu kama nilikatiwa mimi,* it fits me exactly, just as if it had been measured for me (or, I had been measured for it). *Tulikatiwa maneno,* we had our matters settled. *Katiwa notisi,* be summoned. Rp. of Prep. **Katiana,** e.g. settle accounts together, strike a balance, i.e. by striking out items on both sides. Cs. **Katiza,** cause to cut (be cut, &c.), or Inten. cut (end, decide abruptly, vigorously, sharply, &c.). *Katiza maneno,* break off (interrupt, stop, apply closure to) a discussion. *Walikatiziwa vyakula,* their supplies were deliberately stopped. Rp. **Katana,** cut each other, e.g. *wanakatana visu* (or *kwa visu*), they are fighting with knives. Rd. **Katakata,** cut to pieces, make mincemeat of; also hurt, e.g. *tumbo langu linakatakata* (or *kakata,* which see) my stomach hurts (just as though it were being cut in pieces). **Kata,** n. but usu. **Kataa,** a cutting, piece, part, portion, section, fraction, and of a literal cut or cutting, but fig. e.g. (*a*) part of plantation, *kataa ya shamba,* a plot; (*b*) part of a house, *kataa ya nyumba,* a room, an apartment, one of the screened-off divisions in a native hut, or *kataa ya* *chumba*, an alcove, recess, part of a room; (*c*) *kataa ya kitabu*, part of a book, section, leaf, page (cf. *jusuu, ukurasa*); also of a country, 'quarter, district', *kata ya nchi*; (*d*) lengths of rope, string, silk, &c., as sold in shops, i.e. hank, skein, coil. **Kato**, n. *ma-* a cutting, fragment, thing cut or broken off. **Mkata**, n. *wa-*, **Mkataji**, n. *wa-* one who cuts. **Mkate**, n. *mi-* something cut, and so, (1) any kind of lump, or separate piece, *mkate wa tumbako*, a plug or cake of tobacco. *Mkate wa nyuki*, a piece of honeycomb, but esp. (2) a loaf, cake, bun, biscuit, or anything similar, and used commonly of European bread. Various kinds are distinguished as *mkate wa ngano*, bread made of wheat flour; *mkate wa mofa*, or *mofa* only, a cake of millet meal, baked in an oven; *mkate wa kumimina*, a cake made of batter, fritter, &c. When *mkate* is used of European bread, the crust (*ganda la mkate*) is distinguished from the crumb (*nyama ya mkate*). Sometimes *mkate wa nyuki* is used to describe honeycomb. **Mkati**, n. *wa-* one who cuts, a cutter. **Mkato**, n. *mi-* (1) a cutting, incision, amputation, cut; (2) effect of cutting, a slit, crack, crevice; (3) a fraction, piece, esp. a separate part of a native house, a division, apartment, room—made by partition or screen only (*kiambaza*); (4) fig. a cutting down or away, cutting short, reduction, retrenchment; (5) a short, abrupt, decisive act or method. *Fanya kwa mkato*, like *mkataa*, act quickly, decisively, at a word. (Cf. *pasua, tema*. Ar. قط to cut, or Bantu *-kanta*, to cut.)

Kataa,* n. See under **Kata.**

Kataa,* v. refuse, reject, decline, say 'no'. Ps. **Kataliwa.** St. **Katalika.** Prep. **Katalia**, e.g. refuse, refuse credence to, decline acceptance from, say 'no' to, &c. Cs. **Kataza**, prohibit, forbid, deter, cause to refuse, refuse peremptorily. Followed by Neg. Subj., *Kataza watu wasifanye ghasia*, prohibit the people from making confusion. (Cf. also *gombeza, zuia, komesha*, &c., all of which are followed by Neg. Subj.). **Kataa**, a. final, decisive, conclusive. *Neno hili kataa*, this is the final word. **Katazo**, n. *ma-* prohibition, contradiction, objection. **-katavu**, a. obstinate, argumentative, contradictious. **Makataa** also **Mkataa**, n. and adv. (1) what is settled, final decision, end of an affair; (2) in a fixed, firm, decided way, e.g. *neno hili mkataa, sitakwenda*, this is my final word, I will not go. **Mkatavu**, n. *wa-* an obstinate, argumentative, sullen person. (Ar. قطع prevent, speak decisively, قطعا certainly, without doubt.)

Katabahu,* Arabic—lit. he wrote it —usually at the end of letters, with the name of the writer. (Cf. *kitabu, mkataba*.)

Kata dole, n. the name of a bird, Grosbeak weaver, *Amblyospina albifrons*, also called *yombiyombi* and *kwaru*.

Katani,* n. hemp, sisal fibre, also what is made from it, coarse sacking, rope, &c. The plant is called *mkatani*, n. *mi-* also **mkonge.** (Ar. كتان.)

Katara, n. any old vehicle, cycle, motor-car, &c., and so often applied to a motor lorry or motor bus which carries passengers, which are often old, dilapidated vehicles. (Cf. *kataa*, v.)

-katavu, a., **Katazo,*** n. *ma-*. See under **Kataa.**

Kati, n. and adv. also **Katikati**, and (with *ya*) prep. middle, centre; among, between, inside, in the middle of, amidst, surrounded by. *Kati ya nyumba*, in the middle of the house. *Kata katikati*, cut asunder (through the middle). *-a kati* and *-a katikati*, central, middle. *Wakati wa kati*, the intervening period, interval. *Weka katikati*, place in the centre. Also *kati na kati*. **Katika**, prep. The root meaning is 'in', but it can mean, to 'in' or, from 'in', as well as, at 'in'. (*a*) of place—in, at, to, towards, into, from (in), out of, away from, in the midst of, on, e.g. *tuliingia katika shamba*, we went into the plantation. *Tulitoka katika shamba*, we came out of the plantation. *Wanakaa katika mashamba*, they live in the plantations. *Nilikuwamo katika hatari nyingi*, I was in the midst of many dangers. *Andika katika karatasi*, write on a paper. *Jenga nyumba katika mlima*, build a house upon a mountain. (*b*) of time—in, at, during, whilst, e.g. *nilikuwa katika kusema*, I was in the act of speaking. *Katika kuenda alianguka*, whilst going, he fell. (*c*) in general—in, engaged in, to, in the direction of, from, e.g. *alikuwa katika kazi*, he was engaged in work. (*d*) in the matter of, in reference to, concerning, as to, about, e.g. *katika habari zile*, with reference to (about, concerning, &c.) those affairs. (*e*) in the locative use, it is equivalent to *-ni* termination, e.g. *katika nyumba*, is the same as *nyumbani*. *Katika sanduku—sandukuni*, &c. (Cf. *ndani*.)

Katiba,* n. ordinance, custom, natural (or original) constitution, destiny, doom—from the idea of binding and permanent force of Muhammadan law as written in the Koran. **Katibu**, n. a writer, amanuensis, clerk (cf. *karani, mwandishi*); also **Katibu**, v. (1) write; (2) take on agreement, bind on contract, e.g. *nilimkatibu kwa miaka mitatu*, I made an agreement with him for 3 years. Rp. **Katibiana**, e.g. *tukatibiane*, let us draw up a contract. **Kitabu**, n. *vi-* a book. (Ar. the *ki-* being part of the root, but treated as a noun of the *ki-* class by analogy.) **Kitiba**, n. custom, habit, character, i.e. what is preordained according to the Muhammadan point of view. **Mkataba**, n. *mi-* what is written, book, statute, contract, engagement. (Cf. *andika, chuo*. Ar. كتب.)

Katika, prep., **Katikati**, n. and adv., and prep. See under **Kati.**

Katikiro, n. an office messenger. In some places, e.g. Uganda, a chief adviser to the native ruler. (Cf. *tarishi*.)

Katili,* n. *ma-*, and a. also **Mkatili**, n. *wa-*, murderous person, bloodthirsty, cruel man, a ruffian; cruel, bloodthirsty, murderous. **Ukatili**, n. cruelty, bloodthirstiness, &c. (Cf. *ua, dhalimu, fisha*. Ar. قتل.)

Katiti, a. invar. dim. like *kadogo*, exceedingly small, minute, infinitesimal, tiny. Also adv. in a very small degree.

Katiza, v., **Kato**,* n. *ma-*. See under **Kata, v.**

Katu,* n. a kind of gum, imported and sold in small dark-red lumps chiefly for chewing with betel. See *tambuu, uraibu*. (Hind. كتها catechu.)

Katua, v. polish, brighten, clean by rubbing, esp. of brass, silver, copper, and other metals. Ps. **Katuliwa.** St. **Katuka.** Prep. **Katulia.** *Majivu ya kukatulia visu*, ashes to clean knives with.

Kauka, v. (1) become dry, dry up, be parched. *Nchi imekauka*, the earth is parched. *Sauti imemkauka*, his voice is dried up, he is hoarse. (2) become stiff, hard, i.e. of joints, a corpse, &c. Prep. **Kaukia**, dry with (for, off, &c.), e.g. *sakafu imekaukia maji*, the water has dried off the cement roof (or floor, pavement, &c.). Rp. of Prep. **Kaukiana**, be all dried up, be absolutely stiff. Cs. **Kausha**, dry, cause to dry up, parch. Prep. **Kaushia**, dry for (with, at, &c.). **Kausha**, n. also **Kikausha**, n. an unlucky ill-omened person, one who brings bad luck, who causes a person's property, &c., to wither, disappear, be destroyed. **-kavu, a.** (1) dry, parched, waterless, barren. *Nchi kavu,* dry land, as opp. to *bahari,* sea. *Kuni kavu,* dry firewood. *Nguo kavu,* dry clothes. Prov. *maji mafu, mvuvi mkavu,* at neap tides the fisherman gets little. (2) satirical, sarcastic, impudent, deceitful, intrepid, nonchalant. *Mtu mkavu,* a sly deceitful person. *Mkavu wa macho,* impudent, intrepid, nonchalant person. Also *mwenye macho makavu.* (3) stiff, hard, e.g. used of joints, dead body, &c., i.e. rigor mortis. **Kikavu** also **Kikaufu,** n. and adv. dryness, in a dry manner. **Ukavu,** n. dryness, humour, intrepidity, nonchalance. *Ukavu wa macho,* an unconcerned, fearless, cool, unabashed look, or character, imperturbability. (Cf. *yabis, -gumu.*)

Kauleni,* n. See under **Kauli.**

Kauli,* n. (1) sentence, expression; (2) expressed opinion, narrative, account, advice. *Kauli tatu zilizosemwa,* three accounts were given. *Tufuase kauli za walimu wetu,* let us follow the opinion of our teachers. *Kauli ile ilimwudhi,* that expression vexed him. **Kauleni,** n. a person who cannot be trusted, one who is two-faced, double-tongued, i.e. *mwenye kauli mbili.* (Cf. *neno, shauri, habari.* Ar. قول.)

Kaumu,* n. a crowd, many together. *Kaumu ya watu,* a crowd of people, many people together; a particular lot of people. (Cf. *umati, jumla, kundi, akina.* Ar. قوم.)

Kaumwa, n. calumba root, root of the *mkaumwa,* n. *mi-,* the root is used for making medicine for dysentery and stomach ailments, *Jateorhiza palmata.*

Kauri,* n. a cowrie shell. For various kinds, cf. *dondo, kululu, kete. Kauri* is also used to describe china, *vyombo vya kauri,* as opp. to earthenware, *vyombo vya udongo.* (Hind. كوڑي.)

Kausha, v. and n. See under **Kauka.**

Kauta, n. dust, grit. (Cf. *mavumbi, uvumbi.*)

-kavu, a. See under **Kauka.**

Kawa, n. (— and of size *ma-*) (1) a dish cover, conical in shape, made of plaited grass. Prov. *Tulingane sawasawa kama sahani na kawa,* let us be to each other as a dish and its cover, i.e. in harmony, fit together. (2) mildew, mould.

Kawa, v. be delayed, tarry, linger, delay, loiter, take a long time, be behind time, be late. Prep. **Kawia,** same as *kawa*; also **Kawilia,** delay for (on account of, at, about, &c.). Cs. **Kawilisha,** cause to delay, keep back, make late. Cs. **Kawisha,** put off, make stand over, adjourn, e.g. *kawisha kodi,* get in arrears for rent (tax). **Ukawa,** n. and **Ukawio,** n. delay. (Cf. *usiri, ahiri, chelewa, limatia.* Prob. Cv. of *kaa, kaua* elided to *kawa.*)

Kawadi,* n. also **Kuwadi,** a procurer, a pander, a pimp. (Ar. قود.)

Kawaida,* n. (sometimes *kaida* is heard), regulative principle, fundamental rule, usage, custom, system. *Fuata kawaida,* follow the usual, recognized custom. *Mambo ya kawaida,* regular (customary, common, everyday) affairs, not out of the ordinary. (Cf. *desturi, kanuni, ada, kiada.* Ar. قواعد.)

Kawe, n. dim. of *jiwe,* which see.

Kawia, v., **Kawilia,** v., **Kawisha,** v. See under **Kawa,** v.

Kaya, n. (1) *ma-* a kind of shell-fish; (2) a village, perh. not strictly Swahili, but generally known.

Kayamba, n. a rattle—dry grain, &c., shaken inside a flat case of reeds, or the seed pod of the flamboyant tree or other such tree. (Cf. *mkakaya.*)

Kayaya, n. trouble, difficulty. (Cf. *matata.*)

Kaza, v. (prob. a Cs. of *kaa,* v.) (1) fix, make fast, fasten, tighten; (2) grip, hold tight, fit tightly; (3) use force (in), exert energy, act with a will, emphasize, accentuate. *Kaza kamba,* make a rope fast. *Kaza mbio,* run hard. *Kaza kuimba,* sing with a will. Ps. **Kazwa.** St. and Pot. **Kazika.** Prep. **Kazia,** e.g. *kazia macho,* rivet the gaze upon. Cs. **Kazisha.** Rp. **Kazana,** (1) hold each other, make a mutual effort, make an effort; (2) hold together, be compact, be firm (stiff, hard). *Kazana na,* adhere to, stick to. **Kazi,** n. see under separate heading. **Kazo,** n. *ma-* a pressing tight, holding hard, grip. **Kikaza,** n. *vi-* a thing which tightens, strengthens, holds together, &c. **Kikazo,** n. *vi-* (1) like *kikaza*; (2) a tightening up, a strengthening; (3) stress, accent. **Mkazi,** n. *wa-*, e.g. *Mungu ni mkazi wa ulimwengu,* i.e. God is the holder up (firm supporter) of the world. **Mkazo,** n. *mi-* (1) using force, tension, effort, energy, pressure, exertion; (2) stress, accent, emphasis (in a word). *Mkazo mkuu,* strong accent. *Mkazo mdogo,* weak accent. (Cf. *bidii, jitihadi, juhudi.*)

Kazi, n. (1) work, labour, employment, occupation, profession, business, function, a job; (2) hard work, toil, strain, effort, exertion; (3) normal action, habit, regular duty, routine; (4) skill, art, decoration, e.g. *mkeka wa kazi,* a sleeping-mat of fine work, coloured, &c., as contr. to *mkeka wa mfuto,* an ordinary plain one. *Kofia ya kazi, kanzu ya kazi.* (5) use, usefulness, i.e. *kazi yake nini kitu hiki?* what is this thing used for? *Tupa hiki sina kazi nacho tena,* throw this away, I have no further use for it. *Kazi bure,* labour in vain, effort thrown away. *Ni kazi yake,* he is responsible for it, or it is his usual custom, what he always does, what can be expected from him. *Fanya (tenda) kazi,* work. *Nguo hii ni kazi ya Wahindi,* this cloth (garment) was made by Indians. *Kazi ya mkataba,* contract work, work by contract. *Nakwenda kazini,* I am going to work. *Kazi ya kijungu jiko* (or *chungu meko*), an expression meaning work which provides one with only a bare living, i.e. hand-to-mouth existence. (The derivation of this word is uncertain—it may be a plur. of *ukazi,* see under *kaa,* v. or it may be from Hind. كاج, Pers. كار, or Ar. كد; the final *r* or *d* could have become *z* through the influence of an added closed vowel *i*—see *timazi.*) The word *kazi* in the expression *kofia (kanzu, mkeka,* &c.) *ya kazi* may have an entirely different derivation, and is prob. from Ar. قز floss silk, silk; from the silk embroidery worked on a garment, and hence used for all decorative work.)

Kazoakazoa, n. a term of abuse (perh. from *zoa* and *-ka,* which see), i.e. a wretched gutter-scraper.

Ke!* int. used only in the phrase, *Ke bado?* What, not yet? (Ar. لُ.)

-ke, a. (1) of the female sex, female, feminine; (2) like a woman, timid, stupid. **Mke,** n. (*wake*), **Mtu mke,** n. (*watu wake*), **Mtu wa kike,** n. (*watu wa kike*), but practically always **Mwanamke,** n. (plur. *wanawake*), are all used of 'woman' generally, in respect of sex simply. In relation to the male sex, *mke* has the definite meaning of 'wife, married woman', and is then distinguished from *mwanamke,* which denotes an irregular connexion, e.g. *mkewe waziri alikuwa mwanamke wake Abunawasi,* the vizier's wife was Abunawasi's paramour. *Wake* as a noun plur. of *mke,* usually takes for distinctness pronouns of the form in *z-*, i.e. *wake zake,* his wives rather than *wake wake. Watoto wanawake,* or *wa kike,* girls. *Bata jike,* a female duck. *Moyo wa kike,* a womanly (i.e. usu. 'timid, stupid') character. **Jike,** n. *ma-* and a. female animal. *Punda jike,* an ass. *Bata jike,* a duck. **Kike,** n. and adv.

(seldom *vike* in plur., for the usu. *-a kike*, or *vijike*) a female of any kind, anything of feminine style, womanly behaviour (usu. meaning weakness, timidity, foolishness), like a woman, in a feminine way, e.g. *watoto wa kike*, girls. *Fanya kike*, act like a woman. *Sauti ya kike*, a shrill treble voice. **Kuke**, n. and **Kuuke**, n. the female kind, feminine status or condition—used only in a few adverbial phrases. *Mkono wa kuke*, the left hand, as the (usually) weaker, also *wa kike*—but commonly *wa kushoto*. Opp. to *mkono wa kuume*. *Kukeni*, on the female side, by the mother. *Ujamaa wa kukeni*, relatives on the mother's side, in the female line. **Uke**, n. (1) womanhood, female condition, status, characteristics—but commonly for distinctness *utu uke*; (2) condition (privilege, duties) of being a wife, e.g. *uke na ume umekwisha*, (we) have ceased to be husband and wife; (3) for the vulgar *kuma*, vagina. (Contr. *ume*.)

Kebe, n. *ma-* amplic. of *mkebe*.

Kebehi,* v. (1) revile, insult, disgrace, e.g. *alimkebehi mbele za watu*, he insulted (disgraced, reviled, &c.) him in public; (2) question a person slyly about his affairs out of idle curiosity, with the desire to hear some shameful rumour about him confirmed, e.g. of a man hearing that a certain woman is a prostitute questioning her slyly to find out if it is true, not with the intention of having dealings with her, but to satisfy his idle curiosity. (Cf. *kashifu, tukana, aibisha*. Ar. قبح.)

Kefu,* adv. much less, much more, not to mention. *Yeye amekubali kwenda, kefu wewe*, he has agreed to go (but you a much less important person won't agree to go). (Cf. *sembuse*. Ar. قفي.)

Kefu!* int. also **Kefule!** and **Sefule!** expressing disgusted surprise, indignation, aversion. (Ar. قنا and كفل.)

Kefu,* n. See under **Kifu**.

Kefule!* int. See **Kefu!** int.

Kefyakefya, v. tease, annoy, nag at, depress, discourage, put out of heart. (Cf. *sumbua, tesa, chokoza, udhi*.)

Kejekeje, a. slack, not taut. (Cf. *kajekaje, pwaya, legea*.)

Kejeli,* v. (1) treat a person in a familiar manner, make fun of him, make a fool of him, e.g. knowing that a person is in need, question him about his needs and then promise to help him, knowing all the while that you cannot help him, moreover having no intention of doing so; (2) question a person about his affairs as though knowing nothing about them, but knowing all about them, just for the sake of seeing whether he will tell the truth about them. (Cf. *dharau, simanga, mzaha*. ? Ar. هجل play the fool in talk, attack the reputation of a person.)

Kekee, n. (1) a boring tool, brace and bit; (2) a kind of silver bracelet, usually broad and flat, fastened by a clasp or bolt. (Cf. *kikuku, bangili, urembo*.)

Keketa, v. cut as with something blunt or anything hard or tough, or with a saw-like motion. **Mkeketo**, n. *mi-* used of things of equal size, i.e. cut the same length; also of people who are the same size, build, &c.

Kekevu, n. (1) hiccup (cf. *chechevu, kwikwi*); (2) brave, strong. (Cf. *hodari*.)

Kelb,* n. dog—seldom heard and then only as a term of abuse. **Kalab**, n. rabies, hydrophobia. (Cf. *mbwa*. Ar. كلب.)

Kelele, n. *ma-* a shout, shouting, uproar, noise. *Piga kelele*, shout, give a shout. *Nena kwa kelele*, or *kikelele*, make a loud remark. *Makelele!* as an int. ordering silence, i.e. Make less noise! Be quiet! Silence! (Cf. *chub! huss! usu! buu! nyamaza!* (or plur.

nyamazeni!) *kimya!* **Ukelele,** n. (*kelele* and *ma-*) a cry, &c., like *kelele.* (Ar. ? قلل diminish, lessen.)

Kem ?* interrog. adv. How much? How many? e.g. in requiring price; *Kem? Wauzaje? Kiasi gani?*—all meaning 'How much?'. (Cf. *kima.* Ar. كم.)

Kemba, v. strip off the skin, peel, as of cassava, &c. (Cf. *menya, ambua, chuna.*)

Keme, n. See under **Kemea.**

Kemea, v. scold, rebuke, speak loudly (roughly) to, snub. **Keme,** n. a call, noise. **Ukemi,** n. shout, call, cry. (Cf. *karipia, laumu, nenea, ambilia,* and *ukelele, unyeme.*)

Kenda, n. and a. nine, *-a kenda,* ninth. (Cf. *tisa,* equally common.)

Kende, n. *ma-* the scrotum, testicle. (Cf. *pumbu, hasua, korodani.*)

Kenga, v. deceive, cheat, make a fool of, play tricks on. (Cf. *danganya, zuzua.*)

Kenge, n. a large lizard, large water lizard, monitor lizard.

Kengee, n. (1) the flat part of a cutting instrument, blade of a knife, sword, spearhead, &c., frequently used of an old blade worn to a thin point by much use; (2) the sun's rays. **Ukengee,** n. same as *kengee.* (Cf. *bapa,* and contr. *makali* and *machinjioni,* edge, *mafutuni,* back, *manoleo,* ring, dividing blade, and haft, and *mpini, kipini,* handle, of such instruments.

Kengele, n. (— and *ma-* of size), a bell. *Piga* or *gonga kengele,* ring a bell. (Cf. *njuga.*)

Kengemeka, v. reproach, make charges against, find fault with, question suspiciously, accuse. (Cf. *suta, laumu, shutumu, shtaki.*)

Kengeua, v. turn aside, i.e. leave the straight road and take a bad one, turn from the right way, backslide. St. **Kengeuka.** Cs. **Kengeusha.**

Kengewa, n. a kind of hawk or kite. (Cf. *mwewe.*)

Kengeza, v. squint. **Kengeza,** n. *ma-* squinting, a squint, e.g. *makengeza ya macho. Mwenye makengeza,* one who squints. (Cf. *kengeua.*)

Kenua, v. (1) show the teeth in laughing, also (2) draw back the lips and show the teeth, a sign of contempt or scorn.

Kenyekenye, adv. absolutely, entirely. (Cf. *kabisa.*)

Kera, v. worry, tease, annoy, vex. **Kero,** n. trouble, annoyance, disturbance, vexatious conduct. (Cf. *sumbua, udhi, kereketa, kereza.*)

Kereketa, v. (1) cause an irritating sensation, esp. in tongue or throat, have a rough taste, cause a choking feeling. *Roho yangu inanikereketa kwa sababu ya kutafuna tumbako,* my throat is irritated from chewing tobacco. (2) fig. annoy, be too much for, e.g. *na likukerekete,* may that stick in your gizzard, you cannot give an answer to that, &c. (Cf. *kera, kereza.*)

Kerem-kerem, n. the name of a bird, Bee-eaters, *Merops.*

Kereng'ende, n. (1) red-legged partridge, francolin; (2) a kind of dragon-fly.

Kereza, v. (1) saw into, cut into with a saw (rasp, file, &c.), make or cut a notch in; (2) cut in a lathe, turn; (3) *kereza meno,* grind the teeth; (4) to work, as of a machine. **Mkereza,** n. *wa-* one who turns with a lathe, a turn. **Kerezo,** n. a machine for turning, a lathe. (Cf. *kera, kereketa.* Bantu *-kela,* cut, or Cs. from Ar. جرز grind (teeth).)

Kero, n. See under **Kera,** v.

Kesha, v. remain awake, keep awake, stay up at night, not to sleep, watch, keep watch. *Kesha kucha,* stay awake until morning. Prep. **Keshea,** stay up for, keep night watch with, nurse all night. Cs. **Keshesha,** keep a person awake. Rp. **Keshana,** remain awake together. (Cf. *kaa macho.*)

Kesha, n. *ma-* also **Mkesha,** n. *mi-*

night watch, vigil. *Siku ya kesha la mwisho,* the last night of a formal mourning (*matanga*). *Mvua ya kesha,* a shower of rain which is very local.

Kesho, n. and adv. tomorrow, the next day, the day after. *Kesho yake,* the following day. **Kesho kuchwa** (and **Kutwa**), the day after tomorrow. *Kushinda kesho kutwa,* the third day, also called *mtondo.*

Kesi,* n. a case (criminal or civil), a lawsuit, &c. *Kesi ya jinai,* a criminal case. *Sikiliza kesi,* hear a case. (Eng. Prob. adopted because of its similarity to *kisa* (2).)

Keta, v. knock down and hurt. *Alimketa,* he knocked him down and hurt him.

Kete, n. (1) a small kind of cowrie. Also a game played with these shells. *Meno kama kete,* teeth like cowries—a point of beauty (cf. *kauri*). (2) *ma-* a string (of beads, &c.). Two *makete* one *timba*; ten *makete* five *timba* one *fundo.* (Cf. *kata,* of which it may be a noun made from the old perfect, *kete.*)

Keti, v. (1) (in poet. *kelcti*), sit down, take a seat; (2) dwell, live, remain, stay, reside. *Tafadhali uketi,* please take a seat. (Cf. *kaa kitako,* meaning strictly, squat in the native way.) Ps. **Ketiwa.** Prep. **Ketia,** e.g. *kiti cha kuketia,* a seat to sit on. Cs. **Ketisha,** cause to remain, keep, preserve. (Cf. *kaa.*)

Keu, n. (1) *kupiga keu,* chew the cud; (2) see under *keua.*

Keua, v. straighten a pole for building by cutting a notch in it and inserting a wedge or small piece of wood. This is also called *kuutia mti mafuta.* **Keu,** n. a stroke made with an axe, i.e. to straighten a pole, &c. (See also **Keu.**)

kh. Many Swahili words are taken from Arabic originals beginning with the sound *kh-*. These will be found under *h* in this dictionary, representing the simple aspirate to which they all become assimilated in proportion as they become naturalized among Africans. On the other hand, the *kh* sound is often used by persons imitating or influenced by Arabic pronunciation, and sometimes in words in which it never existed.

Ki-. Many words beginning with *Ki-* are nouns made from verbs or diminutives of other nouns. These will be found with their definitions under the verb or noun, and here a reference to them only will be found. For the significance of *ki-* as a formative particle and *-ki-* as a tense prefix, see the Grammars.

Kia, n. (*via*) (1) door bar (cf. *kiwi, pingo, komeo*); (2) a joint of the leg or arm; (3) anything used as a lid for covering a cooking-pot.

Kia, v. step over, as of a log, &c. (Cf. *kiuka, chupa.*)

Kiada,* adv. in an orderly, distinct, intelligible way. *Sema kiada,* speak slowly and distinctly. (Cf. *kawaida.* Ar. قاعد or قيد diligence, regard carefully.)

Kiaga, n. *vi-*. See under **Aga,** v. (B).

Kiali, n. *vi-* dim. of *mwali* n. (4).

Kialio, n. *vi-* (1) dim. of *walio*; (2) *kialio cha mvua,* rain which falls just when people are going to bed.

Kiambaza, n. *vi-*. See under **Wamba.**

Kiambo, n. *vi-* household, establishment, village. (Cf. *mji.*)

Kiamshakinywa, n. See under **Amka.**

Kianga, n. *vi-*, **Kiangaza macho,** n., **Kiangazi,** n. See under **Anga,** n.

Kiango, n. *vi-*. See under **Anga,** v.

Kiapo, n. *vi-*. See under **Apa.**

Kiarabu,* n. and adv. See under **Mwarabu.**

Kiasi,* n. (A) and adv. (1) a measure, quantity, amount (cf. *kadiri, kipimo*); (2) moderation, self-control, temperance (cf. *kadiri, kujizuia*); (3) a little, a small (moderate) amount (cf. *kidogo*); (4) *kiasi cha sehemu,* numerator, in arithmetic. Common in inquiring price. *Kiasi gani?* How much? What is the price? *Mtu wa kiasi*, a temperate person, a man of moderation. *Alimpa kiasi*, he gave him a little. As adv. of quantity, time, or space—'a little', e.g. *neno hili limeanza kiasi*, this business began some time ago. *Alikwenda kiasi*, he went a little way, or he went a short time ago. (Ar. قاس, the radical *ki-* being treated as a prefix as in *kitabu*.)

Kiasi,* n. (B) *vi-* the charge of a gun, cartridge. (Cf. *risasi*.)

Kiatu, n. *vi-*. See under **Kwata.**

Kiazi, n. *vi-* a sweet potato—root of a kind of convolvulus, *Ipomea batatas*. The leaves, also used as a vegetable, are called *mriba*, *mtolilo*, and *matembele*. Different kinds are known as *kiazi sena* (white), *kiazi kindoro* (red), *halimtumwa*, *kwata jeupe*, *kwata jekundu*, *kirehani*, &c. **Kiazi kikuu**, *vi-* yam, edible roots, different sorts are: *kinana*, *mviringo*, *madole*, *mwendachi*, &c. *Kiazi cha kizungu*, the common European potato.

Kibaazi, n. *vi-* dim. of *mbaazi*, which see, applied to several plants and shrubs. (1) fish poison plant, a short-lived perennial plant up to 15 ft. tall with racemes of white or reddish mauve pea-like flowers and fairly large hairy pods; the fresh green stems and leaves are pounded and used as a fish poison, also medicinally, *Tephrosia Vogelii*; (2) a perennial herb up to 3 ft. tall with small white pea-like flowers and small dark brown hairy pods, *Tephrosia noctiflora*; (3) an annual or short-lived perennial herb up to 3 ft. tall with dense spikes of small yellow flowers and pea-like pods, *Crotalaria emarginata*; (4) a perennial semi-prostrate herb with pinkish mauve flowers and grey leaves, *Tephrosia ehrenbergiana*; (5) a shrub or small tree with leathery grey green leaves and yellow flowers in short terminal racemons and small sausage-shaped fruits which split open exposing a number of bright red seeds, *Cadaba farinosa*.

Kibaba, n. *vi-* (1) a common dry measure, about a pint, or a pound and a half of grain. A *kibaba* is half a *kisaga*, and a quarter of a *pishi*. *Kibaba cha tele*, a full, heaped-up measure. *Kibaba cha mfuto*, a measure to the top only, i.e. *kilichofutwa*. Prov. *Haba na haba hujaza kibaba*, grain upon grain fills the measure, or many a little (or pickle) makes a mickle. (Cf. *haba*.) (2) dim. of *baba*, which see. (? Ar. باب measure.)

Kibafute, n. a children's game of guessing what is hidden in the hand.

Kibago, n. *vi-* a stool. (Cf. *kiti*.)

Kibahaluli,* n. *vi-* (1) a small torch of twisted grass, or paper spill, such as is used for lighting a pipe, &c. (Cf. *kimwenge*. ? Ar. بهل small quantity.) (2) a foolish person, a small-witted person who usu. does foolish actions. (Cf. *mjinga*, *mpumbavu*. Ar. بهالة stupidity.)

Kibakuli,* n. *vi-* dim. of *bakuli*.

Kibali,* n. See under **Kubali.**

Kibanda, n. *vi-* dim. of *banda*.

Kibano, n. *vi-*, **Kibanzi**, n. *vi-*. See under **Bana.**

Kibama, n. *vi-* a cake made of flour and bananas.

Kibao, n. *vi-*. See under **Bao.**

Kibapara, n. *vi-* (1) a pauper, destitute person, used in contempt; (2) an old garment used to throw on anyhow; (3) a kind of small cap.

Kibaramwezi, n. *vi-* a children's toy, a windmill made from the fronds of the coco-nut palm fixed to the end of a piece of the midriff. (Cf. *kititia*.)

Kibarango, n. *vi-* (1) dim. of *mbarango*; (2) also used of a stumpy, thick-set person.

Kibarua,* n. *vi-* dim. See under **Barua.**

Kibata, n. *vi-* dim. of *bata*.

Kibatari,* n. *vi-* a small lamp made of a tin in which is placed oil and a floating wick. (Pers. بتيل wick for lamp.)

Kibatobato, n. See under **Batobato.**

Kibavu, adv., **Kibavubavu**, adv. See under **Bavu.**

Kibawa, n. *vi-* dim. of *bawa.*

Kibe, n. a noise, shout, &c. (Cf. *ukelele, ukeme.*)

Kibeberu, n. *vi-* (1) dim. of *beberu*; (2) a rush, *Scirpus* sp.

Kibemasa, n. a children's game like hide-and-seek.

Kiberenge, n. *vi-* (1) a light locomotive, trolley, used on railway line; (2) a prostitute. **Berenge**, *ma-* the carriages of a train, either passenger or goods.

Kiberiti,* n. *vi-* (*kibiriti* is also heard), sulphur, a match, a firework. *Kiberiti* is used of one match, also of a whole boxful, but sometimes one match is referred to as *kijiti cha kiberiti*, and the whole box as *ganda la kiberiti*, a term used also for the empty matchbox. (Ar. كبريت.)

Kibeti, n. *vi-* (*kibete* is also heard), an undersized creature (man, beast, bird), a dwarf, or bantam. (Cf. *mbilikimo.*)

Kibia, n. *vi-* (1) a small cooking-pot or pan, or its lid, an earthenware cover; (2) a basin which is put under the *mbuzi*, i.e. scraping utensil, to catch the grated coco-nut, *chicha.* (Cf. *mkungu, bunguu.*)

Kibibi, n. *vi-* dim. of *bibi.*

Kibinadamu, n. and adv. See under **Bin.**

Kibindo, n. *vi-*. See under **Bindo.**

Kibinja, n. *vi-*. See under **Ubinja.**

Kibiongo, n. *vi-* a person bent by age or infirmity, bowed, round-shouldered.

Kibirikizi, n. *vi-* a proclamation, e.g. *kupiga kibirikizi*, make an announcement, proclaim. (Cf. *mbiu, tangaza.*)

Kibiriti.* See **Kiberiti.**

Kibisi, n. dabchick or little grebe, *Poliocephalus ruficollis.*

Kibla,* n. (1) north; (2) the direction of Mecca, the point to which Muhammadans turn in prayer. Also **Kibula.** (Cf. *kabili.* Ar. قبلة.)

Kibobwe, n. *vi-*. See **Kibwebwe.**

Kibofu, n. *vi-* the urinary bladder. **Bofu**, n. *ma-* amplic.

Kibogoshi, n. *vi-* a small bag made of skin, a leather bag, used to carry miscellaneous articles on a journey, money, gunpowder, &c. (Cf. *mfuko, mkoba.*)

Kibogoyo, n. *vi-* a person who is toothless, or has but few teeth.

Kiboko,* n. *vi-* (1) a hippopotamus, also sometimes *boko*, of larger size; (2) a strip of hippo hide, formerly used for inflicting judicial punishment on offenders, now replaced by a cane; (3) small zigzag ornament embroidered in silk on a *kanzu* round the neck. See **Kanzu.** (? Pers. the *ch-* being treated as a prefix as in *kiasi, kitabu*, &c. چابك whip.)

Kibonde, n. *vi-* dim. of *bonde.*

Kibonge, n. *vi-* dim. of *bonge.*

Kibua, n. *vi-* (1) dim. of *bua*; (2) anything light in weight, pithy; (3) a garden which has been cultivated, left, and returned to. (Cf. *dimba.*)

Kibubutu, n. *vi-* a stump, i.e. of a tree, the tail of an animal which has been docked, or of a limb which has been amputated, &c. (Cf. *butu* and *butua.*)

Kibudu,* adv. *Kufa kibudu*, die a natural death, of people and animals. Also used sometimes of an animal killed without the killer observing the Muhammadan ritual; or of a person who professes no religion, dying. (Ar. كأد adversity, calamity, &c.)

Kibuhuti,* n. (1) grief, sorrow, distress; (2) foreboding, fear of things about to happen. (Cf. *huzuni, majonzi, hofu, butaa.* Ar. بهت perplex, distress, with *ki-* prefix.)

Kibula,* n. See under **Kibla.**

Kibuluu,* n. (1) a kind of cassava

(cf. *muhogo*); (2) **a.** blue in colour. (Eng. blue.)

Kibumba, n. *vi-* dim. of *bumba.*

Kibunguu, n. *vi-* dim. of *bunguu.*

Kibunzi, n. *vi-* (1) the end of the year; (2) a sanded board, used for predicting future events, or for divining generally (cf. *ramli, bao*); (3) anything light in weight, insignificant; (4) a children's game; (5) a cob of maize. (Cf. *gunzi.*)

Kiburi,* n. pride, arrogance, conceit, haughtiness. *Piga (fanya) kiburi*, show off, be ostentatious, play the grandee. *Mtu asiye na kiburi na watu*, one who does not treat people in a discourteous (contemptuous, off-hand) way, (for proper pride, see under *fahari*). **Takabari, v.** be proud, give oneself airs, play the grandee. Though not correct, the Rf. form *jitakabari* is often heard, also a Cs. *jitakabarisha.* (Ar. كبر and تكبر.)

Kiburuji,* n. *vi-* dim. of *buruji.*

Kibuyu, n. *vi-* dim. of *buyu.*

Kibuzi, n. *vi-* dim. *mbuzi.*

Kibwana, n. *vi-* dim. of *bwana.*

Kibwe, n. *vi-* dim. of *jiwe.*

Kibwebwe, n. *vi-* a broad strip of calico, wound tightly round the waist, esp. by women, for support during work, sometimes called *kibobwe.*

Kibwengo, n. (1) one of the numerous kinds of *ngoma* used in exorcism of spirits; (2) an evil spirit said to live in large trees, also in the sea, which gives off a shining light.

Kibweta, n. *vi-* dim. of *bweta.*

Kibwiko, n. *vi-* a club-foot, a deformed foot. (Cf. *kiguu.*)

Kicha, n. *vi-* a bunch, bundle, of palm leaf strips, vegetables, &c.

Kichaa, n. craziness, lunacy, madness. *Ana kichaa*, he is crazy. *Umaskini wake umemtia kichaa*, his poverty has driven him mad. (Cf. *wazimu.*)

Kichaani, n. *vi-* an erect, rather rigid, annual herb 6–18 in. tall with terminal spikes of crimson, scarlet, pink, or white flowers, *Striga elegans.*

Kichaazi, n. *vi-* a kind of banana. (Cf. *ndizi.*)

Kichaga, n. *vi-* a kind of store or receptacle for storing grain, &c., on a raised platform. **Uchaga, n.** same as *kichaga.* (Cf. *ulingo.*)

Kichaka, n. *vi-* dim. of *chaka.*

Kichala, n. *vi-* bunch, cluster of fruit.

Kichalichali, adv. See **Chali.**

Kichane, n. *vi-* dim. of *chane.* See under **Chana.**

Kichangamko, n. *vi-*. See under **Changamka.**

Kichanganyiko, n. *vi-*. See under **Changa, v.** (A).

Kichango, n. *vi-* dim. of *chango.*

Kichanio, n. *vi-*. See under **Chana.**

Kichea, n. See under **Cha, v.** (B).

Kicheche, n. *vi-* dim. of *cheche.*

Kichefuchefu, n. See under **Chefuka.**

Kicheko, n. *vi-*. See under **Cheka.**

Kichele, a. and in some places **Kichelele**, bare, naked; easily seen or understood; wide, uncovered, e.g. *alitoka kichele kuzimu hakuna nyota*, he went out stark naked in broad daylight (i.e. after the sun was up and the stars had disappeared). *Fedha za kichele*, small change, i.e. which can be counted and understood, as contr. with a note or coin of greater value, the value of which cannot be easily understood by some natives.

Kichelema, n. (1) used of cassava, potatoes, &c., which when cooked are watery and not floury as they are liked; (2) *vi-* also heard for *kiselema*, which see.

Kichembe, n. *vi-* dim. of *chembe.*

Kichepe, n. *vi-* e.g. *vichepe vya vitambaa*, cloth worn soft and threadbare.

Kichichi, adv. *Kukata kichichi*, cut with a sawing motion, or with a blunt knife. (Cf. *chikicha, keketa.*)

Kichikichi, n. *vi-*. See under **Chikichi.**

Kichinja mimba, n. *vi-*. See under **Chinja.**

Kichinja udhia, n. a common weed with a rose-like flower, a supposed cure for headaches, *Dissotis prostrata.*

Kichinjo, n. *vi-*. See under **Chinja.**

Kichipukizi, n. *vi-*. See under **Chipua.**

Kicho, n. *vi-*. See under **Cha,** v. (A).

Kichocheo, n. *vi-*, **Kichocho,** n. *vi-*. See under **Chocha.**

Kichochoro, n. *vi-*. See under **Chochoro.**

Kichoma mguu, n. *vi-*, also **Kichoma nguo,** n. *vi-* (1) Black Jack, an annual herb with yellowish flowers and barbed seeds, *Bidens pilosa*; (2) a perennial tussock grass, *Heteropogon contortus.*

Kichomi, n. *vi-*. See under **Choma,** v. (A).

Kichomo, n. *vi-*. See under **Choma,** v. (A) and (B).

Kichopa, n. *vi-*. See under **Chopa.**

Kichoro, n. *vi-*. See under **Chora.**

Kichozi, n. a name applied to sun birds. (Cf. *chozi.*)

Kichuguu, n. *vi-* and **Chuguu,** n. *ma-* of larger size, a white ant hill. Also sometimes **Kisuguu,** n. *vi-*.

Kichungu, n. *vi-* (1) dim. of *chungu*; (2) adv. bitterly, from *-chungu,* which see.

Kichupa, n. *vi-* dim. of *chupa.*

Kichwa, n. *vi-* (1) the head; (2) the upper part, top; (3) principal thing, important part or person, prime mover, leader, author, beginning, chief point, source; (4) anything resembling a head; (5) pain in the head; (6) obstinacy, pride, headiness. *Kichwa wazi,* bare head, bareheaded. *Nina kichwa,* or *naumwa kichwa,* I have a headache. *Kuwa na kichwa, kufanya kichwa,* to be headstrong (presumptuous, refractory, proud). *Kichwa kikubwa,* big head, swelled head, pride, arrogance, obstinacy. *Jipa kichwa, pata kichwa,* be proud, &c. *Mwenye kichwa,* a proud, obstinate person. *Kwa kichwa kikubwa,* in a presumptuous, headstrong way. *Kichwa kichwa,* topsy turvy, upside down. *Kichwangomba,* turning head over heels, a somersault.

Kidachi,* n. and adv. See under **Dachi.**

Kidaka, n. *vi-* (1) dim. of *daka*; (2) a coco-nut in the first stage of growth on the flower stem, before it becomes *kitale* (see *nazi*); (3) of the uvula—called *kidaka tonge,* that which catches (or receives) the lump of food, see under *daka,* v.; (4) dumbness. (Cf. *ububu.*)

Kidamu, v. and n. *vi-*. See under **Kadamu.**

Kidanga, n. *vi-* and a. of fruit in a very early stage of formation, before it is even *-changa,* e.g. *limau kidanga, embe kidanga.*

Kidani, n. *vi-* a neck ornament, necklace, collar of gold, silver, beads, &c., often chainwork, with large open links. (Cf. *mkufu* and *urembo.*)

Kidari, n. *vi-* breast, chest—of men and animals, but usu. of animals and birds. (Cf. *kifua* of man only.)

Kidato, n. *vi-* *vidato vya ngazi,* the rungs of a ladder. (Cf. *kipawa, kipandio.*)

Kidau,* n. *vi-* (1) dim. of *dau*; (2) an ink-well or pot, which is also *kidawa.* (Ar. دواة.)

Kidawa,* n. *vi-*. See (2) under **Kidau.**

Kidawati,* n. *vi-* dim. of *dawati.*

Kidazi, n. baldness, a bald patch on the head. (Cf. *upara.*)

Kidei, n. See **Kideri.**

Kidemu, n. *vi-* dim. of *demu.*

Kideri, n. a disease, a kind of cholera, which attacks fowls and cattle.

Kidevu, n. *vi-*. See under **Udevu.**

Kidhabidhabina,* n. *vi-*. See **Mdhabidhabina.**

Kidhi,* v. grant, give to, satisfy, e.g. *Mungu ndiye anayekidhi haja* (or *ni mkidhi haja*), God is the granter (satisfier) of all needs. *Amekidhi maombi yako,* he has given you (granted) what you asked or prayed for. Prep. **Kidhia.** Cs. **Kidhisha.**

Ps. **Kidhiwa. Mkidhi,** n. *wa-* one who grants, who gives to, a title of God, *Mkidhi haja,* the Granter of needs. (Ar. قضي.)

Kidiku, n. *vi-* a broken piece, strip, &c., i.e. of a pencil, broken knife, stick, &c.

Kidimbwi, n. *vi-* dim. of *dimbwi.*

Kidimu, n. *vi-* a fowl with naturally ruffled feathers or with featherless neck. Some people refuse to eat such fowls, they say they have a disease. (Cf. *mangisi.*)

Kidimu msitu, n. *vi-* a wild citrus fruit tree, *Citrus* sp.

Kidingapopo, n. the name given to a relapsing fever, dengue fever.

Kidiri, n. a squirrel. (Cf. *kindi.*)

Kidividivi, n. *vi-* an ear ornament. (Cf. *bali, nti.*)

Kidogo, form of *-dogo.*

Kidokezi, n. *vi-*, **Kidoko,** n. *vi-*. See under **Dokeza.**

Kidole, n. *vi-* a finger, toe. Distinguished by *kidole cha mkono,* a finger; *kidole cha mguu,* a toe; and these further, *kidole gumba,* the thumb; *kidole cha shahada,* forefinger; *kidole cha kati* or *kikubwa,* middle finger; *kidole cha kati ya kando,* fourth finger. *kidole cha mwisho,* little finger. **Dole,** n. *ma-* (1) a large finger; (2) a clumsy person; (3) a single banana fruit, i.e. one of a cluster (*chana*) on a large fruit stem (*mkungu*). **Udole,** n. (*ndole*) finger, toe, like *kidole. Udole* is also used sometimes for the nail of a finger and claw of an animal implying bigness or clumsiness. Also for a person who is weak and slender, e.g. *fulani kama udole.* (Cf. *ukucha, chanda.*)

Kidomo, n. *vi-*. See under **Mdomo.**

Kidonda, n. *vi-* dim. of *donda.*

Kidondo, n. *vi-* usu. used in the plur., kindling, small scraps of firewood used for starting up a fire.

Kidonge, n. *vi-* dim. of *donge.*

Kidotia, n. *vi-* also **Kilotia,** a child's cap. (Cf. *kofia.*)

Kidoto, n. *vi-* (1) blinker—like a small basket, or a small patch or bandage of cloth fastened over a camel's eyes while working a mill; (2) a small drinking-vessel.

Kidu,* n. the hole or place in a canoe in which the mast is placed. (Cf. *kiwida* of which this appears to be a corruption.)

Kidude,* n. *vi-* dim. of *dude.*

Kidudu,* n. *vi-* dim. of *dudu.*

Kidudusi, n. *vi-*. See under **Duduka.**

Kidugu, n. *vi-* and adv. See under **Ndugu.**

Kiduku, n. *vi-* the common duiker. (Cf. *funo.*)

Kidundu, n. *vi-* the forehead. (Cf. *kipaji.*)

Kidungadunga, n. *vi-*. See under **Dunga.**

Kidurango, n. *vi-* a dwarf. (Cf. *kibete, mbilikimo.*)

Kidurusi, n. *vi-* a termite hill. (Cf. *chuguu.*)

Kidusi, n. (1) the smell of a wild animal or fish; (2) an unusual smell or flavour in anything.

Kiduta, n. *vi-* a hill, rising ground, elevation.

Kielekezo, n. *vi-*, **Kielelezo,** n. *vi-*, **Kielezo,** n. *vi-*. See under **Elea,** v. (B).

Kiembe, n. *vi-* (1) for *chembe* (2), which see; (2) dim. of *embe.*

Kiendeleo, n. *vi-*. See under **Enda.**

Kieneo, n. *vi-*, **Kienezo,** n. *vi-*. See under **Enea.**

Kienge, n. *vi-* dim. of *mwenge.*

Kifa, n. *vi-* (1) see under **Fa,** v.; (2) nipple of a gun, pan of a matchlock.

Kifaa, n. *vi-*. See under **Faa.**

Kifabakazi, n. Nandi flame tree, a much branched tree up to 40 ft. tall with large brilliant scarlet flowers and woody pods containing winged seeds, *Spathodea nilotica.*

Kifaduro, n. whooping cough.

Kifafa, n. fits, convulsions, epilepsy.

Kifalme, n. and adv. See under **Mfalme.**

Kifandugu, n. the coccyx, some Muhammadans say that this bone never rots, even in the grave.

Kifani, n. *vi-*, **Kifano**, n. *vi-*. See under **Faa**.

Kifaranga,* n. *vi-* dim. of *faranga*.

Kifaransa.* See under **Faransa**.

Kifaru, n. *vi-* dim. of *faru*, a rhinoceros.

Kifauwongo, n. *vi-* lit. the death shammer, (1) sensitive plant, a scandent perennial herb with thorny stems and small heads of pinkish purple flowers, the leaves closing up when touched, *Mimosa pudica*; (2) an annual herb 3 to 12 in. tall with a terminal rosette of leaves and small yellow or pinkish flowers, *Biophytum sensitivum*; (3) also applied to insects which sham death when touched.

Kifefe, n. See under **Ufefe**.

Kificho, n. *vi-*. See under **Ficha**.

Kifidio, n. *vi-*. See under **Fidi**.

Kifijo, n. *vi-* shout of joy, applause, &c., often used in plur. *vifijo*.

Kifiko, n. *vi-*. See under **Fika**.

Kifo, n. *vi-*, **Kifu**, n. *vi-*. See under **Fa**.

Kifu,* v. be sufficient (for), suffice, satisfy. *Vitu vya kukifu*, things in sufficiency. Prep. **Kifia**, e.g. *amenikifia haja yangu*, he satisfied my wish. **Kefu**, n. and **Kifu**, n. a sufficient quantity, a full amount, abundance, e.g. *amekula kefu yake*, he has eaten his fill. (Cf. *kidhi*, *tosha*, *ridhisha*. Ar. كفي.)

Kifua, n. *vi-* (1) breast, bosom, chest, usu. of man only (cf. *kidari*); (2) any chest affection, cough, pleurisy, pneumonia, &c. *Hawezi kifua*, he has a chest complaint. *Kifua kikuu*, consumption. (3) dim. of *fua*, a small round wooden platter. *Kifua chake nyumba ya udongo, haihimili vishindo*, said of a quick-tempered person who cannot bear to be put out. **Mafua**, n. plur. chest symptoms, chest complaint (cold in the chest and head, bronchitis, &c.). (Cf. *fuu*, v. and *pafu*.)

Kifuasi, n. *vi-*. See under **Fuata**.

Kifudifudi. See under **Fudifudi**.

Kifuka, n. *vi-* an erect herb up to 5 ft. tall with numerous heads of small reddish blue daisy-like flowers, *Vernonia cinerea*.

Kifukizo, n. *vi-*. See under **Fuka**.

Kifuko, n. *vi-*. dim. of *mfuko*.

Kifuku, n. See under **Fuka**.

Kifulifuli. See under **Fudifudi**.

Kifumba, n. *vi-*, **Kifumbu**, n. *vi-*. See under **Fumba**, v.

Kifumufumu, n. a kind of cassava. (Cf. *muhogo*.)

Kifundo, n. *vi-* dim. of *fundo*. See under **Funda**, v. (D).

Kifunga mbuzi, n. *vi-* lit. the goat fastener, an annual or short-lived perennial tussock grass up to 12 in. tall, *Eleusine indica*.

Kifungo, n. *vi-*. See under **Funga**.

Kifungu, n. *vi-* dim. of *fungu*.

Kifungua (*kinywa*), (*mimba*), n., **Kifunguo**, n. *vi-*. See under **Funga**.

Kifunifuni, adv. See **Kifudifudi**.

Kifuniko, n. *vi-*. See under **Funika**.

Kifuo, n. *vi-* (1) a stake fixed in the ground with a pointed end for ripping off the husk of coco-nuts (cf. *fua*, v. (3)); (2) dim. of *mfuo*, a small groove, line, or mark.

Kifupa, n. *vi-* dim. of *mfupa*.

Kifupi, adv. and n. See under **-fupi**.

Kifurushi,* n. *vi-* dim. of *furushi*.

Kifusi, n. *vi-* dim. of *fusi*. See under **Fusa**, v. (A).

Kifuu, n. *vi-*. See under **Fuu**, n. (B).

Kiga, n. *vi-* the thigh of an animal when killed, the ham. (Cf. *paja*.)

Kigae, n. *vi-* dim. of *gae*.

Kigaga, n. *vi-*. See under **Gaga**.

Kigagazi, n. nausea, a sick feeling. (Cf. *kichefuchefu*.)

Kigambo, n. *vi-*. See under **Amba**, v. (A).

Kiganda, n. *vi-* dim. of *ganda*, n. See under **Ganda**, v.

Kigango, n. *vi-* dim. of *gango*. See under **Ganga**, v.

Kiganja, n. *vi-* the palm of the hand, also **Ganja**, n. *ma-*.

Kigasha, n. *vi-* the forearm, i.e. *kigasha cha mkono.*

Kigawanye, n. *vi-*, **Kigawanyo**, n. *vi-*, **Kigawe**, n. *vi-*, **Kigawo**, n. *vi-*. See under **Gawa**, v.

Kigego, n. *vi-* a child which develops its upper teeth first, or which is born in an abnormal manner, or which develops in an abnormal manner, and is therefore considered unlucky. (Cf. *chura, chimbi, chimvi.*)

Kigelegele, n. *vi-*, also **Ugelegele**, a peculiar high-pitched trill, shrill scream—used by women esp. as a sign of joy or triumph, welcome on return, at a birth, wedding, &c. (Cf. *kelele, shangwe, kifijo.*)

Kigeregenja, n. *vi-* also **Kigereng'enza**, (1) a very small splinter, broken piece, fragment, chip; (2) a very small piece of pot, broken plate, glass, &c. (Cf. *gae.*)

Kigesi, n. *vi-*, also **Kigezi**, n. *vi-* an anklet. See **Kugesi.**

Kigeugeu, n. a. and adv. See under **Geua.**

Kigezo, b. *vi-*. See under **Geza.**

Kigingi, n. *vi-* a tent peg or similar peg or stake, e.g. for tethering an animal, &c. (Sometimes heard as *kigwingwi.*)

Kigodo, n. rice flour mixed with sugar and grated coco-nut. (Cf. *bumbwi, bwimbwi.*)

Kigoe, n. *vi-*. See under **Ngoeka.**

Kigogo, adv. and n. *vi-* dim. of *gogo.*

Kigogota, n. *vi-* the woodpecker, also called *gogota* and *gongonola.*

Kigoli, n. *vi-* a girl—of one just growing up, almost marriageable, between *mtoto* and *mwali.* (Cf. *msichana.*)

Kigomba, n. *vi-* dim. of *mgomba.*

Kigombegombe, n. a kind of fish, not considered good eating by Europeans.

Kigongo, n. *vi-* dim. of *gongo.*

Kigong'ota, n. same as *kigotagota, kigogota,* and *king'oto.*

Kigono, n. *vi-*. See under **Gona.**

Kigosho, n. *vi-* bend, crook, curve, esp. when abnormal, a deformity. *Kigosho cha mkono,* a deformed arm, or one bent by some disease or accident. *Mwenye kigosho cha miguu,* a knock-kneed person. *Fimbo hii ina kigosho,* this stick has a crook in it. (Cf. *kombo, pinda.*)

Kigotagota, n. same as *kigong'ota, kigogota,* and *king'oto.*

Kiguba, n. *vi-*. See **Kikuba.**

Kigudulia, n. *vi-* dim. of *gudulia.*

Kigugu, adv. and n. *vi-* dim. of *gugu.*

Kigugumizi, n. See under **Gugumia.**

Kiguguta, n. *vi-* dim. of *guguta.*

Kigulio, n. *vi-* also **Gulio**, n. *ma-* a market, for the commoner *soko.*

Kigumba, n. *vi-* the head of an arrow or spear.

Kigunda, n. *vi-* dim. of *gunda.*

Kigundu, n. used to describe anybody whose buttocks stick out more than is usual. (Cf. *shuri.*)

Kiguni,* n. *vi-* dim. of *guni.*

Kigunzi, n. *vi-* dim. of *gunzi.*

Kigutu, n. *vi-* dim. of *gutu.*

Kiguu, n. *vi-*. See under **Mguu.**

Kiguzo, n. *vi-* dim. of *nguzo.*

Kigwaru, n. *vi-* a growth, said to be like a wart or pimple on the clitoris of a woman. It is said to cause the woman either to be childless, or if she has children they die at birth or when still young; also she may cause the death of her husband. The *waganga* have an operation to remove the growth. (Also called *kisukumi* and *kinyakuzi.*)

Kigwe, n. *vi-* dim. of *ugwe,* small cord, string, braid, piping on edge of dress, tape, a rein. (Cf. *kitani, uzi, kamba.*)

Kigwingwi, n. *vi-* same as *kigingi.*

Kihame, n. *vi-*. See under **Hama.**

Kiharusi,* n. apoplexy. (Ar. خرس be dumb, with *ki-* prefix.)

Kihasho,* n. *vi-* dim. of *hasho.*

Kiherehere, n. (1) palpitation, confused movement, e.g. *kiherehere cha moyo,* palpitation of the heart; (2) trepidation, bustle, anxiety.

Kihero,* n. *vi-* (1) dim. of *hero*; (2) a trough for putting grass in as fodder for cattle.

Kihindi, n. and adv. See under **Mhindi.**

Kihongwe, n. *vi-* a kind of donkey, from the Nyamwezi, Iramba, and Masai countries, used for carrying loads. Often called *punda kihongwe.*

Kihori,* n. *vi-* dim. of *hori.*

Kihoro, n. a great grief because of bereavement, or great loss of property, &c. *Amekufa kihoro,* he died of grief. (Cf. *majonzi, huzuni.*)

Kihunzi, n. *maneno ya kihunzi* or *kihunzi cha maneno,* speech in which the last syllables of the words are put first, *kinyume.*

Kiinamizi, n. *vi-*. See under **Ina,** v.

Kiingereza,* n. and adv. See under **Mwingereza.**

Kiini, n. *vi-* innermost part of a thing, and so (1) kernel or stone of fruit, e.g. the inner part of a clove (*karafuu*) when the outer skin is removed after soaking in water; (2) the yolk of an egg, *kiini cha yai*; (3) the heart or hard core of a tree—also called *moyo wa mti,* esp. if soft or pithy; (4) pupil of the eye (cf. *mboni*). **Kiini macho,** n. *vi-* a conjurer, a conjurer's trick, sleight of hand, jugglery. Distinguished from *uganga,* e.g. *huyu si mganga ni kiinimacho,* this man is not a real medicine man, but a juggler. *Mganga alifanya kiinimacho,* the medicine man used a juggler's trick. (Cf. *ini, moyo,* and *macho.*)

Kiinikizo, n. *vi-*. See under **Ina,** v.

Kiinua, n. *vi-*. See under **Ina,** v. *Kiinua mgongo,* a present given on completion of a task, a back raiser.

Kiislamu,* v. See under **Silimu.**

Kiitikio, n. *vi-*, **Kiitiko,** n. *vi-*. See under **Ita.**

Kijaa, n. *vi-* (1) the stones used for grinding corn, &c.; (2) a vessel full to the brim, see under *jaa,* v.

Kijakazi, n. *vi-* dim. of *mjakazi.*

Kijaluba,* n. *vi-* dim. of *jaluba.*

Kijamanda,* n. *vi-* dim. of *jamanda.*

Kijambia,* n. *vi-* (1) dim. of *jambia*; (2) a gusset (of a shirt, *kanzu,* &c.).

Kijana, n. *vi-* dim. of *jana,* but more usually used than *jana,* a youth, &c. See under **Jana,** n. (A).

Kijani, n. *vi-* dim. of *jani.*

Kijembe, n. *vi-* dim. of *jembe.*

Kijeraha,* n. *vi-* dim. of *jeraha.*

Kijia, n. *vi-* dim. of *njia.*

Kijicho, n. *vi-*. See under **Jicho.**

Kijichwa, n. *vi-* dim. of *kichwa.*

Kijidudu, n. *vi-*. See under **Dudu.**

Kijiguu, n. *vi-* dim. of *mguu.*

Kijiji, n. *vi-* dim. of *mji.*

Kijike, n. *vi-* dim. of *jike,* a young female, human or other.

Kijiko, n. *vi-* (1) dim. of *mwiko*; (2) dim. of *jiko.*

Kijimbi msitu, n. *vi-* the mangrove kingfisher (Pemba), *Halcyon senegaloides.*

Kijimo, n. *vi-* a dwarf. (Cf. *kibeti, mbilikimo.*)

Kijineno, n. *vi-* dim. of *neno.* See under **Nena,** v.

Kijinga, n. and adv. See under **-jinga.**

Kijinga, n. *vi-* dim. of *kinga,* a small firebrand.

Kijini, n. *vi-* dim. of *jini.*

Kijino, n. *vi-* (1) dim. of *jino*; (2) a small fish like whitebait. (Cf. *dagaa, nyambuo, ushimbu.*)

Kijio, n. *vi-*. See under **Ja.**

Kijiri, n. See **Chichiri.**

Kijiti, n. *vi-* dim. of *mti.*

Kijito, n. *vi-* dim. of *mto.*

Kijitu, n. *vi-*. See under **Mtu.**

Kijivi, n. and adv. See under **Iba.**

Kijivu, n. and a. (1) see under *jivu*; (2) a wooden socket in which the handle of a native drill turns. (Cf. *kekee.*)

Kijiwe, n. dim. of *jiwe.*

Kijogoo, n. *vi-* (1) dim. of *jogoo*; (2) a kind of fish.

Kijoli, n. *vi-* dim. of *mjoli.*

Kijombo, n. *vi-* dim. of *chombo.*

Kijongo, n. *vi-* a hump-backed person, &c., like *kigongo.*

Kijoyo, n. *vi-*, **Kijoyojoyo,** n. *vi-*. See under **Moyo.**

Kijukuu, n. *vi-* great grandchild, dim. of *mjukuu*, which see.

Kijumba, n. *vi-* dim. of *nyumba*.

Kijumbamshale, n. applied to swallows and swifts. (Cf. *mbayuwayu*.)

Kijumbe, n. *vi-* dim. of *mjumbe*, a special secret messenger, a go-between, a match-maker. (Cf. *mjumbe*.)

Kijungu, n. *vi-* dim. of *chungu*, i.e. small cooking-pot.

Kijusi, n. *vi-* (1) see under **Ujusi**; (2) a small kind of lizard. (Cf. *mjusi*.)

Kijuso, n. *vi-* dim. of *uso*.

Kijusu, n. *vi-* a foetus (human) of four months' old. (Cf. *kilenga*.)

Kijuto, n. *vi-* for usual *kijito*, dim. of *mto*, a small river.

Kijuujuu, adv. and n. See under **Juu**.

Kijuvi, n. *vi-* and adv. See under **Jua, v.**

Kikaango, n. *vi-*, **Kikango**, n. *vi-*. See under **Kaanga**.

Kikaimati,* n. *vi-* (1) a kind of gruel made of wheat flour; (2) a kind of round fritter of wheat flour fried in fat. (Cf. *andazi*, *kitumbua*. From Ar. لقمة kind of fritter.)

Kikaka, n. and adv. See under **Kakakaka**.

Kikalasha,* n. *vi-* dim. of *kalasha*.

Kikale, adv. See under **-kale**.

Kikambo, n. and adv. See under **Kambo**.

Kikanda, n. *vi-* dim. of *kanda*, n.

Kikande, n. a fish, kind of sole.

Kikanza, n. See under **Kaanga**.

Kikao, n. *vi-*. See under **Kaa, v.**

Kikapu, n. *vi-* a wide-mouthed flexible basket of plaited leaf-strips or grass, with two small handles, used for all purposes. **Kapu**, n. *ma-* a large *kikapu*. (Other kinds of baskets and bags are: *kanda*, *jamanda*, *tunga*, *dohani*, *pakacha*, *ungo*, *kiteo*, *kung'uto*, *kifumbu*, and cf. *mfuko*.)

Kikaramba, n. *vi-* an old person, used as a scornful expression.

Kikariri,* n. and adv. See under **Kariri**.

Kikasha,* n. *vi-* dim. of *kasha*.

Kikasiki,* n. *vi-* dim. of *kasiki*.

Kikaufu, n. and adv., **Kikausha**, n. *vi-*, **Kikavu**, n. and adv. See under **Kauka**.

Kikawe, n. dim. of *jiwe*.

Kikaza, n. *vi-*, **Kikazo**, n. *vi*. See under **Kaza**.

Kike, n. and adv. See under **-ke**.

Kikebe, n. *vi-* dim. of *mkebe*.

Kikero, n. *vi-* a nose ornament, nose ring or pendant. (Cf. *hazama*, *kishaufu*.)

Kikeukeu, n. See **Keukeu**.

Kikia, n. *vi-* dim. of *mkia*.

Kikiki, adv. firmly, e.g. *funga kikiki*, fasten firmly.

Kikingio, n. *vi-*, **Kikingo**, n. *vi-*. See under **Kinga**.

Kikiri,* n. wrestling, struggling, pushing, and shoving. (Cf. *kakara*, *kukuru*.) **Kikirika**, v. St. wrestle, push and shove, be in the act of wrestling, struggling. (Cf. *buburusha*. Ar. كركر rolling about.)

Kikisa, v. speak in a hesitating, confused, broken way, be unintelligible or half-understood, puzzle, mystify. *Jambo hili lakikisa*, this business is difficult, hard to get at. *Fulani anakikisa maneno*, So-and-so cannot get his words out clearly. (Cf. *gugumiza*, *goteza*.)

Kiko, n. *vi-* tobacco pipe, used of an ordinary pipe and also of a hookah, the latter consisting of the *kiko* proper, i.e. a coco-nut shell partly filled with water, and two tubes of wood or reed (*digali*, *mdakali*), one leading from the bowl (*bori*) holding tobacco (*tumbako*) into the water, the other (*shilamu*) from the *kiko* to the mouthpiece through which the smoke is drawn. The bubbling of the water is called *malio ya kiko*. Other simpler pipes consist of a hollow reed and earthenware bowl only, e.g. *toza*. (Cf. *buruma*, *kikororo*, *mtemba*.)

Kiko, verb-form, (it) is there, the pfx. *ki* and locative *ko*.

Kikoa, n. *vi-* (1) a meal eaten in common, provided by each of those who join in it by turns, a common table, a mess, boarding together; *kula kikoa*, to have meals in common (contr. *kula bia*, where each person provides a share at each meal). *Leo kikoa changu*, it is my turn to provide the meal to-day.—Also used for the feasts prepared by wizards and witches, said to be human flesh either of a child killed, or part of a corpse dug up from a grave, i.e. the child or person, &c., given up in turn by the wizards for their feast. (2) a collection made for a newly married couple; (3) a football team; (4) dim. of *koa*.

Kikoba, n. *vi-* dim. of *mkoba*.

Kikofi, n. *vi-*. See **Kofi**.

Kikohozi, n. *vi-*. See under **Kohoa**.

Kikoi, n. *vi-* white loin-cloth with coloured border in cotton or silk.

Kikoka, n. *vi-* blade or shoot of a grass used as forage. **Ukoka**, n. a fine, creeping kind of grass, largely collected and used as fodder for horses, donkeys, and cattle.

Kikoko, n. *vi-* dim. of *koko*, *mkoko*, and *ukoko*, a bit of hard dried stuff, and so of a scab or scurf.

Kikomba, n. *vi-*. See under **Komba**, v.; also dim. of *komba*, n.

Kikombe, n. *vi-*, **Kikombo**, n. *vi-*. See under **Komba**, v.

Kikomo, n. *vi-*. See under **Koma**.

Kikondo, n. *vi-* (1) a kind of banana (cf. *ndizi*); (2) dim. of *mkondo*.

Kikondoo, adv. and n. *vi-* dim. of *kondoo*.

Kikongwe, adv. and n. *vi-*. See under **Konga**, v. (A).

Kikono, n. *vi-* dim. of *mkono*.

Kikonyo, n. *vi-* like *kikono*, e.g. of a stalk, *vikonyo vya karafuu*, clove-stalks.

Kikope, n. *vi-* eyelid, cf. *kope*.

Kikopo, n. *vi-* (1) dim. of *kopo*; (2) see under **Kopa**, v.; (3) in the expression *mtoto wa kikopo*, of a young ruffian, vagabond. (Cf. *mhuni*.)

Kilopwe, n. *vi-* an annual herb with twining or trailing stems and heads of blue flowers, *Jacquemontia capitata*.

Kikora, n. *vi-* (1) see under **Kora**, v.; (2) the stem of the *mwaa*, i.e. the Hyphaene or Dwarf palm.

Kikore, n. *vi-* (1) a rich, noted person (cf. *tajiri*, *maarufu*, *mashuhuri*); (2) a new plantation or garden.

Kikorokoro, n. *vi-*. See **Vikorokoro**.

Kikorombwe, n. *vi-* signal cry or call—made by blowing into the hand or through the fingers.

Kikoromeo, n. *vi-*. See under **Koroma**.

Kikororo, n. *vi-* a hookah, a water-pipe for smoking. (Cf. *kiko*, *buruma*, *mtemba*.)

Kikosi, n. *vi-* (1) see under **Kosi**; (2) company, band, troop, esp. of soldiers or armed men. (Cf. *kundi*, *jeshi*, *umati*.)

Kikota, n. *vi-*. See **Kikoto** (3).

Kikotama, n. *vi-* dim. of *kotama*.

Kikoto, n. *vi-* (1) a whip of plaited grass, leaf-strips, or bark-fibre; (2) plait of hair; (3) the stem of the millet plant, some of which contain sweet juice and are chewed like sugar-cane, sometimes called *kikota*.

Kikozi, n. *vi-*. See **Kozi**.

Kikuba,* n. *vi-* (1) a bundle or packet of aromatic herbs, &c., worn on the breast by some women for their perfume (? Ar. كبا frankincense); (2) dim. of *kuba*.

Kikucha, n. *vi-* dim. and **Kikuchia**, n. *vi-*. See under **Ukucha**.

Kikuku, n. *vi-* (1) ring, usually of metal, worn on the arm or leg, armlet, bracelet, anklet; (2) *kikuku cha kupandia farasi*, a stirrup; (3) dim. of *kuku*.

Kikuli, n. horror, fright. (Cf. *kitisho*, *kioja*.)

Kikulia, n. *vi-*. See under **Kua**.

Kikumbatio, n. *vi-*. See under **Kumbatia**.

Kikumbo, n. *vi-*. See under **Kumba**, v. (A).

Kikumi, n. *vi-* the word adopted for a ten-cent piece, i.e. a piece worth ten (cents). (Cf. *kitano*, for a five-cent piece.)

Kikunazi, n. *vi-* (obscene), a euphemism for a certain part of the female genitals.

Kikundi, n. *vi-* dim. of *kundi.*

Kikundu, n. *vi-* (1) dim. of *mkundu*; (2) haemorrhoids, piles. (Cf. *bawasiri, futuri.*)

Kikungu, n. *vi-* dim. of *mkungu,* n. (3).

Kikunjo, n. *vi-*. See under **Kunja.**

Kikuta, n. *vi-* dim. of *ukuta.*

Kikuti, n. *vi-* (1) dim. of *kuti*; (2) see under **Kuta,** v. (A).

Kikuto, n. *vi-* (1) anything rolled up, a roll, i.e. a sleeping-mat rolled up for a journey, &c.; (2) hyena, for the common *fisi.* (Cf. *kingugwa.*)

Kikuukuu, n. and adv. See under **-kuukuu.**

Kikwapa, n. *vi-*. See under **Kwapa.**

Kikwaru, n. *vi-* cock's spur. (Cf. *kipi.*)

Kikwata, n. *vi-* a much branched shrub or small tree up to 15 ft. tall with white flowers and oblong 2- to 4-seeded pods, *Acacia mellifera.*

Kikwata, adv. *kwenda kikwata,* see **Kwata.**

Kikwato, n. *vi-* dim. of *ukwato.*

Kikwi, n. *vi-* (*zikwi*) a thousand, rarely used and only in poetry. (Cf. *elfu.*)

Kikwifukwifu, n. hiccup, sobbing after crying. (Cf. *kitefutefu.*)

Kila,* a. every (as a rule with a singular noun only, and unlike other adjs. in Swahili with its noun following). *Kila mtu,* every one. *Kila siku,* daily, day by day. *Kila aendako,* wherever he goes. *Kila atakapo,* whenever he likes. (Ar. كلّ.)

Kilaji, n. *vi-*. See under **La.**

Kilalanungu, n. *vi-* a perennial herb with creeping stems, cordate leaves, and white spathes, growing on forest floors at low altitudes, *Callopsis Volkensii.*

Kilalio, n. *vi-*, **Kilalo,** n. *vi-*. See **Lala.**

Kilango, n. *vi-* dim. of *mlango.*

Kile, a. (1) dem. that; (2) Imper. form of *-la,* v. e.g. *kitoto kile kikile kile kileji,* let that little child eat that cake.

Kilegesambwa, n. (1) the knee-cap, also called *pia ya mguu*; (2) an old saying *kilege sambwa* (*nisiambwe*), meaning 'How can I live (or be) and not be spoken evilly of?'

Kileji, n. *vi-* a round flat cake made from wheat flour or rice flour.

Kilele,* n. *vi-* top, point, peak, pointed end, e.g. *kilele cha mlima,* the top of the mountain. Also of plants and trees. *Kilele cha mnazi kilichanua,* the shoot of the coco-nut tree blossomed. **Kileleta,** n. *vi-* the summit of a hill or mountain. (Cf. *nguu.* ? Pers. كلال summit of mountain.)

Kilema, n. *vi-*. See under **Lemaa.**

Kilemba, n. *vi-* (1) a cloth worn as a wrapper round the head, a turban —the style of folding and wearing being according to the rank, dignity, &c., of the wearer, often of silk, and costly. *Piga kilemba,* wear a turban. *Vunja kilemba,* take off or unfold a turban. (2) fig. gratuity at the end of a job, apprenticeship, course of teaching, &c. (cf. *ada, bakshishi, ufito*); (3) also, fig. reputation, praise, e.g. *alimpiga kilemba cha ukoka,* he praised him falsely, flattered him, made him think himself an important person, &c.; (4) crest, e.g. *kilemba cha jogoo,* cock's comb. (Cf. *upanga, shungi, kishungi, undu.*) **Kilemba cha bwana,** n. an annual weed with heads of orange or scarlet flowers, *Emilia sagittata.* **Mkilemba,** n. *wa-* one who has earned a turban, i.e. by completing a job or a course of instruction, and so denotes a successful candidate, prizeman, graduate, &c. (Cf. follg.)

Kilembwa, n. *vi-* a point, end, e.g.

kilembwa cha titi, the nipple of the breast. (Cf. *chuchu*, and prec.)

Kilembwe, n. *vi-* great-great-grandchild. (Cf. *kining'ina, kijukuu, mjukuu. Mjukuu, kitukuu, kilembwe, kining'ina*—grandchild, great-grandchild, great-great-grandchild.

Kilemea nembo, n. *vi-* a shrub or scandent plant with dark-green opposite leaves and clusters of white flowers in the axils of the leaves, *Cremaspora africana*.

Kilendo, n. a kind of fish.

Kilenga, n. *vi-* a foetus (human) of four months' old. (Cf. *kijusu*.)

Kilenge, n. *vi-* a children's game played by throwing four pieces of stick.

Kileo, n. *vi-*. See under **Lewa**.

Kileti, n. *vi-* (1) metal rowlock, crutch, for an oar (cf. *kishwara, makosi*); (2) stick used for twisting in native rope-making.

Kilifu,* n. *vi-* usu. *difu, ma-* which see.

Kilihafu, n. *vi-* first stomach in quadrupeds, the maw, belly, paunch.

Kilili, n. *vi-* (1) dim. of *ulili*; (2) a pulpit.

Kilima, n. *vi-* dim. of *mlima*.

Kilimbili, n. *vi-* the upper arm, i.e. above the elbow.

Kilimi, n. *vi-*. See under **Ulimi**.

Kilimia, n., **Kilimo**, n. *vi-*. See under **Lima**.

Kilinda, n. *vi-*. See under **Linda**.

Kilindi, n. *vi-* a place of deep water, a deep channel, a deep. Cf. *Kilindini*, the harbour at Mombasa.

Kilindo, n. *vi-*. See under **Linda**.

Kilinge, n. *vi-* (1) mystery, puzzle, trick, an innuendo. *Maneno ya kilinge*, dark unintelligible utterance. (2) a secret meeting of wizards, also the place where spirits are exorcized; (3) a place for dancing, playing cards, &c.

Kilingo, n. *vi-* (1) see under *linga*; (2) a platform erected in a plantation for the watchers who guard the crops against birds and animals. **Ulingo**, n. *ma-* is also used in the same sense. (Cf. *kilindo*, and *dungu, jukwaa*.)

Kilinzi, n. *vi-* a strap of beads worn round the wrist.

Kilio, n. *vi-*. See under **Lia**.

Kilo,* n. a kilogramme (almost as common as *ratli* in use in Tanganyika Territory).

Kilometa,* n. a kilometre (used on the railways in Tanganyika Territory).

Kilotia, n. *vi-*. See **Kidotia**.

Kilua, n. a kind of sweet-smelling flower. (Cf. *ua*.)

Kiludhu,* n. velvet. (? Ar. لاذة red china silk.)

Kiluwiluwi, n. *vi-* the larva of an insect, mosquito, &c., also a tadpole.

Kima, n. (A) a kind of monkey.

Kima,* n. (B) *vi-* (1) price, value, e.g. *kima chake kadiri gani?* How much is it? (cf. *kem*); (2) measure, stature, height, but **Kimo**, n. *vi-* is in much commoner use, (1) measure, stature, height, depth, but the latter is usually *kina*, which see; (2) a measuring rod, tape, foot rule. *Kimo cha mtu*, a man's height. *Akupita kimo*, he is taller than you (cf. *kipimo*). (3) the front or back piece of a *kanzu*, sometimes called *badani*. (Ar. قامة stature, قيمة price, كم what quantity.)

Kima,* n. (C) minced meat, i.e. *mchuzi wa kima*, gravy made with minced meat. (Pers. and Hind. قيمة.)

Kimaada, a. regular, proper, genuine.

Kimacho, adv. See under **Jicho**.

Kimako, n. See under **Maka**.

Kimaji, adv. and a. See under **Maji**.

Kimanda, n. *vi-* (1) an omelette; (2) an oath or trial in which the parties are given bread to eat, the guilty person is supposed not to be able to swallow the bread.

Kimanga, n. and adv. See under **Manga**.

Kimangari, n. *vi-* an annual or perennial herb with rose-coloured flowers, parasitic on the roots of grasses, *Rhamphicarpa veronicaefolia.*

Kimango, n. *vi*-, and **Mango**, of larger size, a round stone used for grinding flour, snuff, &c.

Kimashamba, n. and adv. See under **Shamba.**

Kimasomaso, n. pretence, i.e. *kufanya kimasomaso*, to try to get out of a difficulty, argument, tight corner, by trickery, e.g. by pretending not to have heard argument, or not to understand or to have forgotten, &c.

Kimatu, n. young locust. (Cf. *nzige, maige, funutu, tunutu.*)

Kimau, n. *vi*- a tunic with short sleeves, such as is worn by native police, soldiers, office messengers, &c.

Kimavi cha kuku, n. goat-weed used as a vegetable in some places, *Ageratum conyzoides.*

Kimba, n. *vi*- (1) dead body, corpse, for the usual *maiti* (cf. *mfu, mzoga*); (2) heap of dung, animal or human. (Cf. *mavi, kinyesi.*)

Kimbaombao, n. See under **Bao.**

Kimbia, v. run away, fly (from), escape (from). *Adui walikimbia*, the enemies fled. *Mtoto alimkimbia simba*, the child ran away from (escaped from) the lion. Ps. **Kimbiwa**, be run away from, be escaped from. St. and Pot. **Kimbika**, e.g. allow of running (escape, &c.). Prep. **Kimbilia**, run to (for, in, after &c., but *not* as a rule, run away *from*), overtake, take refuge with, have recourse to, fall back upon, go on an errand for; e.g. *mbuzi hawa watakimbia kumkimbilia mama yao*, these goats will run off to find their dam. *Kimbilia roho*, run for (to save) one's life. *Kimbilia fedha*, run races for money. With *-ji-* e.g. *watu walijikimbilia*, the people took to their heels—of a promiscuous, shameful flight, every one for himself. Ps. **Kimbiliwa**, be run to (for, after, &c.), be a refuge (asylum, resource), and St. and Pot. **Kimbilika.** Cs. **Kimbiliza**, cause to run on, make go fast, hurry, hasten, do in a hurry, do rashly (precipitately, carelessly) —like *endeleza*, but more emphatic, e.g. *kimbiliza maneno*, talk too fast, talk recklessly (foolishly, at random, without thinking). *Kimbiliza jipu*, open an abscess too soon, treat it prematurely. *Kimbiliza udongo*, be quick with the clay, before it gets too dry and hard to use. *Kimbiliza kazi*, hurry on the work. Cs. **Kimbiza**, cause (encourage, allow, &c.) to run, put to flight, allow to escape, help in escaping, drive away, pursue. *Alikimbiza roho yake*, he saved his soul. *Akimbiza mtoto asije akauawa*, he saves the child from being killed. *Kimbiza punda*, run in front of a donkey, as a slave used to do before his master, when riding. With Rf. *ji*- hide oneself away, be hidden, be out of view, e.g. *alijikimbiza*, he hid himself. Prep. of Cs. **Kimbizia**, e.g. *amenikimbizia watu wangu*, he has got all my men to run away from me. Rp. of Cs. **Kimbizana**, e.g. *watu walikimbizana*, the people encouraged each other to run away, or to push on quickly. **Kimbilio**, n. *ma*- (1) a place of refuge, or to hide in; (2) fig. help, assistance, salvation. **Kimbio**, n. and adv. at running pace, with speed, at full speed, hastily, also *kimbiombio* (cf. *mbio*). **Kimbizi**, n. and adv. (1) similar to *kimbio*; (2) anything which causes speed, haste, &c. **Mkimbizi**, n. *wa*- (1) one who runs away, fugitive, runaway, deserter, truant; (2) one who causes to run, pursuer, hunter, persecutor, also one who runs in front of a donkey so that it will follow. (Cf. *upesi.*)

Kimbimbi, n. hair standing on end because of fear or cold, &c., the condition of being cold with fright, goose flesh.

Kimbio, n. and adv., **Kimbizi**, n. and adv. See under **Kimbia.**

Kimbugibugi, n. *vi*- an annual or short-lived perennial grass up to 1 ft. tall, the very small seeds of which are eaten in times of famine, *Dactyloctenium aegyptium.*

Kimbunga, n. *vi-* typhoon, hurricane, esp. the famous and exceptional typhoon at Zanzibar on April 15, 1872, often used as an epoch in reckoning time. (Cf. *dhoruba, tufani, chamchela.*)

Kimburu, n. *vi-* a semi-wild cat. (Cf. *shume.*)

Kimea, n. *vi-*, **Kimelea,** n. *vi-*. See under **Mea.**

Kimene, n. See under **Mena.**

Kimenomeno, n. See under **Jino.**

Kimerimeti, n. *vi-*, **Kimeta,** n. *vi-*, **Kimetameta,** n. *vi-*, **Kimeti,** n. *vi-*, **Kimetimeti,** n. *vi-*. See under **Meta.**

Kimia, n. *vi-* a circular casting-net—of light fine twine. Also used to describe 'netting, network, lace, cambric', &c., i.e. *nguo ya kimia, -a kimia,* of network, netted. (Cf. *wavu, jarifa.*)

Kimio, n. *vi-*. See under **Umio.**

Kimkumku, n. (1) madness; (2) a lie. (Cf. *wazimu, kichaa, -wongo.*)

Kimo, n. *vi-*. See under **Kima,** n. (B).

Kimoyo, n., also **Kimoyomoyo.** See under **Moyo.**

Kimrima, n. and adv. See under **Mrima.**

Kimu,* v. (1) begin prayers in a mosque; (2) maintain, supply with food, clothing, necessaries (cf. *ruzuku*); (3) keep harping on a particular matter. **Mkimu,** n. *wa-* (1) a person who supplies another with the necessaries of life, who looks after another; (2) one who is careful, who looks after things with great care; (3) one who keeps harping on a particular matter. (Cf. *ruzuku, lisha, tunza, chukua.* Ar. قام stand, carry on (a matter), maintain.)

Kimulimuli, n. *vi-*. See under **Mulika.**

Kimwa, v. become wearied, get cross, be disgruntled, lose one's temper, be sulky. *Kimwa kwa chakula* (*njia, kazi,* &c.), be put out by one's food (journey, work, &c.). **Mkimwa,** n. *wa-* an obstinate, bad-tempered, sulky person. **Ukimwa,** n. sulkiness. (Cf. *kinai, choka, sumbuka, nuna.*)

Kimwitu, n. *vi-* and adv. See under **Mwitu.**

Kimwondo, n. *vi-* (1) a shooting star, a meteor; (2) a foolish person, simpleton. (Cf. *mjinga.*)

Kimya, n. and adv. (1) silence, stillness, absence of noise; (2) quietness, calm, reserve. As adv. silently, without noise. Prov. *Kimya kingi kina mshindo mkuu,* much silence has a mighty noise. *Nyamaza kimya,* hold one's tongue, be perfectly silent. *Mtu wa kimya* or *kimyakimya,* a very quiet, reserved person. (Cf. *tulia, nyamaa.*)

Kina, pfx. or n. used as pfx. See under **Akina.**

Kina, n. *vi-* (1) a rhyme, a terminal assonance, a similar final syllable, *kuwa na vina,* to have rhymes—of lines of poetry. *Tia vina,* make rhymes, rhyming endings. *Mashairi ya vina,* rhyming verses. (Cf. *guni,* for absence of rhyme, blank verse.) (2) depth, e.g. *kina cha bahari,* a deep place in the sea. *Bahari ina kina,* the sea is very deep. (Cf. *kilindi.*)

Kinaganaga, adv. personally, clearly, in detail. *Nilimweleza kinaganaga,* I explained to him personally, in detail, &c.

Kinagiri, n. *vi-* an ornament, usually of gold, like a large bead bored through the middle and worn on a chain or string.

Kinai,* v. (1) be content, be self-satisfied, be independent, want no sympathy or help, be self-sufficient, be self-contained. Hence, often (2) in the sense, of being conceited, offensive, independent, or of active dislike, i.e. be disgusted, be surfeited, dislike, have loathing, e.g. of food, *amekinai,* he has had enough, he has had a full meal, (or of a sick man) he has no appetite, he revolts from food. Rf. *jikinai,* feel quite satisfied, or secure, be boastful, vaunt oneself. Cs. **Kinaisha**, satisfy, surfeit, glut, disgust, nauseate, revolt. *Chakula hiki kinanikinaisha*, this food revolts me. *Atakukinaisha siku moja*, you will have enough of him one day. *Kujikinaisha ubora*, to vaunt one's perfections. **-kinaifu**, a. of one who has had enough, does not desire or need anything, and so (1) moderate, self-controlled, sober, independent; (2) self-sufficient, contemptuous, cold, supercilious, unsociable. **Kinaya**, n. self-content, independence, selfish isolation, a supercilious air, insolence. **Mkinaifu**, n. *wa-* a satiated, self-satisfied person, an independent person. **Ukinaifu**, n. self-sufficiency, independence, fastidiousness, self-satisfaction, conceit. (Cf. *shiba, ridhisha, chukiza, jisifu, jivuna, kiasi, upweke, baridi*. Ar. قنع.)

Kinamasi, n. (1) mucilage, slime, slimy substance or fluid. *Mafuta yanafanya kinamasi*, the oil is getting thick and sticky. (2) marsh, wet slippery soil. (Cf. *utelezi, utope*, and follg.)

Kinamo, n. See under **Nama**.

Kinana, n. a kind of yam. (Cf. *kiazi kikuu*.)

Kinanasi, n. *vi-* a perennial herb with grass-like leaves, *Anthericum* sp.

Kinanda, n. *vi-* (1) a stringed instrument of the kind commonest in East Africa, a kind of banjo or guitar. Extended to mean piano, organ, and almost any similar European instrument of music. *Piga kinanda*, play the banjo, &c. (Cf. *ngoma*.) (2) Kersten's Weaver Finch, also called *binti Chuma*.

Kinara,* n. *vi-* (1) see under **Nurisha**; (2) a small ornament in the embroidery worked in silk on the collar of a native dress (*kanzu*), i.e. *vinara vya shingo*. (Hind. کناری).

Kinaya,* n. See under **Kinai**.

Kinda, n. *ma-* also sometimes **Mkinda**, *mi-* and *wa-* young one, esp. of birds, a chick, also of animals, but not of man, e.g. *kinda la farasi*, a foal. Sometimes a. e.g. *mnazi mkinda* (also *kinda la mnazi*), a young coco-nut tree. (Cf. *mtoto, mwana, ndama*.)

Kindakindaki, adv. aloft. *Kuchukuliwa kindakikindaki*, to be carried aloft. (Cf. *juujuu*.)

Kindi, n. a squirrel. (Cf. *kidiri, komba*.)

Kindoro, n. (1) a kind of red dye; (2) a kind of red sweet potato; (3) a kind of red cap, formerly only worn by elders and chiefs.

Kindu, n. fruit of the *mkindu*, which see.

Kindugu, n. and adv. See **Kidugu** under **Ndugu**.

Kinembe, n. *vi-* the clitoris. (Cf. *kisimi*.)

Kinena, n. *vi-* middle of the body between the groins. **Nena**, n. *ma-* the groins.

Kinga, v. is used of the effect of what is interposed between two objects, as a protection or defence. (1) act as a screen against, ward off, parry, check, stop, interpose, get in the way of, intercept, catch; (2) fig. contradict, oppose, obstruct; (3) act as a screen to, cover, be a defence to; (4) fig. help, assist, protect. *Kinga, jiwe hili linaanguka*, guard (yourself) this stone is falling. *Nimeukinga mwili wangu kwa ngao*, I have protected my body with a shield. *Mungu amenikinga*, God has protected me. *Kinga mvua*, keep off the rain, also catch rain-water (in a vessel). *Kinga jua*, keep off the sun. Ps. **Kingwa**, (1) be screened (warded) off; (2) be used as a screen; (3) be screened (protected). St. **Kingika**. Prep. **Kingia**, e.g. *ngao ya kukingia silaha*, a shield to keep off weapons. Cs. **Kingiza**, usually protect, defend. *Kingiza na mvua*, protect from the rain. *Jikingiza*, defend oneself. Rp. **Kingana**, (1) protect each other; (2) oppose each other, with arguments, force, &c. Stc. **Kingama,** (1) be interposed, lie across, be in the way, act as a screen; (2) obstruct, baffle, thwart. *Gogo limekingama njiani,* a log blocks the way. *Njia nyingine inakingama njia ya mbele,* another path cuts across the road leading straight on. Prep. **Kingamia,** e.g. *nyoka amenikingamia njiani,* a snake has stopped me on the road. Cs. **Kingamisha,** inten. frustrate, stop altogether, block. Rp. **Kingamana,** e.g. *tumekingamana mimi na yeye,* he and I have had a (friendly or stormy) interview, we encountered each other. Cs. of Rp. **Kingamanisha,** cause to get in each other's way, made difficulties among. Cs. (2) **Kinza,** which see. **Kinga,** n. (— and sometimes *vinga*), something interposed, and which has different effects accordingly, e.g. (1) a check, a stopper, a fender, a fence, a guard, a screen, a shelter—and so either (2) protection, defence, assistance, or (3) obstruction, difficulty, misfortune, limitation, e.g. *kinga cha moto,* or *kinga* only, a fireguard, i.e. commonly firebrand, brand used as a guard, rather than 'a fender'. Prov. *Kinga na kinga ndipo moto uwakapo,* firebrand on firebrand, then it is the fire burns. *Kinga cha maji,* or *kinga* alone, a long blade of grass or leaflet tied round the stem of a tree to collect the rain trickling down and direct it to a water-jar. *Kinga ya jicho,* a blinker. **Kingilizi,** n. *ma-* anything which protects or catches. **Kingio,** n. and **Kingo,** n. screen, hand-screen, shade, lamp-cover, shield, &c. **Mkinga,** n. *mi-* anything that stops, obstructs, or diverts something else, e.g. *mkinga wa maji,* see **Kinga.** Also *wa-* a person who stops, obstructs, diverts, &c. **Mkingamo,** n. *mi-* a crossing, being athwart, obstructing, in the way. *Njia ya mkingamo,* a cross-road. **Mkingiko,** n. *mi-* a cross-pole laid on the top of upright posts to carry the lower ends of the rafters in building a native house. **Ukingo,** n. (*kingo*), (1) act (means, manner, &c.) of warding off—and so used variously of a screen in a house, an awning to keep off the sun, a fence for directing game to a trap, a barricade of trees across a road, a parapet, or balustrade, &c.; (2) edge, rim, margin, verge, border, e.g. of a river, precipice, pit, &c., edge of a squared or chamfered board. (Cf. *pinga, zuia, epa.*)

Kingaja, n. *vi-* (1) armlet or bracelet of seeds, beads, &c.; (2) the back of the hand.

Kingalingali, n. and adv. on the back, face upwards. *Lala kingalingali,* lie on the back. *Anguka kingalingali,* fall backwards. (Cf. *chalichali, kitanitani.*)

Kingama, v., **Kingamana,** v. See under **Kinga.**

Kinganga, n. a kind of drum, a small *msondo.*

Kingilizi, n. *ma-*. See under **Kinga.**

Kingio, n., **Kingo,** n. See under **Kinga.**

Kingoe, n. *vi-* dim. of *ngoe.* See under **Ngoeka.**

Kingojeo, n. *vi-*, **Kingojezi,** n. *vi-*, **Kingojo,** n. *vi-*. See under **Ngoja.**

King'ong'o, n. (1) speaking nasally, as with the nose pinched; (2) sometimes heard for *ng'ong'o.*

Kingoringori, adv. See under **Njorinjori.**

King'oto, n. the woodpecker, also called *kigogota, kigotagota,* and *gongonola.*

Kingozi, n. the old dialect of Swahili, esp. as formerly spoken at Malindi, Pate, and the northward towns of the Zanzibar coast, now only poetical and hardly intelligible. Hence now used of 'difficult, half-understood speech'.

Kingugwa, n. *vi-* the large spotted hyena, also *simba marare* and *shundwa.* (Cf. *fisi.*)

Kingune, n. *vi-* a tree stunted in growth. *Kingune cha mnazi,* a stunted coco-nut tree.

Kini, Kinika,* v. be sure, be certain, be ascertained—apparently from Ar. *yakini* (which see), treated mistakenly as a form of a verb *kini*. (Ar. يقن.)

Kining'ina, n. *vi-* great-great-grandchild. (Cf. *kijukuu, kilembwe*, and *ning'inia*, rock, dandle.)

Kinjorinjori, n. and adv. (1) a particular way of cutting the hair, leaving one long tuft, i.e. *kukata kinjorinjori*; (2) lengthwise. See **Njorinjori.**

Kinofu, n. *vi-* dim. of *mnofu*.

Kinokero, n. *vi-* a gazelle. (Cf. *paa*, n.)

Kinongo, n. *vi-* a perennial more or less branched herb up to 4 ft. tall with dense spikes of white or yellow-white woolly flowers which are used for stuffing pillows, *Aerva lanata*.

Kinono, n. *vi-*. See under **Nona.**

Kinou, n. *vi-*. See under **Noa.**

Kinu, n. *vi-* (1) a wooden mortar, made of a hard block of wood hollowed out in the centre, used for pounding and cleaning grain, and crushing and mixing vegetable food generally. Also for extracting oil. The wooden pestle is called *mchi*, and the operation usually *kutwanga*. (2) it is extended to metal mortars, e.g. *kinu cha chuma*, an iron mortar, and also is used of any kind of mill, machine for crushing, &c. *Kinu cha moshi*, a steam mill. *Kinu cha kushindikiza* a crushing mill, whether of oil-seeds or sugar-cane. *Kinu cha mkono*, hand mill. *Kinu cha kusagia*, a grinding (flour) mill. (3) hub of wheel, also sometimes called *kikombe*.

Kinubi,* n. *vi-* and adv. (1) a kind of harp, used in their dances by the *Wanubi*, i.e. Sudanese (or Nubians) settled on the coast. Also (2) the Sudanese language; (3) in the Sudanese style. *-a Kinubi*, of the Sudanese kind. (Ar. نوبى Nubian.)

Kinuka Jio, n. Marvel of Peru, 4 o'clock flower, *Miribilis jalapa*. Roots and seeds are poisonous.

Kinukamito, n. used to describe a restless person, one who is continually moving his residence, or divorcing and marrying. (Cf. *inuka* and *mto*.)

Kinundu, adv. and n. *vi-*. See under **Nundu.**

Kinungu, n. *vi-* dim. of *nungu*.

Kinwa, n. *vi-*. See **Kinywa** under **Nywa.**

Kinyaa, n. *vi-*. See under **Nyara, v.**

Kinyago, n. *vi-*. See under **Unyago.**

Kinyakuzi, n. *vi-* same as *kigwaru*, which see. (Cf. also *kisukumi*.)

Kinyama, n. *vi-* dim. of *mnyama* and *nyama*, and *adv.*

Kinyamkela, n. *vi-* (1) a kind of evil spirit, to be propitiated at crossways, a storm devil; (2) the spirit which is in and causes a whirlwind. (Cf. *chamchela*.)

Kinyangalele, n. *vi-* the top, summit, i.e. of a hill, tree, &c. (Cf. *kilele, nguu*.)

Kinyegele, n. *vi-* kind of a small animal, skunk. (Cf. *cheche, nyegere*.)

Kinyeleo, n. *vi-*. See under **Nya.**

Kinyemi, n. and a. something good, pleasing, acceptable. Prov. *Kipya kinyemi kingawa kidonda*, a novelty has its charms, even though it be a sore.

Kinyenyevu, n. See under **Nya.**

Kinyenyezi, n. condition of being dazzled. (Cf. *kiwi*.)

Kinyerenyere, adv. gentle, with a gliding motion, slowly. (Cf. *pole, nyinyirika*.)

Kinyesi, n. *vi-*. See under **Nya.**

Kinyevu, n. *vi-* (1) see under **Nya**; (2) see under **Nyea.**

Kinying'inya, n. *vi-* same as *kining'ina*, which see.

Kinyo, n. *vi-*. See under **Nya.**

Kinyonga, n. *vi-* (1) chameleon, see under **Nyonga, v.**; (2) see under **Nyonga, n.**

Kinyonge, n. and adv., **Kinyongo**, n. *vi-*. See under **Nyonga, v.**

Kinyong'onyo, adv. and n. *vi-*. See under **Nyong'onyea.**

Kinyozi, n. *vi-*. See under **Nyoa**.

Kinyuma, n. and adv. See under **Nyuma**.

Kinyumba, n. and adv. See under **Chumba**.

Kinyumbu, n. *vi-* dim. of *nyumbu*.

Kinyume, n. and adv. See under **Nyuma**.

Kinyunga, n. flour mixed into a dough with water.

Kinyunya, n. *vi-* a little cake, a bit of cake, a sweetmeat. (Cf. *nyunyiza*, sprinkle, *nyunyo* and *andazi*.

Kinywa, n. *vi-*, **Kinywaji**, n. *vi-*, **Kinyweleo**, n. *vi-*, **Kinyweo**, n. *vi-*, **Kinywewa**, n. *vi-*. See under **Nywa**.

Kinza, v. (a Cs. form of *kinga*, shown separately for convenience), object, contradict, deny, oppose, rebel, obstruct. Rp. **Kinzana**, object, stand in the way, oppose, contradict each other. *Kinzana na mtu*, dispute with a person. **-kinzani**, a. refractory, combative, obstructive. **Kinzano**, n. *ma-* objection, obstruction, contradiction. **Mkinzani**, n. *wa-* an obstructionist, &c. **Ukinzani**, n. (*kinzani* and *ma-*), obstructiveness, contentiousness, petulance, objection, contradiction. (Cf. *pinga, kaidi, bisha, shindana, zuia.*)

Kiogajivu, n. name of a bird, the blue roller. (Cf. *oga* and *jivu.*)

Kioja, n. *vi-*. See under **Roja**.

Kiokosi, n. *vi-*. See under **Okota**.

Kiokozi, n. *vi-*. See under **Okoa**.

Kiolezo, n. *vi-*. See under **Oleza**.

Kiomo, n. and adv. See under **Omo**.

Kiongozi, n. *vi-*. See under **Ongoa**.

Kiongwe, n. *vi-*. See **Kihongwe**.

Kionja, n. *vi-*, **Kionjo**, n. *vi-*. See under **Onja**.

Kionyo, n. *vi-*. See under **Ona**.

Kioo, n. *vi-* (1) a piece of glass, *kioo cha kujitazamia*, or *kioo* alone, a mirror. *Kioo cheupe*, clear, white glass. (Cf. *bilauri*. Prob. formerly *kiolo* from *ola.*) (2) a fish-hook. (Cf. *ndoana.*)

Kiopoo, n. *vi-*. See under **Opoa**.

Kiosha, n. *vi-*, **Kiosho**, n. *vi-*. See under **Osha**.

Kiota, n. *vi-*, **Kioteo**, n. *vi-*, **Kioto**, n. *vi-*. See under **Ota**, v. (C).

Kioza, n. See under **Oza**.

Kipa, n. *vi-*. See under **Pa**, v.

Kipaa, n. *vi-* (1) see under **Paa**, v. (A); (2) for *kipara*, which see.

Kipago, n. *vi-* the rung of a ladder, a step in a staircase.

Kipaji, n. *vi-* (1) see under **Pa**, v.; (2) part of the forehead (*paji*), see under **Paji**; (3) a sweet-scented cosmetic, applied to the brows, an ornamental patch of colour, a brow ornament; (4) a small projection on the side of the *mjusi*, worked on the front of a native dress (*kanzu*), also called *kiguu*.

Kipaka, n. *vi-* dim. of *paka*, n.

Kipakacha, n. *vi-* dim. of *pakacha*.

Kipakasa, n. *vi-*. See under **Paka**, v. (A).

Kipaku, n. *vi-* dim. of *paku*. See under **Paka**, v. (A).

Kipamba, n. *vi-*. See under **Pamba**, n.

Kipambo, n. *vi-*. See under **Pamba**, v.

Kipa mkono, n. See under **Pa**, v.

Kipande, n. *vi-* (1) a small bit, piece, slip, part, of anything (cf. *fungu, sehemu, kitambo, kidogo, kato*); (2) an instrument, tool, utensil (cf. *ala, chombo, kitu, samani*). *Kipande cha nyama*, a piece of meat. *Vipande vya kupimia*, surveying instruments. (3) used esp. of (*a*) a light wooden rammer used in hardening a concrete or mud floor or roof; (*b*) a card on which a monthly labourer's daily task is marked. *Kazi ya kipande*, work by the ticket, i.e. on which each day's work is recorded. **Pande**, n. *ma-* (1) a big piece (part, side), block, mass, lump, e.g. *pande la chuma*, a bar (or lump) of iron; *pande la mti*, a block of wood; *pande la mtu* (also *kipande cha mtu*) big man. **Mpande**, n. *mi-* rarely used, same as *kipande* and *upande*. **Pandikizi**, n. *ma-* a big piece. *Pandikizi la mtu*, a giant. **Upande**, n. (*pande*) a piece, a portion, a certain part, a side, a direction, region, district, place, part of a town or country, e.g. *weka upande*, put aside, on one side. *Kwenda upande*, go sideways, go askew, go wrong. *Mambo yamekwenda upande*, things have gone all wrong. *Kuwa upande*, to be slanting, askew, out of the level or straight. *Pande za bara*, the mainland region. *Pande zote*, on all sides. *Upande wa chini*, lee-side—in sailing, *upande wa juu*, weather side. *Upande wa fulani*, on so-and-so's side, i.e. in a discussion, quarrel, &c. Also used as measure of cloth, i.e. a conventional piece or length, two yards. (Note: *mpande*, *kipande*, and *pande* seem to be sometimes used in contrast, with reference to size, but not clearly differentiated.)

Kipandikizo, n. *vi-*. See **Pandikizo** under **Panda**, v. (B).

Kipandisho, n. *vi-*. See under **Panda**, v. (A).

Kipanga, n. *vi-* (1) dim. of *upanga*; (2) a horse fly, a biting fly; (3) name of a bird, Dickinson's Falcon, *Falco Dickinsoni*.

Kipango, n. *vi-* dim. of *pango*.

Kipao, n. *vi-*. See under **Paa**, v. (A).

Kipapa, n. *vi-*. See under **Papa**, v. (A).

Kipapae, n. black magic, witchcraft, but that which is caused by suggestion or other means than administering charms, medicine, poison, &c. (Cf. *uchawi*, *uramali*.)

Kipapatiko, n. *vi-*, **Kipapato**, n. *vi-*. See under **Papa**, v. (A).

Kipara, n. *vi-*. See under **Para**, n. (B).

Kipasuasanda, n. *vi-* name of a bird, screech owl, nightjar, *pwaju*, *mraruasanda*, *gawa*. It is considered to be a bird of evil omen. (Cf. *pasua* and *sanda*.)

Kipato, n. *vi-*. See under **Pata**.

Kipatu, n. *vi-* dim. of *patu*.

Kipawa, n. *vi-* (1) dim. of *upawa*; (2) a gift, see under **Pa**, v.; (3) a rung of a ladder. (Cf. *kipago*, *kipandio*.)

Kipele, n. *vi-* dim. of *upele*.

Kipemba, n. *vi-* a sort of coco-nut tree, the young coco-nuts of which are yellow in colour; used very much in making medicine by the *waganga* (medicine men).

Kipendo, n. *vi-*. See under **Penda**.

Kipenga, n. *vi-* a whistle, such as are used by the police. (Cf. *filimbi*, *mluzi*, *miunzi*.)

Kipengee, n. *vi-*, also **Kipengele**, n. *vi-* (1) side-path, by-path, way round, side-channel, out of the straight or usual course; (2) evasion, subterfuge, shift, indirect means of obtaining an object, dodge, device, wile. *Maneno yake haya vipengee*, these statements of his are evasive (shuffling, deceitful). Also **Pengee**, n. *ma-* with the same meanings. *Maneno yake hayana mapengee* (*vipengee*), his statement is straightforward. (Cf. *hila*, *udanganyifu*.)

Kipenu, n. *vi-*. See **Upenu** which is more commonly used.

Kipenyo, n. *vi-*. See under **Penya**.

Kipeo, n. *vi-* (1) see under **Pea**, v. (A); (2) a small brush, from *pea*, v. (B).

Kipepeo, n. *vi-*. See under **Pepa**.

Kiperea, n. *vi-* a small canoe capable of holding two persons only. (Cf. *mtumbwi*, *ngalawa*.)

Kipete, n. *vi-*, **Kipeto**, n. *vi-*. See under **Peta**, v. (A).

Kipi, n. *vi-* a cock's spur, i.e. *kucha la* (or *mwiba wa*) *nyuma katika kisigino cha jogoo*, the spur behind at the cock's heel. (Cf. *kikwaru*.)

Kipia, n. *vi-* (1) the top of a hill or tower, pinnacle; (2) the posts or supports of the ceiling of a house.

Kipigi, n. *vi-* a small stick to throw up into a tree to knock down fruit, but usu. *kipiki*. See under **Piga**.

Kipigo, n. *vi-* See under **Piga**.

Kipiki, n. *vi-*. See **Kipigi** under **Piga**.

Kipila, n. *vi-* a curlew, also called *sululu*.

Kipilipili, n. (1) a kind of fish considered to be good eating by Europeans; (2) n. and adv. like a peppercorn, e.g. *nywele za kipilipili*, hair of a short woolly kind, growing in small tufts. **Kipilipili mwitu,** n. *vi-* a branched shrub about 2 to 3 ft. tall with violet blue flowers, *Thunbergia hookeriana.*

Kipimio, n. *vi-*, **Kipimo,** n. *vi-*. See under **Pima.**

Kipinda, n. and adv. an animal which has died a natural death, a carcass. (Dist. *mzoga*, dead body of animal, and *maiti*, human corpse.) *Kufa kwa kipinda*, die a natural death.

Kipindi, n. *vi-*, **Kipindo,** n. *vi-*, **Kipindupindu,** n. *vi-*. See under **Pinda.**

Kipingili, n. *vi-*. See under **Pingua.**

Kipingo, n. *vi-* (1) see under **Pinga,** v.; (2) an armlet or bracelet or anklet of beads or pearls.

Kipingu, n. *vi-*, **Kipingwa,** n. *vi-*. See under **Pinga.**

Kipini, n. *vi-* (1) handle, haft, holder —of tools, knife, sword, hoe, &c.; (2) small stud or button-like ornament worn chiefly in a hole in the side of the nose, but worn by some women in the ear also. (Cf. *kipuli, jasi, urembo.*) **Mpini,** n. *mi-* used like (1) of *kipini* for a handle, &c. **Pini,** n. *ma-* of larger size, same as *kipini.*

Kipipa,* n. *vi-* dim. of *pipa.*

Kipira, n. *vi-* (1) dim. of *mpira*; (2) a carpenter's moulding-plane, *kipira cha mviringo* (cf. *landa*); (3) a projecting moulding.

Kipito, n. *vi-*. See under **Pita.**

Kipofu, n. *vi-*. See under **Pofua.**

Kipokee, adv. See under **Pokea.**

Kipolepole, (1) n. *vi-* a kind of butterfly; (2) adv. from *-pole*, i.e. in a very slow (calm, gentle) way.

Kipondo, n. *vi-*, **Kipondwe,** n. *vi-*. See under **Ponda.**

Kiponya, n. *vi-*. See under **Poa.**

Kipooza, n. *vi-*. See under **Pooza.**

Kipopo, n. *vi-* dim. of *popo.*

Kipopoo, n. *vi-* dim. of *popoo.*

Kipora, n. *vi-* dim. of *pora.*

Kiporo, n. *vi-* food left over from evening till next morning, also called *uporo.*

Kipozamataza, n. *vi-* the clapper lark.

Kipuku, Kipukupuku, adv. See under **Pukuta.**

Kipukusa, n. *vi-* (1) see under **Pukuta**; (2) an insect which bores holes in timber; (3) a kind of banana.

Kipukute, n. *vi-* a kind of banana.

Kipuli, n. *vi-* a small ornament, often crescent shaped, worn in the ear as a pendant. (Cf. also *jasi, shamili, kipini, puleki.* Hind. بهلى.)

Kipumba, n. *vi-* same as *kibumba,* dim. See under **Bumba.**

Kipumbu, n. *vi-*. See under **Pumbu.**

Kipumziko, n. *vi-*. See under **Puma.**

Kipungu, n. *vi-* also **Pungu,** n. *ma-* (1) the name of a fish; (2) an eagle; (3) the osprey.

Kipunguo, n. *vi-*, **Kipunguzi,** n. *vi-*. See under **Punga,** v. (C).

Kipunjo, n. and adv. See under **Punja.**

Kipupa, n. and adv. See under **Pupa.**

Kipupwe, n. the cold season, i.e. June, July, and August; cold weather.

Kipure, n. a small bronze wing dove.

Kipusa, n. *vi-* a tusk of the rhinoceros when not fully grown.

Kipwa, n. *vi-*. See under **Pwa.**

Kipwe, n. the Senegal Bush Shrike, *Dryoscopus senegalensis.*

Kipwepwe, n. a disease of the skin causing red spots or blotches thought to be caused by lice (*chawa*).

Kirago, n. *vi-*. See under **Rago.**

Kirahi,* n. See under **Karaha.**

Kiraka,* n. *vi-* and adv. (1) a piece, spot, patch different from the rest or the surroundings, colour in spots or patches, e.g. *nguo ya kiraka,* patched, ragged clothes. *Mapwaji ya kiraka,* patches left by the receding tide. *Kirakaraka,* anything variegated, mottled, dappled, speckled, spotted, e.g. of birds and animals.

Also (2) fig. used of hiding a person's faults, e.g. *anamtilia kiraka tu*, he is helping him by hiding his faults. **Marakaraka,** a. with patches, stripes, spots, and so of colour, mottled, speckled, variegated. **Raka,** n. *ma-* amplic. of *kiraka*. (Cf. *doa, paku*. Ar. رقع to patch.)

Kiranja, n. *vi-* the title given to the first boy circumcised in a group, who is also treated as the leader of the group.

Kirehani, n. a kind of sweet potato. (Cf. *kiazi*.)

Kirembo, n. *vi-* and adv. See under **Remba.**

Kiri,* v. acknowledge, admit, accept, assent, state formally, confess, allow, aver, ratify. Often in legal documents, e.g. *nimekiri mimekubali kwamba*, I do hereby formally acknowledge and agree that, &c. *Kiri makosa*, confess offences. *Kiri deni*, admit a debt. Ps. **Kiriwa.** St. and Pot. **Kirika.** Prep. **Kiria.** Cs. **Kirisha,** e.g. obtain formal consent, extract confession, allow ratification, &c. Rp. **Kiriana. Ukiri,** n. acknowledgement, confession, admission. (Cf. *kubali, idhini, ungama*. Ar. اقر.)

Kiriba,* n. *vi-* water-skin, i.e. the skin of an animal made into a bag, and used for carrying water; sometimes also used for a water-bottle, i.e. such as are used on *safari*, &c. (Ar. the *ki-* belonging to the root, as in *kitabu*, قربة.)

Kirihi,* v. See under **Karaha.**

Kirimba, n. *vi-* (1) a cage (for bird or animal); (2) *kirimba cha mlango*, the top or bottom piece of the frame of a door (or window), sill, lintel, threshold. (Cf. *kizimba, tundu, kizingiti*.)

Kirimu,* v. See under **Karama.**

Kiroboto, n. *vi-* a flea.

Kiroja, n. *vi-*. See under **Roja.**

Kirugu, n. *vi-* (1) the wall-plate of a house, the top of the walls or of a cement roof; (2) the height of the walls of a house. (Cf. *matungizi*.)

Kiruhu,* n. See **Kiruu.**

Kirukanjia, n. *vi-*. See under **Ruka.**

Kirukia, n. *vi-* leafy parasitic plants growing on trees, very striking when in flower, ranging in colour from greens through whites, yellows, pinks, to very dark red, *Loranthus* spp. (Cf. *ruka*.)

Kirumbizi, n. *vi-* (1) a large bird, described as being like a goose (cf. *umbia*); (2) a kind of dance in which the dancers fight with sticks.

Kirungu, n. *vi-* dim. of *rungu*.

Kirusu, n. a mixture of a kind of gruel made of millet flour (*makomba*) and the sprouting seeds (*kimea*), ready to make beer (*pombe*).

Kiruu,* n. blind rage, rage which is like madness. (A corruption in form and meaning of Ar. كره (see *karaha*), or Ar. قهر rage, fury, cf. the form *kiruhu* in which the consonants have become transposed.)

Kisa,* n. *vi-* (1) story, account, report, history, narrative; (2) statement of case, reason alleged, cause, explanation; (3) affair, matter, business, subject of report, e.g. *nipe kisa chako*, tell me your story, i.e. all about yourself. *Visa vingi*, many stories, a complicated business, endless difficulties. *Alimpiga bila kisa*, he hit him without a reason. (Cf. *hadithi, habari, neno*.) Also (4) like *kiini*, the innermost part, e.g. *kisa cha koko*, the kernel inside a fruit-stone. **Mkasa,** n. *mi-* an event, happening, news, either good or bad. (Cf. *tukio, jambo*. Ar. قصة.)

Kisafu, n. *vi-* same as *kilihafu*, which is more common.

Kisaga, n. *vi-* (1) a dry measure of about a quart, equal to two *kibaba*, or half a *pishi* (cf. *saga*); (2) a kind of weevil?

Kisagalima, n. *vi-* a hoe which has

become small, ground down, through much use. (Cf. *kiselema*, also *saga*, *lima*.)

Kisagaunga, n. *vi-* a kind of whitish coloured crab, which runs about the sea-shore and into the water, where it digs itself into the sand. (Cf. *saga*, *unga*.)

Kisahani,* n. *vi-* dim. of *sahani*.

Kisaki, adv. See under **Saki**.

Kisalisali,* n. (1) gonorrhoea, also (2) bilharzia. These two diseases are thought to be identical by the uneducated native, owing to the similarity of their symptoms. (Cf. *kisonono*, *kichocho*. Perhaps a redupl. of Ar. سل with prefix *ki-*, see the form سلالة gonorrhoea.)

Kisambare, n. *vi-* Lobelia, an annual or perennial prostrate weed with small blue flowers, *Lobelia fervens*.

Kisamli, n. *vi-* the Pemba coco-nut or king coco-nut palm, only used for drinking. Also called *kitamli*.

Kisamvu, n. a vegetable made from the leaves of the cassava plant. (Cf. *muhogo*.)

Kisanduku, n. *vi-* dim. of *sanduku*.

Kisango, n. *vi-* a divining board. (Cf. *ramli*.)

Kisarawanda, n. *vi-* the cloth spread on the bed on the night of marriage, to ascertain whether the bride is a virgin. Should she prove to be a virgin, the cloth is shown and it is said that *arusi imejibu*.

Kisasa, n. and adv. See under **Sasa**.

Kisasi,* n. *vi-* vengeance, revenge, retaliation, requital, compensation for harm done, damages. *Toa* (*lipa*) *kisasi*, suffer vengeance, pay (for harm done). *Weka kisasi*, lay up vengeance. *Ondoa kisasi*, take vengeance. *Toza* (*lipiza*, *twaa*) *kisasi*, exact vengeance or compensation, &c. *Twaa kisasi cha ndugu yangu*, avenge my brother. (Ar. قصاص.)

Kiselema, n. *vi-* a hoe or anything which has become small or worn down through much use, e.g. pencil, knife, mortar, &c. Prov. *Usidharau kiselema chalima kikapita jembe zima*, do not despise a worn hoe, it is able to cultivate and even surpass a sound one. (Cf. *kichelema*.)

Kisetiri,* n. *vi-*. See under **Stiri**.

Kiseyeye, n. a complaint of the teeth, tender gums with bleeding, prob. scurvy.

Kisha, adv. See under **Isha**.

Kishada, n. *vi-* dim. of *shada*.

Kishamba, n. and adv. See under **Shamba**.

Kisharifu,* n. also **Msharifu**, Natal Pigmy Kingfisher, *Ispidina picta*.

Kishaufu,* n. *vi-*. See under **Shaua**.

Kishaushi,* n. *vi-* same as *kishawishi*, n. *vi-*. See under **Shawishi**.

Kishazi,* n. *vi-* dim of *shazi*.

Kishenzi,* n. and adv. See under **-shenzi**.

Kishiki cha buga, n. *vi-* a perennial twining and climbing plant with small greenish yellow flowers, roots used medicinally, *Cissampelos Pariera*.

Kishiku,* n. *vi-* stump of a tree, log. **Shiku**, n. *ma-* of larger size than *kishiku*. (Cf. *kisiki*, *gogo*. Ar. شق.)

Kishimo, *vi-* dim. of *shimo*.

Kishina, n. *vi-* (1) dim. of *shina*; (2) the name of a dance.

Kishinda, n. *vi-*, **Kishindo**, n. *vi-*. See under **Shinda**.

Kishoka, n. *vi-* dim. of *shoka*.

Kishona nguo, n. *vi-* a perennial tussock grass up to 2 ft. tall with strongly awned glumes, *Heteropogon contortus*. (Cf. *shona* and *nguo*.)

Kishoroba,* n. *vi-* a narrow strip of anything, a narrow space, or patch, e.g. the paths in a plantation. *Amelima kishoroba*, he has cultivated a narrow strip of land. *Amenyoa kishoroba*, he has shaved his head making narrow lines, i.e. has made partings. **Ushoroba**, n. same as *kishoroba*. (? Ar. ضرب cut off.)

Kishubaka,* n. *vi-* dim. of *shubaka*.

Kishungi, n. *vi-* dim. of *shungi*.

Kishupi, n. *vi-* a kind of matting bag.

Kishutuo, n. *vi-*. See **Kisutuo.**

Kishwara,* n. *vi-* a loop of rope, such as is used to hold an oar (like a row-lock) in a boat, or (in a box lid, &c.) to lift by. (Cf. *kitanzi, shalaka, kileti.* Ar. صور bend, with *ki-* prefix.)

Kisi,* v. (1) consider critically, estimate, calculate, make a guess, form an opinion on, guess. Frequently used in the Prep. Form **Kisia**, guess at (for, by, &c.), approximate. (Cf. *fikiri, kadiri, bahatisha, hesabu, pima.*) (2) as a nautical term, shift, make a change in. *Kisi tanga*, shift the sail over, tack, put about. (Cf. *pindua, bisha.*) **Kisi**, n. *ma-*, also **Makisio**, n. plur. a guess at, estimation, approximation, &c. (Ar. قيس.)

Kisibau,* n. *vi-* a waistcoat worn open in the front. Described as *kisibau cha mikono*, i.e. sleeved; *kisibau cha kikwapa*, or *cha kwapa*, i.e. sleeveless—the usual kind; *kisibau cha bitana*, i.e. lined; *kisibau cha mfuto*, i.e. in common plain style. Made of all kinds of materials and colours, and worn over the *kanzu*, now comparatively rare except as a kind of uniform for house boys, messengers, &c. (Prob. a corruption and confusion of Ar. جبة vest or jacket with wide sleeves, and سبجة sleeveless dress or shirt, with prefix *ki-*. In some places the prefix is dropped and *zibau* is heard.)

Kisibiti,* n. *mboga za kisibiti*, cummin caraway seed. (Ar. سبت ?, with *ki-* prefix indicating similarity.)

Kisichana, n. *vi-* dim. of *msichana*.

Kisigino, n. *vi-* heel, elbow, further distinguished as *kisigino cha mguu*, and *kisigino cha mkono*. (Cf. *kifundo, kiwiko.*)

Kisiki, n. *vi-* (1) log, stump, trunk of a fallen tree; (2) also sometimes used as a euphemism for a prostitute. (Cf. *kishiku gogo, shina*, and *malaya.*)

Kisikusiku, adv. and n. (1) at night, in the dark (cf. *usiku, siku*); (2) a shove, push, jostling.

Kisima, n. *vi-* well, water-hole, water-pit, place where water is drawn.

Kisimbo, n. *vi-* sometimes used for *msimbo*, n. which see.

Kisimi, n. *vi-* clitoris. (Cf. *kinembe.*)

Kisio, n. *ma-*. See under **Kisi.**

Kisirani,* n. anything considered of ill omen or evil portent; mishap, misfortune. (Cf. *baa, balaa, mkosi, mdhana, mchimvi*, and dist. *kasirani.* Prob. from Ar. كسر wreck, break.)

Kisiwa, n. *vi-* an island. **Siwa**, n. *ma-* a large island, but very rarely used.

Kisogo, n. *vi-* nape of the neck, back of the head. Prov. *akupaye kisogo si mwenzio*, he who turns his back on you is not your friend. *Kumlamba mtu kisogo*, to make contemptuous or derisive signs behind a person's back. (Cf. *kogo, kikosi.*)

Kisokoto, n. *vi-* (1) see under **Sokota;** (2) a *ngoma* used in the exorcism of spirits.

Kisombo, n. *vi-* a dish of beans and cassava, &c., beaten or mashed up into a thick soup or paste. (Cf. *kipondwe, mseto.*)

Kisonge, n. *vi-* (1) a kind of *ngoma* used in exorcism of spirits; (2) see *msonge.*

Kisongo, n. *vi-*. See under **Songa.**

Kisonono, n. See under **Sonoa.**

Kisozi, n. *vi-* sometimes also *chozi* name of a small bird, sun-bird.

Kisu, n. *vi-* a knife, of any sort, often used with such verbs as *toa, futa*, take out, draw, *tia*, apply, *noa*, sharpen, *futika*, stick in the girdle, put up, *chomoa*, draw, take out, *chomeka*, sheathe. *Kisu kikali*, a sharp knife. *Kisu butu*, a blunt, dull knife. *Kisu hiki hakipati*, this knife does not cut, it is blunt. *Wewe kisu sisi nyama*, you are the knife, we are the meat, i.e. do what you will with us. *Kisu cha kukunja*, a pocket-knife, a clasp-knife. **Jisu**, n. *ma-* a large knife. **Kijisu**, n. *vi-* a very small knife.

(Cf. *jambia, shembea, kotama, kijembe, sime, buchari,* and *msumeno.*)

Kisua,* n. *vi-* (1) any kind of garment, suit of clothes, &c. Also (2) to describe a person well dressed, of striking appearance, *yeye ni kisua,* he is a fine figure. *Amevaa kisua,* he is well dressed. (Cf. *kisuto, nguo, vazi, malidadi.* Ar. كسوة a garment, the *ki-* being treated as though it were a prefix, cf. *kitabu.*)

Kisuguu, n. *vi-* a white-ant hill, but usu. *kichuguu* and *chuguu.* (Cf. *kidurusi.*)

Kisukari,* n. and adv. (1) see **Sukari;** (2) a kind of very sweet banana.

Kisukuma, n. *vi-*, **Kisukumi,** n. *vi-*, **Kisukumizi,** n. *vi-*. See under **Sukuma.**

Kisuli,* n. dizziness, vertigo, mental confusion. **Kisulisuli,** n. *vi- upepo wa kisulisuli,* a whirlwind. (Cf. *chamchela, kinyamkela,* and *kizunguzungu, wasiwasi, kisunzi, kisusuli.* Ar. دوخة giddiness, with *ki* prefix.)

Kisumari,* n. *vi-* dim. of *msumari.*

Kisunzi, n. dizziness, vertigo. (Cf. *kisuli, kizunguzungu.*)

Kisunzu, n. *vi-* dim. of *sunzu.*

Kisusi, n. *vi-* one of the smaller slopes of a thatched roof, running up under the edge of the larger. (Cf. *kipaa.*)

Kisusuli,* n. *vi-* (1) a scorpion (cf. *nge*); (2) a kind of kite (toy) (cf. *kishada, portangi, tiara*); (3) anything whirling about and dazing the eye, a whirling gust, a windmill. *Kisusuli cha mchanga,* a sandstorm. (Ar. دوخة giddiness, with *ki* prefix.)

Kisutu,* n. *vi-* a kind of *kanga* (cloth) which see, used very much for weddings, also as a screen or partition in a native house to hide the bed, &c. (Ar. same root as *kisua.*)

Kisutuo, n. *vi-* food received after a task has been completed.

Kiswahili,* n. and adv. See under **Mswahili.**

Kita, v. (1) be firm, taut, stand firm, e.g. as a man does when he is standing up against somebody in a fight, or when he places his arm firmly on a table, &c.; (2) place firmly, stick firmly in the ground. *Kita mkuki,* stick a spear upright in the ground. (Cf. *dinda, simama, kaza.*)

Kitaa, (1) n. *vi-* dim. of *mtaa;* (2) a kind of fish.

Kitabu,* n. *vi-* a book. (Ar. كتاب the *ki-* being part of the root but treated as a pfx. by analogy. Cf. *mkataba, katiba, katabahu,* and *msahafu, chuo.*)

Kitadali, n. *vi-* an annual or perennial erect or prostrate herb with reddish-green leaves and clusters of small yellowish-green flowers, *Euphorbia hirta.*

Kitangaa, n. *vi-* dim. of *tagaa.*

Kitakataka, n. *vi-*. See under **Taka,** n.

Kitakizo, n. *vi-*, **Kitako,** n. *vi-* and adv. See under **Tako.**

Kitale, n. *vi-* a young coco-nut in the second stage of development, between a *kidaka* and *dafu,* see **Nazi.**

Kitalu, n. *vi-* (1) a fence or wall either of stone or wood surrounding a yard, courtyard, or garden; (2) a walled or fenced-in enclosure, courtyard, or garden. (Cf. *ua, ugo.*)

Kitambaa, n. *vi-*. See under **Tambaa,** n.

Kitambi, n. *vi-* (1) a length or piece of cloth, usu. of the kind used for head-wear, as a kind of turban—defined as *kitambi cha kilemba*—also worn round the waist, and as a loincloth; (2) *mwenye kitambi,* a very corpulent person; (3) *kitambi cha tumbo,* mesenteric membrane; (4) see under **Tamba,** v. (Cf. *tambaa.*)

Kitambi cha maskini, n. *vi-* an edible plant like spinach when cooked, *Talinum cuneifolium.*

Kitambo, n. and adv. (1) a piece, a little, usually of time, a short period, e.g. *alikaa kitambo,* he remained a short time. *Kitambo kidogo,* after a little, soon, presently. *Kitambo cha* *chuo*, a school session. (Cf. *kip ınde, kidogo, kipindi, muda.*) (2) also of stature, length, a certain length or height. *Kutoka hapa hata mjini ni kitambo*, from here to the town is some distance. **Tambo**, n., **Utambo**, n. length, distance, height, like *kitambo*.

Kitamli, n. *Mnazi wa kitamli*, a kind of coco-nut tree, the nuts of which are only used for drinking, i.e. *dafu*.

Kitana, n. *vi-*. See under **Chana**.

Kitanda, n. *vi-*, **Kitandawili**, n. *vi-*, **Kitandiko**, n. *vi-*. See under **Tanda**.

Kitanga, n. *vi-* (1) a small piece of matting circular in shape, used as a prayer-mat (cf. *msala*), to lay out food on, or goods for sale; (2) the palm of the hand, *kitanga cha mkono*; (3) the scale or pan of a balance, *kitanga cha mizani*; (4) a kind of dance, *kitanga cha pepo* (cf. *ngoma*); (5) dim. of *tanga*, n. which see.

Kitangangaya, n. a children's game like hide-and-seek. (Cf. *kibemasa.*)

Kitango, n. *vi-* (1) see under **Tanga**, v.; (2) dim. of *tango*, n.; (3) a bit of string, lace, shoe-lace, tuft on a mattress, used for fastening things up or together.

Kitangulizi, n. *vi-*, **Kitanguo**, n. *vi-*. See under **Tangua**.

Kitani, n. flax, anything made of flax, &c., e.g. string, linen. (Ar. كتان.)

Kitanitani, adv. on the back, backwards—of position. (Cf. *kichali.*)

Kitano, n. *vi-* the word adopted for a five-cent piece, i.e. a piece worth five cents (Cf. *kikumi, -tano.*)

Kitanzi, n. *vi-*. See under **Tanda**.

Kitanzu, n. *vi-* dim. of *tanzu*.

Kitao, n. *vi-* dim. of *tao*.

Kitapo, n. *vi-*. See under **Tapa**, v.

Kitara,* n. *vi-* a curved sword, scimitar. (Cf. *upanga, sime, jambia*. Hind. كتار.)

Kitasa, n. *vi-* (1) a box, door, or cupboard-lock (cf. *kufuli*, a padlock); (2) a buckle, fastening of a belt (cf. *bizimu*); (3) *kuvunja kitasa*, is sometimes used euphemistically for deflowering a virgin; (4) dim. of *tasa*, small metal pot.

Kitata, n. *vi-* (1) see under **Tata**, v.; (2) a splint (for bandaging a broken limb, &c.). (Cf. *ganga.*)

Kitatange, n. *vi-* (1) a bright-coloured sea-fish with spines, a sea porcupine; (2) a person who incites others to quarrel, one who stirs up strife among others. (Appar. from *tatanga*, a Cont. form of *tata.*)

Kitawa, n. and adv. See under **Tawa**.

Kitawi, n. *vi-* (1) dim. of *tawi*; (2) a kind of weed; (3) a tool used in weaving.

Kitaya, n. *vi-* dim. of *taya*.

Kite, n. (1) a cry of pain, a sigh, a moan, a groan; *piga kite*, groan, sigh (cf. *guna*); (2) trust, liking affection. *Hana kite naye*, he has no liking for him, he does not trust him. (3) strain, bear down, e.g. as a woman at childbirth, &c. *Piga kite mama, ujikomboe*, bear down mother, and so deliver yourself.

Kitefu, n. See under **Kitefutefu**.

Kitefute, n. *vi-* the cheek-bone. (Cf. *kituguta.*)

Kitefutefu, n. (1) sobbing, as before or after crying; (2) also **Kitefu**, anything soft or smooth. (Cf. *teketeke.*)

Kiteku, n. *vi-*. See under **Tekua**.

Kitelemsho, n. *vi-*. See under **Telea**.

Kitembe, n. and adv. (1) a defect in speech, a lisp, thick utterance. *Piga (sema) kitembe*, speak with lisp, in a thick indistinct way as if there was something in the mouth (cf. *utembe*); (2) dim. of *tembe*.

Kitembwe, n. (1) a vegetable fibre; (2) a kind of fish. **Utembwe**, n. fibre from the leaf-stalk of various palms, used as string. (Cf. *ugomba, ununu, uzi, unanasi, utembo.*)

Kitendawili, n. *vi-*, **Kitende**, n. *vi-*, **Kitendo**, n. *vi-*. See under **Tenda**.

Kitengele, n. *vi-* (1) stripe, band of colour, &c. (cf. *mfuo, mlia*); (2) a small round disk of cloth or leather used in making mattresses. (Cf. *kitango* (3).)

Kiteo, n. *vi-*. See under **Uteo**.

Kitete, n. *vi-* dim. of *tete*.

Kitetefu, n. See **Kitefutefu**.

Kitetemeko, n. *vi-*, **Kitetemo**, n. *vi-*. See under **Tetema**.

Kithiri,* v. get to be more, do in addition, cause to be more, increase, grow. *Mtende umekithiri kuzaa*, the date tree has borne more than ever. Prep. **Kithiria**. Cs. **Kithirisha**, make more, increase, &c. (Cf. *zidi*. Ar. كثر.)

Kiti, n. *vi-* (1) a native stool, seat. Hence a seat or chair of any kind. *Kiti cha kifalme*, a throne. (2) a person who is being exorcized is referred to as the *kiti*. The exorcist (*mganga wa pepo*) is said to call the spirit and make him sit on the head of the person being exorcized (*humpandisha*). (Cf. *chuchia, punga, lema, pepo, mteja*.) (3) headquarters, place of residence of a chief, &c.

Kitiba,* n. *vi-*. See under **Katiba**.

Kitimbi, n. *vi-* a mischievous act, trick, artifice, stratagem, an act which causes hurt, damage, bad luck. (Cf. *chimvi* under *chimba*.)

Kitimiri,* n. (1) name of the dog in the Seven Sleepers' story; (2) name of an evil spirit. The consonants are sometimes written as a kind of charm on letters to ensure safe delivery. (Ar. قطمير.)

Kitinda, n. (from the verb *tinda*, not in use in its simple form, except in Kimvita, but cf. *tindika*). *Kitinda mimba*, the last, youngest child, lit. the ending of conception. (Cf. *chinja*.)

Kitisho, n. *vi-*. See under **Tisha**.

Kitita, n. *vi-* (1) dim. of *tita*; (2) n. and adv. cash down, ready money; (3) in a large quantity, in abundance, &c. *Amepata fedha kwa kitita*, he has money in abundance (cash in hand).

Kititi, n. and adv. (1) dim. of *titi*, which see; (2) an ailment of the female breasts; (3) a small hare, leveret; (4) *kititi cha bahari*, the depth of the sea. As adv. (also *kitita*) (1) fully, wholly, altogether, all at once, at one time, e.g. of money, cash, ready money; *kukutana na mtu kititi*, meet with a person suddenly, unexpectedly, i.e. without pre-arrangement; (2) straight up, upright, in an erect position. *Genge limesimama kititi*, the cliff rose up perpendicularly. *Mti umesimama kititi*, the tree stood straight up, was perpendicular (cf. *kita*).

Kititia, n. *vi-* a child's toy, a windmill, made out of palm fronds. (Cf. *kibaramwezi, titia*.)

Kititimo, n. *vi-*. See under **Titima**.

Kito, n. *vi-* a precious stone, gem, jewel. (Cf. *johari, almasi*.)

Kitobo, n. *vi-*. See under **Toboa**.

Kitobosha, n. *vi-* a kind of fritter or dumpling made of flour with sugar or honey and fried in fat. **Tobosha**, n. *ma-* amplic.

Kitobwe, n. *vi-*. See under **Toboa**.

Kitoeleo, n. *vi-*. See **Kitoweo** under **Towea**.

Kitokono, n. *vi-* also **Tokoni**, **Tokono**, the coccyx.

Kitoleo, n. *vi-*. See under **Toa**, v. (A).

Kitoma, n. *vi-* (1) a small round pumpkin, the outer rind or shell of which is dried, hollowed out, and used as a vessel for liquids, i.e. water, milk, also snuff, &c.; (2) descriptive of orchitis, hydrocele. (Cf. *boga*, pumpkin, and *mshipa, pumbu*.)

Kitone, n. *vi-*. See under **Tona**.

Kitonge, n. *vi-* a small rounded mass, a small lump or ball, e.g. of rice or other food, as taken in the fingers and eaten by natives. **Tonge**, n. *ma-* same as *kitonge*, but of a larger size. (Cf. *donge*.)

Kitongo, adv. sideways, obliquely. *Tazama kitongotongo*, look askance. (Cf. *tongoza*, and *upande, mshazari, kitongoji*.)

Kitongoji, n. *vi-* small village, hamlet. *Watu walio nje mashamba vitongojini*, all the people who are out in the country villages. (Cf. *kijiji* under *mji*.)

Kitopa, n. *vi-* a small plaited leaf package of turkish delight.

Kitoria, n. *vi-* edible fruit of the *mtoria*, *Landolphia patersiana.*

Kitororo, n. *vi-* the Zanzibar Golden-rumped Barbet, *Pogoniulus bilineatus.*

Kitoto, n. *vi-* and adv. See under **Mtoto.**

Kitovu, n. *vi-* the navel, the umbilical cord, also anything resembling the navel, i.e. in the centre, a button-like thing, i.e. the hub of a wheel, &c.

Kitoweleo, n. *vi-*, **Kitoweo**, n. *vi-*. See under **Towea.**

Kitu, n. *vi-* (1) a thing, esp. a sensible, material object, but also what is an object to the mind; (2) substance, what a thing is made of, matter. *Mtu ni kitu, lakini si kitu*, a man may be regarded as a thing, but he is not (only) a thing. *Pana kitu kama hasira?* is there such a thing as anger? *Si kitu*, it is nothing, no matter. (Cf. *haidhuru, mamoja*). *Hapana kitu*, there is nothing, nothing at all, nought. *Kitu gani hiki?* What is this? *Kitu chake ni chuma*, its substance is iron. (Cf. *mtu* and *utu*. The idea of 'substance' is often conveyed by the abstract forms beginning with *u-*, and *nyama* is also used, chiefly of organic substances.)

Kitua, n. *vi-* (1) dim. of *mtua*, a tree, the fruit of which (*matua*) is used for making medicine; (2) a kind of cassava. (Cf. *muhogo.*)

Kitubio, n. *vi-*. See under **Tubu.**

Kituguta, n. *vi-* the cheek-bone. (Cf. *kitefute.*)

Kituka, n. *vi-* small clump of trees, thicket. (Cf. *kichaka.*)

Kituko, n. *vi-*. See under **Tukia.**

Kitukuu, n. *vi-* a great-grandchild. (Cf. *mjukuu.*)

Kitulizo, n. *vi-*. See under **Tua.**

Kitumba, n. *vi-* dim. of *mtumba* and *tumba*, n.

Kitumbo, n. *vi-* and adv. See under **Tumbo.**

Kitumbua, n. *vi-* a small round fritter made of rice flour, fried in fat. (Cf *andazi.*)

Kitumwa, n. *vi-* and adv. See under **Tuma.**

Kitunda, n. *vi-* (1) dim. of *tunda*, n.; (2) a chess pawn.

Kitundu, n. *vi-* dim. of *tundu.*

Kitunga, n. *vi-* (1) dim. of *tunga*, n.; (2) *kofia ya kitunga*, a kind of tarboosh.

Kitungule, n. *vi-* a hare. (Cf. *sugura.*)

Kitunguu, n. *vi-* (1) an onion, *Allium cepa*; (2) shallot, *Allium ascalonicum.* **Kitunguu soumu**, n. garlic, *Allium sativum.*

Kituo, n. *vi-*. See under **Tua.**

Kitutumi, n. *vi-*. See under **Tutuma.**

Kitwana, n. *vi-* dim. of *mtwana*, a boy or youth of the slave class, also used in a derogatory sense, brat, scamp, rascal.

Kitwangomba, n. *vi-*. See **Kichwa-ngomba** under **Kichwa.**

Kitwea, n. loneliness, solitariness. (Cf. *upweke, ukiwa.*)

Kitwitwi, n. *vi-* applied to nearly all the smaller waders, esp. the common Sandpiper.

Kiu, n. absence of water, drought, want of water, thirstiness, thirst. *Kuwa na kiu, kuona kiu*, to be thirsty. *Komesha kiu*, quench thirst. *Kiu ya maji*, lack of water. (Cf. *kwiu, nyota.*)

Kiua, n. *vi-* (1) see under *ua*, v.; (2) dim. of *ua*, n.; (3) a kind of fish; (4) an eyelet-hole, buttonhole, esp. the holes made in embroidering white skull caps (cf. *kofia*); (5) *kiua mwitu*, a kind of tree with a beautiful flower, common in Pemba.

Kiuaji, n. *vi-*. See under **Ua, v.**

Kiuka, v. step over, get (leap, pass, jump) over, surmount. (Cf. *kia, chupa, ruka, vuka.*)

Kiuma, n. *vi-*. See under **Uma.**

Kiumambuzi, n. the goat-biter, a kind of black lizard which lives in burrows in the earth. (Cf. *uma* and *mbuzi.*)

Kiumbe, n. *vi.* See under **Umba.**

Kiumbizi, n. *vi-*. See **Kirumbizi** and **Umbia.**

Kiumbo, n. *vi-* a pot in which a potter keeps his tools. (Cf. *umba* and *mfinyanzi*.)

Kiume, n. and adv. See under **Ume.**

Kiunda, n. *vi-*. See under **Unda.**

Kiunga, n. *vi-*, **Kiungo**, n. *vi-*. See under **Unga**, v.

Kiunguja, n. and adv. the dialect of Swahili used in Zanzibar city and neighbourhood, as contrasted with the kindred dialects of the coast (*Kimrima*), of Mombasa (*Kimvita*), and Lamu (*Kiamu*). As adv. 'of the Zanzibar kind'. (Cf. *Unguja*.)

Kiungulia, n. *vi-*, **Kiunguza**, n. *vi-*, **Kiunguzo**, n. *vi-*. See under **Ungua**, v. (B).

Kiungwana, n. and adv. See under **Mwungwana.**

Kiuno, n. *vi-* loin, flank, waist, the part just above the hips (*nyonga*) and groin (*kinena*). In building, an abutment. *Jambia kiunoni na bakora mkononi*, dagger at waist and stick in hand. *Kucheza kiuno*, to dance a ventral dance such as is taught to young girls by the *somo* and the *nyakanga* at the advent of puberty.

Kiunza, n. *vi-*, **Kiunzi** n. *vi-*. See under **Unda.**

Kiva, n. unity, acting in unison. (Cf. *umoja*.)

Kivazi, n. *vi-*. See under **Vaa.**

Kivi, n. *vi-* (1) elbow; (2) sometimes heard for *kiwi*, which see.

Kivimba, n. *vi-*, **Kivimbe**, n. *vi-*, **Kivimbo**, n. *vi-*. See under **Vimba**, v. (A).

Kivinyovinyo, n. *vi-* and adv. See under **Vinya.**

Kivivu, adv., **Kivivuvivu**, adv. See under **-vivu.**

Kivo, n. (also *kizo*) an abundance, surplus, a great deal. (Cf. *wingi*.)

Kivukizo, n. *vi-* (1) see under **Vua**, v. (C); (2) sometimes heard for *kifukizo*, see under **Fuka.**

Kivuko, n. *vi-*. See under **Vua**, v. (C).

Kivulana, n. *vi-* and adv. See under **Mvulana.**

Kivuli, n. *vi-* (1) a shadow, a shady place; (2) sometimes used to mean a ghost, apparition. **Jivuli**, n. *ma-* amplic. **Mvuli**, n. *mi-* a shady place, shade of a tree, &c. **Mwavuli**, n. *mi-* an umbrella, sunshade. **Uvuli**, n. shade, shadiness—in general.

Kivumanyuki, n. *vi-* a branched perennial herb or shrub up to 5 ft. tall with opposite leaves and heads of tubular red or dark mauve flowers, *Pentas purpurea*.

Kivumanzi, n. *vi-* a small bell, such as may be used for fastening round the neck of a cat, &c.

Kivumbasi, n. a strong-smelling herb, with spikes of greenish-white flowers, sometimes used to keep off mosquitoes, &c.—a kind of basil, *Ocimum canum*, and spp. (Cf. *mrehani*.)

Kivumbi, n. *vi-* and adv. See under **Vumbi.**

Kivumi, n. *vi-*, **Kivumo**, n. *vi-*. See under **Vuma.**

Kivunde, a. See under **Vunda.**

Kivunga, n. *vi-*, *kivunga cha nywele*, long hair, a long thick crop of hair. Also *vunga la nywele*.

Kivunjajungu, n. *vi-*, **Kivunjo**, n. *vi-*. See under **Vunja.**

Kivuno, n. *vi-*. See under **Vuna.**

Kivusho, n. *vi-* (1) see under **Vua**, v. (C); (2) also heard for *kifusho*, see under **Fuka.**

Kivyao, n. *vi-*, **Kivyazi**, n. *vi-*. See under **Vyaa.**

-kiwa, a. solitary, alone, desolate, abandoned, outcast (with prefix *m-* and *wa-*, of persons, *pa-* of place, but without prefix for things—*nyumba kiwa, shamba kiwa*, &c. **Mkiwa**, n. *wa-* (1) a solitary, destitute, friendless person, a poor man; (2) a bereaved person. **Ukiwa**, n. solitariness, loneliness, abandonment, desolation, state of being uninhabited. (Cf. *upweke, -hame, ganjo*.)

Kiwaa, n. *vi-* dim. of *waa*, n.

Kiwamba, n. *vi-*. See under **Wamba.**

Kiwambaza, n. *vi-*. See **Kiambaza** under **Wamba.**

Kiwambo, n. *vi-*. See under **Wamba.**

Kiwanda, n. *vi-* (1) a plot of ground for working in, i.e. a yard covered or uncovered, shed, workshop. *Akatiwa kiwandani kushona nguo*, he was put in a workshop to learn tailoring. (2) *kiwanda cha mayai*, an omelette; (3) dim. of *uwanda*, i.e. a small plot of wilderness, ground. (Cf. *uwanda*, and dist. from *kiwanja* and *uwanja*.)

Kiwango, n. *vi-* (1) see under **Wanga**; (2) a kind of cowrie shell.

Kiwanja, n. *vi-* a place of ground, e.g. for building a house on, for playing games on (football, hockey, cricket, &c.), for a dance, a golf-green, &c. *Nitakuuzia nyumba yangu, lakini kiwanja si changu*, I shall sell you my house, but the plot is not mine. (Cf. *uwanja*, and dist. *kiwanda*.)

Kiwara,* n. *vi-* a plain, a large piece of ground. (Cf. *uwanda, mbuga*. Ar. كِرَة.)

Kiwavi, n. *vi-* (1) see under **Wawa**; (2) a perennial herb with long slender twining stems and stinging hairs, (i) *Tragia furialis*, (ii) *T. Scheffleri*.

Kiwe, n. *vi-*. See under **Jiwe**.

Kiweko, n. *vi-*. See under **Weka**.

Kiwele, n. *wi-* milk-gland of a female animal, udder. (Cf. *ziwa*.)

Kiwembe, n. *vi-* dim. of *wembe*. See under **Jembe**.

Kiweo, n. *vi-* thigh, ham, hip; used in the butchery trade for the region between the *kinena* and *paja*, which see. *Paja* is more generally used for human beings. (Cf. *kiga*.)

Kiwete, n. *vi-* and adv. (1) lameness, crippled condition; (2) a crippled person, a cripple; (3) in a lame, halting, crippled way. *Kwenda kiwete*, walk lamely. *-a kiwete*, crippled. *Yu kiwete*, or *ana kiwete*, he is lame. (Cf. *kilema, kiguu, chechemea*.)

Kiweto, n. *vi-* a hen that does not lay eggs.

Kiwewe, n. *vi-* a confused feeling induced by joy, astonishment, fear, &c. *Alikuwa na kiwewe, hakuweza kusema vizuri*, he was so confused that he was not able to speak properly.

Kiwi, n. (A) *vi-* a stout stick, bar of wood, set against a door inside as a fastening, &c., usually set upright in a bolt-hole. (Cf. *komeo, pingo*.)

Kiwi, n. (B) (1) state of being dazed, unable to see clearly, i.e. *kiwi cha macho*. *Jua lafanya kiwi cha macho*, the sun blinds, dazzles. *Haoni usiku, ana kiwi*, he does not see at night, his sight is defective. (2) fig. *kumtia mtu kiwi*, to cheat a person. **Ukiwi**, n. condition of being dazzled by a glare, of not being able to see clearly.

Kiwida,* n. *vi-* a hole in the beam of a dhow, &c., into which the mast is fixed. (Cf. *kiyunga*. Pers. كاده piece of wood in which pivot turns.)

Kiwiko, n. *vi-*, *kiwiko cha mkono*, the wrist; *kiwiko cha mguu*, the ankle. (Cf. *kisigino, kifundo*.)

Kiwiliwili, n. *vi-*. See under **Mwili**.

Kiwimawima, adv. See under **Wima**.

Kiwimbi, n. *vi-* dim. of *wimbi*.

Kiwingu, n. *vi-* dim. of *wingu*.

Kiwiwi, n. same as *kiwi*, n. which see.

Kiyama,* n. the general resurrection of the dead, as conceived by Muhammadans. (Cf. *ufufuo*. Ar. قيامة.)

Kiyambaza, n. *vi-*. See **Kiambaza** under **Wamba**.

Kiyana,* n. *vi-* an earthenware dish used for cooking. (Cf. *mkungu wa tanu*, under *chungu*. Ar. اناء vessel, with *ki-* prefix.)

Kiyoga, n. *vi-* dim. of *uyoga*, a little mushroom or similar fungus, toadstool, whether edible or not. **Uyoga**, n. mushroom, used as a collective noun. **Yoga**, *ma-* amplic.; but *uyoga* is the common term.

Kiyowe, n. *vi-*. See under **Yowe**.

Kiyunga, n. *vi-* the hole in the beam of a dhow, &c., into which the mast is fixed. (Cf. *kiwida*.)

Kiyuyu, n. *vi-* a shrub up to 12 ft. tall with fleshy green branches which contain a milky latex, used as a fish poison, *Synadenium carinatum*.

Kiza, n. sometimes heard for *giza*, which see.

Kiza, v. See **Ikiza**.

Kizalia, n. *vi-*. See under **Zaa**.

Kizamiadagaa, n. a name for the kingfisher, also called *mdiria* and *mtilili*. (Cf. *zama* and *dagaa*.)

Kizao, n. *vi-*, **Kizazi**, n. *vi-*. See under **Zaa**.

Kizee, n. *vi-* and adv. See under **Mzee**.

Kizembe, n. and adv. See under **-zembe**.

Kizibo, n. *vi-*. See under **Ziba**.

Kizidishe, n. *vi-*, **Kizidisho**, n. *vi-*. See under **Zidi**.

Kizimba, n. *vi-*, also **Kizimbi**, n. *vi-* a cage with bars, coop for fowls, &c. (Cf. *kirimba, tundu*.)

Kizimwe, n. *vi-*. See under **Zima**, v.

Kizimwi, adv. and n. *vi-*. See under **Zimwi**.

Kizinda, n. *vi-*, also **Kisinda**, hymen. *Weka kizinda*, preserve virginity. *Tomoa kizinda*, deprive of virginity. (Cf. *zinda, ungo, ubikira*.)

Kizingo, n. *vi-*, **Kizingia**, n. *vi-*. See under **Zinga**.

Kizingiti, n. *vi-* (1) top or bottom piece of the frame of a door or window, threshold, sill, lintel; (2) bar of a river, reef, or rocks, natural dam, weir. *Mlango wa kizingiti*, opening in a bar or reef, sluice, floodgate. (Cf. *mlango, kimandu, mwimo, kirimba*.)

Kizingo, n. *vi-* (1) see under **Zinga**; (2) sand from the sea-shore. (Cf. *mchanga*.)

Kizio, n. *vi-* a half of anything round, e.g. half of a coco-nut.

Kiziwi, n. *vi-* (1) a deaf person; (2) used of a coco-nut which has dried up and has no nut inside it. **Ukiziwi**, but usu. **Uziwi**, n. deafness. (For form, cf. *kipofu, kizee, kibiongo, kilema, kiwete*.)

Kizizi, n. *vi-* dim. of *zizi*.

Kizo, n. See **Kivo**.

Kizuio, n. *vi-*, **Kizuizi**, n. *vi-*, **Kizuizo**, n. *vi-*. See under **Zuia**.

Kizuizui, n. a children's game like blind man's buff. (Cf. *bui*.)

Kizuka, n. *vi-*. See under **Zua**.

Kizuli, n. sometimes heard for *kisuli*.

Kizungu, n. and adv. See under **Mzungu**.

Kizunguzungu, n. *vi-*. See under **Zungua**.

Kizushi, n. *vi-*. See under **Zua**.

Kizuu, n. *vi-* a kind of evil spirit, said to be capable of being employed by witches and wizards to enter houses in the form of a rat and kill people by devouring their livers. They are said to be the spirits of people thought to be dead, but who were in reality spirited away by magic. (Cf. *zua*.)

K.m. abbrev. for *kwa mfano*, for example.

Ko, as a separate word only appears in such a phrase as *ko kote*, wherever, under whatever circumstances. For the use of *-ko-* as a pfx. see grammars.

Koa, n. *ma-* (1) a band of thin metal plate, esp. as worn for ornament on the neck or arm, e.g. *koa la fedha*, a silver armlet, *koa la shingo*, a neck-ring (sometimes broadened into a crescent shape in front). (Cf. *furungu, kikuku*, and for ornaments generally *urembo*.) (2) (— and *ma-*) a snail, a slug. *Ute wa koa*, the slime of a snail. (Cf. *konokono*.) (3) a leather strap. **Kikoa**, n. *vi-* dim. **Ukoa**, (*koa*) same as *koa* (1) and (3).

Koa, v. (1) be sharp, e.g. *kisu kinakoa*, the knife is sharp; (2) be pleasing, be pleasant, of food, conversation, &c., but this is usu. *kolea*, which see.

Koba, n. *ma-* (1) amplic. of *mkoba*; (2) *fanya koba*, be convex, i.e. of a sail bellying out with the wind, &c. (Cf. *mkoba* and *kubaza*.)

Kobe, n. *ma-* (1) a land tortoise; (2) a name applied to a man who breaks his fast in the month of Ramadhan. *Huyu ni kobe leo*, this man is *kobe* to-day, i.e. he has broken his fast. (Cf. *kasa, ng'amba*.)

Koboa, v. sometimes heard for *goboa*, which see.

Kobwe, n. (1) a kind of bean, like *kunde*; (2) a loud clapping with hollowed hands, or with the hands on the biceps, i.e. *kupiga kobwe*, used in dances when the *wachawi* (wizards) summon one another at night; (3) a kind of snail.

Koche, n. *ma-* the edible fruit of the *mkoche*, which see.

-kocho, a. clever, expert (cf. *hodari*, *bingwa*, *stadi*); adv. and **Kochokocho**, in large quantities. *Miti inazaa kochokocho*, the trees bear abundantly.

Kodi,* v. rent, lease, hire, e.g. a house, plantation, &c. Cs. **Kodisha**, (1) let on hire, lease; also (2) hire, take on lease, &c. **Kodi**, n. rent, tax, customs-duties. **Mkodi**, n. *wa-* one who hires or lets on hire. (Cf. *ushuru*, *panga*, v. Hind. كر tax or fee, or Pers. كرد stack or heap of corn, i.e. as a tithe.)

Kodoa, v. esp. with *macho*, open the eyes wide, stare, glare. Prep. **Kodolea**, e.g. *kodolea* (*macho*), stare at, gaze at fixedly with eyes wide open. *Kwa nini unanikodolea macho?* Why are you staring at me? (Cf. *ng'ariza*, *kaza macho*, *angaza*.)

Kodwe, n. small stone, used as a marble in games—as are *korosho* and *komwe*. (Cf. *jiwe*, *mbwe*.)

Koeka, v. catch hold of anything with a hook on the end of a stick, &c., more usu. *ngoeka*, which see. *Kukoeka mwari*, is used of a *somo* making definite arrangements so that an initiate will be under his (or her) charge.

Kofi, n. *ma-* (1) flat of the hand, the palm extended or upturned; (2) a blow with the open hand, slap, box on the ear; (3) as much as can be held on the palm of the upturned hand. *Piga kofi*, slap, box the ear. *Piga makofi*, clap the hands. **Kikofi**, n. *vi-* same as (1) and (3) of *kofi*. **Ukofi**, n. (*kofi*), same as (1) and (3) of *kofi*. (Cf. *mkono*, *chopa*, *konzi*, and for handful, *ukufi*.)

Kofia,* n. cap, usu. a fez of red cloth, or of white linen often elaborately stitched. Used also of any foreign head-cover. *Vaa kofia*, put on a cap. *Vua kofia*, take off a cap. *Kofia ya bulibuli*, a white embroidered skull-cap, also called *kofia ya kazi*. *Kofia ya kitunga*, a kind of tarboosh. (Ar. كوفية.)

Koga, n. mould, blight, mustiness. *Fanya* (*ota*) *koga*, get mouldy (blighted). (Cf. *kutu*, *kizimwe*, and dist. *ukoga*.)

Koga, v. make a show, display, show off. Also sometimes heard for *kuoga*, to bathe. **Makogo**, n. plur. e.g. *makogo ya macho*, side-looks. **Mkogo**, n. *mi-* a showing off, display, e.g. of a youth showing off on a bicycle by doing tricks, &c.

Kogo, n. (1) the part of the skull which projects at the back, the back of the head, occiput. (Cf. *kikosi*, *kisogo*.) (2) a string of beads, worn by some women round the loins. (Cf. *utunda*, *kondavi*.)

Kohl,* n. antimony used for beautifying the eyes. **Mkahale**, n. *mi-* a pencil for applying antimony to the eyes. (Ar. كحل.)

Koho,* n. Vulturine Fish-Eagle, *Gypohierax angolinsis*. (Hind. كوهي falcon, species of hawk.)

Kohoa, v. cough. Cs. **Kohoza**, e.g. *jikohoza*, cough on purpose, as a sham, to attract attention, to deceive a person, &c. **Kikohozi**, n. *vi-* a coughing, fit of coughing. **Kohoo**, n. *ma-* expectoration, sputum, phlegm coughed up. **Kohozi**, n. *ma-* same as *kohoo*. **Ukohozi**, n. coughing, expectoration, sputum, phthisis, any chest affection causing coughing. (Cf. *belghamu*, *kifua*.)

Koikoi, n. *ma-* (1) a kind of evil spirit (cf. *pepo*); (2) the name applied to heron or stork.

Koja, n. (1) a neck ornament, a ring with disks or coins attached worn round the neck (cf. *koa, urembo*); (2) a kind of metal pot. (Cf. *kopo, sufuria.*)

Kojoa, v. urinate, make water. Prep. **Kojolea.** Cs. **Kojosha,** also **Kojoza,** e.g. *dawa ya kukojosha,* a diuretic. **Mkojo, n.** (sometimes Plur. *mi-*) micturition, urine, also *choo cha mbele, choo kidogo.* **Mkojozi, n.** *wa-* one who cannot or does not control his urine, one who wets his bed. **Kojojo, n.** *ma-* a sea slug, bêche-de-mer. **Kojozi,** n. (1) urine; (2) a kind of banana said to cause much urine; (3) a person who has difficulty in controlling his urine. (Cf. *nya, tabawali.*)

Koka, v. (1) heap up ready to set on fire, set on fire; (2) warm oneself at a fire (cf. *ota moto*); (3) also sometimes heard for *kuoka,* to bake.

Koko, n. (— and *ma-*) (1) stone of a fruit but more frequently *kokwa* is heard—the kernel being *kiini*; (2) bush, undergrowth, jungle, such as in a mangrove swamp. *Mbwa koko,* a bush dog, i.e. in a semi-wild state. *Kaa makoko,* small mud-crabs. (Cf. *mkoko.*) (3) the testicles, i.e. *koko* (or *kokwa*) *za pumbu.*

Kokoa, v. sweep up, collect together in a heap—of dust, rubbish, &c., i.e. *kokoa taka.* Ps. **Kokolewa,** e.g. *mchanga unakokolewa na maji,* the sand is being swept away by the water. (Cf. *soa, fagia, kumba, chukuliwa.*)

Kokoleka, v. cackle—of a hen, crow —of a cock.

Kokomea, v. fix a thing in its place, fix with a wedge, &c. (Cf. *kongomea, pigilia, kaza.*)

Kokomoa, v. (1) retch violently, belch; (2) fig. blurt out, burst out with. St. **Kokomoka,** used in the same way as *kokomoa.* (Cf. *foka, bubujika, tapika.*)

Kokona, v. clean oneself with grass, leaves, &c., after evacuation; used also of a dog dragging its hindquarters on the ground for the same purpose.

Kokorocha, v. See **Korocha.**

Kokota, v. drag, haul, tug at, pull along, draw. *Kokota gari,* draw a cart. *Kokota roho,* used of slow painful breathing. *Kokota maneno,* of slow dragging speech, difficult articulation. *Kokota kazi,* work slowly. *Jikokota,* move slowly, reluctantly, with difficulty. Cs. **Kokoteza,** e.g. *kokoteza kazi,* work slowly, whether from care or laziness. Ps. **Kokotwa.** St. and Pot. **Kokoteka.** Prep. **Kokotea.** **Mkokoto, n.** *mi-* (1) a dragging, a hauling, a pull; (2) the mark of something dragged along. **-kokotevu, a.** dragging, dilatory, slow. (Cf. *kokoto, buruta, vuta.*)

Kokoto, n. *ma-* often in the plur. small stones, esp. with reference to use as material, e.g. *makokoto ya kupigilia,* for use in concrete. *Makokoto ya kutomelea,* for use in plastering. They are sometimes classed according to size as compared with common fruits, e.g. *makokoto ya ndimu* (lime size), *ya malimau* (lemon size), *ya nazi* (coco-nut size).

Kokwa, n. (— and *ma-*) stone of a fruit. (Cf. *koko.*)

Kole, n. *ma-* (1) a branch of a coco-nut palm; (2) see under **Koleza, v.** (B).

Kolea, v. (1) be properly seasoned, have a flavour, and (2) fig. have point (force, meaning). *Samli imekolea katika chakula,* the food has been flavoured with ghee. *Mbona chai yangu haikukolea sukari?* Why has my tea not had (enough) sugar put in it? *Ubishi wake haukukolea,* his joke fell flat. Cs. **Koleza,** (1) flavour food; (2) *koleza moto,* make up a fire, make it burn up (with oil, shavings, &c.). (Cf. *kora, unga,* **v.,** *kiungo, kitoweo.*)

Kolego, n. *ma-* a spade or shovel.

Kolekole, n. name of a large kind of fish.

Koleo, n. (— and *ma-*) (1) a smith's tool for handling his work, a pair of tongs, also any similar instrument, pliers, pincers, &c. Prov. *Kusima* *koleo si mwisho wa uhunzi*, cooling the tongs is not the end of the job. (2) a notch in an arrow (held on the string with fingers).

Koleza, v. (A). See under **Kolea.**

Koleza, v. (B) apprehend a person or property for debt. **Kole**, n. a person seized in place of a brother or relation who has committed an offence or is in debt, and has absconded: *kukamata mtu kole*, to arrest or seize a person for the reason described.

Koli, n. a ship's papers. (? Ar. كلاء safe anchorage.)

Koma, n. *ma-* the edible fruit of the *mkoma*, which see.

Koma, n. the spirit of a dead person, believed to exist in the grave, and appear to relatives in dreams. (Cf. *mzimu, ngoma.*)

Koma, v. cease, come to an end, stop, decease. Also sometimes Act. bring to an end, close. Prov. *Lisilo na mkoma hujikoma lilo*, what has no one to end it, ends of itself. *Walipokoma nusu ya njia*, when they ended half of the journey. *Koma usije*, stop, don't come any further. Cs. **Komesha**, make stop, bring to an end, thwart, forbid, kill—usually implying some force or abruptness. *Komesha maneno*, stop conversation, cut short a debate. (Folld. by Neg. of Subj. Cf. *kataza.*) **Kikomo**, n. *vi-* (1) stop, stopping, stoppage, place or time of stopping, cessation, end; (2) *kikomo cha uso*, forehead, brow. **Mkoma**, n. *wa-* one who stops, ceases, comes to an end. **Komo**, n. *ma-* same as *kikomo*, **Ukomo**, n. (*komo*) act (manner, time, place, &c.), of coming to a stop, end, halting-place, goal, end part, limit, destruction, death. *Ukomo wa njia* (*kisa*), end of road (story). *Ukomo wa bahari*, seashore. *Ukomo wa uso*, forehead. (Cf. *isha, nyamaa, tindika, maliza.*)

Komaa, v. (1) be fully ripe, be full grown (developed, matured) and so (2) be past the prime, fall off, begin to lose powers, decline, become demoralized. Cs. **Komaza**, unduly stimulate, over-excite, make game of, mock. *Usinene nakukomaza*, do not say I am talking improperly with you. (Cf. *pea, balehe, -zima*, prob. a Dur. form of *koma*, v.)

Komafi, n. *ma-* fruit of the tree *mkomafi*, which see. Wooden clogs (*mitalawanda*) and donkey-cart wheels are made from the wood of this tree in Zanzibar.

Komakanga, n. name of a little black-and-white finch.

Komamanga, n. *ma-* pomegranate, the fruit of the *mkomamanga*.

Komanguku, n. a herb, *Crotalaria senegalensis*. The fruits are used for flavouring curries.

Komanya, v. know, understand, comprehend. Cs. **Komanza**, (1) make a person understand, &c., also (2) show a person something wonderful, something he has never seen before, astonish.

Komba, n. (1) a small racoon-like animal, galago—common on the coast and in Zanzibar, and very destructive to coco-nuts, also very noisy at nights as it makes a sharp unpleasant barking noise; (2) a kind of fish, not considered good eating by Europeans.

Komba, v. scrape out, hollow out, clean out, e.g. *komba ngoma*, make a drum (by hollowing it out). *Komba dafu*, scrape out the nutty part of a young coco-nut. Cf. *dafu la kukomba*, a coco-nut full of milk, but beginning to form the soft nutty substance inside. *Komba chungu*, clean out a pot *Komba mtu mali*, clean a man out of his money, ruin, impoverish. St. **Kombeka**, be cleaned or cleared out. Prep. **Kombea.** D. Prep. **Kombelea.** St. and Pot. **Kombeleka**, e.g. *amekombeleka mali*, he has lost every penny he had. Cv. **Komboa**, (1) scrape out, but with special meaning of ransom, redeem, deliver, make compensation for, pay for. *Nitamkomboa mtu aliyeuzwa,* I will redeem the man who was sold. *Komboa deni,* pay a debt, compensate a creditor. *Komboa dhamana,* surrender to bail. *Niliiweka rehani saa yangu, nataka kuikomboa,* I placed my watch in pawn, now I want to redeem it. (2) make hollow, convex, hence, make crooked, warp, put out of shape, give a turn or twist to, and so fig. cause difficulty to, thwart, hamper, give trouble to. *Amelikomboa sanduku langu,* he has redeemed my box, also, possibly, he has put my box out of shape. Ps. **Kombolewa.** St. and Pot. **Komboka,** e.g. (1) be redeemed; (2) be crooked, or hollowed out. Prep. **Kombolea,** e.g. *mali ya kukombolea,* money for a ransom. Cs. **Komboza,** (1) cause to ransom; (2) make crooked, &c. **Kikomba,** n. *njaa ya kikomba* (or *kukomba*), ravenous hunger, that makes a man scrape up and sweep off everything. Also *kikomba cha njaa,* intense hunger. **Kikombe,** n. *vi-* a vessel scraped or hollowed out, and so dim. of *kombe,* a small dish, cup, basin, mug, of any material—the common word used for a cup. *Kikombe cha chai* (*bilauri, fedha*), a teacup (wine-glass, silver cup). **Kikombo,** n. *vi-* and adv. a small crooked, hook-shaped, or curved thing, e.g. a small curved gouge-shaped tool; also a small bend, curve, irregularity, deflection, defect, fault, flaw. As adv. in a crooked, irregular way. **Kombe,** n. (— and *ma-*) (1) anything hollowed or scraped out, flat and slightly curved, and also (2) an instrument for scraping or hollowing. Hence various meanings: (1) a large dish, pan, or platter of earthenware, charger (cf. *kikombe*); (2) bivalve shell-fish and their shells, such as oysters, &c., *kombe ya pwani* (cf. *kome, konokono, kauri*); (3) shoulder-blade, *kombe la mkono,* also an empty skull, *kombe la kichwa* (cf. *kichwa, bufuu, fuvu*); (4) a gouge, scraper, e.g. *miiba na kombe za kunichoma,* thorns and sharp edges to hurt me. Also of the fluke of an anchor, *bawa ya makombe mawili,* a European anchor with two flukes. (5) also used of medicines prepared by Muhammadan teachers, by writing certain texts from the Koran on a plate, this is then washed off with water, and the water is drunk as a medicine. **Kombo,** n. *ma-* (1) a scrap, a scraping, a bit of food remaining over; (2) like *kikombo,* twist, turn, crook, crookedness, deviation from the straight or standard, defect, fault, ill temper, awkwardness, difficulty, sticking-point. *Mti huu ni kombo,* or *una kombo,* this tree is all crooked. *Hapana kombo,* there is no difficulty, it is all straightforward, plain sailing. *Mimi, ni kombo nayo,* as for me, I just cannot do it (that is where I stick). (3) escape, acquittal, pardon, e.g. *-pa kombo,* grant pardon. **Kombozi,** n. *ma-* see *ukombozi* below. **Mkombozi,** n. *wa-* one who ransoms (buys back, gets out of pawn, recovers a deposit), a redeemer, hence, a title of Jesus Christ. **Ukomba,** n. also **Ukombe,** n. (1) a curved tool, used for hollowing out by cutting and scraping, e.g. for native wooden mortars, drums, measures, canoes, &c.; (2) a small spoon of earthenware, or of wood. **Ukombo,** n. (*kombo*), (1) curve, bend, crook; (2) the fee given by a parent to a teacher at the end of his son's training in school. **Ukombozi,** n. (1) rescue, ransoming, redemption, ransom, fine.

Kombamoyo, n. *ma-* a long thin straight pole, used as a rafter in constructing the roof of native huts, carrying the cross-pieces (*fito* or *pao*) and thatch (*makuti, nyasi, majani,* &c.).

Kombati, n. thin poles used in building native houses, to fill in spaces between the larger poles. (Cf. *wasa.*)

Kombe, n. See **Komba,** v.

Kombeo, n. *ma-* a sling made from rope, fibre, cloth, for throwing stones. (Cf. *teo,* and for catapult, *manati, panda.*)

Kombo, n. *ma-*, **Komboa,** v. See under **Komba,** v.

Kombora,* n. *ma-* a bomb, a shell, also a mortar for throwing bombs. (Ar. قنبرة.)

Kombozi, n. See under **Komba,** v.

Kome, n. (— and *ma-*) a kind of shell and shell-fish. *Kome za pwani,* univalves. (Cf. *kombe* under *komba,* v.)

Komea, v. bolt, bar, fasten with a *komeo.* Prep. **Komelea,** e.g. *ufunguo wa kukomelea,* a key to remove a bolt. Cs. **Komeza.** Ps. **Komewa.** St. **Komeka.** Cv. **Komoa,** (1) unbar, i.e. remove the *komeo*; (2) fig. shame, disgrace, and used in the sense of *Nitakukomoa,* I will rend you asunder, I will be your undoing; (3) used of freeing a person from an evil spirit, i.e. *kukomoa pepo.* **Komeo,** n. *ma-* bar, bolt, latch (of wood), for fastening a door, window, a kind of native lock. **Komoo,** n. act of freeing a man from an evil spirit, *siku ya komoo,* day of exorcizing a spirit. (Cf. *funga, pingo, kiwi.*)

Komeo, n. *ma-* (1) see under **Komea;** (2) a creek, an inlet of the sea. (Cf. *hori, ghuba.*)

Komo, n. *ma-*. See under **Koma,** v.

Komoa, v., **Komoo,** n. See under **Komea.**

Komwe, n. *ma-* seed of a tree *mkomwe,* used as counters in playing games.

Kona,* n. a second house kept by a man for meeting his paramour without the knowledge of his wife. (? Ar. كن keep concealed, home, asylum.)

Konda, v. grow thin, become lean, be emaciated, get into a low condition of health or body, pine. Prep. **Kondea,** become thin because of, pine for. Cs. **Kondesha,** cause to get thin, wear out, dispirit, cause to pine (languish). *Jikondesha,* worry oneself by brooding, taking a matter too much to heart. (Cf. *nywea, nyorora, churuzika.*)

Kondavi, n. *ma-* a broad belt of beads worked in a pattern, worn by some women under their outer dress. (Cf. *shegele, ushanga, utunda.*)

Konde, n. *ma-* (1) fist, closed hand. *Piga konde,* strike with fist (knuckles of the closed hand). *Piga moyo konde,* take courage, cheer up, make a bold resolve (cf. *ngumi, konzi*). (2) the palm of the hand (cf. *kitanga*); (3) a field-clearing, cultivated piece of ground, garden which has been cultivated before. *Lima konde,* till a plot of ground (cf. *shamba*). (4) a date-stone, the stone inside fruit. (Cf. *kokwa.*)

Kondo, n. (1) *kondo ya nyuma,* after-birth; (2) *siku za kondoni,* the period of a woman's rest after giving birth; (3) an old word for war, strife, difficulty, seldom used now except in poetry. (Cf. *mkondo, zalio, vita.*)

Kondoo, n. a sheep. *Chunga kondoo,* tend sheep. *Manyoya ya kondoo* (or *sufu*), fleece. *Kondoo dume,* ram. *Kondoo jike,* ewe. **Kikondoo,** n. *vi-* and adv. (1) dim. of *kondoo*; (2) like a sheep, unresisting, meekly, calmly.

Konga, v. (A) grow old, get feeble with age. *Mzee huyu amekonga, hawezi kufanya kazi,* this old man is weak with age, he cannot work. Cs. **Kongesha,** make old, add to the age of, wear out, e.g. with nagging or abuse. Ps. **Kongwa.** Cv. **Kongoa.** St. of Cv. **Kongoka,** e.g. be old, *mtu huyu amekongoka,* this man is now old. Hence **Kongoja,** v. walk feebly, like an old man (with difficulty) totter, stagger. Prep. **Kongojea,** e.g. *fimbo ya kukongojea,* a stick to steady one's steps with. *Jikongojea,* prop oneself, steady oneself, as with a stick. *Nipe gongo langu, mkongojo, nipate kujikongojea,* give me my staff, the *mkongojo,* so that I may steady myself. **Kikongwe,** n. *vi-* and adv. a person bent and bowed with age, a very old person. And as adv. like an old person. **-kongwe,** a. old, worn out, aged, past work. **Mkongwe,** n. *wa-* an old person. **Mkongojo,** n. *mi-* a staff used as a prop or crutch for an old man or weakly person. **Ukongojo,** n. (*kongojo*), same as *mkongojo*. **Ukongwe,** n. extreme old age. (Cf. *uzee*.)

Konga, v. (B) take a sip of water, get a drop of, used of water to allay, not quench, thirst. *Nipe maji nikonge roho,* give me a little water to revive myself.

Kongoa, v. draw out, cut out, extract, disengage. *Kongoa misumari,* draw out nails. *Kongoa jino,* extract a tooth, but usu. *ng'oa jino. Walikongoa pembe,* they cut out the (elephant's) tusk. Prep. **Kongolea,** take to pieces, break up, e.g. a frame of any sort, a box, a boat, &c. *Mashua yote ilikongolewa vipande vipande,* the whole boat was taken to pieces. *Kongolea sanduku,* open a case for (with, &c.). St. and Pot. **Kongoka,** e.g. *shoka limekongoka,* the axe has come off its handle. (Cf. *ng'oa.* Note: this is a Cv. form with reversive meaning from a verb *konga,* join, gather, &c., not now used in Swahili. See *kongamana* which is from a Cv. form not reversive in meaning.)

Kongoja, v. See under **Konga, v.** (A).

Kongoka, v. See under **Kongoa.**

Kongomana, v. be joined, be assembled, meet together, be heaped (gathered, piled) together, e.g. *sharti mkongomane,* you must be united, *Vyuma hivi vimekongomana kwa kutu,* these pieces of iron are stuck together with rust. Cs. **Kongomanisha,** gather, assemble, unite, weld, heap together, agglomerate. Prep. **Kongomea,** fasten up, nail, put together. *Alizikongomea nguo zangu katika sanduku,* he fastened up my clothes in a box. **Kongomeo,** n. *ma-* a fastening. (Cf. *ng'oa, kuta, kusanya.* Note: this is from a Cv. form of *konga,* join, gather, &c., not now used in Swahili. See **Kongoa** which is a Cv. form of the same verb, but with reversive meaning.)

Kongomeo, n. *ma-* (1) see under **Kongomana;** (2) the larynx. (Cf. *koromeo.*)

Kongoni, n. the hartebeest, topi, gnu, also called *nyumbu.*

Kongonyoa, v. break off, pluck off, as fruits from a tree, wring off the head of a bird, &c. (Apparently a Cv. form of Cs. of *kongoa.*)

Kongoro, n. an old bull (cattle).

Kongosho, n. the pancreas, sweetbread.

Kong'ota, v. beat in order to make even, as of a skin, metal, &c. (Cf. *babata.*)

Kongoti, n. (1) a stork, or heron; (2) a game in which one of the players dresses up as a stork, by means of stilts and grass, &c.

Kongowea, v. greet, salute, accost, but with excessive humility or show. (Cf. *mwezi kongo,* under *kongo.*)

Kongozoka, v. straighten out anything that is bent or crooked, i.e. the arm, leg, &c. (Prob. from *konga,* v. (C).)

Kongwa, n. (A) *ma-* a forked stick, a slave-stick, i.e. a stick or pole with a forked end in which the slave was secured with an iron cross-pin. (Cf. *panda,* n.)

Kongwa, n. (B) a herb, good fodder. *Commelina* sp.

Kongwe, n. (1) a lead in singing. *Toa kongwe,* start a song, give a lead, lead off (cf. *bwaga wimbo*). (2) a perennial herb with stems 2 to 8 ft. long with small yellow, blue, mauve, or lilac flowers, *Aneilema aequinoctale*; (3) a perennial herb up to 3 ft. tall with small blue or dull purple flowers, *A. sinicum.*

-kongwe, a. See under **Konga, v.** (A).

Konje, n. a small animal like a fox. (Cf. *kala.*)

Konjo, n. See **Konzo.**

Kono, n. *ma-.* See under **Mkono.**

Konoa, v. See **Konyoa.**

Konokono, n. (1) *ma-* a snail (cf. *koa*); (2) (—) sweet sop, a shrub or small tree with edible fruits, *Annona squamosa.*

Konsonanti,* n. the word adopted for a consonant for use in text-books and school lessons. (Eng.)

Kontinenti,* n. *ma-* the word adopted for a continent, for use in text-books and school lessons. (Eng.)

Konya, n. a child's game.

Konya, v. wave, swing, sway. (Cf. *punga, suka.*)

Konyeza, v. make a covert sign to, i.e. in order to attract notice, warn, give a hint to, e.g. *konyeza kwa macho*, raise the eyebrows, wink. *Konyeza kwa mkono*, make a significant gesture. **Konyeza**, n. *ma-* also **Ukonyezo** (*konyezo*), a hint, suggestion, warning, secret sign, esp. with the eyes or hands, a wink, shrug of the shoulders. (Cf. *ashiria, onya.*)

Konyoa, v. break off, pluck off, tear off, esp. with some instrument, e.g. of removing the grains from a cob of maize by pounding, i.e. *konyoa mahindi. Konyoa embe*, peel a mango with a knife. *Konyoa maungo*, dismember, quarter.

Konzi, n. *ma-* (1) closed fist. *Piga konzi*, rap with the knuckles, with the back of the hand, on the head. (2) a fistful, as much as can be taken up in the fist with the fingers nearly closed. *Konzi ya maji yamtosha kunywa mtoto*, a fistful of water is sufficient for a child to drink. (Cf. *konde, ngumi, kofi, chopa.*)

Konzo, n. *ma-* large stick, stake, pole, with the end pointed and hardened with fire, used as a weapon, hunting-spear, or in pitfalls set for large animals. **Mkonzo**, n. *mi-* smaller than *konzo*. **Ukonzo** (*konzo*) same as *konzo*. Sometimes this word is heard as *konjo*. (Cf. *mkuki.*)

Koo, n. *ma-* (1) throat; ailment of the throat; mucus from the throat, expectoration (cf. *kohoo* under *kohoa*); (2) of a breeding-animal or bird, e.g. *koo la kuku*, a breeding-fowl. *Koo la mbuzi*, a breeding-goat. (3) a mistress, a paramour. (Cf. *umio, roho*, and dist. *mkoo, ukoo.*)

Koongo, n. *ma-* hole dibbled or dug with a hoe for planting seeds.

Kopa, n. *ma-* (1) a slice of dried cassava (*muhogo*). Seldom used in the sing. Also dried bananas (*ndizi*). (Cf. *ubale.*) (2) hearts in a pack of playing-cards. (Cf. *karata*, Port. *copa*, hearts in cards.)

Kopa, v. (1) get food or money on credit, borrow for trading purposes, i.e. on promise to account for according to agreement, negotiate for a loan on credit. *Kopa mali* (*nguo, fedha*), borrow goods (cloth, cash). (2) swindle, cheat, defraud, get on false pretences, e.g. *amenikopa mali yangu yote*, he has cheated me of all my property. Ps. **Kopwa**, (1) i.e. (of things) be borrowed; (2) (of persons) be swindled. Prep. **Kopea**. (1) borrow for (from, with, &c.); (2) cheat by (for, with &c.). *Nimekukopea nguo kwa Banyani kwa shilingi mbili, kwa muda wa miezi miwili*, I have borrowed cloth for you from the Banyani for two shillings on credit of two months. Cs. **Kopesha**, lend, supply goods on credit (to), advance as a loan, e.g. *mlipe mtu kadiri akukopeshavyo*, pay a man as much as he advances to you. (Cf. *azima, karidhi*, and *punja, danganya*). **Kikopo**, n. *vi-* and adv. (1) a borrowing, &c.); (2) impudence, cheating, shamelessness in dealing. **Kope**, n. *ma-* a loan, something borrowed. **Kopo**, n. *ma-* same as *kope*. **Mkopeshi**, n. *wa-* one who supplies goods or capital on credit for commercial purposes, a lender. **Mkopi**, n. *wa-* (1) one who borrows goods or money, e.g. to trade with; (2) a swindler, impostor, knave. **Mkopo**, n. *mi-* (1) act (process, method, &c.) of borrowing, also (2) of swindling. **Ukopi**, n. (*kopi*), (1) borrowing and not repaying, knavery, cheating, deceit, fraud; (2) thing borrowed, loan, advance.

Kope, n. (— and *ma-*) (1) see under **Kopa**, v.; (2) the burnt end of the wick of a lamp or candle; (3) the eye-lashes, but generally not distinguished from the eyelid. *Kwa kope la juu na chini*, in the twinkling of an eye. **Kikope**, n. a disease of the eye inflammation of the eyes. **Ukope**, n. (*kope*) a hair of the eyelashes.

Kopesa, v. *kopesa macho*, wink. (Cf. *kope, pepesa, macho*.)

Kopo,* n. *ma-* (1) see under **Kopa**, v.; (2) used very generally of any vessel of metal (esp. of tin, zinc, sheet iron), can, mug, pot, jug, cup, &c. Used also of other metal articles, e.g. *kopo la maji*, a gutter, rain-spout. (Cf. *tasa, sufuria, kikombe, chombo, chungu*. Ar. كوب cup, &c., without a spout or handle, or Port. *copo*, cup, glass, &c.)

Kora, v. (sometimes heard as *kola*), please, satisfy, be on good (comfortable, confidential) terms with, be loved by. *Chakula hiki kimenikora*, this food has satisfied me. Ps. **Korwa**, e.g. be loved by, have one's wishes met by, be pleased with. **Kikora**, n. joy, rejoicing. (Cf. *kolea*, which appears to be derived from the same root, but one is usu. pronounced with an *r*, the other with an *l*.)

Kora manza, v. do an evil act, worthy of punishment.

Korani,* n. also **Kurani**, the Holy Book of the Muhammadans, the Koran. (Cf. *sura*, chapter; *juzuu, qya*, short section; and *hitimu*. Ar. القرآن.)

Kore, n. a plantation, garden, cultivated field. (Cf. *shamba*.)

Korho,* n. a kind of eagle or large bird of prey. (Ar. جدايه a kite.)

Korija,* n. a score, a lot of twenty, twenty together. Used in selling poles, strings of beads, lengths of cloth, &c. (Hind. كورى.)

Koroboi,* n. (1) a kind of rifle (prob. from Eng. carbine); (2) native mission boys (or girls) who were taken from slavery (said to be derived from Eng. 'call a boy'); (3) a small lamp without a chimney.

Korocha, also Rd. **Korochakorocha**, v. poke about, like *chokoa*, which see.

Korodani,* n. (1) the sheave of a pulley. (Cf. *roda, kapi, gofia*. Pers. كر hawser, rope, and دان container.) (2) scrotum, testicles. (Cf. *makende, hasua, pumbu*. Pers. قرر testicle, and دان container.)

-korofi,* a. (1) evil-minded, tyrannical, destructive, malignant, brutal, savage; (2) inauspicious, of ill-omen, unlucky. *Mkorofi sana huyu*, he is a destructive person. *Ndege korofi*, an evil (inauspicious, unlucky) omen. **Korofika**, v. be treated brutally, be ruined. Cs. **Korofisha**, treat with cruelty, bring to ruin. **Mkorofi**, n. *wa-* (1) an evil-minded, malignant, brutal, tyrannical person, a monster, a brute; (2) one who brings bad luck, misfortune. **Ukorofi**, n. (1) evil temper, malignity, savagery, brutality, tyranny, &c.; (2) bad omen. (Ar. قرف loathe, abhor.)

Korofindo, n. a muzzle-loading musket.

Koroga, v. (1) stir, stir up, mix by stirring (of liquids). *Koroga maji*, make water muddy by stirring. (2) fig. stir up strife, e.g. *koroga fitina*, begin trouble, agitate. **Mkoroga**, n. *wa-*, **Mkorogaji**, n. *wa-*, **Mkorogi**, n. *wa-* a stirrer, i.e. (1) maker of discord, an agitator, firebrand; (2) a blunderer, bungler. **Mkorogo**, n. *mi-* (1) a stirring, mashing, mixing of ingredients, &c.; (2) a causing of discord, agitation, disturbance of peace, blundering, bungling. **Ukorogefu**, n. (1) mixing; (2) untidiness, &c.; (3) disturbance. (Cf. *tibua, buruga, vuruga, pigisha, fuja, chafua*.)

Korokoni,* n. a guard-room, a lock-up, a watching-post, e.g. such as a camp-fire at night, &c. (Turk. قوقون.)

Koroma, n. *ma-* a coco-nut just becoming ripe, the milk drying, the nutty part formed and hardening, between the stages of *dafu* and *nazi*. (Cf. *nazi*.)

Koroma, v. snore, snort, groan, and of similar sounds. **Koroma**, n. and **Koromo**, n. *ma-* a snore, snoring, a snort. **Kikoromeo**, n. *vi-* the Adam's apple. (Cf. *zoloto*.) **Koromeo**, n. the larynx, also the food-passage, *amenaswa na kokwa la embe katika koromeo*, the stone of the mango stuck in his throat. **Mkoromaji**, n. *wa-* one who snores as a rule. **Mkoromo**, n. *mi-* an act of snoring or snorting.

Koromeo, n., **Koromo**, n. *ma-*. See under **Koroma**.

Korongo, n. *ma-* (1) name of a crane or similar long-legged bird, applied to the larger species of heron, and so fig. as a nickname for a long, lean person; (2) water channels made by rainy-season streams, often very large, a ravine, a donga.

Kororo, n. *ma-* (1) the crested guinea-fowl, *Guttera pucherani*, the common sort being *kanga*; (2) an ailment, i.e. swelling in the throat; (3) sound of heavy breathing, snore.

Korosho,* n. *ma-* cashew nut, from the tree *mbibo*, *mkanju*, or *mkorosho*. (Cf. *bibo*, *dunge*. ? Port. *caraco*, stone, kernel.)

Korota,* v. snore, snort. (Cf. *koroma*, *forota*. Pers. قرط noise made in swallowing water.)

Korowai, n. a kind of rice. (Cf. *mchele*.)

Koroweza, v. (1) increase the difficulty of a task, make trouble, puzzle; (2) catch, i.e. a ball, person, &c. Prep. **Korowezea**, i.e. *amenikorowezea kazi yangu*, he has bungled my work. **Makorowezo**, n. plur. bungling work, confusion.

Korti,* n. *ma-* a court of law, criminal or civil. (Cf. *baraza*, *hukumu*, *sheria*. Eng. court.)

Kosa, v. (1) make a mistake (as to), do wrong (to), offend (against), go astray (in), blunder, err; (2) fail to get (hit, find, attain), miss (a mark), fall short, be deficient, be defective; (3) lack, be without, lose, suffer loss of, e.g. *nimekosa*, I have failed, done wrong, sinned. *Hamkunikosa hata siku moja*, you never treated me badly (failed in duty to me) in any particular. *Mtu akikosa mali hawi mtu mbele ya watu*, a man without money is not a man in the sight of men. *Amemkosa nduguye*, he has lost his brother, or, he has done some wrong to his brother. *Kosa njia*, miss the road. *Kosa mnyama*, miss (shooting) an animal. *Kosa shabaha*, miss a target (mark, aim). *Kosakosa*, make a series of blunders. Ps. **Koswa**. St. and Pot. **Koseka**, e.g. be done wrongly. Rp. of St. and Pot. **Kosekana**, e.g. be missed, be wanting, be not to be had, fail. *Mungu hakosekani wala hafi*, God never fails (is absent) or dies. *Neno hili limekoseka*, this affair has been bungled. Prep. **Kosea**, offend (against) about, &c.), *kosea sheria*, commit a legal offence, but often used of making only a slight error. Cs. **Kosesha**, cause to do wrong, mislead. Rp. **Kosana**, e.g. miss each other, quarrel, treat each other badly, disagree. **Mkosaji**, n. *wa-* one who always makes mistakes or errs continually, a sinner. **Kosa**, n. *ma-* mistake, a miss, error, fault, failing, failure, defect, wrongdoing, sin. *Si kosa lake*, it is not his fault. *Tia kosani*, blame, accuse. *Sahihisha makosa*, correct mistakes. **Mkosi**, n. has a spec. meaning, see **Mkosi**. **-kosefu**, a. full of (given to, liable to) mistakes, erroneous, defective, &c. **Ukosefu**, n. *ma-*, **Ukosekana**, n. *ma-* failure (to obtain, reach, get) lack, want, deficiency, defect, faultiness, shortcoming.

Kosha,* n. sweet palm wine. (Cf. *tembo*. Hind. كس kind of sweet beverage.)

Koshi,* n. *ma-* slipper without the back part. (Cf. *kiatu, sapatu*. Pers. كوش shoe or slipper.)

Kosi, n. *ma-*, **Kikosi**, n. *vi-*, and **Ukosi**, n. (*kosi*) back of the neck, nape, e.g. *vunja kosi*, break the neck. Also coat collar. (Cf. *kogo, kisogo*.)

Kota, n. *ma-* (1) a crook, bend, crooked condition, e.g. *kota la miguu*, crooked legs (cf. more usually *kombo*, and *matege*); (2) sweet stalks of a kind of millet, chewed like sugar-cane, also **Kikota**, n. *vi-*. (Cf. *bua, mtama*.)

Kota, v. sometimes heard for *kuota* (*moto*), which see.

Kotama, n. a thin curved broad-bladed knife, used in getting palm wine (*gema tembo*), esp. for cutting a thin slice from the growing shoot to enable the sap to flow more freely. **Kikotama**, n. *vi-* dim. (Cf. *upamba, kisu, jambia, kijembe, gema*.)

Kote, a. form of *-ote*, all, agreeing with locative.—As adv. *kote, kote kote*, under all circumstances, everywhere, on all sides.

Koti,* n. *ma-* a coat, a jacket. (Eng. coat.)

Koto, n. (1) see **Kikoto**; (2) a gift given by a father to a teacher on entering his child into a school; (3) a large hook used for catching sharks.

Kotokoto, n. See under **Okota**.

Kotwe, n. the white-backed duck (Pemba), *Thalassornis leuconotus*.

Kovu, n. (— and of size *ma-*) a scar, mark of a wound or injury.

Kowana, n. a kind of fish, considered good eating by Europeans.

Koya, v. be glad, rejoice at getting something, or achieving some object, rest after effort, e.g. of finishing school, coming out of the initiation rites, &c.

Kozi, n. also **Kikozi**, n. *vi-* (1) East African Goshawk, *Astur tachiro*. Also applied to the Black Sparrow, *Accipiter melanoleucos*; (2) the fibrous sheath of the coco-nut palm. (Cf. *kumbi la mnazi*.)

Ku-. For the use of *ku-* and *-ku-* see the Grammars.

Kua, v. (1) grow, grow up, get large, increase, become great—used of the growth of men and animals (but *ota* and *mea*, usual of plants, and similar growths). Prov. *Mtoto umleavyo ndivyo akuavyo*, as you bring up a child, so does he grow up. Prep. **Kulia**, (1) grow up in (at, by, for, &c.), e.g. *mtoto amekulia hapa*, this child has grown up here. Also (2) be (too) great for, be heavy to, burden, be hard on, e.g. *neno hili limemkulia kubwa, zito*, this thing has grown too much for him, it is big and weighty. *Mambo haya yamenikulia taabu*, these affairs have grown to be a burden to me. Cs. **Kuza**, make great, enlarge, magnify, increase, glorify, prosper. **Kikulia**, n. *vi-* a thing or person that has grown up at a place—not born at a place, which is *kizalia*. **-kulivu**, a. (1) easily tired or discouraged or beaten; lacking grit (spirit, perseverance), remiss, weak-kneed, poor spirited; (2) oppressive, burdensome, tiresome, fatiguing. **-kuza**, a. well grown, fine, big of its kind—of things capable of growth. *Yule paka mkuza sana*, that is a very fine cat. **Mkulivu**, n. *wa-* (1) a slack, idle, lazy person; (2) one who is tiresome, a bore. **Ukulivu**, n. (1) being tired, remissness, yielding; (2) oppressiveness, being overwhelming or too much, &c. (Cf. *-kuu, -kubwa, -kuukuu, tukuka, tukuza*, and *-legevu, -zembe*.)

Kuba,* n. (1) vaulted roof, arched structure, cupola, dome, such as sometimes built over graves of Muhammadan saints or sheiks; (2) see under **Kikuba**. **Kikuba**, n. *vi-* dim. of *kuba*; *-a kikuba*, like a dome, dome-like. (Ar. قبة.)

Kubali,* v. accept, approve, acknowledge, assent (to), agree (to), welcome. Ps. **Kubaliwa.** St. and Pot. **Kubalika,** e.g. be acceptable, be capable of acceptance. Prep. **Kubalia,** accept from (about, at, &c.). Cs. **Kubalisha,** force to accept, procure acceptance by, win over, persuade, &c. Rp. **Kubaliana,** be on good terms. **Kabuli,** n. also **Kibali, Ikibali,** and **Ukubali.** (1) acceptance, sanction, favour, assent. **Takabali,** v. same as *kubali.* (Cf. *pokea, patana, kiri, ridhi, idhini.* Ar. قبل.)

Kubaza,* v. swell out, belly out, as of a sail filled with wind, &c. (? Cs. made from Pers. کُب a rising, swelling, cf. also *mkoba* and *koba.*)

Kubazi,* n. *ma-* a kind of sandal with ornamental work on the front. (Cf. *kiatu, koshi, mtalawanda, ndara.* ? Ar. مكعب kind of shoe (often treated as a plur., and عز magnificent, &c.)

-kubwa, a. (1) great, big, large, spacious, extensive, e.g. *nyumba kubwa,* a large house. *Shamba kubwa,* an extensive estate, a large plantation. *Kisu kikubwa,* a large knife. (2) great in power (influence, rank, importance, &c.), important, significant. *Bwana mkubwa, bibi mkubwa,* is a usual term of respectful address or reference. *Neno limekuwa kubwa halikataliki,* this has become urgent, it cannot be met with a negative. *Asiyesikia mkubwa huona makubwa,* he who disregards a superior usually finds serious consequences. (3) elder, oldest, e.g. *ndugu yangu mkubwa* (or simply *mkubwa wangu*), my elder brother. (4) *-kubwa* is used with a noun or another adjective simply to intensify its meaning, as having a quality in a marked way or high degree, like the adv. *sana,* e.g. *mwizi mkubwa,* a regular thief. *Mtu huyu ni mlevi mkubwa,* this fellow is an utter drunkard. **Mkubwa,** n. *wa-* superior, chief, manager, director, &c. **Ukubwa,** n. greatness, whether (1) materially; big, bulky, huge, or (2) morally; high, powerful, important, weighty. (Cf. *-kuu, kua, tukuza.*)

Kubwebwe, adv. *kupiga kubwebwe,* to throw with a sling. (Cf. *kombeo, panda, teo.*)

Kucha, n. *ma-* amplic. of *ukucha,* and its plur.

Kucha, v. Infin. of *cha,* v.

Kuchewa, see under **Cha,** v. (A) and (B).

Kuchi, n. kind of fowl; the cocks are used in some places as fighting-cocks.

Kuchwa, see under **Chwa,** v.

Kudu,* n. (1) worthiness of blame because of not treating a person with the respect to which he is entitled (Ar. قود requital); (2) a kind of fish.

Kudura,* n. strength, power, might —but only in reference to God, i.e. *kudura ya Mungu,* the power, might of God. **Makadara,** n. strength, power, influence. (Cf. *nguvu, uwezo.* Ar. قدر.)

Kufuli,* n. (— and *ma-*) a padlock. (Cf. *kitasa.* Ar. قفل.)

Kufuru,* v. See under **Kafiri.**

Kugesi, n. anklets, also **Kigesi, Kigezi.**

Kuguni, n. See **Kongoni.**

Kuhani,* n. *ma-*. See under **Kahini.**

Kuje? interrog. (colloquial) How goes it? How's things? See under **Kuko.**

Kuke, n. also **Kuuke, Kuukeni,** see under **-ke, a.**

Kuko, (1) n. a. and adv. that, there, that there, e.g. *huko ni kuzuri,* that is nice there. *Kupika kuko kwapendeza,* that way of cooking pleases. *Kwenda kuko,* to go yonder. So, *kwa kuko, -a kuko, kuko huko,* just there, on that spot. (2) verb-form, there is there, there is, it is there. **Kukoje?** interrog. (colloquial) How are things? How is that place?

Kuku, n. (1) a fowl, hen. *Mtoto wa* (*mwana wa, kinda la*) *kuku,* a chicken, also *faranga, kifaranga. Koo la kuku,* a breeding-fowl. **Kuku ziwa,** n. the African moorhen, *Gallinula chloropus,* also applied to other water-fowl; (2) n. a. and adv. this here, this, here, e.g. in the phrase, *kuku huku,* just here, in this very place. (Cf. *kuko.*)

Kukurika,* v. (1) be anxious, distressed, excited, busy oneself; (2) wrestle, struggle. **Kukuru,** n. (1) anxiety, distress; (2) wrestling, struggling. (Cf. *kakara, hangaika, shughulika.* Ar. كركر.)

Kukusa, v. (1) be neglectful, superficial, flighty, inattentive; (2) attempt to remove a difficulty or a quarrelsome person, &c. (Cf. *puruka.*)

Kukuta, v. (1) shake off water after getting wet, as a bird or dog (cf. *kung'uta*); (2) pant for breath. (Cf. *tweta, hema.*) Dur. **Kukutaa,** be dry, hard, stiff. St. **Kukutika,** be dry, i.e. have the water shaken off. **Kukutu,** adv. e.g. *kukauka kukutu,* to be absolutely dry (or hard).

-kukuu, a. sometimes heard for *-kuukuu.*

Kula,* a. sometimes heard for *kila,* which see.

Kulabu,* n. a hook, hooked instrument, grapnel, of various kinds. Used for holding work in position, e.g. by tailor, blacksmith, and on board ship, for fastening clothes, &c. *Ulimi wangu umetiwa kulabu, hauwezi kunena,* my tongue has had a hook put in it, it cannot speak. (Cf. *ndoana, kiopoo, upembo, ngoe.* Ar. كلاب.)

Kulasitara, n. applied to certain species of Heron, perhaps strictly to the Black Heron, *Melanophoyx ardesiaca,* from its habit of spreading its wings, when seizing its prey. (Cf. *la,* v., and *setiri.*)

Kule, used as (1) n. 'that' used indefinitely, *kule ni mbali,* that is a long way off; (2) a form of *-le,* agreeing with Infin. or noun in *ku-*; (3) adv. there, in (from, to) that position, &c. Sometimes reduplicated *kule kule,* just there. Also pronounced *kule-e-e,* the final vowel raised in pitch and prolonged in proportion to the distance indicated.

Kuli,* n. *ma-* a labourer on a wharf or on board ship. (Hind. قلي Eng. coolie.)

Kulia, v. (1) see under **Kua, v.;** (2) *lia,* prep. form of *la,* v.

Kulihali,* adv. i.e. *kila hali,* in all circumstances, in any case. (Ar.)

Kuliko, relative verb-form (1) that which is, which is, referring to Infin. e.g. *kufa kuliko bora,* the mode of dying which is best; (2) where there is, the *ku,* of general reference, e.g. *peponi kuliko raha,* in Paradise where there is rest; (3) esp. common in comparisons 'than' after an adjective, 'where there is' being equivalent to 'as compared with', e.g. *yeye mkubwa kuliko nduguye,* he is bigger (taller, older) than his brother; also (4) in the general sense, 'as to, as regards', e.g. *kuliko bei ya vitu,* as regards the price of things.

-kulivu, a. See under **Kua, v.**

Kulula,* v. beat, surpass, excel. (Cf. *shinda, pita.* Ar. كلال?)

Kululu, n. *ma-* (1) a large kind of cowrie, a tiger-cowrie, so little valued that it is used in the expression, *fulani amepata kululu,* so-and-so has got something of no value; (2) a kind of insect rather like a grasshopper which burrows into the earth.

Kulungu, n. a species of antelope, bushbuck, the female is called *mbawala.*

Kuma, n. vagina. (Cf. *uke, utupu, kisimi, ubikira, kizinda.*)

Kumba, n. *ma-* (1) i.e. *kuti la kumba,* a whole coco-nut leaf with the fronds plaited all along each side of the central rib. Used for light fences, and enclosures, back-yards. (2) see under *kumba,* v. (Cf. *kuti.*)

Kumba, v. (A) push, shove, press

against, jostle, attack, e.g. *alikumbwa na simba,* he was sprung upon by a lion. St. and Pot. **Kumbika.** Cs. **Kumbiza,** e.g. push off on to, transfer to. *Adamu alimkumbizia mkewe,* Adam put it off on his wife. Rp. **Kumbana,** jostle each other, hustle. (Cf. *sukuma.*) **Kikumbo,** n. *vi-* a thrust, shove, jostling. *Piga kikumbo,* thrust away, shove aside, push by, nudge with the elbow. *Pigana vikumbo,* of rough hustling, horseplay. **Kumbo,** n. *ma-* same as *kikumbo.* **Mkumbizi,** n. *wa-* a rough hustling, jostling fellow. **Ukumbizi,** n. a pushing off, thrusting aside.

Kumba, v. (B), clear out, take away all, make a clean sweep (of), glean, bail out water (as from a boat), *kumba maji.* Sweep out a place and collect rubbish, *kumba taka. Walikumba biashara yote ya tumbako,* they monopolized the whole traffic in tobacco. Ps. **Kumbwa.** St. and Pot. **Kumbika.** Prep. **Kumbia,** e.g. *mwizi amenikumbia mali,* a thief has carried off everything I had. **Mkumbizi,** n. *wa-* one who cleans up, makes a sweep of anything, a gleaner. **Kumba,** n. *-a kumbakumba,* miscellaneous, promiscuous, of all and any sort. **Mkumbo,** n. *mi-* a sweeping clean, a thorough removal, wholesale devastation, a cleaning off. **Kumbo,** n. *ma-* devastation, depopulation, wholesale destruction. **Ukumbizi,** n. (*kumbizi*), a cleaning away, sweeping up, making a clean sweep.

Kumbakumba, a. See under **Kumba,** v. (B).

Kumbati, n. See **Kombati.**

Kumbatia, v. clasp in the arms, embrace. **Kumbatiwa.** St. **Kumbatika.** Cs. **Kumbatisha.** Rp. **Kumbatiana,** embrace each other. **Kikumbatio,** n. *vi-* an embrace. (Prob. Prep. of Ten. form of *kumba,* v. (A), with restricted meaning. Cf. *shika, pambaja.*)

Kumbe, adv. expressing astonishment, pleasant or unpleasant, surprise, esp. of something happening the reverse of what was expected. Lo and behold! What do you think! For a wonder, all of a sudden.

Kumbi, n. *ma-* also **Kumvi** (1) the fibrous husk or sheath of various plants, esp. of the coco-nut, arecanut, &c. *Kumbi* is used collectively (i.e. of the material generally), but the plur. is commonly used. Single fibres are called *uzi* (plur. *nyuzi*). husks are commonly buried in pits on the shore or in a wet place, till the fibres are loosened. They are then taken up, beaten out, and cleaned, and are called *makumbi ya usumba.* (2) or *ukumbi,* a name for the initiation or circumcision school. (Cf. *jando.*)

Kumbikumbi, n. white ants in the flying stage, when they first issue in swarms from the ground. Some people catch them, roast them, and eat them as a relish. (Cf. *mchwa.*)

Kumbo, n. See under **Kumba,** v. (A) and (B).

-kumbufu, a. See under **Kumbuka.**

Kumbuka, v. call to mind, remember, think of, bear in mind, brood over, i.e. mental attention directed usually to the past, or a subject connected with it. Ps. **Kumbukwa.** Prep. **Kumbukia,** direct the memory (or, attention) to. *Silikumbukii,* I do not recall it. *Amenikumbukia kitabu changu,* he recollected my book for me, reminded me of it. Cs. **Kumbusha,** remind, put in mind (of). (Cf. *fahamu,* of memory, and *tambua* of recognition.) **-kumbufu,** a. having a good memory, thoughtful. **Kumbuko,** n. *ma-* (1) memory. *Ana makumbuko mengi ya kale,* he has many memories of ancient times. (2) in the Sing. faculty of memory, e.g. *ana kumbuko zuri,* he has a good memory. **Kumbukumbu,** n. (— and *ma-*) mention, remembrance, memorial, parting gift, souvenir, anything that recalls another thing to mind. *Kumbukumbu ile imeniacha kufikiri kwetu,* that incident (smell, tune, &c.) made me think of home. **Kumbusho,** n. *ma-* something which recalls to mind, a reminder, memorial, souvenir. **Ukumbuko,** n. *ma-* a calling to mind, remembering. **Ukumbusho,** n. same as *kumbusho.*

Kumbwaya, n. (1) a kind of drum standing on legs. *Ngoma ya kumbwaya,* is a special kind of dance, the *kumbwaya* drum, however, is used in other dances. (2) a *kanzu* without sleeves.

Kumbwe, n. *ma-* a snack, a mouthful of food, a taste. Colloquial. *Kumbwe na kinyweo,* something to eat and drink.

Kumi, n. and adv. (plur. *ma-*) ten, the highest simple numeral of Bantu origin used in Swahili. Also used of the three divisions of a month, a decade. *Kumi la kwanza (la kati, la mwisho),* the first (middle, last) decade. *-a kumi,* tenth. **Kikumi,** n. *vi-* the word adopted for a ten-cent piece, i.e. a piece worth ten (cents). (Cf. *kitano* for a five-cent piece.)

Kumoja, n. See under **Moja.**

Kumpuni, n. See **Kampani.**

Kumunta, v. same as *kung'uta,* v. which is more usual.

Kumunto, n. same as *kung'uto,* which is more usual.

Kumvi, n. *ma-* also plur. of *ukumvi.* See **Kumbi.**

Kuna, v. scratch. Used of allaying irritation rather than laceration or wounding (cf. *papura, piga makucha*), e.g. *kuna kichwa,* scratch the head. *Kuna ngozi,* scratch the skin. Also of coarse grating, e.g. *kuna nazi,* grate a coco-nut, i.e. extract the nutty part from the shell with an instrument called *mbuzi.* Ps. **Kunwa.** Prep. **Kunia,** e.g. *mbuzi ya kukunia nazi,* a coco-nut grater. **Kuno,** n. *ma-* what is produced by scraping, a scraping. *Makuno ya nazi,* grated coco-nut. **Mkuno,** n. *mi-* act (method, time, &c.) of scratching, scraping, grating. (Cf. *kunyua,* prob. a Cv. form.)

Kuna, verb-form. (1) there is, there are (*ku* of general reference); (2) it has, they have, *ku* agreeing with Infin. The negative form *hakuna* is one of the commonest expressions for a simple negative, 'there is not, nothing, no'. *Kuna nini?* What is there? What is the matter? *Kunako,* there is (there), that is so, in reference to the query *kuna?* *Kufa kuna maumivu,* death involves suffering. *Kuna* supplies one way of expressing abstract existence. *Kuna Mungu?* Is there a God? Does God exist? *Kunaye,* He exists. Also *kunaye* may mean 'it depends on him' (it is with him).

Kunazi,* n. *ma-* the small edible fruit of the tree *mkunazi,* the Chinese date or jujube tree, *Zizyphus jujuba.* **Kikunazi,** n. *vi-* (obscene) a euphemism for part of the female genital organ. (Pers. قونج.)

Kunda, n. *ma-* (1) a green vegetable like spinach (cf. *mchicha, mayugwa*); (2) a kind of pigeon. (Cf. *njiwa, hua.*)

Kundaa, v. be short, stunted, small of stature, dwarfed, e.g. *mtu aliyekundaa,* a stunted man, a dwarf. (Cf. *via.*)

Kunde, n. plur. of *ukunde,* a kind of bean, produced by the plant *mkunde,* which see.

Kundi, n. *ma-* a number of things (usually living things) together, crowd, troop, group, flock, herd, swarm, &c. *Makundi makundi,* in troops, in large bodies, in masses. **Kikundi,** n. *vi-* dim. (Cf. *umati, kusanyiko, kikosi, jeshi.*)

Kunga, n. (— and *ma-*). See under **Kunga,** v. (A) and (B).

Kunga, v. (A), used of various processes of sewing, hem, make a border trim, embroider, e.g. *kunga mshono,* make a stitched seam on band. *Kunga nguo,* put a border, trimming, or stitched edge to a cloth. *Kunga utepe,* with similar meaning. Ps. **Kungwa.** Prep. **Kungia.**

Kunga, v. (B) teach confidential matters, i.e. in the *jando*. **Kunga,** n. (— and *ma-*) (1) a secret, wile, subterfuge, trick, device, e.g. *kunga za moyo,* secret thoughts, private reflections. *Mtumi wa kunga haambiwi maana,* he who conveys a secret message is not told its meaning. *Kazi haifai ila kwa kunga,* work is no good, unless you have been taught the art. (2) esp. of confidential and private instruction on matters unfit for open mention, e.g. sexual subjects, sometimes called *malango* and *mizungu,* or *kunga za mwituni* (*za nyumbani, za jandoni, za miyomboni*). **Kungwi,** n. *ma-* is the person who assists in giving teaching in the initiation school. The circumciser is called *ngariba,* the assistants *makungwi.* **Mkunga,** n. *wa-* (1) a midwife, sometimes called *mzalishi*; (2) confidential adviser, esp. an older friend who gives advice to unmarried women, and makes all arrangements for them at the time of their marriage, receiving various fees and presents from the bridegroom for doing so. (Cf. *somo.*) **Ngungwi,** n. same as *kungwi* above. **Ukunga,** n. the work (pay, art, &c.) of a midwife, midwifery. **Ukungwi,** n. the work (pay, art, &c.) of a *kungwi,* see above. (Cf. *siri, msiri, nyakanga, mshongo.*)

Kunge, n. (A) mist rising from the ground, fog. **Kungu,** n. also **Ukungu,** mist, fog, haze.

Kunge, n. (B) the hard centre of a tree. (Cf. *ngarange.*)

Kungu, n. *ma-* (1) an edible stone fruit from the tree *mkungu.* The stone contains a kernel rather like an almond, of which children are fond. (Cf. *mkungu.*) (2) a large cooking-pot (cf. *chungu*) capable of holding more than 2 *pishi*; (3) a kind of fish considered good eating by Europeans; (4) see under **Kunge,** n. (A); (5) see **Kulungu.**

Kungugu, n. mist, fog. (Cf. *ukungu, kungu.*)

Kungumanga, n. a nutmeg, fruit of the *mkungumanga.* (Lit. the Arabian *kungu,* cf. *manga.*)

Kunguni, n. a bug. **Kunguni mgunda,** n. a kind of insect which attacks the roots of growing crops.

Kunguru, n. *ma-* (1) a carrion crow, black with white on the back and shoulders, Pied crow, *Corvus albus*; (2) a kind of checked cotton material.

Kung'uta, v. (1) shake out, shake off, sift by shaking, winnow; (2) test severely, scrutinize, examine; (3) fig. beat severely, e.g. *kung'uta mavumbi* (*mvua*), shake off the dust (rain). *Jikung'uta,* shake oneself. *Kung'uta mabawa,* shake out the feathers, of a bird basking in the sun. *Walilipeleka jamvi uani wakalikung'uta,* they took the matting into the yard and they shook it. **Kung'uto,** n. *ma-* a kind of basket used as a sieve, or for tossing and winnowing grain. **Mkung'uto,** n. *mi-* a shaking off, a sifting, a beating off, i.e. of chaff, dust, &c. (Cf. *kumunta, kumunto,* and *pepeta.*)

Kunguwala, v. also **Kungwala,** v. stumble, strike the foot against a stone, &c. (Cf. *kwaa.*)

Kungwi, n. *ma-*. See under **Kunga,** v. (B).

Kungwia, n. a kind of dance.

Kuni, n. plur. of *ukuni,* firewood.

Kunja, v. fold, wrap up, crease, wrinkle, tumble, make a mess of, e.g. *kunja uzi,* wind up thread. *Kunjakunja uzi,* tangle thread. *Kunja uso,* knit the brows, frown. *Kunja mabawa,* fold the wings. *Jikunja,* shrink, cower, flinch. *Kisu cha kukunja,* a clasp-knife. Ps. **Kunjwa.** St. and Pot. **Kunjika,** e.g. be folded be easy to fold, admit of folding. Prep. **Kunjia,** e.g. wrap up for (with, in, &c.). Cs. **Kunjisha.** Rp. **Kunjana,** e.g. *nguo imekunjana kwa upepo,* the cloth has been ruffled up by the wind. Stc. **Kunjama,** seldom used, but the Rp. **Kunjamana** is common: be folded, wrinkled, creased, e.g. *kukunjamana uso*, knit the brows, frown, and so, *uso umekunjamana*. Cv. **Kunjua**, unfold, unwrap, smooth out, spread open. *Kunjua nguo*, lay out a cloth. *Kunjua miguu*, stretch the legs out. *Kunjua uso*, smooth the brows, smile, look pleased. *Jikunjua*, be cordial, be open. Ps. **Kunjuliwa**. St. and Pot. **Kunjuka**. Prep. **Kunjulia**. **Kikunjo**, n. *vi-* a crease, a fold, hem, &c. **Kunjo**, n. *ma-* fold, wrinkle, crease, e.g. *makunjo ya mshipi*, the folds (i.e. loops) of a fishing-line. **-kunjufu**, a. open, serene, unclouded genial, amiable, merry. *Mtu mkunjufu*, a genial man. So with *uso* (face), *moyo* (heart, temper). **Mkunjo**, n. *mi-* a folding, a creasing, a turning over, a fold. **Ukunjufu**, n. cheerfulness, gladness, good temper, geniality (of mind and manner). (Cf. *pinda, kunyanzi, kunyata*, and *changamka*, and Pers. كنج wrinkle, pleat, &c.)

Kuno, n. *ma-*. See under **Kuna**.

Kunradhi,* v. a common phrase of polite apology—pardon me, excuse me, by your leave, no offence meant. Often strengthened by *sana*. *Kunradhi sana*, with your kind permission, I humbly beg pardon. (Cf. equivalent *uwe* (or *mwe radhi*), and *radhi, utafadhali*. Ar. كون راض be content.)

Kununu, n. *ma-* empty husk or spike of grain, i.e. *kununu la mawele*, a spike of bullrush-millet with no grain on it. (Cf. *pepe*.)

Kunyanzi, n. *ma-* a fold, wrinkle, crease. (Cf. *kunja, kunyata*.)

Kunyata, v. draw together, cause to shrink, compress. Seldom occurs except with Rf. *ji*, in the sense of cower, shrink together, esp. as an attitude of fear, pain, or supplication. *Jikunyata kama maskini*, humble oneself like a beggar. *Jikunyata kwa baridi*, double up with cold. *Jikunyata uso*, have an offended, disgusted look. (Cf. *kunja, kunyanzi*.)

Kunyua, v. (1) scratch at, give a scratch to, e.g. to hurt or to attract notice; (2) call by a secret sign, give a private hint to, &c. *Kunyua kidole*, hurt the finger, by a scratch, implying more than a simple *kuna*, scratch. (3) bite a piece off. Ps. **Kunyuliwa**. St. and Pot. **Kunyuka**, e.g. *kunyuka kwa mti*, get scratched by a tree in passing it. (Cf. *papura, piga mtai*. A Cv. form of Cs. of *kuna*, v.)

Kuo, n. *ma-* (1) furrow, trench, hollow, hole, i.e. made by hollowing out. *Makuo ya kuku*, holes scratched by fowls. Usu. (2) a bed or row of seedlings, &c.; (3) a plot of ground marked out by a furrow or line drawn on the ground, and given to a man to cultivate. (Cf. *ngwe*, same marked by a cord.) Hence *nyosha kuo*, mark out on piece of ground; *ongeza* (*punguza*) *kuo*, enlarge (reduce) a plantation. (Cf. *shimo, koongo, handaki, mfuo*.)

Kupa,* n. *ma-* one of the side-pieces forming a pulley (*kapi, gofia*), enclosing the sheave (*roda*). (Cf. *korodani*. Ar. قب cross-beam of pulley or its axle-hole.)

Kupe, n. a cattle- or dog-tick. *Kama kupe na mkia wa ng'ombe*, like a tick and a cow's tail—of things adhering closely. The spirillum tick is *papasi*.

Kupia, v. (1) wink, blink, the eye; (2) nod from drowsiness. (Cf. *pesa, kopesa, pepesa*.)

Kupua, v. (1) shake out, shake off, throw off, let fall, drop on the ground (by a push, jerk, &c.), e.g. *kupua nguo*, throw off the clothes. *Kupua mbu*, drive off mosquitoes. (2) spill, pour out, e.g. *kupua wino*, spill ink; (3) hit or strike (as with a stick), e.g. *alimkupua mkwaju wa mgongo*, he hit him on the back with tamarind stick. Ps. **Kupuliwa**. St. and Pot. **Kupuka**, (1) e.g. fig. be cast off, be a fugitive (outcast); (2)

get up or go out with a rush. **Mkupuo,** n. *mi-* (1) a shove, push, shaking or pushing off, a getting rid of, or letting drop; (2) fig. water or food which is able to be swallowed in one gulp, a gulp. **Mkupuzi,** n. *wa-* one who pushes, shoves, hits, &c., one given to horse-play.

Kura,* n. a lot, i.e. in casting lots. *Piga kura,* cast lots. (Ar. قرع.)

Kurani,* n. See **Korani.**

Kurea, n. a small bird—grey kingfisher, also called *mtilili, kizamiadagaa, kisharifu.*

Kuro, n. a water-buck.

Kuru,* n. (1) a solid cylindrical body, hollowed is *mzinga*; (2) the side of a Zanzibar pice (coin) on which is depicted a pair of scales or balances. (Ar. كرة ball, round body.)

Kuruba,* n. a bend, e.g. in a road, &c. (Cf. *kombo.* Ar. عقرب make crooked.)

Kurubia,* v. and **Kurubisha,** sometimes heard for *karibia, karibisha,* which see.

Kurumbizi, n. the Golden Oriole, *Oriolus oriolus.* (Cf. *kirumbizi* and *umbia.*)

Kurupuka, v. be startled, roused, surprised, e.g. as of animals hearing a noise, &c. Cs. **Kurupusha,** startle, rouse. *Jikurupusha,* rouse oneself.

Kurunzi,* n. a searchlight, also used for an electric torch. (Ar. قرص disk of sun or moon.)

Kururu, n. small white crabs, many of which are usu. seen on the beach.

Kuruta, v. smooth by rubbing, esp. of cleaning or smoothing rope after it has been twisted. (Cf. *guruta.*)

Kuruwiji, n. the Zanzibar Sombre bulbul, *Andropadus insularis.*

Kusa, v., **Kusanya,** v., **Kusanyiko,** n. *ma-*, **Kusanyo,** n. *ma-*. See under **Kuta,** v. (A).

Kushoto, n. and adv. the left side, the left-hand position. *Mkono wa kushoto,* the left hand, as opp. to *mkono wa kuume* (*wa kulia*). *Kaa kushotoni,* sit on the left side. (Cf. *ku* in *kumoja, kuzimu, kuke,* &c.)

Kusi,* n. southerly wind, south monsoon—prevailing from May to October approx. Hence also of the season, and of the southerly direction. *Kusini,* the south quarter, to (from, in) the south. *-a kusini,* of the south, southerly. Contr. *kaskazi,* the north wind, &c. (Prob. a very ancient word dating from the early days of trading on the east coast, and perh. from the same source as Cush, in Hebrew mythology the first son of Ham, and used for the peoples regarded as his descendants, and the land in which they lived, i.e. it was used for Ethiopia, the whole country south of Egypt. In Assyrian this word was Kusu and Kos in Egyptian. The earliest travellers travelling to the regions south of Egypt would probably regard themselves as going to, and into Kush, Kos, Kusu, &c.)

Kustabani,* n. a thimble, also heard as *kastabini* and *subana.* (Ar. كستبان.)

Kusudi,* v. intend, purpose, propose, design, aim at, usu. in the Prep. **Kusudia,** with the same sense. *Kusudia safari,* resolve on an expedition. *Kusudia kwenda,* intend to go. Ps. **Kusudiwa.** St. **Kusudika.** Cs. **Kusudisha. Kusudi,** n. *ma-*, **Makusidio,** n. intention, purpose, aim, object, end. *Kwa kusudi,* on purpose, intentionally, deliberately, wilfully. (Cf. *kwa moyo, kwa nafsi.*) **Kusudi,** adv. also **Makusudi,** like *kwa kusudi.* And as conj. with Infin. or Subjunct. on purpose to, in order that (to), with the object of, e.g. *aliondoka kusudi aende* (or *kwenda*) *Ulaya,* he started with the intention of going to Europe. (Cf. *shauri, maana, nia, mradi.* Ar. قصد.)

Kusuru,* v. (A) accomplish by effort, difficulty, self-denial, deny oneself anything in order to gain an object. (Ar. قسر force, compel.)

Kusuru,* v. (B) shorten, e.g. as of

a Muhammadan saying more than one of the prescribed prayers at one time, i.e. *kusali kusuru*. (Cf. *kasa, kasoro*. Ar. قصر.)

Kuta, n. plur. of *ukuta*.

Kuta, v. (A) come upon, meet (with), chance on, hit on, find. *Nilimkuta hawezi* (*hayuko*), I found him ill (absent). *Kuta mashaka*, meet with (experience) difficulties. Ps. **Kutwa**. St. **Kutika**. Prep. **Kutia**. Cs. **Kutisha**, also sometimes **Kusha** and **Kusa**, cause to come on, bring upon, involve in. *Nimemkusa mashaka*, I have got him into trouble. Rp. **Kutana**, meet together, assemble, collect, hold a meeting, be crowded. (Cf. *songa, barizi*.) *Jeshi limekutana*, the crowd is dense, or has met together. *Nilikutana naye mjini*, I met him in the town. St. **Kutanika**, be met together, be assembled, meet. D.Cs. (from *kusa*) **Kusanya**, collect, gather together, bring together, assemble, amass, make a pile or heap of, e.g. *kusanya watu*, collect people. *Kusanya jeshi*, form an army. *Kusanya mali*, amass wealth. Ps. **Kusanywa**. St. **Kusanyika**, be gathered together. Rp. **Kusanyana**, e.g. meet together by common consent. **Kikuti**, n. *vi-* chance, hap, luck, an incident, occurrence. *Kikuti chema*, a happy chance, happening. **Kusanyo**, n. *ma-*, **Kusanyiko**, n. *ma-* a collecting together, gathering, crowd, &c. **Kutano**, n. *ma-* a meeting together, meeting, &c. **Mkusanya**, n. *wa-* a collector, a gatherer together, convener. **Mkusanyo**, n. *mi-* a gathering together, meeting, &c. **Mkutano**, n. *mi-* (1) meeting, gathering, council, committee, &c.; (2) confluence, concurrence, coincidence. **Mkuto**, n. *mi-* (1) a meeting with, a lighting upon, a finding; (2) a fold, like *kunjo*. *Kunja nguo mkuto*, fold up a dress.

Kuta, v. (B) *kuta mayai*, lay eggs. (Cf. *taga*.)

Kuta, v. (C) become satisfied with food. (Cf. *shiba*, which is more common.)

Kutaa, v. wither, dry up, as of grass in the hot dry season. (Cf. *nyauka, kauka*.)

Kutana, v., **Kutano**, n. *ma-*. See under **Kutana**, v. (A).

Kuti, n. *ma-* (1) a coco-nut leaf, whether green or dry; (2) a coco-nut leaf prepared for use in different ways, e.g. (*a*) *kuti la kumba* (and *fumba*), the whole leaf with the fronds on either side simply plaited together, used in making light fences, enclosures, shelters of any kind; (*b*) *kuti la pande*, with the fronds all plaited together on one side, similarly used; (*c*) *kuti la viungo*, lengths of the leaf-rib (*upongoo*) or of stick about 3 ft. long with all the fronds attached to it and brought to one side. These form the usual roofing material of native houses on the coast where coco-nut trees grow, and are a regular article of sale. **Kikuti**, n. *vi-* dim. **Ukuti**, n. (*kuti*) a side frond of the coco-nut leaf. (Cf. *mnazi*. Ar. خضرة verdure, vegetation.)

Kutu, n. rust. *Chuma kimeota* (*kimefanya*) *kutu*, the iron has become rusty.

Kutua, v. also **Gutua** give a jerk to, pull suddenly, cause a shock to, dislocate. *Kutua kamba*, jerk a rope. St. **Kutuka**, e.g. fig. be shaken, startled, frightened, shocked. Cs. **Kutusha**, startle, frighten. **Mkutuo**, n. *mi-* a jerk, fright, shock. (Cf. *kupua, shtuka, tuka*.)

Kutuzi, n. evil smelling perspiration, such as that of some people's armpits, also called *kikwapa*.

-kuu, a. great. Seldom simply 'big', i.e. of merely physical size or material greatness, but implying some moral or sentimental element of pre-eminence, authority, and excellence. *-kubwa*, on the other hand, means 'big, large, extensive', though also used to include and denote the natural effects of great size, i.e. authority, weight, influence, impressiveness. Thus (1) 'great, powerful, having natural or representative authority', &c. *Wakuu kwa vijana*, is a common contrast, 'old and young, great and small' (also *wakubwa kwa wadogo*). (Cf. *mkuu* below.) *Bustani kuu*, a great (grand, fine) garden. *Kiazi kikuu*, a yam, often of great size in East Africa. (2) noble, pre-eminent, high-class, excellent, influential; (3) over-great, presuming on greatness, excessive, unnatural, outrageous, beyond the proper bounds of a decorum (self-control, human nature), e.g. *maneno makuu*, presumptuous, boastful words *Taka makuu*, aim too high, be over-ambitious. *Piga makuu*, give oneself airs, be arrogant, make a great show. *Hana makuu*, he is unassuming, civil spoken, humble person—sometimes in contrast to *-kuu* in other sense, e.g. *makuu mengi lakini hana makuu*, he has many great qualities, but he never makes too much of them. **Mkuu**, n. *wa-* (1) a great person (in wealth, position, power, &c.), a grandee; (2) ruler, head, master, governor, &c. **Ukuu**, n. greatness—but more in a moral than material sense. (Cf. *kua*.)

Kuuke, n. and **Kuukeni**, n. See under **-ke**, a.

-kuukuu, a. worn out, old, past work, useless from old age. **Kikuukuu**, n. and adv. a worn out thing, old, useless, past work. (Cf. *-kongwe*, *-chakavu*, *-bovu*, and *kua*.)

Kuume, n., **Kuumeni**. See under **-ume**.

Kuungo, n. a small white stone used by potters for smoothing the clay when shaping the articles he is making. (Cf. *finyanga*.)

Kuungu, n. See **Kulungu**.

Kuvu, n. mould, blight. (Cf. *koga*.)

Kuvuli, n. *mkono wa kuvuli*, the right hand—for *mkono wa kuume* or *mkono wa kulia*.

Kuwa, v. Infin. of *wa*, the verb 'to be' which see. Also as a n. being, existence, i.e. of pure existence. *Mwenye kuwa*, the existing one, as a title of God, the Self-existing. Conj. that, and with *kwa* or *ya*, for, because. *Kwa kuwa umefanya hivi, utajuta*, because you have done that you will regret it. *Alisema (ya) kuwa amechoka*, he said that he was tired.

Kuwadi,* n. sometimes heard for *kawadi*, which see.

Kuwi, n. a kind of fish with black and white spots, considered to be good eating by Europeans.

Kuwili, n. and adv. See under **-wili**.

Kuyu, n. the fruit of the *mkuyu*, the fig-mulberry tree.

Kuza, v. (1) see under **Kua**, v.; (2) sometimes heard for *kuuza*, to sell, and for *kuuza* (*kuuliza*), to ask.

-kuza, a. See under **Kua**, v.

kuzi,* n. *ma-* an earthenware pitcher or jug, larger than a *gudulia*, with handle or handles and a narrow neck. (Cf. *mtungi*, *chombo*. Ar. كوز.)

Kuzimu, n. See under **Mzimu**.

Kuzumburu, n. a small bird with a long tail and a crest.

K.v. abbrev. for *kama vile*, such as, for instance.

Kwa, prep. (*ku-* combined with the prepositional element *-a*). This is the most common and comprehensive of the Swahili preps. It is used (*a*) to express with, of the instrument used, likewise any other prep. used in English to indicate the instrument, e.g. *alipigwa kwa jiwe* (or *alipigwa jiwe*), he was struck by a stone. Note: the agent is *na*, e.g. *alipigwa kwa kisu na fulani*, he was struck with a knife by so-and-so. *Tulitazama kwa darubini*, we looked through a telescope. *Nitaufungua kwa ufunguo*, I shall open it with a key. *Andika kwa kalamu na wino*, write with pen and ink. (*b*) Object, purpose, or use—in this connexion it can be generally translated by the word 'for' in English, e.g. *alinijia kwa shauri*, he came to me for advice. *Haifai kwa chakula*, it is no use for food. (*c*) Manner or means, and in this connexion, may be translated by a variety of English words, e.g. *alinijia kwa siri*, he came to me in secret. *Je, ulikwenda kwa gari la moshi au kwa miguu?* Did you travel by train or go on foot? *Andika kwa Kiswahili*, write in Swahili. *Tafsiri kwa Kiingereza*, translate into English. *Nilitambua tabia yake kwa mambo yake*, I knew his character by his actions. (*d*) With a noun denoting a person, it indicates locality, at, to, or from, e.g. *anakaa kwa Ali*, he lives at Ali's place. *Nitakwenda kwa Jumbe*, I shall go to the chief. *Umetoka kwa nani?* From whom have you come? *Barua imetoka kwa ndugu yangu*, a letter has come from my brother. *Toka kwa fulani*, come from so-and-so's place. *Kaa kwa fulani*, remain or live at so-and-so's place. Note: *kwa* cannot be used with proper names of places, e.g. *ninakwenda kwa Ali akaaye Mombasa*, I am going to Ali who lives at Mombasa, but, *ninakwenda Mombasa anapokaa Ali*, I am going to Mombasa where Ali lives. (*e*) Frequently used with the invariable part of the Poss. Pron. i.e. *kwangu, kwako, kwake*, &c., indicating place, circumstances, &c., e.g. *kwao hawana njaa*, where they live (at their place) they have no famine (or, shortage of food). *Kwetu kuzuri*, our place (circumstances, &c.) is pleasant. (*f*) *Kwa* is commonly used to form adverbs and conjunctions from nouns, verb infinitives, and even pronouns, e.g. *kwa hila*, stealthily, sneakingly. *Kwa siri*, privately. *Kwa kutambaatambaa*, creepingly. *Kwa kuwa* (*sababu, ajili, hiyo*), because. *Kwa sababu* (*ajili*) *ya*, because of. *Kwa haraka*, in haste, hastily. *Kwa habari hizi*, at (about, on account of) these news. *Wakastaajabu kwa maneno yake*, and they were astonished at his words. (*g*) Sometimes it may be translated as 'always', e.g. *alikula* (*chakula*) *kile kwa kile*, he always ate the same sort of food, i.e. never changed his diet, as opp. to, *alikula* (*chakula*) *kile kile*, he ate that same (i.e. very) food. (*h*) With Interrog. *Kwa nini?* Why? *Kwa sababu gani?* Why? (*i*) With fractions and percentages: *kumi kwa moja*, ten to one. *Tano kwa nane*, five-eighths. *Mia kwa tano* (*kumi*, &c.). Five (ten, &c.) per cent. (*j*) Sometimes it may be translated as—with, and, as well as, e.g. *wali kwa mchuzi*, rice with gravy. *Wakubwa kwa wadogo, wanawake kwa wanaume*, great and small, women as well as men.

Kwaa, v. (1) strike the foot (against an object), stumble, knock, be stopped by a sudden obstacle; (2) fig. falter, hesitate, be brought to a stop or check, get into difficulty. *Kwaa na jiwe* or *jiweni*, knock the foot against a stone. Prov. *Heri kukwaa kidole kuliko kukwaa ulimi*, better the stumble with the toe than the tongue. Cs. **Kwaza**, cause to stumble, make difficulties for, &c. Also Inten. *dau limekwaza maweni*, the boat struck hard on the rocks. Rp. **Kwazana**, knock against each other. Stc. **Kwama**, (1) become jammed, stick fast, come to a deadlock, be gripped, be squeezed; (2) fig. be in a fix, get into difficulties. *Maneno yalimkwama kooni*, the words stuck in his throat. *Mlango umekwama*, the door has stuck fast. Prep. **Kwamia**. Cs. **Kwamisha**, cause to jam, make stick fast, put in difficulty, &c. *Mti huu umenikwamisha mkono*, this tree has got my hand fixed in it. Cv. **Kwamua**, get out of a tight place, set free, disengage, clear, loose. Prep. **Kwamulia**. **Kwao**, n. *ma-*, **Kwazo**, n. *ma-* a stumbling-block, obstruction to the feet. *Njia ya kwao*, a rough road, stony path. (Cf. *kunguwaa, kunguwala, fungwa, naswa, kamatwa, fungua, nanua.*)

Kwa heri! Good-bye! adieu! the usual leave-taking at any time or season. (Cf. *heri.*)

Kwaje? (*kwa je*) How? What way? By what means? &c. *Kwaje hufanya hivi?* How is it you do this, i.e. why, or in what way?

Kwaju, n. See under **Mkwaju.**

Kwajuka, v. lose colour, beauty, shrivel, shrink, become spoiled, be no longer pleasant to the eyes. (Cf. *fifia, chujuka.*)

Kwake, n. (1) his (hers, its) circumstances (position, house, &c.); (2) adv. idiomatic equivalent of *kwa yeye*, to (from, at, with) him (her, it), to his house, &c.; (3) form of a. *-ake*, agreeing with the Infin. and locatives ending in *-ni.*

Kwako, n. adv. and a. same as *kwake*, but relating to 2 Pers. Sing., i.e. *wewe*, you.

Kwakura, v. scratch in the earth. *Simba hukwakura chini, lakini huparura mtu.* When a lion scratches the ground the word *-kwakura* is used: when he scratches a person the word *-parura* is used.

The same action of 'scratching' in each case but expressed by a different word.

Kwale, n. francolin, partridge—including several species.

Kwama, v. See under **Kwaa.**

Kwamba, conj. See under **Amba,** v. (A).

Kwamua, v. See under **Kwaa.**

Kwanga, n. a rock-rabbit. (Cf. *wibari, pelele.*)

Kwangu, n. adv. and a. same as *kwake*, but relating to 1 Pers. Sing.

Kwangua, v. scrape, remove a coating, crust, or anything adhering (solid or liquid), e.g. *kwangua matope*, clean mud off (boot, &c.). *Kwangua chungu*, scrape the burnt off the cooking-pot. *Kwangua kucha*, pare the nails. *Kwangua maji*, scrape up a remnant of water in a waterhole. Prep. **Kwangulia.** (Cf. *komba, paruza.*)

Kwani? slang—(1) adv. interrog. for *kwa nini?* What for? Why? For what reason? (Cf. *mbona.*) (2) conj. for, because. (Cf. *kwa sababu, kwa maana, kwa ajili, kwa kuwa.*)

Kwanua, v. and **Kwanyua,** tear down, rip (split, strip) off, e.g. of branches, leaves, fruit. Ps. **Kwanuliwa.** St. **Kwanuka,** e.g. *panda ya mti imekwanuka kwa mtu mzito*, the fork of the tree has been split down by a heavy man. (Cf. *nyakua, pasua, rarua, ambua.*)

Kwanza, Infin. of *anza*, which see.

Kwao, n. adv. and a. same as *kwake*, but relating to the 3 Pers. Plur.

Kwao, n. *ma-*. See under **Kwaa.**

Kwao, n. Brown-headed parrot, *Poicephalus fuscicapillus.*

Kwapa, n. *ma-* the armpit. *Futika (chukua) kwapani*, tuck (carry) under the arm. *Kisibau cha kwapa*, a sleeveless waistcoat. **Kikwapa,** n. *vi-* (1) same as *kwapa*; (2) the perspiration of the armpit; (3) the smell of the perspiration of the armpit, also called *kutuzi*; (4) the gore or gusset of a native dress, under the armpit.

Kwapua, v. See **Kwepua.**

Kwarara, n. Hadad ibis, *Hagedashia hagedash.*

Kware, n. See **Kwale.**

-kware, a. See under **Ukware.**

Kwaresima,* n. the season of Lent. (A contraction of Quadragesima.)

Kwaru, n. Grosbeak weaver, also called *yombiyombi, katadole.*

Kwaruza, v. (1) scrape, grate, whether of action, movement (scrape along, move with difficulty), or sound (be harsh, be grating); (2) grate, be of a coarse, gritty, rough kind, e.g. *chombo kimekwaruza mwamba*, the vessel has grazed a rock. *Mchele huu unakwaruza*, this rice is gritty to the taste. *Njia ya kukwaruza*, a rough, stony road. **Mkwaruzo,** n. *mi-* (1)

a scraping, a grating; (2) track or trail of something scraping along, i.e. *mkwaruzo wa nyoka*, the trail of a snake. (Cf. *paruza, para, kwangua, kwaza*, and contr. *laini.*)

Kwasi, v. make rich. **-kwasi**, a. rich, wealthy, opulent. **Mkwasi**, n. *wa-* a rich, wealthy person. **Ukwasi**, n. wealth, opulence, riches, the condition of being wealthy. (Cf. *tajiri*, and contr. *maskini, fukara, mkata.*)

Kwata, adv. (1) also *kikwata, piga kwata*, go a long journey, on foot. **Kwata**, n. drill, parade, manœuvre; (2) *kwata jeupe* and *kwata jekundu* are kinds of sweet potatoes. (Cf. *kiazi.*) **Kiatu**, n. *vi-* native shoe, sandal—and used of any kind of shoe. *Kiatu cha ngozi*, leather sandal, flat sole with cross-strap and small thong (*gidamu*) between the toes. (Cf. *kubazi, njuti, staka, ndara, koshi, sapatu.*) *Kiatu cha mti*, a kind of wooden clog, worn indoors, and held on by a peg (*msuruaki*) between the toes. Known as *mtalawanda*, from the wood used. *Kiatu cha kihindi* (*kizungu*), Indian (European) shoe. *Mshona viatu* or *mshoni wa viatu*, a shoemaker. **Kwato**, n. *ma-* also plur. of **Ukwato**, the cloven hoof of an animal. **Liwato**, n. (also sometimes *liwado*), the butt end of a thing, i.e. of a rifle, &c. (Cf. *liwata, nyata.*)

Kwatua, v. clean. *Kwatua shamba*, clean a plantation of weeds. *Jikwatua*, clean oneself, tidy oneself up, make oneself smart and tidy.

Kwaza, v. See under **Kwaa**.

Kwazi, n. a large bird which catches and eats fish, a fish-eagle.

Kwazo, n. *ma-*. See under **Kwaa**.

Kwea, v. go up, get on the top of, mount, climb, ascend, rise, e.g. *kwea mnazi* or *mnazini*, climb a coco-nut tree. *Kwea mlima* (*farasi*), mount a hill (a horse). *Kwea chombo*, get on board a vessel. Ps. **Kwelewa**. St. and Pot. **Kweleka**. Prep. **Kwelea**, e.g. *kamba ya kukwelea*, a rope to climb with. Cs. **Kweza**, cause to go up, set up, raise, put one thing on another. *Kweza mashua*, haul a boat high on the beach. *Kweza bei*, raise the price of an article. *Kweza mataruma ya gurudumu*, set the spokes in a wheel. *Kweza nguo*, lift the dress. *Jikweza*, boast, vaunt oneself. Rp. of Cs. **Kwezana**. (Note: this verb and its derivatives should be used carefully, as in some places they are frequently used in an obscene sense.) **Kwelea**, n. i.e. *kwelea ya mawimbi, mawimbi ya kwelea*, a swell, rolling waves, as dist. from breakers. **Kweleo**, n. *ma-* a peg stuck in a tree, or notch cut in for climbing purposes. **-kwezi**, a. creeping, climbing, e.g. of a plant, &c. **Mkweo**, n. *mi-* a climbing, or mounting up or upon. **Mkwezi**, n. *wa-* one who climbs, mounts up, esp. one who climbs coconut trees to knock down coco-nuts, as a business. **Ukwezi**, n. the work, fee, &c., of a *mkwezi*. (Cf. *panda*, v. and deriv.)

Kweche, n. an old worn-out, broken-down vehicle of any description. (Prob. onomatopoeic.)

Kwekwe, n. (— and *ma-*), weeds. *Lima kwekwe*, weed a plantation or garden.

Kwelea, n. See under **Kwea**.

Kweleo, n. (1) see under **Kwea**; (2) sometimes heard for *koleo*, pliers, pincers, &c.

Kweli, n. and adv. truth, truthfulness, reality, genuineness, certainty. *Kwa kweli si kwa ubishi*, seriously, not in fun. Prov. *Kweli iliyo uchungu si uwongo ulio mtamu*, an unpleasing truth is better than a pleasing falsehood. *-a kweli*, true, truthful, genuine. As adv. truly, really, certainly, genuinely. **Ukweli**, n. truthfulness, &c. (Cf. *hakika, yakini, halisi.*)

Kwembe, n. the Crowned hornbill, *Lophoceros melanoleucos*, also called *fimbi* and *hondo*. **Kwembe maji**, the African Woolly-necked stork, *Dissoura episcopus*.

Kweme, n. seed of the plant *mkweme*, very rich in oil.

Kwenda, v. Infin. of *enda*, which see.

Kwenu, n. adv. and a. same as *kwake*, but relating to the 2 Pers. Plur.

Kwenye, form of *-enye*, which see.

Kwenzi, n. the name applied to the starling, *Sturnidae*.

Kwepua, v. snatch, take by force, steal, filch. **Mkwepuzi**, n. *wa-* a thief, one who steals by snatching and running away. (Cf. *pokonya, bekua, iba*.)

Kwesha, v. fix, make secure, e.g. as of a handle in a hoe, &c.

Kweta, v. shuffle along on the buttocks. (Cf. *sota, sowera, sombera*.)

Kwetu, n. adv. and a. same as *kwake*, but relating to 1 Pers. Plur.

Kweu, n., **Kweupe**, n. See under **Eua**.

-kwezi, a. See under **Kwea**.

Kwikwi, n. hiccup. *Kwikwi ya kulia*, convulsive sobbing. (Cf. *kitefutefu*.)

Kwinini,* n. quinine. (From Eng.)

Kwisha, v. Infin. of *isha*, v. which see.

Kwiu, n. hunger or longing, esp. for meat; meat hunger. (Cf. *kiu, hamu, uchu, shauku, tamaa*.)

K.w.k. abbrev. for *kadha wa kadha*.

L

L represents, as a general rule, the same sound as in English, but it sometimes has cerebral qualities which make it almost like *r*, in fact, the two sounds *r* and *l* can in many cases said to be interchangeable. The same individual may pronounce the same word, sometimes with *l*, and sometimes with *r*, e.g. one hears *lipuka* and *ripuka*, *telemka* and *teremka*, *mpila* and *mpira*, &c. Therefore, words not found under *l* or spelt with an *l*, should be looked for under *r*, or as though spelt with an *r*.

An *l* sound has generally been dropped when a vowel is written twice, and also between two vowels coming together. In the derived forms of verbs based on the Prep. form, the *l* returns *pendea, pendelea, pendeleza*, &c. In some words it is evanescent, e.g. *mlango* or *mwango*; *ufalme* or *ufaume*. For the use of *l* as a prefix, and for the changes which take place when it is preceded by a nasal, the Grammars should be consulted.

La!* int. No! Not so! By no means!. often followed by another negative. *La, hapana*; *la siyo*, &c. (Cf. *siyo, sivyo, hakuna, hapana, hasha*. Ar. لا.)

La, v. (1) eat, consume—of food generally. *Watu walikula*, the people ate. (2) use, use up, require for use or efficiency (as material, time, &c.) (Cf. *tumia, chukua*.) *Itakula fedha* (*saa nzima, siku nyingi*), it will take money (a whole hour, several days). (3) wear away, diminish, spend (materials, means, money). *Kutu inakula chuma*, rust eats (wears away) iron. The Infinitive form *kula* is used as the root-form in certain tenses as is the case with other monosyllabic verb-forms. *La* is rarely used as the imperative, as a rule the Infinitive is used *kula*, sing. *kuleni*, plur. Ps. **Liwa**, be eaten, &c. St. and Pot.

Lika, be eatable, be fit for food, be eaten, be worn through. *Kitu hiki hakiliki*, this substance is not edible. *Chuma kinalika*, iron rusts away, or is being worn down. Prep. **Lia**, eat for (with, in, &c.). *Amemlia mwenzi wali wake*, he has eaten up his friend's rice. *Tumeliana siku zote*, we have always had our meals together. Rf. *jilia*, eat selfishly (for his own purpose, &c.). *Mwana mpotevu amejilia mali ya baba yake*, the prodigal son has wasted his father's goods (like a fool, wilfully). *Mkono wa kulia*, the eating hand, the right hand. *Chumba cha kulia*, the dining-room. *Kijiko cha kulia*, a spoon to eat with. Rp. **Lana**, all join in eating, eat together, eat each other, wear each other away. *Magurudumu haya yanalana*, these two wheels are wearing each other down. Cs. **Lisha**, (1) cause to feed, feed, keep (animals), graze, pasture. *Lisha ng'ombe na mbuzi*, keep (or feed) cows and goats. *Lisha mbuzi majani*, feed the goats on grass. *Watu wanalisha kinu miwa*, people are feeding the sugar-cane into the mill. *Ng'ombe wanalishwa na mchungaji*, the cows are being fed (or tended) by the herdsman. (2) Inten. eat, browse, feed on. *Kondoo kulisha majani*, sheep browse on grass. D.Cs. **Lishisha**, make to eat, feed with. *Lishisha* (or *lishiza*) *sumu*, administer poison to. **Chakula**, n. *vya-* something to eat, food, victuals, provender, a meal, e.g. *kitu cha kula*. *Chakula cha asubuhi*, breakfast, i.e. *chamshakinywa*. *Chakula cha mchana* (*cha adhuhuri*), midday meal, lunch. *Chakula cha jioni*, evening meal, dinner, supper. **Kilaji**, n. *vi-* (1) food; (2) anything that eats, corrodes, &c. **Malaji**, n. plur. food, quality or character of food. **Malisha**, n. plur., and **Malisho**, n. plur. pasturage, grazing-ground, paddock, forage, food for cattle. **Mlisha**, n. *wa-*, **Mlishi**, n. *wa-* (1) one who feeds or has care of animals or other creatures, and hence, fig. (2) leader of a congregation, pastor. **Mlisho**, n. *mi-* (1) a feeding, giving food, rearing, supporting. *Mlisho wa samaki*, baiting for fish. *Mlisho wa mshipi*, putting bait on the fishing-line, bait. (2) name for the month called in Arabic *Sha'ban*, i.e. the month before the fast of Ramadhan. **Mla**, n. *wa-* governed by noun following, an eater, consumer, devourer. *Mla watu*, a cannibal, *mla ng'ombe*, &c. **Mlaji**, n. *wa-* an eater, one addicted to eating certain things. **Mlo**, n. food. **Ulaji**, n. act of eating, customary diet, method of eating. Provs. *Ulacho ndicho chako, kilichobaki ni cha mchimba lindi*, that which you eat is yours, what is left is for the grave-digger (the heir). *Mlaji ni mla leo, mla jana kalani?* The eater is he who eats to-day, the eater of yesterday, what has he eaten? i.e. you can't eat your pie and have it. **Ulio**, n. a platter or vessel to eat from.

Laabu,* v. play with, entertain with. **Leba**, n. deceit, untruthfulness, slyness with intent to deceive. **Lebu**, v. cheat. (Cf. *chezea*, *furahisha*, *teremesha*. Ar. لعب.)

Laana,* n. *ma-* a curse, imprecation, oath. **Laani**, v. curse, swear (at), damn. Ps. **Laaniwa**. St. **Laanika**. Cs. **Laanisha**, cause to curse, get cursed, bring a curse on. **-laanifu**, a. (1) given to cursing; (2) accursed. **Maleuni** and **Maluuni**, the accursed, Satan. (Cf. *Shetani*.) **Mlaanifu**, n. *wa-* (1) like *mlaanizi*, also (2) an accursed person. **Mlaanizi**, n. *wa-* one who curses, swears, uses bad language. **Ulaanifu**, n. a cursing, being cursed. **Ulaanizi**, n. a cursing, character of cursing or using imprecations. (Cf. *apiza*. Ar. لعن.)

Labda,* adv. perhaps, it seems so, no doubt, probably, possibly. *Labda mvua itakunya leo*, perhaps it will rain to-day. (Cf. *yamkini*, *huenda*, *yawezekana*. Ar. لا بد.)

Labeka!* int. also **Lebeka!** At your service! Yes, sir (madam)!—in answer to a call, coming! I am here! A common reply of a slave or inferior to a master's call, and often pronounced *ebe, ebee, labe,* and simply *bee.* (Cf. *saa, inshallah, eewallah.* Ar. لبيك.)

Ladha,* n. the taste or flavour of anything, whether pleasant or unpleasant, but usually the former. (Cf. *onja, harufu.* Ar. لذ.)

Ladu,* n. a sweetmeat made up in hard round balls, consisting of flour or fine grain mixed with treacle, ginger, pepper, &c. (Hind. لدو.)

Lafidhi.* See **Lafudhi.**

Lafua, v. See under **Lapa.**

Lafudhi,* n. accent, pronunciation, style of speech. *Lafudhi ya maneno,* a good accent in speaking. (Cf. *ufasaha, nahau.* Ar. لفظ.)

Laghai,* v. cheat, deceive, beguile, esp. with persuasiveness. **-laghai,** a. and n. deceitful, false, sly, dishonest. As a noun, and also **Mlaghai,** n. *wa-* a cheat, sly dishonest person, one who cheats with persuasiveness. Ar. راوغ employ a ruse, or Pers. لاغ deception, fraud, &c.)

Laha,* n. a sheet of paper. (Rarely used, cf. *karatasi, ukurasa.* Ar. لوح tablet, slab.)

Lahamu,* v. and n. See **Lehemu.**

Lahaula,* n. and int. (1) blasphemy. *Kila lahaula hufuatwa na adhabu ya Mungu,* every blasphemy is followed by God's punishment; (2) as an expletive: Well I never! What next! God forbid! Also used on hearing a person blaspheme or use unseemly words. (Ar. لا حولة an abbrev. of 'there is no power nor strength but in God', &c.)

Laika, n. *ma-* also **Ulaika,** n. *ma-* short downy hair, as on the hands and human body generally (but see *vuzi*). Also down of birds. (Cf. *unywele, unyoya,* and dist. *malaika,* an angel.)

Laiki,* v. become, be fitting, be suitable, be proper, e.g. *matendo yake yanamlaiki,* his actions are just what you would expect of him. **Laiki,** n. what is becoming, fitness, fitting, proper, e.g. *mambo aliyotenda si laiki yake,* his actions were not what one would have expected of him, they did not become him. (Cf. *faa, agia.* Ar. لاق.)

Laini,* a. and **-lainifu,** a. (1) of things: smooth, supple, soft, flexible, pliable, of delicate texture, thin, fine (cf. *-ororo, -embamba*); (2) of persons: facile, gentle, good-humoured (cf. *-pole, taratibu*). *Nguo laini,* smooth, fine cloth. *Mchanga laini,* fine sand. Also sometimes as a v. smoothen, but usu. **Lainisha** Cs. smoothen, make smooth. *Lainisha nguo hizi kwa pasi,* smooth these clothes with an iron. St. **Lainika,** (1) be smoothed, be made smooth; (2) fig. be softened, be appeased. *Ndipo moyo wake ulipolainika,* then his heart was softened. Ps. **Lainiwa. Ulaini,** n. and **Ulainifu,** n. softness, flexibility, smoothness, tenderness, gentleness (of accent, manner, &c.). (Ar. لين.)

Laiti!* int. Oh that, if only, would that—esp. of regret for what is past or impossible, and then used with verbs in the Past or Conditional Tenses. But also of hope, with the Present, e.g. *laiti safari yangu ingalikwisha!* oh that my journey had come to an end! *Laiti (kwamba) tulifika jana!* would that we had arrived yesterday! (Ar. ليت.)

Lake, a. form of *-ake,* which see.

Laki,* n. and a. a hundred thousand, a lac. (Hind. لاكه.)

Laki,* v. meet, go to meet, esp. in a friendly, complimentary, ceremonial way. But also sometimes used of going to meet with intent to harm, &c. *Alinilaki kwa fimbo,* he met me with a stick (i.e. to beat me with). *Waliwalaki kwa matusi,* they met them with abuse. (Cf. *kuta, onana na, pokea.* Ar. لاقى.)

Lakini,* conj. but, yet, however, nevertheless. (Cf. *walakini, ila, bali.* Ar. لٰكن.)

Lakiri,* n. sealing-wax. (Port. *lacre.*)

Lako, a. form of *-ako,* which see.

Lala, v. (1) lie, lie down, go to bed; (2) sleep, go to sleep; (3) settle down, fall, collapse; (4) lie flat, be spread out, be horizontal. Also *lala usingizi,* go to sleep. *Nyumba imelala,* the house has fallen down. *Nchi yote yalala sawasawa,* the whole country is a flat plain. *Chumba cha kulala,* a bedroom. Prep. **Lalia,** sleep (or lie) on, in, at, &c. *Lalia matanga,* sleep in a house of mourning. St. and Pot. **Lalika,** be fit (or possible) for sleeping in. *Hakulaliki nyumbani kwa jasho,* it is impossible to sleep indoors because of the heat. Cs. **Lalisha** and **Laza,** cause to lie down, put to bed, lay flat or horizontal. *Jilaza,* rest oneself, take a siesta. Rp. **Lalana,** sleep with each other, used of sexual intercourse only. (Note: *lala* with an object pfx., i.e. as act. and *lalana,* are used of coition.) Examples: *Mtu wa kulalia nyumba,* a caretaker, night watchman. *Mkeka mpya usiolaliwa,* a new mat which has never been slept upon. *Lala uamke,* may you sleep (and wake), i.e. may you sleep well. *Lala unono,* sleep in comfort. *Lala macho,* lie awake. *Lala chali* (*kifudifudi, mgongoni, kingalingali, kibavu, kitumbo,* &c.) lie on the back (face down, on the back, on the side, on the stomach, &c.). *Lala zamu,* sleep by turns, also 'keep watch'. *Lala kigogo,* sleep like a log. *Lala chini,* sleep on the ground, also, collapse, fall down. (Cf. *sinzia, pumzika, jinyosha, gona.*) **Kilalio,** n. *vi-* (1) the evening meal; (2) bedding, a bed, &c., anything on which to lie. **Kilalo,** n. *vi-* (1) camping- or sleeping-place on a journey; (2) a sleeping-shelter, e.g. a few sticks resting on forked uprights, and carrying some grass as a covering; (3) dim. of *ulalo,* see below. **Malalo,** n. plur. sleeping-things, i.e. place, arrangements, bedding and things to lie on. **Malazi** and **Malazo,** n. plur. things to sleep on, bedding, place to sleep in, &c., like *malalo.* **Mlalavi,** *n. wa-* a restless sleeper, one who turns over and over in sleep or sleeps in a restless manner. **Mlazi,** n. *wa-* (1) one who puts people to bed, or soothes them to sleep, i.e. of a mother and a child; (2) one who is accustomed to sleep in a certain place is *mlazi wa huko.* **Ulalo,** n. (*malalo*), (1) place (time, accessories, manner) of lying down or sleeping, camping-place, bed; (2) something lying or laid down, e.g. a tree or plank laid as a bridge across a stream.

Lalaika, v. cry and complain because of hunger, pain, &c. (Cf. *lalamika.*)

Lalama, v. ask for mercy (of), make an appeal (to), cry out, beg one's pardon, lament, confess lamenting one's fault. *Mwizi alilalama mbele ya bwana wake apate msamaha,* the thief begged before his master for forgiveness. Ps. **Lalamiwa.** St. **Lalamika,** be made to appeal for mercy, be reduced to submission, be beaten—and so, beg for mercy, cry out for quarter, like *lalama.* Prep. **Lalamia,** e.g. *mdaiwa alimlalamia mdai,* the debtor threw himself on the mercy of the creditor. Cs. **Lalamisha,** make cry out, bring to terms, force to confess defeat. **Lalamiko,** n. *ma-* often used in the plur. pleadings for mercy, &c. **Ulalamishi,** n., **Ulalamizi,** n. (*lalamizi*) supplication, humble appeal, begging for mercy. (Cf. *omba, kiri, ungama, lilia.*)

Lamba, v. (sometimes *ramba* is heard, see note on *L*) lick, lick up with the tongue. *Lamba makombo ya sahani*, lick up the scraps on the plate. *Kumlamba mtu kisogo*, to put out the tongue as a sign of contempt when some one's back is turned. Ps. **Lambwa.** Prov. *Mkono mtupu haulambwi*, an empty hand is not licked. St. and Pot. **Lambika.** Prep. **Lambia**, lick with (for, off, &c.), e.g. *lambiwa damu mkononi*, have the blood licked off the hand. Cs. **Lambisha**, e.g. *mlambishe utamu*, give him a taste of it (so that he may want it again). Prep. of Ten. of Prep. **Lambitia**, desire anything so much that one's mouth waters, i.e. makes one lick one's lips. **-lambilambi**, a. soft, possible to be licked or picked off. **Mlamba**, n. *wa-* one who licks. **Ulambilambi**, n. i.e. *ulambilambi wa dafu*, condition of a coco-nut, when the nutty part is just forming, still soft and can be picked or licked off.

Lami,* n. pitch, tar, and sometimes used for any dark viscous stuff. (Ar. Steingass has 'زفت pitch, of which there are three kinds: *rūmī* (Greek) . . .', i.e. رومى and as *r = l*, hence *lami*.)

Landa, n. See **Randa.**

Landa, v. (1) resemble very closely, be like, be on the same level. *Mwana huyu anamlanda baba yake*, this boy resembles his father. Rp. **Landana**, e.g. *kuta hizi mbili zinalandana*, these two walls are equal in height. (Cf. *fanana, lingana, -wa sawasawa*, also see **Randa**, v.)

Lango, n. *ma-* (1) amplic. of *mlango*, which see; (2) *malango*, n. plur. is also used of secret instruction given to girls and boys on growing up. (Cf. *kunga, jando, unyago, mizungu.*)

Langu, a. form of *-angu*, which see.

Lao, a. form of *-ao*, which see.

Lapa, v. finish off hastily, eat ravenously. Cv. **Lafua**, like *lapa*, but Inten. be very greedy, wish to eat everything. St. of Cv. **Lafuka**, be insatiable. **Mlafi**, n. *wa-* a voracious eater, glutton, gormandizer. **Ulafi**, n. gluttony, voracious eating, gormandizing. (Bantu *-lapa*, swallow greedily. Cf. also Ar. طلف glutton.)

Lasi,* n. a kind of silk, tussore. (Pers لاس coarse silk.)

Latamia, v. bring up a child, rear, educate. (Cf. *atamia*, but perh. from Ar. لطم to slap.)

Latifu,* n. goodness, gentleness. (Cf. *pole, -ema.* Ar. لطف.)

Latitudo,* n. latitude, adopted for use in text-books and school lessons. (Eng.)

Laula,* used with *kama, laula kama*, if not, unless. *Siwezi kumaliza kazi hii laula kama nitapata msaada*, I cannot finish this work unless I get help. (Rarely used, cf. *isipokuwa, ila.* Ar. لولا were it not for.)

Laumu,* v. reproach, find fault with, reprove, upbraid, blame, accuse. Ps. **Laumiwa.** St. **Laumika.** Prep. **Laumia.** Cs. **Laumisha**, Intens. scold, rebuke sharply. Rp. **Laumiana. Laumu**, n. *ma-* but usu. **Lawama**, n. *ma-* reproach, charge, blame, reproof, guilt. (Cf. *karipia, kemea, suta, shtaki, hatia, nenea.* Ar. لوم.)

Launi,* n. likeness, kind, shape, colour, esp. of countenance—very rarely used. (Cf. *mfano, namna, sura, rangi.* Ar. لون colour, kind.)

Launi,* v. walk about. (Eng. go the rounds.)

Lavani,* n. vanilla. (Prob. same word with syllable transposed.)

Lavya, v. See under **Lawa.**

Lawa, v. come out, seldom used except with Rf. *jilawa*, get up or go out, very early in the morning. Cs. **Lavya**, put out, reveal—seldom used. St. **Lauka**, rise early. Prep. **Laukia**, rise early for . . .; surprise early in the morning. (Cf. *jidamka, mapema, toka, ondoka.*)

Lawalawa, n. a kind of sweetmeat, prob. from *lowa*, which see.

Lawama, n. *ma-*. See under **Laumu.**

Lawiti,* v. commit sodomy. (Cf. *fira*. Ar. لوظي.)

Laza, v. See under **Lala.**

Lazima,* n. necessity, obligation, surety, bail, responsibility, e.g. *chukua lazima*, bail, go bail. *Ni lazima juu yako*, it is obligatory on you. *Ni lazima uende*, you must go. **Lazimu**, v. be obligatory (on), be a necessity (to), be binding (on), make responsible, put pressure on. *Sheria imemlazimu*, the law has bound him, forced him. *Amekulazimu*, he has made you responsible, he has made it binding on you, he has bound you. Ps. **Lazimiwa**, be bound, be under an obligation, be responsible, &c. Prep. **Lazimia.** Cs. **Lazimisha**, inten. put strong pressure on, force, compel. *Jilazimisha na*, devote oneself to, accept full responsibility for. (Cf. *shurutisha, sharti*, Ar. لزم.)

-le, (1) final characteristic of a. dem. 'that' (see *yule, wale, kile*, &c.); (2) sometimes a contraction of *lake*, e.g. *jinale*, his name. (Cf. *-lo* for *lako*); (3) subjunct. of *la*, v. eat.

Lea, v. bring up, rear, nurse, educate. Prov. *Mwana umleavyo ndivyo akuavyo*, as you bring up a child, so he grows up. Ps. **Lelewa** (not *lewa*, prob. to dist. from *lewa*, v. be drunk), *amelelewa vema*, he has been well brought up. **Malezi**, n. plur. rearing, bringing up (both of nurture generally, and of education), training. *Malezi mazuri*, good breeding, good education, accomplishments. **Mlezi**, n. *wa-* a nurse, governess, tutor, one engaged in the rearing or training of a child. **Ulezi**, n. act (trade, work, pay) of one who has care of children, e.g. a nurse, tutor, guardian, &c.

Leba,* n. See under **Laabu.**

Lebasi,* n. clothes, raiment, wearing apparel, for the common *mavazi, nguo*. (Ar. لباس.)

Lebeka.* See **Labeka.**

Lebu,* v. See under **Laabu.**

Lega, v. also **Legalega**, waver, totter, shake, be rickety, be loose, as of a tooth or anything not fixed firmly. *Jino hili linalegalega*, this tooth is loose. Prep. **Legea**, v. (1) be loose (slack, relaxed, soft, pliable); (2) be faint (weak, remiss), flag, yield, give in, e.g. of the effects of illness, hunger, exhaustion, &c.—or of a rope being slack, &c. Cs. **Legeza.** loosen, slacken, exhaust, cause to yield, &c. **-legevu**, a. slack, relaxed, weak, soft, yielding, remiss, inattentive, idle, limp. **Mlegevu**, n. *wa-* a slack, remiss, careless, negligent, inattentive person. **Ulegeo**, n. and **Ulegevu**, n. (1) slackness, relaxed condition, exhaustion, limpness, weakness; (2) remissness, carelessness, negligence, inattention. (Cf. *dhoofu, -vivu, -zembe, -tepetevu, nyong'onyea.*)

Legeni,* n. a large metal vessel used for cooking *mkate wa kumimina*. (Ar. لكن.)

-legevu, a., **Legeza.** See under **Lega.**

Lehemu,* v. solder, apply solder, repair with solder. Ps. **Lehemiwa.** St. **Lehemika.** Prep. **Lehemia.** Cs. **Lehemisha. Lehemu**, n. solder. *Tia lehemu*, apply solder, &c. (Cf. *tindikali*. Ar. لحم.)

Lekea, v. See under **Elekea, v.** also for derivatives, *lekeana, lekeza*, &c.

-lekevu, a. See under **Elea, v.** (B).

Lela,* n. a night—seldom used for usu. *usiku*. (Ar. ليل.)

Lelam.* See **Lilam.**

Lele, n. *ma-* amplic. of *kilele.*

Lema, n. a variant of *ndema*, which see.

Lema, v. exorcize spirits, as the *waganga* do. (Cf. *chuchia, punga, pepo, mleja, kiti.*)

Lemaa, v. be disfigured, be mutilated, be maimed. *Mtu yule alilemaa baada ya ugonjwa wa ukoma,* that man was disfigured after leprosy. Cs. **Lemaza,** maim, mutilate, disfigure, cripple. **Lemaa,** n. defect, deformity, disfigurement, blemish, mutilation. *-enye lemaa,* deformed, maimed, crippled, &c., but the common form is **Kilema,** n. *vi-* (1) a deformity, defect, blemish; (2) a deformed or disfigured person, a cripple. *Kilema cha jicho,* a one-eyed man, i.e. *chongo.* (Cf. *kiwete, kiziwi, kipofu, kibiongo.*)

Lemba, n. *ma-* amplic. of *kilemba.*

Lemba, v. (1) sometimes heard for *remba,* which see; (2) take by force or by trickery. (Cf. *danganya, punja, hadaa.*)

Lembea, v. reach down something from a height for somebody, i.e. as fruit on a tree, &c.

Lemea, v. also sometimes **Elemea,** (1) press forward, go on steadily, push on; (2) press upon, rest heavily upon, lie on the top of; (3) oppress, be burdensome, discommode. *Lemea mbele,* press on faster. *Lemea njia,* push on a journey. *Mzigo unamlemea,* the load is tiring him, is heavy for him. *Kasha lililemea juu ya kasha,* one box rested on another. Ps. **Lemewa,** be burdened, be oppressed, &c. Cs. **Lemeza,** e.g. pile up, place a load on, and so, oppress, burden. Rp. of Cs. **Lemezana.** Rp. **Lemeana,** lie on (lean on, rest against, press) each other. (Cf. *pagaa, elemea, gandamiza.*)

Lenga, v. also sometimes **Linga,** (1) aim at (with a rifle, &c.), take aim, *lenga shabaha,* aim at a target; (2) cut in slices, i.e. *lenga muhogo,* cut cassava into slices (to dry it for making into flour or storing). Ps. **Lengwa.** Prep. **Lengea.** Rp. **Lengana.** (Cf. *linga, elekeza, lekeza.*)

Lengalenga, v. be tearful, be near to crying. *Machozi yanamlengalenga,* his eyes are full of tears.

Lengelenge, n. *ma-* a blister, pustule. *Fanya (toka, tokwa na) malengelenge,* get blistered.

Lenu, a. form of *-enu,* which see.

Lenye, a. form of *-enye,* which see.

Lenyewe, a. form of *-enyewe,* which see.

Lenzi,* n. a lens, the word adopted for use in text-books and school lessons. (Eng.)

Leo, n. and adv., to-day, this day, the present time. Also *siku ya leo,* to-day. *Leo hivi, hivi leo,* this very day. *Si leo,* not to-day, long ago. *Si -a leo,* old, out of date. *Leo alfajiri (mapema, asubuhi, adhuhuri,* or *saa sita, alasiri, jioni, mchana, usiku),* to-day at daybreak (early morning, twelve noon, afternoon, evening, during the day-time, night). *Leo siku ya nane...,* to-day is the eighth day since . . . *Leo kabla ya kesho,* to-day before to-morrow, i.e. this very day. *Tangu (toka, tokea, mwanzo) leo,* from to-day. Prov. *Juzi na jana si kama ya leo,* the (affairs of the) day before yesterday and (of) yesterday are not like those of to-day, i.e. you cannot judge what will happen by what has happened previously. **Leoje,** some considerable time, e.g. *amefika leoje,* he has been here some time.

Lepe, n. *ma-* drowsiness, faintness, a heavy slumberous condition. *Lepe la usingizi,* sleepiness, drowsiness. *-enye lepe,* drowsy. *Huyu ni lepe,* this man is drowsy, he is hard to rouse. (Cf. *usingizi, uzito, sinzia.*)

Leso,* n. (— and *ma-*) handkerchief —of printed calico, often worn round the neck or on the head. *Leso ya* (or *la*) *upande mmoja,* the 'scarf' of commerce, one piece of it forming a *kanga,* i.e. a woman's dress. *Leso ya* (or *la*) *kushona,* handkerchief, two pieces of three handkerchiefs each being sewn together to make a *kanga*; coloured handkerchiefs, 12 of them form one piece of cloth. *Leso seno,* cheap handkerchiefs of white and black print. (Sometimes *ankachifi* and *angajifi* are heard, from the English. Port. *lenco.*)

Leta, v. bring, fetch, supply, cause to come to where a person is, thus supplying a Cs. of *-ja*, come. Examples: *leta maneno* (*shauri, daawa*), bring a request (a case, an action). *Leta vita*, bring war, wage war, begin a war. *Leta udaku*, make objections, protest. *Leta baina* (*hakika, ushuhuda, ushahidi*), prove (demonstrate, bring evidence, &c.). Used in an idiomatic way, e.g. *Ataleta nini?* What can you expect from him? *Mtu akaaye na wevi ataleta nini kama si wivi?* What can you expect from a man who associates with thieves, except that he also be a thief? Ps. **Letwa**, be brought. Note the idiom *maji yamekwenda kuletwa*, lit. water has gone to be brought, for, some one has gone to bring water. St. rarely used. **Leteka.** Prep. **Letea.** Ps. of Prep. **Letewa**, have (a thing) brought to. *Waliletewa chakula*, they were brought food. Rp. **Letana.** Rp. of Prep. **Leteana**, e.g. *leteana barua*, exchange letters, correspond. (Cf. *chukua, peleka, toa.*)

Letu, a. form of *-etu*, which see.

-levi, a., **Levuka**, v., **Levya**, v. See under **Lewa.**

Lewa, v. be drunk (giddy, intoxicated), stagger, sway, reel, wave to and fro. *Lewa kwa pombe*, be drunk on beer. *Lewa kwa bahari*, of the effects of sea-sickness—be giddy. Also Rd. *lewalewa*, reel and stagger, used also of loose branches of a tree swaying. *Mashua yalewalewa*, of a boat tossing on a rough sea. Cs. **Levya**, make drunk, intoxicate, cause to reel, make stagger, make giddy. *Jilevya*, make oneself drunk, get intoxicated. Also Rd. *levyalevya*. St. of Cv. **Levuka**, get sober, become steady—in manner, gait, &c. Cs. **Levusha**, make sober, steady, &c. **Kileo**, n. *vi-* (1) state or case of intoxication, staggering, reeling, &c., but usu. (2) anything intoxicating or narcotic, e.g. *pombe, mvinyo, tembo, bangi*, &c. *Kileo kimempata*, he is under the influence of liquor. **-levi**, a. drunken, intoxicated, given to drinking. **Mleo**, n. *mi-* reeling, staggering, unsteady gait. Also *mleoleo*, of uncertain wavering movement. **Mlevi**, n. *wa-* a drunken person, but usu. a drunkard. **Ulevi**, n. *ma-* (1) a state of drunkenness, intoxication, giddiness, staggering, reeling; (2) an intoxicant. *Ulevi wa bahari*, sea-sickness. (3) the plur. *malevi*, is used of drunkenness, i.e. drunken habits, acts, &c. **Uleoleo**, n. a state midway between consciousness and unconsciousness, of a patient recovering from an anaesthetic, &c. **Ulewalewa**, n. state of swaying or staggering. (Cf. *wayawaya, yumbayumba, pepesuka, mrama.*)

Li, for the various functions of *li* as a pfx., tense pfx., &c., see Grammars.

Lia, v. (1) sound, make a sound (the most general word for sound of any kind, in animate or inanimate nature); (2) utter a cry, cry out (for joy, sorrow, pain, &c.); (3) mourn, weep. *Chuma chalia kikipigwa na nyundo*, iron rings if it is beaten with a hammer. *Panalia wazi*, the place sounds hollow. *Ndege wanalia*, the birds are singing. *Bunduki zalia*, guns are going off (sounding). *Lia machozi*, shed tears, cry. *Lia ngoa* (*uwivu*), cry from jealousy. Prep. **Lilia**, cry to (for, at, with, &c.), sound in harmony with, &c. *Jililia*, bewail oneself. Ps. of Prep. **Liliwa**, be mourned for, &c. Cs. **Liza**, cause to sound, make cry, cause (or be the occasion of) crying. *Liza bunduki*, fire off a gun. *Jiliza*, pretend to cry, sham sorrow, shed mock tears. Rp. **Liana**, e.g. of harmonious sounds, or general mourning, &c. Rp. of Cs. **Lizana**, weep together, make each other weep, make each other utter a sound. **Kilio**, n. *vi-* (1) sounding, a sound, crying, weeping, mourning, a cry, scream, shout, dirge; (2) a subject for mourning, a sad thing; (3)

dim. of *mlio*, see below. **Lio**, n. *ma-* amplic. of *mlio*, a very loud sound, a roar. **Malizano**, n. plur. mourning, of many together, a general wailing. **Malizi**, things causing sound, things rustling, making a noise. **Mlia**, n. *wa-* a crier. *Mlia choyo*, a grumbler. *Mlia wivu*, a jealous person. **Mlio**, n. *mi-* a sound—in the widest sense, a cry, a note, weeping. Used of all kinds of objects, animate and inanimate, yielding a sound. *Mlio wa mtoto*, a child's crying. *Mlio wa simba*, a lion's roar. *Mlio wa bunduki*, the report of a gun. *Mlio wa ndege*, a bird's singing. *Ngoma yenye milio saba*, a drum with seven notes. **Mlizi**, n. *wa-* (1) one who cries or makes a noise, also (2) one who causes another or anything to make a noise. **Ulizi**, n. *ma-* bawling, squealing, shouting, screaming, loud cry. (Cf. *toa sauti, paaza sauti, vuma, nguruma, imba, kishindo.*)

Libasi,* n. See **Lebasi**.

Licha, conj. and *licha ya*, prep. not only ... but more than, used when the act (circumstance, thing, &c.) being used for the purpose of comparison, contrast, &c., is larger, of greater value, stronger, of more importance, &c., than the act, &c., under consideration—often used with *hata*, e.g. *licha ya senti moja, hata kumi nitakupa*, not only one cent (will I give you), but I will give you ten. *Licha ya huyu kushindwa na mambo haya, hata wenye akili wameshindwa nayo*, not only has he been beaten by these affairs, but even clever people have been beaten by them. *Licha ya kukupiga wewe, hata kaka yako nitampiga*, not only will I beat you, but I will even beat your elder brother (who is stronger than you). *Licha ya vitu hafifu kukosa bei, hata vitu bora havipati bei siku hizi*, not only is it impossible to get a good price for inferior articles, but even superior articles bring no price at present. (Prob. derived from a verb *licha*, leave, allow, permit, &c., now superseded by *acha*. Cf. (1) *likiza*, with the same meaning, also *leka* in other dialects, and (2) the idiomatic use of *acha*, which can be used in almost every case where *licha* is used. *Licha ya senti moja, hata kumi nitakupa*, could well be rendered by *acha senti moja, hata kumi nitakupa*. (Cf. *sembuse* used in the same way, but when the act, &c., being used for the purpose of comparison, contrast, &c., is less than the one under consideration.)

Liga, n. (— and *ma-*) poison, any medicine which makes one sick, feeble, or weak. **Liga**, v. poison, weaken the health or cause illness by poison. *Zamani wachawi waliwaliga adui zao*, in the olden days the witch doctors poisoned their enemies. (Cf. *sumu* and *sumisha.*)

Lihamu, v. and n. also **Lihimu**.* See **Lehemu**.

Lijamu,* n. bit (of a horse, donkey, &c.). *Seruji na lijamu na vigwe*, saddle, bit, and reins, but usually all are included in the word *matandiko*. (Ar. لجام.)

Lika, v. See under **La**, v.

Likiza, v. (rarely used. Cf. *acha* and *ruhusu*, which are usual.) (1) give leave (respite, relief, holiday) to, release, let go; (2) dismiss, send away, make go, not allow to stay. Thus *likiza mtoto*, may mean (1) give a boy a holiday, or (2) wean a child. (Cf. *achisha.*) Ps. **Likizwa**. Prep. **Likizia**. Cs. **Likizisha**. Rp. **Likizana**. **Likizo**, n. *ma-* holiday, relief, &c. (Cf. *acha, ondosha, ruhusu*, and *licha.*)

Liko, n. same as *diko*, which see.

Likwama, n. *ma-* a cart drawn by men. These carts are often very old and cumbersome, prob. hence the name from *kwama*. (Cf. *hamali, kweche.*)

Lila na fila,* a saying: for good and bad, whether or no—also cf. Prov.

Lila na fila haitangamani, 'perhaps' and 'actuality' are not compatible, (Cf. Ar. لعل perhaps, may be, and فعل deed, misdeed.)

Lilam,* n. also **Lilamu, Lelam,** an auction, public sale, also sometimes the place where an auction is held. Used with the verb *nadi*, i.e. *nadi katika lilam*, sell by auction, but *nadi* and the n. *mnadi* are more common. (Cf. *nadi, mnadi, dalali.* ? Hind.)

Lima,* n. in the expression *lima ya arusi*, or *wali wa lima*, wedding feast. (A corruption of Ar. وليمة, wedding banquet, dinner party.)

Lima, v. hoe, cultivate or work land (used of the native mode of cultivation, and nowadays of ploughing also). Ps. **Limwa.** St. and Pot. **Limika,** e.g. be fit for cultivation, arable. Prep. **Limia,** e.g. *jembe la kulimia*, a hoe to dig with. *Nilimlimia shamba*, I cultivated a plantation for him. Cs. **Limisha,** cause to hoe, cultivate, plough, get hoeing done (used of the overseer, *msimamizi*), give permission to begin hoeing (used of the master, Agricultural Officer, rain-makers, &c.). **Kilimia,** n. the Pleiades (constellation). Prov. *Kilimia kikizama kwa jua huzuka kwa mvua, kikizama kwa mvua huzuka kwa jua*, when the Pleiades set in sun (sunny weather) they rise in rain, when they set in rain they rise in sun. Used of the time to begin cultivating. **Kilimo,** n. *vi-* (1) hoeing, and so the care of a plantation generally, i.e. cultivation, agriculture; (2) products of cultivation, produce, crops. **-limaji,** a. engaged in agriculture. **Makulima,** n. plur. implements or operations of agriculture. **Mkulima,** n. *wa-* (*-ku-* inserted to dist. from *mlima*) a cultivator, agriculturist, field labourer, peasant, &c. **Mlimaji,** n. *wa-* same as *mkulima.* **Mlimo,** n. *mi-* same as *kilimo.* **Ulimaji,** n. (*ma-*) method (process, fee, &c.) of cultivation, agriculture: and *malimaji*, apparatus, and things used in cultivation.

-limaji, a. See under **Lima.**

Limatia, v. be delayed, remain behind, be late, be too long. Ps. **Limatiwa.** Cs. **Limatisha.** (Cf. *chelewa, kawia, -siri.*)

Limau,* n. *ma-* a lemon, fruit of the *mlimau.* (Hind. ليمو.)

Limbika, v. (1) put aside until a thing increases, or leave to increase, grow in quantity, quality, ripeness, &c.; (2) allow time for, wait for; (3) bear with, be patient to, show consideration for. *Limbika nywele*, let the hair grow. *Limbika kucha*, let the nails grow. *Limbika maji*, wait for water, at an exhausted or slow-running well. *Limbika ndizi*, wait for bananas to ripen. *Limbika watu*, not to overwork people, treat with consideration. Ps. **Limbikwa,** be left on, &c. *Nazi hulimbikwa juu ya mnazi mpaka ziive*, the coco-nuts are left on the tree until they ripen. Prep. **Limbikia,** spare for somebody, put aside for. *Mtu huyu amewalimbikia watoto wake mali*, this man has put aside money for his children. Cv. **Limbua,** eat the first-fruits of a new crop, enjoy for the first time. St. **Limbuka,** do or get anything for the first time, use for the first time, come to the end of waiting for, get the result of waiting (care, consideration, prudence), enjoy a looked-for advantage, have a first taste of pleasure deferred, enjoy the first-fruit, get the benefit of, &c. *Mwenye shamba amekwenda kulimbuka katika shamba lake*, the owner has gone to taste the first-fruit of his estate. Ps. **Limbukwa,** be enjoyed by, be used for the first time, &c. Prep. **Limbukia,** enjoy oneself (at, with, for, &c.). Cs. **Limbusha,** reward waiting, give a foretaste of, satisfy hope deferred, yield the wished-for result, answer expectations. **Limbiko,** n. *ma-* same as *mlimbiko*, see under. **Limbukeni,**

used as a noun—people enjoying a thing or experience for the first time. **Limbuko**, n. *ma-* same as *mlimbuko*, see under. **Mlimbiko**, n. *mi-* (1) a waiting for something, taking turns, a turn (in waiting); (2) a store, reserve, treasure, a saving-up little by little over a period of time. *Mlimbiko wa fedha*, a reserve of funds. **Mlimbuko**, n. *mi-* (1) the using anything or experiencing anything for the first time; (2) the first-fruits, reward for waiting, fulfilment of hope, foretaste of reward. (Cf. *zao, weka, akiba.*)

-limi, a. See under **Ulimi**.

Limki,* v. (used very rarely, and only in the negative sense), have a want, have a deficiency, have a defect, be wanting, be deficient, fail, want. (Cf. *kosa, toa* (B). Ar. لمق efface, blot out.)

Limuka, v. be sly, be cunning, be crafty. *Mtu huyu amelimuka sana*, this man is very sly. Cs. **Limusha**, cause to become sly, play a trick on somebody. *Tuliwalimusha adui vitani*, we played a trick (devised a stratagem) on our enemies in the battle. **Limuko**, n. *ma-* a trick, stratagem. (Cf. *hila, danganya, hadaa.* Cf. *elimu* from which this appears to be derived with a restricted sense.)

Linda, v. (1) defend, protect, guard, watch, keep safe; (2) keep off, fend off, guard against, watch for. *Linda ndege*, watch against birds. *Linda kingojo* (*zamu*), guard, be a sentinel, be on sentry duty. *Jilinde, nami nitakulinda*, defend yourself and I will defend you. Ps. **Lindwa**. St. **Lindika**. Prep. **Lindia**, guard (defend, watch, protect) for, &c. Cs. **Lindisha**, cause to watch, &c. Rp. **Lindana**, defend one another. **Lindo**, n. *ma-* watching-place, station, post (to guard). **Kilinda**, n. *vi-* (governing a noun following), a guard, protector, e.g. *kilinda chozi*, the rear-guard, the pendulous end of a cluster of banana fruits, with a pearly drop of moisture at the tip. **Kilindo**, n. *vi-* (1) act (process, means, &c.) of guarding, protection, guard, charge, care. *Tu katika kilindo cha Mungu*, we are in God's keeping. (2) a watchman's platform in a plantation; (3) a shelter (from rain, sun, &c.); (4) a basket with a lid of bark, wood, or skin. **Mlinda**, n. *wa-* (governing a noun following), a guard, watchman, &c., e.g. *mlinda nyumba*, a caretaker of a house. **Mlinzi**, n. *wa-* guardian, protector, keeper, guard, watchman, sentinel, &c. **Ulinzi**, n. watching, guardianship, method (means, fee, &c.) for guarding. (Cf. *tunza, hifadhi.*)

Lindi, n. *ma-* (1) amplic. of *kilindi*, which see; (2) *lindi la choo*, a cesspool. (Cf. *shimo.*)

Lindo, n. *ma-*. See under **Linda**.

Linga, v. (1) make equal, put side by side in order to match or compare, suit, level, smooth, straighten, harmonize; (2) be equal, be like, suit, harmonize, fit. *Linga bunduki*, level a gun, take aim. (Cf. *lenga* and *elekeza.*) *Linga nguo*, try on clothes, be measured for clothes. *Linga kichwa*, of a movement in dancing—bending the head forward and sweeping round. Ps. **Lingwa**. St. and Pot. **Lingika**. Prep. **Lingia**. Rp. **Lingana**, be level with one another, match, be like, harmonize—also make a suitable reply. *Tulingane sawasawa kama sahani na kawa*, let us be to each other as a plate and its cover (i.e. let us be in harmony). Rp. of Stc. **Lingamana**, be in a state of concord, harmony, complete agreement. Cs. of Rp. (1) **Linganya**, make equal, suit, match, harmonize, tune (an instrument). St. and Pot. **Linganyika**, be equal, &c. Cs. of Rp. (2) **Linganisha**, compare, put together two things in order to compare them or make them fit, &c. St. **Linganika**. **Kilingo**, n. *vi-* a pattern, example, &c. **-linganifu,** a., also **-linganyifu,** a. agreeing, matched, similar, suitable, apt, harmonious, regular. **Mlingano,** n. *mi-* likeness, &c. **Ulinganifu,** n. also **Ulinganyifu,** a. correspondence, harmony, comparison, suitableness, aptness, convenience. **Ulingano,** n. like *mlingano* above. (Cf. *sawazisha, fananisha.*)

Lingwa, v. be twisted in a thing, tripped up, puzzled, &c. *Alilingwa na nyasi akaanguka,* he was caught in the grass and fell.

Lini? adv. interrog. When? At what time? (Cf. *wakati gani? saa ngapi? saa ipi?*)

Lio, n. *ma-*. See under **Lia.**

Lipa, v. (1) pay, give in payment, repay, make a return for, recompense, compensate, reward; (2) have to pay, suffer (for). *Lipa deni,* pay a debt. *Nikulipe mema yako uliyonitendea,* let me pay back your kindness to me. *Lipa kisasi,* take vengeance, i.e. pay back. *Lipa kodi (ushuru),* pay tax (interest, custom's duty). Ps. **Lipwa.** St. and Pot. **Lipika.** Prep. **Lipia,** pay on behalf of, avenge, &c. Cs. **Lipisha** and **Lipiza,** make pay, exact a return from, &c. *Lipiza kisasi,* take vengeance on. *Jilipiza,* pay oneself by force, take as one's due, and with *kisasi,* avenge oneself on. **Lipizi,** n. *ma-* forced payment, exaction, vengeance, extortion. **Lipo,** n. *ma-* payment, recompense, revenge, allotment. **Majilipio,** n. plur., **Majilipizi,** n. plur., **Majilipo,** n. plur. repayment, requital, revenge. **Mlipa,** n. *wa-* governing noun following, a payer, one who pays. **Mlipaji,** n. *wa-* one who pays. **Mlipizi,** n. *wa-* one who extracts payment, causes to pay. *Mlipizi kisasi,* an avenger. **Ulipizi,** n. forcing payment, exaction, vengeance. (Cf. *toa, toza, kabidhi, tuza, jazi, ridhi.*)

Lipu, n. plaster (in building). (Hind. ليپ.)

Lipuka, v. (1) take fire suddenly, burst into flames, flare up, explode; (2) also fig. burst into a temper, &c.

Lisani,* n. used of the flap under the opening of a *kanzu* in front. (Ar. لسان tongue.)

Lisasi,* n. See **Risasi.**

Lisha, v. See under **La, v.**

Liwa,* n. a sweet-scented wood of the tree *mliwa,* a kind of sandalwood. It is ground and mixed with water and used as a perfume and as a cooling lotion for the skin. (Cf. *sandali,* also *msagaliwa,* under *saga.* Ar. ألوة a fragrant wood.)

Liwado, n. See **Liwato** under **Liwata.**

Liwali,* n. *ma-* also sometimes **Wali,** a headman, usually an Arab, appointed by the Government to deal with the affairs of the Muhammadan community. **Uliwali,** n. status, &c., of a *liwali.* (Cf. *tawala.* Ar. والٍ.)

Liwata, v. tread on, tread under foot. **Liwato,** n. the butt end, i.e. the part which is put on the ground. (Cf. *kanyaga, vyoga,* and *kwata* and *kiatu* from the same root.)

Liwaza, v. soothe, comfort, quieten. **Liwazo,** n. *ma-* comfort, condolence, anything that soothes. (Cf. *tuliza, tumbuiza, fariji.*)

Liza, v. (1) see under **Lia, v.**; (2) cause to buy, induce to buy, sell to, but rarely used. (Cf. *uza.*)

Liza, also **Riza.** See **Reza.**

Lo, a. relative, 'which, that'. Only used independently in such phrases as *kasha lo lote,* any box whatsoever. *Hakufanya (neno) lo lote,* he did nothing at all.

-lo, a. short form of *lako,* appended sometimes to a noun, e.g. *jinalo,* your name, i.e. *jina lako.*

Lo! Loo! int. of pleasure, wonder, horror, &c.—the intensity of feeling being represented by the indefinite prolongation of sound. Also *Lo salale! Loo salaalee! Lo masalale!*

Lodi, n. See **Rodi.**

Loga, n. (sometimes *roga,* see note on *l*), bewitch, use enchantment on, place under a spell or charm, practise black magic against with intention to do harm. Ps. **Logwa.** Rv. **Logoa,** deliver from a spell, remove a spell or witchcraft. **Mlozi,** n. *wa-* wizard, sorcerer, for the more usual *mchawi.* **Ulozi,** n. witchcraft, sorcery, enchantment, &c. (Cf. *uchawi, uganga, mwanga, pagaza.*)

Loja, v. see **Roja.**

Loma, n. a badger, ant-bear.

Londea, v. (1) look for, want; (2) hang around hoping to be invited to food, &c. Generally to hang around some one hoping for what may be got. Try to win over a woman's affection and possess her. (Cf. *pandia, mpandiaji.*) (3) sponge for food and drink. *Huja mara nyingi kulondea,* he is very often hanging around to see what he can get. Ps. **Londewa,** e.g. *mwanamke yule analondewa na huyu,* that woman is being sought after (pursued) by this fellow. Rp. **Londeana.** Cs. **Londesha** play the coquette. *Anajilondesha sana kwangu, lakini simtaki,* she comes around making herself cheap at my place, but I won't have anything to do with her. Rp. of Cs. **Londeshana.** (Cf. *dusa, doea, doya.*)

Longitudo,* n. longitude, the word adopted for use in text-books and school lessons. (Eng.)

Lonjo, a. tall, of people only. **Mlonjo,** n. *mi-* a stilt. Stilts are used in various games.

Lonyo, n. See under **Ona.**

Loo! int. See **Lo!**

Lopoka, v. See **Ropoka.**

Lote, a. form of *-ote* all.

Lovulovu, n. See under **Lowa.**

Lowa, v. get wet, be soaked (drenched, saturated), be damp. St. **Loweka,** (1) get wet—same as *lowa,* and (2) make wet, drench, souse, soak, e.g. *loweka nguo,* put clothes to soak. (3) be nonplussed, not be able to answer. (Cf. *shangaa, fadhaika, pumbaa.*) Ps. **Lowekwa,** be wetted, drenched, soaked, &c. Rp. **Lowana,** all get wet together. Stc. **Lowama,** be in a wet condition, be soaked, &c. Cs. **Lowanisha,** soak, put to soak, drench, &c. **Lawalawa,** n. a sweetmeat, any kind of confectionery, pudding, &c., saturated with sugar or honey. Also *lowalowa* and *lovulovu. Huu si wali tena ni lawalawa,* this is no longer rice, it is saturated. *Yu lovu kwa ulevi* (*kwa damu*), he is saturated with drink (blood). **-lowefu,** a. wet, moist, damp, soaking, &c. (Cf. *tia maji, rutuba, chovya, bambika, majimaji, chepechepe, unyevu.*)

Lowela, v. remain in a place, i.e. having come to a place on a visit only, decide to remain. **Mlowezi,** n. *wa-* a person who visits a place and then settles there. (Cf. *selelea.*)

Lozi,* n. *ma-* an almond, fruit of the *mlozi.* (Ar. لوز.)

Ludha,* n. See **Ladha.**

Lugha,* n. language, speech. *Lugha ya Kiswahili* (*Kiingereza, kikwetu*), the Swahili language (English, native, i.e. of our country). (Cf. *maneno,* and the use of *ki-,* e.g. *ki-* prefixed to the name of a tribe, nation, &c., denotes the language, also characteristics, mannerisms, &c., of the tribe, nation, &c. Ar. لغة.)

Luja,* n. (1) thief, robber, pickpocket; (2) deep thought. *Yumo katika luja,* he is deep in thought. (Cf. *mwizi, mkwepuzi, mawazo, fikira.* Ar. لص a thief, and لجه deep sea.)

Lukuki,* n. a number so large as to be uncountable. (Hind. لاكه a lac. plur.)

Lukuma,* food, sometimes used in the sense of a bribe, e.g. *lukuma yako, basi nifanyizie hivi,* here is a morsel for you, so do so-and-so for me. (Ar. لقمة morsel, mouthful.)

Lulu,* n. a pearl. *Zamia* (*vua*) *lulu,*

dive for pearls. *Bora kama lulu,* as beautiful as a pearl. As a type of perfection, *lulu* is playfully used in salutation: *Hujambo kama lulu?* Are you as well as a pearl (is beautiful)? **Lulumizi,** n. mother of pearl. (Ar. لؤلؤ.)

Lumba, v. (1) question; (2) make a speech, relate in a serious fashion. St. **Lumbika. Mlumbaji,** n. *wa-* a questioner, orator. **Malumbano,** n. plur. cross-questioning, &c. (Cf. *simulia, hadithia, hoji.*)

Lumbwi, n. a chameleon. (Cf. *kigeugeu, kinyonga.*)

Lundika, v. be piled up, one on top of the other, accumulate. Ps. **Lundikwa.** (Cf. *kusanya, panganya.*)

Lungo, n. an old word for *ungo,* which see, heard in the saying *peku lungo,* which see.

Lungu, n. See **Rungu.**

Lungula, v. treat with violence, extort money from, threaten, rob, blackmail. **Mlungula,** n. *mi-* (1) a bribe, blackmail, *kula mlungula,* take a bribe; (2) plur. *wa-*, a blackmailer, an extortioner, a robber. (Cf. *honga, rushwa, nyang'anya.*)

Luteka, n. a word used by native troops for manœuvres.

M

M represents the same sound as in English. But besides this purely consonantal sound, it includes also a semi-vowel sound, very common in Swahili; capable of bearing an accent and so of being treated as a distinct syllable.

M as a simple independent syllable, is a verb-form '(you) are', used like other personal prefixes for *ni*, agreeing with the Pronoun of 2 Pers. Plur., e.g. *ninyi m watu wazuri,* you are fine people. For *M* and *Mw-* as a formative, prefix, &c., see the Grammars.

Ma- as an initial syllable (1) is in most words of Arabic origin the Arabic formative of verbal nouns and particles, but from its identity of form it is sometimes treated by Swahili instinct as the Bantu formative of the plural of the *Ma-* class of nouns (cf. same tendency as to the formative *Ki,* e.g. *kitabu,* plur. *vitabu*). (2) As a formative proper in Swahili, *ma-* is (*a*) the plur. pfx. of the *ma-* class of nouns and adjectives agreeing with them (other than pronominal adjectives, these having *y-* for *ma-*), (*b*) an amplic. pfx. Thus many nouns have practically two plurals, expressing different degrees of size or importance, e.g. *pete,* in the *n* class, is a ring of moderate size; but *pete,* plur. *mapete,* rings of unusual size. (*c*) After the plur. pfx. of most foreign words, even when the sing. is treated as belonging to the 1st class, but the tendency is growing, to place such nouns in the 1st class with the plur. *wa-*. Words beginning with *Ma-*, not found under *ma-*, may be looked for under the letter following *ma-*, or under *u* followed by that letter.

Maabadi,* n., **Maabudu, n.** See under **Abudu.**

Maadam,* conj. (1) when, while, since; (2) since, if, seeing that, because. *Maadam umekuja, basi, kaa,* seeing that you have come, very well, remain. *Maadam amtaka,* when (as long as) he wants him. (Cf. *madhali, dumu.* Ar. ما دام.)

Maadili,* n. See under **Adili.**

Maafa,* n. See under **Afa.**

Maafikano,* n., **Maafikiano.** See under **Afiki.**

Maafu,* n. See under **Afu.**

Maagano, n. plur. See under **Aga,** v. (A) and (B).

Maagizo, n. plur. See under **Aga,** v. (B).

Maaguzi, n. plur. See under **Agua.**

Maakuli* n. victuals, food. (Cf. *chakula.* Ar. ماكل.)

Maalum,* a. recognized, known, particular, proper, special, peculiar. (Cf. *hasa, halisi, kanuni,* and *elimu* from the same root. Ar. معلوم.)

Maamkio, n. plur., **Maamkizi.** See under **Amka.**

Maamuma,* n. also **Mahamuna,** an utter fool, blockhead, simpleton, ignoramus. (Cf. *mjinga, baradhuli.* Ar. مأمون.)

Maamuzi, n. plur. See under **Amua.**

Maana,* n. (1) cause, reason, sake, consideration; (2) meaning, import purpose, intention; (3) reasonableness, sobriety, sense, e.g. *kwa maana (ya),* because (of), on account of, for the sake of considering (that). *Tia maanani,* keep in the mind, ponder, reflect on. *Maneno ya maana,* statements of importance, worth considering. *Wanaume wenye maana,* manly, sensible men. *Asiyejua maana, haambiwi maana,* he who does not know the meaning will not be told it. *Niambie maana yake nini?* Tell me what it means. *Mazungumzo yasiyo na maana,* foolishness, meaningless gossip. Often (4) as conj., because, in order to (that). (Cf. *sababu, ajili.* Ar. معنى.)

Maandalio, n. plur., **Maandamano,** n. plur., **Maandamizi,** n. plur., **Maandazi,** n. plur. See under **Andaa.**

Maandikio, n. plur., **Maandiko,** n. plur., **Maandishi,** n. plur. See under **Andika.**

Maangalizi, n. plur. See under **Anga,** n.

Maangamizi, n. plur., **Maangamizo,** n. plur. See under **Angamia.**

Maanguko, n. plur. See under **Anga,** v.

Maao, n. plur. See under **Waa,** v.

Maapizo, n. plur. See under **Apa.**

Maarasi,* n. a pole with a load, e.g. tin of water at each end, carried on the shoulders. (Cf. *mzegazega, mpiko.* Ar. مرس a halter.)

Maarifa,* n. See under **Arifu.**

Maarubu,* n. reason, purpose, intention, often a second reason for doing anything, i.e. an ulterior motive, but not necessarily a bad one. (Cf. *matilaba, madhumuni, sababu.* Ar. مأربة.)

Maarufu,* a. See under **Arifu.**

Maasi, n., **Maasum,*** n. See under **Asi.**

Maawio, n. plur. See under **Waa, v.**

Maazimio,* n. plur. See under **Azimu,** v. (B).

Maazimo, n. plur. See under **Azima,** v.

Mabaya, n. plur. See under **-baya.**

Mabishano, n. plur. See under **Bisha.**

Mabomoko, n. plur. See under **Bomoa.**

Mabotea, n. plants which grow up of their own accord in a garden, i.e. without seeds having been planted.

Mabruki,* n. See under **Baraka.**

Maburudisho, n., **Maburudu,*** n. See under **Baridi.**

Maburuzo, n. See under **Buruta.**

Machachari, n. plur. See under **Chachari.**

Machafuko, n. plur. See under **-chafu.**

Machela,* n. litter, sling or hammock for carrying a person. (Cf. *susu.* Port. *machila.*)

Macheleo, n. plur. See under **Cha,** v. (A).

Macheo, n. plur. See under **Cha,** v. (B).

Machi,* n. the month of March. (Eng.)

Machinjioni, n., **Machinjo,** n. plur. See under **Chinja.**

Macho, n. plur. See under **Jicho.**

Machozi, plur. of *chozi.*

Machubwichubwi, n. plur., also **Matubwitubwi,** mumps.

Machugachuga, n. See under **Chugachuga.**

Machukio, n. plur., **Machukizo,** n. plur. See under **Chuki.**

Machunga, n. plur., **Machungani,** n. plur. locative. See under **Chunga,** v. (A).

Machwa, n. plur., **Machweo,** n. plur. See under **Chwa.**

Madadi,* n. preparation of opium, made up into little pellets for smoking. (Cf. *afyuni, bangi, kasumba.* ? Ar. مدد auxiliaries (i.e. to smoking.)

Madaha,* n. airs, graces, fascinating manners. *Fanya* (*piga*) *madaha,* show off, make a display—of personal attractions. (Cf. *madahiro.* Hind. مدهو.)

Madahili,* n. plur. See under **Dahili.**

Madahiro,* n. elegance, gravity of gait, &c. *Kujitia madahiro,* be proud, put on airs, vaunt oneself. *Kutia madahiro,* add elegance, add decoration, e.g. on an article after it is really finished. (Cf. *madaha.* Ar. مظاهره.)

Madai,* n. plur. See under **Daawa.**

Madakata, n. plur. dry leaves which fall of their own accord.

Madanganyo, n. plur. See under **Danganya.**

Madaraka,* n. plur. See under **Daraka.**

Madenda, n. saliva which trickles from the mouth of some people in their sleep, &c.

Madende, n. an affected style of singing, with trills, quavers, protracted notes, &c. (Cf. *madoido.*)

Madevu, n. amplic. of *udevu.*

Madhabahu, n., **Madhabuha,*** n. See under **Dhabihu.**

Madhali,* conj. (1) while, when, since; (2) since, if, seeing that, because. *Madhali umefanya hivi, basi ni shauri lako,* since you have done that very well, its your own affair. (Ar. Cf. *maadam, sababu, kwa kuwa,* also **Mithali** from the same root, but in this form the *th* is always voiced.)

Madhara,* n. See under **Dhara.**

Madhehebu,* n. (1) customs, ideas, tenets, usages; (2) sect, denomination, party, persuasion. (Cf. *desturi, kawaida, kanuni.* Ar. مذاهب).

Madhii,* n. the clear viscid discharge of the male organ when sexually excited. (Ar. مذى.)

Madhilifu,* n. See under **Dhila.**

Madhubuti,* a. See under **Dhibiti.**

Madhumuni,* n. intention, purpose. (Cf. *makusudi, nia, maazimio, maarubu.* Ar. مضمون.)

Madifu, n. plur. of *difu.*

Madini,* n. metal—of any kind. (Cf. *chuma, shaba, bati, risasi, dhahabu, fedha.* Ar. معدن.)

Madoadoa, n. See under **Doa.**

Madoido, n. embellishment. *Tia madoido,* embellish, beautify, and in singing, put in trills, add notes which are not in the original tune. (Cf. *madende.*)

Madole matano, n. an epiphytic fern growing on walls and trees, *Polypodium phymtodes.*

Maduhuli,* n. income, wages, revenue. (Cf. *mshahara, faida, uchumi.* Ar. مدخول.)

Maduyuni,* n. See under **Deni.**

Maelekeo, n. See under **Elea** v. (B).

Maelezi, n. plur. See under **Elea,** v. (A).

Maelezo, n. plur. See under **Elea,** v. (B).

Maendeleo, n. plur., **Maenenzi,** n. plur. See under **Enda.**

Mafa, n. plur. See under **Fa.**

Mafaa, n. plur. See under **Faa.**

Mafamba, n. (1) underhand dealings, such as judgement in a lawsuit got by bribery; accounts which have been tampered with, made up evidence; (2) secret matter, difficult to understand.

Maficho, n. plur. See under **Ficha.**

Mafu, n. plur. See under **Fa.**

Mafua, n. plur. See under **Kifua.**

Mafuatano, n. plur. See under **Fuata.**

Mafukizo, n. plur., **Mafukuto,** n. plur. See under **Fuka.**

Mafunde, n. See **Mavunde.**

Mafundisho, n. plur. See under **Funda,** v. (C).

Mafungia, n. plur., **Mafungulia,** n. plur. See under **Funga.**

Mafunjo, n. plur. reeds such as grow by the sides of lakes and in marshes, sedge, papyrus.

Mafuriko, n. plur. See under **Fura.**

Mafusho, n. plur. See **Fuka.**

Mafuta, n. plur. (1) oil, fat, grease (of any kind). *Mafuta ya nyama,* fat, lard, dripping (also **Shahamu,** animal fat). Butter is commonly distinguished as *siagi* or *samli,* ghee. *Mafuta ya taa,* common paraffin oil; *mafuta ya uto,* semsem oil; *mafuta ya mbarika,* castor oil; *mafuta ya nazi,* coco-nut oil. Olive oil is in some places known as *halzeti* or *mafuta ya halzeti.* (Ar. زيت oil.) (2) *kutia mti mafuta,* is used of making a notch in a crooked pole and inserting a wedge or piece of wood in it, in order to straighten it. (Cf. *shahamu,* for animal fat, and *keua,* for (2).)

Mafutu, n. anger, i.e. *ana mafutu,* he is angry. (Cf. *kasirika, hasira.*)

Mafutuni, n. the back of a knife as opp. to *makali* or *machinjioni,* the cutting edge.

Mafuu, n. (1) craziness, silliness, half-witted state (cf. *kichaa, wazimu*); (2) plur. of *fuu.*

Mafya, n. plur. of *jifya.*

Mafyeko, n. plur. See under **Fyeka.**

Magadi, n. (1) soda; (2) plur. of *gadi.*

Magamaga, v. (1) walk very quickly; (2) straddle, walk with the legs apart as though the inside of the legs were chafed.

Magangao, also **Magaogao,** n. plur. ruin, desolation, e.g. as of a battle-field, &c.

Mageuzi, n. plur., **Mageuzo,** n. plur. See under **Geua.**

Magharibi,* n. (1) time of sunset, Muhammadan evening prayers; (2) place of sunset, the west. (Cf. *mashariki, kaskazi, kusi.* Ar. مغرب.)

Mago, n. plur. a variant of *makago,* plur. of *kago,* which see.

Magombezi, n. plur., **Magombezo,** n. plur. See under **Gomba.**

Magubiko, n. plur. See under **Gubika.**

Mahaba,* n. See under **Hebu, v.**

Mahabusi,* n. a prisoner awaiting trial, and the place where such prisoners are kept. (Ar. محبوس.)

Mahakma,* n. See under **Hukumu.**

Mahala,* n. See **Mahali.**

Mahali,* n. (1) place, position, situation, and fig. place of honour; (2) region, district, country (cf. *nchi*); (3) room, space, interval (cf. *nafasi*). *Mahali* is the only noun in Swahili meaning 'place', the only word with which the pfx. *p-* (*pa-, po-*) in reference to space is regularly associated, and as a rule means 'place, position' only. *Mahali hapa* (*pale*), this (that) place. *Kila mahali,* every place, everywhere. *Mahali pa*, in the place of, instead of. *Wakamwendea pale mahali pake*, and they went to him at his place there. *Aniweka mahali*, he puts me in a place, i.e. treats me with distinction. (Ar. محل.)

Mahame, n. plur. See under **Hama.**

Mahameli,* n. velvet. (Ar. مخمل.)

Mahamuna,* n. See **Maamuma.**

Maharagi,* n. plur. See **Maharagwe.**

Maharagwe,* n. plur. See **Haragwe**, a kind of beans.

Maharazi,* n. a shoemaker's awl. (Ar. مخرز.)

Mahari,* n. marriage settlement, money or property paid to the wife's relations, or settled on the wife, dowry. (Dist. *mahali*. Ar. مهر.)

Maharimu,* n. See under **Haramia.**

Mahashumu,* a. and n. See under **Heshima.**

Mahati,* n. a carpenter's gauge for marking lines. Also a marking cord, ruddle. (Ar. مخط pencil, ruler (for drawing lines).)

Mahazamu,* n. See **Hazamu.**

Mahdi,* n. a cradle, a bed—rarely heard for the usual *kitanda*. (Cf. *mede* (1) which is probably a corruption of the same word. Ar. مهد.)

Mahindi,* n. plur. See **Hindi.**

Mahiri,* a. skilful, clever, quick, adept, adroit, artful, tactful. *Fundi mahiri*, a clever craftsman. **Umahiri**, n. skill, cleverness, tact, &c. (Cf. *bingwa, stadi, waria*. Ar. ماهر.)

Mahitaji,* n. See under **Hitaji.**

Mahluki, Mahluku,* n. See under **Huluku.**

Mahoka, n. plur. (1) a kind of evil spirits; (2) frenzy, mania, madness. (Cf. *shetani, pepo, wazimu.*)

Mahonyo, a. free, gratis, e.g. *mali ya mahonyo*, property given free.

Mahsai,* n. See **Maksai.**

Mahsusi,* a. See under **Husu.**

Mahututi, a. serious, difficult, used of distresses, illness, &c. *Taabu mahututi*, great difficulty. *Ugonjwa mahututi*, serious illness, at death's door. Also used in the expression *akili mahututi*, of weak intellect. (Ar. محطوط laid low, or be intensely hot, violent, difficult.)

Maige, n. plur. young locusts. (Cf. *nzige, kimatu, tunutu*. From the same Bantu root as *nzige*, but cf. also Pers. ملخ locust.)

Maili,* n. a mile (Eng. mile. Cf. *inchi, futi, yadi.*)

Maisha, Maishilio,* n. See under **Ishi.**

Maiti,* n. a dead body, corpse—usually human only. Also, a dead person, i.e. *mtu maiti*. (Cf. *mauti*, also *mzoga, pinda, mfu, kimba*. Ar. ميت.)

Maizi, v. know, understand, recognize. (Cf. *jua, tambua, fahamu.*)

Majadi,* n. See under **Jadi, n. (B).**

Majahabu,* n. See under **Jahabu.**

Majaliwa,* n. plur. See under **Jalia.**

Majani, n. (1) plur. of *jani*; (2) *majani ya mwaka*, n. used as a green vegetable, *Ipomaea maritima*.

Majaribu,* n. plur. See under **Jaribu.**

Majengo, n. plur., **Majenzi**, n. plur. See under **Jenga.**

Majeruhi,* n. and a. See under **Jeruhi.**

Maji, n. water, or what resembles water, (1) in general—liquid, fluid, moisture, damp; (2) in particular—secretion, juice, sap, &c., treated as plur. of *ma-* class, with no singular, e.g. *teka maji*, draw water (from a well, water-hole, &c.). *Maji ya baridi* (*matamu, ya mvua, ya moto, ya chumvi, ya bahari*), cold water (fresh, rain, hot, salt, sea). *Maji bamvua* (*makuu*) or *maji kujaa*, spring tide. *Maji mafu* or, *maji ya mbande*, neap tide. *Maji ya moto*, (1) hot water, (2) a kind of light red or yellow ant, which bites. *Kama maji*, (1) fluid, liquid; (2) fluent, flowing—of ready speech.

Used also in virtual compounds, *mja maji*, one who arrives by sea, a stranger, newcomer. *Mwana maji*, a sailor, sea-faring man. *Maji ya shahada*, water poured (by Muhammadans) into a small hole at the head of a grave, when filled in. Also as a., *maji, majimaji*, wet, damp. Also used in the sense of being absolutely tired or exhausted, e.g. in a liquid state, i.e. nothing solid left. *Tu maji kwa kazi hii*, we are just like water because of this work. *Yu maji kwa maswali; ameulizwa na kujibu hata amekwenda kapa*, he is just like water with the questions he has been asked and has answered until there is nothing left in him (he is left without anything), and has gone away beaten (cf. *kapa*). *Ali yu maji, anadaiwa kope si zake. Wadeni wamemsimamia kama Izraili*, Ali is in a liquid state (he has nothing solid left, he is done for), he is being sued for a debt which is not his. His creditors are standing over him like the angel of death. The expression *kunywa maji* (drink water) is used with the meaning, 'go on strike, disobey, rebel'.

In describing the depth of water: *maji ya magotini* (or *mafuti*), water up to the knees; *maji ya kiunoni*, water up to the loins, &c. *Maji ya kilindi*, deep water. *Maji matulivu*, smooth, still water. *Maji maangavu*, clear, transparent water. *Pimamaji*, a water-level, used by builders. **Kimaji**, adv. and a., like water, wet, damp, watery, swampy. Also *-a kimaji*. **Umaji, Umajimaji**, n. being fluid, being watery, wet, damp, moisture, humidity.

Majibizano,* n. plur., **Majibu**, n. plur. See under **Jawabu.**

Majilio, n. plur. See under **Ja.**

Majilipio, n. plur., **Majilipizi**, n. plur., **Majilipo**, n. plur. See under **Lipa.**

Majilisi,* n. See under **Jilisi.**

Majira,* n. (1) time, period, season. *Majira ya mvua*, the rainy season (cf. *wakati, pindi*). (2) course of a ship—in navigation; (3) also used of a watch keeping time, e.g. *saa imepotea majira*, or *haina majira*, the watch does not keep good time. (Cf. *jiri, njia, mwendo*. Ar. مجرى.)

Majisifu,* n. plur. See under **Sifa.**

Majivu, n. plur. ashes, of burnt material. See **Jivu.**

Majivuno, n. plur. See under **Vuna.**

Majnun.* See **Majununi.**

Majonzi, n. (also sometimes heard as *mayonsi*), sorrow, grief, mourning, sadness. *Fanya* (*ona*) *majonzi*, be sorrowful, sad. (Cf. *ghamu, huzuni, simanzi, sikitiko*. ? Ar. مايوس.)

Majuni,* n. a preparation of opium, Indian hemp, &c., with sugar and other ingredients made up into a sweetmeat—strongly intoxicating. (Cf. *afyuni, madadi, kasumba*. Ar. معجون.)

Majununi,* n. (1) buffoon, jester; (2) madman (cf. *punguani, wazimu, mwenye kichaa*); (3) foolish conversation which causes amusement or ridicule, such as might be expected from a madman. (Ar. مجان.)

Majusi,* n. *ma-* astrologer. (Ar. مجوس.)

Majuto, n. plur. See under **Juta.**

Maka,* n. Mecca. (Ar. مكة.)

Maka, v. be astonished, be surprised, make an exclamation of astonishment or surprise. Cs. **Makisha. Kimako**, n. astonishment, surprise. (Cf. *shangaa, tunduwaa, duwaa.*)

Makaa, n. plur. coal, charcoal. See **Kaa, n.**

Makaakaa, n. the palate of the mouth. (Cf. *kaakaa.*)

Makadara,* n. See under **Kudura.**

Makafara,* n. See under **Kafara.**

Makala,* n. a written article, treatise. (Ar. مقالة.)

Makali, n. See under **-kali.**

Makamasi, n. plur. See under **Kamasi.**

Makamu,* n. and a. See under **Kaimu.**

Makani,* n. place, dwelling-place, residence, home. (Cf. *kao, makazi.* Ar. مكان.)

Makao, n. See under **Kaa, v.**

Makasi,* n. a pair of scissors, usu. *mkasi, mi-.* (Ar. مقاص.)

Makataa,* n., **Makatazo,** n. See under **Kataa.**

Makazi, n. plur. See under **Kaa, v.**

Makeke, n. trouble, annoyance, boasting, bragging, showing off. (Cf. *majivuno, malata.*)

Makelele, n. plur. See under **Kelele.**

Makengeza, n. plur. See under **Kengeza.**

Makeruhi,* a. a variant of *makuruhi.*

Maki,* n. thickness, stoutness. *Nguo za maki,* thick clothes. (Cf. *unene.* Ar. عمق.)

Makini,* n. and a. strength of character, dignity, serenity, and as a. quiet, calm, amenable, well-behaved, gentle, composed. *Roho makini,* a quiet disposition. *Fanya kwa makini,* do in a gentle, calm, dignified manner. (Cf. *-pole, -tulivu.* Ar. مكين.)

Makiri,* n. a cleat on the side of a native vessel, for fastening a rope. (Ar. مقر firm stand, &c.)

Makisi,* n., **Makisio,** n. See under **Kisi.**

Makiwa, n. plur. of *ukiwa,* used as a salutation when visiting a house of mourning. *Makiwa!* or *makiwani!* The answer being *yamepita,* if the corpse has been buried, or *tunayo,* if it is still in the house.

Makogo, n. plur. See under **Koga.**

Makolokolo, n. plur. bag and baggage, utensils, goods, chattels, &c. (Cf. *vikorokoro.*)

Makomba, n. a kind of gruel made from millet flour used in the preparation of native beer. (Cf. *pombe, kimea.*)

Makopa, n. plur. dried cassava, whether raw or cooked. (Cf. *muhogo.*)

Makoroa,* n. a knot tied in the rope of the anchor of a native vessel. (Cf. *mangrini.* Ar. مقرن what joins two things.)

Makororo, n. plur. (1) swollen glands in the throat; (2) the sound made when breathing with difficulty, or when a person is dying, *kuvuta makororo,* breathe with difficulty.

Makorowezo, n. plur. See under **Koroweza.**

Makosekano, n. plur. See under **Kosa.**

Makosi,* n. plur. loops of rope through which the oars of a boat are passed, used instead of rowlocks. (Cf. *kileti, kishwara.* ? Ar. مقاص cross-beam in which others are inserted.)

Makoza,* n. (1) the testicles (cf. *pumbu, hasua, kende,* prob. corruption of Ar. خصية testicle); (2) ivory armlets or bracelets. Both seldom heard. (Cf. *kikuku, bangili.*)

Maksai,* n. a castrated animal, bullock, gelding. *Ng'ombe maksai,* a bullock. (Cf. *hasi* and *towashi.* Ar. مخصى.)

Maksusi.* See **Mahsusi** under **Hususa.**

Makubazi,* n. plur. leather sandals with ornamentation. (Cf. *kiatu, staka, ndara, mtalawanda.* ? Ar. مكعب kind of shoe, and عز magnificent, &c.)

Makufuru,* n. See under **Kafiri.**

Makuli,* n. See **Maakuli.**

Makulima, n. plur. See under **Lima, v.**

Makungu, n. plur. signs of dawn, daybreak. (Cf. *ukungu.*)

Makupwa, n. plur. See under **Pwa.**

Makuru,* n. ointment, sticking plaster. (Ar. مرهم liniment, note the transp. of consonants.)

Makuruhi,* n. See under **Karaha.**

Makusanyiko, n. plur. See under **Kuta, v.**

Makusudi,* n., **Makusudio,** n. See under **Kusudi.**

Makutano, n. plur. See under **Kuta.**

Makuti, n. plur. See under **Kuti.**

Makuu, n. See under **-kuu.**

Makwa, n. (1) notches or holes cut in the top of an upright post to carry a cross-piece; (2) a prop, shore; (3) pieces of timber put in the bottom of a boat to prevent the cargo getting wet from the bilge.

Malaika,* n. (1) a messenger, an angel, a good spirit; (2) a baby. (Cf. *mtoto mchanga*, and dist. *malaika*, plur. of *laika*, down, fur. Ar. ملائكة.)

Malaji, n. plur. See under **La, v.**

Malalamiko, n. plur. See under **Lalama.**

Malale, n. sleeping-sickness, i.e. *ugonjwa wa malale*. (Cf. *mbung'o, chafuo*. Prob. from *lala*, but cf. Ar. ملال weariness, languidness.)

Malalo, n. plur. See under **Lala.**

Malango, n. plur. See under **Mlango.**

Malaria,* n. i.e. *homa ya malaria*, malaria fever. (Eng.)

Malau, n. inquiry into an offence, curiosity regarding an offence. (Cf. *shauri, utafiti, daawa*.)

Malaya,* n. a prostitute, either male or female (cf. *danguro, kahaba*, Pers. لايه prostitute); (2) a short garment worn by some women. (Ar. ملاية kind of garment.)

Malazi, n. plur., **Malazo, n.** See under **Lala.**

Malele, n. orchilla weed, *Rocella tinctoria*, used as a dye, and a regular article of commerce in East Africa.

Maleleji, n. and **Malelezi**, plur. the season of uncertain and changing winds between the monsoons and during the rains, also called *tanga mbili*. (Cf. *msimu, kusi, kaskazi*, prob. from *lala*.)

Malendalenda, n. mucus-like faeces, watery stools. (Cf. *choo, mavi, kinyesi*.)

Malenga, n. (1) a professional singer, employed to lead the singing in dances, concerts, &c. (perhaps at first the name of a well-known singer); (2) native beer (*pombe*) before it has had the fermenting agent added.

Maleuni,* a. See under **Laana.**

Malevi, n. plur. of *ulevi*. See under **Lewa.**

Malezi, n. plur. See under **Lea.**

Malhamu,* n. See **Marhamu.**

Mali,* n. property, goods, wealth, riches, possession. *Ni mali ya*, it is the property of. *Mtu wa mali*, a rich man. *Mali ya watu* (or *ya mwenyewe*), it is some one else's property, it is not mine. *Mali inayoondoka* (*isiyoondoka*), movable (immovable) property. There is a game called *mali ya mdimu*, guessing an unseen striker. (Ar. مال.)

Malidadi,* n. (1) one who dresses neatly, cleanly; also (2) a showily dressed person, fop, dandy, coxcomb. **Umalidadi**, n. (1) display of dress or ornaments, fine, neat dressing, and (2) overdressing, dandyism, foppery. (Ar. ملدان freshness, &c., or Pers. مالیدن rub, polish, furbish, &c.)

Maliki,* n. See under **Miliki.**

Maliki,* v. make a beginning of, set to work on, start a job, e.g. of construction, cultivation, &c. *Maliki shamba*, begin to clear, or hoe, a plantation. *Maliki kuunda chombo*, begin to construct a ship. Ps. **Malikiwa.** Prep. **Malikia.** Cs. **Malikisha. Maliki**, n. (1) planks used for beginning to build a dhow; (2) see under **Miliki.** (Ar. ملك.)

Malimati, n. also **Maliumati**, food eaten after a Muhammadan service for remembrance of the dead, in the first ten days of the third month after Ramadhan. (? *mali ya maiti*.)

Malimbiko, n. plur., **Malimbuko**, n. plur. See under **Limbika.**

Malimwengu, n. See under **Ulimwengu.**

Malindi, n. (1) a flap or small apron

of beads worn by a string round the loins by some native women (cf. *kondavi*); (2) see under **Lindi.**

Malipizi, n. plur., **Malipo,** n. plur. See under **Lipa.**

Malisha, n. plur., **Malisho,** n. plur. See under **La,** v.

Maliumati, n. See **Malimati.**

Maliwato, n. a bath-room, a place for bathing in a house.

Maliwaza, n. plur. See under **Liwaza.**

Maliza, v. (1) complete, finish off, bring to an end, conclude, wind up; (2) abolish, kill, destroy. *Maliza kazi*, finish a job. *Maliza deni*, pay off a debt. *Maliza adui*, annihilate an enemy. Ps. **Malizwa.** St. **Malizika.** Prep. **Malizia.** Cs. **Malizisha.** Rp. **Malizana.** (Cf. *timiliza, kamilisha, isha.*)

Malizano, n. plur., **Malizi,** n. plur. See under **Lia.**

Malki, n., **Malkia,** n. See under **Miliki.**

Malu, n. a kind of antelope.

Malumbano, n. plur. See under **Lumba.**

Maluuni,* n. See **Maleuni.**

Mama, n. mother, female ancestor or parent—of all kinds. *Mama wa kambo*, step-mother. *Mama mkubwa (mdogo)*, mother's elder (younger) sister. *Mama wee!* a cry in pain, sorrow, or surprise. *Mama mzazi*, one's own mother, i.e. who gave one birth. *Mama mlezi (wa kunyonyesha)*, a foster mother.

Mamanua, v. force open or apart, esp. of something fixed at one end, e.g. of piece of firewood partially split. In some places only used of forcing a girl.

Mamba, n. (1) a crocodile; (2) a name of a very dangerous kind of snake.

Mambo, n. (1) plur. of *jambo*, which see; (2) tent-pegs, plur. of *u(w)ambo*. See under **Wamba.**

Mamlaka,* n. (1) authority, dominion, rule, rights of ownership; (2) property, possession, dominions. In the latter sense, *milki*, is more usual. *Sina mamlaka na kitu hiki*, I have no right to (power over) this thing. (Cf. *miliki, enzi, amri, hukumu, nguvu, uwezo.* Ar. مملكة.)

Mamoja, n. See under **-moja.**

Mamsahib,* n. See under **Sahib.**

Manane, n. only in the phrase *usiku wa manane*, the dead of night, in the small hours of the morning. *Usiku huu umekuwa wa manane*, it is dead of night. (Cf. *nane*, eight—of which *manane* is perh. a plural. Thus *usiku wa manane* means 'the night at about 2 a.m.')

Manani,* n. a title of God, the Beneficient. (Ar. منان.)

Manati,* n. a catapult. (Cf. *teo, kombeo, panda.* ? Ar. مناط.)

Manawa, n. a skin disease especially of the hands, which become covered with light-coloured patches. (Cf. *nawa.*)

Manda, n. a kind of bread made from rice flour.

Mandari,* n. a picnic, dance, revel. *Kwenda mandari.* (From same Ar. root as follg.)

Mandhari,* n. appearance, aspect, landscape, prospect, view, scene, show. (Cf. *sura, namna.* Ar. منظر.)

Mandusi, n. See **Ndusi.**

Manemane,* myrrh.

Manena, n. plur. groin—between thigh and belly. (Cf. *kinena.*)

Maneva,* n. a bivouac—used by native dance societies of going into the country and having a feast before a dance. (? Eng. manœuvre.)

Manga, v. eat food without relish, gravy, &c., eat dry food. Prep. **Mangia. Umanga,** n. dry food, food without relish. *Ninakula umanga*, I am eating dry food (i.e. plain, without relish), and so, in poor circumstances.

Manga,* n. a name of Arabia, esp. the region of Muscat in the Persian

Gulf. It is used to describe various objects connected with or derived from Arabia, e.g. *pilipili manga*, black pepper. *Mkomamanga*, pomegranate tree. *Njiwa manga*, a variety of pigeon. (Cf. *Mwarabu, Arabuni.*) **Kimanga**, n. *vi-* adv. of the Arab kind. Hence of the Arab language, &c. (Ar. منقع the sea.)

Mang'amung'amu, n., and **Mang'ang'amu**, n. confusion of mind, fear of the consequences of one's actions, or of being found out in doing something wrong. (Cf. *ng'amua.*)

Manganja, n. plur. small rattles or bells worn on the legs of dancers.

Mangazimbwe, n. an optical illusion, a mirage. (Cf. *mazigazi.*)

Mangharibi,* n. See **Magharibi**.

Mangili,* n. a kind of cat-head or cross-piece for securing a cable, anchor, or rope at the bow of a native vessel. (Ar. مقرن. Cf. *mangrini*, of which this seems to be a variant.)

Mangisi,* n. *Kuku wa mangisi*, a kind of fowl with very long legs and a featherless neck. (Cf. *kidimu*. Ar. منقص defective condition.)

Mango, n. a hard, black, rounded stone used for pounding, smoothing, and polishing. **Kimango**, n. *vi-* dim.

Mangrini,* n. a knot tied in the rope of the anchor of a native vessel. (Cf. *makoroa*. Ar. مقرن what joins two things.)

Mang'ungumu, adv. secretly, by stealth. (Cf. *siri.*)

Mangwaji, n. plur. finery, foppery, showy dress or appearance, foolish display. (Cf. *umalidadi, ulimbwende.*)

Mani,* n. a weight, about three pounds. (Ar. منا.)

Manii,* n. semen. (Cf. *shahawa*. Ar. منى.)

Manja, n. Pemba White-eye, name of a bird, *Zesterops vaughani*, also called *shige-la-manjano*.

Manjali,* n. one of the ropes of a front sail. (Ar. جر.)

Manjano, n. turmeric—used as a yellow colouring material for ornament, and also in curry powder. *Rangi ya manjano*, yellow colour. *Rangi ya manjano mabivu*, orange colour.

Manjorinjori, n. plur. See under **Njorinjori**.

Manju, n. an expert at composing songs and leading the singing at dances.

Manoleo, n. plur. the metal shoulder of a knife, i.e. between the blade and the haft. (Cf. *noa.*)

Manong'onezo, n. plur., and **Manong'ono**, plur. See under **Nong'ona**.

Manowari,* n. a man-of-war. (Eng.)

Mansuli,* n. a kind of woollen material, used for dress and as a coverlet. (Ar. مسوح a coarse hair- or woollen-material.)

Manufaa,* n. See under **Nafuu**.

Manukato, n. plur., **Manuko**, n. plur. See under **Nuka**.

Manukuu,* n. a copy, transcript, translation, imitation, rarely used. (Cf. *nakili.*)

Manyonyota, n. See under **Nyonyota**.

Manyoya, n. plur. of *nyoya*.

Manyunyu, n. See under **Nyunya**.

Manza, n. trouble, crime, offence, legal process, litigation, dispute. (Cf. *daawa, shauri.*)

Manzili,* n. circumstances, position, as given by God. Anything sent by God, including revelations, &c. (Ar. منزلة.)

Maokozi, n. plur. See under **Okoa**.

Maombi, n. plur., **Maombo**, n. plur., **Maombolezo**, n. plur., **Maomvi**, n. plur. See under **Omba**.

Maondokeo, n. plur., **Maondoleo**, n. plur. See under **Ondoa**.

Maongezi, n. plur. See under **Ongea**, v. (A).

Maongezo, n. plur. See under **Ongea**, v. (B).

Maongozi, n. plur. See under **Ongoa**.

Maonji, n. plur., **Maonjo**, n. plur. See under **Onja**.

Maono, n. plur., **Maonyo**, n. plur. See under **Ona**.

Maowidha,* n. a variant of *mauidha*, which see.

Maozi, n. plur. See under **Oa**.

Mapafu, n. plur. of *pafu*.

Mapaji, n. plur. See under **Pa, v.**

Mapakio, n. plur., **Mapakizi**, n. plur. See under **Paka**, v. (A).

Mapalio, n. plur., **Mapalilio**, n. plur., **Mapalizi**, n. plur. See under **Paa**, v. (B).

Mapambano, plur. See under **Pambana**.

Mapana, n. plur. See under **-pana**.

Mapatanisho, n. plur., **Mapatano**, n. plur., **Mapatilizo**, n. plur., **Mapato**, n. plur. See under **Pata**.

Mapema, adv. in good time, early, soon. *Asubuhi na mapema*, early in the morning. (Cf. *jilawa, jidamka*.)

Mapendano, n. plur., **Mapendeleo**, n. plur., **Mapendezi**, n. plur., **Mapendo**, n. plur., **Mapenzi**, n. plur. See under **Penda**.

Mapepe, n. plur. empty husks of grain, empty (barren) ears of grain.

Mapepeta, n. plur. a preparation of immature rice. (Cf. *pepeta*.)

Mapigano, n. plur. See under **Piga**.

Mapinduzi, n. plur. See under **Pinda**.

Mapishi, n. plur. See under **Pika**.

Mapiswa, n. plur. unmeaning nonsense, drivel, silliness.

Mapokeo, n. plur. See under **Pokea**.

Maponea, n. plur., **Maponyea**, n. plur., **Maponyo**, n. plur. See under **Poa**.

Mapooza, n. plur. See under **Pooza**.

Maposo, n. plur. See under **Posa**.

Mapoza, n. plur. See under **Poa**.

Mapune, n. See under **Pua**, v.

Mapurendi,* n. plur. epaulettes, sometimes applied to decorations, gold braid, &c., of a uniform. (Corruption of same word, for *l* becoming *nd* cf. *peremende*.)

Mapuzo, n. plur. See under **Puza**.

Mapwa, n. plur., **Mapwaji**, n. plur. See under **Pwa**.

Mapyoro, n. See under **-pyoro**.

Mara,* n. and adv. (1) a time, a single time, a turn, an occasion, an occurrence; (2) at once, immediately. *Mara moja*, (1) once; (2) at once, immediately, but it is better to use *mara* only, or *mara hiyo*, to avoid ambiguity. *Mara mbili*, twice. *Mara nyingi*, often, repeatedly. *Mara kwa mara*, time after time, often. *Mara mara*, at intervals, at times, occasionally. *Mara hii*, at once, on the spot, also, this once, this time. *Mara chako, mara changu*, now yours, now mine—a riddle to which the answer is *mali*, wealth. (Cf. *safari zamu*, which are sometimes syn. Ar. مرة once, مر course, succession.)

Maradhi,* n. sickness, disease—in general. (Cf. *uele* and *ugonjwa*. For particular diseases cf. *homa, ndui, safura, surua, tetewanga* (*tetekuwanga*), *ukoma, baridi yabisi, sekeneko, kaswende, kisonono, kichocho, kifua, mafua*. Ar. مرض.)

Maradufu,* n. See under **Rudufu**.

Marahaba!* int. used as a common rejoinder to the salute of an inferior, dependant, or younger person. (Ar. مرحبا.)

Marahamu,* n. See **Marhamu**.

Marakaraka, a. See under **Kiraka**.

Marasharasha, n., **Marashi**,* n. See under **Rasha**.

Mardudi,* n. (1) repudiation, rejection; (2) the second time of doing a thing, e.g. go over a sum the second time in order to find an error, &c. (Cf. *rudi*. Ar. مردود rejected, refuted, ردد ponder, repeat.)

Marehemu,* n. and a See under **Rehemu**.

Marejeo,* n. plur. See under **Rejea**.

Marembo, n. plur. See under **Remba.**

Marendarenda, n. See **Malendalenda.**

Marhamu,* n. ointment, plaster, glue, any sticky substance. (Cf. *lehemu, mafuta, bandiko.* Ar. مرهم.)

Maridhawa,* a. in abundance, plenty, sufficient. (Cf. *ridhi, -ingi, tele.* Ar. رضوان.)

Marigedi,* n. a large cooking-pot of copper. (Cf. *sufuria.* Ar. مراجل.)

Marijani,* n. *Marijani ya fedhaluka,* red coral. (Cf. *fedhaluka, matumbawe.* Ar. مرجان.)

Marika, n. plur. of *rika.*

Marimba, n. a kind of native-made xylophone.

Marinda, n. plur. a skirt, the pleats of a skirt or similar pleats, i.e. of a loose cover of a settee, &c.

Maringo, n. plur. See under **Ringa.**

Marini,* a. pleasing in appearance, bright, smart, blooming. (Cf. *-zuri.* ? Ar. مرن practised, trained.)

Marisaa,* n., also **Marisau,** shot, i.e. for firearms. (Cf. *rasisi, risasi, kiasi.*)

Marmar,* n. marble. (Ar. مرمر.)

Marudi,* n., **Marudio,** n. See under **Rudi.**

Marufaa,* n. See under **Rufaa.**

Marufuku,* a. See under **Rufuku.**

Marugurugu, n. and a. small swellings, lumps, e.g. *mtu akijikuna, hufanya marugurugu ya mwili,* if a man scratches himself (as when stung), he raises swellings on his body. (Cf. *matuutuu.*)

Masa, n. evil. (Cf. *uovu.*)

Masahaba,* n. plur. the special friends and companions of Muhammad. (Ar. Cf. *sahibu.*)

Masaibu,* n. See under **Sibu, v.** (C).

Masakasaka, n. plur. dry leaves, twigs, &c., which have fallen from trees.

Masalala! Masalale!* int. See **Salala** (2).

Masalio, n. plur. See under **Saa, v.**

Masalkheri,* the common Arabic evening salutation, good evening—as *sabalkheri,* for the morning. (Ar. مساء الخير.)

Masamaha,* n. See under **Samehe.**

Masango, n. wire, esp. thick brass wire, used for making rings, bracelets, anklets, &c., for adornment. (Cf. *masoka, udodi.*)

Masaa, n. plur., **Masalio,** n. plur., **Masao,** n. plur., **Masazo,** n. plur. See under **Saa, v.**

Masega, n. *Masega ya nyuki,* honeycomb.

Mashairi,* n. plur. of *shairi,* which see.

Mashaka,* n. great hardship, trouble, difficulty, danger, distress. (Dist. *shaka.* Ar. مشقة.)

Mashambizo, n. the cloths with which a corpse is washed.

Mashapo, n. plur. dregs, lees, sediment, e.g. of squeezed fruits, grains, herbs, &c. (Cf. *masira, mashata, masimbi, mashudu.*)

Mashariki,* n. the East. *-a mashariki,* eastern, easterly, oriental. (Cf. *magharibi,* and syn. *matlai macheo, maao, uche wa jua.* Ar. مشرق).

Mashata, n. the remains of seed, &c., after the oil has been skimmed off; also any thick liquid with a lot of sediment, i.e. like thick gravy, &c. (? Ar. شطا.)

Mashendea, n. plur. rice cooked as a kind of gruel, or thinly, as for invalids.

Mashindano, n. plur. See under **Shinda.**

Mashine,* n. (or *mashini*), a machine, an engine of any description, sometimes used for a locomotive. (Eng. cf. *cherehani.*)

Mashobo,* n. showiness of dress, character of showing off. (Cf. *umalidadi, mkogo.* Ar. شاب youth.)

Mashono, n. plur. See under **Shona.**

Mashtaka,* n. plur. (seldom used in the sing.) charges, accusations, reproaches. See under **Shtaki.**

Mashua,* n. boat, boats—built of boards, &c., not hollowed out in native fashion. (Cf. *chombo.* Hind. مچهوا.)

Mashudu,* n. plur. the remains of seed, &c., after the oil has been pressed out. (Cf. *mashapo, masimbi.* Ar. شد to compress.)

Mashuhuri,* a. famous, renowned, celebrated, well-known, notorious. (Cf. *maarufu, -enye sifa, -bayana.* Ar. مشهور.)

Mashumushumu,* n. (1) an evil occurrence; (2) evil recoiling on a person, e.g. witchcraft employed by him, &c. (Ar. مشوم unlucky, inauspicious.)

Mashuzi, n. See under **Shuta.**

Masia,* n. *Enda masia,* walk about with the mind preoccupied, or in agitation, or with vexation, &c. (? Ar. مسح walk apace.)

Masifu,* n. See **Sifa.**

Masihara,* n. play, jest, light matter, e.g. *kujenga nyumba si masihara,* the building of a house is not play, it is not to be taken lightly. (Cf. *mchezo, mzaha.* Ar. مسخر laugh at, mock.)

Masihiya,* n. also **Mmasihiya,** n. *wa-* a Christian. **Masiya,** n. Christ. *-a masiya,* Christlike. (Ar. مسيحي.)

Masika, n. the season of the greater rains, when the hot north monsoon gives way to the cooler south. Corresponds to autumn in northern latitudes.

Masilaha, n. and **Masilahi,*** n. See under **Suluhu.**

Masimango, n. See **Simanga.**

Masimbi, n. plur. the remains after the oil has been pressed out of seeds, or after straining beer, liquid, &c. (Cf. *mashudu, mashapo.*)

Masimbulio, n. plur., **Masimbulizi,** n. plur. See under **Sumba.**

Masingizio, n. plur. See under **Singizia.**

Masiya,* n. See under **Masihiya.**

Masizi, n. plur. soot, grime, i.e. the black smoky grime that forms on a cooking-pot.

Maskani,* n. See under **Sakini.**

Maskini,* n. (1) a poor man, beggar—used descriptively, and also, (2) in pity or contempt, a hapless, luckless, miserable individual; (3) one who has no home or belongings, and often applied to a blind man or cripple, *maskini wa Mungu.* **Umaskini,** n. poverty, wretchedness, misery. (Cf. *fukara, mwombaji, mnyonge.* Ar. مسكين.)

Masoka, n. (1) thick iron or brass wire (cf. *masango*); (2) an evil spirit. (Cf. *mahoka, pepo, shetani.*)

Masomaso, adv. sometimes heard for *macho,* wide awake, with the wits about. (Cf. *macho,* and dist. *kimasomaso.*)

Masombo, n. girdle, consisting of a long piece of cloth wound round the waist. (Cf. *mshipi, ukumbuu, kibwebwe.*)

Masomo, n. plur. See under **Soma.**

Masongo, n. plur. See under **Songa.**

Mastakimu,* n. See under **Stakimu.**

Masua,* n. giddiness. (A form of *mbasua* which see. Cf. *kizunguzungu, kisulisuli.*)

Masuko, n. plur., and **Masukosuko.** See under **Suka.**

Masuluhu,* n. See **Suluhu.**

Masumbulizi, n. plur., **Masumbuo,** n. plur. See under **Sumba.**

Masuo, n. See under **Sua.**

Masurufu,* n. See under **Sarafu.**

Masuto, n. plur. See under **Suta.**

Mata, n. plur. of *uta,* native shooting-weapons, bows and arrows. (Cf. *upindi, mshale.*)

Mataajabu,* n. See under **Ajabu.**

Matabwatabwa, n. plur. anything

which has been pounded until it is soft and liquid, anything like gruel. *Matabwatabwa ya wali*, thin watery gruel made of rice.

Matafuni, n. plur. See under **Tafuna.**

Matagataga, adv. See under **Taga**, n.

Matakwa, n. plur. See **Taka**, v.

Matamalaki,* n. See under **Miliki.**

Matamvua, n. plur. See under **Chambua.**

Matana, n. leprosy, for the more common *ukoma*. (Cf. *jethamu*.)

Matandiko, n. See under **Tanda.**

Matanga, n. plur. (1) plur. of *tanga*, a sail, which see; (2) a formal mourning—usually in the plur. *matanga*, lasting from three or four to ten days, during which friends sleep in the mourner's house. *Kaa* (*weka*, *andika*) *matanga*, remain in (arrange a) mourning. *Ondoa* (*vunja*) *matanga*, go out of (end) mourning.

Matangamano, n. plur. See under **Changa**, v. (A).

Matanguko, n. plur., **Matanguo**, n. plur. See under **Tangua.**

Mataruma,* n. plur. of *taruma*.

Matata, n. plur. See under **Tata.**

Mate, n. plur. of *ute*, spittle, spitting, saliva. *Tema mate*, spit, expectorate.

Matege, n. plur. bow legs. *Mwenye matege*, a bow-legged person. (Cf. *chege*.)

Mateka, n. plur. (1) booty, prey, plunder, and esp. (2) captive in war, slave—used as sing. and plur. (Cf. *teka*.)

Matembele, n. leaves of the sweet-potato plant, used as a vegetable. (Cf. *kiazi*.)

Matembezi, n. plur. See under **Tembea.**

Matemo, a. and adv. (1) crooked, slanting, oblique (cf. *mshazari*); (2) see **Tema.**

Matendo, n. plur. See under **Tenda.**

Matengemano, n. plur. See under **Tengema.**

Matengenezo, n. plur. See under **Tengenea.**

Matengu, n. plur. (1) legs of a table (usually *matendegu*); (2) the outriggers of a canoe, *ngalawa* (usually *mirengu*).

Mateso, n. plur. See under **Tesa.**

Matetezi, n. plur., **Mateto**, n. plur. See under **Teta.**

Matezo, n. plur. See under **Tega.**

Mathalan.* See under **Mithali.**

Mathali,* n. See **Mithali.**

Mathubuti,* n. and a. See under **Thabiti.**

Matibwitibwi, n. See under **Tibua.**

Matiko, n. (1) hardening or tempering of metal. *Tia matiko*, harden, temper. *Fundi amelitia matiko shoka langu*, the smith has tempered my axe. So *tilika* (*pata*, *ingia*) *matiko*—of the metal. (2) plur. of *utiko*, which see.

Matilaba,* n. desire, wish, purpose. *Matilaba na mradi*, desire and intention. Sometimes used like *maarubu*, as a second motive, for doing anything, i.e. an ulterior motive, not necessarily a bad one. (Cf. *kusudi*, *nia*, *madhumuni*. Ar. مطلوب.)

Matilo,* n. a rope from the after-part of the yard to the masthead, to give greater security in a high wind. (Ar. متل firm, strong, &c.)

Matimutimu, n. See under **Timka.**

Matindi, n. half-grown maize (*muhindi*).

Matiti, n. (1) *enda matiti*, trot, go at a trot—of an animal (cf. *telki*, *mbio*); (2) plur. of *titi*, which see.

Matlaa,* but usu. **Matlai**, n. sunrise, the east, east wind, morning wind. (Cf. *mashariki*. Ar. مطلع.)

Matokeo, n. plur. See under **Toa**, v. (A).

Matongo, n. discharge from the eyes. *Mwenye matongo ya macho*, a person whose eyes run from weakness or disease. **Utongo**, n. same as *matongo*.

Matope, n. plur. See under **Tope.**

Matu,* adv. *Kuenda matu*, to go

with a perplexed, amazed gait as though astonished or afraid. (Ar. مات.)

Matukano, n. plur. See under **Tukana.**

Matuko,* n. plur. airs, graces, pleasing gait and manners. (Cf. *madaha, maringo.* ? Ar. طوق power, ability, range of mind.)

Matule,* n. (1) see under **Tule**; (2) a reception room or place for receiving company. (Cf. *sebule, majilisi.* Ar. تل reclining posture, with *ma-* of place.)

Matumatu, grasshoppers, young locusts, not yet in the flying stage. (Cf. *tunutu, maige, nzige.*)

Matumbawe, n. plur. coral stone in the intermediate stage, between actual formation and complete fossilization—a white, light, compact stone, used esp. on account of its lightness in concrete roofs; and being comparatively soft, it is also cut to form a projecting support for plaster string-courses.

Matumbo, n. plur. of *tumbo*, used of the intestines and stomach as a whole. See under **Tumbo.**

Matumishi, n. plur., **Matumizi**, n. plur. See under **Tuma.**

Matungizi, n. plur. (1) the level top of a wall or of a concrete roof, &c. (cf. *kirugu*); (2) see under **Tunga.**

Matunguu, n. wild cardamom, *Aframomum angustifolium.* (Cf. *kitunguu.*)

Matusi, n. plur., **Matushi**, n. plur. See under **Tusha.**

Matwana, n. a motor-lorry or motor-omnibus for carrying passengers. (Cf. *kweche.*)

Maudhiko,* n. See under **Udhi.**

Mauguzi, n. plur. See under **Ugua.**

Mauidha,* n. good advice, teachings, exhortations. (Ar. وعظ.)

Mauja,* n. (1) agitation, danger, misfortune, &c.; (2) a wave. (Ar. موج a wave, ماج be agitated.)

Maujudi,* n. things which are obtainable, or which are known from previous experience, or which are actually in one's possession. (Ar. موجود.)

Mauko, n. plur. See under **Uka.**

Maulana,* n. Lord, sir, a title of God. (Cf. *Mola.* Ar. مولانا.)

Maulidi,* n. birthday celebrations, esp. of Muhammad. (Ar. مولد.)

Maulisho, n. plur. See under **Ua, v.**

Maulizo, n. plur. See under **Uliza.**

Maumbile, n. plur. See under **Umba.**

Maumivu, n. plur. See under **Uma, v.**

Maundifu, a. sometimes used of very high tides, i.e. *maji maundifu.* (Cf. *bamvua.*)

Maungo, n. plur. See under **Unga, v.**

Maunzi, n. plur. See under **Unda.**

Mauri, n. plur. kind of hornet or stinging fly. (Cf. *dondoro.*)

Mauti,* n. death. *Patwa na (kutwa na, patikana na) mauti*, die. (Cf. *maiti, ufu, kifo.* Ar. موت.)

Mauwidha,* n. See **Mauidha.**

Mauzauza, n. (1) juggling, conjuring tricks, puzzles, illusions. (Cf. *mazingaombwe.*) (2) bewilderment, confusion of mind. (Cf. *wasiwasi.*)

Mava, n. a cemetery, a place where people are buried. (Cf. *makaburini, mazikoni, ziara.*)

Mavalio, n. plur., **Mavazi**, n. plur. See under **Vaa.**

Mavi, n. plur. (no sing.), (1) dung, excrement; (2) dross (of metal), scoria, e.g. *mavi ya chuma*, iron-workers' refuse, slag; *mavi ya nyota*, star droppings—used of bright metallic, sparkling stone, mica, &c. (cf. *ulanga*); (3) a coarse term of abuse and contempt, like *mawe*, rot, humbug, nonsense, trash.

Mavilio, n. plur. See under **Via.**

Mavu, n. a hornet. (Cf. *nyigu.*)

Mavumi, n. plur. See under **Vuma.**

Mavunde, n. plur. also **Mavunde-**

vunde, (1) broken, scattered, ragged clouds, a cloudy, overcast sky; (2) things which have become rotten or stale and smelly (cf. *vunda*); (3) fatigue, weariness, stiffness in the joints (cf. *mavune* (2)).

Mavune, n. (1) plur. see under **Vuna**; (2) stiffness in the joints, fatigue, weariness.

Mavunga, n. *mavunga ya nywele*, a thick crop of hair on the head.

Mavungu, n. plur. animals killed or caught in a hunt. (Cf. *mawindo*.)

Mavuno, n. plur. See under **Vuna**.

Mavusho, n. plur. See under **Vua**, v. (C).

Mavuzi, n. plur. the hair under the armpits and of the pudenda, considered to be particularly unclean by many tribes, and usu. kept shaved off.

Mawazo, n. plur. See under **Waza**.

Mawe, n. (1) plur. of *jiwe*. *Mawe ya mizani*, the weights of a pair of scales; (2) a coarse term of abuse and contempt like *mavi*, rot, humbug, nonsense, rubbish.

Mawele, n. plur. bullrush millet, *Pennisetum malacochaete* and other edible species. **Uwele**, n. same as *mawele*. **Mwele**, n. *mi-* the plant which bears *mawele*.

Maweo, n. plur. See under **Waa**, v.

Mawese, n. the oil of the oil-palm, *mchikichi*.

Mawingu, n. plur. of *wingu*.

Mayonsi,* n. See **Majonzi**.

Mayowe, n. plur. of *yowe*.

Mayugwa, n. plur. the leaves of the taro plant *jimbi*, a green vegetable like spinach when cooked.

Mayungiyungi, (1) plur. of *yungiyungi*, a water-lily; (2) honeycomb. (Cf. *kamba ya asali, masega, mazana*.)

Mazali and **Mazalani**.* See under **Mithali**.

Mazao, n. plur. See under **Zaa**.

Mazeka,* n. buglers (in a band, &c.). (Eng. music?)

Mazeru, n. See under **Zeru**.

Maziada,* n. plur. of *ziada*, **Mazidio**, n. plur., **Mazidisho**, n. plur. See under **Zaidi**.

Maziga, n. (1) a censer, a vessel for burning incense in (cf. *kifukizo*); (2) an earthenware dish, casserole.

Mazigazi, n. an optical illusion, a mirage. (Cf. *mangazimbwe*.)

Maziko, n. plur. See under **Zika**.

Mazimbwezimbwe, n. darkness, dullness. (Cf. *giza*.)

Mazingaombwe, n. juggling, tricks, conjuring, puzzle, optical illusions.

Mazingaumbo, n. sometimes heard for *mazingaombwe*.

Mazingazinga, n. plur., **Mazingira**, n. plur. See under **Zinga**.

Mazishi, n. plur. See under **Zika**.

Maziwa, n. (1) plur. of *ziwa*, which see; (2) milk; (3) *maziwa ya watu wawili*, dragon's blood (sap of a tree).

Mazoea, n. plur., **Mazoezi**, n. plur., **Mazoezo**, n. plur. See under **Zoea**.

Mazu,* n. kind of banana. (Cf. *ndizi*. Ar. موز banana.)

Mazuka, n. plur. See under **Zua**.

Mazungumzo, n. plur. See under **Zungumza**.

Mb-, a common plural prefix of nouns beginning with *u, w, uw, ub* in the singular, usually representing a change according to the phonetic laws of Swahili from original *n* sound. Words not found under *mb* may therefore be looked for under *u, uw, w, ub*.

Mba, n. (1) a kind of skin disease, causing irritation and subsequently scaling; (2) also applied to scurf in the hair. (Cf. *choa, dasi, rupia, uwati*.)

Mbaamwezi, n. See **Mbalamwezi**.

Mbaazi, n. *mi-* (1) a shrub bearing a yellow laburnum-like blossom and pods containing an edible pea (pigeon pea), *Cajanus cajan*; (2) the peas of this shrub. *Mbaazi mwitu, Eriosema psoraleoides*.

Mbacha, n. *mi-* an old worn small mat. Prov. *Usiache mbachao kwa msala upitao*, do not leave your old mat for a praying-mat which passes, i.e. do not desert your old friend for a new one who may not be permanent.

Mbadhiri, n. *wa-*, **Mbadhirifu**,* n. *wa-*. See under **Badhiri**.

Mbago, adv. *kwenda mbago*, to go separately, as two people who have quarrelled.

Mbahili,* n. *wa-*. See **Bahili**.

Mbala, n. also **Mbaa**, sometimes heard for *mbawala*, a bush-buck.

Mbalamwezi, n. moonshine, bright moonlight, full moon (prob. plur. of *uwala wa mwezi, uwala mwezi*. Cf. *waa*, v.)

Mbalanga,* n. a skin disease, esp. of the hands which become covered with light- or dark-coloured patches. There are two kinds, *nyeupe* (white). and *nyeusi* (black). (Cf. *manawa*, Ar. بلقاء spotted.)

Mbalasi,* n. See **Balasi**.

Mbalehe,* n. *wa-*. See under **Balehe**.

Mbali, adv. (1) far, far off, apart, on one side, distant (in place or time), long ago, long after, e.g. *rangi mbalimbali*, of different colours, many coloured, variegated. *Mambo haya ni mbalimbali kabisa*, these things are diametrically opposed *Watu hawa wanakaa mbalimbali*, these people live in different places—also used of people being on bad terms with each other. (2) also *mbalimbali*, distinct, separate, different, contrary, opposite; (3) with the Prep. form of verb, 'altogether, completely, quite', e.g. *ulia mbali*, kill outright. *Potelea mbali*, perish utterly—a common imprecation, 'go and be hanged'. *Tupia mbali*, throw quite away. With *ya* or *na*, is used as a prep. far from, distant from—in time, space, or quality. *Anakaa mbali na sisi*, he lives at some distance from us. With *-a* as an a., e.g. *safari ya mbali*, a long journey. **Umbali**, n. is sometimes used, distance, being distant.

Mbalungi,* n. *mi-* (1) the pomelo, shaddock, *Citrus decumana*; (2) grapefruit tree, *Citrus grandis*. **Balungi**, n. *ma-* fruit of the *mbalungi*. (Pers. بالنگ citron.)

Mbamba, n. *mi-* (1) see under **Bamba**, n.; (2) a plant with thorny branches, poisonous, *Euphorbia* sp.

Mbambakofi, n. *mi-* a good timber-tree, like mahogany, *Afzelia quanzensis*. In other dialects called *mkongo, mkora, mkola, mtame, mbarikia*.

Mbambangoma, n. *mi-* a shrub with long spines, *Fagara* sp.

Mbamia,* n. *mi-* Okra, Lady's fingers, *Hibiscus esculentus*. The unripe pods are used as a vegetable, the fruit is *bamia, ma-*. (Cf. *mbinda*. Ar. بامیا okra.)

Mbande, n. sometimes used of neap tides, &c. *Maji ya mbande*. See under **Maji**.

Mbandiko, n. *mi-*, **Mbanduko**, n. *mi-*. See under **Bandika**.

Mbangi,* n. *mi-* the Indian hemp, bhang, *Cannabis sativa indica*. Oil is obtained from the seeds, fibre from the stems, and the well-known narcotic. (Cf. *afyuni, majuni*.) **Bangi**, n. leaf of the *mbangi*, often chewed or smoked, and used in various sweet preparations—a strong intoxicant. Pers. بنگ.)

Mbango, n. (1) a kind of wild pig with projecting tusks (cf. *ngiri, nguruwe, gwase*); (2) a slang term for money.

Mbanjo, n. *mi-*. See under **Banja**.

Mbano, n. *mi-*. See under **Bana**.

Mbao, n. plur. of *ubao*. See under **Bao**.

Mbaraka,* n. *mi-*. See under **Baraka**.

Mbaramba, n. See **Mramba**.

Mbaramwezi, n. See **Mbalamwezi**.

Mbarango, n. *mi-* a stout club, cudgel. **Kibarango**, n. *vi-* dim.

Mbarapi, n. the sable antelope.

Mbari, n. family, relations, clan. *Yeye ni mtu wa mbari yangu*, he is a member of my tribe (clan, family).

Mbarika, n. *mi-* the castor oil plant—also applied to certain trees with seeds which when dry split open with a crack. From the verb *alika.* (Cf. *mbono mdogo.*)

Mbaruti, n. *mi-* the Mexican Poppy, *Argemone mexicana*, an annual herb with yellow flowers, used medicinally.

Mbashiri,* n. *wa-*. See under **Bashiri.**

Mbasua,* n. giddiness, craziness. (Ar. صما stupid.)

Mbata, n. coco-nut in the final state of ripeness and dryness, when the nutty part inside gets loose from the shell, commonly used for copra. (Cf. *mnazi* and *mchokoo.*)

Mbati, n. plur. of *uwati*, the poles laid along the top of a wall, or of side-posts, supporting the rafters on which the roof rests.

Mbavu, n. (1) plur. of *ubavu*, which see; (2) strength, e.g. *sina mbavu kupigana naye*, I have not sufficient strength to fight with him. **Mbavuni**, adv. by the side (of), alongside, on the sides (skirts, flanks). *Mbavuni mwa mlima*, on the flanks of the mountain. *Alimganda mbavuni*, he stuck to his side—kept close to him. (Cf. *kando, upande.*)

Mbawa, n. plur. of *ubawa.*

Mbawala, n., **Mbawara**, n. a bush-buck.

Mbawawa, n. a kind of fish, not considered good eating by Europeans.

Mbayana,* n. *wa-*. See under **Baini.**

Mbayuwayu,* n. applied to swallows and swifts. (Cf. *kijumba mshale.* Pers. بالوایة.)

Mbazazi,* n. *wa-*. See under **Bazazi.**

-mbea, a. See under **Umbea.**

Mbega, n. a monkey with long black silky hair, white on the shoulders. The Colobus monkey. (Cf. *kima.*)

Mbegu, n. (1) seed, germ, that from which a plant grows; (2) breed, race, stock. A wider term than *chembe*, *punje* (a single grain, a separate small thing), and including what is planted and set to grow, i.e. bulbs, roots, seedlings, cuttings, &c. Fig. of the germ of a disease.

Mbeja,* n. *wa-* a person who is neat, smart, well dressed, careful of appearance. *Mbeja wa kano*, a fine muscular man, athlete. **Ubeja**, n. smartness, neatness, good athletic appearance in a man. (Pers. بجا in place.)

Mbeko, n. See **Mbeleko** under **Eleka.**

Mbele, adv. and n. (1) of place,—before, in front, on the near side, on the far side, forward, beyond; (2) of time—long ago, previously, in the past, in the future, hereafter; (3) fig. in the front, in prominent place (as to rank, quality, value, &c.). *Mbele* is often used with *ya* or *za* (never *na*) in the above sense, and also (4) in the presence (of), in view of, and so, as compared with, e.g. as a noun, 'something before', *huna mbele wala nyuma*, you have nothing before or behind you, no prospects or resources, you are utterly destitute. *Neno hili nitakueleza mbele*, I will explain this matter to you presently. *Tuendelee mbele*, let us go forward. *Alikuja mbele*, he arrived previously. *Si mumewe mbele ya sheria*, he is not her husband according to the law. *Dunia si kitu mbele ya jua*, the world (earth) is nothing compared with the sun. *Akiba ya mbeleni*, a provision for the future. But note: *mbele* with the locative, *mbeleni*, is frequently used as a euphemism for the genital organs, both male and female. *Mbele* is the plural of *ubele*, or *uwele*, which in some dialects is a breast, hence its prepositional use with *za*, as well as *ya*. The seeming vagueness of *mbele*, as meaning 'on the near side' and 'on the farther side' and also 'before' and 'after' in time, is generally removed by the context suggesting the point of view. If the idea of movement onward, progression, is suggested by the circumstances or only present in the mind, then *mbele* is usually 'on the farther side, farther on, after', e.g. *mbele ya mlima*, beyond the mountain, otherwise *mbele* may equally well mean 'in front of, before'. *Alisimama mbele ya mlima*, he stopped on this side of the mountain, in front of it. *Hufunga mbele ya sikukuu*, there is a general fast before the festival. (Cf. *kabla, nyuma, baada.*) **Umbele**, the future, a place in front, &c., presumption, forwardness.

Mbeleko, n. See under **Eleka.**

Mbelewele, n. pollen.

Mbembe, n. *wa-*, **Mbembelezi**, n. *wa-*, **Mbembezi**, n. *wa-*. See under **Bemba.**

Mbenuko, n. *mi-*. See under **Benua.**

Mbezi, n. *wa-*. See under **Beza.**

Mbibo,* n. *mi-* the cashew apple and nut tree, *Anacardium occidentale.* The apple is called **Bibo**, n. *ma-*; the nut which grows at the end of the apple, **Korosho.** The tree is also called *mkorosho, mkanju.* (Port. *bibo.*)

Mbigili, n. *mi-* a thorny brier-like shrub, *Tribulus terrestris.* Its leaves are used as a vegetable. **Mbigiri mke**, n. *mi- Pedalium murex.* **Mbigiri mume**, n. *mi- Pretrea zanzibaricum.*

Mbiha, n. *mi-* a perennial herb with pale yellow flowers, *Abutilon zanzibaricum.*

Mbili, a. form of *-wili*, which see.

Mbilikimo,* n. a name by which the pigmy races of Central African forest regions are known on the coast, a dwarf. (Ar. بلا without, and قيمة stature, see *kimo.*)

Mbilimbi, n. *mi-* the cucumber tree, *Averrhoa bilimbi*, bearing acid fruit like small cucumbers which are used in native chutneys.

Mbilingani,* n. *mi-* the egg plant, 'mad apple' or brinjal, *Solanum melongena.* The fruit is called **Bilingani**, n. *ma-* and is used as a vegetable. (Pers. بادنگان.)

Mbinda,* n. *mi-* the okra, lady's finger plant, *Hibiscus esculentus.* The fruit is called **Binda**, n. *ma-*. Also called *mbamia.* (Hind. بهندى.)

Mbingiri, n. *mi-* a plant, the green stems of which are stirred up with milk and yolk of egg and used as an aphrodisiac.

Mbingu, n. plur. of *uwingu.* See under **Wingu.**

Mbini,* n. *wa-*. See under **Bini.**

Mbinja, n. plur. of *ubinja* and *uwinja*, whistling. *Piga mbinja*, give a whistle. *Endeleza mbinja*, make a long whistle. (Cf. *ubinja, mluzi.*)

Mbinu, n. See under **Benua.**

Mbio, n. and adv. (1) act of running, running with speed, fast. *Piga mbio*, run. *Enda mbio*, go quickly. Rd. *mbiombio*, at full speed. (Cf. *kimbia, upesi, hima.*) (2) a kind of cassava. (Cf. *muhogo.*)

Mbiomba, n. a maternal aunt. (Cf. the more usu. *shangazi*).

Mbirambi,* n. used only in the semi-Arabic expression of condolence to a mourner, or bereaved person, or after great personal loss, viz. *mbirambi zako.* Also in the form of *bi rabi zako*, e.g. *hunena, bi rabi zako. Hujibu, zimepita*, the usual words are 'thy (sorrow) be with the Lord', and the usual reply, 'they are over'. Also **Rambirambi**, in the same way. (Cf. *makiwa, pole.*)

Mbishi, n. *wa-*, **Mbisho**, n. *mi-*. See under **Bisha.**

Mbisi, n. See **Bisi.**

Mbiu, n. (1) a buffalo's horn—sometimes beaten as a musical instrument; (2) also formerly blown to call public attention, and so meaning a proclamation. *Piga mbiu*, give public notice, announce. *Ilipokwisha mbiu*, when the proclamation had been made. Prov. *Mbiu ya mgambo ikilia ina jambo*, when the buffalo-horn sounds, there is something of importance. (For horn cf. *pembe*, for proclamation *hubiri, tangaza, habari, ilani.*)

Mbiya, n. only used in the phrase *tia mbiya*, transplant seedlings. (Cf. *pandikiza* under *panda*, v. (B).)

Mbizi, n. a dive, diving. *Piga* (*enda*) *mbizi*, dive. *Hodari sana kwenda mbizi*, a first-rate diver. (*Mbizi* is used mainly of the plunge itself. Professional diving is described by *zama*, which see.)

Mbobo, n. fertility, abundance, cheapness.

Mboga, n. *mi-* (1) a large edible gourd, *Cucurbita moschata*, which is called *boga, ma-*; (2) when treated as belonging to the *N* class, is a general term for garden produce, edible vegetables of all kinds, including the above; hence (3) anything used as a relish for eating with rice, *ugali*, &c., even though it be meat or fish. (Various other vegetables are *dodoki, nyanya, mumunye, figili, bamia, bilingani, jimbi, kiazi, tango, uwatu, mchicha, yugwa, kisamvu.*)

Mbogo, n. a buffalo. (Cf. *nyati.*)

Mbokora, n. a narrow calabash used for drinking beer from. (Cf. *kiparia, kitoma.*)

Mbolea, n. manure, dung, richness of soil. (Cf. *samadi, rutuba.*)

Mbomoshi, n. *wa-*. See under **Bomoa**.

Mbona, adv. interrog., why? what for? for what reason? Also sometimes used in a non-interrog. sense, e.g. *mbona si vizuri mkikaa na kuwasengenya wenzenu*, don't you see that it is not good to sit and slander your companions. (Perh. from *ona.*)

Mboni, n. See under **Ona**.

Mbono, n. *mi-* the physic-nut plant, *Jatropha curcus* much used for making hedges. Its seeds yield oil. **Mbono mdogo**, n. *mi-* the castor-oil plant, *Ricinus communis*, also called *mbarika*. **Mbono pembe**, n. *mi-*, *Jatropha multifida*. **Mbono wa kizungu**, n. *mi-* a name given to the frangipane tree, also called *msanapichi, mjinga.*

Mboo, n. penis. (Cf. *dhakari, uume.*)

Mboza, n. *mi-* a tree, *Sterculia cinerea*, up to 25 ft. tall with star-shaped fruits which split open, exposing numerous black seeds with yellow axils. The bark of the younger trees makes excellent string and rope.

Mbu, n. mosquito.

Mbuai, a. invar. savage, wild, rapacious. *Mnyama mbuai*, a beast of prey. (Cf. *ua, mwuaji*; perh. for *mbuaji*. See also syn. *-kali, katili, -a mwitu.*)

Mbuga, n. steppe.

Mbuge, n. *wa-*. See under **Bugia**.

Mbugi, n. small bells, sometimes fastened to children's legs so that should they stray away, they will be heard. (Cf. *njuga.*)

Mbugu, n. *mi-* a kind of creeper, creeping plant. (Cf. *mbungo.*)

Mbuguma, n. a cow that has calved.

Mbuji,* n. *wa-*. See **Mmbuji** under **Umbuji**.

Mbuki, n. *wa-*. See under **Buki**.

Mbukulia, n. *wa-*, **Mbukuzi**, n. *wa-*. See under **Bukua**.

Mbulia, n. *mi-* a plant which has grown of its own accord, i.e. without being planted. (Cf. *mbotea.*)

Mbulu, n. *wa-* a person who says meaningless things because of madness or weak intellect.

Mbulukwa, n. *wa-* a person who is not in his proper senses. *Fanya mbulukwa*, play the fool. (Cf. *mbulu* and *puruka.*)

Mbungati, n. *mi-* the sausage-tree, *Kigelia pinnata*, also known as *mwegea, mnyegea, mvongonya*. The roasted fruits are put into native beer to ferment it.

Mbungo, n. (A) *mi-* a tree with an edible fruit like a medlar, *Landolphia florida*, also called *mbugu*.

Mbungo, n. (B) or **Mbung'o**, a tsetse fly, also called *chafuo*.

Mbungu, n. an eland. (Cf. *pofu.*)

Mbuni,* n. (1) an ostrich; (2) *wa-*, verbal noun of *buni*, v.; (3) *mi-*, a coffee-plant, the berries are *buni*, or *buni za kahawa*, and the beverage, *kahawa*. (Ar. بن coffee-beans.)

Mbura, n. *mi-* a tree with small yellow flowers and edible fruits the size of a plum, *Parinari curatellaefolium*.

Mburuga, n. magic or divining for finding out an offender, by using the *bao* or *ramli*.

Mburugo, n. *mi-*. See under **Buruga.**

Mburukenge, n. See **Kenge.**

Mbururo, n. *mi-*, **Mbuuzo,** n. *mi-*. See under **Burura.**

Mbuya, n. (1) a prostitute, a paramour, a woman living with a man who is not her husband (cf. *hawara*); (2) a companion or abettor in any evil undertaking.

Mbuyu, n. *mi-* the baobab or calabash tree, *Adansonia digitata*—often of enormous girth in proportion to the height, producing a large nut (*buyu*), the hard shell of which is used for drawing water, and the kernel (*ubuyu*, a dry biscuit-like substance with an acid taste) for flavouring food. The witch-doctor's name for the tree is *mkuu hapingwa*.

Mbuzi, n. (1) a goat, *mbuzi mwitu*, Klipspringer; (2) an instrument for grating coco-nut, i.e. a piece of iron with serrated edge fixed in a board.

Mbwa, n. a dog. *Mbwa wa mwitu*, a jackal, or wild dog. *Mbwa koko*, a bush-dog, the common pariah or half-wild dog of a reddish fox-like kind, living in the plantations near towns in a semi-domesticated state.

Mbwago, n. *mi-*. See under **Bwaga.**

Mbwanda, n. *mi-* the sword-bean, edible, *Canavalia ensiformis*. *Kula mbwanda*, an expression meaning get pleasant things, rejoice, be glad. (Cf. *mwande*.)

Mbwe, n. See under **Jiwe.**

Mbwedu, n. *wa-* and *mi-*, a man or thing which causes disgust, an abnormal man or thing. (Cf. *dubwana*.)

Mbweha, n. See **Bweha.**

Mbwende, n. a sort of small apron made of beads worn by some women underneath their ordinary dress. (Cf. *shegele, malindi, kondavi*.)

Mbweu, n. belching, eructation. *Piga* (*enda*) *mbweu*, belch. (Cf. *teuka*.)

Mbwoji, n. *mi-* a spring, i.e. of water. (Cf. *bubujiko, chemchemi, bwaga*.)

Mcha, n. *wa-*. See under **Cha,** v. (A).

Mchachatochachato, n. slow and careful walking.

Mchafuko, n. *mi-*. **Mchafuzi,** n. *wa-*. See under **-chafu.**

Mchago, n. *mi-* the end of a bedstead, where the head rests. (Cf. *kitanda*.)

Mchaguzi, n. *wa-*. See under **Chagua.**

Mchai, n. Lemon grass, *Cymbopogon citratus* (cf. *mzumai*); also tea bush.

Mchaji, n. *wa-*. See under **Cha,** v. (A).

Mchakacho, n. *mi-*. See under **Chakacha.**

Mchakuro, n. *mi-*. See under **Chakura.**

Mchamvya, n. *mi-* another name for *mchocha*, a tree with yellow edible berries.

Mchana, n. (no plur.) day as opposed to night (*usiku*), daytime, daylight. *Mchana* and *usiku* together make one day or period of twenty-four hours. An evening salutation is *Za mchana?* i.e. *Habara za mchana?* How have you been to-day?—with the invariable response, *Njema*, quite well. Also as a reply to a kind of challenge at night. One says *Usiku?* night? (i.e. enemy). To which the reply is *Mchana!* daylight! (i.e. peace). *Mchana kuchwa* (and *kutwa* the whole day long, like *usiku kucha*, the whole night long. *Mchana* is also used in a more limited sense, midday, noon, also *mchana mkuu*, i.e. the height of day (and commonly *adhuhuri* and *jua kichwani*). *Mchana mdogo*, the period before and after the midday hours. *Chakula cha* *mchana*, the meal eaten about mid-day. The commonest divisions of time are: *alfajiri*, when the first signs of light appear; *mapambazuko* and *kucha*, dawn; *asubuhi*, forenoon (including *mafungulia ng'ombe*, between 8 a.m. and 9 a.m.); *adhuhuri*, noon; *alasiri*, afternoon, about 3 p.m.; *jioni*, evening, till dark; *usiku*, night; *usiku wa manane*, dead of night, in the small hours of the morning.

Mchanga, n. (no plur.) sand. *Mchanga mnene*, coarse sand. *Mchanga mwembamba*, fine sand. *Mchanga mtifu*, loose, dry, dust-like sand. *Chembe ya mchanga*, a grain of sand. and perh. *uchanga*.

Mchanganyiko, n. *mi-*, **Mchanganyo**, n. *mi-*. See under **Changa**, v. (A).

Mchango, n. *mi-* (1) see under **Changa**, v. (A); (2) intestinal worms, *mchango wa tumbo*, but more frequently *chango ya tumbo*.

Mchanjo, n. *mi*. See under **Chanja**.

Mchanyato, n. *mi-*. See under **Chanyata**.

Mchapo, n. *mi-*. See under **Chapa**, v.

Mchawi, n. *wa-* a wizard, a witch, one of either sex who practises the black arts, a sorcerer, a magician. Contr. *mganga*, whose art is in the main under the control of, and allowed by, the community, e.g. *huyu ni mganga, kisha ni mchawi, wala hawezekani*, he's a medicine-man, and what's more, a wizard, and we cannot put up with him. **Uchawi**, n. witchcraft, sorcery, black arts, magic. (Cf. *loga, mwanga, uramali, mburuga*.)

Mche, n. *mi-* seedling, slip, shoot, cutting, young plant, e.g. *mche huu ni mti gani?* What tree is this cutting of? (Dist. *mchi* and *mchu*.)

Mchea, n. *wa-*, **Mcheaji**, n. *wa-*. See under **Cha**, v. (A).

Mcheche, n. *mi-* (1) like *cheche*, a spark, small drop, or piece, see *checha*, v.; (2) spine of a porcupine.

Mchegamo, n. *mi-*. See under **Chegama**.

Mchekecho, n. *mi-*. See under **Chekecha**.

Mchekele, n. *mi-* a wild olive tree. The cultivated olive tree is **Mzeituni**.

Mchekeshaji, n. *wa-*, **Mchekeshi**, n. *wa-*, **Mcheko**, n. *mi-*. See under **Cheka**.

Mchele, n. *mi-* rice—collectively, the grain as gathered and cleaned of the husk. The plur. is seldom used. *Mchele* has also a wider sense, i.e. 'cleaned grain' in general, hence *mchele wa mtama*, millet grain, and *mchele wa mpunga*, defining it as 'rice-grain'. Different sorts of rice are known locally as: *sena, bungala, shindano, karafuu, kapwai, kifungo, madevu, mwanga, sifara, uchukwi, korowai, meli*, &c. (Dist. *mpunga*, the rice-plant, growing rice, and the various kinds of cooked rice: *wali, uji, ubwabwa, mashendea*.)

Mchelea, n. *wa-*, **Mcheleaji**, n. *wa-*. See under **Cha**, v. (A).

Mchelema, n. See **Chelema**.

Mchengo, n. *mi-*. See under **Chenga**.

Mchenza, n. *mi-* the mandarin-orange tree, *Citrus nobilis*, the fruit is *chenza*.

Mcheshi, n. *wa-*. See under **Cheka**.

Mcheza, n. *wa-*, **Mchezaji**, n. *wa-*, **Mchezi**, n. *wa-*, **Mchezo**, n. *mi-*. See under **Cheza**.

Mchi, n. *mi-* a pestle, a pole of hard wood used for pounding grain, &c., in a wooden mortar (*kinu*).

Mchicha, n. a common plant with edible leaves used as a vegetable, like spinach, *Amaranthus* spp.

Mchikichi, n. *mi-* the oil-palm, *Elaeis guineensis*, bearing the fruit *chikichi*. The oil from the seeds is called *mawese*.

Mchikicho, n. seasoning, i.e. salt, pepper, lemon, &c., mixed together to put into food. (Cf. *kiungo*.)

Mchimbi, n. *wa-*, **Mchimvi**, n. *wa-*. See under **Chimba**.

Mchinjadamu, n. a kind of banana. (Cf. *ndizi*.)

Mchinjaji, n. *wa-*. See under **Chinja**.

Mchinjiko, n. cord made of the fibre

of the baobab tree, fastened round their breasts by some women when they are suckling a child.

Mchinjo, n. *mi-*. See under **Chinja.**

Mchiririko, n. *mi-*, **Mchirizi**, n. *mi-*. See under **Chiririka.**

Mchocha, n. *mi-* a tree with yellow edible berries, also called *mchamvya.*

Mchocheo, n. *mi-*, **Mchocho**, n. *mi-*. See under **Chocha.**

Mchochoni, n. *mi-* a plant with tuberous roots, eaten after removing the poison contained in them, *Dioscora* sp.

Mchochoro, n. *mi-*. See under **Chochoro.**

Mchochota, n. See under **Chochota.**

Mchokocho, n. *mi-*. See under **Chokoa.**

Mchokochore, n. *mi-* a tree, when its flowers open the natives say that the rains are over. **Mchokochore dume**, n. *mi-* (called *mtakawa dume* in Pemba) a common weed *Waltheria americana* with clinging seeds, smaller and rounder than those of the *mchokochore jike* (see below). *Mchokochore jike* n. *mi-* (also called *Mtakawa jike*), a common weed, *Urena lobata*, with burr-like seeds. The stem yields a good fibre, often used for tying cattle. Note: The two weeds *Mchokore jike* and *mdume* are nearly always found together, hence they are generally considered man and wife. *Urena* being the female and *Waltheria* the male.

Mchokoo, n. *mi-* (1) see under **Chokoa;** (2) a name for *mbata* (copra).

Mchokozi, n. *wa-*. See under **Chokoa.**

Mchomo, n. *mi-*. See under **Choma**, v. (A) and (B).

Mchongelezi, n. *wa-*, **Mchongezi**, n. *wa-*, **Mchongo**, n. *mi-*. See under **Chonga.**

Mchongoma, n. *mi-* (1) a kind of euphorbia; also a thorny hedge shrub, sometimes called *mlimbolimbo*; (2) Governor's plum, *Flacourtia indica.* (Cf. *chonga.*)

Mchoo, n. the rains which occur about July to September.

Mchopozi, n. *wa-*. See under **Chopa.**

Mchorachora, n. *wa-*, **Mchoro**, n. *mi-*, **Mchorochoro**, n. *mi-*. See under **Chora.**

Mchoroko, n. *mi-* a plant which produces an edible green gram, called *choroko, Phaseolus mungo.*

Mchoshi, n. *wa-*. See under **Choka.**

Mchoto, n. *mi-*. See under **Chota.**

Mchovu, n. *wa-*. See under **Choka.**

Mchovya, n. *wa-*, **Mchovyo**, n. *mi-*. See under **Chovya.**

Mchu, n. *mi-* a kind of mangrove with tough whitish wood, *Avicennia marina.*

Mchukuzi, n. *wa-*. See under **Chukua.**

Mchumba, n. *wa-*. See under **Chumba.**

Mchumbururu, n. a sword-fish. (Cf. *chuchunge.*)

Mchunaji, n. *wa-*, **Mchuni**, n. *wa-*. See under **Chuna.**

Mchunga, n. *wa-*, **Mchungaji**, n. *wa-*. See under **Chunga**, v. (A).

Mchunguti, n. *mi-* a tree usually called *msunguti,* which see.

Mchunguzi, n. *wa-*. See under **Chunga**, v. (B).

Mchungwa, n. *mi-* the tree which bears a sweet orange, *Citrus aurantium.* The fruit is called *chungwa, ma-*.

Mchuuzi, n. *wa-*. See under **Chuuza.**

Mchuzi, n. *mi-* any kind of gravy, soup, sauce, broth, esp. as used to flavour a dish of rice or other cooked grain.

Mchwa, n. white ants—of a small but destructive kind. (For other varieties of ants, cf. *chungu, siafu, maji moto, sisimizi, kumbi.*)

Mdaa, n. *mi-* a plant used for producing a black dye, also called *msirisha, Euclea fruticosa.*

Mdaawa,* n. *mi-* and *wa-*. See under **Daawa.**

Mdachi,* n. *wa-* a German. **Kidachi**, n. and adv. the German language, of the German kind. **Udachi**, n. Germany. (German *Deutsch*, sometimes *Jeremani* is used.)

Mdadisi, n. *wa-*. See under **Dadisi**.

Mdago, n. *mi-* a kind of weed, with pink or light-reddish flowers, *Adenium coetaneum*.

Mdahalo,* n. *mi-*. See under **Dahili**.

Mdai,* n. *wa-*, **Mdaiwa**, n. *wa-*. See under **Daawa**.

Mdakale,* n. *mi-* the stem of a pipe for smoking opium. (From same root as *digali*, i.e. Ar. رضع to suck.)

Mdakizi, n. *wa-*, **Mdako**, n. *mi-*, **Mdaku**, n. *wa-*, **Mdakulizi**, n. *wa-*. See under **Daka**.

Mdalasini,* n. *mi-* the cinnamon tree, *Cinnamomum zeylanicum*, also its bark. (Ar. دار صينى.)

Mdambi, n. giant heath, *Erica* sp.

Mdanganyi, n. *wa-*, **Mdanganyifu**, n. *wa-*. See under **Danganya**.

Mdanzi, n. *mi-* the bitter-orange tree, *Citrus bigaradia*, the fruit is called *danzi*, *ma-*.

Mdarabi,* n. *mi-* the rose-apple tree, *Eugenia jambosa*. (? Pers. دار a tree, and آب splendour, &c.)

Mdeki,* n. *mi-* a ramrod. *Shindilia bunduki kwa mdeki*, load a gun with a ramrod. (Ar. مدك.)

Mdengu,* n. *mi-* a plant which bears a small edible bean or pea, lentils. (Cf. *adesi*. Pers. دانگو.)

Mdeni,* n. *wa-*. See under **Deni**.

Mdesha, n. *mi-* a shrub or tree with white flowers and milky latex, *Conopharyngia* sp.

Mdewere, n. native spinach. See **Mchicha**.

Mdhabidhabina,* n. *wa-* liar, cheat, deceitful person, one who spreads evil or false reports. (Ar. ذبذب swing to and fro.)

Mdhalimu,* n. *wa-*. See under **Dhalimu**.

Mdhamini,* n. *wa-*. See under **Dhamana**.

Mdhana,* n. bad luck, a bad omen, anything which brings bad luck or misfortune. (Ar. ظان one who renders others suspect.)

Mdila,* n. *mi-* coffee-pot. (Cf. *buli*, for teapot. Ar. دل.)

Mdimu,* n. *mi-*. See **Mndimu**.

Mdiria, n. a kingfisher, also called *kizamiadagaa* and *mtilili*.

Mdirifu,* n. *wa-* a person in easy circumstances, neither too poor nor too rich. (Ar. ? ظريف elegant, skilful.)

Mdodoki,* n. *mi-* (1) a loofah, the fruit is eaten young in curries, and used as a vegetable, *Luffa acutangula*; (2) also *L. cylindrica*, used in curries and as a vegetable, and the ripe fruit is retted for sponges. The fruit is called *dodoki*. **Mdodoki wa Kibanyani**, n. a flowering shrub, *Capparis galeata*.

Mdoea, n. *wa-*. See under **Doea**.

Mdomo, n. *mi-* (1) a lip; (2) beak, bill (of a bird); (3) fig. anything lip-like, i.e. a similar organ, a projection, overhanging part. *Mdomo wa pande*, a hare-lip. *Piga mdomo*, pout—also, make a long speech, be garrulous—but usually *domo*, is used in this sense. **Domo**, n. *ma-* (1) large lip, large beak; (2) protuberance, projection, thing resembling a beak, overhanging crag, &c.; (3) brag, boasting, cant. *Piga domo*, let the tongue wag, brag, boast. (4) garrulity. *Domo kaya*, one who lets out secrets, a blabber. **Kidomo**, n. *vi-* (1) dim. of *mdomo*; (2) daintiness in food, e.g. *mwenye kidomo*, a fastidious person with regard to eating.

Mdomwa, n. a game in which people stand in two rows facing each other, they then jump up and down, at the same time clapping their hands. The opposites in the two rows must always come down with opposite feet, i.e. if one comes down on the right foot, his opposite must come down on the left foot, &c. (Cf. *tinge*.)

Mdongea, n. *mi-* a cloth to throw over the shoulders. (Cf. *mtandio.*)

Mdono, n. *mi-*. See under **Dona.**

Mdoshi, n. *mi-* a kind of pedal or treadle, working the part of a native loom which raises the threads of the warp alternately. (Cf. *Juma, kitanda.*)

Mdoya, n. See under **Doya.**

Mduara,* n. See **Duara.**

Mdubira,* n. *wa-* a person who always appears to have bad luck, everything he attempts fails. (Ar. رزية calamity.)

Mdudu,* n. (1) *wa-* see under **Dudu**; (2) a shrub with large tuber roots only eaten in time of famine, *Thylachium africanum.*

Mdukizi, n. *wa-*, **Mdukuo**, n. *mi-*. See under **Dukiza.**

Mdumu, n. *mi-* can, pot, jug, mug, esp. of metal, also **Dumu**, n. *ma-*.

Mdundo, n. *mi-*. See under **Dunda.**

Mdundugo, n. a kind of medicine or charm said to make one invulnerable, so that one cannot be harmed by bullets from a rifle, &c.

Mdunzidunzi, n. *wa-* a spy, detective, one who prys into the affairs of other people.

Mduriani, n. *mi-* or **Mdoriani**,* n. *mi-* the durian tree, bread-fruit tree, *Durio zibethinus.* Also called *Mfenesi wa kizungu.* (Malay *duri.*)

-me- for use as a tense infix, see Grammars. Prob. derived from the old perfect of the verb, *mala*, finish, which was *mele.* (Cf. *-ta-* future tense infix from *-taka*, and *-to-* negative of infinitive from *to(w)a.*)

Mea, v. 'grow' as a vegetable or plant—of plant life, but also of parts of the animal organization, which resemble plants in growth, i.e. hair, teeth, nails, &c. Also in a quasi-active sense, e.g. *buu likamea mbawa*, and the grub grew wings. Prep. **Melea**, grow in (on, by, &c.), grow as a parasite of, and also in a quasi-passive sense, be grown over, be overgrown, e.g. *shamba langu linamelea*, my plantation is overgrown (with weeds, &c.). Cs. **Melesha**, cause to grow (from the Prep. form to avoid confusion with *meza*, swallow). **Mmea**, n. *mi-* anything possessing vegetable life, or growth resembling it, plant, shoot, sucker, sprout, &c. **Mimea**, n. plur. vegetation in general. **Mmelea**, n. *mi-* that which grows at (in, on) some place or thing, a creeper, a parasite shrub. **Kimea**, n. *vi-* (1) dim. of *mmea*, also (2) the seeds of grain which are sprouted and then used for making beer. **Kimelea**, n. *vi-* a plant which grows of itself, a self-grown plant, an indigenous plant, generally applied to a vegetable parasite.

Mede,* n. (1) a small bedstead, used as a seat for guests. (Perhaps a corruption of Ar. مهد a cradle, bed. See *mahidi.* (2) goal, winning post, bay of safety in certain games. (Ar. أمد goal, limit, end, term.)

Mega, v. (1) break off a piece, take a bit, esp. with fingers or teeth—of taking a share of food, a help from a common plate or dainty; (2) fig. of breaking off in other ways, i.e. the sea and erosion. Ps. **Megwa.** St. **Megeka.** Prep. **Megea.** Cs. **Megesha**, e.g. invite to take a bite, ask to help himself. Rp. **Megana**, of general consent or common action. **Mego**, n. *ma-* a piece, a bit, a morsel, a bite, a helping, esp. of food. **Mmego**, n. *mi-* the act of breaking off or biting of a piece of food, &c.

Mei,* n. May, the month. (Eng.)

Meka, v. (1) be red hot, glow as of red-hot iron or fire; (2) be red, as of a wound, &c. Rd. *mekameka*, sparkle, shine, glitter. (Cf. *metameta.*)

Meko, n. plur. of *jiko.*

Meli,* n. (1) the word used for any steamship, whether carrying cargo or passengers; (2) goods imported by ship, and so a kind of rice, cloth, &c. (Eng. mail.)

Melikora, n. a kind of rice.

Melimeli,* n. a kind of thin cloth, muslin. (Hind. ململ.)

Mema, n. plur., a form of *-ema*.

Membe, n. a bird, the whimbrel, *Numenius phaeopus*.

Memeteka, v., also **Memetuka**, v. sparkle, shine, twinkle, as of the stars. (Cf. *umeme*.)

Mena, v. despise, scorn, hate. **Kimene**, n. pride, disdain. (Cf. *dharau, chukia, beza, kiburi*.)

Mende, n. (1) a cockroach; (2) a euphemism for one who practises sodomy, prob. because *mende* is called *mdudu wa choo*.

Mengi, a. form of *-ingi*.

Meno, n. plur. of *jino*.

Mentari,* n. tweezers, used for depilation. (Ar. منتاخ for change of final خ to *r* see *vinjari*.)

Menya, v. (1) shell, husk, peel, e.g. sugar-cane, &c.; (2) beat, pound. *Nilimmenya sana*, I gave him a sound thrashing. (Cf. *ambua, chambua, pua, twanga, ponda*.)

Menzili,* n. See **Manzili**.

Meremeta, v. sparkle, shine. (Cf. *metameta*.)

Merikebu,* n. a ship, esp. of foreign construction, as contr. with the native vessel *chombo*. Seldom used now except when referring to sailing-vessels. For steamers the usu. word is *meli*. (Cf. *rekebu*. Ar. مراكب.)

Meta, v. and **Metameta**, shine, sparkle, glitter, be bright, &c., e.g. of polished metal, fire-flies, stars, &c. St. **Meteka**, e.g. *upanga humeteka kote kote*, the sword is bright all over. Cs. **Metesha**, make shine, polish. **Kimeta**, n. *vi-*, also **Kimete**, n. *vi-*, and **Kimetameta**, n. *vi-* sparkling, sparkle, glitter, lustre, shining. *Kimeta cha jua*, sparkling radiance of the sun. *Kimeta cha upanga*, the glitter of a sword. Also in the forms *kimeti, kimetimeti, kimerimeti*, of anything sparkling, spangle, tinsel, and esp. of fire-flies, glow-worms, &c. (Cf. *meka, memeteka, memetuka*, also *mulimuli, mulika*, and of steady light *ng'aa, anga*.)

Methalani, conj., **Methali**,* n. See under **Mithali**.

Meza,* n. a table, raised wooden bench, school form. *Mezani* (of Europeans) at a meal, at dinner—also dining-room, mess-room, i.e. *chumba cha kulia*. (Pers. ميز and Port. *mesa*.)

Meza, v. swallow, swallow up. Ps. **Mezwa**. St. **Mezeka**.

Mfaa, n. *mi-* centre-piece of native door, fixed to one valve, the other closing against it, i.e. *upanga wa mlango*.

Mfadhili,* n. *wa-*. See under **Fadhili**.

Mfagio, n. *mi-* a fibre plant used for brooms, *Sida carpinifolia*. (Cf. *fagia*.)

Mfalme, n. *wa-* king, chief, ruler. **Ufalme**, n. (*falme*) (1) chieftainship, kingship, royalty; (2) sway, rule, dominion; (3) sphere of dominion, kingdom. (Cf. *enzi, mamlaka, ukuu, utawala*.)

Mfano, n. *mi-*. See under **Faa**.

Mfanya, n. *wa-*, **Mfanyi**, n. *wa-*. See under **Fanya**.

Mfaransa,* n. *wa-*. See under **Faransa**.

Mfariji,* n. *wa-*. See under **Faraja**.

Mfarika,* n. *wa-* a young animal, goat, sheep, &c., grown but not yet breeding. (Ar. فراخ young of birds and animals.)

Mfariki,* n. *mi-* and *wa-*. See under **Faraka**.

Mfarishi,* n. *mi-* a kind of thin quilted mattress, a quilt. (Ar. فراش a pallet.)

Mfaruku, n. *wa-*. See under **Faraka**.

Mfasa, n. *mi-* a tall herb with blue daisy-like flowers, *Veronica obconica*.

Mfasiri,* n. *wa-*. See under **Fasiri**.

Mfenesi,* n. *mi-* the jack-fruit tree, *Artocarpus integra*, a single fruit of which often weighs over 20 lb.

edible fruits and useful timber. The seeds also are eaten cooked or raw. The fruit is called **Fenesi**, n. *ma-*. **Mfenesi wa kizungu**, n. *mi-*, *Artocarpus communis*, the fruit of this tree is appreciated for its seeds which resemble those of the jack-fruit and are used in the same way. *Mfenesi punda*, a tree which bears a fruit not so sweet as the ordinary type. *Mfenesi tende*, a tree which bears very sweet fruit.

Mfereji,* n. *mi-* a ditch, water-channel, trench dug for carrying off water or for irrigation. (Ar. فرج.)

Mfichachani, n. a kind of banana. (Cf. *ndizi*.)

Mfichaji, n. *wa-*, **Mfichifichi**, n. *wa-*. See under **Ficha**.

Mfidhuli, n. *wa-*. See under **Fidhuli**.

Mfigili,* n. *mi-* a kind of radish plant, with an edible root, *Raphanus sativus*. The roots are called **Figili**, n. *ma-*. (Ar. فجل.)

Mfiko, n. *mi-*. See under **Fika**.

Mfilisi, n. *wa-*, **Mfilisika**,* n. *wa-*. See under **Filisi**.

Mfinyanzi, n. *wa-*. See under **Finyanga**.

Mfinyo, n. *mi-*. See under **Finya**.

Mfiraji,* n. *wa-*. See under **Fira**.

Mfisadi,* n. *wa-*. See under **Fisadi**.

Mfisha, n. *wa-*, **Mfishaji**, n. *wa-*. See under **Fa**.

Mfitini,* n. *wa-*. See under **Fitina**.

Mfiwa, n. *wa-*. See under **Fa**.

Mfiwi, n. *mi-* the plant producing the lima bean, *Phaseolus lunatus*. The beans are edible and are called **Fiwi**, n. **Mfiwi mafuta**, n. *mi-* the Bonavist bean plant, *Dolichos lablab*, the beans of which are edible.

Mfo, n. *mi-* a torrent, rain-fed stream, flood, also the channel or bed of a torrent. *Mfo mkavu*, dry bed of a torrent. *Leo kumeshuka mfo, hakupitiki*, to-day a flood has come down, it is impossible to cross. *Mto ulikuwa na mfo*, the river was in flood. (Cf. *mto, furika*.)

Mforsadi,* n. *mi-* the mulberry-tree, *Morus alba*. The fruit is called **Forsadi**. (Ar. فرصاد.)

Mfu, n. *wa-*. See under **Fa**.

Mfua, n. *wa-* and *mi-*. See under **Fua**.

Mfuasi, n. *wa-*. See under **Fuata**.

Mfufu, n. *mi-*, also **Mfuu**, n. *mi-* a tree bearing small black edible berries called **Fuu**, *Vitex cuneata*.

Mfufuaji, n. *wa-*. See under **Fufua**.

Mfufumaji, n. *mi-* a kind of tree.

Mfufuzi, n. *wa-*. See under **Fufua**.

Mfuga, n. *wa-*, **Mfugaji**, n. *wa-*, **Mfugo**, n. *mi*. See under **Fuga**.

Mfujaji, n. *wa-*. See under **Fuja**.

Mfuko, n. *mi-* a bag, pocket—a general term, with dim. **Kifuko**, n. *vi-* and amplic. **Fuko**, n. *ma-* a large bag, travelling bag, saddle-bag—sometimes used for the womb. (Cf. *tumbo, mji*. Various kinds of bags are *fumba, gunia, kanda, mtumba*.)

Mfukuaji, n. *wa-*. See under **Fukia**.

Mfukuto, n. *mi-*. See under **Fuka**.

Mfukuzi, n. *wa-* (1) see under **Fukia**; (2) also under **Fukuza**.

Mfulizo, n. *mi-*, **Mfululizo**, n. *mi-*. See under **Fua**.

Mfuma, n. *wa-*, **Mfumaji**, n. *wa-*. See under **Fuma**.

Mfumba, n. *wa-*, **Mfumbaji**, n. *wa-*. See under **Fumba**.

Mfumbati, n. *mi-* the side-piece of the frame of a native bedstead. See **Kitanda** under **Tanda**.

Mfumbi, n. *mi-* a trench or channel dug to carry away rain-water.

Mfumbua, n. *wa-*, **Mfumbuaji**, n. *wa-*. See under **Fumba**.

Mfumi, n. *wa-*, **Mfumo**, n. *mi-*. See under **Fuma**, v. (A).

Mfumo, n. *wa-* and old name for a chief. (Cf. *jumbe, mtawala*.)

Mfumua, n. *wa-*, **Mfumuaji**, n. *wa-*. See under **Fuma**, v. (A).

Mfundishi, n. *wa-*. See under **Funda**, v. (C).

Mfundo, n. *mi-*. See under **Funda**, v. (D).

Mfune, n. *mi-* a straight tall tree with

a white bark, also called *mgude*, *Sterculia appendiculata*.

Mfunga, n. *wa-*, **Mfungizo**, n. *mi-*, **Mfungo**, n. *mi-*, **Mfunguo**, n. *mi-*, **Mfungwa**, n. *wa-*. See under **Funga.**

Mfuniko, n. *mi-*. See under **Funika.**

Mfununu, n. *mi-* a kind of tree.

Mfunza, n. *wa-*, **Mfunzaji**, *wa-*, **Mfunzi**, *wa-*. See under **Funda**, v. (C).

Mfuo, n. *mi-* (1) see under **Fua**, v.; (2) a groove, crease, mark made by drawing a line, stripe, band of colour, &c.; (3) a carpenter's tool for making broad holes; (4) a furrow dug under a bed to receive the water when a corpse is being washed; (5) a furrow, e.g. *chora mifuo*, plough furrows.

Mfupa, n. *mi-* a bone. *Mifupa*, a skeleton. *Mifupa mitupu*, a mere skeleton, i.e. very emaciated. **Kifupa**, n. *vi-* dim. **Fupa**, n. *ma-* amplic. a large bone. *Fupa la kichwa*, the skull, also called *fuu* or *fuvu*. *Fupa jororo*, (large) cartilage. **Ufupa**, n. bony substance, cartilage, gristle.

Mfuradi,* n. a verse of poetry. (Cf. *shairi, beti*. Ar. مفرد.)

Mfure, n. *mi-* a kind of wooden platter.

Mfuria,* n. also *kanzu ya mfuria*, an Arab garment, a sort of loose cloth coat, with a collar, but no sleeves. (Ar. فروة tunic with turned-up sleeves.)

Mfurungu,* n. *mi-* the citron-tree, *Citrus medica*. Also shaddock. The fruit is **Furungu**, n. *ma-*. (From same root as *balungi*.)

Mfuto, n. *mi-*. See under **Futa**, v. (A).

Mfuu, n. *mi-* a tree bearing a small black edible berry, also called *mfufu*.

Mfyatuko, n. *mi-*. See under **Fyata.**

Mfyeka, n. *wa-*. See under **Fyeka.**

Mfyozaji, n. *wa-*, **Mfyozi**, n. *wa-*. See under **Fyoza.**

Mfyuso, n. *mi-*. See under **Fyata.**

Mgaagaa, n. *wa-* and *mi-*. See under **Gaagaa.**

Mgahawa,* n. *mi-*. See **Mkahawa.**

Mgambo, n. *mi-*. See under **Amba**, v. (A).

Mganda, n. *mi-* (1) a bundle, a sheaf, e.g. of rice or other crop. (See **Ganda**); (2) a kind of drum.

Mganda wa simba, n. *mi-* a kind of custard apple. (Cf. *mtopetope, mstafeli, mtomoko.*)

Mgandisho, n. *mi-*, **Mgando**, n. *mi-*. See under **Ganda.**

Mganga, n. *mi-* a shrub up to 12 ft. tall with fleshy green branches which contain a milky latex, used as a fish poison, *Synadenium carinatum*.

Mganga, n. *wa-*. See under **Ganga.**

Mgangajale, n. *mi-* a kind of tree.

Mgangaungo, n. *mi-* a tree from which the colour used for smearing sifting trays is obtained.

Mgange, n. *mi-* same as *mkabilishemsi*, which see.

Mgango, n. *mi-*, **Mganguzi**, n. *wa-*. See under **Ganga.**

Mgaragazo, n. *mi-* confusion, muddle. (Cf. *chafuko, fujo, ghasia.*)

Mgawanya, n. *wa-*, **Mgawanyi**, n. *wa-*, **Mgawanyo**, n. *mi-*, **Mgawo**, n. *mi-*. See under **Gawa.**

Mgema, n. *wa-*, **Mgemi**, n. *wa-*, **Mgemo**, n. *mi-*. See under **Gema.**

Mgeni, n. *wa-*. See under **-geni.**

Mghafala,* n. *mi-*. See under **Ghafilika.**

Mghalaba,* **n.** See under **Ghilibu.**

Mgiligilani,* n. *mi-* the coriander plant, *Coriandrum sativum*. Oil is extracted from the seeds and the leaves and fruit are used for curries. (Ar. جلجلان.)

Mgogoro, n. *mi-* (1) an obstacle, obstruction, e.g. a stone or tree in the road; (2) difficulty, nuisance, trouble, worry. (Cf. *zuio, taiizo, shida, kwao.*)

Mgomba, n. *mi-* (1) the banana plant, *Musa sapientum*, bearing the fruit *ndizi* (which see), and producing a strong fibre, called **Ugomba**; (2) the plantain, *Musa paradisiaca*; (3) *wa-* see under **Gomba.**

Mgombakofi, n. *mi-* a tree found in swamps, *Typhonodorum lindleyanum*. The roots are called *majimbi*. Also called *mtongonya*.

Mgombezi, n. *wa-*. See under **Gomba**.

Mgombwe, n. *mi-* bull's-mouth shell (*Cassis rubra*).

Mgomvi, n. *wa-*. See under **Gomba**.

Mgongo, n. *mi-* (1) the back, back part, backbone—of man or animal; (2) of things resembling the back, anything raised, ridge, hump, edge. *Geuka* (*elekeza, -pa*) *mgongo*, turn the back—in fear, contempt, &c. (Cf. *-pa kisogo.*) *Lala mgongoni*, lie on the back. (Cf. *kichalichali, kitanitani.*) *Mgongo wa nyumba*, ridge of a roof. *Nyumba ya mgongo*, a house with a ridge-roof. (Cf. *paa.*) *Njia ya mgongo*, a raised path, causeway. *Mgongo wa mwitu*, a thick line of trees, a forest ridge. *Kinyosha* (*kiinua*) *mgongo*, a back straightener, i.e. a gratuity after a hard job. **Gongo**, n. *ma-* amplic. use of thick dense ridges, humps, &c. (1) seam in a cloth; (2) hump (of a camel) (cf. *nundu*); (3) dense wood, thicket, *gongo la mwitu*, where trees are thickest in a forest. *Gongo la mlima*, a broad hill. **Jongo**, n. *ma-* (1) amplic. (for *ji-ongo*), a large high back, ridge, high projection; (2) a seam—in sewing. *Jongo nene*, a large projecting seam. (3) an ailment accompanied by pains in the joints, like rheumatism. **Kigongo**, n. *vi-* dim. *mwenye kigongo*, or *kigongo*, a hunchback, a deformed man. **Kijongo**, n. *vi-* dim. a hump-backed person, &c., like *kigongo*. (Cf. *maungo, kibiongo.*)

Mgoni, n. *wa-*. See under **Gona**.

Mgonjwa, n. *wa-*. See under **-gonjwa**.

Mgono, n. *mi-* a kind of fish-trap. (Cf. *dema.*)

Mgoto, n. *mi-*. See under **Gota**.

Mgude, n. *mi-* a very tall tree with whitish bark. Also called *mfune*.

Mgulabi,* n. *mi-* the litchi fruit-tree, *Nephelium lappasceum*. (Pers. گلابی.)

Mgumba, n. *wa-* (1) a sterile man, one who begets no children, hence (2) a lonely man. (Cf. *gumba.*)

Mgumio, n. *mi-*. See under **Guma**.

Mgunda, n. *mi-* a plantation, for the commoner *shamba*.

Mgunga, n. (1) *wa-* see under **Gunga**; (2) *mi-* a species of acacia.

Mguno, n. *mi-*. See under **Guna**.

Mgunya, n. *wa-* a native of the coast district between Mombasa and the river Juba.

Mguruguru, n. See **Guruguru**.

Mguruto, n. *mi-*. See under **Guruta**.

Mguso, n. *mi-*. See under **Gusa**.

Mguu, n. *mi-* (1) the leg—of man or any kind of living creature, and esp. the lower part of it, the foot; (2) anything resembling a leg, in shape or function. *Enda kwa miguu*, go on foot, walk. *Shika miguu* (*ya*), make obeisance (to), become a subject or dependant (of). *Panua* (*tanua*) *miguu*, take long strides, also, open the legs. **Guu**, n. *ma-* (1) amplic. of *mguu*, anything resembling a leg or foot of man or animal; (2) *tia guu*, cause trouble, annoyance, &c. **Kiguu**, n. *vi-* dim. (1) a leg or foot disabled or shortened by injury or disease, &c., a stump, club-foot; (2) a person disabled or disfigured, one who walks lame, crippled, unable to walk; (3) anything like a leg or leg-shaped. **Mjiguu**, n. *mi-* (1) a large foot or leg; (2) a person with an extra large foot or long leg.

Mgwaru, n. *mi-* the cluster bean plant; an erect herb cultivated as fodder, *Cyamopsis psoraloides*. The beans are **Gwaru**, n. *ma-*.

Mgwisho, n. *mi-* a fly switch, the tail of an animal tied to the end of a stick used for keeping off flies. (Cf. *mwengo* (2).)

Mhabeshi,* n. *wa-*, also **Habeshi**, n. *ma-*, an Abyssinian.

Mhadimu,* n. *wa-*. See under **Hadimu.**

Mhajiri,* n. *wa-*. See under **Hajiri.**

Mhalbori,* n. *mi-* a strip of lining under the ornamental silk stitching down the front of a *kanzu*. (Ar. محل place, and Pers. بر bosom.)

Mhali,* n. See **Muhali.**

Mhambarashi, n. *mi-*. See **Mpweke.**

Mhamishi, n. *wa-*. See under **Hama.**

Mhanga, n. *wa-* (1) an animal described as being about the same size as a sheep, which is said to dig the holes in which porcupines live, as they are said to be unable to dig; (2) any animal killed as a sacrifice or offering to spirits, &c. (Cf. *kafara.*)

Mhanuni,* n. *mi-*. See **Mhina.**

Mharabu,* n. *wa-*. See under **Harabu.**

Mharagi,* n. *mi-*. See **Mharagwe.**

Mharagwe,* n. *mi-* a bean plant. The beans are **Haragwe,** n. *ma-*. (? Pers. خرقي a kind of grain.)

Mharibifu,* n. *wa-*. See under **Harabu.**

Mharita,* n. *mi-* the soapberry tree, *Sapindus saponaria*. The seeds are used as a substitute for soap, esp. for washing the hair and garments made of silk. (Hind. ريٹھا.)

Mharuma,* n. *mi-* a coloured woollen shawl, sometimes worn as a turban, much favoured by Muhammadan teachers and that type of native. (Ar. مخرم embroidered, chased.)

Mhashiri,* n. *mi-* a strong beam, to which the mast is secured in a native vessel. (Cf. *mwashiri*, which appears to be a variant from the same root. Ar. صارى cross-beam with *m* prefix.)

Mhasi,* n. *wa-*. See under **Hasi.**

Mhenga, n. *wa-* (1) the chief of the *kungwi*, which see; (2) an elder who sits on a native council, or who is trusted to give sound advice.

Mhenzerani,* n. *mi-* a plant producing a thin kind of cane, called *henzerani*. (Ar. خنزران.)

Mhimili,* n. *mi-* and *wa-*. See under **Hamali.**

Mhina,* n. *mi-* the henna plant, *Lawsonia inermis*. The leaves when steeped in water make a red dye which is used for staining the fingers, feet, beard, &c. Also called *mhanuni*. (Ar. حنا.)

Mhindi,* n. *wa-* a native of India. (Sometimes heard for *muhindi* which is usu. maize.) **Kihindi,** n. and adv. anything Indian, esp. an Indian language. *-a kihindi*, Indian, of the Indian kind. **Uhindi,** n. India, also **Bara Hindi.**

Mhirabu,* n. *mi-* the apse of a mosque, which shows the direction of Mecca, i.e. in which to turn during prayers. (Ar. محراب.)

Mhisani,* n. *wa-*. See under **Hisani.**

Mhitaji,* n. *wa-*. See under **Hitaji.**

Mhogo,* n. *mi-*. See **Muhogo.**

Mhoro, n. *mi-* a wooden spear, pointed stick, used for putting in game-traps, &c. (Cf. *mkonjo, konzo.*)

Mhubiri,* n. *wa-*. See under **Hubiri.**

Mhulihuli, n. *mi-* a large tree with small edible fruits, *Sorindeia Madagascariensis*.

Mhuni,* n. *wa-*. See under **Huni.**

Mhunzi, n. *wa-* a worker in metals or stone, a smith, a stone-cutter. Usually defined by the word following, e.g. *mhunzi wa chuma* (*fedha, bati*), a blacksmith (silversmith, tin-worker), (but silversmith, goldsmith, jeweller, &c., is usu. *sonara*). *Mhunzi wa mawe*, a stone-cutter, carver in stone. **Uhunzi,** n. work (pay, &c.) of a blacksmith. (Cf. *fua.*)

Mia,* n. and a. a hundred, one hundred. *-a mia*, hundredth. *Mia kwa moja*, one per cent. *Mia mia*, hundreds, in hundreds—of a large indefinite quantity. **Miteen,** two hundred. (Ar. مئة.)

Miaa, n. plur. also **Miyaa.** See **Mwaa.**

Miadi,* n. a promise, esp. with reference to a particular time or date. (Cf. *ahadi.* Ar. ميعاد.)

Mialamu,* n. (1) a mark, the marks of a fold, i.e. *mialamu ya kilemba,* the marks of the folds of a turban; (2) stripe, band of colour, esp. in dress material. Sometimes heard as *mwalamu,* with plur., *mi-.* (Cf. *alama.* Ar. معلم.)

Miayo, n. plur. a yawn. *Kupiga* (or *kwenda*) *miayo,* to yawn.

Mikaha,* n. See **Nikaha.**

Mikambe, n. plur. *Kupiga mikambe,* in bathing, duck down and throw one leg over the other so as to strike the water with it, a game played in the water.

Mikasi,* n. See **Mkasi.**

Mila,* n. custom, habit, propensity, usage. (Cf. *kawaida, desturi, zoezi.* Ar. ملة.)

Milele,* n. and adv. eternity, perpetuity. *-a milele,* continual, never ending. As adv. always, perpetually, for ever. *Maisha na milele,* for life and for ever, for ever and ever. **Umilele,** n. perpetuity, eternity. (Cf. *daima, sikuzote.* ? Ar. مرر unbroken duration of time from مر or ملا be complete, &c.)

Milia, n. plur of *mlia,* but used as a., striped. *Punda milia,* a zebra.

Milihoi, n. a kind of evil spirit. (Cf. *pepo, shetani.*)

Miliki,* v. possess, be owner (ruler, king) of, rule, exercise authority over. Ps. **Milikiwa.** Prep. **Milikia,** e.g. hold in trust for, be regent for, rule in (for, with, &c.). Cs. **Milikisha,** put in possession, make king or ruler. **Matamalaki,** n. rule. **Maliki,** n., and **Malki,** n. a king, ruler, sovereign (usu. *mfalme*). **Malkia,** n. queen, female sovereign. **Milki,** n. possession, property, dominion, kingdom. **Tamalaki,** v same as *miliki.* (Cf. *tawala, mfalme.* Ar. ملك.)

Milioni,* n. and adv. a million. (Eng.)

Mimba, n. conception, pregnancy, embryo. *Shika* (*chukua, tunga, -wa na*) *mimba,* be (or become) pregnant, conceive. *Tia mimba,* cause to be pregnant. *Haribu mimba,* cause miscarriage, miscarry. Also of plants, *mtama unafanya mimba,* the millet is just forming in the ear. (Cf. *himila, uzito.*)

Mimbari,* n. a pulpit—in a mosque. (Ar. منبر.)

Mimi, pron. of 1 Pers. Sing., I, me. Also often *miye. Mimi mwenyewe, mimi nafsi yangu,* or *bi nafsi yangu,* I myself. *-angu mimi,* my own.

Mimina, v. (1) pour out, pour, spill—of anything in a fluid state, and so (2) run into a mould, cast. *Amemimina samli chomboni,* he has poured some ghee into a vessel. *Mkate wa kumimina,* a kind of confectionery. Ps. **Miminiwa.** St. **Miminika,** e.g. be poured out, overflow, used fig. of a crowd of people, *watu walimiminika kwenda kutazama,* crowds of people went to see. Prep. **Miminia.** Cs. **Miminisha. Miminiko,** n. *ma-* something poured out, a casting.

Min,* prep. in Arabic, used in such words as *minghairi, mintarafu, minajili,* &c. Ar. من from, of, for.)

Minajili,* conj. because of, for the reason, for the sake. (Cf. *min* and *ajili, kwa sababu.*)

Mindi, n. a name for the Duiker, also called *funo.*

Minghairi,* conj. without, not having, except. (Cf. *min* and *ghairi, bila, pasipo.*)

Minika, v. hem, turn up a cloth and hem it. (Cf. *pinda.*)

Mintarafu,* conj. concerning, with regard to, regarding, on behalf. (Cf. *min* and *tarafu, juu ya.*)

Minya, v. press, squeeze, squeeze out.

Rp. **Minyana.** (Cf. *finya, kama, kamua.*)

Minyara, n. plur. a kind of Euphorbia with milk-like sap, much used as a hedge plant and for making circular enclosures for cattle and to protect houses from the wind, &c., *Euphorbia tirucalli.*

Mio, n. (1) plur. of *umio*; (2) ma-amplic. form of *umio*, e.g. *mio la mnyama*, the throat-passage of an animal.

Miongo, n. plur. of *mwongo.* **Miongoni,** plur. loc. form from *mwongo*, number, account, reckoning. Used in *miongoni mwa*, as a prepositional phrase, in the number of, among, from among, on the side of, in the party of, i.e. *katika hesabu ya. Hawa si miongoni mwetu*, these are not among our people. *Hesabu za miongo*, decimal sums.

Mirathi,* n. inheritance, heritage—for the more usual *urithi*, which see under **Rithi.**

Mirengu, n. plur. of *mrengu.*

Mirimo, n. plur. the secrets of the medicine men, wizards, &c.

Misili.* See **Mithali.**

Miski,* n. musk, or similar perfume. (Ar. مسك.)

Misko,* n. Moscow, and used for Russia.

Misri,* n. Egypt. (Ar. مصر.)

Miteen,* n. and a. See under **Mia,** n.

Mithali,* n. also frequently **Methali,** n. a likeness, resemblance, emblem, similitude, parable, proverb, allegory. *Watu wengine hutumia mithali katika mazungumzo yao*, some people use proverbs (allegories, &c.) in their conversation. *Mithali ya*, like, resembling, a likeness of, and so (2) as, like, just as if, for instance—same as the commoner *kama. Ni mithali ya kuwa ameua mtu*, it is as if he has killed a man. **Madhali** (from the same Ar. root, but the *th* is always voiced) conj. as, since, because, e.g. *umesema haji, basi madhali haji na tuende sisi kwake*, you say he is not coming, very well, since he is not coming let us go to him. (Cf. *maadam, kwa kuwa.*) **Mathalan,** conj. also **Methalan,** for instance, for example, &c., e.g. *haiwezekani kuepuka hali iuliyokwisha pata kwa asili yetu, mathalan mtoto kwa wazazi wake au mtu kwa kabila lake*, it is impossible to avoid the condition (circumstances, &c.) which we have got by our origin, for example, a child from his parents or a man from his tribe. **Mithilisha,** v. compare. *Ni upuzi kujaribu kumithilisha habari za tembo na nyoka; maana wanahitilafiana kabisa*, it is foolishness to try to compare an elephant with a snake, because they are entirely different. Other forms of the above may be heard in which the *th* is changed to *dh, s*, and even *z*, also in which the vowels are changed, e.g. *mazalani, mazali, mizali, midhali, misili*, &c. (Ar. مثل.)

Miuja,* n. danger, misfortune, calamity. (Cf. *mauja.* Ar. ماج.)

Miunzi, n. plur. of *mwunzi*, which is seldom used, whistling, a whistle. *Piga miunzi*, whistle. (Cf. *ubinja, mbinja, msonyo.*)

Miwani,* n. a pair of spectacles, eye-glasses. (Ar. معاينة seeing with one's own eyes.)

Miyaa, n. plur. See under **Mwaa.**

Miye, pron. 1 Pers. Sing., same as *mimi*, I, me. (Cf. *weye, yeye, siye.*)

Mizali,* n., **Mizili,** n. See under **Mithali.**

Mizani,* n. (1) weighing machine, balance, scales. The pan is called *kitanga*, the beam of the scales *mtange*, and the weights, *mawe.* (2) the pendulum, or balance, regulating a machine, clock, watch, &c. **Uzani,** n. weighing, weight (by measure). (Cf. *kapani.* Ar. ميزان.)

Mizungu, n. plur. (1) conjuring, jugglery (cf. *kiinimacho*); (2) smartness, any way of getting out of a difficult position or danger, a ruse; (3) the teachings given to young girls when they reach the age of puberty, or in the initiation rites. (Cf. *mzungu.*)

Mja, n. *wa-*. See under **Ja.**

Mjafari,* n. *mi-* (1) the flame-tree, *Erythrina tomentosa.* A small tree with dense racemes of scarlet flowers and beaded pods. (2) a shrub or tree with small greenish-yellow flowers, *Fagara* sp. (Ar. جعفرى.)

Mjakazi, n. *wa-*. See under **Ja.**

Mjali, n. See **Ujali.**

Mjane, n. *wa-* (1) a bereaved person, male or female, a widow, a widower; (2) a bachelor, spinster, one who is not yet married or who is living in a single state. **Ujane**, n. the unmarried state—of bachelor, spinster, widow, or widower. (Cf. *mseja, useja, kapera.*)

Mjango, n. an empty, useless visit, i.e. ineffectual, on which one gets nothing. *Amepata mjango leo,* he has got nothing to-day.

Mjanja, n. *wa-*. See under **-janja.**

Mjarabati,* a. See under **Jaribu.**

Mjarari,* n. See **Mjari** and **Ujari.**

Mjasiri,* n. *wa-*. See under **Jasiri.**

Mjasusi,* n. *wa-*. See under **Jasusi.**

Mjeledi,* n. *mi-* whip (of leather), thong, strap. *Piga (tia) mijeledi,* beat with a whip. (Cf. *jalidi.* Ar. جلد.)

Mjengo, n. *mi-*, **Mjenzi**, n. *wa-*. See under **Jenga.**

Mji, n. *mi-* (1) village, hamlet, town, city, i.e. a collection of human dwellings, irrespective of number. Used with and without preps. *Toka (ondoka,* &c.) *katika mji,* or *mjini,* or *mji* only. So *enda (fika,* &c.) *katika mji,* or *mjini* or *mji.* (2) middle of a piece of cloth; (3) after-birth, placenta, and sometimes of the womb itself. **Kijiji**, n. *vi-* dim. of *mji.* (Cf. *kitongoji, kiambo, kaya.*)

Mjiari,* n. *mi-* tiller-rope. Also *ujari.* (Ar. اجر.)

Mjibu,* n. an affable, pleasant, accessible person. (Cf. *wajibu.*)

Mjiguu, n. *mi-* and *wa-*. See under **Mguu.**

Mjiko, n. (1) lower bowel, rectum (cf. *mkundu, kinyo*); (2) piles, haemorrhoids (cf. *bawasiri, futuri, kikundu*); (3) the condition of standing firm as one does when attacked or when one expects danger. (Cf. *jika, kita.*)

Mjima, n. *wa-*. See under **Ujima.**

Mjinga, n. (1) *wa-*. See under **Jinga;** (2) *mi-* the frangipane-tree, *Plumiera acuminata,* also called *mbono wa kizungu, msanapichi.*

Mjio, n. *mi-*. See under **Ja.**

Mjoho,* n. *mi-* the velvet apple-tree, *Diospyros* sp. (Cf. *joho.*)

Mjohoro, n. *mi-* the ironwood-tree, *Cassia siamea,* which bears yellow flowers and black pods.

Mjoja, n. *mi-* a kind of tree used for making canoes, also called *mjoo.*

Mjoli, n. *wa-* fellow slave, member of the same establishment, fellow servant.

Mjomba, n. *wa-* (1) uncle, nephew—the term being used by each of the other, but only of the uncle on the mother's side. (The uncle on the father's side is called *baba mkubwa,* or *mdogo,* according as he is older or younger than the father. Contr. *amu* (Ar.), uncle on the father's side.) (2) a native name for a Swahili—the Swahili region being called **Ujomba,** and the language **Kijomba.**

Mjombakaka, n. a large kind of lizard.

Mjombo, n. a kind of fish described as *chewa mkubwa,* considered to be good eating by Europeans.

Mjoo, n. *mi-*. See **Mjoja.**

Mjuba,* n. See under **Ujuba.**

Mjukuu, n. *wa-* grandchild, or other relation of the second generation, grand-nephew (or -niece), second cousin (male or female). (Cf. *kijukuu.*)

Mjumbe, n. *wa-* messenger, go-between, deputed person, ambassador, delegate, representative. **Ujumbe,** n. (1) a message, delegation, &c.; (2) status, fee, &c., of a messenger—see also *jumbe*.

Mjume,* n. *wa-* a skilled workman who executes ornamental work, engraving, inlaying, &c., on weapons and personal ornaments. *Mjume wa visu*, a high-class cutler. **Mjumu,** or **Njumu,** inlaid work, ornamental decoration with various materials, e.g. studding with metal, brass nails, &c. *Kasha kubwa la njumu*, a large chest ornamented with metal, brass studs, &c. **Ujume,** n. the art (profession, wages, &c.), of a *mjume*; high-class metal-work, cutlery, &c.

Mjusi, n. *mi-* (1) a lizard—of the smaller sort, of which there are many varieties (for larger kinds cf. *guruguru, kenge*); (2) a lizard-shaped ornament worked in silk stitches on the front of a *kanzu*; (3) a kind of complaint which causes the nose to bleed.

Mjuvi, n. *wa-*, **Mjuzi,** n. *wa-*. See under **Jua,** v.

Mkaa, n. (1) *wa-* see under **Kaa, v.**; (2) *mi-* the candlenut-tree; the bark is used medicinally as an astringent, *Aleurites moluccana*.

Mkaajabali, n. *mi-* a shrub or small tree with silvery leaves and small pinkish-white flowers, *Pemphis acidula*.

Mkaaji, n. *wa-*. See under **Kaa, v.**

Mkabala,* adv. See under **Kabili.**

Mkabidhi,* n. *wa-*. See under **Kabidhi.**

Mkabilishemsi,* n. *mi-* an edible herb, *Gynandropsis gynandra*, also used for making medicine for the eyes and ears. Other names are *mwangani* and *mgange*. (Cf. *kabili* and *shemshi*.)

Mkadamu,* n. *wa-*. See under **Kadamu.**

Mkadi,* n. *mi-* a screw pine with a strongly scented flower, *Pandanus Kirkii*. **Mkadi dume,** n. *mi-* a screw pine, see *msanaka*. (Ar. كاذى dwarf palm.)

Mkaguo, n. *mi-*, **Mkaguzi,** n. *wa-*. See under **Kagua.**

Mkahaba,* n. See **Kahaba.**

Mkahale,* n. *mi-*. See under **Kohl.**

Mkahawa,* n. *mi-* coffee-house, restaurant, café. Also sometimes heard as *mgahawa*. (Cf. *kahawa*.)

Mkaidi,* n. *wa-*. See under **-kaidi.**

Mkaja, n. *mi-* cloth worn by women round the body, esp. after childbirth —one of the presents usually made to the bride's mother at marriage.

Mkakamavu, n. *wa-*. See under **Kakamka.**

Mkakasi, n. (1) a cylindrical metal box with a lid, used for keeping things in, such as perfume (*uturi*), &c., a vanity box; (2) see **Mkasasi.**

Mkakaya,* n. *mi-* the flamboyant, *Delonix regia*. (Pers. اقاقيا acacia.)

Mkale, n. *wa-*. See under **-kale.**

Mkalimana, n. a kind of banana. (Cf. *ndizi*.)

Mkalimani,* n. *wa-*, **Mkalimu,** n. *wa-*. See under **Kalima.**

Mkalio, n. *mi-*. See under **Kaa, v.**

Mkamachuma, n. *mi-* a kind of tree.

Mkamba, n. (1) a sickness accompanied by coughing, a sore chest, and ulcers in the throat; (2) *mi-* see under **Kamba** (C).

Mkambala, n. *mi-* a medium-sized tree with thorny trunk and branches, *Acacia brosigii*.

Mkamshi,* n. *mi-* a ladle, a kind of wooden spoon used for stirring and for ladling out gravy, &c. (Cf. *upawa*. Hind. چمچى.)

Mkana, n. *wa-*. See under **Kana, v.**

Mkandaa, n. *mi-* a kind of mangrove, *Ceriops candolliana*—the bark is used for tanning and furnishes a red dye. The hard straight trunks supply largely the *boriti* of commerce, i.e. poles used for carrying the concrete roofs in house-building. (Cf. *mkoko, msinzi, miwi*.)

Mkando, n. *mi-*. See under **Kanda.**

Mkangaja, n. *mi-* a tree which bears clusters of a small kind of mandarin orange, called **Kangaja, n.** *ma-*. (Cf. *mchenza.*)

Mkangazi, n. *mi-* mahogany, *Khaya nyasica*, also known locally as *mtondo, mwovu, mavu, mbawa, nyalulasi.*

Mkanju,* n. *mi-* the cashew apple-tree, *Anacardium occidentale*, also called *mbibo* and *mkorosho.* (Hind. كاجو.)

Mkano, n. *mi-* (1) see under **Kano**; (2) see under **Kana, v.**

Mkanya, n. *wa-*, **Mkanyo, n.** *mi-*. See under **Kana, v.**

Mkarafuu,* n. *mi-* the clove-tree, *Eugenia aromatica.* The cloves are called *karafuu.* When very small they are called *thamra*, when a little larger *misumari* (nails), and when fully grown *mavi ya panya* (rats' dung). **Mkarafuu maiti,** n. *mi-* the camphor-tree, *Cinnamomum camphora.* (Ar. قرنفل.)

Mkaragazo, n. *mi-* (1) a very heavy shower of rain; (2) a kind of tobacco of inferior quality.

Mkarakala, n. *mi-* a timber-tree, *Bridelia* sp., generally an indicator of good soil, also called *mkarati* and *mtututu.*

Mkarati, n. *mi-* a kind of tree. See **Mkarakala.**

Mkarimu,* n. *wa-*. See under **Karama.**

Mkasa,* n. *mi-*. See under **Kisa.**

Mkasama,* n. *mi-* (1) see under **Kasimu**; (2) a kind of cassava. (Cf. *muhogo.*)

Mkasasi,* n. *mi-* a fine tree but useless for timber, sometimes called *mkakasi. Uzuri wa mkasasi ukipata maji basi*, the *mkasasi* is a fine tree, but all it yields is sap. (Ar. قصاص kind of tree.)

Mkasi,* n. *mi-* a pair of scissors. (Ar. مقص, see also *makasi.*)

Mkasiri, n. *mi-* a tree the bark of which is used to dye nets black, *Phyllanthus floribundus.*

Mkasisi mkiwa, n. *mi-* a twining herb. *Cissampelos pareira.* Leaf and root are used for making a medicine for fever and dysentery.

Mkata,* n. (1) see under **Kata, v.**; (2) a poor man. *Ni mkata, sina mbele wala nyuma*, I am a poor man, with nothing before or behind me. *Mkata hana kinyongo*, a poor man cannot afford to have whims.

Mkataa,* n. and adv. See under **Kataa.**

Mkataba,* n. *mi-*. See under **Katiba.**

Mkataji,* n. *wa-*. See under **Kata.**

Mkatale,* n. *mi-* stocks, instruments for confining a prisoner or demented man by the feet. (Ar. مقطرة.)

Mkatani,* n. *mi-* (1) the sisal hemp plant, *Agave sisalana*, also called *mkonge*; (2) Mauritius hemp, *Furcreae gigantea.* The fibre and also material made from it is called *katani.* (Cf. *mkonge.* Ar. كتان.)

Mkatavu,* n. *wa-*. See under **Kataa.**

Mkate,* n. *mi-*, **Mkati,** n. *wa-*. See under **Kata.**

Mkatili,* n. *wa-*. See under **Katili.**

Mkato,* n. *mi-*. See under **Kata, v.**

Mkaumwa,* n. *mi-* Columba root, *Jateorrhiza palmata*, used for making medicine for dysentery and stomach ailments. (Perhaps corruption of Columba.)

Mkavu wa macho. See under **Kauka.**

Mkazi, n. (1) *wa-* see under **Kaa, v.**; (2) see under **Kaza.**

Mkazo, n. *mi-*. See under **Kaza.**

Mke, n. *wa-* a woman, a female, also *mwanamke.* Used alone, *mke* means distinctively 'wife' in contrast with *mwanamke. Mume ni kazi, mke ni nguo*, the husband works, the wife dresses. (See under *-ke.*)

Mkebe,* n. *mi-* pot, can, canister, mug (for drinking and other purposes), a cigarette case. *Mkebe wa ubani*, a pot for keeping or burning incense in. (For other kinds, cf. *chungu, chombo, kopo.* Ar. كوب with *m* prefix or مكب.)

Mkeka, *mi-* a mat (usually of the kind used for sleeping on). Hence *kama kitanda kupata mkeka*, like a bedstead getting a mat, i.e. of natural completion, the final touch. These mats are oblong, made of certain leaves (*ukindu*), slit into strips, plaited, and stained various colours. The strips (*ukili*) are sewn together, and bound round the edge. Their manufacture is the ordinary occupation of women when not engaged in cookery or other household work. *Mikeka* are described as *ya kulalia*, for sleeping on; *ya rangi*, with coloured stripes; *ya mfuto*, of the common cheap kind; *ya kazi*, plaited in patterns. (Other kinds of mats are *jamvi, msala, kitanga, utanga.*)

Mkeketo, n. *mi-*. See under **Keketa.**

Mkekewa, n. *mi-* a sprawling common weed with prickly stems, which often climbs to the tops of trees, *Smilax kraussiana*, also called *mkwanguachare.*

Mkenge, n. *mi-* a general term applied to Albizzia trees such as *Albizzia glabrescens, A. Petersiana*, &c.

Mkereza, n. *wa-*. See under **Kereza.**

Mkesha, n. *mi-*. See under **Kesha.**

Mkewe, n. for *mke wake*, his wife. So, *mkeo*, your wife, i.e. *mke wako.*

Mkia, n. *mi-* a tail. *Suka mkia*, wag the tail. *Mkia wa mjusi*, lines of silk stitching running up the front of a *kanzu*, from the ornament called *mjusi.*

Mkichaa, n. *wa-* a crazy person, madman, but usually *mwenye kichaa* is used.

Mkidhi,* n. *wa-*. See under **Kidhi.**

Mkiki, n. a kind of fish not considered good eating by Europeans.

Mkilemba, n. *wa-*. See under **Kilemba**, n.

Mkilungwana, n. *mi-* Zanzibar rubber-tree, *Landolphia Kirkii*, also called *mpyo.*

Mkimbizi, n. *wa-*. See under **Kimbia.**

Mkimu,* n. *wa-*. See under **Kimu.**

Mkimwa, n. *wa-*. See under **Kimwa.**

Mkinaifu,* n. *wa-*. See under **Kinai.**

Mkinda, n. (1) see under **Kinda**; (2) a dance used in the initiation ceremonies of young girls.

Mkindu, n. *mi-* the wild date palm, *Phoenix reclinata*; the leaves are used for fibre, also when they are split (*ukindu*) for weaving mats, &c. **Ukindu**, n. (*kindu*) material from the *mkindu*, i.e. leaf used for plaiting, and fibre for string. **Kindu**, n. fruit of the *mkindu.*

Mkinga, n. *mi-*, *wa-*. See under **Kinga.**

Mkingabale, n. *mi-* a flowering shrub, *Pentas carnea.*

Mkingamo, n. *mi-*, **Mkingiko**, n. *mi-*. See under **Kinga.**

Mkingiri, n. *mi-* a shrub, *Dichrostachys glomerata*, with spikes of yellow and pinkish-purple flowers. Used medicinally esp. in cases of snakebite.

Mkingu, n. *mi-* a lac-bearing tree, *Albizzia lebbek.*

Mkinzani, n. *wa-*. See under **Kinza.**

Mkirika, n. *mi-* a useful hedge plant, *Ehretia* sp.

Mkirizi, n. *mi*. See **Mchirizi** under **Chiririka.**

Mkitamli, n. *mi-* the Pemba coconut or king coco-nut palm, *Cocos mucifera*, only used for drinking. In some places called *kisamli.*

Mkiwa, *wa-*. See under **-kiwa.**

Mkizi, n. *mi-* cuttle-fish.

Mkoba,* n. *mi-* a bag, pouch, wallet—sometimes made of the entire skin of a small animal. *Mawimbi ya mkoba*, bag-like waves, i.e. smooth swelling waves, not like breakers. *Kifungua mkoba*, the fee paid to a medicine man (*mganga*), who usu. keeps his paraphernalia in a *mkoba*. *Kufunga mkoba*, said of the medicine men during the month of Ramadhan, because they do not exorcize spirits during that month. (Cf. *kuba, kubaza.* Ar. كب provision-bag.)

Mkoche, n. *mi-* the hyphaene or dwarf palm, also called *mwaa* and *mkoma*. **Koche**, n. *ma-* the edible fruit of the *mkoche*.

Mkodi, n. (1) a kind of spirit (cf. *pepo*); (2) see under **Kodi**.

Mkodo, n. (1) a kind of spirit (cf. *pepo*); (2) **Mkodo wa paka**, n. *mi-* a shrub or small tree with yellow flowers, *Grewia glandulosa*.

Mkoe, n. *mi-* a scandent or climbing annual herb, *Pergularia extensa*. It has white flowers and soft spiny pods containing seeds covered with soft silky hairs. The stems and leaves contain a latex, and the plant is used medicinally as an emetic.

Mkogo, n. *mi-*. See under **Koga**.

Mkojo, n. *mi-*, **Mkojozi**, n. *wa-*. See under **Kojoa**.

Mkoko, n. *mi-* (1) a kind of mangrove much used for firewood where found, with red bark used for dyeing, *Rhizophora mucronata* (cf. *msinzi*, *mkandaa*, *muwi*); (2) the cocoa-tree, *Theobroma cacao*.

Mkokoto, n. *mi-*. See under **Kokota**.

Mkole, n. *mi-* a tree with a small red, edible fruit. Its fibre is used for producing a soapy substance, used by some women for washing their hair, also as a lubricant in certain ways, e.g. in *punyeto*, and as a medicine for dysentery.

Mkoma, n. *mi-* the hyphaene or dwarf palm, also called *mkoche* and *mwaa*.

Mkoma, n. *wa-* (1) see under **Koma**; (2) sometimes heard for a leper, instead of the more usual *mwenye ukoma*.

Mkomafi, n. *mi-* (1) a tree with red wood, *Carapa moluccensis*; (2) a much-branched tree up to 30 ft. tall with hard brown fruits the size of a grapefruit, only found growing on muddy sea-shores and in mangrove swamps, *Xylocarpus moluccensis*.

Mkomamanga, n. *mi-* the pomegranate, *Punica granatum*. The fruit, which is edible, is called **Komamanga**, n. *ma-*.

Mkombo, n. *mi-* the handle of a rudder. (Cf. *kana*.)

Mkombozi, n. *wa-*. See under **Komboa**.

Mkombwe, n. *mi-* also **Mkomwe**, n. *mi-* a kind of creeper; its seeds are used as counters in certain games.

Mkomo, n. *mi-*. See **Mkomwe**.

Mkomoka, n. a kind of cassava. (Cf. *muhogo*.)

Mkomwe, n. *mi-* (1) a kind of climbing plant, *Caesalpinia cristata*; the seeds are used as counters, &c., in playing *bao* and other games, (2) a kind of powder used in witchcraft, said to cause the death of a person should he tread on the place where it has been hidden. See also **Mkombwe**.

Mkondo, n. *mi-* current, flow, rush, passage, run, e.g. of water in a river or poured on the ground; of air through a door or window, i.e. a draught; of the wake of a ship, a track, run of an animal. *Mkondo wa nyasi*, a track through rushes, showing where people have passed.

Mkonga, n. *mi-* trunk of an elephant, sometimes called *mkono wa tembo*, and *mwiro*.

Mkonge, n. *mi-* (1) a large aloe-like plant used for fibres, *Sansevieria* spp.; (2) a kind of fish. **Mkonge dume**, n. *mi-* sisal hemp, *Agave sisalana*. Also called *mkatani*. **Ukonge**, n. (*konge*) sisal fibre.

Mkongojo, n. *mi-*, **Mkongwe**, n. *wa-*. See under **Konga**, v. (A).

Mkonjo, n. *mi-* sometimes heard for *konzo*, which see.

Mkono, n. *mi-* (1) the arm of a human being, esp. of the lower arm, and the hand. *Tia mkono*, sign. *Mwenye mkono mrefu*, one whose authority is far-reaching, also a thief. *Ana mkono mzuri*, he writes a good hand. *Mkono wake mwepesi*, he is clever with his hands, also he cannot be trusted, he steals. (2) of a corresponding member in animals, front paw. Cf. *mkono wa tembo*, an elephant's trunk (also a kind of banana). (3) of what resembles an arm, as projecting, spreading, grasping, &c., e.g. *mkono wa sufuria*, the handle of a saucepan, *mikono ya mto* (*bahari*), branches of a river, creeks of the sea; (4) as a convenient measure, from finger-tips to elbow, a cubit, same as *dhiraa*, 18 inches, i.e. a double span, half a yard. Also in various figurative senses: *kupa mkono*, to give the hand, i.e. greet, congratulate, condole with, assist, take leave, take an oath, &c. *Mkono wa msiba*, condolence in grief. *-pa* (*acha*) *mkono*, die. *Fulani ametupa* (*ametuacha*) *mkono*, So-and-so has taken leave of us, i.e. died. *Mkono wa kuume* (*wa kulia*), the right hand (eating hand). *Mkono wa kushoto*, the left hand. **Kikono**, n. *vi-* dim. (1) small arm or hand, short or defective arm, stump of the arm, e.g. *ana kikono*, he has lost a hand (arm); (2) anything resembling a small hand, e.g. projecting prow of a vessel, guard of a sword-handle, small stalk or tendril of plants and flowers, tentacle or feeler of fish or insect. **Kono**, n. *ma-* amplic. of *mkono*, something that projects, sticks out, e.g. a handle, a shoot, or sprig of a plant. **Ukono**, n. (*kono*) used of the tendrils by which plants grasp or cling to anything, and of other hand-like objects.

Mkono wa simba, n. *mi-* a shrub or small tree, *Cordia* sp.

Mkonzo, n. *mi-*. See **Konzo**.

Mkoo, n. *wa-* a slut, slattern, a dirty untidy person, male or female.

Mkopeshi, n. *wa-*, **Mkopi**, n. *wa-*, **Mkopo**, n. *mi-*. See under **Kopa**.

Mkoria, n. *mi-* a shrub or small tree, *Cordia* sp.

Mkorofi, n. *wa-*. See under **Korofi**.

Mkoroga, n. *wa-*, **Mkorogaji**, n. *wa-*, **Mkorogi**, n. *wa-*, **Mkorogo**, n. *mi-*. See under **Koroga**.

Mkoromaji, n. *wa-*, **Mkoromo**, n. *mi-*. See under **Koroma**.

Mkorosho,* n. *mi-* the cashew apple-tree, *Anacardium occidentale*, also called *mbibo* and *mkanju*; the nuts are called *korosho*, which see.

Mkosaji, n. *wa-*. See under **Kosa**.

Mkosi, n. a bad omen, bad luck. (Cf. *kisirani*. ? Ar. from قاصّ punish).

Mkota, n. *mi-* sweet sorghum, *Sorghum saccharatum*. The stalks are chewed for the sugar, and also sugar is extracted.

Mkristo,* n. *wa-* a Christian. **Kikristo**, adv. in a Christian-like method, &c. *-a Kikristo*, Christian. **Ukristo**, n. Christianity, the condition, manner, &c., of being a Christian.

Mkubwa, n. *wa-*. See under **-kubwa**.

Mkudhumani,* n. *mi-* a tree rather like pomegranate.

Mkufu, n. *mi-* a chain, usually metal, of a light kind, worn as an ornament. (Contr. *mnyororo*.)

Mkufunzi, n. *wa-*. See under **Funda**, v. (C).

Mkuki, n. *mi-* a spear. *Chomeka mkuki*, stick a spear in the ground, *chomoa mkuki*, withdraw a spear. (For the iron head cf. *chembe*, *kengee*; for the shaft, *mti*, *uti*; for the butt end, *tako*.)

Mkuku, n. *mi-* (1) the keel—of a boat or ship (dist. *kuku*, fowl); (2) a large woody climber, *Salacia* sp.

Mkule, n. a garfish, sometimes called *chuchunge*.

Mkulima, n. *wa-*. See under **Lima**, v.

Mkulivu, n. *wa-*. See under **Kua**.

Mkulo, n. *mi-* a strainer for straining grated coco-nut. (Cf. *kifumbu*.)

Mkumbi, n. *mi-* a tree from the bark of which a yellow dye is made, used for staining *ukili*, also called *mwungamo*.

Mkumbizi, n. *wa-*. See under **Kumba**, v. (A) and (B).

Mkumbo, n. *mi-*. See under **Kumba**, v. (B).

Mkumbuu, n. *mi-* (1) cincture, sash; (2) the shoulder-strap of a soldier's equipment, i.e. the strap crossing the chest from shoulder to waist.

Mkunazi,* n. *mi-* the Chinese date or jujube-tree, *Zizyphus jujuba*, bearing a small edible stone fruit like a cherry. The fruit is called **Kunazi. Kikunazi,** n. *vi-* is sometimes used as a euphemism (obscene) for part of the female genital organs. (Pers. قونج.)

Mkundaji, n. a kind of fish which is said to cause a rash if eaten.

Mkunde, n. *mi-* the shrub bearing a runner bean, edible, *Phaseolus vulgaris*. The bean is called **Ukunde** (*kunde*).

Mkundu, n. *mi-* the anus, orifice of the bowel. **Kikundu,** n. *vi-* piles, haemorrhoids. (Cf. *bawasiri, mnyo, futuri.*)

Mkunga, n. (1) *wa-* see under **Kunga,** n. (B); (2) *mi-* an eel.

Mkungu, n. *mi-* (1) the Indian almond-tree, *Terminalia catappa*; both the fruit and nut are edible. The fruit is called **Kungu.** The ordinary almond-tree is *mlozi*. (2) the fruit-stem or pedicel of a banana plant carrying the whole head of fruit; (3) see under **Chungu,** n. (A).

Mkunguma, n. *mi-* a kind of tree, *Sorindeia usambaraensis*, up to 30 ft. tall with long pendulous racemes of pink or yellow flowers.

Mkungumanga, n. *mi-* lit. the Arabian *mkungu*, the nutmeg-tree, *Myristica fragans*, bearing the **Kungumanga,** n. nutmeg.

Mkunguni, n. *mi-* (1) a tree, *Terminalia Fatraea*, from which pestles are made; (2) a firm strong stick; (3) *wa-* an idle, lazy person. **Ukunguni,** n. laziness, idleness. (Cf. *ubwete, uvivu.*)

Mkungupwa, n. *mi-* a shrub with white fragrant flowers, *Guettarda speciosa*, a useful fuel tree.

Mkunguru, n. also **Ukunguru,** n. the fever or illness which attacks a new-comer at a place, after a change of residence and diet; sickness of acclimatization.

Mkung'uto, n. *mi-*. See under **Kung'uta.**

Mkunjo, n. *mi-*. See under **Kunja.**

Mkuno, n. *mi-*. See under **Kuna.**

Mkunungu, n. *mi-* a tree, *Fagara* sp., with compound leaves, and scattered prickles on the stem and leaves; the young leaves are eaten as a vegetable.

Mkuo, n. *mi-* an ingot, lump, or bar of cast or unwrought metal, pig (of iron), rough casting.

Mkupuo, n. *mi-*, **Mkupuzi,** n. *wa-*. See under **Kupua.**

Mkuranga, n. *mi-* a waterless tract of country. (Cf. *jangwa.*)

Mkuro, n. *mi-* (1) see **Mkulo**; (2) cry (of an animal or person), the sound made by an animal pawing or scraping the ground in anger.

Mkurufunzi, n. *wa-*. See under **Funda,** v. (C).

Mkurugenzi, n. *wa-* a leader, a pioneer, a person of importance, one who is learned in affairs above his fellows. **Ukurugenzi,** n. leadership, condition, &c., of being a pioneer. (From the same roots as *mkuu* and *enda.*)

Mkurungu, n. *mi-* a tree with good timber, *Pterocarpus Chrysothrix*.

Mkururo, n. *mi-* a following, i.e. of people following after each other, a string of people, &c.

Mkuruti, n. *mi-*. See **Mkarati.**

Mkuruzo, n. *mi-* a piece of string, tape, &c., for fastening a garment or the neck of a bag, by drawing it.

Mkusanya, n. *wa-*, **Mkusanyi,** n. *wa-*, **Mkusanyiko,** n. *mi-*, **Mkusanyo,** n. *mi-*, **Mkutano,** n. *mi-*, **Mkuto,** n. *mi-*. See under **Kuta,** v. (A).

Mkutuo, n. *mi-*. See under **Kutua.**

Mkuu, n. *wa-* (1) see under **-kuu**; (2) **Mkuu hapingwa,** n. *mi-* see under **Mbuyu.**

Mkuwadi,* n. impotence, i.e. sexual. (Cf. *kawadi.*)

Mkuyati,* n. medicine which restores virility, an aphrodisiac, a tonic. (Ar. مقيت nourishing.)

Mkuyu, n. *mi-* the fig mulberry or wild fig-tree, *Ficus sycamorus*, bearing the edible fruit **Kuyu**.

Mkwachuro, n. a disease of coconuts; the husk of the nut splits and a thick sticky juice exudes.

Mkwadi,* n. *wa-*. See **Kawadi**.

Mkwaju, n. *mi-* the tamarind-tree, *Tamarindus indica*. It is a good timber tree, and the fruits, **Kwaju**, are used in curries and in a preparation together with *katu*, for cleaning copper and brass.

Mkwakwa, n. *mi-* a creeping plant, *Landolphia florida*, with an edible fruit like a medlar. Also called *mbungo* and *mbugu*.

Mkwakwara, n. *mi-* a tree, *Boerhavia repens*, the leaves of which are sometimes used as a vegetable. Also called *mkwayakwaya*.

Mkwamba, n. *mi-* a kind of thorny bush, *Securinega*, which looks rather like a henna bush.

Mkwanguachare, n. *mi-*. See **Mkekewa**.

Mkwara, n. *mi-* a tree, *Millettia bussei*, much used for firewood and for sticks for fighting.

Mkware, n. *wa-*. See under **Ukware**.

Mkwaruzo, n. *mi-*. See under **Kwaruza**.

Mkwasi, n. *wa-*. See under **-kwasi**.

Mkwayakwaya, n. *mi-*. See **Mkwakwara**.

Mkwe, n. (*wakwe*), used of near connexions by marriage, father- (or mother-) in-law, son- (or daughter-) in-law.

Mkweme, n. *mi-* a climbing plant, *Telfairia pedata*, with large seeds which provide an oil suitable for cooking. The fruit is called **Kweme**, and is used as a medicine.

Mkweo, n. (1) *mi-* see under **Kwea**; (2) *wa-* for *mkwe wako*, see **Mkwe**.

Mkwepuzi, n. *wa-*. See under **Kwepua**.

Mkwezi, n. *wa-*. See under **Kwea**.

Mkwiji, n. (1) *mi-* a long narrow cylindrical cloth bag or poke, used for keeping money in; (2) *wa-* sometimes heard for *gwiji*, which see.

Mkwiro, n. *mi-* a drumstick, used with some kinds of native drums.

Mla, n. *wa-*. See under **La**, **v.**

Mlaanifu, n. *wa-*, **Mlaanizi**, n. *wa-*.* See under **Laana**.

Mladi,* n. *mi-* a thin piece of stick used by cloth weavers to tighten the threads. (? Ar. ملد stretch.)

Mlafi, n. *wa-*. See under **Lapa**.

Mlaghai,* n. *wa-*. See under **Laghai**.

Mlaji, n. *wa-*. See under **La**, **v.**

Mlala, n. *mi-* the hyphaene or dwarf palm, also called *mkoche* and *mwaa*.

Mlalangwa, n. *mi-* a tree, *Ficus bussei*, with dark leathery leaves and small fig-like fruits.

Mlalavi, n. *wa-*. See under **Lala**.

Mlama, n. *mi-* applied to various species of *Combretum*, which are employed in native snake-bite remedies.

Mlamba, n. *wa-* (1) see under **Lamba**; (2) sometimes heard for *mramba*, the name of a bird; (3) *mi-* a kind of very tall baobab-tree.

Mlamu, n. *wa-* brother-in-law, sister-in-law. (Cf. *mwamu*.)

Mlandawa, n. *mi-* the banyan-tree.

Mlandege, n. *mi-* a parasite often found on clove-trees, *Ficus natalensis*, and other spp.

Mlangali, n. *mi-* a kind of euphorbia tree.

Mlangamia, n. *mi-* a parasite which grows on cloves and other vegetation, *Cassytha filiformis*.

Mlango, n. *mi-* (1) door, doorway, gate; (2) entrance, means of access, fee for entrance; (3) anything resembling a door, e.g. a pass (in hills and mountains), a channel (across a bar), a strait, estuary, mouth of a river; (4) fig. of a man's relation to his family, social attitude, circle of acquaintances, branch of a family. *Mlango wake mzuri*, he is a kind, hospitable, sociable person. *Wote walioko katika mlango wetu*, all who belong to our circle. Prov. *Penye wimbi na mlango ni papo*, the channel and the breaker are close together, i.e. safety and danger. *Mlangobahari*, a strait. *Mlango wa maarifa*, *mi-* one of the five senses, i.e. through which perception or knowledge is got. *Mlango*, is also used for a chapter of a book (cf. *sura*). Native doors are commonly of two kinds: (1) a single door made of pieces of *mwale* (i.e. mid-rib of a large raphia palm-leaf) set side by side with two cross-pieces passed through them, making a light screen, tied or propped in the doorway; or (2) a double or folding door of two boards (*ubao*) turning inwards on projecting tongues of wood fitting in socket holes in the top and bottom of the frame. One board carries a centre strip (*mfaa* or *upanga*) to cover the space between the valves when closed. The frame consists of side-pieces (*mwimo* or *mhimili*) and top and bottom pieces (*kizingiti*). **Lango**, n. *ma-* (1) amplic. of *mlango*, (2) the plur. *malango*, is used of the secret instruction given to girls and boys on growing up. **Kilango**, n. *vi-* dim.

Mlariba, n. *wa-* a usurer, a money-lender (Ar. Cf. *riba*, usury, interest, and syn. *faida*.) The first syllable is perh. *mla*, one who eats, a consumer.

Mlasa, n. *mi-* a shrubby herb, *Hibiscus micranthus*, with red, pink, or white flowers.

Mlazi, n. *wa-*. See under **Lala**.

Mle, (1) adv. there within—like *kule*, *pale*; (2) form of the pronominal a. *-le*, 'that' agreeing with a noun in the locative form, e.g. *nyumbani mle*, in that house; (3) subjunct. 2 Pers. Plur. of *la*, (that) you may eat.

Mlegevu, n. *wa-*. See under **Lega**.

Mleli, n. *mi-* the long tail-feathers of a cock or any bird, sometimes used as adornment at dances, &c., hence, fig. *fulani ametoa mleli*, so-and-so has put out a tail-feather, i.e. he is prospering.

Mlembe, n. *wa-* the honey bird.

Mlenge, n. a game played by throwing four pieces of stick, stalk, &c., and watching how they fall.

Mlengu, n. *mi-* an outrigger of a canoe. (Cf. *ngalawa*, *ndubi*, *mtengo*.)

Mleo, n. *mi-*, **Mlevi**, n. *wa-*. See under **Lewa**.

Mlezi, n. (1) *wa-* see under **Lea**; (2) *mi-* a baby's swinging cot; (3) a complaint in which the glands swell, esp. those of the neck (cf. *tezi*, *hijabu*, *halula*); (4) the bullrush millet plant, the grain being called *ulezi*.

Mlia, n. (1) *wa-* see under **Lia**; (2) *mi-* a stripe (line, band) of colouring. Used in the plur. as a. *Punda milia*, a zebra.

Mlilana, n. *mi-* a sort of mangrove, *Sonneratia caesolaria*, with pithy stems which are used for fibre.

Mlima, n. *mi-* a mountain, high hill, long steep ascent. *Milima*, *milima mingi*, *mfululizo wa milima*, or *safu ya milima*, a mountain range. *Mshikano wa milima*, a mountain mass. *Mlima mrefu* (or *mkubwa*), a high mountain. **Kilima**, n. *vi-* dim. a hill.

Mlimaji, n. *wa-*. See under **Lima**, v.

Mlimau,* n. *mi-* the lemon-tree, *Citrus limonum*, bearing the fruit **Limau**, *ma-*. (Pers. and Hind. ليمو.)

Mlimbiko, n. *mi-*. See under **Limbika**.

Mlimbolimbo, n. *mi-* a useful hedge plant with thorns. See **Mchongoma**. It has a sticky white sap, **Ulimbo**, which is used for bird-lime.

Mlimbuko, n. *mi-*. See under **Limbika**.

Mlimi, n. *wa-*. See under **Ulimi**.

Mlimo, n. *mi-*. See under **Lima**, v.

Mlimwengu, n. *wa-*. See under **Ulimwengu**.

Mlinda, n. *wa-*. See under **Linda**.

Mlingano, n. *mi-*. See under **Linga**.

Mlingoti, n. *mi-* mast—of a vessel. *Mlingoti wa maji*, bowsprit, also called *dasturi*. *Mlingoti wa mbele*, foremast, also called *wa omoni*. *Mlingoti wa galme*, mizzen mast. The mast rests on the false keel (*msitamu*) and is fixed by a beam (*fundo*) and two longitudinal timbers (*mwashiri*). *Mlingoti* is sometimes used as an obscene euphemism in songs, &c., for the penis.

Mlinzi, n. *wa-*. See under **Linda**.

Mlio, n. *mi-* (1) see under **Lia**; (2) a piece of stick used for twisting the rope binding a bundle of firewood, in order to tighten it.

Mlipa, n. *wa-*, **Mlipaji**, n. *wa-*, **Mlipizi**, n. *wa-*. See under **Lipa**.

Mlipu, n. *mi-* a herb, which together with *mnyamata* and *mpendeupendapo*, is used for making love potions.

Mlisha, n. *wa-*, **Mlishi**, n. *wa-*. See under **La**, v.

Mlishangwa, n. *ni-* a tree, with a fruit which is not edible.

Mlisho, n. *mi-*. See under **La**, v.

Mliwa,* n. *mi-* a tree with a fragrant aromatic wood, *Spirostachys africana*. See **Liwa**. (Ar. لوة a fragrant wood.)

Mlizamu,* n. *mi-* a spout for carrying water off a house-top, or eaves, commonly called *kopo*, in Zanzibar. (Cf. *mrizabu*. Ar. مزراب water-course, note the trans. of *z* and *r*, and *m* for *b*.)

Mlizi, n. *mi-*. See under **Lia**.

Mlo, n. See under **La**, v.

Mlombo, n. *mi-* a kind of vegetable.

Mlomo, n. *mi-* a variant of *mdomo*, which see.

Mlongama, n. *mi-* a tree from the bark of which a yellow dye is made.

Mlonge, n. *mi-* a tree, the leaves of which are used as a vegetable. (Cf. *pombo*.) The fruit when young is called *singu* (*singh*), and is eaten by some people, esp. by a class of Indian, hence the name.

Mlongo, n. *wa-* and *mi-* a variant of *mwongo*, which see.

Mlonjo, n. *mi-* See under **Lonjo**.

Mlowezi, n. *wa-*. See under **Lowela**.

Mlozi,* n. (1) *mi-* the almond-tree, bearing **Lozi**, *ma-*; (2) *wa-* see under **Loga**, v. (Ar. لوز a nut.)

Mlumbaji, n. *wa-*. See under **Lumba**.

Mlungula, n. *wa-* and *mi-*, also **Mlungura**. See under **Lungula**.

Mluzi, n. *mi-* a whistle, made with the mouth. **Mluziluzi**, n. *mi-* a forest tree the seed pods of which make a whistling noise when there is a wind blowing.

Mmaka, n. *mi-* a name for the frangipane-tree. (Cf. *msanapichi*, *mbono wa kizungu*.)

Mmakanuka, n. *mi-* a climbing weed, *Nidorella microcephala*.

Mmasihiya,* n. *wa-*. See under **Masihiya**.

Mmavimavi, n. *mi-* a kind of tree, *Celtis Durandii*, its flowers have a very unpleasant smell, hence the name.

Mmbea, n. *wa-*. See under **Umbea**.

Mmbuji, n. *wa-*. See under **Umbuji**.

Mmea, n. *mi-*. See under **Mea**.

Mmego, n. *mi-*. See under **Mega**.

Mmelea, n. *mi-*. See under **Mea**.

Mmoja, n. one person, a person, a certain man. See **-moja**.

Mmoyomoyo, n. *mi-* same as *mmwaka*, which see.

Mmumunye, n. *mi-* bottle-gourd plant, *Lagenaria vulgaris*. The gourd which is like a vegetable marrow is used as a vegetable. The gourds are sometimes hollowed and dried and used as vessels for water, &c. Also called **Mmung'unye**, n. *mi-*.

Mmung'unye, n. *mi-* same as *mmumunye*.

Mmunina, n. See **Muminina**.

Mmwaka, n. *mi-* a tree, *Sapindus saponaria*, the roots of which are used as a stomach medicine, and the fruits as a substitute for soap, also called *mmoyomoyo* and *mharita*.

Mna, verb-form, (1) there is (within); (2) you (plur.) have.

Mnaanaa,* n. *mi-*. See **Mnanaa**.

Mnada, n. *mi*, **Mnadi,*** n. *wa-*. See under **Nadi.**

Mnafiki,* n. *wa-* a hypocrite, pretender, impostor, liar. **Unafiki**, n. hypocrisy, dissembling, deceit. (Cf. *mwongo*. Ar. نفاق.)

Mnajimu,* n. *wa-* an astrologer. **Unajimu**, n. astronomy, astrology. (Ar. منجم.)

Mnajiri, n. *mi-* a kind of tree, sometimes also called *mkono wa pongi.*

Mnajisi,* n. *wa-*. See **Najisi.**

Mnana, n. (1) the Golden Weaver Finch (*Ploceus aureoflavus*); (2) a kind of yellow dye used for staining the leaf-strips for making mats, &c. (*ukili*).

Mnanaa,* n. *mi-* mint, *Mentha viridis*, in some places confused with *mrenaha.* (Ar. نعنع.)

Mnanasi,* n. *mi-* the pineapple plant, *Ananas comosus.* The fruit is called **Nanasi**, n. *ma-*. **Unanasi**, n. the inside of the pine-apple plant and so usually a strong fibre obtained from it, and used as sewing thread. (Pers. اننانس.)

Mnandi, n. the Cormorant, *Phalacrocorax* sp.; (2) the yellow weaver bird.

Mnara,* n. *mi-*. See under **Nurisha.**

Mnasara,* n. *wa-* also **Mnasarani**, n. *wa-* Nazarene, used of Christians by Muhammadans. (Cf. *masihiya.* Ar. نصراني.)

Mnaso, n. *mi.* See under **Nasa.**

Mnavu, n. *mi-* a kind of solanum, *Solanum nigrum* and *S. nodiflorum*; the stalks and leaves are edible.

Mnavunavu, n. *mi-* in some places, the name given to the Cape Gooseberry plant.

Mnawili,* n. See under **Nauli.**

Mnazaa,* n. *wa-*. See under **Nazaa.**

Mnazi,* n. *mi-* coco-nut tree, *Cocos nucifera.* The tree-stem is little used, except for stout posts or props, but when cut down the soft nutty substance at the top, from which the leaves and blossoms grow, is eaten as a delicacy (*moyo wa mnazi, kilele cha mnazi*). The other principal parts and products are the leaf, *kuti*, fruit, *nazi*, fibre, *kumvi* and *kumbi*; and the sap called *tembo.* The trees are distinguished as *mkinda*, i.e. young, not yet bearing; *mume*, male, and *mke*, female. **Nazi**, n. a coco-nut. *Nazi* is the most general descriptive term, but seven stages in its development are distinguished under the names: (1) *upunga*, the first forming of the fruit on the flower stem; (2) *kidaka*, a young nut; (3) *kitale*, a half-grown nut; (4) *dafu*, full grown and full of milk (*maji*), also of *ulambilambi*, and *tonga*; (5) *koroma*, when the milk is decreasing, and the nutty part forming; (6) *nazi*, fully ripe, no milk, and nut hardening; (7) *nazi kavu*, the nutty part dry and separating from the shell (cf. *mbata*). Also *joya*, a nut full of white spongy nut-substance; *kizimwe* (or *kiziwi*) without milk or nut; *makumbi*, the fibrous husk, *kifuu* and *ufuu* the hard inner shell (dist. *kifuo*, a stake used for ripping off the husk); *kizio*, half a nut (when broken in two). As a rule *nazi* are only gathered, i.e. fully ripe fruit, and the nutty part used for cooking (cf. *tui, chicha, mbuzi*) or dried and sold as copra. *Mafuta ya nazi*, coco-nut oil. Prov. *Nazi mbovu harabu ya nzima*, a bad coco-nut spoils the good ones. (See also *tembo, gema, kuti.* Perh. a corruption of Ar. and Pers. نارجيل a coco-nut-tree.)

Mndimu,* n. *mi-* the lime tree, *Citrus aurantifolia.* **Mndimu mtamu**, is the sweet lime-tree, *Citrus limetta.* The fruit is called **Ndimu.** (Pers. and Hind. ليمو.)

Mndunga, n. a kind of bitter cassava. (Cf. *muhogo.*)

Mnena, n. *wa-*, **Mnenaji**, n. *wa-*, **Mneni**, n. *wa-*, **Mnenea**, n. *wa-*. See under **Nena.**

Mng'ambu, n. *mi-* a tree with good timber of a reddish colour.

Mng'ao, n. *mi-*, **mng'ariza**, n. *wa-*, **Mng'arizo**, n. *mi-*. See under **Ng'aa.**

Mngazija, n. *wa-* a native of the Great Comoro Island. (Anzwani, Moali, and Maotwe are the other islands in the group.) **Kingazija**, n. *vi-* and adv. the Ngazija dialect, of the Ngazija kind, according to the Ngazija way, &c.

Mng'oaji, n. *wa-*. See under **Ng'oa.**

Mngoja, n. *wa-*, **Mngoje**, n. *wa-*, **Mngojezi**, n. *wa-*. See under **Ngoja.**

Mng'ongo, n. *mi-* a kind of tree, *Sclerocarya caffra*, with fruits which are eaten in times of famine. In some places children suffering from whooping-cough (*kifaduro*) are made to go round one of these trees singing and chewing cooked maize. After going round the tree they take the maize out of their mouths and throw it at the tree shouting, 'Here we leave our whooping-cough.'

Mnguri, n. *mi-* a shoemaker's mallet.

Mngurumizi, n. *wa-*. See under **Nguruma.**

Mnili,* n. *mi-* the indigo plant, *Indigofera tinctoria*, which furnishes indigo dye. (Ar. نيل.)

Mnimbi, n. a kind of very large fish.

Mninga, n. *mi-* a tree, *Pterocarpus bussei*, with excellent timber, also known locally as *muhagata, mtumbati, mkunguru*, and *pagata*.

Mnjugumawe, n. *mi-* the Madagascar or Bambara ground-nut, *Voandzeia subterranea*. The nuts which are edible are called *njugumawe*. They are so hard when ripe that considerable soaking is necessary before use.

Mnjugunyasa, n. *mi-* the monkey nut, peanut, ground-nut, *Arachis hypogaea*. These nuts are used for eating, for flavouring food, and also for producing oil, which is called *mafuta ya karanga*. Many are exported for soap making, salad oil, &c. The nuts are called **Njugu**, but very often **Karanga**, though the latter name is probably only correct for them when they are roasted. (Cf. *kaanga*.)

Mno, adv. very much, too much, excessively, exceedingly, beyond measure. Sometimes combined with other adverbs of similar meaning, *sana mno, mno ajabu*, very exceedingly, wonderfully much.

Mnofu, n. *mi-* flesh, meat, fleshy part, as opp. to bone, i.e. *nyama tupu*, all meat. **Kinofu**, n. *vi-* a scrap of meat. **Nofu**, n. a lean piece of meat, i.e. all flesh, no fat or bone. **Nofoa**, v., and **Nyofoa**, v. strip off flesh from bone.

Mnoga, n. *mi-* the leaf of the tobacco plant.

Mnong'onezi, n. *wa-*, **Mnong'oni**, n. *wa-*, **Mnong'ono**, n. *mi-*. See under **Nong'ona.**

Mnubi,* n. *wa-* a Nubian. (Cf. *Kinubi*. Ar. نوب Nubian.)

Mnukauvundo, n. *mi-* a shrubby herb, *Cassia occidentalis*, the leaves of which if rubbed in the hands make an unpleasant smell; used for making medicine in which to bathe young children.

Mnukio, n. *mi-*, **Mnuko**, n. *mi-*. See under **Nuka.**

Mnumanuma, n. *wa-* a person who is always employing black magic, evil charms, &c. (Cf. *mshirikina*.)

Mnuna, n. *wa-*, **Mnunaji**, n. *wa-*. See under **Nuna.**

Mnunda, n. *wa-*. See **Nunda.**

Mnuni, n. *wa-*, **Mnuno**, n. *mi-*. See under **Nuna.**

Mnunuzi, n. *wa-*. See under **Nunua.**

Mnyaa, n. *mi-*. See under **Mwaa.**

Mnyakuzi, n. *wa-*. See under **Nyaka.**

Mnyama, n. *wa-* an animal, beast. Sometimes used fig. of a stupid brutish man. **Nyama**, n. (1) often used in the same way as *mnyama*; (2) meat, flesh; (3) body, substance, matter, chief constituent, e.g. *nyama ya mkate*, crumb as opp. to crust (of bread), *nyama ya embe*, the flesh of a mango-fruit; (4) with plur. *ma-* amplic. a very large animal. **Kinyama**, n. *vi-* dim. and adv. in a brutish manner, like an animal. **Unyama**, n. the nature of a beast, being like a beast, brutishness, stupidity, &c. (Cf. *hayawani.*)

Mnyamata, n. *mi-* a perennial herb, *Pseudarthria Hookeri*, with small whitish pea-shaped flowers, used in the preparation of love potions together with *mlipu* and *mpendeupendapo.*

Mnyamavu, n. *wa-*. See under **Nyamaa.**

Mnyangalika, n. *wa-* a useless, foolish person. See under **-nyangalika.**

Mnyang'anyi, n. *wa-*. See under **Nyang'anya.**

Mnyanya, n. *mi-* the native tomato plant, *Lycopersicum cerasiforme*, also used for the English tomato plant, *Solanum lycopersicum*. **Mnyanya mshumaa**, n. *mi-* the plant bearing the long red tomato, *Lycopersicum pyriforme*. The fruit is called **Nyanya.** (Cf. *mtunguja, mtungule.*)

Mnyapara, n. *wa-* (sometimes heard as *mnyampara*), head of a body of men, (caravan, expedition, army), or of a part of it, headman—whether of porters or armed guard. (Cf. *msimamizi.*)

Mnyara, n. *mi-* a kind of euphorbia.

Mnyaufu, n. See under **Nyauka.**

Mnyegea, n. *mi-* the sausage-tree, *Kigelia pinnata*, also called *mbungati, mwegea, mvongonya*, and in some places *mranaa.*

Mnyenyekeo, n. *mi-*, **Mnyenyekevu**, n. *wa-*. See under **Nyenya.**

Mnyeo, n. *mi-*. See under **Nyea.**

Mnyevu, n. *mi-*. See under **Nya.**

Mnyima, n. *wa-*, **Mnyimaji**, n. *wa-*, **Mnyimo**, n. *mi-*. See under **Nyima.**

Mnyiri, n. *mi-* arm, tentacle, feeler of the cuttle-fish, commonly *mkono* or *mkia wa pweza.*

Mnyofu, n. *wa-*. See under **Nyoka**, v.

Mnyonge, n. *wa-*. See under **Nyonga**, v.

Mnyonyore, n. *mi-* Barbados pride, *Caesalpinia pulcherrima.*

Mnyoo, n. *mi-* intestinal worm. (Cf. *chango.*)

Mnyororo, n. *mi-* (1) a chain; (2) fetters, prison, confinement, jail. (Cf. *silisila, pingu.*)

Mnyozi, n. *wa-* for the common *kinyozi*. See under **Nyoa.**

Mnyunyo, n. *mi-*. See under **Nyunya.**

Mnywa, n. *wa-*, **Mnywaji**, n. *wa-*. See under **Nywa.**

Mnywanywa, n. *mi-* salt bush, *Pluchea Dioscorides* and *Suaeda monica.*

Mnywo, n. *mi-*. See under **Nywa.**

Mo, for the use of *mo* as a relative pron., &c., see Grammars. As a separate word it only occurs in such a phrase as *mo mote*, in whatever place, wherever.

Moali, n. the island Mohilla in the Comoro group, where the Wangazija live.

Moduleta,* n. a modulator, the word adopted for use in text-books and school lessons on music. (Eng.)

Mofa,* n. (1) a small oven made of clay used in some of the Arab dhows; (2) a small, hard, round kind of bread made from millet flour and baked in a *mofa* oven. (Ar. ميفى hearth for baking bread.)

Mogo, n. *mi-*. See under **Oga.**

Moja, n. (the number) one, one as an abstract. *Kumi na moja*, ten and one, eleven. *Moja kwa moja*, straight on, continuously, without a break. *Mia kwa moja*, one per cent. **-moja**, a. (1) one, a single, a certain, an individual; (2) one in kind, similar, identical; (3) one in feeling, agreeing, harmonious, of one kind. *Mtu mmoja*, an individual, a certain man. *Nguo moja*, one cloth, the same kind of cloth. *Moyo mmoja*, concord, harmony, so *hali moja, shauri moja*. *Namna moja na kile*, the same pattern as that one. Various plural forms occur, e.g. *vitu* *vingi vimoja*, many separate, single things. *Watu si wamoja*, people are not all alike. *Mtu na mwanawe, watu wamoja maskini*, a man and his son, both equally poor. *Mamoja*, often with *yote* or *pia* added, all one, all the same, all alike, to express indifference. *Mamoja kwangu*, it's all one to me, I do not care, never mind. (Cf. *haidhuru, -mojawapo*, any one whatever.) *-moja moja*, one by one, *njoni mmoja mmoja*, come singly, individually, come separately, one by one. *Mmoja wetu*, one of us. *Mmoja wa kwetu*, one of our party, one from our village or country. **Kumoja**, n. one kind. *Kazi zetu hazina kumoja*, our occupations are not all of one kind, a form of *-moja* agreeing with Infin. adv. on one side, from one point of view, i.e. *-kali kumoja*, with one sharp edge. **Pamoja**, the form agreeing with the *pa* class and locatives is used as an adv., all together, unanimously, at one time (or place). *Pamoja na*, together with, at the same place (time), as in company of. **Umoja**, n. oneness, unity, identity, concord.

Mola,* n. a title of God, 'Lord', used chiefly by Muhammadans. (Ar. مولى). **Maulana**, n. our Lord. (Cf. *Mungu, Allah, Rabi, Bwana*. Ar. مولانا.)

Moma, n. *ma-* puff-adder, also called *pili* or *piri*.

Moma, v. be spread quickly over a large area, i.e. a river in flood, a forest fire, disease like erysipelas, &c.

Mombasa, n. the Arab name of the island and town of Mombasa, in Kenya Colony, the port is now usually called Kilindini, but few ships go to Mombasa. The Kenya and Uganda railway which now reaches Kampala, begins at Kilindini. The native name of the island is *Mvita*, and the dialect of Swahili spoken in and near Mombasa, is called *Kimvita*.

Mombee, n. also **Mwombei**, Bombay.

Momonyoka, v. See under **Monyoa**.

Mo mote. See under **Mo**.

Monyoa, v. break off, pull off, as ripe bananas off a bunch, &c. St. and Pot. **Monyoka**, v. also **Momonyoka**, v. (1) be broken off; (2) break off, as of coast erosion, bricks or mortar falling off an old building, &c., of very ripe bananas falling off the bunch and similar things.

Mori, n. (1) a heifer. *Mori ya ng'ombe*, a heifer. (2) great bravery, anger, or ferocity, such as of male animals when fighting for the females; (3) medicine which is said to cause a man to be angry, fierce, &c.; (4) tallow, fat of animals. (Ar. مرعة fat, and مراء quarrel, dispute.)

Moris, n. Mauritius.

Morita, n. also **Morta**,* a short span, i.e. from the thumb to the forefinger; a long span, i.e. from the thumb to the little finger is *shibiri*. (? Corruption of Ar. ترز a short span.)

Moshi, n. *mi-* (1) smoke, steam; (2) soot, lamp-black. *Moshi wa moto*, the smoke of a fire. (3) a distilled liquor made from bananas. **Gari la moshi**, n. *ma-* a locomotive. **Joshi**, n. amplic. thick black, much smoke. (Cf. *oka, mvuke, masizi*.)

Mosi, n. (the number) one, seldom heard now except in the name for Saturday, i.e. *Jumamosi*, the first day of the month *mwezi mosi*, and the first month, after the fast of Ramadhan, *mfunguo mosi*. *-a mosi*, first, but *-a kwanza*, is generally used.

Mota,* n. a motor. **Motaboti**, n. a motor-boat. **Motakaa**, n. a motor-car. (Eng.)

Mote, a. and **Mwote**, form of *-ote*, all, agreeing with nouns having the locative termination *-ni*, e.g. *mjini mote*, in the whole town. *Mo mote*, in whatever place, wherever.

Moto, n. (A) (*mioto*). See under **Ota**, v. (C).

Moto, n. (B) (*mioto*). See under **Ota**, v. (D).

Moyo, n. *mi-* (plur. *nyoyo* is sometimes heard, esp. in Zanzibar and Mombasa) (1) the heart (the physical organ); (2) the heart, feelings, soul, mind, will, self; (3) inmost part, core, pith, centre; (4) courage, resolution, presence of mind; (5) special favourite, chief delight; (6) desire, hope. *Jipa moyo; piga moyo konde*, take heart, pluck up courage. *Tia (simika, kuza) moyo*, encourage, cheer, hearten. *Shuka moyo, legea moyo*, be depressed. *Moyo mchache*, lack of courage, a faint heart. *Shupaza moyo*, harden the heart. *Moyo wa jipu*, the core of an abscess. *Moyo wa mnazi*, the soft, nutty core at the top of a coconut tree, from which the leaves and blossoms grow, eaten as a delicacy. *Huyu ndiye moyo wake*, he (or she) is his great pet. *-a moyo*, voluntary, willing. *Sema (fanya) kwa moyo*, speak (act) voluntarily, readily. Also *sema kwa moyo*, say by rote, repeat without a book or reminder. *Kutoka moyoni*, is used in the sense of 'to cease to interest', e.g. when the newness of a thing has worn off, &c. **Choyo**, n. (no plur. but usually takes concords of Sing. of *ki-* class), avarice (shown either in getting or keeping), greediness, covetousness, a grasping nature, miserliness, &c. *Mwenye choyo*, a grasping, niggardly person. *Kuwa na choyo*, to be covetous, grudge. *Lia choyo*, cry for (disappointed) greediness. **Kijoyo**, n. *vi-* dim. of *moyo*, like *kimoyo* (see under), also inclination, hankering—not quite so strong as *choyo* (see prec.). *Sebusebu na kijoyo ki mumo*, of a person who half-likes a thing, he likes it, but is not quite sure about it. **Kijoyojoyo**, n. *vi-* (1) like *kijoyo*; (2) a person of a childish nature, fond of trifling with small unimportant matters. **Kimoyo**, n. also **Kimoyomoyo**, n. something affecting the heart, e.g. (1) heart ailment, heart disease; (2) a feeling, esp. fear, indignation, passion; (3) a term of endearment, favourite, sweetheart. **Uchoyo**, n. same as *choyo* (above). (Cf. *roho, bahili, tamaa, unyimivu.*)

Mpagazi, n. *wa-*. See under **Pagaa.**

Mpaji, n. *wa-*. See under **Pa, v.**

Mpaka, n. *mi-*. See under **Paka, v.** (B).

Mpaka, n. *wa-*, **Mpakaji**, n. *wa-*, **Mpakato**, n. *mi-*, **Mpaki**, n. *wa-*, **Mpakizi**, n. *wa-*. **Mpako**, n. *mi-*, **Mpakuzi** n. *wa-*. See under **Paka, v.** (A).

Mpalilio, n. *mi-*, **Mpalilizi**, n. *wa-*, **Mpalio**, n. *mi-*, **Mpalizi**, n. *wa-*. See under **Paa, v.** (B).

Mpamba,* n. *mi-* the cotton plant. *Gossypium* sp. **Pamba**, n. cotton, lint. (Cf. *pamba*, n. Pers. پنبه.)

Mpamba, n. *wa-*, **Mpambaji**, n. *wa-*. See under **Pamba, v.**

Mpambano, n. *mi-*. See under **Pambana.**

Mpambauke, n. *mi-* a shrub with aromatic leaves and greenish-yellow flowers, *Lippia asperifolia.*

Mpambe, n. *wa-*, **Mpambi**, n. *wa-*. See under **Pamba, v.**

Mpanda, n. *wa-*. See under **Panda, v.** (A) and (B).

Mpanda, n. *mi-* usu. *panda*, n. which see.

Mpandaji, n. *wa-*. See under **Panda, v.** (A) and (B).

Mpande, n. *mi-* usu. *upande* or *kipande*, which see.

Mpando, n. *mi-*. See under **Panda, v.** (A) and (B).

Mpanga, n. *wa-*, **Mpangaji**, n. *wa-*, **Mpangishaji**, n. *wa-*, **Mpangishi**, n. *wa-*, **Mpango**, n. *mi-*. See under **Panga, v.**

Mpanje, n. *mi-* a kind of banana. (Cf. *ndizi.*)

Mpanzi, n. *wa-*. See under **Panda, v.** (B).

Mpapai,* n. *mi-* the pawpaw, edible fruit, *Carica papaya.* The leaves and juices rubbed on meat make it tender, and are so used by cooks. The fruit contains pepsin. Sometimes it is called *mpapayu*. The fruit is called **Papai**, *ma-*. **Mpapai mwitu**, n. *mi- Melochia melissifolia*. (Hind. پپیا.)

Mpapatiko, n. *mi-*. See under **Papa**, v. (A).

Mpapindi, n. *mi-* a palm, *Cycas Thouarsii*, resembling the areca palm, but which grows in forests and has small red berries; its seeds are ground into flour and used in times of famine.

Mpapuro, n. *mi-*. See under **Papura**.

Mparamuzi, n. *mi-* name of a tree difficult to climb, because of its height and straightness. It exudes a gum which becomes hard. This gum is dissolved and used as a medicine. It is said to make the seminal fluid thick and thus cause child-bearing. Also called *mfune* and *mgude*.

Mparuzi, n. *wa-*, **Mparuzo**, n. *mi-*. See under **Para**, v.

Mpasi, n. *wa-*. See under **Pata**.

Mpasua, n. *wa-*. See under **Pasua**.

Mpasuasanda, n. *wa-* a nightjar. (Cf. *mraruasanda*.)

Mpasuko, n. *mi-*. See under **Pasua**.

Mpatanishi, n. *wa-*. See under **Pata**.

Mpato, n. *mi-* (1) see under **Pata**; (2) a float used for showing the position of a fishing-net, and keeping it extended, usually called *chelezo*.

Mpayukaji, n. *wa-*. See under **Paya**.

Mpea,* n. *mi-* the avocado pear-tree, *Persea americana*, also sometimes called *mpera wa kizungu*. (? Port. *pera*, a pear.)

Mpekecho, n. *mi-*, **Mpeketevu**, n. *wa-*, **Mpeketo**, n. *mi-*, **Mpeko**, n. *mi-*, **Mpekuzi**, n. *wa-*. See under **Pekecha**.

Mpelekwa, n. *wa-*. See under **Peleka**.

Mpelelezi, n. See under **Peleleza**.

Mpemba, n. *mi-* a kind of cassava. See **Muhogo**.

Mpenda, n. *wa-*, **Mpendelevu**, n. *wa-*, **Mpendi**, n. *wa-*. See under **Penda**.

Mpendeupendapo, n. *mi-* a shrub used for making love potions. See **Mlipu** and **Mnyamata**.

Mpendwa, n. *wa-*. See under **Penda**.

Mpenyezi, n. *wa-*, **Mpenyezo**, n. *mi-*. See under **Penya**.

Mpenzi, n. *wa-*. See under **Penda**.

Mpepea, n. *mi-*, **Mpepetaji**, n. *wa-*. See under **Pepa**.

Mpera,* n. *mi-* the guava tree, *Psidium Guajava*. **Mpera wa kizungu**, n. *mi-* the rose-apple tree. (Cf. *mdarabi*. Port. *pera*.)

Mpeta, n. *mi-* cloves which have fallen from a tree.

Mpetaji, n. *wa-* same as *mpepetaji*, which see.

Mpevu, n. *wa-*, **Mpevushi**, n. *wa-*. See under **Pea**, v. (A).

Mpiga, n. *wa-*, **Mpiganisho**, n. *mi-*, **Mpigano**, n. *mi-*, **Mpigi**, n. *wa-*, **Mpigo**, n. *mi-*. See under **Piga**.

Mpiga kalulu, n. *mi-* a thorny tree with sweet-scented mimosa-like flowers.

Mpikaji, n. *wa-*. See under **Pika**.

Mpiko, n. *mi-* (1) see under **Pika**; (2) a stick or pole to carry or sling loads on; (3) a lever. (Cf. *wenzo*.)

Mpilipili,* n. *mi-* red or white pepper plant, *Capsicum annuum*. **Mpilipili hoho**, n. *mi-* bird, guinea or African pepper plant, *Capsicum frutescens*. **Mpilipili manga**, n. *mi-* the black pepper plant, *Piper nigrum*. (Pers. پلپل.)

Mpima, n. *wa-*, **Mpimaji**, n. *wa-*, **Mpimo**, n. *mi-*. See under **Pima**.

Mpinchi, n. *mi-*. See **Mpingi**.

Mpindani, n. *wa-*, **Mpindano**, n. *mi-*, **Mpinduzi**, n. *wa-*. See under **Pinda**.

Mpingani, n. *wa-*. See under **Pinga**.

Mpingi, n. *mi-* a large thorny tree, *Ximenia americana*, which grows on the steppes. It bears oval red tart edible fruits.

Mpingo, n. *mi-* the ebony-tree, *Diospyros ebenum* and *Dalbergia melanoxylon*.

Mpini, n. *mi-* amplic. of *kipini*.

Mpinzani, n. *wa-*. See under **Pinza**.

Mpira, n. *mi-* (1) a tree producing india-rubber; (2) the substance india-rubber; (3) a ball of india-rubber, and hence a ball of any material—used of cricket ball, tennis ball, football, &c.; (4) a bicycle or motor-car tyre, the inner tube being called *mpira wa ndani*, and the outer cover, *mpira wa nje*. *Gema mpira*, draw off the sap from a rubber-tree. *Mpira wa kuponda*, india-rubber got by boiling the roots of trees. *Kucheza mpira*, to play football.

Mpishi, n. *wa-*. See under **Pika.**

Mpofu, n. an eland, also **Pofu.** Also sometimes heard instead of *kipofu*, a blind man.

Mpokeaji, n. *wa-*, **Mpokezi**, n. *wa-*. See under **Pokea.**

Mponda, n. *wa-*. See under **Ponda.**

Mpondo, n. *mi-* (1) see under **Ponda**; (2) a pole for pushing a vessel in shallow water, a punting-pole. Also **Pondo**, n. *ma-*, and **Upondo.**

Mponyi, n. *wa-*. See under **Poa.**

Mpopoo,* n. *mi-* (1) the areca palm, *Areca catechu*, bearing the betel-nut. **Popoo**, n. (1) the betel-nut, which is used for making the chewing mixture *uraibu*, which see (Pers. يريل); (2) see under **Popoa.**

Mpororo, n. *mi-* (1) Indian file. (Cf. *sanjari*.); (2) a line of tribal tattoo marks down the length of the nose. (Cf. *nembo*.)

Mposa, n. *wa-*, **Mposaji**, n. *wa-*, **Mposeaji**, n. *wa-*, **Mposo**, n. *mi-*. See under **Posa.**

Mpotevu, n. *wa-*, **Mpotezi**, n. *wa-*, **Mpoto**, n. *mi-*, **Mpotoe**, n. *wa-*, **Mpotovu**, n. *wa-*. See under **Pota.**

Mpozi, n. *wa-*. See under **Poa.**

Mpujufu, n. *wa-*. See under **Pujua.**

Mpukuti, n. See under **Pukuta.**

Mpumbavu, n. *wa-*. See under **Pumbaa.**

Mpunga, n. *mi-* the rice plant, *Oryza sativa*; also the rice while still growing or in the husk. When husked it is called *mchele*; when cooked in the ordinary way, *wali*. Different kinds of rice plants are known locally as: *afaa, gamti, sena, meli, bungala*, &c.

Mpungate, n. *mi-* a kind of cactus, prickly pear, *Opuntia* sp.

Mpungufu, n. *wa-*. See under **Punga**, v. (C).

Mpupu, n. *mi-* (1) the cowitch bean plant, *Mucuna pruriens*, useful for green manure; (2) the sword bean, *Canavalia ensiformis*.

Mpurukushani, n. *wa-*. See under **Pura**, v. (B).

Mpurule, n. *mi-* a shrub, *Chenopodium* sp., the seeds and leaves are edible, the oil is used as a medicine for hookworm. The seeds are also burned and mixed with oil as a medicine for thrush.

Mpururo, n. *mi-*. See under **Pura**, v. (A).

Mpuzi, n. *wa-*. See under **Puza.**

Mpwa, n. *wa-* son or daughter of sister, a nephew or niece.

Mpweke, n. *wa-* a lone, solitary man, one without any relations. See **-pweke.**

Mpweke, n. *mi-* (1) a short thick stick, bludgeon; (2) a hard kind of tree from which walking-sticks are made, sometimes called *mhambarashi*.

Mpya, form of *-pya*, which see.

Mpyo, n. *mi-* the Zanzibar rubber-tree, *Landolphia Kirkii*, also called *mkilungwana*.

Mpyoro, n. *wa-*. See under **-pyoro.**

Mraba,* n. *mi-* (1) what is fourfold, square, a square, rectangle, a right-angle. Also of squares laid out for planting, garden beds. *-a miraba minne*, rectangular. *Mtu wa miraba minne*, a square-built, stout man, of medium stature. *Piga miraba katika shamba*, lay out beds for cultivation in a plantation. (2) jam, preserve. *Mraba wa tangawizi*, preserved ginger. (Ar. مربع square, form. مربى preserve.)

Mrabaha,* n. royalty, fee paid to a chief by a trader for the right of trading in a place, e.g. the Sultan of Zanzibar used to levy the sum of

9 reale (1 reale was valued at about Sh. 4) on each *frasila* (35 lb.) of elephant ivory brought to the coast from inland, as *mrabaha*. (Ar. ربح profit.)

Mradi,* n. *mi-* intention, plan, resolve. (Cf. *nia, kusudi.*) Also conj. well, and so, accordingly, and then. (Cf. *basi, kisha, ndipo.* Ar. مراد.)

Mrama,* n. *mi-* pitching, tossing, rolling—the motion of a ship at sea, e.g. *mrama wa chombo. Enda mrama,* roll, toss, pitch, &c., of a ship. (Cf. *msukosuko.* Ar. رمى.)

Mramba, n. the Glossy-backed Drongo, *Dicrurus adsimilis,* also called *mbaramba.* **Mramba mweupe,** n. the Golden Oriole, *Oriolus oriolus,* also called *kirumbizi*; **Mramba mweusi,** the Pemba Glossy Starling, *Lamprocolius corruscus,* also called *kwenzi.*

Mranaa,* n. *mi-* (1) see **Mrenaha**; (2) sometimes applied to *mwegea,* the sausage-tree.

Mrao,* n. *mi-* (1) fuse for a gun, match for lighting the powder in a matchlock, a small twisted bit of combustible fibre from a suitable tree. *Bunduki ya mrao,* a matchlock gun. *Kufuatia mirao,* go to war (? Ar. رمى throwing); (2) the cool season, harvest time. (? Ar. ملاح hoar frost.)

Mrarua, n. *wa-*. See under **Rarua.**

Mraruasanda, n. *wa-* lit. a shroud tearer, the nightjar, also called *kipasua sanda* and *pwaju.* ;This bird, and also the wood owl, *bundi,* are considered to be birds of bad omen. (Cf. *rarua, pasua,* and *sanda.*)

Mraruo, n. *mi-*. See under **Rarua.**

Mrasharasha,* n. *mi-*. See under **Rasha.**

Mrashi,* n. *mi-* (1) see under **Rasha**; (2) a kind of tree, the litchi, also called *mgulabi,* which see.

Mratabu,* n. *mi-* the Sapodilla plum-tree, *Achras zapota.* The latex is used for chicle, the basis of chewing-gum, in Malay and elsewhere. (Ar. رطب moisten, refresh.)

Mrehani,* n. *mi-* Sweet basil, *Ocimum basilicum.* The leaves are used as a scent, sometimes worn by women in a sort of locket suspended round the neck. (Ar. ريحان.)

Mrejaa,* n. See under **Rejea.**

Mrembe, n. *mi-* a sharp-pointed wooden spear. (The German military spiked helmet (*pickelhaube*) used to be referred to as *mrembe* by natives in Tanganyika Territory.)

Mrembo, n. *mi-* and *wa-*. See under **Remba.**

Mrenaha,* n. *mi-* a plant, *Datura metel,* the dried flowers are smoked like tobacco for chest and lung complaints by Indians. The seeds are very poisonous. (Ar. رنح dizziness.)

Mrengu, n. *mi-* an outrigger or a native canoe, usu. *rengu, ma-*.

Mreno,* n. *wa-*. See under **Reno.**

Mrera, n. lines of ornamental stitching on the collar of a woman's *kanzu,* or a *kisibau,* usually of red silk.

Mriba, n. *mi-* a leaf of the sweet potato plant, used as a vegetable. (Cf. *kiazi.*)

Mridhia,* n. *wa-*. See under **Radhi.**

Mrihani,* n. *mi-*. See **Mrehani.**

Mrihi, n. *mi-* a tree, *Brachystegia edulis,* used for making canoes, also for building houses, sometimes called *mriti.*

Mrija, n. *mi-* (1) a small kind of reed —often used as a pipe, also for drinking with, making musical instruments, &c.; (2) a pipe, tube, piping.

Mrima,* n. the coastland of East Africa—the name used by people inhabiting the islands off the East Coast, e.g. Zanzibar. **Mmrima,** n. *wa-* a coast dweller, i.e. *Swahili.* **Kimrima,** n. and adv. the language spoken by the coast dwellers, i.e. *Swahili,* also the manner, &c., of the coast dwellers. (Ar. مرماة dangerous deserts, far lands.)

Mrithi,* n. *wa-*, **Mrithisha,** n. *wa-*, **Mrithishi,** n. *wa-*. See under **Rithi.**

Mriti, n. *mi-* same as *mrihi*, which see.

Mrizabu,* n. *mi-* a drain or channel leading from a tap or tank, for washing hands, &c., as the water passes. (Cf. *mlizamu*. Ar. مرزاب water course, note the trans. of *r* and *z*.)

Mroho,* n. *wa-*. See under **Roho.**

Mronge, n. *mi-* the horse-radish tree, *Moringa pterigosperma*. The green pods are used for flavouring curries and as a vegetable, and the roots as a substitute for horse-radish.

Mrongo, n. *wa-* (1) sometimes heard for *mwongo*; (2) one who has been through the initiation rites, and is versed in matters of sex. (Contr. *msungo*.)

Mrua,* n. *wa-* also n. (—), (1) a pleasant person, one with pleasing manners; (2) pleasing manners, honour, respect, reverence, &c. (Cf. *murua*. Ar. مروة.)

Mruba,* n. *mi-* a leech, used sometimes by the *waganga* (medicine men), instead of cupping.

Mrugaruga, n. *wa-* an irregular soldier, a native levy, also a messenger or retainer of a native chief. Sometimes *rugaruga, ma-*.

Mruko, n. *mi-*. See under **Ruka.**

Mrungura, n. *mi-* (1) see under **Lungula**; (2) a kind of large drum, used to call people together, and also sometimes together with other drums, used for dances.

Mrututu,* n. sulphate of copper, bluestone, blue vitriol, often used as a caustic for sores. In some places cooked with gruel (*uji*) and eaten as a medicine for yaws (*buba*). (? Ar. مرطيس a blue medicinal stone.)

Msaada,* n. *mi-*. See under **Saidia.**

Msafa,* n. *mi-* a line, row, series—more commonly *safu*, which see.

Msafara,* n. *mi-*. See under **Safiri.**

Msafihi, n. *wa-*, **Msafii,** n. *wa-*.* See under **Safihi.**

Msafiri,* n. *wa-*. See under **Safiri.**

Msaga, n. *wa-*, **Msagaliwa,** n. *wa-*. See under **Saga.**

Msago, n. *mi-* (1) see under **Saga**; (2) a kind of dance.

Msaha,* n. *mi-* an iron crowbar. (Cf. *mtaimbo, mshamo, mwuo*. Ar. مسحاة a poker.)

Msahafu,* n. *mi-* a book (blank, written, or printed), esp. the Koran, the Book, the Muhammadan Bible. Also sometimes a page or leaf of a book. **Sahifa,** n., **Sahifu,** n. a page, layer. (Cf. *kitabu, chuo*. Ar. مصحف the Koran, صحيفة a written page.)

Msahala,* n. a purgative medicine, salts, &c. (Ar. مسهل.)

Msahau, n. *wa-*, **Msahaulifu,** n. *wa-*, **Msahaulizi,** n. *wa-*.* See under **Sahau.**

Msaji,* n. *mi-* the teak-tree, *Tectona grandis*. (Ar. ساج.)

Msaka, n. *wa-*, **Msakaji,** n. *wa-*. See under **Saka.**

Msakalawa, n. *wa-* a native of Madagascar.

Msakamo, n. *mi-*, **Msako,** n. *mi-*. See under **Saka.**

Msala,* n. *mi-* (1) see under **Sala**; (2) a private place, bath, closet, lavatory—like *faraghani*. *Yuko msalani*, he is engaged, he is in the lavatory.

Msalaba,* n. *mi-*. See under **Sulibi.**

Msalani,* n. locative of *msala* (2) which see.

Msalata,* n. *wa-*. See under **Salata.**

Msalihina,* n. *wa-*. See under **Salihi.**

Msalimina, n. *wa-*, **Msalimu,*** n. *wa-*. See under **Silimu.**

Msaliti,* n. *wa-*. See under **Salata.**

Msamaha,* n. *mi-*. See under **Samehe.**

Msamba, n. *mi-* described as *mshono wa kati ya miguu*, i.e. the suture between the legs, the perineum, also called *kitako*. Prov. *Njia mbili zilimshinda mzee fisi, alipasuka msamba,* two ways defeated the old hyena, (and in trying to follow them) he split in two.

Msambale, n. *mi-* a flowering shrub, *Lobelia fervens,* rice-plot weed.

Msambia, n. *mi-* a tall tree, *Pachystela brevipes,* with dark red to black plum-like edible fruits.

Msameha, n. *wa-*, **Msamehe,** n. *wa-*, **Msameheji,** n. *wa-*.* See under **Samehe.**

Msamilo, n. *mi-* a wooden head-rest, used by some natives as a pillow.

Msana,* n. *mi-*. See under **Sana, v.**

Msanaa,* n. *wa-*. See under **Sanaa.**

Msanaka, n. *mi-* a screw pine, *Pandanus* sp., its leaves are used for fibre, also called **Mkadi dume.**

Msanapichi, n. *mi-*, also **Msanapiti,** n. *mi-* the frangipane-tree, *Plumeria acuminata.* Also called *mjinga, mvurtangi, mbono wa kizungu.*

Msandali,* n. *mi-* the sandal-wood tree, *Santalum album.* (Ar. صندل.)

Msandarusi,* n. *mi-* the gum-copal tree, *Trachylobium verrucosum.* (Ar. سندروس.)

Msangao, n. *mi-*. See **Mshangao** under **Shangaa.**

Msani, n. *wa-*, **Msanii,** n. *wa-*.* See under **Sanaa.**

Msapata,* n. a kind of dance. (Port. *sapatear,* a dance.)

Msaro, n. *mi-* a kind of thorny tree.

Msasa, n. *mi-* (1) a plant or shrub, *Ficus* sp., with rough leaves which are used as sandpaper for smoothing wood; (2) sandpaper, emery paper.

Msasi, n. *wa-*. See under **Saka.**

Msazo, n. *mi-*. See under **Saa, v.**

Msegese, n. *mi-* a tree, *Bauhinia Thonningii,* the timber of which is used for making the legs of bedsteads. The roots are used as a medicine for bronchitis, the bark for making a red dye, and the pods as a substitute for soap. Also called *mbambangoma.*

Mseja, n. *wa-* a bachelor, a man living in the unmarried state. **Useja,** n. (1) the condition of living without a wife, bachelorhood; (2) a kind of small beads threaded as a necklace.

Msema, n. *wa-*, **Msemaji,** n. *wa-*, **Msemi,** n. *wa-*, **Msemo,** n. *mi-*. See under **Sema.**

Msengenyaji, n. *wa-*, **Msengenyi,** n. *wa-*, **Msengenyo,** n. *mi-*. See under **Sengenya.**

Msetiri,* n. *wa-*. See **Mstiri** under **Stiri.**

Mseto, n. *mi-*. See under **Seta.**

Msewe, n. *mi-* (1) a sort of rattle, fastened to the leg, to make a jingle when dancing (cf. *njuga*); (2) a kind of large drum.

Mshabaha,* n. *mi-*. See **Shabaha, n.**

Mshahara,* n. (— and sometimes *mi-*) monthly wages, regular salary. (Cf. *ujira.* Ar. مشاهرة monthly payment.)

Mshairi,* n. *wa-*. See under **Shairi.**

Mshakiki,* n. *mi-* (1) a spit, skewer; (2) a bit of meat toasted over embers on a skewer, also *mshikaki.* (Cf. *kijiti, kibanzi.* Ar. شقق.)

Mshale, n. *mi-* an arrow. For various parts cf. *chembe* (iron head), *wano* (shaft), *manyoya* (feathers), *koleo* (notch). *Mshale wa sumu,* a poisoned arrow. **Kishale,** n. *vi-* dim. Both sometimes used fig. *mshale wa nuru,* a ray of light.

Mshambakuche, n. *mi-* a kind of thorny tree.

Mshamo, n. *mi-* a stick used for digging holes, crowbar. (Cf. *mtaimbo, mwuo, msaha.*)

Mshangao, n. *mi-*. See under **Shangaa.**

Msharafu,* n. *wa-*. See under **Sharifu.**

Mshari,* n. *wa-* an evil person, one who brings ruin, mischief, strife, ill luck, destruction, &c. **Shari,** n. evil, malice, ill luck, disaster, adversity, mischief. Opp. to *heri. Mtu wa shari,* same as *mshari. Jahazi ya shari,* an unlucky vessel. *Hawana shari na wageni,* they do not molest strangers. *Taka shari,* defy, challenge. *Nimekuja kutaka shari,* I have come to bid you defiance. *Mtaka shari simwepe,* I do not refuse a challenge. *Mambo ya shari,* adversity, malicious acts, &c. (Cf. *ukorofi, jeuri, kisirani.* Ar. شر.)

Msharifu,* n. the Natal Pigmy Kingfisher, *Ispidina picta,* also called *kisharifu.* (Cf. *sharifu.*)

Msharika,* n. *wa-*. See under **Shiriki.**

Mshaufu,* n. *wa-*. See under **Shaua.**

Mshauri,* n. *wa-*. See under **Shauri.**

Mshazari,* n. and adv. (1) crooked, slanting, oblique, out of the straight or level, sloping, on one side; (2) the cylindrical part of a worked skullcap, the top piece is called *kahafi.* (Cf. *upande, kikombo.* Ar. شزر.)

Mshelisheli,* n. *mi-* the breadfruit-tree, *Artocarpus incisa.* The fruit is cut into sections and fried or boiled. Sometimes it is cooked with sugar and cardamoms. This is a distinct species from the *mfenesi wa kizungu,* which has broader leaves and much deeper dentition. (From Seychelle, the island.)

Mshemali,* n. *wa-* a northern Arab, i.e. one who comes from Muscat and the Persian Gulf. (Ar. شمال.)

Mshenga, n. *wa-* a go-between, a person who arranges a betrothal on behalf of another.

Mshenzi,* n. *wa-*. See **-shenzi.**

Mshihiri,* n. *wa-* an Arab from Sheher in South Arabia, usu. engaged in manual trades and labour, fishing, &c.

Mshika, n. *wa-*, **Mshikano,** n. *mi-*. See under **Shika.**

Mshikaki,* n. *mi.* See **Mshakiki.**

Mshiki, n. *wa-*, **Mshikilizo,** n. *mi-*, **Mshikizo,** n. *wa-*. See under **Shika.**

Mshinda, n. *wa-*, **Mshindaji,** n. *wa-*, **Mshindani,** n. *wa-*, **Mshindanizi,** n. *wa-*, **Mshindano,** n. *mi-*, **Mshinde,** n. *wa-*, **Mshindi,** n. *wa-*, **Mshindikizo,** n. *mi-*, **Mshindilio,** n. *mi-*, **Mshindio,** n. *mi-*, **Mshindo,** n. *mi-*, **Mshindwa,** n. *wa-*. See under **Shinda.**

Mshipa, n. *mi-* used rather vaguely of minor organs of the body not commonly distinguished by natives, blood-vessel, nerve, vein, artery, and of any pain, ache, disease, or affection of them—ache, swelling, throbbing, fullness of blood, e.g. *mshipa umempiga fundo,* there is a knot (obstruction, clot) in his vein—of aneurism, &c. *Maradhi ya mshipa,* neuralgic pain, sciatica, and similar pains. *Mshipa unamtambaa mwilini,* of creeping or shooting pains in the different parts of the body. *Mshipa unapiga* (*unapuma, unatukutika, unauma*) the vein, or pulse, beats (throbs, is irregular, hurts). *Kanda mshipa,* feel the pulse. Also used for hernia, hydrocele, described as *mshipa wa maji, mshipa wa ngiri,* &c. Because of the general meaning of this word, the following have been adopted for text-books and school lessons on physiology, &c., artery, *arteri*; aorta, *aorta*; vein, *vena*; nerve, *neva*; capillary, *kapilari*; muscle, *musuli.*

Mshipi, n. *mi-* (1) a narrow strip of stuff (cloth, webbing, &c.) used as a belt, girdle, waist-band, halter—also used of braces, suspenders, &c.; (2) a fishing-line.

Mshirazi,* n. *wa-* a man from Shiras in Persia, also used of their descendants, many of whom are settled on the east coast.

Mshirika, n. *wa-*, **Mshiriki,*** n. *wa-*, **Mshirikina,** n. *wa-*. See under **Shiriki.**

Mshokishoki, n. *mi-* the Rambutan-tree, which bears a good fruit, *Nephelium lappaceum.* The fruit is **Shokishoki,** n. *ma-*.

Mshona, n. *wa-*, **Mshonaji,** n. *wa-*. See under **Shona.**

Mshongo, n. *wa-* an erotic, passionate person, male or female. (Cf. *kware.*)

Mshoni, n. *wa-*, **Mshono,** n. *mi-*. See under **Shona.**

Mshtaka, n. *mi-*, **Mshtaki**, n. *wa-*, **Mshtakiwa,*** n. *wa-*. See under **Shtaki.**

Mshtarii,* n. the planet Jupiter. (Ar. المشتري.)

Mshtiri,* n. *wa-* a buyer, one who makes the final bid at an auction. (Cf. *mnada, mzabuni, lilamu.* Ar. مشتر.)

Mshtuo, n. *mi-*, **Mshtuko,*** n. *mi-*. See under **Shtua.**

Mshubiri,* n. *mi-*. See **Msubili.**

Mshuko, n. *mi-*. See under **Shua.**

Mshuku,* n. *mi-* tobacco for chewing. (Prob. from Ar. شوق fill with longing, cf. *uraibu.*)

Mshumaa,* n. *mi-* a candle. *Kinara cha mshumaa*, a candlestick. *Washa mshumaa*, light a candle. *Zima mshumaa*, extinguish a candle. (Ar. مشمع.)

Mshupavu,* n. *wa-*. See under **Shupaa.**

Mshuru,* n. *mi-*. See under **Shulu.**

Mshurutisho,* n. *mi-*. See under **Shuruti.**

Mshushio, n. *mi-*, **Mshusho**, n. *mi-*. See under **Shua.**

Msia, n. *mi-*. See **Mzia.**

Msiba,* n. *mi-*. See under **Sibu**, v. (C).

Msibu,* n. *wa-*. See under **Sibu**, v. (A), (B), and (C).

Msichana, n. *wa-* a young girl who has reached puberty but is not yet married. (Cf. *mwanamwali.*) **Kisichana**, n. *vi-* a young girl who has not yet reached puberty.

Msidari,* n. *mi-* a species of lotus-tree. (Ar. سدر.)

Msifu,* n. *wa-*. See under **Sifa.**

Msiga, n. *mi-* a tree with small white flowers; the younger branches are used as tooth-brushes, *Dobera loranthifolia.*

Msikiaji, n. *wa-*, **Msikilivu**, n. *wa-*. See under **Sikia.**

Msikiti,* n. *mi-* a mosque. (? Pers. مزکت from Ar. مسجد.)

Msikivu, n. *wa-*, **Msikizi**, n. *wa-*. See under **Sikia.**

Msikundazi, n. *mi-* a tree, *Xylocarpus moluccensis*, the timber of which is used for making boats.

Msikwao, n. *wa-* one who has no home, a vagrant, a wanderer, i.e. *si kwao*—seldom used.

Msilimu,* n. *wa-*. See under **Silimu.**

Msimamizi, n. *wa-*. See under **Simama.**

Msimbo, n. *mi-* (1) bad reputation, bad character, bad name; (2) an adopted name, i.e. to hide identity, &c., also *kisimbo*, n. *vi-*.

Msimu,* n. *mi-* (1) the north-east monsoon; (2) a season, i.e. *msimu wa karafuu* (*pamba, mpunga*, &c.), the clove (cotton, rice, &c.) season, esp. used of a good season; (3) pattern, kind, sort, esp. of something new or strange. (Ar. موسم season, and سمى name, repute, kind.)

Msimulizi,* n. *wa-*. See under **Simulia.**

Msindi, n. *mi-* a kind of mangrove, usu. called *mkoko.* (Cf. *msinzi, simba ulanga, mkandaa.*)

Msindikizo, n. *mi-*. See under **Sindikiza.**

Msindusi, n. *mi-* a kind of tree, *Croton* (*eucroton*); the pounded bark is used for making poultices for swellings.

Msinga, n. *mi-* a tall tree with very light wood, *Trema guineensis.* The roots are used for making a medicine for chest complaints.

Msingefuri, n. *mi-*. See **Mzingefuri.**

Msingi, n. *mi-* a trench, ditch, cutting made in the ground, e.g. round a house for carrying off water, &c., but esp. of the foundation for a stone house. *Piga* (*weka*) *msingi*, lay a foundation. *Msingi* is the word adopted for the key, in music.

Msinji, n. *mi-*. See **Msingi.**

Msinzi, n. *mi-* a kind of mangrove tree, *Bruguiera gymnorrhiza*, and *Rhizophora mucronata*, usually known as *mkoko*, much used for firewood where found, with a red bark used for dyeing. Also used for making boats. (Cf. *mkandaa, muwi, mkoko.*)

Msio, n. *mi-* a piece of soft coral stone used for massage and rubbing perfumed ointment, &c., into the skin. (Cf. *singa, chua.*)

Msiri,* n. *wa-*. See under **Siri.**

Msirimbo, n. *mi-* a line of bad writing.

Msirisha, n. *mi-* a plant used for producing a black dye, *Euclea multiflora*, also called *mdaa* and *msizi*.

Msisimko, n. *mi-*. See under **Sisima.**

Msitamu,* n. *mi-* kelson or inner keel, to which the foot of the mast and ribs of a vessel are secured. (Cf. *mkuku, keel.* Ar. سطام a bolt.)

Msitiri,* n. *wa-*. See **Mstiri** under **Stiri.**

Msitu, n. *mi-* land covered with thick bushes, undergrowth, small trees, thorn-bush. *Mwitu* is a forest with large trees.

Msizi, n. *mi-* a plant from which black dye and ink is made, usu. called *mdaa*, also *msirisha*.

Msoa, n. *mi-* a large company of people, such as those travelling together. (Cf. *kundi, msafara.*)

Msokoto, n. *mi-*. See under **Sokota.**

Msolo, n. *mi-* a thorny shrub, *Caesalpinia cristata*, with yellow flowers. The seeds **Solo**, which are contained in oblong prickly pods, are used as counters in playing games.

Msoma, n. (1) *wa-* see under **Soma**; (2) *mi-* a kind of dance.

Msomaji, n. *wa-*. See under **Soma.**

Msombo, n. *mi-* a mixture of grains and other ingredients cooked for food, a mash, also called *mseto*.

Msomeshaji, n. *wa-*, **Msomeshi**, n. *wa-*, **Msomo**, n. *mi-*. See under **Soma.**

Msonde, n. *mi-* a kind of drum, long and of large size—also called *gogo*.

Msondo, n. *mi-* (1) a kind of large, long drum; (2) one of the dances in the girls' initiation rites; (3) the sound of a large drum, or of a cannon, &c.; (4) a long kind of tarboosh, such as is worn by the native police, prob. because of its being like the *msondo* drum.

Msonga, n. *wa-*, **Msongano**, n. *mi-*. See under **Songa.**

Msonge, n. *mi-* (1) see under **Songa**; (2) a round-shaped hut is called *nyumba ya msonge*, or *ya kisonge*.

Msongi, n. *wa-*, **Msongo**, n. *mi-*. See under **Songa.**

Msono, n. *mi-*, **Msonyo**, n. *mi-*. See under **Sonya.**

Mstaarabu,* n. *wa-*. See under **Staarabu.**

Mstadi,* n. *wa-*. See under **Stadi.**

Mstafeli,* n. *mi-* the soursop, *Annona muricata*, see also *mtopetope, mtomoko*, which are not always distinguished from each other by natives; also *mtopetope mwitu, mganda wa simba*. **Mstafeli wa kizungu**, n. *mi-*, *Anona squamosa*, also **Mstafeli gao**, n. *mi-*. **Mstafeli ajemi**, n. *mi-* the bullock's heart, *Annona reticulata*. **Mstafeli mwitu**, n. *mi-*, the wild custard-apple tree. (Hind. سيتاپهل fruit of Sita.)

Mstahivu,* n. *wa-*. See under **Staha.**

Mstaki,* n. *wa-*. See **Mshtaki** under **Shtaki.**

Mstamu,* n. *mi-*. See **Msitamu.**

Mstarehe,* n. *wa-*. See under **Raha.**

Mstari,* n. *mi-* a line, a line ruled or marked, a row. *Piga* (or *andika*) *mstari*, draw a line. (Cf. *safu, mfuo, alama.* Ar. مسطرة.)

Mstatili,* n. *mi-* an oblong. (Cf. *mraba, duara.* Ar. مستطيل.)

Mstiri,* n. *wa-* (1) see under **Stiri**; (2) also sometimes used for *mshtiri*, which see.

Mstuo, n. *mi-*, **Mstuko**, n. *mi-*. See **Mshtuo** and **Mshtuko** under **Shtua.**

Msuani, n. *mi-* a shroud or grave-cloth used for burying women. (Cf. *sanda.*)

Msubili,* n. *mi-* the aloe plant, *Aloe spicata,* and other spp. of which there are about ten in East Africa. (Ar. صبر.)

Msubukuo, n. *mi-*. See under **Subukua.**

Msufi,* n. *mi-* the cotton- or kapok-tree, *Bombax rhodognaphalon* and *Ceiba pentandra.* **Msufi wa bara,** n. *mi-* lalang grass, *Imperata cylindrica.* **Sufi,** n. and **Usufi,** n. kapok. (Ar. صوف wool.)

Msuka, n. *wa-*. See under **Suka.**

Msuka, n. *mi-* the spike of a native hoe (*jembe*)—the part of the iron head which is fixed in the handle (*mpini* or *kipini*). (Cf. *jembe.*)

Msukani,* n. *wa-* a steersman, *mshiki usukani.* **Usukani,** n. (*sukani*) rudder, and steering-gear in general, of a boat, ship, motor-car, bicycle, &c. Of a ship, the tiller or handle is called *kana*; the tiller-rope, rudder-line, *ujari* (plur. *njari*). The steersman is sometimes called *rubani,* the usual name for a pilot. A steering-wheel, *cherehe* (*gurudumu,* or *duara*). (Ar. سكان rudder.)

Msukano, n. (1) *mi-* see **Msukwano**; (2) see under **Suka.**

Msuki, n. *wa-* usu. *msusi.* See under **Suka.**

Msuko, n. *mi-* (1) see under **Suka**; (2) a tree, the leaves of which are made into a medicine. (Cf. *jimbo.*)

Msukosuko, n. *mi-*. See under **Suka.**

Msukumizi, n. *wa-*. See under **Sukuma.**

Msukwano, n. *mi-* the shaft and barrel of a drill (*kekee*) used by native carpenters. (From *suka,* or cf. Ar. مسكن house, and similarly used of *nyumba,* i.e. *nyumba ya randa,* the stock of a plane.)

Msuli,* n. *wa-* name given to Arabs from the Persian Gulf who come in dhows with the north-east monsoon (*msimu*) and, after trading, return with the south-west monsoon (*kusi*). (? Ar. ساحل coast, with *m-* prefix.)

Msuluhisha, n. *wa-*, **Msuluhishi,** n. *wa-*, **Msuluhivu,*** n. *wa-*. See under **Suluhu.**

Msumari,* n. *mi-* a nail, large pin, or anything similar in appearance or use. *Kuipigilia* (*kuikongomea*) *sanduku misumari,* to nail down a box. *Kongoa* (sometimes *ng'oa*) *misumari,* draw out nails. *Msumari* (also *mwiba, kiuma*) *wa nyuki,* a bee's sting. (Ar. مسمار.)

Msumbufu, n. *wa-*. See under **Sumba.**

Msumeno, n. *mi-* a saw. *Piga msumeno,* use a saw. *Kata kwa msumeno,* cut with a saw. *Noa msumeno,* set a saw. *Msumeno wa kitanda,* frame-saw, large ones being used at saw-pits, and for plank cutting. The frame is called *kitanda,* or sometimes *farasi.* *Msumeno wa kamba,* a fret-saw. *Unga wa msumeno,* saw-dust. (From *kisu* and *meno, msu-* a large knife, and *meno,* teeth.)

Msungo, n. *wa-* a youth of either sex unversed in the matters of sex, or uncouth in manners, &c.; one who does not understand properly the teachings given in the initiation rites. **Usungo,** n. state of being untrained or uncouth in sexual affairs. (Contr. *mrongo.*)

Msungululu, n. *mi-* a poisonous plant, *Strophanthus eminii,* used for medicinal purposes, and perhaps in the preparation of arrow poison, also called *mtondo.*

Msunguti, n. *mi-* (1) a knotty thorn tree, *Acocanthera longiflora,* with red flowers and a purple coloured fruit. Natives use the roots, the bark for dye, also the wood, leaves, and seeds for making a poison for arrows. (2) anything strongly flavoured, i.e. strong tobacco, tea, coffee, beer, &c. (Sometimes called *mchunguti,* and prob. connected with *-chungu.*)

Msunobari,* n. *mi-* used of imported

fir and pine timber, also sometimes of the flamboyant, which is also called *mkakaya*, and the ironwood-tree, *Cassia siamea*. (Ar. صنوبر pine tree.)

Msuraki, n. *mi*, also **Msuruaki**, n. *mi-* the wooden peg in a kind of clog (*mtalawanda*) used by some women indoors, passing between the toes and so holding the clog on the foot.

Msusi, n. *wa-*. See under **Suka.**

Msusu, n. *mi-* (1) a kind of tree; its roots are used as a medicine; (2) the tail-feathers of a bird.

Msuto, n. *mi-* (1) see under **Suta**; (2) sometimes used for *msutu* and *kisutu*, which is the usual name. See **Kisutu.**

Msuzo, n. *mi-* handle of wood by which the upper stone is turned, in grinding grain between two stones.

Mswahili,* n. *wa-* the general name given to a native of the east coast of Africa, from the Arabic for east coast. In the hinterland, sometimes called *mwungwana*, a gentleman, prob. a small god. Often used of any native who wears a *kanzu* or professes to be a Muhammadan. **Kiswahili**, n. and adv. the Swahili language, according to the Swahili manner, kind, &c. **Uswahili**, n. the Swahili country, i.e. the coastal belt. (Ar. سواحل.)

Mswaki,* n. *mi-* (1) applied to a number of trees and shrubs, the twigs of which when chewed at the end are used as tooth-brushes. The most popular are *Salvadora persica* and *Dobera loranthifolia*. (2) a tooth-brush, a piece of twig, the end of which is chewed until the fibres form a sort of brush, used for brushing the teeth. (Ar. مسواك.)

Mtaa,* n. *mi-* division of a town, quarter, district, parish. *Kaa mtaa mmoja*, live in the same district, be neighbours. *Mtaa wa* (*Waswahili, Wahindi, Wazungu*) the quarter (of the town) of the (Swahili, Indians, Europeans). (Prob. from Ar. موطن fixed abode, treated as a locative. Cf. *utani, tania*.)

Mtaala,* n. See under **Taali.**

Mtaalamu,* n. *wa-*. See under **Elimu.**

Mtaawa, n. *wa-*. See **Mtawa** under **Tawa.**

Mtabiri,* n. *wa-*. See under **Tabiri.**

Mtafara,* n. *mi-*. See **Mtafura.**

Mtafitafi,* n. *wa-* a blabber, go-between, tale-bearer. (Ar. تفتاف.)

Mtafiti,* n. *wa-*. See under **Tafiti.**

Mtafuno, n. *mi-*. See under **Tafuna.**

Mtafura,* n. *mi-* crupper—the strap fastened to the saddle passing under the tail of a horse, donkey, &c. (Ar. طفر.)

Mtago, n. *mi-*. See under **Taga.**

Mtahamari,* n. *wa-* a drunkard—seldom heard. (Ar. خمر wine.)

Mtai, n. *mi-* a scratch, a slight cut. *Piga mtai*, make a scratch, scarify. (Cf. *papura, chora, toja, piga, ukucha*, also *mfuo*.)

Mtaimbo, n. *mi-* an iron crowbar, lever, bar. Also *mtalimbo, msaha, mwuo*.

Mtajiri,* n. *wa-*. See under **Tajiri.**

Mtaka, n. *wa-*. See under **Taka, v.**

Mtakadamu,* n. *wa-*. See under **Kadamu.**

Mtakaso, n. *mi-*, **Mtakatifu**, n. *wa-*. See under **Takasa.**

Mtakawa, n. *mi-* the yellow tulip-tree which supplies good timber, *Thespesia populnea*. **Mtakawa dume**, see **Mchokochore dume. Mtakawa jike**, see **Mchokochore jike.**

Mtalalishi,* n. *wa-*. See under **Talalishi.**

Mtalawanda, n. *mi-* (1) a tree, *Mimusops densiflora*, from which wooden clogs, fish-traps (*madema*), and the outriggers of canoes are made (*matengu*); (2) the tulip-tree, *Markhamia zanzibarica*; (3) a wooden clog.

Mtali, n. *mi-* a bangle, a broad kind of anklet, usually made of silver.

Mtalimbo, n. *mi-*. See **Mtaimbo.**

Mtama, n. *mi-* millet, Kaffir corn, sorghum—a food staple in many parts of East Africa. *Mtama mtindi*, young half-grown millet. *Mtama tete*, millet with grain formed but not fully ripe. The stalk is *bua, ma-*, and of a sweet kind, *kota, ma-*. Various kinds are known locally as *felefele, jebele nyeupe, jebele nyekundu, fumba, kipaji, kibakuli, runzi nyeupe, runzi nyekundu, shungi, karachi*, &c. For other kinds of grain see *uwele, ulezi, wimbi, ngano, shayiri, kimanga, mchele*. (Bantu *-tama*, grain, or Ar. مطعم, food.)

Mtama wa bibi, n. a kind of bird.

Mtamani,* n. *wa-*. See under **Tamani.**

Mtamba, n. *mi-* a female animal that has not yet borne young. *Mtamba wa ng'ombe*, a heifer. Sometimes *mori ya ng'ombe*. (Cf. *mfarika*.)

Mtambaa, n. *wa-*, **Mtambaa jongoo**, n. *mi-*, **Mtambaa panya**, n. See under **Tambaa**, v.

Mtambala, n. *mi-* a kind of *ukunde* (which see).

Mtambazi, n. *wa-*. See under **Tambaa**, v.

Mtambatamba, n. *wa-*. See under **Tamba.**

Mtambika, n. *wa-*, **Mtambikaji**, n. *wa-*, **Mtambiko**, n. *mi-*. See under **Tambika.**

Mtambo, n. *mi-* (1) a trap with a spring action. Hence of any contrivance or machine with a similar movement. *Mtambo wa bunduki*, the lock (or action) of a gun. *Mtambo wa saa*, a clock (or watch) spring. *Tega mtambo*, set a trap. (2) the sides of a weaving-frame (*kitanda cha mfumi*).

Mtambua, n. *wa-*. See under **Tambua.**

Mtambuu,* n. *mi-* the betel plant, *Piper betel*. (Cf. *uraibu*. Hind. and Pers. تامبول.)

Mtambuzi, n. *wa-*. See under **Tambua.**

Mtanashati,* n. *wa-*. See under **Tanashati.**

Mtanda, n. *wa-*, **Mtande**, n. *mi-*, **Mtandio**, n. *mi-*, **Mtando**, n. *mi-*. See under **Tanda.**

Mtanga, n. *wa-*, **Mtangatanga**, n. *wa-*. See under **Tanga**, v.

Mtangawizi, n. *mi-* the ginger plant, *Zingiber officinale*. **Tangawizi**, n. ginger.

Mtangazaji, n. *wa-*, **Mtangazi**, n. *wa-*. See under **Tanga**, v.

Mtange, n. *mi-* the beam of a pair of scales for weighing with. (Cf. *mizani*.)

Mtango, n. *mi-* (1) native cucumber, edible, *Cucumis sativus, Cucumis metuliferus*, and *Cucumis melo*; (2) see under **Tanga**, v.

Mtangulizi, n. *wa-*. See under **Tangulia.**

Mtani,* n. *wa-*. See under **Tania.**

Mtapisho, n. *mi-*. See under **Tapika.**

Mtapo, n. *mi-* (1) name of a plant, an ornamental shrub, a kind of cycad, *Cycas Thouarsii*; (2) ore, i.e. of iron, gold, silver, &c.; (3) see under **Tapa**, v.

Mtasbihi,* n. *mi-* wild canna, Indian shot, *Canna bidentata*. The seeds are used as beads, esp. for Moslem rosaries, hence the name. (Ar. تسبيح.)

Mtashi, n. *wa-*. See under **Taka**, v.

Mtata, n. *mi-* an ornamental plant from which good firebrands are made, *Acalypha* sp.; also called *gonasokola*.

Mtatago, n. *mi-*. See under **Tataga.**

Mtatio, n. *mi-*, **Mtatizo**, n. *mi-*. See under **Tata.**

Mtawa, n. *wa-*. See under **Tawa.**

Mtawala, n. *wa-*, **Mtawalaji**, n. *wa-*, **Mtawali,*** n. *wa-*. See under **Tawala.**

Mtawalia,* adv. also **Mtawalio,** consecutive, prolonged, in succession, i.e. *siku tatu mtawalio*, three days in succession. (Ar. متوال consecutive.)

Mtawanya, n. *wa-*, **Mtawanyo**, n. *mi-*. See under **Tawanya.**

Mtazamo, n. *mi-*. See under **Tazama.**

Mteba, n. *mi-* a widespread scandent climbing plant, with scarlet berries, *Flagellaria guineensis*. The stems are used in rain-making ceremonies.

Mtego, n. *mi-*. See under **Tega.**

Mteja, n. *wa-* a person who is being exorcized by a *mganga*; also one who has already been exorcized and now belongs to a sort of guild (*mwana chama*) which assists in the exorcism of spirits. (Cf. *pepo, punga.*)

Mteka, n. *wa-*. See under **Teka.**

Mtelemko, n. *mi-*. See under **Telea.**

Mtema, n. *wa-*. See under **Tema**, v. (A) and (B).

Mtemba, n. *mi-* a pipe for smoking tobacco. (Cf. *kiko, buruma, toza, kikororo.*)

Mtembezaji, n. *wa-*, **Mtembezi**, n. *wa-*. See under **Tembea.**

Mtembo, n. *mi-* (1) the shoots of the sugar-cane, or any other plant, used for planting out; also the top shoot of the coconut-tree; (2) crack in the hard skin of the soles of the feet caused by *buba* (yaws) and other diseases, sometimes called *uyabisi*.

Mtemi, n. *wa-* (1) see under **Tema**, v. (A) and (B); (2) title of a native chief in some of the tribes in Tanganyika Territory, and well known now at the coast.

Mtemo, n. *mi-*. See under **Tema**, v. (A) and (B).

Mtenda, n. *wa-*, **Mtendaji**, n. *wa-*. See under **Tenda.**

Mtende, n. *mi-* the date palm, *Phoenix dactylifera*. The fruit is called **Tende.**

Mtendo, n. *mi-*. See under **Tenda.**

Mtenga, n. *wa-*. See under **Tenga**, v. (A).

Mtenga, n. *mi-* a pole used for carrying a load between two men, one end is carried on the shoulder of each man and the load is slung in the middle. (Cf. *mpiko* and *tenga.*)

Mtenge, n. *mi-* an outrigger of a canoe. (Cf. *mlengu, ndubi, ngalawa.*)

Mtengenezaji, n. *wa-*. See under **Tengenea.**

Mtengo, n. *mi-*, **Mtengwa**, n. *wa-*. See under **Tenga**, v. (A).

Mtenzi, n. *wa-*. See under **Tenda.**

Mteo, adv. *kupika mteo*, to cook food by boiling, but remove it from the fire before it is properly done, parboil.

Mtepe, n. *mi-* a native sailing-vessel, with a very long projecting prow, upright mast, and square matting sail. Constructed with wooden pegs and cord, at coast towns north of Mombasa, Lamu, &c., and used by the *Wagunya* in their trading voyages.

Mtepetevu, n. *wa-*. See under **Tepeta.**

Mteremeshi, n. *wa-*, **Mteremezi**, n. *wa-*, **Mteremo**, n. *mi-*. See under **Terema.**

Mtesa, n. *wa-*, **Mtesaji**, n. *wa-*, **Mtesi**, n. *wa-*. See under **Tesa.**

Mtetaji, n. *wa-*. See under **Teta.**

Mtete, n. *mi-* a reed, usually *utete* (*matete*).

Mteteaji, n. *wa-*. See under **Teta.**

Mtetemeko, n. *mi-*, **Mtetemo**, n *mi-*. See under **Tetema.**

Mteua, n. *wa-*, **Mteule**, n. *wa-*, **Mteuzi**, n. *wa-*. See under **Teua.**

Mti, n. (A) *mi-* (1) a tree—of any kind, and in any state; (2) tree-material, i.e. wood, timber; (3) a tree or part of a tree, prepared for use—pole, post, palisade. *-a mti*, of wood, wooden. *Merikebu ya mti*, a wooden ship. *Nyumba ya mti*, a house of timber. *Mlango wa mti*, a wooden door. *Kijiko cha mti*, a wooden spoon. *Kibanzi cha mti*, a wooden spit or skewer. *Mti kati*, a post to which a prisoner used to be secured by fetters on his feet. (Cf. *mkatale.*) **Kijiti**, n. *vi-* dim. a small tree, bush, shrub, small pole, piece of wood, peg, stick. **Jiti**, n. *ma-* amplic. a large tree, a trunk of a tree, piece of wood. **Ujiti**, n. (*njiti*) any tall, slender tree. **Uti**, n. (*nyuti*) (1) stem, trunk, portion of a tree or shrub; and (2) fig. of the backbone, *uti wa maungo* (or *wa mgongo*), as the central support of the human frame. Also (3) the wooden part, shaft of a spear (*uti wa mkuki*), &c.; (4) a small bit of wood, a chip, splinter, e.g. matchwood. (Cf. *kiti.*)

Mti, n. (B). *Maradhi ya mti, uele wa mti*, denotes sores of a scrofulous or gangrenous kind.

Mtia, n. *wa-*. See under **Tia.**

Mtihani,* n. (— and *mi-*) an examination, esp. of a school examination. (Ar. امتحان.)

Mtii, n. *wa-*, **Mtiifu,*** n. *wa-*. See under **Tii.**

Mtikiso, n. *mi-*. See under **Tikisa.**

Mtikiti, n. *mi-* water-melon, *Citrullus vulgaris*. The melon is called **Tikiti**, *ma-*, often *tikiti maji*.

Mtilili, n. *mi-* a name for the kingfisher, also called *kizamiadagaa* and *mdiria.*

Mtima, n. *mi-* heart, seldom used now. (Cf. *moyo.*)

Mtimaji, n. *mi-* a tree, *Trichilia emetica*, the seeds of which contain oil suitable for cooking or for the manufacture of soap. Also called *mkungwina.*

Mtimbi, n. *wa-*, **Mtimvi**, n. *wa-*. See under **Chimba.**

Mtinda, n. *wa-*. *Mtinda mimba*, the last child a woman is able to bear. Lit. the finishing of conception. (Prob. from same root as *-chinja.*)

Mtindi, n. (1) buttermilk—also described as *mtindi wa maziwa*, or *maziwa ya mtindi*; (2) a name given to any kind of intoxicating liquor, i.e. *pombe, tembo, ulevi*, &c.

Mtindo, n. *mi-* (1) sort, shape, size, pattern, cut; (2) a special sort, a good kind, extra quality; (3) conclusion, end. *Nguo hii ya mtindo*, this is a special (unusual, superfine) cloth. *Mtindo wa kusi*, the end of the (season of the) south wind. *Mwanangu ni mtindo wa yule*, my son is just like him. *Mambo haya ni mtindo wa peke yake*, these affairs are of a special kind, there are none like them. (Cf. *mtinda* and *chinja.*)

Mtini,* n. *mi-* the fig-tree, *Ficus carica*, edible fruits. (Ar. تين.)

Mtipitipi, n. *mi-* a climbing plant or creeper, *Abrus precatorius*, bearing small red seeds with a black dot which are poisonous but ornamental. The roots and leaves are used in native medicine. The seeds are sometimes called *macho ya tipitipi*, i.e. the eyes of the bird called *tipitipi*, the white-browed coucal.

Mtiriri, n. *wa-* (1) an erotic man or woman (cf. *mkware*); (2) when used of a child, a restless, irresponsible, untrustworthy child. (Cf. *mtukutu.*)

Mtiririko, n. *mi-*. See under **Tiririka.**

Mtishaji, n. *wa-*. See under **Tisha.**

Mtiti, n. *mi-* a species of owl. (Cf. *bundi, mpasuasanda.*)

Mtitio, n. *mi-*. See under **Tita.**

Mti wa mstari, n. *mi-* a kind of sweet potato, *Ipomaea repens.*

Mto, n. (A) *mi-* (1) a river, small or large, rivulet, brook, stream, &c.; (2) creek, inlet, estuary, arm of the sea, i.e. *mto wa bahari*. *Mto wa mkono*, a branching river, delta. *Mto mkavu*, a river bed, dry channel. *Mkono wa mto*, affluent, branch of a river. *Mto waenda kasi* (or *kwa kasi*), the river runs swiftly. *Vuka mto*, cross a river. *Kata mto*, go upstream. *Fuata mto*, go downstream. *Mto haupitiki*, the river is impassable. *Ukingo wa mto*, the side of a river. **Jito**, n. *ma-* amplic. a large river, lake (cf. *ziwa*), also sometimes *juto*, as if from a root *uto*. **Kijito**, n. *vi-* dim. small river, brook, stream, rivulet, sometimes *kijuto.*

Mto, n. (B) *mi-* a cushion, pillow. (Cf. *takia.*)

Mtoa, n. *wa-*, **Mtoaji**, n. *wa-*. See under **Toa**, v. (A).

Mtoamali, n. *mi-* a kind of tree.

Mtoaulimi, n. *mi-* a kind of tree, *Rauwolfia* sp., also called *mwango.* (Cf. *toa*, v. (A) and *ulimi.*)

Mtobwe, n. *mi-* a scandent shrub, *Strophanthus courmonti*, from which a favourite kind of walking-stick is made—white and possessing the quality of bending and keeping any curve it is bent to, like lead. (Cf. *mkwaju.*)

Mtofaa,* n. *mi-* the rose-apple tree, *Eugenia jambosa*, also called *mpera wa kizungu* and *mdarabi*. Also the Malay apple-tree, *Eugenia malaccensis*, which is also called *mtomondo*. The fruit is edible. (Ar. تفاح apple.)

Mtohara,* n. *wa-*. See under **Tahiri.**

Mtoki, n. *mi-*. See under **Toa,** v. (A).

Mtokoso, n. *mi-*. See under **Tokosa.**

Mtokwe, n. *mi-* custard-apple tree, also called *mtopetope* and *mtomoko.*

Mtolilio, n. *mi-* a leaf of the sweet potato plant, used as a vegetable. (Cf. *kiazi.*)

Mtombo, n. *mi-*. See **Mtembo** (1) and **Mtombwe** (1).

Mtombwe, n. *mi-* (1) the heart or centre of the sprouting shoot of a palm tree, coco-nut or other (cf. *mtembo, kilele*); (2) painful cracks or sores in the soles of the feet, usually caused by yaws or syphilis. (Cf. *mtembo, yabis.*)

Mtomo, n. *mi-*. See under **Tomea.**

Mtomoko, n. *mi-* the bullock's heart tree, *Anona reticulata*. (Cf. *mtopetope, mstafeli, mganda wa simba, mtokwe.*)

Mtomondo, n. *mi-* (1) the Malay apple-tree, bearing edible fruits, *Eugenia malaccensis*, also called *mtofaa*; (2) a tree which grows beside streams, *Barringtonia racemosa.*

Mtondo, n. *mi-* (1) the third day following, the series being: *leo*, to-day; *kesho*, to-morrow; *kesho kutwa* (or *kuchaw*), the day after to-morrow; then *mtondo*, the third day. The fourth day is called *mtondo goo*, or *kushinda mtondo*. (2) See **Msungululu.**

Mtondoo, n. (1) *mi-* a large tree, *Calophyllum inophyllum*, bearing the fruit *tondoo*, with a seed rich in oil. Medicinal; (2) an old musket; (3) a thimble. (Cf. *subana, kastabini*); (4) a sail-maker's palm made of bark. (Cf. *dopa.*)

Mtonga, n. *mi-* (1) a shrubby herb, *Solanum obliquum*; (2) a tree, *Strychnos Engleri*; (3) a tree with fruit about the size and colour of an orange containing an abundant edible pulp and large seeds, *Strychnos spinosa.*

Mtongonya, n. *mi-* a tree, another name for which is *mgombakofi*, which see.

Mtongotongo, n. *mi-* a kind of euphorbia with poisonous sap, *Euphorbia abyssinica.*

Mtongoza, n. *wa-*, **Mtongozi,** n. *wa-*. See under **Tongoza.**

Mtopetope, n. *mi-* the sweetsop, sugar apple, *Anona squamosa*. (Cf. *mstafeli, mtomoko, mganda wa simba.*) **Mtopetope mwitu,** n. *mi-* the wild custard-apple, *Anona senegalensis.*

Mtoria, n. *mi-* a large liana, East African rubber-tree, *Landolphia petersiana*, which bears an edible fruit called **Kitoria,** n. *vi-*.

Mtoro, n. *wa-*. See under **Toroka.**

Mtoto, n. *wa-* implies generally what is (A) in an early stage of development, or (B) in a subordinate position, and includes the following meanings. A. child, young person, offspring, offshoot, descendant, e.g. *mtoto mwanamume (mume, wa kiume)*, male child, son, boy. *Mtoto mwanamke (wa kike, mke)*, a female child, daughter, girl. An *mtoto* remains so till the age of about 7 years, or about 15 years—next becoming a *kijana* which see. *Mtoto mchanga*, a very young child, a baby. *Mtoto wa watu*, is used to describe a person of good birth, or a good family, &c. The offspring of any animal is called *mtoto*, e.g. *mtoto wa ng'ombe*, a calf; *mtoto wa mbuzi*, a kid; *mtoto wa kuku*, a chicken. For offshoot of plants cf.

watoto wa mgomba, the young shoots springing from the roots of a banana plant. *Mtoto* is also used of morbid growths, e.g. *mtoto wa jicho*, of a growth near the eye. But cf. B: (1) dependant, subordinate, follower, servant, ward, member of a household in relation to its head. This sense is quite irrespective of age. (2) *mtoto* is also extended to inanimate objects of all sorts, whose function is of a subordinate kind, such as a motor-car trailer, side-car of a motor-cycle, &c., but in this case it is sometimes treated as a *mi-* noun, i.e. with plural *mitoto*, e.g. *mtoto wa meza*, the drawer of a table; *mtoto wa kasha*, shelf or inner compartment in a box; *mtoto wa kitasa*, a ward of a lock; *mtoto wa mto*, a tributary of a river; *mtoto wa parafujo*, the worm (thread) of a screw; *mtoto wa randa*, the iron wedge used to secure the cutting-iron in a plane. **Kitoto**, n. and adv. *vi-* dim. of *mtoto*, a small child, baby, like a child, foolishly. **Toto**, n. *ma-* amplic. like *mtoto*, but commonly either (1) of size, a big, fine child; or (2) of some object resembling a child or offspring, e.g. *toto la ndizi*, the fruit bud on a banana stalk; *toto la meza*, the drawer of a table. **Utoto**, n. state (characteristics, condition) of a child or dependant, childhood, dependence. (Cf. *kijana, mwana*.)

Mtoza, n. *wa-*. See under **Toa**, v. (A).

Mtu, n. *wa-* (1) a person, a human being, an individual, one of the human race, a man; (2) a dependant, servant, slave, follower, adherent, e.g. *mtu mume*, a male; *mtu mke*, a female, usually *mwanamume, mwanamke*. *Mtu wangu*, one of my servants. *Mtu wa nani?* Who does he belong to? *Mtu gani?* Of what tribe is he? *Si mtu*, not a man, no one. *Hakuna mtu*, there is no one, nobody. *Mtu* and *watu* are used to point a number of contrasts, each illustrating the content of the idea. Thus (1) *mtu, si watu*, one person, not many persons; (2) *mtu, si mnyama*, a human being, not a beast; (3) *mtu, si kitu*, a living personality, not a chattel; (4) *mtu*, a mere man, a man as isolated and helpless. *Nimekuwa mtu tu*, of one conscious of his own existence only, ignorant of all his surroundings, 'I was a simple nonentity'. (5) *mtu*, a man as possessed of intrinsic worth, e.g. *sisi hatukuwa watu mbele yao*, we did not count as men in their eyes. (6) *mtu*, in an emphatic sense, a person of rank, importance, and consideration, e.g. *mtoto wa watu*, a well-born, (well-connected) person, a person of position. (7) *watu*, people in general, the average man. *Mimi mtu kama watu*, I am a common man; *mimi mtumtu tu*, I am only an ordinary person. (8) *watu*, other people, as distinct from the self, esp. as to ownership, e.g. *kwenda kwiba tango la watu*, to go and steal other people's cucumbers. *Fedha hii ya watu*, this money is not mine. (9) *watu*, public opinion, society. *Watu husema hivi*, it is common (popular, general) opinion. (10) *mtu* is often used to denote the possession of a certain attribute, or condition, e.g. *tukawa watu wa kufa tu*, we were as good as dead (entirely at the mercy of an enemy, or mortally wounded). *Si mtu wa kwenda naye*, he is not a man to go with, a fit companion. **Jitu**, n. *ma-* amplic. a very big man, a giant, an ogre. **Kijitu**, n. *vi-* dim. a little man. Also in contempt, manikin, or in disgust, e.g. *ewe kijitu kiovu!* Oh, you wicked wretch! **Utu**, n. human nature, humanity, manhood, membership in the human race. *Utu ume*, manhood, as contr. with *utu uke*, womanhood. Also used to indicate the finer qualities of humanity, i.e. gentleness, goodness, &c *Mwenye utu*, a human, gentle, considerate, kind, person. *Pande la mtu*, or *pandikizi la mtu*, an abnormally large man, a giant, an ogre. (Cf. *mwanadamu, binadamu.*)

Mtua, n. *mi-*. See under **Mtunguja**.

Mtuatua, n. *mi-* a kind of Solanum. See **Mtunguja**.

Mtubwi, n. *mi-* the yam, edible roots, *Dioscorea* sp.

Mtuchi, n. *mi-* a disease of the stomach. Cancer?

Mtukufu, n. *wa-*. See under **Tukuka**.

Mtukutu, n. *wa-*. See under **Tukusa**.

Mtula, n. *mi-*. See **Mtunguja**.

Mtule, n. *wa-*. See under **Tule**.

Mtulinga, n. *mi-* the collar-bone.

Mtulivu, n. *wa-*. See under **Tua**.

Mtulwa, n. *mi-*. See **Mtunguja**.

Mtumba, n. *mi-* (1) a bale, bag, or bundle, e.g. of cloth or other goods, made up as a load for a caravan-porter, and so (2) in general, a load, a man's burden. **Tumba**, n. *ma-* amplic. (Cf. *mzigo, robota, tumbo.*)

Mtumbako,* n. *mi-* the tobacco plant, *Nicotina tabacum.* The prepared tobacco is *tumbako*, and chewing tobacco is *shuku*. (Pers. تنباك.)

Mtumbati, n. *mi-* a good timber tree, also called *mninga*, which see.

Mtumbuizi, n. *wa-*. See under **Tumbuika**.

Mtumbuu, n. *mi-* a sprat.

Mtumbwi, n. *mi-* a native canoe, made all in one piece of a dug-out tree trunk, often a hollowed log of the mango tree, without outriggers, but sometimes with a small mast and sail. (Cf. *kiperea, tumbua, tumbo, tumba*, and for other kinds of boats *ngalawa, dau, mashua.*)

Mtume, n. *mi-*, **Mtumishi**, n. *wa-*, **Mtumo**, n. *mi-*, **Mtumwa**, n. *wa-*, **Mtumwaji**, n. *wa-*. See under **Tuma**.

Mtundu,* n. *wa-* (1) a mischievous, troublesome person, a restless, sly, tricky person (cf. *mtukutu*); (2) when used of a child, a spoilt precocious child, one who never keeps still. **Tundu**, a. mischievous, obstinate, perverse, self-willed, troublesome, restless, precocious. **Tundua**, v. spoil a child by letting it have its own way. **Utundu**, n. mischief, slyness, precocity, &c. (Pers. تند bold, impetuous; rough, quarrelsome.)

Mtunduizi, n. *wa-* See under **Tunduia**.

Mtunga, n. *wa-*, **Mtungaji**, n *wa-*. See under **Tunga**.

Mtungi, n. *mi-* an earthen pitcher—the commonest kind of water-jar of this baked earthenware, mostly plain and made by hand, but also imported with colour and ornamentation. Water-jars of various shapes and kinds are *balasi, kasiki, kuzi, gudulia*, &c. **Tungi**, n. *ma-* amplic.

Mtungo, n. *mi*. See under **Tunga**.

Mtunguja, n. *mi-* a name of a shrub, *Solanum bojeri*, with a fruit which is edible when young, but poisonous when grown; it is a common weed. The fruit and roots are boiled and used as a medicine for syphilis and yaws, and as a poison for dogs. In some places the fruit is stuck on the end of a finger which is sore, but esp. with a whitlow. Also known as *mtungule* in some places, which, however, more often refers to the European tomato; also as *mtua, mtula, mtulwa, mtura, mtuatua*, and as *mnyanya mwitu.*

Mtungule, n. *mi-* the European tomato plant, *Solanum lycopersicum.* Also called *mnyanya*. The fruit is **Tungule**, n. *ma-* but it is usu. called *nyanya*.

Mtunguo, n. *mi-*. See under **Tunga**.

Mtupa, n. (1) *wa-*. See under **Tupa**, v.; (2) *mi-* a general term applied to most plants which are used as fish poisons: (1) a leafless twining succulent herb, *Cynanchum sarcostemmatoides*, with thin stems which contain a milky latex, common to the coast; (2) a leafless succulent tree, *Euphorbia tirucalli*, with small yellow green flowers and trilocular fruits; used medicinally and as a protective hedge on account of its very caustic latex which on entering the eyes causes a temporary blindness; (3) a shrub, *Tephrosia vogellii*, with greyish-green leaves and white or purple pea-like flowers and woody hairy pods; (4) *mtupa wa porini*, a tree, *Mundulea sericea*, with purple pea-like flowers. It is used as a fish poison and is said to be so strong that fish poisoned by it are often eaten with fatal results. (5) *mtupa wa pwani*, a shrub, *Sophora tomentosa*, with silvery branches, pea-like flowers, and yellow pods, found only on sandy sea-shores in sheltered situations. The stems and leaves of these plants are pounded and broken up and either thrown direct into a pot-hole in a river, or else placed in a matting bag with some stones and thrown into fresh or salt water. The toxic contents of the leaves and stems are dissolved in the water and cause fish to float stomach upwards on the surface in an intoxicated condition, when they are immediately caught.

Mtupio, n. *mi-*, **Mtupo**, n. *mi-*. See under **Tupa**, v.

Mturituri, n. *mi-*. See **Mtipitipi**.

Mtutu, n. *mi-* the barrel of a rifle, also called *mwanzi, kasiba*.

Mtutumo, n. *mi-*. See under **Tutuma**.

Mtututu, n. *mi-* a good timber tree, sometimes called *mkarakala*.

Mtwa, n. *wa-* a dwarf, pigmy. (Cf. *mbilikimo, kibeti*.)

Mtwaa, n. *wa-*. See under **Twaa**.

Mtwana, n. (1) *wa-* a male slave; also used in a derogatory sense, rascal, rogue, ill-bred person, &c.; (2) a pole used for strengthening the mast in native vessels. **Kitwana**, n. *vi-* dim. a boy or youth of the slave class, also used in a derogatory sense like *mtwana*. **Twana**, n. *ma-* same as *mtwana*, but usu. with a derogatory sense. (Cf. *mwana, kijana, matwana*.)

Mtwango, n. *mi-*, **Mtwanzi**, n. *wa-*. See under **Twanga**.

Mtweto, n. *mi-*. See under **Tweta**.

Mu, for the uses of *mu* as a prefix, &c., see Grammars.

Mua, n. *mi-*. See **Muwa**.

Muaa, n. *mi-*. See **Mwaa**.

Muawana,* n. See under **Auni**.

Muda,* n. space of time, period, set term, fixed interval. *Muda wa*, for the space of, during. *Muda wa chuo*, a school term. *Muda kitambo*, a short time. *Muda mzima*, a considerable time, full time. *Alinipa muda wa miezi mitatu nimlipe*, he gave me a term of three months in which to pay him. (Cf. *mudu*, v. and *muhula, wakati, majira, nafasi, huku*. Ar. مدة.)

Mudir,* n. a chief, village headman, used in Zanzibar and Pemba only. **Mudiria**, n. the district of a Mudir. (Ar. مدير.)

Mudu,* v. (1) stretch, extend. It is commonly used in Rf. form, *jimudu*, stretch oneself, move one's limbs—as a sick person recovering or for relief, but usually in the sense of (2) be temperate, have self-control, be equal to (a task, &c.), tolerate, bear with; (3) and also used of a person in easy circumstances. (Ar. مدّ spread, extend.)

Mufti,* a. superior, pleasing, elegant, i.e. of clothes. (Eng.)

Muhagata, n. *mi-*. See **Mninga**.

Muhali,* n. anything difficult, impossible, unreasonable, absurd, unobtainable, &c., or only possible or obtainable with great difficulty. *Anitaka muhali*, he wants me to do something (or give something) quite out of the question. *Nifanyeje, ni huo muhali tu*, used in the sense of, What am I to do? I do not do this because I like it, but to please (somebody). (Ar. محال unreasonable.)

Muharamu,* the fourth month of the Muhammadan year. (Ar. محرم.)

Muhashamu,* a. See under **Heshima**.

Muhebi, n. and **Muhibu.*** See under **Hebu**, v.

Muhimu,* n. a. See under **Hima.**

Muhina, n. blood from the nose. (Cf. *damu.*)

Muhindi,* n. *mi-* Indian corn plant, maize, *Zea mays*. Also the grain. Single cobs are called *gunzi, kigunzi, bunzi*, and the grains when separated *mahindi. Unga wa mahindi*, maize flour.

Muhogo,* n. *mi-* the cassava or manioc plant, *Manihot aipi*, producing the edible roots, also called in their natural state and collectively *muhogo*. Very large roots are called *hogo, ma-*. The roots are eaten after being roasted or boiled, or are cut into strips (cf. *kopa, ubale*) and dried; then when wanted, pounded and boiled. There are many varieties known locally as *Binti Ali, Binti Athmani, kifumufumu, kibuluu, mndunga* (a bitter kind), *mpemba, mkasama, mkomoka, mbio, mzungu, shina rupia, sogea, usiniombe, bungala, kindoro, nangwa*, &c. There is a very bitter *muhogo* which requires to be dried before being eaten, also varieties which are poisonous, used for planting on the edges of a *muhogo* plot, in order to protect it from the ravages of pigs and other animals fond of *muhogo*. (Prob. through Port. from native Brazilian *mandioca*, cf. with manioc.)

Muhtasari,* n. abridgement, abstract, summary, précis. *Muhtasari ya mafundisho*, a syllabus (of instruction). (Ar. مختصر.)

Muhula,* n. space of time, period, interval. (Cf. *muda*. Ar. مهل.)

Muhuri,* n. seal, signet, crest, armorial bearing. *Tia muhuri*, seal, set seal to, confirm, sign. (Ar. مهر.)

Mujibu,* n. See under **Wajibu.**

Mulika, v. shine, gleam, throw (make, show) a light. *Akumulikaye mchana, hukuunguza usiku*, who lights you by day, sets fire to you by night. Prep. **Mulikia**, bring light for, make a light with, e.g. *nimulikie chini*, light me downstairs. Cs. **Mulikisha. Kimulimuli**, n. *vi-* fire-fly, glow-worm.

Mumbi, n. the bittern(?) described as a large bird which makes a noise like a drum. It is considered to be a bird of evil omen, hence the saying, *utakula mumbi*, you shall meet with misfortune or trouble.

Mume, n. (*waume*). See under **Ume.**

Mumiani,* n. a dark-coloured gum-like substance used by some Arabs, Indians, and Swahili as a medicine for cramp, ague, broken bones, &c. It is used as an outward application, also when melted in ghee for drinking as a medicine. It is said to be brought from Persia, but many natives firmly believe that it is dried or coagulated human blood taken from victims murdered for the purpose, and when a rumour is started that *mumiani* is being sought for, the natives in a town are filled with terror and seldom go out of their houses after sunset. (Pers. موميانى a medicine, substance with which mummies are preserved.)

Muminina,* n. a true believer, i.e. a Muhammadan. (Cf. *imani, amini*. Ar. مؤمن.)

Mumo, adv. dem. of reference, inside; also *mumo humo*. **Mumu**, adv. dem., usually with *humu*, i.e. *mumu humu*, just inside this very place (in these circumstances), just in here.

Mumunya, v. also **Munya**, v. break in small pieces, esp. in the mouth, i.e. mumble, munch, suck, prepare for swallowing, e.g. like a toothless person or donkey. St. **Mumunyika**, (1) be broken up, munched, crumble away; (2) be friable, easily crumbled or triturated, e.g. like bad mortar.

Mumunye, n. *ma-* a kind of gourd resembling a vegetable marrow, used as a vegetable. The rind when hard and dry is used as a vessel to hold fluids, like *boga* and *buyu*. The plant is *mmumunye*.

Munda, n. (*miunda*) (1) a harpoon, for spearing large fish (cf. *chusa*); (2) a piece of planking used in wooden construction. (Cf. *unda*.)

Mundu, n. (*miundu*) a sickle, bill-hook, chopper. (Cf. *panga, parange*.)

Mungu, n. (*miungu*) (1) God, a god; (2) providence, luck, accident—used to describe anything unaccountable or unexpected. Words connected with *Mungu* are *Mwenyezi Mungu*, i.e. *mwenye ezi Mungu*, Almighty God. *Omba Mungu*, pray to God, also *omba kwa Mungu*—*ombea* being usu. 'pray for, intercede'. *Shukuru Mungu*, be resigned, accept the inevitable, submit—seldom of felt or active gratitude. *Shiriki Mungu*, be wholly given to God—the strongest expression for a religious life (cf. *shiriki*), and when pressed to its extreme, i.e. union or sharing the nature, repudiated by Muhammadans, as impious and inconceivable. (Cf. *shiba Mungu*.) *Mungu akijalia*, God willing—for the common Ar. *Inshallah*. *Mungu akuweke*, May God provide for you (bless you), is often used, also *Mungu akubariki*. *Mbaraka wa Mungu*, God's blessing. *Maskini wa Mungu*, a destitute person, esp. of a blind man, cripple, &c. *Mola* is sometimes used for God, but seldom *Allah*. **Umungu**, n. deity of God, divinity, divine essence, or nature of a personal god. **Uungu**, n. deity in general, and so as conceivable attributable to other than God Himself, Dist. from *Umungu*. (Cf. *Mola, Allah, Rabi*, and various titles of God.)

Mung'unya, v. break in small pieces, &c., same as *mumunya*, which see.

Mung'unye, n. *ma-* a kind of gourd, same as *mumunye*, which see.

Munkari,* n. a wicked, bad, malevolent person. (Ar. منكر wicked, &c.)

Munya, v., also **Munyamunya**, same as *mumunya*, which see.

Munyi, a form of *mwenye*. See **-enye**.

Munyu, n. salt, sometimes used for the more common *chumvi*. (Cf. *chunyu*.)

Muo, n. (*miuo*), a wooden stake used to dig up stones, &c., with, or as a lever, often with an iron point. (Cf. *mtaimbo, mchokoo*.)

Muradi,* n. and conj. See **Mradi**.

Muru, n. a kind of native medicine used for stomach trouble of children; also mixed with aloes and other ingredients and used for putting on swellings.

Murua,* a. nice, pleasing, beautiful, elegant. (Cf. *mrua*. Ar. مرؤ refined manners.)

Musimu,* n. See **Msimu**.

Mustarehe,* n. See under **Raha**.

Musuli,* n. a muscle, the word adopted for use in text-books and school lessons. (Eng.)

Mutasari,* n. See **Muhtasari**.

Mutribu,* n. See under **Tarabu**.

Muujibu,* n. See under **Wajibu**.

Muujiza,* n. *mi-*. See **Mwujiza**.

Muumba, n. (*waumba*), **Muumbizi**, n. *wau-*. See under **Umba**.

Muumishi, n. *wa-*. See under **Umika**.

Muunda, n. *mi-*. See **Munda**.

Muundi, n. (*miundi*), *muundi wa mguu*, the shin, shin-bone, between knee and ankle.

Muungo, n. (*miungo*). See under **Unga, v.**

Muungu, n. (*miungu*). See **Mungu**.

Muuya,* n. (*miuya*). See **Mauja**.

Muwa, n. (*miwa*), the sugar-cane, *Saccharum officinarum*. There are several different kinds, *bokoboko, bungala, nyeusi, sena*, &c.

Muwi, n. (*miwi*), a kind of mangrove, *Bruguiera gymnorrhiza*. (Cf. *mkoko, msinzi, mkandaa*.)

Muyombo, n. *mi-*. See **Myombo**.

Muziki,* n. music of any description. (Eng. music.)

Mvao, n. *mi-*. See under **Vaa**.

Mvi, n. (1) grey hair. *Mwenye mvi*, a grey-haired old man. *Ndevu za mvi*, grey beard. *Nywele za mvi*, grey hairs. (2) *mi-* an arrow.

Mviko, n. *mi-*. See under **Vaa.**

Mvinje, n, *mi-* the Whistling Willow, Beef-Wood, *Casuarina equisetifolia*, a tall fir-like tree used for masts for dhows, &c.

Mvinyo,* n. wine, spirits, esp. the latter, the former being *divai*. (Port. *vinho.*)

Mviringo, n. *mi-* (1) see under **Viringa**; (2) a kind of yam. (Cf. *kiazi, mtubwi.*)

Mviru, n. *mi-* a tree, *Vangueria adulis*, with edible fruits about the size of pomegranates, containing two or three stones. The roots are used for making medicine for stomach complaints.

Mvita, n. the Swahili name for the town and island of Mombasa. Also **Mmvita**, an inhabitant of Mombasa, and **Kimvita**, n. and adv. the language spoken there, of the manner, kind, &c., of Mombasa.

Mvivu, n. *wa-*. See under **-vivu.**

Mviza, n. *mi-* a kind of evergreen tree used in magic and medicine making. It is said that if an offering is placed under the tree by a person, who meanwhile chews some of its leaves and forms a wish in his mind, that wish will be granted. Also, if its wood is burnt, wild animals will not come near.

Mvo, n. *mi-*. See **Mfo.**

Mvongonya, n. *mi-* the sausage-tree, see *mwegea, mnyegea, mbungati, mranaa*, all of which are names for the same tree.

Mvua, n. rain. *Mvua kubwa* (*nyingi*), heavy rain. *Mvua ya mwaka*, a slight rainfall, usually in August. *Mvua ya mawe*, hailstones. *Kunya* (but usu. *kunyesha*) *mvua*, to rain. *Mvua imenyesha*, it has rained. (Cf. *masika, kifuku, mvuli, manyunyu.*)

Mvua, n. *wa-*. See under **Vua**, v. (B).

Mvugamkubwa, n. *mi-* a flowering annual, *Senecio* sp.

Mvugulio, n. (1) air in a compressed space, e.g. a coco-nut, which comes out when it is pierced; (2) a bribe: (3) a hint, such as is asked for by a diviner when a person goes to consult him.

Mvuje, n. *mi-* a tree, the gum of which is evil smelling, *Asafoetida*. The gum is dissolved in water and used by some people to put under their pillow; it is said to ward off evil dreams. Some also put it under the pillow of small children to prevent the spirits taking the child away and leaving an albino (*zeru* or *zeruzeru*) in its place. It is also used for flavouring. (Cf. *papuri.*)

Mvuke, n. *mi-* vapour produced by heat; steam, perspiration. (Cf. *fuka.*)

Mvuko, n. *mi-*. See under **Vua**, v. (B).

Mvukuto, n. *mi-* bellows—used by native smiths, i.e. two leather bags alternately inflated by hand. (Cf. *mfua, fuka.*)

Mvulana, n. *wa-*, also **Mvuli**, n. *wa-*, a young unmarried man, a bachelor. **Kivulana**, n. *vi-* and adv. dim. a boy, a youth. **Uvulana**, n. age, condition, &c., of a young unmarried man, youthfulness, bachelorhood. (Cf. *kijana.*)

Mvule, n. *mi-* East African teak-tree, *Chlorophora excelsa*, having a good timber which is used for making doors, windows, furniture, &c.

Mvuli, n. (1) the lesser rains, the short rainy season, i.e. November in Zanzibar and adjacent places, when the north monsoon begins to set in (cf. *masika, mvua*); (2) *wa-* a young unmarried man (cf. *mvulana*); (3) see under **Kivuli.**

Mvuma, n. *wa-*. See under **Vuma.**

Mvumanyuki, n. *mi-* a shrub, *Premna chrysoclada.*

Mvumatiti, n. See **Vumatiti.**

Mvumba mkuu, n. *mi-* a herb with aromatic leaves, *Ocimum suave.* (Cf. *vumba, mvumbasi, kivumbasi.*)

Mvumbasi, n. *mi-* a herb with aromatic leaves, *Ocimum* sp., a little larger than *kivumbasi.* (Cf. *vumba.*)

Mvumo, n. *mi-* (1) the Deleb palm, Palmyra palm—a palm with a slightly bottle-shaped stem up to 60 ft. tall crowned with a head of large fan-shaped leaves. The fruits are large, brown, globular, and are edible. A wine is obtained from the palm. *Borassus flabellifera*, var. *aethiopium*. (2) see under **Vuna.**

Mvunaji, n. *wa-*. See under **Vuna.**

Mvungu, n. *mi-* a hollowed-out place, a hollow, hole, empty space, cavity, concavity—e.g. a hole in a tree, the space under a bedstead, i.e. *mvungu wa kitanda*. Prov. *mtaka cha mvunguni huinama*, he who wants what is under a bed stoops for it. Also sometimes used for the armpit (cf. *kwapa*) and the belly, i.e. *sehemu katikati ya nyonga na utupu*, the region between the hip-bones and the pubes. **-vungu,** a. hollow, having a cavity, concave.

Mvuni, n. *wa-*. See under **Vuna.**

Mvunja, n. *wa-*, **Mvunjo,** n. *mi-*. See under **Vunja.**

Mvuo, n. *mi-* (1) see under **Vaa;** (2) also under **Vua,** v. (B).

Mvurtangi, n. *mi-* the frangipane-tree, also called *msanapichi*.

Mvuruga, n. *wa-*, **Mvurugaji,** n. *wa-*, **Mvurugo,** n. *mi-*. See under **Vuru.**

Mvushaji, n. *wa-*, **Mvushi,** n. *wa-*. See under **Vua,** v. (C).

Mvuto, n. *mi-*. See under **Vuta.**

Mvuvi, n. *wa-*. See under **Vua,** v. (B).

Mvyele, n. *wa-* an old woman. (Cf. *kizee*.)

Mw- for *mw-* as a prefix, &c., see Grammars.

Mwaa, n. (with the plural *miwaa*, *miaa*, and *miyaa*), (1) the Hyphaene or Dwarf palm, furnishing the leaves which are generally used as a material for mats, bags, baskets, coarse cord, and string, also called *mkoma*, *mkoche*, and *mlala*. *Hyphaena coriacea* and *H. crinita*. (2) a leaf-blade of this palm. The blade is divided into two parts, *chane*, and each part slit into three, the central piece being the finest material for plaiting, the outsides for coarser kinds. (Cf. *ung'ongo*, *utangule*, *ukindu*, *ukili*, *chana*, *suka*.)

Mwabudu,* n. *wa-*. See under **Abudu.**

Mwadhini,* n. *wa-*. See under **Adhini.**

Mwafa,* n. *mi-* same as *afa*, which see.

Mwafaka,* n. *mi-*. See under **Afiki.**

Mwafu,* n. *mi-* wild jasmine, *Jasminum mauritianum*, the blossoms are called *afu*. (? Ar. افا scent, with *mw-* prefix.)

Mwaga, n. v. pour out, pour away, spill, waste, empty out. Ps. **Mwagwa.** St. and Pot. **Mwagika,** be spilt, be scattered, &c. Prov. *Maji yaliyomwagika hayazoleki*, spilt water cannot be picked up. Used fig. of people, i.e. of a crowd dispersing, e.g. *watu walimwagika* or *walijimwaga*, the people dispersed, went their ways. Prep. **Mwagia,** pour out on (from, &c.). **Mwago,** n. *mi-* a pouring out, spilling, loss.

Mwago, n. *mi-* (1) see under **Aga,** v. (A) and (B); (2) see under **Mwaga.**

Mwaguzi, n. *wa-*. See under **Agua.**

Mwajimbo, n. *wa-* (1) one concerned in a case, one 'in the know', i.e. used after saying something concerning a particular person or persons in a company, to give the hint that he or they only are concerned; (2) a person confined to the house undergoing medical treatment, perh. from *jimbo*, which see.

Mwaka, n. (*miaka*) a year. Two ways of reckoning years are in use in the coast towns, (1) the lunar year of twelve lunar months, *Ramadhani* being counted as the first month—and about 355 days. This is the Muhammadan religious year, and beginning ten days earlier each year has no correspondence with the seasons. (2) the solar year, with 365 days, the first day of the year being called *siku ya mwaka*, and kept as a popular festival, the last *kigunzi*, and the days being reckoned by decades (*miongo*). It is of Persian origin, and used for nautical and agricultural purposes. *Mwaka wa jana* (or *mwaka jana*) last year. *Mwaka wa juzi* (or *mwaka juzi*), the year before last. *Mwaka wa kesho* or (*ujao*) next year. *Mwaka kwa mwaka, kila mwaka*, year by year, annually. *Miaka nenda na miaka rudi*—many years. *Mwakani*, in a year's time—but often indefinitely, some day or other, sooner or later. *Mvua ya mwaka*, light rains which fall usually in August, between the two rainy seasons. The seasons on the coastal belt near Zanzibar are more or less regular and well defined. Zanzibar lying about 7° south of the equator, the sun is overhead about October 21 and February 21. These dates are followed by periods of calm, light, variable winds, and rains—the greater rains called *masika*, come chiefly in April, the lesser rains *mvuli*, in November. When the sun is in the south the north wind blows, and the heat is greatest, i.e. in December, January, and February. This is called *kaskazi, msimu* or *kiangazi*. When the sun is in the north the south wind blows, and the heat is less, i.e. from June to October. This is called *kusi*, and includes *kipupwe*, or cool period in June and July, following the heavy rains, and the *demani* in September and October. The times of calms and light winds are called *maleleji* or *tanga mbili*. For other divisions of time see *mwezi* and *siku*. (Cf. *waka* and *chaka*, the hot season.)

Mwake, Mwako, forms of *-ake, -ako*, which see.

Mwako, n. *mi-*. See under **Waa,** v.

Mwalamu,* n. (*mialaamu*). See **Mialamu.**

Mwale, n. *mi-* the Raphia palm. The mid-ribs are used for making native doors, windows, &c., *Raphia monbuttorum.*

Mwali, n. (1) (*wali*) a girl or boy before or while in the initiation rites; (2) *mwanamwali, wa-* or *mwali*, a virgin, a maiden; (3) a pelican; (4) (plur. *nyali*), flame, tongue of fire. (Cf. *ulimi wa moto* (4) is from Ar. مولع.)

Mwaliko, n. (*mial-*). See under **Alia** and **Alika.**

Mwalimu,* n. (1) (*walimu* and *waalimu*) a learned man, a teacher, a schoolmaster, esp. Muhammadan official teacher attached to a mosque. *Mwalimu mshauri*, a visiting, helping, Jeanes teacher. (2) sometimes applied to the navigator or chief officer of a coastal steamer. (Cf. *mkalimu, elimu.* Ar. معلم a teacher, master, علم navigation.)

Mwalishi, n. *wa-*. See under **Alia** and **Alika.**

Mwamali,* n. See under **Amali.**

Mwamana, n. *wa-*, **Mwamini,** n. *wa-*, **Mwaminifu,*** n. *wa-*. See under **Amana.**

Mwamba, n. *mi-* (1) a rock, a mass of rock, a very large stone, a reef; (2) in building, a ridge pole or wall-plate, i.e. a transverse pole, resting on the top of poles forming the side or roof of a native house. **Kimwamba,** *vi-*, or **Kijimwamba,** n. *vi-* dim.

Mwambao, n. *mi-* and *wa-*. See under **Ambaa.**

Mwambaji, n. *wa-*, **Mwambi,** n. *wa-*. See under **Amba.**

Mwambo, n. *mi-*. See under **Wamba.**

Mwambula, n. *mi-* a perennial herb, *Plumbago zeylanica*; its roots are poisonous.

Mwamizi, n. *wa-*. See under **Amia.**

Mwamu, n. (*waamu*) (also sometimes *mlamu, wa-*) brother-in-law, sister-in-law. (Cf. *wifi.*)

Mwamua, n. *wa-*, **Mwamuzi,** n. *wa-*. See under **Amua.**

Mwana, n. (*wana* and *waana*). See under **Jana.**

Mwanafunzi, n. *wa-*. See under **Funda**, v. (C).

Mwanamimba, n. an ailment of women, of the womb.

Mwanamizi, n. *wa-* a kind of crab, a hermit crab, also called *nyamizi*.

Mwanamke, n. (*wanawake*) a woman. See under **-ke**.

Mwanamume, n. (*wanaume*) a man. See under **-ume**.

Mwanasesere, n. *wa-* a doll, child's toy, usu. made out of a cucumber and grass, &c. (Cf. *bandia*.)

Mwanashanga, n. the north-west wind.

Mwandaliaji, n. *wa-*, **Mwandamano**, n. *mi-*, **Mwandamizi**, n. *wa-*, **Mwandamo**, n. *mi-*, **Mwandani**, n. *wa-*, **Mwandao**, n. *mi-*, **Mwandazi**, n. *wa-*. See under **Andaa**.

Mwande, n. In the expression—*kula mwande*, get nothing, be disappointed. (Contr. *mbwanda*.)

Mwandikaji, n. *wa-*, **Mwandiki**, n. *wa-*, **Mwandiko**, n. *mi-*, **Mwandishi**, n. *wa-*. See under **Andika**.

Mwanga, n. (1) *wa-* see under **Anga**, n. and v.; (2) *mi-* see under **Anga**, n.; (3) a kind of rice.

Mwanga, n. *mi-* the African arrowroot plant, *Tacca pinnatifida*.

Mwangachaa, n. *mi-* a kind of tree, *Cerbera Manghas*.

Mwangalizi, n. *wa-*. See under **Anga**, n.

Mwangamizi, n. *wa-*. See under **Angama**.

Mwangani, n. *mi-* another name for the tree *mkabilishemsi* and *mgange*.

Mwangao, n. *mi-* a clove epiphyte. (Cf. *kirukia, kimelea*.)

Mwangati, n. *mi-* the African cedar tree, *Juniperus procera*.

Mwangavu, n. *wa-*, **Mwangaza**, n. *mi-*, **Mwangazi**, n. *wa-*. See under **Anga**, n.

Mwango, n. *mi-* (1) see under **Anga**, v.; (2) a kind of tree, *Rauwolfia* sp., also called *mtoaulimi*; (3) sometimes heard for *mlango*.

Mwangu, n. form of *-angu*, which see.

Mwangushi, n. *wa-*, **Mwanguzi**, n. *wa-*. See under **Anga**, v.

Mwangwi, n. *mi-* an echo.

Mwani, n. (*miani*), seaweed (in general).

Mwanya, n. *mi-* a gap, hole, notch, narrow pass, small opening, cleft, crevice. *Mlima wenye mianya*, a hill with ravines. *Mwanya wa meno*, a gap between teeth. (Cf. *pengo, ufa*.)

Mwanzi, n. *mi-* a bamboo, *Bambusa* spp., hence of other kinds of reed and cane, and things resembling them in appearance or use, e.g. a pipe or tube of any kind, a musical pipe, flageolet, flute, tube of a telescope. *Mwanzi wa pua*, the nostril. *Mwanzi wa bunduki*, the barrel of a gun.

Mwanzo, n. *mi-*. See under **Anza**.

Mwao, n. (*miao*), (1) a piece of wood used as a support, prop, or strut; (2) pieces of board placed in the bottom of a dhow, &c., to prevent the cargo getting wet from the bilge; (3) libel, scurrilous reports, *kuwekwa mwao*, to have libellous, &c., things said about one.

Mwao, a form of *-ao*, which see.

Mwapaji, n. *wa-*, **Mwapishi**, n. *wa-*, **Mwapizi**, n. *wa-*. See **Apa**.

Mwarabu,* n. *wa-* Arab. One from the south coast of Arabia is known as *mshihiri*, from the north, i.e. the Persian Gulf, *mshemali*. **Uarabu**, n. Arabia. **Kiarabu**, n. and adv. the Arabic language, something of the Arabic kind, in the Arab way. (Ar. عرب.)

Mwari, n. *wa-* and *mi-*. See under **Mwali**.

Mwaridi, n. *mi-* the rose bush, *Rosa damascena*. The flower is **Waridi**, and the perfume **Halwaridi**. (Ar. وردة.)

Mwarita,* n. *mi-*. See **Mharita**.

Mwasha, n. *wa-*. See under **Waa**, v.

Mwasherati,* n. *wa-*. See under **Asherati**.

Mwashi, n. *wa-*. See under **Aka, v.**

Mwashiri,* n. *mi-* one of the longitudinal timbers which support the mast (*mlingoti*) in a native vessel. (Cf. *mhashiri*. Ar. صارى cross-beam, with *mw-* prefix.)

Mwasi,* n. *wa-*. See under **Asi.**

Mwata, n. small worms dug up on the beach, a good bait for fishing. (Cf. *chambo, daa.*)

Mwatuko, n. *mi-*. See under **Atua.**

Mwavi, n. *mi-* (1) a kind of acacia, *Erythrophloeum guineense*, the bark of which is poisonous and provides a dark red colouring matter. The bark is steeped in water and administered in certain trials by ordeal. (2) a trial by ordeal, i.e. *kula mwavi*, take an oath and drink a preparation of poison to substantiate it.

Mwavuli, n. *mi-*, also sometimes **Mwamvuli**, *mi-* an umbrella, sunshade. (Cf. *kivuli, mvuli*, and *tapa.*)

Mwawadhi, n. *wa-*, and **Mwawazi**,* n. *wa-*. See under **Awadha.**

Mwayo, n. *mi-* seldom heard except in the plur. a yawn. *Piga, enda miayo*, yawn.

Mwaza, n. *wa-*, **Mwazi**, n. *wa-*. See under **Waza.**

Mwazimo, n. *mi-*. See under **Azima, v.**

Mwede, n. *mi-* an aromatic shrub, *Lantana salvifolia*, with small purple edible fruits.

Mwega, n. *mi-*, **Mwegamu**, n. *wa-*. See under **Egama.**

Mwegea, n. *mi-* the sausage-tree, also called *mvongonya, mnyegea, mwegea, mranaa.*

Mwehu, n. lunacy, madness. Sometimes a verb, **Ehuka**, is used, i.e. be seized with madness.

Mweko, n. *mi-*. See under **Weka.**

Mwele, n. (A) (*waele*), a sick person a bedridden patient, an invalid, a cripple. **Uele**, n. sickness. (Cf. *mgonjwa* and dist. follg.)

Mwele, n. (B) (*miwele*), the bullrush millet plant, *Pennisetum malacochaete* and other edible species. The grain is called **Wele**, n. *ma-*. (Cf. *ulezi, wimbi*, and dist. prec.)

Mwelea, n. a kind of fish not considered to be good eating by Europeans.

Mweleko, n. *mi-*. See under **Eleka.**

Mwelewa, n. *wa-*, **Mwelezo**, n. *mi-*. See under **Elea**, v. (B).

Mwembe,* n. *mi-* the mango-tree, *Mangifera indica*. The wood is used for making canoes, mortars, &c. The fruit is called **Embe**, different kinds are known locally as *dodo, boribo, mviringe, maji, tango, shindano, sikio la punda, kinoo, kongwa, kiarabu, mali, maburuki, mawazo, ngwangwa, bwanashoka*, &c. **Mwembe wa kizungu**, the Otakeite apple, *Spondia mangifera*. (Hind. آنب.)

Mwenda, n. *wa-*. See under **Enda**, also for compound nouns made from it, i.e. *mwenda wazimu, mwendanguu.*

Mwendachi, n. a kind of yam. (Cf. *kiazi.*)

Mwendeleo, n. *mi-*, **Mwendelezi**, n. *wa-*, **Mwendeshaji**, n. *wa-*, **Mwendeshi**, n. *wa-*, **Mwendo**, n. *mi-*. See under **Enda.**

Mwene, n. See **Mwenye** under **-enye.**

Mwenea, n. *wa-*. See under **Enea.**

Mwenendo, n. *mi-*, **Mwenenzi**, n. *wa-*. See under **Enda.**

Mweneza, n. *wa-*, **Mwenezi**, n. *wa-*. See under **Enea.**

Mwenge, n. *mi-* a torch, a fire-brand, a wisp of straw or grass for carrying fire or light, such as the torches used by fishermen at night.

Mwengero, n. the portion of palm wine which belongs to the owner of a coco-nut-tree when it is tapped by somebody who has hired the right of tapping it.

Mwengo, n. (1) kind of scent; (2) a tail of a horse, donkey, mule, giraffe, or elephant, used in certain dances. (Cf. *mgwisho.*)

Mwenu, form of *-enu*, which see.

Mwenye, n. (*wenye*), **Mwenyeji**, n. (*wenyeji*). See under **-enye**.

Mwenyewe, n. (*wenyewe*). See under **-enyewe**.

Mwenyezi, n. See under **Ezi**.

Mwenzi, n. (*wenzi*). See under **Enda**.

Mwere, n. *mi-* a kind of wild kapok or cotton plant, *msufi mwitu*.

Mwerezi,* n. *mi-* the cedar-tree, *Pygeum africanum*. (Ar. ارز with *mw-* prefix.)

Mwetu, n. form of *-etu*, which see.

Mwewe, n. a bird of prey, a kind of kite or hawk, which carries off chickens, &c. The African kite, *Milvus migrans*.

Mweza, n. *wa-*. See under **Weza**.

Mwezekaji, n. *wa-*, **Mwezeko**, n. *mi-*. See under **Ezeka**.

Mwezi, n. *mi-* (1) the moon; (2) a month, i.e. a lunar month; (3) menses (also *damu* and *hethi*, which see). (1) *mwezi mkubwa* (*mpevu, kamili, duara, wa mviringo*), full moon. *Mwezi mdogo* (*kongo, mchanga, mpya, mwandamo*), new moon. *Mwanga* (*mwangaza*) *wa mwezi*, moonshine, also *mbalamwezi*. *Mwezi wapasua wingu, wachimbuka, waleta anga*, the moon pierces the cloud, it bursts forth, it sheds light. (2) Each month begins when the new moon is first seen, or 30 days from the last new moon. *Mwezi mwandamo, mwandamo wa mwezi, mwezi kongo*, new moon, the beginning of the month. *Mwezi mpungufu*, a month of 29 days. *Mwezi kamili*, a full month of 30 days. The month beginning when *Ramadhani* ends is considered the first month, and called *mfunguo mosi*, i.e. the first non-fasting month. The next are called (*mfunguo*) *pili* (or *wa pili*), *tatu* (*wa tatu*), &c., to *kenda* (*wa kenda*), the ninth month—the remaining three having the Arab names *Rajabu, Shaabani* (*Shabani* or *mlisho*), *Ramadhani* (*mwezi wa mfungo*). The other Arab names are sometimes used in letters and in giving dates; but are not commonly known. The month is divided variously into (1) weeks, or quarters, i.e. four sets of 7 days, *juma, ma-*. *Mwezi ni majuma manne*, the month is 4 weeks. But the weeks are reckoned independently of the months, the week and the month not necessarily beginning together. (2) decades, *kumi, ma-* or *mwongo miongo*, i.e. three sets of 10 days, called *kumi la kwanza, la kati*, and *la mwisho*, the days in each being counted as *mwezi mosi*, the first day of the month, *mwezi pili*, the second day, and so on—also *mwezi wa mosi, wa pili*, &c. *Mwezi ngapi?* or *siku ya mwezi ngapi* (or *wa ngapi*)? What day of the month is it? (3) halves, the full moon being the middle point, the first half being called *mwezi nje*, or *mwanga mkubwa*, the second *mwezi ndani* (*mchimbu*) or *giza*. (4) in letters, documents, agreements, &c., the days are usually reckoned straight on from 1 to 30, and are commonly designated by the number only e.g. *ishirini Shabani*, the 20th of *Shabani*. *Mosi Ramadhani*, the first of *Ramadhani*. (See also *mwaka, siku, tarehe*.)

Mwia, n. *wa-*. See under **Wa**, v.

Mwiba, n. (*miiba*), (1) any small sharp-pointed thing, e.g. a thorn, prickle, spur, sting, fish-bone, spine, sharp splinter, nail, defined by context or qualifying word, as *mwiba wa nyuki*, a bee's sting. *Mwiba wa samaki, wa nge*, &c.

Mwibaji, n. *wa-*. See under **Iba**.

Mwiga, n. *wa-*, **Mwigaji**, n. *wa-*. See under **Iga**.

Mwigo, n. (1) *mi-* see under **Iga**; (2) *wa-* a large kind of dove. (Cf. *njiwa, hua*.)

Mwijiko, n. *mi-*. See **Mjiko**.

Mwiko, n. (A) (*miiko*) a spoon, or instrument resembling it, e.g. a mason's trowel. **Kijiko**, n. *vi-* dim. (Cf. *mkamshi, upawa*.)

Mwiko, n. (B) (*miiko*) something

deliberately abstained from, by order of a doctor, or for considerations of health, taboo, totem, &c. *Mwiko wa nyama*, abstention from meat. *Mwiko wa vileo*, teetotalism. *Shika mwiko*, live by rule, diet oneself. *Shikeni mwiko, msionane na make zenu*, keep the rules, and abstain from your wives. *Vunja mwiko*, do something which is taboo. *Kumvunjia mtoto mwiko*, to break a taboo to (for, &c.) a child, i.e. break a taboo and by doing so, harm a child.

Mwiku, n. food left over for the morning from the previous evening's meal. (Cf. *bariyo*.)

Mwili, n. (*miili*), a body, human or animal, and usually a living body, a whole body, including the head and limbs. Also the trunk of the body, without the head. **Kiwiliwili**, n. *vi-* and adv. variously used as (1) the body in general, of man, animals, and birds, &c., like *mwili*; (2) the main part of the body, the trunk, i.e. not with the head or limbs, or both; (3) a part of the body, member, limb; (4) bulk, girth, size (cf. *kivimbe, unene*). *Viwiliwili vyangu vyote vizima*, all my members are whole. *Kiwiliwili chake chapataje?* What does its bulk come to? What does it measure round? As adv., in a bodily form. Obs. *m-wili*, is a possible form of *-wili*, twofold, double, two, and so perh. of the body as characterized by pairs of limbs, symmetrical sides.

Mwima, n. *wa-* (1) see under **Wima**; (2) *mi-* a party of women who are arranging a funeral (*maziko*).

Mwimba, n. *wa-*, **Mwimbaji**, n. *wa-*, **Mwimbishi**, n. *wa-*. See under **Imba**.

Mwimo, n. (*miimo*). See under **Wima**.

Mwina, n. *mi-* a hole, deep place, pit. (Cf. *kina, shimo, lindi*.)

Mwinamishi, n. *wa-*, **Mwinamo**, n. *mi-*. See under **Ina**, v.

Mwinda, n. *wa-*, **Mwindaji**, n. *wa-*. See under **Winda**, v.

Mwingajini, n. *mi-* an edible herb, *Cassia occidentalis*.

Mwingambuu, n. *mi-* a kind of tree, *Pluchea Dioscorides*.

Mwingamo, n. *mi-*. See **Mkumbi**.

Mwingasiafu, n. *mi-* the sword bean, *Canavalia ensiformis*; the bean is edible; also known as *mbwanda*. (Cf. *winga* and *siafu*.)

Mwingereza,* n. *wa-* an Englishman. **Kiingereza**, n. *vi-* and adv. (1) the English language; (2) after the English style, &c. **Uingereza**, n. England, Great Britain.

Mwingilizi, n. *wa-*, **Mwingizaji**, n. *wa-*, **Mwingizi**, n. *wa-*. See under **Ingia**.

Mwinuko, n. *mi-*. See under **Ina**, v.

Mwinyi, n. See **Mwenye**.

Mwinzi, n. *wa-*. See under **Winda**, v.

Mwiro, n. *mi-* an elephant's trunk. (Cf. *mkonga, mkono wa tembo*.)

Mwisho, n. *mi-*. See under **Isha**.

Mwislamu, n. *wa-*. See under **Silimu**.

Mwita, n. *wa-*, **Mwitaji**, n. *wa-*, **Mwito**, n. *mi-*. See under **Ita**.

Mwitu, n. (— and *miitu*), forest, implying large trees and close together. *Mwitu mnene* (also *gongo la mwitu*), a thick, dense forest. *-a mwitu*, wild, savage, untamed. *Mnyama wa mwitu*, a wild animal. *Gugu mwitu*, a weed. (Cf. *msitu*, thick underwood, jungle, *nyika*, open grassy forest sparsely covered with trees, also *pori, pululu*.) **Kimwitu**, n. dim., and adv. of the forest, wild, uncultivated kind, or manner.

Mwivi, n. (*wevi*). See under **Iba**.

Mwivu, n. *wa-*. See under **-wivu**.

Mwiwa, n. *wa-*. See under **Wa**, v.

Mwizi, n. (*wezi*). See under **Iba**.

Mwoga, n. *wa-*. See under **-oga**, a. and **Oga**, v.

Mwogaji, n. *wa-*, **Mwogeleaji**, n. *wa-*, **Mwogo**, n. *mi-*. See **Oga**, v.

Mwogofyo, n. *mi-*. See under **Oga**, a.

Mwoka, n. *wa-*, **Mwokaji**, n. *wa-*, **Mwoko**, n. *mi-*. See under **Oka**.

Mwokosi, n. *wa-*, **Mwokotaji**, n. *wa-*, **Mwokoti**, n. *wa-*. See under **Okota**.

Mwokozi, n. *wa-*. See under **Okoa**.

Mwomba, n. *wa-*, **Mwombaji**, n. *wa-*, **Mwombezi**, n. *wa-*, **Mwombi**, n. *wa-*, **Mwombolezi**, n. *wa-*. See under **Omba**.

Mwongea, n. *wa-*, **Mwongezi**, n. *wa-*. See under **Ongea**, v. (A).

Mwongo, n. *mi-* (1) number, reckoning, rank. Usually in plur. *Hamo katika miongo yao*, he is not one of them, and in the phrase *miongoni mwa*, used prepositionally, among the number of, on the side of, form among. (2) a period of time, esp. a decade, sometimes used as a division of the Swahili month (see *mwezi*, and syn. *kumi*). *Hesabu za miongo*, arithmetic of tens, hence, decimals.

Mwongo, n. (*wawongo*). See under **-wongo**.

Mwongofu, n. *wa-*, **Mwongozi**, n. *wa-*, **Mwongozo**, n. *mi-*. See under **Ongoa**.

Mwonjo, n. *mi-*. See under **Onja**.

Mwonzi, n. *mi-* a sunbeam, ray of light.

Mwosha, n. *wa-*, **Mwoshaji**, n. *wa-*, **Mwosho**, n. *mi-*. See under **Osha**.

Mwozi, n. *wa-*. See under **Oa**.

Mwua, n. *wa-*, **Mwuaji**, n. *wa-*. See under **Ua**, v.

Mwuguzi, n. *wa-*. See under **Ugua**.

Mwuja,* n. *mi-*. See **Mauja**.

Mwujiza,* n. *miu-* anything wonderful, extraordinary, supernatural, a wonder, a surprise, a miracle. (Cf. syn. *ajabu*, *mzungu*, *shani*, *kioja*. Ar. معجز.)

Mwulimwengu, n. *wa-*. See **Mlimwengu** under **Ulimwengu**.

Mwumba, n. *wa-*, **Muumba**, n. *wa-*, **Mwumbaji**, n. *wa-*. See under **Umba**.

Mwumbi, n. See **Mumbi**.

Mwumikaji, n. *wa-*. See under **Umika**.

Mwumini,* n. See **Mwamini** under **Amana**.

Mwumishi, n. *wa-*. See under **Umika**.

Mwumizi, n. *wa-*. See under **Uma**.

Mwunda, n. *wa-*, **Mwundaji**, n. *wa-*, **Mwundi**, n. *wa-*, **Mwundo**, n. *mi-*. See under **Unda**.

Mwungama, n. *wa-*, **Mwungamaji**, n. *wa-*, **Mwungamishi**, n. *wa-*. See under **Ungama**, v. (B).

Mwungamo, n. *mi-* (1) see under **Ungama**, v.; (2) a tree from which a yellow dye is made, sometimes called *mkumbi*.

Mwungo, n. *mi-*. See under **Unga**, v.

Mwungwana, n.* *wa-* a freeman, formerly commonly contrasted with *mtumwa*, slave. One relatively high in the social grade, and so, a person of good breeding, an accomplished, civilized person. In the hinterland, often used of any person who professes to be a Muhammadan and wears a *kanzu*. **Kiungwana**, n. the speech, bearing, characteristics of a freeman (gentleman, lady). Also the name given in the hinterland sometimes for *Kiswahili*. *-a kiungwana*, well-bred, educated, civilized. **Uungwana**, n. usu. contracted to **Ungwana**, n. condition (status, rank, quality) of a freeman, commonly contrasted formerly with that of a slave. Now usually denoting a relatively high social grade —and so, good breeding, education, accomplishments, civilization, in contrast with *ushenzi*, barbarism.

Mwunzi, n. *wa-*. See under **Unda**.

Mwunzi, n. *mi-* usually in the plur., i.e. *miunzi*, whistling.

Mwuo, n. *mi-* a sharp-pointed stick used for digging holes.

Mwuza, n. *wa-*, **Mwuzaji**, n. *wa-*. See under **Uza**.

m.y. abbreviation for *maana yake*.

Myaa, n. *mi-* Hyphaene or Dwarf palm. See **Mwaa**.

Myahudi,* n. *wa-* a Jew, Hebrew. Sometimes **Yahudi**, n. *ma-*, and **Myuda**, n. *wa-* are used. **Uyahudi**, n. the land of the Jews. **Kiyahudi**,

n. and adv. the Jewish language, according to the Jewish custom, religion, &c. (Ar. يهودي.)

Myombo, n. *mi-* a kind of tree, *Brachystegia* sp. In some places the bark is used for making a kind of cloth, and young girls are given instruction on sexual matters under one of these trees, hence the expression, *kupelekwa myomboni*, be taken for sexual instruction. (Cf. *jando, unyago, ukumbi.*)

Myombo kamba, n. *mi-* a creeper which gives a kind of india-rubber.

Myugwa, n. *mi-* the taro plant, *Colocasia antiquorum* and *indica*. The root is called *jimbi* and is edible. The leaves **Mayugwa** are like spinach when cooked.

Myunani, n. *wa-* an ancient Greek. **Kiyunani,** n. and adv. the ancient Greek language, after the ancient Greek style, &c. **Uyunani,** n. ancient Greece. (Ar. يوناني.)

Mzaa, n. *wa-*. See under **Zaa.**

Mzaanyuma, n. *mi-*, also **Mzalianyuma,** n. *mi-* lit. it which bears later or behind, applied to a kind of euphorbia, *Phyllanthus Niruri*. The roots are boiled and used for making medicine for gonorrhoea (*kisonono*). (Cf. *zaa, nyuma.*)

Mzabibu,* n. *mi-* the grape vine, *Vitis vinifera*. The fruit is called **Zabibu,** which is also applied to raisins. **Mzabibu mwitu,** n. *mi-* (1) *Heeria mucronata*; (2) *Ampelocissus grantii*. (Ar. زبيب.)

Mzabuni,* n. *wa-*. See under **Zabuni.**

Mzaha,* n. *mi-* fun, joke, ridicule, derision. *Jina la mzaha*, a nickname. *Fanya mzaha*, do in fun. *Fanyizia mzaha*, make fun of, make a mock of, treat disrespectfully, scornfully, &c. (Ar. مزاح.)

Mzalia, n. *wa-* **Mzalisha,** n. *wa-*, **Mzalishi,** n. *wa-*, **Mzaliwa,** n. *wa-*. See under **Zaa.**

Mzama, n. *wa-*, **Mzamaji,** n. *wa-*. See under **Zama,** v.

Mzambarau, n. *mi-* the Java plum-tree, *Syzygium jambolanum*. The fruit which is like a damson and edible is called *zambarau*. (? Port. *jambalao.*)

Mzamia, n. *wa-*, **Mzamio,** n. *mi-*, **Mzamishi,** n. *wa-*, **Mzamisho,** n. *mi-*, **Mzamo,** n. *mi-*. See under **Zama,** v.

Mzandiki,* n. *wa-*. See under **Zandiki.**

Mzao, n. *mi-* and *wa-*, **Mzawa,** n. *wa-*, **Mzazi,** n. *wa-*. See under **Zaa.**

Mzee, n. *wa-* (1) an old person, an elder, *wazee wa mji*, the elders of a village, members of a native court, &c.; (2) a parent; (3) an ancestor. **Kizee,** n. *vi-* and adv. (1) an old person, or thing, esp. an old woman, crone, hag; (2) in antiquated style, old-fashioned. *-a kizee*, antique, old, old-fashioned. *Enda kizee*, walk like an old person. **Uzee,** n. being old, old age. **-zee,** a. aged, old—of animate objects—others being described as *-a kale, -a siku nyingi, -kuukuu*. (Cf. *zaa.*)

Mzegazega,* n. (1) a water carrier who carries two tins of water, one on each end of a pole carried across the shoulders; (2) *mi-* one of the tins so carried. (Ar. زقرق or زكرك from the peculiar gait caused by the swinging of the tins.)

Mzeituni,* n. *mi-* the olive-tree, *Olea europea*. (Ar. زيتون.)

Mzembe, n. *wa-*. See under **-zembe.**

Mzengwe, n. *mi-* a secret council or meeting.

Mzia, n. a kind of eel-like fish.

Mzibo, n. *mi-*. See under **Ziba.**

Mzigo, n. *mi-* a load, a burden, esp. of such a load as a caravan porter (*mpagazi*) carries on his head, i.e. from 50 to 60 lb. weight. Also fig. of a sorrow, bereavement, infirmity. *Mizigo ya kutafuta*, odd jobs of porterage. *Twika mzigo*, shoulder a load (i.e. place on the head or shoulders). *Tua* (*panga*) *mzigo*, lay down a load. *Funga mizigo*, prepare for a journey, pack, make preparations (for any undertaking). *Bwaga mzigo*, throw a load on the ground. (Cf. *mtumba*, *mpagazi*.)

Mziko, n. *mi-*. See under **Zika.**

Mzikoziko, n. *mi-* Ipecacuanha, an emetic is made from its roots, *Psychotria* sp.

Mzima, n. *wa-* (1) see under **-zima**, a.; (2) see under **Zima**, v.

Mzimu, n. *mi-* (1) spirit of a dead person, spirit of an ancestor. When a man dies he is said to become a *mzimu*. He has no body, and is thought to be able to have certain powers over living people, and is able to visit them with disease. The relations of the dead man sometimes build a small hut where offerings and prayers are made to the spirit, sometimes a rock, cave, tree, or ruin is used for this purpose, and the offerings are pieces of cloth, beads, small coin, flour, &c. This is called *tambiko*, which see. (2) a native place of worship, i.e. where offerings and prayers are made to the spirits, whether of ancestors or others. Usually a rock, cave, tree, or ruin, and the offerings are rags of calico, cooking-pots, flour, beer, and occasionally small coin. *Peleka kitu kuzimuni*, go and make an offering, i.e. *kutambika*, which see. (3) a kind of white earth used for smearing the *wali* (see *mwali*) while in the initiation rites. **Kuzimu**, n. state (place, condition) of departed spirits of the dead, the grave, the lower world. *Enda kuzimuni*, die and be buried. *Chungulia kuzimuni*, look into the other world, i.e. be at death's door. *Kuzimu kuna mambo*, the world of spirits has its wonders. (Cf. *zimwi*, and perh. *wazimu*, also *ahera*, *peponi*.

Mzimzi, n. *mi-*. See **Msinzi.**

Mzinduko, n. *mi-*. See under **Zindua.**

Mzinga, n. *mi-*. See under **Zinga.**

Mzingativu, n. *wa-*. See under **Zingatia.**

Mzingefuri,* n. *mi-*. See under **Zingefuri.**

Mzingile, n. *mi-*, **Mzingo**, n. *mi-*. See under **Zinga.**

Mzinifu,* n. *wa-*, **Mzinzi**, n. *wa-*. See under **Zini.**

Mzio, n. *mi-*. See under **Zia.**

Mzira, n. a kind of fish, baracouta, good for eating.

Mzishi, n. *wa-*. See under **Zika.**

Mziwanda, n. *wa-* the last child a woman is able to bear. (Cf. *kitinda mimba*.)

Mziwaziwa, n. *mi-* umbrella grass, *Cyperus alternifolius*.

Mzizi, n. *mi-* (1) a root, rootlet, the small root-fibres of a tree; (2) perh. from the use of roots in native medicine, 'a doctor's prescription, dose, medicine', described according to the way it is to be used, e.g. *wa kuchoma*, to be heated; *wa kusaga*, to be pulverized; *wa kuchanjia*, for inoculation; *wa kutafuna*, to be chewed; *wa kuchemsha*, to be boiled, &c. *Amepigwa* (*amechomekewa*) *mzizi*, he has been bewitched. (Cf. *mwiko*, *shina*, *dawa*.)

Mzizimizi, n. *wa-*. See under **Zizima**, v. (B).

Mzizimo, n. *mi-*. See under **Zizima**, v. (A).

Mzo,* n. *mi-* (1) a measure of weight or dry measure, viz. 10 *frasila*, or 60 *pishi*, i.e. about 350–60 lb.—equivalent to *jizla*; (2) a large quantity. (Ar. مز measure, quantity.)

Mzofafa,* adv. on tiptoe, with a strut, proudly. (Ar. زفوف striding apace.)

Mzoga, n. *mi-* carcass, dead body—usually of a human body, corpse, i.e. *maiti*. (Cf. *mwili*, *pinda*.)

Mzomari,* n. a kind of grass with sweet-smelling roots, used as a perfume. (? From Ar. ضمران sweet basil, from the smell.)

Mzomeo, n. *mi-*. See under **Zoma.**

Mzozo, n. *mi-*. See under **Zoza.**

Mzuhali,* n. *wa-* a lazy, unpunctual person, one who is always late. (Ar. زحل remain behind.)

Mzuka, n. *wa-* and *mi-*. See under **Zua.**

Mzumai,* n. *mi-* (1) Khus khus grass, *Vetiveria zizanioides*; also called *mchai*; (2) a bead of a rosary (*tasbihi*), the seed of a tree. (Cf. *mzomari.*)

Mzumbao, n. astonishment, bewilderment. *Pigwa* (*shikwa*) *na mzumbao*, be nonplussed, bewildered. (Cf. *shangaa, duwaa.*)

Mzumire,* n. a kind of fish not considered good eating by Europeans. (Ar. زمير kind of fish.)

Mzungu, n. (A) *wa-* a European. The name given to the picture cards in a pack of playing-cards. The Queen is *mzungu wa mbili*, Jack, *mzungu wa tatu*, and the King, *mzungu wa nne*, so called because the Queen scores 2, the Jack 3, and the King 4. **Kizungu** n. and adv. a European language, in European style. *Sema Kizungu*, speak a European language. *Vaa Kizungu*, wear European dress, *-a Kizungu*.

Mzungu, n. (B) *mi-* (1) something wonderful, startling, surprising, ingenuity, cleverness, a feat, a trick, a wonderful device; (2) any device or expedient for getting out of a difficulty; (3) instinct in animals, insects, &c. *Kila dudu ana mizungu yake*, each insect has its own instinct. (4) in the plural, usu. the teachings given to young girls when they reach puberty or in the initiation rites. (5) a kind of cassava. (Cf. *muhogo.*) **Uzungu**, n. strangeness, wondrousness, novelty. **-zungu**, a. strange, wonderful, clever, extraordinary.

Mzunguko, n. *mi-*, **Mzungushi**, n. *wa-*, **Mzungusho**, n. *mi-*. See under **Zungua.**

Mzushi, n. *wa-*. See under **Zua.**

Mzuwanda, n. *wa-*. See **Mziwanda.**

Mzuza, n. *wa-*, **Mzuzi**, n. *wa-*. See under **Zua.**

Mzuzu, n. *wa-* (1) see under **Zua**; (2) *mi-* name of a kind of banana which is cooked when unripe and tastes rather like potato. (Cf. *ndizi.*)

N

N represents the same sound as in English, except that when it is the initial letter of a monosyllabic noun, it is a semi-vowel and takes the accent, e.g. *ncha, nchi, nne, nso, nti*, &c., which are pronounced almost as though the *n* were *in*. For the phonetic changes caused by *n* in combination with other consonants, see the Grammars.

Na is a particle used as a conj., prep., and with a verbal significance, with the general idea of connexion, association, or the opposites. Like *kwa* and *katika* it is one of the commonest particles in Swahili.

1. As a conjunction. (*a*) *na*, simply connective, 'and', but con-

nective mainly of nouns, pronouns, or their equivalents, not commonly of sentences, or adjectives, which in Swahili usually follow each other without separate connective particles, e.g. *Mimi na wewe*, I and you. *Baba na mama*, father and mother; e.g. *wapikieni na nyama wapeni wale washibe walale*, cook for them, and give them meat, so that they may eat and be satisfied, and go to sleep. (The common connectives of paragraphs are *hata* and *basi*.) Even when beginning a paragraph, *na* is as a rule in close connexion with a noun. When used to connect two verbs, when the verbs are quite distinct in mood, tense, &c., e.g. *omba na utapewa*, ask and you will receive, &c., the latter verb is commonly in the Infinitive (i.e. a noun) form, the force of the inflexions of the first verb, mood, tense, person, &c., being, however, carried on to the second, e.g. *moyo wangu waniambia, Soma na kusali*, my heart says to me, Read and pray. (*b*) *na* qualifies, and corrects, 'and yet, withal, even'—connexion suggesting some difference—whether with nouns or verbs. *Na tungoje basi*, let us even wait. *Akala na nguruwe*, he ate even pork. *Na* is thus commonly used with pronouns, after a verb, with an idiomatic force qualifying the verb rather than the pronoun, e.g. *njoo nawe*, do come along, I wish you would come, lit. come even you. *Kafa naye*, he is actually dead.

2. As a preposition, the main idea of *na* is connexion or association, i.e. 'with', whether in thought, place, or time, but is inclusive of many correlative ideas, e.g. disconnexion, distance as well as nearness, reciprocation, separation as well as union, subtraction as well as addition, i.e. 'from' as well as 'with, by, to', e.g. *alikwenda na baba yake*, he went with his father (also, 'he went and (so did) his father', or 'his father went also', or 'even his father went'). Thus (*a*) *na* is the characteristic preposition of the Agent with a passive verb. *Aliuawa na adui*, he was killed by an enemy, the instrument being denoted by *kwa*. But *na* may be used of any active force, and also of the instrument. *Alishikwa na homa*, he was seized with fever. *Alipigwa na fimbo*, he was beaten with a stick—also *kwa fimbo*, or *fimbo* alone. Also in other passive constructions, e.g. *alitokwa na damu*, he bled. (*b*) *na* is used with adjectives and adverbs in consonance with its main idea, e.g. *sawa na*, equal to; *mbali na* (or *ya*), distant from, different from; *karibu na* (or *ya*), near to; *pamoja na*, together with. (*c*) *na* is frequently connected with the Rp. form of verbs (which appears to be formed with it), *shindana na*, contend with, *agana na*, take leave of; *tengana na*, be divided from; *achana na*, depart from.

3. *Na* has a very common and important use in connexion, and in combination, with the verb *-wa*, be, and those other forms, including the person-prefixes, which are regularly used with the meaning of *-wa* (see *wa*), especially *li* with the relative, and the person-prefixes, *ni, u, a, o, i, li, zi, ma, ya, pa, ku*, &c. With all these *na* is used (and too commonly to need illustration) to express (*a*) having, (*b*) being, existing. Thus (*a*) *-wa na*, &c., have, lit. be with, e.g. *alikuwa na mali*, he had property. *Kitabu alicho nacho*, the book which he has. *Sina nguvu*, I have no strength. *Ana afya? Anayo*, has he health? He has (it). (*b*) *-wa na*, be, exist. *Palikuwa na mtu*, there was a man. *Kuna nini?* What is the matter? What is there? *Hakuna kitu*, there is nothing. In some negative phrases *na* seems to lose all trace of its connective meaning and prepositional force, and to represent itself the force of a verb, e.g. *hakuna*,

there is not. In all cases *na* is very commonly compounded with the pronouns (*nami, nawe, naye, nasi,* &c.), and with the relative forms of other prefixes (e.g. *nayo, nalo, nazo, napo, nako,* &c.). For the uses of *na* as a Pers. Prefx. and tense-prefix, &c., see the Grammars.

Naam,* (1) a common affirmative particle, Yes, Certainly, I understand, It is so; (2) also as interrog. I beg your pardon, what did you say? (Cf. *ndiyo, vema, enhee.* Ar. نعم.)

Nabihi,* v. remember, perceive. Cs. **Nabihisha,** cause to remember. **Tanabahi,** v. (1) be awake to, give attention (to), turn the mind to, carefully notice and consider, form a conclusion (about); (2) be on the alert, be ready; (3) understand. (Cf. *kumbuka, tafakari, fahamu.* Ar. نبه and تنبه.)

Nabii,* n. *ma-* a prophet, a preacher of righteousness, one who foretells the future. Used of Adam, Noah, Abraham, Jesus, and others as well as Muhammad. (Cf. *bashiri, tabiri, sibu.* Ar. نبي.)

Nadhari,* n. (1) look, glance; (2) attention, consideration; (3) choice, discretion, judgement, common sense. *Nadhari yako* (or *kwako*), it is for you to choose. *Sina nadhari,* I have no choice. **Tanadhari,** v. beware, take care, be on one's guard, be discreet, &c. (Cf. *mtazamo, fikira, busara, uchaguo, hiari.* Ar. نظر.)

Nadhifu,* a. clean, neat, well kept. *Nyumba yake nadhifu sana,* his house is in very good order. Sometimes heard as a verb, also a Cs. form **Nadhifisha,** make clean, make neat, &c. **Unadhifu,** n. neatness, cleanliness, good order. (Cf. *safi, safidi.* Ar. نظف.)

Nadhiri,* n. vow, solemn promise, dedication of something to God. *Weka nadhiri,* make a vow. *Ondoa* (*timiza, tekeleza*) *nadhiri,* fulfil (perform) a vow. (Cf. *kiapo, ahadi.* Ar. نذر.)

Nadi,* v. (1) call, summon, announce publicly, proclaim; (2) hold a sale (or public auction), hawk about the streets (but this is usu. *tembeza*). *Watu wananadi vitu kwa makelele,* people are having a noisy sale. Cs. **Nadiwa.** Prep. **Nadia. Mnada,** n. *mi-* (1) an auction, sale; (2) public notice. *Mnadani,* a sale-room, place of auction. *Tia mnadani,* put up for sale. *Mnada wa sultani unanadiwa,* a proclamation of the sultan is being made. **Mnadi,** n. *wa-* an auctioneer, announcer, i.e. *mnadi sala,* one who calls to prayer. (Cf. *tangaza.* Ar. نادى.)

Nadra,* a. uncommon, rare, scarce. (Cf. *haba, ghali, -chache, kidogo.* (Ar. ندر.)

Nafaika,* v. See under **Nafuu.**

Nafaka,* n. corn, grain—in general, including rice, maize, millet, &c. (Cf. *ngano, mpunga, mahindi,* &c. Ar. نفقة sustenance.)

Nafasi,* n. (1) breathing time, space, room, opportunity, leisure, relief, spare time; (2) interval, e.g. as in music, &c. *Sina nafasi,* I have no time, I am too busy. **Nafisi,** v., usually **Nafisisha,** accommodate with money, relieve, put in easy circumstances. Rf. *jinafisisha,* make oneself comfortable. St. **Nafisika,** get out of poverty, become well off, be relieved. **Nafsi,** n. vital spirit, breath, soul, self, person, individuality, essence. Generally used to emphasize personality, e.g. *mimi nafsi yangu* (*bi nafsi yangu*), I myself. *Walichukizwa nafsi zao,* they were deeply offended. **Tanafusi,** v. breathe, draw breath, recover breath. (Cf. *pumzika, roho.* Ar. نفس soul, self, تنفس breathe, نفس be precious.)

Nafidhi,* v. save, help. (Cf. *saidia, okoa, hifadhi.* Ar. نافذ effective.)

Nafisi, v., **Nafisisha,** v., **Nafsi,*** n. See under **Nafasi.**

Nafuu,* n. profit, advantage, gain, progress, assistance, e.g. in money or food, for a journey; also of improvement in health, convalescence. *Amepata nafuu,* he has got better (like *hajambo*). **Manufaa,** n. plur. (1) useful things, provisions, tools necessary for a particular work, clothing, &c.; (2) use, usefulness. **Nafaika,** and **Nufaika,** v. get profit, gain, prosper. (Cf. syn. *riziki, vifaa, faida.* Ar. نفع.)

Nahau,* n. explanation, unfolding of meaning, and so (1) grammar, syntax; (2) fig. excuse, quibble, subterfuge. *Usiniletee maneno ya nahau,* don't try to get round me with fine words, or quibbles. *Kila neno lina nahau yake,* every word has its meaning, for the more common *maana, tafsiri, elezo.* Also for 'grammar'. (Cf. *sarufi.* Ar. نحوي.)

Nahodha,* n. *ma-* (1) captain—of a vessel; (2) a name for the Heron. (Ar. ناخذاة.)

Naibu,* n. *ma-* deputy. **Niabu,** n. *kwa niabu ya,* on behalf of, in the place of. **Unaibu,** n. deputyship. (Ar. نائب.)

Nairuzi,* n. the Persian festival on the first day of the new year. (Pers. نوروز.)

Najisi, -najisi,* a. generally, unclean, dirty, impure, profane; strictly, anything which makes a person unclean until he has purified himself by ceremonial washing (*tawadha*). **Najisi,** v., also **Najisisha,** defile, contaminate, pollute, cause ceremonial uncleanness. **Mnajisi,** n. *wa-* an unclean, profane, impure person. **Unajisi,** n. ceremonial uncleanness, filth, profanity, &c. (Cf. *-chafu.* Ar. نجس.)

Nakala,* n. See under **Nakili.**

Nakawa,* a. clear, good-looking, in sound condition, of fine quality—of persons and things. *Mtu nakawa,* a good-looking, healthy person. *Pembe nakawa,* good sound ivory. **Jinaki,** used only as a Reflex. verb-form: consider oneself pure, good, &c., and so take a pride in oneself, be proud, boast, &c. (Cf. *-ema, -zima, -zuri.* Ar. نقى.)

Nakidi,* n. cash, ready money, payment on the spot. (Cf. *taslimu.* Ar. نقد.)

Nakili,* v. copy, transcribe, translate. Ps. **Nakiliwa.** St. and Pot. **Nakilika.** Prep. **Nakilika.** Cs. **Nakilisha. Nakala,** a copy, a single book, i.e. one of an edition. **Nakili,** n. a copy, an imitation, a translation, duplicate. *Nakili ya waraka,* copy of a letter, sometimes, *nakala, nakli, nuku, nukulu, manukuu.* (Cf. *fuatisha.* Ar. نقل.)

Nakisi,* v. reduce, i.e. of wages, &c. **Nakisi,** n. reduction, deficit, blemish. (Cf. *upungufu, kasoro.* Ar. نقص.)

Nako, for *na huko,* and there.

Nakshi,* n. carving, carved ornament, fine chisel-work, engraving, and used of any ornamentation of similar appearance, e.g. fancy work, embroidery. *Piga (kata, chora) nakshi,* carve, adorn with carving (embroidery, &c.). **Nakshi,** v. carve, engrave, adorn with carving, &c. Prep. **Nakshia.** (Cf. *chora, pamba, tema.* Ar. نقش.)

Naksi,* v. See **Nakisi.**

Nakudi.* See **Nakidi.**

Nakulu,* n. and v. See **Nakili.**

Nama, v. (1) be flexible, pliable, e.g. as a cane, &c.; (2) be plastic, e.g. as clay, &c.; (3) be sticky, stick, adhere. **-nama,** a. pliable, flexible, &c. *Mti mnama,* a flexible, pliable tree or stick. **Kinamo,** n. flexibility, pliability, plasticity. *Udongo wa kinamo,* clay.

Namba,* n. (sometimes *nambari*) a (single) number, e.g. the number which marks an object, person, &c. Used frequently in grading things, *namba ya kwanza*, first quality, &c. In arithmetic, *namba tasa*, a prime number; *namba isiyo tasa*, a number which is not prime. (Eng. number.)

Nami, for *na mimi*, and I, even me.

Namna,* n. example, sample, pattern, model, sort, kind. (Cf. *aina, mtindo, jinsi, msimu.* Pers. نمونه.)

Namua, v. draw away, disengage, get out of a difficulty, take out of a trap, set free. (Cf. *tegua, nasua, okoa.*)

Nanaa,* n. mint. See **Mnanaa.** (Ar. نعنع.)

Nanasi,* n. *ma-* pine-apple. See **Mnanasi.** (Pers. اناناس.)

Nane, -nane, n. and a. eight, *-a nane*, eighth. (Perh. *nne na nne.*)

Nanga,* n. an anchor—properly of the four-fluked pattern but commonly used for European two-fluked anchor which is also called *baura. Tia (puliza) nanga*, cast (let go) anchor. *Ng'oa nanga*, weigh anchor. (Pers. لنگر.)

Nang'anika, v. be fat, shine as though smeared with fat.

Nani, pron. interrog. What person (persons)? Who? *Jina lako nani?* What is your name? *-a nani?* whose?

Nanigwanzula, n. a small lizard, also called *mjusi kafiri.*

Nanua, v. force apart, widen or open by force. St. **Nanuka**, be split open, as of anything split by the heat of the sun drying it.

Nao, for *na hao*, or *na wao*, and these, and they.

Napukia, v. be flexible, elastic, bend, yield to pressure without breaking. (Cf. *nyumbua.*)

Nargisi,* n. a bulb plant rather like an onion with white flowers, also its flowers. (Ar. نرجس narcissus.)

Nasa, v. get hold of, catch in a trap, hold fast. Ps. **Naswa.** St. and Pot. **Nasika.** Prep. **Nasia.** Cs. **Nasisha.** Cv. **Nasua**, take from a trap, let go free from a trap, &c. Ten. **Nata**, be sticky, adhere, stick. *Utomvu wa fenesi hunata sana*, the sap of the jackfruit is very sticky. Rp. **Natana**, stick together. **Mnaso**, n. *mi-* a holding fast, a trapping, also a trap. (Cf. *tega, ambata, ganda.*)

Nasaba,* n. pedigree, genealogy, lineage. **Nasibu**, v., also Cs. **Nasibisha**, trace one's lineage. *Jinasibu kuwa ndugu*, claim (for oneself) to be a brother. (Cf. *ukoo, jadi.* Ar. نسب.)

Nasaha,* n. a request or petition for forgiveness, for pardon. **Nasihi**, v. (1) give good advice (to), counsel wisely; (2) beg for forgiveness or pardon. **Nasiha**, n. a sincere friend, faithful counsellor, wise adviser. (Ar. نصح.)

Nasi, for *na sisi*, and we, with us.

Nasibu,* n. chance, fortune, luck, accident, destiny. *Kwa nasibu*, accidentally, not on purpose, by chance. *Bahati nasibu*, a raffle, lottery. (Ar. نصيب.)

Nasiha, n., **Nasihi,*** v. See under **Nasaha.**

Nasua, v. See under **Nasa.**

Nasuri,* n. a fistula. (Ar. ناسور.)

Naswi. See **Nasi.**

Nata, v. See under **Nasa.**

Nauli,* n. fare, charge for freight (or conveyance), passage money. **Nauli**, v. hire, pay fare for passage (carriage, &c.). Cs. **Naulisha**, let for freight (carriage, conveyance), charter, be a ship's broker. **Mnawili**, n. an agreement for shipping. (Ar. ناولون.)

Navya, v. See under **Nawa.**

Nawa, v. wash the hands and face, also used of washing the hands before food. Ps. **Nawiwa.** St. **Nawika.** Prep. **Nawia**, wash with (at, by, &c.). *Maji ya kunawia*, water for washing with. **Cs. Nawisha,** also **Navya,** *nawisha watu mikono,* i.e. bring people water for them to wash, esp. before a meal.

Nawiri,* v. See under **Nuru.**

Naye, for *na yeye,* and her (he), even him (her). *Mjinga ni mtu naye,* a fool is, after all, a man.

Nazaa,* v. quarrel, contend. Prep. **Nazia.** Rp. **Naziana. Nazaa,** n. a quarrel, contention, noise, confusion, feud. **Mnazaa,** n. *wa-* a quarrelsome person, one who does a disgraceful action. (Ar. نازع.)

Nazi.* See under **Mnazi.**

Ncha, n. tip, point, end, extremity, e.g. of a knife, branch, cord, &c. *Hakuna refu lisilo na ncha,* there is nothing so long that it has no end. *Habari ya uwongo ina ncha saba,* a false story has seven endings, i.e. can be told in many ways. *Ncha ya kalamu,* the point of a pencil. In Geography, *ncha ya kaskazini (ya kusini),* the North (South) Pole. (Cf. *kikomo, mwisho, mpaka,* and dist. *nta.*)

Nchi, n. (1) country, district, land, region. *Nchi yetu, nchi ya kwetu,* our country, fatherland. *Nchi za bara,* the regions of the continent, also the hinterland. *Nchi za Ulaya,* the countries of Europe. (Cf. *ulaya, wilaya, upande.*) (2) land, ground, dry land, i.e. *nchi kavu,* as opp. to the sea, *bahari. Piga katika nchi* (or *chini*), throw to the ground, dash down. *Chini ya nchi,* under ground. *Nchi sawa,* level country. (Cf. *bara.*) (3) the earth, the inhabited world. *Pembe za nchi,* the corners of the earth, i.e. remotest parts of the world. Never of the actual substance or materials of the ground, i.e. soil, earth, which is *udongo.* (Cf. *dunia, ardhi, ulimwengu, chini.*)

Ndago, n. nut grass, *Cyperus rotundus,* a troublesome weed, the tubers are used medicinally. **Ndago mwitu,** n. papyrus grass, *Cyperus papyrus,* also called *njaanjaa.*

Ndakaka, n. long thin poles used in thatching a roof with grass. (Cf. *fito, pao.*)

Ndama, n. the young of cattle, esp. a calf. Sometimes used as *ndama ya ng'ombe,* calf; *ndama ya mbuzi,* kid; *ndama ya kondoo,* lamb, but as a rule other than cattle are referred to as *mwana,* &c. (Cf. *mnyama, mtamba, mwanambuzi,* &c.)

Ndani, adv. within, inside, in the heart. Contr. *nje. Ndani ya,* prep. inside of, within. *-a ndani,* internal, inner, secret, heartfelt. *Kwa ndani,* internally, in the inside, in the heart, secretly. **Undani,** n. secrecy, a secret grudge. (Cf. *katika, kati.*)

Ndara, n. a plain leather sandal. (Cf. *kiatu, makubazi.*)

Ndaro, a. e.g. *maneno ya ndaro,* bragging, boasting speech.

Ndau, n. a vessel for bailing water out of a boat. (Cf. *sila, upo, kumba maji.* Prob. a variant of *ndoo,* see also *dau.*)

Ndege, n. (1) a bird; (2) an omen; (3) *ndege ulaya,* the name often used for an aeroplane of any description. *Ndege za anga,* birds of the air. *Ndege njema (mbaya),* a good (bad) omen. *Ndege aliruka juu,* the bird flew upward. *Tusimtilie ndege,* do not let us obstruct him (by anything which might be a bad omen). **Kidege,** n. *vi-* dim. (Cf. *nyuni.*)

Ndema, n. See **Dema.**

Ndere, n. *Unga wa ndere,* a sort of powder which, if put on the face, is said to attract one of the other sex desired; a love charm.

Nderemo, n. See under **Terema.**

Nderi, n. a large black bird of prey with a long bill, said to attack caravans sometimes.

Ndevu, n. plur. of *udevu,* which see.

Ndewe, n. (1) a hole pierced in the lobe of the ear, i.e. *ndewe ya sikio,* to hold an ornament, sometimes of great size; (2) the lobe of the ear. (Cf. *toja.*)

Ndezi, n. (1) the name of a kind of rat; (2) drowsiness. (Cf. *sinzia.*)

Ndiga, n. a thorny shrub with tuber roots only eaten in time of famine, *Dioscorea dumetorum*. It is poisonous unless it has been boiled in two or three changes of water.

Ndigano, n. east-coast fever (cattle).

Ndilo, emphat. for *ni hilo*, that is it.

Ndimi, (1) plur. of *ulimi*, which see; (2) emphat. for *ni mimi*, it is I.

Ndimo, emphat. for *ni humo*, it is in there.

Ndimu,* n. a lime, the fruit of the lime-tree, *mdimu*, or *mndimu* (Hind. ليمو).

Ndinyi, emphat. for *ni ninyi*, it is you (plur.).

Ndio, emphat. for *ni hao* (*huo*), it is they (it).

Ndipo, emphat. for *ni hapo*, it is there or then. *Ndipo nilipompiga*, it was there (or then) that I struck him.

Ndiposa, conj. therefore—seldom heard except in Kimvita.

Ndisi, emphat. for *ni sisi*, it is we.

Ndivyo, emphat. for *ni hivyo*, it is in this (or that) manner; these very things, &c.

Ndiyo, emphat. for *ni hiyo*. *Ndiyo* is one of the commonest forms of simple affirmation, 'yes, it is so'.

Ndizi,* n. banana, plantain, the fruit of the *mgomba*. The fruit-stalk with the whole head of fruit is called *mkungu*, a cluster or bunchlet on it *chana* (*tana*), a single fruit *dole*. There are many varieties known locally as *kisukari, kipukusa, msuzu, mchanga, mkono wa tembo, bungala, paka, kiguruwe, kizungu, bokoboko, kikondo, kichaazi, mfichachani, mlalimana, mchinjadamu, tongo*, &c. (Perh. from Ar. موز treated as belonging to the *Mu-*, *Mw-* class.)

Ndoa. See under **Oa**.

Ndoana, n. a fish-hook.

Ndoero, n. name of a bird, the crab-plover (Pemba), *Dromas ardeola*.

Ndogoro, n. a water buck.

Ndole, n. plur. of *udole*. See under **Kidole**.

Ndondi, adv. *Kupigana ndondi*, to fight with fists, box. (Cf. *ngumi*.)

Ndongoa, n. the custom in some places of killing an ox or goat in front of the house of a dead person before carrying the corpse to the grave.

Ndonya, n. a circular plug of light wood worn in the upper lip, esp. by the Makonde women in the south of Tanganyika, the Wiha in Portuguese East Africa, and the Nyasa.

Ndoo, n. a bucket, a pail. (Prob. a variant of *ndau*, see also *dau*.)

Ndoto, n. See under **Ota**, v. (B).

Ndorobo,* n. tsetse-fly. (Cf. *mbung'o, chafuo*.)

Ndovu, n. an elephant, usu. known at the coast as *tembo*.

Nduara, n. a kind of fish not considered good eating by Europeans.

Ndubi, n. an outrigger of a canoe. (Cf. *ngalawa, mlengu, mtengo*.)

Ndugu, n. (1) brother, sister, cousin, relation, fellow tribesman (citizen, countryman). Further defined as *ndugu mume* (or *wa kiume*), brother; *ndugu mke* (or *wa kike*), sister. *Ndugu baba mmoja mama mmoja*, full brother, with the same father and mother. *Ndugu tumbo moja*, brother with the same mother, half-brother (at least). *Ndugu wa kunyonya*, foster-brother. *Ndugu wa kupanga*, a brother by arrangement (cf. *panga*). (2) a birthmark; (3) *Donda ndugu*, a malignant kind of ulcer. **Kidugu**, n. and adv. (1) dim. of *ndugu*, little brother; (2) in a fraternal way, like brothers. *Kupendana kidugu*, to love as brothers. **Udugu**, n. brotherhood, kinsmanship, being of the same family, clan, or tribe. All of these words are often used in a very loose way of any friend.

Ndui, n. plur. small-pox (*udui*, a single pustule).

Nduli, n. and a. (1) a savage person, a killer, murderous, blood-shedding; (2) the angel of death, *Izraili*. (Perh. from *ua* (*ula*), kill.)

Ndumakuwili, n. a blind-worm, it is believed by some to have a mouth at both ends, hence its name. (Cf. *uma* and *kuwili*.)

Ndume, n. See under **-ume**.

Ndumiko, n. See under **Umika**.

Nduni, n. a novelty, a new thing, a strange and wonderful thing which pleases.

Ndusi, n. also **Mandusi**, a box, i.e. in which to put clothing, &c.

Nduu, n. ground-nuts, used in Kimvita, elsewhere *njugu*, which see.

Ndwele, n. sickness, Kimvita, elsewhere *uele*, which see.

Ndweo, n. pride, arrogance. (Cf. *kiburi*.)

Neema,* n. (1) ease, affluence, comfort; (2) bounty, favour, help, grace. Esp. of providential blessings, plenty, a good harvest, abundance of food. *Nchi ile ina neema nyingi*, that is a favoured country, a good one to live in. *Imemshukia neema kubwa kwa Mungu*, a great mercy has descended on him from God. *Neema ya Mungu*, the grace of God. **-neemevu**, a. plentiful, abundant. **Neemeka**, v. live at ease, have plenty, be in comfortable circumstances, possess property, get good profits. Cs. **Neemesha**, make rich, provide well for. **Uneemevu**, n. abundance, plentiful supply. (Ar. نعمة.)

Neli,* n. a tube, a pipe—usu. *mrija* and *mwanzi*. (Hind. نلي.)

Nema, v. bend, give way, yield. St. **Nemeka**, e.g. of graceful dancing. Cs. **Nemesha**, cause to bend. (Cf. *nepa* and *inama*.)

Nembo, n. a tribal mark, usually a kind of tattoo. (Prob. a plur. of *urembo*, which see.)

Nemsi,* n. good name, honour—rarely heard. (Ar. ناموس.)

Nena, n. *ma-* the groin. See **Kinena**.

Nena, v. (1) speak, articulate, utter, say; (2) speak of, mention, name, declare. Ps. **Nenwa**. St. and Pot. **Neneka**. (1) be spoken, be mentioned; (2) be utterable, be such as can be expressed in words, be fit for mention, &c. *Mambo yasiyoneneka*, unutterable, indescribable things. *Neno hilo halineneki*, that word is not in use, is not a possible word. Prep. **Nenea**, e.g. speak against (for, to, with, &c.), but in common usage *ambia* regularly takes its place for 'speak to, say to', and *nenea* (when not defined by the context) is used for 'speak against, rebuke, scold', hence *neneana*, speak against each other, accuse each other, &c. Cs. **Nenesha** and **Neneza**, cause (provoke) to speak, e.g. *walinenezana kwa maneno mabaya*, they exasperated each other by abuse. Rp. **Nenana**, speak of each other, and so commonly, quarrel, abuse each other. **Kijineno**, n. *vi-* a silly little speech, child's prattle. **Neno**, n. *ma-* (1) a word, utterance, expression, message; (2) assertion, objection, argument, plea, point; (3) thing, fact, matter, affair, cause, case; (4) a serious matter, difficulty, danger, trouble. The plural **Maneno**, is also used for (1) language, speech—in general, and (2) consultation, discussion, argument, trial, debate, e.g. *sikufanya neno*, I did nothing. *Ukiona neno, usinene neno; ukinena neno, litakujia neno*, if you see anything, do not say anything; if you say anything, something will happen to you. *Fanya maneno*, hold a discussion, argue, debate. *Mtu wa maneno mengi*, a talkative, argumentative person. *Maneno ya Kiswahili*, the Swahili language. *Hana neno*, he has nothing to say, he has no complaint to make. *Mnisaidie nisione neno njiani*, help me that I may not find difficulty in the road. **Mnena**, n. *wa-* (followed by another noun) one who speaks, or who has the power of speech. **Mnenaji**, n. *wa-*, and **Mneni**, n. *wa-* a speaker, a professional orator, an eloquent person. **Mnenea**, n. *wa-* (1) a pleader, interceder, one who speaks for or to the advantage of another; (2) a critic, opponent, one who speaks against or in rebuke of another. **Unenaji**, n. art (power, practice) of speaking, eloquence, fluency. **Uneni**, n. power of speech, speaking, articulation. (Note: *Sema* is used exactly like *nena* of rational speech, and in most other senses. But (1) with a person-object, *nena* means mention, *sema*, speak against, rebuke, abuse (like *amba*). (2) *sema* has often the meaning 'talk, converse', *nena* rarely. *Ambia* with a person-object regularly takes the place of both *nena* and *sema*, when the meaning is simply, speak to, say to).

Nenda. See under **Enda**.

-nene, a. (1) thick, stout, fat, plump, broad; (2) full, whole, complete. *Sauti nene*, a deep voice. **Nenepa**, v. become fat (stout, corpulent) of persons, but *nona* of animals. Cs. **Nenepesha**, make stout, &c. **Unene**, n. stoutness, thickness, corpulence. For the significance of the term *-pa*, i.e. *nene-pa*, see note under *pa*.)

Neno, n. *ma-*. See under **Nena**.

Nepa, v. incline downwards, bend down, be bent down, dip, drop (of a rope), sag. *Bakora hii inanepa sana*, this stick bends very much. *Kisu chanepa*, the knife (blade) bends. Cs. **Nepesha**, cause to bend, bend (by pressure, &c.). (Cf. *nema, inama, pinda*.)

Nesa, v. (1) bend, as of a twig, &c. (cf. *nepa*); (2) beat, as with a stick. *Nilimnesa kofi*, I boxed his ears.

Neva,* n. a nerve—the word adopted for use in text-books and school lessons on anatomy, physiology, &c. (Eng. nerve.)

Ng' represents the velar nasal, i.e. the sound of *ng* in the English word 'sing'. In many Bantu languages the symbol ŋ has been adopted for this sound, thus avoiding the cumbersome combination of three symbols.

Ng'aa, v., also **Ng'ara**, be bright, glitter, gleam, shine. Cs. **Ng'aza**, make shine. **Mng'ao**, n. *mi-* (1) brightness, blaze, lustre, glare; (2) fig. clearness, perspicuity. *Mng'ao wa maneno*, lucidity of statement. **Mng'ariza**, n. *wa-* with or without *macho*—one who has glowing, glaring eyes, and so to some, one suspected of sorcery, malignity, evil intent. **Mng'arizo**, n. *mi-* like *mng'ao*, *Mng'arizo wa macho*, glowing, radiant look, or glaring, gleaming eyes. **Ung'aro**, n. brightness, lustre, light.

Ngabu, n. a gouge—a carpenter's tool, same as *bobari*.

Ngadu, n. a kind of crab. (Cf. *kaa*.)

Ng'akia, v. snarl and show the teeth, as of a dog.

Ngalawa, n. a small dug-out canoe with outriggers.

Ngama, n. (1) the hold of a vessel, i.e. in a native vessel amidships; (2) the faeces passed by people (also animals) sometimes when *in extremis*, or which is forced out when the corpse is being washed preparatory to burial; (3) a kind of whitish clay.

Ng'amba, n. a kind of hawk's-head turtle, from which tortoise-shell is procured. *Piga (pindua) ng'amba*, is used to describe pouncing on a harmless person and robbing him. *Chuma cha ng'amba*, the shell of the hawk's head turtle. (Cf. *kasa*.)

Ngambi, n. agreement of people of a place to act together for the common good, e.g. in order to prevent their crops being destroyed by pest, &c. (prob. from *amba*, v. (A)).

Ng'ambo,* n. one of two opposite sides or positions, the other side, the farther side, e.g. of a river or creek. *Ng'ambo ya huku*, the side, this side. *Ng'ambo ya pili*, the other, farther side. (Perh. from Ar. جنب side, see *ngamia* for somewhat similar form.)

Ngamia,* n. a camel. A common

term of abuse, like *ng'ombe, mbuzi,* i.e. idiot, fool—the camel being regarded as a type of stupidity. (Ar. جمل camel, for somewhat similar form see *ng'ambo,* also *jinsi* which is sometimes heard as *ginsi.*)

Ng'amua, v. find out, get to know, realize. (Cf. *tambua, fahamu, maizi.*)

Ng'anda, n. (1) a handful, as much as can be held with the fingers, esp. of something sticking together, as *ugali*; (2) the planet Venus (cf. Ar. *Zuhura*); (3) the pips on playing-cards, e.g. *ng'anda ya saba,* the seven in a suit, also heard as *nganda* and *ganda.*

Ng'ang'ama, v. clutch hold of, as of a swinging branch of a tree, &c.

Ng'ang'anaa, v. become stiff and dry by being left in the sun or cold.

Ng'ang'ania, v. beg earnestly, beseech, go on begging or worrying persistently until one gets what one wants.

Ngano, n. (1) a story, a tale, narrative, fable (cf. *kisa, hadithi*); (2) wheat, i.e. the grain. (Cf. *nafaka.*)

Ngao, n. (1) shield, buckler; (2) face, or front, of a house. Also of the rear, *ngao ya nyuma. Kifua cha ngao,* a bosom like a shield—point of beauty. **Kigao,** n. *vi-* dim. of (1).

-ngapi, interrog. How many? *Watu wangapi?* How many people? *Saa ngapi?* What o'clock is it?

Ngara, n. (1) the male blossom of the maize plant; (2) a hide, skin.

Ng'ara, v. See under **Ng'aa,** also for derivatives.

Ng'arange, n. the hard centre or heart of a tree.

Ngariba, n. one who circumcises, a professional circumciser. (Cf. *tahiri, ukumbi.*)

Ng'ariza, v. Cs. of *ng'ara.* See under **Ng'aa.**

Ngawa, n. civet cat, i.e. *paka wa zabadi.* (Cf. *fungo, zabadi.*)

Ngazi, n. a ladder, set of steps, stairs, i.e. *ngazi ya kupandia. Ngazi ya noti,* a scale in music. The rungs of a ladder are called *kipandio, vi-, kipago, vi-* and *kipawa, vi-.* (Cf. *kwea, panda, daraja.*)

Ngazija, n. the great Comoro Island. **Mngazija,** n. *wa-* a Comoro man. **Kingazija,** n. and a. the Comoro language, after the style of the Comorians.

Nge, n. See **Ng'ge.**

Ngedere, n. a small black monkey—also called *kima.* (Cf. *tumbili, mbega, nyani.*)

Ngema, sometimes heard for *njema,* which see.

Ngeu, n. (1) a line used by carpenters for marking work, a ruddle, so called from the red chalky earth applied to make the mark; (2) red chalky earth, red ochre; (3) a wound on the head caused by a stick, and the bleeding from the wound.

Ng'ge, n. a scorpion, usually spelt *nge.*

Ngiri, n. wild boar—commonly *nguruwe wa mwitu. Mshipa wa ngiri,* used to describe a swollen scrotum, hernia. (Cf. *mshipa.*)

Ngisi, n. a kind of cuttle-fish. *Wino wa ngisi,* the dark fluid emitted by cuttle-fish. *Kifuu cha ngisi,* cuttle-fish bone.

Ng'o, and **Ng'oo,** an expression of contempt, derision, or of absolute refusal.

Ng'oa, v. root up, dig out, pull up. *Ng'oa mti,* root up a tree. *Ng'oa jino,* extract a tooth. *Ng'oa macho,* gouge out the eyes. *Ng'oa hema,* strike a tent. *Ng'oa safari,* start on a journey. Ps. **Ng'olewa.** St. and Pot. **Ng'oka,** be rooted out. *Moyo umening'oka,* my heart jumped into my mouth. Prep. **Ng'olea. Mng'oaji,** n. *wa-* one who digs out, roots up, extracts, &c. *Mng'oaji meno,* dentist.

Ngoa, n. desire, passion, lust, jealousy. *Timiza ngoa,* satisfy the passions. *Lia ngoa,* weep for jealousy. (Cf. *hawa, shauku, ashiki, tamaa, wivu, ghera.*)

Ngoe, n. See under **Ngoeka.**

Ngoeka, v. take hold of anything, e.g. fruit on a tree, &c., with a forked or hooked stick, in order to pluck it. (Also sometimes heard as *koeka.*) **Goe, Goya,** same as *ugoe,* see below. **Kigoe,** n. *vi-,* and **Kingoe,** n. *vi-* (1) a small hooked or forked stick or pole, used for pulling down branches of trees, in order to pluck the fruit; (2) the term used for golf clubs. **Ngoe,** n. amplic. of *kingoe.* **Ugoe,** n. hooking a foot round an opponent's leg in wrestling in order to trip him up, e.g. *kupiga ugoe, kumwangusha mtu kwa ugoe.*

Ng'ofu, n. roe of a fish.

Ngogo, n. a kind of small fish with a spiny back.

Ngoja, v. wait, wait for, await, stay for, remain. *Ngoja mlango,* wait at a door, act as a doorkeeper. *Ningoje,* wait for me—also *ningojee.* Prep. **Ngojea,** wait for (at, with, &c.), be patient with, &c., e.g. *mngojee bwana aje,* wait for the master to come. Cs. **Ngojeza,** e.g. keep waiting, delay, adjourn. Rp. **Ngojeana,** wait for each other, wait all together. **Kingojeo,** n. *vi-,* **Kingojezi,** n. *vi-,* and **Kingojo,** n. *vi-* act (time, place, &c.) of waiting or watching, watch, guard, guard-station, post, sentry-go, turn of watching, e.g. *linda kingojo,* keep watch. **Mngoja,** n. *wa-,* **Mngoje,** n. *wa-,* one who waits at a place (occupies a station, is on guard), sentinel, guard, keeper. *Mngoja mlango,* a hall porter, door-boy, gate-keeper. **Mngojezi,** n. *wa-* keeper, caretaker, guardian, watchman. **Ngojo,** n. waiting-place, station, &c., like *kingojo.* **Ungoje,** n., and **Ungojezi,** n. a waiting (for), being in attendance on, service, a keeping watch, wages for attendance (waiting, watching).

Ngojamaliko, n. applied to the African Green-backed Heron, and other smaller species of Heron, and also probably the little bittern.

Ngojo, n. See under **Ngoja.**

Ngoma, n. a drum. As the usual accompaniment of all merrymaking, and ceremonial, *ngoma* is extended to include (1) any kind of dance; (2) music in general. *Piga (chapua) ngoma,* beat a drum. *Cheza (ingia) ngoma,* join in a dance. *Ngoma ya kucheza,* dancing for amusement. *Ngoma ya kupunga (pepo),* dance for the exorcizing of a spirit. Prov. *Ngoma ikilia sana, haikawii kupasuka,* when a drum sounds loud, it will soon burst. (Drums are of many sizes and patterns, and these as well as the accompanying dances and modes of beating vary with every tribe, and with the different occasions of their use.) **Goma,** n. *ma-* amplic. **Kigoma,** n. *vi-* dim. Some of the drums are called *tari, msapata, dandalo, kiumbizi, msondo, vumi, chapuo, kumbwaya, kitanga, kishina, msoma, mganda.* Some of the musical instruments are: *kinanda, santuri, kinubi, zeze, zumari, toazi, upato, kayamba, panda, baragumu, filimbi, fidla.* The following are some of the dances used when spirits are being exorcized: *dungumaro, kigala, kisomali, pungwa, punda, ng'ombe, kisonge, lengwe, kiganda, kinyika, kipemba, kitumbatu, kinyamkera, mali kwa mali, likunda, lewa, kibulushi, mkondo, shehe, kilua, kibisa, koikoi, mkodi, kisokota, kaputa, machinju, kimwera, kingindo, kibwengo, ununguli, marombo, kisanga, kirua, kumba, kitimiri.*

Ng'ombe, n. ox, cow, cattle. Defined as *ng'ombe dume,* and *fahali,* or *ng'ombe fahali,* a bull. *Maksai,* an ox, bullock. *Ng'ombe jike,* a cow. *Ndama ya ng'ombe,* a calf. *Mtamba, mori,* or *mfarika,* a heifer. *Ng'ombe tasa,* a barren cow. *Kukama ng'ombe,* to milk a cow. Prov. *Wawili hula ng'ombe,* two can manage to eat an ox. Also used as a term of insult, idiot, blockhead, like *ngamia* and *mbuzi.*

Ngome, n. (1) fort, fortress, stronghold, castle; (2) an escarpment. (Cf. *gereza, boma, husuni, buruji.*)

Ng'onda, v. cure fish, by cutting it in strips and drying it in the sun. Ps. **Ng'ondwa. Ng'onda,** n. fish which has been sliced and dried in the sun.

Ng'ong'a, v. (1) make a sign of contempt or derision behind a person's back (cf. *lamba kisogo*); (2) buzz round as flies do round a dead animal or filth.

Ng'ongo, n. plur. of *ung'ongo,* which see.

Ng'ong'ona, v. gnaw, as of gnawing a bone, &c. (Cf. *guguna, ng'ota.*)

Ngono, n. plur. See under **Gona.**

Ng'oo! int., also **Ng'o!** and **Nyoo!** expressing utter contempt, a derisive or contemptuous refusal.

Ngoringori. See under **Njorinjori.**

Ng'ota, v. (1) gnaw, as of gnawing off the seeds of a cob of maize, or meat off a bone (cf. *ng'ong'ona*); (2) tap, knock, rap, i.e. of the woodpecker pecking (hence its name, *king'oto*), or of mason roughing a wall by knocking it with a hammer, chisel, &c., preparing it for refacing.

Ngovi, n. sometimes used for *ngozi,* but usu. *govi* (1) an uncircumcised man; (2) the prepuce. **Ngozi,** n. skin, of any animal, hide, leather. *Chuna ngozi,* take the skin off, skin, flay. *Tengeneza ngozi, fanyiza ngozi,* tan hides.

Ngozi, n. See under **Ngovi.**

Nguchiro, n. a mongoose.

Ngumbaru, n. an adult, a grown-up person, one who is no longer a child. (Cf. *-zima.*)

Ngumbi, n. See **Kumbikumbi.**

Ngumi, n. fist. *Piga ngumi,* strike with the fist, give a cuff to.

Ng'ungwe, n. (1) a furrow made in which to plant seeds; (2) a portion of a field measured out for a man to cultivate. (Cf. *ngwe.*)

Ngungwi, n. See **Kungwi** under **Kunga,** v. (B).

Nguo, n. (A) (1) cloth, as material, i.e. any woven fabric, of cotton, flax, silk, &c., but commonly cotton cloth, calico; (2) a cloth, a piece of cloth, for whatever purpose, e.g. *nguo ya meza,* a tablecloth; *nguo za kitanda,* bed clothes; *nguo za kuugulia,* mourning or hospital dress; (3) clothes, a garment of any kind. *Vaa nguo,* put on clothes, dress oneself. *Vika nguo,* clothe (another). *Vua nguo,* take off clothes, undress. *Fuma nguo,* weave cloth. *Tanda nguo,* (1) prepare the web in weaving, (2) spread cloth (cf. *tanda*). *Sifa ya nguo ni pindo,* the merit of a cloth is the (coloured, embroidered) border. Various kinds of cloth are known as *nguo asili,* in commerce 'grey sheeting', *nguo maradufu,* grey drilling. *Amerikani, kaniki, bendera, bafta, hudhurungi, satini, gamti, joho, ulaili, hariri, shashi,* &c. For articles of dress, cf. (1) for men, *kikoi, kanzu, kisibau, koti, fulana, kilambi, kilemba, kofia, shuka, gwanda, joho, suruali, mfuria, shati.* (2) for women, *shiti, kisutu, kanga, leso, kanzu, suruali, dusamali, kaniki, buibui, marinda, barakoa, ukaya, shela.* Cf. *uo* and *chuo* prob. from the same root.

Nguo, n. (B) the name of a kind of a bird which is said to be of ill omen.

Nguri, n. a shoemaker's tool, a kind of mallet. (Cf. *pondeo,* under *ponda.*)

Nguru, n. name of a fish, the king fish; of good quality for eating and often of a large size, sold fresh, and also dried and cured with much salt, when it has a very powerful smell.

Nguruma, v. make a rumbling or roaring noise—of any loud and deep sound, e.g. roar of a lion, thunder, roar, growl, rumble. **Mngurumizi,** n. *wa-* one who grumbles, growls. *Simba ni mngurumizi,* the lion is a roarer. **Ngurumo,** n. a loud, roaring, rumbling sound, growl. *Leo kunapiga ngurumo,* it is thundering to-day. *Mshindo wa ngurumo,* a clap of thunder. (Cf *koroma, tutuma, vuma.*)

Nguruwe, n. a pig, hog, swine. *Nguruwe wa mwitu*, a wild pig. *Nguruwe jike*, a sow. Prov. *Nguruwe aendealo, ndilo atendalo*, what a pig goes for, that he does. Also of a loose, immoral character, *yule nguruwe aliyetaka kufisidi nyumba*, that vile wretch, who wanted to violate a home.

Nguu, n. (1) the summit of a hill or mountain. (Cf. the more usual *kilele*.) (2) in the expression *mwendanguu*, of one who utterly despairs.

Nguva, n. dugong, manatee.

Nguvu, n. force, strength, power—in general. Thus (1) strength of body, muscular, physical power, strength of mind, or character, ability, energy, vehemence, or mere mechanical strength, force, impetus, momentum, solidity, stability, pressure; (2) authority, supremacy, influence, importance, weight, earnestness; (3) exercise of force, compulsion. *Tia (pa) nguvu*, strengthen, consolidate, establish. *Fanya (toa) nguvu*, use (put forth, exert) strength, exercise authority. *Neno la nguvu*, an effective, forcible statement, command. *Kwa nguvu*, (1) by force (strength, ability, energy, &c.); (2) in a high degree, strongly, earnestly; (3) reluctantly, under compulsion, against the will, e.g. *alikubali kwa nguvu*, he consented under pressure. (Cf. *bidii, uwezo, ezi, kudura, makadara, shawishi, shurutisha*.)

Nguyu, n. the knuckle, the foot above the knuckles.

Nguzi, n. a hole in the bottom of a boat or vessel, for letting water out, i.e. *tundu katika mkuku*.

Nguzo, n. (1) pillar, supporting column, post, prop, buttress, palisade, pale, pole; (2) fig. assistance, support, evidence, fundamental principles. Forms of prayer are *nguzo za sala*. *Nguzo za imani*, articles (pillars) of faith, creed. In house building *nguzo* are the poles forming the sides and supporting the roof. **Kiguzo**, n. *vi-* dim. and lit. or fig. support, prop, comfort, assurance, &c. (Cf. *mti, mhimili, mwimo*, and *tumaini, egemeo*.)

Ng'wafua, v. snatch a piece of flesh, i.e. as of a dog or wild animal. (Cf. *nyofoa*.)

Ngwe, n. (perh. plur. of *ugwe*), a measured plot, or patch of ground, whether (1) a bed or row of young plants, &c., or (2) an allotment, ground assigned for cultivation, or for a task. (Cf. *kuo*, and perh. *ugwe*, of the line used in measuring.)

Ngwea, v. (1) become thin, emaciated; (2) shrink. (Cf. *konda, nywea, finyaa, sinyaa*.)

Ngwena, n. a crocodile, but the usu. word is *mamba*.

Ni, is used simply as a copula, without distinction of person or number, or definite indication of time, though usually equivalent to the present tense of the verb *wa*, 'be', i.e. I am (was), you are (were), he (she, it) is (was), we (you, they) are (were), e.g. *yeye ni mwema*, he is a good man. *Ni hivi tu*, it is just so. *Nyumba ni tupu*, the house is empty. For *ni-*, *-ni*, and *-ni-*, as a prefix, see Grammars.

Nia,* v. have in mind, think of, purpose, intend, resolve. **Nia**, n. (1) intention, purpose, resolve; (2) thought, idea; (3) mind, conscience, heart, character, disposition. *Nia njema (safi)*, a good disposition. *Nia mbovu*, bad intention (conscience, &c.). (Cf. *ania, nuia*, from same root, and *kusudia, waza, moyo, dhamiri, mradi*. Ar. نوى.)

Niabu,* n. See **Naibu**.

Nikaha,* n., also sometimes **Nikahi**, marriage—esp. with reference to formalities, ceremonial, &c., betrothal, espousals, marriage settlement, e.g. *humfungia nikaha humwoza*, he makes a match for her, and gives her in marriage. *Akamwoa kwa nikaha*, and he married her in due form. *Fungisha nikaha*, perform the marriage ceremony for. *Sikiliza (shuhudia) nikaha*, attend (attest) a marriage, said of the congregation present at the mosque. (Cf. *ndoa, arusi, maozi*. Ar. نكح.)

Nikwata, n. a kind of small lizard, the type found frequenting houses indoors.

Nili,* n. indigo. See **Mnili**. (Ar. نيل.)

Nina, n. mother—only used in poetry and in certain obscene phrases like *kuma nina*. (Cf. *mama, nyoko*.)

Nina, verb-form, I have.

Ninga, n. (1) Deland's green pigeon, *Vinago delalandii*; (2) a female personal name. **Ninga wa bahari**, n. applied to certain sea birds.

Ning'inia, v. sway, swing, wave to and fro, dandle (a child), rock, e.g. of tree, *matawi yananing'inia*, the branches swing to and fro. Cs. **Ning'iniza** and **Ning'inisha**. **Kining'ina**, n. *vi-* great-great-grandchild. (Cf. *kijukuu, kilembwe*, and *wayawaya, yumbayumba*.)

Nini, pron. interrog. what?—often subjoined to verbs in the contracted form *-ni*. *Wataka nini?* What do you want? *Ya nini? Kwa nini?* Why? What for? *Kunani?* sometimes used for *kuna nini?* What is the matter? *Hujambo nini?* Are you well, (or) what?

Ninyi, pron. of 2nd Pers. Plur. you, ye. Often subjoined to verbs in the unreduplicated form *-ni*, e.g. *njoni*, come (ye). *Nitakupigeni*, I will beat you. *Kwa herini*, good-bye all of you.

Nipo, verb-form, I am here.

Nira,* n. a yoke (for oxen). (Ar. نير.)

Nisha, n. or **Nishaa,*** starch—rarely heard for the usu. *wanga*. (Ar. نشا.)

Nishani,* n. a medal, decoration, badge, &c. *Askari waliopigana vitani walipewa nishani*, the soldiers who fought in the war received medals. (Ar. نشان.)

Njaa, n. hunger, craving for food, lack of food, famine. *Nina (naona) njaa*, I am hungry. *Shindisha kwa njaa*, starve. *Njaa inaniuma*, I feel the pangs of hunger. *Njaa ya leo ni shibe ya kesho*, hunger to-day means (i.e. hopes for) plenty to-morrow. (Dist. *jaa*, dust-heap.)

Njaanjaa, n. papyrus grass See **Ndago mwitu**.

Njama, n. a secret council or meeting. (Cf. *mzengwe, faragha*.)

Njana, n. a kind of fish not considered good eating by Europeans.

Nje, adv. outside—opp. to *ndani*. *-a nje*, external, outside, outer, outward. *Nje ya*, outside of, on the surface of. *Kwa nje*, outwardly, on the outside.

Njegere, n. a kind of small pea, pigeon pea.

Njeku, n. a small undersized bull.

Njema, a. form of *-ema*. Often used as an adv. in rejoinders, like *vema*, Good! Very well! Certainly! (Cf. *vema, taibu, inshallah*.)

Njia, n. path, road, way, means, &c. See under **Ja**.

Njiwa, n. Lesser Red-eyed Dove, and applied generally to other doves.

Njombo, n. name of a fish barred with black and yellow.

Njongwanjongwa, adv. (of walking) softly with long stealthy steps, as when tracking something or following a person secretly.

Njoo, Njoni, v. See under **Ja**.

Njorinjori, a. and n. *ma-* (1) tall. *Mtu njorinjori*, a very tall man. (2) also a man with many tribal marks on his face; it usually refers to a Nubian. **Kingoringori**, adv. lengthwise, **Manjorinjori**, n. plur. used to described tall people of other tribes, e.g. Nubians. (Cf. *-refu*.)

Njozi, n. vision, apparition. (Cf. *ndoto, ota, ruya*.)

Njuga, n. a small bell, worn as an

ornament, and at dances. (Cf. *kengele.*)

Njugu, n. ground-nut. Two varieties are (1) *njugumawe*, which are hard, and (2) *njugunyasa*, often called *karanga*, the peanut. The plant is called *mnjugu*.

Njujumu, n. same as *njumu*. See under **Mjume**.

Njukuti, n. plur. of *unjukuti*.

Njumu, n. See under **Mjume**.

Njuti,* n. a shoe of European make and shape. (Cf. *kiatu*. Hind. جوتی.)

n.k., abbreviation for *na kadhalika*.

Nne, n. and a. four. As a n. always disyllable, and pronounced almost like *inne*. As an a. the semi-vowel property of the first *n* is not so pronounced, but it is still retained. *Watu wanne*, four people. *-a nne*, fourth. *Kumi na nne*, fourteen. (Cf. Ar. *aroba*, also often used.)

Noa, v. sharpen, make sharp, whet, give an edge to—of metal tools, weapons, knives, &c. Ps. **Nolewa**. St. and Pot. **Noleka**, e.g. take an edge, be capable of taking an edge. Prep. **Nolea**, e.g. *jiwe la kunolea*, a whetstone. Cs. **Nolesha**. **Kinoo**, n. *vi-* a whetstone. **Noleo**, n. *ma-* (1) any instrument for sharpening, i.e. a whetstone, grindstone, strop, knife-sharpener; (2) a ferrule, metal ring round the haft of a tool. In the Plur. *manoleo*, the back edge of a knife, &c., i.e. the part which does not cut (cf. *mafutuni*). **Noo**, n. *ma-* amplic. of *kinoo*.

Nofo, a., **Nofoa**, v., **-nofu**, a. See under **Mnofu**.

Nokoa,* n. *ma-* the second man in authority over a plantation, under the *msimamizi*, and over the *kadamu*, sub-overseer, assistant. (? Pers. نوکر servant, &c.)

Noleo, n. *mu-*. See under **Noa**.

Nomi,* adv. full up to the brim. (Cf. *pomoni*, *jaa*. Ar. نمی grow, increase, &c.)

Nona, v. get fat, usually of animals (*nenepa* of man). Cs. **Nonesha**. **-nono**, a. fat, sleek, plump, well-fed —of animals (*-nene* properly of human beings) and things, e.g. *maisha nono*, a life of luxury. *Ng'ombe wanono*, fat cattle. **Kinono**, n. *vi-* a fatted animal, a fatling. **Unono**, n. (1) fatness—of animals, and so (2) richness, comfort, luxury. A common expression of good wishes is *ishi* (*lala*) *unono*, may you live (sleep) in comfort.

Nonea, v. kiss. (Cf. *busu*.)

Nondo, n. (1) a kind of moth; (2) a kind of snake, sometimes called *tuwanyika*.

Nonga, v. be disagreeable, wear out a person's patience with much talk, also Cs. **Nonza**, used in the same way. **Nongwa**, n. disagreeableness, spite, an act which gets somebody into mischief or causes trouble. *Ana nongwa*, he is disagreeable, has a secret grudge, &c.

Nongo, n. perspiration, the dirt which is rubbed off the body when one perspires.

Nong'ona, v. whisper, speak under one's breath (in a low tone). Cs. **Nong'oneza**, address in a whisper, whisper to. Rp. **Nong'onezana**, whisper to each other. **Manong'onezo**, n. plur. **Manong'ono**, n. plur. See **Mnong'ono** below. **Mnong'onezi**, n. *wa-*, and **Mnong'oni**, n. *wa-*, a whisperer. **Mnong'ono**, n. *mi-* (1) whispering, a whisper; (2) a rumour, secret information, &c. **Nong'onong'o**, n. and **Unong'onezi**, n. (1) whispering; (2) a rumour.

Nongwa, n. See under **Nonga**.

-nono, a. See under **Nona**.

Nonza, v. See under **Nonga**.

Noo, n. *ma-*. See under **Noa**.

Noti,* n. (1) a bank or Treasury note; (2) a note in music—adopted for use in text-books and school lessons. (Eng.)

Notisi,* n. the common word used for a summons to a court of justice,

&c. *Kukata notisi,* to take out a summons. *Kukatiwa notisi,* to be summoned. (Eng. notice).

Novemba,* n. November. (Eng.)

Nso, n. a kidney. (Cf. *figo, buki.*)

Nswi, n. an old word for fish, now usually *samaki.*

Nta, n. wax, beeswax—collected by natives from *mizinga* (which see) and used in barter or sold to merchants.

Nti, n. an ear ornament. (Cf. *kidivi-divi, bali.*)

Nufaika,* v. See under **Nafuu.**

Nuhusi,* n. See **Nuksi.**

Nuia,* v. have in mind, consider, purpose, intend, form a resolution, form a wish in the mind, &c. Ps. **Nuiwa.** Prep. **Nuilia,** resolve as to, form a good resolution about. Cs. **Nuiza,** (1) cause to have in mind, instruct, but also (2) intens. fix the mind on some particular desire, wish, &c., as when offering incense for a particular purpose, i.e. *kutia ubani na kunuiza,* to put in incense and form a wish. The wish may be for good or for evil. *Mchawi alimwambia anuize na huku yeye anaomboleza,* the wizard told him to form his wishes while he prayed earnestly (on his behalf to the spirits). *Kunuiza uchawi,* to place a spell or witchcraft on somebody by wishing. (Cf. *nia, ania* from the same root, and *azimu, taka, omboleza, kusudi, wazo, dhana, fikira, moyo, dhamira, mradi.* Ar. نوى.)

Nujumu,* n. See **Jumu** and **Mnajimu.**

Nuka, v. (1) give out a smell, smell, but esp. (when used alone) of a bad smell, stink; (2) nauseate, repeat (of food), e.g. *chakula hiki kinaninuka,* this food disagrees with me, it repeats, nauseates. (Cf. *puzia.*) Prep. **Nukia,** have a sweet smell. D.Prep. **Nukilia.** Cs. **Nukiliza,** smell out, follow by scent, e.g. *mbwa hodari wa kunukiliza,* excellent sporting dogs, dogs with a good sense of smell. Cs. **Nusa** and **Nukiza,** use the sense of smell, smell, smell out, and so of dogs hunting, scent, follow by scent—and of taking snuff. *Tumbako ya kunusa,* snuff. **Nukato,** n. *ma-* anything having a sweet smell, odour, perfume, scent (see *-to*). **Mnukauvundo,** n. a kind of evil smelling grass. **Mnukio,** n. *mi-* a sweet smell, perfume. **Mnuko,** n. *mi-* a bad smell. **Nuko,** n. *ma-* a smell, aroma.

Nuksani, n., **Nuksi,** n., also **Nuhusi,*** n., bad luck, a quarrel, a mischievous action. (Ar. نحوس.)

Nukta,* n. a dot, point, mark, spot, vowel sign. (In Arabic writing) mark of punctuation (comma, fullstop, &c.); (2) a second (of time). (Ar. نقطة.)

Nuku, v., **Nukulu,*** v See under **Nakili.**

Numbi, n. a draught of fishes

Nuna, v. grumble, show discontent, complain, be sullen, sulk. *Nuna uso,* look discontented (sulky). Prep. **Nunia,** be sulky about, complain of (to, &c.). Cs. **Nunisha,** put in a bad temper, cause to grumble, &c. Rp. **Nuniana,** sulk together, complain of each other. **Mnuna,** n. *wa-*, **Mnunaji,** n. *wa-*, and **Mnuni,** n. *wa-* a grumbler, one who complains (sulks, is discontented). **Mnuno,** n. *mi-* grumbling, discontent, complaint, sulkiness. (Cf. *nung'unika, guna.*)

Nunda, n. (1) a fierce animal, beast of prey; (2) a semi-wild town cat; (3) used also to describe a cruel, bloodthirsty man; (4) used to describe anything very heavy, e.g. *kitu hiki ni nunda,* this thing is extraordinarily heavy.

Nundu, n. protuberance, boss, lump, hump, esp. of the hump of native cattle, which is considered a delicacy. *Achinjaye ng'ombe atoa nundu akampa jumbe,* he who kills an ox takes the hump and presents it to the chief. *Nundunundu,* or *kinundunundu,* humpy, lumpy. **Kinundu,** n. *vi-* dim. and adv.

Nunge, n. a leper settlement. (Prob. originally the name of a place where a settlement was made, now applied generally to such settlements.)

Nungu, n. (1) a porcupine; (2) a globe fish, usu. called *bunju*.

Nung'unika, v. murmur, grumble, show discontent, complain. Prep. **Nung'unikia,** grumble at (about, to, &c.). **Nung'uniko,** n. *ma-* grumbling, murmuring, complaint. (Cf. *nuna, guna*.)

Nungunungu, n. a porcupine. See **Nungu.**

Nunua, v. buy, purchase, bargain about, make a bid for. *Nunua bia* (or *shirika*), buy jointly, combine to buy. Ps. **Nunuliwa.** St. and Pot. **Nunulika.** Prep. **Nunulia,** buy for (with, at, &c.). *Amenunuliwa shamba*, he has had an estate bought for him. Cs. **Nunuza,** e.g. cause (press, invite, persuade) to buy. **Mnunuzi,** n. *wa-* a buyer, customer, purchaser. **Ununuzi,** n. buying, purchase, bargaining, bidding (for an article), custom, price. (Cf. *zabuni, mshtiri*.)

Nunuza, v. help a child to teethe by rubbing its gums.

Nurisha,* v. See under **Nuru.**

Nuru,* n. light, brightness, illumination. *Tia nuru*, brighten, illuminate, make bright (clear, intelligible). *Toa nuru*, give out light, shine. Used of a bright expression or complexion, e.g. *nuru ya uso ikampotea*, he lost his happy expression. *Wanawake hao nuru yao sawasawa*, these women are equally good looking. **Nurisha,** v. cause to shine, make bright, give light to. **Kinara,** n. *vi-* (1) dim. of *mnara*, see follg.; (2) a candlestick. **Mnara,** n. *mi-* (1) a lighthouse; (2) tower, minaret, steeple. **Nawiri,** v. shine, but only used of a person's countenance. *Uso wake unanawiri*, her face shines, i.e. is healthy looking, pleasant. (Cf. *mulika, angaza*. Ar. نور.)

Nusa, v. See under **Nuka.**

Nusra,* n. See **Nusura.**

Nusu,* n. a half, a part, a portion, a bit. *Nusu* is often used in a very loose way of any fraction of a whole, but in arithmetic it is used strictly to denote one half. *Nusu kidogo*, a little bit. *Kata nusu nusu*, cut in halves (pieces, bits). *Gawa nusu kwa nusu* (or *nusu bi nusu*), divide in halves. *Nusu . . . nusu*, partly . . . partly. *Nusushilingi*, the name adopted for a fifty-cent piece. *Nusudunia*, a hemisphere. Ar. نصف half.)

Nusura,* adv. almost, nearly, within a little, e.g. *amenitukana nusura kunipiga*, he has abused me almost to the point of striking. (Ar. ? نسرة strip of skin or flesh.)

Nusura,* n. aid, help. **Nusuru,** v. help, assist, defend, preserve—esp. of God's help. *Mungu ameninusuru*, God has helped me. St. **Nusurika,** be helped, be saved, be delivered out of a difficulty. (Cf. *auni, saidia*. Ar. نصر.)

Nwa, v. See **Nywa.**

Ny, represents the palatal nasal which is as near as possible the sound of *ni* in the English word 'companion'.

Nya, v. (1) discharge, emit, let fall, drop of something fluid or semi-fluid, but restricted almost entirely to the passage of excreta and, when used alone, of urine; (2) of rainfall, be discharged. *Kunya mvua*, to rain. *Kunya mavi* (*damu*), pass to faeces (blood). *Mvua imekunya leo*, it has rained to-day. *Mvua yanya*, rain is falling. *Inakunya* it is raining. Prep. **Nyea,** discharge a drop on (with, to, &c.), e.g. of a child fouling its mother. *Asifuye mvua imemnyea*, he who praises rain has had it (i.e. it has rained for (or on) him. Cs. **Nyesha,** (1) of rain: *Mungu amenyesha mvua nyingi*, God has caused much rain to fall. In some places *nyesha* is used of rain falling, e.g. *mvua imenyesha*, rain has fallen (prob. to avoid the use of *nya* and its association with excreta); (2) e.g. *nyesha mtoto*, attend to a child at stool. The Cv. form *nyua* has probably become contracted to *nywa*, and is reversive in meaning, i.e. drink up, absorb, &c. This form, together with its derivatives are shown separately under *nywa* for convenience of reference. (For a similar contraction see *cha* and its Cv. *chwa*.) **Kinyeleo**, n. *vi-* a pore (of the skin). **Kinyesi**, n. *vi-* excretum. **Kinyenyevu**, n. *vi-* but usually **Kinyevu**, n. *vi-* dampness, humidity. **Kinyo**, n. *vi-* the anus. (Cf. *mkundu*.) **Mnyo**, n. *mi-* the act of discharging faeces or urine; or of rain, a shower. **Mnyevu**, n. damp, wet, moisture. **Nyeleo**, n. *ma-* like *kinyeleo*, a pore of the skin. **Nyesi**, n. *ma-* same as *kinyesi* above. **-nyevu**, a. moist, wet, damp, humid. **Unyaji**, n. method, &c., of passing or discharging fluid, excreta, &c. **Unyeleo**, n. *ma-* same as *nyeleo*. **Unyesi**, n. (*manyesi*) passing excreta, excretion, excrement, urine. **Unyevu**, n. dampness, moisture, absorbability.

Nyaa, n. finger-nail, usu. *kucha*.

Nyaenya, n. a kind of fish not considered very good eating by Europeans.

Nyafua, v. sometimes heard for *nofoa* and *nyofoa*, which see.

Nyaka, v., and Cv. form **Nyakua**, catch in the hands, snatch up, tweak, pluck with the fingers, twitch—also filch, pilfer. **Mnyakuzi**, n. *wa-* (1) one who snatches, one who is quick at catching in the hands; (2) a filcher, a thief who grabs or snatches a thing and runs away with it, shop-lifter, pickpocket. **Unyakuzi**, n. filching, grabbing, snatching.

Nyakanga, n. the chief of the *kungwi*, which see. (Cf. also *mhenga*.)

Nyakua, v. See under **Nyaka**.

Nyalio, n. plur. of *walio*, which is seldom used, (1) pieces of stick placed inside at the bottom of a cooking-pot to prevent the food from burning; (2) a kind of fish-trap (cf. *uzio*); (3) see under **Alia**.

Nyama, n. See under **Mnyama**. **Nyamafu**, n. a dead animal. (Cf. *mnyama* and *fa*, v. die, and *mzoga*.)

Nyamaa, v. be silent, stop talking, hold one's tongue, be (become) quiet, die away, cease, be still—used not only of talking and noise, but of anything violent, troublesome, or painful, e.g. of mental or bodily suffering, &c., e.g. *kichwa kiliniuma sasa kimenyamaa*, my head was aching but now it has ceased. Prep. **Nyamalia**, e.g. be quiet to (for, in, &c.). Cs. **Nyamaza**, usu. Inten., i.e. keep quiet, refrain from noise, repress oneself, and in the Imperat., Silence! Hold your tongue! Also in the same way as *nyamaa*, be silent, &c. Prep. **Nyamazia**, make quiet for (with, &c.). *Mchezo wa kunyamazia mtoto*, a toy to keep the child quiet. D.Cs. **Nyamazisha**, reduce to silence, make quiet, calm, still. **-nyamavu**, a. silent, quiet, still, reticent, reserved. *Mtu mnyamavu*, a man who says very little, keeps to himself. *Panyamavu*, a quiet spot. **Unyamavu**, n. silence, quiet, repose, taciturnity.

Nyamafu, n. See under **Nyama**.

-nyamavu, a., **Nyamaza**, v., **Nyamazisha**, v. See under **Nyamaa**.

Nyambua, v. (1) pull in pieces, tear into bits, take off in strips, peel off; (2) fig. reproach, make charges against, find fault with, &c. (Cf. *suta, sibabi*.) St. **Nyambuka**, come to pieces, fall into bits, be peeled off, e.g. of over-ripe fruit, over-cooked meat, &c. Cs. **Nyambuliwa**. (Cf. *ambua, chambua*, and dist. *nyumbua*.)

Nyambuo, n. a small fish like whitebait. (Cf. *dagaa, kijino*.)

Nyamizi, n. See **Mwanamizi**.

-nyangalika, a. used as an evasive or contemptuous epithet of what is difficult, impossible, or unfit to describe, a sort of —, a what-do-you-call-it, a nondescript. *Kitu kinya-*

ngalika, a nondescript thing. *Mnyangalika gani huyu?* What sort of wretch is this?

Nyang'amba, n. a kind of sweetmeat, round, made of arrowroot.

Nyang'anya, v. take by force, steal, plunder, rob—with the thing stolen, or person robbed, as object. *Amemnyang'anya mali*, he has robbed him of money. *Alinyang'anya yule mtoto*, he kidnapped that child, or, he robbed that child. Ps. **Nyang'anywa**. St. and Pot. **Nyang'anyika**. Prep. **Nyang'anyia**. Cs. **Nyang'anyisha**. Rp. **Nyang'anyana**. **Mnyang'anyi** n. *wa-* robber, thief, highwayman, burglar. Commonly implies a larger scale of action than *mwizi*, which includes mere petty thieving and pilfering. **Unyang'anyi**, n. robbery, carrying off by force, abduction, brigandage, lawless depredation.

Nyangumi, n. a whale.

Nyangwa, n. plur. of *wangwa*.

Nyani, n. an ape, a baboon. (Cf. *kima*.)

Nyanya, n. (1) tomato, fruit of the *mnyanya*; (2) grandmother.

Nyanya, v. cause to be prominent, protrude, put out, raise up. *Aliunyanya mkono wake, akachukua upanga*, and he put out his hand, and took a sword. The more usual form is the Cv. **Nyanyua**, raise up, lift. St. and Pot. **Nyanyuka**, be prominent, rise above the rest, stick up, stick out. Prep. **Nyanyia**, is usu. restricted to, use trickery, artfulness, cunning, &c., in getting anything.

Nyanyasa, v. tease, annoy, molest, treat disrespectfully or rudely, hurt the feelings of. (Cf. *sumbua*, *udhi*, *chokoza*, and *nyarafu*.)

Nyanyia, v., **Nyanyua**, v., **Nyanyuka**, v. See under Nyanya, v.

Nyapa, v. often Rd. *nyapanyapa*, stalk or creep after, follow by stealth, by bending down and taking cover, &c., as when stalking game, &c. (Cf. *nyemelea*, *vizia*, *nyatia*.)

Nyara, n. plur. (1) booty, spoils, plunder—persons or things, taken in war, by violence or trickery. *Teka (kula) nyara*, take captive. (Cf. *teka*.)

Nyara, v. be ashamed, be put to shame because of disgust felt or expressed by another at one's dirty habits, clothes, home, &c. *Fulani amenyara*, so-and-so feels ashamed (because somebody is disgusted with him). **Nyarafu**, v. be disgusted, feel disgust, avoid contact with a person because of his filthiness, disgusting habits, surroundings, &c.—also used of things which cause disgust. Ps. **Nyarafiwa**, like *nyara*, be ashamed, &c. **Kinyaa**, n. (1) filth, anything which causes a feeling of disgust, e.g. excrement; (2) the disgust felt by a person because of anything filthy. *Moyo wangu huona kinyaa kwa ajili ya fulani*, I feel disgusted (sick) because of so-and-so (i.e. his filthiness, &c.) **Unyaa**, n. disgust felt by a person because of anything filthy, like *kinyaa* (2). **Unyarafu**, n. (1) disgust, disdain, abhorrence felt because of anything filthy; (2) superiority, pride, aloofness, &c., felt by a person over another who is dirty. (Cf. *unyanya*, prob. a dur. form of *nya*.)

Nyasi, n. *ma-* a reed, long coarse grass, lalang grass, *Imperata cylindrica*. Also plur. of *unyasi*.

Nyata, v. go silently (quietly, stealthily), steal along, slink, skulk, sneak, e.g. of a wild beast's stealthy walk, or of a hunter stalking. Prep. **Nyatia**, creep up to, steal upon, stalk (of a hunter). Cv. **Nyatua**, used of a child just beginning to walk, moving its feet too quickly. **Nyatunyatu**, adv. stealthily, &c. (Cf. *nyemelea*, *tambalia*, *gundulia*, *nyapanyapa*.)

Nyati, n. the African buffalo, also called *mbogo*.

Nyatua, v., **Nyatunyatu**, adv. See under **Nyata**.

Nyauka, v. dry up, be withered shrivel—with heat, or drought,

Mnyaufu, n. e.g. *mnyaufu wa mwili*, pining away of the body. **Unyaufu,** n. condition of being dried up, shrivelled, &c., and as of pining, languishing. (Cf. the more common *kauka.*)

Nyayo, n. plur. of *wayo*, which see.

Nyea, v. (1) prep. form of *nya*, which see; (2) cause a tickling or itching sensation, tickle, itch. *Upele unaninyea*, the eruption itches. Ps. **Nyewa,** be made to itch, be irritated, tickled, also feel sexual excitement. (Cf. *nyega.*) **Kinyevu,** n. *vi-* a tickling, itching, tingling sensation. **Mnyeo,** n. *mi-* a tickling, prickling, itching sensation, a creeping feeling, craving. *Mnyeo wa njaa*, the pricks, pangs of hunger. Also of prurience. **Unyeo,** n. itching, tickling, &c. (Cf. *washa*, also *nyega*, *nya*, which appear to be closely connected.)

Nyega, v. cause to itch or tickle, cause sexual excitement, excite prurient desire. Cs. **Nyegesha,** Inten. (also *nyegeresha*, *nyengeresha*). **Nyege,** n. (sometimes *unyege*) itching, tickling, irritation, but almost entirely confined to sexual excitement, prurient desire, and in animals, heat. (Cf. *nya*, *nyea.*)

Nyegere, n. a small animal rather like a mongoose, skunk. (Cf. *cheche.*)

Nyegeresha, v. See under **Nyega.**

Nyekenya, v. (1) decompose, as a dead body does with the heat; (2) turn gangrenous, also used of a sore which does not heal; (3) wriggle about, used of maggots in filth, &c.

Nyeleo, n. *ma-*. See under **Nya.**

Nyemelea, v. go quietly up to, steal up to, creep upon, stalk (a wild animal or bird), surprise. Ps. **Nyemelewa,** e.g. be approached by stealth, be taken by surprise. (Cf. *nyapa*, *nyatia.*)

Nyemi, n. and a. See under **Kinyemi.**

Nyendea, v. stalk, follow stealthily. (Cf. *nyemelea*, *nyatia*, *nyapanyapa.*)

Nyenga, n. a kind of large flat fish. (Cf. *taa.*)

Nyenga, v. talk a person into telling, extort an admission from, pump with questions. Ps. **Nyengwa.** Prep. **Nyengea.** Cs. **Nyengesha.** (Cf. *nyenya.*)

Nyengeresha, v. See under **Nyega.**

Nyenje, n. a kind of cricket, also called *chenene*, *nyenze*.

Nyenya, v. (cf. *nyenga*, v.) talk a person into telling, talk over, extort an admission from, urge, extract news, pump with questions. Ps. **Nyenywa.** St. and Pot. **Nyenyeka,** be talked over, give way to pressure, submit, hence **Nyenyekea,** act with submission (humility, reverence, respect) towards, be polite (obsequious, cringing, &c.) to, be humble, defer to, e.g. *kijana amemnyenyekea baba yake*, the young man has treated his father with due deference. Prep. **Nyenyelea,** get at a secret, &c., whence, Cs. **Nyenyeleza,** introduce quietly, slip in secretly. Cs. and Inten. **Nyenyesha.** Rp. **Nyenyana.** Ps. of St. **Nyenyekewa.** Cs. of St. **Nyenyekesha,** e.g. teach humility to, humiliate, &c. **Mnyenyekeo,** n. *mi-* deference, a humble attitude, reverence, &c. **Mnyenyekevu,** n. *wa-* a humble, quiet, deferent person. **-nyenyekevu,** a. humble, servile, obsequious, &c. **Unyenyekeo,** n., **Unyenyekevu,** n. humility, self-abasement, submission, reverential awe, obsequiousness, servility, cringing.

Nyenyere, n. a kind of very small black ant, also called *sisimizi*.

Nyenze, n. a cricket, also called *nyenje*, *chenene*.

Nyenzo, n. plur. of *wenzo*. See under **Enda.**

Nyerere, n. brass or copper wire worn round the arms as an ornament. (Cf. *udodi.*)

Nyerereza, v. hide one's actions so as to deceive, camouflage.

Nyesha, v., **Nyesi,** n. *ma-*. See under **Nya.**

Nyeta, v. be teasing (tiresome, hard

to please, unsatisfied, never content), be ill-mannered (disrespectful, arrogant), swagger. Prep. **Nyetea,** (1) be disrespectful to (about, &c.); (2) see **Jetea.** Cs. **Nyetesha,** cause to be troublesome, impertinent, &c. **Unyeti,** n. being tiresome, irritability, sensitiveness, causing irritation, conceit, spite, misconduct. (Cf. *deka.*)

Nyeusi, n. (1) a form of *-eusi*; (2) a kind of sugar-cane. (Cf. *muwa.*)

-nyevu, a. See under **Nya.**

Nyewa, v. See under **Nyea.**

Nyie, pron. for *ninyi -ye,* you (plur.), you there.

Nyigu, n. *ma-* a large wasp, a hornet. (Cf. *mavu.*)

Nyika, n. *ma-* open, bare, treeless wilderness, open forest with high grass, a barren, desolate region, contr. with *mwitu,* e.g. *tukaenda mwitu na nyika, mwitu na nyika,* we went on and on, through woods and wastes, forest and field. (Cf. *pori, pululu, jangwa.*)

Nyima, v. withhold (from), keep back (from), deprive, refuse, not give, esp. of what is due, a person's right, e.g. wages, a debt, e.g. *ana haki ya kupewa, lakini amemnyima kusudi,* he has a right to be paid, but he has kept it back purposely. Ps. **Nyimwa. Mnyima,** n. *wa-,* **Mnyimaji,** n. *wa-* a niggard, a stingy, mean person. **Mnyimo,** n. *mi-* act of withholding what is due, a niggardly, stingy act. **-nyimivu,** a. and **-nyiminyimi,** a. niggardly, stingy, miserly, &c.

Nyinyiha, v. shine as though rubbed with oil or fat. (Cf. *nang'anika.*)

Nyinyirika, v. move with a gliding motion, like a snake or trickle of water. (Cf. *tiririka.*)

Nyinyoro, n. a bulbous plant which throws up a large head of red flowers.

Nyinywi. See **Ninyi.**

Nyiririka, v. same as *nyinyirika.*

Nyiza, n. strips of palm leaf when dyed, ready for plaiting. (Cf. *ukili.*)

Nyoa, v. (1) shave off—of hair only. Ps. **Nyolewa.** Prep. **Nyolea,** e.g. *wembe wa kunyolea nywele,* a razor to shave off the hair; (2) take off the leaves of maize cobs. **Kinyozi,** n. *vi-* also rarely **Mnyozi,** n. *wa-* a barber, hairdresser. **Unyozi,** n. art (profession, fee, &c.) of a barber, haircutting, shaving. (Cf. *nyonyoa.*)

Nyoe, n. a kind of green grasshopper found in maize cobs before the grain begins to form. Also called *nyonye.*

Nyofoa, v. See under **Mnofu.**

-nyofu, a. See under **Nyoka.**

Nyoka, n. serpent or snake of any kind; also applied to tapeworms (cf. *tegu*), and intestinal worms (cf. *chango*). **Joka,** n. *ma-* amplic. a large snake, a dragon. **Kijoka,** n. *vi-* dim.

Nyoka, v. (1) become straight (extended, laid out in a straight line), be straightened; (2) fig. be straightforward, be honest (practical, steadfast, effective). Cs. **Nyosha,** make straight, &c. Ps. **Nyoshwa.** Prep. **Nyoshea.** Rp. **Nyoshana,** e.g. *nyosha mkono,* put out the hand. *Jinyosha,* stretch oneself, take one's ease, rest, &c. *Nyosha mgongo,* straighten the back, on completion of a job. **-nyofu,** a. (1) straight, extended, stretched out; (2) usually fig. straightforward, honest, upright, trustworthy, e.g. *mtu mnyofu,* an honourable man. *Maneno manyofu,* plain, direct statements. **Unyofu,** n. (1) straightness, being straight, extension; (2) straightforwardness, honesty, uprightness.

Nyoko, n. an old word for 'your mother' now seldom used except in one of the commonest terms of obscene abuse, '*kuma nyoko*'. (Cf. *mama, nina, kuma.*)

Nyonga, n. plur. of *unyonga,* but also used as a sing. the hip, the part where the thigh (*paja*) and flank (*kiuno*) meet. Prov. *Uchungu wa mtoto u katika nyonga ya mama yake,* the trouble with a child is on the mother's hip—native women often carry a child astride on the hip. **Kinyonga,**

n. *vi-* complaint. **Unyonga,** n. (*nyonga*) (1) hip; (2) hip-complaint, lameness due to disease or injury of the hip.

Nyonga, v. (1) twist, twist the neck of, strangle, throttle; (2) vex, harass, worry; (3) as an Intr. twist, wriggle, move from side to side. Ps. **Nyongwa.** Prep. **Nyongea.** St. **Nyongeka.** Cs. **Nyongesha.** Cv. **Nyongoa,** straighten out twists, used esp. of stretching oneself after being in a cramped or bent position for some time. **Kinyonga,** n. *vi-* a chameleon. (Cf. *kigeugeu, lumbwi.*) **Kinyonge,** n. and adv. state of wretchedness, abject, destitution, degradation, &c. **Kinyongo,** n. *vi-* of a mental or moral twist, (1) fancy, whim, scruple, fad; (2) ill feeling, grudge, bitterness, spite, resentment. *Usifanye kazi kwa kinyongo,* do not work unwillingly, as if against the grain. Prov. *Mpenzi hana kinyongo,* a lover has no scruples (or faults). *Mwenye kinyongo,* a hypochondriac, faddy person. **Mnyonge,** n. *wa-* a humble, abject, low, debased person. **-nyonge,** a. of a low order, (degree, or kind), low, mean, base, degraded, servile, insignificant, vile. *Lia kinyonge,* cry in a feeble, helpless way. **Nyongea,** n. an illness of children, rickets (cf. *chira*). **Unyonge,** n. condition of being mean (vile, abject, low, lowly), meanness, poverty, feebleness, insignificance. In plur. low acts, conditions, &c. (Cf. *hafifu, duni, -baya, dhaifu.*)

-nyonge, a., and **Nyongea,** n. See under **Nyonga,** v.

Nyongeza, n. plur. of *uongezo.* See under **Ongea.**

Nyongo, n. bile. *Kutumbukia nyongo,* is sometimes used fig. of things losing their pleasantness. *Safari imetumbukia nyongo,* i.e. the journey has been spoiled, i.e. through some misfortune, &c.

Nyongoa, v. See under **Nyonga,** v.

Nyong'onyea, v. be languid, be weary, become slack and weak. **Kinyong'onyo,** n. *vi-* and adv. (1) anything which causes fatigue, slackness, or weakness of the body; (2) tiredness, weakness, fatigue, &c., and as adv. in a slack, weary, tired way. **Unyong'onyevu,** n. sometimes contracted to **Unyogovu,** weariness, languidness, slackness, or weakness of the body.

Nyono, n. See under **Gona.**

Nyonya, v. suck the breast—said of a child or animal. *Nyonya titi la mama,* suck the mother's teat. *Ndugu wa kunyonya,* foster brother (or sister). **Mtoto mnyonya,** a babe suckling. Cs. **Nyonyesha,** suckle, give suck to, put to the breast. **Nyonye,** n. a mother's breasts, a word used by small children.

Nyonye, n. (1) see under **Nyonya;** (2) a kind of green grasshopper found in the cobs of maize before grain begins to form. (Cf. *nyoe.*)

Nyonyo, n. seeds of the castor-oil plant, *mbono.*

Nyonyoa, v. pluck out hair (feathers, wool, &c.), pluck a bird, shave unskilfully (pulling instead of cutting). *Mninyonyoeni manyoya,* pluck out my feathers. Ps. **Nyonyolewa,** e.g. *ngozi ya kondoo isiyonyonyolewa manyoya,* a sheepskin with the wool on. St. and Pot. **Nyonyoka,** e.g. *kima amenyonyoka manyoya pia,* the monkey has all its hair plucked off. Prep. **Nyonyolea.** Cs. **Nyonyosha,** used fig. nag, constantly harass, worry, tease. (Cf. *unyoya* and *nyoa.*)

Nyonyota, v. drizzle, **Manyonyota,** n. plur. drizzle, light rain. (Cf. *nyotanyota, nyunyu.*)

Nyonyotoka, v. be over-cooked, be falling to pieces from being over-cooked. (Cf. *nyambuka* under *nyambua.*)

Nyoo! int. of derision, contempt, &c. See **Ng'oo.** Sometimes a verb is made from this int., i.e. when a person has got the better of another, he frequently pulls a face and says

Nyoo! in derision; should the other turn the tables on him, he may turn round and say, *Nyoo! na wewe ume-nyoka!* i.e. I can now say *nyoo!* to you.

Nyorora, v. become thin, lean, emaciated through illness—of animals and humans. (Cf. *churuzika, konda, nywea.*)

Nyosha, v. See under **Nyoka,** v.

Nyota, n. (1) a star. *Nyota hazionekani mchana,* the stars are not visible in the daylight. (2) sometimes heard for thirst (cf. *kiu*); (3) luck, either good or bad. *Fulani amezaliwa na nyota nzuri,* so-and-so was born lucky.

Nyotanyota, v. drizzle, used of drizzling rain. (Cf. *nyonyota, nyunyu.*)

Nyote, a common contraction for *ninyi nyote,* you all, all of you. Cf. *sote,* for *sisi sote. Ninyi wote,* commonly for 'both of you (two)'.

Nyotoa, v. (1) smart, feel raw—of a sore; (2) make thin—of an illness, e.g. *homa imemnyotoa,* the fever has made him thin. St. **Nyotoka,** become thin, because of fever, &c.

Nyoya, n. *ma-* also plur. of *unyoya,* a hair, a single feather, a piece of wool, an animal's hair. *Manyoya* is used generally of the external covering—wool, hair, feathers—of the bodies of birds and animals, more particularly of the smaller body feathers of birds (contr. *ubawa, mbawa,* sometimes used of the wing feathers), and of short hair in animals (cf. *singa* of long straight hair) —down, both of birds and animals, being *malaika. Nywele* is regularly used of human hair. **Unyoya,** n. (*nyoya*), a fibre of wool, or animal's hair, or down, &c., of birds. (Cf. *nyoa, nyonyoa.*)

Nyoyo, n. sometimes heard for plur. of *moyo,* which see, esp. in Zanzibar and Mombasa.

Nyua, n. plur. of *ua,* which see.

Nyuka, v. hit, beat. (Cf. *piga.*)

Nyuki, n. a bee. *Asali ya nyuki,* honey. Prov. *Nyuki huenda na maua yake,* the bee goes with its flowers. *Fadhili ya nyuki ni moto,* a bee's thanks is fire, i.e. all the thanks the bee gets is fire, referring to the custom of smoking bees out of their hives in order to get their honey. **Uki,** n. honey.

Nyukua, v. pinch with the fingers, pluck. Rp. **Nyukuana,** pinch or pluck each other, i.e. as children do in play.

Nyuma, adv. after, behind, (1) of a place—behind, at the back of, whether (*a*) on the farther side of, beyond, or (*b*) after, in the rear of; (2) of time (*a*) hereafter, in the future, (*b*) behind, in the past. For the apparent vagueness of meaning cf. *mbele,* in which also the meaning is decided by the context and implied mental attitude. *Watu wabaya wataondoka nyuma yangu,* may mean 'bad people will rise up after me' (when I am gone, in the future—if of time; or behind me, in my rear—if of place). *Mambo ya nyuma,* may mean (1) the future, *mambo ya baadaye, mambo ya mbele,* or (2) the past, *mambo yaliyopita, yaliyokwisha zamani, yaliyokuwa mbele. Rudi nyuma,* go back. *Kaa nyuma,* sit behind. *Huko nyuma,* often means 'meanwhile, to resume'—of returning to a point in a story. *-a nyuma,* behind, in the rear, in the past, in the future. *Nyuma ya,* after, behind, in the rear of, beyond. **Kinyuma,** n. and adv. but usu. **Kinyume,** the back part, the rear, behind, the contrary, backwards, after time, late, in a contrary way. *Kwa kinyume,* backwards, to the rear. *Habari ya kinyume,* later, subsequent news, also, contrary news, contradictory news. *Kinyume changu,* behind me, also something quite the opposite to what I am. *Maneno ya kinyume,* a kind of puzzle-language, the last syllable of each word being made the first.

Nyuma, n. plur. of *uma,* n. See under **Uma,** v.

Nyumba, n. See under **Chumba**.

Nyumbu, n. (1) a mule; (2) hartebeest, topi, and gnu, also called *kongoni*.

Nyumbua, v. used of handling a flexible, elastic, adhesive substance—bend, draw out, stretch, manipulate without breaking. St. **Nyumbuka**, be flexible (elastic, bend, yield to pressure) without breaking. (Cf. *pinda, kunja, napukia, nama*.)

Nyundo, n. a hammer. (Cf. *unda*.)

Nyungunyungu, n. (1) ulcerous cracks or sores on the feet, between the toes, &c. *Miguu yangu imefanya nyungunyungu kwa jasho*, my feet are ulcerated with the heat. (2) also the name of a worm.

Nyuni, n. a bird, but usu. *ndege* is used.

Nyunya, v. drizzle, rain gently. (Cf. *nyonyota, nyotanyota*.) Cs. **Nyunyiza**, sprinkle. Ps. **Nyunyizwa**. Prep. **Nyunyizia**. D.Cs. **Nyunyizisha**. Rp. **Nyunyizana**. **Mnyunyo**, n. *mi-* act (method, &c.) of sprinkling. **Nyunyu**, n. *ma-* mostly used in the plur. *manyunyu*, sprinkled liquid, sprinklings, drizzle, light rain.

Nywa, v. (prob. a Cv. form of *nya*, i.e. *nyua* contracted into *nywa*, with an opposite meaning) 'drink, absorb, suck up, exhaust, consume', either of liquids or fig. of other things—corresponding to *-la* eat. Ps. **Nywewa**, be drunk up, be absorbed, dwindle, pine away, be consumed, dissolve away, evaporate, vanish. St. and Pot. **Nyweka**, e.g. (1) be drunk up, &c.; (2) be capable of (fit for) being drunk, be good for drinking purposes. Prep. **Nywea**, (1) drink at (with, for, to, &c.), e.g. *kope la kunywea*, a mug to drink from. Sometimes also in a Ps. sense, e.g. *kila siku mkewe huzidi kunywea*, every day his wife gets thinner. *Nyama imenywea*, the meat has dried up (in cooking). (2) be absorbed, e.g. *maji yamenywea*, the water has dried up, is absorbed. Cs. **Nywesha**, cause to drink, furnish drink to, supply with water, &c. **Jinywa**, n. *ma-* amplic. of *kinywa*, below a large mouth, esp. as an insulting term, e.g. *ziba jinywa lako*, stop that great mouth of yours, shut up. **Kanwa**, n. *ma-* sometimes heard for *kinywa* follg. **Kinywa**, n. *vi-* the mouth (as organ of drinking) of man, animals, insects, &c. (of birds usually *mdomo*). Also 'something to drink, a beverage', but this is usually *kinywaji*. *Kinywa* (or *kionja*) *mchuzi*, the hair on the under-lip, the imperial, place where the imperial grows, lit. the gravy drinker. *Kinywa wazi*, open mouth, with open mouth, open mouthed. **Kinywaji**, n. *vi-* something to drink, a beverage liquid for drinking purposes. **Kinyweleo**, n. *vi-* a pore (of the skin), also *kinyeleo*. **Kinyweo**, n. *vi-* (1) same as *kinywaji*; (2) a drinking-vessel of any description. **Kinywewa**, n. *vi-* same as *kinywaji*, but seldom heard. **Mnywa**, n. *wa-* and **Mnywaji**, n. *wa-* one who drinks, a drinker. **Mnywo**, n. *mi-* (1) a drink, act of absorbing; (2) a mouthful of water. **Nyweleo**, n. *ma-* and **Unyweleo**, n. *ma-* a pore of the skin, same as *kinyweleo*. **Unywaji**, n. method, &c., of drinking, absorbing, liquid, moisture, &c.

Nywea, v. shrink, shrivel, recoil, or curl up, e.g. as of a dog when frightened, or a leaf when dry. See prep. of **Nywa**.

Nywele, n. plur. of *unywele*.

Nyweleo, n. *ma-*, **Nywesha**, v. See under **Nywa**.

Nzige, n. a locust, the young are called *tunutu, funutu, maige*, and *vimatu*.

Nzigunzigu, n. a butterfly. (Cf. *pepea*.)

O

O represents *o* as in 'pole' when long; when short it is similar to the *o* in 'pot'.

Oa, v. take a wife, marry a wife—of the man only. Ps. **Oawa** (seldom used), be married—of the man only. Ps. **Olewa,** be married—of the woman only. St. and Pot. **Oleka,** of the woman only—be married, be marriageable. Prep. **Olea,** marry with (for, at, in, &c.) of gifts, accessories, place, &c., for marrying. Cs. **Oza,** cause (allow) to marry, perform the ceremony of marriage. Used of parents, friends concerned, persons assisting, the official, &c., and even of the bridegroom, 'get for wife, take in marriage'. Prep. **Ozea.** Ps. of Cs. **Ozewa.** D.Prep. of Cs. **Ozelea,** marry to (with, at, &c.). D.Cs. **Ozesha,** *uniozeshe mtoto wako,* allow me to marry your daughter. Rp. **Oana,** of the couple marrying, and of intermarriage generally, of families, tribes, &c. **Maozi,** n. plur. giving in marriage, arrangements for bringing about a marriage. **Mwozi,** n. *wa-* one who gives in marriage, or who performs the ceremony. **Ndoa,** n. marrying, marriage—often treated as a plur. noun, *ndoa zangu,* my marriage. **Uozi,** n. *ma-* act of marrying, celebration of a wedding, esp. of the religious ceremony at a mosque, but applicable to the part of the parents, bridegroom, or celebrant. (Cf. *arusi, nikaha,* and *posa,* and dist. *oza,* v. (A).)

Oama, v. sometimes heard (Kimvita) for *lowama,* which see.

Ofisa,* n. *ma-* officer, i.e. the English word as pronounced by a native. **Ofisi,** n. an office.

Oga, v. bathe, wash the whole body, take a bath. *Koga* is often used as the root (i.e. *ku-oga*). Prep. **Ogea,** e.g. *maji ya kuogea,* water to bathe with, and *pakuogea,* a bathing-place, a bath-room. *Chakogea,* a vessel to bathe in, a bath, i.e. of the European kind—otherwise *kiogeo, birika* (and cf. *hamamu*). D.Prep. **Ogelea,** is used specially of swimming. Cs. **Ogeleza** and **Ogelesha,** make (cause, teach) to swim. St. and Pot. **Ogeleka,** e.g. *hapaogeleki hapa,* it is not possible to swim here. Cs. **Ogesha,** e.g. take (send, order), to bathe, or bathe, as a mother, a child, &c. Rp. **Ogana,** all bathe together. **Chakogea,** i.e. *cha kuogea,* bath, vessel for bathing in. **Mogo,** n. *mi-* sometimes heard for *mwogo,* see below. **Mwoga,** n. *wa-*, **Mwogaji,** n. *wa-*, a bather. **Mwogeleaji,** n. *wa-* a swimmer. **Mwogo,** n. *mi-* act (manner, &c.) of bathing. *Siku ya mwogo,* the day on which the boys who have been circumcised go to bathe for the first time after the ceremony.

Oga, a. cowardly, timid, nervous, easily frightened. **Ogopa,** v. be afraid (of), fear, feel fear. (For the significance of the *-pa* termination, i.e. *oga-pa,* see note under *pa.*) Ps. **Ogopwa.** Prep. **Ogopea,** e.g. *mama humwogopea mtoto akiwa mgonjwa,* a mother fears for her child if he is sick. *Unamwogopea nini?* Why are you afraid of him? Cs. **Ogofya,** and sometimes **Ogofisha,** frighten, terrify, alarm, threaten, menace. **Mwoga,** n. *wa-* a coward, a timid person, &c. **Mwogofyo,** n. *mi-* threatening, denunciation, a threat. **Ogofyo,** n. *ma-* menace, threat, denunciation. **Woga,** n. cowardice, fear, timidity, shyness. *Woga mkubwa,* panic. *Fanya (ona, ingiwa na) woga,* be frightened. **Wogofya,** n. (*nyogofya* and *ma-*) causing fear, threat, menace, terrifying. (Cf. *hofu, tisha.*)

Ogelea, v. See under **Oga,** v.

Ogofisha, v., **Ogofya,** v., **Ogofyo,** n. *ma-*, **Ogopa,** v. See under **Oga,** a.

Oka, v. roast, toast, bake, i.e. prepare by applying fire only, not with water. Of pottery, burn, bake. *Oka mkate,* bake bread. Ps. **Okwa.** St. **Okeka.** Prep. **Okea.** Cs. **Okesha.** **Joko,** n. *ma-* oven, kiln, esp. of potter's work, a place for baking earthen vessels. **Mwoka,** n. *wa-*, and **Mwokaji,** n. *wa-* a baker, one who bakes. *Mwoka mkate,* a baker of bread. **Mwoko,** n. *mi-* act (process, &c.) of baking, roasting. (Cf. *pika, choma, kaanga,* and *moshi.*)

Okoa, v. save, rescue, deliver, preserve. Ps. **Okolewa.** St. and Pot. **Okoka.** Prep. **Okolea.** Cs. and Inten. **Okoza,** e.g. exert oneself to save, rescue, &c. Rp. **Okoana.** **Kiokozi,** n. *vi-* act (means, way, &c.) of recovering, and so reward for finding something lost or for saving something from danger. Also of persons, one who saves, rescuer, preserver, but this is usu. *mwokozi.* **Maokozi,** n. plur. (1) deliverance, preservation, and also (2) the means of deliverance. **Mwokozi,** n. *wa-* one who saves, a saviour, rescuer, preserver, deliverer. *Mwokozi wetu,* our Saviour, deliverer. **Wokovu,** n. deliverance, rescue, escape, salvation. (Cf. *opoa, ponya.*)

Okota, v. (prob. Ten. of *okoa,* v. with restricted meanings), (1) pick up, take up with the fingers, hands, &c.; (2) light upon, come across, find by chance, get without exertion or anticipation, e.g. of fishing, *wakiokota nguva hugawana,* if they come across a dugong, they divide it. Ps. **Okotwa.** St. and Pot. **Okoteka,** e.g. *maji yaliyomwagika hayaokoteki,* spilt water cannot be picked up. Prep. **Okotea.** Cs. **Okotesha.** Rp. **Okotana.** Rp. of Prep. **Okoteana.** **Kiokosi,** n. *vi-* a reward for finding something lost. (Cf. *utotole.*) **Kotokoto,** n. money got by supplementary work, i.e. out of business hours. **Mwokosi,** n. *wa-*, **Mwokotaji,** n. *wa-*, and **Mwokoti,** *wa-* one who picks up, one who finds by chance. **Uokotaji,** n. picking up (payment, reward, &c.) for picking up, finding, &c. (Cf. *zoa, kuta, vumbua, pata.*)

Oktavo,* n. an octave in music—adopted for use in text-books and school lessons. (Eng.)

Oktoba,* n. October. (Eng.)

Ola, v. look at, seldom used. (Cf. *tazama* and *oleza,* also *kioo,* prob. from same root.)

Ole,* n. usu. with a pron. adj. as an exclamation of woe, pity, i.e. *Ole wangu!* woe is me! *Ole wao!* how sad for them! *Mwenye ole,* a melancholy, sad, despondent person. (Ar. ويل disaster, woe, &c.)

Oleleza, v. See under **Oleza.**

Olewa, v. See under **Oa.**

Oleza, v., and **Oleleza,** v. make straight (even, level) with—and so follow a pattern, copy, imitate. *Oleza kitu na kitu kingine,* make one thing like another. **Kiolezo,** n. *vi-* a pattern, sample—not often used. (Cf. *fuatisha, linganisha, sawazisha, iga, namna, kielelezo, mfano,* and *ola* prob. from the same root.)

Omba, v. beg (for), be a beggar, pray (to), request, ask (of)—with either person asked, or thing asked, as object, or both. Thus *omba mtu,* ask a person. *Omba mtu kitu*, ask a person for a thing. Also *omba kitu kwa mtu*, ask a thing of a person, e.g. *niliomba nguo kwa bwana*, I asked my master for clothes. *Ndivyo tuombavyo*, so we pray—a common rejoinder on hearing good news. Ps. **Ombwa.** St. and Pot. **Ombeka,** e.g. be asked, be a proper request. Prep. **Ombea,** usually in a restricted sense, e.g. ask on behalf of, plead for, intercede for, or petition against, rather than ask for (i.e. to have) or ask of (i.e. from). Thus *kumwombea kwa Mungu*, to intercede for him with God, is more usual than *kuombea baraka za Mungu*, ask for God's blessings, or simply *kuombea Mungu*, pray to God. Cs. **Ombesha (Ombeza),** e.g. cause to beg, instruct in prayers, &c. Rp. **Ombana.** Cv. *omboa*, not in use, but the following form is derived from it—**Omboleza,** (1) bewail, lament, in a ceremonial way. Used of formal chanting of dirges, &c. (2) beseech for, beg earnestly for, pray in detail, i.e. mentioning one's needs one by one. Cs. of St. **Ombokeza,** repeat the words of an oath before swearing or taking an oath. **Maombi,** n. plur. **Maombo,** n. plur., also **Maomvi,** n. plur. prayers, entreaties, requests, intercessions. (Cf. *haja, dua, sala.*) **Maombolezo,** n. plur. (1) loud wailing, lamentations, mourning, dirges; (2) earnest, sincere prayer, prayer in detail, i.e. mentioning one's needs one by one. **Mwomba,** n. *wa-* one who asks (begs, prays) governing a noun following. *Mwomba dua*, one who makes a special petition. *Mwomba Mungu*, a person of prayer, a devout person. **Mwombaji,** n. *wa-* (1) one given to praying; (2) a beggar, a professional beggar, a mendicant. **Mwombezi,** n. *wa-* one who begs on behalf of (or against) another, an intercessor, pleader, advocate—also opponent. **Mwombi,** n. *wa-* one who makes a petition (or prayer), a petitioner, a supplicant. **Mwombelezi,** n. *wa-* a suppliant, mourner, &c. **Uombaji,** n. *ma-* begging as a practice or profession, repeated or importunate requests. **Uombezi,** n. *ma-*, and **Uombi,** n. *ma-* begging, praying, intercession, supplication, entreaty, prayer.

Ombasha,* n. lance-corporal—formerly used in what is now Tanganyika Territory by the Germans for that rank—not generally known now. (Cf. *shaushi, bishaushi,* and *soli*. Turk. اناباش.)

Ombojea, v. be soft because of being over-cooked or over-ripe.

Ombokeza, v., **Omboleza,** v., **Ombolezo,** n. *ma-*. See under **Omba.**

Ombwe, n. edge, brink—usu. *ushi na ombwe*, as of a well, seashore, &c. (Cf. *ukingo.*)

Omekeza, v. pile up, arrange by placing one thing on top of another. (Cf. *panganya.*)

Omo,* n. *ma-* forepart of ship, bows, prow—also called *gubeti*. *Pepo za omo*, winds that carry forward, a wind astern, a fair wind. **Kiomo,** n. *vi-* dim. and adv. straight ahead. (Ar. اماه ahead, or Ar. عومة navigation.)

Omoa, v. (1) dig up, dig out, break up, e.g. of breaking up soil with crowbars, &c.; (2) fig. disturb, weaken, cause trouble in, make confusion; (3) bring to light, reveal, show, begin, set on foot, e.g. *omoa udongo*, break up earth. *Omoa vita*, bring about war. Prep. **Omolea.** Ps. **Omolewa,** e.g. Prov. *Mti huomolewa na matunda yake*, a tree is dug up with its fruit, i.e. digging up a tree involves the fruit also. St. and Pot. **Omoka.** Cs. **Omosha.** (Cf. *chimbua, fukua, tekua, vumbua,* and perh. *umua.*)

Ona, v. used on any mode of perception by the senses or the mind, and hence with a wide range of meanings, viz. 1. of the senses: (1) of sight. *Ona* alone and unqualified by context usually means, see with the eyes, as contr. with other senses, e.g. *kusikia si kuona,* hearing is not the same as seeing. *Ona* (Imperat.) look, use your eyes (contr. *tazama,* fix your gaze upon, contemplate, *angalia,* observe, attend to). By a curious inversion *ona* is sometimes used for 'be transparent', e.g. *nguo hii inaona,* this cloth is transparent, i.e. one can see through it, it sees. (2) of the other senses, e.g. *naona harufu,* I smell a smell. *Naona kishindo,* I hear a noise, or I feel a shock. *Naona mti huu mgumu,* I feel this wood is hard. *Naona utamu wake,* I taste its flavour. *Naona kiu (njaa),* I am thirsty (hungry). (3) get to see, come on, find (cf. follg.). 2. of mental perception, of all kinds: (1) of feelings, very commonly with defining noun, e.g. *ona taabu (huruma, hasira, umivu, furaha, haya, mashaka, huzuni,* &c.), feel (experience) distress (pity, anger, hurt, joy, shame, doubt, sorrow, &c.). A common expression is *Waonaje?* How are you? How do you feel? What do you think? (2) of other mental faculties: observe, think, be of the opinion, notice, discern, judge, consider, expect, fancy, imagine, e.g. *naona,* very commonly alone, I think so, certainly, probably, possibly, it is likely, perhaps. *Naona nyani kusema,* I observe an ape speaking. *Naona utaona ajabu kuona barua hii,* I think you will feel surprise at seeing this letter. Rf. *jiona,* (1) feel oneself, e.g. *najiona nipo kwetu,* I feel myself quite at home, am quite at ease; (2) commonly of affectation, self-conscious pride, &c., i.e. be conceited (arrogant, ostentatious, affected), e.g. *anajiona,* he is conceited, proud of himself, showing off. **Ps. Onwa,** of all the senses in the Act. St. and Pot. **Oneka,** e.g. (1) be seen, &c.; (2) be perceptible (vision, audible, tangible, &c.). Rp. of St., and Pot. **Onekana,** i.e. come into view, become visible, be apparent, be perceptible, appear, appear like (as if), seem to be. Prep. **Onea,** e.g. (1) see, feel, &c., with (for, at, by, in, against, &c.), e.g. *nataka kujionea,* I want to see for myself. *Namwonea chuki,* I am offended with him. *Usimwonee makosa,* do not visit his errors upon him. (2) Commonly used alone in the restricted sense of an active expression of ill feeling against, i.e. bully, ill treat, harass, persecute, oppress. *Wale ndugu wakamwonea ndugu yao,* and those brothers bullied their younger brother. Ps. **Onewa,** be ill treated, persecuted. Rp. **Oneana,** tease each other, as well as 'feel towards each other'. D.Prep. **Onelea,** (1) like *onea,* but Inten.; (2) feel towards, have the impression or opinion about. Cs. **Onya,** (1) cause to see, show, display, e.g. *nilimwonya njia,* I showed him the road, but esp. (2) warn, admonish, reprove, e.g. *nilimwonya asiende,* I warned him not to go. *Onyaonya kwa mikono,* warn by waving the hands (arms), gesticulate. St. and Pot. **Onyeka,** be warned, be capable of being warned, be amenable to warning, admonition, &c., e.g. *nilimwonya, lakini haonyeki,* I warned him, but he does not heed warnings, or was not in a position to see my warnings. D.Cs. also Cs. of St. **Onyesha,** cause to see, show, point out, demonstrate, make clear, exhibit, place on view. Note: the simple Cs. form *onesha* is never used. Ps. **Onyeshwa,** be shown. Prep. **Onyeshea.** Ps. **Onyeshewa,** have a thing shown to one. Rp. of Cs. **Onyana,** of mutual warning. Rp. of Dir. **Onana,** (1) see each other, hence (2) meet each other—often of friendly meetings. *Onana uso kwa uso,* meet face to face. *Tulionana nao njiani,* we met with them in the road. *Kwa heri ya kuonana,* good-bye till we meet again. **Kionyo,** n. *vi-* secret warning, hint, suggestion. **Lonyo,** a. fine, showy, specially grand, i.e.

mwenzetu ametuonyesha nguo za lonyo, our companion has shown us some very showy (smart, fine) clothes. **Maonyo,** n. plur. warnings, advice, hints, suggestions. **Mboni,** n. (1) *mboni ya jicho*, the seeing part of the eye, i.e. the apple or pupil of the eye, also described as *mwana wa jicho*; (2) anything precious; (3) a present given as a reward for finding something lost, also given by a hunter, fisherman, &c., to the head of his village. **Oneo,** n. *ma-* unkind treatment, persecution, bullying. **-onevu,** a. ill feeling, oppressive, given to ill treating or bullying, &c. **Ono,** n. *ma-* thought, feeling, perception, something seen, felt, perceived by the senses, &c. **Uonevu,** n., and **Uonyo,** n. (*maonyo*) warning, exhortation, remonstrance. **Wonyesho,** n. showing, exhibition, demonstration, pointing out, &c. **Wonyeshano,** n. showing, exhibiting, demonstration, &c., to each other. (Cf. *mbona*, prob. from the same root.)

Ondoa, v. (1) start off, set going off; (2) take (put, send, move) away, remove, take out of the way, set aside, dismiss; (3) do away with, abolish, finish off, conclude. *Uniondoe nisimame*, start me (help me) to get up. *Shauku nyingi huondoa maarifa*, great desire overrides prudence. *Daraka ya kuondoa au kuweka*, responsibility for removing or establishing. *Ondoa nadhiri* (*ahadi*), fulfil a vow, discharge a promise. *Ondoa matanga*, bring funeral ceremonies to an end. *Ondoa dhambi*, remit sin. Ps. **Ondolewa.** St. and Pot. **Ondoka,** e.g. (1) go away, make a move, get out of the way, start off, set out (on a journey), depart, withdraw, retire; (2) rise up, get up, stand upright (as the first step to going off, &c.), e.g. often in beginning a story, *paliondoka* (or *paliondokea*) *mtu*, a man went (began, made a start). *Ondoka mbele yangu*, get out of my way. *Ondoka katika ulimwengu*, depart from this world, die. *Alikuwa amelala, akaondoka, akakimbia*, he was lying prostrate, but he rose up and fled. Prep. **Ondokea,** (1) get on in the world, prosper, e.g. *ameanza kuondokea*, he has begun to prosper; (2) make a move for (against, at, with, &c.), get out of the way of, esp. of rising up before, as a sign of respect, e.g. *haondokewi*, no respect is shown him; (3) rise up, swell, protrude, stand out, become prominent, e.g. *maziwa yaanza kumwondokea*, her breasts begin to swell. D.Prep. of St. **Ondokelea,** rise up and leave a place. Prep. **Ondolea,** e.g. send (take, put) away for (by, with, at, &c.), i.e. remove from, deprive of, rid of, condone, forgive, &c. *Ondolea heshima*, disgrace, degrade. *Ondolea mashaka*, rid of difficulties. *Ondolea huzuni*, comfort, cheer. *Ondolea dhambi*, absolve from sin. *Ondolea hatia*, acquit. Rp. **Ondoana.** Rp. of Prep. **Ondoleana.** Cs. **Ondosha,** Inten. send off, dispatch, dismiss, cause to go away, do away with. *Ondosha nanga*, get up an anchor (commonly *ng'oa*). *Ondosha mtumishi*, dismiss a servant, or dispatch on an errand. **Ondokeo,** n. *ma-* usu. in the plur. (1) prospering, succeeding in life, &c.; (2) departure, going away, taking leave; (3) rising up, respectful salute. **Ondoleo,** n. *ma-* usu. in the plur. taking away, removal. *Maondoleo ya dhambi*, remission (forgiveness) of sins. (Cf. *toa*, *weka*, *twaa*, in various senses.)

Onea, v., **Oneka,** v., **Onekana,** v., **Oneo,** n. *ma-*, **-onevu,** a. See under **Ona.**

Ongea, v. (A) spend time, talk, gossip, idle, converse, pass time, waste time. **Maongezi,** n. plur. talk, conversation, gossip, amusement, pastime. *Weka maongezi*, prepare for a long chat. **Mwongeza,** n. *wa-*, **Mwongezi,** n. *wa-* a gossip, one fond of talking, an expert conversationalist. (Cf. *zungumza.*)

Ongea, v. (B) increase, become more, seldom used in the Dir. form. Cs. **Ongeza**, increase, add to, make greater, multiply, magnify, enlarge. *Ongeza maneno*, make a lengthy (or additional) speech. *Ongeza urefu*, lengthen. Ps. **Ongezwa.** St. and Pot. **Ongezeka**, e.g. be added to, increase, multiply. Prep. **Ongezea**, add to (for, with, &c.) *Tumeongezewa mshahara*, we have had an increase to pay. Rp. **Ongezana. Ongezo**, n. *ma-* usu. in the plur. addition, increase, supplement, increment. **Nyongeza**, n. (plur. of *uongeza*, not in use), addition, appendix, supplement, increment. (Cf. *zidisha, zidi.*)

Ongeza, v., **Ongezo**, n. *ma-*. See under **Ongea**, v. (B).

-ongo, a. See **-wongo** under **Mwongo.**

Ongoa, v. cause to go right, guide, lead, set right, reform, correct, convert, make successful, prosper. *Ongoa mtoto*, give a child a good training. *Useme naye hata umwongoe*, talk to him till you convert him. *Ongoa mbele*, lead forward. *Ongoa njia*, make the road straight, take a straight course on. Ps. **Ongolewa.** St. and Pot. **Ongoka**, e.g. become straight, be set right, be well taught, prosper, be reformed, be converted, &c. *Vilimo vyao havikuongoka*, their plantings did not turn out well. *Ongoka moyo*, become a reformed character. *Mti umeongoka*, the pole has become straight. Prep. of St. **Ongokea**, e.g. *mwaka huu watu wameongokewa*, this year people have been prosperous (cf. *fanikiwa*). *Ongokea Mungu*, be turned (directed) to God. Prep. **Ongolea**, (1) similar in use to *ongoa*, e.g. *ongolea mtoto*, get a child to be tractable. *Mungu amemwongolea kazi*, God has granted success to his labours; (2) rhyme. Cs. **Ongoza**, Inten. make go right, drive forward, carry on vigorously, lead. *Ongoza kazi*, do good work. *Ongoza maneno*, give a good turn to a discussion, clear up a statement. *Ongoza kuku*, drive fowls along a road. Rp. of Cs. **Ongozana**, cause each other to follow in the right way, follow after each other. Rp. **Ongoana. Kiongozi**, n. *vi-* act (means, way, &c.) of directing; but usu. a guide on the road, director, leader of a caravan, also reward for such services, guide's fee. **Maongozi**, n. plur. direction, superintendence, management, administration, arrangements. *Maongozi ya Mungu*, Providence, divine dispensation. **Mwongofu**, n. *wa-* one who is directed, instructed, put in the right way—and so in religion, i.e. *mwongofu wa dini*, a convert, a proselyte. *Mwongofu wa kazi*, a proficient in an art, good workman. **Mwongozi**, n. *wa-* one who shows the right way (guides, leads) and so, a skilled workman who can show others how to work (cf. *fundi*), or a guide, pilot (cf. the usual word, *kiongozi*). **Mwongozo**, n. *mi-* (1) direction, help to go in the right way, example, &c.; (2) manual, text-book, commentary, &c. **-ongofu**, a. reformed, converted, led aright, well-conducted, well-trained, successful. **Wongofu**, n. righteousness, uprightness. (Cf. *unyofu, nyosha, adili, onyesha.*)

Ongopa, v., **Ongofya**, v. See under **-wongo.**

Ongoza, v. See under **Ongoa.**

Onja, v. (1) taste, take a taste of; (2) try, test, examine. *Onja uone*, taste and see—if a thing is good. *Onja mitego*, inspect traps. Ps. **Onjwa.** St. **Onjeka.** Prep. **Onjea**, e.g. *mwiko wa kuonjea asali*, a spoon to taste honey with. Cs. **Onjesha. Kionja**, n. *vi-* that which tastes, i.e. *kionja mchuzi*, a name given to the imperial, or under-lip, i.e. the gravy taster, like *kinywa mchuzi*. **Kionjo** n. *vi-* a little taste, a small sample, a trial. **Mwonjo**, n. *mi-* a tasting, a trial, also **Onji**, n. *ma-*, and **Onjo**, *ma-* with the same sense.

Ono, n. *ma-*, **Onya**, v., **Onyesha**, v., **Onyo**, n. *ma-*. See under **Ona**.

Onza, v. wound, hurt, torment, vex. (Cf. *jeruhi, choma, udhi, sumbua.*)

Opoa, v. (1) take (fetch, pull, draw) out; (2) fig. save, rescue, deliver, e.g. *opoa ndoo kisimani*, fish a bucket out of a well. *Opoa sumu*, get poison out of the system—by medicine. Ps. **Opolewa**. St. and Pot. **Opoka**, be saved (rescued, cured). Prep. **Opolea**, e.g. *chuma cha kuopolea*, an iron hook (to pull with). Cs. of Prep. **Opoleza**. Cs. **Oposha**. **Kiopoo**, n. *vi-* anything used for taking up, fishing up, as from a well or pit—a pole or stick with a fork, hook, gaff. (Cf. *koeka, ngoeka.*)

Orodha,* n. a list, inventory, catalogue, invoice, time-table, &c. *Orodha za kuzidisha*, multiplication tables. *Orodha za hesabu*, tables of weights and measures. *Orodha ya majina*, a list of names, register. (Ar. عرض.)

Orofa,* n. upper room, upper floor (story, flat) of a house. *Nyumba ya orofa tatu*, a house with three upper rooms or stories. (Ar. غرفة.)

-ororo, a. soft, smooth, velvety, tender. *Nguo nyororo*, a soft fabric. *Godoro jororo*, a soft mattress. *Mwili mwororo*, soft flesh. (Cf. *laini, -anana*, and *nyorora*. Contr. *-gumu*, hard.)

Osha, v. wash, the most general term for washing anything, but for several kinds of washing see *fua, nawa, chamba, tawadha, chanyata*, &c. *Osha mwili (maiti)*, wash the body (a dead body). Ps. **Oshwa**. St. and Pot. **Osheka**, e.g. be washed, be washable, stand washing. *Nguo hizi haziosheki*, these materials are not washable. Prep. **Oshea**, e.g. *unioshee sahani hizi*, wash these plates for me. *Mahali pa kuoshewa maiti*, a place for washing corpses. Cs. **Osheza**. **Kiosha**, n. *vi-* that which washes, e.g. *kiosha miguu*, that which washes the feet—name of a wedding fee for particular service. **Kiosho**, n. *vi-* act (place, means, &c.) of washing. **Chosho**, n. a place for washing, same as *josho*. **Josho**, n. *ma-* (for *ji-osho*), a bathing-place, a place for washing. **Mwosha**, n. *wa-*, **Mwoshaji**, n. *wa-* (1) one who washes—in general, but also (2) esp. of one who is engaged to wash a corpse, and prepare it for burial, an undertaker—sometimes one of the three, who each take a part. *Mwosha naye huoshwa*, the washer (of corpses) is himself washed (i.e. one day a corpse). **Mwosho**, n. *mi-* act (place, manner, &c.) of washing. (Cf. *oga*, v.)

Ota, v. (A) grow, sprout, spring up—usually of vegetable life, or growth resembling it, e.g. of nails, hair, teeth, &c. (So also *mea*, but of animal growth usually *kua*.) *Mihindi inaota*, the maize is springing up. *Simba huota nywele za shingo*, lions grow manes, i.e. *ota* in a semi-active sense. Prep. **Otea**. Cs. **Otesha**, e.g. cause to grow, tend, cherish, rear vegetable growth. **Oteo**, n. *ma-* vegetable growth, &c. **Woto**, n. growing (as a vegetable), vegetation. (Cf. *mabotea.*)

Ota, v. (B) (1) dream, have a dream; (2) be in a dreamy, dozing state, be half awake, be silly—often with *ndoto*, following. Prep. **Otea**, dream about. Rp. **Otana**, dream about each other. Cs. **Otesha**, cause to dream. **Ndoto**, n. a dream, dreaming.

Ota, v. (C) sit by (in, for), squat down at, often with *jua*, i.e. *ota jua*, bask in the sun, or *moto, ota moto*, sit close to a fire, warm oneself. Prep. **Otea**, like *ota*, and also esp. lie in wait, form an ambush, look out for. Stc. **Otama**, squat, sit, be in a sitting or squatting position. Prep. **Otamia**, sit on, i.e. as a hen on eggs (cf. *atamia*). **Joto**, n. amplic. of *moto* (see below), great heat, inflammation, pyrexia. **Kiota**, n. *vi-*, also **Kioto**, n. *vi-*, sitting-place of a bird, nest, roost, fowls' laying-place. **Kioteo**, n. *vi-* ambuscade, ambush, lurking-place. **Moto**, n. (*mioto*) (1) fire, flame, a fire, a conflagration; (2) heat, warmth, inflammation, temperature; (3) fig. zeal, ardour, energy, vehemence, martial spirit, intensity, fierceness. *Koka moto*, prepare a fire. *Washa moto*, light a fire. *Ota moto*, sit by the fire, warm oneself. *Pekecha moto*, light a fire by means of firesticks. *Paa moto*, take out live coals from the fire. *Pata moto*, get hot. *Pasha moto*, warm up, heat. *Choma moto*, burn. *Chochea moto*, stir up a fire. *Zima moto*, put out a fire. Prov. *Dawa ya moto ni moto*, fire must be met with fire. *Askari wa adui walikuwa moto siku za vita*, the soldiers of the enemy were very fierce during the war. *Wanawake walikuwa moto, jinsi walivyopambwa*, the women were pleasing because of the way in which they were adorned. *-a moto*, hot, warm, energetic, fiery, &c. *Kazi moto*, strenuous, eager work. *Maji ya moto* (often heard) *maji moto* only, (1) hot water; (2) a large red ant, living in trees, is so called. **Oteo**, n. *ma-* ambush, lying in wait. **Ujotojoto**, n. heat, warmth. **Umoto**, n., and **Umotomoto**, n. heat, warmth, vehemence, fury. **Vimoto**, adv. heatedly, with energy, energetically, &c. **Woto**, n. getting warm, basking, warmth.

Ota, v. (D) make marks on the body, as by beating with a stick. *Fimbo zimemwota mgongoni*, the stick has made marks on his body. **Moto**, n. *mi-* marks on the body, as though made by a stick.

Otama, v. See under **Ota**, v. (C); also **Atamia**.

-ote, a. all, all the, the whole (of). Takes the forms *sote* and *nyote* when associated with the pronouns *sisi*, *ninyi*. *Sisi sote*, all of us, we all. *Ninyi nyote*, all of you. *Ninyi nyote wawili*, both of you. *Nyumba yote*, all the house, the whole house. *Nyumba zote*, all the houses. *-ote* is generalized by combination with a corresponding separate relative form, e.g. *mtu ye yote*, any man whatever. *Watu wo wote, neno lo lote*, &c. (Cf. *awaye yote, kiwacho chote*.) 'All', in the sense of 'every individual', is denoted by *-ote -moja -moja*, e.g. *vitu vyote kimoja kimoja*, every thing singly. *Waambie watu wote na waje mmoja mmoja*, tell all of the people to come one at a time. (Cf. *kila*.)

Otea, v. See **Ota**, v. (A), (B), and (C).

Oteo, n. *ma-*. See under **Ota**, v. (A) and (C).

-ovu, a. bad—usually in a moral sense, wrong, unprincipled, wicked, evil. If required to agree with nouns not of the *wa* class, then usually *-a uovu*, e.g. *nyumba za uovu*, wicked houses, not *nyumba ovu*. Prov. *Mema na maovu ndio ulimwengu*, the world is a mixture of good and bad. Contr. *-bovu* apparently from the same root, but of physical condition, e.g. *nyumba mbovu*, dilapidated houses. Also cf. *-baya*, which includes the meanings of *-ovu* and *-bovu*. **Ovu**, n. *ma-* often in the plur. *maovu*, wickedness, badness, wrong, injustice, &c. **Uovu**, n. wickedness, badness, evil, corruption.

Ovyo, a. and adv. used of trash, useless articles, rubbish, what is common and valueless. As adv. anyhow, recklessly, hazard, at random, extravagantly, foolishly, carelessly. *Mpanda ovyo hula ovyo* he who plants in a haphazard fashion eats also what is haphazard or rubbish. (Perh. cf. *-ovu*.)

Owama, v. sometimes heard for *lowama*, which see.

Oya, n. (for *uoya* and *woya*) (*nyoya*), a handful, i.e. as much as is able to lie on the palm of the hand. (Cf. *gao, ukufi, konzi*.)

Oza, v. (A) (1) go bad, rot, putrefy,

spoil, be corrupt. *Tia dawa isioze,* use medicaments to prevent putrefaction, use antiseptics, embalm (a corpse). Prov. *Samaki mmoja akioza, ni mtungo pia,* if one fish rots, it is the whole string. Prep. **Ozea.** Cs. **Ozesha.** **Kioza,** n. state of a putrid thing, putridity, gangrene. *Mtu huyu ana kioza ndani,* this man is rotten inside. **Wozo,** n. (*u-ozo*) decay, rottenness, &c. (Cf. *-ovu, -bovu,* and perh. *mbolea.*)

Oza, v. (B). See under **Oa.**

P

P represents the same sound as in English.

Pa (1) is the form of the preposition *-a,* of, agreeing with *mahali,* and nouns with the locative termination *-ni,* e.g. *mahali pa kukaa,* a place to stay at. *Mjini pa mgeni,* in the foreigner's town. (2) used alone (not as a preposition) after *mahali,* represents the verb-form *ni,* is, e.g. *mahali hapa pa pema,* this place is a good one. For the use of *pa-* as a prefix, see Grammars. Note: in a few cases *-pa* suffix is used to make verbs from adjectives Cf. *-nene, nenepa*; *-oga, ogopa*; *-wongo,* (*w*)*ongopa*; *-kali, karipa* (for *kalipa*).

Pa, v. give to, bestow on, present with. Unless used in the Infinitive, *pa* must necessarily have an object pfx. This restriction of use leads to the use of *toa* (A) in its place when all reference to a person as object is omitted, i.e. in the sense 'give, give away, bestow, distribute, present'. But *toa* is vague, and means 'take away' as well as 'give', e.g. *aliitoa nguo,* he presented the garment, or he removed, took away the garment. *Ilitolewa,* it was given, or it was withdrawn. See *toa,* v. (A). *-pa mgongo,* turn the back on, *-pa uso,* face, *-pa radhi,* content, satisfy, *-pa mkono,* congratulate, condole with. *-pa salamu,* salute. Rf. *jipa,* varies with the idea attached to the Rf., e.g. *jipa ujinga,* play the fool, be purposely silly. *Jipa mali,* be a grandee, make a foolish show. *Jipa moyo,* take heart, gain courage. *Jipa salama,* consider oneself safe. *Jipa ubwana,* domineer, tyrannize, and so on. Ps. **Pewa,** with a personal subject only, be given, be presented with, receive as a gift, e.g. *nimepewa,* I have been given (a present, &c.). St. **Peka,** seldom used. Prep. **Pea** or **Pia** (and there is a St. **Palika** as if from *palia,* rarely used), give to, &c. *Sumu umenipiani?* why have you given me poison? Rp. of Prep. **Peana,** e.g. *peana mikono* (*salamu*), conclude a bargain, exchange greetings. Cs. none in use. Rp. **Pana,** e.g. *ahadi* (*mikono, zawadi*), make mutual promises (engagements, presents). **Kipa,** n. *vi-* that which gives, governing a noun following, e.g. *kipa mkono,* a fee given at a wedding for special attendance. *Kipa imara,* that which gives strength, hence, used by some Christian bodies for the rite of Confirmation. **Kipaji,** n. *vi-* (1) a presentation, a present, donation, gift. *Kipaji cha Mungu*, a gift of God. **Kipawa**, n. *vi-* a gift. **Mpaji**, n. *wa-* donor, giver, benefactor, a generous, liberal person. But esp. of God, e.g. *mpaji na kupa ni Mungu*, the real (only) giver is God—also *mpaji asiye-pewa*, He who always gives and never receives. **Paji**, n. *ma-* like *kipaji*, also offerings, i.e. the offerings to the spirits, in *kutambika*, which see. **Uapo**, n. and **Wapo**, n. rarely used, a giving, a gift. **Upaji**, n. giving, free giving, liberality, open-handedness, bounty, gift, esp. of God, as the Giver.

Paa, n. a gazelle, esp. of the very small species, an impala.

Paa, v. (A) go up, ascend, mount, rise—like *panda*, which is more common, and cf. *kwea*. *Usingizi ulini-paa*, sleep left me. *Sikukuu ya Ku-paa*, the name given to the festival of the Ascension. Prep. **Palia**. St. and Pot. **Palika**. Cs. **Paaza**, **Paza**, and **Paliza**, raise, cause to rise. *Paaza (paliza) sauti*, lift up the voice, speak in a loud tone. *Paza pumzi*, draw the breath in, inhale (*shusha pumzi*, exhale). Cv. **Paua** used in special sense of preparing the roof of a native hut, viz. fixing the cross-sticks (*pao*) to which the thatch is fastened. *Paua nyumba*, fix rafters on a house. Ps. **Pauliwa**. St. **Pa-uka**. Prep. **Paulia**. **Kipaa**, n. *vi-* dim. of *paa*, (1) a small roof, roof of a shed, &c., (2) one of the sides of the four-sided roof of a native hut, usually one of the smaller slopes, overlapped by the larger ones (*ma-paa*). *Kipaa cha mbele (cha nyuma)*, the front (back) slope of a roof. (Cf. *kisusi*.) **Kipao**, n. *vi-* act (means, way) of mounting up. **Mpalio**, n. *mi-* a rising in the throat or nostril, a choke. **Paa**, n. *ma-* (1) the sloping thatched side of a native roof—the smaller sides or ends being *kipaa*; (2) the roof of a hut (in general). Thus *paa la makuti*, a roof of coco-nut-leaf thatch. *Paa la mgongo*, a gable roof. *Mapaa manne*, a four-sided roof. **Pao**, n. *ma-*, also *upao (pao)* (sometimes heard as *pau*), (1) long thin pole used in making the roof of a native hut, laid across the larger poles (*kombamoyo*) used as rafters, and carrying the thatch, and hence (2) long thin pieces of iron, whether flat or round, e.g. *pao za chuma*, rod iron, iron bars. (Cf. *paraga, paramia*.) Note: the deriv. of *pao* is doubtful. It may be derived from Port. *pao*, stick, cudgel, pole, wood, &c. Cf. *bao* in this respect.

Paa, v. (B) (also *para*, which see), scrape off, scrape up, e.g. *paa samaki* or *magamba ya samaki*, clean a fish for cooking by scraping off the scales. So of potatoes, gum copal, &c. *Paa moto*, convey fire, by getting a live ember on a sherd, i.e. *twaa moto kwa kigae*. *Paa nchi*, scrape, paw the ground, e.g. as a horse. *Paa karata*, clear off the cards, i.e. win a game. (Cf. *para*.) Ps. **Pawa**. St. **Palika**. Prep. **Palia**, (1) as above, e.g. *uni-palie samaki*, clean the fish for me. (2) also esp. of cleaning ground under cultivation, i.e. which has been once hoed, i.e. 'collect weeds off, hoe the surface of the ground'. D.Prep. **Palilia** is used of the subsequent operations, piling grass (rubbish, weeds) in heaps, or round the roots of trees or plants, &c. Cs. **Paliliza**, (1) employ in cleaning-work; (2) fig. stir up feeling, e.g. *paliliza ugomvi*, raise a quarrel. (Cf. *chochelea, vu-mbulia*.) Cs. **Paaza** and **Paraza**, used of coarse grinding of grain, or pounding with a pestle and mortar (as contr. with *saga*, fine grinding between millstones). Rp. **Paana**. **Mapalio**, n. plur. time, place, process of hoeing, i.e. not the first hoeing (*lima*) but the cross-hoeing, cleaning the ground between trees or growing crops. **Mpalilio**, n. *mi-*, also **Mpa-lio**, n. *mi-*, like *mapalio*. **Mpalilizi**, n. *wa-*, **Mpalizi**, n. *wa-* one who hoes up the soil and weeds among growing crops. **Palizi**, n. *ma-* weeds which have grown in a cultivated plantation. *Kulima palizi*, like *palilia*. (Cf. *kuna, komba*, v.)

Paanda, n. See **Panda**, n.

Paaza, v. Cs. of *paa*, v. (A) and (B).

Pacha, v. (1) bear (grow) more than one shoot (plant, &c.) from one seed, i.e. like rice, also of the banana plant which sends off shoots from the main plant, send off shoots; (2) of fruit, bear, growing in clusters, not singly. St. **Pachika**, secure in a particular position, i.e. between two things, fix, stick, e.g. *pachika mshale*, adjust an arrow to the bowstring. *Pachika kisu mshipini* (*kiunoni*), stick a knife into the girdle (at the waist, i.e. between the body and belt or loin-cloth). *Shada la maua la kujipachika sikioni*, a small bunch of flowers to wear over the ear, i.e. between head and ears. Rf. *Jipachika*, sit astride of, bestride. Ps. **Pachikwa**. Cs. **Pachisha**. Rp. **Pachana**, grow in clusters. Cv. **Pachua**, take out anything which has been placed in position between two or more things. **Pacha**, n. (— and *ma-*) (1) a twin, one of twins; (2) something resembling another, counterpart. *Zaa* (*zaliwa*) *pacha*, bear (be born) twins. *Pachapacha*, like twins, similar, e.g. *nyumba hizi ni pachapacha*, these houses are a pair, exactly alike. (3) a bifurcation, cross-roads, also anything similar of form, e.g. *pacha za vidole*, the spaces between the fingers. *Njia pacha*, a place where two or more roads meet. Also **Pachipachi**, with the same meanings. And with *ya*, as a Prep. *pachipachi ya*, in between two things, in the space between. (Cf. *futika, chomeka, kati*.)

Padre,* n. *ma-* a clergyman, a priest. (Cf. *kasisi, kuhani*. Port.)

Pafu, n. *ma-* a lung. (Cf. *yavuyavu, buhumu*, and *punu* of the living organ.)

Pagaa, v. (1) carry—esp. as a load, on head or shoulders, but also more generally, e.g. of charms worn on the neck; (2) used of the influence or power of an evil spirit over a person, possess (i.e. perh. carry along against his will). Ps. **Pagawa**, e.g. *amepagawa na pepo*, he is possessed by a spirit. Cs. **Pagaza**, e.g. (1) cause to carry a load, engage as a porter; (2) bring evil on, i.e. illness, calamity, an evil spirit; (3) followed by *kwa*, nonplus, dumbfound, astound, e.g. *alitupagaza kwa maneno yake*, he dumbfounded us with his statement; (4) *pagaza maneno, alitupagaza maneno*, he made us hear his words, whether we would or not. **Mpagazi**, n. *wa-* carrier, bearer, caravan-porter. **Pagao**, n. *ma-* a charm (against possession by a spirit, or other calamity). (Cf. *kago, hirizi, talasimu*.) **Upagazi**, n. (1) work (profession, pay, &c.) of a caravan porter; (2) witchcraft, being bewitched or possessed by a spirit. (Cf. *chukua, beba*.)

Pagua, v. See **Pogoa**.

Pahali,* n. See **Mahali**.

Paipu,* n. used of a motor horn, claxon, ship's siren, or anything similar. *Kupiga paipu*, to sound a horn. (Eng. pipe.)

Paja, n. *ma-* thigh, ham, of human beings and animals. Also plur. of **Upaja**, with the same sense. (Cf. *kiweo*.)

-paji, a. See under **Pa**, v.

Paji, n. *ma-* (1) see under **Pa**, v.; (2) *paji la uso*, forehead. Also called *kikomo cha uso*, and **Kipaji**, n. *vi-*.

Paka, n. (— and *ma-* of size) a cat. *Paka dume*, a tom-cat. *Paka shume*, or *shume la paka*, large tom-cat. A half-wild cat in a town is sometimes called *mnunda* or *nunda*. **Kipaka**, n. *vi-* dim.

Paka, v. (A) apply, lay (on), spread (on), usually of some greasy or adhesive substance, i.e. daub, smear, anoint, paint on, e.g. *paka mtoto* *mafuta*, smear a child with oil (ointment). *Paka rangi*, paint. *Paka chokaa*, plaster, also whitewash. *Paka udongo*, plaster with mud (clay, earth). Dur. **Pakaa**, same as *paka*. Ps. **Pakwa.** Rp. **Pakana** (but see under **Paka**, v. (B)). Prep. **Pakia**, (1) e.g. of an instrument used for painting, &c.; (2) put (take) on board a vessel, cart, train, &c.—of passengers or cargo. Load up, embark, stow, pile up. *Wakaunda merikebu wakapakia vyakula*, and they built a vessel and loaded it with food. Ps. **Pakiwa**, (1) be spread (with), daubed, &c.; (2) be loaded, have on board. D.Prep. **Pakilia**, usually (1) ship or load goods (a cargo, passengers, &c.) to (for, in, by, &c.); (2) lay upon, charge up, laid to the charge of, put on the shoulders of, blame, and more generally, pile up, make heaps of. Cs. of D.Prep. **Pakiliza**, with same meanings as *pakilia* in an Inten. sense. Rp. of D.Prep. **Pakiliana** (1) load one on top of another, pile up in heaps, and (2) of mutual recrimination, countercharges, &c. Ten. **Pakata**, usually restricted to—hold a child or anything on the knee, lap, or shoulder. Ps. of Ten. **Pakatwa.** St. and Pot. of Ten. **Pakatika**, e.g. *mtoto huyu hapakatiki, hufurukuta*, there is no holding this child, he is so restless. Prep. of Ten. **Pakatia.** Cs. of Ten. **Pakatisha.** Cs. of Dir. **Pakaza**, Inten. apply, lay on, smear, rub on, e.g. *hupakaza mtoto dawa mwili mzima*, they smear the child's whole body with medicaments. Cs. of Prep. **Pakiza**, get freight stowed on board, see to shipping, cargo, load on a cart or train, &c., contract for freight, with either the vessel (cart, vehicle, boat, &c.) loaded or the cargo (load, freight) as object. *Pakiza gari*, load a cart. *Pakiza nazi*, ship coco-nuts. *Vitu vipakizwavyo*, exports. *Jipakiza*, take on one's own conscience, charge oneself with, undertake, be responsible for. Rp. of Prep. **Pakiana**, (1) of people getting themselves on board or huddle togethe on board; (2) daub or smear one another, &c. Cv. **Pakua**, (1) take off what has been put on or applied, e.g. take out, take off, unload; (2) commonly used of taking cooked food off the fire—dish up, serve up, bring to the table; (3) remove honey from a hive. Ps. of Cv. **Pakuliwa.** St. and Pot. of Cv. **Pakulika**, e.g. be fit for serving up, &c. Prep. of Cv. **Pakulia.** Cs. of Cv. **Pakulisha.** Rp. of Cv. **Pakuana. Kipakasa**, n. *vi-* one of the presents given to a bride by the bridegroom on the day of the marriage. **Kipaku**, n. *vi-* small spot, speck, patch of colour or coloured stuff, e.g. used of mottled or speckled colouring of animals and birds. *-a kipaku*, or *kipaku* alone, mottled, speckled, e.g. *kuku kipaku*, a speckled fowl. *Kipakupaku*, in the same sense. **Mapakio**, n. plur. **Mapakizi**, n. plur. (1) arrangements connected with shipping and dispatch of goods, conveyance on board, payment of freightage, &c.; (2) goods shipped, cargo, freight, &c. **Mpaka**, n. *wa-*, **Mpakaji**, n. *wa-*, and **Mpaki**, n. *wa-* a plasterer, a painter, i.e. *mpaka chokaa*, a plasterer, *mpaka rangi*, a painter. **Mpakato**, n. *mi-* (1) something applied, stuck on, e.g. a patch, a plaster, a bandage, &c.; (2) act of holding anything on the knee or lap, &c. **Mpakizi**, n. *wa-* (1) a shipper, a stevedore, one who sees goods or freight put on board a ship, train, cart, &c.; (2) also same as *mpakaji*. **Mpako**, n. *mi-* a plastering, plaster. *Mpako wa rangi*, applying paint, painting. **Mpakuzi**, n. *wa-* (1) one who unloads a ship, train, &c.; (2) one who serves up food. **Paku**, n. *ma-* amplic. of *kipaku*. **Upakio**, n. **Upako**, n. and **Upakizi**, n. (1) applying, plastering, &c.; (2) loading a ship, train, &c., placing goods on board; (3) freight, freightage. **Upakuzi**,

n. unloading, taking off anything applied, ladling out, serving out, distribution, esp. of food.

Paka, v. (B) (prob. from same root as above, but given separately for convenience because of the apparently different meaning), make the boundaries of, fix the bounds of. *Paka shamba*, make the bounds of a plantation. No Ps. or other derivatives are in use except Rp. *pakana* (which rather points to this verb being identical with *paka*, v. (A), the derivatives of which have become restricted or extended in use as shown). Rp. **Pakana**, have a common boundary, be adjacent, adjoin, be next to each other—with a Cs. **Pakanisha**, lay out side by side, cause to adjoin. **Mpaka**, n. *mi-* boundary, limit, border, term. *Piga* (*weka*) *mpaka*, fix a boundary, lay down a limit. *Ruka mpaka*, trespass, break bounds, also, go too far, i.e. be presumptuous, &c. *Mpaka mmoja*, adjacent, bordering, adjoining. Also used as a prep. up to, to, as far as, till, until, to the time of—like *hata*. *Alifika mpaka kwetu*, he came as far as our country. *Nikae mpaka lini?* how long am I to remain? (Cf. *hata*, *hadi*, *upeo*.)

Pakaa, v. See under **Paka**, v. (A).

Pakacha, n. *ma-* (1) a light basket—used for carrying fish or fruit, &c., make by plaiting part of a coco-nut leaf (cf. *kikapu*); (2) also *pakaja*, night-robber, one who waylays passers-by. (Cf. *mwizi*, *mnyang'anyi*.) **Kipakacha**, n. *vi-* dim. of (1).

Pakaja, n. *ma-*. See **Pakacha** (2).

Pakana, v. See under **Paka**, v. (B).

Pakanga, n. rue, wormwood.

Pakanya, n. *ma-* money or present given as compensation, or to end a quarrel or ill feeling.

Pakasa, v. twist thread, string, or rope. (Cf. *pota*, *sokota*.)

Pakata, v., **Pakaza**, v. See under **Paka**, v. (A).

Pake, a. form of *-ake*, his, her.

Paketi,* n. a packet, e.g. of cigarettes. (Eng. packet.)

Pakia, v., **Pakiza**, v. See under **Paka**, v. (A).

Pako, a. form of *-ako*, which see.

Paku, n. *ma-*, **Pakua**, v. See under **Paka**, v. (A).

Pakuogea, n. sometimes **Pakogea**, i.e. *mahali pa kuogea*, a place to wash in, bathroom. See under **Oga**, v.

Palahala, n. sable antelope.

Palama, v. See **Parama**.

Pale, form of the dem. *-le*, agreeing with *mahali* and locatives in *-ni*, that, that yonder. As an adv. there, in that spot, then, at that time. So *pale pale*, on the spot, at once, just then, just there. *Pale* indicates distance, and great distance is indicated by prolonging the last vowel and raising the pitch of the voice proportionately, i.e. *pale-e-e*.

Palia, v. See under **Paa**, v. (A) and (B).

Palilia, v., **Palizi**, n. *ma-*. See under **Paa**, v. (B).

Palikuwa, v. Past tense of *-wa*, v. be, with pfx. *pa*, of place. Often with *na* in narrative, e.g. *palikuwa na mtu*, there was once a man.

Pamba,* n. (1) cotton, the produce of the cotton plant *mpamba*, lint. *Nguo ya pamba*, cotton cloth, calico. (2) Sometimes used for the common *pambo* (which see), ornament, &c. **Kipamba**, n. *vi-*, also **Upamba**, n. a small bit (tuft, plug, patch), of raw cotton (cotton-wool, lint), e.g. for medical application. (Pers. پنبه.)

Pamba, v. (1) adorn, deck out, decorate, embellish—and of a house, furnish, fit for occupation; (2) cover, e.g. *wadudu wameupamba mti*, the insects have covered the tree; (3) also in certain senses, arrange, prepare. *Pamba maiti*, prepare a corpse for burial. *Jipamba*, put on a gay dress (ornaments, &c.). Ps. **Pambwa**. St. and Pot. **Pambika**. Prep. **Pambia**, adorn for (to, &c.), also give a finishing touch to, finish off, e.g. a dish of food for the table. Cs. **Pambisha,** e.g. undertake to decorate, furnish, &c. Rp. **Pambana,** dress each other, decorate each other, &c., but usu. extended in meaning, see below. Cv. **Pambua,** remove adornment, disfigure, disfurnish, &c. Ps. **Pambuliwa.** St. **Pambulika.** Prep. **Pambulia.** Cs. **Pambulisha. Kipambo,** n. *vi-* an ornament, ornamental work, a fitting, furniture of a house. *Nyumba hii haina kipambo,* this house is unfurnished, i.e. has no nice things in it. **Mpamba,** n. *wa-* governing a noun following, one who adorns, a decorator. **Mpambaji,** n. *wa-* (1) one who makes a habit of decorating, &c.; (2) an undertaker, one of the professional attendants who with the *mwosha,* prepares a dead body for burial. **Mpambe,** n. *wa-* a person who is dressed up in finery, one bedecked with ornaments, in showy costume, esp. of the small girls dressed up on the day of a wedding and told off to wait on the bridegroom and to fan him. **Mpambi,** n. *wa-* a decorator, of a house, person, &c., e.g. a lady's maid, valet, &c. **-pambe,** a. adorned, dressed up, decorated. **Pambo,** n. *ma-* ornament, decoration, embellishment, and so of a house, fittings, furniture—of dress, finery, jewellery, fine clothes, &c. (Includes any kind of personal and other adornment.) **Upambo,** n. decoration, adornment, furnishing a house, furniture, decorations. (Cf. *vaa, funika, andaa,* also *pambana* and *pambazua.*

Pambaja, v. (1) embrace, clasp with the arms, as a mother her child on her lap or thigh; (2) obtain food or clothing by one's own efforts, little by little (also *pambanya*). **Pambaja,** n. an embrace. *Piga pambaja,* embrace. (Cf. *kumbatia.*)

Pambana, v. come together, get into contact, whether pleasant or otherwise, thus of ships. (1) go abreast, lie alongside, but usually (2) collide, fall foul of each other, jostle together. Prep. **Pambania.** Cs. **Pambanisha,** e.g. (1) set side by side, bring together, exhibit, compare; (2) set in contrast, cause conflict (opposition, contradiction, confusion) in (or among), e.g. *pambanisha maneno,* make conflicting statements, show to be contradictory, &c., and of persons, make trouble between, set at variance. Cs. (2) **Pambanya,** (1) browbeat, contradict, or prevaricate, speak with a loud blustering voice so as to confuse people; (2) get together little by little until the amount required is got. (Cf. *pambaja.*) Cv. **Pambanua,** put together for purposes of comparison, and so discriminate, pick out, distinguish, select, clear up, explain. Ps. **Pambanuliwa.** St. **Pambanuka.** Prep. **Pambanulia. Mapambano,** plur. contact, comparisons, collisions. **Mpambano,** n. *mi-* a colliding, confronting, encounter. **Upambano,** n. *ma-* comparison, collision, quarrel. **Upambanuzi,** discrimination, power (character, inclination) to select, choose, discriminate. (Prob. from *pamba,* the root-meaning of which appears to be, put together, bring into contact. Cf. also forms under *pambazua.*)

Pambanya, v. (1) see under **Pambana,** v.; (2) obtain food or clothing by one's own efforts, little by little, like *pambaja* (2).

Pambauka, v., **Pambauko,** n. *ma-*. See under **Pambazua.**

Pambazua, v. make clear, explain, e.g. *pambazua maneno,* speak plainly, make a case clear. St. **Pambazuka** is chiefly used in a purely physical sense, of the dawn—become clear, get light, be daytime. *Kumepambazuka,* morning has come. Prep. **Pambazukia,** dawn upon, e.g. *tumepambazukiwa,* dawn has risen upon us, it has found us asleep, we are late in getting up. **Pambauko,** n. *ma-*

dawn, light of morning. **Pambazuko,** n. *ma-* dawn, light of morning. (Cf. *weupe, asubuhi, alfajiri, pamba, pambua.* Prob. a Cv. of Cs. form of *pamba,* see note under *pambana.*)

-pambe, a. See under **Pamba, v.**

Pambizo, n. *ma-,* also **Pembizo,** margin, edge, outskirts, &c., e.g. the suburbs of a town or village. (Cf. *kiunga, kando*). *Weka kitabu katika pambizo la meza,* place the book on the edge of the table.

Pambo, n. *ma-,* **Pambua,** v. See under **Pamba, v.**

Pamoja, a. form of *-moja*—agreeing with *mahali,* and locatives in *-ni,* one, the same. Also as adv., at one place, at one time, all together, unanimously. *Pamoja na,* together with, at the same place (time) as, in company of.

Pana, verb-form—agreeing with *mahali,* there is, it has.

-pana, a. broad, wide, flat, level. *Nchi pana pana,* a flat country, a plain. (Cf. *sawa, uwanda, tambarare.*) *Bahari pana pana,* broad, open sea. **Panua,** v. make broad, broaden, widen, spread apart, open out. *Panua miguu,* put legs apart, also, take long strides. Ps. **Panuliwa.** St. **Panuka.** Prep. **Panulia. Mapana,** n. plur. the wide or broad part of a thing, flat side, breadth, width, diameter. *Meza hii ina mapana,* this table is broad. **Upana,** n. width, breadth. (Cf. Pers. and Hind. پہن wide, broad.)

Panapo, verb-form, where there is (are, was, were), or, there is (are, was, were) there—according as *-po* represents the relative or demonstrative.

Panda, n. (— and *ma-*) (1) parting, division, fork, bifurcation, e.g. *njia panda,* or *njia ya panda,* the place where roads meet, cross-ways. *Panda za mto,* branches (arms) of a river. *Panda za mti,* arms of a tree. *Kijiti cha panda,* a forked stick, for getting fruit from a tree, &c.; (2) a cross-piece, e.g. short arm of a cross (transept of a church, &c.); (3) a catapult, i.e. made of a piece of forked stick; (4) a trumpet. *Piga panda,* blow a trumpet. (5) *jongoo panda,* see under *jongoo.* (Cf. *pacha.*)

Panda, v. (A) (1) go up, ascend, climb, mount, get upon, ride upon (cf. *kwea*); (2) fig. rise (of price), increase (in number, weight, quantity, &c.) (cf. *zidi*); (3) cover (of a male animal); (4) be steep, i.e. *mlima huu umepanda sana,* this mount is very steep. *Panda chomboni,* go aboard a vessel (also *ingia*). *Chombo kimepanda pwani* (*mwamba*), the vessel has run ashore (on a rock). *Panda farasi* (*juu ya farasi*), mount a horse, get on horseback. Also used of possession by a spirit, e.g. *atampanda huyu shetani,* this evil spirit will come out of him. *Pepo atapanda kichwani,* the spirit will rise to his head, of the stage in exorcism when the exorcist causes the spirit to come to the head of the patient. *Panda mti* (*katika mti*), climb up a tree. Ps. **Pandwa.** St. and Pot. **Pandika.** Prep. **Pandia,** (1) get up with (to, by, &c.). *Ngazi ya kupandia,* a ladder to go up by. (2) hang around sponging for food and drink. Cs. **Pandisha,** also **Panza,** cause to go up, raise, hoist, increase. *Panza mtambo* (*wa bunduki*), cock the trigger of a gun. *Amekipanza chombo mwambani,* he has run the vessel on a rock. *Panza suruali,* pull up the trousers, i.e. to avoid a muddy place, &c. *Mganga alimpandisha shetani kichwani,* the medicine man caused the evil spirit to mount to the head. Rp. **Pandana,** get on one another, and so, overlap, cross each other, lie across each other. Rp. of Cs. **Pandishana. Kipandio,** n. *vi-* dim. e.g. rungs of a ladder, &c. **Kipandisho,** n. *vi-* something which causes to rise, hence used for a sharp sign in music. **Mpanda,** n. *wa-* (governing a noun following), and

Mpandaji, n. *wa-* (1) a climber; (2) a sponger, i.e. one who hangs round sponging for food and drink. **Mpando,** n. *mi-* a climbing, mounting, ascent. **Pandio,** n. *ma-* means (act, method) of climbing, e.g. steps cut in the stem of a coco-nut palm. **Upandaji,** n. climbing, ascending. (Cf. *kwea, paa,* v. (A), and *rondea.*)

Panda, v. (B) sow, plant, set in the ground (whether seed or plant). Ps. **Pandwa.** St. and Pot. **Pandika.** Prep. **Pandia.** Cs. of St. **Pandikiza,** plant out, e.g. of seedlings from a nursery into the plantation, &c. **Mpanda,** n. *wa-* (governing a noun following), **Mpandaji,** n. *wa-*, and **Mpanzi,** n. *wa-* a planter, one who plants. **Mpando,** n. *mi-* act (process, method, &c.) of planting, time or season of planting. Also of a row or line of plants, cuttings, seeds, &c., e.g. *mipando kumi ya mihindi,* ten rows of maize. **Pandikizo,** n. *ma-* (1) act of planting out, i.e. seedlings grown in a nursery; (2) seedlings planted out from a nursery, &c. **Pando,** n. *ma-* like *mpando.* **Upandaji,** n., also **Upanzi,** n., planting, sowing seeds, &c.

Pande, n. *ma-* (1) see under **Kipande**; (2) *kupiga pande,* to become vexed, be arrogant, bad tempered.

Pandikiza, v. See under **Panda,** v. (B).

Pandikizi, n. *ma-*. See under **Kipande.**

Pandikizo, n. *ma-*, **Pando,** n. *ma-*. See under **Panda,** v. (B).

Pandio, n. *ma-*. See under **Panda,** v. (A).

Panga, n. *ma-* (1) matchet, a kind of large knife used for cutting trees, bush, &c. (cf. *mundu*); (2) a kind of shell-fish, bivalve with broad, flat, sharp-edged shell; (3) plur. of *upanga.*

Panga, v. (1) generally set in line, put in order, arrange, also (2) hire, rent, take for use on hire, e.g. *panga mizigo,* set down loads in a row, or in a special order. *Jina la kupanga,* an adopted name, nickname. *Panga askari,* draw up soldiers in line. *Panga udugu* (*urafiki, umama, ubaba,* &c.), arrange brotherhood (friendship, motherhood, fatherhood, &c.), used of arranging with a person to be to him as a brother (friend, son, or daughter, &c.). This type of friendship, &c., which is not now so strong as it used to be, involves all the privileges, responsibilities, &c., of the relationship concerned. *Ndugu* (*rafiki, mama, baba*) *wa kupanga,* a brother (friend, mother, father, &c.) by arrangement. *Nimempanga udugu,* I have arranged a friendship with him (of the particular sort of friendship explained above). *Panga nyumba* (*chumba*), rent a house (a room). (3) stick up for one's rights, show fight in order to ensure one's position, rights, &c. Ps. **Pangwa,** (1) be arranged, &c.; (2) be let on hire, of a house, &c. St. and Pot. **Pangika.** Prep. **Pangia.** Cs. **Pangisha,** (1) often Inten. e.g. *pangisha watu karamuni,* see that the guests are duly arranged at a feast; (2) hire, take for use on hire; also let out on hire. *Nimempangisha nyumba,* I have let a house to him, or I have rented a house from him. *Unipangishe,* allow me to hire. Rp. **Pangana,** e.g. (1) of people arranging themselves in rows, as soldiers, guests, &c. Also *pangana safu,* fall into line, dress, of soldiers. (2) *pangana urafiki,* &c., of people arranging friendship, &c., with each other. D. Prep. **Pangilia,** set in rows upon rows, i.e. interpose, intersperse, put in between rows, put in alternate places, e.g. *pangilia mapando,* plant crops in regular order or rotation. Rp. of D. Prep. **Pangiliana,** succeed in regular order or rotation. Cv. **Pangua,** remove or disarrange what has been set in order. Cs. **Pangusa** (seldom *pangusha*), Inten. usu. of sweeping or dusting or removing dust, e.g. *pangusa vumbi ka ka vyumba hivi,* remove the dust from these rooms. *Pangusa vyombo* dust the furniture. Ps. **Panguswa**, St. **Pangusika.** Prep. **Pangusia.** (Cf. *futa, sugua, ondoa.*) **Mpanga,** n. *wa-*, **Mpangaji,** n. *wa-* usu. a tenant, one who takes on hire. **Mpangishaji,** n. *wa-*, **Mpangishi,** n. *wa* one who lets on hire. **Mpango,** n. *mi-* (1) act (process, manner, time, &c.) of arranging, setting in order, placing in line, marshalling; (2) act (terms, method, &c.) of hiring, renting, &c. **Pangilio,** n. *ma-* interposition, succession, alternation, rotation, e.g. *mapangilio ya mapando,* rotation of crops. Also a lode or vein of metal, &c., enclosed in rock. *pangilio la madini.* **Upangaji,** n. like *mpango,* also rent, money paid for hire.

Panga za wazuka, n. a herb, *Achyranthes* sp., the juice of the leaves is used as a medicine for dysentery.

Pange, n. *ma-* a kind of large biting fly, a gadfly.

Pangilio, n. *ma-*. See under **Panga,** v.

Pango, n. (— and of size *ma-*) a hollowed-out place, natural recess, cave, grotto, den, hole, lair of an animal, esp. of a large one. **Kipango,** n. *vi-* dim. e.g. as of a rat hole, &c. (Cf. *shimo, tundu, uvungu.*)

Pangu, a. form of *-angu,* which see.

Pangua, v., **Pangusa,** v. See under **Panga,** v.

Pania, v. double up, turn up, fasten up, used of clothing, e.g. *pania mikono ya koti,* turn up the sleeves of the coat. *Pania suruali,* turn up the trouser legs. *Pania kanzu,* double up a *kanzu* and tuck the bottom part round the waist, to prevent it from trailing, or getting wet in grass covered with dew, &c.

Panja, n. *ma-* the temples, side of the forehead where the hair recedes.

Panju, n. a kind of fish not considered good eating by Europeans.

Panua, v. See under **-pana.**

Panya, n. (— and of size, *ma-*) a rat—of any common kind. **Kipanya,** n. *vi-* dim. a young rat, a mouse. Prov. *Paka akiondoka panya hutawala,* when the cat is away, the rat rules. *Panya ya mkono,* children stretch out their arm and strike quickly the muscle of the upper arm, and a movement is seen, this is called *panya ya mkono.* (Cf. *buku.*)

Panza, n. the coco-nut left in the shell after the soft part has been scraped out.

Panza, v. See under **Panda,** v. (A).

Panzi, n. *ma-* (1) a grasshopper; (2) a flying fish.

Pao, a. form of *-ao,* which see.

Pao,* n. *ma-* (1) see under **Paa,** v. (A); (2) (—) clubs, in cards. (Port. *pao.*)

Papa, adv. used to strengthen *hapa* (which see). Thus *papa hapa,* just here, at this very place, at this very time, now, on the spot.

Papa, n. a shark. Different sorts are: *jodari, kapungu, kinengwe, papa upanga, sansuri,* &c. Dried shark, *papa kavu,* is a favourite relish, and largely imported.

Papa, v. (A) (1) tremble, palpitate, flutter, e.g. of the heart—and so (2) be agitated, doubtful, anxious. *Papa roho,* have a throbbing of the heart, e.g. after running, or a fright, &c. Prep. **Papia,** usu. restricted to hurry over anything, eat voraciously, greedily, in a hurry without regarding or waiting for others. St. of Ten. **Papatika,** flutter, move convulsively, flap the wings wildly, e.g. of a fowl. **Kipapa,** n. *vi-* a fluttering, convulsive movement, palpitation, &c. **Kipapatiko,** n. *vi-*, **Kipapatio,** n. *vi-* little flapping object, feathery waving end, e.g. of a fin or feather. **Mpapatiko,** n. *mi-* fluttering, throbbing. **Papara,** n. haste. *Mbona una papara?* why are you in such a hurry? **Papatiko,** n. *ma-* (1) like *mpapatiko;* (2) the arm, or part of a bird or fowl on which the wing grows. **Papio,** n. (1) unnecessary haste, agitation;

(2) greediness, covetousness. **Papo,** n. *ma-* a throb, flutter, palpitation, e.g. of the heart, *papo la moyo.* (Cf. *pupa.*)

Papa, v. (B), allow exudation, be porous, let through (a liquid), i.e. as of the mud walls of a house, a porous earthenware vessel, used for cooling water, &c. To absorb water is *nywa* and *sharabu.* (Cf. *rishai.*)

Papai,* n. *ma-* a pawpaw, fruit of the *mpapai,* which see. (Hind. پپیا.)

Papara, n. See under **Papa,** v. (A).

Papasa, v. (1) stroke with the hand, touch gently, rub lightly; (2) grope about, feel about, feel one's way in the dark with hands spread out. Ps. **Papaswa.** St. and Pot. **Papasika.** Prep. **Papasia.** Cs. **Papasisha.** Rp. **Papasana.**

Papasi, n. *ma-* the Spirillum tick, *Ornithodoros moubata,* which infects with Spirillum tick fever, *homa ya papasi.*

Papatika, v., Papatiko, n. *ma-.* See under **Papa,** v. (A).

Papatua, v. (1) remove the husk or shell (of a vegetable or fruit), e.g. *papatua maganda ya mbaazi,* shell beans; (2) shine, be bright, be clean and white. St. and Pot. **Papatuka,** go away, come off, e.g. *nipapatuke,* clear off from me, leave me alone.

Papayuka, v. same as *payuka,* which see under **Paya.**

Papi, n. plur. of *upapi,* which see.

Papia, v., **Papio,** n., **Papo, n.** *ma-.* See under **Papa,** v. (A).

Papo, adv. related to *papa,* adv. (which see), with *hapo* following, i.e. *papo hapo,* also *papo kwa papo,* in that place or time referred to, there, then.

Papura, v. tear, claw, scratch, lacerate, rend in pieces, e.g. of wild beasts, birds of prey, thorns, combatants. *Papura uso kwa makucha,* scratch the face with the nails (or claws). Also fig. of quarrels, abuse, &c. St. and Pot. **Papurika.** Ps. **Papuriwa.** Prep. **Papuria. Mpapuro,** n. *mi-* a scratching, a scratch, esp. with nails or claws.

Papuri,* n. *ma-* a thin cake flavoured with asafoetida. (Cf. *mvuje.* Hind. پاپڑ.)

Para,* n. (A) *ma-* a cake of semsem. (Hind. پوری.)

Para, n. (B) (1) see under **Para, v.;** (2) baldness, a bald patch on the head. (Cf. *paa,* n.) *Para la kichwa,* a bald, or shaved head. **Kipara,** n. *vi-* dim. a clean-shaved patch, a bald place on the head, a tonsure. *Mtu wa kikoa asipolipa ana kipara cheupe,* a member of a mess (or club), if he does not pay, has a bald patch, i.e. is a marked man. **Upaa,** n. but usu. **Upara,** n. (1) the crown of the head; (2) baldness.

Para, v., also **Paa, v.** (B) which see, scrape. Prep. **Paria,** scrape with (for, &c.); sometimes used for getting money, &c., by gambling. Rd. **Parapara,** e.g. of a horse pawing the ground. Cs. **Paaza** and **Paraza.** Cv. **Parua,** but usu. **Parura,** scratch, scrape. Cs. **Paruza,** Inten. (1) be rough, be grating, graze, grind coarsely; (2) fig. be harsh (to), be un- (feeling towards); (3) rub, of a rough thing, i.e. *paruza kiberiti,* strike a match. Ps. **Paruzwa.** Prep. **Paruzia.** Rp. **Paruzana,** e.g. of boats, &c., scraping against each other. **Mparuzi,** n. *wa-* one who does not work smoothly, a bungler. **Mparuzo,** n. *mi-* a scraping, rough work, bungling, &c. **Para,** n. a scraping, sliding, gliding. **Paruparu,** adv. roughly, coarsely—used of rough, untidy work, wanting care and finish.

Parafujo,* n. a screw, i.e. nail with a spiral groove, also *msumari wa parafujo, msumari wa hesi, skrubu.* (Port. *parafuso.*)

Paraga, v. swarm up a tree, climb by grasping with arms and legs. **Parago,** n. *ma-* a stick used for sitting on when picking cloves. (Cf. *sombea, paa,* v.)

Parakacha, n. the sound made by dry leaves, &c., rustling.

Parama, v. be lacking, be wanting (i.e. essential qualities, of expected or proper sentiments, &c.); be sterile, unfertile, barren, esp. of trees. *Mnazi umeparama*, the coco-nut is barren. *Uso wake umeparama* (used of a person at a mourning ceremony (or entertainment, &c.) who does not show that he is sorry (or pleased, &c.). *Usingizi uliniparama*, I lacked sleep, sleep left me at night, I could not sleep. (Cf. *kosa.*) Note: the Prep. **Paramia** seems to have a reversive meaning, i.e. (1) catch hold of, e.g. a man grappling with an opponent in a fight. *Usingizi ulimparamia*, he was overtaken by sleep. (2) scale, mount, climb over (wall, tree, &c.), also used of climbing on to a vehicle, e.g. *watoto waliparamia nyuma ya gari*, the children climbed on to the back of the cart; (3) interrupt a person speaking (cf. *dakiza*); (4) quarrel, attack with words, i.e. *usiniparamie kwa maneno.* (Cf. *paa, paraga.*)

Parange, n. *ma-* a large, broad-bladed knife or matchet, used for clearing forest, &c. (Cf. *panga, ukengee, mundu.*)

Parapanda, n. the last trump, the trumpet which shall be sounded on the last day. (Cf. *panda*, n. (4).)

Parare, n. a kind of large grasshopper with barbed legs.

Paraza, v. See under **Paa**, v. (B).

Paria, v. See under **Para**, v.

Paru,* n. *ma-* a kind of sweetmeat made of sugar mixed with opium. (Hind. پارو.)

Parua, v., **Paruparu**, adv., **Parura**, v., **Paruza**, v. See under **Para**, v.

Pasa, v. See under **Pata**.

Pasaka,* n. the Passover, *Sikukuu ya Pasaka*, the Festival of the Passover, Easter. (Hebrew, introduced by Christian missions.)

Pasha, v. See under **Pata**.

-pasi, a. See under **Pata**.

Pasi,* n. (—, or *ma-*) (1) an iron—for ironing clothes. *Piga pasi*, iron clothes (Hind.). (2) in common use in some places for a passport or road pass. (Eng.)

Pasina, verb-form used in the same way as *pasipo*, which see.

Pasipo, verb-form (person pfx. of place *pa-*, negative sign *si*, relative of place or time, *-po*), 'where there is not' used most frequently in a prepositional sense 'without'. *Pasipo hofu*, without fear, fearless, safe. *Pasipo nguo*, without clothes. (Cf. *bila, pasina, minghairi.*)

Pasiwe, verb-form, negat. subjunct. of *wa*, v. 'be', may there not be, that there may not be, without there being.

Pasua, v. cleave, split, tear, rend, burst, blow in pieces, saw in two, make a cut in. Ps. **Pasuliwa**. St. **Pasuka**. Prep. **Pasulia**. **Mpasua**, n. *wa-* i.e. *mpasua mbao*, a sawyer, one who cuts boards. One who cleaves, rends, tears, &c. **Mpasuko**, n. *mi-* a crack, split, tear, rent, &c. (Cf. *kata, rarua, chenga, chanja, tema.*)

Pata,* n. a hinge. (Cf. *bawaba*. Hind. پات.)

Pata, v. the general meaning is 'get' with a wide range of application to persons and things. Thus (1) get, obtain, find, catch, get hold of, seize, secure, attain; (2) get to be, get at, get to, reach, find means to effect a purpose, succeed in doing; (3) happen to, come upon; (4) be the victim of, suffer, experience, e.g. *pata mali*, get rich. *Pata faida*, get profit. *Pata hasara*, suffer loss. *Pata nguvu*, get strong. *Pata homa*, get fever—thus *nimepata homa*, I have got fever, or *homa imenipata*, fever has seized me, or *nimepatwa na homa*, I am seized with fever. *Pata nchi*, reach a country. *Jiwe likampata mtoto*, the stone hit the child. *Kisu hakipati*, the knife is blunt, it will not cut. *Kisu chapata,* the knife cuts. Of time, *hawakupata mwezi mmoja, ila walisikia Sultani amefariki,* they did not pass a month before they heard the Sultan was dead. *Haukupata mwaka,* before a year passed, also, less than a year. Sometimes *kupata* is used absolutely as a kind of conjunction. *Kupata njiani mwenzetu akakamatwa na simba,* as it happened, on the way our companion was seized by a lion. *Pata* is common in connexion with another verb, in a semi-auxiliary sense, like *kwisha,* e.g. *pata kujua,* get to know, find out. *Nimepata kufanya,* I have succeeded in doing it, I have done it. And in the Subjunctive, it often has the force of a final conjunction, 'in order to, so as to, to get to, so that', e.g. *akaenda apate kuona,* and he went in order to see. Ps. **Patwa,** e.g. be got, be seized, be a victim, suffer, esp. of calamity, illness, &c., e.g. *patwa na homa,* be attacked by fever. *Patwa na hasira,* be seized with fury. *Patwa na msiba,* be the victim of a misfortune, be bereaved. Also used of an eclipse, *mwezi (jua) umepatwa,* the moon (sun) is got hold of, i.e. eclipsed. St. and Pot. **Patika,** e.g. (1) be got; (2) be gettable, be to be had, be procurable, be obtainable—but this is usu. **Patikana.** *Patika kosani,* be caught in fault. *Fedha hazipatikani siku hizi,* money is not obtainable at present. (Cf. *adimika.*) Prep. **Patia,** e.g. get for (by, with, in, &c.)—also often, get up to, overtake, attain to. D. Prep. **Patilia,** e.g. *patilia hasira,* get angry with. Cs. **Patiliza,** without a noun, cause to get—usu. of some unpleasant consequence, i.e. visit something upon, take vengeance on, remember something against, punish. *Mungu alimpatiliza Farao maovu yake,* God visited Pharaoh for his iniquities. Rp. of Cs. of D.Prep. **Patilizana,** of angry recrimination, each trying to inflict something on the other. Cs. (1) **Pasa,** used in a restricted way, concern, befit, be due (to), behove, be a duty, be binding, be of obligation. Often used in an impersonal way, e.g. *yapasa, imepasa,* it is right, it is a duty, it is proper. Also *imenipasa,* it is my duty, I am bound, lit. it has got me—Inten. *Imekupasaje?* How does it concern you? Cs. **Paswa,** e.g. *tumepaswa kwenda,* it is our duty to go. Prep. **Pasia,** e.g. *ada zilizompasia jumbe,* the customary privileges of the chief. *Jamaa zake waliompasia,* the relations who had a claim on him. *Kila neno lililompasia maiti,* every proper attention to the corpse. Ps. of Prep. **Pasiwa.** *Amepasiwa adhabu,* he is liable to punishment. Cs. **Pasisha,** cause to get, bind upon, and so inflict, e.g. *pasisha hukumu,* pass sentence on, give judgement on, condemn. Rp. **Pasana,** be bound to each other, be under mutual obligations, belong to each. (Cf. *bidi, juzu, wajibu, wia, funga.*) Cs. (2) **Pasha (Patisha** and **Patiza),** cause to get, cause to have, &c. *Pasha moto,* make warm, heat. *Pasha fedha,* give (lend) money to. *Baridi imekupasha homa,* cold has given you fever. *Nitampasha habari,* I will inform him (cause him to have the news). Rp. **Patana,** get each other—commonly used as 'come to terms, strike a bargain, agree, be reconciled, work harmoniously, harmonize, correspond'. Cs. of Rp. **Patanisha,** reconcile, arrange terms between, make peace among, bring to agreement, pacify. **Kipato,** n. *vi-* anything got, receipts, earnings. **Mpatanishi,** n. *wa-* a peacemaker, reconciler, one who brings people to terms, settles quarrels and difficulties, a negotiator. **Mpato,** n. *mi-* a getting, a procuring, &c. **-pasi** a. given to acquiring things, money-making, avaricious, ambitious, pushing. *Mtu mpasi,* one who acquires things, money, &c., in large quantities, an ambitious, avaricious, pushing person. **Patanisho,** n. *ma-* (1) act of agreement, reconciliation; (2) anything causing agreement, &c. **Patano,** n. *ma-* usu. in the plur. *mapatano,* agreement, contract, understanding, conspiracy, alliance. **Pato,** n. *ma-* something got, an acquisition, usu. in the plur. *mapato,* gains, receipts, profits, income, revenue, &c. **Upataji,** n. buying power, value, cost, price. **Upatilivu,** n. reproach, blame—whether as inflicted or incurred. **Upatilizo,** n. *ma-* blaming, reproaching, punishing, visiting on offences.

Patana, v., **Patanisha,** v., **Patanisho,** n. *ma-*, **Patano,** n. *ma-*. See under **Pata,** v.

Patasi,* n. a chisel. (Cf. *juba, chembeu.*)

Patikana, v., **Patiliza,** v., **Patisha,** v., **Patiza,** v., **Pato,** n. *ma-*. See under **Pata,** v.

Patu, n. *ma-*. See **Upatu.**

Patwa, v. *Kupatwa mwezi (jua),* eclipse of the moon (sun). See under **Pata,** v.

Pau, n., **Paua,** v. See under **Paa,** v.

Pauni, n. a pound—weight or value. (Eng. pound.)

Pawa, n. plur. of *upawa,* which see.

Paya, v., and Rd. **Payapaya,** talk foolishly (idly, indiscreetly, unintelligibly, &c.), talk nonsense, blurt out secrets, blab, be delirious. St. of Cv. **Payuka,** with same sense as *paya.* Cs. **Payusha,** e.g. *tembo limempayusha,* palm-wine has loosed his tongue. *Homa inampayusha,* fever makes him delirious. **Mpayukaji,** n. *wa-* a gossip, chatterer. **Payo,** n. *ma-* foolish talk, chatter, nonsense, gossip, blabbing; also of wandering of the mind, delirium. *Mwenye payo,* a talkative, gossiping person. *Ana payo,* he is always talking, lets out secrets, does not control his tongue. *Sema mapayo,* talk idly, mischievously, &c. **Upayukaji,** n. indiscreetness in talking, &c.; incoherence, incoherency.

Paza, v. See under **Paa,** v. (A) and (B).

Pazia,* n. *ma-* (1) a curtain, screen (of calico, &c.), awning (cf. *chandalua*); (2) *pazia la tumbo,* sometimes used for the diaphragm. (Cf. *kiwamba moyo* under *wamba.* ? Pers. پرس curtain, veil.)

Pea, n. a rhinoceros, for the commoner *kifaru,* and *faru.*

Pea, v. (A), become fully grown, be completely developed, attain to the highest point (limit, acme of perfection). The St. form *pevuka* made from the adj. *-pevu* is almost entirely used in this connexion. **Pevua,** v. (1) develop fully, ripen, bring to perfection, hasten the maturity of. Hence (2) over-stimulate, excite unduly, pervert, teach bad ways to, corrupt. *Jipevua,* make a man of oneself, behave like a grown-up person or big man, swagger, be conceited, brag. St. **Pevuka,** be fully grown, be completely developed, &c. Cs. **Pevusha. Kipeo,** n. *vi-* (1) the highest or furthest point, apex, top, end, culmination; (2) ideal, best example, standard of excellence. *Kipeo cha macho,* furthest limit of vision, horizon. **Mpevu,** n. *wa-* one who is fully grown, an adult. **Mpevushi,** n. *wa-* a corrupter of morals, esp. of the young, lit. one who ripens, brings to maturity, forces growth. **-pevu,** a. full-grown, ripe, adult—of plant or animal growth. *Mwili mpevu,* sound, healthy well-developed body. *Uchawi mpevu,* the acme of witchcraft. **Upeo,** n. *(peo)* like *kipeo. Upeo wa macho,* as far as the eye can see, the limit of vision, horizon, e.g. *jangwa kubwa upeo wa macho yake,* a great waste extending as far as he could see. *Kupita upeo,* very extreme, beyond all bounds. Used as adv., to the utmost, thoroughly, as much as possible, e.g. *piga upeo,* give a sound beating to. *Furahi upeo,* be filled with joy, be enraptured. **Upevu,** n. ripeness, maturity, &c.

Pea, v. (B), sweep, for the commoner *fagia*. Prep. **Pelea. Kipeo**, n. *vi-* a small brush for sweeping with.

Pecha, adv. in a halting, crippled, staggering manner, i.e. *kwenda pecha*, to walk in a halting, crippled manner.

Peka, n. but usu. **Peke**, condition of being single, singular, alone, lonely, isolated, unique, different from every thing else. Used only with a possessive adjective following, and attaching to an object, state of action, the attribute of singleness, loneliness, uniqueness, e.g. *mimi peke yangu*, I alone, I only, I myself. *Nguo hii ni ya peke yake*, this cloth is the only one of its kind. *Wakaa peke yako*, you live alone. So *peke yetu* (*yenu*, *yao*). **-a peke yake** or **-a pekee**, single, alone, unique. *Mtu wa pekee*, a solitary man. *Mwenda pekee*, a person (or animal) who is solitary, or who always goes alone. **Upekee**, n. **Upweke**, n. condition of being alone, solitariness. *Amekufa upweke*, he died alone, unattended. *Safari ya upweke haifai*, it is not a good thing to travel alone. Prov. *Upeka* (or *upweke*) *ni uvundo*, loneliness is disgusting.

Pekecha, v. (from a root *peka*, drill, bore, not now used in Swahili, but is in some Bantu languages, e.g. Nyanja), produce, or affect, by turning something with the hands and so (1) bore a hole, drill, i.e. *pekecha tundu*, with a pointed knife, drill, &c., twirled by rubbing between the palms of the hands; (2) produce fire, i.e. *pekecha moto*, by firesticks, one stick (*wimbombo* or *upekecho*) twirled between the palms of the hands, the point turning in a hole in another stick (*ulindi*); (3) fig. excite bad feeling, bore, exasperate, e.g. by abuse, noise, or sorcery, &c.; (4) make a mess of, spoil, e.g. *pekecha kazi*, bungle a job (cf. *burunga*, *chafua*, *fuja*); (5) gnaw, hurt, ache, e.g. *mifupa yangu inanipekecha*, my bones are aching. St. **Peketeka** (for *pekecheka*—for the use of *t* for *ch* see note on *ch*) (1) be drilled, bored, as by a pointed instrument; (2) be confused, mixed up, slack, stirred up. *Matunda haya yamepeketeka*, this fruit is soft (mixed up, mushy). *Mtoto huyu, mbona anapeketeka?* Why is this child slack? (used when the slackness is affected by arrogance, pride, &c.) (contr. *-tepetevu*). (3) be arrogant, scornful, be high and mighty. Prep. **Peketekea**, treat with scorn, be insulting (or contemptuous) to. Cv. **Pekua**, (1) scratch up, scratch about, e.g. like a hen; (2) search diligently; (3) be inquisitive, be curious, prying; (4) colloquial—decamp, run away. Ps. **Pekuliwa**. St. of Prep. **Pekulika**. Prep. **Pekulia**, hunt for, pry into, &c. **Mpekecho**, n. *mi-* (1) a twirling, a stirring; (2) a disturbance, agitation, fomenting of discord in any way; (3) an insistent inquiry into a person's affairs. **Mpeketevu**, n. *wa-* (1) an arrogant, proud, boasting person; (2) one who excites bad feeling in any way, e.g. by abuse, noise, witchcraft, &c. **Mpeketo**, n. *mi-* a stirring up of trouble, discord, &c. **Mpeko**, n. *mi-* an instrument, piece of stick, &c., used for stirring. **Mpekuzi**, n. *wa-* (1) one who picks and scratches (like a fowl); (2) an inquisitive, prying person. **-peketevu**, a. (1) scornful, provoking, making discord; (2) mixed up, stirred up, mushy. **-pekuzi**, a. curious, inquisitive, prying. **Upekecho**, n. (*pekecho* and *ma-*) (1) drilling, turning a boring tool, but esp. manner of making fire by twirling one stick in a hole in another; (2) ache or gnawing pain in the bones; (3) fig. annoyance, vexatious conduct; (4) a stick used for making fire, as above. **Upeketevu**, n. contempt, arrogancy, &c. **Upekuzi**, n. (1) inquisitiveness, prying manner, criticism; (2) curiosity.

Pekee, n. See under **Peka**.

Pekesheni,* v. (1) investigate, search; (2) eavesdrop; (3) get by cheating, in an underhand manner. (Eng. inspection.)

Peketeka, -peketevu, a., **Pekua,** v. See under **Pekecha.**

Peku lungo, n. used only in the saying: *lililopata peku na lungo litapata. Peku* is an old worn-out sifting basket, *lungo* (*ungo*) is one being used. Hence: what happened to *peku* shall also happen to the *ungo*—all things grow old.

-pekuzi, a. See under **Pekecha.**

Pele, n. plur. of *upele.*

Pelea, v. (1) prune, as of trees; (2) prep. of *pea,* v. (B).

Peleka, v. cause to go, send, take, convey, conduct, transmit, move, &c., both of persons and things. Dist. *tuma,* which see, in the direct form, is limited to persons. *Nitatuma mtu kupeleka mzigo kwako,* I will employ a man to convey a load to your house. *Nitapeleka mtu na mzigo,* I will send a man with a load. *Peleka mkono,* move the hand in a given direction, apply the hand, set to work. *Kitu kipi kilichokupeleka dukani?* which thing caused you to go to the shop? i.e. what did you go to buy? Ps. **Pelekwa.** Prep. **Pelekea,** send to (for, by, in, &c.). Rp. of Prep. **Pelekeana,** send to each other. Rp. **Pelekana,** accompany each other, all go together. Cs. **Pelekeza,** cause to send, &c., also *pelekeza kidole,* point with the finger. **Mpelekwa,** n. *wa-* one sent, a messenger.

Pelele, n. a rock-rabbit, hyrax. (Cf. *wibari, kwanga.*)

Peleleza, v. spy out, reconnoitre, secretly examine, pry into, be curious (or inquisitive) about. *Peleleza nchi,* spy out a country. *Peleleza siri,* pry into secrets. Ps. **Pelelezwa.** Prep. **Pelelezea. Mpelelezi,** n. *wa-* (1) one who investigates, reconnoitres, examines, &c.; (2) a spy, scout, tracker, eavesdropper. **Upelelezi,** n. spying, eavesdropping, scouting, &c.

Pelezi, n. *ma-* blunt places or gaps, in a knife or axe, &c. (Cf. e.g. as *pengo.*)

Pemba, n. an island near Zanzibar, famous for its cloves.

Pemba, v. (1) grasp with a hook, grapple, hook down, e.g. of fruit, *pemba embe,* get mangoes down with a stick with a crook at the end; (2) cheat, deceive, beat by trickery, outwit; (3) question a person until he is trapped; (4) taste with the tongue, lick. (Cf. *onja, lamba.*) **Upembo,** n. (*pembo*) curved end, hook, crook, a hooked stick, &c., e.g. for pulling down fruit from a tree.

Pembe, n. (1) horn, of an animal—also the substance generally; (2) tusk of an elephant, also ivory generally. (Cf. *kalasha, buri* for tusks of different sizes—*buri,* the larger); (3) a projection, angle, corner; (4) a side, e.g. of a room, plantation, &c.; (5) various articles of horn, esp. powder-flask. *Pembeni,* in a corner. *-a pembe, -enye pembe, pembepembe,* with angles (corners, projections). *Pembe za dunia,* the uttermost parts of the land, quarters of the globe. *Pembe za mwaka,* the seasons of the year. *Pembemraba,* a right angle. *Pembebutu,* an obtuse angle. *Pembekali,* an acute angle. **Upembe,** n. the upper corner of the triangular sail of a native vessel of the common kind.

Pembea, v. swing, sway, rock, balance, oscillate. Cs. **Pembeza,** set swinging, rock to and fro. **Pembea,** n. swing, see-saw. *Kiti cha pembea,* a rocking-chair. (Cf. *ning'inia, wayawaya, yumbayumba.*)

Pembeja, v. persuade with fine words or promises, deceive with plausible statements, usu. implying deceit.

Pembejo, n. the thigh and side, the hams. (Cf. *paja, kiweo.*)

Pembizo, n. See **Pambizo.**

Pembo, n. plur. of *upembo.*

Pembua, v. (1) sift, winnow; (2) fig.

sort out, choose, select. (Cf. *pepeta*, and *chagua*, *teua*, *pambanua*.)

Penda, v. like, love, choose, wish, will. Ps. **Pendwa**. St. and Pot. **Pendeka**, e.g. be loved, be lovable, be popular, &c. Cs. of St. **Pendekeza**, cause to be loved, excite affection for. *Jipendekeza*, make oneself pleasant, ingratiate oneself. Prep. **Pendea**, love for (on account of, with, in, &c.). Ps. of Prep. **Pendewa**, e.g. *pendewa uzuri*, be loved for beauty. D.Prep. and Inten. **Pendelea**, have a special liking (predeliction, bias, propensity) for, be partial to, favour, often used in the sense of favouring unjustly, i.e. to the loss or damage of others. Ps. **Pendelewa**. St. **Pendeleka**. Cs. **Pendeleza**, cause to favour, recommend to favour, prepossess in favour (of), recommend. Cs. of Dir. **Pendeza**, please, be pleasing (popular), attractive, amiable, &c.), cause to like (love, prefer). Ps. **Pendezwa**. Prep. **Pendezea**, please with (for, in, &c.). Ps. **Pendezewa**, be pleased with (something), be pleased. D.Cs. **Pendezesha**, cause to please, make popular, &c. Rp. of Cs. **Pendezana**, be mutually agreeable. Cs. of Rp. of Cs. **Pendezanisha**. Rp. **Pendana**, love each other. Cs. **Pendanisha**, cause to be friends, reconcile. **Kipendo**, n. *vi-* act (trait, manifestation, &c.) of affection, kindness, love. **Kipenzi**, n. *vi-* a beloved object, a favourite, darling, pet. **Mapendezi**, n. plur. things, circumstances, &c., which give pleasure, happiness. **Mpenda**, n. *wa-*, **Mpendi**, n. *wa-* governing a following noun, one who likes, &c., e.g. *mpenda kula*, one who likes eating, a glutton. **Mpendelevu**, n. *wa-* one given to favouritism, a biased person. **Mpendwa**, n. *wa-* one who is liked, loved, a favourite. **Mpenzi**, n. *wa-* (1) one who is beloved, a dear, favourite; (2) one who loves, a lover. **-pendelevu**, a. inclined to favour, biased. **-pendevu**, a. kind, loving. **Penzi**, n. *ma-* (1) love, liking, pleasure, wish, will; (2) that which is loved, liked, &c. The plur. **Mapenzi** is used in the sense of love, liking, inclination, desire, will, wish, purpose. **Upendaji**, n. habit of liking or loving something. **Upendano**, n. *ma-* mutual love. **Upendeleo**, n. *ma-* having a special liking, bias, inclination, favour, favouritism. **Upendelevu**, n. (1) as *upendeleo*, but also admits of a Ps. sense; (2) being favoured, being liked. **Upendezi**, n. *ma-* (1) being agreeable (amiable, pleasing, lovable), pleasantness; (2) being pleased, happiness, delight. **Upendo**, n. (*pendo* and *ma-*) act (manner, &c.) of loving, liking, affection, love. **Upendwa**, n. *ma-* being loved, liked. **Upenzi**, n. *ma-* (1) loving, liking, desiring, willing, resolving. Also (2) Ps. being loved, liked, &c.

Penga, v. blow the nose.

Pengee, n. See under **Kipengee**.

Pengi, a form of *-ingi*, many.

Pengo, n. *ma-* (1) gap, notch, hole, vacant space; (2) fig. defect, flaw, e.g. of a gap between teeth. *Ana pengo*, he has lost a tooth.

Peninsula,* n. the English word, adopted for use in text-books and school lessons on Geography. (Eng.)

Pentekote,* n. the word used for the season of Pentecost. (Greek, introduced by Christian missions.)

Penu, n. (1) plur. of *upenu*, which see; (2) form of *-enu*.

Penua, v. open a little, draw aside or open, e.g. a person's legs or clothing. (Cf. *panua*.)

Penya, v. penetrate, make a way into, get inside, enter, pass into like *ingia*, but implying more effort, or purpose, difficulties in the way. *Penya mwituni*, make one's way through a forest. Ps. **Penywa**. St. and Pot. **Penyeka**. Prep. **Penyea**, e.g. *tundu la kupenyea*, a hole to get in by. Cs. **Penyeza**, and sometimes **Penyesha**, cause to go into, force into, insinuate, introduce (by stealth, force, stratagem, &c.). Hence of slipping money into the hand of another, putting an idea into the mind of another, and so of bribery, undue influence, &c. *Nilimpenyezea fedha, akanipatia haki,* I bribed him and he got me justice. *Penyeza bidhaa katika nchi,* introduce trade goods into a country, i.e. by stealth, or by avoiding customs duty. **Kipenyo,** n. *vi-* a hole through which something is passed, a thing which is passed through, i.e. the peg of a top, axis of a globe, &c. **Mpenyezi,** n. *wa-* (1) one who introduces, causes to enter or penetrates, brings in, and esp. in an underhand secret way, hence (2) a traitor, smuggler, illicit trader, secret agent, one who gives bribes. **Mpenyezo,** n. *mi-* (1) an introducing, a penetration; (2) a bribe. **Penyenye,** n. *ma-* secret matters. **Penyo,** n. *ma-* like *kipenyo,* but amplic. **Upenyezi,** n. (*penyezi,* and *ma-*) (1) secret, underhand illicit action; (2) bribery, smuggling, giving commissions—also (3) insinuation, suggestion.

Penye, form of *-enye.*

Penyenye, n. *ma-.* See under **Penya.**

Penyewe, form of *-enyewe.*

Penyo, n. *ma-.* See under **Penya.**

Penzi, n. *ma-.* See under **Penda.**

Pepa, v. with the general meaning, sway, reel, stagger, totter, &c., with many derived forms developed in more or less restricted senses. Prep. **Pepea,** (1) fan, wave (like a fan), wave about in the air, make a current of air, e.g. *wapambe humpepea bwana arusi,* the attendants fan the bridegroom. *Pepea mainzi,* keep flies off with fans. *Pepea bendera,* wave a flag about. *Pepea vitambaa,* flourish pieces of cloth. *Pepea moto kwa kipepeo,* blow up the fire with a fan; (2) also used of ripening fruit by artificial means. (Cf. *vumbika.*) Ps. **Pepewa,** be fanned, wafted about. D.Prep. **Pepelea,** fan for (with, &c.). *Pepelea mwana wali upate kupoa,* fan the child's rice for him to make it cool. St. of Cv. of Prep. (note *r* for *l*) **Peperuka,** be carried away by a current of air, blown away, wafted, fly off, soar up. *Nguo ilipeperuka kwa upepo,* the cloth was carried away by the wind. Cs. **Peperusha,** blow away. Cs. of *pepa,* with restricted meaning **Pepesa,** blink the eye, shut and open the eye, hence also, keep the eye clear or steady, as in taking aim, i.e. *pepesa jicho kushika shabaha,* blink the eye in order to be able to take a good aim. (Cf. *kopesa.*) St. of Inten. of Cs. **Pepesuka,** shake, totter, reel to and fro, be shaken in the air, wind-tossed, caused to fly away, caused to wave about. Ten. **Pepeta,** winnow, sift, separate husks, chaff, &c., from grain by shaking and tossing in the air with a flat basket, e.g. *pepeta mchele, wishwa utoke,* sift to get out the husks. (Cf. also *peta.*) Ps. **Pepetwa.** St. and Pot. **Pepeteka.** Prep. **Pepetea.** Cv. of Dir. **Pepua,** sift, winnow, like *pepea* and *pepeta.* **Kipepeo,** n. *vi-* (1) a small fan; (2) a butterfly; (3) a kind of flat fish. **Mpepea,** n. *mi-* a light breeze. **Mpepetaji,** n. *wa-* one who sifts or winnows grain, &c. **Pepe,** n. *ma-* empty husk of grain, empty (barren) ear. **Pepeo,** n. *ma-* amplic. of *kipepeo,* and plural of *upepeo,* a large fan, punkah. Also to describe a winnowing machine, vane on a tower, &c. **Pepeta,** n. *pepeta za mpunga,* grains of rice heated, and then pounded—sometimes mixed with sugar. **Pepo,** n. (1) genus of disembodied spirits. *Pepo mwema,* a good spirit. *Pepo mbaya* (or *shetani*), an evil spirit. *Pagawa na pepo,* be possessed by a spirit. *Punga pepo,* exorcize, expel a spirit, by native methods, i.e. dancing, ceremonies, beating drums of different sorts, &c. *Mwenye pepo,* possessed person. *Pepo atapanda,* that spirit will come forth, i.e. *mganga kupandisha pepo* *kichwani*, the medicine man causes the spirit to mount to the head. (Cf. *punga, mteja.*) Various names of kinds of spirits are: *jini, shetani, milihoi, zimwi, kinyamkela, kilima, dungumaro, mahoka, koikoi, kitimiri, kizuu, kizuka, pungwa, mkasia,* &c. (2) the region of spirits, spirit world, unseen world, place of departed spirits, paradise. *Pepo za kesho,* the world to come, the life beyond the grave. *Pepo ya leo,* this world's rest. (3) much wind, a strong, high wind; (4) Plur. of *upepo*; (5) *pepo punda,* tetanus, lockjaw. **Peponi,** n. loc. paradise, in paradise, at rest. *Kama ameingia peponi,* (a man) as happy as if in paradise. **Upepeaji,** n. See **Upepezi,** below. **Upepeo,** n. (*pepeo,* and *ma-*) a fan, punkah. **Upepezi,** n. fanning, the act of fanning, e.g. of the bride and bridegroom at the wedding, by children in attendance for that purpose. **Upepo,** n. (*pepo*), wind, breeze, draught, fresh air, i.e. of a light movement of air—the plur. *pepo* being used of high wind, a gale. *Upepo mwanana* (*mwororo*), gentle (soft) breeze, zephyr. *Punga upepo,* take fresh air, go for a change, fan oneself. *Kaa upeponi,* sit in a draught. *Upepo wa kawaida,* prevailing wind.

Pepetua, v. See **Popotoa,** for which it is sometimes heard.

Pepo, n., **Peponi,** n. See under **Pepa.**

Pepo punda, n. (1) a kind of evil spirit; (2) lockjaw, tetanus.

Pepua, v. See under **Pepa.**

Pera,* n. *ma-* guava, fruit of the tree *mpera.* (Port. *pera,* a pear.)

Perema, n. a disease in which the glands of the neck swell, mumps. (Cf. *machubwichubwi, matubwitubwi.*)

Peremende,* n. *ma-* (1) peppermint, also applied to any sort of boiled sugar sweets. (Eng. peppermint.) (2) a plot to get somebody into trouble. (Cf. *fitina.* ? Eng. parliament.)

Pesa,* n. (— and *ma-*) (1) a pice, the Indian quarter anna, or 3-pie piece. The two plurals differ a little in use, like pence (*pesa*) and pennies (*mapesa*). 64 pice are one rupee. (2) money—in general, in Zanzibar, and often still heard on the mainland. *Hana pesa,* he is a poor man. *Pesa hapana,* I have no money. *Robo pesa,* a pie, i.e. one-third of a pice. (Hind. پیسا.)

Pesa, Pesapesa, v. look about, look here and there. (Cf. *pepesa.*)

Peta, v. (A) bend round, bend, bow, curve, fold over, wrap up, make like a ring. *Peta ufito,* bend a switch into a bow. *Peta mguu,* bend the leg. *Peta suruali,* turn up the trousers (usu. *pania suruali*). *Peta nguo,* roll up clothes. *Peta uso,* put on an angry look, bend the brows, frown. Ps. **Petwa.** St. and Pot. **Peteka.** Cs. **Petesha,** bend round, make into a ring. Rp. **Petana,** be bent round, be bowed, form a ring (a circle, a hoop). Cv. **Petua,** turn round, turn over bottom upwards (upside down), upset, capsize. St. and Pot. **Petuka.** Prep. **Petulia.** Ps. **Petuliwa.** Cs. **Petusha.** Stc. **Petamana,** be bent round, be formed into a ring, be made into a hoop, or circle. Cs. **Petemanisha,** make into a hoop (circle), bend round, give a curve to. **Kipete,** n. *vi-* a small ring, ferrule, circlet. **Kipeto,** n. *vi-* bag (with flap or cover), case, receptacle, cover, parcel, packet. *Kipeto cha barua,* letter case. **Pete,** n. (— and for large size, *ma-*) (1) a ring, hoop, staple, circle. *Kama pete na kidole,* like ring and finger—of close contact and attachment. *Pete ya sikio,* earring. (2) the holes bored in women's ears in which plugs of coloured paper are worn, are also called *mapete, toga mapete,* bore holes in the ears. **Peto,** n. (— and of large size, *ma-*) a bag, matting-sack, e.g. used for carrying stones and sand, &c. **Upeto,** n.

(*peto*) folding, fold, roll, something rolled up, package, bundle.

Peta, v. (B), clean or sift grain by shaking in a tray. (Cf. *pepa, pepeta.*)

Pete, n. (— and *ma-*), **Petamana, v., Peto, n.** (— and *ma-*). See under **Peta, v.** (A).

Petroli,* n. petrol—in common use. (Eng.)

Petu, a form of *-etu,* which see.

Petua, v. See under **Peta, v. (A).**

Peupe. See under **Eua.**

Peusi. See under **-eusi.**

-pevu, a., Pevua, v., Pevuka, v. See under **Pea, v.** (A).

Pewa, v. See under **Pa, v.**

Pezi, n. *ma-* (1) fin of a fish; (2) crookedness, obliqueness. (Cf. *mshazari, upandeupande.*)

-pi, (1) in combination with Pers. pfx. forms an interrog. adj. who? which? what? e.g. *mtu yupi?* which person? *Mti upi?* which tree? *Kitu kipi?* which thing? Also suffixed to verbs, with the meaning 'how?' 'in what way?', e.g. *nitawezapi?* how shall I be able? Also with *wa-* pfx. *wapi?* in the sense of 'it was of no use', 'quite impossible', e.g. *nilijaribu, nikajaribu tena, lakini wapi?* I tried, and I tried again, but it was not possible. And (2) colloquially contracted for *wapi,* e.g. *unakwendapi?* or *wendapi?* for *unakwenda wapi?* where are you going?

Pia, a. and adv. all, the whole, complete, quite, altogether. Often with *-ote,* giving it emphasis, e.g. *watu wote pia,* all the people without exception. *Nitakupa yote pia,* I will give you the whole lot. As an adv. often in rejoinders (1) all of it, that too, that as well; (2) exactly so, just so. *Nitwae hizi? Pia.* Am I to take these? Yes, all of them, or those as well.

Pia, n. (1) a top, i.e. the toy, a humming-top or whipping-top; (2) a reel, such as used on spinning machines; (3) *pia ya mguu,* the knee-cap.

Picha,* n. a picture, a photograph. *Andika picha,* draw a picture. (Eng. picture. Cf. *sanamu,* used for an image, statue, &c.)

Piga, v. strike, beat, hit, give a blow. This is the common *definite* meaning of *piga.* But *piga* in the Direct Act. form has an *indefinite* use, which is at once one of the commonest and most characteristic features of the Swahili language, and also difficult to describe. It is used with a great number and variety of nouns to express the act, action, or effect, which the noun itself most naturally suggests; and even when another verb exists conveying this meaning, *piga* is nevertheless often substituted for it with a peculiar significance and flavour of its own. This is no doubt connected with the original idea of *striking,* but 'striking' in different aspects—sometimes suggesting its mode, i.e. the suddenness, forcibleness, effectiveness of a stroke, and sometimes the effect on the mind or senses, of what is striking, sensational, moving. It is impossible to enumerate all the nouns with which *piga* is commonly, or may be used, or the most appropriate rendering—depending (as they would do) largely on the context in each case, and a knowledge of the alternative verbs for which *piga* is in any particular instance purposely substituted (1) the proper use of a tool (in place of simple *tumia, endesha,* &c.), e.g. *piga bomba,* work a pump; *piga randa,* plane (wood); *piga pasi,* iron (clothes); *piga picha,* photograph; *piga kinanda,* play an organ, piano, musical instrument; *piga kengele,* ring a bell; *piga chapa,* print (a book); *piga kura,* cast lots; *piga bao,* take omens with a divining board; (2) construction, execution, giving form to something, e.g. *piga fundo,* tie a knot; *piga kilemba,* wear a turban; *piga mbinda* (*winda*), adjust the loin-cloth, i.e. tuck it up and fasten it between the thighs; *piga mstari,* draw a line; *piga bandi*, hem, run, in sewing; *piga ponta*, stitch; (3) of a sudden forcible action, e.g. *piga mbio*, run; *piga mwendo*, beat time (in music); *piga kelele*, shout; *piga kofi*, give a box on the ear; *piga miayo*, yawn; *piga mbizi*, dive; *piga mluzi*, whistle; *piga teke*, kick; *piga pembe*, butt; *piga domo*, bite (of a serpent) also, make a lot of noise with chatter, be garrulous; *piga mikambe*, lash out with the legs in a game in the water; *piga hodi*, ask admittance. (4) of producing a showy, sensational effect, *piga makuu*, play the grandee; *piga ubwana*, domineer, tyrannize; *piga umalidadi*, wear finery, and simply *piga nguo*, show off clothes; *piga kiburi*, show conceit; *piga pua*, turn up one's nose, carry one's head high; *piga umeme*, lighten (of lightning); *piga moyo konde*, take courage. Other examples are: *piga mikono*, gesticulate; *piga mabawa*, flap the wings; *piga fatiha*, perform a religious ceremony; *piga magoti*, kneel down; *piga moto*, set fire to; *piga uvivu*, waste time by idling; *piga mafungu*, divide into lots; *piga marufuku*, publicly forbid; *piga shauri*, take formal counsel; *piga shabaha*, take aim; *piga vita*, declare (wage) war. Ps. **Pigwa.** St. and Pot. **Pigika.** Prep. **Pigia**, e.g. strike for (with, at, in, &c.). D.Prep. Inten. **Pigilia**, used of a special operations, i.e. *pigilia sakafu*, beat a concrete roof or floor, with rammers (*vipande*) till hard, lit. beat away at. Cs. **Pigisha**, cause to beat about, flap, wave, e.g. *pigisha tanga*, let the sail flap; *pigisha kiapo*, administer an oath; *pigisha nguo na upepo*, air clothes; *pigisha chombo*, make a vessel pitch, rock, toss; *pigisha maji*, stir up water—with inten. force. Rp. **Pigana**, hit each other, fight. Cs. of Rp. **Piganisha**, cause to fight, set fighting, or fight hard. St. and Pot. **Piganika.** Ps. of Rp. of Prep. **Piganiwa**, be fought for (about, with, in, &c.). **Kipigi**, n. *vi* (usually *kipiki*, or *piki*, or *pikipiki*) a little stick to beat with or throw. **Kipigo**, n. *vi-* stroke, blow, shot. **Mpiga**, n. *wa-*, **Mpigi**, n. *wa-* verbal of *piga*, in all its manifold uses, one who strikes, uses, &c. **Mpiganisho**, n. *mi-* collision, encounter, conflict. **Mpigano**, n. *mi-* same as *pigano*. **Mpigo**, n. *mi-* act (mode, &c.) of striking, &c. **Pigano**, n. *ma-* fighting, battle, skirmish, beating each other. **Pigipigi**, n. *ma-* see *pikipiki*. **Pigo**, n. *ma-* (1) blow, stroke, beat, e.g. *aliwafundisha mapigo ya ngoma*, he taught them the proper beats of the drum; *pigo mbili* (*tatu*, &c.), two (three, &c.) pulse measure. (2) calamity, plague, &c. **Upigano**, n. *ma-* fighting, contest, rivalry. In plur. battle, riot, brawl.

Pigipigi, n. See **Pikipiki** under **Piki.**

Pigo, n. *ma-*. See under **Piga.**

Pika, v. cook, prepare by the use of fire, dress (food), but usually by boiling, boil (water). Ps. **Pikwa.** Prep. **Pikia**, cook for (with, in, &c.). St. and Pot. **Pikika.** Ps. of Prep. **Pikiwa**, be cooked for, have a cook. Cs. **Pikisha**, get some one to cook, get something cooked. **Mpikaji**, n. *wa-* but more usually **Mpishi**, n. *wa-* a cook. **Mpiko**, n. *mi-* act (process, method) of cooking, see *upishi*. **Upishi**, n. (*pishi*, and *ma-*) act (method, means, profession, &c.) of cooking, wages of a cook. Prov. *Upishi ni kuni*, cooking means firewood.

Piki, n. *ma-*, also **Pikipiki**, n. *ma-* (1) a stick used for throwing into a tree to knock down fruit; (2) in some places *pikipiki* is used of a motor cycle—from the sound it makes! **Kipiki**, n. *vi-* dim. a small stick for throwing.

Piku,* v. (1) win a trick at cards, or win a game; (2) excel in any way, i.e. beauty, skill, &c. **Piku**, n. *ma-* a trick in card games. (Port. *pacau*, sort of card game.)

Pilao,* n. a dish of boiled rice, cooked with ghee, raisins, &c. (Pers. پلاو.)

Pili, n. an adder (also *piri*).

Pili, a. *-a pili,* the second, next. *-a pili yake,* the next to him (or her). *Mara ya pili,* the second time. (Cf. *mara mbili,* twice.) *Kwa pili,* the other side, over the page. *Ya pili,* secondly, next—after *kwanza,* first, in the first place. (Cf. *-wili.*)

Pilipili,* n. pepper, seeds and pods of the *mpilipili. Pilipili manga,* black (Arab) pepper. *Pilipili hoho,* red pepper, capsicum. (Cf. *mpilipili.* Pers. پلپل.)

Pima, v. measure, weigh, test, criticize in the sense of finding out worth or value. *Pima urefu,* measure the length. *Pima mchele,* weigh rice. *Pima mayai,* test eggs. *Pima maji,* take soundings. *Pima kazi,* examine (criticize) work. Ps. **Pimwa.** St. and Pot. **Pimika.** Prep. **Pimia,** *pishi ya kupimia,* a measure to measure with. *Pimiwa nguo,* have cloth measured out to one, receive a measure of cloth, also be measured for a garment. Cs. **Pimisha,** cause to be measured, superintend measuring, &c. **Kipimio,** n. *vi-* a thing to measure with, hence scale of a map or plan. **Kipimo,** n. *vi-* thing for measuring, measure, a weight, amount measured. *Kipimo cha urefu,* measurement of (length), linear measure; *cha upana,* (breadth); *cha kimo,* (height); *cha ukubwa,* (cubic measure); *cha uzito,* (weight); *cha nafasi,* (cubic contents); *cha eneo,* (area, i.e. square measure); *cha wakati,* (time); *cha ujazo,* (liquid or capacity). **Mpima,** n. *wa-*, **Mpimaji,** n. *wa-* one who measures, a surveyor, &c. **Mpimo,** n. *mi-* (1) act (mode, means, &c.) of measuring; (2) payment for measuring. **Pima,** n. a fathom, two yards, the stretch of a man's arms—equal to four cubits (*mkono, dhiraa*) or eight spans (*shibiri*). **Pimamaji,** n. a water level, spirit level, also **Pimasharazi. Upimaji,** n. weighing, criticism (of books, lessons, &c.). (Cf. Pers. پیما (in comp.) measuring, measurer, weigher.)

Pinda, v. (1) bend, twist, fold, bend up, strain, put a strain on, make tense (stiff, hard); (2) hem. *Pinda upinde,* bend a bow. *Pinda upindo,* make a hem. *Jipinda,* (1) exert oneself; (2) be convulsed, i.e. *pinda-pinda maneno.* Ps. **Pindwa.** St. and Pot. **Pindika,** be bent or bendable. Prep. **Pindia,** bend for (with, by, &c.). Cs. **Pindisha.** Rp. **Pindana,** be bent together, be stiff, be tense, have cramp. *Pindana mguu,* have a club foot. Stc. **Pindamana,** be bent together, curved, contracted, tense, twisted, gnarled, convulsed, &c. Cv. **Pindua,** (1) turn over, give a different direction to, reverse position of, upset, overturn, capsize; (2) change (into something quite different), turn (into), transform. *Pindua mtumbwi,* overturn a canoe. *Pindua chombo,* change course. *Pindua vyombo,* upset the utensils. Ps. **Pinduliwa,** be turned over (into, &c.), e.g. *alipinduliwa gogo,* he was turned into a log. St. and Pot. **Pinduka,** be upset, &c., be changed (into), become, take a new direction. *Lilipopinduka jua kichwani,* when the sun passed the meridian. Prep. of St. **Pindukia,** (1) climb from one side (of a wall, &c.) to the other; (2) also used in the sense of being expert, arrant, &c. *Mwizi wa kupindukia,* an arrant thief, an expert thief. Prep. **Pindulia.** Cs. **Pinduza,** *pinduza dau huko na huko,* turn a boat first on one side, then on the other—to get the water out. **Kipindi,** n. *vi-* (1) a portion of time, period, e.g. *kila kipindi, kipindi chote,* all times, at all times, constantly, always. *Kipindi cha adhuhuri,* noon. *Kwa vipindi,* at times, periodically; also, by fits and starts, irregularly.

-a vipindi, periodical, regular. *-a kipindi*, temporary. Also adv. *Kipindi*, for a time, a short time. (Cf. *kitambo*, *kidogo*, and *kipande*.) (2) a fixed time, a regular hour. *Tangu asubuhi hata jioni ni vipindi kumi na viwili*, from morning to evening there are twelve hours. *Vipindi vya kusali*, the five regular hours of prayer. *Kipindi cha somo*, a lesson-period. (3) fit, attack, paroxysm of sickness, anger or emotion generally. *Homa ya vipindi*, recurrent (or, intermittent fever). *Kipindi cha hasira*, a fit of anger. **Kipindo**, n. *vi-* a wrapper, esp. a folding cloth for a corpse before placing it in the shroud (*sanda*). Also a fold (in a garment), pocket, purse, &c. **Kipindupindu**, n. *vi-* descriptive of a violent seizure, convulsions, cholera, or other disease—from the effect—also used of an epidemic. **Mpindani**, n. *wa-* a person bent or crooked by stiffness or disease. **Mpindano**, n. *mi-* a bending together, folding together, a stiffening. *Mpindano wa mshipa*, cramp. **Mpinduzi**, n. *wa-* one who turns things upside down, a revolutionist, a disturber of peace. **-pindani**, a. obstinate, unyielding, stiff. **Pindi**, n. (— and *ma-*) (1) a bend, twist, turn, curve, winding, fold, coil, ring; (2) a space or division of time, a time (of something), hour (in a general sense) like *kipindi*, e.g. *pindi za asubuhi*, morning hours. *Pindi ya chakula*, meal-time. *Pindi za mchana*, times (divisions) of the day. *Wajua pindi atakapokuja?* Do you know the time when he will arrive? *Pindi ya muwa*, a ring on a sugar-cane. *Nyoka anapiga mapindi*, the snake is coiling up itself. *Mapindi ya mto*, windings of a river. Also as conj. when, if, supposing, although, i.e. at the time when, giving time for, allowing time for. **Pindo**, n. *ma-* selvedge, border of a cloth or garment, folded edge, hem. **Pindu**, n. *ma-* turning, tumbling, somersault. **Pinduani**, n. and a. (1) obstinate, revolutionary; (2) an obstinate, revolutionary person, one who upsets things, matters, &c. **Pinduli**, n. *ma-* something which causes revolution, and hence the pendulum of a wall clock. (Note: this may be a corruption of the Eng. word 'pendulum', but associated with *pinda!*) **Pinduo**, n. *ma-* a change, an upsetting, an alteration in procedure, affairs, &c. **Pindupindu**, n. and adv. cholera, convulsions, &c., and as adv. upside down, rolling over, &c. *Alianguka pindupindu*, he fell down head over heels, or rolled over and over. **Upindani**, n. (*pindani*), stiffness, obstinacy. **Upinde**, n. (*pinde*) a bending, a bend, a being bent, a thing bent, but commonly a bow (for shooting, the weapon) only. *Pinda upinde*, bend a bow. *Upinde wa mvua*, a rainbow. **Upindo**, n. *ma-* same as *pindo* and *kipindo*. **Upinduzi**, n. *ma-* upsetting, overturning, capsizing, revolution, habit of turning things about, revolutionary spirit, habit, traits, &c.

Pinda, n. *ma-*. See under **Kipinda**.

Pindamana, v., **-pindani**, a., **Pindi**, n. (— and *ma-*), **Pindo**, n. *ma-*, **Pindu**, n. *ma-*, **Pindua**, v., **Pinduani**, a. and n., **Pinduka**, v., **Pindukia**, v., **Pinduli**, n. *ma-*, **Pinduo**, n. *ma-*, **Pindupindu**, n. and adv. See under **Pinda**, v.

Pinga, v. (see also *pinza*), (1) cause (be, make) an obstruction, put in the way, obstruct, stop the way, block, thwart, check, oppose, contradict. *Jipinga*, put oneself in the way, oppose. *Pinga mlango*, fasten (close, bar) the door. *Pinga shikio la chombo*, *pinga chombo kwa shikio*, i.e. use the rudder to check, shape the course of a vessel. *Pinga njia*, block the road. (2) bet, lay wager. Ps. **Pingwa**. St. and Pot. **Pingika**. Prep. **Pingia**, e.g. *pingia mlango*, close the door against, or, put a bar across the door, secure the door. **Cs.**

Pingisha. Rp. **Pingana,** (1) oppose each other; (2) bet against each other, challenge each other. *Pingana na mtu,* come to cross purposes with a person. Stc. **Pingama,** and Rp. **Pingamana,** be in a position of obstructing, of opposing, &c. Cs. **Pingamisha.** Cs. of Rp. **Pingamanisha,** obstruct, thwart, use as an obstacle, or bar—like *pinga,* but with Inten. force, of active, intentional opposition. **Kipingo,** n. *vi-* bar, peg (keeping something in place), barrier, obstruction. **Kipingu,** n. *vi-* dim. of *pingu,* see below. **Kipingwa,** n. *vi-* a door-bar, bolt. **Mpingani,** n. *wa-* an obstructionist, a stubborn opponent. **Pingamizi,** n. *ma-* that which obstructs, person or thing, a difficulty, obstacle, check, stop. **-pingani,** a. obstructive, contradictory, causing difficulty—usually of persons. **Pingo,** n. *ma-* barrier, obstruction, bar, e.g. a door-bar. **Pingu,** n. (— .nd *ma-*) (1) a fetter, and plur. fetters, i.e. two rings fastened round the leg at the ankle, and connected by an iron bar; (2) also, of a cord fastened round the ankles to assist in climbing a tree; (3) handcuffs; (4) *pingu za sikio,* a round piece or disc of wood, often ebony, worn in the lobe of the ear by the women of some tribes (cf. *jasi, kipini*); (5) a charm, i.e. for keeping off evil. (Cf. *hirizi, kago.*)

Pingili, n. See under **Pingua.**

Pinginyika, v. move the buttocks with a circular motion when walking or dancing. (Cf. *finginyika* and *vinginyika.*)

Pingo, n. *ma-*, **Pingu,** n. (— and *ma-*). See under **Pinga.**

Pingua, v. cut into pieces, cut up, cut in lengths, e.g. of sugar-cane. Ps. **Pinguliwa.** Prep. **Pingulia.** **Kipingili,** n. *vi-* a ring marking a knot or joint in a plant, e.g. in sugar-cane. Also the part between the knots or joints, e.g. part of the leg between the knee and ankle, the shin. Anything similar in form. **Pingili,** n. *ma-* amplic.

Pini, n. (— and of size *ma-*) haft, handle—in which a tool or instrument is inserted. **Kipini,** n. *vi-* dim.

Pinza, v. (a Cs. or Inten. of *pinga*), obstruct, stop the way, thwart, check, oppose, contradict, like *pinga.* (Cf. *kinga* and *kinza.*) **-pinzani,** a. obstructive, contradictory, causing difficulty. **Mpinzani,** n. *wa-* an obstructionist, stubborn, opponent, one who contradicts or opposes. **Upinzani,** n. obstruction, habit, trait, action, &c., of obstructing, opposing, thwarting, &c.

Pipa,* n. *ma-* cask, barrel, tub, butt. Dim. **Kipipa,** n. *vi-* (Port. *pipa,* a pipe, i.e. 2 hogsheads, or Hind. پيپا.)

Pirikana, v. be strong, well knit, muscular.

Pisha, v. See under **Pita.**

Pishi, n. (1) a measure of capacity for solids, i.e. grain, &c. a dry measure—equal to 4 *kibaba* (which see), i.e. about half a gallon; (2) it is also used as a measure of weight corresponding generally to the above, about 6 lb.; (3) the vessel used as a measure. *Kwa mizani au kwa pishi,* by weight or measure, i.e. of capacity.

Pisho, n. *ma-* cautery, mark made by cautery.

Piswa, v. become silly, foolish, doting. **Piswa,** n. *ma-* foolishness, dotage. (Cf. *kichaa, pumbaa,* v.)

Pita, v. (1) pass, go on, go by, pass by (on, in front of, off, away, over, beyond); (2) fig. surpass, overpass, excel, exceed, outstrip, be too much for. *Pita njia,* go along a road. *Mto wapita,* the river is flowing by. *Mambo yaliyopita,* past events, the past. *Mtu wa kupita,* a passer-by, a wayfarer, a passing traveller. *Yapita cheo,* it passes bounds, is excessive. Hence *kupita cheo* used as adv. beyond all bounds, extravagantly, abnormally. *Kupita,* as conj. more than—in comparisons (cf. *kuliko*). *Yule mrefu kupita mimi*, he is taller than I. *Pita juu*, fly through the air. Used (like *enda*) with *zangu, zako, zake*, &c. *Napita zangu*, I am going away. *Piteni zenu*, (Imperat.) go away, pass on. Also in semi-Cs. sense, *njia zinazopita watu*, paths which people pass along. *Shamba linalopita maji*, a garden with a running stream. Ps. **Pitwa.** St. and Pot. **Pitika,** be passed, be passable, be able to be surpassed, &c. *Njia inapitika*, the road is passable. Hence **Pitikana,** be able to be passed (surpassed). *Haipitikani*, it is unsurpassable. Prep. **Pitia,** (1) pass by (away, from, to, &c.); (2) pass by on purpose, or by accident, and so slight, neglect, omit; (3) pass away from the mind, be forgotten. *Nilipitiwa*, I forgot, it passed from my memory. D.Prep. **Pitilia,** pass right by, pass quite away from, be utterly forgotten by, wholly surpass, and with *mbali* (which see), e.g. *amewapitilia mbali*, he has completely outstripped them. *Nimepitiliwa*, I have quite forgotten. Rp. of Prep. **Pitiana,** e.g. of commercial or social intercourse, pass to (or from) each other, be on good terms, be in constant contact with each other, &c. Cs. **Pitisha,** or more commonly **Pisha,** (1) cause to pass, guide, conduct; (2) let pass, make room for, allow passage; (3) put away (aside, off) oust, neglect, reject, &c. *Pisha wakati*, spend time. *Pisha mchana* (*masika*), pass away the day (the rainy season). *Mito haipishi*, the rivers do not allow crossing—like *haipitiki*. *Pishwa tohara*, be put through the ceremony of circumcision. Prep. of Cs. **Pishia.** Rp. of Cs. **Pishana,** pass by each other, i.e. by overtaking, allow each other to pass. Rp. **Pitana,** pass by each other, overlap. **Kipito,** n. *vi-* a passing by or through, a way through, a passage, pass, &c. **Pito,** n. *ma-* (1) way (means, &c.) of passing, a passage; (2) amplic. of *kipito*. (Cf. *njia, kijia, kichochoro*.)

Plau,* n. a plough—adopted for use in text-books and school lessons on agriculture to distinguish from native implements of agriculture. (Eng. plough.)

Po is a form of the demonstrative prefix *pa*, of place—the *o* (*a*) either denoting reference or relative distance, 'there', (*b*) or else giving it the force of a relative pronoun, 'where'. (1) As a demonstrative *-po* is used of position in time, as well as place, and also of circumstances generally, and commonly occurs (*a*) in the adv. *hapo, papo*, (*b*) affixed to *ndi-* or the person-pfxs. or parts of the verb *-wa*, and its equivalents, e.g. *yupo*, he is there (here). *Ndipo alipo*, that is where he is, &c. *Alikuwapo*, he was there, &c. (2) as a relative, with verb-forms generally, referring (*a*) to *mahali*, understood, (*b*) of place, time, or circumstances, 'where, when, as, if, supposing, in case'. As a separate word *po* only appears in such phrases as *po pote*, in whatever place, wherever it be.

Poa, v. become cool, and so (a temperature being a common symptom of illness) improve in health, become well, be cured. *Wali umepoa*, the rice has cooled. *Amepoa ugonjwa*, he has recovered from his sickness. *Hasira yake ilipoa*, his anger cooled down. Prep. **Polea.** *Mambo yamenipolea*, affairs have become cooler (better) for me. **Pona** (for other forms in which *n* is interposed between two vowels as a kind of derived form, see *faa, fana*; *pua, puna*) (1) become safe, escape, be rescued (saved, delivered); (2) get a living, subsist, preserve one's life, live; and esp. (3) get well (from illness), recover health, be convalescent, regain strength. Prep. **Ponea,** (1) be saved by (with, for, at, &c.); (2) live on, be supported by, depend for subsistence (whether food, necessaries, or occupation). *Unaponea nini?* What are you living on? *Aliponea maji siku sita,* he lived on water six days. *Aliponea mizizi wakati wa njaa,* he ate roots and was saved over the famine. *Cha kuponea,* subsistence, means of living. Cs. of Dir. **Poza,** (1) cool, make cool; (2) cure, heal, comfort, quieten, &c. *Mganga amenipoza ugonjwa wangu,* the doctor has cured my sickness. *Alikuja akanipoza moyo,* he came and comforted me. *Alimpa tunzo kupoza uchungu wake,* he gave him a present to cool his bitterness. Cs. of *pona,* **Ponya,** save, deliver, rescue, cure, restore to health, evade danger, &c. *Uniponye wa jua, nitakuponya wa mvua,* protect me (in the time—*wakati*) of sun, and I will protect you (in the time) of rain. *Jiponya!* Mind yourself! Look out! (Cf. *jihadhari, simile, habedari.*) Cs. **Ponyesha,** sometimes used like *ponya* and *poza.* St. of Cs. and Pot. **Ponyeka,** *haiponyeki kabisa,* it is absolutely incurable. Cv. *ponyoa* is not in use, but St. of Cv. is—**Ponyoka,** slip away, slide out, escape—of secret, unnoticed or unexpected movements. *Mtu aliponyoka makutini, akaanguka,* a man slipped off the thatch and fell. *Bilauri imeniponyoka mkononi,* the glass has slipped out of my hand. Cs. **Ponyosha,** cause to fall, let slip from one's hand, &c. Prep. of Cs. **Ponyoshea,** cause to fall, let slip from one's hand, &c., e.g. *alimponyoshea kuku chembe za mtama,* she let some grains of millet fall from her hand for the fowl. **Kiponya,** n. *vi-* something which preserves or cures, a remedy. *Kiponya cha njaa,* the remedy of hunger, i.e. food. **Maponea,** n. plur. means of subsistence, livelihood, food. **Maponyea,** n. plur. means of curing (rescuing, &c.). *Matikiti ndiyo maponyea njaa,* water melons are what save from starvation, i.e. as the last resource in a drought. **Maponyo,** n. plur. (1) helping things, drugs, medicines, means of saving; (2) getting well, a cure, rescue, preservation. **Mapoza,** n. plur. remedies, means, or appliances for healing. **Mponyi,** n. *wa-*, **Mpozi,** n. *wa-* (1) one who cures, a physician, one who gets another out of danger, difficulties, &c. *Mpozi ni Mungu,* God is the (real) physician. Native medicine-men are usually called *mganga*; European doctors, *daktari* or *tabibu*; (2) one who cools, comforts, &c. **Uponyi,** n. (*ponyi*), means of saving, way of escape, rescue, cure. (Dist. *pooza.*)

Pochi,* n. *ma-* a sort of chain bangle worn on the wrist by some women. (? Pers. and Hind. پیچ a coil.)

Podo, n. (— and *ma-*) quiver, arrow-case, commonly of wood. (Cf. *ala, uo.*)

Pofu, n. an eland, also *mpofu.*

-pofu, a. See under **Pofua.**

Pofua, v. spoil, cause to fail, ruin, blight—but esp. of sight, blind, deprive of sight. *Amempofua macho,* he has destroyed his eyes. Ps. **Pofuliwa.** St. and Pot. **Pofuka.** Prep. **Pofulia.** Cs. and Intens. **Pofusha,** used in the same way as *pofua.* **Kipofu,** n. *vi-* and adv. (1) a blind person, in a blind state or way, blindly. *Mtoto kipofu haoni,* the child is blind, he does not see. *Mtu huyu ni kipofu,* this man is blind. **Mpofu,** n. *wa-* rarely heard, a blind person, the usual word is *kipofu.* **-pofu,** a. spoiled, bereft, lacking something—and esp. of lack of sight, blind, i.e. *pofu wa macho. Labda nitakuwa pofu,* I shall perhaps become blind, but usu. *kipofu* is used. **Upofu,** n. deprivation, ruin, loss, but esp. of loss of sight, blindness, i.e. *upofu wa macho.*

Pogo, n. and adv. See under **Pogoa.**

Pogoa, v. lop, prune, cut away branches or leaves. Ps. **Pogolewa.** Prep. **Pogolea,** cut with (for, &c.),

e.g. *kisu cha kupogolea*, a pruning-knife. **Pogo**, n. and adv. (perh. plur. of *upogo*) lopsidedness, a one-sided awry condition, e.g. *wana pogo za nyuso zao*, they have their faces awry. *Kwenda pogo*, walk in an unequal, limping way. *Tazama pogo*, squint, leer. **Pogoo**, n. *ma-* a branch cut off a tree. (Cf. *tawi, tanzu.*) **Upogo**, n. (*pogo*) condition of being cut awry, i.e. one-sided, in unequal parts, being awry, distorted, zigzag. Of the eyes —squinting. As adv. *upogoupogo*, from side to side, zigzag.

Pojo, n. a green gram, usu. called *choroko*.

Poka, v. take by violence, steal away, rob (of), abduct. *Wanataka kupoka mke wangu*, they want to carry off my wife. Ps. **Pokwa**, *nimepokwa upanga*, I have been robbed of my sword. Prep. not in use, as the direct form has a prepositional meaning, also, there is a verb *pokea*, derived from another verb, *poka*, receive. Rp. **Pokana**, rob each other. Cv. **Pokonya** (from *pokoa*), take away by force, rob, plunder, abduct, ravish.

Pokea, v. (1) receive, accept, take in the hand; (2) take in, welcome, entertain, receive as guest; (3) fig. accept, assent to, agree with. *Wakawapokea mizigo*, they took their loads from them, i.e. in a friendly way, they relieved them. *Tulikwenda kwao wakatupokea vizuri*, we went to their place and they received (welcomed) us well, i.e. gave us hospitality. *Mtu akikupa kitu, pokea kwa mikono miwili*, if a person gives you a thing, take it with two hands. *Hatukuweza kuyapokea maneno yao*, we were not able to receive (agree with) their statements. Ps. **Pokewa.** Prep. **Pokelea**, receive for (on behalf of, in the place of, &c.). Cs. of Prep. **Pokeleza**, cause to accept. Cs. **Pokeza**, cause to receive, give to, put in the hands of. Rp. of Cs. **Pokezana**, also Cs. **Pokezanya**, *pokezana mizigo*, take turns in carrying loads. *Pokezana mshahara*, take turns in drawing wages, a custom among some people: perhaps four or five agree *kupokezana mshahara*, one man draws the wages of the four or five men one month, another the next month, and so on. **Kipokee**, adv. turns, turn and turn about. **Mpokeaji**, n. *wa-*, **Mpokezi**, n. *wa-* one who receives, a receiver, recipient. **Pokeo**, n. *ma-* thing received, often used in the plur. *Mapokeo* (1) receipts, also (2) in the sense of traditions, customs, &c., passed down from father to son, or from chief to chief, &c. (Cf. *kabidhi, twaa, kubali, karibisha.*)

Pokonya, v. See under **Poka.**

-pole, a. mild, meek, gentle, sober-minded, amiable, kind—opp. to *-kali*, of temper generally. *-a upole*, is more common in the same sense. *Pole* is used as an adv., gently, softly, quietly, slowly, &c. Often Redupl. *polepole*. Frequently used to sooth or encourage or express sorrow, condolence after an accident, shock, misfortune, bad news, &c.—be calm, take it quietly, don't excite yourself, never mind. *Tulikwenda kuwapa pole*, we went to condole with them. *Pole bwana* (to a person who has stumbled, hurt himself, &c.). **Upole**, n. gentleness, kindness, meekness, slowness of movement. The quality implied holds a high place in native estimation, esp. as to Europeans—contr. *ukali*, and cf. *-ema, -anana, taratibu, kiasi.*)

Polisi,* n. *ma-* a policeman. (Eng.)

Pombe, n. a native beer—an intoxicant made from many kinds of grain and some fruits, e.g. bananas, by fermentation. In the earlier stages of manufacture, while sweet and unintoxicating, it is called *togwa*. (Cf. *kileo, ulevi*, under *lewa*, v.)

Pombo, n. applied to the leaves of any suitable plant or tree used as a vegetable, which when cooked are viscous.

Pombogea, v. also **Pombojea**, v. fail, be a failure, e.g. of a ceremony, dance, &c. (Cf. *pooza*.)

Pomboo, n. (— and *ma*-) porpoise. *Pomboo huzama na kuibuka* (or *kuzuka*), porpoises dive and reappear.

Pomoka, v. variant for (1) *bomoka*, and (2) *poromoka*, which see.

Pomoni, adv. choke-full, crowded, filled to overflowing. *Vitu vilijaa pomoni*, (the place) was choke full of things. *Watu walijaa pomoni*, the people filled the place.

Pona, v. See under **Poa**.

Ponda, v. (1) crush by pounding or beating, pound to pieces, beat small, pulverize—usually with wooden pestle and mortar (cf. *kinu mchi*) Dist. *twanga*, properly used of the same process applied to cleaning grain, i.e. removing the husks, *saga*, of grinding grain to flour by millstones, pressure, attrition. Thus *twanga* is used of rice, maize, millet, &c., *ponda* of such seeds as pepper, curry (*bizari*), and also leaves of cassava, &c.; (2) fig. crush, take all life and spirit away from, break down, dispirit; also (3) of being run over or crushed by a motor-car or other vehicle, &c. Ps. **Pondwa.** St. and Pot. **Pondeka**, (1) be crushed, beaten down, pulverized; (2) capable of being broken in pieces. Prep. of St. **Pondekea**, e.g. *mtama umepondekea chini*, the millet is crushed down to the ground. Rp. of Prep. **Pondekeana**, e.g. of stalks of millet crushed and bruised against each other. Prep. **Pondea**, e.g. *amenipondea pilipili kinuni*, she pounded the peppercorns for me in a mortar. Cs. **Ponza**, (1) cause to be crushed, &c., but esp. (2) put in danger, risk, speculate with, make a venture, do by hazard, be reckless. *Aliponza roho yake*, he took his life in his hand, i.e. did (an action) to the danger of his life (or soul). (Cf. *hatirisha*, *bahatisha*.) **Kipondo**, n. *vi*- dim. of *pondo*, see below. **Kipondwe**, n. *vi*- food consisting of something pounded or crushed, a mash, e.g. of cleaned grain and grated coco-nut mixed together in a mortar. **Mponda**, n. *wa*- governing a noun following, one who crushes, breaks to pieces. *Mponda mali*, a spendthrift, prodigal. **Mpondo**, n. *mi*- act of crushing, &c. **Pondeo**, n. *ma*- a kind of millet used by shoemakers. (Cf. *nguri*.) **Pondo**, n. *ma*- a punting-pole, for pushing a boat or canoe along shallow water. *Maji ya pondo hayataki tanga*, shallow water does not require a sail, also sometimes **Upondo**, n. (*pondo*).

Pongea, v. recover from a serious illness, a difficult position, a dangerous undertaking, &c. Cs. **Pongeza**, used in the sense of condole with, congratulate, salute a person who has recovered from a serious illness, &c. **Pongezi**, n. congratulations on recovery from illness, &c. (Cf. *hongea*, under *honga*, v. of which *pongea* appears to be a variant.)

Poni* n. *weka poni*, pledge, pawn a thing. **Poni**, v. (sometimes) pledge, pawn. (Cf. *rehani*. Eng. pawn.)

Pono, n. name of a fish, said to be often in a torpid state. *Ana usingizi kama pono*, he is as sleepy as a *pono*.

Ponoa, v. (1) strip off, e.g. of bark from a tree, get the fibres out of bark; (2) wipe off, e.g. oil or liquid from the skin. (Cf. *pua*, v.)

Ponta,* n. back-stitch—in sewing. *Piga ponta*, sew a back-stitch, e.g. of a wristband or cuff. (Port. *ponto*.)

Ponya, v., **Ponyeka**, v., **Ponyoka**, v. See under **Poa**.

Ponza, v. See under **Ponda**.

Pooza, v. (1) become useless, withered, paralysed, impotent. *Mwenye kupooza*, a cripple, an impotent man. (2) be spoiled, lose beauty, appearance, fail, &c. *Mambo yamepooza*, things have not gone well, they have gone awry. *Walipoondoa vyombo nyumbani, nyumba ilipooza*, when they removed the furniture from the house, it became bare, uncomfortable, it lost its appearance, &c. Cs. **Poozesha**, of the effect of illness, cripple, disable. (Cf. *chakaa, fifia, umbua.*) **Pooza**, n. *ma-* something undeveloped, withered, dried up, arrested in growth, esp. of fruit fallen from a tree in a half-formed, withered state. **-pooza**, a. undeveloped, withered. **Kipooza**, n. *vi-* paralysis, deadness, a paralysed person, a withered dried-up thing. Also adv., in a withered (dead, helpless) state. **Upooza**, n. deadness, numbness.

Popo, n. (— and of size *ma-*) a bat, also often used for moths and butterflies. **Kipopo**, n. *vi-* dim.

Popoa, v. knock down fruit from a tree with a stone, stick, &c. Prep. **Popolea**, e.g. *fimbo ya kupopolea*, a stick to knock fruit from a tree. **Mpopoo**, n. *mi-* act of knocking anything down with a stick, stone, &c. (Cf. *pura*, v. (B).

Popolea, v. (1) see under **Popoa**, v.; (2) *tui la kupopolea*, see under **Tui.**

Popoo,* n. (1) the areca nut, fruit of the *mpopoo*. Cut in thin slices, it is much used for chewing with *tambuu*, &c. See *uraibu*. (Pers. پوپل.) (2) a ball of iron or lead, bullet.

Popotoa, v. wrench, twist, strain, distort. *Popotoa mkono*, twist the hand—so as to make the joints crack. Ps. **Popotolewa**, e.g. *mlango ulifungwa ukapopotolewa*, the door was fastened and then wrenched open. St. and Pot. **Popotoka**, of a sprained ankle, &c. Prep. **Popotolea.** Cs. **Popotosha.** (Cf. *pota, tegua.*)

Pora, n. *ma-* a young cockerel, not yet old enough to crow.

Pori,* n. *ma-* steppe, wilderness, uninhabited wilds, grassy without trees. (Ar. بورة waste land.)

Poroja, n. porridge, or anything of similar consistency. *Wali poroja*, rice cooked with too much water. *Poroja la chokaa*, watery mortar. **Poroja**, v. be watery, like gruel.

Porojo, n. *ma-* (1) light conversation, idle chatter, also (2) an idle chatterer, one conversationally gifted.

Poromoa, v. knock down, cause to fall. *Jiporomoa*, roll or rush down a slope. St. and Pot. **Poromoka**, glide or slip down in a mass, or with a rush (like an avalanche, cataract, or stone-slide), be poured out, gush out like a flood, be discharged, rush down, fall in a shower, or fit of terror, collapse. *Poromoka mnazi*, slide down a coco-nut tree. *Poromoka mlima*, rush down a hill. *Poromoka* is used of a banana plant bending down with its load of fruit. Prep. **Poromokea.** Cs. **Poromosha**, and *pomosha*, e.g. like *poromoa*. *Poromosha nazi*, shower down coco-nuts from a tree. *Poromosha mavi*, empty the bowels. *Aliporomosha sanduku*, he let the box come down with a rush. **Poromoko**, n. *ma-* (1) place of sudden descent, precipice, steep place, face of a cliff; (2) shower, fall, discharge, rush, e.g. of stones, water, &c. *Maporomoko ya mto*, cataracts, rapids. *Maporomoko ya maji*, waterfalls.

Posa, v. ask in marriage, become a suitor for, woo—the person addressed being the parent or relation in the first place. Ps. **Poswa.** St. and Pot. **Poseka.** Prep. **Posea**, e.g. *mali ya kuposea*, money to arrange a marriage with, to marry on. Cs. **Posesha**, *mtu wa kuposesha*, a matchmaking person. Rp. **Posana**, agree about a marriage. **Maposo**, n. plur. proposals or arrangements for marrying, wooing. **Mposa**, n. *wa-*, and **Mposaji**, n. *wa-*, a suitor, one who makes a proposal of marriage to parents. **Mposeaji**, n. *wa-* one who proposes on behalf of another. **Mposo**, n. *mi-* proposal of marriage, wooing. **Posa**, n. marriage settlement, gifts, arrangements, &c., with a view to marriage. **Uposo**, n. *ma-* application for a wife, proposal of marriage, present sent to bride's relations.

Posha, v. (1) give rations to, supply

with daily food, serve out supplies to; (2) use, give for nothing, without pay, e.g. *sikupata mshahara, nimeposha nguvu zangu bure,* I received no wages, I have used my strength for nothing. Prep. **Poshea.** Ps. **Poshwa.** Cs. **Posheza. Posho,** n. (—and *ma-*) rations, daily supply of food, clothing, maintenance, e.g. such as is given to porters on a journey, labourers on a plantation, soldiers, a wife, &c.

Poso, n. *ma-*. See under **Posa.**

Posta,* n. used of reference to the Post Office and its services. *Nyumba ya posta,* a post office. *Kupeleka barua kwa posta,* to send a letter by post. (Eng. post.)

Pota, v. twist, esp. of twisting the strands of flax, cotton, &c., to make string, twine, rope. (Cf. *sokota, pakasa.*) The Prep. and its derivatives are restricted in meaning, see *potea,* given separately for convenience of reference. Cv. **Potoa,** (1) twist, put out of the straight, make crooked (curved, slanting, &c.), turn aside, give a twist to; (2) fig. ruin pervert, spoil, corrupt. *Potoa kazi,* spoil work. *Potoa maneno,* pervert words. *Jipotoa,* behave extravagantly, ruin oneself, e.g. by over-dressing, bad habits, drink, &c. Ps. **Potolewa.** St. and Pot. **Potoka,** be crooked, twisted, spoiled, perverted—also be wrong-headed, eccentric, cranky, perverse. Prep. **Potolea.** Cs. **Potosha,** Inten. pervert, &c. *Amempotosha mtoto,* he has perverted the child, led him astray, led him into bad habits, &c. **Mpoto,** n. *mi-* a twisting, of rope, &c. **Mpotoe,** n. *wa-*, **Mpotovu,** n. *wa-* a wrong-headed, wilful, perverse, wayward, headstrong, unprincipled person—contr. of *mwongofu.* **-potoe,** a. out of the straight, crooked—but usu. in the fig. sense, perverted, perverse, spoilt, headstrong, depraved. **-potovu,** a. used generally like *-potoe,* but with Act. as well as Ps. force. *-potovu wa mali,* prodigal, wasteful. *-potovu wa akili,* wrong-headed. **Upote,** n. (*pote*) thong, bowstring—of sinew or twisted string. **Upotoe,** n. but usu. **Upotovu,** n. caprice, wilfulness, obstinacy, wickedness, perversion, perverseness.

Pote, a form of *-ote,* all.

Potea, v. (Prep. of *pota,* which see, with restricted application) (1) go astray, get lost, wander, be at fault, be ruined, perish; (2) fig. fall away, deteriorate, go to ruin, become reprobate; (3) be scarce. *Potea* is the common word for material and moral loss, failure, and ruin. Frequently used with an obj. pfx. as if a Prep. form. *Kisu kimenipotea,* I have lost my knife, for *nimepotewa na kisu. Akili zimempotea,* he has lost his senses. Prov. *kupotea njia ndiko kujua njia,* to lose your way is to know your way. *Fedha zimepotea siku hizi,* money is scarce at present. Ps. **Potewa,** e.g. incur the loss of, *kupotewa na mali,* to lose money. Prep. **Potelea,** not often used, except in the common imprecation, *potelea mbali,* go and be hanged. Cs. **Poteza,** cause to perish, throw away, ruin, corrupt, spoil, abuse, use wrongly. Prep. of Cs. **Potezea,** e.g. *alimpotezea maneno,* he quite refuted (thwarted, perverted) his statements. Rp. of Cs. **Potezana.** Rp. **Poteana,** of several objects, get scattered, lose each other. **Mpotevu,** n. *wa-* a destructive, wasteful, person. **Mpotezi,** n. *wa-* one who spoils, ruins, wastes, corrupts, misleads, destroys, &c. In many ways like *mpotovu.* **-potevu,** wasteful, destructive, ruinous, &c. **Upotevu,** n. (1) destructiveness, waste, ruin, vandalism; (2) Ps. being lost, wandering, perishing, delusion.

Potoa, v., **-potoe,** a., **-potovu,** a. See under **Pota.**

Povu, n. *ma-* scum, froth, foam, a bubble, lather. *Povu la sabuni,* soap lather. *Povu la bahari,* foam on the sea. *Fanya povu,* foam, froth. *Mpa-*

ka povu lipande, till scum forms on the surface.

Poza, v. See under **Poa**.

Pua, n. (A) the nose—and used to describe what resembles (or is supposed to resemble) the nose, e.g. apex of an arch. *Mwanzi wa pua*, nostril, also *tundu la pua*. *Piga pua*, snort. *Sema kipua, semea puani*, speak as though the nose were pinched. *Ujinga huo wa kuacha kinywa kutia puani*, the stupidity of using the nose for the mouth.

Pua,* n. (B) steel, tempered iron—also *pua ya chuma, chuma cha pua*. *Tia pua shoka*, temper the edge of an axe. (Cf. *matiko*. Pers. پور steel.)

Pua, v. wipe the face with the palm of the hand. Rd. *puapua*, slice, take slices off. (Cf. *lenga*.) Note: this word is sometimes used for *pura*, which appears to be from a separate root. **Puna** (for similar cases where *n* is interposed as a kind of derived form, see *faa, fana*; *poa, pona*) (1) wipe the face with the palm of the hand, wipe or scrape off perspiration; (2) scrape off, peel, e.g. *puna ganda la mti*, strip the bark off a tree. *Puna ngozi*, scrape a skin clean—of fat, hair, &c. *Puna ndizi*, strip the the skin off a banana. Also used in the same way as *fidua*, i.e. draw back the foreskin. Ps. **Punwa**. St. and Pot. **Punika**. Prep. **Punia**. Cs. **Punisha**. Cv. **Punua**, same as *puna*. Cs. (2) *punya*, is not in use, but a noun made from it is, i.e. *punyeto*. **Mapune**, n. plur. a disease of the skin. **Punyeto**, n. masturbation (for the significance of *-to* terminal, see *-to*). *Fanya* (*piga*) *punyeto*, masturbate, also sometimes used for sodomy. (Cf. *futa, menya, matuutuu, marugurugu*.)

Puchua, v. See **Pujua**.

Pugi, n. wood-dove, also *Pugiwanda*, *Turtur afer*. **Pugikikombe**, Tambourine dove, *Typmanistria tympanistria*.

Puju, n. unicorn fish, considered to be good eating by Europeans. It has a thick skin which has to be stripped.

Pujua, v. (sometimes heard as *puchua*), (1) take the skin off, remove the outside covering, abrade, e.g. *pujua muhindi* (*embe*), e.g. of a cob of maize, or the rind of a mango, i.e. strip off with the fingers (cf. *koboa*, when an instrument is used)—not of the skin of animals, which is *chuna*; (2) separate grain from chaff after pounding; (3) with Rf. pfx. *jipujua*, (1) bruise oneself; (2) fig. bare onself, cast off shame, lead a mean, beggarly, shameful life. Ps. **Pujuliwa**. St. **Pujuka**. Prep. **Pujulia**. **Mpujufu**, n. *wa-* (also *mpujuzi*), a mean, abased, shameful person, one with filthy habits, who uses filthy words, &c. **-pujufu**, a. (also *-pujuzi*), shameless, beggarly and in Act. sense, wasteful, prodigal.

Puku, n. a field rat or mouse.

Pukuchua, v., **Pukupuku**, adv., **Pukusa**, v. and n., **Pukuso**, n., **Pukutua**, v. See under **Pukuta**.

Pukuta, v. shake off like a bird or animal shaking off water; strip off, like grains off a cob of maize, St. and Pot. **Pukutika**, fall off in showers, as leaves when withered, or fruit when ripe, also of rice when cooked so that the grains are dry, not watery. Cf. **Pukutisha**, e.g. *pukutisha umande*, wait, give time, for the dew to fall. *Pukutisha mkate*, crumble bread, let fall the crumbs. *Pukutisha jasho*, drop with sweat. *Uso wake unapukutisha jasho*, sweat is dropping from his face. Cf. **Pukutua**, but often **Pukuchua**, same as *pukuta*. Cs. **Pukusa**, (1) cause to fall in showers, cause to shower down in quantities, make shed fruit; (2) throw money about, make liberal presents; (3) make a congratulatory visit to—with presents, &c. **Pukusa** is used of e.g. stripping the grains off a cob of maize, leaves or fruit from a tree, giving money to a crowd, destroying lives wholesale (of an epidemic). *Twende tumpukuse*, let us go and offer our congratulations (presents) to him. But, *aliupukusa mkoma mzima*, he shook all the fruit off the *mkoma* tree. Ps. **Pukuswa.** Prep. **Pukusia.** Cs. **Pukusisha. Kipuku,** adv. also **Kipukupuku,** adv. in showers, in numbers, wholesale, like leaves falling, e.g. of the effect of an epidemic in killing people, i.e. *maradhi ya kipuku* (*pukupuku*). *Watu wanakufa kipuku*, people are dying like flies. **Kipukusa,** n. *vi-* (1) something shed, cast, dropped, e.g. horns of an animal, but esp. of leaves or fruit self-detached or early shed; (2) dim. of *pukusa*; (3) a kind of boring insect; (4) a kind of banana. **Mpukuti,** n. a slang term for money. (Cf. *mbango*.) **Pukupuku,** adv. lit. in showers like *kipuku*, and so, in quantities, wholesale, plentifully. *Jaa pukupuku*, be full to overflowing, e.g. of a measure full till the grain runs over. **Pukusa,** n. a kind of banana; also **Pukuso,** n. a present given at a wedding, or when a youth reaches puberty or comes out of the initiation school; a congratulatory present. **Pukute,** n. (1) lit. that which is showered down, or in a condition resembling such; (2) used of rice, when cooked so that every grain is loose and separate, i.e. *pukute ya wali*, or *wali wa pukute*.

Puleki,* n. a spangle, tinsel ornament (Pers. پولک scales of a fish.)

Pulika, v. listen, for the more common *sikiliza*.

Puliza, v. (sometimes heard as *puza*), (1) blow with the mouth, puff—and with an object, blow up, fill with air. *Puliza pumzi*, fill with breath. *Puliza mpira*, blow up a ball (tire). *Puliza moto*, blow up a fire. *Panya hupuliza aumapo*, a rat blows when it bites—so many natives believe; they say it blows so that the person being bitten will not feel it at the time. Also used of blowing on a sore place, to deaden the smart, and fig. of a man who, after using bitter, strong language, follows it up by a kind or gentle expression—to take the sting out! (2) pay out a rope, as when letting a bucket into a well, an anchor down, a fishing-line into the sea—also used of playing a fish after it is hooked. *Puliza kishada*, let a kite go up, i.e. pay out the cord in order to fly it. (3) irritate, itch. *Koo linapuliza*, the throat is tickling, irritating. (4) cast a spell, e.g. *mchawi hupuliza*, the wizard casts a spell. *Puliza mafundo*, make a spell (either for good or bad) by tying charms, &c., in knots in a string, and forming a wish while tying the knot. Ps. **Pulizwa.** St. and Pot. **Pulizika.** Prep. **Pulizia,** e.g. (1) blow into, blow up; (2) pay out a rope, &c. (for, in), e.g. *amepulizia mshipi samaki baharini*, he has let down his line to a fish in the sea.

Pululu, n. *ma-* wilderness, uninhabited country, forest. (Cf. *pori*.)

Puma, v. throb, pulsate—like the pulse, heart, &c., e.g. of an abscess, the head in illness. (Cf. *purita*.) Cv. **Pumua,** (1) draw breath, breathe, live; (2) get breath, rest, find relief, have breathing time. Cs. **Pumuza.** St. **Pumzika,** get breath, rest oneself take a holiday, stop working. *Pumzika udhia*, have a respite from annoyance. *Pumzika kazi*, rest from work. Prep. **Pumzikia,** e.g. *mahali pa kupumzikia*, a resting-place. Cs. **Pumzisha,** cause (invite, allow) to rest. **Kipumziko,** n. *vi-* act (place, time, means, &c.) of taking rest, resting-place, recreation time, refreshment, relief. **Pumu,** n. *ma-* (1) breathing organ, lung, esp. of a living animal; (2) any affection of the lung, chest complaint, asthma. **Pumzi,** n. breath, breathing, respiration. *Paza* (*pandisha, vuta*) *pumzi*, draw in breath, fill the lungs. *Shusha* (*toa*) *pumzi*, empty the lungs. *Kokota pumzi* (or *roho*), draw the breath with difficulty. **Pumzikio,** n. *ma-*, **Pumziko,** n. *ma-* place (time, mode, &c.) of resting. **Upumuo,** n., **Upumzi,** n. same as *pumzi*.

Pumba, n. (— and *ma-*) (1) lump, rolled-up piece, clod of earth, packet. *Mapumba ndani ya uji,* lumps in the gruel. (2) chaff of grain; (3) excretion under the foreskin. (Cf. *chicha.*) **Kipumba,** n. *vi-* dim. (Cf. *donge.*)

Pumbaa, v. (1) be speechless, because of astonishment, fear, &c.; (2) be foolish, silly, weak-minded, negligent. *Pumbaa kazi,* take no pains about a job, do it carelessly, be idle. Cs. **Pumbaza,** (1) nonplus, cause to be speechless, because of astonishment, &c.; (2) befool, make a fool of, treat as a fool, deceive, play jokes upon. *Jipumbaza,* be stupid on purpose, pretend to be a fool. Ps. **Pumbazwa.** St. and Pot. **Pumbazika,** be made a fool of, be duped, e.g. *pumbazwa njia,* miss the way by carelessness. *Msiende mkapumbazika,* do not go and be foolish. **Mpumbavu,** n. *wa-* a fool, dupe. **-pumbavu,** a. foolish, stupid, ignorant. **Upumbavu,** n. folly, stupidity, ignorance.

Pumbu, n. (— and *ma-*) (1) scrotum, and plur. testicles; (2) affection of the scrotum, hernia, orchitis, &c. *Kokwa za (mayai ya) pumbu,* testicles. **Kipumbu,** n. *vi-* (1) dim.; (2) affection of the scrotum, hernia. (Cf. *korodani, kende.*)

Pumu, n. *ma-*, **Pumua,** v., **Pumzi,** n., **Pumzika,** v., **Pumzikio,** n. *ma-*, **Pumziko,** n. *ma-*, **Pumzisha,** v. See under **Puma.**

Puna, v. See under **Pua,** v.

Punda, n. (1) donkey, ass. *Punda kihongwe,* a mainland donkey, in contrast to the large white Muscat donkey. **Punda milia,** zebra. (2) a kind of dance used in exorcism of spirits. *Pepo punda,* tetanus, lockjaw.

Punde, adv. a little, just a little, somewhat, within a little time, just now (then), presently, soon, e.g. *niliona sijambo punde,* I felt a little better. *Mrefu punde,* a little taller. *Atapita punde hivi,* he will come shortly. *Umefika punde,* you have arrived lately. *Punde kwa punde,* little by little. (Cf. *kidogo, kitambo,* and opp. *sana, zaidi.*)

Punga, n. plur. of *upunga.*

Punga, v. (A) (1) wave, swing, sway, move to and fro, as of a fan, &c., use or cause a rhythmical motion. Thus *punga upepo,* put the air in motion, with a fan, &c., hence used of taking a change of air, *nakwenda pwani kupunga upepo,* I am going to the sea-shore for a change of air (also *punga hewa*). *Punga mikono,* wave the arms, i.e. as a signal or when walking. **Ps. Pungwa.** St. and Pot. **Pungika.** Prep. **Pungia,** *pungia mkono (kitambaa, nguo),* wave the hand (cloth, dress) to, signal to, &c. Cs. **Pungisha.** *Unipungishe upepo,* fan me. (Cf. *suka, tikisa, pepea.*)

Punga, v. (B) exorcize spirits, use of the whole ceremonial of native exorcism—dancing, drumming, incantations, e.g. *punga pepo,* exorcize a spirit, and with personal object *kupunga mtu,* put a person through the ceremony of exorcism. The man who directs the ceremony, i.e. the *mganga, mpunga pepo,* usually begins with the word *tawireni* or *taileni* (perh. from Ar. تعويل cry for help, with *-ni* of plural), a kind of formula as though making a request to the powers and the other *waganga* who may be present not to interfere with the proceedings or prevent the work from going well. He ends with *tailetai uganga una Mungu* (perh. from Ar. نولة magic, enchantment, &c.), which appears to mean, the work is now finished, but God is the one who has the power of curing. Those who have been exorcized are called *mteja, wa-* and they form a kind of guild which assists at other ceremonies. The ceremony consists of drumming and dancing, during which the *mganga* is said to call the spirit into the head of the patient (*pandisha* or *chuchia pepo kichwani*) and the head of the person is referred to as the *kiti cha pepo*, the seat of the spirit. Ps. **Pungwa.** St. **Pungika.** Prep. **Pungia.** C. **Pungisha. Pungwa**, n. a kind of dance used in the exorcism of spirits. (Note: this verb is identical with the prec.—the exorcism of spirits involves swaying to and fro, cf. *chuchia.*)

Punga, v. (C) decrease, but esp. of heat of the sun. *Jua limepunga*, the heat of the sun has decreased—of towards sunset. Cv. **Pungua**, grow less, diminish, abate, fall, decrease, e.g. *maumivu yamepungua*, the hurt has grown less. *Upepo umepungua*, the wind has diminished. *Akili zimempungua*, he has lost his mental powers. St. **Punguka**, grow smaller, get less, diminish, abate, fail. Prep. of St. **Pungukia**, e.g. *anapungukiwa mali*, his resources are failing him. Cs. **Punguza**, (1) make less, reduce, shorten, diminish, &c.; (2) discount. *Punguza bei*, lower the price. *Jipunguza*, humble, depreciate oneself. **Kipunguo**, n. *vi-* act (case, means, &c.) of lessening, diminution, defect, deficiency, short allowance. **Kipunguzi**, n. *vi-* discount. **Mpungufu**, n. *wa-* one lacking in sense, strength, &c. **Punguani**, n. *ma-* (1) a person who is mentally deficient, a simple person, an idiot (cf. *mpumbavu, mjinga, wazimu*); (2) a half-breed. (Cf. *suriama.*) **-pungufu**, a. defective, wanting, diminished, scanty. *Mpungufu wa mali*, short of money. *Mwezi mpungufu*, an incomplete month, i.e. one of 29 days. **Pungufu**, n. *ma-* defect, deficiency, something wanting, flaw. **Upungufu**. n. (*pungufu* and *ma-*), also **Upunguo**, n. *ma-* becoming less, abatement, decrease, deficiency, defect.

Pungu, n. (1) a kind of fish; (2) an eagle or other large bird of prey. Also **Kipungu**, n. *vi-*.

Pungua, v., **Punguani**, n. *ma-*, **-pungufu**, a. and n. *ma-*, **Punguka**, v., **Punguza**, v. See under **Punga**, v. (C).

Pungwa, n. See under **Punga**, v. (B).

Punja, v. cheat, swindle, by giving short measure, less than what is due, &c. Ps. **Punjwa.** St. and Pot. **Punjika.** Prep. **Punjia. Kipunjo**, n. *vi-* and adv. short measure, short weight, &c., i.e. something which has been withheld from a sale, &c., also, adv. with deceit, slyly, in a cheating manner. *Nilimwuliza kipunjo*, I questioned him slyly. (Cf. *hadaa, danganya, kopa, karamkia.* Prob. a Cs. or Inten. form of *punga*, v. (C).)

Punje, n. a grain, i.e. a single grain—of corn, maize, &c. *Punje moja ya mtama*, a grain of millet. (Cf. *chembe.*)

Punju, n. also sometimes **punyu**, a medicine prepared by wizards, said to be made from the heart of a snake and a lizard called *guruguru* mixed with certain things got from trees and plants and from the graves of people; these are all ground to powder and put over a fire. If mixed with food the preparation is said to cause constant coughing and a fatal illness.

Punua, v., **Punyeto**, n. See under **Pua**, v.

Puo, n. See under **Puza.**

Pupa, n. eagerness, haste, effort, zeal, eager desire. *Fanya pupa ya kwisha kazi*, be eager to finish work. *Pupa ya kula*, greediness, voracity. *Kula kwa pupa*, to eat greedily. Prov. *Mtaka yote kwa pupa hukosa yote*, he who wants everything in a hurry loses everything. **Kipupa**, n. *vi-* and adv. unseemly haste, over-eagerness, greediness, &c. (Cf. *choyo, bidii, tamaa, papa.*)

Pura, v. (A) (1) beat, beat out, e.g. as of washing clothes in the native fashion; (2) shell peas or beans by stripping them out of the pod with the thumb, strip off grains of corn, &c., by pulling the stalk through the hand, the fingers being held together to strip off the grains. (Note: the Rf. *jipura*, is used for to masturbate, and the Rp. *purana*, sometimes of coition, also of fighting each other.) Cv. **Purura,** (1) rub off, strip off, e.g. by pulling a stalk or branch through the hand and so stripping off fruit, &c.; (2) spin out, let thread off a reel by allowing it to pass through the fingers, e.g. as of a boy paying out the string of a kite, &c. Prep. **Pururia,** spin out to (for, &c.); and in a colloquial way, spin a yarn, tell a tale. St. **Pururika,** (1) be rubbed off, stripped off; (2) be spun out. **Mpururo,** n. *mi-* (1) a rubbing or stripping off, &c.; (2) a spinning out, as of thread, &c.; (3) also used of a single file, of people or animals, following each other. (Cf. *msago, sanjari.*)

Pura, v. (B) knock down fruit from a tree by throwing sticks or stones. (Cf. *popoa.*) Cs. **Purusha.** St. and Pot. **Puruka,** (1) be knocked off; (2) fly off, be scared away as of birds when startled. Cs. of Cv. of St. **Purukusha,** (1) cause to fly off, and (2) fig. treat with contempt, slight, make light of, be offhand with. *Purukusha maneno,* talk heedlessly, discuss superficially, speak indistinctly or in a muddling way to evade discussion, &c. *Purukusha sikio,* listen inattentively. Rf. *jipurukusha,* be flighty, superficial, neglectful, inattentive, pretend not to understand or to have forgotten, or to be not concerned in a matter. Ps. **Purukwa,** used esp. in the sense of be out of one's senses, be temporarily insane, &c. **Mpurukushani,** n. *wa-* a careless, negligent person, one who does things in a hasty, slipshod manner. **Purukushani,** n. negligence, superficial treatment, a hasty, careless manner. *Fanya kazi purukushani,* work carelessly. **Upurukushani,** n. **Upurukusho,** n. carelessness, inattention, &c.

Pure,* n. a dish made from maize and beans (*kunde*) boiled together. (Hind. پوري.)

Purendi, n. *ma-* used in the plur. See **Mapurendi.**

Puruka, v., **Purukusha,** v., **Purukushani,** n. See under **Pura,** v. (B).

Purupuru, a. sportive, frolicsome, playful.

Purura, v. See under **Pura,** v. (A).

Pusa, v. cease, of rain, e.g. *mvua imepusa,* the rain has stopped.

Puta, v. beat soundly, flog, thrash. Sometimes heard as *buta.* Ps. **Putwa.** St. **Putika.** (Cf. *piga, chapa, gonga.*)

Puza, v. (1) sometimes heard for *puliza*; (2) be silly, foolish, nonsensical, esp. in talk—gossip, flirt. *Puza kazi (maneno),* work (talk) in a silly way. Rf. *Jipuza,* play the fool, be good for nothing. St. **Puzika,** in the same sense. *Siku zote anapuzika na wanawake,* he is always fooling with women. Cs. **Puzisha,** e.g. amuse, entertain, make sport for (or of). Prep. **Puzia.** **Mpuzi,** n. *wa-* one who is foolish, flippant, careless, loose—in conduct, conversation, &c., a gossip, flirt, babbler, gadabout. **Puo,** n. *ma-*, **Puzo,** n. *ma-* nonsense, foolish talk, silly behaviour. **-puzi,** a. foolish, &c. **Upuzi,** n. folly in talk or conduct, dissipation, gossip, nonsense, mere fun.

Puzia, v. (1) repeat (of food); (2) sometimes heard for *pulizia.* See under **Puliza.**

Puzo, n. *ma-*. See under **Puza.**

Pwa, v. dry, become dry, dry up, esp. of the ebb of the tide, e.g. *bahari inakupwa,* the sea is ebbing; *maji yapwa,* the tide is going out. Prep. **Pwea,** e.g. of the voice, be dry, hoarse, *sauti imenipwea, nimepwewa na sauti,* I am hoarse—and of swelling, subside, go down. *Uvimbe umepwea,* the swelling has subsided.

D.Prep. **Pwelea**, like *pwea*, but also esp. in Ps. and St. forms, of ships running aground, be high and dry, go ashore. *Chombo kimepwelea mwambani*, the vessel has gone aground on a reef. Cs. of Prep. **Pweleza**, (1) cause to dry up; (2) run aground. Cs. **Pwesha**, e.g. *Mungu amepwesha maji*, God has dried up the water, caused it to go down. Also *pwesha jipu*, reduce the swelling of an abscess or boil. **Makupwa**, n. plur. shore, rocks, &c., left uncovered at low tide. **Kipwa**, n. *vi-* rock, dry patch (left by receding tide), a shallow place. **Mapwa**, n. plur., **Mapwaji**, n. plur. coast, foreshore, part affected by tides, but usually used in the locative, i.e. **Pwani**, shore, coast, esp. the part affected by the tide, e.g. *Kilwa pwani yake hupwa sana*, at Kilwa the tide runs out a long way. *Hiyo pwani nchi nzuri*, this coast land is a fine country. *Oga pwani*, bathe on the sea-shore. Also generally used in reference to the coastal strip in contr. to the hinterland. *Pwani na bara*, the coastal strip and the hinterland. *Pwani* is now treated as though it belonged to the N class of nouns, not as a locative.

Pwaga, v. pound rice in a mortar in order to remove the husks.

Pwagu, n. a thief, used in the expression, *pwagu na pwaguzi*, a thief and a bigger or more expert one, i.e. when thief meets thief.

Pwaguzi, n. See under **Pwagu**.

Pwaju, n. a nightjar, *Caprimulgus* sp. (Cf. *kiruka njia.*)

Pwani, n. See under **Pwa**.

Pwata. See under **Pweteka**.

Pwaya, v. be loose, or loose fitting, as of a ring, clothes, &c. (Cf. *legea, cheza.*)

Pwea, v. See under **Pwa**.

Pweke, n. and a. solitariness, alone. *Mimi ni pweke*, I am by myself—commonly *peke yangu*. **Upweke**, n. being alone, solitariness, independence, singleness, singularity. *Upweke ni uvundo*, loneliness is disgusting. (Cf. *peka.*)

Pwelea, v., **Pwelewa**, v., **Pweleza**, v. See under **Pwa**.

Pweteka, v. only heard in the Rf. *jipweteka*, throw oneself down in a sitting position, sometimes *jipweteka pwata*, is heard.

Pweza, n. a cuttle-fish.

Pwita, v. throb, pulse, as of the heart, also of the throbbing of an abscess, sore, &c. *Jipu hili linapwita sana*, this boil (abscess) is throbbing very much. (Cf. *puma.*)

-pya, a. new, fresh, recent, novel, modern. (Opp. to *-a kale, -a zamani, -kuukuu, -zee.* (Cf. for 'young in age', *mtoto, -dogo*; for 'novel, strange', *-geni*; for 'fresh in condition, not fully matured', *-bichi.*) **Upya**, n. (1) newness, freshness, recency, novelty, strangeness; (2) former condition of newness, &c., e.g. *kuirudishia nyumba upya*, restore a house to its former new condition.

-pyoro, a., also **-pyororo**, a. of one who uses obscene language, one who cannot be trusted, one who deceives, exaggerates, &c. **Mapyoro**, n. plur. deceitfulness, exaggeration, double-dealing. **Mpyoro**, n. *wa-* (1) a two-faced person, a swindler, betrayer, one who deceives by exaggeration; (2) one who uses obscene language.

R

R is used to represent (i) the Bantu *r* sound, i.e. the cerebral fricative which in Swahili may perhaps be described as a sound between *l* and *r*. Nearly all words of Bantu origin beginning with this sound will be found under *L*. (ii) the Arabic *r* sound, which is somewhat stronger than the English *r*, but in Swahili is often assimilated to the Bantu *r*. Nearly all the words given under *R* will be seen to be of foreign origin. The rolled or guttural *r* is only used in imitation, conscious or unconscious, of Arabic pronunciation, esp. of *ghain*. Though not always careful to distinguish *r* and *l*, in fact the same person may pronounce the same word sometimes with *r*, and sometimes with *l*, the Swahili recognizes the difference, and preserves it as a rule in words where needed to make the meaning clear, e.g. *hali*, condition, *hari*, sweat, and in demonstratives such as *yule*.

Rabi,* n. master, lord, but only used by Muhammadans referring to God, and some Christians referring to God or Jesus Christ. (Cf. *bwana, Mola, Mungu*. Ar. رب.)

Rabishi,* v. confuse, nonplus, put in disorder or confusion, distract. *Maneno yake yamenirabishi akili zangu*, his words nonplussed me. St. and Pot. **Rabishika**, e.g. *mahali hapa pamerabishika*, this place is in disorder. *Nimerabishika*, I am perplexed. Ps. **Rabishiwa.** Prep. **Rabishia**, e.g. *amenirabishia kazi zangu*, he has made a mess of my work for me. Rp. **Rabishana. Rabsha,** n. confusion, commotion, disorder, noise, quarrelling. *Kulikuwa na rabsha njiani*, there was a disorderly crowd in the street. (Cf. *zahama, vurugu, ghasia, ukelele, wasiwasi, fujo.* ? Ar. ربس. See the form ارتبس to be mixed.)

Rada,* n. See **Rudi.**

Radhi,* n. (1) pardon, apology, contentment, acquiescence; (2) blessing. *Radhi ni kubwa kuliko mali*, (a parent's) blessing is more than wealth. *Radhi* is the word used to express a father's blessing when dying. It means that he is contented with his son's life and conduct. *Amempa mwana wake radhi yake*, he has given his son his blessing (when father is dying). *Hana radhi ya baba yake*, he has not had his father's blessing (father being dead). This is a terrible condemnation! *Uniwie radhi!* Pardon me! *Taka radhi*, ask pardon. **-radhi**, a. contented, satisfied, willing, consenting. *Yu radhi*, he is satisfied, reconciled. Also common in the Arab. form, *kunradhi*, pardon me. **Ridhi**, v. please, content. Prep. **Ridhia**, acquiesce, approve, accept. St. and Pot. be satisfied, &c. Cs. **Ridhisha**, cause to be content, satisfy, please, win approval of. *Ameniridhishia baba yangu*, he has satisfied my father on my account. Rp. **Ridhiana**, be mutually satisfied. **Maridhia**, a. contented, satisfied, agreeable. **Mridhia**, n. *wa-* a pleasant, affable, amiable person. **Ridhaa**, n. acceptance, agreement. **Taradhia**, v. be in need of, desire, ask for, beg. **Uradhi**, n. (1) feeling or making (giving) satisfaction, complacency; (2) active approval, kindness, condescension, assent, authorization, sanction; (3) amends, apology, payment of claims or damages, satisfaction of demands. (Cf. *kubali, pokea, idhini, tulia, kinai.* Ar. راض from rt. رضى.)

Radi,* n. clap of thunder, thunderbolt. *Piga radi*, thunder. *Mngurumo wa radi*, thunder. *Nilisikia radi* (or *ngurumo ya radi*), I heard thunder. *Mnazi huu ulipigwa na radi*, this coco-nut tree was struck by lightning. *Kumepiga radi leo*, it has thundered to-day. (Cf. *mngurumo, umeme*. Ar. رعد.)

Rafardha,* n. propeller of a ship, more commonly *jembe, ma-* (? from Ar. ارفض to disperse).

Rafiki,* n. (— and *ma-*) friend. **Kirafiki**, adv. in a friendly way, &c. **Urafiki**, n. friendship. *Fanya urafiki*, make a friendship, be friendly. *Vunja urafiki*, break off a friendship. (Cf. *mwenzi, mwandani, mpenzi, sahibu, msiri, somo, muhibu, shoga*. Ar. رفيق.)

Rafu,* n. shelf, wall at the back of a recess. (Cf. *shubaka*. Ar. رفّ.)

Ragai, n., **Raghai,*** n. usu. heard as *laghai*, which see.

Rago, n. *ma-* a camp. *Piga rago*, make a camp. (Cf. *kambi, kituo*.) **Kirago**, n. *vi-* (1) dim. of *rago*; (2) a kind of sleeping-mat. (Cf. *mkeka*.)

Raha,* n. rest, repose, peace, bliss, comfort. *Ona raha*, enjoy happiness, be at ease, be comfortable. *Kaa raha mustarehe*, live in perfect comfort and peace. **Starehe**, v. be at rest (comfortable, undisturbed), live in peace and quietness, be still. *Starehe* (Imperat.), used commonly as a form of courtesy on a meeting, or entering a room, 'keep your seat, pray do not move, do not disturb youself'. Cs. **Starehesha**, make comfortable, give rest to, refresh, relieve, tranquillize. **Mustarehe** (or *mstarehe*), n. state of rest, repose, calm—esp. in the phrase *raha mustarehe*, i.e. absolute, complete repose, also as a. cosy, comfortable. **-starehefu**, a. comfortable, peaceful, tranquil, calm. (Cf. *amani, utulivu, furaha, kimya, neema*. Ar. راحة.)

Rahimu,* a. an attribute of God in the sense of His mercifulness, used commonly when some request or need has not yet been fulfilled to express the idea that God in His mercy will one day still fulfil it. *Mungu Rahimu Karimu!* is the expression used in this sense: The merciful and bountiful God. (Cf. *rehema*. Ar. رحمة.)

Rahisi,* a. cheap, easy, light (in sense of easy), e.g. *kazi rahisi*, light work. *Njia rahisi*, an easy road or method. *Itakuwa rahisi kwako*, it will be easy for you. **Rahisi**, v. scorn, belittle, debase. *Amemrahisi*, he has belittled him. *Amejirahisi*, he has made himself cheap. St. and Pot. **Rahisika**, become cheap, depreciated, gone off. Prep. of St. **Rahisikia**, e.g. *karafuu zimemrahisikia*, cloves have become cheap for him. Cs. **Rahisisha**, make cheap, bring down the price. *Wamemrahisishia kitu hiki apate kukinunua*, they have lowered the price for him so that he might buy the article. Rp. **Rahisiana**, e.g. *wamerahisiana*, they have degraded one another, belittled one another. **Urahisi**, n. also sometimes **Rahisi**, is used with the effect of a noun, but rather in an adverbial way. *Ukitaka rahisi kila siku utachelewa!* if you want a bargain every day, you will not get far! *Rahisi inavunja upishi*, 'cheaply' spoils things, i.e. destroys the art of cooking. *Urahisi wake ulinipeleka kukinunua*, its cheapness led me to buy it. (Cf. *-epesi*. Ar. رخيص.)

Rai,* n. (A) (1) opinion, view, way of thinking; (2) suggestion. *Kwa (katika) rai yangu naona njia hii ni bora*, in my opinion this is the best way. (Cf. *ona, fikiri, waza*. Ar. رأي.)

Rai,* n. (B) health, strength, good bodily condition, e.g. *sina rai siku hizi*, I am off condition these days. (Ar. ربيع.)

Rai,* v. (A), also **Rairai**, be obsequious to, often in an insincere sense with a view to obtaining some favour, play the hypocrite, flatter. *Alimrairai hata akapata mradi wake*, he flattered him until he got what he wanted. Ps. **Raiwa.** St. and Pot. **Raika,** e.g. *aliraiwaraiwa hata akaraika*, he was flattered and flattered until he gave in, acceded, &c. **Urai,** n. flattery, cunning. (Ar. رأى.)

Rai,* v. (B) give food to, put food into the mouth of, as a sign of affection or respect. (Ar. رى.)

Raia,* n. a subject, e.g. of the king. **Uraia,** n. citizenship, the condition or state of being a subject. (Ar. رعية.)

Rajabu,* n. (1) the seventh month of the Muhammadan year, regarded as especially sacred on account of being the month of the Prophet's journey to Jerusalem and thence to heaven. The 27th day of *Rajabu* is Miraj, which is observed as the anniversary day of the journey. (2) a common personal male name given esp. to boys born in *Rajabu*. (Ar. رجب.)

Rajamu,* n. mark, stamp, trademark, but usu. *chapa* is used in this sense. (Ar. رجم mark the tomb with a stone.)

Rajua,* n. hope, e.g. *hana rajua ya kupata kazi hii*, he has no hope of getting this work. (Ar. رجو.)

Rajua,* v. change the mind, put off, defer. (Cf. *ghairi, ahiri*. Ar. ارجا.)

Raka,* n. *ma-* amplic. of *kiraka*, which is more common.

Rakaa,* n. the act of bowing with the hands on the knees during Muhammadan prayers; *enda rakaa*, is to perform the act. *Amesali rakaa mbili*, he bowed twice with his hands on his knees. **Rukuu,** v. bow with the hands on the knees during prayer, after the manner of the Muhammadans. (Ar. ركع.)

Rakibu,* n. a good rider (man). **Rakibu,** v., also **Rekebu,** mount, ride. *Alimrakibu punda*, he rode on a donkey. Ps. **Rakibiwa,** be ridden, mounted. St. and Pot. **Rakibika,** *punda huyu harakibiki*, this donkey is unridable. **Rakibia,** ride for, &c. Cs. **Rakibisha,** also **Rekebisha,** (1) put together; assemble; (2) set a watch right; (3) make to ride or mount. *Rekebisha kitanda hiki*, put this bed together. *Rekebisha saa yako kwa saa ya mnarani*, put your watch right by the clock in the tower. *Alinirakibisha punda wake*, he made me ride his donkey. *Rakibisha ngazi hapa*, put the ladder up in position here. Ps. of St. **Rakibishwa,** e.g. *baisikeli hii ilirakibishwa hapa*, this bicycle was put together here. Ps. of Prep. of Cs. **Rakibishiwa,** e.g. *nilirakibishiwa baisikeli yangu na fundi*, my bicycle was assembled for me by a mechanic. Cs. of St. of Cs. **Rakibishika,** e.g. *baisikeli haijarakibishika bado*, the bicycle has not yet been properly assembled. Rp. of Cs. **Rakibishana,** e.g. *walirakibishana punda*, they helped one another to mount. **Tarakibu,** n. sketch, pattern, design. (Cf. *panda, kwea, tengeneza, tunga, unga, panga*, and *kielezo, sanamu, namna*. Ar. ركب.)

Ramadhani,* n. the last month of the Muhammadan year. A month of fasting between dawn (1½ hours before sunrise) and sunset. Also common personal name of males, esp. of boys born in this month. (Ar. رمضان.)

Ramani,* n. map, chart, also heard as *rahamani*. (? Ar. رقم numerical signs, &c.)

Ramba,* n. (1) a kind of Madagascar cloth of fine plaited grass with coloured stripes; (2) a kind of knife used by shoemakers. (Hind. رنبى.)

Ramba, v. See **Lamba.**

Rambaza, v. (1) cruise around looking for fish (fishermen's word); (2)

go hunting around for a strumpet. *Wanarambaza samaki*, they are cruising (e.g. edges of reefs) for fish. Ps. **Rambazwa.** St. and Pot. **Rambazika**, e.g. *samaki hurambazika hapa*, fish may be found here by hunting round. (Cf. *ambaa.*)

Rambirambi,* n. (always plur.) words of condolence to bereaved people. *Rambirambi zako.* I sympathize with you in your bereavement. *Mpe rambirambi zake.* Condole with him. (Cf. *makiwa*, pole. Ar. Cf. also *mbirambi.*)

Rambitia, v. See **Lambitia** under **Lamba.**

Ramia,* n. a bullet. *Bunduki ya ramia kumi*, a magazine rifle carrying ten rounds. (Cf. *risasi, kiasi.* Ar. رمية a throw, hit.)

Ramisi,* v. enjoy (amuse) oneself. **Ramsa,** n. a place crowded with people merry-making, e.g. as at a fair, where games are being played, &c. (Pers. رامش cheerfulness, singing for joy.)

Ramli,* n. soothsaying from figures in sand. *Piga ramli*, divine, take the omens. *Mpiga ramli*, fortune-teller. *Bao la kupiga ramli*, a board covered with sand used by fortune-tellers and diviners. (Cf. *bao, uramali.* Ar. رمل soothsaying from figures in sand.)

Ramsa,* n. See under **Ramisi.**

Ramu,* n. plot of land for house-building. *Nimenunua nyumba na ramu yake*, I have bought a house and the plot on which it stands. Seldom heard except in Zanzibar, elsewere *kiwanja* is used. (? Ar. رم moist ground.)

Ramuka, v. attack each other in war. (Cf. *shambulia.*)

Randa,* n. a carpenter's plane. *Piga randa*, plane. (Pers. رنده.)

Randa, v. (1) dance (of men) in a way symbolizing courage, or showing off; (2) walk about, stroll; (3) also heard for *landa*, resemble, which see. Prep. **Randia,** used fig. of trying to get something by slyness. Rp. of Prep. **Randiana.** St. and Pot. **Randika,** e.g. *leo kunarandika*, it is possible to dance (*randa*) to-day (i.e. the conditions are favourable, the men are ready and the weather suitable). Cs. **Randisha.** Prep. of Cs. **Randishia.** Rp. of Cs. **Randishana,** e.g. *walirandishana kwa muda mkubwa kabla ya kupigana*, they made one another dance around for a long time before they fought. Prep. **Randishiana,** e.g. *walirandishiana watoto wao*, they made their children dance for one another. Rd. **Randaranda,** dance about. (Cf. *tamba.*)

Rangi,* n. colouring matter, pigment, paint, dye, stain, colour or tint. *Tia* (*paka*) *rangi*, dye, stain, paint. *-enye rangi*, coloured. *-enye rangirangi*, of various colours. *Geuka rangi*, change colour. *Rangi ya buluu* (*ya samawi, ya kahawia, ya kijani kibichi, ya kijivu, ya zambarau, ya manjano*), blue (sky blue, brown, green, grey, violet, yellow). *Rangi nyeupe* (*nyeusi, nyekundu*), white (black, red). (Hind. and Pers. رنگ.)

Rarua, v. tear, rend—used regularly of a wild animal tearing its prey, also of clothes. Ps. **Raruliwa.** Prep. **Rarulia.** St. and Pot. **Raruka,** e.g. *kila nivaapo kanzu yangu inararuka*, every time I put on my *kanzu* it gets torn (i.e. by itself because it is too tight, &c.). *Kitambaa hiki kinararulika upesi*, this cloth is easily torn. Rp. **Raruana,** tear each other, also abuse each other, cut each other. **Mrarua,** n. *wa-* one who tears, &c. *Simba ni mrarua mnyama*, the lion is one who tears an animal (its prey). **Mraruo,** n. *mi-* an act of tearing. **Raruo,** n. *ma-* tearing, rending, &c.

Rasha,* v., also Rd. **Rasharasha,** (1) daub on, paint, whitewash, &c.; (2) do anything superficially. Prep. **Rashia,** sprinkle, (1) used in the same way as *rasha*, also, *amenirashia* *chumba chokaa*, he has whitewashed the room for me. *Rashia maji hapa*, sprinkle some water here. (2) make smooth, i.e. finish off the surface of a mud wall. Ps. **Rashwa.** Ps. of Prep. **Rashiwa.** St. **Rashika.** Cs. **Rashisha. Marasharasha,** n. plur. sprinkling, showers, drizzle of rain, sprinkled perfume, &c. **Marashi,** n. plur. scent, liquid perfume. (Cf. *tibu, liwa, manukato.*) **Mrasharasha,** n. *mi-* same as *rasharasha*, see below. **Mrashi,** n. *mi-* a long-necked glass or metal bottle or flask, used for sprinkling scent. **Rasharasha,** n. *ma-*, **Urasharasha,** n. *ma-* light drizzling rain. *Inaanguka rasharasha tu*, it is only drizzling. (Cf. *nyunya.* Ar. رشّ and for (2) Ar. راز plasterer of walls.)

Rasi,* n. cape, head, promontory. *Rasilmali*, assets, capital, principal, property; *rasilmali ya akiba*, reserved capital; *rasilmali ya mafungu*, share capital. *Sheikh rasi*, the chief person in any club or *ngoma.* Met. *Chafi, rasilmali yake utumbo!* All he has is his own guts! i.e. he hasn't a cent. in the world! (Ar. رأس.)

Rasimu,* v. (1) make a first bid at an auction. To bid is *kuzabuni*, to make a final bid is *kushtiri.* (2) to value, i.e. estimate the value of; (3) make a copy of (but usually *nakili* or *fuatisha*). Ps. **Rasimiwa,** e.g. *nyumba hii imerasimiwa shilingi* 2,000, this house has been valued at Sh.2,000, or, a first bid of Sh.2,000 has been made for this house. Prep. **Rasimia,** e.g. *nirasimie meza hii*, value this table for me, or make a first bid to me for this table. St. and Pot. **Rasimika.** Cs. **Rasimisha. Rasimu,** n. a drawing, plan, design. (Ar. رسم engrave, &c., also fix a fee, &c.)

Rasisi,* v. plate with tin. Ps. **Rasisiwa,** e.g. *sufuria yangu imerasisiwa*, my cooking-pot has been plated with tin. Prep. **Rasisia.** St. and Pot. **Rasisika.** Cs. **Rasisisha. Risasi,** lead, solder, tin, bullet. *Piga risasi*, shoot. *Tia risasi*, (1) tin-plate; (2) load a rifle. *Tia risasi sufuria yangu*, tin-plate my cooking-pot. **Marisaa,** n. plur., also **Marisau,** shot, i.e. for fire-arms. (Ar. رصاص.)

Rasmi,* a. official, e.g. *nguo za rasmi*, official dress, uniform, livery, also special dress, one of good quality. (Ar. رسمي.)

Rasuli,* n. (— or *ma-*) prophet, apostle, messenger, envoy. **Risala,** n. message, occasionally used to mean messenger. (Cf. *mtume.* Ar. رسول.)

Ratibu,* v. arrange, put in order. *Ameratibu mambo haya vizuri*, he has arranged these matters nicely, but usu. Cs. *ratibisha* would be used in this sense. Ps. **Ratibiwa.** Prep. **Ratibia.** St. and Pot. **Ratibika.** Cs. **Ratibisha. Taratibu,** n. (1) arrangement, method, system, neatness, order. *Taratibu ya masomo*, a timetable (of lessons). (2) quietness, slowness, gentleness. *Fanya taratibu*, be orderly, quiet, &c., also seek a way of accomplishing something. *Kwa taratibu*, and *taratibu*, as adv. in a regular, steady, quiet, slow, easy-going way. Also as a. and sometimes *-taratibu*, quiet, slow, regular, systematic, &c. *Mtaratibu hushinda mwenye nguvu*, a quiet orderly, methodical person usually accomplishes more than a man with strength (violence, &c.). **Utaratibu,** n. like *taratibu*, but more in the sense of orderly, quiet, &c., character or action. (Ar. رتب.)

Ratli,* n., also **Ratili,** 16 *wakia*, 1 lb. (Ar. رطل.)

Raufu,* a. gentle. *Mtu raufu*, or *wa raufu*, a gentle person. **Uraufu,** n. compassion, gentleness. (Cf. *-pole.* Ar. رؤوف.)

Rausi,* v. nautical term, trim sail. (Ar. ? رواس.)

Reale,* n. See **Riale.**

Ree,* n. *ma-* ace (at cards). (Port. *rei.*)

-refu, a. long, tall, high, deep. Sometimes a v. is made, **Refusha,** make long, tall, &c. **Marefu,** n. plur. length. **Urefu,** n. length, tallness, height, depth, distance. *Urefu wa kwenda juu (chini)*, height (depth).

Rega, v., **Regarega,** v., **Regea,** v. See **Lega, Legalega, Legea** under **Lega.**

-regevu, a. See **-legevu** under **Lega.**

Rehani,* n. (sometimes heard as *rahani*, but apt to confuse as the latter is the locative form of *raha*, which see), pledge, security, mortgage. *Mshika rehani*, pawnbroker. *Weka rehani*, mortgage, place in pawn. (Cf. *amana, poni.* Sometimes heard for *rihani*, which see. (Ar. رهن.)

Rehe,* n. See **Riahi.**

Rauka, v. See under **Lawa.**

Rehema,* n. mercy, pity, compassion, fellow feeling. *Amekwenda katika rehema ya Mungu*, he has died. **Rehemu,** v. pity, have mercy on, commiserate, and as a euphemism, end the life of, grant rest to. St. **Rehemika.** Prep. **Rehemia.** Cs. **Rehemisha,** show mercy to, bless, prosper. **Marehemu,** n. and a. one who has found mercy, used as a euphemistic term of reference to a deceased person, the late, the departed, the defunct. *Marehemu baba yangu*, my deceased father. (Ar. رحم and مرحوم deceased (person).)

Rejareja,* a. See under **Rejea.**

Rejea,* v. go back, return, turn back, refer to, relate to, revoke, begin again, e.g. *rejea nyuma*, retreat. *Walirejea kumwudhi*, they began again to worry him. *Yafaa kurejea kamusi*, it is better to refer to the dictionary for this matter. *Amerejea mkewe*, he has remarried his wife (after a divorce). St. and Pot. **Rejeka,** e.g. *huyu harejeki*, this person is incorrigible. Ps. **Rejewa,** e.g. *amerejewa na ugonjwa wake*, he has a return of his old illness. Cs. **Rejesha** and **Rejeza,** repay, correct, call off (a dog, &c.), return. Prep. of Cs. **Rejeshea** and **Rejezea,** e.g. *awarejeshee makosa yao*, he is to correct their mistakes. Ps. of Cs. **Rejezwa** and **Rejeshwa.** Rp. of Cs. of Prep. **Rejesheana (Rejezeana),** e.g. *wamerejesheana fedha*, they returned their money to one another. St. of Cs. **Rejesheka (Rejezeka),** be returnable, *kitu hiki kinarejesheka*, this thing is returnable. *Mwanamke anarejesheka bado*, the woman is still remarriageable. **Mrejaa,** n. *bei ya mrejaa*, trade by commission, see follg. **Rejareja,** a. returnable, i.e. used in the expression *biashara ya rejareja, uza rejareja* (or *mrejaa*), of selling retail, the goods being obtained by the retail seller on the understanding that those unsold may be returned. **Rejeo,** n. *ma-* (often used in plur.) return. *Marejeo yake yatakuwa saa mbili*, he will be back at eight o'clock. *Po pote atakapokwenda marejeo yake hapa*, wherever he goes, this is the place to which he returns. Prov. *Mwenda omo na tezi, marejeo ni ngamani*, one who goes from the bow to the stern must pass through the bilge. (Cf. *rudi.* Ar. رجع.)

Rekebisha,* v. See follg.

Rekebu,* v. and Derivative forms, *rekebisha*, &c., used in some places instead of *rakibu*, which see. (Ar. ركب.)

Reli,* n. railway, train. *Njia ya reli*, railway track—in common use. (Eng. rail.)

Remba, v. adorn, decorate, make beautiful. Ps. **Rembwa.** St. **Rembeka.** Prep. **Rembea.** Cs. **Rembesha.** Rp. **Rembana.** Cv. **Rembua,** disfigure, spoil the beauty of, also in the term *rembua macho*, show the whites of the eyes, i.e. as a sign to women. St. **Rembuka**, be disfigured, exhausted. Prep. of St. **Rembukia**, e.g. *mgonjwa amenirembukia kwa ghafula*, the patient has become suddenly worse (to me), i.e. giving me more anxiety and trouble. Prep. **Rembulia**, e.g. *amemrembulia macho*, she made a sign with her eyes to him. Cs. **Rembusha.** Rp. of Prep. of Cs. **Rembushiana**, of making signs with the eyes to one another. **Kirembo**, n. *vi-* and adv. any small article of adornment, decoration, beauty, &c.; in fine style, dressed up, &c. **Mrembo**, n. *mi-* (1) same as *rembo*, follg.; (2) *wa-* a person who dresses well, who wears finery. **Rembo**, n. *ma-* ornament, ornamental markings (form, colour). **Urembo**, n. *ma-* (also perh. a plur. *nembo*) adornment, ornamentation, finery, display, esp. of dress or person, e.g. the delicate black lines sometimes painted on the face to heighten a light complexion. *Piga* (*fanya*) *urembo*, make a display, dress oneself up. *Urembo wa Mungu*, the glorious work of God, i.e. the Universe, Cosmos. For various kinds of personal ornament see *mkufu, mtali, furungu, bangili, kekee, kikuku, kipini, kipuli, kingaja, koa, useja, jasi, kipaji, dalia, ndonya, shamili, sarafu, azama, pete*. Note: the form *nembo* is usually confined to tribal marks, usually in a kind of tattoo.

Renga, v. cheat, make a fool of. Ps. **Rengwa.**

Rengu, n. *ma-* an outrigger of a canoe. (Cf. *ndubi, ngalawa.*)

Reno,* a. Portuguese. **Mreno**, n. *wa-* a Portuguese. **Kireno**, adv. and n. the Portuguese language, after the Portuguese style, &c. **Urend**, n. Portugal. (Port. *Reino.*)

Rewa, n. a large signal drum.

Riahi,* n., also **Rihi**, gas in the stomach. *Chakula cha riahi*, food which causes flatulence. *Kumwondoshea mtu riahi*, to get rid of flatulency for some one. *Mshipa wa rihi*, hernia. (Ar. ريح.)

Riale, Riali or **Reale**,* n. a dollar (worth varying according to variety), now only heard in stories.

Riaria,* v. seek, watch. (Cf. *tafuta, vizia*. Ar. رأرأ.)

Riba,* n. usury, interest on money or property, e.g. *kula riba*, to practise usury. *Kopesha kwa riba*, lend at interest. *Mla riba*, usurer. *Kulipa* (or *kutoa*) *riba*, pay interest. (Ar. ربا.)

Ridhaa, n., **Ridhi**, v., **Ridhia**,* v. See under **Radhi.**

Riha,* n. an odour. (Cf. *harufu*. Ar. ريح.)

Rihani,* n. sweet basil, a sweet-scented herb. *Rihani ya Kipate*, a variety from the island of Pate. *Rihani ya Kiajemi*, a variety from Persia. The plant is *mrihani*. (Ar. ريحان.)

Rihi,* n. See **Riahi.**

Rijali,* n. a man. Seldom used except in the sense of implying real manliness. *Rijali huyu!* He is a real man! (Ar. رجال.)

Rika, a. and n. *ma-* of same age, time of life, contemporary, person of same age, an equal, of those who were in the same initiation rites, &c. *Rika moja*, of the same age. *Hawa ni marika*, they are contemporaries.

Riksho,* n. *ma-* a rickshaw. (Japanese, introduced with the vehicles.)

Rima, n. *ma-* a pit dug for catching large animals.

Rimbua, v. See **Limbua.**

Rinda, n. *ma-*. See **Marinda.**

Rindima, v. (1) roar as of thunder, waterfall, drum (like *nguruma*); (2) fig. hit, strike, e.g. *fulani alimrindima mwenziwe ngumi*, so-and-so struck his companion with his fist. **Rindimo**, n. *ma-* noise of thunder, waterfall, drum, &c., e.g. *rindimo la ngoma*, the rolling, booming of a drum.

Ringa, v. (1) put on airs, walk with

swagger; (2) set one's cap at. Prep. **Ringia**, e.g. *amemringia huyu*, she has set her cap at him. Ps. of Prep. **Ringiwa**. **Maringo**, n. plur. airs, graces, graceful gait, swagger, &c. (Cf. *randa*.)

Ripoti,* n. report, account—in common use. (Eng. report.)

Ripuka, v. See **Lipuka**.

Risala,* n. See under **Rasuli**.

Risasi,* n. See under **Rasisi**.

Rishai,* v. (1) be wet, moist, cool; (2) exude moisture. **Warishai**, n. and a. a vessel for cooling water in, and as a. damp, humid, moist. (Cf. *papa*, v., *rutuba*, *-nyevu*. Ar. رشح.)

Risiti,* n. a receipt—in common use. (Cf. *stakabadhi*. Eng.)

Ritadi,* v. See under **Rudi**.

Rithi,* v. inherit. *Amerithi mali nyingi kwa baba yake*, he was left (or he inherited) much property from his father. *Ameurithi ugonjwa ule kwa mama yake*, he has inherited that disease from his mother. *Alimrithi ukhalifa*, he succeeded him in the Khalifate. Ps. **Rithiwa**, only used of the deceased person in question, it cannot, for example, be used as equivalent of 'he was left' in the first example above. *Amerithiwa na mwanawe*, he was succeeded (i.e. his property was inherited) by his son. *Nyumba hii irithiwe na mwanawe*, this house is to go to his son. St. and Pot. **Rithika**, e.g. *mali haya yanarithika*, this property passes down through the family. Cs. **Rithisha**, distribute the estate of a deceased person according to law (as is done by an administrator). *Uvivu hurithisha umaskini*, laziness engenders poverty. Prep. **Rithia**. Rp. **Rithiana**, e.g. *kawa wanarithiana*, these people inherit one another's property, used also to signify close family relationship. **Mirathi**, n. inheritance, for the usual *urithi*. **Mrithi**, n. *wa-* an heir, legatee, inheritor. **Mrithisha**, n. *wa-*, **Mrithishi**, n. *wa-* an executor—of a will. **Urithi**, n. (*rithi*), inheritance, a heritage, bequest, legacy. (Ar. ورث.)

Riza,* n., also **Liza**, a door chain. (Ar. رزة.)

Riziki,* n. necessaries of life, means of subsistence, food, maintenance, by some Muhammadans restricted to God's providence, the necessities of life regarded as His gift. Fate, destiny, e.g. *hii ndiyo riziki yake*, this is his destiny. **Ruzuku**, v. supply with necessaries of life, provide for, maintain, support, used commonly of God's providential care for His creatures, i.e. bless, preserve. By some Muhammadans, used only of God's providence. Ps. **Ruzukiwa**, e.g. *ameruzukiwa watoto wengi*, he has been blessed with many children. **Tarazaki**, v. same as *ruzuku*. (Ar. رزق.)

Robo,* n. a fourth part, quarter; *kasa robo* or *kasoro robo*, three-quarters. *Saa tano kasa* (or *kasoro*) *robo*, 4.45. (Ar. ربع.)

Robota,* n. *ma-* packet, parcel, bundle, bale. *Robota la tambuu*, a bundle of 25–30 betel-nut leaves as sold in the bazaar. *Robota la pamba*, a bale of cotton. (Cf. *bunda*, *tumba*. Ar. ربطة.)

Robu,* n. used only in the expression, *maziwa ya robu*, curds. (Ar. روب.)

Roda,* n. sheave of a pulley, pulley. (Cf. *korodani*, *gofia*, *abedari*. Port. *roda*.)

Rodi,* n., also **Lodi**, (1) a swaggering, pompous person, one who puts on airs, but esp. one who wears a monocle; (2) a monocle. **Urodi**, n. pomposity, swagger, &c. (from Eng. Lord, the word being connected in the native mind with pomposity and a monocle!)

Roga, v. See **Loga**.

Rogoa, v. See **Logoa** under **Loga**.

Roho,* n. (1) soul, spirit, life, vital

principle. *Kila kiumbe chenye roho,* every living creature. (2) breath. *Kata roho,* die, *amekata roho,* he is dead. (3) throat. *Kaba roho,* seize by the throat. (4) character, individuality. *Roho yake njema,* he is good, trustworthy, &c. *Kila mtu ana roho yake,* every person has his own personality. (5) greediness, gluttony, avarice. *Una roho,* you are greedy. *Fanya roho,* be greedy. Sometimes *uroho* is used in this sense, e.g. *kula kwa uroho,* eat greedily. **Mroho,** n. *wa-* a greedy, avaricious, covetous person, one who eats hastily, or more than his share when invited to food, also one who frequents other people's houses in the hope of being invited to food. (Cf. *rondea, lapa, choyo.* Ar. روح.)

Roja,* v. marvel, be astonished. *Niliroja kuonana naye hapa,* I marvelled at seeing him here. **Kiroja,** n. *vi-,* also **Kioja,** something that astonishes or terrifies, an oddity, a curiosity, a portent, a bugbear, monster. (Cf. *kitisho, shani, ajabu, maafa, dude, dubwana.* (? Ar. رجّ agitate.)

Rojorojo, a. thick, as of food. *Nifanyie mchuzi (wa) rojorojo,* make me some thick gravy. **Rojorojo,** n. gravy.

Rok,* n. the gigantic bird of eastern tales (Arabian Nights). (Ar. رخ.)

Rondea, v., Rondesha, v., &c. See **Londea.**

Rongaronga, v. (1) implore, beseech (cf. *omba, sihi*); (2) carry carefully, e.g. a thing which is already damaged in a way so as not to damage it further.

Rongera, n. native beer before it is fermented. (Cf. *togwa.*)

Rongofya, v. See under **-wongo.**

Ronjo, a. See **Lonjo.**

Ropoka, v. blather, talk without thinking, e.g. *amekaa pale anaropoka tu,* he sits there talking nothing but nonsense. Ps. **Ropokwa,** e.g. *aliropokwa na maneno mengi,* lots of thoughtless talk came from him. Prep. **Ropokea.** Cs. **Ropokesha,** e.g. *mropokeshe,* egg him on and get him started to talk his nonsense. (Cf. *paya.*)

Roshani,* n. balcony, verandah, projecting window. (Pers. روشن.)

Ruba, n. *ma-* a leech.

Rubani,* n. *ma-* a guide, pilot, helmsman. Prov. *chombo cha kuvunja hakina rubani,* fate cannot be avoided, what is predestined is inevitable, lit. a vessel which is to be wrecked has no pilot (helmsman). (Ar. ربّان.)

Rubuni,* v. cheat, deceive, beguile, entice. Ps. **Rubuniwa.** Prep. **Rubunia,** e.g. *amenirubunia mwanangu,* he has cheated my son (for me, i.e. to my loss). Cs. **Rubunisha.** St. and Pot. **Rubunika.** (Ar. غبن.)

Rudi,* v. (1) turn or come back. *Amerudi katika kutembea,* he has come back from walking. (2) give back, send back, reverse, contradict, reply to, repay. *Nirudi fedha yangu,* return to me my money. *Siwezi kurudi lililofanywa,* I cannot reverse what has been done. *Amenirudi neno langu,* he has contradicted me. (3) reprove, correct, keep in order, punish, reform. *Rudi makosa,* correct faults. *Rudi mtoto,* punish a child. (4) shrink. *Nguo hii imerudi,* this cloth has shrunk. Prep. **Rudia,** return to (from, &c.), punish for (with, &c.). St. and Pot. **Rudika,** e.g. *harudiki,* he is not amenable to discipline. *Amri yake hairudiki,* his order is final. Cs. **Rudisha,** give back, send back, repay. *Rudisha utambi wa taa,* turn down the wick of a lamp. Rp. **Rudiana,** correct one another. Rp. of Cs. **Rudishana.** Prep. **Rudishiana,** e.g. *wamerudishiana vitu,* they have returned the things to one another. Ps. of Prep. of Cs. **Rudishiwa,** e.g. *nataka kurudishiwa baki la fedha yangu,* I want my change. **Marudi, n.,** also **Marudio, n.** (1) a return, recompense, a paying back; (2) punishment, discipline, correction. **Rada, n.** punishment, but especially an evil action recoiling on one. **Ritadi, v.** apostasize, backslide, change one's religion. (Ar. ردّ.)

Rudufu,* a. but usually **Maradufu** or *mardufu*, double, twofold. *Nguo hii maradufu*, this cloth is woven with double thread. **Rudufu, v.** double. *Aliziruduf u nyuzi hizi*, he doubled these threads (e.g. in weaving). Prep. **Rudufia.** St. and Pot. **Rudufika,** e.g. *idadi ya watoto imerudufika*, the number of children has become doubled. Ps. **Rudufiwa.** Cs. **Rudufisha** and **Rudufya. Maradufu, n.** a kind of cloth, double in width, also **a.** double, twofold. (Ar. ردف.)

Rufaa,* n. cargo. *Meli ilichukua rufaa*, the ship took cargo. **Rufai, v.** (1) mount; (2) go swiftly, leave a place swiftly. Cs. **Rufaisha,** cause to mount. **Marufaa, n.** (1) part of a native loom—small boards between which the warp is stretched; (2) candlestick, lamp-stand; (3) book rest. (Ar. رفع.)

Rufani,* n. appeal (legal). *Taka chukua) rufani*, appeal in a law case. *Kubali rufani*, allow an appeal. *Batilisha rufani*, dismiss an appeal. *Thibitisha rufani*, uphold an appeal. *Shinda katika rufani*, win an appeal. *Shindwa katika rufani*, lose an appeal. *Mtaka rufani*, an appellant. (Ar. رافع.)

Rufuku,* n. *ma-* prohibition, refusal, always in the plur. *Piga marufuku*, prohibit. *Kuvuta kumepigwa marufuku*, smoking is prohibited. **Rufuku, v.** prohibit, forbid, for the common *kataza*. Ps. **Rufukiwa.** Prep. **Rufukia.** Cs. **Rufukisha.** (? from Ar. فرق separate, determine, by transp.)

Rugaruga,* n. *ma-*, and **Mrugaruga,** n. *wa-* messenger; plain clothes police, levy attached to native chief. (? Ar. روغ act slyly.)

Rugurugu, n. *ma-*. See **Marugurugu.**

Ruhusa,* n. leave, permission, liberty, holiday. *Toa (pa) ruhusa*, give leave. *Omba (taka) ruhusa*, ask leave. *Twaa (pewa, pokea) ruhusa*, take or get leave. **Ruhusu, v.** give leave, permit, allow. Ps. **Ruhusiwa.** St. and Pot. **Ruhusika.** Rp. **Ruhusiana.** Prep. **Ruhusia.** Cs. **Ruhusisha.** (Ar. رخص.)

Rujumu,* v. stone, kill by stoning. Ps. **Rujumiwa.** Prep. **Rujumia.** Cs. **Rujumisha,** e.g. *hili ndilo kosa alilorujumishiwa kwalo*, this is the offence on account of which he was stoned. (Ar. رجم.)

Ruka, v. (1) jump, leap, hop, spring, bound, spout out, fly up, or away, pass through the air. *Ameniruka*, he jumped over me (lit. and fig.), he passed me over (without consideration). (2) pass over or beyond, overstep, trespass, i.e. *ruka mpaka*, go too far, overstep the limit. Ps. **Rukwa,** e.g. *rukwa na akili*, lose one's head. St. and Pot. **Rukika,** e.g. *mto huu unarukika*, this river can be jumped across. Prep. **Rukia,** leap or fly at, attack. Rp. **Rukana,** jump over one another. Cs. **Rusha,** make jump, splash, toss, throw up or off. *Rusha akili*, make lose one's head, startle with fear, &c. *Rusha kishada*, send up a kite. *Punda huyu hurusha*, this donkey throws people. *Amerusha haki yake*, he has deprived him (done him out of) his right. Prep. of Cs. **Rushia.** Rp. of Cs. **Rushana. Kirukanjia, n.** *vi-* (1) the name given to a kind of mouse or shrew; (2) also a small bird—nightjar; (3) a restless person who cannot settle in one place to live. **Kirukia, n.** *vi-* name of a climbing plant.

Mruko, n. *mi-*, also **Ruko**, n. *ma-*, leaping, a leap, overstepping, trespass, omission. **Rusho**, n. *ma-* action or method of throwing up or off, &c.

Ruksa,* n. See **Ruhusa**.

Rukudhu,* v. run into with evil intent, trespass. *Alimrukudhu nyumbani mwake*, he rushed into his house (i.e. the house of some one else) intending to make a scene, swear, fight, &c., insult. Prep. **Rukudhia**. Ps. **Rukudhiwa**. Rp. **Rukudhana**. St. **Rukudhika**. Cs. **Rukudhisha**. (Ar. ركض.)

Rukuu,* v. See under **Rakaa**.

Rula,* n. a ruler, i.e. the instrument for measuring, drawing lines, &c. (Eng. ruler.)

Rum,* n. Turkey, i.e. *Sultani Rum*, the Sultan of Turkey. *Bahariya Rum*, Mediterranean sea. (Ar. روم.)

Rumada,* n. pivot on which a rudder is swung. (Port. *remada*, rowing.)

Rumbi, n. a large jar. (Cf. *chungu, gudulia, kasiki*.)

Rumi,* n. Rome, Roman. *Mrumi, wa-*, a Roman. (Ar. روم.)

Runda, v. (1) be stunted or crippled in growth (cf. *via*); (2) be sullen, sulky, angry.

Rundika, v. See **Lundika**.

Runga, v. gather, be gathered together, esp. in order to hunt.

Rungu, n. (— and of size, *ma-*) knobkerry, any stick with a knob for defensive purpose.

Rungula, v. See **Lungula**.

Rupia,* n. (1) a rupee. *Rupia kwa ya pili*, as alike as two beans. (2) a skin disease. (Cf. *choa*. Hind. روپيه.)

Rusha, v. See under **Ruka**.

Rushd,* n. this word is used in the Courts of Zanzibar to mean 'maturity'. *Amefika miaka ya rushd*, he has attained his majority, he has reached years of discretion. (Ar. رشد rightly guided.)

Rusho, n. *ma-*. See under **Ruka**.

Rushwa, n. bribe. *Toa (penyeza) rushwa*, bribe. *Kula rushwa*, take a bribe. (Cf. *hongo*, and *penyeza*. Ar. رشوة.)

Rusu,* n. a layer, tier. (Cf. *tabaka, safu*. Ar. رصة.)

Rutuba,* n. dampness, moisture. *Chakula hiki ni rutuba ya tumbo*, this food tends to open the bowels. Humidity, also used for humus in soil. *Ardhi hii ina rutuba*, this is good soil. **Rutubisha**, v. make damp, wet, moist; (of food) tend to open the bowels. St. **Rutubika**, (1) be damp, wet, moist; (2) fig. be refreshed, relieved, cooled. Prep. **Rutubishia**. Ps. **Rutubishwa**. (Ar. رطب.)

Ruwaza,* n. a pattern, sample. (Cf. *kilingo, kielezo, kigezo*. Ar. روز to test.)

Ruya,* n. a vision, dream. (Ar. رويا.)

Ruzu,* v. become very poverty stricken, give up hope, be in difficulties. St. **Ruzika**. Ps. **Ruziwa**. (Ar. رزح.)

Ruzuku,* v. See under **Riziki**.

Ruzuna,* n. *dawa ya ruzuna*, a medicine which is a native mixture supposed to cure madness, or children's cough. *Anataka kufanyiwa ruzuna*, he is crazy.

S

S is always pronounced as in Eng. *sit*, never as in *rose*. Some natives do not always clearly distinguish *s* and *sh*, hence different pronunciations of the same word may be heard, and words not found under *S* should be looked for under *Sh*. When *s* or *sh* directly precedes *t*, some natives tend to interpose *i*, e.g. *sitaha*, for *staha*; *sitara* for *stara*; *shitaki* for *shtaki*, &c. *S* is sometimes heard for *th*, e.g. *samani* for *thamani*.

Saa,* n. (1) an hour, a twelfth part of the day or night; (2) time, period of time; (3) a timepiece, watch, clock. *Saa ya mfuko*, a pocket-watch. *Saa ya mkono*, a wrist-watch. A day is reckoned as from sunset (about 6 p.m. where sun time is followed) which is *saa kumi na mbili*, (or *thenashara*) *jioni*, i.e. twelve o'clock in the evening (the twelfth hour of the day), and from it the hours are reckoned on, one, two, three, &c., till 6 a.m. which is called *saa kumi na mbili* (or *thenashara*) *asubuhi*. *Saa ngapi?* What time is it? i.e. how many hours? *Saa moja* (*mbili*, *tatu*, &c.), one (two, three) o'clock, i.e. seven (eight, nine, &c.) English time. *Nusu saa*, half an hour. *Robo saa*, quarter of an hour. *Saa na* (or, *u*) *robo*, an hour and a quarter. *Saa mbili kasoro dakika ishirini*, twenty minutes to two, (twenty minutes to eight, English time) lit. 2 hours less twenty minutes. Note: *kasa* is generally used with *robo* instead of *kasoro*. A particular time of day is often roughly fixed by indicating with outstretched arm the position that the sun will be in at the time and saying *Jua hivi*, the sun thus (Cf. *nukta*, *dakika*, *mchana*, *siku*, *usiku*, *wakati*, *muda*. Ar. ساعة.)

Saa, int. of wonder, impatience, vexation, or merely a reply to a call. *Sema saa!* Speak will you! *Hebu saa*, in remonstrance, don't do that! *Unaniumiza saa!* Look here you are hurting me. Also used as a reply when called, with the meaning, Here I am! Coming at once! (Prob. from the same root as *sasa*, i.e. Ar. ساع the present time, &c.)

Saa, v. remain over, be left over. The Prep. form **Salia**, is commonly used with either the direct or the prep. meaning, remain over (for, to, by, in, &c.). Cs. **Saza**, leave over, cause to remain over, leave unsaid, unfinished, undone, omit. Prep. of Cs. **Sazia**. D.Cs. **Sazisha**. **Masaa**, **Masalio**, **Masao**, **Masazo**, all n. plur. and **Msazo**, n. *mi-*, remains, remnant, what is left over. Sometimes used in the sing. **Salio**, *ma-*, **Sao**, *ma-*, **Sazo**, *ma-*. (Cf. *baki*, *acha*.)

Saanda, n. See **Sanda**.

Saari,* n. price, value, for the common, *bei*, *thamani*, *kiasi*. (Ar. سعر.)

Saba,* n. and a. (sometimes heard as *sabaa*), seven. *-a saba*, seventh. Sometimes for *juma*, a week, e.g. *saba nyingine*, next week. *Saba tatu*, three weeks. **Sabatashara**, seventeen, for *kumi na saba*. *-a sabatashara*, seventeenth. **Sabini**, seventy, *-a sabini*, seventieth. (Ar. سبعة.)

Sababu,* n. and conj. reason, cause, motive. *Toa sababu*, give a reason, assign a cause. *Kwa sababu*, and simply *sababu*, because. *Sababu gani?* Why? For what reason? *Kwa sababu ya*, by reason of, on account of, in consequence of. (Cf. *ajili*, *maana*, *kisa*, &c. Ar. سبب.)

Sabahi,* v. make a morning call on somebody. (Cf. *asubuhi, amkia,* and contr. *tuesha.* Ar. صبح.)

Sabaini,* n. and a. See **Sabini,** under **Saba.**

Sabalkheri,* the common Arab morning salutation, Good morning. (Cf. *asubuhi, heri,* and *masalkheri.* Ar. صباح الخير.)

Sabasi,* n. enmity, discord. (Cf. *uadui, fitina.* Corruption of Ar. صبصب see form تصبصب be hostile towards.)

Sabatashara,* n. and a. See under **Saba.**

Sabidi,* v. put in order, arrange, settle. (Cf. *tengeneza, panga, rekabisha.* (? Ar. ضبط manage, administer, &c.)

Sabiki,* v. go before, lead the way. **Sabiki,** n. cause, reason, precedent. (Cf. *tangulia, takadamu,* and *sababu, kisa, ajili.* Ar. سبق.)

Sabili,* v. permit, remove obstacle, free, loosen, slacken, relax, make room to pass. Prep. **Sabilia. Sabili,** n. permission, freedom, room to pass. **Sabili,** a. free, mobile, unhampered, permissible, clear. (Cf. *ruhusu, huru, legeza, acha.* Ar. سبيل.)

Sabini,* n. and a. See under **Saba.** (Ar. سبعون.)

Sabuni,* n. soap. (Ar. صابون.)

Saburi,* v. also **Subiri,** be patient, wait patiently. **Saburi,** n. also **Subira,** patience, patient waiting, resignation. *Saburi yavuta heri,* patience brings blessing. *Saburi ni ufunguo wa faraja,* patience is the key of comfort. (Ar. صبر.)

Sadaka,* n. a religious offering, sacrifice, alms, act of charity. anything done from a religious motive. (Cf. *sadiki, kafara, dhabihu, tambiko.* Ar. صدقة.)

Sadifu,* a. good, well, right, proper, exact. **Sadifu,** v. turn out to be true (exact, correct, &c.). (Cf. *barabara, -zuri.* ? Ar. سدّ right, true. with adj. ending *-fu.*)

Sadiki,* v. believe, give credence to, accept as true (truthful). Ps. **Sadikiwa.** St. **Sadikika.** Prep. **Sadikia.** Cs. **Sadikisha,** (1) convince, win credence, justify, make out to be true, confirm; (2) inten. believe firmly, trust implicitly. **-sadikifu,** a. (1) prone to believe, credulous; (2) credible, trustworthy, true. **Suduku,** v. (1) verify, ascertain, make sure, prove; (2) accept, concur, usu. in the Prep. **Sudukia,** e.g. *amesudukia maneno yake,* he has proved his words. (Cf. *amini, hakikisha, thibitisha.* Ar. صدق.)

Safari,* n. See under **Safiri.**

Safi,* a. (1) clean, pure, clear, bright, lucid; (2) honest, sincere, disinterested. *Moyo wake safi,* his character is good. *Maneno safi,* clear statements, straightforward account. (3) correct, in order. **Safi,** v. but usu. Cs. **Safisha,** make clean, correct, purify, set to right. Prep. **Safia,** e.g. *amenisafia nia yake,* he has made his intention clear to me. St. and Pot. **Safika. Usafi,** n. cleanliness, correctness, purity. (Ar. صاف.)

Safidi,* v. clean, clear up, put in order, set to rights, arrange neatly, e.g. of a house, effects, or person. Prep. **Safidia.** Cs. **Safidisha.** St. **Safidika,** e.g. *maneno yamesafidika,* the statement is clear, straightforward. **Tasifida,** n. and v. same as *safidi.* **Usafidi,** cleanliness, good order, neatness. (Cf. prec. and *takasa, tengeneza, fanyiza, panga.* Pers. سفيد white, clear, &c.)

Safihi,* v., also **Safii,** abuse, treat in a scornful manner, be arrogant, impudent. **Safihi,** a. impudent, bold, shameless. **Msafihi,** n. *wa-*. **Msafii,** n. *wa-*, a proud, arrogant, insolent, impudent person. **Usafihi,** n. pride, insolence, presumption, arrogance. (Cf. *dharau, takabari, shupaa.* Ar. سلاطة.)

Safii,* v. and a. See under **Safihi.**

Safina,* n. a ship, a vessel, Noah's ark. (Cf. *jahazi, chombo.* Ar. سفينة.)

Safiri,* v. travel, engage in a journey or expedition, sail, start. Prep. **Safiria,** e.g. travel for (in, by, with, &c.). St. and Pot. **Safirika.** Cs. **Safirisha,** send off, dispatch, see start, give farewell greeting to, &c. **Msafara,** n. *mi-*, a caravan, expedition, &c. **Msafiri,** n. *wa-*, a traveller (by sea or land), wayfarer, voyager. **Safari,** n. (1) a journey, voyage, expedition; (2) usu. used for *msafara,* a caravan, company of persons travelling together, an equipped party or expedition. Porters are *wapagazi*; an armed escort, *askari*; a headman, *mnyapara* or *msimamizi*; a guide, *kiongozi.* (3) time, turn, instance, e.g. *safari hii nitakuachilia,* this time I will let you off. *Safari nyingine,* another time. *Fanya safari,* get ready to make a start. *Safari!* Time to start! Right away! **Usafiri,** n. journeying, travelling. (Cf. *enda, sindikiza, aga, mara.* Ar. سفر.)

Safisha,* v. See under **Safi.**

Safu,* n. row, line, rank, series, range. *Panga* (*weka*) *safu,* or *kwa safu,* set in rows. *Miti safu safu,* rows of trees, an avenue of trees. *Safu za taratibu,* regular rows. *Safu ya milima,* a range of mountains. **Msafa,** n. *mi-* same as *safu.* **Safu,** v. arrange in rows, seldom used. (Cf. *mstari, tabaka, rusu, mpango.* Ar. صاف.)

Safura,* n. (1) a disease causing a swollen or dropsical condition; (2) ankylostomiasis. (Cf. *baridi yabisi.* Ar. صفراء bile.)

Saga, v. (1) grind, pulverize, triturate, crush to bits; (2) fig. grind down, oppress, esp. of grinding grain with native millstones, *mawe ya kusagia,* the upper called *mwana,* worked by a handle *msuzo,* on the lower *mama.* (3) together with Rp. **Sagana,** is the term used for lesbianism. *Saga meno,* grind the teeth. Ps. **Sagwa.** St. and Pot. **Sagika.** Prep. **Sagia. Kisaga,** n. *vi-* (1) a dry measure of about a quart, equal to two *kibaba,* or half a *pishi. Nimepimiwa kisaga cha mahindi,* I have had measured for me a quart of maize. (2) a grinding. **Msaga,** n. *wa-* one who grinds, hence, **Msagaliwa,** n. *wa-* lit. one who grinds *liwa,* a kind of aromatic wood which is ground and mixed with water and used as a cosmetic by some women, and so—an impotent male person, engaged as a servant to women. **Msago,** n. *mi-* (1) act (method, &c.) of grinding; (2) see **Sago,** adv. which may be connected. (Cf. *seta, ponda.*)

Sagai, n. javelin, short stabbing spear—of the Zulus and kindred tribes. (Cf. *mkuki, fumo.* ? Ar. زاجل javelin.)

Saghiri,* a. small, little, youngest—seldom heard for the usu. *-dogo.* (Ar. صغير.)

Sago, adv., also **Msago,** following one after the other without pause or interruption, unbroken sequence. (Cf. *sanjari, mfululizo.*)

Sahala,* a. light, i.e. not heavy, easy. **Sahalia,** v. also Cs. **Sahilisha,** make light, make easier. **Tasihili,** adv. quickly, with speed. (Cf. *upesi*), also n. a goodbye, a leave-taking to friends before they set off on a journey. Ar. سهل and تساهل.)

Sahani,* n. dish, plate, &c. **Kisahani,** n. *vi-* dim. a small plate, a saucer. (Cf. for various dishes, &c., *chombo, chungu, bakuli,* &c. Ar. صحن.)

Sahau,* v. forget, fail to remember or call to mind, make a silly mistake. Ps. **Sahauliwa.** St. and Pot. **Sahaulika.** Cs. **Sahaulisha. Sahau,** n. forgetfulness, a lapse of memory. **Msahau,** n. *wa-* a forgetful person,

person with a bad memory, usu. **Msahaulifu**, n. *wa-* also **Msahaulizi**, n. *wa-*. **-Sahaulifu**, a. forgetful, inattentive, absent-minded. **Usahaulifu**, n. forgetfulness. (Ar. سها.)

Sahib,* n. sir, master. **Mamsahib**, n. and **Memsahib**, mistress, lady. (Cf. *bwana, bibi.* Hind. صاحب and Eng. ميم.)

Sahibu,* n. See under **Suhubu.**

Sahifa,* n., and **Sahifu**, n. page of a book, a leaf of a book, for the usu. *ukurasa.* (Cf. *msahafu.* Ar. صحيفة.)

Sahihi,* v. but usu. **Sahihisha**, v. (1) correct, put right; (2) pass as right or valid, attest, sign. Ps. **Sahihiwa.** St. and Pot. **Sahihika. Sahihi**, a. correct, right, valid, genuine, true. *Fanya sahihi*, correct, revise, rectify. **Sahihi**, n. attestation, guarantee, signature. *Tia sahihi*, sign, attest, also as adv. rightly, truly. **-sahihifu**, a. as *sahihi.* **Usahihi**, n. correctness, accuracy, freedom from fault (blemish, or mistake). (Cf. *rekabisha, safisha, tengeneza.* Ar. صح.)

Sahilisha,* v. See under **Sahala.**

Sai,* v. (1) annoy a person so as to make him fight. (Cf. *chokoza.* Ar. سعى calumniate, or ساى stir up enmity.) (2) challenge a person to fight or compete in a game. (Cf. *alika.* Ar. صيح attack.)

Saidi,* n. lord, master, also a common personal male name. When it means lord, as a rule it is spelt *Sayidi, Seyyid, Seyidi,* &c. **Saidina**, n. Our Lord, master, king, &c., Your Majesty. (Cf. *maulana.*) **Saada**, or **Seyyida**, is the fem. Lady, your Ladyship. (Ar. سيد.)

Saidia,* v. aid, help, assist, support, countenance, abet. Ps. **Saidiwa.** St. **Saidika.** Rp. **Saidiana**, e.g. help each other, &c. **Msaada**, n. help, aid, assistance, support. (Cf. *auni, tegemea, shime.* Ar. ساعد.)

Saili,* v. (1) ask, question, examine; (2) often used in the sense of asking in a tactful gentle manner so as not to cause annoyance. Ps. **Sailiwa.** Prep. **Sailia**, e.g. ask about (for, in, &c.). Cs. **Sailisha.** Rp. **Sailiana. Siala**, n. *ma-* a question, inquiry, for the usu. **Swali**, n. *ma-* question, inquiry, interrogation, problem. (Cf. *uliza, hoji, tafiti.* Ar. سال.)

Sairi,* v. (A) coast, hug the shore in a vessel. (Cf. *ambaa.* Ar. سار travel.)

Sairi,* v. (B) beat or pound on the side of a mortar what remains in it. (Ar. ? صار who draws together, or صير a side.)

Saisi,* n. a groom, coachman. (Ar. سائس.)

Saka, v. (1) catch, as of animals in a trap, drive animals into a net or trap, and so hunt—of wild animals and birds, &c.; (2) hunt for, look for carefully. For hunting with firearms, as a rule *winda* is used. Prep. **Sakia.** St. and Pot. **Sakika.** Ps. **Sakwa.** Stc. **Sakama**, (1) stick fast, be caught (held, jammed) as of an animal in a trap or net, and (2) fig. of anything sticking in the throat or feelings, e.g. *maneno yake yamenisakama moyoni*, his words rankled in my heart; a difficulty, perplexity, &c. (Dist. *saki*, v. from a different source.) **Msaka**, n. *wa-*, **Msakaji**, n. *wa-*, and **Msasi**, n. *wa-* a hunter. **Msakamo**, n. *mi-* a sticking-fast, a jamming. **Msako**, n. *mi-* a hunt, a catching in a trap or net. **Usasi**, n. the art (method, fee, &c.) of hunting.

Sakafu,* n. the floor or roof of a flat-roofed stone building, cement or concrete floor. **Sakifu**, v. make a floor, roof, or pavement of concrete. Ps. **Sakifiwa.** Prep. **Sakifia.** Cs. **Sakifisha.** St. **Sakifika.** (Cf. *dari, ezeka, ikiza.* Ar. سقف.)

Sakama, v. See under **Saka.**

Sakara,* v., also St. **Sakarika**, (1) be tired, worn out by thirst, heat, &c.; (2) overeat, eat so much as to feel tired or faint. (Cf. *choka, legea, nyong'onyea.* Ar. سكر be full, and سكرات agony, faintness.)

Sakata, v. hit, beat (cf. *piga*); eat, finish off completely.

Saki,* v. (1) press close, fit tight, e.g. of clothes, stopper of a bottle, &c.; (2) affect deeply, come home to, touch the feelings of, e.g. of unkind words, &c. *Njaa inasaki*, hunger hurts. Ps. **Sakiwa.** Cs. **Sakisha. Kisaki**, adv. tightly, firmly, e.g. *funga kisaki*, fasten, tie, fix firmly. (Cf. *kaza, funga, lemea, bana.* ? Ar. صكّ lock, or سكّ stop, bar, obstruct.)

Sakifu,* v. See under **Sakafu.**

Sakimu,* v. be ill—rarely heard. (Cf. *ugua.* Ar. سقم.)

Sakini,* v. remain in a place, settle down and live in a place. **Maskani**, n. dwelling-place, home, &c. (Cf. *kaa.* Ar. سكن.)

Sakitu,* n. hoar frost. (Ar. صقيع.)

Sakubimbi, n. a trouble-maker, a bearer of tales, a sneak. (Cf. *mfitini, mdakuzi.*)

Sala,* n. prayer. The five prescribed hours of prayer of the Muhammadans are (1) *alfajiri*, at first signs of dawn; (2) *adhuhuri*, noon; (3) *alasiri*, afternoon; (4) *magharibi*, sunset; (5) *isha*, or *esha*, about 8 p.m. **Sali**, v. (1) pray; (2) use the prescribed forms of Muhammadan prayer in public or private. (Dist. *omba* in which the idea of earnest request, begging, is the chief one.) *Sali dua*, offer a special request to, make a petition to God. Prep. **Salia**, pray for, intercede for, &c., e.g. *mtu aliyekufa husaliwa*, prayers are said over a dead person. Cs. **Salisha**, e.g. teach forms of prayer to, lead the prayers—in a mosque or church. Also Inten. engage in worship. **Msala**, n. *mi-* a praying-mat, usually oval, and hence oval or round mats generally. (Cf. *dua, maombi*, and dist. *omba, saili.* Ar. صلى.)

Salaam.* See under **Salamu.**

Salala,* n. (1) meat from near the backbone, the chine, sirloin. (Ar. سرر middle part); (2) also *salale, masalala*, and *masalale*, an exclamation of astonishment &c. (prob. from the Arabic exclamation, God forbid, May God be unwilling, &c. ما شاء الله or, صلى الله عليه و سلم God bless him and give him peace, frequently used after the mention of Muhammad's name).

Salama,* adv. See under **Salamu.**

Salamu,* and **Salaam**, greeting, good wishes, compliments. *Salaam*, is a common greeting used by Arabs, Hindoos, and also by Christians. The full form of the Muhammadan greeting is *Salaam alek* or *aleik* (plur. *alekum* or *aleikum*), peace, safety, be with you—the reply being *wa alek* (*alekum*) *issalaam*, and with you peace—usually accompanied by placing the hand on the heart. **Salamu**, n., also **Salama**, and **Salaam**, safety, security, peace, salvation, sound health. *Toa salamu, pa salamu*, greet. *Peana salamu*, exchange greeting. *Pokea salamu*, receive greeting. *Leta* (*peleka, chukua*) *salamu*, convey greeting. *Salamu ya mkono*, shaking hands, offer of help. *Umsalimu ndugu yako salamu zangu*, give your brother my greetings. *Kwa salamu na amani*, in safety and peace. *Mizinga ya salamu*, a salute with cannon. *Salama salimini*, safe and well, quite safe. A common opening of a letter is: *Kwa fulani salamu sana* (or *salamu nyingi*) *na baada ya salamu* (or *wabadahu*), &c., i.e. To so-and-so, all good wishes, and after good wishes, &c. **Salamu**, a. safe, secure, sound, flourishing, well. **Salimini**, adv. in safety, safely—used in conjunction with *salama*, e.g. *barua yako imenifikia salama salimini*, your letter reached me quite safely. **Salimu**, v. (1) express good wishes to, salute, greet, accost, congratulate, e.g. *fulani anakusalimu*, so-and-so sends his compliments; (2) hand over safely, consign, deliver, rescue; (3) give up, surrender, yield, resign. *Nimesalimu fedha kwa fulani*, I have paid so-and-so his money. *Salimu roho*, give up the ghost, die. Ps. **Salimiwa**. St. **Salimika**, e.g. *salimika ajali*, meet one's fate, come to the appointed end, die. Also, be delivered, rescued, be paid off, &c. Prep. **Salimia**, e.g. *unisalimie baba yako*, give my kind regards to your father. Rp. **Salimiana**. Cs. **Salimisha**, e.g. (1) cause to be safe, save, rescue; (2) give up, hand over, pay, i.e. Inten. *Nitaisalimisha roho yangu*, I shall die. *Mali hii isalimishe mkononi mwa ndugu yangu*, pay this money into my brother's hand. *Salimisha kwa hila*, betray. **Taslimu**, n. direct delivery, prompt (cash) payment, e.g. *nunua taslimu*, buy for ready money, i.e. *mkono kwa mkono*. *Fedha taslimu*, ready money, spot-cash. (Cf. *silimu, toa, kabidhi, ponya, okoa*. Ar. سلم.)

Salata,* n. (1) harshness, unfeeling conduct, sarcasm; (2) adulteration, mixing. **Saliti**, v. (1) be harsh, domineering, sarcastic, bring a charge (against), attack, esp. with the tongue; (2) betray; (3) mix, adulterate. **Msalata**, n. *wa*-, **Msaliti**, n. *wa*- (1) a false accuser; (2) a betrayer, a traitor; (3) a harsh, unfeeling, domineering person. **Tasliti**, v. betray, cause trouble, e.g. *fulani ametasliti hata watu wamegombana*, so-and-so has stirred up trouble until people have quarrelled. (Cf. *changanya, ghoshi, mchongezi*. Ar. سلط and صوالة rubbish, refuse matter.)

Sali,* v. See under **Sala**.

Salia, v. See under **Saa**, v.

Salihi,* a. good, sound, fitting, useful, proper, in good condition. *Mtu salihi*, a man of good (honourable, unblemished) character. **Salihina**, n. also **Msalihina**, n. *wa*- a god-fearing person, a religious, devout person. (Cf. *sahihi, mcha Mungu*, and *suluhu* from which root it is derived. Ar. صالح.)

Salili, n. applied to many species of duck, and also to Pigmy goose. (Cf. *bata*.)

Salimini,* adv., **Salimu**, v. See under **Salamu**.

Salio, n. *ma*-. See under **Saa**, v.

Saliti,* v. See under **Salata**.

Sama,* v. stick in the throat, choke. (Cf. *sakama, kwama*. Ar. صم.)

Samadari,* n. a bedstead of foreign non-African make, of iron or wood. Commonly of Indian beds. (Cf. *kitanda, ulili*. Hind. سامان دار furniture of wood.)

Samadi,* n. manure, cow-dung and ashes mixed. **Simadi**, v. manure a field or garden. (Cf. *mbolea*. Ar. سماد.)

Samaha,* n. *ma*. See under **Samehe**.

Samaki,* n. a fish (of any kind), fish (in general). Some of the commonest are: *papa, nguru, pweza, taa, changu, dagaa, chafi, chewa, furusi, kolekole, kangaja, mkundaji, ngisi, ningu, pono*, n.k. *Kambure* is the commonest fresh-water fish, a kind of barbel. *Samaki mbichi*, fresh fish. *Samaki mkavu*, dried fish. *Samaki ng'onda*, cured fish (sun-dried). *Samaki wa chumvi*, salted fish. *Vua samaki*, fish, catch fish. *Tunga samaki*, tie (hang up) in a row. *Bana* (or *banika*) *samaki*, fasten fish in a cleft stick to bake by a fire. Prov. *Samaki akioza ni mtungo pia*, if one fish goes bad, the whole lot (string) does also. (Cf. *nswi, swi*. Ar. سمكة.)

Samani,* n. implement, tool, utensil, piece of furniture, movable chattel. *Samani za seremala*, carpenter's tools. For the common *chombo, zana*. (Hind. and Pers. سامان.)

Samawari,* n. a kind of urn with a receptacle for charcoal beneath, used by coffee sellers.

Samawati,* n. and **Samawi**, the heavens, the sky, sky-colour, azure, Also *rangi ya samawati* (or *samawi*), sky-blue, blue. (Ar. سموات.)

Sambaa, v. be scattered about, spread about. (Cf. *tawanyika, enea.*)

Sambamba, adv. alongside, abreast, side by side, shoulder to shoulder, in line, parallel. (Cf. *sanjari.*)

Sambusa,* n. a kind of cake containing meat, onion, and pepper. (Pers. سنبوسه.)

Samehe,* v. pardon, forgive, remit, pass over, e.g. of offences, debts, &c. *Nimekusamehe kosa*, I have forgiven your mistake. Ps. **Samehewa.** St. and Pot. **Sameheka.** Prep. **Samehea.** Cs. **Samehesha.** Rp. **Sameheana.** **Msamaha,** n. *mi-* pardon, forgiveness, forbearance, respite. **Msameha,** n. *wa-*, **Msamehe,** n. *wa-*, and **Msameheji,** n. *wa-* a forgiving, merciful person. **Samaha,** n. *ma-* usu. employed in the plur. forgiveness, pardon. (Cf. *achilia, ghofiri.* Ar. سامح.)

Samesame,* n. a kind of red bead. (? Ar. سمسم a kind of red ant.)

Samli,* n. ghee, native butter. (Ar. سمن.)

Sana,* adv. very much, in a high degree—used as an intensive of any kind of action or quality, and translatable accordingly, e.g. *kubwa sana*, very great. *Piga sana*, flog soundly. *Sema sana*, speak loud. *Vuta sana*, pull hard. *Kimbia sana*, run away fast. *Kaa sana*, remain a long time. Often with descriptive nouns, e.g. *mtu mganga sana*, a great medicine man. *Fundi sana*, a good workman. Sometimes doubled for emphasis, *sana sana*, or combined with *mno*, *ajabu*, &c. Also in rejoinder, signifying appreciation, approval—just so, certainly, I understand, quite right, &c. (Ar. سنا sublime, celebrated, eminent, beautiful, &c.)

Sana,* v. forge, as of hoes, hammers, knives, and such like. (Cf. *fua.*) **Msana,** n. *wa-* one who forges, &c., e.g. *msana visu*, a maker of knives. **Usani,** n. forging, i.e. of hoes, hammers, also act (method, fee, &c.) of forging. (Ar. سن.)

Sanaa,* n. art, work of art, skilled handicraft. **Sanaa,** v. make, construct, work with skill, make works of art, &c. **Msanaa,** n. *wa-*, **Msani,** n. *wa-*, also **Msanii,** n. *wa-* one skilled in handicraft, a skilful workman. (Ar. صنع.)

Sanamaki,* n. senna. a laxative, a purgative. (Cf. *msahala, harisha.* Ar. سنامكى.)

Sanamu,* n. image, idol, likeness, statue. *Ibada ya sanamu*, idolatry. *Picha* is generally used to denote a picture, drawing, or photograph, and *sanamu* a statue or photograph. *Andika picha*, draw a picture. *Piga picha* (or *sanamu*) take a photograph. *Chora sanamu*, make a statue. (Cf. *mfano, picha, taswira.* Ar. صنم.)

Sanati,* n. the year, only used in writing the date in letters written in Arabic style, or in documents, &c. (Cf. *tarehe, mwaka.* Ar. سنة.)

Sanda,* n. shroud, winding-sheet, burial cloth—commonly of thin white calico, i.e. *bafta ya kuzikia maiti.* (Cf. *mazishi, satini.* Ar. سند long cloth, also kind of striped stuff.)

Sandali,* n. sandal-wood from the tree *msandali.* (Ar. صندل.)

Sandarusi,* n. gum copal, from the tree *msandarusi.* (Ar. سندروس.)

Sandika, v. throw in one's teeth. (Cf. *sengenya, simanga.*)

Sanduku,* n. (—and of size, *ma-*) chest, box, trunk, case. (Cf. *kasha.* Ar. صندوق.)

Sanifu,* v. do work with skill, compose, invent. **Usanifu,** n. skill, art of composing. (Ar. صنف.)

Sanjari,* adv. (sometimes *chanjari*, and *shanjari*), in Indian file, in column formation, following each other, e.g. of ships in company, a convoy and consort, e.g. *tulifuatana sanjari, mashua zote mbili,* we followed in company with both boats. **Sanjari,** v. follow in line, escort, accompany—of ships. (Ar. انسجر step along in unbroken line. Pers. سنگار ships sailing together. Steere gives *shingari* which seems to support the Pers. derivation).

Sansuri,* n. name of a fish, baracouta.

Santuri,* n. a musical box, gramophone, &c. (Ar. سنطور.)

Sao, n. *ma-*. See under **Saa, v.**

Sapatu,* n. a slipper. (Cf. *kiatu, koshi.* Port. *sapata.*)

Sapa, v., also often Rd. **Sapasapa** (1) tout for customers; (2) make a clean sweep of, i.e. a person's belongings, money, &c. (Cf. *kumba.*)

Sarabi,* n. a mirage. (Cf. *mazigazi.* Ar. سراب.)

Sarafu,* n. (1) coin, small change, money; (2) exchange, rate of exchange; (3) small metal plate worn on the neck or forehead. **Sarifu,** v. spend money, exchange money. **Masarufu,** n., also **Masurufu,** n. (1) provisions taken on a journey (cf. *posho*); (2) money for household expenses, housekeeping money. (Ar. صرف.)

Saraka,* n. a drawer (of a chest of drawers, or of a table) sometimes called *mtoto wa meza.* The whole chest of drawers is *almari.* (Pers. سراچه casket within a larger case.)

Sarara, n. See **Salala.**

Sare,* n. (1) *fina la sare,* the name given to a child just after birth; (2) a draw in a game. *Kuenda sare,* to draw (in a game). (3) used of two things happening simultaneously, i.e. when two men are fighting and each man's stick hits the other man's head at the same time. (Prob. a corruption of *suluhu.*)

Sarifu,* v. (1) arrange, set in order, esp. of language, use words well, grammatically, in good style, i.e. *sarifu maneno kwa uzuri;* (2) see under *sarafu,* n. **Sarufi,** n. grammar. (Ar. صرف.)

Saruji,* n. (1) rubbish of lime when a wall is demolished, concrete, cement, chalk, and sand mixed (Ar. صاروج); (2) saddle, for a horse, but *matandiko* is often used. (Ar. سرج.)

Sasa,* adv. now, at this time, at present, in these days. *Sasa hivi,* directly, immediately, at once. *-a sasa, -a kisasa,* of the present day, fashionable, modern. **Kisasa,** n. and adv. a new, modern, up-to-date thing, a modern fashion. *Vao la kisasa,* a fashionable dress. *Maneno ya kisasa,* current phraseology. (Ar. ساع little while, short time, the present time, reduplicated to emphasize the latter meaning. Cf. *yule yule, kile kile,* &c.)

Sasamlanda, n. a herb, which when pounded and cooked is used as a vegetable.

Sataranji,* n. (1) a kind of sleeping-mat (Ar. سطرنجي); (2) the game of chess. (Ar. شطرنج.)

Satini,* n. grey long-cloth, also a kind of striped material. (Prob. from the same root as *sanda* by transp. Ar. سند.)

Saujika,* v. See **Sawajika.**

Saumu,* n. (A) a fast, fasting, also sometimes as a verb, fast. (Cf. *mfungo, funga.* Ar. صوم.)

Saumu,* n. (B) *kitunguu saumu* (also *somu, thumu*), garlic. (Ar. ثوم).

Sauti,* n. voice, sound, noise—mostly of animals, birds, or instruments, not merely sound. *Toa sauti,* utter a cry. *Paza sauti,* raise the voice, speak loud. *Kwa sauti kubwa,* with a loud voice. *Sauti ya kiume,* a broken (man's) voice. *Sauti ya kitoto,* an unbroken (treble) voice. *Sauti moja,* unison. (Cf. *mlio,* which includes all kinds of sounds, and *uvumi, shindo,* and *ukelele,* of loud sounds. (Ar. صوت.)

Sawa,* a. (1) like, alike, equal, the same; (2) equal, fair, equitable, just, right; (3) level, smooth, even flat, straight. *Sawa na, sawa kama,* equal to, like, just as. *Nchi sawa,* flat country, a plain. *Fanya sawa,* make equal, act fairly, **Sawa,** n. likeness, equality, flatness, &c. *Sawa kwa sawa mimi nawe,* we share equally, have half each. **Sawa,** and **Sawasawa,** adv. equally, just the same. **Sawazisha,** v. cause to be like, equal, even, &c., equalize, compare. Ps. **Sawazishwa. Sawia,** adv. then, at that time, just then, on the spot. *Alipomaliza maneno yake tu na kupigwa sawia,* just as he finished speaking he was struck, i.e. the finishing and the striking occurred together. *Mara tulipoingia nyumbani na mvua kunyesha sawia,* just as we got into the house it began to rain. **Usawa,** n. level, i.e. *usawa wa bahari,* sea-level; likeness, equality, &c. (Cf. *-moja, yule yule, vile vile, linganisha, pambanisha, fananisha.* Ar. ساوى and سوية.)

Sawajika,* v. be marred, disfigured, emaciated from illness, disease, famine, &c. (Cf. *umbuka.* Prob. a St. from Ar. سواد melancholy, black.)

Sawasawa,* adv. See under **Sawa.**

Sawawa, n. a kind of native vegetable.

Sawazisha,* v., **Sawia,*** adv. See under **Sawa.**

Sawiri,* v. form, fashion, make a picture, &c. **Taswira,** n. a picture, likeness, painting, portrait. (Cf. *sanamu, picha.* Ar. صور.)

Sayari,* n. a planet. (Cf. *nyota.* Ar. سيار.)

Sayidi,* n. See **Saidi** and **Seyyid.**

Saza, v., **Sazo,** n. *ma-.* See under **Saa,** v.

Sebule,* n. reception room, waiting room, usu. next to the entrance of a house. (Cf. *baraza* which is usu. outside, and *ukumbi.* ? Ar. صبر be patient.)

Sebusebu,* v. refuse, but really wanting at the same time. (Prob. a redupl. of Ar. صبى incline towards, act childishly.)

Sedeka,* v. be of long duration, such as an illness, &c., *ugonjwa huu unasedeka sana,* this sickness is of long duration. (Ar. سدك cleave to.)

Sefule,* int. of disgust, &c., with meaning, You vile person! Low fellow, &c. (Ar. سفل.)

Sega, n. *ma-* honeycomb. (Cf. *kamba ya nyuki.*)

Sega, v. double up clothes (trousers, &c.) to the knee so as to keep them dry or clean. (Cf. *pania.*)

Segele, n. belt of beads worn by children round the loins. (Cf. *kondavi.*)

Segua, v. See **Sekua.**

Sehemu,* n. part, portion, piece, share, instalment, fraction, *Sehemu za kumi,* tenths, also decimals in arithmetic, *nane kwa tano,* five-eighths, *nane kwa saba,* seven-eighths. *Sehemu za mia,* hundredths, percentages. *Mia kwa tano,* five per cent., *mia kwa kumi,* ten per cent. **Sehemu,** v.—rarely used, divide into portions. (Cf. *gawanya, fungu.* Ar. سهم.)

Sekeneka, v. be syphilized, be infected, ruined, destroyed by syphilis. **Sekeneko,** n. syphilis, but *kaswende* is more commonly used, and sometimes *tego.*

Sekini, n. *kunyoa sekini*, to shave the head leaving a tuft on the crown. (Cf. *denge, kishungi.* ? Ar. سكين a knife.)

Sekua, v. push along, remove by pushing, shoving, &c. (Cf. *sukuma, jongeza, sogeza.*)

Selaha,* n. See **Silaha.**

Selea, v., also Prep. **Selelea**, used in the same way, (1) remain in a place, as a person who visits a town and likes it so much that he remains there and does not return to his country; (2) be attached to, like, as name, town, &c. (Perh. from *selehi.*)

Selea, n. a kind of red bead.

Selehi,* v., also **Suluhi**, improve, make, agree (with), conduce to, serve (for), be of use (to), be fitting for, make peace, reconciled. Cs. **Selehesha**, but usu. **Suluhisha**, reconcile, conciliate, make peace between, cause to agree. **Mseleheshi**, n. *wa-*, **Msuluhishi**, n. *wa-* a peacemaker, arbitrator. (Cf. *patanisha* Ar. صالح and اصلح.)

Selelea, v. See under **Selea.**

Selo,* n. signal of the arrival or departure of a ship, train, &c. (Cf. Eng. Sail ho!)

Sema, v. say, talk, converse, speak. *Sema sana*, speak loud. *Sema na*, talk to, converse with. But *sema*, with an object. Pers. Pfx. means 'speak against, abuse': (cf. *amba*, and *ambia*), e.g. *watu watamsema sana*, people will abuse him soundly. *Jisema* (and *jisemea*), pretend, profess—to be what one is not. Ps. **Semwa.** St. and Pot. **Semeka**, e.g. be said, admit being uttered, pronounced, &c. *Mambo niliyoona hayasemeki*, the things I saw cannot be spoken about. Prep. **Semea**, e.g. speak to, address, say to (contr. *ambia*, which introduces the words used). *Semea puani*, speak with a nasal twang. Cs. **Semesha.** Rp. **Semana**, abuse each other. Rp. of Cs. **Semezana**, hold a conversation together, wrangle. Note: *Husemi* and *useme*, are sometimes used idiomatically as conj. as if, supposing. (Cf. *kama kwamba.*) **Msema**, n. *wa-* one who speaks. **Msemaji**, n. *wa-*, **Msemi**, n. *wa-* (1) a speaker, a narrator; (2) an eloquent person, an orator, a fluent, talkative person. **Msemo**, n. *mi-* act (kind, style, &c.) of speaking, utterance, speech. *Kilichowafunga ni msemo wao wenyewe*, that which convicted them was their own speech. **Usemaji**, n. speaking as a practice or profession, eloquence, fine speech, rhetoric, fluency. **Usemi**, n. speaking, speech, talk, diction, conversation.

Semaa wa taa,* an Arabic expression sometimes heard—hear and obey, to hear is to obey (سمعا, طاعة).

Sembuse, adv. not to mention, let alone, not only . . . but—when the act (circumstance, thing, &c.) being used for the purpose of comparison, contrast, &c., is smaller, of less value, weaker, of less importance, &c., than the act, &c., under consideration (cf. *licha*), e.g. *Senti moja sikupi sembuse shilingi*, I will not give you one cent, much less a shilling. *Kaka yako nitampiga, sembuse wewe*, I will beat your elder brother, let alone you (who are not so strong as he is). (Prob. a contraction of *usiniuze*, old form for *usiniulize*. It would become *sinuze* and *n* and *u* become *mb* by phonetic laws.)

Semitoni, n. See **Toni**—adopted from the English for use in text-books and school lessons on music, a semi-tone.

Semsem,* n. sesame. (Cf. *ufuta.* Ar. سمسم.)

Sena, n. (1) a kind of sugar cane; (2) of sweet potato; (3) of rice.

Senea, v. be blunt, of a knife, tool, &c. (Cf. *butu.*) Cs. **Seneza**, make blunt, and hence, cut or smooth (with an adze) (*tezo, sezo*). **Senezo**, n., also **Sezo**, an adze, usu. *tezo.*

Seng'enge, n. iron wire. *Seng'enge yenye miiba*, barbed wire.

Sengenya, v. calumniate, backbite, attack by secret or underhand insinuations. Ps. **Sengenywa.** Rp. **Sengenyana. Msengenyi**, n. *wa-* a trouble-maker, tale-bearer, &c. **Msengenyaji**, n. *wa-* one accustomed to attack by secret or underhand insinuations, hence, a name for the devil. **Msengenyo**, n. *mi-* evil report, calumny.

Senti,* n. a cent, a one-cent piece.

Senturi,* n. See **Santuri.**

Sepeto,* n. a spade, shovel. (Eng. spade.)

Sepetuka, v. reel to and fro, stagger. (Cf. *seseteka, sesetuka, sesereka, pepesuka.*)

Septemba,* n. September. (Eng.)

Sera, n. (1) fort, fortress, stronghold, castle (cf. *ngome, gereza, boma, buruji.* Ar. سور); (2) bees' wax. (Cf. *nta.*)

Serahangi,* n. (sometimes *serehangi*), headman of a crew, or part of a crew, mate, boatswain. (Pers. سرهنگ.)

Seredani,* n. a brazier. (Pers. ساعور fire, and دان container.)

Seremala,* n. *ma-* a carpenter. **Useremala**, n. occupation, payment, &c., of a carpenter. (Pers. and Ar. سرامد.)

Serikali,* n. Government, public authority, an official. (Pers. سركارى.)

Serifu,* v. See **Sarifu**, under **Sarafu**, n.

Seruji,* n. See **Saruji.**

Sesere, n. also **Mwanasesere**, a doll, usu made out of grass or a kind of cucumber, &c. (Cf. *mtoto wa bandia.*)

Sesereka, v., also **Seseteka, Sesetuka**, reel to and fro, stagger, as of a drunken man. (Cf. *yumba, pepesuka, sepetuka.*)

Seta, v. (1) crush, squash, mash, beat up—usually of things relatively soft, e.g. *seta viazi kwa mwiko*, mash potatoes with a spoon, but also of pounding ingredients together in a mortar; (2) jostle, press (in a crowd). Ps. **Setwa.** Cs. **Setesha**, huddle together. **Mseto**, n. *mi-* a mixture of grains and other ingredients cooked for food, a mash, e.g. *mtama, kunde, viazi.* (Cf. *twanga, ponda, saga, songa, funda.*)

Seti,* n. the sevens in a pack of playing-cards. (Port. *sete.*)

Setiri,* v., and **Stiri**, conceal, hide, cover up, atone for. The deriv. forms usu. follow *stiri* which see. (Ar. ستر.)

Seuze. (Cf. *sembuse* which is more usual.

Seyyid,* n. the title given to the Sultan of Zanzibar. (Ar. سيد.)

Seza, v. same as *seneza*, which see.

Sezo, n., same as *tezo* which see.

Shaba,* n. brass. *Shaba nyekundu*, copper. *Shaba nyeupe*, brass. (Ar. شبة.)

Shababi,* n. a youth. **Ushababi**, n. youth, youthfulness. (Cf. *kijana.* Ar. شباب.)

Shabaha,* n. (A) (1) a target, aim, a mark to aim at; (2) aim (with a weapon), sight (of a gun), e.g. *twaa (piga, lenga) shabaha*, take aim, aim. *Pata shabaha*, hit the target. *Huyu hana shabaha*, he cannot aim properly, he is not a good shot. (Ar. شبح object of vision.)

Shabaha,* n. (B) similarity, likeness. **Shabaha**, adv. like, the same as, e.g. *mnyama shabaha* (or *shabaha ya*) *mbwa*, an animal like a dog. (Cf. *mithali, mfano, kama.*) **Shabihi**, v. be like, analogous to. Rp. **Shabihiana.** *Mtoto huyu anashabihiana na baba yake*, this child is like his father. **Mshabaha**, n. *mi-* likeness, resemblance, similitude, **Shabihi**, n. form, outward appearance of a person, dignity. (Cf. *fanana, lingana landa, mfano, sura.* شابه resemble.)

Shabaki,* n., also **Shabuka,** (1) a quarrelsome, cross-grained person, one who is cunning, who cheats by cunning words; (2) a snare, fishing-net. **Ushabaki,** n. (1) cunning; (2) a snare, a trap, trouble, a quarrel, stratagem, trickery, esp. of words. (Cf. *werevu, mgomvi, mtego.* Ar. شبك entwine; fishing net.)

Shabani,* n., sometimes **Shaabani,** (1) the month of the Muhammadan year next preceding Ramadhan, also called *mwezi wa mlisho,* i.e. the month of feasting; (2) a common personal male name. (Cf. *shiba.* Ar. شعبان.)

Shabihi,* v. See under **Shabaha,** n. (B).

Shabu,* n. alum. (Ar. شب.)

Shabuka,* n. See under **Shabaki.**

Shada,* n. (— and *ma-*) (1) a string, bunch, cluster, e.g. of flowers, beads, &c.; (2) tuft, tassel, rosette. *Shada la ushanga,* a string of beads. *Shada la maua,* a bunch of flowers. **Kishada,** n. *vi-* dim. (Ar. شد.)

Shadidi,* v. hold fast to, fix, use influence, order, direct influence. (Ar. شدّ make effort, &c.)

Shafaka,* n. See **Shufaka.**

Shaghala baghala,* anyhow, indiscriminately, &c. (Cf. *shelabela, ovyo.* ? Hind. Cf. *shughuli,* and بغل on one side, i.e. putting business on one side.)

Shaha,* n. *ma-*, also, **Shehe, Sheki, Sheik** (1) head, headman, chief, councillor; (2) heart, pith—of a coco-nut tree, the crown from which the leaves and flower spring (cf. *kilele*); (3) a minstrel, poet, writer of songs. **Usheha,** n. status, &c., of a councillor, hence, position of respect, formal show of respect, reverence, &c (Ar. شيخ.)

Shahada,* n. (1) a bond, covenant, deed of ratification, testament, evidence; (2) the Muhammadan creed, confession of faith. *Kidole cha shahada,* the forefinger. *Maji ya shahada,* water used ceremonially at a funeral. *Kupiga shahada,* to recite the Muhammadan creed. **Shahidi,** n. *ma-* one who attests or guarantees, a witness, an authority, a martyr. **Shuhuda,** n. *ma-* testimony, evidence, witness, diploma. **Shuhudu,** v. bear witness—but usu. in the Prep. form **Shuhudia,** attest, confirm, give evidence, proof. **Ushahidi,** n., **Ushuhuda,** n. (*shuhuda,* and *ma-*) testimony, evidence, proof. (Ar. شهد.)

Shahamu,* n. fat, lard, grease, i.e. animal fat. (Cf. *mafuta, sifa,* also *nona, nenepa.* Ar. شحم.)

Shahawa,* n. semen. (Cf. *shaua, manii.* Ar. شهوة.)

Shahidi,* n. *ma-*. See under **Shahada.**

Shaibu,* n. a very old person, *mwanamke shaibu ajuza,* a very old woman. (Cf. *kizee, kikongwe.* Ar. شيب.)

Shairi,* n. *ma-* a song, a line of poetry. *Mashairi,* verses, poetry, a poem, a song. *Tunga mashairi,* compose verses. **Mshairi,** n. *wa-* a poet, a writer or composer, of songs, &c. **Ushairi,** n. poetry, the art. (Cf. *utenzi, beti,* and dist. *shayiri,* barley. Ar. شعر and شاعر.)

Shaitani,* n. See **Shetani.**

Shaka,* n. doubt, perplexity, uncertainty, *kuwa na shaka,* to be in doubt, **Shuku,** v. be doubtful, feel scruples, suspect. Prep. **Shukia,** feel doubt about—dist. from Prep. *shuka.* **Shuku,** n. like *shaka,* suspicion, presentiment, doubt, scruple. (Cf. *dhania, tuhumu.* Ar. شكّ. Dist. *mashaka.*)

Shakawa,* n. trouble, difficulty, danger, same as *mashaka.*

Shake,* n. used in the expression, *ingiwa na shake la kulia,* cry with sobbing. (? Ar. شقي be miserable).

Shakevale, n. the African harrier-hawk, *Gymnogenys typicus.* (Cf. *hajivale.*)

Shakiri,* v. be satisfied, esp. with food—a form of *shukuru,* which see. (Cf. *shiba.*)

Shakwe, n. applied to the gulls and terns.

Shalaka,* n. a hole in the gunwale of a boat for securing the loop of rope (*kishwara*) used as a rowlock. **Shaliki,** v. bind lightly or loosely, fix on or in loosely. (Ar. شرك a loop, a snare.)

Shali,* n. a shawl. (Ar. شال.)

Shaliki,* v. See under **Shalaka.**

Sham,* n. Syria. Bahari ya Sham, the Red Sea. (Ar. الشام.)

Shamari,* n. fennel. (Ar. شمر.)

Shamba,* n. *ma-* (1) a plantation, an estate, farm, garden, plot of cultivated ground; (2) the country as opposed to the town. *Enda shamba,* go into the country. *Toka shamba,* come from the country. *Mtu wa shamba,* a rustic, peasant. **Kimashamba, also kishamba,** n. and adv. anything belonging to the plantation or country; countrified, rustic, boorish, rude (unpolished) of language, and manners, &c. (Cf. *kiunga,* and *konde,* and *mgunda,* which are the Bantu words in use. French *champ*—it is very probable that cloves came to Zanzibar from Mauritius where the French introduced them in 1770, as they were introduced to Zanzibar about 25 years later and French ships passed frequently on their way from India. It is also probable that the Arabs learnt, directly or indirectly, how to cultivate cloves from the French. This cultivation would no doubt involve more orderly and extensive agriculture than had been done before, and the French word would be adopted for the plantations. (Cf. French *girofle* for clove, which is undoubtedly connected with the Ar. *karafuu,* also *divai,* which is from the French *du vin.*)

Shambiro,* a. without order, in common use, &c. *Nyumba ya shambiro,* a house in common use, where everybody goes in and out and does what he pleases. (Ar. صبر see form تصبر heap up without measuring.)

Shambulia, v. attack, make an inroad (incursion, invasion, war), upon, rush violently on. **Shambulio,** n. *ma-* sudden attack, rush, incursion. (Cf. *pigia, shindania* (*letea, tolea*), *vita.*)

Shamili,* v. *ma-* an ear ornament. (Cf. *bali.* Ar. شى thing, and ميل hang down.)

Shamiri,* v. (1) load a gun; (2) put together, e.g. fix the legs of a bedstead, table, &c. (Cf. *shindilia.* Ar. شمر see form تشمر make ready for.)

Shamua, v. usu. *chemua,* sneeze, sniff. (Cf. *chafya, enda* (or *piga*), *chafya.*)

Shangaa, v. be astonished, stand and stare, be dumbfounded (with wonder, horror, &c.), be dazed. Cs. **Shangaza,** astonish, strike with wonder, terrify, &c. **Mshangao,** n. *mi-* thrilling excitement, deep sensation, admiration, wonder, perplexity, amazement, bewilderment, stupefaction. **Ushangao,** n. like *mshangao.*

Shangama, n. (1) a kind of shirt with short sleeves made from two pieces only of material, i.e. back and front; (2) a house with ridge roof, i.e. *mapaa mawili.*

Shangazi, n. father's sister, paternal aunt. (Cf. *mama mdogo.*)

Shangilia, v. make rejoicings (for, at) shout or sing with joy and triumph, make demonstrations of enthusiasm, congratulate. Ps. **Shangiliwa,** e.g. be received with triumph (rejoicings, congratulations.) **Shangilio,** n. *ma-* rejoicings, triumph, congratulations. **Shangwe,** n. rejoicing, demonstration of joy (triumph, enthusiasm). (Cf. *shangaa,* *furahia*, and *nyanja*, *sangula*, make happy.)

Shani,* n. startling (rare, unlooked-for) thing or occurrence, a wonder, a novelty, a curiosity, an adventure, a sudden mishap, accident, e.g. *patwa na shani*, have an accident, meet with an adventure. *Nguo za shani*, fine, new clothes, latest fashion. *Mambo haya si shani*, that is nothing to be surprised at, that is no wonder. (Ar. *mwujiza*, *ajabu*, *ibura*, *shangaa*. Ar. شأن.)

Shanjari,* adv. See **Sanjari**.

Shanta,* n. haversack, rucksack, knapsack. (Cf. *mkoba*, *mfuko*. Ar. شنطة.)

Shanuo, n. See **Chanuo** (or perhaps Pers. شانه comb.)

Shapo, n. See **Mashapo**.

Sharabeti,* n. sherbet, often *shebeti*. (Ar. شرابات.)

Sharabu, n. an intoxicating drink (dist. *sharubu*). **Sharabu**, v. absorb, drink up, saturate. (Cf. *nywa*, *rishai*, *papa*, v. Ar. شرب.)

Sharafa,* n. *ma- sharafa la ndevu*, or *ndevu za sharafa*, long flowing beard. (Cf. *-sharifu*.)

Shari,* n. See under **Mshari**.

Sharia,* n. See **Sheria**.

Sharifu,* v. treat with respect, honour, esteem. **-sharifu, a.** honourable, respectable, noble, excellent —originally referred to descendants of Muhammad. **Msharifu**, n. *wa-* **Sharifu**, n. esteemed person. **Usharifu**, n. nobility, excellence, respectability—esp. of rank and character. (Cf. *tukuza*, *heshima*. Ar. شرف.)

Sharika,* n., **Shariki**, v. See under **Shiriki**.

Shariti,* v. tell lies, prevaricate, pervert, change the meaning of. *Fulani anashariti maneno*, so-and-so perverts statements. (Ar. ? شرط tear into pieces, get into a plight, and hence prevaricate.)

Sharti,* n. See under **Shuruti**.

Sharubu,* n *ma-* the moustache. (Ar. شوارب.)

Shashi,* n. a kind of thin muslin, also tissue paper. (Ar. شاش.)

Shashimamishi, adv. proudly, contemptuously, arrogantly. (Ar. شخص lofty, sublime, and مشى walking.)

Shasira,* n. See **Shazia**.

Shata, n. *ma-* lees of coco-nut oil. (? Ar. شطا small splinters.)

Shati,* n. *ma-* an English shirt or similar garment. (Eng. shirt.)

Shatoruma,* n. a shawl, usually worn round the waist by Muhammadans and teachers and that type of person. (Cf. *mshipi*, *mahazamu*, *masombo*. (Pers. شال ترمه a Cashmere shawl.)

Shau,* a. See under **Shaua**.

Shaua,* v. (1) excite desire, and esp. desire which is not gratified, and so, make a display, show off; and (2) deceive, disappoint, delude, flatter, often as Rf. *jishaua*, (1) make a useless show, be silly (lackadaisical, frivolous, flirty) and (3) be disappointed, have a sense of failure. **Kishaufu**, n. *vi-* (1) anything showy, bit of finery, trinket, personal ornament; (2) a nose-ring. (Cf. *azama*.) **Mshaufu**, n. *wa-* (1) one disposed to show off, inclined to frivolity; (2) a shameless person, one without manners. **-shau, a.** and **-shaufu, a.** showy, pretentious, affected, having loose morals, given to frivolity. **Ushaufu**, n. delusiveness, deception, misleading display, disappointing promise. (Note: the adj. *-fu* termination may have been added to the Ar. شهى excite desire, or it may be part of the root شوف to show.)

Shauku,* n. eagerness, strong desire (affection, wish, fondness, liking, longing), sexual passion—it is applicable to good and bad objects, but a stronger word for sexual desire is *ashiki*. *Nina shauku naye*, I am greatly attached to him. *Shauku ya kuzungumza*, passionate fondness for amusement. *Shauku nyingi huondoa maarifa*, strong desire overrides prudence. (Cf. *ashiki*, and syn. *huba, mapenzi, ngoa, tamaa, uchu*. Ar. شاق and شوق.)

Shauri,* n. *ma-* (1) plan, design, intention; (2) advice, counsel; (3) discussion, debate, e.g. *fanya shauri*, consider, deliberate, consult, hold a council, form a plan. *Toa(pa) shauri*, offer (give advice, lay down a plan. *Uliza shauri*, ask advice. *Mwenye shauri, mtu wa mashauri mengi*, a wise, resourceful, clever man, also, a troublesome person, i.e. always in trouble, always in need of advice. **Shauri,** v. ask counsel, get advice, consult. Cs. **Shaurisha,** cause to get advice, get advice for. Rp. **Shauriana,** consult together. **Halmashauri,** n. a committee, advisory body, &c. **Mshauri,** n. *wa-* an adviser, one capable of giving advice, friend, counsellor. The usual name for an Administrative Officer in Tanganyika Territory is *Bwana Shauri*. (Ar. شاور.)

Shaushi,* v. See under **Shawishi.**

Shaushi,* n. corporal, formerly used by the Germans in what is now Tanganyika Territory for native soldiers of that rank. (Cf. *bishausi, ombasha, soli*. (Ar. from Turk. شاويش.)

Shavu, n. *ma-* (sometimes *chafu* and *chavu*) (1) *shavu la uso*, the cheek; (2) biceps, muscle of arm, i.e. *shavu la mkono*; (3) calf of leg, i.e. *shavu la mguu*. Also *shavu la samaki*, gill of fish; *shavu la jogoo*, wattles of a cock.

Shawali,* n. the tenth month according to Islam. (Ar. شوال.)

Shawishi,* v. persuade, coax, entice, tempt, allure. Ps. **Shawishiwa.** Prep. **Shawishia.** St. and Pot. **Shawishika. Mshawishi,** n. *wa-* one who persuades, a tempter, &c. **Kishawishi,** n. *vi-* temptation, lure, attraction. **Shawishi,** n. *ma-* enticement, lure, temptation, &c. **Tashwishi,** n. doubt, perplexity, confusion. (Cf. *vuta, jaribu*. Ar. شوش.)

Shayiri,* n. barley. (Dist. *shairi*. Ar. شعير.)

Shazasi,* n. sal-ammoniac. (? Ar نشادر.)

Shazi,* n. a bunch, cluster, string of anything, i.e. of fish, meat, fruit, &c. **Kishazi,** n. *vi-* dim. (Ar. شاز divided from rest.)

Shazia,* n. (sometimes *shasira* is heard), a long copper or brass needle, used in making mats and mattresses, a bodkin or sail-maker's needle. (A corruption of Ar. شصر.)

Shebaha,* sometimes heard for *shabaha*, which see.

Shebeti,* n. sherbert. See *Sharabeti*.

Shegele, n. See **Segele.**

Sheha,* n. See **Shaha.**

Shehe,* n. See **Sheik.**

Shehena,* n. cargo, freight, load. **Sheheni,** v. have cargo on board, be loaded up—of a ship, e.g. *chombo kimesheheni*, the vessel is full of cargo. Cs. **Sheheneza,** load, fill up with cargo (Ar. شحن).

Sheherasi,* n See **Sheikh rasi,** under **Rasi.**

Sheik,* n. *ma-*, elder, chief, ruler, teacher, an important or influential person. (Cf. *shaha*, and syn. *mkubwa, mkuu, mzee, mwalimu, mfalme*. Ar. شيخ.)

Sheitani,*. See **Shetani.**

Sheki,* n. See **Sheik.**

Shela,* n. (A) a large black veil, usu. a square of black silk, worn over the head by Arab women out of doors. Also called *shela mdeusia*. (Cf. *utaji, dusumali*. Ar. شال.)

Shela,* n. (B) a sword dance. (Ar.

صل sword, see also صول sudden attack.)

Shelabela,* adv. in a lot, just as they are, with all defects, &c., indiscriminately. (Cf. *ovyoovyo, shaghala baghala*. Ar. شيل بيلة.)

Sheleli,* v. sew a seam. (Cf. *shona*. Ar. شلالة.)

Shemali,* n. (1) the left (hand); (2) the north (quarter); (3) the north wind, mist, fog. (Cf. *kushoto, kibla, kaskazi*, and *ukungu*. Ar. شمال.)

Shemasi,* n. *ma-* a deacon. **Ushemasi**, n. office (work, salary, &c.) of a deacon, diaconate. (Cf. *kasisi, padre*. Ar. شماس.)

Shembea,* n. a curved knife. (Cf. *kisu, sime, kotama, buchari*, prob. a form of *jambia*.)

Shemeji, n. a relation by marriage—usu. of the first degree, i.e. wife's (or husband's) brother or sister, brother-in-law, sister-in-law, but frequently used in a loose way of any particular friend of the husband.

Shemeri,* n. a nose-ring of an ox. (Ar. شمر see form اسمر urge to haste.)

Shems l maarifa,* n. the name of a book of medicines. (Cf. follg. and *maarifa*.)

Shemshi,* n. the sun, for the usu. *jua*. (Ar. شمش.)

Shenga,* v. See **Chenga.**

-Shenzi,* a. barbarous, uncivilized, uncouth. **Kishenzi**, n. and adv. anything of a barbarous, rude, uncivilized kind, esp. barbarous language, up-country dialect. *-a kishenzi*, barbarous, uncivilized. **Mshenzi**, n. *wa-* a barbarian, savage, one of the aborigines, a person untouched by civilization. Often used contemptuously by the coast native of those who come from the interior, although they are frequently more cultured and refined than the coast native! **Ushenzi**, n. the condition of an uncivilized person, barbarism, uncouthness, rudeness. (Pers. زنجی or زنج.)

Shere or **Sheri**, n. fun, ridicule, joke, derision. *Kucheza shere*, to make fun of, mock, deride. (Cf. *mzaha, danganya, cheka*. (Ar. ? اشر exulting, rejoicing.)

Sherehe,* n. (1) show, pomp, display; (2) demonstration, rejoicings, cheers, triumph. (Cf. *shangwe, vigelegele, shangilia*. Ar. إنشرح be happy.)

Sheresi,* n. See **Sherisi.**

Sheria,* n. law, a law, and in the locative, *sheriani*, a law court, judicial proceedings. *Sheria ya chuo*, written or statute law. *Sheria ya nchi*, law of the land. *Peleka sheriani*, prosecute. *Enda sheriani*, go to law, litigate. *Mwana sheria*, a lawyer. (Cf. *amri, desturi*. Ar. شريعة.)

Sherifu,* n. *ma-*. See under **Sharifu,**

Sherisi,* n. glue. (Cf. *ambo*. Ar. شراس.)

Sheshe, n. beauty, beautiful, e.g. *kitu cha sheshe*, a beautiful thing. (Cf. *zuri*.)

Shetani,* n. *ma-* (1) an evil spirit, demon, devil, Satan; (2) that which suggests supernatural power, whether evil or simply incomprehensible, e.g. a clever dodge, great skill, conjuring, epilepsy, fits, hysteria. (*Ibilisi, jini, pepo, koma*. Ar. شيطان.)

Shetri,* n. the poop of a dhow, stern part of a vessel. Opp. to *gubeti, omo*, the prow, bow, forepart. (Cf. *tezi*. Ar. شطر part of a thing, see *gubeti*, prow, which also simply means part of a thing.)

Shi-. Note: some natives tend to interpose *i* between *sh* and *t*, so that words not found under *shi* may be looked for under *sht*.

Shiba,* v. (1) have enough to eat or drink, have a full meal, be satisfied with food; (2) sometimes used fig. of being wholly filled with, and so under the influence of something, e.g. *shiba Mungu*, be wholly given to worship and religion, be a devotee. Cs. **Shibisha**, satisfy, feed, fill. **Shibe**, n. fullness, satiety, repletion, completion, finishing touch, e.g. *Shibe ya nyama*, a full meal of meat. (Cf. *shabani*. Ar. شبع.)

Shibiri,* n. a span, from thumb to little finger of the open hand, about nine inches, half a cubit. A short span is *morita*. (Cf. *mkono, dhiraa, morita*. Ar. شبر.)

Shida,* n. (1) hardship, distress, difficulty. *Patwa na shida, -wa na shida, ingia shida*, get into trouble or distress. *Kwa shida*, with difficulty. (Cf. *taabu, dhiki, msiba, matata*. Ar. شدّة.) (2) want, scarceness, rarity, something hard to get. *Siku hizi nyama ni shida*, there is a scarcity of meat at present. *Kwa shida*, scarcely, hardly, seldom, unlikely. (Cf. *adimu, haba, chache*. Ar. قلة وجود = *qillet wegûd*—scarcity, rareness.

Shige la manjano, n. the Pemba White-eye, *Zosterops vaughani*; also called *manja*.

Shika, v. hold fast, take hold of, keep hold on, seize, grasp, keep. A common word with a wide range of application, e.g. (1) get hold on, press hard on, be on the mind, put in difficulties; (2) keep a hold on, persevere in; (3) hold to, keep to, observe, remember, attend to, obey; (4) determine, resolve, make up the mind to; (5) also as Intrans. have a hold, prevail, be urgent, e.g. *shika njia*, take to the road, start, proceed, keep to (follow) a road. *Shika amri*, obey an order. *Shika lako*, mind your own business. *Shika bei*, hold out for a price, haggle, bargain. *Nitakayokuambia shika*, mind you attend to what I shall tell you. *Mvua imeshika*, the rain is set in properly. *Shika miguu ya*, salute, pay honour to . . . submit to, become the slave of. (Cf. *shikamuu*, below.) *Pata shika*, an expression used descriptive of a strenuous game, i.e. of football, &c. *Leo mchezo ulikuwa pata shika*, to-day the game was strenuous, it was striving, i.e. getting and endeavouring to hold. Ps. **Shikwa**, e.g. *shikwa na homa*, have an attack of fever. *Shikwa na deni*, be pressed with debt. St. and Pot. **Shikika**, e.g. *maji hayashikiki*, water cannot be grasped. Prep. **Shikia**, hold by, hold on to, hold for (at, by, in), e.g. *kamba ya kushikia*, a rope to hold by. *Kushikiwa fedha*, to have money held for one, i.e. in the hands of trustees. D.Prep. **Shikilia**, hold on to (in some special way, or obstinately or perseveringly). Cs. of Prep. **Shikiliza**, e.g. tack (in sewing), make hold fast, &c. Rp. of Cs. of Prep. **Shikilizana**, encourage each other to hold on, persevere, &c. Cs. **Shikiza**, cause to hold, make fast (firm, tight) fasten, prop. keep in place, in sewing, tack. *Shikiza nyumba*, prop up a house. *Shikiza mkono*, guide by the hand, e.g. of a scholar writing, &c. Rp. **Shikana**, hold each other, be friends, grapple, form connexion with. Stc. **Shikama**. Rp. of Stc. **Shikamana**, be in a state of firmly holding together, be firm, set, hard, e.g. of mortar, &c. Prov. *Ushikwapo shikamana, ulwewapo* (or *uchwewapo*) *na jua, lala*. When you are pressed, hold together, when you are overtaken by the sun, sleep. Cs. **Shikamanisha**. **Mshika**, n. *wa-* one who holds (governing a noun following), i.e. *mshika usukani*, a steersman, one who holds the tiller. **Mshikano**, n. *mi-* a mass, cluster, e.g. *mshikano wa milima*. **Mshiki**, n. *wa-* same as *mshika*. **Mshikilizo**, n. *mi-*, **Mshikizo**, n. *mi* lit. a causing to hold on to, or together—used of tacking, or basting materials ready for sewing. **Shikamuu** (also shortened to *shikamu, shikam, kamu*, and even *kam* and *muu*), a common salutation used by dependants to superiors, and young people to elders, formerly much used by slaves to masters. In full *nashika miguu yako*, I hold your feet, as a sign of respect, reverence, or of inferiority, submission, &c. **Shikio,** n. *ma-* a thing to hold by, handle, (in a ship rudder. *Mshiki shikio*, a steersman. *Mashikio ya kikapu*, the handles of a basket. **Shikizo,** n. *ma-* (1) fastening, wedge, prop—used for securing something firmly; (2) a tack in sewing. **Ushikamano,** n. a holding fast together, the power or quality of holding fast together, tenacity.

Shiku,* n. *ma-* amplic. of *kishiku*.

Shilamu,* n. the stem of a pipe, leading from the water-bowl to the mouthpiece. (Cf. *buruma, bori, kiko, mrija, mtemba*. Hind. چلم a hookah.)

Shilingi,* n. a shilling. Shillings are current in Kenya, Tanganyika Territory, Zanzibar, and Uganda. One shilling = 100 cents. Other coins are 1-cent piece *senti*, 5-cent piece (called *kitano, vi-*), 10-cent piece (called *kikumi, vi-*), and 50-cent piece (*nusushilingi*). Notes (*noti*) are issued 5-shilling, 10, 20, 50, 100, &c.

Shimbi, n. the lees of native beer or of coco-nut palm-wine, used as yeast.

Shimbika, v. prepare a hook for fishing, tie fast the hook to the line. **Shimbiko,** n. *ma-* (1) a tying fast the hook to the line; (2) the thread used for securing the hook to the line. (Cf. *ndoana, mshipi, vua*, v.)

Shime,* n. used as a call or appeal urging on to further effort. *Haya shime wenzangu tusaidiane*, come my companions, let us put our hearts into it and help each other. (Dist. *sime*. Cf. *haya, mayowe*. Ar. سم attack in proper order.)

Shimiri,* v. do, fit, become, be of avail. *Mavazi yake yamemshimiri*, his clothes fit (suit, become) him. (Cf. *faa*. ? Ar. شمر examine carefully, &c.)

Shimo, n. *ma-* pit, hole, cavity, hollow, excavation—used very generally of small and large holes, mines, quarries, graves, pitfalls, tunnels, inside of a vessel, &c. *Shimo la dhahabu*, a gold mine. *Shimo la sahani*, the hollow of a plate. **Kishimo,** n. *vi-* dim. (Cf. *tundu, chimbo, pango, uvungu*.)

Shina, n. *ma-* root, stem of a tree—including all parts from the rootlets (*mizizi*), to the branches (*matawi*). **Shina rupia**, the name of a kind of cassava. (Cf. *muhogo*.) **Kishina,** n. *vi-* dim.

Shinda, v. (1) overcome, conquer, subdue; (2) surpass, excel, be first (best), win; (3) be over, be left, remain; (4) pass time, keep on, continue, stay for a time (at), stop (in), e.g. *shinda (adui) vitani*, be victorious (over enemies) in war. *Shinda kazi* (or *katika kazi*), carry on work, go on working. *Shinda na njaa*, continue hungry, endure famine. *Shinda shamba*, pay a visit in (stay in) the country, at a country residence. *Amekwenda shinda*, he has gone away for a time (for the day, for a picnic, for a visit). *Maji yashinda kisimani*, water is left in the well, i.e. there is still some left. *Kushinda jana*, used for 'day before yesterday', i.e. continuing over or past yesterday. Ps. **Shindwa,** e.g. *nimeshindwa*, I have been beaten, overcome, of a thing proving too much for one. St. and Pot. **Shindika** (1) be overcome, conquered, &c., but also more commonly as *sindika* in other and apparently different sense; (2) apply force to, but mostly with special senses, e.g. *sindika mafuta*, extract oil by pressure, *sindika miwa*, crush sugar-canes. *Sindika mlango*, partly close the door, close, but not fasten, set ajar. (3) sham sickness, e.g. *Julani anasindika*, so-and-so is shamming sickness. Prep. **Shindia,** D.Prep. **Shindilia,** press, press down, esp.

of ramming a charge home, loading a gun, i.e. *shindilia bunduki. Shindilia chakula kinywani*, stuff food into the mouth. *Shindilia vitu mfukoni*, press things into a bag. Cs. **Shindisha**, and sometimes **Shindiza**, e.g. (1) cause to excel; (2) cause to remain. Thus *shindisha nyumbani*, receive a visitor, take in as a lodger. Also with special Inten. force, *maji ya kushindiza*, flood, inundation. St. of Cs. **Shindizika**, be forced to remain, &c., also used of a knife or crowbar getting spoilt for use by work, blunted, i.e. be defeated for its purpose. Rp. **Shindana**, try to overcome each other, contend, be rivals, dispute, compete. *Shindana sawasawa*, be well matched. Prep. **Shindania**, strive about (for, against, with, &c.), e.g. *shindania fedha*, wager, bet. *Shindania maneno*, oppose, contradict a statement. *Shindania mtungi*, compete for a water-jar. Cs. of Rp. **Shindanisha**, be matched, set to fight (compete, &c.). Rp. of prep. of Rp. **Shindaniana**, e.g. *shindaniana bei*, compete as to price, bid against each other for something. Stc. **Shindama**, rarely if ever used, but Rp. of Stc. **Shindamana**, be firmly pressed together, be compact, fixed fast, i.e. be in a state of being forced together. Prep. **Shindamania**. Cs. **Shindamanisha**. Cs. of St. **Shindikiza** (1) intens. like *shindika*; (2) in a special sense (but usu. *sindikiza*) attend a departing guest or friend to the door, go with him a little way, set off, give a send-off to. (Cf. *safirisha* and *laki*, of going to meet an arriving friend.) Cv. **Shindua**, also **Sindua**, take off, pressure, unfasten; esp. of a door, set ajar, set open. *Shindua maneno*, give vent to utterance, make an opening statement—and so with *akili*. Ps. **Shinduliwa**. St. **Shinduka**, e.g. *maji yameshinduka*, the tide has retreated. **Kishinda**, n. *vi-* verbal from *shinda*, in various senses (1) that which conquers, baffles, is too much for one, e.g. *watu hawa ni vishinda waganga*, these people are a match for the medicine men; (2) a residue, a remainder, esp. of what is left in a vessel, dry or liquid, a quantity less than half of the content, e.g. *kishinda cha maji mtungini*, of a water-jar less than half full. Also a vague measure, a suitable amount for pounding in a mortar (*kinu*), e.g. *vishinda vingapi umetia?* How many measures have you put in? *Kinu tele ni kishinda kimoja*, one measure makes a full mortar, i.e. enough to pound at one time. (Cf. *shinda* with same meaning.) **Kishindo**, n. *vi-* and adv. dim. of *shindo*, shock, blow, outburst, sudden noise, sound of steps (guns, blows, &c.), an agitation, a sensation. *Habari ina kishindo*, news always comes with a kind of shock. **Mshinda**, n. *wa-* verbal of *shinda* in its various senses, one who conquers, remains, &c. **Mshindaji**, n. *wa-* a conqueror, victor, successful competitor or candidate, like *mshinda* and *mshindi*, but the termination *-ji* implies that the action is characteristic. **Mshindani**, n. *wa-* (1) an opponent, rival, antagonist, competitor; (2) a contentious, obstructive, captious person. **Mshindanizi**, n. *wa-*, like *mshindani*, but Inten. **Mshindano**, n. *mi-*, see **Shindano**, below. **Mshinde**, n. *wa-* one who is conquered (the *-e* is the passive termination. Cf. *mtume*. Not often used.) **Mshindi**, n. *wa-* a conqueror, winner, either in war, games, argument, or competition, &c. **Mshindikizo**, n. *mi-*, also **Msindikizo**, act of escorting, escort, retinue. **Mshindilio**, n. *mi-* a pushing, a pressing, application of force. Used of ramming a charge into a gun, clothes into a bag, &c. *Mshindilio wa bunduki*, the charge of a gun. **Mshindio**, n. *mi-* (1) the working of the woof or weft across the warp (*mtande*) in weaving; (2) the woof itself. Used also of the interlacing of plaited strips (*mashupatu*) to form a bedstead (*kitanda*)—*mshindio wa mashupatu*; (3) a meal which must last one whole day. **Mshindo**, n. *mi*- used to describe any act (process, effect), characterized by suddenness, force, violence, &c., and so translated variously by 'shock, blow, stroke, explosion, noise, bang, sensation, burst, thump, crash, outbreak, tumult, roar, &c. *Mshindo wa miguu*, tramp of feet. *Mshindo wa ngurumo*, peal of thunder. *Mshindo wa ngoma*, the noise of a drum. *Mshindo wa bunduki*, the discharge of a gun. Also of a report, rumour, news of a thrilling or sensational kind. Note: *mshindo* being applicable to violent emotion or sensation, is also used of an orgasm in coition. **Mshindwa**, n. *wa*- one who is overcome, beaten, conquered. **Shinda**, n. *ma*- remainder, residue, refuse of oil, seeds, &c., e.g. *shinda la mtungi (kinu)*, what is left in the jar (mortar), a large remainder being *shinda zima (kuu, la kujaa)*. *Gunia hili ni shinda*, this sack is partly full. *Mtungi u shinda la maji*, the jar has some water in it. **-shindani**, a. rivalling, competing, opposing, contesting. **Shindano**, n. *ma*- struggle, competition, race, trial of strength, &c. **Shindikizo**, n. *ma*, and **Sindikizo**, n. *ma*- (1) forcible pressure; (2) a pressing or crushing machine, e.g. oil-press, sugar-mill; (3) act of speeding a parting guest. **Shindo**, n. *ma*- amplic. of *mshindo*, above, which see. *Ukatoka shindo mji wote*, and the whole town was out in a moment. *Enda kwa mashindo*, trot —of a horse. **Ushinda**, n. (*shinda*) same as *shinda*, above, which see. **Ushindani**, n. (*shindani*), rivalry, competition, emulation, contest, fighting. **Ushinde**, n. defeat, state of being conquered. *Asiyekiri ushinde hakuwa mshindani*, one who does not acknowledge defeat has not been a combatant. **Ushindi**, n. (1) a point in dispute, a cause of contention; (2) victory, conquest, overcoming, success.

Shingo, n. (1) neck; (2) objects resembling a neck, e.g. an isthmus. Also (3) fig. of hard, unyielding temper, e.g. *mwenye shingo ngumu*, a stiff-necked person.

Shinikizo, n. *ma*-, also **Sinikizo** (1) pressing, crushing, pulping; (2) a machine or mill for such work, i.e. oil-mill, sugar-mill, &c. (Cf. *Shindikizo* under *shinda*.)

Shira,* n. sail of a vessel—for the common *tanga*. (Ar. شراع.)

Shiraa,* n. the dog star. (Ar. الشعرى).

Shirika,* n. See under **Shiriki**.

Shiriki,* v. (also sometimes **Shariki**), (1) share, have a share in, take part in, be partners (in), be associated (with), act together, do in common, e.g. *shiriki njaa*, come in for a share of famine. *Shiriki katika biashara*, form a commercial partnership (company, joint-stock business). (2) be intimately connected with, be devoted to, be addicted to, e.g. *shiriki kazi*, be heart and soul in a work. *Shiriki ulevi*, be a confirmed drunkard. *Shiriki moyo*, give rein to one's desires, be an utter sensualist. *Shiriki chuo*, be a diligent student. *Shiriki sanamu*, be an idolater. (3) in a deeper sense, of intimate communion, self-identification, communion of spirit and nature, with an object, e.g. *shiriki Mungu*, lead a wholly devoted, saintly, religious life—also share the divine nature. *Shiriki shetani*, be of a diabolic temperament, a sinner of the worst kind. Ps. **Shirikiwa**. Prep. **Shirikia**, e.g. take part in, give a share to, associate with. Cs. **Shirikisha**, e.g. cause (invite, allow, help) to share in, give a share to, &c. Rp.

Shirikiana. **Mshiriki**, n. *wa-*, also **Msharika**, n. *wa-* and **Mshirika**, n. *wa-* a partner, participator, sharer, associate, equal—but *mshiriki* may imply the closest possible identification of interests, communion of life, nature, and feeling. **Mshirikina**, n. *wa-* usu. one who firmly believes in witchcraft and magic. **Shirika**, n. *ma-*, also **Sharika**, n. *ma-* partnership, action in common, common interest, communion, e.g. *Nitajitia shirikani*, I will go shares. *Mali yetu ni shirika*, we are joint owners of our property. Also as adv. in common, together, in partnership. *Fanya kazi shirika*, share a job. **Ushirika**, n (1) partnership, co-operation, sharing; (2) community of interests, common nature, intimate union, commission. (Ar. شارك.)

Shisha,* n. a kind of sand-glass for measuring time, used in some native vessels. (Ar. شيش.)

Shiti,* n. *ma-* printed cotton piece-goods, prints—sold mostly for women's dresses. (Cf. *kisutu, nguo, kanga, leso*. Ar. شيت.)

Shitua, v. See **Shtua**.

Shoga,* n. (1) a term of endearment or familiarity between women (Ar. صفو friendship = محبّة); (2) a catamite; (3) an impotent male person who associates with women, often as a servant. (Cf. *msagaliwa*. Ar. صغار catamite.) **Ushoga**, n. friendship—between women, but also the condition, &c., of (2) and (3) above. (Cf. *jamaa, dada, somo*.)

Shogi,* n. (1) a pannier, a pack-saddle, a large matting bag slung over a donkey's back, and open across the middle (Ar. شوغر basket of palm leaves, or شاغر camel saddle); (2) a pit, &c., in which slaves were hid when they were being searched for. (Ar. شغ go different ways.)

Shogoa,* n. See **Shokoa**.

Shoka, n. *ma-* an axe. *Shoka la bapa*, an adze (also *tezo*). **Kishoka**, n. *vi-* dim.

Shokishoki, n. *ma-*. See under **Mshokishoki**.

Shokoa,* n. forced labour, corvée, conscription, a levy. *Toa katika shokoa*, requisition. *Kamatwa shokoa*, conscripted, caught for forced labour (Pers. شاكار compulsory labour.)

Shombo, n. the natural smell of fish. When it is a bad smell it is *vumba*.

Shomoro, n. a sparrow. A weaver finch, a small yellow bird with a red top-knot.

Shona, v. sew, make (or mend) by sewing. Used of shoemaking as well as tailoring, and all kinds of sewing. **Shona upindo**, hem. Ps. **Shonwa**. St. and Pot. **Shoneka**. Prep. **Shonea**, e.g. sew for (with, &c.). *Sindano ya kushonea*, a needle for sewing with. Cs. **Shonesha**, have sewn, e.g. *shonesha nguo*, get some clothes made, i.e. by a tailor. Cv. **Shonoa**, unsew, undo sewing. St. and Pot. **Shonoka**. Prep. **Shonolea**. **Mshona**, n. *wa-*, **Mshonaji**, n. *wa-*, **Mshoni**, n. *wa-* one who sews, a tailor, &c. *Mshona viatu*, a sandal-maker, a shoemaker. **Mshono**, n. *mi-* sewing, seam. *Pinda mshono*, sew a seam. **Shono**, n. *ma-* usu. in the plur. sewing, type (method, style) of sewing. **Ushoni**, n. *ma-* needlework, sewing, i.e. the art, style, trade, wages, &c., of one who sews, or a tailor, &c. **Ushono**, n. *ma-* type (method, style, &c.) of sewing. (Cf. *bandi, ponta, shuru*.)

Shonde, n. *ma-* (1) dung of animals; (2) dried cake of dung, used in some places for fuel; (3) *kinyongo, undani*.

Shonga, n. persuasion, enticement, incitement. *Tia shonga* (or *chonjo* incite to fight.

Shono, n. *ma-*, **Shonoa**, v. See under **Shona**.

Shore, n. East-coast black-capped

bulbul, *Pycnonotus tricolor*. **Shorekishungi,** n. Paradise fly-catcher, *Tersiphone crustata*. **Shorewanda,** n. Grey-headed sparrow, *Passer griseus*.

Shoroba, n. *ma-* amplic. of *kishoroba*.

Shoti,* n. gallop—of a horse. *Piga shoti, enda kwa shoti*, gallop. *Kumpiga shoti farasi*, to gallop a horse, to make it gallop. Also *piga shoti katika farasi*. (Ar. شوط career.)

Shoto, n. left hand, left-handedness, *Ana shoto*, he is left-handed. *Kushoto*, left hand side. *-a kushoto*, on the left-hand side. (Cf. opp. *kuume*, *kulia*, and Arab. *shemali* opp. to *yamini*.)

Sht—Note: some natives tend to interpose *i* between *sh* and *t*, e.g. *shitaka* for *shtaka*, &c.

Shtaka,* n. *ma-*. See under **Shtaki.**

Shtaki,* v. accuse, charge, complain of, prosecute. Ps. **Shtakiwa.** St. **Shtakika.** Prep. **Shtakia,** e.g. *akamshtakia baba habari za kwake*, she complained to her father about her home. Rp. **Shtakiana.** Cs. **Shtakisha. Mashtaka,** n. plur. seldom heard in the sing. charges, accusations, reproaches. **Mshtaka,** *mi-* charge, accusation, complaint *Fanya mshtaka*, prosecute. **Mshtaki,** n. *wa-* accuser, prosecutor, plaintiff. **Mshtakiwa,** n. *wa-* an accused person, one being complained about. **Shtaka,** n. *ma-* usu. in the plur., see above. **Ushtaki,** n. accusation, prosecution, making complaint. (Ar. تشكى or اشتكى.)

Shtua, v. (also **Stua,** with the same meaning and derivatives made from it), (1) put out of place, move suddenly or violently, sprain, e.g. *shtua mguu*, sprain the foot; (2) startle, surprise, shock; (3) turn over food being cooked, such as rice, meat, &c., so as to prevent it from being burned; (4) turn over grain which has stuck to the bottom of the inside of a mortar (*kinu*) when being pounded. St. **Shtuka,** be sprained, be startled (alarmed, shocked). Cs. **Shtusha,** e.g. *shtusha mshipa*, strain a muscle (tendon). **Mshtuo,** n. *mi-* anything which causes a shock, sprain, &c., said of a child moving in the womb near to delivery. **Mshtuko,** n. *mi-* a shock, sprain, being startled, &c. (Cf. *tegua*. From the same root as *jituka*.)

Shua, v. let down, lower—commonly of launching a boat or ship into the water. Ps. **Shuliwa.** St. **Shuka,** (1) go down, come down, descend, alight, disembark, land; (2) be lowered, depressed, humbled, degraded. *Shuka chini*, go downstairs. *Shuka pwani*, land on the beach, go down to the shore (coast). Prep. **Shulia,** e.g. *vitu vya kushulia*, launching apparatus. Cs. **Shusha,** let down, put ashore, discharge (cargo, &c.). *Shusha pumzi*, breathe out, exhale. *Jishusha moyo*, humble oneself. Note: the Cs. *shusha*, and its Prep. form *shushia*, should be used with caution as they are the words used for an orgasm in coition. **Mshuko,** n. *mi-* (1) descent, coming down, an incline; (2) coming to end, conclusion. Used of the time of coming away from the mosque after any of the usual prayers. *Mshuko wa jua* (*wa magharibi*), time of twilight, just after sunset. **Mshushio,** n. *mi-* and **Mshusho,** n. *mi-* act of bringing down or causing to descend —should be used with caution, see note on *shusha*, v. above. (Cf. *angua*, *inama*, also *chwa* (*chua*), *tua*, and *twa*, in *kutwa* (*kuchwa*).)

Shubaka,* n. *ma-* small window, light-hole, loop-hole, port-hole, embrasure. Sometimes a blind window, a window-like recess in a wall, i.e. above a door, &c. **Kishubaka,** n. dim. (Cf. *dirisha*, *mwangaza*. (Ar. شباك.)

Shudu,* n. *ma-* refuse of seed after it has been crushed for oil, oil-cake. (Ar. شد to compress.)

Shufaka,* n. compassion, tenderness, pity. (Cf. *huruma.* Ar. شفق.)

Shufu,* v. perceive, see, look at. (Ar. شوف.)

Shufwa,* n. even number. An odd number is *witiri.* (Cf. *kifuasi* under *fuata.* Ar. شفع.)

Shughuli,* n. (1) business, occupation, absence of leisure, engagement; (2) trouble, worry, anxiety. *Ana shughuli,* he is busy, engaged. (Opp. to *mchezo, faragha*) e.g. *hatukuja kucheza, tumekuja kwa shughuli,* we did not come to play, we are here for business. *Shughuli za nchi,* public affairs. **Shughulika,** v. be busy (engaged, occupied), have one's hands full, be harassed, hard-worked. Cs. **Shughulisha,** occupy, give trouble to, take up the time of, &c. *Jishughulisha,* trouble oneself, agitate oneself—also pretend to be busy, make excuses (for putting off, not attending to a matter). (Cf. *kazi.* Ar. شغل.)

Shuhuda,* n. *ma-*, **Shuhudu,** v. See under **Shahada.**

Shuhuli, n. the back part of a house. (Cf. *ubati, upenu, kipenu.*)

Shujaa, n. *ma-* a brave man, warrior, hero, champion. **Ushujaa,** n. *ma-* bravery, courage, heroism. The plur. *mashujaa,* heroic deeds, exploits. (Ar. شجاع.)

Shuka, v. See under **Shua.**

Shuka,* n. (— and of size *ma-*) a piece of calico about two yards long, worn as a loin-cloth. **Shuka la kitanda,** a sheet. As a measure, one fathom (*pima*). (Cf. *doti, pima.* Ar. شقة.)

Shukrani,* n. See under **Shukuru.**

Shuku,* v. and n. See under **Shaka.**

Shukuru,* v. (1) thank, give thanks (to), be grateful; (2) take comfort, leave off mourning or grieving, be resigned, become contented. *Shukuru Mungu,* is esp. common in this latter sense, passive acquiescence in things good or bad. **Shukrani,** n. gratitude, thanksgiving, thanks. **Ushukuru,** n. *ma-* (1) thanksgiving, returning thanks, gratitude; (2) resignation, ceasing to feel or care, passive acquiescence. (Cf. *asante.* Ar. شكر.)

Shule,* n. school, also *skuli,* but *chuo,* which see, is better. (Germ.)

Shulu,* n. also **Mshulu** and **Mshuru,** n. *mi-* a kind of sewing, an overstitch. **Shulu,** v. stitch, oversew. (Cf. *shona, darizi.* Ar. شل.)

Shumberere,* n. A kind of hat. (Pemba.) (Port. *sombreiro.*)

Shumbi,* n. (1) deep water, depth; (2) a heap, e.g. *shumbi ya mchanga,* a heap of sand. (Ar. صوب heap; heavy shower.)

Shume,* n. *paka shume,* a semi-wild cat, a large male cat, sometimes called *nunda.* (? Ar. شوْم portentous.)

Shumua, v. See **Chomoa.**

Shumusi,* n. sometimes heard for the Ar. *shems,* sunshine, brightness. (Ar. شمس.)

Shundi, n. a bird, also called *tipitipi, gude,* and *dudumizi,* the white-browed coucal.

Shundwa, n. the large striped hyena, also called *simba marara,* and *kingugwa.* (Cf. *fisi.*)

Shunga, v. drive away, as of fowls when they come round a woman preparing food. *Shunga ng'ombe,* drive cattle. (Cf. *winga, fukuza,* and dist. *chunga.*)

Shungi, n. *ma-* (1) plait of hair, tress, crest, forelock. *Mashungi mawili,* hair dressed in two large plaits or rolls. (2) used of the hair-like silky growth or beard on the ear of some kinds of grain—maize, millet, &c. *Shungi la taa,* a flaring lamp. *Taa inatoa shungi,* the lamp flares. **Kishungi,** n. *vi-* dim. **Ushungi,** n. (*shungi*) (1) handkerchief or cloth worn on the head by some women; (2) a tuft of hair, crest, feathers plume, and so the comb of a cock. (Cf. *denge, undu, kilemba, songo, suko, sokoto.*)

Shupaa, v. (1) be hard, form, well set, compact; (2) be stiff, obstinate, unyielding, peremptory. *Shupaa kwa maneno,* affirm with urgency, insist. Cs. **Shupaza,** harden, render tough, firm, strong—also make obstinate. Rp. **Shupana,** be knit together, strong, well-compacted, stiff, unyielding, obstinate, &c. *Viungo vyake vimeshupana,* his members are tense, hard, i.e. he has good, strong muscles. **Mshupavu,** n. *wa-* (1) a brave, fearless, intrepid, strong person; (2) an obstinate person, a bigot. **-shupavu,** a. (1) firm, compact, well-knit, tough; (2) bigoted, unyielding, &c. **Ushupavu,** n. (1) hardness, toughness, firmness, compactness; (2) resoluteness, pertinacity, obstinacy, bigotry. *Ushupavu wa mwili,* a well-knit, muscular body. *Ushupavu wa maneno,* obstructive, bigoted speech. *Mtu mshupavu,* an obstinate man. (Cf. Ar. شجع vigorous, &c.)

Shupatu, n. *ma-* a narrow strip of plaited grass or leaf, used for lacing bedsteads, or sewn together for mats, bags, &c. (Cf. *ukili.*)

-shupavu, a. See under **Shupaa.**

Shupaza,* n. spades in a pack of playing-cards. (Cf. *karata.* Port. *espada.*)

Shupaza, v. See under **Shupaa.**

Shura,* n. saltpetre in some places known as *chora.* (Pers. شور.)

Shuri,* n. *mtu mwenye shuri,* a person whose buttocks stick out more than those of the average person. (Ar. شور fatness, &c.)

Shuru, v. and n. See **Shulu.**

Shurua, n. See **Surua.**

Shuruti,* v. compel, oblige, stipulate, generally used in the Cs. form. **Ps. Shurutiwa,** e.g. *haikushurutiwa kutoa fedha,* there was no obligation to pay. **Cs. Shurutisha,** also **Shurutiza,** put pressure on, order peremptorily, press with argument, force, compel. Rp. **Shurutiana,** make terms or conditions with each other, bind each other, wager, bet. (Cf. *pingana.*) **Mshurutisho,** n. *mi-* a compelling, a compulsion, stipulation, moral pressure. **Sharti,** n. *ma-* (1) necessity, obligation (actual, practical, rather than moral), absence of choice; (2) binding contract, terms, stipulation, conditions, clause of a legal document; (3) by-law; (4) wager, bet. *Sharti kwenda* (or *uende*), you must go, you have to go. *Fanya sharti,* make a contract, bind oneself. *Maneno ya sharti,* peremptory, incontrovertible language. *Kwa masharti,* under conditions, conditionally. *Masharti ya chama,* the by-laws of a club (association, &c.). *Wekeana masharti shindana* (*pigana*) *kwa masharti,* engage in betting, lay wagers. (Cf. *lazimu, faradhi, juzu, pinga, bidi, mkataba, mapatano, afikana.* Ar. شرط.)

Shusha, v. See under **Shua.**

Shuta, v. break wind. **Shuzi,** n. *ma-* usu. in plur., breaking wind. Prov. *shukrani za punda ni mashuzi,* the gratitude shown by a donkey is the breaking of wind, i.e. that is all you can expect from a donkey or, that is how it shows its gratitude. **Ushuzi,** n. breaking wind. (Cf. *fusa, jamba.*)

Shutumu,* v. abuse, upbraid, reproach, revile, scold, e.g. *watu wanishutumu ubaya bilashi,* people upbraid me for wickedness without cause. Ps. **Shutumiwa.** St. **Shutumika.** Prep. **Shutumia.** Cs. **Shutumisha. Shutumu,** n. *ma-* reproach, railing, abuse, blame. (Cf. *laumu, suta, singizia, karipia.* Ar. شتم.)

Shuzi, n. *ma-*. See under **Shuta.**

Shwari,* n. a calm, calm weather. (Ar. from same root as *mshari,* a calm at sea being ill luck.)

Si, (1) adv. of negation, but always with a word following, which it qualifies—never as an independent negation, no (which is *siyo, sivyo*). *Si mimi*, not I. *Si mrefu*, not tall, &c. *Si* attaches itself so closely to the word qualified as often not only to negative it, but to reverse more or less its meaning. Thus *si vema*, means 'badly', as well as 'not well'. *Si* in comparison indicates the less preferable member, 'rather than', e.g. *jirani ya karibu si ndugu ya mbali*, a neighbour at hand is better than a brother far off. *Si* is commonly combined with (1) the Personal pronouns, e.g. *simi, siye*, &c.; (2) the relative form of person-pfxs., e.g. *sio, sicho, sivyo*, &c. *Siyo* and *sivyo* are commonly used as independent adv. of negation, i.e. 'no, not so'. (Cf. *hakuna, hapana, la.*) (3) as a verb-form, *si* is the negative connective corresponding to *ni*, i.e. 'is not, are not' for all persons, Sing. and Plur., e.g. *wao si watumwa*, they are not slaves. For *si*—as a pfx., &c., see Grammars.

Sia, v. (1) drive away ants (*siafu*) by burning them with a brand of burning grass (sometimes *zia* is used); (2) plant rice by putting the seeds in holes dibbled for the purpose.

Siafu, n. a small reddish-brown ant which bites fiercely. They travel in large swarms and attack all living creatures alike.

Siagi,* n. butter, cream. (Cf. *samli, mafuta*. Ar. صبغ soak bread, &c., in fat, &c.)

Siaha,* n. See under **Sihi.**

Siala,* n. *ma-*. See **Swali**, under **Saili.**

Siasa,* n. and adv. orderliness, gentleness, carefulness, politics; and as an adv. gently, with care, in an orderly fashion. (Cf. *taratibu, polepole*. Ar. سياسة.)

Sibabi,* v. (1) revile, overwhelm with abuse; (2) slander, calumniate. (Ar. سبب.)

Sibu,* v. (A) revile abuse, defame, &c., same as *sibabi*. (Ar. سب.)

Sibu,* v. (B) foretell any event, good or bad which afterwards comes to pass. **Msibu,** n. *wa-* one who foretells an event which afterwards comes to pass. (? Ar. صاب hit the mark.)

Sibu,* v. (C) (1) afflict, bring misfortune (ruin, damage) upon; (2) sometimes used for, happen (to), take place, come to pass. *Ilikusibu lini?* when did it happen to you? Ps. **Sibiwa,** (1) be afflicted; (2) have happened (to); (3) sometimes used of possession by a spirit, e.g. *fulani amesibiwa na shetani*, so-and-so is possessed of a devil. St. **Sibika. Masaibu,** n. affliction, calamity **Msiba,** n. *mi-* calamity, misfortune, untoward accidents, disaster; (2) sorrow, distress of mind, grief; (3) formal mourning, outward signs of sorrow, &c. Used of war, famine, sickness, and minor calamities. *Msiba mkuu (mkubwa, mgumu)*, a great disaster. Frequently refers to a bereavement, i.e. *msiba wa baba yake*, the death of his father. *Vaa nguo za msiba*, wear mourning. *Fanya (ona, ingia, pata, &c.) msiba*, take to heart, grieve (over). *Kwenda kupa mkono wa msiba*, go and make a visit of condolence, offer sympathy, inquire after—after a funeral, misfortune, &c. *Akakaa msiba wa mama yake*, he observed the usual mourning for his mother. Prov. *Hakuna msiba usio na mwenziwe*, misfortune never comes alone. **Msibu,** n. *wa-* one who causes trouble, distress, &c. **Subiani,** n. a kind of evil spirit. (Ar. أصاب assail, smite.)

Sidiboi,* n. one of the native crew of a warship.

Sidiria,* n. a cloth worn by some women just below the breasts to support them, also called *kanchiri*. (Ar. صدرية.)

Sidukia,* v. See **Sudukia,** under **Sadiki.**

Sifa,* n. (A) (1) praise, commendation, flattery, applause; (2) character, reputation, fame, characteristic. *Sifa zake njema,* he is well spoken of. (3) (Grammar) an adjective. **Sifu,** v. praise, commend, flatter, recommend. *Jisifu,* brag, boast. Ps. **Sifiwa.** St. **Sifika.** Prep. **Sifia. Kisifa,** n. *vi-* the word used in some books for an adverb. **Msifu,** n. *wa-* one who praises, recommends, flatters. *Msifu mno,* a gross flatterer, toady, parasite. **Masifu,** n. plur. praises, congratulations. **Majisifu,** n. plur. self-praise, boasting, brag. (Cf. *jiona, jivuna, jigamba.* Ar. صفة.)

Sifa,* n. (B) shark oil, used for caulking vessels. (Port. *cifa,* preparation for painting ship's bottom.

Sifongo,* n., also **Sifunja,** and **Sifonjo,** a sponge. (Variants of the Ar. سفنج.)

Sifu,* n. See under **Sifa.**

Sifuri,* n. (1) brass, for the more usu. *shaba;* (2) a cipher, nought, zero. (Cf. *sufuria.* Ar. صفر.)

Sigareti,* n. a cigar, a cigarette. (Eng.)

Siha,* n. strength, health, good bodily condition. *Hana siha siku hizi,* he has not good health these days, he has no strength. **Sihi,** v. be acceptable, do for the purpose, be suitable. (Cf. *nguvu, siaha, uzima, afya, faa.* Ar. صح be sound, true.)

Sihi,* v. (A) beg humbly, supplicate, beseech, intreat. Ps. **Sihiwa.** St. and Pot. **Sihika,** e.g. be placable, not inexorable, open to appeal. **Siaha,** n. a loud cry. *Lia kwa siaha,* cry bitterly, with much noise. (Cf. *omba, omboleza, lalama.* Ar. صيح call to.)

Sihi,* v. (B). See under **Siha.**

Sihia,* v. *sihia mali,* transfer ownership of property. (Cf. *kabidhi.* Ar. سخا.)

Sihiri,* v. bewitch, fascinate, throw a spell over, have power over, e.g. *mchawi aweza kutusihiri wote tukafa,* a wizard can bewitch us all so that we die. **Sihiri,** n. witchcraft, e.g. *uchawi na sihiri ni kitu kimoja, sihiri* is the same thing as witchcraft. **Usihiri,** n. witchcraft, magic, &c. (Cf. *uramali, pagaa, uchawi.* Ar. سحر.)

Sijafu,* n. wristband or cuff of a native dress, a piece turned in to receive the stitching. (Cf. *kanzu.* Pers. سنجاف border of a garment.)

Sijambo, verb-form. See under **Jambo.**

Sijida,* n. See under **Sujudu.**

Siki,* n. vinegar. (Pers. سِكى.)

Sikia, v. (1) hear; (2) pay attention to, notice, understand, perceive; (3) heed, obey. Mostly of the sense of hearing, but also of other senses except taste, e.g. *nasikia harufu ya samaki,* I smell fish. *Amenisikia maneno yangu,* he has obeyed my order. Ps. **Sikiwa.** St. **Sikika,** e.g. be audible, be noticeable. Prep. **Sikilia,** e.g. listen to (for, with, at). Cs. of Prep. **Sikiliza,** usu. Inten., listen—sometimes in contrast with *sikia,* e.g. *nilimsikiliza simba nisimsikie tena,* I listened for the lion, but did not hear it again. *Sikiliza shauri (kesi),* hear a case. St. and Pot. **Sikilika.** Pot. **Sikilikana,** be audible. Rp. of Cs. of Prep. **Sikilizana,** e.g. cause each other to listen, and so, come to an understanding, agree together. Cs. **Sikiza,** e.g. cause to hear, make understand, make obey. Rp. **Sikizana,** hear each other, agree together, be mutually intelligible, &c. (like *sikilizana*). *Ile lugha yao hatusikizani,* we do not understand each other in that language of theirs. **Msikiaji,** n. *wa-* (1) one who hears, one who is obedient; (2) a hearer, used by some missions of a person who desires to become a catechumen. **Msikilivu**, n. *wa-*, **Msikivu**, n. *wa-* an obedient, well-disciplined person. **Msikizi**, n. *wa-* (1) a hearer, listener, one who attends class or meeting; (2) a follower, obedient person, adherent, a teachable, obedient person, good pupil, good servant. *Mwenyezi Mungu ni msikizi na mjuzi wa kila kitu*, Almighty God hears and sees everything. **Sikio**, n. *ma-* the ear—organ of hearing. *Tega sikio*, listen attentively. *Tia sikioni*, remember, attend to. *Toga sikio*, bore holes in the outer edge of the ear as some women do, for ornaments. (Cf. *ndewe, majasi.*) **-sikivu**, a. and **-sikilivu**, a. attentive, teachable, docile, obedient. **Usikilivu**, n., **Usikivu**, n. (1) attention, hearing, interest, listening, intelligence; (2) docility, obedience. *Usikivu* (*usikizi*) *wa moyo*, interest, i.e. as in a school lesson, &c. **Usikizano**, n. harmony, condition of being in agreement. **Usikizi**, n. same as *usikivu*.

Sikitika, v. be sorry, grieve, feel regret (pity, remorse). Prep. **Sikitikia**, e.g. be sorry for (about, at, in). Cs. **Sikitikisha**, grieve, make sorry. **Sikitiko**, n. *ma-* sorrow, grief, object of pity, cause of sorrow, regret, &c. (Cf. *huzunika, lia, juta.*)

Siku, n. (Plur. of *usiku*, which see) (1) a day, i.e. a period of 24 hours, counted from sunset to sunset, one night (*usiku*) and one day (*mchana*, period of daylight); (2) in a general sense, day, time, e.g. *siku zote*, on all days and as adv. **Sikuzote**, always. *Kila siku*, every day. *Siku hizi*, nowadays, lately, recently, in modern times. *Siku za kale*, days of old, olden times. *Siku kwa siku*, day after day, from day to day. *Sikukuu*, festival, holiday. The usual Muhammadan festivals are: (1) after Ramadhan (*Id-el-Fitr*); (2) *Id-el-Haj*, in the third month after it; (3) 10th of *Muharram*, commemoration of the death of Imam Hussein in the fourth month; (4) *Maulidi*, the birthday of the Prophet, in the sixth month. *Siku ya mwaka*, New Year's Day. (See *mchana, usiku, mwaka.*)

Sila,* n. pail, bucket, dipper, scoop, esp. for bailing water out of a boat. &c. (Cf. the commoner *ndoo, kata*, Pers. سطله.)

Silabi,* n. a syllable, adopted for use in text-books and school lessons. (Eng.)

Silaha,* n. a weapon, arms. *Twaa silaha*, take up arms. (Ar. سلاح.)

Silahi,* n. See **Masilahi** under **Suluhu**.

Sile Maua, n. name of a bird, jacana or lily-trotter, *Actophilus africanus*.

Silika,* n. character, disposition, mien, instinct. (Cf. *tabia, sifa, mwendo*. Ar. سليقة.)

Silimu,* v. become a Muhammadan, be converted to *Islam*. St. **Silimika**. Cs. **Silimisha**, make a Muhammadan. **Kiislamu**, n. and adv. the Muhammadan religion, after the Muhammadan manner, &c. **Msalimina**, n. *wa-*, **Msilimu**, n. *wa-*, and **Mwislamu**, n. *wa-* a Muhammadan. (Cf. *salamu*. Ar. اسلم.)

Silingi,* n. a winch, crane, derrick. (Cf. *winchi*. Eng. sling.)

Silisila,* n. chains, bonds, for the commoner *mnyororo, pingu*. (Ar. سلسلة.)

Sima, n. a stiff kind of porridge made by stirring flour (made from *maize, millet, cassava*) in boiling water, the commoner word is *ugali*.

Simadi,* v. See under **Samadi**.

Simama, v. (The direct form *sima* is not now in use) (1) stand, be standing, i.e. of position, as opp. to sitting or lying (cf. *ondoka*); (2) stand, stand up, rise, i.e. of movement, change of posture (cf. *inuka*); (3) stand, stand still, come to a stand, stop, be stationary, keep in a particular place (cf. *kaa, koma*); (4) be erect, perpendicular, high, steep, elevated (cf. *wima, inuka*); (5) cost (cf. *wakifu*). *Aliondoka akasimama,* he rose and stood up. *Mungu hakusisimama naye,* God did not take his side (support him). *Wali haukusimama tumboni,* the rice was not retained in the stomach. *Mlima umesimama,* the hill is steep. *Maji yamesimama,* the water is motionless, stagnant. Prep. **Simamia,** e.g. stand by (upon, in, for, against, &c.), oppose, obstruct, support—but esp. common in the sense, stand over, overlook, superintend, manage, direct administer. (Cf. *angalia, tazama.*) Cs. **Simamisha,** e.g. (1) make stand, cause to go on with work—also (2) cause to stop, obstruct, thwart; (3) set up, erect, make stand, cause to rise, e.g. *simamisha bei,* stabilize, or fix price. St. and Pot. **Simika,** (1) stand, be set up, be erect, like *simama*; (2) cause to stand, set up erect; (3) cause to prosper, support, uphold; (4) appoint, establish, arrange, e.g. *simika miti* (*mlango*) erect poles (a door). *Mungu akusimike,* God prosper you. *Nisimike mtu awe mkubwa wao,* let me set up a man to be their chief. *Simika mtego,* set a trap. (5) be erect, of the penis (used either of man or organ). (Cf. *disa, dinda.*) Ps. **Simikwa.** Prep. **Simikia,** e.g. *wakamsimikia askari,* and they provided him with a bodyguard. Cs. **Simikisha,** e.g. have a thing set, cause to set up. Cv. **Simua,** place horizontal what was perpendicular, lay down, e.g. *simua mlingoti,* lower a mast (not often used, cf. *shusha, telemsha, weka chini, inamisha*). **Msimamizi,** n. *wa-* an overseer, overlooker, esp. the headman of a plantation, or of a caravan. Also generally, responsible head, director, manager, superintendent, steward, foreman. (Cf. *nokoa, kadamu.*) **Usimamao,** n. the condition of being erect, of standing upright. **Usimamizi,** n. the work (status, pay, &c.) of an overseer, &c. **Usimeme,** n. firmness, stability, strength, uprightness.

Simanga, v. triumph (over), exult (against), cast in the teeth (of), reproach, esp. rejoice over another's misfortune. **Simango,** n. *ma-* triumph or rejoicing over another's misfortune, reproach, also **Usimanga,** n. in the same sense, ill-natured triumph, mockery. (Cf. *dhihaka, mzaha.*)

Simanzi, n. grief, sorrow, depression. (Cf. *huzuni, majonzi,* prob. from *simanga.*)

Simba, n. (— and of size *ma-*), a lion. *Simba dume,* a male lion. *Simba jike,* a lioness. Also as complimentary description of a warrior, fine child, or young man. **Simba marara,** n. the large spotted hyena. (Cf. *kingugwa, shundwa, fisi.*)

Simbi, n. a small cowry shell.

Simbu, n. See under **Sumba,** v. (B).

Simbua, v., **Simbulia,** &c., sometimes heard for *sumbua, sumbulia,* &c., which see under **Sumba,** v. (B).

Sime, n. a large knife, or short two-edged sword, which may be straight or curved, with a blade broadened out near the distal end.

Simika, v. See under **Simama.**

Simile,* int. Make way! Out of the road! By your leave! Often with a word following. *Simile punda* (*ubao, jiwe*), make way for the donkey (plank, stone). (Ar. for *bismillah,* in the name of God. Cf. *inshallah, Ee walla! wallahi,* and syn. *habedari, jihadhari, jitenge.*)

Simiri, v. See **Shimiri.**

Simo,* n. (1) something striking, new, a remarkable occurrence. *Simo mpya imeingia,* a new thing has occurred. (2) kind, sort. **-simo,** a. new, strange. (? Pers. سیما resemblance, similitude.)

Simo, verb-form, I am not in it. Often with the meaning, I am not responsible, it is no concern of mine —Negat. Pfx. of 1 Pers. Sing. with *-mo.*

Simsim,* n. sesame, usu. called *ufuta.* (Ar. سمسم.)

Simu,* n. (A) the telegraph, telegraphic message (news, &c.). (Pers. سيم wire.)

Simu, n. (B) a kind of sprat. (Cf. *dagaa.*)

Simua, v. See under **Simama.**

Simulia,* v. narrate, relate, report, give an account, tell a story. *Alimsimulia habari,* he told him the news. Ps. **Simuliwa.** St. and Pot. **Simulika.** Cs. **Simulisha.** Rp. **Simuliana. Msimulizi,** n. *wa-* one who reports, narrates, gives an account, tells a story, recounts the news, newsman. **Simulizi,** n. *ma-* news, item of news or intelligence. (Cf. *hubiri, hadithia, ambia, habari.* A prep. form of Ar. سمير evening conversation, سمر a story, tale, &c.)

Sina, verb-form, I have not.

Sinasina, v. on the verge of tears, be near to weeping.

Sindano, n. (1) a needle. *Dawa ya sindano,* a medicine given by injection. *Piga sindano,* give an injection. (2) a kind of rice.

Sindika, v. See **Shindika** under **Shinda.**

Sindikiza, v. accompany a parting guest a little way on his road as a gesture of respect, &c. **Msindikizo,** n. *mi-*, and **Sindikizo,** n. *ma-* the act of speeding a parting guest. (Cf. *shindikiza* under *shinda.*)

Sindua, v. See **Shindua** under **Shinda.**

Sine,* n. *ma-* the gum of the teeth. (Cf. *fizi.* Ar. سن.)

Sinema,* n. the cinema—in common use in towns where there are cinematograph theatres. (Eng.)

Singa, v. rub or massage with perfume or aromatic substance, e.g. *singa mwili kwa sandali,* rub the body with perfume of sandal-wood. Ps. **Singwa.** (Cf. *sugua, kanda, chua.*)

Singa, n. plur. of *usinga.*

Singe,* n. a bayonet. (Turk. سونكي).

Singiza, v. pretend, make pretence, allege as excuse, but commonly in the Prep. **Singizia,** make a fictitious, calumnious charge against, slander, insinuate, e.g. *jisingizia ugonjwa,* make a pretence of sickness. *Singizia moto,* lay the blame on the fire. **Ps. Singiziwa. Singizio,** n. *ma-* usu. in the plur. (1) slander, calumny, false insinuation, misrepresentation; (2) pretence, disguise, make-believe, belying facts. (Cf. *-ji-.* Rf. pfx. and *amba.*)

Sini,* n. features, complexion, i.e. of the countenance. (Ar. سحنة.)

Sinia,* n. (— and of size *ma-*), a tray—commonly a circular metal tray for carrying food, &c. (Cf. *sahani, kombe, chano, legeni.* Ar. صينية.)

Siniguse, n. lit. don't touch me—a kind of hollow bead made of very thin glass, usu. of gold or silver colour. (Cf. *kashabu.*)

Sinikizo, n. *ma-*. See **Shinikizo.**

Sinua, v. push over, make lie on the side, make bend over, uproot, e.g. *mti umesinuka,* the tree is bent over or uprooted. (Prob. *simua,* see under *simama.*)

Sinyaa, v. pine away, shrink, shrivel. (Cf. *finyaa, nywea, rudi.*)

Sinzia, v. (1) doze, be drowsy; (2) be inattentive, absent-minded, make a foolish mistake; (3) of a lamp or fire, flicker. This word is used to describe thieves who steal while one of their number distracts the attention of the victim, *wevi sinzia.* Prep. **Sinzilia,** e.g. (1) be sleepy about, be negligent over, fail to observe or pay attention or act properly. Also used to describe a dreamy look of the eyes, e.g. *alinitazama kwa kunisinzilia*, he looked at me with dreamy eyes, i.e. to entice. *Macho ya kusinzilia*, dreamy eyes. (Cf. *usingizi*.)

Sio, n. the powder made by grinding up broken cooking-pots, &c., used for mixing with the clay when making new pots.

Sira,* n. *ma-* dregs, lees. *Sira la tembo*, lees of palm wine. *Masimbi* is a commoner word. (Ar. سر scum.)

Siraji,* n. a lamp, torch—seldom used. (Cf. *taa*. Ar. سراج.)

Sirati,* n. a way or road, but used only by some Muhammadans when referring to the way to heaven or hell. (Ar. سراط.)

Siri,* n. a secret, hidden thing, mystery, puzzle, secrecy. *Mambo ya siri*, secrets. *Kwa siri*, secretly, privately, mysteriously. Sometimes also as a v., e.g. *alijisiri shimoni*, he secreted himself in a hollow. **Msiri**, n. *wa-* a confidential (intimate, bosom) friend, confidential agent (adviser, counsellor). (Cf. *fumbo*, *faragha*, *setiri*, *ficha*, and dist. *usiri*. Ar. سرّ.)

Siri,* v. become, change into—seldom used. (Cf. *-wa*, *geuka*. Ar. صير.)

Siridado, n. insects or dry rot which destroy books, &c. (Ar. سرد bore through.)

Sirika,* n. See **Silika**.

Sirima,* v. (1) wear out one's patience by being kept waiting; make one wait a long time (Ar. صرم stay, abide); (2) smoothen, as the walls of a mud house, &c. (Cf. *rashia*, *sisima*, *lainisha*.)

Sisi, pron. of 1 Pers. Plur. we, us. *Sisi sote*, all of us. *Sisi wote*, commonly of two persons only, 'both of us'. Sometimes *siye* is used for *sisi*. (Cf. *miye*, *weye*.)

Sisima, v. (1) smooth over a surface, i.e. as of the mud walls of a native hut (cf. *lainisha*, *rashia*, *sirima*); (2) startle, cause the blood to run cold, as when one gets a great fright, cause 'goose flesh'; (3) excite, i.e. of the passions. St. **Sisimka**, (1) be smoothed over; (2) be excited, feel the blood race with sexual passion, or feel the blood run cold with fear, have goose flesh. Cv. **Sisimua**, stir up the passions, make the blood race, make the blood run cold with fright, &c. **Msisimko**, n. *mi-* goose flesh, tingling of the blood with fright or sexual passion, &c.

Sisimizi, n. a small black harmless ant. (Cf. *nyenyere*.)

Sisimua, v. See under **Sisima**.

Sisitiza, v. warn or remind over and over again.

Sita,* n. and a., six. *-a sita*, sixth. **Sitashara**, n. and a. sixteen. *-a sitashara*, sixteenth. **Sitini**, n. and a. sixty. *-a sitini*, sixtieth. (Ar. ستّ &c.)

Sita, v. (1) move in an uncertain, undecided way, hang back, dawdle; (2) fig. be in perplexity, be undecided, be in doubt, hesitate. Often Rd. *sitasita*. (Cf. *hangaika*, *kwama*.)

Sitaha,* n. deck, of a vessel. (Dist. *staha*. Ar. سطح roof, platform.)

Sitashara,* n. and a. See under **Sita**.

Sitawi,* v. be in good condition, reach full development, flourish, succeed, go off well, be in full swing, be at the height, e.g. of healthy plants, of social functions, dances (*ngoma*), a feast (*karamu*), a wedding (*arusi*), or of trade (*biashara*). Cs. **Sitawisha**, e.g. cause to flourish, embellish, enhance, prosper, give a finish to. **Usitawi**, n. a flourishing condition, healthy development, full activity, success. (Cf. *fanikiwa*. Ar. استوى ripen.)

Sitiri,* v. See **Setiri** and **Stiri**.

Siti,* n. lady—and in address, my

lady, madam. (Ar. for the common *bibi, mwana* ستّ.)

Sitini,* n. and a. See under **Sita.**

Sivyo, a common form of negative adv., no, not so—negative pfx. with *-vyo* of reference or relative of manner. Often used in asking questions expecting the answer 'yes'.

Siwa, n. *ma-* amplic. of *kisiwa,* which see.

Siwa,* n. a kind of horn used as a trumpet, formerly a special one of wood or ivory was used as a symbol of chieftaincy in certain places. (Cf. *panda, baragumu.* ? From Pers. and Ar. صور trumpet, clarion.)

Siye, Pron. Neg. of 3 Pers. Sing.

Siyo, common form of negative adv., no, not so.

Sizi, n. *ma-* usually in the plur. *masizi,* soot, grime, e.g. from the fire, on a cooking-pot, in a chimney. (Cf. *taka,* and dist. *mzizi.*)

Skeli,* n. a scale. *Skeli ya do,* major scale. *Skeli ya la,* minor scale. *Noti isiyo ya skeli,* an accidental. Adopted for use in text-books and school lessons on music. (Eng.)

Skrubu,* n. a screw. (Eng. screw. Cf. *hesi, parafujo.*)

Skuli,* n. a school, also *shule,* and *chuo*—the latter being preferred. (Eng.)

Slingi,* n. See **Silingi.**

Soda,* n. (1) in common use for soda and mineral waters (Eng.); (2) lunacy, melancholia. (Ar. سوداء.)

Sodawi,* a. See under **Usodawi.**

Sodo,* n. cloth used by women when menstruating. (Ar. صد.)

Soga,* n. *ma-* idle chatter, a chat, conversation. (Cf. *porojo, mazungumzo.* Ar. صغو be attentive, listen to.)

Sogea, n. a kind of cassava. (Cf. *muhogo.*)

Sogea, v. move nearer or further away. *Sogea karibu,* draw near. Prep. **Sogelea.** Rp. of Prep. **Sogeleana,** draw closer together, come nearer to each other. Cs. **Sogeza,** move, either nearer or farther away. (Cf. *jongea, enda,* and *songa* which appears to be from the same root.)

Sogi,* n. See **Shogi.**

Sogonea, v. clean oneself with grass, leaves, &c., after evacuation; used also of a dog dragging its hindquarters on the ground for the same purpose. (Cf. *kokona, sosona.*)

Sogora, n. *ma-* an expert at playing the drum for dances.

Soka,* n. football match or game. (Eng. soccer.)

Soko,* n. *ma-* market, open marketplace, centre of business, mart, emporium. (Cf. *gulio.* Ar. سوق.)

Sokota, v. (1) twist, twine with the fingers, spin, roll with the fingers. Used of thread, yarn, rope, rolling a cigarette, and less properly of the hair (cf. *suka*); (2) of pain, esp. of the stomach, e.g. *tumbo lanisokota,* I have a twisting, griping pain, colic, in the stomach. Ps. **Sokotwa.** St. and Pot. **Sokoteka.** Prep. **Sokotea.** Rp. **Sokotana. Kisokoto,** n. *vi-* dim. of **Msokoto,** n. *mi-* a twisting, also a griping, twisting pain, esp. in the stomach. **Sokoto,** n. *ma-* a twist, something twisted, as twine, string, rope, &c. (Cf. *pota.*)

Soksi,* n. the word used for either socks or stockings. (Eng. socks.)

Sokwe, n. a chimpanzee.

Soli,* n. sergeant major, colour sergeant—formerly used by the Germans in what is now Tanganyika Territory for native soldiers of that rank. (Cf. *shaushi, ombasha.* Turk. صول.)

Soli, adv. face to face, unexpectedly, i.e. *kumkuta mtu soli,* to meet with a person unexpectedly, face to face.

Solo, n. seeds of the *msolo* tree, used as counters in playing *bao* and similar games.

Soma, n. a kind of drum. See **Msoma.**

Soma, v. (1) read, hence (2) go to

school, receive teaching, study. Ps. **Somwa.** St. and Pot. **Someka,** be decipherable. Prep. **Somea,** e.g. *tuliwasomea wazee barua iliyowafikia,* we read the letter which they had received to the old people. Cs. **Somesha,** e.g. send to school, teach, act as a teacher. **Msoma,** n. *wa-* one who reads. *Msoma vitabu,* a reader of books. *Msoma gazeti,* a reader of a newspaper. **Msomaji,** n. *wa-* a regular reader. **Msome-shaji,** n. *wa-*, **Msomeshi,** n. *wa-* one who causes others to read, hence, a teacher, tutor, for the more usual *mwalimu.* **Msomo,** n. *mi-* (1) reading, the act (method, means, &c.) of reading; (2) study, subject of study, lesson, lesson-book. **Somo,** n. *ma-* a reading, a lesson. *Masomo ya chuoni,* the school-lessons. *Tumia maarifa ya somo,* apply a lesson.

Somba, v. carry, esp. of making many journeys to carry a lot of things from one place to another. *Somba mawe* (*mchanga*), carry loads of stone (sand).

Sombea, v., sometimes **Sombera,** move oneself by means of the hands clasping or grasping, e.g. in climbing a tree, or of a cripple who cannot use his legs, moving along the ground on his buttocks by the aid of his hands.

Sombo, n. *ma-* usu. in the plur. *masombo,* a girdle. (Cf. *mahazamu, mshipi, ukanda.*)

Somo, n. (1) *ma-* see under **Soma,** v.; (2) confidential adviser or friend, and so as a term of friendly or familiar address. *Njoo somo,* come along my friend. In coast towns is generally used of a woman who attends a young girl during her first menstruation, and instructs her in affairs pertaining to marriage, &c.; (3) friend and namesake; (4) an assistant at the initiation rites. (Ar. سمى namesake.)

Somu,* n. See **Saumu,** n. (B).

Sonara,* n. a silversmith, goldsmith, jeweller. (Hind. سنار.)

Songa, v. (1) press, press together, press close, throng, meet in a mass; (2) close up by pressure, squeeze, contract, hem in; (3) act on (form, fashion) by pressing; and (4) fig. apply pressure to, urge, press, overwhelm, e.g. *songa mbele,* press forward. *Songa ugali,* make porridge, i.e. stir it till it is stiff. *Songa roho,* throttle, strangle. *Chakula chasonga,* the food chokes. *Watu wanasonga,* there is a crowd, or crush of people. *Njia inasonga,* the road is narrow. *Nguo inasonga,* the dress is too tight. *Siku zinasonga,* the days are approaching. *Mambo yananisonga,* things are overwhelming me, pressing me down. Ps. **Songwa.** St. and Pot. **Songeka.** Prep. **Songea.** Cs. **Songesha.** Rp. **Songana,** press together, crowd together, jostle one another. Stc. **Songama.** Rp. of Stc. **Songamana.** (1) be rolled or pressed together; (2) writhe, e.g. of a snake wriggling and writhing, of clothes rolled up by a high winds, &c.; (3) have a twist or bend, as of a bent stick. Cs. **Songo-meza,** roll or press together, e.g. of folding one's arm in a cloth, coiling up a rope. *Nyoka anajisongo-meza,* the snake is writhing. Cv. **Songoa,** twist together, bind up tight, press together, e.g. *songoa nguo,* wring clothes. *Songoa kuku,* twist a fowl's neck, &c. Cv. of Cs. **Songonyoa,** squeeze together tight, twist hard, wring out—esp. of clothes, also of pain in the stomach, *tumbo lanisongonyoa* (but *sokota* is more common). **Kisongo,** n. *vi-* act (mode, means, &c.) of twisting, esp. an instrument for twisting, tourniquet, &c. **Msonga,** n. *wa-* one who twists or presses. *Msonga mbele,* one who presses forward. **Msongano,** n. *mi-* a twisting or pressing together, a crowd, a mass, of people or things. **Msonge,** n. *mi-* and adv. (something) stirred, twisted, compressed, muddled, jumbled. *Maneno haya ni msongesonge,* these words are all jumbled together, confused. *Nyumba ya msonge.* **Msongi,** n. *wa-* same as *msonga,* above, which see. **Msongo,** n. *mi-* a twisting, stirring, compressing, muddling, &c. **Songo,** n. *ma-* coil, twist (e.g. of a snake). (Cf. *kaza, bana, vuruga,* and *sogea* which appears to be from the same root.)

Soni, n. shame, confusion, modesty. (Cf. *kaya.*)

Sonoa, v. (1) cause hurt or pain; (2) fig. grieve, trouble, disturb, annoy. **Sonona,** (1) be sorry, grieve, regret; (2) be numb with cold, &c.; (3) fig. tremble with rage. St. **Sononeka,** (1) feel hurt, be in pain, ache; (2) fig. be grieved, vexed, troubled. Cs. **Sononesha,** e.g. hurt, cause pain (to) and fig. grieve, vex. **Kisonono,** n. gonorrhoea, various phases being distinguished as *kisonono cha mkojo* (urine), *cha usaha* (pus, matter), *cha damu,* blood. *Ugonjwa wa macho uletwao na kisonono,* gonorrhoeal ophthalmia. *Yabisi iletwayo na kisonono,* gonorrhoeal arthritis. **Usononi,** n. pain, hurt. (Cf. *uma, choma, udhi, sumbua.*)

Sonya, v. make a whistling sound in derision, contempt, &c., usu. in the form *fyonya,* which see. **Msono,** n. *mi-* and **Msonyo,** n. *mi-* a whistling sound made to attract attention, but usu. to express derision or contempt.

Soro, n. See **Solo.**

Sororo, n. a kind of fish considered to be good eating by Europeans. (Prob. *sururu.*)

Sosona, v. same as *kokona,* which see.

Sota, v. move along on the buttocks, as a person who has lost the use of his legs. (Cf. *sombea.*)

Sote, a. form of *-ote,* all, used in agreement with the Pers. pronoun *sisi. Tulikula sote pamoja,* we ate all together. *Twende sote,* let us all go together. *Tu wote,* is commonly used of two persons, we are both; *twende wote,* let us both go.

Sowera, v. (1) go on the hands and buttocks as a lame person who has lost the use of his legs; (2) dance about and show off before others at a dance.

Soza, v. (1) reach, arrive at, meet with, approach, accost. *Soza pwani,* of a vessel, run ashore, be beached, come to land. (2) *soza kidole,* point with the finger.

Spora,* n. a spore—adopted for use in text-books and school lessons when a distinction is desired to be made between seed and spore. (Cf. *mbegu.* Eng. spore.)

St.—Note: some natives tend to interpose *i* between *s* and *t,* e.g. *sitaajabu* for *staajabu,* &c.

Sta-, an Arabic sign of conjugation, retained in several words in Swahili.

Staajabu,* n. *ma-,* and v. with derivatives. See under **Ajabu.**

Staamani,* v. same as *amini,* which see.

Staarabu,* v. usu. in the St. **Staarabika,** get understanding, be wise, know about things, be civilized, e.g. *watu wa nchi hii wamestaarabika kidogo,* the people of this country have a touch of civilization. Cs. **Staarabisha. Mstaarabu,** n. *wa-* a civilized person, one who knows how to behave fittingly. **-staarabu,** a. wise, civilized. **Ustaarabu,** n. knowledge of things necessary for a civilized life, civilization. (Cf. *tamaduni.* Ar. استعرب.)

Stadi,* n. and a. an experienced, capable, skilled person, expert. **Mstadi,** n. *wa-* an expert, skilled, capable, accomplished workman. **Ustadi,** n. skill, expertness, cleverness at a trade, &c. (Cf. *fundi, bingwa.* Ar. مستعد.)

Staha,* n. respect, honour, reverence. **Stahi,** v. give honour to, show respect for, reverence. Ps. **Stahiwa.** Rp. **Stahiana. Mstahivu,** n. *wa-* (1) one who respects, honours, reveres; also (2) one who is respected, honoured. **-stahivu,** a. estimable, honourable, deserving of respect. **Ustahivu,** n. courtesy, deference, respect. (Cf. *tukuza, heshima.* Pers. ستوه.)

Stahabu,* v. See under **Hebu.**

Stahi,* v. See under **Staha.**

Stahiki,* v. and a. See under **Haki.**

Stahili,* v. merit, deserve, be fitting, be proper, be due, e.g. *astahili kupigwa,* he deserves a beating. *Wastahili kumpenda,* you ought to like him. A complimentary greeting on some happy occasion is *stahili salama.* **Astahili,** n. and **Stahili,** n. merit, worthiness, e.g. *si stahili yake;* it is not worthy of him, i.e. he deserves something better, or, he does not deserve it—it is too good for him. **Stahili,** a. worthy, fitting, proper. St. **Stahilika.** Cs. **Stahilisha,** make worthy, deem worthy, declare deserving (suitable, good). *Jistahilisha,* think (make, pretend) oneself worthy, qualified for, &c. **Ustahili,** n. merit, worthiness (of blame, punishment, reward, &c.). (Cf. *stahiki, wajibu.* Ar. استحلال.)

Stahimili,* v. **-stahimilivu,** a. See under **Hamali.**

-stahivu,* a. See under **Staha.**

Staka,* n. a sandal. (Cf. *makubazi, kiatu.*)

Stakabadhi,* v and n. See under **Kabidhi.**

Stakimu,* v. prosper. **Mastakimu,** n. a person's house and circumstances, dwelling, environment. (Cf. *fanikiwa, sitawi,* and *kitende, makao, makazi;* from the same root as *kimu,* which see.)

Stambuli,* Constantinople — also called Rum. (Turk. استانبول.)

Stara,* n. See under **Stiri.**

Starehe,* v., **Starehevu,** a. See under **Raha.**

Stesheni,* n. a railway-station. (Eng.)

Stihizai,* v. See under **Hizaya.**

Stima,* n. a steamer, but as a rule, a steam pinnace; for ocean-going vessels, *meli* is the usual word. (Eng. steamer.)

Stimu,* n. often used for electricity, e.g. *taa za stimu,* electric lights. (Eng. steam.)

Stiri,* v., also **Setiri,** conceal, hide, cover up, atone for. Ps. **Stiriwa.** St. and Pot. **Stirika.** Prep. **Stiria.** Cs. **Stirisha. Kisetiri,** n. *vi-* a cover, screen, screening wall, parapet, partition, hiding-place, retiring-place, closet, &c. **Mstiri,** n. *wa-,* also sometimes *msetiri,* and *msitiri,* one who conceals, a hider, one who covers, veils, disguises. **Stara,** n. covering, concealment, modesty, reserve. Commonly used in connexion with covering of private parts, e.g. *nguo aliyovaa haina stara,* the cloth he wears does not conceal his private parts. (Ar. ستر.)

Stoki,* n. sometimes heard for stocking, but *soksi* is more usual. (Eng. stocking.)

Stua, v., also **Shtua,** put out of place, startle, move suddenly or violently. St. **Stuka,** (1) start, be sprained, be put out of joint; (2) be startled, taken aback, surprised, alarmed, e.g. *mguu wangu umestuka,* my foot is sprained. *Nilistuka kwa hofu,* I started in terror. Prep. **Stukia,** e.g. start (be startled) at. Cs. **Stusha,** e.g. give a jerk to, sprain, startle, terrify, astonish. **Mstuo,** n. *mi-,* **Mstuko,** n. *mi-.* See **Mshtuo** and **Mshtuko,** under **Shtua,** v. (From the same root as *jituka.*)

Sua, v. eject water after rinsing the mouth with it. *Jisua,* retch. **Masuo,** n. plur. water ejected after rinsing the mouth with it. (Cf. *suka, sukutua.*)

Subana,* n. (1) a thimble, also *kastabani;* (2) a small piece of meat. (? Corruption of Ar. كستبان a thimble, a little, trifle.)

Subano,* n. a thimble. (Cf. *subana* (1), *tondoo.*)

Subaya,* n., also **Subahiya,** outside

covering of a bier, used in the better class of funerals, a pall. (Cf. *mazishi*. Ar. سحية covering, veil.)

Subiani, n. a spirit, a large jinnee. See under **Sibu**, v. (B).

Subili,* n. an aloe. (Ar. صبر.)

Subira,* n., **Subiri**, v. See under **Saburi**.

Subu,* v. (A) cast, run molten metal into a mould, i.e. *mimina madini iliyoyeyuka katika kalibu*. Ps. **Subiwa**. St. **Subika**, be cast, of metal. (Ar. صب.)

Subu,* v. (B) sometimes heard for *sibu*, v. (B).

Subukua, v. poke with the finger as a sign of contempt. **Msubukuo**, n. *mi-* a poke with the finger as a sign of contempt. (Cf. *mdukuo*.)

Sudi,* n. luck, fortune, success. (Cf. *bahati, nasibu, nyota*. Ar. سعود.)

Suduku,* v. See under **Sadiki**.

Sudusu,* n. a sixth part, the fraction. (Ar. سدس.)

Suezi,* n. *chuma cha suezi*, a soft kind of iron. Cont. *chuma cha pua*, steel.

Sufi,* n., also **Usufi**, n. the fine soft silky cotton from the pods of the tree *msufi*, kapok. (Ar. صوف wool.)

Sufii,* n. (1) a hermit, dervish; (2) saint, holy person. **Usufii**, n. conduct, life, character of *sufii*. (Cf. *mtawa, walii, mcha Mungu*. Ar. صوفي.)

Sufu,* n., also **Usufu**, n. wool. (Dist. *sufi, kapok*. Ar. صوف wool.)

Sufuria,* n. (— and of size, *ma-*) metal cooking-pot—of copper or iron, sometimes of a very large size. (Ar. صفر copper, brass.)

Sugu, n. See under **Sugua**.

Sugua, v. rub, scrub, scour, clean (smooth, sharpen) by rubbing. Ps. **Suguliwa**. St. **Suguika**, become hard, callous. St. **Sugulika**. Prep. **Sugulia**, e.g. *jiwe la kusugulia visu*, a stone for cleaning and whetting knives. Cs. **Sugulisha**. Rp. **Suguana**. **Sugu**, n. (1) a callosity, place made hard by rubbing or use, a corn (on the foot); (2) callousness, a hard unfeeling nature, e.g. *fanya sugu kwa kazi nyingi*, cause a lump from hard work. *Yu sugu*, he is callous, obstinate, stupid. *Ana sugu*, he has a callosity, &c. **Suguo**, n. *ma-* something to rub with, e.g. a knife-board scraper. **Usugu**, n. obstinacy, callousness, stupidity.

Suhuba, n. See under **Suhubu**.

Suhubu,* v. only used in the Rp. **Suhubiana**, e.g. be friendly with, *si mtu wa kusuhubiana naye*, not a man to make a friend of. **Suhuba**, n. and **Sahibu**, n. a friend, for the common *rafiki*, *suahaba za Mtume Muhammed*, the particular friends of the prophet Muhammad. **Usahibu**, n. and **Usuhuba**, n. friendship, for the common *urafiki*. (Cf. *mpenzi, mwandani, msiri, rafiki*. Ar. صحب.)

Sui,* n. one who is able to endure a great deal of trouble, hardship, one who is hardened. (? Ar. ساعى zealous, energetic, &c.)

Sujudu,* v. bow down (to), prostrate oneself (before), adore, worship. Used regularly of Muhammadan ceremonial of devotion. *Sujudu Mungu*, worship God. **Ps. Sujudiwa**. Prep. **Sujudia**. Cs. **Sujudisha**. e.g. cause to worship, teach worship to, make bow down, turn to God. **Sijida**, n. a callosity made on the forehead by prostration at Muhammadan prayer. (Ar. سجد.)

Suka, v. (1) shake, wag, move quickly to and fro, e.g. *sukasuka mkia*, wag the tail. *Sukasuka maziwa*, churn milk. (2) plait, twist, make by plaiting, e.g. *suka mkeka*, plait a mat. *Suka ukambaa*, plait a cord. *Suka nywele*, plait the hair—regularly of hair-plaiting, often elaborate, of Swahili women. Rd. *sukasuka*, (1) be violently agitated, and (2) fig. cause trouble, e.g. *kumsukasuka mtu,* to cause trouble to a person by saying things about him. Ps. **Sukwa.** St. and Pot. **Sukika.** Prep. **Sukia.** Cs. **Sukisha.** Rp. **Sukana,** e.g. *sukana nywele,* each dress the other's hair. Cv. **Sukua,** untwist, loosen, slacken, e.g. *sukua nazi,* extract the nut from inside a coco-nut. **Masuko,** n. plur. and *masukosuko,* (1) shaking, wagging, moving to and fro quickly, and so generally; (2) agitation, disturbance, a restless state of affairs. Used of the rolling or pitching of a vessel at sea. **Msuka,** n. *wa-* one who plaits, &c. *Msuka nywele,* one who plaits hair. *Msuka mikeka,* a plaiter of mats. **Msukano,** n. *mi-* quarrel, disagreement, i.e. of people, some wanting to do one thing and some the other. **Msuki,** n. *wa-,* see *msuka,* n. *wa-* above and *msusi,* below. **Msuko,** n. *mi-* act, process, style, &c.) of plaiting, a plait. Also of shaking, e.g. of a ship at sea, often Rd. *msukosuko,* with the same meaning as *masukosuko,* see above. **Msusi** n. *wa-* a woman hairdresser, one who plaits women's hair, same as *msuka* and *msuki.* **Ususi,** n. plaiting (style, art, fee, &c.) of plaiting of hair, mats, &c. (Cf. *tikisa, punga, sokota.*

Sukani,* plur. of *usukani.*

Sukari,* n. sugar. *Sukari guru,* half-made sugar, in large lumps, and of dark colour. *Sukari ya mawe,* lump sugar. (Ar. سكر.)

Suke, n. *ma-* the seed-bearing head or ear of various plants, e.g. rice, millet.

Sukua, v. See under **Suka.**

Sukuma, v. (1) push, push away (onward, back, off, &c.), move, drive, thrust; (2) urge, impel, incite, encourage, e.g. *roho yake inamsukuma mbele,* his will impels him onward. *Sukuma gari,* push a cart along Note: this word is also used of rolling out dough. *Mkate wa kusukuma,* a kind of pastry made from dough which has been rolled out. St. **Sukumika.** Prep. **Sukumia.** Ps. **Sukumwa.** Cs. **Sukumiza,** often Inten., e.g. (1) give a vigorous push, or impulse to, throw, thrust away. *Sukumiza rungu,* throw a club. *Sukumiza maradhi,* avert sickness. *Sukumiza pepo,* propitiate (ward off) evil spirits. *Sukumiza dau,* force a boat along. (2) rid oneself of; (3) instigate. Prep. of Cs. **Sukumizia,** thrust on to another, e.g. blame, disaster, sickness, a load. Ps. **Sukumana.** Rp. of Cs. **Sukumizana. Kisukuma,** n. *vi-,* **Kisukumi,** n. *vi-* described as a growth which is said to be like a wart on the clitoris of a woman. A woman so afflicted is said to cause the death of her husband within a short time of marriage, also, she is said to be unable to bear children, or if any are born they die while quite young. The *waganga* perform an operation to remove the growth. Some men are said to have similar growths which cause them to be a menace. *Ana kisukumi,* is said also of a woman who has been married by two or three men in succession all of whom have died within a short time of the marriage; also of a man who has married two or three wives in succession, all of whom have died within a short time of the marriage. **Kisukumizi,** n. *vi-* (1) the same as *kisukumi,* above; (2) a disease or disaster, &c., carried by one person to another. **Msukumizi,** n. *wa-* (1) one who throws blame (sickness, &c.) on to another; (2) an instigator, one who persuades or incites. **Usukumizi,** n. (1) instigation; (2) thrusting or pushing away, &c. (Prob. derived from *suka,* i.e. a Stc. form of Cv.)

Sukutu,* v. be silent, still, quiet—seldom heard. (Ar. سكت.)

Sukutua, v. (1) rinse out the mouth with water, gargle, e.g. before and after eating; (2) fig. eat, consume. *Amesukutua mkate wote*, he has eaten all the bread. Seldom used in deriv. forms. (Prob. a Cv. of Ten. form of *suka*.)

Sulibi,* v. crucify—but usu. in the Cs. form. Ps. **Sulibiwa.** St. **Sulibika.** Prep. **Sulibia.** Cs. **Sulibisha,** cause to crucify (or to be crucified), crucify. **Msalaba,** n. *mi-* a cross, anything in the form of a cross. (Ar. صلب.)

Sulika,* v. feel dizzy. **Sulisuli,** n. dizziness, vertigo. (Cf. *kizunguzungu, kisuli.* ?Ar. ثولة giddiness.)

Sultani,* n. *ma-* king, ruler, chief. *Sultani wa Rum,* the Sultan of Turkey. (In Zanzibar, the Sultan is generally referred to as *Seyyid.*) **Usultani,** n. sultanship. (Ar. سلطان).

Sulu, adv. *Kupiga sulu,* polish, to rub so as to make clean and bright. (Cf. *katua.* Cf. Zulu *sula,* wipe, polish.)

Sulubika,* v. strong, firm, diligent, vigorous, energetic, i.e. of physical energy. **Sulubu,** n. and **Usulubu,** n. firmness, strength, vigour, *Sulubu ya kazi,* energy in work, industry. (Cf. *nguvu, bidii, ushupavu.* Ar. صلب.)

Suluhi,* v., **-suluhifu,** a. See under **Suluhu.**

Suluhu,* v., also **Selehi** and **Suluhi,** put in good condition, improve, make agree (with), conduce to, serve (for), be of use (to), be fitting (for), reconcile, be reconciled. Ps. **Suluhiwa.** St. **Suluhika.** Prep. **Suluhia.** Cs. **Suluhisha,** cause to agree, reconcile, make peace between, conciliate. **Masilaha, Masilahi,** and **Masuluhu,** n. (1) reconciliation, agreement after a quarrel, a compromise; (2) in buying an article, *bei ya masilahi* is a price arrived at after bargaining, in which the buyer gets the article for less than what was asked for at first. **Msuluhisha,** n. *wa-*, **Msuluhishi,** n. *wa-*, **Msuluhivu,** n. *wa-* a peace-maker, reconciler, one who brings to terms, arranges a bargain, ends a quarrel. **-suluhifu,** tending to bring peace, concord, agreement, &c. **Suluhu,** n. (1) peace, agreement to leave off a quarrel, or to come to terms without quarrelling, an armistice; (2) a draw in a game of football, &c. (Cf. *sare.*) **Usuluhi,** n., **Usuluhifu,** n. peacemaking, reconciliation. (Cf. *patanisha, amua.* Ar. صالح make peace, and أصلح repair, improve.)

Sululu, n. or **Sururu,** (1) the curlew, *Numenius arquata*; (2) a pick-axe; (3) a kind of sword-fish.

Sumaku,* n. a magnet, loadstone, e.g. *fulani sumaku, mgumu kukopepesha fedha,* so-and-so is like a magnet, it is difficult to borrow money from him, i.e. it sticks to him. (Ar. سمك.)

Sumba, v. (A) sell off, get rid of at any price, sell under pressure, e.g. of stolen goods, &c. Ps. **Sumbwa.** St. **Sumbika.**

Sumba, v. (B) worry, confuse, seldom used in the Dir. form except in the expression, *kichwa chamsumba* (*kwa mambo fulani,* &c.) he is worried (because of certain things, &c.). Cv. **Sumbua,** discomfort, annoy, trouble, molest, vex, harass, tease, torment. Ps. **Sumbuliwa.** St. **Sumbuka,** e.g. be annoyed, troubled, discomforted, &c. Prep. **Sumbukia,** be troubled about, anxious for, *watoto wanamsumbukia baba,* the children are troubled (worried, anxious about) their father. Prep. **Sumbulia,** (1) give trouble about, make a fuss about (over, to, at, &c.); (2) often used in the sense of make a fuss over what you have done for somebody, i.e. remind him constantly of what you have done to help him when in trouble, &c. (Cf. *simanga.*) Cs. **Sumbusha.** as Inten., e.g. of active, intentional annoyance. Rp. **Sumbuana. Masumbulizi,** n. plur., **Masimbulio,** n. plur., and **Masumbulizi,** n. plur., act of shaming a person by reminding him again and again of any act of kindness shown to him when in difficulty, need, &c., or of by telling others about it. **Msumbufu,** n. *wa-* (1) a troublesome person, one who causes annoyance; (2) one who is full of trouble, troubled, annoyed. **Simbu,** n. same as *masumbulizi,* &c., above. **-sumbufu,** a. (1) troublesome, causing annoyance, &c.; (2) full of trouble, troubled, annoyed. **Sumbuo,** n. *ma-* annoyance, teasing, trouble, in the plur., *masumbuo,* acts of annoyance, annoying habits or character. **Usumbufu,** n. trouble, vexation, annoyance, whether as caused or endured, act. or pass. (Cf. *simbua, udhi, chokoza, taabu, mashaka.*)

Sumisha,* v. See under **Sumu.**

Sumu,* n. poison, *lisha sumu,* or *kwa sumu,* and also sometimes *sumisha,* poison, give poison to. **Sumu,** v. poison, e.g. *atakusumu,* he will poison you. (Ar. سمّ.)

Sumughu,* n. gum-arabic, gum. (Ar. صموغ.)

Sumulia, v. sometimes heard for *simulia,* which see.

Suna,* n. See under **Suni.**

Sungua, v. gather the chaff, &c., when winnowing.

Sungura, n. (1) a hare, represented continually in East African beast stories as owing ascendancy to the power of outwitting all other creatures. Hence (2) a clever, cute person, also an unprincipled, clever rogue. **Kisungura,** n. *vi-* dim. (Cf. *kititi.*)

Sungusungu, n. a large black ant. (Cf. *chungu.*)

Suni,* n. (1) used of what is good, commendable, meritorious, but not absolutely binding or necessary. Hence, good traditions, counsel of perfection, work of supererogation. (2) one of the Sunnite sect. *yeye ni suni,* he belongs to the Sunnite sect. **Suna,** a. good, commendable, meritorious, &c. *Kufa si suna, ni faradhi,* death is not optional, but inevitable. (Ar. صنع.)

Sunobari,* n. deal, pine—wood of the tree *msunobari.* (Ar. سنوبر.)

Sununa, v. be sorry, regret; a form of *sonona.* See under **Sonona.**

Sunza, v. (1) let go grudgingly, give with reluctance; (2) tease, provoke, annoy, e.g. by causeless delay, reluctance, &c.; (3) *kusunza mguu* (or *mkono*), to put the foot (or arm) forward to feel if anything is in the way; (4) *kusunza teo* (or *kombeo*), to throw with a sling.

Sunzu, n. a tuft of hair left on the top of the head when shaving it. (Cf. *denge, kishungi, bwenzi.*)

Sura,* n. (1) form, appearance, look, expression, face, exterior, likeness, general view, prospect. *Sura ya mbingu,* look of the sky, weather; (2) a chapter of a book. (Cf. *uso, tabia, jinsi, mfano, mandhari.* Ar. صورة.)

Suria,* n. *ma-* a concubine, but strictly speaking one who is a slave. **Suriama,** n. *ma-* (1) one born of a concubine; (2) a hybrid, half-caste. **Usuria,** n. condition of being a concubine. (Ar. سرية.)

Surua,* n. measles. (Pers. سرخره measles.)

Suruali,* n. trousers. (Ar. سروال.)

Sururu, n. (1) see **Sululu;** (2) a kind of beetle which destroys coco-nut trees.

Sus,* n. liquorice—very little known. (Ar. سوس.)

Susa,* n. tartar (of teeth), decay (of teeth). (Ar. سوسة worm-hole, &c.)

Susia, v. refuse food, or anything because of pique, or because it disappoints, or is not exactly what was wanted. Take huff and refuse food, &c. (Cf. *zilia.*)

Susu, n. a contrivance for hanging things up in a room, a hanging shelf, a net, a hammock, sometimes used as a child's bed.

Susuika, v. (1) deny having made a charge when confronted by the person about whom the charge was made; (2) keep asking and asking until required information is obtained, apply the 'third degree'.

Susurika, v. go about aimlessly, loiter, waste time. (Cf. *zurura.*)

Susuwaa, v. become dry and hard.

Suta, n. one who has wasted all his money and property and has nothing left.

Suta, v. make charges openly against, charge one openly with deceit or wrongdoing, confront a person who has spread an evil report about one. Ps. **Sutwa.** Cs. **Sutisha.** Rp. **Sutana. Msuto**, n. *mi-* like *suto*, follg. **Suto**, n. *ma-* charges of wrongdoing, made openly against one.

Suuza, v., also commonly contracted to **Suza**, (1) rinse, souse, swill—e.g. the final stage in washing, before drying the clothes or utensils. *Suza mwili*, rinse the body with water to take off the soap after bathing. (2) *suza uji*, make a kind of thin gruel for a sick person.

Swafi,* a. See **Safi.**

Swaga, v. drive cattle along.

Swahili,* n. the Swahili coast. *Mswahili, wa-* a Swahili. *Kiswahili*, the Swahili language. Note: the term Swahili is a very elastic one, and in some places is used for any native who wears a *kanzu* or who is a Muhammadan, even only nominally. (Ar. سواحل.)

Swala, n. Grant's gazelle.

Swali,* n. *ma-*. See under **Saili.**

Swila, n. the spitting cobra. (Cf. *fira.*)

T

T may be pronounced as *t* in English, but in some places, i.e. Mombasa, Tanga, and the north, it is possible to distinguish different varieties of *t*. Many words pronounced with *t* in Mombasa are pronounced with *ch* in standard Swahili, cf. note under *Ch*, and *nchi, ncha, chukua, chupa*, &c., which in Mombasa may be heard as *nti, nta, tukua, tupa*, &c. *T* is difficult to distinguish from *d* in the pronunciation of some natives, therefore words not found under *t* may be looked for under *d*.

-ta- the future tense prefix, see Grammars.

Ta-, an Arabic sign of conjugation, retained in several words in Swahili.

-ta is a formative, the termination of a derived form of the verb, with the significance of contact or tenacity; such forms are shown by the abbreviation Ten. (Cf. *ambata, fumbata, kamata, nata*, &c.)

Taa,* n. (1) a lamp—of any kind.

Washa taa, light a lamp. *Zima taa*, put out a lamp. (? Hind. دِیا lamp, lantern, or Ar. ضوء light, &c.). (2) obedience, see under *Tii*; (3) plur. of *utaa*; (4) sometimes shortened for *taala*, exalted, most high, an Arab title of God (Ar. تع for تعالی); (5) a large flat fish, a skate.

Taabika,* v. be troubled, in distress, anxious, fatigued. Cs. **Taabisha.** Rp. of Cs. **Taabishana. Taabu,** n. trouble, distress, ado, fatigue, toil, travail—also sometimes as a v. for *taabika*, e.g. *hawataabu kitu*, they have no sort of trouble. *Taabu* is often used with a locative, e.g. *mgonjwa taabuni* (often *taabani*), a sick man in great distress, a very sick man. (Ar. تعب.)

Taadabu,* v. See under **Adabu.**

Taadhima, n., **Taadhimika,*** v. See under **Adhama.**

Taadi,* v. See **Tadi.**

Taahari, n., **Taahira,*** n. See under **Ahiri.**

Taajabu,* v. See under **Ajabu.**

Taala,* v. sometimes **Taa**, lit. he is exalted—commonly used in the Arab. phrase, *Allah taala*, God is exalted, God most high—prefixed to letters and formal documents. (Ar. عال and الله تعالی.)

Taalamu,* v. See under **Elimisha.**

Taali,* v. study, learn, be a student. **Mtaala,** n. study, practice, reading. (Cf. *soma*, *jifunza*. Ar. تلا.)

Taamamu,* v. chance a thing, take a chance. (Cf. *bahatisha*. ? Ar. تعميم indefiniteness.)

Taamuli,* n. thought, thoughtfulness, meditation. (Cf. *fikira*. Ar. تأمل.)

Taanasa, n. and v., **Taanisi,*** v. See under **Anasa.**

Taaradhi, v., and **Taaradhia,*** v. cross-question, interfere in a person's affairs, meddle. (Ar. تعرض.)

Taarifa, n. also **Taarifu,*** n. See under **Arifu.**

Taashira,* n. See under **Ashiria.**

Taataa,* v. (1) move restlessly, move about, throw the hands or body about as in sickness, distress, &c.; (2) be bewildered, confused, not know what to do or say. (Cf. *hangaika*, *sitasita*, *gaagaa*, *tapatapa*. Ar. داد dally, &c.)

Taba, n. See under **Tabua.**

Tabaka,* n. anything laid on another—and so, lid, cover, lining (of a dress, &c.), layer, row, stratum, stage, story (of a house). **Tabiki,** v. lie close to, stick to, line, cover, be attached to. Ps. **Tabikwa.** Prep. **Tabikia.** Rp. of Prep. **Tabikiana,** cleave together, e.g. be great friends. Cs. **Tabikisha,** cause to stick to, paste on, glue on, put a lining to. (Ar. طبق.)

Tabakelo,* n. a snuff-box, a tobacco case—made of wood, reed, or horn. (Port. *tabaqueira*, snuff-box.)

Tabakwa, v. be impoverished, poor.

Tabana, v. weave a spell, said of the formula repeated by the *waganga* when they are preparing their medicines, charms, &c. Prep. **Tabania,** put a spell on, prepare or procure a charm for a particular purpose, e.g. *nitamtabania yule mdai wangu asinidai*, I will procure a charm so that the man I owe money to will not sue me. Also used of wizards who are said to beat people and cause them hurt without leaving any marks of the beating. Cs. **Tabanya.** (? Pers. تبانچه a box, blow, slap.)

Tabangatabanga, v. spoil by mixing with anything inferior or bad, adulterate. (Cf. *ghoshi*, *saliti*.)

Tabanya, v. See under **Tabana.**

Tabaradi,* v., also **Tabaridi** and **Tabarudu.** See under **Baridi.**

Tabaruki, v., and **Tabaruku,*** v. See under **Baraka.**

Tabasamu,* v. smile, for common *chekelea*. (Ar. تبسم.)

Tabasuri,* n. See under **Busara.**

Tabawali,* v. urinate, for common *kojoa, nya.* (Ar. تبول.)

Tabia,* n. condition, state, nature. Hence (1) of persons, character, disposition, humour, habits, attainments, gifts; (2) of things, e.g. *tabia ya nchi,* physical features, climate, weather, &c. (Cf. *sifa, madhehebu, moyo, desturi, hali, sura, umbo.* Ar. طبعة.)

Tabibia,* n. (1). See under **Tiba.** (2), v. treat medically, act as doctor to, attend professionally. Ps. **Tabibiwa. Tabibu,** n. *ma-* doctor, physician, medical man. **Tibu,** v. same as *tabibia.* Ps. **Tibiwa.** St. and Pot. **Tibika. Tiba,** n. medicine. **Utabibu,** n. profession (practice, fee, &c.) of a doctor, medical science, doctoring, treatment. (Cf. *mganga, uganga.* Ar. طب.)

Tabiki,* v. See under **Tabaka.**

Tabiri,* v. interpret, explain, expound, e.g. of a fortune-teller, soothsayer, prophet, and so, foretell, predict, interpret a dream. *Tabiri mwaka kwa chuo,* foretell the (events of a) year by a book. Ps. **Tabiriwa.** St. and Pot. **Tabirika.** Cs. **Tabirisha. Mtabiri,** n. *wa-* one who announces or foretells events, a prophet, an interpreter of dreams. **Utabiri,** n. *ma-* interpretation, exposition, explanation, announcement, prediction. (Cf. *fasiri, bashiri, hubiri, eleza.* Ar. تعبير.)

Tabu, n. See under **Tabua.**

Tabua, v. tear off, break off, pluck off. **Taba,** n., **Tabu,** n., and **Tabutabu,** n. a piece broken or torn off, esp. used of the strips of the *mwaa,* i.e. the Hyphaene or dwarf palm, used for plaiting baskets, &c.

Taburu,* n. drill, i.e. of soldiers, &c. (Ar. درب practice, &c., *r* and *b* being transposed.)

Tadaraki, v., and **Tadariki,*** v. See under **Daraka.**

Tadhibiri,* v. (1) put right something that has gone wrong, revise, amend a case which has been settled wrongly or badly; (2) look for, search. Also **Tadubiri,** with same meaning. (Ar. تدبر regard attentively.)

Tadi,* v. transgress, do wrong, offend, be rude, oppress, bully, treat evilly. Prep. **Tadia,** be rude to. **Tadi** and **Utadi,** n. offence, rudeness, aggression, &c., *ingia kwa tadi,* enter rudely (with violence). (Cf. *jeuri, fidhuli.* Ar. تعد.)

Tadubiri, v. See under **Tadhibiri.**

Tafadhali,* v. See under **Fadhili.**

Tafakari,* v. same as *fikiri.*

Tafaraji,* v. also **Tafaruji,** v. seek comfort, look at a pleasant sight, see a new thing, go to an entertainment, &c. **Tafrija,** n. enjoyment, rest, comfort, relaxation, amusement, pleasant entertainment. (Cf. *fariji, anisi.* Ar. تفرج.)

Tafauti,* n. See **Tofauti.**

Tafi, n. same as *tasi,* which see.

Tafiti,* v. pry into, be inquisitive, examine, criticize, &c. **Mtafiti,** n. *wa-* a prying, inquisitive person. **Utafiti,** n. curiosity, inquisitiveness. (Cf. *peleleza, chungua, pekua, dadisi, tafuta.* ? From the same root as *tafuta,* see *fatiisha,* treated as a Cs. form and the final *-sha* dropped. Ar. تفتيش.)

Tafrija,* n. See under **Tafaraji.**

Tafsiri,* v. See under **Fasiri.**

Tafuna, v. chew, nibble, gnaw, masticate food—of men and animals, e.g. *tafuna nyama,* chew meat. *Tafuna miwa* (*mkate*), chew sugar-cane (bread). Ps. **Tafunwa.** Prep. **Tafunia.** Cs. **Tafunisha. Matafuni,** n. plur. chewings, nibblings, things chewed. **Mtafuno,** n. *mi-* act of chewing. (Cf. *guguna, la, mega.*)

Tafuta,* v. (1) search (for), seek, look for; and also (2) search out, get by search, find, obtain. Ps. **Tafutwa.** St. and Pot. **Tafutika.** Prep. **Ta-**

futia, e.g. seek out for (at, by, &c.), search into, look into, look for. Cs. **Tafutisha.** Rp. **Tafutana.** (? From the same root as *tafiti*, see *fatiisha* treated as a Cs. form and the final -*sha* dropped. Ar. تفتش.)

Taga, n. *ma-*, **Tagaa,** n. *ma-*, **Kitagaa,** n. *vi-* bifurcation, either of a tree or a road (cf. *panda*, n.). **Tagaa,** v. (1) walk fast, stride, straddle; (2) be astraddle, astride, e.g. *tagaa mti*, sit (or stand) astride a log; (3) step over, i.e. a log, &c. **Matagataga,** adv. *Enda matagataga*, walk with the legs wide apart, straddle.

Taga, v. lay (an egg) of birds generally—also *taga yai*. Ps. **Tagwa.** Prep. **Tagia.** Cs. **Tagisha.** **Mtago,** n. *mi-* act, manner of laying an egg. **Tago,** n. *ma-* place of laying an egg. (Cf. *kuta, yai, atamia.*)

Taghafali, v., **Taghafaliwa,** v., **Taghafalika,** v., **Taghafalisha,** v.* See under **Ghafilika.**

Tahadhari,* v. See under **Hadhari.**

Tahafifu,* a. See under **Hafifu.**

Tahalili,* n. See **Tahlili.**

Tahamaki,* v. look up, observe, take notice. As an Int. *tahamaki!* (Imperat.) Lo and behold! (Cf. *angalia, tazama.* Ar. تهمك.)

Taharaki,* v. See under **Haraka.**

Taharizi,* n. side-pieces of a *kanzu*, *badani* being the front and back-pieces. (Ar. تخرّص.)

Taharuki,* v. See under **Haraka.**

Tahayari, v., **Tahayarisha,** v., **Tahayuri,** n. See under **Haya,** n.

Tahiri,* v. cleanse—ceremonially, but esp. of circumcision as practised by Muhammadans. Ps. **Tahiriwa.** St. **Tahirika.** Prep. **Tahiria.** Cs. **Tahirisha.** **Tahiri,** n. a ceremonially clean person. **Tohara,** n. (1) purity, cleanness—esp. in a ceremonial sense, i.e. according to Muhammadan rules, e.g. of the purification of a corpse. With reference to details, *tohara* is used as a plur. from **Utohara.** Esp. (2) circumcision. **Mtohara,** n. *wa-* a circumcised person. (Cf. *ukumbi, eua, ngariba.* Ar. طهر.)

Tahlili,* n. funeral song, dirge, coronach—esp. of the recitation of the Muhammadan creed at a funeral. The officiant leads the dirge saying *La illaha ila Lah*, and the people respond. A repetition of the phrase, There is no God but God. (Ar. هلل.)

Tahyati,* n. long life (to you)—used only in salutation. (Ar. تحية from the same root as *hai.*)

Tai, n. a large bird of prey, an eagle or vulture. (Ar. طائر a bird.)

Taibu,* v. be good, be well. St. **Taibika,** be happy. **Taibu,** adv. good, rightly, well, esp. as a common rejoinder of assent or approval, Certainly! Good! Very well! Like *njema, vyema, inshallah, Ee walla.* (Ar. طب.)

Taifa,* n. *ma-* a nation, also a tribe, but this is generally *kabila, ma-*. African tribes are not described by a collective word, but as a number of individuals bearing a tribal name. Thus the *Yao* tribe comprises the *Wayao*; the *Ganda* tribe, the *Waganda*, &c. (Ar. طائفة.)

Taileni, Tailetai, and **Tawireni.** See under **Punga,** v. (B).

Taili,* v. a variant of *talii.*

Taiti,* v. be in need, be poverty stricken. *Nimetaiti*, I am in sore need. **Utaiti,** n. poverty, great need, straightened circumstances. (Cf. *ruzu, uhitaji, mwambo.* ? Ar. داي end of month, i.e. when one's wages are spent.)

Taja, v. name, mention by name, speak of. *Taja jina*, call by name, give a name to, name. Ps. **Tajwa.** St. and Pot. **Tajika,** be named, be mentionable. Prep. **Tajia.** Cs. **Tajisha.**

Tajamala, n., **Tajamali,*** v. See under **Jamala.**

Taji,* n. a crown, coronet. (Cf. *utaji*. Ar. تاج.)

Tajiri,* v., and sometimes **Tijara,** v. get money by trading, get rich. Also St. **Tajirika,** in same sense. Prep. **Tajiria.** Cs. **Tajirisha,** e.g. *jitajirisha*, enrich oneself. **Tajiri,** n. *ma-* a merchant, wholesale trader, capitalist, man of wealth. Prov. *Tajiri na maliye, maskini na mwanawe*, a rich man and his money (are like) a poor man and his son. **Mtajiri,** n. *wa-* same as *tajiri*, n. **Utajiri,** n. riches, wealth, possessions, capital, status of a merchant, &c. (Ar. تاجر.)

Taka, n. (A) dirt, filth, refuse, garbage, rubbish, sweepings. **Takataka,** n. (1) like *taka*; (2) anything of little value, i.e. trifles, odds and ends, scraps, trinkets, fancy articles, miscellany. **Kitakataka,** n. *vi-* a particle of dust, a speck of dirt, a very small (trifling, worthless) thing, a mote. (Cf. *uchafu, jaa*, n., *kipuzi*.)

Taka,* n. (B) a length of calico or cloth, calico or cloth in the piece of about 30 yards. (Cf. *jora*. Ar. طاق.)

Taka, v. (1) feel a want of, want, desire, wish, be inclined; (2) express a want (to), ask, request; (3) be in want of, need, require, (4) (seem to want, and so) have a tendency to, incline to, be on the verge of, be going to (of an imminent result or consequence), e.g. *nataka kwenda*, I want to go—the negative form *sitaki* being the most absolute expression of refusal, I will not. *Taka shauri*, need advice. *Kumtaka mtu mapesa* (or *fedha*), to ask a man for money. Note: a personal object prefix should be used with caution with this verb, as, unless qualified, *kumtaka mtu*, is to want him (or her) sexually. *Inataka kunya* (or *kunyesha*) *mvua*, it is going to rain. Also impersonally, e.g. *inataka unene ujinga na mtu mjinga*, you must speak to a fool in a fool's way. *Mbuzi anataka kufa*, the goat is going to die. Ps. **Takwa.** St. **Takika.** Prep. **Takia,** e.g. ask of (for, from, about, at, against, &c.). Cs. **Takisha** (rare). Rp. **Takana,** want each other (use with caution); also, *takana buriani*, take a final farewell of each other. **Mataka,** n. plur. wantings, desires, inclinations. **Matakwa,** n. plur. (1) things wanted, needs, desires, requests; (2) being wanted, being in request, e.g. *matakwa yangu kuwa mtumishi kila mtu ayajua*, every one knows how I was wanted as a servant, how my services were in request. **Mtaka,** n. *wa-* one who wants, asks, begs, needs, &c. Prov. *Mtaka yote hukosa yote*, he who begs for everything gets nothing. **Mtashi,** n. *wa-* an earnest, importunate suppliant, one whose mind is set on an object, an urgent pleader. **Utashi,** n. strong desire, earnest demand, importunate request, present made to back an appeal. (Cf. *tamani, penda, hitaji, elekea*. Bantu *-taka*, want, lack, desire, and cf. Ar. تاق long for, desire.)

Takabadhi, v., **Takabadhiwa,*** v., See under **Kabidhi.**

Takabali,* v. See under **Kubali.**

Takabari,* v. See under **Kiburi.**

Takadamu,* v. See under **Kadamu.**

Takalifu,* n. See under **Kalifu.**

Takamali,* v. See under **Kamili.**

Takaramu, v., **Takarima,** n., **Takarimu,*** v. See under **Karama.**

Takasa, v. clean, make clean, cleanse, purify, sanctify. Includes all kinds of cleaning. Ps. **Takaswa.** St. and Pot. **Takasika.** Prep. **Takasia,** e.g. *nimemtakasia shamba*, I have cleaned his garden for him. Cs. **Takasisha.** Ten. **Takata,** become clean (clear, white), be cleansed (purified, brightened). *Mbingu zimetakata*, the sky is clear, or *kumetakata*. St. and Pot. **Takatika,** e.g *moyo wake umetakatika*, his mind has been cleaned of its passions, has been calmed. **Mtakatifu**, n. *wa-* a pure, clean person, a saint. **Mtakaso**, n. *mi-* cleansing, a thing cleaned. **-takatifu**, a. cleansed, clean, pure, sanctified, holy. **Takato**, n. *ma-* cleanness, purity, serenity. **Utakaso**, n. cleansing, a thing cleaned. **Utakatifu**, n. cleanliness, purity, material, and moral—and so sanctity, holiness. (Cf. *safisha, eua*.)

Takataka, n. See under **Taka**, n. (A).

-takatifu, a., **Takato**, n. *ma-*. See under **Takasa**.

Takbira,* v. repeat the Muhammadan formula, *Allahu akbar*, God is great. (Ar. تكبير.)

Takia,* n. *ma-* a large cushion. (Ar. متكا.)

Takilifu,* n. See under **Kalifu**.

Tako, n. *ma-* (1) the seat, buttock, ham; (2) the lower part, butt-end of anything, e.g. of a gun, spear, arrow, &c. **Kitakizo**, n. *vi-* end-piece, at the head and foot, for native bedstead (cf. *kitanda*). **Kitako**, n. *vi-* and adv. (1) part of the body between the buttocks (*matako*), the fork or crutch of the legs, perineum, also called *msamba*; (2) haemorrhoids, piles (cf. *bawasiri, kikundu, futuri*); (3) as adv. on the base, or lower end, e.g. *weka pipa kitako*, set the barrel on its end. *Kaa kitako*, (1) sit down, take a seat—in the native way—the usual expression; also (2) remain settled, settle, reside. **Utako**, n. *ma-* same as *tako*.

Takshi,* n. a tarboosh, but usu. *tarbushi*.

Taksiri,* n. fault, defect, offence, deficit, crime. (Cf. *hatia, dhambi, kosa*, which are more usual. Ar. تقصير.)

Takwimu,* n. a calendar. (Ar. تقويم.)

Taladadi,* v. See **Taradadi**.

Talaka,* n. divorce. **Taliki**, v. divorce. Ps. **Talikiwa**. (Ar. طلق.)

Talakeki,* n. a small Arab powder-horn, for carrying a fine-grained powder. (Cf. *pembe*. ? Ar. طلق fire off a gun.)

Talakim,* n. the Muhammadan burial prayers. (Cf. *uradi*. Ar. تلقين.)

Talaleshi,* n. *ma-*, also **Mtalaleshi**, n. *wa-* (1) a prostitute (cf. *malaya, kahaba*); (2) one who seeks for prostitutes, a procurer (cf. *mbembe, kawadi*); (3) an evil malicious person who spreads evil or false reports about others. **Utalaleshi**, n. (1) tale bearing; (2) lasciviousness, carnal passion, prostitution. (? From a Cs. of Ar. دلال lasciviousness, &c.)

Talasimu,* n. *ma-* talisman, charm, magic diagram. (Cf. *hirizi, dawa, kago*. Ar. طلسم.)

Tale, n. *ma-*. See **Kitale**.

Talibisi,* n. a mat fastened round the sides of a heavily laden dhow to prevent the waves from washing in. (Ar. تلبيس.)

Talii,* v. inquire into, look into, examine. (Cf. *chungua, angalia*. Ar. طالع.)

Taliki,* v. See under **Talaka**.

Taliza,* v. smear, plaster—with clay or mortar, so as to give a smooth surface to the wall of a house. Ps. **Talizwa**. (Cf. *rashia, sirima, lainisha*. Ar. طلى cover, anoint, i.e. a Cs. made from it.)

Tama,* v. (A) be finished, come to an end—as a rule *timia* and *isha* are used. **Tama**, a. final, decisive, finishing a matter, e.g. *shauri lake tama, halirudi*, his counsel is final and is never reversed. *Neno la tama*, a final, decisive word. Also as adv. finally, once for all, out and out, wholly. **Tama**, n. end, conclusion, final stage. **Tamati**, used in the sense of Finis, the end, esp. at the end of poems, stories, &c. (Cf. *isha, koma,* and *timu* from same root. Ar. تمّ.)

Tama,* n. (A) dirt, rubbish, filth, dregs. (Cf. *taka,* n. Ar. طم.)

Tama, n. (B) cheek—now only used in the expression *shika tama,* rest the cheek on the hand, sit in a dejected or brooding attitude or in deep thought.

Tama, v. (B) move one's place of abode. (Cf. *hama.*)

Tama la bibi, also **Mtama wa bibi,** Didric cuckoo, *Lamphormorpha Caprius.*

Tamaa,* n. coveted object, longing, desire, lust, ambition, avarice, cupidity, greediness. *Fanya* (*piga, -wa na*) *tamaa,* desire, be ambitious, &c. *Ni mtu wa tamaa, mwenye tamaa, ana tamaa,* he is a covetous ambitious man. *Tamaa ya mali,* love of money, avarice. *Kata tamaa,* despair. *Weka kwa tamaa,* keep waiting (in suspense, unsatisfied). *Shika tamaa,* live in hopes. **Tumai,** v. long for, desire, covet, want, lust after, like. Cv. **Tamauka,** depart, be quiet, be satisfied—used of lust, desire, &c. (Cf. *roho, shauku, taka,* v. Ar. طمع.)

Tamaduni,* v. become civilized. **Utamaduni,** n. refinement, civilization. (Cf. *staarabika.* Ar. تمدّن.)

Tamalaki,* v. See under **Miliki.**

Tamani,* v. long for, desire, covet, want, lust after, like. Ps. **Tamaniwa.** St. and Pot. **Tamanika,** be desired, be desirable, be attractive. Cs. **Tamanisha,** be alluring, seductive, attractive, desirable, rouse the passions, desires, &c. **Mtamani,** n. *wa-* one who desires, an ambitious person, a greedy (lustful) person. **Tamani,** n. desire, longing, lust; also hope, trust. (Cf. *tumaini,* which comes from the same Ar. root but which has retained its original meaning, whereas *tamani* is treated as though derived from *tamaa.* Ar. طمن.)

Tamasha,* n. (— and *ma-*) a spectacle, show, pageant, that which excites wonder (curiosity, amusement). (Cf. *shani, ajabu, mwujiza.* Ar. تماشا.)

Tamati.* See under **Tama, v. (A).**

Tamauka,* v. See under **Tamaa.**

Tamba, v. strut proudly, walk in a swaggering, conceited way, leap, dance—e.g. of warriors returning in triumph from victory. **Kitambi,** n. *vi-* pride, arrogancy. **Mtambatamba,** n. *wa-* one who struts and swaggers, a braggart. **Tambo,** n., and **Utambo,** n. (*tambo*) strutting, swaggering, and (e.g.) of horses, prancing, high action.

Tambaa, n. *ma-* a piece (strip, length) of calico or similar stuff. Usually in the dim. **Kitambaa,** n. *vi-* a piece of calico, a strip, or scrap of any kind of textile fabric for any use, a small cloth, e.g. napkin, towel, duster, handkerchief, bandage, tablecloth—often with a defining phrase. *Kitambaa cha meza* (*cha kufutia mikono, cha kupangusia,* &c.). **Utambaa,** n. (*tambaa*) same as *kitambaa,* but seldom used. Note: *tambaa* and *tambara* are often used for a piece of old cloth, rag, &c. *Alikuwa amevaa matambaa* (or *matambara*), he was wearing old rags. Hence **Tambarajika,** v. be very weak of old age (of things and persons).

Tambaa, v. (1) creep, crawl, move slowly. *Wadudu watambaao,* insects, reptiles. *Ugonjwa unatambaa mwili wote,* the sickness creeps over the whole body. *Mimea inayotambaa,* creeping plants. (1) stretch, i.e. of a plain, be long, drawn out, e.g. *milima inatambaa,* the mountains stretch for a long distance. Prep. **Tambalia,** (2) creep up to, steal upon, e.g. *alimtambalia mpaka kumkaribia,* he crawled up to him till he got near to him (cf. *nyatia, nyemelea*); Cs. **Tambaza,** (1) *tambaza maneno,* speak slowly, drawl; (2) sweep well; (3) drag on the ground, as of a cloth (cf. *kokoteza maneno*). Also **Tambarisha,** drag on the ground, as of one's clothing, &c. **Mtambaa,** n. *wa-, mi-* one who (or which) creeps or crawls—used with various compound nouns: **Mtambaa chini,** n. a snake. **Mtambaa jongoo,** n. *mi-* a tree which is used for making handles of hoes, &c. **Mtambaa panya,** n. *mi-* a pole which is placed along the top of the walls of a native house, on top of the *kirugu,* which see. **Mtambazi,** n. *wa-* any crawling creature, insect, or reptile. **-tambazi,** a. creeping, crawling, of an insect, reptile, or creeping plant. **Tambazi,** n. *ma-* name of a disease which spreads over the body. **Utambazi,** n. (*tambazi*) (1) act (power, means, &c.) of creeping or crawling; (2) mark left in crawling, track, trail. (Cf. follg.)

Tambarare, n. level, plain. *Nchi ya tambarare,* a flat country. (Cf. *tambaa,* v.)

Tambarisha, v. See under **Tambaa.**

Tambavu, n. *ma-* something hung on the shoulders or over the chest, e.g. a charm, amulet (to protect from danger, accident, &c.), also shoulder-straps, bandolier.

Tambaza, v., **Tambazi,** a., **Tambazi,** n. *ma-*. See under **Tambaa,** v.

Tambi, n. (1) macaroni, vermicelli; (2) plur. of *utambi,* which see. (Prob. from *tambaa,* i.e. something long.)

Tambika, v. make offering to propitiate the spirits of the dead (*mizimu*) and ask them not to trouble the living. **Tambiko,** n. *ma-* (1) offering of oxen, goats, fowls, beer, cloth, &c., made to propitiate the spirits of the dead; (2) a totem. **Mtambika,** n. *wa-,* **Mtambikaji,** n. *wa-* one who makes the offering in *tambika.* **Mtambiko,** n. *mi-* act of offering in *tambika.* (Cf. *kafara.*)

Tambo, n. (1) see under **Tamba,** v.; (2) see under **Kitambo;** (3) see under **Tambua;** (4) condition of being well-knit, strong, powerful, e.g. *mtu huyu ana tambo,* or *ni tambo la mtu,* this man is well-knit, powerful.

Tamboa, n. *ma-* testicle. (Cf. *pumbu, korodani, kende.*)

Tambua, recognize, know again, remember, see the meaning of, discern, understand. Ps. **Tambuliwa.** St. and Pot. **Tambulika,** e.g. *mtu wa kutambulika,* a well-known (remarkable, distinguished) person. Pot. **Tambulikana,** be recognizable, be intelligible, be knowable. *Ametambulikana kuwa mwizi,* he has been convicted of thieving. Prep. **Tambulia.** Cs. **Tambulisha,** i.e. make known, expound, explain. Rp. **Tambuana. Mtambua,** n. *wa-,* **Mtambuzi,** n. *wa-* (1) a knowing, clever, well-informed, intelligent person; (2) one able to explain, interpret, fathom difficult problems, &c. **Tambo,** n. *ma-* (from the Dir. form) a puzzle, cryptic saying. **-tambuzi,** a. clever, quick, intelligent, knowing, shrewd. **Utambuzi,** n. (*tambuzi*) (1) mental quickness, intelligence, perception, facility, cleverness, skill; (2) explanation of a difficult problem, answer to a riddle or cryptic saying, &c. (Cf. *tambo* (3), *fahamu, jua, maizi.*)

Tambuu,* n. (1) leaf of the betel-plant, *mtambuu;* (2) a mixture for chewing, of which this leaf is the chief ingredient. (Cf. *uraibu.* Hind. and Pers. تامبول.)

Tambuza, v. used of smith's work—fashion by heat and hammering, beat out, forge, weld, e.g. a broken knife or hoe. Ps. **Tambuzwa.** St. and Pot. **Tambuzika.** Prep. **Tambuzia,** have a thing welded (repaired by a smith), &c.

-tambuzi, a. See under **Tambua.**

Tamia, v. (1) Prep. form of *tama*, v.; (2) sometimes heard for *atamia*, v.

Tamka, v. pronounce, articulate, speak in a formal (emphatic, expressive) way. Ps. **Tamkwa.** Prep. **Tamkia.** St. and Pot. **Tamkika.** Cs. **Tamkisha. Tamko**, n. *ma-* act (style, way, &c.) of speaking, articulation, pronunciation, delivery, speech. *Matamko ya maneno*, ways of pronouncing words. *Tamko la kizungu*, a European accent. (Cf. *taja, sema, lafudhi.*)

-tamu,* a. sweet, pleasant, nice, delightful—of all pleasures, esp. those of sense. *Sukari tamu*, sugar is sweet. *Maneno matamu*, agreeable speech. *Maji matamu*, fresh water, as opp. to salt water. *Tamu?* Is it nice? *Tamu* is also used as an adv., e.g. *kumemkalia tamu*, he has found it agreeable. **Tamutamu**, n. sweets, confectionery, &c. **Utamu**, n. (1) flavour, taste—in general; (2) sweet taste, sweetness, being agreeable to the sense or senses, pleasantness, charm. (Ar. طعم.)

Tamvua, n. *ma-*. See under **Chambua.**

Tana, v. See **Chana.**

Tanabahi,* v. See under **Nabihi.**

Tanadhari,* v. See under **Nadhari.**

Tanafusi,* v. See under **Nafasi.**

-tanashati,* a. clean, neat, well-dressed. **Mtanashati**, n. *wa-* a clean, fresh, well-dressed person. **Utanashati**, n. cleanness, freshness, neatness. (Ar. نشط be active, &c.).

Tanda, v. extend, spread, spread out, be spread out (over). The idea seems to be not of mere extension (*enea*) or dispersion (*tawanya*) but of something that is continuous and covers. Hence several uses, and a large number of derivative forms. *Mbingu zimetanda, kumetanda*, the sky is overcast. *Tanda dagaa*, catch *dagaa* by spreading a large piece of calico in the water, and then when it submerges, dragging it under a shoal of fish, as native women do. Rf. *jitanda*, stretch oneself across (upon, over)—also *jitanda nguo*, cover oneself with a cloth. Dur. **Tandaa**, be spread out over a large area, be open and wide, like a plain. Ps. **Tandwa.** St. **Tandika**—most commonly in an Act. sense, spread out (over), lay out (on), cover (with), e.g. *tandika mkeka kitandani*, spread a mat on the bed. Also *tandika kitanda*, make a bed. *Tandika punda*, harness a donkey, put saddle, &c., on. *Tandika nguo chini*, lay out clothes on the ground. *Tandika majamvi*, spread mats (as carpets), &c. *Wengi waliotandika chini*, many were laid low, i.e. killed. *Mungu ametandika mbingu na nchi*, God spread out the heavens and earth. Ps. of St. **Tandikwa.** Prep. of St. **Tandikia**, e.g. *waliwapa nyumba wakawatandikia*, they gave them houses, and furnished them with mats, &c., for them. Prep. **Tandia.** Cs. **Tandisha**, but usu. **Tandaza**, from *tandaa*, like *tanda, tandika*, but of special objects, e.g. *tandaza mtama*, spread out millet on a mat to dry in the sun, also *tandaza nguo*. Stc. **Tandama**, be in an extended position, be spread out, lie stretched out, e.g. of floating on the water, as a crocodile, log, &c. Prep. of Stc. **Tandamia.** Cs. of Stc. **Tandamisha.** Rp. of Stc. **Tandamana**, of several objects together. Dur. of Ps. **Tandawaa**, be stretched right out, i.e. as of a person reclining, lolling. *Watu wataka kupita, mbona umetandawaa hivyo?* people want to pass, why are you stretched right out in that manner? Cv. **Tandua**, take off (fold up, remove) what is laid on (spread out, &c.), and so of unfurnishing a bed or room, unharnessing an animal, &c. Ps. **Tanduliwa.** St. **Tanduka.** Prep. **Tandulia.** Cs. **Tanduza.** Cv. of Cs. (*tanza*) **Tanzua**, (1) open, uncover, part, i.e. of a curtain or screen.

Tanzua macho, open the eyes. *Tanzua jambo gumu*, explain a difficult matter. (2) get out of a trap made by a noose by slipping the noose. St. **Tanzuka**, (1) like *tanduka*. *Kumetanzuka*, it is clear, fair, fine, i.e. the clouds have dispersed. (2) fig. recover, e.g. *yule mtu alizirai na macho yake yalipomtanzuka . . .*, that man fainted, and when he came to himself . . ., i.e. when his eyes opened. *Mambo hayajatanzuka bado*, matters have not yet improved, i.e. not yet become clear. **Kitanda**, n. *vi-* a wooden frame for stretching something on, esp. a native bedstead, i.e. a frame consisting of two side-pieces (*mfumbati*), two end-pieces (*kitakizo*), resting on four legs (*tendegu, ma-*), and with cord or coconut fibre or plaited grass-strips interlaced across it. The head is called *mchago* or *kichago*, the space underneath (2–3 ft. from the ground) *mvungu*. The place where the body lies is called (*uchago*). Usually a mat only (*mkeka*) is spread on it, sometimes a mattress (*godoro*) and pillows (*mto*) with covers (*foronya*). *Kitanda cha mfumi*, a weaver's frame, a loom, parts and instruments of which are *mdoshi, faraka* or *mfariki, marufaa, kashabu, mladi* (cf. other kinds of bedstead, *ulili, samadari*). **Kitandawili**, n. *vi-* a riddle, conundrum, enigma, &c. (Perh. *ki-tanda-wili*, i.e. a net or web, &c., which catches two ways—cf. *kitendawili*, under *tenda*, some natives say it is one, and some the other.) The common word for propounding a riddle is *tega*, e.g. *Kitandawili!* Here is a riddle! *Tega!* Out with it! *Nyumba yangu kubwa haina taa*, my house is large, but has no lamp. (Ans.) *Kaburi*, the grave. **Kitandiko, n.** *vi-* a spreading, a thing spread, a mantle, anything worn as a covering. **Kitanzi**, n. *vi-* dim. small loop, snare, loop for button, &c. **Mtanda, n.** *wa-* one who spreads, governing a noun following, e.g. *mtanda dagaa*, &c. **Mtande**, n. *mi-* (1) something spread, or stretched out. Hence used of a frame of sticks, or a line on which clothes, &c., are hung to dry. Also a weaver's loom, more accurately called *kitanda cha mfumi*. (2) strip of flesh, or fish, hung up to dry in the sun or by a fire. Also of threads of the warp of a loom, the woof being *mshindio*. **Mtandio, n.** *mi-* a cloth worn by native women over their shoulders (sometimes *kitandio, vi-*). **Mtando, n.** *mi-* a spreading, a stretching out, &c. Also of what is spread out. **Tandabui, n.** (1) caul, i.e. the membrane covering the head of some children at birth (cf. *zalio*); (2) a spider's web (cf. *utando*); (3) used of imperfect sight, e.g. *macho yangu yameingia tandabui* (cf. *tanda* and *bui*, n. (B)). **Tandiko, n.** *ma-* something spread out, but usu. of mats, carpets, &c., e.g. *matandiko ya chumba yaliyotandikwa chini*, the mats with which the room was furnished. Also *matandiko ya kitanda*, bedding; and harness, accoutrements, but only of animals. **Tando, n.** *ma-* (1) something spread out, e.g. *tando la buibui*, a spider's web. *Tando* or *tandu la macho*, a film over the eye, causing blindness. (2) fungus, e.g. *uyoga usio na shina*, mushroom-like growth without stem. **Tanzi, n.** (— and *ma-*) something spread out, hence a loop, noose, slipknot, snare, trap worked by a string, e.g. *tanzi la ukambaa* (*la ugwe*), *la kutegea wanyama*, a noose of cord (or string) for trapping animals. *Tanzi la samaki*, a haul (catch, draught) of fish. *Tanzi la roho*, a halter. **Utando, n.** (*tando*), and **Utandu**, n. used to describe anything spread out, extended, stretched, e.g. (1) a veil, screen, coverlet, tapestry, hangings; (2) a spider's web, *utando wa buibui*; (3) sunset glow; (4) clouded sight, whether a film over the eyes (cf.

chamba cha jicho) or sheer drowsiness; (5) scum, crust, film, e.g. on milk, cream, or on a pot of cooked rice (cf. *ukoko*); (6) swarm of bees or locusts, &c.

Tandabelua,* n. See **Tanta.**

Tandabui, n. See under **Tanda.**

Tandala, n. the greater kudu.

Tandama, v., **Tandamana,** v., **Tandawaa,** v., **Tandaza,** v., **Tandika,** v., **Tandiko,** n. *ma-*, **Tando,** n. *ma-*. See under **Tanda.**

Tandu,* n. a centipede. (Cf. Pers. تندر a spider.)

Tandua, v. See under **Tanda.**

Tanga, n. *ma-* (1) a sail—of a vessel, of matting or canvas. *Tweka tanga,* set (hoist) sail. *Tua tanga,* lower sail. *Kunja tanga,* reef sail. *Matanga kati,* wind abeam. Obs. *tangambili,* of the period of changing winds between the two monsoons, also called *maleleji.* (2) a formal mourning—usually in the plur. *matanga,* lasting from three or four to ten days, during which friends sleep in the mourner's house. *Kaa* (*weka, andika*) *matanga,* remain in (arrange a) mourning. *Ondoa* (*vunja*) *matanga,* go out of (end a) mourning (cf. *msiba*). **Kitanga,** n. *vi-* a small piece of matting, usually circular, used as a praying mat (cf. *msala*), to lay out food on, or goods for sale.

Tanga, v. go to and fro, go from side to side, dawdle, loiter, stroll about, wander. Rd. **Tangatanga,** move in a listless, objectless way. Cs. **Tangisha,** e.g. take for a stroll, cause to idle, &c. Dur. **Tangaa,** be spread abroad, be in vogue, be current, become generally known, be published. *Jina lake limetangaa na ulimwengu,* his name is famous throughout the world. Cs. **Tangaza,** make known, publish abroad, advertise, proclaim. Prep. **Tangazia,** e.g. *amemtangazia aibu yake,* he made his dishonour known. Rp. **Tangasana.** **Kitango,** n. *vi-* gadding about, idling, loitering. **Mtanga,** n. *wa-*, **Mtangatanga,** n. *wa-* one who wanders idly and aimlessly about, an idler, loafer, common tourist, vagabond, tramp. So also **Mtangazaji,** n. *wa-*, **Mtangazi,** n. *wa-* one who makes generally known, proclaims, divulges. **Mtango,** n. *mi-* a loitering, strolling about, idling. **Tangazo,** n. *ma-* a notice, proclamation, advertisement. (Cf. *zurura, enea, vuma, ilani.*)

Tangamana, v. sometimes heard for *changamana,* which see.

Tangamano, n. *ma-* for *changamano,* which see.

Tangawizi, n. ginger, root of the plant, *mtangawizi.*

Tangaza, v., **Tangazo,** n. *ma-*. See under **Tanga,** v.

Tangi,* n. *ma-* a tank, either of metal, or wooden barrel, for storing water, &c. (Eng. tank.)

Tango, n. *ma-* (1) see under *Tanga,* v.; (2) a vegetable, a native cucumber, fruit of the *mtango*; (3) the eaves of a house.

Tangu, prep. since, from—with reference to a time, or less commonly, place, regarded as a starting-point. *Tangu lini alipokuja hapa?* How long ago was it that he came here? *Tangu miaka miwili* (*tangu zamani*), two years ago (a long time ago). *Tangu hapa hata huko,* from here to there. (Cf. *toka, kutoka* used as a prep. and *tangulia.*)

Tangua, v. annul, abolish, annihilate, invalidate, bring to nought, frustrate. *Tangua sheria,* cancel a law. *Tangua ahadi,* revoke a promise. *Tangua ndoa,* annul a marriage. *Tangua urafiki,* break off a friendship. St. **Tanguka.** **Kitanguo,** n. *vi-* act (means, way, &c.) of abolishing, of bringing about a former state of affairs, doing away, bringing to nothing. **Mtanguo,** n. *mi-* like *kitanguo.* **Tanguko,** n. *ma-* annulment, cancellation, anything cancelled or abolished. **Tanguo,** n. *ma-*

abolishing, abrogation, annulling, also annulment. (Prob. from same root as prec. and follg.)

Tangulia, v. (1) go before, go first, precede, take the lead; (2) be beforehand (with), anticipate, forestall. Sometimes *tangulia mbele* and *mbele ya*. *Alitangulia kuniambia*, he was the first to tell me, or he took the initiative in speaking to me. Cs. **Tanguliza**, e.g. cause to go before, send on in advance, prefer, give precedence to. *Tanguliza fedha*, make a payment in advance. *Kujitanguliza*, put yourself forward, hence, self-assertion. **Kitangulizi**, n. *vi-* (1) anything which causes forward movement or which goes first; (2) an odd number (cf. *witiri*). **Mtangulizi**, n. *wa-* one who goes before, leads the way, is pre-eminent or first in anything, and so a leader, ringleader, herald, forerunner, predecessor. **-tangulifu**, a. in advance, before others, but commonly fig. eminent, surpassing, of superior rank (quality). **Utangulizi**, n. *ma-* that which precedes, hence, foreword, introduction, preface. (Cf. *takadamu*, *tangu*, and *tangua*.)

Tani, n. (A) in the adverbial phrase, *kwa tani*, on the back—of position, and in *tanitani*, *kitanitani*, *matanitani*. (Cf. *kichalichali*, *kingalingali*.)

Tani,* n. (B) a ton (weight) adopted for use in text-books and school lessons. (Eng. ton.)

Tania,* v. be familiar with, treat with familiarity, chaff, treat as though of very near kin, or a very great friend. Rp. **Taniana**, treat each other with familiarity. **Mtani**, n. *wa-* one of a family, clan, or tribe, a kinsman, a relation, but not nearer than a cousin on the father's side. Often used in a loose way of a great friend, familiar friend, one with whom you can be on familiar terms; *watani* can abuse each other, or take each other's things, without there being a quarrel. **Utani**, n. kinship, clanship, membership in tribe or race, also in a general way, familiar friendship. *Fanya utani*, like *tania*. **Watani**, n. a person's home, habitation, fatherland, native village, country, &c. (Ar. وطن, reside in, the *wa-* treated as *ua-* of U class nouns, and a verb *tania* made from it.)

Tano, n. and a. *-tano*, five. *-a tano*, fifth. *Jumatano*, Wednesday. See *Juma*. Also sometimes heard for *tanu* or *tanuu*, which see.

Tanta,* n. sometimes heard with *belua*, i.e. *tantabelua*, a disturbance, row, wrangling. (Hind. تانتا, and cf. *belua*.)

Tanua, v. open wide, stretch apart, widen, expand, e.g. *tanua miguu*, take long strides; *tanua kinywa*, open the mouth wide; *tanua mashua*, push off a boat. Ps. **Tanuliwa**. St. and Pot. **Tanuka**. Prep. **Tanulia**. (Cf. *panua*, *tagaa*.)

Tanuru,* n. See under **Tanuu**.

Tanuu,* n., also **Tano**, **Tanu**, and **Tanuru**, native lime-kiln, i.e. limestone piled in a circular heap of logs and burnt. *Choma tanuu*, burn lime. (Ar. تنور.)

Tanzi, n. (— or *ma-*). See under **Tanda**.

Tanzia,* n. news of a death, announcement of a funeral. *Kumpa mkono wa tanzia*, to pay a visit of condolence to him. (Cf. *mbirambi*, *hani*. Ar. تعزية.)

Tanzu, n. *ma-* a bough, but usually *tawi*.

Tanzua, v., **Tanzuka**, v. See under **Tanda**.

Tao, n. *ma-* something curved, e.g. an arc, an arch, a bend of a river, a bay or inlet, the hem round the bottom of a native dress (*kanzu*), e.g. *njia inafanya matao*, the road is winding. *Mwendo wa matao*, (1) the gait of a person walking with bent shoulders or a stoop; (2) a rolling, swaggering gait. **Kitao**, n. *vi-* dim. (Cf. *pindi*, *mzingo*, *kunjo*, *kombo*.)

Tapa, n. *ma-* leaf of the *mvumo* palm, sometimes used as an umbrella.

Tapa, v. (1) shiver, tremble, shudder, jump about convulsively, because of cold, fear, also as a man does when struggling in the water in danger of being drowned; (2) be startled; (3) prevaricate, change one's story, &c., because of fear or because of being confused, &c. Often Rd. *tapatapa*. *Tapa kwa baridi*, shiver with cold. *Mwili wanitapa*, my body is shuddering. (4) bestir oneself, Rf. *jitapa*, jump about—for display. Prep. **Tapia**, (1) go forward quickly or excitedly as though following after something; (2) desire very much, be eager, be greedy. **Kitapo**, n. *vi-* shivering, shaking, trembling, quivering—from cold, fear, illness, &c., e.g. the cold stage of fever. **Mtapo**, n. *mi-* like *kitapo*.

Tapakaa, v. be scattered about, be spread abroad, be here and there, infest, dotted about, e.g. of the stars in the sky, of a flood, robbers, &c. (Cf. *tapanya*, *enea*, *tawanyika*.)

Tapanya, v. scatter about, disperse, throw away, waste, dissipate. *Tapanyamali*, be prodigal. St. **Tapanyika**, e.g. of water in a flood. Rp. **Tapanyikana**, of people dispersing in different directions. Cs. **Tapanyisha**. (Cf. *tapakaa*, *tawanya*, *poteza*.)

Tapika, v. vomit, be sick. Cs. **Tapisha**. **Mtapishi**, n *mi-* an emetic. **Mtapisho**, n. *mi-* a kind of shrub, *Synaptolepis*. **Tapishi**, n. *ma-* (1) vomit; (2) fig. abuse, filthy words. **Tapisho**, n. *ma-* an emetic. **Utapishi**, n. *ma-* (1) causing to vomit, action of an emetic; (2) vomit.

Tapo,* n. *ma-* (1) a lot (troop, number) of men or animals—esp. of a division (detachment, regiment) of fighting men. (A *tapo* would be part of a *jeshi* or *kundi*.) (Turk. توب a division of troops.) (2) a kind of food, rather like the areca-nut (*popoo*) favoured by the Ngazija.

Taraa,* conj. if. *Taraa ukimwona*, if you see him. (Cf. *kama*. Ar. طرا to happen to.)

Taraba,* v. rule by violence. (Ar. ترعاب.)

Tarabe,* n. used to describe a door or window consisting of two valves. (Ar. درب large gate.)

Tarabu,* n. music of the *gambusi*, *zeze*, &c., accompanied by singers. **Mutribu**, n. a player of the *gambusi*, *zeze*, &c. (Ar. طرب.)

Taradadi,* v. (1) waver, hesitate, fluctuate, go here and there, wander about, as one looking for work; (2) turn over and over in the mind. Sometimes used as a n. indecision, weakness of intellect. (Ar. تردّد.)

Taradhia,* v. (1) see under *radhi*; (2) make friendly remonstrances with a person, admonish, reproach. (Ar. تعريض.)

Tarafa, n. and **Tarafu**,* n. a district, parish; part, business, duty, work, task. **Mintarafu**, prep. concerning, about, anent. (Ar. طرف.)

Taraja,* n. See **Taraji**.

Tarajali,* n. an apprentice, for the commoner *mwanafunzi*. (Ar. ترجّل look like a man.)

Taraji,* v. hope, be confident, expect. Ps. **Tarajiwa**. St. and Pot. **Tarajika**. Prep. **Tarajia**, e.g. hope for (about, in, &c.). **Taraja**, n. *ma-* hope, expectation. (Cf. *tumaini*. Ar. ترجى.)

Taraju,* n. a balance, pair of scales, but usu. *mizani*. (Pers. ترازو.)

Tarakanya,* v. search for, by moving things about and looking under them, &c., also of searching for a right word to explain, &c. (? Ar. طرق be piled close together.)

Tarakibu,* n. See under **Rakibu**.

Tarakiki,* a. narrow, slender, for the common *-embamba*. (Ar. ترّق.)

Tarakimu,* n. written numeral, figure. (Ar. ترقيم.)

Tarare, n. a plant sprung up from seed not planted on purpose, which has seeded itself. (Cf. *mabotea*.)

Taratibu,* n. See under **Ratibu.**

Tarawehi,* n. a long prayer said at *Isha*, the Muhammadan hour of prayer after sunset, during the month of Ramadhan. (Ar. تراوح.)

Taraza,* n. border or edging, woven on to turbans or waistcloths, giving the effect of a narrow ornamental braid of silk. **Tarizi,** v. weave a border (to), make an embroidered edging (on). **Tarizo,** n. also sometimes *darizi*, like *taraza*. (Ar. طرز.)

Tarazaki,* v. same as *ruzuku*, which see.

Tarazia,* n. a kind of dance in which the partners *peana chambi*, i.e. one of each sex leaves the ring or line of dancers and meet in the centre, and, after going through certain figures, return again to their places. (Cf. *chando, chobea*. ? Ar. تراجع turning back, returning; from the movement.)

Tarbushi,* n. a tarboosh, a fez, red cap with tassel. (Cf. *kofia*. Ar. طربوش.)

Tarehe,* n. date, annals, chronicle, journal, history, esp. of date of birth, e.g. *tarehe yako imo ndani ya hirizi*, your date (of birth) is inside the charm. (Ar. تاريخ.)

Tari,* n. (1) a kind of small drum; (2) a kind of dance used in exorcism of spirits; (3) trembling, shaking. (Pers. تار.)

Tariki,* n. road, path, way, for the usu. *njia*. (Ar. طريق.)

Tarishi,* n. *ma-* a messenger, postman, courier, swift runner. (Cf. *rugaruga*. Ar. روغ act slyly.)

Tarizi, v., **Tarizo,*** n. See under **Taraza.**

Taruma,* n. *ma-* (1) any piece of wood used to stiffen or strengthen a structure or framework, e.g. ledge, support, strut, spoke of a wheel, rib of a vessel, thwart, &c.; (2) tribal marks, i.e. tattoo marks on the face. (Prob. from the same root as *darumeti*, which see, i.e. Ar. دعامة, an *r* being interposed between *'ain* and *alif* on analogy with two *a*'s. Cf. also *taumu*, in which no *r* appears.)

Tarumbeta,* n. a trumpet or similar instrument. (Eng. 'trumpet' or Port. *tarambote*.)

Tasa,* n. a small metal vessel, cup, jug, mug, basin, saucer, i.e. spittoon, vessel for washing hands before and after meals, &c. (Ar. طاس.)

Tasa,* v. (A) more common in Mombasa and north of Dar-es-Salaam, used with negat. pfxs. only, but not changing the final *a* to *i* in the Present, and only as a kind of auxiliary before another verb in the Infinitive. Be beforehand with, manage (to), get (to), finish (doing), what the following verb implies, e.g. *sitasa kuandika*, I have not yet written.

Tasa, v. (B). See under **Tata.**

Tasa,* a. barren—of any living creature. **Utasa,** n. barrenness, sterility—of produce generally. (Ar. دس not grow, not increase.)

Tasawari,* v. be fully able, be competent. **Tasawari,** n. anything capable of accomplishment. (Ar. تصيير causing to be.)

Tasbihi,* n. (1) praise, ascription of praise to God; (2) a Muhammadan rosary, for recording praises and prayers. *Sali tasbihi*, prayers by a rosary. (Cf. *himidi, sifu*. Ar. تسبيح.)

Tashtiti,* v. tease, provoke. **Tashtiti,** n. and a. teasing, provocation, provocative, harsh, &c. (Ar. تشدید severity, &c.)

Tashwishi,* n. See under **Shawishi.**

Tasi, n. (1) a kind of fish, also called *tafi*; (2) a thing used for cleaning rope after it has been twisted and made.

Tasifida,* v. and n. See under **Safidi.**

Tasihili,* adv. and n. See under **Sahala.**

Taslimu,* n. See under **Salamu.**

Tasliti,* v. See under **Salata.**

Tasua, v. See under **Tata,** v.

Taswira,* n. See under **Sawiri.**

Tata, v. tangle, complicate, confuse. St. **Tatika,** be in a tangle, be complicated, be in confusion. Prep. **Tatia,** (1) make a tangle of; (2) wind up in a skein or ball; (3) puzzle, perplex, make difficulties, e.g. *tatia uzi kijitini,* wind thread on a stick. *Tatia kilemba,* arrange the folds of a turban. Also used of a snake coiling round its prey. Rp. of Prep. **Tatiana.** Cs. (1) **Tasa,** perplex, puzzle, impede, but usu. Cs. (2) **Tatiza,** perplex, puzzle, make curious, intrigue. Rp. **Tatana,** be a tangle, be puzzled, e.g. of interlacing foliage, of tangled wool or thread, of confused statements. Prep. of Rp. **Tatania.** Cs. **Tatanisha,** entangle, complicate, puzzle. Cv. of Rp. **Tatanua,** (1) unravel, unwind; (2) clear up a complication, difficulty, &c. Cv. **Tatua,** (1) disentangle, cut a knot, solve a difficulty; (2) tear, rend, cleave, rip open or apart, e.g. *tatua nguo,* tear clothes (cf. *rarua, pasua, tumbua*). Ps. **Tatuliwa.** St. and Pot. **Tatuka,** be torn, split, rent, &c. Prep. **Tatukia.** Cs. **Tatulisha.** Cv. of Cs. **Tasua,** explain, reveal, make plain. Ps. **Tasuliwa,** e.g. *mtoto hatasuliwi ulimi, akiwa na kitembe,* a child cannot make his speech clear, if he has a lisp. Prep. **Tasulia. Kitata,** n. *vi-* (1) tangle, complication, mess; (2) an impediment in the speech, lisp, &c. *Ana kitata,* he has a lisp. (3) *kitata cha asali,* honeycomb. **Mtatio,** n. *mi-* (1) a coiling (of cord), winding (of thread), an entanglement or mess; (2) that which intrigues, puzzles, excites curiosity, &c. **Mtatizo,** n. *mi-* same as *tatizo,* see under. **Tata,** n. *ma-* usu. in the plur. *matata,* tangle, mess, difficulty, perplexity, &c. *Tata la uzi,* tangled thread. *Tata la maneno,* a puzzling statement. *Matata hayaishi kwake,* he is always in trouble, or he is always causing trouble. **Tatizo,** n. *ma-* entanglement, complication, difficulty. **Utasi,** n. inability or disinclination to speak, an impediment of the speech, being tongue-tied (cf. *kitata* and *tasua* above). **Utata,** n. (*tata*) a kind of wicker fence used for enclosing and catching fish (cf. *uzio*). (Bantu *-tata,* entangle, cf. also Ar. تتع stick, get entangled, confused in speech.)

Tataga, v. (1) make a crossing, esp. with or by means of something, i.e. a tree placed across a river as a bridge, get across, also lay across, as of a tree across a river; (2) walk quickly, i.e. taking long strides; (3) cross by holding on to something, i.e. of holding the arm supports of a bridge when it shakes, &c. **Mtatago,** n. *mi-* (1) a tree placed so as to bridge or dam a stream; something laid astride or astraddle; (2) a going across, gait with long strides, &c. (Cf. *tagaa, ulalo.*)

-tatai,* a. cunning, deceitful. (Ar. تطو.)

Tatana, v., **Tatanisha,** v., **Tatanua,** v., **Tatia,** v., **Tatizo,** n. *ma-*. See under **Tata.**

Tatarika, v. (1) chatter, gabble; (2) crackle, as maize, &c., when being roasted or fried.

Tatu, n. and **-tatu,** a. three. *-a tatu,* third (cf. Ar. *thelatha,* also sometimes used). **Utatu,** n. (1) being triple, threefoldness, trinity; (2) a third part, e.g. *kibaba cha utatu,* a third part of a *pishi,* the usual *kibaba* being *cha nne,* i.e. four to the *pishi.*

Tatua, v. See under **Tata.**

Taufiki,* n. guidance and grace of God, fulfilment of one's wishes, success, prosperity. (Ar. توفيق.)

Taumu,* n. *ma-* prop, shore, support —for a vessel ashore (cf. *tegemeo, mwega.* Ar. دعامه, see also *darumeti* and note under *taruma.*)

Tauni,* n. plague, pestilence, an epidemic, usu. refers to bubonic plague. (Cf. *ugonjwa, maradhi.* Ar. طاعون.)

Taurati,* n. See **Torati.**

Tausi,* n. a peacock, also sometimes called *kibibi.* (Ar. طاؤوس.)

Tawa,* n. (1) a frying-pan, saucepan; (2) a kind of fish not considered good eating by Europeans. (Pers. تاوا.)

Tawa, v. (1) remain indoors, live in seclusion, esp. for a moral or religious object, and so (2) not gad about, live a quiet, moral, religious life. Prep. **Tawia.** Cs. **Tawisha,** e.g. *kijana mwanamke apatapo miaka sita hutawishwa,* a girl when six years old is generally confined to the house. **Kitawa,** n. and adv. devout life (act, character), in a religious way. *Nguo za kitawa,* dress of a devotee, habit of a monk, &c. *Fanya kitawa,* act as a devotee. *Kaa kitawa,* lead a secluded life. **Mtawa,** n. *wa-* (1) one who stays at home, keeps indoors, and so, (2) one who leads a moral self-controlled life, a recluse, a devout religious person. **-tawa,** a. remaining indoors, choosing seclusion, devout, religious. **Utawa.** n. (1) staying in the house, seclusion; (2) a chaste, religious, pious life and character. (? Ar. طوى conceal, fast of one's own accord.)

Tawadha,* v. perform ceremonial ablution—esp. as to the feet, i.e. *tawadha miguu.* (Ar. توضا.)

Tawafa,* n. (1) a candle; (2) a candelabrum. (Cf. *kibatali, mshumaa.*)

Tawakali,* v. See under **Wakala.**

Tawala,* v. become ruler, govern, rule. Ps. **Tawaliwa.** St. **Tawalika.** Prep. **Tawalia.** Cs. **Tawalisha,** but usu. **Tawaza,** e.g. cause to rule, instal as ruler, set on the throne, celebrate the coronation of. **Mtawala,** n. *wa-*, **Mtawalaji,** n. *wa-*, **Mtawali,** n. *wa-* a ruler, a governor. **Utawala,** n. (1) rule, reign, &c.; (2) discipline, i.e. as exercised by a teacher, &c. (Cf. *liwali, miliki.* Ar. تولى.)

Tawanya, v. scatter abroad, disperse, distribute, dissipate, throw away, e.g. *tawanya mbegu* (*mali, adui*), scatter seed (money, enemies). Ps. **Tawanywa.** St. **Tawanyika.** Prep. **Tawanyia.** Cs. **Tawanyisha.** **Mtawanya,** n. *wa-* one who scatters, and so, one who spends freely, an open-handed, liberal person. **Mtawanyo,** n. *mi-* act (manner, &c.) of scattering, of dispersing, of distributing wholesale. **Tawanyiko,** n. *ma-* scattering, wasting, throwing away, dispersion.

Tawasufi,* v. and n. See under **Wasifu.**

Tawaza,* v. See under **Tawala,** v.; sometimes also heard for *tawadha.*

Tawi, n. *ma-* (1) bough, branch (of a tree); (2) stem with growing fruit or grain, bunch, cluster, ear, e.g. *tawi la nazi,* bunch of coco-nuts. *Tawi la mzabibu* (*la mtende*), branch of a vine (of a date-palm). *Ncha* (*shina*) *ya tawi,* tip (stem) of a branch (bunch). **Kitawi,** n. *vi-* dim. **Utawi,** n. (*tawi* and *ma-*) same as *tawi.* (Cf. *tanzu.*)

Tawili,* a. long, tall, for the common *-refu.* **Tawilisha,** v. make long. Ps. **Tawilishwa,** e.g. *shauri hili* *limetawilishwa sana,* this case is taking a long time. **Tuili,** v. be prolonged, be belated. Cs. **Tuiliza,** make late, delay, prolong, like *tawalisha.* **Tuili,** a. long, delayed, &c. (Ar. طويل and طال.)

Tawireni.* See under **Punga,** v. (B).

Taya, n. *ma-* jaw, jaw-bone. *Tia hatamu tayani mwa punda,* put the bridle on the donkey's jaw. **Kitaya,** n. *vi-* dim. but used in the same way as *taya.* **Utaya,** n. bone of the jaw.

Taya,* v. reproach, rebuke, blame. **Tayo,** n. *ma-* reproach, rebuke. (Cf. *taya,* n., and *shutumu, laumu, suta.* Ar. تعيير.)

Tayari,* a. ready, prepared, at hand. *Fanya tayari,* make ready, prepare. **Utayari,** n. readiness, preparedness. (Pers. and Hind. تيار.)

Tayo, n. *ma-*. See under **Taya,** v.

Taz, abbreviation for *tazama,* look at, see.

Tazama, v. look (at), gaze (at), fix the eyes (on), contemplate, examine, observe, test. Ps. **Tazamwa.** St. and Pot. **Tazamika,** e.g. (1) be looked at; (2) be fit to be looked at, be desirable (pleasant) to the eyes, be noteworthy. Rf. *jitazama,* look at one's face in a glass. Prep. **Tazamia,** (1) consult a divining board, take the omens; (2) look into, examine closely, inspect, review, look with, see with. *Darubini ya kutazamia,* a telescope to look through. *Kioo cha kujitazamia,* a glass for looking at oneself with, i.e. a looking-glass, mirror. *Tazamia kazi,* examine work. (3) look forward to, expect. Ps. of Prep. **Tazamiwa,** be examined, looked at (by, with, &c.) be expected. Cs. **Tazamisha,** e.g. attract the eye, draw attention, be attractive (to). Rp. **Tazamana,** look at each other. **Mtazamo,** n. *mi-* an act of looking, gazing. **Tazamo,** n. *ma-* look, glance, gaze. (Cf. *angalia, ona, chungulia, kagua.*)

Teende, n. See **Tende** (2).

-tefu, a soft. *Chakula kitefu,* soft food.

Tega, v. (1) set ready, put in position, prepare, esp. of a trap, and so (2) snare, entrap, decoy, catch, and (3) fig. try to deceive, beguile; also (4) used of preparing certain kinds of charms, witchcraft, e.g. *tega mtego,* set a trap. (5) belch. See under **Teuka.** *Tega sikio,* listen, give ear to, prepare to hear. *Tega kitandawili,* propound a riddle—the challenge being *Kitandawili!* here is a riddle—and the reply, *Tega,* propound it, let us hear it. *Alijitega na uta wake,* he put himself ready with his bow. *Tega ndege kwa tanzi,* snare birds with a noose. Ps. **Tegwa.** St. and Pot. **Tegeka.** Prep. **Tegea.** Cs. **Tegesha.** Rp. **Tegana.** Cv. **Tegua,** let a trap go off, remove a snare or spell, take away what was set ready or specially placed, take off the fire, put out of joint, sprain. Thus: *tegua mtambo,* let off a spring-trap. *Tegua uchawi,* take off a spell —also *tegua tego.* *Tegua mguu,* sprain the ankle. Ps. **Teguliwa.** St. **Teguka.** Prep. **Tegulia.** **Mtego,** n. *mi-* a trap, snare, gin—used of all kinds of devices for snaring animals and birds. **Tego,** n. *ma-* amplic. of *mtego,* a powerful charm, capable of causing disease and death. There are many kinds of *tego,* e.g. *tego la mkeka,* the charm of the sleeping-mat, which is said to cause the mat to stick to the back of a woman who commits adultery. *Tego la mbwa,* which is said to cause a man who commits adultery to be held as a dog is held after copulation. *Tego la kisu,* which is said to have the same effect, and the man and woman committing adultery are so held until the husband who has had the charm prepared takes his knife out of its sheath, &c. **Tezo,** n. *ma-* harm, hurt, &c., caused by witchcraft. (Cf. *nasa guia, kamata,* and dist. *teso.*) (2) carpenter's adze. See under **Tezo.**

Tege, n. *ma-*. See **Chege.**

Tegemea, v. (1) lean upon, rest on, be propped upon; (2) trust (to), find protection (in), rely (upon), e.g. *alimtegemea mkono*, he leaned on his arm. *Nyumba inategemea mti*, the house is supported by a tree. Also with *kwa*, e.g. *tegemea kwa Mungu*, trust to Providence. Ps. **Tegemewa.** Cs. **Tegemeza**, e.g. cause to rest on, prop up, support, buttress, protect, sustain. *Tegemeza chombo*, prop or shore up a vessel. *Tegemeza miguu*, rest one leg on the other. **Tegemeo**, n. *ma-* prop, buttress, support, protection. *Katika mategemeo yangu, hakikupati kitu*, under my protection nothing can get at you. (Cf. *egama, nguzo, himaya, tunza, gadimu.*)

Tego, n. *ma-*. See under **Tega.**

Tegu, n. *ma-* a tapeworm.

Tegua, v., **Teguka**, v. See under **Tega.**

Tehemu,* v. (1) be beaten, overcome, unable, i.e. on account of exhaustion, weariness, &c.; (2) sometimes heard for *tuhuma*, suspect. (Cf. *shindwa* and *shuku.* Ar. تهم.)

Teitei,* n. *ma-* frock, gown.

Teka, v. (1) take, take up, carry off—of water from a well, e.g. *teka maji kisimani*, draw water at a well; (2) plunder, ransack, e.g. *teka mji*, plunder a town. *Teka nchi*, ravage a country. *Teka watu na ng'ombe*, carry off people and cattle. Often *teka nyara*. Ps. **Tekwa**, (1) *kisima kilichotekwa maji*, a well from which water was drawn. *Maji yamekwenda kutekwa kisimani* (some one has gone to draw water at the well), lit. water has gone to be drawn at the well. (2) *tumetekwa*, we are prisoners of war. Prep. **Tekea.** D.Prep. **Tekelea.** Cs. **Tekeza** and **Tekeleza**, Inten. usu. with the meaning of attract, hold spellbound. *Fulani alitutekeleza kwa usemi wake*, So-and-so held us spellbound by his eloquence. Rp. **Tekana.** Ps. of Prep. **Tekewa**, e.g. *tekewa na akili*, be bewildered, lose one's senses, i.e. be robbed of one's senses (like *potewa, rukwa na akili*). **Mateka**, n. plur. (seldom used in the sing.) (1) booty, prey, plunder, and esp. (2) captive in war. **Mteka**, n. *wa-* one who takes away, e.g. *mteka maji*, a water drawer. *Mteka mateka*, one who captures booty, &c.

Tekanya, v. *tekanya miguu*, cross the legs.

Teke, n. *ma-* a kick. *Piga teke*, kick.

Teke, a., also **-teke** and **Teketeke**, (1) soft, yielding, flabby, flaccid; (2) weak, feeble. *Nyama teke*, tender meat. *Mtu teke*, a soft, weak-spirited person. *Muhindi mteke*, maize in a soft, half-ripe state. *Tunda teke*, a soft, over-ripe fruit. Riddle: *Teketeke huzaa gumugumu na gumugumu huzaa teketeke.* Answer: *Mahindi machanga na mahindi makavu*, i.e. the soft bears hard things, and the hard things bear soft. Answer: unripe maize and ripe maize. The meaning being that generation succeeds generation.

Tekea, v. See under **Teka.**

Tekelea, v. (1) arrive (at), reach, come to; (2) be accomplished, be carried through, come to its end, e.g. *wakati umetekelea*, the time has come. *Ahadi imetekelea*, the promise is fulfilled. Ps. **Tekelewa.** Cs. **Tekeleza**, fulfil, execute, carry out. Sometimes *tekeza* is heard. **Tekelezo**, n. *ma-* a fulfilment, a carrying out or accomplishing of a task, promise, &c. (Cf. *fika, timiza.*)

Tekenya, v. tickle. Ps. **Tekenywa.** Rp. **Tekenyana.** **Tekenya**, n. *ma-* a jigger—a burrowing flea, usu. called *funza*. (B. *-tekenya*, shake, tickle.)

Teketa, v. (1) gnaw, as a rat, crunch with the teeth; (2) increase the size of a hole by turning a knife or tool inside of it.

Teketea, v. be consumed, be destroyed, be ruined—commonly in the literal sense and by fire, i.e. *teketea moto* or *kwa moto*, be burnt up—but also of the effects of a storm, *mashamba yote yameteketea*, all the plantations have been destroyed. Cs. **Teketeza**, burn, destroy by fire, ruin. **Uteketevu**, n. destroying, being destroyed, destruction—esp. as by fire, being utterly consumed. **Uteketezo**, n. destruction, burning.

Teketeza, v. See under **Teketea**.

Tekewa, v. See under **Teka**.

Tekeza, v. for *tekeleza*. See under **Teka** and **Tekelea**.

Tekua, v. break down, break up, undermine. **Kiteku**, n. *vi-* an iron tool—for breaking up floors, digging up stones, &c., pick-axe. (Cf. *mtaimbo, sululu*.)

Tele,* n. plenty, abundance, and a. plentiful, many, much, abundant. *Maji tele* or *ya tele*, plenty of water. *Alimpa tele*, he gave him a quantity. (Cf. *-ingi, maridhawa*. Ar. طل abundance.)

Telea, v. come (go) down, descend, disembark, but usu. in the form *telemka*, see below. Cs. **Teleza**, e.g. (1) cause to come down, cause to fall; and so (2) be slippery. Also (3) inten. slip, slide, fall by slipping. *Aliteleza kwa miguu akaanguka*, his feet slipped and fell. *Nchi inateleza*, the ground is slippery. D.Cs. **Telezesha**, cause to slip, make slide. Cv. of Stc. **Telemua**, cause to go down (fall, slip), pull down, &c. St. **Telemka**, go down, descend, slope downwards, run (slide, fall) down a steep place. Cs. **Telemsha**, let down, lower. **Kitelemsho**, n. *vi-* anything which causes a downward movement, hence adopted for the flat sign in music. **Mtelemko**, n. *mi-* a going down, descent, slope. **Telemko**, n. *ma-* act (manner, place, &c.) of going down, descent, slope, declivity, hill, fall of the ground, downward tendency. **Utelezi**, n. a slippery place, slipperiness, anything slippery. (Cf. *shua, angua*.)

Teleka, n. a swallow. (Cf. *shore*.)

Teleka, v. (1) put on the fire—both of cooking-pot and the food in it. Hence (2) cook, boil (water), prepare food. Ps. **Telekwa**. Prep. **Telekea**, e.g. *chungu cha kutelekea maji*, a pot to boil water in. Cs. **Telekeza**, (1) cause to put on the fire, get cooking done, get a meal prepared. *Tulipumzika na kutelekeza*, we rested and had a meal prepared for us. (2) leave, e.g. *tulimtelekeza huko*, we left him there. Cv. **Telekua**, also **Tekua**, take off the fire.

Telemka, v., **Telemko**, n. *ma-*, **Telemua**, v., **Teleza**, v. See under **Telea**.

Teli,* n. gold thread, gold braid. Also *teli ya dhahabu*, gold thread, *teli ya fedha*, silver thread. (Cf. *zari, kigwe, ugwe*. Pers. تله gold fringe or wire.)

Telki,* n. the quick ambling gait of a donkey, half walk, half run. *Enda telki*, step quickly, go at a trot or run. (Hindu دلكي.)

Tema, v. (A) cut, slash, cut up, cut in strips, e.g. with a knife or tool. *Tema kuni* (*miwa*), cut firewood (sugar-cane). *Tema nakshi*, carve. *Tema ulimi*, cut a tenon. Ps. **Temwa**. St. **Temeka**. Prep. **Temea**. Cs. **Temesha**. **Mtema**, n. *wa-*, **Mtemi**, n. *wa-* one who cuts. **Mtemo**, n. *mi-* act (style, &c.) of cutting. **Temo**, n. *ma-* amplic. (Cf. *kata, chanja, pasua*.)

Tema, v. (B) spit out, expectorate. *Tema mate* (*kikohozi*), spit saliva (phlegm). Ps. **Temwa**. St. **Temeka**. Prep. **Temea**. Cs. **Temesha**. **Mtema**, n. *wa-*, **Mtemi**, n. *wa-* one who expectorates. **Mtemo**, n. *mi-* spitting, expectoration.

Tembe, n. (1) a full-grown hen, ready to begin to lay; (2) a flat-roofed house, such as are built in places where thatching and poles suitable for thatching are not obtainable.

Tembea, v. go about, take a walk, stroll, wander, take exercise, go on a tour—usu. for pleasure, but also of a business round. Often used of a loose, unprincipled, immoral way of living, e.g. *amekwenda tembea*, he has gone for a walk. *Akili zake zatembea*, his mind is wandering. Prep. **Tembelea**, e.g. go to visit, call on, walk about in, &c. Rf. *jitembelea*, go for a stroll, go on a pleasure trip. *Fimbo ya kutembelea*, a fancy walking-stick. Rp. **Tembeleana**, call on each other, be on visiting terms. Cs. **Tembeza**, cause to walk about—and so, hawk about for sale, advertise, parade, make a show of, send (employ) to sell goods, show (a stranger) round the town, &c. Prov. *Chema chajiuza, kibaya chajitembeza*, a good thing sells itself, a bad thing is advertised, hawked about. **Mtembezaji**, n. *wa-*, **Mtembezi**, n. *wa-* (1) one who walks about for pleasure or exercise rather than business, an idler, a pleasure-seeker, a tourist, &c. Prov. *Mtembezi ala miguu yake*, one who travels for pleasure lives off his feet. (2) *mtembezi wa bidhaa*, one who hawks goods for sale, a pedlar, a commercial traveller; (3) often in the sense of an immoral, unsteady, gadabout person. **Tembezi**, n. *ma-* but usu. in the plural, *matembezi*, (1) walk, stroll, tour, walking exercise, &c.; (2) gadding about, loose, immoral living, &c. **Utembezi**, n. *ma-* (1) offering for sale, advertising, exhibition of goods—but commonly (2) walking about, like *matembezi*.

Tembo, n. (1) an elephant (cf. *ndovu*). *Mkono wa tembo* (or *mkonga*), trunk of an elephant (also the name of a kind of banana); (2) palm wine, the fermented sap of the coco-nut tree.

Temsi.* n. filigree work. (Ar. تماسّ 'touching one another' = close work.)

Tena,* adv. and conj. then, secondly, further, in addition—also, next, still again, afterwards. A common connective of sentences, like *hata* and *na*, denoting sequence, succession, repetition. *Nimesema tena na tena*, I have said again and again. *Na tena?* and then? What next? *Akampiga tena*, and he hit him again, a second time. (From Egypt. Ar. تانى second, other, again, also, &c., or تن equal, similar, or ثنى repeat, do a second time.)

Tenda, v. do, act, practice. The most common and comprehensive word denoting action, operation, use of energy or force. Often syn. with *fanya*, e.g. *tenda kazi, fanya kazi, tenda vema, fanya vema*, but also broadly contrasted with it, as *do* with *make*, action or operation with production. See *fanya*. The direct stem *tenda*, when used with a direct personal object, denotes not only direct acting upon, or treatment of, but also commonly unfavourable action or bad treatment (cf. a similar use of the Dir. stems *fanya, sema, amba*), and sometimes even bewitch, esp. in the Ps. which see, in contrast to the Prep. form, implying favourable action and treatment, e.g. *akutendaye, mtende*, do harm to him who does harm to you. *Sungura amenitenda leo*, the hare has done (what he liked to) me to-day. Rf. *jitenda*, sometimes Act. as pretend to be, make onself. Ps. **Tendwa**, e.g. (1) *ametendwa mengi*, he has endured much ill treatment; (2) be bewitched. *Fulani ametendwa*, So-and-so has been bewitched. *Ugonjwa wa kutendewa*, sickness caused by witchcraft. St. and Pot. **Tendeka**, e.g. be done, be practicable, and hence Cs. **Tendekeza**, i.e. cause to be practicable, and Rf. *jitendekeza*, (1) get to be able to do, learn by practice, achieve; (2) make a display, show off an achievement. Prep. **Tendea**, e.g. do to (for, on behalf of, with, in, against)—commonly of favourable treatment (see above). Rp. of Prep. **Tendeana.** Cs. **Tendesha** and **Tendeza.** Rp. **Tendana.** **Kitendawili,** n. *vi-* (or *kitandawili?*) riddle, enigma, puzzle, charade, conundrum. The common word for propounding a riddle is *tega,* e.g. *Kitendawili!* Here is a riddle! *Tega!* Out with it! *Nyumba yangu kubwa, haina taa,* my house is large, but has no lamp. (Ans.) *Kaburi,* the grave (? from *ki-tenda-wili,* i.e. *pili,* acting in two ways, but see under *tanda,* v.). **Kitende,** n. *vi-* a person's house, home, surroundings, environment, i.e. all that he has accomplished and prepared (cf. *makao, mastakimu*). **Kitendo,** n. *vi-* act, deed, exploit. **Mtenda,** n. *wa-* a doer, e.g. *mtenda maovu,* an evil worker. **Mtendaji,** n. *wa-* an active (energetic, enterprising, pushing) person. **Mtendo,** n. *mi-* a doing, mode of acting, performing, accomplishing. **Mtenzi,** n. *wa-* one who does things, carries on work, follows a trade, an active, hard-working person. **Tendo,** n. *ma-* (1) amplic. of *kitendo*; (2) *ugonjwa wa matendo,* illness caused by witchcraft. **Utendaji,** n. activity, energy, facility in doing. **Utende,** n. witchcraft (cf. *uchawi*). **Utenzi,** n. activity, action, work, operation, but more commonly this is *utendaji.* (Cf. *bidii, juhudi.*)

Tende, n. (1) fruit of the date palm, *mtende,* a date. Prov. *Rudisha tende Manga,* send dates back to Arabia—of proverbial folly, as dates are largely imported from Arabia. (2) also *teende,* elephantiasis.

Tendegu, n. *ma-* leg of a native bedstead. (Cf. *kitanda.*)

Tendeka, v., **Tendekeza,** v. See under **Tenda.**

Tendeti, n. a kind of pastry. (Cf. *andazi, kipopoo.*)

Tendo, n. *ma-*. See under **Tenda.**

Tenga, n. *ma-* (1) a sea monster, a very large kind of flat-fish with a long tail; (2) a net or crate for carrying things in, slung on a pole between two people, prob. from *tenga,* v. (A).

Tenga, v. (A) separate, set (put, move, take) apart (aside), remove, withdraw, divide off. Rf. *jitenga,* withdraw oneself, move out of the way. Ps. **Tengwa.** St. and Pot. **Tengeka.** Prep. **Tengea.** Cs. **Tengesha.** Rp. **Tengana.** Cv. **Tengua,** (1) separate, &c., as *tenga*; (2) turn aside, go on one side; (3) correct proofs for printing. St. **Tenguka,** be on one side, fall over on one side. **Mtenga,** n. *wa-* governing a noun following, one who separates, &c. **Mtengo,** n. *mi-* a separating, a dividing off, &c. **Mtengwa,** n. *wa-* one who is divided off, separated, put aside, set apart, devoted (to a work or occupation). **Utengo,** n. act (manner, place, time, &c.) of withdrawal, retirement, separation, exclusion, &c.

Tenga, v. (B) alight, as a bird on a branch—usu. *tua.*

Tenge, n. (1) crookedness, e.g. *mti huu una tenge,* this pole is crooked, it has a curve in it; (2) confusion, stir. (Cf. *kombo, ghasia, fujo, wasiwasi.*)

Tengea, v., **Tengelea,** v., **Tengeleza,** v., &c., sometimes heard for *tengenea* and its derivatives, see note under prec.

Tengemaa, v. settle down completely, be at peace. Rp. **Tengemana,** settle down, be at peace, i.e. of people or country after an upheaval, war, famine, &c. **Tengemano,** n. *ma-*, and **Utengemano,** n. settling down after an upheaval, prosperity after a troublesome period, peace after war—used of both people and country. (Note: these forms and those under *tengenea* appear to be derived from a common root *-tenga,* be equal, equalize, not now in use in Swahili.)

Tengenea, v. be settled, be arranged, be in good order, be in a state of comfort (rest, well-being, &c.), e.g.

duka limetengenea, the shop is ready, i.e. stocked, fitted, furnished. *Upepo umetengenea*, the wind is steady. *Chombo kimetengenea*, the vessel is in good order (in trim). Cs. **Tengeneza**, put right, repair, mend, put in order, arrange, correct, settle, bring to a happy conclusion, make comfortable. (Note: of actual construction, and not of repairs merely, *fanya* or *fanyiza* is correct. *Saa ilifanyizwa ikavunjika ikapelekwa kutengenezwa*, the watch was made and it broke and was sent to be repaired.) *Jumbe hakutengeneza mashauri ya nchi yake*, the chief has not settled the affairs of his country. St. of Cs. **Tengenezeka.** Cs. **Tengenezesha**, cause to be mended, repaired, &c. **Mtengenezaji**, n. *wa-* one who puts things right, one who corrects matters, hence, an editor, &c. **Tengenezo**, n. *ma-* arrangement, orderly disposition, administration, regulation. **Utengenezaji**, n. putting to rights, repairing, preparing, method of arrangement, &c., see note under *tengemaa*.

Tengo, n. *ma-* outrigger—of a canoe. (Cf. *ngalawa, mrengu, ndubi.*)

Tengua, v. See under **Tenga.**

Tengura, v. scorn, debase, dishonour. (Cf. *tweza, dharau, beza.*)

Teo, n. a sling for throwing stones. (Cf. *kombeo*, and for catapult, *manati* and *panda.*)

Tepe,* n. *ma-*, also **Utepe**, n. braid, usu. the chevrons worn by noncommissioned officers of the police and native troops. (Eng. tape?)

Tepe, a., also Rd. **Tepetepe**, many. *Alisema maneno tepetepe*, he uttered a great flow of language.

Tepeta, v. be limp, but usu. in the Prep. **Tepetea**, be utterly slack (idle, indolent, listless, unstrung, relaxed). **Mtepetevu**, n. *wa-* lazy, slack, idle, listless person. **Tepete**, a. jelly-like, soft, flaccid, limp, like a ripe banana, &c. **-tepetevu**, a. lazy, listless, &c. **Utepetevu**, n. languor, indolence, slackness, listlessness, lack of interest or energy.

Terafini,* n. turpentine. (Hind. تارپین.)

Terema, v., also Prep. form with same sense **Teremea**, be at ease, be free from care and anxiety, be cheerful (happy, comfortable). St. **Teremeka** (in same sense). Cs. **Teremesha**, e.g. *teremesha mgeni*, make a guest comfortable, at his ease, e.g. cheer up, gladden, relieve, put at ease. **Mteremeshi**, n. *wa-*, **Mteremezi**, n. *wa-* kindly, genial, friendly person, who sets others at their ease. **Mteremo**, n. *mi-* cheerfulness, happiness, comfort, relief from trouble. **Nderemo**, n. same as *mteremo*.

Tesa, v. afflict, cause trouble (pain, anxiety, loss) to, persecute, harass, tease, &c., not of a passing act, but rather over a long period. Ps. **Teswa.** St. **Teseka.** Prep. **Tesea.** Cs. **Tesesha.** Rp. **Tesana.** Cs. of Rp. **Tesanya**, i.e. set at variance (with). **Mtesa**, n. *wa-*, **Mtesaji**, n. *wa-* and **Mtesi**, n. *wa-* one who causes trouble or annoyance, a persecutor. **Teso**, n. *ma-* usu. in plural, *mateso*, suffering, affliction, pain, trial, persecution, adversity. **Utesi**, n. *ma-* sometimes **Utesaji** (1) trouble, distress, annoyance, persecution; (2) strife, quarrelling, antagonism. (Perh. a Cs. form of *teta* with restricted meaning. Cf. *sumbua, udhi, chokoza, adhibu.*)

Teta, v. (1) act or speak strongly, strive, insist—but generally (2) oppose (by word or action), act or speak against, obstruct, contradict, protest, dispute, quarrel, go to law; (3) backbite. Often with *na*, e.g. *ameteta nami*, he disputed with me. Ps. **Tetwa.** St. and Pot. **Teteka.** Prep. **Tetea**, e.g. act (speak) for (against, in, at, &c.), defend, attack, oppose, support. D.Prep. **Tetelea.** Cs. **Teteleza**, cause strife, ill feeling,

&c., between people. Cs. **Tetesha.** Rp. **Tetana,** e.g. quarrel, wrangle, be at enmity. See also **Tesa,** which appears to be a Cs. form. **Mtetaji,** n. *wa-* one given to contradiction, quarrelling, litigation. **Mteteaji,** n. *wa-* one who speaks for or against, a defendant or opponent. **Mtetezi,** n. *wa-* a quarrelsome, argumentative person, one who speaks for, defends another, also one who speaks against or opposes another. **Teto,** n. *ma-* objection, argument, plea, protest. **Utetezi,** n. *ma-* intercession, advocacy, argument or effort for or against, and so also, opposition, obstructiveness. **Uteto,** n. *ma-* debate, argument, quarrelling, scandal, backbiting.

Tete, n. grain fully formed, but not fully ripe or hard. *Tete za mtama* or *mtama tete,* of millet in this stage. **Tetewanga,** n., also sometimes **Tetekuwanga,** chicken pox, from the grain-like eruption. **Tete,** n. *ma-* reeds, *Arundo phragmites.* **Kitete,** n. *vi-* small hollow reed, small pipe. n. *vi-* in some places a small animal —mongoose.

Tetea, v. cackle—of a hen.

Tetekuwanga, n. See **Tetewanga** under **Tete.**

Tetelea, v., **Teteleza,** v. See under **Teta.**

Tetema, v. tremble, shake, quake, quiver. Commonly in the St. **Tetemeka,** e.g. *natetemeka kwa homa,* I shiver with fever, i.e. in the cold stage of malaria. *Nchi inatetemeka,* the earth quakes. **Kitetemo,** n. *vi-*, **Kitetemeko,** n. *vi-* trembling, quivering, shaking, quaking. **Mtetemeko,** n. *mi-*, shaking, trembling, shuddering, shivering, quaking. *Mtetemeko wa nchi,* earthquake. *Mtetemeko wa meno,* chattering of the teeth. **Tetemeko,** n. *ma-*, **Tetemo,** n. *ma-* like *mtetemeko.*

Tetere, n. Ring-necked Dove, *Streptopelia capicola.*

Tetereka, v. (1) stagger, sway to and fro; (2) be spoiled or sprained a little, be slightly disabled.

Tetesi, n. *ma-* a whisper, a rumour, a secret affair.

Tetewanga, n. See under **Tete.**

Teto, n. *ma-*. See under **Teta.**

Teua, v. (1) choose, select, pick out; (2) be dainty, critical, fastidious. Ps. **Teuliwa.** St. and Pot. **Teulika,** for the commoner, *chagua.* **Mteua,** n. *wa-* one who chooses, criticizes, picks and chooses. **Mteule,** n. *wa-* one who is chosen, selected, picked out, and so, choice, of high quality or character. **Mteuzi,** n. *wa-* like *mteua,* a dainty person, a critic, an eclectic, a connoisseur, e.g. *mteuzi haachi tamaa,* i.e. a critic is never satisfied. **-teule,** a. choice, select, eligible, of best quality. **-teuzi,** a. dainty, fastidious, critical. **Uteuzi,** n. choice, choosing, criticizing, fastidiousness, taste, daintiness. (Cf. *chagua.*)

Teuka, v. (1) sometimes heard for *teguka,* see under **Tega;** (2) belch. (Cf. *cheuka.*)

-teule, a., **-teuzi,** a. See under **Teua.**

Tezi,* n. *ma-* (1) stern, poop, of a ship. (Cf. *shetri.* ? Pers. وزى a ship. (2) a tumour, glandular swelling, goitre, wen.

Tezo, n. *ma-* (1) carpenter's adze; (2) see under **Tega.**

Th represents the same sound as *th* in English 'thin'. Some natives are inclined to pronounce this sound as *s.*

Thabiti,* a. (1) firm, proved, constant, strong; (2) resolute, brave, steadfast—of persons and things. **Thibiti,** v. be firm, strong, assured, resolute, steadfast, brave. Cs. **Thibitisha,** make firm, secure, establish, prove. St. **Thibitika.** **Mathubuti,** n. and a. (1) evidence, proof, confirmation, support (cf. *ushahidi*); (2) firm, proved, trustworthy, honest, reliable, effective, decisive (cf. *imara*). **Uthabiti,** n.

firmness, stability, strength, courage, resolution. (Ar. ثبت.)

Thama,* conj. rarely used (1) alike, equally, therewith, at the same time (cf. *mamoja*); (2) then, next, also, too, e.g. *thama wamwonapo na wasipomwona*, alike whether they see him or not. *Thama na wewe*, and you as well. (Ar. ثمّ.)

Thamani,* n. price, value, estimation. *-a thamani*, valuable, precious. **Thamini,** v. value, appraise, put a value on, price. Ps. **Thaminiwa.** St. and Pot. **Thaminika.** Cs. **Thaminisha.** (Cf. *kadiri, kima, bei*, and dist. *samani* and *zamani*. Ar. ثمن.)

Thamra,* n. name given to cloves when just beginning to form (Cf. *mkarafuu*. Ar. ثمر.)

Thawabu,* n. a reward, gift—but esp. as from God. (Cf. for gifts generally, *bakshishi, zawadi, tunzo, jazi, jaza*. Ar. ثوب.)

Thelatha,* n. and a. three—but usually *tatu*. *Thelatha mia*, three hundred. *Thelatashara*, thirteen for *kumi na tatu*. *Thelathini*, thirty. **Theluthi,** a. third (fractional) part. (Ar. ثلاثة, &c.)

Theluji,* n. snow. (Ar. ثلوج.)

Theluthi,* n. See under **Thelatha,** n. and a.

Themani and **Themanya,*** n. and a. eight, but usually *nane*. **Themanini,** n. and a. eighty. *-a themanini*, eightieth. **Themantashara,** n. and a. eighteen, for *kumi na nane*. **Themuni** and **Thumni,** an eighth (fractional) part. (Ar. ثمانية, &c.)

Thenashara,* n. and a. twelve, for *kumi na mbili*. *-a thenashara*, twelfth. **Theneen,** n. and a. two, but usually *mbili, -wili*. (Ar. اثنان, &c.)

Thibiti, v., **Thibitisha,*** v., &c. See under **Thabiti.**

Thubutu,* v. venture, dare, have courage to. *Huthubutu kunipiga*, you dare not strike me. *Sithubutu*, I dare not. Cs. **Thubutisha.** St. **Thubutika.** **Uthubutu,** n. courage, daring. (Ar. ثبت.)

Thumu,* n. garlic, also **Tumu** and **Saumu.** (Ar. ثوم.)

Thumuni,* n. and a. See under **Themani.**

Thurea,* n. (1) a chandelier; (2) the Pleiades. (Cf. *kilimia*. Ar. ثريا.)

Tia, v. (1) put, place, set; (2) apply, use, employ, bring to, bear; (3) cause, effect with, bring about. One of the commonest verbs in Swahili, used freely in all the above senses, translatable according to the sense of the noun with which it is associated, and often forming one verbal notion with it. Synonymous in many senses with *weka*, also very common (which compare), but (generally speaking) in *weka* the action is regarded as ending with itself (i.e. put and leave, put and have done with it), in *tia* the action involves some further effect, or something else affected by it, i.e. put to, apply, add, e.g. *tia maji*, put water (somewhere, in something), add water, dilute. *Tia dawa*, apply medicine. *Tia rangi*, paint. *Tia giza*, darken. *Tia nguvu*, (1) apply force; (2) encourage, strengthen. *Tia nanga*, cast anchor. *Tia ugonjwa*, cause illness, infect with disease. *Tia makali*, sharpen, make sharp. *Tia mashaka* (*matata*), cause (inspire) doubts, perplex. *Tia hofu*, frighten. *Tia adhabu*, sentence (a prisoner). *Tia aibu*, disgrace. *Tia nia* (*moyo*), apply thought, consider seriously—so *tia moyoni* (*maanani*). *Tia askari*, employ soldiers, set a guard. *Tia kazini*, set to a job. *Tia roho*, risk one's life. *Tia mfalme*, call in (appeal to, bring to bear) the chief. *Jitia ugonjwa*, pretend illness. Ps. **Tiwa.** *Tiwa hatiani*, be convicted (of), found guilty. Prep. **Tilia,** e.g. *mbona umenipa mfuko, sina kitu* *cha kuutilia?* why have you given me a bag, I have nothing to put in it. *Wajitiliani maneno hayo?* Why do you thrust yourself into this discussion? D. Prep. **Tililia**, in various operations, e.g. *tililia uzi*, darn. **Tilika**, St. of Prep. Rp. of Prep. **Tiliana**. Cs. **Tilisha**. Rp. **Tiana**. **Mtia**, n. *wa-*, **Mtiaji**, n. *wa-* with noun following, one who puts in or on. *Mtia dawa*, one who applies medicine, &c. **Tilatila**, a. (sometimes *diladila*), of different kinds, i.e. not selected, mixed up. *Anapika vyakula (vya) tilatila*, she is cooking food of different kinds, i.e. all mixed up. Contr. *tolatola*, under *toa*, v. (A).

Tiabu,* n. a game played by throwing up bits of stick, and watching how they fall. (Ar. طاب.)

Tiara,* n. a kite—the child's toy, also called *portangi, kishada, kisusuli*. (Ar. طارة.)

Tiba,* n. (1) see under **Tabibia**, v.; (2) a term of endearment, dear. (Ar. تبع.)

Tibu,* n. perfume, scent, made from sandal-wood ground and mixed with rose water and cloves. (Ar. طيب.)

Tibu,* v. same as *tabibia*, v. which see.

Tibua, v. (1) stir up, make muddy; (2) excite, provoke. *Tibua maji*, stir up the mud in water. St. **Tibuka**. **Matibwitibwi**, n. anything that has been stirred up, e.g. *maji matibwitibwi*, water which has been stirred up and is muddy.

-tifu, a. See under **Tifua**.

Tifua, v. cause to rise like dust, stir up, make dust. **-tifu**, also **-tifutifu**, a. loose, crumbling, dustlike, dusty, e.g. *mchanga mtifu*, fine sand. **Tifu**, n. *ma-* dust, loose dust-like sand, &c. *Fanya tifu*, make a dust.

Tii,* v. obey, submit to, be docile (obedient, submissive). Ps. **Tiiwa**, be obeyed, &c., e.g. *hatiiwi na mkewe*, he is not obeyed by his wife. St. **Tiika**, like *tii*, i.e. be obedient. Cs. **Tiisha**, i.e. reduce to obedience, subdue. **Taa**, n. obedience. **Mtii**, n. *wa-*, **Mtiifu**, n. *wa-* an obedient (submissive, docile) person. **-tii**, a., **-tiifu**, a. obedient, docile, submissive. **Utii**, n. (1) obedience, &c.; (2) discipline, i.e. as exacted from a scholar, &c. (Cf. *sikia, tumikia, nyenyekea*. Ar. طاع.)

Tijara,* v. See under **Tajiri**.

Tike,* adv. exactly, just so, in the same way. (Cf. *ndiyo, hasa*. Ar. دقة.)

Tikisa, v. (1) cause to shake, wave, move to and fro; (2) make restless, agitate, excite, e.g. *tikisa mti, matunda yapate kupukutika chini*, shake a tree so that the fruit drops off. *Tikisa nchi kwa fitina*, disturb a country by rebellion. Ps. **Tikiswa**. St. and Pot. **Tikisika**. Prep. **Tikisia**. Cs. **Tikisisha**. Rp. **Tikisana**. **Mtikiso**, n. *mi-* act (manner, &c.) of shaking, a shaking. (Cf. *tukutiza, suka, tetemesha, punga*.)

Tikita, v. (1) see **Chikicha**; (2) pound or grind finely, i.e. to fine flour; (3) chew properly or masticate well in eating; (4) enjoy sound sleep, e.g. *anautikita usingizi*, he is having a sound sleep. Prep. **Tikitia**. Cs. **Tikitiza**, (1) Inten. grind finely; (2) work the loins with a circular motion, i.e. of the movement taught to girls before marriage and employed often by both sexes in coition, *tikitiza kiuno, chezesha kiuno*, also used in dancing. **Tikitiki**, a., also **Teketeke**, (1) absolutely slack, soft, yielding, like food well masticated; or like ripe fruit; (2) pounded into fine dust or flour.

Tikiti, n. *ma-* (A) (1) a water-melon, fruit of the *mtikiti*, often called *tikiti maji*.

Tikiti,* n. (B) a ticket, pass, chit. (Eng. ticket.)

Tikitiki, a. See under **Tikita**.

Tikiza, v. endure, bear (pain, trouble, &c.). (Cf. *vumilia*.)

Tilatila, a. See under **Tia.**

Tilifika,* v. See under **Tilifu.**

Tilifu,* v. destroy, waste. St. **Tilifika**, decrease, fade away, be lost. Cs. **Tilifisha**, ruin, destroy, &c. (Cf. *potea, poteza, fifia, angamia, angamiza.* Ar. اتلف.)

Tililia, v. See under **Tia.**

Tilisika, v. same as *tiririka*, which see.

Timamu,* n. See under **Timu.**

Timazi,* n. a plummet, i.e. a small stone suspended by a string, used by masons, &c. (Cf. *bildi, chubwi.* Ar. مطمر treated as a plur. and the final *r* changing to *z* under the influence of a final closed *i*.)

Timba, n. (1) a strap of beads, beads threaded together; (2) grain (millet) sprouted with which to make beer. (Cf. *kimea.*)

Timbe, n. lump of cast or unwrought metal. (Cf. *mkuo.*)

Timbi, n. *ma-* (1) sometimes heard for *chimvi*, which see; (2) a bracelet, armlet. (Cf. *bangili, dodi, kekee, kikuku.*)

Timbua, v. stir up maize or millet which is being pounded in mortar, i.e. so that it does not stick to the sides of the mortar. (Cf. *tibua.*)

Timia,* v., **-timilifu**, a. See under **Timu.**

Timka, v. (1) trot, run, amble—of the running movement of an animal; (2) be ruffled, as of hair or feathers. Cs. **Timsha. Timutimu**, n. *ma-*, e.g. *matimutimu ya nywele*, ruffled hair.

Timu,* v. be complete, be ended, but generally used in the Prep. form, i.e. **Timia**, be complete, perfect, whole, finished, fulfilled, accomplished, done, e.g. *wakati umetimia*, the time is ended, is come. So of *kazi, deni*, a task, a debt, &c. *Ahadi imetimia*, the promise is carried out. Prep. **Timilia**, e.g. be finished for, or be finished off, become complete. Cs. of Prep. **Timiliza.** Cs. **Timiza.** **Timamu**, n. (1) completion, completed state, perfected condition; (2) report or intimation of a completed or perfect state, e.g. at the end of a guard, the sentry brings his *timamu* to his superior. **Timamu**, a. complete, perfect. **-timilifu**, a. perfect, complete, finished, consummated. **Utimilifu**, n. perfection. completeness, consummation. (Cf. *kamili, sima.* Ar. تم and تمام.)

Timvi, n. sometimes heard for *chimvi*, which see.

Tinda, n. *ma-* a string of beads long enough to go round the neck.

Tinda, v. See **Chinja**, also **Tindika.**

Tindanga, v. push through a forest or bush from one side to the other, said of people or animals.

Tindi, a. in an unripe stage, half-grown. Used of maize and millet. (Cf. *mtindi* and *-bichi.*)

Tindi, n. *ma-* used for the spokes of a bicycle wheel. (Cf. *njukuti, henzarani.*)

Tindiga, n. thorny herb which grows in swamps.

Tindika, v. be cut off, fall short, fail, be finished, come to an end. Prep. **Tindikia**, e.g. be lacking to, fail to. *Tindikia kuja*, fail to come. *Nimetindikiwa maziwa*, my milk has failed me, has run short. Cs. **Tindikisha.** Rp. **Tindikana**, e.g. be cut off from each other, be separated, alienated. (Prob. from the same root as *chinja*, which bears a specialized meaning, i.e. slay, cut the throat of.) **Tindo**, n. a hard chisel—for cutting metal, &c.

Tindikali,* n. soldering lead, acid used in soldering. (Cf. *lehemu.* Pers. and Hind. تنداب a dissolving fluid, and قلعى tin.)

Tine, n. glans penis.

Tinga, v. (1) shake, vibrate, like a boat, bob up and down, like a buoy in large waves; (2) defeat, e.g. *maneno haya yamemtinga*, these words have defeated him. Rd. *tinga-tinga*, shake, vibrate, &c. Cs. **Tingisha**, cause to shake. St. and Pot. **Tingika. Tingetinge**, n., also **Tingitingi**, a bridge across a river or ravine, prob. because of the shaking or vibration made when crossing it.

Tinge, n. a dancing game, in which the dancers endeavour to keep to a particular order in which they bring their feet to the ground after leaping.

Tingetinge, n., **Tingisha**, v., **Tingitingi**, n. See under **Tinga.**

Tini,* n. a fig, fruit of the *mtini*. (Ar. تينة.)

Tipitipi, n. (1) White-browed Coucal, also called *shundi, dudumizi*, and *gude, Centropus superciliosus*; (2) the small red seeds with black dot of the *mtipitipi*.

Tipwa, a., also Rd. **Tipwatipwa**, well made, healthy, e.g. *mtoto tipwa-tipwa*, a well-built, healthy child.

Tiringa, v. cut notches, e.g. round a stick.

Tiririka, v. glide, trickle, slide along, e.g. of the movement of a snake, of water, &c. **Mtiririko**, n. *mi-* (1) a gliding, trickling, &c.; (2) the mark, track, &c., of anything gliding or trickling. (Cf. *churuzika*.)

Tisa,* n. and a. nine. *-a tisa*, ninth (cf. *kenda*). **Tisatashara**, nineteen. *-a tisatashara*, nineteenth. **Tisini**, ninety. *a tisini*, ninetieth. (Ar. تسع.)

Tisha, v. frighten, overawe, menace, strike with terror, e.g. *alimtisha tu, hakutaka kumwua*, he only frightened him, he did not mean to kill him. Ps. **Tishwa.** St. and Pot. **Tishika.** Prep. **Tishia.** Rp. **Tishana. Kitisho**, n. *vi-* terrifying, something terrifying, a terror, a menace, a fearful thing, an overwhelming danger. **Mtishaji**, n. *wa-* one who terrifies, &c. **Tisho**, n. *ma-* that which terrifies, a menace, a scare. **Utisho**, n. frightening, terrifying, scaring, causing abject terror. (Cf. *hofisha, ogofya, kioja, maafa*.)

Tishari,* n., also **Tishali**, *ma-* a lighter, barge, such as are used in loading and unloading vessels.

Tisho, n. *ma-*. See under **Tisha.**

Tisini,* n. and a. See under **Tisa.** (Ar. تسعون.)

Tisti,* adv. firmly, without moving or wavering. *Simama tisti*, stand firm. (? Ar. تسطيح making flat and level.)

Tita, v. (1) tie up in bundles, i.e. of grass, firewood, &c., i.e. *funga* (*piga*) *tita*; (2) make carry a bundle or load. Prep. **Titia**, tie up bundles, &c., for (with, &c.), but often with Inten. meaning (1) stoop in order to have a load placed on the head; (2) stoop because of a heavy load, and so (3) shake, totter, begin to sink, give way, break up as of a roof the supports of which have become too weak to bear its weight, or of a man staggering under a heavy load, &c. St. **Titika**, (1) carry with difficulty as of a very heavy load; (2) also used of circumstances, illness, &c., overwhelming one. Cs. **Titisha**, (1) cause to tie up in bundles, &c.; (2) make carry a heavy load; (3) make shake, totter, &c. **Kitita**, n. *vi-* a small bundle of grass, firewood, &c. **Mtitio**, n. *mi-* a sinking, tottering, giving way. **Tita**, n. *ma-* a bundle of firewood, grass, &c., a faggot.

Titi, n. *ma-* teat, nipple of breast. **Kititi**, n. *vi-* (1) dim.; (2) an ailment of the female breasts.

Titia, v. See under **Tita.**

Titiga, v. hit, beat, pound. *Kumtitiga mtu*, to hit a person.

Titika, v. See under **Tita.**

Titima, v. (1) roll, rumble—as thunder; (2) make noise, confusion. **Titimka**, rush out to see, as people do when they hear a great shouting or noise (perh. a variant of *tutuma*, which see). **Kititimo**, n. *vi-* (1) a rolling, rumbling sound; (2) confusion.

Tiva, n. Zanzibar Bou-Bou. Also Zanzibar Puffback. *Laniarius ferrugineus*; *Dryoscopus affinis*.

-to a terminal suffix not commonly used, but capable of being added to any appropriate noun or verb-form to denote good quality, high degree, pleasing manner, pleasant sensation, &c. *Manukato*, sweet, high-class perfumes. *Kunyokato*, to be properly straightened. *Kazi yangu ifanyato*, do my work well. *Imbato*, sing well. Cf. also *punyeto*.

Toa, v. (A) one of the commonest verbs in Swahili, with a general idea of put out. (1) show, display, &c., *toa nuru*, shine. *Toa meno*, show the teeth. *Toa taa*, display (or remove) a lamp. *Toa hadithi*, tell a story. *Toa ukali*, show fierceness (bravery). *Toa maua*, put forth flowers, blossom. (2) give, supply, produce—in this sense regularly used for *-pa*, give (in cases where the objective pfx. is absent, and *-pa* therefore cannot be used), e.g. *toa mali*, give money. *Toa gharama nyingi*, lay out large sums. *Toa njia*, grant right of way. Also (3) take out, produce—in contrast with *-pa*, e.g. *akatoa shilingi akampa*, and he took out a shilling and gave it to him. (4) offer, propose, make a plan of, arrange, e.g. *toa salamu*, salute. *Toa shauri*, offer advice. *Toa nyumba*, design a house. *Toa kazi*, supply occupation, work. *Toa masharti*, propose conditions. *Toa siku*, arrange a day. (5) take out, deliver, select, e.g. *toa ndani*, take from within. *Toa hatarini*, save from danger. *Akamtoa nyumbani*, and he turned him out of the house. (6) give up, resign, yield, e.g. *adui wakajitoa*, the enemy surrendered. (7) force out, make come or go out, dismiss, take away. *Toa pumzi*, breathe out. *Mtu huyu ataka kututoa roho zetu*, this man wishes to take our lives. *Toa farasi shoti*, make a horse gallop, get a gallop out of him. *Toa makosa*, remove blemishes, correct mistakes. *Toa mimba*, produce abortion. (8) subtract, the word used in arithmetic for subtraction. Ps. **Tolewa**, e.g. be put out, put forward, put away, be proposed, be rejected, &c. St. **Toka**, (1) come out, appear, be rid (of), be let out; (2) go out, go away, get out, disappear, cease (from)—in this sense syn. with *ondoka*. Used with several constructions, e.g. *toka mjini*, or *toka mji*, go out of the town. *Toka Unguja*, come from Zanzibar. *Toka katika utumwa*, be set free from slavery. *Toka katika chombo*, disembark from a vessel. *Natoka kumwuzia pembe*, I have just been (or come from) selling ivory to him. *Toka!* (Imperat.) Come out! But often of peremptory dismissal. Get out! Begone! Off with you! *Toka* has often a semi-transitive construction, e.g. *anatoka damu*, i.e. he is bleeding. *Damu inamtoka*, blood is coming from him. Thus the same thing may be described by *kutoa moshi* and *kutoka moshi*—according to the prominence of the idea of agency, e.g. of a smoker and his pipe. Ps. form **Tokwa**, e.g. *tokwa na hari* (*damu, machozi, roho*), of perspiring (bleeding, shedding tears, dying). Prep. **Tokea**, e.g. (1) come out to (for, against, in, &c., but *rarely* from, which is usually *toka* only), e.g. *alitoka mji akatokea mji mwingine*, he left the town and appeared at another town. *Alitokewa na malaika*, he was appeared to by an angel, i.e. an angel appeared to him. (2) result (from), be a consequence (of), *mambo mabaya yatokea na mtoto huyu*, evil consequences follow from this child. (3) *tokea* is used simply as 'appear, come on the scene, come out'. *Tokea nje*, come (appear) outside. D.Prep. **Tokelea**, e.g. *nilitokelewa na mgeni*, I was suddenly visited (unexpectedly) by a stranger. Cs. of

D. Prep. **Tokeleza.** Cs. **Tokeza,** (1) cause to come out, make project (or prominent); (2) intens. come out, ooze out, project, protrude, be prominent, e.g. *jiwe latokeza mno,* the stone projects too far. *Jino latokeza nje,* the tooth is forcing its way out. *Sindano inatokeza ncha yake, inatokea upande wa pili,* the needle is getting its point through, it is appearing on the other side. *Mtabiri alitokeza maneno mabaya kwa watu,* the foreteller has predicted bad news to the people. Also used to a person coming in to a place—taking a long time over it. *Tokeza!* show yourself! Rp. **Tokana,** (1) leave each other, part (from), e.g. *huyu ametokana na mkewe,* this man has parted from his wife; (2) result from, have origin in, e.g. *maneno mengi ya Kiswahili yametokana na Kiarabu,* many Swahili words have their origin in Arabic. Prep. **Tolea,** e.g. put out (for, to, from, against, with, &c.), give to, present, offer (to), spend (on)—also take away from, remove from, save from, &c. Thus *kumtolea mali* may mean—spend money on, or take away money from—a person. *Alimtolea* with *meno,* gave him (or showed him, or took from him) his teeth—with *kisimani,* took him out of a well—with *ushairi,* recited him a stanza, &c. Ps. **Tolewa.** Rp. of Prep. **Toleana,** take from each other, give to each other, &c. *Walitoleana matusi,* they abused each other. Cs. **Toza,** collect from, make give up, e.g. *alinitoza kodi,* he collected tax from me, made me pay tax. *Bwana alimtoza adhabu,* the master punished him, i.e. imposed a fine, &c., on him. Rp. **Tozana.** Prep. **Tozea.** Rp. **Toana,** e.g. put each other out (or forward), join in putting (or going) out, e.g. *walitoana katika mji, kwenda vitani,* they made a general move from the town to go to war. **Kitoleo,** n. *vi-* subtrahend, what is subtracted in a subtraction sum. **Mtoa,** n. *wa-,* **Mtoaji,** n. *wa-* one who gives, removes, takes, &c., with meanings as in *toa.* **Mtoki,** n. *mi-* a painful swelling, usually in the groin, but also in the side and under the arm, usually caused by a septic or inflamed sore and accompanied by fever. **Mtoza,** n. *wa-* one who extracts, i.e. tax collector, *mtoza kodi,* &c. **Toka,** prep. **Tokea,** prep. from, out of, away from, starting from, since, e.g. *toka huko,* from yonder, from that time (place). *Toka leo,* from to-day onwards. *Toka zamani,* long since. *Tokea hapo* (and sometimes shortened to *tokeapo*), long ago, from time immemorial. Often combined with *kwa, katika,* to define their meaning, or with locatives in *-ni,* e.g. *toka nyumbani,* from the house. *Toka kwa mfalme,* from the king's presence. **Tokeo,** n. *ma-* (1) place (time, act, mode) of going out (appearing, happening); (2) outlet, pore, e.g. *matokeo ya hari,* pores in the skin (cf. *kitundu, nyweleo*); (3) appearance, apparition, vision (cf. *njozi*); (4) occurrence, result, consequence (cf. *tukio*). **Tolatola,** a. selected. *Vyakula tolatola,* selected foods, contr. *tilatila* under *tia.* **Toleo,** n. *ma-* anything given out, issued, &c. **Utokezo,** n. *ma-* (1) bringing out, displaying, utterance; (2) prominence, appearance. *Utokezo wa maneno,* coming out with words, abrupt utterance, an aggressive speech. **Utoko,** n. mucus (Lat. *e vagina*).

Toa, v. (B) lack, not have, be lacking, not used in the Dir. form except as an auxiliary of negation when combined with other verbs, e.g. *kutoa kufanya* forms the Infinitive of the Negative Conjugation, i.e. not to do, lack doing, and is often shortened to *kutoa fanya* and *kutofanya,* sometimes also used to form a negative of other senses, e.g. *nikipika nikitopika,* whether I cook or not. Prep. and Ps. not in use. St. **Toweka,** be lacking, missing, and hence vanish, disappear, pass out of sight. Cs. **Towesha**, put out of the way, cause to be lacking, ruin. **-tovu**, a. lacking, e.g. *mcha Mungu si mtovu*, one who fears God lacks not. *Huyu ni mtovu wa heshima*, this person lacks honour. **Utovu**, n. lack.

Toasi, n. *ma-* or **Toazi** cymbal, large castanet.

Toba,* n. See under **Tubu**.

Tobo, n. *ma-*. See under **Toboa**.

Toboa, v. bore a hole (in), make a hole (or passage), force a way (through). Ps. **Tobolewa**. St. **Toboka**. Prep. **Tobolea**. **Tobo**, n. *ma-*, also **Tobwe**, n. *ma-* a hole. **Kitobo**, n. *vi-*, **Kitobwe**, n. *vi-* dim. (Cf. *zua*, *pekecha*.)

Tobosha, n. *ma-*. See **Kitobosha**.

Tobwe, n. *ma-* (1) see under **Toboa**, v.; (2) wood of the tree *mtobwe*; (3) simpleton, fool. (Cf. *mjinga*, *mpumbavu*.)

Tofaa,* n. *ma-* fruit of the tree *mtofaa*. (Ar. تفاح.)

Tofali,* n. *ma-* a brick, tile. (Ar. طفال dry loam or clay.)

Tofauti,* n. (1) difference, discrepancy, interval (of space or time); (2) excess, want; (3) blame, quarrel. *Kitu hiki kina tofauti*, this thing is different, not quite what I wanted. *Nina tofauti naye*, I am not quite satisfied with him. *Ana tofauti*, he is not up to the mark, not trustworthy, not qualified. **Tofautisha**, v. Cs. make a difference, cause to be different, treat differently, distinguish. Ps. **Tofautishwa**. (Cf. *pambanua*. Ar. تفاوت.)

Tofoa, v., **Tofua**, v. sometimes heard for *pofua* which see.

Toga, v. pierce (the ear), make incision (for ear ornament). Ps. **Togwa**, e.g. *kutogwa, maana hutiwa mapele katika masikio*, the meaning of *togwa* is, having holes bored in the ears for fixing in ornamental plugs of paper, &c.

Togwa, n. native beer (*pombe*) in the sweet unintoxicating stage, not fermented.

Tohara,* n. See under **Tahiri**.

Tohe, n., or **Toi**, a kind of wild goat.

Toja, v. (1) make incisions (cuts, gashes, &c.), scarify, tattoo, let blood, e.g. *toja mshipa*, open a vein, bleed (cf. *chanja*); (2) drip (cf. *tona*). **Tojo**, n. *ma-* (1) gash, cut, incision, tattoo—whether for ornament, tribal mark, or medical purposes; (2) a drop. (Cf. *tone*.)

Toka, v. and prep., **Tokea**, v. and prep., **Tokeo**, n. *ma-*, **Tokeza**, v. See under **Toa**, v. (A).

Tokomea, v. (1) vanish, disappear, recede from view, extend beyond the range of the eye—e.g. on the sea, *bahari inatokomea*; (2) be destroyed completely; (3) arrive at a place or enter with a rush or with a great noise and confusion. Cs. **Tokomeza**, e.g. reduce to nothing, annihilate. Rp. **Tokomezana**. (Cf. *yoyomea*, *elemea*.)

Tokoni, n. *ma-*, also **Tokono**, n. *ma-* the coccyx. **Kitokono**, n. *vi-* dim.

Tokosa, v. boil, cook by boiling—of food generally. Also of frying in fat or butter, e.g. *tokosa mkate pamoja na samli* (or *kwa samli*), fry a cake in ghee. Of water, *pika* or *chemsha*, is usual. Ps. **Tokoswa**. St. and Pot. **Tokoseka**. Ten. **Tokota**, become boiled (fried), be boiled (boiling, frying), e.g. *chungu chatokota kupata moto sana*, a cooking-pot boils by getting very hot. **Mtokoso**, n. *mi-* act (condition) of boiling.

Tola,* n. a weight about ½ ounce, used for weighing silver, gold, oil, and perfumes. (Hind. تولا.)

Tolatola, a., **Tolea**, v., **Toleo**, n. *ma-*. See under **Toa**, v. (A).

Toma,* v. thrust in, usu. with the Rf. *kujitoma*, to thrust oneself in, burst in. (Cf. *choma*.)

Tomasa,* v. press, feel, knead softly with the fingers—of a soft yielding substance, e.g. of an animals or ripe fruit. (Cf. *papasa, bonyeza, kanda.* Ar. تمس touch.)

Tomba, v. have sexual intercourse, copulate of the male (of animals in general, but commonly avoided as vulgar). Ps. **Tombwa,** of the female. Rp. **Tombana.** (Cf. under *lala.*)

Tombo, n., also **Tomboo** and **Tomboro,** a quail.

Tomea, v. used of mason's work, sticking small stones in mortar on a wall, &c., to bring it to a surface and to strengthen it. Ps. **Tomewa.** Prep. **Tomelea.** Cs. **Tomesha.** Cv. **Tomoa,** break through, pierce, seldom used except of deflowering a virgin. **Mtomo,** n. *mi-* mason's work, i.e. of strengthening plaster work, &c., by reinforcing it with small stones. (Cf. *choma.*)

Tomesha, v. send, set on, e.g. *kumtomesha mbwa,* to set a dog to attack a person or animal.

Tomoa, v. See under **Tomea.**

Tomoko, n. *ma-* fruit of the *mtomoko,* a custard-apple. (Cf. *topetope.*)

Tomondo, n. *ma-* fruit of the *mtomondo.*

Tona, v. fall in drops, drop, drip, form a drop or dot. Also St. **Toneka,** in same sense. Prep. of St. **Tonekea,** drop upon, e.g. *tonekea meza,* drop on the table. Prep. **Tonea.** Cs. **Tonesha,** (1) cause to drip; (2) see under *tonosha.* Rp. **Tonana. Kitone,** n. *vi-* dim. of **Tone,** n. *ma-* a drop of liquid, a dot, a blot.

Tondo, n. (1) a kind of snail; (2) a shell used as an ink-well.

Tondoo, n. *ma-* (1) fruit of the *mtondoo*; (2) a thimble. (Cf. *subana.*)

Tone, n. *ma-.* See under **Tona.**

Tonea, v. (1) see under **Tona;** (2) dress or plait a woman's hair. (Cf. *suka.*)

Tonesha, v. See under **Tona,** also under **Tonosha.**

Tonga, n. *ma-* (1) *tonga la dafu,* a coco-nut when full of milk and in the late stage, when the nutty part is well set and tough; (2) a basket made of canes or reeds.

Tonge, n. (— and *ma-*) a small rounded mass, a small lump or ball, e.g. of rice or other food, as taken in the fingers and eaten by natives. (Cf. *donge.*)

Tongo, n. (1) plur. of *utongo,* see *matongo;* (2) a kind of banana plant (cf. *mgomba*); (3) a deserted village. (Cf. *mahame.*)

Tongo kanga, n. Brown-backed Mannikin, *Spermestes nigriceps.* Also applied to other Mannikin finches. **Tongo pofu,** Bronze Mannikin, *Spermestes cucullatus.* **Tongo simba,** Magpie Mannikin, *Ameuresthes fringilloides.*

Tongoza, v. seduce. Ps. **Tongozwa.** Prep. **Tongozea.** Cs. **Tongozesha.** Rp. **Tongozana. Mtongoza,** n. *wa-,* **Mtongozi,** n. *wa-* one who tries to attract (allure, seduce), e.g. by words, signs, dress, &c., a seducer. **Utongozi,** n. *ma-* (1) vicious propensity, lasciviousness, vicious life; (2) seduction (of women).

Toni,* n. a tone, adopted for use in text-books and school lessons in music. (Eng.)

Tonoa, v. See under **Tona.**

Tonoka, v., also **Tononeka** and **Tononoka,** get fat, flourish, get new health and strength, used of persons, animals, things, and circumstances. Cs. **Tonokesha** or **Tononosha.**

Tonosha, v., also **Tonesha,** v. hurt a sore by knocking against it. St. **Tonoka.**

Top, adv. See under **Topea.**

Topas,* n. *ma-* a street sweeper, scavenger. (? Hind. It is the term used for the bath and lavatory stewards on ships carrying Indian crews.)

Tope, n. (— and *ma-*), also plur. of **Utope,** n. mud, mire, dirt. *Tope nyembamba,* thin, soft mud. *Tope* *nene* (*nzito*), thick mud. *Watu wengi kama tope*—descriptive of a great crowd, thick as mud. (Cf. *topea* with which it may be connected.)

Topea, v. (1) sink in, get into difficulties, get hampered (entangled); (2) fig. plunge into anything, be full of, be steeped in, i.e. vice, &c., e.g. *topea elimu*, be very learned, full of knowledge. Cs. **Topeza**, e.g. of the effect of a heavy load. *Nchi inatopeza miguu yake*, the earth makes his feet stick fast. *Topeza kidole katika mwili*, press the finger deep into the body. Cv. **Topoa**, get out of a difficulty, set free from a spell or charm, extricate, counteract a poison, save from danger, difficult position, &c., e.g. *topoa mtu uganga*, release a man from the power of a charm. *Dawa ya kutopoa*, antidote. Ps. **Topolewa.** Prep. **Topolea.** St. **Topoka**, e.g. *amelala ili umtopoke ulevi*, he is asleep so that his drunkenness may leave him. **Top**, adv. very, in a high degree, i.e. *kunywa* (*kulewa*) *top*, to be very drunk, perh. from Eng. top, i.e. up to the top. (Cf. *zingua*, *opoa*, *vua*, and *zama*, *titia*, *didimia*, *-zito*.)

Topetope, n. *ma-* custard-apple, fruit of the *mtopetope*. (Cf. *tomoko*.)

Topoa, v. See under **Topea.**

Tora, n. (1) a small spear; (2) orderliness. (? Ar. طور corresponding.)

Tora, v. (1) same as *chora*, which see; (2) *tora meno*, pick the teeth (cf. *chokoa*); (3) cackle (as of a hen).

Torati,* n. also **Taurati**, the law of Moses, the Pentateuch. (Ar. توراة.)

Toria, n. *ma-* fruit of the *mtoria*, which see, also **Kitoria**, n. *vi-*.

Toroka, v. desert, run away (from master, home, work, &c.), play truant. *Mtumwa amemtoroka bwana wake*, the slave has run away from his master—also *ametoroka kwa bwana wake*. Ps. **Torokwa**, be deserted, be run away from. Prep. **Torokea.** Cs. **Torosha**, induce to desert, drive into running away, seduce, entice to run away. **Mtoro**, n. *wa-* a runaway, a truant. **Utoro**, n. truancy, desertion.

Tosa, n. *ma-* fruit just ripening, nearly ripe, turning colour, beginning to be soft. *Tosa la embe*, *embe tosa*, a mango getting ripe.

Tosa, v. See under **Tota.**

Toseka, v. See **Tosa** under **Tota.**

Tosha, v. suffice, be sufficient (for), content, be enough (adequate, capable). *Yamtosha kazi yake*, his task is enough for him. Prep. **Toshea**, see also **Toshea, v.** D.Prep. **Toshelea.** Cs. of D.Prep. **Tosheleza**, (1) cause to be sufficient, satisfy, e.g. *maneno yake yalitosheleza baraza*, his statements satisfied the court; (2) also Inten. be sufficient, e.g. *Fulani anatosheleza kwa kazi hii*, So-and-so is sufficient (is able to do) for that work. Prep. of Cs. of Prep. **Toshelezea**, be enough for, &c. *Mchuzi huu utamtoshelezea wali wake*, this gravy will be enough for his rice. *Watu wawili watamtoshelezea kazi yake*, two men will be enough for his work. (Cf. *kifu*, *faa*, and dist. follg.)

Toshea, v. be amazed, astounded, staggered. Also Ps. **Toshewa**, with the same meaning—be struck with amazement. (Cf. *shangaa*, *tunduwaa*, *pumbaa*, *maka*, and dist. *toshea*, prep. form of *tosha*.)

Tota, v. sink down, sink in, be overwhelmed, be drowned. *Tota majini* (*baharini*), sink in water (the sea). *Tota macho*, have the eyes sunken, have lost the eyes (sight). *Merikebu imetota*, the ship has sunk. Prep. **Totea.** Cs. **Tosa**, (1) plunge in water, throw into the sea, cause to sink; (2) prod, poke, e.g. *amenitosa jicho*, he has poked me in the eye. Stc. **Totama**, sink in, used of sewing in the buttons in mattress making—but note—*tota* in some Bantu languages is used for 'to sew'. (Cf. *zama*, *didimia*, *chovya*, *chocha*.)

Toto, n. *ma-*. See under **Mtoto**.

Totoma, v. wander at random, get lost, be off the path. Prep. **Totomea**. (Cf. the more usu. *potea*.)

Totora, v. pick the teeth, pick the nose, also **Tora**, which see. (Cf. *chokoa*.)

-tovu, a. See under **Toa**, v. (B).

Towashi,* n. *ma-* a eunuch. (Pers. طواش.)

Towe, potter's clay. (Cf. *udongo*, *finyanga*.)

Towea, v. use as a relish, i.e. prepare food for the table by adding sauce, curry, gravy, fish, meat, vegetables, &c., to season and flavour it—such addition being *kitoweo*. Prep. **Towelea**, e.g. *towelea wali kwa mchuzi*, flavour boiled rice with gravy. Cs. **Toweza** and **Towesha**. **Kitoweo**, n. *vi-*, **Kitoweleo**, n. *vi-*, also **Toweo**, n. anything eaten as a relish with other food—meat, fish, curry, &c.—the third common ingredient being *mchuzi*, gravy. (Cf. *unga*, v., *kiungo*, and *mboga*, the latter, although it really means vegetable, is frequently used in the same sense as *kitoweo*, for any kind of relish.)

Toweka, v. See under **Toa**, v. (B).

Toweo, n. See under **Towea**.

Toza, n. *ma-* the bowl of a tobacco pipe. (Cf. *kiko*, *buruma*, *kikororo*, *mtemba*.)

Toza, v. See under **Toa**, v. (A).

Tropiki,* n. the tropics, adopted for use in text-books and school lessons. (Eng.)

Tu, adv. only, just, exactly, simply, no more, merely, barely—always following the word it refers to, and used with nouns as well as adjs. and verbs, e.g. *mtoto tu*, a mere child, *kidogo tu*, just a little, *giza tu*, utter darkness. (Cf. *-tupu*, e.g. *giza tupu*, utter darkness.)

Tua,* n. (1) fate, destiny; (2) disgrace, stain, blemish. (Cf. *ila*, *waa*. Ar. طوح to perish, and طوخ disgrace.)

Tua, v. (A) (1) put down, set down; (2) fig. cause to settle, stop, decide, e.g. *tua mzigo*, put down a load. *Tua tanga*, lower sail. *Maneno yale yalimtua asiingie*, those words stopped him, so that he did not go in, or settled him not to go in. (3) as Intrans. settle down, rest, halt, bivouac, encamp, stop for the night; (4) go down, settle down, set, e.g. *jua likatua*, and the sun set. (Cf. *chwa*, *twa*, from *chua* or *tua*?) *Ndege alitua*, the bird alighted. Ps. **Tuliwa**. St. **Tulika**. Prep. **Tulia**, (1) be quiet, be calm, settle down; (2) fig. become quiet (tranquil, peaceful), reform, give up bad ways, take to a settled life, cease from anger (grief, excitement, passion), e.g. *Tulia!* (Imperat.), Be quiet! *Moyo wake umemtulia*, or *ametuliwa moyo*, he has calmed down. *Bahari inatulia*, the sea is going down. *Uso wa kutulia*, a tranquil, peaceful expression. *Chakula hakimtulii*, the food does not agree with him, i.e. he cannot digest it. Ps. of Prep. **Tuliwa**, be settled down, &c., in the senses given above. D.Prep. **Tulilia**, e.g. *Maneno haya yamekutulilia?* Have you got the matter settled? Ps. **Tuliliwa**, e.g. *tumetuliliwa na habari hizi*, we are pleased (content, reassured) by this news. Rp. of D.Prep. **Tuliliana**, come to an agreement or settlement among each other. St. **Tulilika**. Cs. **Tuliza**, bring to rest, pacify, settle, relieve pain, comfort, bring to a better mind, effect a reform in. Ps. **Tulizwa**. Rp. **Tulizana**, (1) comfort, quiet each other; (2) settle down, e.g. *bahari haikutulizana*, the sea did not settle down. *Wametulizana*, they have settled down, become quiet, also, they kept each other quiet, comforted, pacified each other. Ps. of Prep. **Tuliziwa**, e.g. *ametuliziwa moyo*, he has been tranquillized. Rp. **Tuana**, settle down together, all join in setting things in order, agree,

&c. Stc. **Tuama**, be in a settled state, settle down, subside. e.g. of muddy water clearing itself. *Acha maji yatuame yawe safi*, leave the water to settle and get clear. *Mambo yanatuama*, matters are settling themselves. Cs. **Tuamisha. Kitulizo**, n. *vi-* a quietening influence, anodyne, like *tulizo* below. **Kituo**, n. *vi-* (1) stopping, resting, cessation, respite, remission, quiet; (2) a stopping-place, encampment, time for rest, stage in a journey; (3) a stop, pause (e.g. in talking, music, writing, &c.), a note of punctuation, end of a sentence. *Roho yake haina kituo*, his spirit is always uneasy. *Hana kituo*, he is always on the move (cf. opp. *kitango*). *Maneno yasiyo kituo*, talk without breaks or pauses. *Piga kituo*, form an encampment. **Mtulivu**, n. *wa-* a gentle, quiet, reserved, reliable person. **Tuli**, adv. quiet, still, e.g. *kusimama tuli*, to stand still, quiet. **-tulivu**, a. quiet, tranquil, peaceful, composed, gentle, docile, e.g. *maji matulivu*, standing tranquil water. *Watu watulivu*, quiet peaceful people. **Tulizo**, n. *ma-* a quieting, soothing, means of soothing, relief, comfort, sedative. **Utulivu**, n. quietness, rest, peacefulness, gentleness, composed manner of mind. **Utuvu**, n. gentleness, good manners, orderliness, quietness of mien. (Cf. *upole, makini*.)

Tua, v. (B) sometimes heard for *chua*, v. which see.

Tuama, v., **Tuana**, v. See under **Tua**, v.

Tubu,* v. repent, be penitent, feel remorse, mend one's ways. A punished child says, *nimetubu*, I am sorry, I will not do it again. Prep. **Tubia**, e.g. *tubia kosa*, repent of a fault; *tubia Mungu*, repent before God. Cs. **Tubisha**, e.g. correct, chastise, bring to a penitent state of mind. **Kitubio**, n. *vi-* act of penitence, also used of penance. **Toba**, n. repentance, penitence, regret, remorse. (Cf. *juta, sikitika*. Ar. توب.)

Tuesha, v. (1) pay an evening visit to, call on at night, bid good-night to. (Prob. a Cs. form of *tua*, which see, esp. in the sense of *tua*, of setting of the sun. Contr. *amkia*, of morning call.) (2) used of a man with more than one wife visiting one of them out of turn at night.

Tufani,* n. storm, gale, tempest, hurricane, e.g. of rain, wind, and thunder together. (Cf. *kimbunga, dhoruba*. Ar. طوفان.)

Tufe,* n. (— and *ma-*) a ball, a game of ball. *Cheza tufe*, play at ball, e.g. cricket, tennis, golf. *Mpira* is almost generally used now in preference to *tufe*. (Ar. طوف.)

Tuguu, n. *ma-* a kind of mat on which women do the grinding of grain. (Cf. *utanga*.)

Tuhuma,* n. See under **Tuhumu**.

Tuhumu,* v. suspect, accuse, reproach. Ps. **Tuhumiwa**. St. **Tuhumika**. Prep. **Tuhumia**. Rp. **Tuhumiana**. Cs. **Tuhumisha**. **Tuhuma**, n. suspicion, accusation. (Cf. *shuku, dhania*. Ar. توهّم.)

Tui, n. the creamy juice or milk got by grating the nutty part of a coconut (cf. *kuna, mbuzi*), mixing it with water and straining it through a sieve or bag (*kifumbu, kung'uto*, or *kiteo*), leaving only *machicha*, which is thrown away. *Inzi kufia tuini si hasara*, a fly does not mind dying in coco-nut cream. *Tui bubu*, is the juice squeezed out without passing water through the grated coco-nut. *Tui la kupopolea*, is the juice obtained by passing the grated coco-nut with water through *kifumbu*. *Tui* is much used for cooking, esp. rice. (Cf. *kasimile*.)

Tuili,* v. See under **Tawili**.

Tuka, n. post supporting the projecting eaves in front of a native house, post of a verandah. (Commonly *nguzo, kiguzo.*)

Tukana, v. curse, use abusive language (to), abuse, revile, insult, call bad names. Ps. **Tukanwa.** St. **Tukanika.** Prep. **Tukania.** Cs. **Tukanisha,** e.g. inten. treat with scorn. *Jitukanisha kwa watu,* expose oneself to public derision, i.e. voluntarily incur abuse in public. Rp. **Tukanana. Tukano,** n. *ma-* generally in the plural, *matukano,* abuse, abusive expressions. (Cf. *tusi, sema, amba.*)

Tukia, v. happen (to), occur (to), present itself, come to pass. *Jambo limenitukia leo,* a thing has happened to me to-day. *Atajitukia yuko mjini,* he will find himself in the town. Ps. **Tukiwa,** e.g. *nilitukiwa na udhuru,* opportunity presented itself to me. Cs. **Tukiza. Kituko,** n. *vi-* (1) a feeling (object, cause, &c.) of fear, a terror, horror, fright, alarm, esp. of things caused by witchcraft, e.g. *inatia watu vituko vya hofu,* it causes people alarm. *Mtu ana (ameingiwa na) kituko,* the person is frightened. *Vituko vikutishavyo,* terrors which alarm you. **Tukio, n.** *ma-* occurrence, event, accident. (Cf. *kitisho, shtuo, hofu, kioja, afa.*)

Tuku, n. a kind of fish considered to be good eating by Europeans.

-tukufu, a. See under **Tukuka.**

Tukuka, v. become exalted, grand, glorious, &c. Cs. **Tukuza,** make exalted, magnify, glorify, aggrandize, place in high position, give all honour to. Ps. **Tukuzwa.** Rp. **Tukuzana. -tukufu,** a. exalted, grand, glorious, majestic. **Mtukufu,** n. *wa-* an exalted person. **Utukufu,** n. exalted state or station, majesty, glory, aggrandizement. (Cf. *adhimisha, heshima, kuza, -sharifu.*)

Tukusha, v. cause to shake, make restless, agitate. Ten. **Tukuta,** be restless, nervous, always on the move, be tiresome, petulant. St. **Tukutika,** e.g. move tremulously, tremble, quiver with excitement, shudder, be in a flutter. Cs. **Tukutiza,** Inten. (1) cause to quiver, shake, &c.; (2) should be used with caution as it is also the motion made by women during coition (*chezesha kiuno*) taught them in the puberty rites. **Mtukutu,** n. *wa-* restless, troublesome, petulant person. **Tukutiko,** n. *ma-* tremor, tremulous movement, nervous excitement, e.g. *tukutiko la moyo,* fluttering of the heart, excited feeling. **Tukuto, n.** *ma-* same as *tukutiko.* **-tukutu, a.** restless, nervous, excitable, petulant, troublesome, e.g. of children. **Utukutu,** n. (1) restlessness, nervousness, tremulousness; (2) playfulness, petulance, fidgeting, mischievousness, e.g. of a child. (Cf. *tikisa.*)

Tukuza, v. See under **Tukuka.**

-tule,* a. low, of low estate. **Matule,** n. wretchedness, disgrace, misery. **Mtule,** n. *wa-* a poor man. **Utule,** n. poverty, wretchedness. (Cf. *umaskini, unyonge, ufukara, ukata.* Ar. طلا beggar.)

Tuli, adv., **Tulia,** v., **-tulivu,** a., **Tuliza,** v., **Tulizo,** n. *ma-*. See under **Tua,** v.

Tuma, v. employ (a person), send (a person), give work to, e.g. *tuma mtu kazi* (*kwa kazi, kufanya kazi*), set a person to work. *Tuma mtu mahali* (*mjini, Mombasa, kwenda safari*), dispatch a person to a place (to the town, to Mombasa, on an expedition). Ps. **Tumwa,** i.e. be employed, be under orders, be on service (an errand, a job, a particular duty). St. and Pot. **Tumika,** e.g. (1) be engaged, be in service, be under orders, be used (in a general sense); (2) be disengaged, free to be employed, capable of service, be usable, available, &c. (see note below). The St. applies to things as well as persons. Pot. **Tumikana,** be capable of (free for, fit for, available for) service or use. Prep. of St. **Tumikia,**

be used or available by, be at the service of, and so commonly, obey, be obedient to, be servant to. Ps. **Tumikiwa,** have a service done, be obeyed. Cs. of St. **Tumikisha,** cause to obey, reduce to obedience, take as a servant. Prep. **Tumia,** use a person or thing, make use of, employ, e.g. *alitumia mali sana,* he spent money extravagantly. *Kisu kiki kinatumiwa,* this knife is being used. *Tumia maarifa ya somo,* apply a lesson, hence application of a lesson. (Note: *tumia tumiwa* and *tumika* should be used with caution as it is in common use (1) with object pfx. in a sexual way, i.e. of sexual intercourse, also sodomy, and (2) without object pfx. of a woman menstruating, e.g. *anatumia.*) D. Prep. **Tumilia,** e.g. use for (with, in, against, &c.). *Jitumilia,* spend selfishly, waste. *Tumilia mbali,* use up, consume entirely. Rp. of Prep. **Tumiana.** Cs. **Tumisha** and **Tumiza,** (1) cause to employ, make send; (2) commonly inten. give a special or urgent task to, impose a duty, give a charge to. *Wale ng'ombe aliowatumiza wamekuja,* those oxen he sent for have come. *Tutatumiza watu wa mji,* we will give work to the people in the town. Rp. **Tumana. Kitumwa,** n. and adv. *vi-* (1) dim. of *mtumwa,* which see; (2) service, what is servile or degrading. *Fanya kitumwa,* act as a slave. *-a kitumwa,* of a slavish, servile kind. **Matumishi,** n. plur. service, a servant's work. **Matumizi,** n. plur. (1) acts of use, using, employment; (2) things used, requisites, conveniences, e.g. food, clothes, firing, &c. *Hana matumizi nayo,* he has no use for them. *Sina matumizi leo,* I have nothing with which to buy food (necessities) to-day. **Mtume,** n. *mi-* one who is employed or sent, a messenger, an emissary, but esp. of Muhammad, i.e. the Apostle, and also of the chief characters of the Old Testament, Moses, Job, and others. It is the word adopted for the Christian Apostles also. **Mtumishi,** n. *wa-* a paid servant, hired domestic, house-servant. **Mtumo,** n. *mi-* employment, using, use, &c. **Mtumwa,** n. *wa-* one who is employed or sent, but usually in the special sense of bond-servant, slave, one who is the property of another. **Mtumwaji,** n. *wa-* rarely used, one who is regularly employed, or sent, an agent, a messenger, i.e. *mtumwa,* without the limitation to slaves. **Tume,** n. (1) messenger, envoy, employee, representative, servant, e.g. *wale wazee, tume za Mbega,* the old men, Mbega's envoys. Used like *mtume,* of Muhammad, as apostle of God. Also (2) occupation, task, errand, business. *Tume zangu zimekwisha,* my duties are finished. **Tumo,** n. *ma-* same as *mtumo,* which see. **Utume,** n. being employed (sent, used), status (fee, message, &c.) of one sent. **Utumi** and **Utumo,** n. employment (sending, using)—both meaning employment, use, service, errand, wages for service. **Utumishi,** n. (*tumishi* and *ma-*), **Utumizi,** n. *ma-* like *utume,* i.e. being used, or using, act of service, use, employment, work (duties, pay, &c.) of a servant, e.g. *katika matumishi yangu,* in my service. *Kitu cha utumizi,* a handy article, an implement, utensil, tool. *Matumizi mengi,* many uses, much service. **Utumwa,** n. state of being used or employed—but esp. of slavery, forced service, being used as a tool, or instrument merely. *Tia utumwani,* enslave. *Toa utumwani,* emancipate. (Cf. *peleka.*)

Tumai,* v. See under **Tamaa.**

Tumaini,* v. hope, trust, expect, be confident, be trustful, rely on. *Natumaini una afya,* I hope you are well. *Namtumaini mtu huyu,* I trust this man. Ps. **Tumainiwa.** St. and Pot. **Tumainika.** Prep. **Tumainia,** e.g. hope in, confide in, rely on. Cs.

Tumainisha, e.g. raise the hopes of. **Tumaini,** n. *ma-* usu. in the plur. confidence, trust, expectation, hope. **-tumaini,** a. confident, sanguine, hopeful. **-tumainifu,** a. (1) reliable, capable of being trusted; (2) confident, trusting, hopeful. (Ar. اطمان be free from disquietude, trust implicitly, &c.)

Tumba, n. (— and *ma-*) (1) outer case, cover; (2) case, or bale, of goods, e.g. the unopened bud of a flower, *matumba ya mawaridi*, rosebuds. *Tumba la chuo*, cover of a book, also its thickness. *Tumba la mwezi*, the halo surrounding and encasing the moon, and *tumba la uso*, the effect produced by oiling the face. *Tumba la mchele*, a bag of rice. *Tumba la nguo*, a bale of cloth, amplic. of *mtumba*, which see. **Utumbavu,** n. a swelling, bulging, rising up. (Cf. *tumbo, tumbua.*)

Tumbako,* n. tobacco. *Vuta tumbako*, smoke. *Nusa tumbako*, take snuff. *Tafuna tumbako*, chew tobacco. The forms in which it is made are known as *mkate*, cake; *ukambaa* (rope-like), twist; *pumba*, lump; *mshuku*, a plug or pinch of chewing tobacco. (Hind. تمباکو.)

Tumbasi, n. abscess, for common *jipu*.

Tumbawe, n. *ma-* coral rock in the intermediate stage between coral and rock—white and massive, but light and not fully consolidated. Used largely (from its lightness) for concrete roofs, also for cornices, being easily cut to shape, and for lime-burning.

Tumbili, n. name of a small light-coloured monkey. Also **Kitumbili.** (Cf. *kima, nyani, ngedere.*)

Tumbo, n. *ma-* (1) stomach, belly, abdomen, womb; (2) anything resembling the stomach in shape—a swelling, protuberance; (3) or in capacity—inside of a vessel, receptacle, hold (of a ship); (4) pain or disease in the abdominal region, colic, stomach-ache, diarrhoea, stoppage, &c., e.g. *tumbo la kuhara* (*la kuendesha*), diarrhoea, looseness of the bowels; *tumbo la kuhara damu*, dysentery. Also of pregnancy, *ana tumbo*, or *tumbo kubwa*, she is pregnant. *Ndugu tumbo moja*, children of the same mother. The expression *tia tumbo* or *mtumbotumbo*, or *tumbo moto* is used in the sense of causing confusion of mind, disconcert, worry, &c. Plur. **Matumbo,** guts, entrails, bowels, i.e. contents of the lower part of the body. **Kitumbo,** n. *vi-* and adv. (1) dim. of *tumbo*; (2) obesity, a large abnormal stomach (cf. *kikono, kiguu*, of malformation or maiming); (3) as an adv. *lala kitumbotumbo*, lie stomachwise, on the stomach. **Utumbo,** n. contr. with *tumbo*, as meaning (1) gut, i.e. the substance or material of the intestine; (2) the gut proper, the intestine. (Cf. *tumbo, tumbua.*)

Tumbua, v. (1) disembowel, rip up, cut open, make a hole (in), perforate; (2) lay open, display. *Tumbua kindu*, rip a leaf into strips. *Tumbua jipu*, lance a boil. Ps. **Tumbuliwa.** St. **Tumbuka,** e.g. (1) have a cut or hole made in; (2) burst out, break open. *Jipu limetumbuka*, the abscess has broken. *Mahali pa chombo palipotumbuka*, the place in the vessel, which was ripped open Prep. of St. **Tumbukia,** esp. in sense (1) break out into, burst suddenly into, of a sudden rush or fall, e.g. *ametumbukia kisimani*, he has tumbled into the well; (2) get suddenly involved in, be caught or strangled in. Cs. **Tumbukiza,** thrust into, push into, e.g. a well, pit, &c. Prep. **Tumbulia,** (1) lay open for (to, at, with, against); (2) thrust out the eyes, i.e. stare at with wide open eyes. *Nilikuambia, Fanya kazi yako, nawe wanitumbulia macho*, I said to you, Go on with your work, and you glare at me (cf. *kodolea macho, ng'ariza macho*). Cs. of

Prep. **Tumbuliza.** Cs. **Tumbuza,** (1) inten. force a way through, penetrate, come out on the other side of, e.g. *tumbuza mwitu,* pass through a forest; *jua limetumbuza,* the sun has burst out (cf. *penya* and *chimbuza*); (2) glare at, like *tumbulia.* Rp. **Tumbuana.** (Cf. *tumba, tumbo, pasua, kata, fungua, funua.* A Cs. form of *-tumba,* swell out, not now in use in Swahili.)

Tumbuika, v. be soothed by being sung to. Cs. **Tumbuiza,** soothe by singing, make a soothing sound with or without words, sing to, sing by turns. *Tumbuiza kwa nyimbo* (*kwa maneno mazuri*), soothe by songs (by gentle words). **Mtumbuizi, n.** *wa-* one who soothes by singing songs. **Tumbuizo, n.** *ma-* lullaby, ditty, refrain of a song, a soothing melody. **Utumbuizi, n., Utumbuizo, n.** singing a lullaby, soothing by singing, singing a refrain in a dance.

Tumbukia, v., Tumbulia, v., Tumbuliza. See under **Tumbua.**

Tumburujika, v. (1) be absolutely decayed and rotten, be decomposed; (2) same as *tumbuka,* which see, under *tumbua.*

Tumbuu,* n. an iron fastener consisting of a chain, hasp, and staple used for fastening doors and windows. (Cf. *liza, riza.* ? Pers. تنبه bar of a door.)

Tumbuza, v. See under **Tumbua.**

Tume, n., Tumia, v., Tumika, v., Tumiwa, v., Tumo, n. *ma-*. See under **Tuma.**

Tumu,* n. (1) a fast, fasting, e.g. of Ramadhan, *mwezi wa tumu,* the fasting month, for *saumu* (cf. *mfungo, saumu*); (2) garlic, also heard as *thumu.* Ar. صوم fast. ثوم garlic.)

Tuna, v. (1) puff out, swell out; (2) show anger, be petulant (arrogant), e.g. *tuna mashavu,* swell out the cheeks. **Jituna,** bluster, brag (cf. *jivuna*). Ps. **Tunwa.** St. **Tunika.** Prep. **Tunia.** Cs. **Tunisha,** e.g. (1) offend, enrage; (2) puff out, flatter. (Cf. *fura.*)

Tunda, n. *ma-* (1) a fruit of any kind, a product of a tree, plant, vegetable, &c.; (2) beads worn by some women round their loins. (Cf. *utunda.*)

Tunda, v. pluck fruit, flowers, &c. Used at Tanga and in the north, as a rule instead of *chuma,* v.

Tundama, v. Stc. settle down, gather, accumulate, e.g. as water at bottom of a well or hole. Cs. **Tundamisha.** (Cf. *tungama, tuama.*)

Tundika, v. hang up, suspend—but clear of walls, &c., not touching anything (contr. *angika, tungika*), e.g. *tundika bendera,* hang up a flag (cf. *tweka*). Ps. **Tundikwa.** Prep. **Tundikia.** Cs. **Tundikisha.** Cv. **Tundua,** take down anything which has been hung up or is suspended. **Tunduo,** *ma-* an act of taking down. **Tundiza, v.** begin to ripen, of fruit, &c.

Tundu, n. (— and *ma-*) hole, hollow, passage, hollow receptacle, and hence of several objects, den or lair of a wild animal, snake, &c., nest of a bird, a cage of any kind, a basket of open wicker-work. *Tundu ya pua,* nostril. Dim. **Kitundu, n.** *vi-*. *Fanya tundu,* bore a hole. *Tundutundu,* full of holes, e.g. describing trellis-work, lattice, network, &c., or of moth-eaten clothes. *Tundu* is the most general word for 'hole'. (Cf. *shimo,* which is generally bigger, *pango, kitobwe, ufa, mwanya.*)

-tundu, a. See under **Mtundu.**

Tundua, v. (1) see under *tundika;* (2) see under *mtundu.*

Tunduia, v. keep a watchful eye on, look out for, spy out, lie in wait for, e.g. of a doctor, *akiugua mtoto hutaweza kumtunduia,* if the child is ill, you will not be able to attend him. **Mtunduizi, n.** *wa-* a spy, a scout. **Tunduizi, n.** one who watches, guardian, spy. **Utunduizi, n.** spying out, watchfulness, &c. (Cf. *chungua, angalia, tunza, peleleza.*)

Tunduo, n. **ma-**. See under **Tundika.**

Tunduwaa, v. be still, silent, motionless, e.g. of one amazed, deceived, fascinated, deep in thought. Cs. **Tunduwaza.** (Cf. *duwaa, shangaa, pumbaa*).

Tunga, n. (1) a round flat basket, used for sifting husks, &c., from grain by tossing (cf. *kitunga* and *chunga,* v. (B)); (2) tail-bones of a skate (*taa*); (3) *mwendo wa tunga* or (*matunga*), a prancing gait, i.e. like somebody showing off.

Tunga, v. (1) put together, put in order, put in a row; (2) form by arranging, compose, bring materials or ingredients together, construct, connect, make, e.g. (1) *tunga nyama kijitini,* put bits of meat in a row on a skewer. *Tunga samaki,* string fish together, or put them on a stick. *Tunga ushanga,* string beads. *Tunga maua,* tie flowers together, make a garland or nosegay. *Tunga sindano, tunga uzi* (*katika sindano*), are both used of threading a needle. (2) *tunga mayai,* form eggs—also Intrans. *mayai yametunga,* the eggs are hard set—the contents having taken form. *Mtama unatunga,* the millet (grain) is forming. *Tunga mimba,* conceive, form an embryo. *Tunga chuo* (*mashairi, nyimbo, maneno*), compose a book (poetry, songs, essay). *Tunga usaha,* form matter, suppurate, e.g. of an abscess. Ps. **Tungwa.** St. **Tungika,** (1) not only as above, i.e. be put together, be formed, but (2) with the further sense, be hung up, be suspended, be connected with, be dependent on; and (3) sometimes Trans. e.g. *tungika paa,* put on a roof. Ps. **Tungikwa** (cf. *angika, tundika*), e.g. *alitungikwa tanzi la roho,* he was hung up by a noose round the neck. Prep. of St. **Tungikia.** Prep. **Tungia,** e.g. *umetungia* (*uzi*) *sindano,* you have threaded the needle. Cs. **Tungiza,** (1) put in order; (2) cause to follow after or in order; *tungiza ukuta,* build up the wall from the floor-level (cf. *tungizi* below). *Gari la moshi linatungiza behewa,* the engine pulls the carriages after it, e.g. causes them to follow. *Fulani anatungiza watu,* So-and-so has people following after him (in Indian file). Rp. **Tungana.** Stc. **Tungama,** be in a firm, compacted state, be formed like a clot, congeal, get thick, e.g. *damu inatungama,* the blood is clotting. *Nyuki wanatungama,* the bees are forming a cluster. Rp. of Stc. **Tungamana,** hold together, be connected, agree, be in a settled, peaceful state, be in harmony. Cs. **Tungamanisha,** make agree, bring into harmony, &c. Cv. **Tungua,** (1) unform, disconnect, take to pieces; (2) unstring, take down, let down, e.g. *tungua madafu,* get down coco-nuts. *Tungua roho,* discourage, dishearten. *Nguo za kutungua,* ready-made garments. (3) fig. depress, depreciate, degrade. Ps. **Tunguliwa.** St. **Tunguka,** e.g. be let down, be taken down, sink, be depressed, &c. Prep. **Tungulia.** Cs. **Tunguza. Mtunga,** n. *wa-*, **Mtungaji,** n. *wa-* arranger, constructor. **Mtungo,** n. *mi-* a putting together, arranging in a row (and in other sense of *tunga,* v.), also of things put together in a row. Used esp. of fish, *mtungo wa samaki* or *mtungo* only, a string or stick of fish, i.e. fish on a string or stick. *Mtungo mkubwa,* a great lot (haul, catch) of fish. *Mtungo wa habari,* a composition, essay. **Kitungo,** n. *vi-* dim. **Mtunguo,** n. *mi-* a ready-made garment, i.e. 'off the peg'. **Tungo,** n. *ma-* amplic. of *mtungo,* i.e. way of forming, composition, device, things in a row. **Tungizi,** n. *ma-* usu. in the plur. (1) the level of the floor and walls of a house, i.e. above which the walls are built; (2) arrangements of the thoughts, inventions, &c. **Utungaji,** n. (1) ability to compose,

&c.; (2) act of arranging, composition. **Utungo**, n. (1) composing, arranging, literary composition (novel, essay, &c.); (2) form, fashion, build, make, mould, plan; (3) idea, proposal, design, fancy; (4) invention, figment; (5) a series, succession, chain, line (of ideas, objects, &c.).

Tungama, v., **Tungamana**, v. See under **Tunga**, v.

Tungi, n. *ma-* amplic. of *mtungi*.

Tungika, v., **Tungiza**, v., **Tungizi**, n. *ma-*, **Tungo**, n. *ma-*. See under **Tunga**, v.

Tungua, v. (1) see under **Tunga**, v.; (2) *tungua usingizi*, get sleep, i.e. of a sick man or one very tired, e.g. *je! leo ulitungua usingizi? La, sikuutungua hata kidogo.* Did you get any sleep to-day? No, I did not sleep a wink.

Tunguja, n. fruit of the *mtunguja*.

Tungule, n. *ma-*. See under **Mtungule**.

Tunguri, n. a small gourd in which native medicine-men (*waganga*) keep their medicines.

Tunguridi, n. Brown's Red-faced Weaver Finch, *Pyletia afra*.

Tuni,* n. a tune, adopted for use in text-books and school lessons. (Eng.)

Tunu, n. See under **Tunuka**.

Tunuka, v. and **Chunuka**, (1) set the heart on, treasure, prize, long for, have special affection for, make a treasure of, e.g. *namtunuka mtu huyu*, I have set my heart on this man; (2) get something which has been longed for. Ps. **Tunukwa**. Prep. **Tunukia**, e.g. make a present to. *Tunukia kofia*, give a cap to. *Tunukia msikiti*, make a gift to a mosque. Rp. **Tunukana**. **Tunu**, n. something rare, choice, valuable—keepsake, a souvenir, an heirloom, a special present, treasure, a rare sight, a curiosity. **Utunu**, n. quality of being rare, choice, valuable. (Cf. *hedaya, kioja, tunzo, tuzo*, see also *chunuka*.)

Tunutu, n. also **Funutu**, the young of locusts.

Tunza, v. treat with care or affection; (1) guard, protect, care for, tend, keep safe; (2) attend to, observe, examine, keep an eye on; (3) make a present to, but usu. *tuza*, e.g. *tunza kazi*, work with care. *Tunza mtoto*, mind a child. *Tunza akili*, keep the brain clear, use the wits. Ps. **Tunzwa**. St. and Pot. **Tunzika**. Prep. **Tunzia**. Cs. **Tunzisha**. Rp. **Tunzana**. **Tunza**, n. (— and *ma-*), **Tunzo**, n. (— and *ma-*), (1) care, attention, guardianship; (2) things cared for, belongings. *Akamletea kijana na tunza zake*, and he brought him the youth and his belongings. (3) gift, present, reward, but this is often *tuzo*. **Utunzaji** and **Utunzi**, n. caring for, looking after, protecting (and sometimes plur. *matunzaji*). *Utunzaji* (*utunzi*) *wa watoto*, welfare of children, child welfare. **Utunzo**, n. (*tunzo* and *ma-*) care, guardianship, &c., like *tunza*. (Cf. *tunu, tunuka*.)

Tupa, n. a file—for metal, i.e. *tupa ya chuma*. A flat file is called *tupa ya msumeno*; a rasp for wood, *tupa ya tunga*.

Tupa, v. (1) throw, cast, fling, e.g. a spear, stone, &c.; *Ametutupa mkono*, he has thrown us (his) hand, is a phrase frequently used with the meaning, he has (is) died (dead). (2) throw away, cast off, desert, abandon. *Tupa jicho*, throw a glance. *Tupa mtoto*, abandon a child. Ps. **Tupwa**, e.g. *nimetupwa*, I am an outcast. St. and Pot. **Tupika**, be thrown, often in the sense of being thrown down carelessly. Prep. **Tupia**, e.g. throw at (from, with, to)—also sometimes pass on to, refer to, e.g. *Sultani kumtupia waziri maneno*, the Sultan usually refers matters to his prime minister. D.Prep. and Inten. **Tupilia**. Rp **Tupana**. Rp. of Prep. **Tupiana**. **Mtupa**, n. *wa-* with a noun follg. one who throws, e.g. *mtupa mkuki*, a spear thrower. **Mtupio,** n. *mi-* (1) act of throwing down, esp. carelessly; (2) *vazi la mtupio,* a well-worn garment which is just thrown on anyhow. **Mtupo,** n. *mi-* (1) an act of throwing, &c.; (2) distance of a throw, e.g. *mtupo wa jiwe,* as far as a stone can be thrown. (Cf. *acha, rusha, peleka, piga, vurumisha.*)

-tupu, a. (1) empty, bare, void, naked; (2) mere, sheer, bare, by itself (themselves), unmixed, pure, without change or adulteration; (3) meaningless, worthless, vain, devoid of content, e.g. *mikono mitupu,* empty hands, empty-handed. *Miguu mitupu,* bare feet, barefoot. *Mtu mtupu,* just a man, a mere man, one who has nothing. *Uwongo mtupu,* a sheer, downright falsehood. *Watu weusi watupu,* none but black people. *Maneno matupu,* idle talk, nonsense. Sometimes indeclinable, e.g. *vyakula vitamu tupu* (or *vitupu*), nothing but nice food. Obs. *-tupu,* includes 'unclothed, naked', but to denote nakedness in a vulgar sense, *utupu* or *tupu* is used as an indeclinable adj. e.g. *huyu yu utupu,* this person is naked. *Mtu tupu,* a naked person. A less vulgar word is *uchi.* **Utupu,** n. (1) bareness, emptiness, simplicity, being unmixed, purity. Not common, because of the commoner meaning (2) nakedness, nudity—in a vulgar sense, and (3) sexual organs, e.g. *wanaume wanakwenda utupu, hawavai nguo,* the men go naked, wearing no clothes.

Turubali,* n. a tarpaulin, ground sheet of a tent, canvas, &c. (Corruption of same word.)

Turufu,* n. a particular card chosen out of a pack which is the suit which must be followed; a trump in cards. (Eng. 'trumps' or Port. *trunfo.*)

Turufu,* v. scorn, slight, despise, treat with contempt. (Cf. *dharau, beza, fyoza.* Ar. ازرف.)

Turuhani,* n. (1) tare, allowance made in weighing for package, vehicle, &c.; (2) something thrown in with a sale, a bonus, gift with a sale. (Pers. زرخان exempt from tax, &c.)

Turuki,* n. *ma-,* also **Turki, Mturki,** *wa-* a Turk. **Uturuki,** Turkey. **Kituruki,** Turkish language, after the Turkish style, &c. (Turk. ترك.)

Tusha, v. annoy, put in a bad temper, rouse resentment, lower, degrade, humiliate, hold in contempt, treat contemptuously. *Jitusha,* disgrace oneself—by unworthy conduct. Ps. **Tushwa.** St. **Tushika.** Prep. **Tushia.** Cv. **Tushua,** with same meaning as *tusha.* **Tushi,** n. *ma-,* **Tusi,** n. *ma-,* and **Tusu,** n. *ma-,* filthy words, words which cause annoyance, which rouse resentment, insulting language or conduct, abuse. (Prob. a Cs. form of Bantu *-tuka,* abuse, curse. Cf. *chuki* and *chukia.*)

Tusi, n. (1) see under **Tusha,** v.; (2) a litter, palanquin, sedan, sling, or hammock for carrying a person. (Cf. *machela, jeneza.*)

Tusu, n. *ma-.* See under **Tusha.**

Tuta, n. *ma-* a raised bed for planting, a long ridge of earth with deep furrows on either side.

Tuta, v. (A) beat, throb, as of the heart.

Tuta, v. (B), (1) pile up; (2) carry. Prep. **Tutia,** (1) fill up a pit or hole with rubbish, level a road; (2) carry for (with, &c.). St. **Tutika,** carry many loads from one place to another, i.e. one after the other.

Tutu! int. leave it alone!

Tutu, n. (1) a kind of small drum; (2) a small bird like a dove; (3) a swelling, but cf. *tutuu* under *tutuma,* v.

Tutuka, v. rise in small swellings. Stc. **Tutuma,** swell up, bubble up, boil up, and fig. be puffed up, swell up, e.g. with pride, anger, &c. St. **Tutumka,** swell, i.e. of the face or body, also like *tutuma.* Cv. **Tutumua,** (1) e.g. *jitutumua,* brag, boast, puff oneself up; (2) make a great effort as when trying to lift a heavy load, i.e. swell with effort. St. of Cs. **Tutuzika**, rest after making an effort, rest for want of breath. **Tutuo**, n. *ma-* (1) haste in doing, impatience, greediness (cf. *haraka*, *pupa*); (2) loud boasting (cf. *majisifu*). **Tutuu**, n. *ma-*, also **Tuutuu**, n. *ma-*, a wart or hard swelling. (Cf. *tuta*, v. (B).)

Tutuma, v. (1) see under **Tutuka**, v.; (2) make a rumbling (muttering, grumbling, growling) sound, e.g. thunder, the bowels, &c. **Kitutumi**, n. *vi-* anything which causes a rumbling sound. **Mtutumo**, n. *mi-* a low distant roll or rumbling sound, as of thunder, an earthquake, waterfall, boiling water.

Tutumka, v., **Tutumua**, v., **Tutuo**, n. *ma-*. See under **Tutuka**.

Tutusa, v. grope about in the dark, looking for something, or feeling one's way.

Tutuu, n. *ma-*, **Tutuzika**, v., **Tuutuu**, n. *ma-*. See under **Tutuka**, v.

Tuwanyika, n. a kind of snake, also called *nondo*.

Tuza, v. make a present (to), give as a reward (to). *Mumewe alimtuza mganga mchele*, her husband gave the doctor a present of rice. Ps. **Tuzwa**, e.g. get a present. **Tuza**, n. and **Tuzo**, n. a present, esp. of a reward for success. See **Tunzo** under **Tunza**.

Tuzua, v. disgrace, put to shame. (Cf. *aibisha*, *hizi*, *tahayarisha*, *tusha*.)

Twa, v. See **Chwa**.

Twaa, adv. still, silent, e.g. *alilala twaa*, he lay still and silent.

Twaa, v. (1) take (to oneself), take away (from another), carry away (from another), take off, receive, accept, obtain. (Syn. with *pokea*, *pewa*, *chukua*, *pata*, *shika*.) *Alitwaa miji mingi*, he seized (got possession of) many towns. (2) also used in the sense of taking a woman, e.g. *twaa mwanamke*, lie with a woman. *Twaa bikira*, deflower a virgin. Rp. **Twaana**, (1) take each other, of a man and woman; (2) be like, resemble each other—sometimes with *sura*, *uso*, of personal resemblance, also Rp. of Cs. **Twazana**, in the same sense. (Cf. *fanana*, *lingana*.) Ps. **Twawa**, but more usu. of the Prep. **Twaliwa**, (1) be taken, seized, received, also (2) be robbed of, have something taken from (or for) one, lose. St. and Pot. **Twalika**. Prep. **Twalia**, take (receive) from (for, with, at, &c.), rob of, relieve, rid a person of, take on behalf of, &c. Rp. of Prep. **Twaliana**. **Mtwaa**, n. *wa-*, also **Mtwaaji**, n. *wa-* one who takes or carries off.

Twaana, v. See under **Twaa**.

Twana, n. *ma-*. See under **Mtwana**.

Twanga, v. (1) clean grain by pounding in a mortar, pound in order to get off the husks; (2) fig. beat, give a beating to, fig. beat down, as in price, &c. Ps. **Twangwa**. St. and Pot. **Twangika**. Prep. **Twangia**. Cs. **Twangisha**. **Mtwango**, n. *mi-* act (place, or manner, &c.) of pounding with pestle and mortar. **Mtwanzi**, n. *wa-* one who pounds grain.

Twaza, v. vaunt oneself, be proud, arrogant, show oneself off. (Cf. *takabari*, *jivuna*.)

Twazana, v. See under **Twaa**.

Tweka, v. hoist up, raise up, i.e. *tweka bendera*, hoist a flag; *tweka tanga* (or simply *tweka-*), hoist a sail. Ps. **Twekwa**. Prep. **Twekea**. (Cf. *twika*, usually used of loads only.)

Twesha, v. (1) for *tuesha*, which see; (2) sometimes heard for *tweza*, v. which see.

Tweta, v. pant, gasp, catch the breath—of any irregular or difficult breathing. Prep. **Twetea**. **Mtweto**, n. *mi-* panting, gasping. (Cf. *kokota roho*, *vuta pumzi*.)

Tweza, v. humble, bring low, degrade, debase, dishonour, humiliate. (Cf. *aibisha*, *tahayarisha*, *dhii*, *aziri*, *hizi*, *tuzua*.)

Twiga, n. a giraffe. *Twiga mdogo*, a name for the Gerenuk.

Twika, v. like *tweka*, but usu. only of lifting loads on to the head or shoulder. *Jitwika*, lift on to one's own head. Cs. **Twisha**, e.g. *nitwishe mzigo huu*, put this load on to my head (or shoulder) for me. **Twisho**, n. a round pad for putting on the head under a load. (Cf. *kata*.)

U

U represents the sound of *oo* as in 'fool', or *u* in 'put'. **Uu** is written when the sound is very marked and sustained, as in *kuukuu*, dist. *kuku*.

U is commonly pronounced as *w* before the vowels, *a*, *e*, *i*, and *o*, so that words not found under *u* may be looked for under *w*.

U is used independently: (A) as a verb-form (1) 'you are', agreeing with the pronoun of the 2nd person sing. i.e. *wewe*, or (2) 'it is', agreeing with the singular of the *mw-*, *mi-* class, and of the *u* class, e.g. *mzigo u mzito*, the load is heavy. (B) occasionally as conj., 'and', e.g. *tatu u nusu*, three and a half. (Cf. Ar. *wa*.)

U! Int. expressive of contempt and derision; a jeering exclamation.

Ua, n. (A) (*maua*) a flower. *Chuma maua*, pick flowers. *Toa maua*, come into flowers. (Cf. *chanua*. Dist. follg.)

Ua, n. (B) (*nyua*) (1) an enclosure, commonly an open court or backyard attached to a house, and fenced with sticks, plaited leaves, or a hedge. Also (2) a fence of this kind, i.e. *ua wa nyasi* (*miti*, *makuti*, *mabua*), a fence of grass (sticks, leaves, stalks). (Cf. *uga*, *ugo*, *kiwanja*, *kitalu*, *boma*.)

Ua, v. kill, destroy life. Ps. **Uawa.** Prep. **Ulia**, (1) kill with (for, &c.); (2) Inten. e.g. *ulia mbali*, kill outright, kill off entirely. *Umwulie kisu*, kill him with a knife. Prov. *Fimbo uliyo nayo ndiyo uuliayo nyoka*, the stick you have with you is the one with which you kill a snake, i.e. make the best of what you have. *Amemwulia nduguye*, he has killed his brother (for him, i.e. to his disadvantage, in pursuance of a blood feud). Rp. **Uana.** (Syn. *fisha*, *chinja*.) **Kiua**, n. *vi-* that which kills. **Kiuaji**, n. *vi-* something deadly, something that kills, e.g. beast of prey, snake, poison, firearms, &c. **Maulisho**, n. anything likely to cause death. **Mwua**, n. *wa-* a killer. **Mwuaji**, n. *wa-* a murderer, assassin, slayer. **Uuaji**, n. (sometimes plur. *mauaji*) murderousness, savagery, bloodshedding, massacre.

Uadui,* n. See under **Adui.**

Uaguzi, n. See under **Agua, v.** (A) and (B).

Uaili,* n. See under **Aili.**

Uajemi, n. Persia, Iran. **Kiajemi**, n. and adv. the Persian language, after the Persian manner, style, &c. (Ar. العجم.)

Uajizi,* n. See under **Ajazi.**

Uambukizo, n. See under **Amba, v.** (B).

Uamini, n., **Uaminifu**,* n. See under **Amana.**

Uana, n. See under **Jana.**
Uanafunzi, n. See under **Funda**, v. (C).
Uandamano, n., **Uandamizi**, n. See under **Andaa.**
Uanga, n. See under **Anga**, v.
Uangalifu, n., **Uangalizi**, n. See under **Anga**, n.
Uangamizi, n. See under **Angamia.**
Uangavu, n. See under **Anga**, n.
Uapo, n. (*nyapo*) (1) see under **Apa**; (2) see under **Pa**, v.
Uarabu,* n. See under **Mwarabu.**
Uasherati,* n. See under **Asherati.**
Uashi, n. See under **Aka**, v.
Uasi,* n. See under **Asi.**
Uaskari,* n. See under **Askari.**
Uati, n. (*mbati*) the pole which lays on top of the walls of a native house, wall-plate. (Cf. *mtambaa panya*.)
Ubaba, n. See under **Baba.**
Ubadhiri, n., **Ubadhirifu**,* n. See under **Badhiri.**
Ubadili, n., **Ubadilifu**.* See under **Badala.**
Ubahili,* n. See under **Bahili.**
Ubaini, n., **Ubainifu**,* n. See under **Baina.**
Ubale, n. (*mbale*) strip, slice, piece, e.g. *mbale za muhogo*, cassava cut in pieces lengthways—called also *kopa, ma-*, when dried. The process of cutting is *lenga* (also *kata*) *mbale*. **Mbale**, n. *mi-* same as above but of larger slices. **Bale**, n. *ma-* same, but of largest slices of all.
Ubalehe,* n. See under **Balehe.**
Ubalozi,* n. See under **Balozi.**
Ubamba, n. (*bamba*), **Ubambo**, n. See under **Bamba**, n.
Ubango, n. (*bango*), (1) the leathery sheath of betel-nuts; (2) a kind of reed.
Ubani,* n. (1) frankincense, brought from India. It is different from *udi* (which see) which comes from Barawa, and is a tree, i.e. *ubani* is a gum, but *udi* pieces of wood of an odoriforous kind; (2) fig. customary fee, footing. *Toa ubani*, pay a customary fee. *Aliambiwa atoe ubani, na ubani ulikuwa shilingi mbili*, he was told to pay the usual fee, which was two shillings, i.e. of a doctor's fee, an apprentice's fee paid to his master, &c. (Ar. لبان.)
Ubao, n. (*mbao*). See under **Bao.**
Ubapa, n. (*bapa*). See under **Bapa.**
Ubaradhuli,* n. See under **Baradhuli.**
Ubaridi,* n. See under **Baridi.**
Ubashiri,* n. See under **Bashiri.**
Ubati, n. (*bati*), an addition to a house, wing, outhouse, lean-to. Used as a kitchen, &c. (Cf. *kipenu, shuhuli*.)
Ubatili,* n. See under **Batili.**
Ubatizo,* n. See under **Batiza.**
Ubavu, n. (*mbavu*), a rib. Plur. side of the body, or anything corresponding to it in relative position, e.g. skirt (slope, flank) of a mountain, side wing (of an army, &c.). *Mbavuni mwa*, at the side of, on the flanks of. **Bavu**, n. *ma-* amplic., see also under **Bavu**, n.
Ubawa, n. (*mbawa*), a wing. *Funua mbawa*, spread out the wing. See also under **Bawa.**
Ubawabu,* n. See under **Bawaba.**
Ubaya, n. *ma-*. See under **-baya.**
Ubayana,* n. See under **Baini.**
Ubazazi,* n. See under **Bazazi.**
Ubeja,* n. See under **Mbeja.**
Ubeleko, n. See under **Eleka.**
Ubembe, n., **Ubembelezi**, n. See under **Bemba.**
Ubeti,* n. (*beti*), verse, stanza, strophe. (Cf. *shairi*. Ar. بيت.)
Ubichi, n. See under **-bichi.**
Ubikira,* n. See under **Bikira.**
Ubilisi,* n. See under **Bilisi.**
Ubinadamu,* n. See under **Bin.**
Ubinda, n. manner of girding up the loin-cloth by passing the ends between the legs and tucking them into the fold round the waist. *Alipiga ubinda kama Baniani*, he girded himself with his loin-cloth in Hindu style. Also called *winda* and *upati*.

These words are also used for the method of putting on a baby's napkin. (Cf. *bindo.*)

Ubingwa, n. See under **Bingwa.**

Ubini,* n. See under **Bini.**

Ubinja, n. (*mbinja*), also **Uwinja**, a whistling noise, whistle, i.e. the act or sound of whistling. *Piga mbinja*, whistle. (Cf. *mluzi, miunzi*, and dist. *ubinda, winda.*) **Kibinja**, n. *vi-* a whistle, either sound or instrument. (Cf. *filimbi, kipenga.*)

Ubishi, n. (*mbishi* and *ma-*). See under **Bisha.**

Ubivu, n. See under **-bivu.**

Uboi,* n. See under **Boi.**

Ubongo, n. brain substance, brain, marrow. **Bongo**, n. *ma-* brain, marrow. *Bongo lake si barabara*, his mind is not quite right.

Ubono, n. (*mbono*). See under **Mbono.**

Ubora,* n. See under **Bora.**

Ubovu, n. See under **-bovu.**

Ubozi, n. See under **Boza.**

Ubua, n. (*mbua*). See under **Bua.**

Ububu, n. See under **Bubu.**

Ubuge, n. See under **Bugia.**

Ubugu, n. (*mbugu*), the long stem of any creeping-plant which can be used as a substitute for cord, e.g. stems of the *mbungo, mtoria*, and *mkunguzi*, but esp. of the latter. It serves to fasten together the stakes used in building a hut or fence, and for binding loads. (Cf. *mbungo, kamba.*)

Ubukuzi, n. See under **Bukua.**

Uburidisho,* n. See under **Baridi.**

Ubutu, n. See under **Butu.**

Ubuyu, n. See under **Mbuyu.**

Ubwabwa, n. (1) gruel, pap, e.g. rice, esp. as made for babies who have no teeth or for invalids, boiled with water enough to make a paste, or (2) much less usually, of a very small quantity of rice cooked without coco-nut juice. *Ubwabwa wa mtoto mtamu*, a child's gruel is nice—a riddle to which the answer is, *usingizi*, sleep.

Ubwana, n. See under **Bwana.**

Ubwete, n. laziness, idleness. (Cf. *ukunguni.*)

Uchache, n. See under **-chache.**

Uchachu, n. See under **Chacha.**

Uchafu, n., **Uchafuko**, n. *ma-*. See under **-chafu.**

Uchaga, n. a raised stage used for storing grain on. (Cf. *utaa, ghala, uchala, kichaga.*)

Uchago, n. See **Chago.**

Uchaguo, n., **Uchaguzi**, n. See under **Chagua.**

Uchaji, n. See under **Cha**, v. (A).

Uchakacho, n. See under **Chakacha.**

Uchala, n. a raised stage for storing grain on. (Cf. *uchaga.*)

Uchale, n. cut, incision, gash. *Ndugu wa uchale*, a blood brother. (Cf. *chanja.*)

Uchanga, n. (1) see under **-changa**; (2) see under **Mchanga.**

Uchango, n. (*chango*) (1) see under **Changa**, v. (A); (2) see under **Chango.**

Uchanjaa, n. open ground, plain, wilderness. (Cf. *uwanja.*)

Uchao, n. See under **Cha**, v. (B).

Uchawi, n. See under **Mchawi.**

Uche, n., **Ucheachea**, n. See under **Cha**, v. (B).

Uchechefu, n. fewness, e.g. *niliona watu wengi njiani, uchechefu wao haupungui mia moja*, I saw many people in the road, not fewer than 100, lit. their fewness was not less than 100.

Uchekechea, n. a collection of small, unimportant, insignificant people or things.

Uchengelele, n. *ma-*, also **Ujengelele**, small intestines, but also used as a euphemism (obscene) for penis. (Cf. *uchango, mboo, uume.*)

Ucheo, n., **Uchoo**, n. a piece of land prepared ready for planting.

Uchepechepe, n. See under **Chepechepe.**

Ucheshi, n. See under **Cheka.**

Uchi, n. nakedness, nudity, a vulgar word, the sexual organs (cf. *utupu*). Used adverbially, *kwenda uchi*, to go naked. Also as a. *washenzi walikuwa uchi*, the savages were naked. *Uchi wa nyama*, stark naked. **Koa uchi**, n. a slug.

Uchimvi, n. See under **Chimba.**

Uchipuko, n. (*chipuko*). See under **Chipua.**

Uchochoro, n. *ma-*. See under **Chochoro.**

Uchokozi, n. See under **Chokoa.**

Uchoo, n. See **Ucheo.**

Uchomozi, n. See under **Choma**, v. (B).

Uchongelezi, n., **Uchongezo**, n. See under **Chonga.**

Uchongo, n. (1) see under **Chonga**, n. (B); (2) discharge from a weak or diseased eye. (Cf. *utongo*.)

Uchovu, n. See under **Choka.**

Uchoyo, n. See under **Moyo.**

Uchu, n. (1) fondness, longing, e.g. *uchu wa samaki* (*embe*), a craving for fish (mangoes). *Mtoto huyu ana uchu wa kitoweo*, this child is very fond of meat. (2) sexual desire, lust: in this sense regarded as a vulgar boorish word. (Cf. *shauku, tamaa, ashiki, utamanifu*.)

Uchukuti, n. (*chukuti*), also **Ujukuti**, central part, or midrib, of coco-nut leaf. (Cf. *ukuti, kuti*.)

Uchukuzi, n. See under **Chukua.**

Uchumba, n. See under **Chumba.**

Uchumi, n., **Uchumo**, n. See under **Chuma**, v.

Uchungu, n. See under **-chungu.**

Uchunguzi, n. See under **Chunga**, v. (B).

Uchuro, n. See under **Chura**, v.

Uchusichusi, n. See **Utusitusi.**

Uchuuzi, n. See under **Chuuza.**

Udachi, n. See under **Mdachi.**

Udadisi, n. See under **Dadisi.**

Udago, n. (*ndago*), nut grass, *Cyprus rotundus*, a weed which spreads very rapidly by means of long roots, bearing black tubers which quickly send up shoots. These tubers are a favourite food with wild pigs, and are also used medicinally.

Udaktari,* n. See under **Daktari.**

Udaku, n., **Udakuzi**, n. See under **Daka.**

Udalali,* n. See under **Dalali.**

Udamisi,* n. See under **Damisi.**

Udanganyifu, n. *ma-*. See under **Danganya.**

Udara, n. (*ndara*) used in the plur. as a rule, *viatu vya ndara*, sandals with broad leather straps across the instep.

Udekuaji, n. See under **Dekua.**

Udelele, n. saliva which sometimes trickles from the mouth of children or very old people. (Cf. *udende, mate, ute*.)

Udende, n. saliva, same as *udelele*.

Udevu, n. (*ndevu*) a hair of the face, of the beard and whiskers. In the plur. used with the meaning of beard, *mwenye ndevu*, bearded. Also *ndevu za mashavuni*, whiskers. Of the moustache *mashurubu* is the usual word. **Devu**, n. *ma-* amplic. **Kidevu**, n. *vi-* chin. *Ndevu zamwota kidevuni*, a beard is growing on his chin.

Udhahiri,* n. See under **Dhahiri.**

Udhaifu,* n. See under **Dhaifu.**

Udhalilifu,* n. See under **Dhalili.**

Udhalimu,* n. See under **Dhalimu.**

Udhamini,* n. See under **Dhamana.**

Udhani,* n. (1) see under **Dhana**; (2) sometimes heard for *uzani*, which see.

Udhanifu,* n. See under **Dhana.**

Udhi,* v. give trouble, annoy, harass, vex, pain, grieve. Prep. **Udhia**, e.g. *neno hili latuudhia watoto wetu*, this matter is annoying our children. Ps. **Udhiwa.** St. **Udhika**, usu. in the sense of to be angry, inconvenienced, e.g. *niliudhika sana*, I was very angry. Cs. **Udhisha.** (Cf. *sumbua, tesa, chokoza, onea, taabisha*.) **Adha**, n. but usu. **Udhia**, n. trouble, annoyance, difficulty, bother, confusion, disturbance, uproar, riot, e.g. *usifanye udhia*, don't make such a noise. **Udhiko**, n. *ma-* trouble, annoyance, vexation, i.e. *hali ya kuudhika*. (Cf.

usumbufu, ghasia, makelele. Ar. (اذى).

Udhihirifu,* n. See under **Dhahiri.**

Udhiki,* n. See under **Dhii.**

Udhiko,* n. *ma-*. See under **Udhi.**

Udhilifu,* n. See under **Dhila.**

Udhu,* n. state of ceremonial purity, e.g. *nitajitia udhu nisali,* I will purify myself for prayer. Also *kaa kwa udhu,* i.e. *kaa kwa adabu nzuri,* a common expression, live an orderly respectable life. (Ar. وضوء.)

Udhuru,* n. (1) excuse, pretext, reason; (2) need, want, e.g. *ninao udhuru wa rupia moja,* I am in need of one rupee. Also, *nilikuwa na udhuru nawe,* I needed you (i.e. for a specific purpose, e.g. to help with some work). (3) occasion, opportunity, emergency, e.g. *nilikuwa na udhuru wa kukutaka,* I had a reason for asking you. *Hana ruhusa kutembea bila udhuru,* he is not allowed to go walks without occasion. *Toa udhuru,* offer an excuse. *Tolea udhuru,* make an excuse for. Sometimes used as a verb **Udhuru,** make excuse, esp. in the Rf. *jiudhuru,* i.e. *usijiudhuru,* don't excuse yourself. (Cf. *hoja, sababu, dharura.* Ar. عذر.)

Udi,* n. (1) aromatic aloe wood—used for fumigation (*fukizo*) (cf. *ubani, uvumba.* Ar. العود); (2) a musical instrument like a banjo. (Ar. عود.)

Udibaji,* n. See under **Dibaji.**

Udobi,* n. See under **Dobi.**

Udodi, n. (*dodi*). See **Dodi.**

Udogo, n. See under **-dogo.**

Udohodoho, n. but usu. used in adverbial sense, e.g. *nitatumia fedha udohodoho,* I shall spend economically, i.e. *kidogo kidogo.*

Udole, n. See under **Kidole.**

Udongo, n. earth, esp. used of thick soil or clay, *udongo wa kufinyanga,* potter's clay. *Katika nchi hii uko udongo wa namna nyingi,* in this country there are many kinds of soil.

Udufu, n. See under **Dufu.**

Udugu, n. See under **Ndugu.**

Udui, n. See under **Ndui.**

Udusi, n. also **Ujusi,** n. (1) matter, pus; (2) a bad smell.

Uduvi, n. (*nduvi* and *uduvi*) prawn. Also called *kamba ndogo.* Also applied to small green fly common at the coast in certain seasons.

Uele, n. (*maele*) sickness, illness, esp. of a severe and crippling kind which confines the patient to bed. *Uele wa macho,* ophthalmia. *Uele wa viungo,* rheumatism. **Mwele,** n. (*waele*) a sick person. (Cf. *ugonjwa, maradhi, mgonjwa,* and dist. *uwele, mawele.*)

Uelekeo, n., **Uelekevu,** n. See under **Elea,** v. (B).

Uendeleo, n. *ma-*, **Uendelezi,** n. *ma-*, **Uendo,** n. (*mwendo, nyendo*). See under **Enda.**

Ufa, n. (*nyufa*), a crack, split, slit, cleft, rent, tear, or similar aperture. *Fanya* (*tia*) *ufa,* crack. Prov. *Usipoziba ufa, utajenga ukuta,* if you neglect a crack, you will have to build a wall, the Swahili equivalent of 'A stitch in time saves nine'.

Ufadhili,* n. See under **Fadhili.**

Ufafanuzi, n. See under **Fafanisha.**

Ufagio, n. See under **Fagia.**

Ufahamivu, n., **Ufahamu,*** n. See under **Fahamu.**

Ufalme, n. (*falme*). See under **Mfalme.**

Ufananaji, n., **Ufanani,** n., **Ufanisi,** n. See under **Faa.**

Ufaransa,* n. See under **Faransa.**

Ufarisi,* n. See under **Farisi.**

Ufasaha,* n., **Ufasihi,** n. See under **Fasaha.**

Ufasiki,* n. See under **Fasiki.**

Ufefe,* n. weakness, uselessness. **Kifefe,** n. (1) like *ufefe*; (2) a weak, useless person. (Ar. اففا.)

Ufidhuli,* n. See under **Fidhuli.**

Ufidio, n., **Ufidiwa,*** n. See under **Fidi.**

Ufifi, n., **Ufifilizi,** n. See under **Fifia.**

Ufilisi,* n. See under **Filisi.**

Ufinga, n. sometimes heard for *ufu-nga*, which see.

Ufinyanzi, n. See under **Finyanga.**

Ufisadi,* n. See under **Fisadi.**

Ufitina,* n. See under **Fitina.**

Ufito, n. (*fito*), (1) a small stick used as a walking-stick (cf. *bakora, fimbo*); (2) long thin piece of stick, rod, lath, or anything similar in appearance, e.g. thin bar of metal, *ufito wa chuma*, rod iron, iron bar (cf. *upao*). Often of the thin straight sticks used on roofs of native huts to carry the thatch, laid crosswise horizontally on the rafters, also sticks similarly placed horizontally in walls of huts and fences, on which the mud is plastered or grass, &c., tied. (3) a present given by a father to a teacher when entering his son into a school.

Ufizi, n. (*fizi*), gum, of the jaw.

Ufu, n. See under **Fa.**

Ufuaji, n. (sometimes plur. *mafuaji*). See under **Fua.**

Ufuasi, n. (*fuasi* and *ma-*). See under **Fuata.**

Ufufuko, n., **Ufufuo**, n. See under **Fufua.**

Ufukara,* n. See under **Fakiri.**

Ufuke,* n. poverty, necessity, need. (Cf. *umaskini, ufukara*. Ar. فاقة.)

Ufukizo, n. *ma-*. See under **Fuka.**

Ufuko, n. (*fuko*), (1) sandy margin of the sea-shore about high-water mark, i.e. *maji ya bahari yakomapo* (where the sea ceases), including the whole shore to low-water mark. Prov. *Ulichokiacha pwani, kakingoje ufukoni*, the thing you left on the shore, go and wait for it on the high-water mark (cf. *ufuo*). (2) the fine white sand of the shore. (Cf. *ufukwe*.)

Ufukuto, n. *ma-*. See under **Fuka.**

Ufukwe, n. see also **Ufuko**, (1) the fine white sand formed by the beating of waves on the shore (cf. *fua*, v.); (2) poverty. (Cf. *ufukara*.)

Ufumbi, n. (*ma-*) depression between hills, valley bottom, for the more common *bonde*.

Ufumwale, n. fibre, esp. from the raffia palm. (Cf. *mwale, ulembo*, and *nyuzinyuzi*.)

Ufundi, n. See under **Funda**, v. (C).

Ufunga, n. (*funga*), a stone bench or seat of masonry, usu. against the wall in front of a house, for the reception of visitors.

Ufungu, n. (1) relationship, connexion; (2) relations, kinsmen, collectively, e.g. *ufungu wangu unakuja*, my relations are coming. (Cf. *ukoo, ndugu, jamaa*.)

Ufunguo, n. (*funguo*). See under **Funga.**

Ufunuo, n. See under **Funika.**

Ufuo, n. (1) hollow made in the floor beneath the bed on which a corpse is laid, to receive the water when the corpse is washed; (2) the sand or beach at high-water mark; (3) origin, beginning.

Ufupa, n. See under **Fupa.**

Ufupi, n., **Ufupisho**, n. *ma-*. See under **-fupi.**

Ufuraha,* n. a small box, made of tin or silver as a rule, in which the lime is kept which is used in the chewing mixture *uraibu*. (Cf. *kijaluba*. Ar. اورة mixture.)

Ufurufuru,* n. See under **Fura.**

Ufusho, n. but usu. *mafusho*. See under **Fuka.**

Ufusio, n. See under **Fusa**, v. (A) and (B).

Ufuta, n. (1) simsim, or semsem, gingelly, the oil of which is called *mafuta ya uto*—the seeds are used for flavouring food, *Sesamum indicum*; (2) Rozelle, edible fruit and leaves, and the stem is used for fibre, *Hibiscus sabdarifu*.

Ufuu, n. See under **Fuu**, n. (B).

Ufyozi, n. See under **Fyoa.**

Uga, n. an open space in a town or round a house, a threshing-floor, e.g. *alifika ugani panapo ile nyumba*, he arrived at the open place where the house stood. (Cf. *uwanja, kiwanja*.)

Uga, v. bellow, of a bull.

Ugaga, n. also **Ugwagwa**, tartar on teeth. (Cf. *ukoga.*)

Ugale, n. the soft white part of wood, opp. to *kiini*, which see. **Gale**, n. *ma-* as above.

Ugali, n. a stiff porridge, made of maize, millet, or cassava flour. (Cf. *sima.*)

Ugandamano, n., **Ugandisho**, n., **Ugando**, n. See under **Ganda.**

Uganga, n. *ma-*, **Uganguzi**, n. See under **Ganga.**

Ugavu, n. a net for trapping animals or fish. (Cf. *wavu.*)

Uge, n. also **Ugea**, n. fat, grease, which has stuck to the inside of a vessel, e.g. *chungu hiki chanuka uge*, this pot smells greasy.

Ugege, n. the grating, dry feeling on the teeth such as is caused by eating acid fruit or similar things. (Cf. *ukakasi.*)

Ugelegele, n. See under **Kigelegele.**

Ugema, n. See under **Gema.**

Ugeni, n. See under **-geni.**

Ugeuzi, n. See under **Geua.**

Ughaibu,* n. See under **Ghaibu.**

Ughoshi, n., **Ughushi**,* n. See under **Ghoshi.**

Ugimbi, n. (*ngimbi*), beer, intoxicating liquor. (Cf. *pombe, ulevi.*)

Ugo, n. (*nyugo*) enclosure, fenced courtyard, also the fence surrounding it. (Cf. *ua, kiwanja.*)

Ugoe, n. (*ngoe*). See under **Ngoeka.**

Ugolo, n. snuff, ground tobacco, also used for chewing. (Cf. *mshuku.*)

Ugomba, n. See under **Mgomba.**

Ugombo, n. a kind of banjo, *piga ugombo*, play a banjo.

Ugomvi, n. (*gomvi, magomvi*). See under **Gomba.**

Ugoni, n. (*ngono*). See under **Gona.**

Ugonjwa, n. *ma-*. See under **-gonjwa.**

Ugono, n. See under **Gona.**

Ugozi, n. algae, the green scum which grows on stagnant water. (Cf. *ngozi, ugaga.*)

Ugua, v. (1) become sick, fall ill, be in pain, be ailing; (2) wail, groan. Prep. **Ugulia**, e.g. *nguo za kuugulia*, hospital dress. *Anauguliwa*, he has sickness in his house. Cs. **Uguza**, attend in sickness, as nurse, treat or doctor a sick person. **Mwuguzi**, n. (*wauguzi*) one who tends or has the care of the sick, medical attendant, nurse. **Uuguzaji**, n. *ma-*, **Uuguzi**, n. *ma-* nursing the sick, care of the sick, operations (material, means, &c.) of nursing.

Ugumu, n. See under **-gumu.**

Ugundi, n. a sort of brown powder obtained by scraping *gubi*, i.e. base of leaf-stem of coco-nut palm, and used as a cure for sores.

Uguza, v., **Uguzi**, n. *ma-*. See under **Ugua.**

Ugwagwa, n. See under **Ugaga** and **Gaga.**

Ugwe, n. (*ngwe* and *nyugwe*), string, small cord, and anything used as such. **Kigwe**, n. *vi-* dim. of above, braid, piping on the edge of a dress, a rein, &c. (Cf. *kitani, kamba.*)

Uhaba,* n. See under **Haba.**

Uhafifu,* n. See under **Hafifu.**

Uhai,* n. See under **Hai.**

Uhaini,* n. See under **Haini.**

Uhaji,* n. (1) see under **Haja, n.**; (2) *kuingia uhaji*, an expression used of a person becoming a Muhammadan, esp. by the way of circumcision. (Cf. *tohara.*)

Uhali,* n. See under **Hali.**

Uhalifu,* n. (*halifu* and *mahalifu*). See under **Halifu.**

Uhamaji,* n. See under **Hama.**

Uharabu,* n. See under **Harabu.**

Uharamia,* n. See under **Haramia.**

Uharara,* n. See under **Harara.**

Uharibifu,* n. See under **Harabu.**

Uhasama,* n. See under **Hasimu.**

Uhasi,* n. See under **Hasi.**

Uhasidi,* n. See under **Hasidi.**

Uhawara,* n. See under **Hawara.**

Uhayawani,* n. See under **Hayawani.**

Uheri,* n. See under **Heri.**

Uhiana,* n. See under **Hini.**

Uhindi,* n. See under **Mhindi.**

Uhitaji,* n. See under **Hitaji.**
Uhodari,* n. See under **Hodari.**
Uhondo, n. a big feast, generous entertainment.
Uhuni,* n. See under **Huni.**
Uhunzi, n. See under **Mhunzi.**
Uhuru,* n. See under **Huru.**
Uhusiano,* n. See under **Husu.**
Uhusuda,* n. See under **Hasidi.**
Uigaji, n. See under **Iga.**
Uingereza,* n. See under **Mwingereza.**
Uislamu,* n. See under **Silimu.**
Uizi,* n. See **Wizi** under **Iba.**
Uja, n. See **Mja** under **Ja.**
Ujahili,* n. See under **Jahili.**
Ujaji, n. (1) see under **Ja**; (2) see under **Jaji.**
Ujaka, n. (1) a kind of native spinach (cf. *mchicha*); (2) small mushrooms. (Cf. *uyoga.*)
Ujali,* n. also **Mjali, n.** *mi-* a lamp wick, for the common *utambi.* (Hind. جلا burnt.)
Ujalivu, n. See under **Jaa, v.**
Ujamaa,* n., **Ujamii,** n. See under **Jamaa.**
Ujamu,* n. a piece of rope passed through the nose or nose-ring of an ox. (Cf. *lijamu, shemeri.* Ar. لجام.)
Ujana, n. See under **Jana, n.** (A).
Ujane, n. See under **Mjane.**
Ujanja, n. See under **-janja.**
Ujapojapo, n. a narrow country path. (Kipemba. Cf. *ujia, kijia* under *ja,* v.)
Ujari,* n. (*njari*), tiller-rope in a native vessel. Sometimes heard as *mjaro.* (Ar. جر.)
Ujasiri,* n. See under **Jasiri.**
Ujasusi,* n. See under **Jasisi.**
Ujazi, n. See under **Jaa,** v., and **Jaza.**
Ujengelele, n. See **Uchengelele,** of which this is a variant.
Ujenzi, n. *ma-*. See under **Jenga.**
Ujeuri,* n. same as *jeuri,* which see.
Uji, n. gruel or soup, usually made of rice mixed with water and drunk from cups or bowls, esp. as an early morning meal, i.e. breakfast. It is the thinnest of all gruels or porridges made, *ubwabwa* being the next, then *mashendea,* while *ugali* is the stiffest of all. *Kunde* beans are often added, and in this case sugar is put in. If the gruel is made of rice only coconut juice and salt are added, and it is called *uji wa mapande.* If ground rice is used, coco-nut juice is not added, and it is called *uji wa maji.* Sugar is sometimes added in this case. (Cf. *ubwabwa, ugali, mashendea,* and *wali.*)
Ujia, n. (*njia, majia*). See under **Ja, v.**
Ujima, n. (1) work done with the assistance of neighbours, e.g. in building a house, planting, or harvest —a common native practice repaid by a beer-drinking or by similar help on occasion; (2) a company of men hired or engaged for the speedy dispatch of business. **Mjima, n.** *wa-* one who gives friendly help.
Ujinamizi, n. See under **Ina.**
Ujinga, n. See under **-jinga.**
Ujini,* n. See under **Jini.**
Ujio, n. (*majio*). See under **Ja, v.**
Ujira,* n. See under **Ajiri.**
Ujirani,* n. See under **Jirani.**
Ujitahidi,* n. See under **Jitahidi.**
Ujomba, n. See under **Mjomba.**
Ujotojoto, n. See under **Ota,** v. (C).
Ujuba,* n. fearlessness, also violence, tyranny, oppression, &c., e.g. *alifanya ujuba sana kwenda nyumba kama ile,* he displayed great fearlessness in going to a house like that. **Mjuba,** n. *wa-* a fearless person, also a violent, tyrannical, oppressive person. (Ar. عجب wonder, marvel.)
Ujuhula,* n. See under **Jahili.**
Ujuizi, n. sometimes heard for *ujuzi.*
Ujukuti, n. (*njukuti*) (1) the midriff of the coco-nut palm leaf; (2) sometimes used for the spokes of a bicycle wheel.
Ujumbe, n. See under Mjumbe and Jumbe.

Ujume, n. See under **Mjume.**

Ujusi,* n. (1) natural defilement of childbirth as affecting both mother and child and everything that comes into contact with them until both have been washed ceremonially according to Muhammadan usage seven days after the birth of the child; (2) the strong natural unpleasant smell of animals (cf. *udusi, kidusi*); (3) *kufa ujusi*, die a natural death, used of animals only; and fig. of persons pining for something or desiring something inordinately, e.g. *nafa ujusi kwa sababu sipati haja yangu*, I am inclined to die because I cannot get what I want. **Kijusi**, n. *vi-* an act (case, instance, &c.) of defilement, a particular legal (ceremonial, physical) impurity. (Cf. *unajisi, uchafu*, and for purification, *eua*. Ar. نجس defiled.)

Ujuvi, n., **Ujuzi**, n. See under **Jua**, v.

Uka, v. go away (seldom used). **Mauko**, n. plur. (1) departing, departure; (2) death. Also sometimes used in the old perfect as a formula at the beginning of stories *Paukile*, there arose (happened), i.e. once upon a time. (Cf. *ondoka, toka, enda.*)

Ukaaji, n. See **Kaa**, v.

Ukaango, n. (*kaango*). See under **Kaanga.**

Ukabaila,* n. See under **Kabaila.**

Ukabidhi,* n. See under **Kabidhi.**

Ukadirifu,* n. See under **Kadiri.**

Ukafiri,* n. See under **Kafiri.**

Ukafu, n. (1) froth or foam (cf. *povu*); (2) the dryness of the teeth after eating unripe acid fruits, &c. (Cf. *ukamvu, ukakasi.*)

Ukago, n. See under **Kaga.**

Ukaguzi, n. See under **Kagua.**

Ukahaba,* n. See under **Kahaba.**

Ukaidi,* n. See under **Kaidi.**

Ukaimu,* n. See under **Kaimu.**

Ukakasi, n. the dryness of the teeth after eating unripe acid fruit, &c. (Cf. *ukamvu, ukafu.*)

Ukakaya, n. narrowness, extent, surface. (Cf. *wembamba, eneo.*)

Ukali, n. *ma-*. See under **-kali.**

Ukalifu,* n. See under **Kalifu.**

Ukambaa,* n. (*kambaa*), cord of plaited leaf-strips, like *shupatu*. (Cf. *kamba*, of coco-nut fibre.)

Ukambi, n. measles, but usually *surua*.

Ukame, n. See under **Kame.**

Ukamili, n., **Ukamilifu**, n. See under **Kamili.**

Ukamio, n. (*kamio*). See under **Kamia.**

Ukamvu, n. the dryness of the teeth after eating unripe acid fruit. (Cf. *ukakasi, ukafu.*)

Ukanda, n. (*kanda*) a strip of leather, strap, thong, e.g. *ukanda wa kupigia*, a scourge. *Ukanda wa kuvalia suruali*, a trouser-belt. *Ukanda wa uta*, a bow string. (Cf. *ugwe.*)

Ukando, n. (*kando*). See **Kando.**

Ukano, n. (*kano*). See under **Kano.**

Ukao, n. (*kao*). See under **Kaa**, v.

Ukarimu,* n. See under **Karama.**

Ukasasi, n. a variant of *ukakasi*, which see.

Ukashifu,* n. See under **Kashifa.**

Ukata, n. See under **Mkata.**

Ukatili,* n. See under **Katili.**

Ukavu, n. See under **Kauka.**

Ukawa, n., **Ukawio**, n. See under **Kawa**, v.

Ukaya, n. (*kaya*), a long piece of thin blue calico or blue or black muslin or fine silk of various colours, rolled up and wound round the head and under the chin, leaving two long ends, formerly worn by married women of the poorer class, but now rapidly passing out of use and worn only by a few old women who cleave to the fashions of former days.

Ukazi, n. See under **Kaa**, v.

Uke, n. See under **-ke.**

Ukelele, n. (*kelele* and *ma-*) a cry, shout, exclamation, noise of voices. (Cf. *ukemi* and *kelele.*)

Ukemi, n. See under **Kemea.**

Ukengee, n. See under **Kengee.**

Uketo, n. depth. (Cf. *kina, kilindi.*)

Uki, n. honey. (Cf. *nyuki*, a bee, also *asali.*)

Ukigo, n. (*kigo*), a fence, hedge, enclosure. (Cf. *boma, ua, kitalu.*)

Ukiki, n. a kind of bird, the Green Coucal, *Ceuthmochares Aereus*.

Ukili, n. (*kili*) a narrow length of plaited leaf-strip of the wild date palm (*mkindu*). Such lengths when sewn together form the mats called *mkeka, mi-*. *Suka ukili*, plait *ukili*. (Cf. *mkindu, mkeka.*)

Ukilia, v. intend, determine, purpose, have a design, think about a thing diligently, e.g. *Saidi alimwukilia Ali kwa kumtilia fitina*, Saidi had designs upon Aii, with the view to causing him trouble. *Anaukilia vita*, he is intent upon war. (Perh. D.Prep. of *uka*, v. which see. Cf. *nia, azimia, kusudia.*)

Ukimwa, n. See under **Kimwa.**

Ukinaifu,* n. See under **Kinai.**

Ukindu, n. (*kindu*). See under **Mkindu.**

Ukingo, n. (*kingo*). See under **Kinga.**

Ukinzani, n. (*kinzani* and *ma-*). See under **Kinza.**

Ukiri,* n. See under **Kiri.**

Ukiwa, n. See under **-kiwa.**

Ukiwi, n. See under **Kiwi.**

Ukiziwi, n. See under **Kiziwi.**

Uko, verb-form, you are (it is) there.

Ukoa, n. (*koa*). See under **Koa.**

Ukofi, n. See under **Kofi.**

Ukoga, n. used of accretions or incrustations, such as tartar on the teeth, scum on water, scurf on the skin, &c. (Cf. *ukoko, ugaga, ukafu.*)

Ukohozi, n. *ma-*. See under **Kohoa.**

Ukoja, n. (*koja*) a necklace of beads. See **Koja.**

Ukoka, n. a fine, creeping kind of grass, largely collected and used as fodder for horses, donkeys, and cattle. (Cf. *majani, unyasi.*) *Ukoka mkavu*, hay. **Kikoka**, n. *vi-* blade or shoot of above.

Ukoko, n. (1) used of the hard-burnt caked rice or other food at the bottom of a cooking-pot, or on the top of the pot, which is often dry and scorched owing to the custom of pouring away the water when the food is sufficiently cooked and heaping live embers on the lid of the pot; (2) used of accretions. **Kikoko**, n. *vi-* dim. of above, a bit of hard dried stuff, and so a scab or scurf. (Cf. *ukoka, ukoga.*)

Ukoma, n. leprosy, considered of such ill omen in some places that when the word is mentioned it is customary to spit on the ground. (Cf. *matana, balanga, balasi.*)

Ukomba, n. (1) see under **Komba**, v.; (2) a young coco-nut with soft kernel.

Ukombe, n. (*kombe*), **Ukombo**, n. (*kombo*), **Ukombozi**, n. See under **Komba, v.**

Ukomo, n. (*komo*). See under **Koma.**

Ukonge, n. See under **Mkonge.**

Ukongojo, n. (*kongojo*), **Ukongwe**, n. See under **Konga, v. (A).**

Ukonjo, n. same as *ukonzo*, which see.

Ukono, n. See under **Mkono.**

Ukonyezo, n. (*konyezo*). See under **Konyeza.**

Ukonzo, n. (*konzo*). See under **Konzo.**

Ukoo, n. (*koo*), (1) relationship, kinship, affinity, ancestry, pedigree, descent, family (cf. *ujamaa, udugu, utani, akraba, nasaba*); (2) uncleanness, slovenliness, filth, dirt. (Cf. *mkoo.*)

Ukope, n. (*kope*). See under **Kope.**

Ukopi, n. See under **Kopa.**

Ukorofi, n. See under **Korofi.**

Ukorogefu, n. See under **Koroga.**

Ukosefu, n. *ma-*, **Ukosekano**, n. See under **Kosa.**

Ukosi, n. (*kosi*). See under **Kosi.**

Ukuba,* n. (1) a bad smell (Ar. قبح foulness, &c.); (2) a bad omen, misfortune, curse, evil fortune, e.g. *usitutie ukuba*, don't bring us ill luck, addressed to some one who is tempting fate by gambling or other improper action, e.g. homosexuality, or to one who has a disease which renders his presence obnoxious, e.g. leprosy. (Ar. عقبى requital.)

Ukubali,* n. See under **Kabili.**

Ukubwa, n. See under **-kubwa.**

Ukucha, n. (*kucha*), nail (of finger or toe), claw. *Piga ukucha*, scratch, claw. **Kikuchia**, n. *vi-* a small piece torn off the root of the finger- or toe-nail. **Kucha**, n. *ma-* amplic. claw (of a lion), talon (of an eagle).

Ukufi, n. (*kufi*) as much as will lie on the flat of the hand, handful. *Punje za mtama zinazopata ukufi*, as much millet as would lie on the hand. So generally, a very small quantity, e.g. *umenipa ukufi tu*, you have given me a mere handful, addressed to one who has given short measure or been parsimonious. (Cf. *kofi.*)

Ukufuru,* n. *ma-*. See under **Kafiri.**

Ukukwi, n. a species of thin, green, harmless snake, usu. found in trees, also called *ukuti.*

Ukulima, n. *ma-*. See under **Lima.**

Ukulifu, n. See under **Kua.**

Ukumbi, n. (*kumbi*), porch, vestibule, outer hall, ante-room, room first entered in going into a house or hut. *Ingia* (*tiwa*) *kumbini*, is a euphemistic expression for being circumcised, i.e. to be kept indoors for a fixed period. Hence *kumbi* for *tohara*, e.g. *alimtia mtoto wake kumbi*, he had his son circumcised. This does not apply to people in the hinterland where the boys are generally taken into the forest and do not return to their homes until the end of the initiation ceremonies. (Cf. *jando, unyago.*)

Ukumbizi, n. (*kumbizi*). See under **Kumba, v.** (A) and (B).

Ukumbizo, n. an outside veranda. (Cf. *ukumbi, baraza, ufunga.*)

Ukumbuko, n. *ma*, **Ukumbusho**, n. *ma-*. See under **Kumbuka.**

Ukumbuu, n., also **Ukumbuo** (*kumbuu*), a sash, a belt. Used for a sash which is worn across one shoulder, e.g. the insignia of an order, &c., or as part of a uniform worn by soldiers, messengers, janitors, &c. (Cf. *ukanda, sombo, hazamu, mshipi.*)

Ukumvi, n. (*kumvi*), (1) empty ear, spike, or head of grain-bearing plant, rice, millet, &c., without the grain; husk, bran, chaff (cf. *wishwa, kapi,* and *kumbi*); (2) a single grain (cf. *punje*). **Kumvi**, n. *ma-* husk or sheath of various vegetable products, maize, rice, &c., i.e. *kumvi la muhindi*, the sheath of the maize plant (enclosing the ear, *suke*). *Kumvi la mpunga*, &c. (Cf. *kununu.*)

Ukunde, n. See under **Mkunde.**

Ukunga, n. See under **Kunga**, n. (B).

Ukungu, n. (*kungu* and *ma-*) (1) damp, moisture, mouldiness, mildew, e.g. *nyumba hii ina ukungu*, this house is mouldy. *Chakula hiki kimeota ukungu*, this food has gone mouldy. *Mkate unafanya ukungu*, the bread is getting mildewed. (2) fog, mist, vapour, esp. of morning, called *ukungu wa alfajiri*, and evening, and so of twilight, e.g. *ukungu unatanda* (*unakuja, unawamba*), the dawn is spreading.

Ukunguni, n. See under **Mkunguni.**

Ukunguru, n. See under **Mkunguru.**

Ukungwi, n. See under **Kunga, v.** (B).

Ukuni, n. (*kuni*), a stick of firewood. *Chanja* (*pasua*) *kuni*, cut firewood.

Ukunjufu, n. See under **Kunja.**

Ukurasa, n. (*kurasa*), sheet or strip of paper, leaf or page of a book. (Cf. *karata, karatasi.* Ar. كراسة.)

Ukurugenzi, n. See under **Mkurugenzi.**

Ukuruti, n. sometimes **Ukurutu**, small pimples. (Cf. *upele.*)

Ukuta, n. (*kuta*) any stone or masonry wall, i.e. *ukuta wa mawe*. (Dist. *boma*, which may or may not be a wall, *kiambaza*, a partition wall, commonly of sticks and plaster, *kitalu*, wall of a court or enclosure.)

Ukuti, n. (*kuti*) (1) a side frond of a coco-nut leaf, the whole leaf being **Kuti**, n. *ma-*; (2) *nyoka ukuti*, a long thin green tree snake, so named because owing to its colour it is indistinguishable from the fronds when hiding in a coco-nut tree. Also called *ukukwi*. (3) children's game in which they join hands and go quickly round in a circle.

Ukuu, n. See under **-kuu.**

Ukwaju, n. (*kwaju*) a tamarind, fruit of the *mkwaju*.

Ukware, n. lascivious love, carnal lust, but usu. of uncontrolled, excessive lust. **-kware**, a. carnal, lascivious, erotic. **Mkware**, n. *wa-* a lascivious person, either male or female, a prostitute, a person of easy and carnal habits, also of a female animal when in heat. (Cf. *uchu, ashiki, ufasiki, ukahaba*.)

Ukwasi, n. See under **Kwasi.**

Ukwato, n. (*kwato*), hoof (solid, of horse, donkey, zebra, &c.), part of a cloven hoof (of cow, &c.). *Mguu wa ng'ombe una kwato mbili*, a cow's foot is cloven, i.e. in two parts. *Piga ukwato*, stamp (of a horse, &c.). (Cf. *kwata, liwata, nyata, kiatu*.)

Ukwe, n. See under **Mkwe.**

Ukweli, n. See under **Kweli.**

Ukwezi, n. See under **Kwea.**

Ulaanifu,* n., **Ulaanizi**, n. See under **Laana.**

Ulabibu,* n. perseverance, sustained effort. (Cf. *ujitahidi, bidii*. Ar. لبيب.)

Ulafi, n. See under **Lapa.**

Ulaika, n. See under **Laika.**

Ulaini, n., **Ulainifu,*** n. See under **Laini.**

Ulaiti,* n. See **Ulayiti** under **Ulaya.**

Ulaji, n. (*malaji*). See under **La.** v.

Ulalamishi, n., **Ulalamizi**, n. See under **Lalama.**

Ulalo, n. (*malalo*). See under **Lala.**

Ulambilambi, n. See under **Lamba.**

Ulanga, n. See under **Anga**, n.

Ulaya,* n. (1) a land, esp. if not further defined, Europe. *Ulaya wa Waamerikani*, America. *Ulaya wa Waarabu*, Arabia. *Ulaya wa Waingereza*, England, &c. (2) a district, in this sense it is usually *wilaya*, which see. **Ulayiti**, n. European textile stuff, used of a very light inferior kind of unbleached cotton cloth, lighter than *amerikani*. It is used especially in the manufacture of cheap loin-cloths (*shuka*), but is used also for making shirts, sails, &c. *Kamba ulayiti*, hemp rope, not of coco-nut fibre, which is *kamba*. (Ar. ولاية.)

Ule, dem. pron. that.

Uledi,* n. cabin boy, kitchen boy on a dhow. His duties are to keep the boat clean, to cook for the crew, and to row the dinghy for the latter when they go ashore. Also a common personal male name. (Ar. ولد).

Ulegeo, n., **Ulegevu**, n. See under **Lega.**

Uleoleo, n., **Ulevi**, n., **Ulewalewa**, n. See under **Lewa.**

Ulezi, n. *ma-*. (1) See under **Lea, v.**; (2) bullrush millet, eleusine. (Cf. *mawele, wimbi*.)

Ulia, v. See under **Ua**, v.

Ulili, n. (1) a shrine or place where blood-offerings are made to spirits. It is constructed inside the houses of witch doctors (*waganga*), rises to a height of twelve feet, and has a platform at the top, to which a ladder inside gives access. The framework is made of bamboo, and the walls are covered with paper, e.g. *pepo yuko ulilini, anakunywa damu*, the spirit is in the *ulili*, he is drinking blood. The blood is usually that of a goat, supplied by the person on whose behalf the witch doctor is interceding with the spirit. (2) a bedstead, with turned legs. **Kilili**, n. *vi-* dim.

Ulimaji, n. *ma-*. See under **Lima, v.**

Ulimbo, n. birdlime, gum, glue. *Ulimbo ni utomvu wa kutegea ndege*, *ulimbo* is a sticky stuff for catching birds with. *Utomvu wa fenesi*, the sticky stuff from a jack-fruit is generally used. **Mlimbolimbo**, n. *mi-* a kind of euphorbia with a thick white sticky juice, used for making hedges. *Penye urembo ndipo penye ulimbo* (but usually *urimbo* to agree with *urembo*), where there is beauty, there is generally a catch, fascination is generally a snare.

Ulimbwende, n. dandyism, showy dress or manner, coxcombry. (Cf. *umalidadi*.)

Ulimi, n. (*ndimi*) (1) the tongue—of man and animals generally, and also (2) of objects resembling it, a projection (cf. *mdomo*), e.g. 'tenon' in carpentering; (3) *ulimi wa moto*, a tongue of flame, esp. of a conflagration seen in the distance. Prov. *Ulimi hauna mfupa*, the tongue has no bone, i.e. nothing stable, reliable. *Kama ulimi na mate*, like tongue and saliva, of things inseparable. *Ulimi hauna dawa*, the tongue is incurable. *Ulimi wake ndio uliomchongea*, his own tongue betrayed him. *Uji wa moto haupoi kwa ncha ya ulimi*, the tip of the tongue does not cool hot gruel. **Kilimi**, n. *vi-* (1) dim.; (2) a bad or abusive style of speaking; (3) the uvula. **-limi**, a. talkative, chatting, long-winded. **Mlimi**, n. *wa-* a fluent person, a babbler, a talkative person. (Cf. *mwenye domo*, under *mdomo*.)

Ulimwengu, n. (*ma-*), (1) the world in general, the whole creation, universe, visible things; (2) the sky, e.g. *ulimwengu umetakata*, the sky is clear; (3) the inhabited world, earth, globe, e.g. *ulimwengu tunaokaa sisi*, the world we live in; (4) the present world, i.e. *kuwapo ulimwenguni*, to be alive, as opp. to the next world, which is *peponi, kuzimu, ulimwengu wa huko* (*wa baadaye, ujao*), e.g. *najiona si mtu wa ulimwengu tena*, I feel I have not much longer to live, said by an old man about to make his will. (5) the world in a moral sense, the world as worldly, the world as transitory, unstable, evil, e.g. *mema na mabaya ndiyo ulimwengu*, it takes bad and good to make the world. *Mtu wa ulimwengu*, a worldly person (but not as a rule with quite the same connotation as the English 'a man of the world', see below). (6) the environment, each man's own surroundings (circle, circumstances). *Ametengeneza ulimwengu wake*, he has feathered his nest. Plur. *malimwengu*, usu. worldly affairs, worldly pleasures or interests. **Mlimwengu**, n. *wa-* (1) an inhabitant of the earth, a living person, and (2) esp. one who takes things calmly, a happy-go-lucky person (rather different from the English 'worldly man'), e.g. *mwalimu huyu ni mlimwengu sana*, this teacher takes things calmly. *Mlimwengu ni mwanawe*, a man's (chief worldly interest) is his child. (3) also, a man of the world, a worldly man. (Prob. a confusion of Ar. لمعان luminousness, and عالميان people, inhabitants of the world.)

Ulindi, n. the male stick of firesticks (the female is called *wimbombo*). See **Pekecha**.

Ulinganifu, n., **Ulingano**, n., **Ulinganyifu**, n. See under **Linga**.

Ulingo, n. (*lingo* and *ma-*), a platform in a plantation, for a watchman in charge of crops. **Kilingo**, n. *vi-* dim. of above. (Cf. *kilindo, dungu*.)

Ulinzi, n. See under **Linda**.

Ulio, n. See under **La**, v.

Ulipizi, n. See under **Lipa**.

Ulitima,* n. also heard as *ultima*, and *uritima*, (1) unemployment, distress of circumstances, poverty, need. *Mtu huyu ameshikwa na ulitima*, this man has got into the grip of unemployment. (2) the last round in a game of cards called *wahid usitini*. (Port. *ultimo*, for other traces of Port. card games nomenclature, cf. *karata, ree, shupaza, pao, uru*, &c.)

Uliwali,* n. See under **Liwali**.

Uliza, v. question, interrogate, inquire (of, about), ask, ask about (not 'ask for', which is *omba, taka*), demand, e.g. *nilimwuliza hali*, I asked him about his health, how he was. *Nitauliza kisa hiki*, I will ask about this matter. Ps. **Ulizwa**, e.g. be questioned. *Kuulizwa uwongo*, is often used of asking about something while knowing all about it, to see if the person asked will tell the truth. *Siwezi kuulizwa uwongo*, i.e. you can't catch me that way, I know you are asking to see if I tell the truth. St. **Ulizika**, seldom used. Prep. **Ulizia**, e.g. ask on behalf of, e.g. *nenda ukaniulizie sababu*, go and demand on my behalf to have a reason given. Rp. **Ulizana**. **Ulizo**, n. *ma-* question, inquiry, interrogation. (Cf. *saili, hoji, dadisi.*)

Ulizi, n. *ma-*. See under **Lia.**

Ulodi,* n. See under **Rodi.**

Ulozi, n. See under **Loga.**

Uluzi, n., also **Mluzi**, n. *mi-* and **Mwunzi**, n. *mi-*, a whistle made with the lips or with a whistle.

Uma, v. cause pain, injure, hurt, bite, sting, e.g. *mdudu huyu anauma*, this insect stings (bites); *meno (kichwa, tumbo) yaniuma*, my teeth (head, stomach) are paining me. Ps. **Umwa**, be bitten, feel pain, ache, smart, be ill, suffer, e.g. *naumwa jino*, I have toothache. *Mwalimu anaumwa leo*, the teacher is ill to-day. St. **Umika** rarely used, cf. *umika*, of medical cupping. Prep. **Umia**, e.g. cause pain to (at, with, in, by, &c.), and also feel pain (like *umwa*), be injured (in this sense more frequently used than *umwa*), e.g. *nyuki ameniuma, nami nimeumia*, a bee has stung me, and I am hurt. *Alianguka garini, akaumia vibaya*, he fell from a cart and was badly hurt. *Nimeumia macho*, I have a pain in my eyes. *Simba alimwumia mwituni (kichwani)*, the lion bit him in the forest (on the head). Cs. **Umiza**, usu. Inten. or of intentional infliction of pain, hurt, cause to feel pain. *Ameniumiza kusudi*, he has hurt me deliberately. Rp. of Cs. **Umizana**, e.g. *acheni! msiumizane*, stop! don't hurt one another. Rp. **Umana**, hurt each other, e.g. *msiumane meno*, do not hurt one another (fight) with your teeth. *Meno ya mbwa hayaumani*, a dog's teeth do not hurt each other, i.e. blood is thicker than water. Cs. **Umanisha. Kiuma**, n. *vi-* anything that bites, stings, or hurts, esp. *kiuma mbuzi*, a kind of lizard which bites men and beasts, also like *uma*, n. see below. **Mwumizi**, n. *wa-* one who hurts, causes pain, injuries. **Uma**, n. (*uma, nyuma, mauma*), (1) a metal point, skewer, pointed tool, awl, punch; (2) sting (of an insect or reptile) (in this sense *msumari* or *mwiba* is the usual word); (3) fork. **Umizi**, n. *ma-* causing of hurt, injury, pain. **Umo**, n. *ma-* hurting, bite, sting, i.e. the effect rather than the cause. **Umivu**, n. *ma-* used almost invariably in the plur.—pain, ache, smarting, suffering. *Maumivu mengi sana*, agony. (Cf. *choma, washa*, and *uchungu, uchomi.*)

Umahiri,* n. See under **Mahiri.**

Umaji, n. and **Umajimaji**. See under **Maji.**

Umalidadi, n. See **Malidadi.**

Umana, v. (prob. Rp. of *uma*, v. with restricted meaning), close, fit together, e.g. of folding doors, windows, shutters, &c. *Madirisha haya hayaumani*, these windows won't close. Prep. **Umania**, close for. *Mlango wa nyumba yangu hauniumanii*, the door of my house won't close for me, i.e. I cannot close it. Cs. **Umanisha**, join together, cause to close, e.g. *umanisha mtego*, set a trap.

Umande, n. dew, damp cool air of the morning or evening, mist, fog. (Cf. *ukungu, unyevu.*)

Umanga,* n. See under **Manga.**

Umanisha, v. See under **Uma** and **Umana.**

Umaskini,* n. See under **Maskini.**

Umati,* n. (1) a great many people, a crowd, e.g. *kulikuwa na umati wa watu leo,* there was a large gathering of people to-day; (2) the people of, followers of, e.g. *umati wa Muhammadi,* Muhammadans, Islam. *Umati wa Kristo* (*wa Isa*), Christians. *Umati wa Musa,* Jews. (Cf. *watu, akina, kundi, jamii.* Ar. أمّة.)

Umba, v. give form to, shape, fashion, create, make—but in most places used only of God. The word used regularly of the divine creation. *Mungu aliuumba ulimwengu,* God created the world. *Hukujiumba wewe, uliumbwa na Mungu,* you did not create yourself, you were created by God. Ps. **Umbwa.** St. **Umbika,** e.g. *ameumbika vizuri,* he has a fine figure, is handsome, beautiful. Prep. **Umbia,** e.g. *tumeumbiwa dunia tukae,* the world was created for us to live in. *Tumeumbiwa pepo tukaingie,* paradise was made for us to go to. (Cf. *huluku.*) Cv. **Umbua,** take away the form of, and so (1) spoil the look of, deface, deform, disfigure; (2) depreciate, degrade, demoralize, corrupt, e.g. *asiyeweza kutuumba, kutuumbua hawezi,* he who cannot create us cannot uncreate (corrupt) us; (3) break up (spoil), i.e. change the appearance of the land, e.g. *nakwenda kuumbua shamba langu,* I am going to loosen up the soil of my plantation. Ps. **Umbuliwa.** St. **Umbuka,** e.g. *umbuka mwili,* of the body disfigured by disease, &c. Prep. **Umbulia.** Rp. **Umbuana,** revile one another, take away each other's character. **Kiumbe,** n. *vi-* a created thing, a creature, but usually limited to the rational, or at least animate, creation, e.g. *pana wanyama wawili na kiumbe kimoja,* there are two animals and one man. *Mti umeumbwa kuwa kiumbe, lakini si kiumbe, na mnayama si kiumbe, mtu ni kiumbe,* a tree is a creature like a *kiumbe,* but it is not strictly a *kiumbe,* nor is an animal a *kiumbe,* but only man. **Muumba,** n. (*waumba*), also **Mwumba,** n. *wa-* and **Mwumbaji,** n. *wa-,* one who creates, makes, fashioner, esp. as a title of God, the Creator of the world, i.e. *Muumba yote.* **Muumbuzi,** n. *wa-* one who disfigures, destroys, reviles, abuses, &c. **Umbile,** n. *ma-* used almost invariably in the plur.—created state, original condition, natural constitution—but *umbo* is more usual. **Umbo,** n. *ma-* shape, form, natural condition (appearance, constitution). *Umbo la Adamu aliloumbwa mbele,* the form of Adam in which he was originally created. *Umbo la mtu mbali, na la mnyama mbali,* men and animals have a different constitution. Also used like *methali,* e.g. *umbo lake limefanana na kiziwi,* or *ana umbo la uziwi,* he is like a deaf person. *Najiona umbo la uziwi,* I feel like a deaf person. (Cf. *asili, namna, tabia, methali.*)

Umbali, n. See under **Mbali.**

Umbea, n. telling tales, tale-bearing, spreading scandal, e.g. *mtoto huyu anajizoeza umbea,* this child is accustoming himself to tale-bearing. **Mmbea,** n. (*wambea*), a tale-bearer, gossip, scandalmonger, e.g. *mtoto huyu mmbea sana,* this child is a great tell-tale. **-mbea,** a. false, untrue. (Cf. *-wongo.*)

Umbele, n. See under **Mbele.**

Umbia, v. (1) soar about, glide round (cf. *kirumbizi* or *kiumbizi,* the name of a bird); (2) flare up, as the flames of a fire.

Umbile, n. *ma-,* **Umbo,** n. *ma-.* See under **Umba.**

Umbu, n. *ma-* a sister or half-sister if mentioned by a brother, or a brother or half-brother if mentioned by a sister, not used by sister to sister, or brother to brother.

Umbua, v. See under **Umba.**

Umbuji,* n. grace, elegance, pleasing appearance, accomplishments—

of dress, manner, &c. **Mmbuji** n. *wa-* an elegant, well-dressed person. (Prob. from the same root as *mbeja*, i.e. Ar. مبهج causing joy, cheering.)

Ume, n. (1) male nature (sex, condition, characteristics), e.g. manliness, courage, pluck, potency—but commonly *utu ume*, for manhood generally, and *kiume* for qualities and character, e.g. *ume wa leo na kesho*, true courage lasts for more than a day. *Anajipa lakini hana ume*, he boasts, but he is impotent. (2) condition of a husband, e.g. *ume na uke umekwisha*, of having ceased to be husband and wife. **-ume**, a. (1) of the male sex, male, masculine; (2) like a man, virile, strong, courageous, prudent; (3) of things—strong, firm, reliable, big. *Mtu mume*, man generally, in respect of sex simply. (Cf. *mume*, *mwanamume* below.) *Mnazi mume*, the male coco-nut tree—comparatively unfertile. *Mahindi maume*, small inferior grains of maize. *Maume*, manly deeds, prowess, e.g. *ajetea maume*, he brags of his strength. *Kijana kiume*, a young man. **Dume**, n. *ma-* and a. a male, esp. of animals and plants. *Dume la farasi* (or *farasi dume*), a stallion. *Bata dume*, a drake. *Ng'ombe dume*, a bull. *Dume la punda* (or *punda dume*), a jackass. *Dume la mnazi* (or *mnazi dume*), a male coco-nut tree. The plur. when used generally denotes something extra large, i.e. *mang'ombe madume*, big bulls. **Kiume**, n. and adv. (rarely used in the plural, which is expressed as a rule by *-a kiume* and *dume*, a male, something of the male kind, manly behaviour, bearing, fashion, way, proceeding, &c.), courage, strength, prudence, spirit, heroism. *Watoto wa kiume*, boys (also *watoto wanaume*). *Fanya kiume*, act like a man, show spirit, be brave. *Sauti ya kiume*, a bass, deep voice. *Vaa kiume*, wear a man's clothes, dress like a man. **Kuume**, n. (like *ume* and *kiume* of sex, but more generalized), (1) the male kind (status, condition); (2) right-hand side, right hand. Used (like *kuke*) only in a few adjectival and adverbial phrases. *Mtu huyu ni ndugu yangu wa kuumeni*, this man is a relation of mine on the father's side. *Mkono wa kuume*, the right hand (also *mkono wa kulia*, the hand used in eating, as opp. to *mkono wa kushoto*). *Kaa kuumeni*, sit on the right-hand side, also on the men's side, i.e. at a feast where the men sit on one side and the women on the other. *Wa kuume haukati wa kushoto*, the right hand does not cut the left. (Cf. *ku-* in *kushoto*, *kumoja*, *kuzimu*, *kuvuli*.) **Mume**, n. (*waume*) for *mtu mume*, a male, a man. Used alone *mume* means distinctively husband, in contrast with *mwanamume*, which, if used in relation to the female sex, denotes an irregular connexion. **Mwanamume**, n. (*wanaume*), a man, see above. Also *watoto wanaume*, boys. **Ndume**, n. and a. a plur. form of *uume* (i.e. for *ulume*) sometimes used as both sing. and plur. (1) a male animal, as contr. with man; (2) a man, in respect of manly character and qualities, rather than of sex or individuality, but as a rule *dume* is used. **Uume**, n. for the vulgar *mboo*, penis, male organ of generation. (Cf. *dhakari*, *uchi*, *utupu*.)

Umeme, n. lightning, electricity. *Unamulika* (or *kunamulika*) *umeme*, it lightens. (Cf. *memeteka*, *metameta*.)

Umika, v. (1) cup, apply a cupping instrument, draw blood by cupping. The horn of a ram or goat is commonly used. When it is thought that a sufficient amount of blood has come into the horn, it is then put into a vessel with water to be examined. *Mwumishi ameniumika leo*, the cupper has cupped me to-day. *Aliniumika pembe mwilini*, he applied a horn to my body. (2) tap, apply a vessel to a tree for the purpose of tapping the sap, e.g. *niliumika kibuyu mnazini*, I applied a calabash to a coco-nut tree for the purpose of tapping it; (3) apply a vessel to the lips, and so, take a long draught, e.g. *Juma aliyaumika maziwa*, Juma took a long drink at the milk (i.e. out of a calabash). Ps. **Umikwa.** Prep. **Umikia**, e.g. *tumenunua pembe za kuumikia*, we have bought cupping horns. Cs. **Umikisha**, e.g. employ as a cupper, cause (persuade, compel) to be cupped. Cv. **Umua**, (1) used as Rv. of above in all senses, e.g. take off the cup, &c. *Mwumizi ameumua pembe zake*, the cupper has taken off his horns. *Niliumika kibuyu mnazini, kesho nitakiumua*, I applied a calabash to the coco-nut tree to catch the sap, to-morrow I will take it off. Also used in a special sense (2) see also under **Umua, v.** Ps. **Umuliwa.** St. **Umuka**, e.g. *pembe imeumuka*, the cupping-horn has dropped off. **Muumishi**, n. *wa-*, **Mwumizi**, n. *wa-*, **Mwumikaji**, n. *wa-* a professional cupper. **Umiko**, n. also **Ndumiko**, n. a cupping instrument, usu. a horn, commonly known as *pembe ya kuumikia*. Also *chuku*. **Uumikaji**, n., **Uumizi**, n. the art (process, fee, &c.) of cupping.

Umilele,* n. See under **Milele.**

Umio, n. (*mio*), internal throat, throat-passage—including both alimentary and air passages. *Mio za mtu ni mbili*, a man has two passages in his throat. *Umio wa pumzi*, the windpipe. **Kimio**, n. *vi-* dim. of above, also something in the throat, and so (1) uvula; (2) a throat affection, used to describe quinsy, croup, abscess in the throat, enlarged uvula or tonsils, &c. **Mio**, n. *ma-* amplic. of *umio*, e.g. *mio la mnyama*, the throat of an animal. (Cf. *koo, roho, shingo*.)

Umito, n. (1) heaviness or swelling of the feet of a pregnant woman; (2) heaviness or idleness of a man whose wife is pregnant, thought by some to be caused by his wife's condition.

Umivu, n. *ma-*, **Umiza**, v., **Umizi**, n. *ma-*, **Umo**, n. *ma-*. See under **Uma.**

Umo, verb-form, you are (it is) **in.**

Umoja, n. See under **Moja.**

Umoto, n. See under **Ota**, v. (C).

Umri,* n. time of life, age. *Umri wake unapataje?* How old is he? *Umri mkubwa*, an advanced age. (Cf. *uzima, maisha*. Ar. عمر.)

Umua, v. (1) see under **Umika, v.**; (2) take by craft (from), deprive (of), steal away, e.g. honey from bees, woman from husband, &c.; (3) cast metal in a mould; (4) put yeast or leaven into flour to make it rise, *umua unga wa mikate*, put yeast in bread-flour. St. **Umuka**, (1) see under **Umika, v.**; (2) rise up, e.g. *unga wa mkate umeumuka*, the flour has been leavened, and so has risen; (3) swell up, rise, i.e. of waves and breakers. Prep. **Umulia.**

Umungu, n. See under **Mungu.**

Una, n. a kind of fish.

Una, verb-form, you have, it has. *Una nini?* what is the matter with you?

Unadhifu,* n. See under **Nadhifu.**

Unafiki,* n. See under **Mnafiki.**

Unaibu,* n. See under **Naibu.**

Unajimu,* n. See under **Mnajimu.**

Unajisi,* n. See under **Najisi.**

Unanasi,* n. See under **Mnanasi.**

Unda, v. (A) construct, make, build, put together, esp. of wooden structures requiring skill, e.g. shipbuilding, but also of other materials. *Unda chombo*, build a dhow. *Unda dema*, construct, repair a fish-trap. *Merikebu ile iliundwa ya dhahabu*, that ship was built of gold. Ps. **Undwa.** St. **Undika.** Prep. **Undia**, e.g. *mti huu ukiundiwa una maisha sana*, this wood if used in shipbuilding is specially durable. Cs. **Undi-**

sha, e.g. order a ship to be built, give (or take) a contract for ship-building. **Kiunda**, n. *vi-* a kind of trap (cf. *mtego*). **Kiunza**, n. *vi-* a board laid to protect a corpse when placed in the grave, also called *mlango wa maiti*, the dead man's door. The *kiunza* is placed so as to close the *mwana ndani*, i.e. the recess made in the side of the grave to receive the corpse, to prevent the earth and stones from coming into contact with the corpse. **Kiunzi**, n. *vi-* a wooden frame or structure, esp. of ship-wright's work, the hull of a vessel. **Mwunda**, n. *wa-*, **Mwundaji**, n. *wa-*, **Mwundi**, n. *wa-*, **Mwunzi**, n. (*waunzi*), one who constructs, esp. of woodwork. **Mwundo**, n. *mi-* a shape, form, &c. **Uunzi**, n. (*maunzi*) construction, (fee, method, &c.) of construction, esp. of woodwork.

Unda, v. (B) remove honey from a bee-hive.

Undani, n. a secret grudge. (Cf. *ndani*.)

Undu, n. (*nyundu*), comb of a cock (*jogoo*). (Cf. *shungi, kilemba*.)

Uneemevu,* n. See under **Neema**.

Unenaji, n. See under **Nena**.

Unene, n. See under **-nene**.

Uneni, n. See under **Nena**.

Unga, n. anything powdered or ground small, esp. grain of any kind, powder, flour, meal, &c. *Unga wa mbao* (*wa mti*), sawdust. *Unga wa ndere*, a powder made by witch doctors for the purpose of bewitching people. (Cf. *ndere*.)

Unga, v. (1) make a joining, join, join together, connect, make by joining, unite, form connexion (with), compound, combine; (2) used also of mixing ingredients skilfully, e.g. *unga chakula*, season food. *Unga dawa*, compound medicine. *Unga tambuu*, make a chewing mixture (cf. *uraibu*). Also *unga mbao*, join planks. *Unga mfupa*, set a bone. *Unga kamba na jiwe*, put a stone and rope together, i.e. in drawing water at a well. *Unga hesabu*, add, mix together. Ps. **Ungwa**. St. and Pot. **Ungika**. Pot. **Ungikana**. Prep. **Ungia**. Cs. **Ungisha**. Rp. **Ungana**. Stc. **Ungama**. Rp. of Stc. **Ungamana**, be joined together, united, connected, coherent, interdependent. Cv. **Ungua**, disjoin, disconnect, cut in two, pull apart. St. **Unguka**. Prep. **Ungulia**. **Kiunga**, n. *vi-* (1) anything which joins, e.g. a link, &c.; (2) suburb of a town, suburban residence, outskirts, place adjacent. *Ana kiunga chake na nyumba yake mjini*, he has an estate (garden) in the suburbs, and a house in town. *Anakaa kiungani*, he lives in the outskirts of the town. The *kiunga* is often an orchard, fruit or pleasure garden. **Kiungo**, n. *vi-* (1) act (method, means, &c.) of joining, a joining, link, connecting part, connexion, amalgamation. Hence (2) a joint of the animal frame, a member of the body, i.e. *kiungo cha mwili*. *Viungo vimeachana*, the joints have come apart. Also *achana viungo*, loosen the joints, of a man lying at ease—so too *jitupa viungo*, of a sprawling attitude. *Makuti ya kiungo*, or *viungo*, coco-nut leaves prepared for use as a thatch. (3) something which seasons, gives a taste or relish to, food, e.g. sauce, pickle, salt, vinegar, &c. (i.e. *mchuzi, achali, chumvi, siki*). **Muungo**, n. *mi-*, **Mwungo**, n. *mi-* a joining together, a joint, e.g. *mwungo wa kufuli*, to describe a dovetail joint, lit. a lock-joining. **Ungo**, n. *ma-* (1) a joining, a joint, and (of the body) a member, a part—usually *kiungo, vi-*, but the plur. *maungo* is regularly used (*a*) of the limbs of the body collectively and so of the body as a whole, e.g. *maungo yote yanatetemeka*, the whole body is shaking. *Maungo wazi*, stripped to the skin, bare body. *Ana maungo*, he has a fine (well-knit, well-developed, muscular) frame—of a strong athletic man. (*b*) back,

back-bone, in a similar inclusive sense, also *uti wa mgongo*, i.e. the stem on which the limbs grow, e.g. *juu ya maungo ya farasi*, on horseback. *Ameshuka maungoni mwa mama yake*, he has got off his mother's back. (Cf. *mgongo*.) (2) the hymen. (*a*) *vunja ungo*, begin to menstruate. (*b*) fig. of a tree beginning to bear fruit.

Ungama, v. acknowledge, confess, admit, allow, grant, concede. *Ungama wizi*, confess a robbery (see also Stc. of *unga*, v.). Ps. **Ungamwa**. St. **Ungamika**. Prep. **Ungamia**. Cs. **Ungamisha**, induce to confess, hear a confession. **Mwungama**, n. *wa-*, **Mwungamaji**, n. *wa-* one who acknowledges (admits, confesses) wrongdoing. Used as a title of Muhammad, also for penitents in the confessional. **Mwungamishi**, n. *wa-* one who invites (receives, extorts) confession, &c., a confessor. **Mwungamo**, n. *mi-* acknowledgement of obligation, confession, admission of guilt. **Ungamo**, n. *ma-* confession, concession, admission. **Uungamaji**, n. condition or state of one who confesses.

Ungamana, n. See under **Unga**, v.

Ungamo, n. (1) *ma-* see under **Ungama**, v.; (2) a yellow stuff, used as a dye, from the shrub *mwungamo*.

Ungana, v. See under **Unga**, v.

Unga'ro, n. See under **Ng'aa**.

Ungi, n. sometimes heard for *wingi*, which see.

Ungo, n. *ma-* (1) see under **Unga**, v.; (2) (*ma-* and *nyungo*) a round flat basket used for sifting grain.

Ungoje, n., **Ungojezi**, n. See under **Ngoja**.

Ung'ongo, n. (*ng'ongo*), a strip of palm-leaf, esp. of the wild date palm *mkindu*; one of the coarser strips next to the mid-rib, used for sewing together the plaits for a mat, or basket, or for the binding round the edge. Prov. *Mtu aliyeumwa na nyoka akiona ung'ongo hushtuka*, a man who has been bitten by a snake starts even if he sees an *ung'ongo*, i.e. once bitten twice shy. (Cf. *mwaa, ukindu, ukili*.)

Ungu, n. (*nyungu*). See under **Chungu**.

Ungua, v. (A). See under **Unga**, v.

Ungua, v. (B) be scorched, scalded, or hardened, damaged with fire, burnt. *Nyumba imeungua moto*, the house has been (more or less) burnt, damaged by fire. Ps. **Unguliwa**. St. and Pot. **Ungulika**, e.g. (1) be hardened with fire; (2) be combustible. Prep. **Ungulia**, e.g. (1) apply fire to, bake (pottery); (2) also used of the burning sensation of heartburn, indigestion. Cs. **Unguza**, burn, scorch, scald. **Kiungulia**, n. *vi-* stomachic disorder causing eructation or belching. Also *kiungulia cha moyo*, heartburn (cf. *cheu*). **Kiunguza**, n. *vi-*, also **Kiunguzo**, n. *vi-* something which burns, causes the sensation of burning, as fire, acid, &c.

Unguja, n. Zanzibar—island and city. *Unguja mkuu*, Great Zanzibar is now a small village on the same island south of the capital. **Kiunguja**, n. and adv. the dialect of Swahili spoken in Zanzibar, and adv. used generally of anything peculiar to Zanzibar, e.g. dress, customs, &c.

Unguza, v. See under **Ungua**, v. (B).

Ungwana, n. See **Uungwana** under **Mwungwana**.

Unong'onezi, n. (*nong'onezi*). See under **Nong'ona**.

Unono, n. See under **Nona**.

Ununu, n. fibre from the inner skin of the stalk of a coco-nut leaf. *Puna ununu*, strip the fibre.

Ununuzi, n. See under **Nunua**.

Unyaa, n. See under **Nyara**, v.

Unyago, n. dancing and other ceremonies connected with the initiation of children of both sexes into tribal rights, as of adult age. Used also of other grotesque dances, i.e. mummery, acting, farce. *Amekwenda* *unyagoni*, she has gone to be initiated. **Kinyago**, n. *vi-* the paraphernalia used in the *unyago*, but esp. a dressed-up grotesque figure, mock-ghost, masks and images. *Cheza kinyago*, play at *unyago*, play at ghosts, dress up—of any kind of acting, theatricals, farce. (Cf. *jando*.)

Unyaji, n. See under **Nya.**

Unyakuzi, n. See under **Nyaka.**

Unyama, n. See under **Mnyama.**

Unyamavu, n. See under **Nyamaa.**

Unyang'anyi, n. See under **Nyang'anya.**

Unyanya, n. disdain, feeling of superiority over another, drawing back from, avoiding (because of pride, superiority, &c.), or because of disgust, &c. (Cf. *nyara*, v.)

Unyarafu, n. See under **Nyara**, v.

Unyasi, n. (*nyasi* and *ma-*) a blade of coarse grass, a flag-like reed, much used in thatching. **Unyasi wa kizungu**, Vetiver grass.

Unyaufu, n. See under **Nyauka.**

Unyayo, n. (*nyayo*), sometimes heard for *wayo* (*uayo*), which see.

Unyege, n. See under **Nyega.**

Unyele, n. See **Unywele.**

Unyeme, n. a call, noise. (Cf. *ukelele*, *ukemi*.)

Unyende, n. also **Unyenje**, a cry. *Kupiga unyende*, to cry out loudly for fear.

Unyenyekeo, n., **Unyenyekevu**, n. See under **Nyenya.**

Unyenyezi, n. condition of being hazy, blurred, indistinct, &c., i.e. of things at a distance which can only be seen with difficulty or indistinctly. *Kuona kitu kwa unyenyezi*, to see a thing with difficulty, indistinctly.

Unyeleo, n. (*nyeleo* and *ma-*). See under **Nya.**

Unyeo, n. See under **Nyea.**

Unyesi, n. See under **Nya.**

Unyeti, n. See under **Nyeta.**

Unyevu, n. See under **Nya.**

Unyo and **Unyounyo**, adv. together, close, e.g. *fuatana unyounyo*, follow each other very close together.

Unyofu, n. See under **Nyoka**, v.

Unyogovu, n. See under **Nyong'onyea.**

Unyonga, n. (*nyonga* and *ma-*). See under **Nyonga**, n.

Unyonge, n. See under **Nyonga**, v.

Unyong'onyevu, n. See under **Nyong'onyea.**

Unyoya, n. (*nyoya* and *ma-*) a fibre of wool, or animal's hair, or down. See under **Nyoya.**

Unyozi, n. See under **Nyoa.**

Unyumba, n. See under **Chumba.**

Unyushi, n. (*nyushi*). See under **Ushi.**

Unywaji, n. See under **Nywa.**

Unywele, n. (*nywele*) a hair, when used alone, properly of human hair—but *nywele za singa*, long straight, soft hair, is used of the hair of Europeans, and of some animals when of similar kind, e.g. horse-hair, mane of a lion, &c. *Nywele za kipilipili* (*za kusokota, za kusongamana*), describes the woolly, tufty, wiry hair of natives. *Nywele za ukoka*, fairly straight hair with a wave in it. The hairy (furry, woolly) coat of almost all animals is described as *manyoya*. (Cf. *usinga, unyoya*, also *ulaika, udevu, uvuzi, ukope, ushi, panja, shungi, mvi*.)

Unyweleo, n. See under **Nywa.**

Uo, n. (*nyuo*) cover, case, scabbard, sheath. *Uo wa kisu*, sheath of a knife (usu. *ala*). *Uo wa kitabu*, cover, binding of a book (usu. *jalada*). (Cf. *chuo* and *nguo*, prob. from the same root.)

Uombaji, n., **Uombezi**, n. *ma-*, **Uombi**, n. *ma-*. See under **Omba.**

Uonevu, n. *ma-*, **Uonyo**, n. (*onyo* and *ma-*). See under **Ona.**

Uovu, n. (*maovu*). See under **-ovu.**

Uozi, n. *ma-*. See under **Oa.**

Upaa, n. See under **Para.**

Upagazi, n. See under **Pagaa.**

Upaja, n. (*paja* and *ma-*) thigh, ham. *Upaja wa tanga*, broad bulging side of a sail. Also **Paja**, which see. (Cf. *kiweo, kiga*.)

Upaji, n. See under **Pa**, **v.**

Upakio, n., **Upakizi**, n. *ma-*, **Upako**, n., **Upakuzi**, n. *ma-*. See under **Paka**, v. (A).

Upamba, n. (*pamba*) (1) see under **Pamba**, n.; (2) a small billhook, a knife with a broad, flat, thin blade, used in getting palm wine (*tembo*)—also called *kotama*; (3) tusk of a boar, wart-hog, &c. (Cf. *gema*.)

Upambano, n. *ma-*, **Upambanuzi**, n. *ma-*. See under **Pambana**.

Upambo, n. *ma-*. See under **Pamba**, **v.**

Upana, n. *ma-*. See under **-pana**.

Upandaji, n. See under **Panda**, **v.** (A) and (B).

Upande, n. (*pande*). See under **Kipande**.

Upanga. n. (*panga*) (1) a sword. Also (2) a flat, wooden sword-shaped instrument, used by weavers to tighten each thread of the woof in weaving. *Upanga wa feleji*, a long, straight, two-edged sword. *Upanga wa imani*, a short sword with a kind of cross hilt. *Bapa la upanga*, flat of the sword. *Makali ya upanga* or *machinjioni*, the edge. *Maungo ya upanga* (or *mafutuni*), the back of a sword. *Futa* (or *chomoa*) *upanga*, draw a sword. *Futika* (or *chomeka*) *upanga*, sheath a sword. *Upanga wa suruali*, crease of trousers. *Mtu mwenye upanga wazi*, a bloodthirsty person (cf. *sime*, *kitara*). (3) a batten of wood on one of the wings of a double door, to prevent them passing each other (cf. *mfaa*); (4) comb of a cock, *upanga wa jogoo* (cf. *undu*.)

Upangaji, n. See under **Panga**.

Upanzi, n. See under **Panda**, **v.** (B).

Upao, n. (*pao*). See under **Paa**, **v.** (A).

Upapasa, n. a kind of bread or cake made from cassava and coco-nut juice (*tui*).

Upapi, n. (*papi*), long narrow strip, flat or rounded, of wood or metal, a long lath or bar, beading, edging, border. Of clothes, a gore, a gusset.

Upara, n. See under **Para**, **n.**

Upataji, n. See under **Pata**.

Upati, n. the method of wearing a loin-cloth as the Banyans do, i.e. tucked up between the legs to form a sort of divided skirt or loose trousers. (Cf. *winda*, *ubinda*.)

Upatilivu, n., **Upatilizo**, n. *ma-*. See under **Pata**.

Upatu,* n. (*patu*, and of size *ma-*) (1) a round metal, dish-shaped gong, with the edges turned up; (2) gifts put on a plate for the bridal pair at a wedding. **Kipatu**, n. *vi-* dim. of (1). (Hind. پات.)

Upau, n. See **Upao** under **Paa**, **v.** (A).

Upawa, n. (*pawa*), a flat, shallow ladle—usually of a part of a coco-nut shell fixed on a short stick as handle. (Cf. *kata*, a deeper kind of ladle.)

Upayukaji, n. See under **Paya**.

Upekecho, n. (*pekecho* and *ma-*). See under **Pekecha**.

Upekee, n. See under **Peka**.

Upeketevu, n., **Upekuzi**, n. See under **Pekecha**.

Upele, n. (*pele*) eruption, pimples, pustules, a breaking out of the skin. The word generally used for scabies. **Kipele**, n. *vi-* dim.

Upelelezi, n. See under **Peleleza**.

Upembe, n. See under **Pembe**.

Upembo, n. (*pembo*). See under **Pemba**.

Upendaji, n., **Upendano**, n. *ma-*, **Upendeleo**, n. *ma-*, **Upendelevu**, n., **Upendezi**, n. *ma-*, **Upendo**, n. (*pendo* and *ma-*), **Upendwa**, n. *ma-*. See under **Penda**.

Upenu, n. (*penu*) space outside a native hut covered by the projecting frame and thatch of the roof, and often enclosed so as to form a small lean-to or sleeping-place. Hence any similar appendage to a house. **Kipenu**, n. *vi-* dim. (Cf. *ubati* and *shuhuli*.)

Upenyezi, n. (*penyezi* and *ma-*). See under **Penya**.

Upenzi, n. *ma-*. See under **Penda.**
Upeo, n. See under **Pea, v.** (A).
Upepeaji, n., **Upepeo**, n. (*pepeo* and *ma-*), **Upepezi**, n., **Upepo**, n. (*pepo*). See under **Pepa.**
Upesi, n. See under **-epesi.**
Upeto, n. (*peto*). See under **Peta, v.** (A).
Upevu, n. See under **Pea, v.** (A).
Upigano, n. *ma-*. See under **Piga.**
Upimaji, n. See under **Pima.**
Upinda, adv. *kufa upinda*, die a natural death. **Upinda**, v. die, of dying a natural death. (Cf. *kufa, fariki.*)
Upindani, n., **Upinde**, n. (*pinde*), **Upindo**, n. (*pindo*), **Upinduzi**, n. *ma-*. See under **Pinda.**
Upinzani, n. See under **Pinza.**
Upishi, n. (*pishi* and *ma-*). See under **Pika.**
Upo, n. (*nyupo*), a dipper, for bailing water out of a boat, &c., commonly a calabash (*buyu*) or can (*kopo*). (Cf. *upawa, kata, sila.*)
Upofu, n. See under **-pofu.**
Upogo, n. (*pogo*). See under **Pogoa.**
Upole, n. See under **-pole.**
Upondo, n. See **Ponda.**
Upongoo, n. (*pongoo*), central rib or stem of a coco-nut or similar leaf. (Cf. *kuti.*)
Uponyi, n. (*ponyi*). See under **Poa.**
Upooza, n. See under **Pooza.**
Uporo, n. food left over from evening till next morning, also called *kiporo.*
Uposo, n. See under **Posa.**
Upote, n. (*pote*), thong, bowstring—of sinew or twisted string, i.e. *ugwe wa mikano ya ng'ombe.* (Cf. *ugwe, ukanda,* and *pota.*)
Upotevu, n. See under **Potea.**
Upotoe, n., **Upotovu**, n. See under **Pota.**
Upumbavu, n. See under **Pumbaa.**
Upumuo, n., **Upumzi**, n. See under **Puma.**
Upunga, n. (*punga*), stage in the growth of a fruit-bearing tree or plant, when the flower is full blown, and the embryo fruit beginning to form. At the coast, esp. of coco-nut. (Pl. *punga*, the male flowers) but also used of maize, millet, &c., and obs. *mpunga*, of rice, while still on the plant.
Upungufu, n. (*pungufu* and *ma-*), **Upunguo**, n. See under **Punga, v.** (C).
Upupu, n. cow-itch—the mucuna bean, covered with velvet-like glossy hairs which are extremely irritating to the skin.
Upurukushani, n., **Upurukusho**, n. See under **Pura, v.** (B).
Upuzi, n. See under **Puza.**
Upweke, n. See under **Peka.**
Upya, n. See under **-pya.**
Uradhi,* n. See under **Ridhi.**
Uradi,* n. prayers said at a Muhammadan burial. Sometimes heard as *auradi*. *Kuvuta uradi* (*auradi*), to finger the beads of a rosary after praying. (Cf. *talakim*. Ar. اوراد.)
Urafiki,* n. See under **Rafiki.**
Urahisi,* n. See under **Rahisi.**
Urai,* n. See under **Rai, v.** (A).
Uraia,* n. See under **Raia.**
Uraibu,* n. strictly anything one is accustomed to and cannot do without, but only applied to a chewing-mixture very popular at the coast and commonly called *tambuu*, from the betel leaf in which it is wrapped and chewed. The ingredients are lime (*chokaa*), tobacco (*tumbako*), chips of areca-nut (*popoo*), and often a red gum (*katu*), and cloves (*karafuu*). The gum and areca-nut colour the saliva expectorated a blood-red colour (*utembe*), and also dye the teeth. (Cf. *tambuu*. Ar. غائب things longed for.)
Uramali,* n. black magic, but used of that caused by incantations, not by administration of poison or charms, &c. Perh. of the magic found out by divining, i.e. *ramli*. (Cf. *ulozi, uchawi, usihiri*, and *ramli* which is apparently from the same Ar. root.)

Urambirambi, n. See **Ulambilambi** under **Lamba**.

Urari,* n. equality, proportion, evenness, balance—a technical term used in accounts. *Urari wa hesabu*, balancing an account. *Fanya urari*, strike a balance. *Gawa kwa urari*, divide in proportion. (Ar. عرار.)

Urasharasha,* n. *ma-*. See under **Rasha**.

Uraufu,* n. See under **Raufu**.

Urefu,* n. See under **-refu**.

Urembo, n. (*rembo* and *ma-*). See under **Remba**.

Urithi,* n. (*rithi*). See under **Rithi**.

Urodi,* n. See under **Rodi**.

Urongo, n. sometimes heard for *uwongo*. See under **-wongo**.

Uru,* n. diamonds in a pack of cards. (Cf. *karata*. Port. *ouru*.)

Urujuani,* n. violet—the colour. (Pers. ارجوان.)

Urukususu,* n. cough medicine. (Cf. *sus*. Ar. عرق سوس liquorice root.)

Urumo,* n. poverty, straitened circumstances. *Shikwa* (*pigwa*, *patwa*) *na urumo*, be in straitened circumstances. (Cf. *utaiti*, *ufukara*, *mwambo*. Ar. عرم bring calamity upon.)

Usafari,* n. See under **Safiri**.

Usafi,* n. See under **-safi**.

Usafidi, n. See under **Safidi**.

Usafihi,* n. See under **Safihi**.

Usafiri,* n. See under **Safiri**.

Usaha,* n. matter (from abscess, wound, &c.), pus, discharge, e.g. *kidonda kinatoka usaha*, the sore is discharging pus. (Ar. وسخ foul.)

Usahaulifu,* n. See under **Sahau**.

Usahibu, n. See under **Suhubu**.

Usahihi,* n. See under **Sahihi**.

Usani,* n. See under **Sana**, v.

Usanifu,* n. See under **Sanifu**.

Usare, n. (1) blood-brotherhood, e.g. *udugu wa kuchanjia uchale* (prob. for *uchale*); (2) being of the same pattern, see **Sare**.

Usasi. See under **Saka**.

Usawa,* n. See under **Sawa**.

Useja, n. (1) see under **Mseja**; (2) a collar of beads.

Usemaji, n., **Usemi**, n. See under **Sema**.

Useremala,* n. See under **Seremala**.

Ushababi,* n. See under **Shababi**.

Ushabaki,* n. See under **Shabaki**.

Ushahidi,* n. (*shahidi*). See under **Shahada**.

Ushairi,* n. See under **Shairi**.

Ushakii,* n. bravery, courage. (Cf. *ushujaa*, *ujasiri*. Ar. شقى doings of a robber, murderer, &c.)

Ushanga, n. (*shanga* and *ma-*, but also used collectively), a bead, beads in general. *Shanga* in relation to beads singly, *mashanga* collections of beads, bead articles. *Ushanga mwingi*, a quantity of beads. Beads are sold in strings, *timbi*, *kete*, or bunches, *shada*, *fundo*, and formerly supplied the place of money in the interior.

Ushangao, n. See under **Shangaa**.

Usharifu,* n. See under **Sharifu**.

Ushaufu,* n. See under **Shaua**.

Usheha,* n. See under **Sheha**.

Ushemasi,* n. See under **Shemasi**.

Ushenzi,* n. See under **Shenzi**.

Ushi, n. (*nyushi*) (1) eyebrow; (2) any ridge (projection, roughness) resembling an eyebrow, e.g. string-course of a wall, cornice, hedge, &c.; (3) brink, edge, e.g. of a well, &c. (cf. *ombwe*). **Unyushi**, n. (*nyushi*), a hair of the eyebrow.

Ushikamano, n. See under **Shika**.

Ushimbu, n. shrimps. (Cf. *uduvi*.)

Ushinda, n., **Ushindani**, n., **Ushinde**, n., **Ushindi**, n. See under **Shinda**.

Ushirika,* n. See under **Shiriki**.

Ushoga,* n. See under **Shoga**.

Ushoni, n. *ma-*, **Ushono**, n. *ma-*. See under **Shona**.

Ushoroba, n. See under **Kishoroba**.

Ushtaki,* n. See under **Shtaki**.

Ushuhuda,* n. See under **Shahada**.

Ushujaa,* n. *ma-*. See under **-shujaa.**

Ushukuru,* n. *ma-*. See under **Shukuru.**

Ushungi, n. (*shungi*). See under **Shungi.**

Ushupavu, n. See under **Shupaa.**

Ushuru,* n. taxation, tax, customs duty, rate, rent, &c. *Toa* (*lipa*) *ushuru*, pay taxes. *Toza ushuru*, collect taxes. (Cf. *ashara*. Ar. عشر.)

Ushuzi, n. See under **Shuta.**

Usi, n. a grass bearing a kind of cotton.

Usia,* v. direct, commission, order, charge—and esp. of a solemn, serious, weighty command, e.g. last directions on starting on a journey, a religious exhortation, giving the terms of a will. Thus of dying father, *enyi watoto wangu nitawausia*, my children I will give you my last directions. *Alimwusia nyumba*, he bequeathed a house to him. Ps. **Usiwa.** St. **Usika.** Prep. **Usilia,** e.g. give orders concerning (to, &c.). Cs. **Usisha.** Rp. **Usiana.** **Usia,** n. *ma-* solemn charge, last will and testament, warning, exhortation, commission. *Alifanya usia*, he made a will. *Ndilo usia langu*, that is my final charge, will. **Wasii,** n. *ma-* executor, trustee, i.e. one named in a will or nominated as such. **Wosia,** n. last will and testament. (Cf. *agiza*. Ar. وصى.)

Usihiri,* n. See under **Sihiri.**

Usikilivu, n., **Usikivu,** n., **Usikizano,** n., **Usikizi,** n. See under **Sikia.**

Usiku, n. (*siku*), a night (in counting the plural, *siku* is used, i.e. the nights, not the days being counted, but sometimes *masiku* is heard), night time, i.e. the twelve hours of darkness, from 6 p.m. to 6 a.m. where sun time is kept. *Siku nne* is really four nights, the days not being taken into consideration in counting, although one hears *siku nne, mchana na usiku*. *Usiku wa manane*, midnight. *Usiku kucha*, the whole night long. (Cf. *siku, mchana*.)

Usimamao, n., **Usimamizi,** n. See under **Simama.**

Usimanga, n. See under **Simanga.**

Usimeme, n. See under **Simama.**

Usinga, n. (*singa*), a single hair—of the long, straight kind, of men and certain animals.

Usingizi, n. sleep. *Lala usingizi*, go to sleep. *Usingizi mzito*, deep sleep. *Hana usingizi*, he is a light sleeper. *Usingizi ulinipaa* (*uliniparama*), sleep left me. *Shikwa na usingizi*, feel sleepy. (Cf. *sinzia, lepe*.)

Usiniombe, n. a kind of cassava. (Cf. *muhogo*.)

Usira, n. a powder made from the burnt skin of an animal, used as a charm for protection against that particular animal. Also a medicine for headache, &c.

Usiri,* v. stay, delay, be detained, also commonly St. **Usirika,** be detained, delayed, behindhand. **Usiri,** n. detention, delay, being late, lagging behind, e.g. *mwanzo huwa na usiri*, starting always seems slow to come. *Usifanye usiri*, don't procrastinate. (Cf. *kawia, shelewa, ahiri, uzuhali, limatia*. Ar. سر remain.)

Usita, n. a street, way, path. (Cf. *njia, ujia*.)

Usitawi,* n. See under **Sitawi.**

Usitu, n. a narrow length of plaited leaf-strip. Strips are sewn together to make mats, baskets, &c. (Cf. *ukili*.)

Uso, n. (*nyuso*), (1) face, countenance, expression (cf. *sura*); (2) front, surface, exterior, e.g. *uso wa nyumba*, the front of a house. *Vunja uso*, disgrace, discourage. *Kunja uso*, express sorrow, anger, &c., frown. *Kunjua uso*, of pleasure, good humour. *Uso kwa uso*, face to face. *Usoni pa*, in the presence of. *Uso wa ardhi*, the surface of the earth.

Usodai,* n. same as *usodawi*.

Usodawi,* n. pride, superciliousness, disdain. **Sodawi,** a. proud, supercilious, arrogant. (Ar. صد aversion.)

Usoka, n. *ma-* brass wire—in general, or a small piece of wire. **Masoka,** thick brass or iron wire. (Cf. *masango*.)

Usono, n. (1) friendship; (2) rest, sleep.

Usononi, n. See **Sonoa.**

Ustaarabu,* n. See under **-staarabu.**

Ustadi,* n. See under **-stadi.**

Ustahiki,* n. See under **Haki.**

Ustahili,* n. See under **Stahili.**

Ustahimili,* n., **Ustahimilivu,** n. See under **Hamali.**

Ustahivu,* n. See under **Stahi.**

Usu! int. Hush! Silence! Make less noise! (Cf. *kelele*.)

Usubi, n. a small biting gnat, midge, sandfly.

Usufi,* n. See under **Msufi.**

Usufii,* n. See under **Sufii.**

Usufu,* n. wool, contr. *sufi*, kapok.

Usugu, n. See under **Sugu.**

Usuhuba,* n. See under **Suhubu.**

Usukani,* n. (*sukani*) rudder, and steering-gear in general, of a boat, ship, motor-car, bicycle, &c. **Msukani,** n. *wa-* a steersman. (Ar. سكان.)

Usukumizi, n. See under **Sukuma.**

Usultani,* n. See under **Sultani.**

Usulubu,* n. See under **Sulubika.**

Usuluhi,* n., **Usuluhifu,** n. See under **Suluhi.**

Usumba, n. fibres of the coco-nut husk after being soaked and cleaned for use in making string, cord, &c. Also *makumbi ya usumba*. (Cf. *kumbi*.)

Usumbufu, n. *ma-*. See under **Sumba.**

Usungo, n. See under **Msungo.**

Usuria,* n. See under **Suria.**

Ususi, n. See under **Suka.**

Ususu, n. a passage in a house, a corridor.

Uswahili,* n. See under **Mswahili.**

Uta, n. (*nyuta*), a bow, and plur. *mata*, bow and arrows, i.e. the weapon complete. (Cf. *upindi, ugwe, upote*.)

Utaa, n. (*taa*), a stage, raised and covered, to put grain on for storage and drying. (Cf. *uchaga*.)

Utaba, n. See under **Tabua.**

Utabibu,* n. See under **Tabibia.**

Utabiri,* n. *ma-* See under **Tabiri.**

Utadi,* n. See under **Tadi.**

Utafiti,* n. See under **Tafiti.**

Utagaa, n. (*tagaa*), branch of a tree. (Cf. *tawi, tanzu*.)

Utaiti,* n. See under **Taiti.**

Utaji,* n. a piece of calico or stuff of any kind used by women and men as a covering of the head, whether to conceal the features, protect from the sun, or as an ornament, a veil. (Cf. *taji, shela, dusamali, ushungi*. Pers. تاج crown.)

Utajiri,* n. See under **Tajiri.**

Utakalifu,* n. See under **Kalifu.**

Utakaso, n., **Utakatifu,** n. See under **Takasa.**

Utako, n. See under **Tako.**

Utaleleshi,* n. See under **Talaleshi.**

Utamaduni,* n. See under **Tamaduni.**

Utambaa, n. *ma-*. See under **Tambaa,** n.

Utambazi, n. See under **Tambaa,** v.

Utambi, n. (*tambi*) (1) wick of a candle or lamp; (2) stuff for a turban; (3) membrane enclosing the bowels. (Cf. *tambi, kitambi*.)

Utambo, n. (*tambo*) (1) see under **Tamba;** (2) see under **Kitambo;** (3) the swinging handle of a pail, iron pot, &c. (as contr. with *mpini* or *kipini*, of a knife; *mkono*, of a saucepan; *shikio*, of a basket, &c.

Utambuzi, n. See under **Tambua.**

Utamu, n. See under **-tamu.**

Utamvua, n. See under **Chambua.**

Utanashati,* n. See under **Tanashati.**

Utando, n., **Utandu,** n. See under **Tanda.**

Utanga, n. (*tanga*) a kind of mat on

which women do the grinding of grain. (Cf. *tuguu.*)

Utangule, n. the leaves of the fan-palm cut into narrow strips for plaiting. (Cf. *ung'ongo, ukili.*)

Utangulizi, n. *ma-*. See under **Tangulia.**

Utani,* n. See under **Tania.**

Utanzu, n. (*tanzu*, and of size, *ma-*) a branch of a tree. (Cf. *tagaa, tawi.*)

Utapishi, n. *ma-*. See under Tapika.

Utaratibu,* n. See under **Ratibu.**

Utari,* n. (*tari*) string of an instrument, leather thong, cord, rope. (Ar. اوتار, plural of وتر.)

Utasa, n. See under **Tasa.**

Utashi, n. See under **Taka, v.**

Utasi, n., **Utata**, n. (*tata*). See under **Tata.**

Utatu, n. See under **Tatu.**

Utawa, n. See under **Tawa.**

Utawala,* n. See under **Tawala.**

Utawi, n. (*tawi* and *ma-*). See **Tawi.**

Utaya, n. See under **Taya.**

Utayari,* n. See under **Tayari.**

Ute, n. (*mate*) (1) thick, sticky, viscid fluid, e.g. saliva, mucus, lather. *Ute wa yai*, white of egg. *Tema mate*, expectorate. (2) saliva which comes to one's mouth—mouth-watering. (Cf. *uto, mate*, and dist. *uta, mata.*)

Uteatea, n. See **Ucheachea** under **Cha, v.** (B).

Uteketevu, n., **Uteketezo**, n. See under **Teketea.**

Utelezi, n. *ma-*. See under **Telea.**

Utembe, n. the chewed refuse of the mixture called *tambuu* or *uraibu*, which is expectorated. It is of a blood-red colour.

Utembezi, n. See under **Tembea.**

Utembo, n. fibre from the leaf-stalk of various palms, used as string, cord, &c. (Cf. *utembwe, ufumwale.*)

Utembwe, n. same as *utembo*, which is more common. (Cf. *ufumwale.*)

Utendaji, n., **Utende**, n. See under **Tenda.**

Utengemano, n., **Utengenezaji**, n. See under **Tengenea.**

Utengo, n. See under **Tenga.**

Utenzi, n. (*tenzi*) (1) see under **Tenda**; (2) a poem, esp. of a religious kind, an old story told in verse. (Cf. *shairi.*)

Uteo, n. (*teo*) a tray made of plaited leaf-strips, used for sifting grain. **Kiteo**, n. *vi-* dim. *Kiteo cha mfiwa*, a tray of food sent by neighbours to a bereaved person. (Cf. *ungo.*)

Utepe,* n. (*tepe* and *ma-*) a narrow strip of cloth, band, fillet, ribbon, tape, badge on the arm (of a soldier). *Amepata utepe*, he has been given a stripe (chevron, &c.). (? Eng. tape.)

Utepetevu, n. See under **Tepetea.**

Utesaji, n., **Utesi**, n. See under **Tesa.**

Utete, n. (*tete* and *ma-*) stalk or stem of a reed or grass, used as a pipe, or musical instrument. **Kitete**, n. *vi-* dim.

Utetezi, n. *ma-*, **Uteto**, n. *ma-*. See under **Teta.**

Uteuzi, n. *ma-*. See under **Teua.**

Uthabiti,* n. See under **Thabiti.**

Uthubutu,* n. See under **Thubutu.**

Uti, n. (*nyuti*). See under **Mti.**

Utii,* n. See under **Tii.**

Utiko, n. (*matiko*) roof-ridge of a thatched house, and so, ridge-tile or anything so used.

Utimbi, n. See **Uchimvi** under **Chimba.**

Utimilifu,* n. See under **Timu.**

Utimvi, n. See **Uchimvi** under **Chimba.**

Utingo, n. bus conductor, the boy who usually assists on a motor-car or taxi, or who is learning to drive.

Utiriri, n. elusiveness, being provoking. (Cf. *tiririka.*)

Utisho, n. (*tisho*). See under **Tisha.**

Utitiri, n. chicken lice.

Uto, n. oil, any thick oily fluid. Not usually employed by itself. *Mafuta ya uto*, semsem oil. *Uto wa tui la nazi*, oil from coco-nut juice.

Utohara,* n. See under **Tahiri.**

Utokezo, n., **Utoko**, n. See under **Toa, v.** (A).

Utomvu, n. thick viscid sap or juice from a plant. (Cf. *uto, ulimbo.*)

Utondoti, n. (1) repetition; (2) a silver ornament worn by some women on the chest.

Utongo, n. *ma-* discharge from the eyes. (Cf. *chongo, matongo.*)

Utongozi, n. *ma-*. See under **Tongoza.**

Utope, n. *ma-*. See under **Tope.**

Utoro, n. See under **Toroka.**

Utosi, n. (*tosi*) crown of the head.

Utoto, n. See under **Mtoto.**

Utotole, n. a reward for finding something lost. (Cf. *kiangaza macho, kiokosi.*)

Utovu, n. See under **Toa, v. (B).**

Utu, n. See under **Mtu.**

Utukufu, n. See under **Tukuka.**

Utukutu, n. See under **Tukuta.**

Utule, n. See under **Tule.**

Utulivu, n. See under **Tua.**

Utumbavu, n. See under **Tumba.**

Utumbo, n. (*tumbo* and *ma-*). See under **Tumbo.**

Utumbuizi, n., **Utumbuizo**, n. See under **Tumbuika.**

Utume, n., **Utumi**, n., **Utumishi**, n. *ma-*, **Utumizi**, n. *ma-*, **Utumo**, n., **Utumwa**, n. See under **Tuma.**

Utunda, n. (*tunda*) a string of beads, worn by some women round the loins, i.e. *utunda wa ushanga.* (Cf. *kondavi.*)

Utundu, n. See under **Mtundu.**

Utunduizi, n. See under **Tunduia.**

Utungaji, n. and **Utungo**, n. See under **Tunga, v.**

Utungu, n. same as *uchungu*, but only used of the pains at childbirth, birth pangs, labour, i.e. *utungu wa kuzaa* (*wa uzazi*).

Utunu, n. See under **Tunuka.**

Utunzaji, n., **Utunzi**, n., **Utunzo**, n. (*tunzo* and *ma-*). See under **Tunza.**

Utupa, n. the juice of a kind of euphorbia, *mtupa*, used as a fish poison.

Utupu, n. See under **-tupu.**

Uturi,* n. perfume, scent, attar (from same root), &c., also sometimes called *usuri.* (Ar. عطر.)

Utusitusi, n. darkness, cloudiness, mistiness. (Contr. *ucheachea* under *cha*, v. (B).)

Utuvu, n. See under **Tua.**

Uuaji, n. See under **Ua, v.**

Uuguzi, n. *ma-*, **Uuguzaji**, n. *ma-*. See under **Ugua.**

Uume, n. See under **Ume.**

Uumikaji, n., **Uumizi**, n. See under **Umika.**

Uungamaji, n. See under **Ungama.**

Uungu, n. See under **Mungu.**

Uungwana, n. See under **Mwungwana.**

Uunzi, n. See under **Unda.**

Uvimbe, n. See under **Vimba, v. (A).**

Uvimbizi, n. *ma-*. See under **Vimba, v. (B).**

Uviringo, n. See under **Viringa.**

Uvivu, n. See under **-vivu.**

Uvoo, n. an armlet of ivory or beads. (Cf. *kikuku.*)

Uvuguvugu, n. See under **-vuguvugu.**

Uvukizo, n. See **Ufukizo** under **Fuka.**

Uvukuto, n. See under **Vukuta, also Ufukuto** under **Fuka.**

Uvulana, n. See under **Mvulana.**

Uvuli, n. See under **Kivuli.**

Uvumba, n. an odoriferous gum used for perfume and incense. (Cf. *udi, ubani*, and *fukizo.*)

Uvumbi, n. See under **Vumbi.**

Uvumbuaji, n., **Uvumbuzi**, n. See under **Vumbika.**

Uvumi, n. *ma-*, **Uvumo**, n. *ma-*, **Uvumilivu**, n. See under **Vuma.**

Uvundo, n. See under **Vunda.**

Uvungu, n. See under **Mvungu.**

Uvunjifu, n., **Uvunjo**, n. See under **Vunja.**

Uvuno, n. See under **Vuna.**

Uvunzovunzo, n. the state of being well worn or used very much. (Cf. *vunja.*)

Uvurungu, n. See **Mvungu.**

Uvushi, n. See under **Vua, v. (C).**

Uvusho, n. *ma-*. See under **Vua, v. (C)**, also **Ufusho** under **Fuka.**

Uvutano, n., **Uvuto,** n. See under **Vuta.**

Uvuvi, n. See under **Vua,** v. (B).

Uvuvio, n. See under **Vuvia.**

Uvuzi, n. *ma-*, also **Vuzi,** n. *ma-*, a hair from under the armpits or the pudenda, considered particularly unclean by most tribes, and either shaved regularly or plucked out. (Dist. *unywele,* hair, and *fuzi,* shoulder-blade.)

Uvyazi, n. See under **Vyaa.**

Uwakili,* n. See under **Wakala.**

Uwambo, n. (*mambo*). See under **Wamba.**

Uwanda, n. (*nyanda*) an open space, i.e. (1) in towns—public square, space before houses; (2) in the country —open ground, plain, wilderness. *Uwanda wa juu,* a plateau. (Cf. *uwanja, kiwanja.*)

Uwanja, n. (*wanja*), court, enclosure, open space in front of a house, or among houses. (Cf. *kiwanja, uwanda.*)

Uwasho, n. See under **Waa,** v., also under **Wawa.**

Uwati, n. (1) an eruption on the skin; (2) plur. *mbati,* which see.

Uwatu, n. the herb fenugreek, *Trigonella Foenum-graecum,* its fruits are used for flavouring curries.

Uwazi, n. See under **Wazi.**

Uwaziri,* n. See under **Waziri.**

Uwazo, n. See under **Waza.**

Uwele, n. (*mawele*), bullrush millet, the grain produced by the plant *mwele.* (Dist. *uele,* sickness.)

Uweza, n., **Uwezo,** n. See under **Weza.**

Uwidha,* n. See under **Mauidha.**

Uwili, n. See under **-wili.**

Uwinda, n. sometimes heard for *winda,* n. which see.

Uwindaji, n., **Uwindo,** n. See under **Winda,** v.

Uwingu, n. (*mbingu*). See under **Wingu.**

Uwinja, n. See **Ubinja.**

Uwinzi, n. See under **Winda,** v.

Uwivi, n. See **Wivi** under **Iba.**

Uwivu, n. See **Wivu.**

Uwizi, n. See **Wizi** under **Iba.**

Uwongo, n. See under **-wongo.**

Uya, v. return, for the more common *rudi.*

Uyabisi,* n. See under **Yabisi.**

Uyahudi,* n. See under **Yahudi.**

Uyoga, n. the generic term for fungus, mushrooms, whether edible or not. Also **Kiyoga,** n. *vi-*.

Uza, v. (A) sometimes heard for *uliza,* which see.

Uza, v. (B) sell. *Nataka kuuza nyumba yangu,* I want to sell my house. Ps. **Uzwa.** Prep. **Uzia,** sell to (for, in, at, with, by, &c.). *Nilimwuzia nyumba,* I sold a house on his behalf, also, I sold a house to him. Note: some old people still use a form **Liza,** for selling to another, e.g. *nilimliza nyumba,* I sold him a house. St. **Uzika,** i.e. be for sale. Pot. **Uzikana.** D.Prep. **Uzilia.** Prep. of Rp. **Uziana,** sell to each other. Cs. of Rp. **Uzanya,** be for sale. **Mwuza,** n. *wa-*, **Mwuzaji,** n. *wa-* a salesman, one who sells. *Mwuza tumbako,* a tobacco seller. (Cf. *nadi, zabuni, nunua,* and *gulio* from same root.)

Uzandiki,* n. See under **Zandiki.**

Uzani,* n. weighing, weight (by measure). **Mizani,** n. scales, a balance for weighing things. (Cf. *pima.* Ar. وزن.)

Uzanya, v. See under **Uza,** v. (B)

Uzao, n., **Uzazi,** n. See under **Zaa.**

Uzee, n. See under **Mzee.**

Uzembe, n. See under **-zembe.**

Uzi, n. (*nyuzi*), thread, cotton, string, fibre—and similar objects, e.g. small sinew, ligature, a thin stripe, a fine beading. **Nyuzinyuzi,** fibre. **-a** *nyuzinyuzi,* fibrous, stringy, &c.

Uzima, n. See under **-zima.**

Uzimbezimbe, n. the condition of being withered, slack, useless, impotent. (Cf. *-zembe, pooza.*)

Uzinge, n., **Uzingo,** n. See under **Zinga.**

Uzini, n., **Uzinifu,** n., **Uzinzi,** See under **Zini.**

Uzio, n. (*nyuzio*), a fish-trap, consisting of a fence of upright sticks fastened together, and used for enclosing an area, sometimes very large, on a sloping tidal shore, and preventing the escape of fish as the tide falls. **Zio**, n. *ma-* amplic. (Cf. *kichaga, utata, dema, mgono.*)

Uzishi, n. See under **Zika.**

Uzito, n. See under **-zito.**

Uziwa, n. See under **Ziwa.**

Uziwi, n. See under **Kiziwi.**

Uzohari,* n. hurry over work, scamping of work, &c., the opposite of idleness. (Cf. *haraka, bidii.* Ar. زحر strain in breathing.)

Uzua,* v. remove from office or rank, but usu. *uzulu.*

Uzuhali,* n. gentleness, slowness. (Cf. *upole.* Ar. عهول.)

Uzuio, n. *ma-*, **Uzuizi**, n. *ma-*. See under **Zuia.**

Uzuka, n. See under **Zua.**

Uzulu,* v. remove from office, dismiss, cause to abdicate, dethrone, depose, degrade. *Uzulu kazini* or *katika kazi,* discharge from work. *Jiuzulu,* resign an office, abdicate, retire. Ps. **Uzuliwa.** Prep. **Uzulia.** Cs. **Uzulisha. Uzulu**, n. *ma-* abdication, dismissal, discharge. (Cf. *ondoa, ondosha, toa, shusha, tusha.* Ar. عزل.)

Uzungo, n. See under **Zungua.**

Uzungu, n. See under **Mzungu**, n. *mi-*.

Uzuri, n. See under **-zuri.**

Uzushi, n., **Uzuzi**, n. See under **Zua.**

Uzuzu, n. See under **Zuzua.**

V

V represents the same sound as in English. But it is not clearly distinguished from *f* in some words, partly, no doubt, under the influence of Arabic, which has only the *f* sound. Hence words not found under *v* may be looked for under *f*.

Vaa, v. put on, dress in, clothe oneself, dress. *Amevaa nguo nzuri,* he is wearing fine clothes. *Alivaa,* he wore. *Hajavaa,* he is not dressed yet. Ps. **Valiwa**, (1) of things, be worn; (2) of persons, be dressed. St. **Vika**, is used as Act. clothe (with), cause to wear, dress (in). *Hamlishi wala hamviki,* he does not provide him with food or clothing. Ps. of St. **Vikwa**, be clothed (with). Prep. **Valia**, e.g. (1) put on with (for, in, &c.), but esp. (2) put on something by the way of addition to ordinary clothes—and so dress oneself up, wear fine clothes—and of a soldier, put on accoutrements, e.g. *mshipi wa kuvalia nguo,* a belt to secure one's clothes with. *Amevalia leo,* he has on his best clothes to-day. *Walivalia nguo za kiraia,* they disguised themselves as ordinary citizens. Also in fig. sense, *neno hili lajivalia,* this matter stands on its merits. Rp. **Valiana.** Cs. **Valisha**, but usu. *vika,* as above, also **Visha**, cause to wear, give clothes to, &c. *Mvishe aende zake*, dress him so that he may go. *Vika* is used rather in the sense of to provide with clothes, i.e. clothe habitually, whereas *visha* and *valisha* are used of the actual act of dressing. Cv. **Vua**, take off clothes, undress, unclothe oneself, strip, both Act. and St.—with or without *nguo* expressed. Used of any article of dress, e.g. *vua kofia*, take off a cap, or even *vua miwani*, take off a pair of spectacles. Ps. **Vuliwa**, (1) of clothes, be taken off; (2) of person, be undressed, stripped. St. **Vuka**, e.g. *nguo zote zimemvuka*, all his clothes have come off him. Prep. **Vulia**, take off for (from, in, with, &c.). Cs. **Vulisha**, e.g. make take off clothes, force (induce, allow) to undress. Rp. **Vuana. Kivazi**, n. *vi-* dress, clothes, style of dress. *Kivazi chake kizuri*, he dresses well. **Mvao**, n. *mi-* style of dressing, &c., like *vao* below. **Mviko**, n. *mi-* act (style, &c.) of dressing, clothing, a garment, dress. **Mvuo**, n. *mi-* a taking off of clothes, a stripping. **Valio**, n. *ma-* extra apparel, accoutrement, ornament, addition to usual dress. **Vao**, n. *ma-* style of dressing, mode of wearing, something worn, dress. **Vazi**, n. *ma-* generally used in the plur. raiment, apparel, robes. **Vulio**, n. *ma-* clothes laid aside or not in use, cast-off (old, rotten) clothing, the cast skin or slough of snakes, &c.

Vama, v. (1) lie heavy on, cut into, as of a rope which is tied tightly. Prep. **Vamia**, used in the same way as *vama*, also (2) pounce upon, advance with a rush upon, e.g. *simba alimvamia*, the lion pounced upon him; (3) snatch hastily or greedily; (4) lie upon, recline upon, press upon, e.g. *amevamia mto*, he is lying on a pillow. *Mtoto alimvamia mama yake*, the child rested upon its mother. (Prob. Stc. of *vaa*, with restricted meaning.)

Vao, n. *ma-*. See under **Vaa.**

Varangavaranga, v. interrupt rudely, introduce discord into a friendly conversation. *Usivarangevarange maneno yetu, uache tupatane*, do not bring discord into our conversation, leave us in concord.

Vazi, n. *ma-*. See under **Vaa.**

Vema, a. and adv. See under **-ema.**

Vena,* n. a vein, adopted for use in text-books and school lessons on physiology and anatomy, &c. (Eng.)

V.h. abbreviation of *vivi hivi* and *vivyo hivyo*.

Vi, verb-form, they are, e.g. *vyakula hivi vi ghali*, this food is dear, taking the place of *ni*, or Pres. Indic. of *wa*, be for *vi-* as a prefix, see Grammars.

Via, v. fail of full development (completion, perfection), and so (1) be stunted, cut short, half-done, unfinished, blighted, underdone, spoilt, e.g. *chakula kimevia*, the food is underdone. *Amevia huyu*, he is stunted. *Yai limevia*, the egg has gone bad. Also (2) fig. be a failure, lack life, be of a low type, be backward, stagnate. Prep. **Vilia**, stagnate, stop running, e.g. of blood. *Damu imevilia ndani kwa ndani*, the flow of blood has been completely stanched. Cs. **Viza**, e.g. (1) cut short, make stop, stanch, interrupt, break off, keep back (work, progress, growth), e.g. *ameviza kazi*, he has spoilt the work; (2) curse, destroy, e.g. *Mungu akuvize*, may God curse you; (3) put a spell on, i.e. of wizards and witches. Ps. of Cs. **Vizwa.** Prep. of Cs. **Vizia**, spoil work for, frustrate, balk, try to prevent success or completion of, but commonly used in a more limited sense, waylay, set an ambush for, be on the watch for, beleaguer, beset, keep an unfriendly eye on, molest, harass, e.g. *amenipiga kwa kunivizia*, he has lain in wait for me and beaten me. Ps. **Viziwa.** Rp. **Viziana. Vilio**, n. *ma-* stopping short, stagnation, but esp. of blood, e.g. *mavilio ya damu*, bruises, contusions. **Viza**, a. and n.

ma- bad, i.e. *yai viza* or *yai la viza*, also *viza la yai*, an addled egg used by wizards in their witchcraft.

Viboko, n. the fancy-work along the edges of an embroidered seam, e.g. *mshono wa darizi*.

Vidondo, n. (plur. of *kidondo*, seldom used), small chips of wood used as kindling for lighting a fire. (Cf. *dondoa*.)

Vifaa, n. plur. of *kifaa*, which see under *faa*.

Vifijo, n. plur. whistling, shouting, noises of approval or joy, applause. (Cf. *vigelegele*.)

Vigumu, adv. See under **-gumu**.

Vije? interrog. How's things? How goes it? (Colloquial.)

Vika, v. See under **Vaa**.

Vikorokoro, n. plur. (not used in sing.) goods and chattels, utensils, bag and baggage, belongings, also *makolokolo*.

Vikwa, v. See under **Vaa**.

Vile, a. dem. (1) agreeing with plur. of *ki-* class; (2) adv. thus, in that way, so. *Vile vile*, just the same, just so, as before, equally. (Cf. *vivi hivi, vivyo*.)

Vilia, v., **Vilio**, n. *ma-*. See under **Via**.

Vimba, v. (A) swell, expand, be distended (puffed out, swollen, bloated, stuffed). Prep. **Vimbia**, e.g. *nimekula hata nimevimbiwa*, I have eaten so much that I am stuffed. Cs. **Vimbisha**, cause to swell, e.g. *jivimbisha*, gorge oneself with food, eat gluttonously. **Kivimba**, n. *vi-*, but usu. **Kivimbe**, n. *vi-*, a swelling, a protuberance, girth, circumference, bigness of anything round. *Kivimbe cha mti*, girth of a tree. Also **Kivimbo**, n. *vi-* with the same meanings (cf. *mzingo*). **Uvimbe**, n. (1) state of being swollen, puffed out, distension, protuberance, projection, inflation; (2) girth, circumference, but in this sense *kivimbe* is more often used. **Vimbizi**, n. *ma-* pains from overeating, or from eating greedily.

Vimba, v. (B) thatch a house or hut, for the common *ezeka*. Cv. **Vimbua**, take off the thatch of a house, for the more common *ezua*. **Uvimbizi**, n. *ma-* the thatching of a house.

Vimbizi, n. *ma-*. See under **Vimba**, v. (A).

Vimoto, adv. See under **Ota**, v. (C).

Vinara, n. plur. of *kinara*, which see.

Vingine, **Vinginevyo**, forms of *-ingine*.

Vinginyika, v. (1) wriggle like a worm or maggot; (2) move the buttocks with a circular motion when dancing or walking. (Cf. *nyonganyonga, nyekenya, finginyika*.)

Vingirika, v. See **Fingirika**.

Vinjari,* v. (1) cruise about, be on the watch, search about—but esp. of ships or boats. *Manowari ya vinjari*, a cruiser, a ship on patrol. (2) loiter about, e.g. *anavinjari, hataki kuja*, he is loitering about, he refuses to come. (Ar. فنشخ lag behind, &c., *f* = *v*, and for change of final خ to *r* see *mentari*.)

Vinya, v., also Rd. **Vinyavinya** (1) crush food—but esp. for small children and sick people, e.g. *vinyavinya ndizi hizi umlishe mtoto*, crush these bananas so as to give the child a meal (cf. *ponda, seta*); (2) dandle in the arms, i.e. *vinyavinya mtoto* (cf. *bembeleza*); (3) tremble, of the lips, eyelids, muscles, &c. **Kivinyovinyo**, n. *vi-* and adv. (1) used to describe anything wagging, or quivering, e.g. of an animal's tail, the trembling or quivering of a muscle, &c.; (2) confusion of mind, hesitancy, &c. (Dist. *finya*.)

Viringa, v. become round, form a curve or bend, be rounded (spherical). Cs. **Viringisha**, make round (curved, bent). Rp. **Viringana**, (1) be round; (2) used of a well-built man, i.e. *ameviringana*. **Mviringo**, n. *mi-* roundness, a round shape, anything round, a circle, a curve, a ring, a washer. **Mviringano,** n. *mi-* anything round or spherical. **Uviringo,** n. roundness. (Cf. *duara, mzingo, pete.*)

Virugu, n. plur. (Sing. seldom used) (1) anger (cf. *hasira*). *Virugu vya mbele,* sudden anger. (2) roughness of the skin, e.g. as a result of the bites of flies. Also *virugurugu* and *marugurugu* of large size.

Visha, v. See under **Vaa.**

Vita, n. sometimes treated as *N* class, sometimes as plur. of *ki-* class: (1) war, battle, fighting; (2) contest, struggle, wrangle, dispute. *Fanya (piga) vita,* make war, fight. *Leta vita,* raid, invade. *Alika vita,* challenge to battle, issue a summons to soldiers, call to arms, muster an army—so *kusanya vita, funga vita,* engage in war, commence operations. *Vita vikubwa* or *vita kuu,* a great battle. (Cf. *mapigano,* and in poetry often *zita.*)

Vitio, n. plur. a kind of growth said to occur on the genitals of man or woman, same as *kisukumi,* which see.

Vitoleo, n. plur. See under **Toa,** v. (A).

Vivi, a. only in the phrase *vivi hivi,* i.e. agreeing with plur. of *ki-* class, these very, just these, and as adv., just so, in the very way.

Vivia, v. blow with the mouth, e.g. a fire, &c. (Cf. *puliza, vuvia.*)

Vivinyuka, v. wriggle, i.e. like a worm or maggot. (Cf. *vinginyika.*)

-vivu, a. (1) idle, slack, remiss, indolent, slow (cf. *-legevu, -zembe*); (2) blunt, e.g. *kisu kivivu,* a blunt knife (cf. *butu*). **Kivivu** and **Kivivuvivu,** adv. in an indolent, languorous way, e.g. *alimtazama kivivuvivu,* he looked at him with half-closed eyes, in a languorous way. **Mvivu,** n. *wa-* an indolent, slack, lazy person. **Uvivu,** n. idleness, slackness, negligence, sloth, laziness, indolence. (Cf. *ulegevu, utepetevu.*)

Vivyo, a. of ref. i.e. in the manner mentioned before. **Vivyo hivyo,** in exactly the same way as before.

Viza, n. and a., **Vizia,** v. See under **Via.**

Vokali,* n. a vowel, adopted for use in text-books and school lessons. (Eng.)

Volkeno,* n. a volcano, adopted for use in text-books and school lessons. (Eng.)

Vongonya, n. *ma-* the fruit of the *mvongonya,* sausage-tree.

Vua, v. (A) see under **Vaa.**

Vua, v. (B) fish, catch fish, try to catch fish—with or without *samaki* expressed, e.g. *vua baharini,* engage in sea-fishing. *Vua samaki,* catch fish. *Vua kwa mshipi, kwa dema,* &c., fish with a line, a trap, &c. Prep. **Vulia,** e.g. *ndoana ya kuvulia,* a fish-hook. Ps. **Vuliwa. Mvua,** n. *wa-*, **Mvuvi,** n. *wa-* a fisherman, proverbially quarrelsome over their fish, and so *nyumba ya wavuvi,* a noisy, quarrelsome household. **Mvuo,** n. *mi-* act of fishing, catch of fish; place of fishing, fishing-ground. **Vuo,** n. *ma-* catch of fish, e.g. *kukasirika kwa vuo baya kama lile,* to be vexed at such a bad catch of fish as that. **Uvuvi,** n. act (manner, &c., of fishing), a fisherman's calling, fee for fishing, &c.

Vua, v. (C), save, preserve, get out of a difficulty. *Avuaye yu karibu,* a preserver is at hand. *Mungu atakuvua, inshallah utavuka,* God will save you, and if he will you will be safe. St. **Vuka,** (1) be saved, escape, be preserved, e.g. *waliosimama vitani wakavuka,* those who stood firm in the fight and escaped alive; (2) pass safely through or over, and so, simply, pass through (of a forest), get to the other side (of a hill), &c.; (3) most commonly in the more specialized sense, get safely across, cross over, be ferried over, pass over —of crossing a river, creek, or channel in a canoe or ship. Prep. **Vukia,** e.g. cross by (in, with, at,

&c.), e.g. *tulivukia chini*, we crossed on our feet, by wading. *Chombo cha kuvukia*, a ferry-boat. Cs. **Vukisha** and **Vusha**, cause (allow, induce) to cross, convey across (through, past), ferry over. Rp. **Vukana.** (Dist. *fuka*, sometimes heard as *vuka.*) **Kivukizo**, n. *vi-* means of crossing, &c., same as *kivuko*, follg. **Kivuko**, n. *vi-* (1) act (place, time, means, &c. of crossing, e.g. a river, marsh, &c.), crossing-place, ford, ferry; also ferry fare, e.g. *kivuko chake kiasi gani?* How much does it cost to get across? *Kivuko kikavu*, an isthmus connecting two pieces of land. (2) also in fig. sense, e.g. *kivuko cha bahati*, a lucky escape. **Kivusho**, n. *vi-* (1) act of ferrying or putting across, &c.; (2) fare for ferrying. **Mvuko**, n. *mi-* crossing, ferry, ford. **Mvushaji**, n. *wa-*, **Mvushi**, n. *wa-* (1) a ferryman; (2) a preserver. **Vusho**, n. *ma-* anything which puts one across a place, i.e. ford, &c., or saves one, &c. **Uvushi**, n., **Uvusho**, n. a ferryman's calling; act (time, place, means, &c.) of carrying across, ferrying, also fee for carrying across.

Vua, v. (D) bail out water, as from a boat. (Cf. *kumba.*)

Vua, v. (E), *vua macho*, throw a glance or raise the eyes. (Cf. *inua macho, tupa macho.*)

Vuata, v. put or hold between the teeth and the lower lip, of tobacco, sugar, &c., e.g. *usivuate tumbako Ramadhani, utafungua*, do not put a quid of tobacco in your mouth during Ramadhan or you will break your fast. Tobacco is pounded like snuff and then put in the cheek or under the lower lip, and chewed; it is then called *mshuku.*

Vuaza, v. (1) make a cut in, cut, pierce; (2) fig. hurt, give pain (to), e.g. *vuaza mnazi*, cut the flower-stem of a coco-nut tree—to get the sap (*tembo*). Cf. the commoner word, *gema. Kisu kimenivuaza*, the knife has cut me. *Neno hili lavuaza*, this matter is painful. Ps. **Vuazwa.** (Cf. *kata, choma, chanja, toja, gema.*)

Vue, n. a thicket of long grass.

Vugaza, v. put to (a door). (Cf. *shindika*, and dist. *funga*, close completely.)

Vugo, n. *ma-* a horn played upon by beating it.

-vuguvugu, a. tepid, lukewarm, neither cold nor hot. **Uvuguvugu**, n. (1) lukewarmness, tepidity, i.e. neither cold nor hot; (2) stuffiness, heat of a crowded room, fug; (3) confusion. (Cf. *ghasia, fujo.*)

Vuja, v. (1) allow liquid to pass in or out, leak, let in, let out; (2) of a liquid, pass in, pass out, ooze out, leak out (on, in), e.g. *mashua yavuja* (*yavuja maji*), *maji yavuja mashuani*, the boat leaks. *Nyumba inavuja*, the house is letting in rain. Prep. **Vujia**, e.g. *mvua imenivujia*, the rain has come in on me. St. **Vujika**, e.g. *ukuta unavujika*, the wall is being spoilt by a leak—by water getting in. (Cf. *chuja, chuza.*)

Vuka, v. See under **Vaa, Vua, v.** (C), and also **Fuka.**

Vuke, n. *ma-* vapour, steam, a drop of condensed steam, the steam of perspiration from the body, e.g. *vuke lake linanuka vibaya*, the steam from his body has a bad smell. **Mvuke**, n. *mi-* vapour produced by heat, steam, perspiration. (Prob. from *fuka*, but always pronounced with a *v.*)

Vukizo, n. *ma-*. See **Fukizo** under **Fuka.**

Vukuta, v. work bellows, with or without *mivua*, bellows. **Mvua**, n. *mi-*, **Mvuo**, n. *mi-* bellows. **Uvukuto**, n. the working of bellows. (Often heard as *fukuta, mfua*, and *mfuo.*)

Vukuto, n. *ma-*. See **Fukuto** under **Fuka.**

Vuli, n. the season of the lesser rains, November and December in Zanzibar and the adjacent coast. The showers at this time of the year are very local.

Vulio, n. *ma-*. See under **Vaa.**

Vuma, v. (1) usually of any low indistinct sound, i.e. roar, growl, rumble, hum, buzz, rustle, e.g. of wind, thunder, wild beasts, insects, drums, e.g. *bahari inavuma*, of the roaring of breakers on a reef. *Upepo unavuma leo*, the wind blows hard to-day. (2) fig. rumour, be in the air, be a subject of common talk, e.g. *mambo haya yanavuma mjini*, these matters are the talk of the town; (3) work hard, used esp. of carpenters or others engaged in hard manual labour, perhaps from the sound of the tools, or as we say, 'the work fairly hummed', e.g. *nimevuma toka asubuhi mpaka jioni*, I have worked hard from morning till evening; (4) in a specialized sense, lose (in card-playing), e.g. *tulicheza karata jana, tukavuma*, we played cards yesterday, and we lost. Ps. **Vumwa.** St. **Vumika**, e.g. be rumoured, be talked about, become famous or notorious. *Alivumika kwa uganga*, he was famed for medical skill. Prep. **Vumia.** D.Prep. **Vumilia**, used in a special sense connected with (3) above, persevere in, bear, endure, suffer, tolerate. Ps. **Vumilika.** Cs. **Vumilisha.** Rp. **Vumiliana** (cf. *stahimili, chukua*). Cs. **Vumisha**, (1) cause to make a noise; (2) make well known, celebrate; (3) win (in card playing), i.e. make one's opponents lose. Also Inten. *Simba alivumisha mlio mkuu*, the lion uttered a furious roar. Rp. **Vumana. Kivumi**, n. *vi-*, **Kivumo**, n. *vi-* (1) rumbling sound; (2) rumour, report, hearsay; (3) reputation i.e. *ana kivumi kibaya*, he has a bad reputation. **Mvuma**, n. *wa-*, **Mvumi**, n. *va-*, one who mutters, hums, &c. **Mvumo**, n. *mi-* (1) a rumbling, muttering sound; (2) a report, rumour; (3) a rubber or win (in cards); (4) the borassus palm, perh. from the rumbling sound made by its leaves in the wind. **Uvumi**, n. (1) any low indistinct sound, such as rumbling, roaring, humming, buzzing, murmuring; (2) common talk, rumour, report, gossip, fame. **Uvumilivu**, n. endurance, perseverance, patience, fortitude (cf. *ustahimili, saburi*). **Uvumo**, n. *ma-* a rumbling, humming noise. **Vumo**, n. *ma-* a loud rumbling roar, hum, roll of a drum, &c., also the name of a drum.

Vumatiti, n. (1) a kind of owl, also called *bundi*; (2) in some places the name given to the bittern.

Vumba, n. *ma-* a bad smell, always connected with fish. *Ananuka vumba la samaki*, he has a nasty smell of fish. *Vumba la papa*, an evil odour of dried shark. (Cf. *vunda, shombo, uvundo, udusi.*)

Vumbi, n. *ma-* dust, a mass (collection, cloud) of dust, fine powder, sediment, muddiness in water. **Kivumbi**, n. *vi-* and adv. (1) a particle of dust, like dust, dusty; (2) a dust-storm, sand-storm; (3) fig. a crowd of people in confusion, ado, fuss and noise (cf. *fujo, ghasia*). **Uvumbi**, n. dust, dust as a substance, a grain of dust, dust collectively, dustiness. *Tifua uvumbi*, stir up dust, also *piga uvumbi*, make a dust.

Vumbika, v. (1) pile up, cover up, i.e. of fruit put in earth, ashes, leaves, embers, &c., to ripen it, store coconuts for seed. *Tuvumbike mbegu hizi, zitufae kwa kupanda*, let us cover up these seeds that they may serve us for sowing. (2) confine to the house, e.g. *Fulani hujivumbika nyumbani*, So-and-so seldom goes out, he remains in the house. *Amemvumbika mkewe nyumbani*, he has hidden his wife in the house, i.e. will not allow her out often. Ps **Vumbikwa**, e.g. (1) *ndizi hizi haziliki, ila kwa kuvumbikwa*, these bananas are not fit for eating, unless they are covered up to ripen; (2) fig. *amevumbikwa na homa*, he is so ill with fever that he is unconscious. Prep. **Vumbikia.** Cs. **Vumbikisha.** D.Prep. of Dir. form, **Vumbilia**, Inten. stir up, excite, get mixed up in a quarrel, brawl, war. Ps. **Vumbiliwa.** St. **Vumbilika.** Cv. **Vumbua,** (1) disclose, bring to light, uncover, and so discover, explore, open up, hunt out, invent, come upon, &c., e.g. *vumbua nchi,* explore a country. *Vumbua njia,* find a road. (2) stir up, like *vumbilia,* i.e. *vumbua vita.* Ps. **Vumbuliwa,** e.g. *tulivumbuliwa na adui zetu,* we were taken unawares by our enemies. St. **Vumbuka.** Prep. **Vumbulia.** Cs. **Vumbusha,** e.g. Inten. come on suddenly, waken up with a start. **Mvumbua,** n. *wa-,* **Mvumbuaji,** n. *wa-,* **Mvumbuzi,** n. one who discovers, opens up, brings to light, an explorer, inventor, &c. **Uvumbuaji,** n., **Uvumbuzi,** n. discovery, exploration, &c. **Vumbuo,** n. *ma-* act of discovery, exploring, &c. (Cf. *fumba,* and derivatives.)

Vumbu, n. *ma-* a lump in flour, esp. wheat flour. (Cf. *donge.*)

Vumbua, v., **Vumbulia,** v., **Vumbuo,** n. *ma-.* See under **Vumbika.**

Vumburuka, v. start or move suddenly, esp. when sleeping (said of animals). Cs. **Vumburushu,** e.g. *mwindaji alivumburusha kulunga,* the hunter started up an antelope. (Cf. *bumburusha,* also *vumbusha* under *vumbika.*)

Vumilia, v., **Vumisha,** v., **Vumo,** n. *ma-.* See under **Vuma.**

Vuna, v. (1) gather a crop, reap, get in a harvest of any kind; (2) fig. reap profit, get an advantage, profit. Hence the expression *jivuna,* boast oneself, brag, swagger, show off, give oneself airs, be conceited (cf. *jiona, jigamba*). Ps. **Vunwa.** St. and Pot. **Vunika.** Prep. **Vunia,** e.g. reap for (with, at, &c.). *Nimemvunia shamba lake,* I have got in his crops for him. Cs. **Vunisha,** e.g. employ in reaping, contract for harvesting. *Yafaa tuvunishe buni,* we ought to have the coffee harvested (cf. *chuma, faidi*). **Kivuno,** n. *vi-* a harvest, profit, something worth having, but more usually *vuno.* **Majivuno,** n. plur. boasting, bragging, self-laudation. **Mavune,** n. plur. (seldom used, see *mavuno* below) that which is harvested or reaped. Sometimes used fig. of outcome, result, consequences, effect. **Mavuno,** n. plur. (1) time (place, process, results, &c.) of harvesting, reaping crops; (2) profit generally, gain, exploitation. *Mavuno ya nyuki,* bee harvest, i.e. honey. **Mvunaji,** n. *wa-,* **Mvuni,** n. *wa-* one who gathers in a crop, a reaper, &c. **Uvuno,** n. harvesting, reaping, gathering crops, getting profits. *Nchi hii haina uvuno,* this country is not fertile.

Vunda, v. be high, of meat which has been laid by, so that it is smelling somewhat, but is still fit to eat, at any rate in the opinion of the native. *Nyama mbichi au ya kuvunda,* fresh or high meat. **Kivunde,** a. *ugali wa kivunde,* porridge made from flour of cassava which has been steeped until fermentation has begun. **Uvundo,** n. a bad smell, stink, stench. *Chungu vundo,* a large, evil-smelling sort of ant. **Vunde,** n. *ma-* anything which has become high and is smelly. (Dist. *oza,* and cf. *nuka.*)

Vundarega, v. break through, as of animals through the forest or of getting into a plantation and destroying crops by stamping and rolling.

Vunga, n. *ma-* a bunch. *Vunga la nywele,* a thick crop of hair.

Vungavunga, v. (1) break up small (of soil); (2) crumple, e.g. *usizikunje nguo hizi vyema, uzivungevunge tu,* do not fold these clothes up properly, crumple them only. *Vungavunga karatasi,* crumple up paper. (3) used of careless work generally, e.g. of builders, *hawakujenga vizuri, wamevungavunga tu,* they have not built well, they have put up a jerry building. *Atakuvungavunga kwa maneno,* he shall bewilder you with words (confuse, nonplus, &c.). (Prob. from same root as *vunja.*)

-vungu, a. See under **Mvungu.**

Vunja, v. (1) break, break down (up, in pieces, into, through, out of, off, away), and so (2) spoil, damage, destroy; (3) put a stop to, balk, frustrate, e.g. *usikivunje kitambaa changu*, do not spoil my cloth, i.e. disarrange it after it has been ironed and folded nicely. *Vunja kilemba*, take off a turban, i.e. unfold the folds. *Vunja jungu*, break a cooking-pot (used of the final feast or carnival before the month of Ramadhan, during which month these things are forbidden). *Vunja thamani*, destroy the value, depreciate, disparage. *Vunja uso*, put to shame, bring dishonour on, insult openly. *Vunja mwendo*, be a drag, spoil a days' march, make delay. *Vunja shilingi*, change a shilling, i.e. into smaller coinage. *Vunja ungo*, deflower, ravish, also begin menstruation (the meaning is restricted to the beginning of puberty). *Vunja baraza*, dismiss a meeting. *Vunja merikebu*, wreck a vessel. *Vunja nyumba*, pull down a house. *Vunja moyo*, discourage, dishearten. *Vunja adui*, defeat an enemy. *Vunja mwitu*, break through, force one's way through a forest. *Vunja mtoto*, harm a child (used of harm supposed to be the result of the parents breaking the restrictions imposed by native custom between a child's birth and weaning (cf. *chira*). Ps. **Vunjwa.** St. and Pot. **Vunjika**, e.g. *jahazi imevunjika*, the vessel is wrecked. Also be fragile, e.g. *sahani hizi zavunjika upesi*, these plates are very fragile. Prep. **Vunjia**, e.g. *vunjiwa mwiko*, be released from a taboo (or diet). Cs. **Vunjisha**, e.g. *vunjisha shilingi*, have a shilling changed. Rp. **Vunjana** (cf. *ponda, piga, haribu, komesha*). **Kivunjavunja**, n. *vi-* a mantis, also *vunjavunja* and *kivunja jungu*, from a superstition that should any one happen to kill one, he will break the next article he touches. **Kivunjo**, n. *vi-* (1) act (means, way, &c.) of breaking; (2) an instrument for breaking such as a hammer, stone, crowbar, &c. **Mvunja**, n. *wa-* one who breaks, destroys, &c. **Mvunjo**, n. *mi-* act (time, manner, &c.) of breaking or destroying, &c. **Uvunjifu**, n. destructiveness, vandalism, destruction, devastation, broken condition, wreck. **Uvunjo**, n. breaking, &c. **Vunjajungu**, see *kivunjavunja* above. **-vunjifu**, a. destructive, prone to destroying.

Vuo, n. (1) a medicine for vapour bath or inhalation prepared from the roots and leaves of trees, either boiled or steeped; (2) see under **Vua**, v. (B).

Vura, v. drag out, pull out, extract, as grass from a bundle, &c., usually *chopoa*, which see.

Vuru, adv., also **Vuruvuru**, descriptive of anything spinning and making a humming sound, i.e. a top, &c.

Vuruga, v. (1) stir up, stir, stir round (about), mix by stirring, (2) fig. stir up the feeling of, excite, exasperate. Rd. **Vurugavuruga**, very commonly used, and in a variety of senses. *Vuruga maji*, stir up water (i.e. make it turbid). *Vuruga karatasi*, disarrange papers. *Vuruga mkate*, crumble bread. *Vuruga nguo*, crumple clothes. Ps. **Vurugwa.** St. and Pot. **Vurugika**, be in a stirred-up, mixed-up condition, also used of things in a mouldering (decaying, crumbling) condition, be completely decomposed or putrefied, e.g. *kitu hiki kinaoza, hata kinavurugika*, this thing is decaying, and even going to pieces. *Nimevurugika*, I am utterly exhausted, I have gone all to pieces. Also used of wounds and sores in a bad, festering condition. Prep. **Vurugia.** Cs. **Vurugisha.** Cv. **Vurujua**, make soft by pounding, squeezing, &c. Stc. **Vuruma**, i.e. *tulipita katika maji (umande) yakavuruma*, we passed through the water (dew) and it was stirred up. Cs. of Stc. **Vurumisha,**

cause a thing to be stirred up, to buzz round and round, i.e. *vurumisha jiwe*, hurl a stone so that it goes round and round and makes a humming sound. Fig. *jivurumisha*, cast oneself headlong; also burst in upon, i.e. enter without waiting for permission, e.g. *askari walijivurumisha ndani, wakamkamata*, the police burst in and arrested him. **Mvuruga**, n. *wa-*, **Mvurugaji**, n. *wa-* one who stirs up, causes strife or confusion, a destructive person, &c. **Mvurugo**, n. *mi-* (1) messing, muddling, mixing up, mixture, (2) of unripe fruit in a squashy, messy condition. **Vuruguvurugu**, n. (1) confusion, e.g. *mambo haya yana vuruguvurugu*, these affairs are puzzling; (2) *nyumba ile imejaa vuruguvurugu*, that house is full of confusion. (Cf. *ghasia, machafuko.*)

Vusha, v. See under **Vua**, v. (C).

Vuta, v. (1) draw, pull, drag, strain, stretch, have an effect upon; (2) change, pervert, give a new direction (meaning, aspect) to; (3) have an influence on, charm, entice, tempt, allure, lead astray. *Ngoma hii inavuta watu wengi*, this dance attracts many people. Also with various special applications, e.g. *vuta makasia*, pull oars, row, and *vuta mashua*, row a boat. *Vuta maneno*, put a strain on words, i.e. strain their meaning. *Vuta tumbako*, smoke. *Vuta maji*, bale out water. Sometimes heard for *futa*, e.g. *vuta upanga*, but see *futa*, v. Ps. **Vutwa**. St. and Pot. **Vutika**, e.g. be pulled, be capable of being stretched or altered. Pot. **Vutikana**. Prep. **Vutia**, or particular operations, e.g. in plaiting. *Amenivutia kazi ile*, he enticed me into that work. *Vutia roho*, struggle for breath. Cs. **Vutisha**, e.g. *alinivutisha tumbako*, he made me smoke. Rp. **Vutana**, pull each other. **Mvuto**, n. *mi-* act (manner, &c.) of drawing. Also in other senses of the verb, pulling, influence, persuasion, perversion. *Mvuto wa maji* (*upepo*), current of water (air) (cf. *mkondo*). **Uvutano**, n. mutual attraction or influence, i.e. force of gravity. **Uvuto**, n. attraction, force, influence, &c.

Vuvia, v. blow with the mouth or bellows (cf. *puliza, vivia*). **Uvuvio**, n. blowing; (fig.) vanity, boastfulness. (Cf. *majivuno, majisifu*, &c.)

Vuvumka, v. grow up fast, develop quickly, shoot up—of vegetation and also animal life, e.g. of mangoes, children, of dough rising (cf. *umuka*). Cs. **Vuvumsha**, e.g. *nilimvuvumsha kwa chakula*, I fed him and made him grow up quickly. (Cf. *chipua, kua, mea.*)

Vuvuwaa, v. (1) be tepid, lukewarm, of water and liquids; (2) be silent as of a person who has no thoughts or opinion on the subject under discussion. (Cf. *vuguvugu, duwaa.*)

Vuzi, n. *ma-*, also **Uvuzi**, hair of the armpits and pudenda. Considered by most natives to be particularly unclean and kept shaved or plucked.

V.v. abbreviation of *vile vile*.

Vya, prep. of, the form agreeing with plur. of the *Ki-* class.

Vyaa, v. bear children or fruit. **Kivyao**, n. *vi-*, **Kivyazi**, n. *vi-*, **Uvyazi**, n. These forms are sometimes heard for *zaa*, v., *kizao, vi-, kizazi, vi-, uzazi*, &c., which see.

Vyake, **Vyako**, **Vyangu**, **Vyao**, forms of *-ake, -ako, -angu*, and *-ao*, which see.

Vyema. See under **-ema**.

Vyenu, **Vyetu**, forms of *-enu* and *-etu*, which see.

Vyero, n. a fish-trap. (Cf. *uzio*.)

Vyo, relative particle, only used separately in *vyo vyote*, whatever. For its use as pfx. see Grammars.

Vyoga, v. tread upon, trample upon, crush, used of feet, hands, or vehicle, &c. (Cf. *seta, kanyaga.*)

Vyote, form of *-ote*, all.

W

W represents the same sound as in English, before a vowel it sometimes represents the pfx. *u*.

Wa, (1) prep. of—form agreeing with sing. and plur. of the *Wa* class, and sing. of the *Mi* and *U* classes; (2) verb-form, they are, agreeing with plur. of the *Wa* class, e.g. *watumwa wa rahisi*, slaves are cheap; (3) conj. Arab. and—occurs sometimes, esp. in written Swahili, letters, documents, &c., and in combination, e.g. *wabadahu, wasalaam, wakatabahu*; (4) sometimes used in the sense of 'son of' (cf. *bin*). *Hamisi wa Juma*, Hamisi son of Juma. For *wa-* as pfx. see Grammars.

Wa, v. be, become, take place, exist, occur, happen. (Being monosyllabic in root, the *ku-* sign of the infinitive is retained in certain tenses.) (1) the common use of the simple verb *-wa*, in all tenses and moods, is to connect Subject and Predicate in a sentence, and to supply an auxiliary in forming compound tenses—like the verb 'to be' in English. (2) the meaning 'become' is only clear in connexion with the sign of the Present tense Definite, *-na*, e.g. *jua linakuwa kali*, the sun is becoming scorching, the Perf. tense, *-me-*, e.g. *amekuwa mgonjwa*, he has become sick, he is ill, and the Narrat. Tense *-ka-*, e.g. *cheche la moto lilimpiga jichoni, aka wa kipofu*, a burning spark struck him in the eye, and he became blind. (3) Concrete existence, i.e. being as a fact, actual being or taking place, is expressed by *-wa*, e.g. *mambo haya yamekuwa*, these things have actually taken place, and are now, and hence are facts; and also absolute existence, so far as a Swahili conceives it, e.g. *mwenye kuwa*, as a title of God, the Self-existent, He who is. *Ndiye awaye*, it is he who is (exists). Obs. however, that *-wa* is rarely used at all in any sense in the Pres. Positive, and not often in the Pres. Negative, e.g. *yuwa*, he is, *siwi*, I am not, *hamwi*, you (plur.) are not. As a copula, it is (1) either simply omitted —or its place is taken by (2) *ni* for all persons and numbers, or by the personal pfx. (*ni, u, tu, wa*, &c.) used as independent forms, or (3) by use of the root *li* but only in combination with a relative pfx. *Li* is another form of the Bantu verb to be, *aliye, uliye, kilicho, vilivyo*, &c., he who is, you who are, it which is, they which are. Simple existence is also expressed by *na* in certain combinations (see *na* (3) for this, and also *-wa na*, as corresponding to the English verb 'have'). Prep. **Wia** and **Wea** (1) with the usual prepositional relations, be to (for, with, in, &c.), e.g. *kazi hii inaniwia ngumu*, this work is hard on me, i.e. I find it hard. *Uniwie radhi*, be kind to me, pardon me. (N.B. the D.Prep. form is also used, *uniwilie radhi*.) (2) with a special and definite sense, viz. be a creditor of, have a claim on, have in one's debt—both in the Act. and Ps. Thus *ananiwia* commonly means,

I owe him money; *namwia*, he owes me money. So in the Ps. form, *nawiwa naye*, I am his debtor; and *awiwa nami*, he is my debtor, e.g. *wote wenye kumwia wakutane*, let all his creditors hold a meeting. The form **Wea** and the D.Prep. **Welea** is sometimes used alone for 'be good for, be in favour of, be useful to, turn out well for, be the property of, or turn ill for, harm'. This is an old form rarely heard nowadays. No Cs. in use. Rp. **Wiana**, e.g. be to each other, be mutually indebted or under obligations. **Mwia**, n. *wa-* a creditor. **Mwiwa**, n. *wa-* a debtor.

Waa, n. *ma-* spot, patch of colour (light or dark), mark, speck, e.g. *kuku mwenye mawaa*, a speckled fowl. (Dist. *doa*, which may be used of an accidental blot or stain as well as of natural markings.) **Kiwaa**, n. *vi-* (1) dim; (2) used of bad sight, e.g. *ana kiwaa*, his vision is blurred, he is not able to see distinctly. (Cf. prec. and *kiwi*, also *kipaku*.)

Waa, v. shine brightly, blaze—i.e. of the sun or moon, but not often used (cf. *ng'aa*). St. **Waka**, in general use, (1) blaze, burn brightly, be lighted, show a flame. *Kuni kavu huwaka upesi*, dry sticks catch fire quickly. (2) fig. of things, temper, &c., e.g. *mchanga unawaka kwa jua*, the sand is burning with the sun's heat. *Hasira yake iliwaka*, his anger burned, i.e. he was angry. Prep. **Wakia**, e.g. *moto unajiwakia*, the fire is lighting up of itself (accidentally). Cs. **Washa**, kindle, cause to burn, set fire to, light, e.g. *washa taa, moto*, light a lamp, fire. Ps. **Washwa**. St. and Pot. **Washika**, be lighted, burn. *Taa ya namna hii inawashika upesi*, a lamp of this sort lighted quickly. Prep. **Washia**, e.g. *uniwashie taa*, light the lamp for me. Pot. **Washikana**, be inflammable, be capable of being lighted. **Maao**, n. plur. (for *mawao*), **Maawio**, **Maweo**, and also **Mawio**, sunrise, the Orient, east. **Mwako**, n. *mi-* blaze, flame, blazing, burning. *Mwako wa moto* (*jua*), blaze of a fire (the sun). **Mwasha**, n. *wa-* one who lights, e.g. *mwasha taa*, a lamp-lighter. **Uwasho**, n. lighting. (Cf. similar forms under the verb *wawa*, with the meaning of irritation, smart, &c.)

Waadhi,* n. also **Mauidha**, n. a sermon, solemn exhortation, esp. in a religious sense. (Cf. *hotuba*, lecture, sermon, used in a much wider sense. Ar. وعظ.)

Waaidha.* See under **-aidha**.

Waama,* conj. further, moreover, then. (Cf. *tena, basi, kisha*. Ar. و and عما.)

Waba,* n. cholera. (Cf. *kipindupindu*. Ar. وبا.)

Wabadahu,* Ar. for *na baada ya haya*, in letters, 'and after this, and next', following on the complimentary preface and introducing the substance of the letter. The Swahili equivalent is more often used now. (Cf. *wa* (3), and *baada*. Ar. وبعده.)

Wadi,* n. (A) son of, like *bin*, and *wa* for *mwana wa*; seldom used. **Wadinasi**, a man of good birth. (Cf. *mtoto wa watu*. Ar. ولد الناس.)

Wadi,* n. (B) watercourse, bed of a torrent, ravine—seldom used. (Ar. واد, a dale.)

Wadi,* v. the Dir. form is seldom used, complete a time, keep to a time, be up to time. As a rule the Prep. form is used. **Wadia**, be fully time (for), be in good time (for). *Wakati wa kurudi kwetu umewadia*, it is fully time we went home. **Wadi**, n. appointed time, e.g. *wadi wetu umetimia*, our time has fully come, i.e. a time previously agreed upon. (Ar. واعد, make an appointment.)

Wafiki,* v. See **Afiki**.

Wahadi,* n. sometimes heard for *hadi* and *ahadi*.

Wahedi,* n. and a. one—the numeral —often used, as well as Bantu *mosi*, *-moja*. *Wahedi u sitini*, a very popular card game, the aim being to have cards which give a score of sixty-one or over at the end of the game, can be played by two, four, or six players, only one pack being used. There is a special system of scoring, in which the cards have not all the same value as are usually assigned to them in Europe and America, e.g. the seven scores ten points, and is called *seti* (or *jike* or *mke*). **Wahedu,** adv. alone, only. (Cf. *pekee*. Ar. احد one, وحد be alone.)

Wahi,* v. be in time, be prompt (ready, forward) to act, e.g. *hakuwahi kufika mjini*, he had not time to get to the town (when), i.e. before he got to the town. *Aliwahi kumkaribisha*, he was ready to welcome him. Used also impersonally, e.g. *leo haiwahi, jua linakuchwa*, there is not time to-day, the sun is setting. (Ar. وحى haste, hurry.)

Waima,* also **Waina,** conj. if not, otherwise, for the usu. *kama sivyo*. (Ar. وان.)

Wajibia,* v. See under **Wajibu.**

Wajibu,* n. what is right, fitting, proper, suitable; and so in moral sense, duty, obligation, due courtesy. *Wajibu wako*, what is expected of you, worthy of you. *Mtoto wajibu ni kuwaheshimu wazee wake*, a child should be respectful to his parents (elders). Also sometimes as v., i.e. be proper, be a duty, be an obligation. Prep. **Wajibia.** Cs. **Wajibisha.** *Mambo mabaya, ndiyo yaliyowajibisha kuuawa*, it's a bad case, that is why he deserves to be put to death. **Mujibu,** n., also **Muujibu,** n. that which is according to (law, custom, &c.), that which concerns or is a duty, or appertains to. *Mujibu wa sheria*, according to law. (Cf. *suna, bidi, pasa*. Ar. وجب.)

Wajihi,* n. form, appearance. *Unamjua Ali? Utaweza kuniambia wajihi wake?* Do you know Ali? Can you tell me what he looks like? **Wajihi,** v. appear, present oneself, visit, meet face to face, interview, salute. *Walimwajihi Seyyid*, they appeared before the Sultan. Rp. **Wajihiana,** meet face to face. *Shuka pwani tuwajihiane*, come down to the shore and let's have it out—said by one man to another when a quarrel has broken out between them in the street. (Cf. *onana, onekana, kutana, sura*. Ar. واجه meet one, and وجه face, surface.)

Waka, v. See under **Waa,** v. dist. *aka*.

Wakaa,* n. a time, a single time, e.g. *wakaa tatu za chakula*, the three meals, the three times of eating. (Cf. *wakati, mara, zamu*. Ar. وقع happen, occur.)

Wakala,* n. agency, appointment, commission, power of attorney, e.g. *unayo wakala*, have you a power of attorney (appointment, power to act, &c.). **Wakili,** n. *ma-* agent, steward, representative, commissioner, barrister, manager (under proprietor). *Wakili wa mshtaki*, prosecutor (in the sense of a prosecuting counsel). Also sometimes as v., act as agent, &c. Cs. **Wakilisha,** appoint as agent, commission, entrust to as an agent. *Nikisafiri nitamwakilisha nyumba yangu*, if I go away I shall leave my house to his care. **Tawakali,** v. put trust in, have confidence in, rely on, take courage, hope, e.g. *tawakali kwa Mungu*, trust in God. **Uwakili,** n. condition (employment, methods, salary, &c.) of an agent or representative, stewardship. (Cf. *mjumbe, karani, naibu*. Ar. وكل.)

Wakati,* n. (*nyakati*), time (in general), season, period of time, point of time, sufficient time, opportunity. *Njoo kesho, wakati haujafika bado* come to-morrow, it is not time yet. (Cf. *saa, muda, muhula, zamani,* and *pindi, kitambo.* Ar. وقت.)

Wake, (1) pron. his, hers, its, from *-ake*; (2) plur. of *mke,* females, wives, see under *-ke.*

Wakf,* n. something set apart for religious purposes, consecrated, devoted to a holy use, esp. of land or other gifts assigned to a mosque for its expenses, pay of the minister, &c., or land left by will for use as burial ground, i.e. *wakf ya misikiti,* and *wakf ya makaburi. Weka (fanya) wakf,* set apart for religious purposes, &c. (Ar. وقف.)

Wakia,* n. an ounce (weight)—formerly reckoned in Zanzibar as the weight of an Austrian silver dollar piece, i.e. *ni uzito wa reale,* and as sixteen to the pound weight (*ratli*). (Ar. اوقية.)

Wakifu,* v. stand, stop, but usu. referring to cost, be priced at, cause expense. Prep. **Wakifia,** cost to (a person). Cs. **Wakifisha,** forbid, prevent, stop, cause to stop. (Cf. *gharimia* and *simama* (4) used in the same way. Ar. وقف, stop, stand, cost.)

Wakili,* n. See under **Wakala.**

Wako, (1) a. form of *-ako,* your; (2) verb-form, they are (there).

Wala,* conj. nor. Used (1) after a negative, repeating, not reversing it, and so often translatable 'or'; (2) itself repeated, *wala . . . wala,* neither . . . nor . . . (cf. *au, ama*). **Walakini,** (1) conj. but, however, nevertheless, notwithstanding (Ar. ولكن); (2) sometimes used as a noun, defect, a lacking. *Nyumba hiyo ina walakini,* that house has a defect. Cf. the English use of 'but', e.g. 'It's all right, but—', i.e. there is a 'but' about it. **Walau,** adv., also **Alau,** even, at least, though, anyhow, at any rate, notwithstanding, e.g. *humwachii walau kitu kidogo,* you do not leave him even a little. *Uganga walau wa mvua,* at least rain-medicine. Often used with *kama,* e.g. *watu wa nchi ile walau* (or *alau*) *kama wana chakula kingi, hukipoteza,* the people of that country, even though (or if) they have plenty of food, waste it. (Ar. لا, and ولى.)

Wale, (1) adj. pronom. those—form of *-le*; (2) subjunct. of *la,* v. that they may eat.

Wali,* n. (A) cooked rice, i.e. rice so cooked that each grain is whole and separate, though soft and thoroughly cooked. The staple dish of the people of the coast towns. *Wali ni sultani ya chakula, walawazwa katika kiti,* cooked rice is the king of foods, it is placed on a royal throne, i.e. on a raised stool serving as a table. Rice cooked with too much water is *wali mlepelepe* or *majimaji.* (Also cf. *pilau, poroja la wali, uji, ubwabwa, matabwatabwa, mashendea,* and see *mchele* and *mpunga.* Prob. a corruption of Ar. وليمة, banquet, &c., cf. *wali wa lima* under *lima,* n.)

Wali,* n. (B) *ma-,* but usu. *liwali,* which see.

Walii,* n. *ma-* a holy person, a saint, a dervish, a calender, i.e. member of a sort of Muhammadan religious order. Also used less commonly like *malaika,* an angel, e.g. *paka akajifanya walii sana,* and the cat set up as a great saint. *Mungu akamshushia walii,* and God sent down an angel to him. (Cf. *sufii, mtawa, malaika.* Ar. ولى.)

Walima,* n. See **Wali wa lima** under **Lima,** n.

Walimwengu, n. plur. See under **Ulimwengu.**

Walio, n. (*nyalio*) (1) usu. in the plur. bits of stick put crosswise at the bottom of a cooking-pot to prevent the contents from burning; (2) a kind of wattle fence for trapping fish; (3) see under **Alia.** (Cf. *uzio, utata, tando,* and dist. *walio,* verb-form, they who are.)

Wallahi!* also **Wallai!** a common Swahili oath, By God! not considered profane by Muhammadans. (Ar. والله.)

Wama, v. but usu. Prep. **Wamia,** stretch oneself on the ground or before a fire, bend over a fire.

Wamba, v. spread (bind, stretch, fix) over, overlay, overspread, overcast, e.g. *wamba kitanda kwa mashupatu,* cover a bedstead with cords interlaced. *Wamba ngoma kwa ngozi,* stretch a skin tightly on a drum. Also in an Intrans. sense, e.g. *ukungu umewamba,* a mist hangs over the earth. *Umewamba mlango,* you have blocked the door—of one who has barred the way with arms and legs. *Ngalawa inawamba,* of a canoe which is broadside on the waves, having broken loose from its moorings or which has drifted on to the shore. *Fulani amewamba,* used of a person who has spent his wages and is now in need of money. **Kiambaza, n.** *vi-* a wall as made by natives, i.e. a screen or framework of sticks fastened to upright poles and filled up with kneaded earth and stones, but also applied to any wall of a house (cf. *ukuta, kandika*). **Kiwamba, n.** *vi-* anything stretched like a net, screen, &c., or for stretching things on, i.e. a little frame, support, &c. **Kiwambo, n.** *vi-* act (process, means, &c.) of making one thing cover another, and esp. of the thing which covers, overlays, or is stretched over another, a diaphragm, e.g, the *kiwambo* of a drum (*ngoma*) is the skin stretched tightly over it, *ngozi iliyowambiwa ngoma. Kiwamba cha makuti,* a screen of coco-nut leaves. *Kiwambo cha kitanda,* the lacing of a bed-frame with cord, &c. *Kiwambo cha moyo* or *kiwambamoyo,* the diaphragm. **Mwambo, n.** condition of being in need of money, used particularly of the last few days of the month when a person's wages have been spent and none remain, i.e. *siku za mwambo.* **Uwambo, n.** (*mambo*) (1) act (manner, operations, &c.) of stretching over, &c.; (2) the laced cords of a native bedstead; (3) the bone of a bird's wing, i.e. on which the feathers and membrane are fixed; (4) in the plur. usu. means tent-pegs, pegs for fixing anything stretched out, e.g. a hide stretched out to dry, &c. (Cf. *tanda.*)

Wambe, n. dust which comes from millet when it is being winnowed.

Wambiso, n. See under **Amba, v.** (B).

Wamia, v. See under **Wama.**

Wana, (1) verb-form, they have; (2) plur. of *mwana,* which see.

Wanadamu, n. plur. of *mwanadamu,* which see.

Wanda, n. (*nyanda*) a finger's breadth, about one inch, used sometimes in measuring. (Cf. *chanda.*)

Wanda, v. get fat, become stout, used chiefly in expressing astonishment, e.g. *Loo! amewanda barabara!* I say, he has become fat! (cf. *nenepa, nona*). Cs. **Wandisha.**

Wanga, n. (1) arrowroot, used alike of the plant itself, *Maranta arundinacea,* the roots, and the flour prepared from the roots; (2) starch, as starch is extracted from arrowroot; (3) a sweet confection, made of arrowroot and other ingredients, some of which may be intoxicating.

Wanga, v. (A) count, reckon, but *hesabu* is the usual word. **Kiwango, n.** *vi-* (1) number, a number; (2) importance, account, dignity, position, and hence (3) behaviour or duties &c., proper to a position, province, sphere of action. *Ni kiwango changu kusema,* it is my duty (it is proper for me) to speak. *Kiwango cha mtumwa,* the position of a slave.

Wanga, v. (B) (1) cut, as of a tree in

order to get the honey stored in it; (2) hurt, give pain. (Cf. *umiza.*)

Wangavu, n. See under **Anga, n.**

Wangu, form of *-angu*, which see.

Wangwa, n. (*nyangwa*) (1) waste, bare ground, sandy wilderness (cf. *jangwa*); (2) the sandy or muddy tracts which are covered by the sea at high tide, hence lagoon, tidal flats.

Wanja, n. *wanja wa manga*, antimony, used by women to blacken the eyebrows, mostly imported from Arabia. (Cf. *dalia, manjano.*)

Wano, n. *ma-* (1) wooden part, or shaft, of a spear, arrow, harpoon, &c., also called *uti*; (2) the four sticks sometimes used in divining. (Cf. *bao, ramli.*)

Wao, (1) pron. of 3rd Pers. Plur. they, denotes only persons and animals; (2) a. pronom. their, form of *-ao*.

Wapi? (1) pron. interrog. of place, where? and colloquially How? How so? e.g. *nilijaribu lakini wapi?* I tried, but could I? (with the sense that it was not possible). Often shortened to *-api* and *-pi*, and appended to verbs, e.g. *wendapi?* where are you going? (2) a form of *-pi*, which, agreeing with plur. of *Wa* class.

Wapilia,* v. smell strongly of scent, be heavily scented. (Ar. وبيل unwholesome, of atmosphere, &c.)

Wapo, (1) verb-form 'they are here'; (2) used in connexion with *-moja*, e.g. *mmojawapo*, some one or other. *Kimojawapo*, one or other of the things. (3) n. see under **Pa, v.**

Waraka,* n. (*nyaraka*), (1) a written communication, a letter (of correspondence), certificate, deed, title-deed, document. *Andikiana waraka*, correspond by letter. *Waraka ni nusu ya kuonana*, a letter is next to seeing each other (cf. *barua, hati, cheti*); (2) a cigarette paper. (Ar. ورق.)

Wargi,* n., also **Warigi**, n, a kind of intoxicant. (Cf. *sarambo.* ? Ar. ولغ give to drink, lap up.)

Wari,* n. (1) a yard (measure), half a fathom (*pima*), equal to two cubits (*dhiraa, mikono*); (2) valve of a bicycle or motor-car tire. (Derivation of (1) Pers. وار, a measure. Derivation of (2) a corruption of Eng. valve.)

Waria, n. a skilled workman, artisan. Often coupled with a defining word, *seramala waria, mwunzi waria*, &c. *Jahazi hii inaundwa na waria wengi*, this vessel is being built by a number of shipbuilders (riveters). The *waria* is below the *fundi*, who is the master craftsman, and may have several *waria* under him, hence, *waria* really means a 'journeyman' as opposed to *mwanafunzi*, 'apprentice', and *fundi*, 'boss'. *Fundi na waria wake*, a craftsman and his mates. (Cf. *bingwa, stadi, fundi.*)

Waridi,* n. a rose. Also as a., *mawaridi*, attar of roses. *Maji mawaridi*, water scented with roses for the toilette and bath. **Mwaridi, n.** *mi-* a rose bush. (Ar. ورد.)

Warishai,* n. See under **Rishai.**

Warithi,* n. *ma-* an heir. (Ar. but very rarely heard, the Bantuized form *mrithi* being in regular use, see under *rithi.*)

Wasa,* n. (A) used collectively for the small sticks or lathes which are put in to reduce the spaces between larger ones in the framework of the wall or roof of a native house. Strong selected rods are always stuck in the ground at fairly wide intervals first, then rods are fastened to those with rope horizontally so as to form crossbars. *Wasa* are the more slender rods which are inserted afterwards, preparatory to applying mud or *makuti*. (Ar. عصا a stick.)

Wasa, n. (B) *ma-* drizzle, fine rain, i.e. *wasa la mvua.*

Wasa,* v. sometimes heard for *asa*, v. forbid.

Wasaa,* n. room, space, freedom, means, leisure, opportunity. *Kuwa* *na wasaa*, to be comfortable, satisfied, be in easy circumstances. *Leo sina wasaa*, I have no time to-day. (Cf. *nafasi*. Ar. وسع.)

Washa, v. See under **Waa, v.**, also under **Wawa.**

Wasia,* v. sometimes heard for *usia*, v. which see.

Wasifu,* v. describe, explain. **Tawasifu**, v. give information, i.e. as to a person's character, &c. **Tawasufi**, n. moderation, temperance, good character. (Ar. وصف.)

Wasii,* n. *ma-*. See under **Usia.**

Wasili,* v. arrive, reach, come to, get to destination, be delivered to be received. Often followed by *kwa, katika, hata*, and locative in *-ni*, e.g. *wasili kwake* (*Unguja, hata nyumbani, kisiwani*), arrive at his house (at Zanzibar, at the house, at an island). Ps. **Wasiliwa.** Prep. **Wasilia**, e.g. *barua yako imeniwasilia*, your letter has reached me. Cs. **Wasilisha**, e.g. cause to arrive, send. Prep. of Cs. **Wasilishia**, e.g. *kumwasilishia kitu*, to convey something to him. **Wasili**, n. receipt, income, credit side of cash account. *Cheti cha wasili*, a receipt (cf. *stakabadhi*). Also as a., *barua yako wasili*, your note (is) duly received. (Cf. *fika, pata*. Ar. وصل.)

Wasiwasi,* n. doubt, perplexity, scruple, infatuation, disquiet, esp. when caused by moral want of balance, weakness of character, yielding to temptation. *Fanya wasiwasi*, feel irresolute. *Tia wasiwasi*, confuse the mind (conscience). *Ukamwingia wasiwasi yule kijana*, and that young man was filled with perplexity. (Cf. *mashaka, tashwishi, fadhaa*, and dist. *wasiwasi*. Ar. وسواس.)

Wastani,* n. and a. middling, average, moderate, medium, between extremes. (Cf. *kadiri, kiasi*. Ar. وسط.)

Watani,* n. See under **Tania.**

Wavi, n. See under **Wawa.**

Wavu, n. (*nyavu*), a net—used for fish, game, &c. *Wavu wa kulalia*, a hammock. *Wavu wa chuma*, wire netting. *Tanda wavu, tega wavu*, set a net—to catch something. (Cf. *jarife, juya, kimia.*)

Wawa, v. itch. 'I am itchy' can be expressed in two ways, (1) *mwili wangu unawawa*; (2) *mwili unaniwawa*. St. **Waka**, smart, burn, hurt (as by burning, &c.), be inflamed. *Ulimi wangu unawaka kwa pilipili*, my tongue smarts with the pepper. Cs. **Washa**, irritate, sting, cause a burning sensation. *Majani haya yawasha sana*, these leaves sting badly. Ps. **Washwa**, e.g. *ukimgusa mdudu huyu utawashwa sana*, if you touch this insect (beetle, &c.) you will suffer severe irritation, esp. of hairy caterpillars, contr. *uma* used of insects armed with stings, and even those which bite. **Kiwavi**, n. *vi-* (1) a nettle, sea nettle; (2) a chrysalis; (3) a large hairy caterpillar, the hairs of which irritate very much if they penetrate the skin. **Uwasho**, n. irritation, inflammation. *Najikuna sana kwa ajili ya uwasho*, I scratch myself a great deal on account of irritation. **Wavi**, n. amplic. of *kiwavi*, above. (Note the second *w* in *wawa* disappears in the derived forms which are made from *waa*, hence the similarity with those shown under *waa*, v. which see.)

Waya,* n. (*nyaya*) an earthen dish for baking cakes in. (Cf. *chungu*. Ar. وعاية.)

Wayawaya, v. (1) sway to and fro, stagger, totter, reel, e.g. of a tree loaded with fruit, a man from weakness, &c.; (2) be heavy with fruit or leaves, be bearing abundantly. **Wayowayo**, n. reeling, staggering; hesitating. (Cf. *lewa, sita, yonga, yugayuga, yumba, ning'inia.*)

Wayo, for *u-ayo*, n. (*nyayo*) (1) sole of the foot; (2) footprint, track of the foot. **Unyayo** (*nyayo*) is a common form, used as above, also fig. *unyayo wa taabu*, proverbially of great effort, e.g. of a persistent search for something.

Wayowayo, n. See under **Wayawaya.**

Waza, v. (1) suppose, fancy, imagine; (2) reflect, ponder, meditate, have mind. *Waza Mungu*, is used of religious meditation, deep inward heart-searching. Ps. **Wazwa.** St. and Pot. **Wazika.** Prep. **Wazia**, e.g. *niliwazia kumwandikia barua, lakini sikuwahi*, I thought of writing him a letter, but I had not time. Cs. **Wazisha**, used Inten. but very rare. Rp. **Wazana.** Cv. **Wazua**, only heard in the phrase *waza na kuwazua. Niliwaza na kuwazua, mwisho nilipata njia ya kufaa*, I thought this way and that way, and in the end I discovered a way out. **Mwaza**, n. *wa-*, **Mwazi**, n. *wa-* one who thinks, supposes, fancies, &c., a thinker. **Uwazo**, n. imagination. **Wazo**, n. *ma-* thought, fancy, idea, notion, supposition. *Yu katika mawazo yake*, he is abstracted, buried in thought, absent-minded. (Cf. *dhani, nia, fikiri, kumbuka, zingatia.*)

Wazi, a. (1) open, bare, uncovered (of clear passage, free access, room inside, open book, &c.). *Mlango wazi*, open door. *Njia wazi*, open road. *Kichwa wazi*, bare head. *Panalia wazi*, it sounds hollow (cf. *tupu*). (2) fig. open, manifest, evident, clear, plain; in this sense frequently Rd. *waziwazi* (cf. *dhahiri, baini*). **Uwazi**, n. openness, clearness, distinctness, intelligibility. (Ar. واضح clear, manifest, or Bantu *vali*, open place, *v* = bilabial fricative which in Swahili may become *w*, and *i* = closed vowel which would cause *l* to become *z*.)

Wazimu, n. madness, mania, hallucination, desperation, infatuation, e.g. *ana wazimu*, he is mad. *Fanya wazimu*, act madly. *Tia wazimu*, make mad. *Ingiliwa na wazimu*, go mad. *Nimemtafuta hata nusura kuingiliwa na wazimu*, I have searched for him till I am nearly mad. *Mwenda wazimu*, or *mwenye wazimu*, a madman. (Cf. *mzimu*, perh. *wazimu* is connected and means lit. possession by evil spirits.)

Waziri,* n. *ma-* chief officer of state under a sovereign, prime minister, secretary of state. **Uwaziri**, n. office (dignity, duties, pay, &c.) of a minister or chief secretary of a monarch. (Ar. وزر.)

Wazo, n. *ma-*, **Wazua**, v. See under **Waza.**

-we, a. form of *wake*, his, her, its—affixed to nouns, e.g. *mwanawe*, his son. *Mwenziwe*, his companion. (So *-le, -ze*, and *-ye.*)

Wea, v. See under **Wa, v.**

Wee, for *wewe, weye*, you—pron. of 2nd Pers. Sing., but only used in addressing children or inferiors, and even then usually avoided by polite people; it is the sort of expression one would use to a dog, donkey, &c.

Wehu, n., madness. See under **Mwehu**, (Cf. *kichaa, wazimu, mafuu.*)

Weka, v. one of the very common Swahili words, with the general sense 'place, put, set', and a great variety of applications, e.g. (1) put in position, set fast, place firm, e.g. *weka ulimwengu*, of the creation. *Weka msingi*, lay a foundation. *Kikao tulichomweka*, the position in which we placed him. (2) put down, put off, lay aside, e.g. *weka silaha*, lay down weapons. *Weka mzigo*, put down a load. (3) put off, delay, adjourn, esp. *weka hukumu*, defer judgement. *Tutaweka shauri hili mpaka Jumamosi*, we shall put off this discussion until Saturday. (4) reserve, store up, keep for future use, e.g. *weka akiba*, lay up a store, save up. *Weka chakula*, keep food (in a safe, cupboard, &c.). (5) in a special sense, preserve intact, keep whole, &c. *Weka kizinda,* preserve virginity. A common form of pious wish or blessing, *Mungu akuweke,* as we say, 'May the Lord help and keep you', sometimes with *heri* added, 'God bless you'. (6) dedicate, devote to a certain purpose, e.g. *weka wakf,* devote to religious purposes; (7) make place for, accommodate, have room for, contain, make comfortable, e.g. *ulimwengu wote haumweki,* the world is too small for him. *Nyumba hii hainiweki,* this house does not suit me, is not comfortable. (8) entrust, deposit, commit, allot, assign, e.g. *weka fedha* (*heshima, amana*), give money (honour, a pledge); (9) appoint, institute, e.g. *weka mfalme,* set a king on his throne; (10) establish, found, lay down, e.g. *weka desturi,* establish a custom. *Weka sheria,* enact a law. *Kiwekwacho na Mungu, mwanadamu hawezi kukiondoa,* what God has established, man cannot annul. Ps. **Wekwa.** St. and Pot. **Wekeka,** e.g. *mpunga huu unawekeka mpaka mwakani,* it is possible to put aside this rice till next year. Prep. **Wekea,** put aside for (with, &c.), e.g. *nimemwekea shilingi kumi,* I have committed ten shillings to his keeping, also I have put aside ten shillings for him. *Wekea heshima,* pay honour to. *Wekea wakf,* dedicate to. *Niliwekewa amana,* I had something entrusted to me. Rp. of Prep. **Wekeana,** e.g. *wekeana masharti,* place conditions on each other, also bet together. *Wekeana heshima,* exchange compliments, treat each other with due respect. Cs. **Wekesha** and **Wekeza,** seldom used. Rp. **Wekana,** e.g. *tuliwekana kuonana Jumamosi,* we arranged to meet again on Saturday. **Kiweko,** n. *vi-* (1) act, &c., of placing, place for putting, placing, resting, position; (2) pedestal, base, rest socket, &c. *Kiweko chake kilikuwa kwa upole,* he put it down gently. *Hapo ndipo kiweko chake,* this is its proper place. **Mweko,** n. *mi-* a putting aside (off, down, away, &c.). **-wekevu,** a. giving to putting aside, hence thrifty, careful, also miserly. **Weko,** n. *ma-* (1) place for putting something, stand, magazine, base, pedestal; (2) piece of metal used for welding. *Tia weko,* weld.

Wekevu, n. sometimes heard for *welekevu,* see under **Elea, v.** (B); also a. see under **Weka.**

Weko, n. *ma-.* See under **Weka.**

Wekua, v. sometimes heard for *ekua,* which see.

Wekundu, n. See under **-ekundu.**

Wele, n. *ma-.* See under **Mwele, n.** (B).

Welea, v. See under **Wa, v.**

Weledi,* a. and n. skill, cleverness; skilful, clever. (Cf. *hodari, ustadi, bingwa.* Ar. ولد, cf. ذا ولد he is a sharp fellow, or an abstract noun made from Ar. لضو be experienced, skilful, &c.)

Welekeo, n. (for *uelekeo*), **Welekevu,** n. (for *uelekevu*). See under **Elea, v.** (B).

Wema, n. See under **-ema.**

Wembamba, n. See under **-embamba.**

Wembe, n. (*nyembe*). See under **Jembe.**

Wembembe, n. very small bees which build in door-locks and other small apertures in houses, a wild bee.

Wendeleo, n., **Wendelezo,** n., **Wendo,** n., **Wenendo,** n. See under **Enda.**

Wenga, v. (1) come out in a rash after eating certain kinds of fish or flesh, e.g. of a person who has eaten what is taboo for him (cf. *mwiko, mzio*); (2) harm; (3) dislike.

Wengi, n. form *-ingi,* which see.

Wengu, n. the spleen. (Cf. *bandama.*)

Weni, n. a stinging plant, from which a cure for sores is made.

Wenu, a. form of *-enu,* yours.

Wenzi, n. (*u-enzi*), (1) friendliness, friendly association, companionship;

(2) plur. of **mwenzi**, companion, see under **Enda.**

Wenzo, n. (*nyenzo*). See under **Enda.**

Wepesi, n. See under **-epesi.**

Werevu, n. See under **-erevu.**

Wetu, a. form of *-etu*, ours.

Weu, n. (*nyeu*), **Weuo**, n., **Weupe.** See under **Eua.**

Weusi, n. See under **-eusi.**

Wevi, n. plur. of *mwivi*. See under **Iba.**

Wewe, pron. of 2 Pers. Sing. you—also **Weye.** In sudden emphatic address often combined with *ee*, *Ewe!* You there! I say, you!

Weweseka, v. talk in sleep, or in delirium, or unconsciously. Cs. **Wewesesha**, e.g. *ile picha niliyoona sinema* (cinema) *iliniwewesesha usiku kucha*, that picture I saw at the cinema made me talk all night long in my sleep.

Weye, pron. See under **Wewe.**

Weza, v. (1) be able, be strong, be capable, have strength. The forms of the Negative Present, *siwezi*, *huwezi*, &c., are regularly used in the special sense, I am sick (ill, unwell, &c.) (see under *jambo*); (2) have power (means, liberty, opportunity, occasion, option, &c.), with an Infinitive following, e.g. *aweza kwenda*, he has strength to walk, leave to go, &c. *Naweza kumpiga*, I can beat him. (3) get mastery over, control, overcome, defeat, subdue — with nouns. *Simba alimweza*, the lion overcame him (cf. *shinda*, *funga*). (4) be able to bear, endure, tolerate, e.g. *ukali wako hawauwezi*, they cannot bear your tyranny (cf. *vumilia*, *stahimili*, *chukua*). Rf. *jiweza*, have power over oneself (or in oneself, of oneself), have self-control, be temperate. Hence *jiwezea*, be able to get on (to manage, do for oneself), be independent, self-sufficient. Ps. **Wezwa**, e.g. *amewezwa*, he has been beaten. St. and Pot. **Wezeka**, e.g. be practicable, possible, permissible, probable—and also more commonly **Wezekana**, e.g. *haiwezekani*, it is not feasible. *Hawezekani*, he is invincible, beyond all control, or not to be endured. Prep. **Wezea.** Cs. **Wezesha**, e.g. empower, give authority (leave, strength, means, &c.) to. Rp. **Wezana. Mweza**, n. *wa-* one who is able, possessed of power over (or to do), a ruler. *Mweza nchi*, the ruler of a country. *Mweza mwenyewe*, his own master, an independent power. *Mweza yote*, supreme over all things, Almighty—a title of God. Also *mweza kwetu*, ruler of our world. **Uweza**, n., **Uwezo**, n. (1) being able—and so (2) strength, might, power, capacity, authority, ability, faculty. (Cf. *nguvu*, *enzi*, *mamlaka*, *amri*, *akili*.)

Wezi, n. plur. of *mwizi*. See under **Iba.**

-wi, a. bad, an old word seldom used now. *Mtu huyu mwi sana*, this man is very wicked. *Simba ni mnyama mwi sana*, the lion is a very harmful animal. Prov. *Kazi mbi si mchezo mwema*, bad work rather than good play.

Wia, v. (1) get warm, seethe, begin to get hot, of water, &c.; (2) see under **Wa**, v.

Wibari,* n. a hyrax, rock-rabbit. (Cf. *kwanga*, *pelele*. Ar. وبار.)

Widhaa,* n. *ma-* sometimes heard for *waadhi*, which see.

Wifi, n. sister-in-law, i.e. brother's wife, or husband's sister. *Wifi* is used by women of 'in laws'; *shemeji* is used by men of 'in laws'.

Wika, v. crow—of a cock. *Jogoo lawika*, the cock crows. Prov. *Likiwika lisiwike kutakucha*, whether the cock crows or not, it will dawn.

Wiki,* n. a week in common use, esp. in Zanzibar. (Cf. *juma*. Eng.)

Wilaya,* n. parish, district, province. (Cf. *ulaya*. Ar. ولاية.)

-wili, a. of second numeral, two, a pair of, together, both. *Mara mbili*, twice. *Upanga mkali kuwili*, a two edged sword. *Walikwenda wawili*, they went together, or they both went. *Wote wawili*, both. **Kuwili**, n. and adv. the double kind, in a double way, in two ways. *Kisu chenye makali kuwili*, a knife with two sharp edges. *Anatajwa kuwili*, he has two names. **Uwili**, n. being twofold, duality, dualism, doubleness. (Cf. *pili*.)

Wima, n. uprightness, being perpendicular, standing up. *Kwa wima*, perpendicularly. **Wima**, v. be erect, straight. **Imaima**, adv., **Kiwimawima**, adv. in an erect position, upright, perpendicular, steep, e.g. of a steep hill, precipice, &c. *Simama wima* (or *kiwimawima*), stand upright. **Mwima**, n. *wa-* one who stands upright. **Mwimo**, n. *mi-* an upright or side piece of a door or window frame.

Wimbaji, n. (for *uimbaji*). See under **Imba.**

Wimbi, n. *ma-* a wave. *Hapana maji yasiyo na mawimbi*, there is no water without waves. *Kila chombo na wimbile*, every vessel has its waves to meet. *Mawimbi ya kuumuka*, breakers. *Mawimbi ya kwelea*, storm waves, high seas. **Kiwimbi**, n. *vi-* and adv., dim. of *wimbi*, wavelet, ripple, eddy. As adv., like a wave, undulating, with ridges, hillocks, &c.

Wimbo, n. (*nyimbo*). See under **Imba.**

Wimbombo, n. the male stick in firesticks, the female is called *ulindi*.

Winchi,* n. a winch, crane, derrick. (Cf. *silingi*. Eng. winch.)

Winda, n. manner of girding the loins by tucking the loin-cloth between the legs and fastening the ends to the fold round the waist. (Cf. *ubinda*.)

Winda, v. (1) hunt—of game in general, animals, birds, large and small, with weapons, nets, dogs, &c. (cf. *saka*); (2) search for a thing quietly and secretly, also of seeking for an enemy to take revenge, pursuing a flying foe or fugitive. *Nitamwinda mpaka tuonane*, I will hunt him till we meet. Rp. **Windana**, e.g. *watu hawa wanawindana*, these people are hunting each other. **Mwinda**, n. *wa-*, **Mwindaji**, n. *wa-*, **Mwinzi**, n. (*wawinzi*), a hunter, one who pursues. **Windo**, n. (— and *ma-*) what is got by hunting, booty, prey, a hunter's bag. **Windo**, n. same as *uwindo* below. **Uwinda**, n., **Uwindaji**, n., **Uwindo**, n., and **Uwinzi**, n. art (profession, method, payment, &c.) of hunting.

Windo, n. (— and *ma-*). See under **Winda, v.**

Winga, v. drive away, chase away. *Upesi, winga kuku hawa*, quick, chase away these fowls. (Cf. *fukuza*.)

Wingi, n. form of *-ingi*.

Wingu, n. *ma-* cloud—or what resembles a cloud. *Wingu la mvua*, rain cloud. *Wingu la moshi*, cloud of smoke. Thick cloud is called *nene*, *zito*, *kubwa*, *jeusi*. *Wingu la giza*, a dark cloud (cf. *ghubari*, *mavunde*). **Kiwingu**, n. *vi-* dim. **Uwingu**, n. (*mbingu*) (1) the sky, cloud region, upper air, heaven; (2) cloudiness, darkness, gloom. Plur. *mbingu*, the skies, heaven is much the most usual form, and is sometimes used as sing. *Mbingu ikanena kwamba mimi bora*, Heaven said that I am best. *Mbingu saba*, the seven heavens. *Kumefanya uwingu mkubwa*, there is a great gloom. The plur. is often used with the locative *-ni*, *mbinguni*, heaven, i.e. the abode of God and his angels.

Wino,* n. ink. *Kidau cha wino*, inkstand, inkpot. *Wino mwekundu*, red ink. (Ar. لون colour.)

Wishwa, n., **Wiswa**, n. chaff, husks, bran. (Cf. *kumvi*, *kapi*.)

Witiri,* n. odd—of a number, i.e. not even. (Cf. *kitangulizi* under *tangulia*. Ar. وتر.)

Wito, (1) infection, infectiousness, contagion. *Pata wito*, be infected. *Ndui ina wito sana*, smallpox is very infectious, but the usual word is *ambukizo*, see under **Ambua**, v. (2) casting—of metal in a mould; also a mould for casting. (cf. *subu*); (3) see under **Ita**.

Wituri,* n. See **Witiri**.

Wiva, v. sometimes used for *iva*, which see.

Wivi, n. See under **Iba**.

-wivu, a. jealous, envious. **Mwivu**, n. *wa-* a jealous person. **Wivu** (for *uwivu*), jealousy, envy. *Lia wivu*, cry for jealousy. (Cf. *husuda, kijicho.*)

Wiwa, v. See under **Wa**, v.

Wizi, n. See under **Iba**.

Wo, (1) relative form, used independently only in such phrases as *watu wo wote*, whosoever (plur.), any people whatsoever. *Mti wo wote*, any tree whatsoever. *Wimbo wo wote*, any song. (2) contracted form of *wako*, and subjoined to nouns, generally shortened to **-o**, e.g. *mwanao*, your son.

Woga, n., **Wogofya**, n. *ma-*, **Wogofyo**, n. *ma-*. See under **-oga**, a.

Wokovu, n. See under **Okoa**.

-wongo, a. false, untrue, lying, pretended, sham, deceitful, but *-a uwongo* is the form commonly used. **Mwongo**, n. (*wawongo*), a liar, impostor, inventor of falsehoods, deceiver, perverter of the truth. **Ongopa**, v. tell a lie. Cs. **Ongofya**, Inten. mislead, tell a lie. Sometimes *rongopa* and *rongofya* are heard, just as *urongo* is sometimes heard for *uwongo*. For the function of the suffix *-pa*, i.e. *(w)ongo-pa*, see note under *pa*. **Uwongo**, n. falseness, falsehood, a lie, lies, untruth, deception, sham, fraud, delusion, pretence. *Sema* (*toa*) *uwongo*, tell a lie. *Alilia kwa uwongo*, he shed crocodile's tears. Used also like an adj. *kufa uwongo*, to sham being dead (cf. *kifauwongo*, a name given to the sensitive plant, and also to some insects). Prov. *Njia ya uwongo ni fupi*, lies do not go far.

Wongofu, n. See under **Ongoa**.

Wonyesho, n., and **Wonyeshano**, n. See under **Ona**.

Worodha.* See **Orodha**.

Wosia,* n. and v. sometimes heard for *usia*, which see.

Wote, a. form of *-ote*, all, the whole agreeing with sing. of *Mi-* and *U* class nouns, and plur. of *Wa* class. *Twende wote*, let us all go, but commonly of two persons, i.e. let us both go, or go together. *Twende sote*, let us all go. *Wote wawili*, both of them, both together.

Woto, n. See under **Ota**, v. (A) and (C).

Wozo, n. See under **Oza**, v. (A).

Y

Y represents the same sound as in English, i.e. a semi-vowel or consonantal *i* before another vowel.

Ya, prep. form of *-a*, of, e.g. *nyumba ya mgeni*, the stranger's house; *makasha ya mbao*, boxes of wood, &c. Also the form used most generally for 'of' whenever the reference is indefinite and general, e.g. *ya nini?* why?

ya kwamba, that (conj.); *ya kuwa*, because, in that, &c. Thus it is used continually with adverbs to form prepositional phrases, e.g. *mbele ya*, before; *juu ya*, above; *chini ya*, below; *nje ya*, outside, &c. (But cf. *mbali na*, far from; *karibu na*, near; *mkabala wa*, opposite, &c.)

Ya, verb-form, they are, e.g. *makasha ya tayari*, the boxes are ready—and so in place of *ni*, or the present tense of *wa*, v. which see.

Yaa!* int. used esp. *Yaa Rabi!* Oh God! (Ar. يا.)

Yaani,* conj. that is, that is to say, I mean. (Cf. *ndiyo*. Ar. يعني.)

Yabisi,* a. and **Yabis**, dry, hard, e.g. *udongo yabisi*, hard, parched earth. *Baridi yabisi*, rheumatism. Sometimes heard as a v., with a St. **Yabisika**, in the same sense, be hard, dry. **Uyabisi**, n. (1) dryness, hardness, stiffness; (2) fig. disobliging conduct, rudeness, reserve, e.g. *uyabisi wa maungo*, of rheumatism, and *uyabisi wa tumbo* (or *choo*), costiveness. (Cf. *-kavu*, *-gumu*, *-shupavu*, *ubaridi*. Ar. يبس.)

Yadi,* n. a yard (measure). (Eng.)

Yahe,* n. (1) the ordinary people, e.g. *sisi akina yahe*, we of the common herd; (2) brother, friend. (Cf. *ahi*. Ar. اخ.)

Yahom,* a nautical term for straight ahead, *upepo wa yahom*, is a following wind. (Ar. امام ahead.)

Yahudi,* n. *ma-* also **Myahudi**, n. *wa-* a Jew, Hebrew. **Kiyahudi**, n. and adv., the Hebrew language; after the Hebrew kind, &c. **Uyahudi**, n. Palestine. (Ar. يهود.)

Yai, n. *ma-* an egg. *Taga yai*, lay an egg. *Atamia mayai*, sit on eggs. *Yai bichi*, fresh, uncooked egg. *Yai viza* (*bovu*), bad (addled, rotten) egg. *Yai la kutokosa*, boiled egg. *Yai la kukaanga*, fried egg. *Angua mayai*, hatch out eggs. Also *mayai ya pumbu*, the testicles.

Yaika, **v.** See **Yeyuka**.

Yake, **a.** pronom. form of *-ake*, his, her, its.

Yakini,* n. truth, certainly, assurance, proof, e.g. *najua yakini ya habari*, I know the truth of the matter. *Kwa yakini*, really and truly. *Wataka yakini gani?* What sort of proof do you want. **Yakini**, a. true, certain, proved. **Yakini**, **v.** be sure. *Nayakini kukuja jana kwangu*, I am sure you did not come to my house yesterday. Prep. **Yakinia**, resolve on, make up one's mind, be sure of, determine on. *Nimeyakinia kwenda shamba*, I have resolved to go to the country. Ps. **Yakiniwa**. St. **Yakinika**, e.g. *maneno uliyosema yanayakinika*, what you said is certain. Cs. **Yakinisha**, e.g. *niliweza kuliyakinisha neno lake*, I was able to establish his word. (Cf. *hakika*, *kweli*, *azimia*, *kusudia*, *thubutisha*. Ar. يقن.)

Yako, (1) a. pronom. form of *-ako*, your, yours; (2) verb-form, they are (there).

Yakuti,* n. ruby, sapphire. (Cf. *johari*, *kito*. Ar. ياقوت.)

Yale, a. form of *-le*, those.

Yamini,* n. (1) right hand; (2) solemn oath sworn with the right hand on the Koran. Thus take a solemn oath is *twaa* (*piga*, *apa*, *la*), *yamini*, e.g. *naweza kula yamini ya kuwa simjui*, I can solemnly swear that I do not know him. *Nimemlisha yamini*, I have made him swear an oath. (Cf. *mkono wa kulia*, *kiapo*, *apa*. Ar. يمين.)

Yamkini,* n. sometimes heard as **Yumkini**, possibility. **Yamkini**, a. possible, likely, probable, e.g. *mambo haya ni yamkini*, these things are possible. **Yamkini**, **v.** be possible (likely, probable). *Je, itayamkini kulia bure wewe?* Will it be likely you should cry for nothing? St. **Yamkinika**, with the same meaning, usually in the negative, e.g. *maneno haya hayamkiniki*, these words are not plausible. *Haiyamkiniki*, it is impossible. (In Ar. an impersonal form of the verb, but in Swahili treated as above, like *yakini*. Cf. *weza, wezekana*. Ar. امكانة.)

Yangeyange, n. the Little Egret, *Egretta garnetta*; also the white form of the Red Sea Reef Heron, *Demigretta schistacea*.

Yangu, a. pronom. form of **-angu**, my, mine.

Yao, a. pronom. form of **-ao**, their, theirs.

Yasi,* n. a yellow powder from India used by women as a cosmetic, more often called *dalia*. (Cf. also *liwa*. ? Ar. ميس yellowish white.)

Yasini! int. a scornful, disdainful, and often insulting reply, as a rule only used by women: Why should I? It's not worth the trouble, &c.

Yasini,* n. a certain chapter from the Koran, used in making charms, so called because of the letters ي *ya* and س *sin* which appear at the beginning of the chapter.

Yasmini,* n. a cultivated kind of jasmine, *Jasminum Sambac*. (Cf. *afu*. Ar. ياسمين.)

Yatima,* n. a fatherless, motherless, or orphan child. (Cf. *mkiwa*. Ar. يتيم.)

Yavuyavu, n. *ma-* and a. (1) lungs; (2) jelly-fish (cf. *pafu, buhumu, pumu*). As a. descriptive of anything of a sponge-like nature.

Yaya,* n. *ma-* a child's nurse, an ayah, either male or female. *Kila mtoto na yaya wake*, every child with its nurse. (Cf. *mlezi*. Hind. from Port. *aia*.)

Yaya, a. a form of the a. *haya*, used only in combination with it for emphasis, i.e. *yaya haya*, just these very things. So, *lili hili, sisi hizi, vivi hivi*, &c. **Yayo**, a. the relative corresponding to *yaya*, e.g. *yayo hayo*.

Ye, (1) relative pfx. sing. referring to persons and animals. Only used independently in such phrases as *ye yote*, any one whatsoever, whosoever. (2) shortened for *yake* and subjoined to nouns and adverbs, e.g. *nyumbaye*, his house. *Baadaye*, after that. (3) used in a form of the personal pronouns, except *wao*, i.e. *miye* for *mimi*, *siye* for *sisi*, &c.; (4) for further uses as a pfx. see Grammars.

Yee, pron. sometimes heard for *yeye*.

Yetu, Yenyewe, Yenye, Yenu, forms of *-etu, -enyewe, -enye*, and *-enu*.

Yeye, pron. 3 Pers. Sing., he, she, him, her.

Yeyuka, v. melt, become fluid, melt away. Cs. **Yeyusha**, cause to melt, melt, make a solution. Also used metaphorically, e.g. *furaha yangu iliyeyuka*, my joy melted away. **Myeyuko**, n. *mi-* act (method, &c.) of melting. **Myeyusho**, n. *mi-* a solution.

Yo, (1) relative pfx. used independently in *yo yote*, whatever, any whatsoever; (2) shortened for *yako*, yours, and subjoined to nouns, e.g. *babayo*, your father; (3) for other uses as a relative, &c., see Grammars.

Yoga, n. *ma-*. See under **Kiyoga**.

Yombiyombi, n. Grosbeak Weaver, *Amblyospina albifrons*, also called *kata dole*. (Cf. *kwaru*.)

Yonga, v. sway, bow or bend down, stagger under a weight or from feebleness, &c., e.g. *miti inayonga kwa upepo*, the trees are bending with the wind. *Jahazi inayonga*, the vessel is rolling. *Mwendo wake wa kuyonga, lakini mlevi hupepesuka, hutaka kuanguka*, his gait is unsteady but a drunken man reels and he nearly falls. *Mtu mrefu huyonga anapokwenda*, a tall man bends forward as he goes, i.e. he does not hold himself erect. Cs. **Yongesha,** e.g. *upepo huyongesha miti,* the wind bends the trees. (Cf. *yugayuga, yumba, wayawaya, sita, lewalewa.*)

Yongoa, v., and **Yongoja,** v. be carried shoulder high or on the back of some one, i.e. as the bride and bridegroom in some tribes, and also the initiates when they leave the initiation rite.

Yote, a. form of *-ote,* all, agreeing with sing. of *N* class nouns, and plur. of *Mi* and *Ma* class nouns.

Yowe, n. *ma-* a loud cry, shout, scream, esp. of call for help. *Piga yowe,* give a shout. *Kitanda cha mayowe,* a name given in play to a native bedstead from the creaking it makes. **Kiyowe,** n. *vi-* dim. used in the same way as *yowe.* (Cf. *kelele, kilio, kigelegele, shime, hoihoi.*)

Yoyomea, v. arrive at a place or enter with a rush, or with great noise and confusion. (Cf. *tokomea.*)

Yu (1) pfx. of 3 Pers. Sing. referring to a person, common in some dialects —but in Zanzibar and the adjacent coast (except Mombasa) not usual in verb-form, and only before the present tense sign of one or two monosyllabic verbs, e.g. *yuna,* he has, sometimes heard for *ana*; *yuaja,* he comes, sometimes heard for *aja, anakuja.* (2) he (she) is—used as 3 Pers. Sing. Pres. Tense of the verb 'to be' instead of *a* which is never used independently, but only in combinations, e.g. *Abdallah yu mvivu,* Abdallah is lazy. **Yuko,** verb-form, he (she) is (there). **Yule,** a. form of *-le,* that (person). **Yumo,** verb-form, he (she) is within. **Yupi,** a. form of *-pi,* who? **Yupo,** verb-form, he (she) is here. (3) *Yu* also appears in the three Dem. adj. forms as applied to the 1st. Class names, e.g. *huyu, huyo, yule.*

Yua, v. wobble, e.g. *mshale unayua,* the arrow is not flying straight. Seldom used. Rd. *yuayua,* wander about, stray. *Hana kazi ila kuyuayua tu mjini,* he has nothing to do but wander about the streets. This form is more frequently used than the Dir.

Yugayuga, v. reel, stagger. *Mlevi yule anayugayuga sana,* that drunken man is staggering a lot.

Yuko, Yule. See under **Yu.**

Yumba, v. sway, wave to and fro, stagger, e.g. of trees, a balanced pole, a drunken or feeble person. *Matawi ya miti huyumba kwa upepo,* boughs of trees sway with the wind. Rd. *yumbayumba* is often used.

Yumkini.* See **Yamkini.**

Yumo. See under **Yu.**

Yungayunga, n. also **Nyungu-nyungu,** a worm.

Yungiyungi, *ma-* a large blue or white variety of water-lily, *Nymphaea stellata.*

Yupi, Yupo. See under **Yu.**

Z

Z represents the same sound as in 'zeal' in English. A few words spelt and pronounced by some people as though they contained *z* will be found under *dh* or spelt with *dh* in this dictionary.

Za, for the uses of *za* as a termination see Grammars.

Za, prep. form of *-a*, of.

Zaa, v. denotes vital reproduction, the whole process or a stage in it, of male or female, in any region of organic life—thus bear offspring, produce fruit, procreate, beget, have children, be pregnant, give birth to, be delivered (of a child), be fruitful (productive, fertile). *Watu wa nchi ile huzaa sana*, the people of that country are very prolific. *Miembe hii inazaa mno*, these mango trees are bearing very much fruit. *Amezaa mtoto*, he has begotten a child, or she has given birth to a child. Ps. **Zawa**, but the Ps. of Prep. is more usual, i.e. *zaliwa*. *Siku ya kuzaliwa kwangu*, my birthday. St. **Zalika.** Prep. **Zalia**, e.g. bear to (for, by, at), &c. *Mkewe alimzalia mtoto*, his wife bore him a child. Obs. *amezaliwa mtoto*, may mean (1) a child has been born, or (2) he has had a child born to him, e.g. *alizalia hapa*, he has had children here. Cs. **Zalisha**, cause to bear (to be born), beget, fertilize, make productive, assist at childbirth, act as midwife, &c. Rp. **Zaana** and **Zaliana**, breed together, multiply. **Kizalia**, n. *vi-*, **Kizao**, n. *vi-* produce, production, offspring, that which is born in a given place, home-born, indigenous, native, e.g. of home-born slaves (cf. *kikulia*, *kimelea*). **Kizazi**, n. *vi-* any part or step in causing birth, or being born, procreation, generation. Usually (1) birth, production of offspring, being born. *Haya niliyoandika ya kizazi cha Buge*, this is my account of the circumstances of Buge's birth. *Ana kizazi*, he has birth, he is a man of good family. (2) that which is born, a birth, offspring, whether individually 'a child, a young one' or collectively 'a generation'. *Kizazi hiki*, the present generation. **Mzaa**, n. *wa-* one who begets, or gives birth to. *Mzaa bibi*, great-grandmother, i.e. the bearer of the grandmother. **Mzalia**, n. *wa-* with Ps. sense, one born at (or in) a place, a native of a given spot, and formerly esp. a home-born slave, one born in the house or country of his master. **Mzalisha**, n. *wa-*, **Mzalishi**, n. *wa-* a midwife (cf. *mkunga*). **Mzaliwa**, n. *wa-* one born (at), e.g. *mzaliwa huko* (or *wa huko*), one born there, a native. **Mzao**, n. *wa-* and *mi-* child, offspring, descendant. **Mzawa**, n. *wa-* same as *mzaliwa*. **Mzazi**, n. *wa-* (1) one who begets, or bears offspring, a parent (male or female); (2) used to distinguish between a parent and other relative, i.e. *mama* (*baba*) *mzazi*, mother (father), to distinguish from aunt or uncle; used also of a woman recently delivered, and (3) a prolific parent, whether human or animal. **Zalio**, n. *ma-* (1) like *kizalia*, also (2) a caul (cf. *tandabui*). **Zao**, n. *ma-* fruit, produce, product, offspring, product in arithmetic. **-zazi**, a. fruitful, productive. **Uzao**, n. *ma-* product, production, offspring. **Uzazi**, n. (1) reproduction at any stage, production of fruit, or offspring; (2) parentage (of man or animal, male or female), begetting, procreation, childbirth, delivery, confinement; (3) reproductive power, fruitfulness, fertility, fruit-bearing; (4) produce, offspring—but this is usually *mazao*. *Chango la uzazi*, umbilical cord.

Zaba,* v. hit, beat. *Kuzaba kofi*, to box the ears. (Cf. *piga*. ? Ar. صاب.)

Zabadi,* n. civet, musk—substance taken from the civet cat, *ngawa*, and used in perfumes. **Zabidi**, v.

take civet from the civet cat. (Ar. زدبا.)

Zabibu,* n. raisin, grape. **Mzabibu,** n. *mi-* a grape vine. *Tawi la mzabibu,* a branch of a vine. (Ar. زبيب.)

Zabidi,* v. See under **Zabadi.**

Zabuni,* v. bid at an auction. **Mzabuni,** n. *wa-* a bidder at a sale. (Cf. *mnada, mushtiri, nunua.* Ar. زبون a customer.)

Zaburi,* n. a psalm, the psalter. (Cf. *utenzi.* Ar. زبور.)

Zafarani,* n. saffron. (Ar. زعفران.)

Zafe,* n. slime, slipperiness. (Ar. زيف pitch.)

Zagaa,* v. shine, glisten, give light, illuminate. Ps. **Zagawa,** e.g. be lighted up, be enlightened. Cs. **Zagaza,** cause to shine. *Nuru ya jua inazagaa,* the sun gives forth its light. (Cf. more usual *ng'aa, mulika.* Ar. زغره stare, glare.)

Zahali,* n. the planet Saturn. (Ar. زحل.)

Zahama,* n. also **Zahimu,** n. (1) confusion, noise; (2) oppression, distress. (Cf. *ghasia, kishindo.* Ar. زحم to crowd, press.)

Zaidi,* adv. more, in addition, in a greater degree or quantity. *Zaidi ya (kuliko, kama),* more than, besides. Also as n. *zaidi ya habari,* further news. **Zidi,** v. (1) become more (greater, larger, taller, longer, &c.), grow, increase, multiply, be more and more. With an Infinitive following it is very often best translated by the adverb 'more' or a comparative adverb, e.g. *anazidi kwenda,* he is going faster (or farther). *Azidi kujua,* he knows better. *Habari inazidi kuenea,* the news goes on spreading. *Zidi* also means 'do more', e.g. *nizidi kumpiga?* shall I beat him more? *Uzidi kuifikiri,* give more thought to the matter. Obs. *mambo yamezidi,* things have become worse and worse. (2) be the greater, have more power (than), outstrip, gain on (in a race), be superior (to), e.g. *hao ndio watuzidio sisi,* these are the persons who surpass us (are better than we, more powerful, &c.). *Adui zao waliwazidi,* their enemies were their overlords. (3) get the better of, beat, overwhelm, reduce to straits, e.g. *kazi imenizidi sana,* the work has become too much for me, is too much for me. This meaning is more clearly shown in the Ps. **Zidiwa,** e.g. (1) be surpassed; (2) very often 'be beaten by, be put in difficulties by', and so, be in want of help about, e.g. *nimezidiwa,* I am in difficulty, or, with *fedha,* I am in want of cash, or, with *karatasi,* I have run short of paper, &c. *Tulizidiwa na mvua,* the rain got the better of us. Prep. **Zidia,** e.g. increase to, grow upon. Sometimes Act. *Mungu awazidie afya,* may God grant them continuance of health. Cs. **Zidisha,** cause to be greater, multiply, the word used for multiplication in Arithmetic (cf. *ongeza*). Prep. of Cs. **Zidishia,** e.g. *Mungu alimzidishia baraka,* God increased his blessings. **Kizidishe,** n. *vi-* multiplicand. **Kizidisho,** n. *vi-* multiplier. **Zaidana,** n., **Zaidi,** n., an increase, addition, increment, bonus, e.g. *ziada la msaada,* additional help. Prov. *Hakuna zaidi mbovu,* there is no increase which is bad. **Zawadi,** n. present, gift, keepsake. **Ziada,** n. *ma-,* **Zidi,** n. *ma-,* **Zidio,** n. *ma-,* **Zidisho,** n. *ma-* all used occasionally for 'increase, addition, bonus, augmentation, supplement', &c. (Cf. *ongeza,* and for presents, *bakshish, hedaya, tunzo, tuzo.* Ar. زاد Note: *zawadi* may be derived from Ar. زواد provender, see similar use of *lukuma,* or from زود increase, growth.)

Zaini,* v. cheat, deceive, persuade to do wrong. (Cf. *danganya, shawishi.* ? Ar. دنى mean, low, contemptible.)

Zaka, n. (A), also **Zakati**,* n. tithe, offering to religious purposes. (Cf. *sadaka*. Ar. زكاة.)

Zaka,* n. (B) a quiver for arrows. (Cf. *podo*. Ar. زكة arms, armour.)

Zake, Zako, a. forms of *-ake* and *-ako*, his (her, its), and yours.

Zalia, v., **Zalio**, n. *ma-*. See under **Zaa**.

Zama,* n. See under **Zamani**.

Zama, v. (1) sink in a fluid, be immersed, dive, be drowned, sink down; (2) fig. plunge (into), be immersed (in), be overwhelmed (by), e.g. *kilimia kikizama kwa jua, huzuka kwa mvua*, if the Pleiades set in fine weather they will rise in wet. *Zama katika elimu* (*katika bahari ya maneno*), plunge into study (into the sea of words, e.g. dictionary). Prep. **Zamia**, e.g. *zamia lulu*, dive for pearls. Cs. **Zamisha**, e.g. engage as a diver, contract for diving, immerse, drown (cf. *tota, didimia, zizimia*). **Kizamia dagaa**, n. *vi-* a name applied to various birds which dive for small fish, esp. the malachite kingfisher. **Mzama**, n. *wa-* one who sinks or dives in water. **Mzamaji**, n. *wa-* a diver by profession, e.g. of those who dive for coins in harbours when passenger ships are in. **Mzamia**, n. *wa-* one who dives for something, esp. *mzamia lulu*, one who dives for pearls. **Mzamio**, n. *mi-* a diving for something, style (act, &c.) of diving into water. **Mzamishi**, n. *wa-* one who employs divers. **Mzamisho**, n. *mi-* causing to sink, plunging in water, employment of divers. **Mzamo**, n. *mi-* diving, a dive, a plunging into water.

Zamani,* n. (1) time, period, epoch, e.g. *zamani moja*, at a certain time—commonly in the plur. *Zamani za kale*, ancient times. *Zamani za Harun al-Rashid*, in the time of Harun al-Rashid. *Zamani hizi*, nowadays. *Zamani zetu*, our own times. (2) ancient times, antiquity, the past. Thus as adv. long ago, in ancient days, some time past, or merely already, before, e.g. *alikuja zamani*, he came some little time ago; but *nimemwona zamani*, I have seen him before. *Nimelipa deni ile zamani*, I have already paid that debt. Sometimes it is shortened, *zama*, as though the *-ni* was a locative, or in confusion with *zamu* (Cf. *wakati*. Ar. زمن.)

Zambarau,* n. (1) a small fruit somewhat resembling a damson or sloe, fruit of the *mzambarau*, which see; (2) also used as a. of colour, i.e. purple.

Zamburu, n. *ma-* a kind of fish found in mangrove swamps.

Zamu,* n. (1) properly, a six hours' spell of work, or watching; (2) period of duty or occupation, e.g. sentry, patrol, turn, innings. *Zamu yangu*, it is my turn. *Ngoja zamu, kaa zamu, keti zamu, shika* (*linda*) *zamu*, all phrases used for keeping watch. *Waliwekana zamu, wengine kulala, wengine kukesha*, they arranged watches amongst themselves, some to sleep, some to remain awake. (Cf. *kingojo, kesha, linda*. Ar. زام.)

Zana,* n. fittings, apparatus, gadgets, &c. *Zana za vita*, munitions. *Zana za chombo*, a boat's fittings. (Cf. *vyombo, vifaa*. ? Ar. زين adornment, or صنعة, صناع art, handicraft.)

Zandiki,* v. be a hypocrite, pretend to be what one is not. **Mzandiki**, n. *wa-* a hypocrite, liar. **Uzandiki**, n. hypocrisy, falseness, deceit. (Cf. *mnafiki, mwongo*. Ar. زنديق.)

Zangu, a. form of *-angu*, my, mine. Obs. *naenda* (or *nakwenda*) *zangu*, I am going my way, i.e. away, on. (Cf. *enda*.)

Zao, (1) n. *ma-* see under **Zaa**; (2) a. form of *-ao*, their, theirs.

Zaraa,* n. Arabic for *kilimo*, agriculture. (Cf. *lima*, v. Ar. زرع.)

Zarambo,* n. a spirit distilled from palm wine, *tembo*. (Pers. زراب golden-water, wine.)

Zari,* n. gold thread (braid, brocade). (Pers. زر gold.)

Zartari,* n. a kind of herb put in tea to give it a pleasant flavour and smell.

Zatiti,* v. put in order, put ready, arrange, prepare, provide. *Zatiti vyombo vya safari*, place ready the things required for the journey. (Cf. *tengeneza, andaa, weka tayari.* (Ar. حاضر.)

Zawa, v. See under **Zaa.**

Zawadi,* n. See under **Zaidi.**

Zawaridi,* n. the Java sparrow, *Padda oryzivora.* (Ar. ضوارب.)

-zazi, a. See under **Zaa.**

-ze, subjoined to a noun, shortened form of *zake*, his, her, its, e.g. *nduguze*, his brothers.

Zebaki,* n. mercury, quicksilver. (Ar. زئبق.)

Zebe,* n. (1) a fool. (Cf. *mpumbavu, bozi, baradhuli.* Ar. صبى act childishly.) (2) one who practises sapphism. (Prob. from *zubu.*)

-zee, a. See under **mzee.**

Zefe,* n. a row. *Watu walijipanga zefe*, the people arranged themselves in rows. (Cf. *mstari*, prob. a corruption of *safu*, which see.)

Zege,* n. (1) a dome, cupola (cf. *kuba*); (2) concrete, reinforced concrete. (Cf. *saruji.*)

Zeituni,* n. an olive. The tree is **Mzeituni,** n. *mi-*. (Ar. زيتون.)

Zelabia,* n. also **Zilabia,** n. a twist, i.e. a light pastry made in the form of a horseshoe. The chief ingredients used are flour, ghee, and sugar. (Hind. جلیبی.)

Zema, a. an occasional form of *-ema*, good, for *njema.*

-zembe, a. slack, idle, indifferent, remiss, negligent. **Kizembe,** n. and adv. idling, slack (remiss, negligent) conduct or act; in an idle, negligent manner. **Mzembe,** n. *wa-* an idle, remiss, negligent person. **Uzembe,** n. slackness, idleness, indifference, negligence.

Zengea, v. search for.

Zenu, Zenye, Zenyewe, Zetu, a. form of *-enu, -enye, -enyewe*, and *-etu.*

Zeri,* n. balm. (Cf. *marhamu.*)

Zeru, n. and **Zeruzeru,** n. *ma-* an albino—thought by some to be substituted for the proper children by evil spirits, or to be children conceived by a woman while menstruating.

Zeze, n. (1) a native stringed instrument, a kind of banjo or guitar; (2) pod of the *mzeze* tree, or *mkakaya* (flamboyant), used as a rattle, also called *kayamba.*

Zi, verb-form, they are, taking the place of *ni*, or Pres. Tense of the verb 'to be'. *Nyumba hizi zi nzuri*, these houses are good. For its uses as a pfx. see Grammars. Obs. *zizi hizi*, these very, just these.

Zia, v. (1) hate, detest, abhor (cf. *zira*); (2) sow rice seeds and then cover with earth (not just scatter them); (3) drive away with firebrands, as people do biting ants (*siafu*); (4) give sentence, pronounce as with authority; (5) also *zira*, abstain from certain food, &c., because of a taboo, or for medical reasons (cf. *mwiko*). Cs. **Ziza,** put on a diet, forbid certain food, &c. **Mzio,** n. *mi-* a taboo, either for medical reasons or because of totemism.

Ziada,* n. *ma-*. See under **Zaidi.**

Ziara,* n. *ma-* (1) tomb, burying-place, monument, cenotaph (cf. *kaburi*); (2) visit, pilgrimage. **Zuru,** v. visit, go on a visit to. In some places esp. used of visiting a grave, e.g. *zuru kaburi* or *katika kaburi. Enda kuzuru*, go to pay a call. Ps. **Zuriwa.** St. **Zurika.** Prep. **Zuria,** e.g. *atanizuria katika kaburi ya mtume*, he will pay a visit for me to the tomb of the prophet, i.e. Muhammad. Cs. **Zuruza,** cause to visit, often used in the sense of send on a long errand by giving misleading directions. (Cf. *amkia*. Ar. زار.)

Ziba, v. fill up a hole (crevice, opening of any sort)—and so, stop up, cork, plug, dam, fill up, close, shut off. *Ziba chupa*, cork a bottle. *Ziba masikio*, plug up one's ears. Ps. **Zibwa**. St. **Zibika**, e.g. *mfereji umezibika*, the pipe has become choked up. Pot. **Zibikana**. Prep. **Zibia**, e.g. fill up with (for, in, &c.). *Alimzibia chombo chake*, he patched up the hole in his boat for him. Cs. **Zibisha**. Rp. **Zibana**, e.g. stop itself up, get stopped up, get filled up. Cv. **Zibua**, unclose an opening, remove a stopper or plug, uncork, clear a hole, open (a closed aperture). Ps. **Zibuliwa**. St. **Zibuka**. Prep. **Zibulia**. **Kizibo**, n. *vi-* (1) anything used to stop a hole or opening, a stopper, plug, cork, bung, &c., and (2) fig. of what is used merely for filling a hole, i.e. a stop-gap, padding, temporary expedient. **Mzibo**, n. *mi-* (1) a stopping up, closing a hole (path, passage, &c.), a plug, a stopper, bung, &c. Also (2) fig. a check, a stop, a deadlock. **Zibo**, n. *ma-* a stopper, plug, cork, anything that stops an opening.

Zidi, n. *ma-*, **Zidio**, n. *ma-*,* **Zidi**, v. See under **Zaidi**.

Zidua, v. extract, draw out, as nails with pincers, &c. (Cf. *kongoa, ng'oa*.)

Ziga, n. *ma-* a vessel into which burning embers are put, i.e. to warm a sick person, &c., sometimes used as a censer.

Zika, v. bury, assist in burying, attend a funeral. Ps. **Zikwa**. Prep. **Zikia**, e.g. bury in (with, for, &c.). *Sina fedha ya kuzikia*, I have no money for funeral expenses. Cs. **Zisha**, undertake, arrange (manage, pròvide), attend to or at a funeral. **Maziko**, n. plur. burial, funeral, and with the locative, *mazikoni*, sometimes used for a cemetery, place of burial (cf. *makaburini, mava, ziara*). **Mazishi**, n. plur. preparations for burying, attendance at a funeral, things used at a burial, e.g. *sanda, kiunza, pamba, ubani*, &c. **Mziko**, n. *mi-* act (manner, &c.) of burial. **Mzishi**, n. *wa-* one who has to do with a burial, and so (1) a friend who attends it, esp. a trusted, intimate, bosom friend, as being relied on for securing decent burial; (2) an undertaker, who manages the burial, or a grave-digger. **Uzishi**, n. act (method, fee, &c.) for burying.

Ziki,* n. *kanzu ya ziki*, a kanzu with a collar, i.e. with white stitching round the neck, but not the usual red silk embroidered stitching. (Cf. *kanzu*. Ar. زيق collar, of shirt, &c.)

Zikwi, n. See **Kikwi**.

Zile, n. form of *-le*, those.

Zilebia,* n. See **Zelabia**.

Zilia, v. refuse anything because of pique, take the huff. (Cf. *susia*.)

-zima, a. whole, sound, unhurt, entire, alive, perfect, in good health, full grown, adult, e.g. *mimi mzima*, I am quite well. *Watu wazima*, grown-up people, i.e. people in the prime of life, as opposed to *vijana*, young people up to the age of thirty or so. *Mtu mzima kabisa*, an old man, a polite way of expressing *mkongwe*, which see. *Fungu zima*, a whole heap. *Samaki mzima*, a live fish, also a whole fish. **Uzima**, n. (1) life, vitality, health, vigour, soundness; (2) being full grown, adult age, full development; (3) completeness, wholeness, totality, full dimensions, freedom from injury (defect, harm). *Uzima* can also be used of 'life, lifetime', but this is commonly *maisha*. (Time of life, age, is *umri*.) **Utu uzima**, n. full age, manhood, years of discretion. (Cf. *hai, kamili, pevu, maisha, siha*.)

Zima, v. repress, quench, quell, extinguish, put out, rub out—in both literal and fig. senses, but with a limited range of application (the idea being not merely to restrain, put a check on (*zuia*), nor to stop access, close an avenue or passage (*ziba*), nor to bring to an end, destroy (*komesha*), but rather stop by active repression, turning back on itself, e.g. of a fire, *zima moto*, put out a fire—the commonest use, but also of light, *zima taa*, and also *zima nuru*; of thirst (hunger), *zima kiu* (*njaa*); of life and consciousness, *zima roho*. *Zima maneno*, rub out words (but cf. much commoner *futa*). Also fig. *zima ugomvi* (*hasira*), &c., quell a quarrel (anger, &c.). Ps. **Zimwa.** St. **Zimika,** e.g. *taa imezimika*, the lamp has gone out. Prep. **Zimia,** e.g. put out for (by, in, with, &c.), and in a special sense, *zimia*, faint (cf. *zirai*), e.g. *yule mtu aliyeumia amezimia*, that person who was hurt has fainted. Often with *roho*, *zimia roho*. Cs. **Zimisha,** also used as Inten. Cv. **Zimua,** used with similar meanings as *zima*, but esp. reduce the intensity, strength, sweetness, &c., of something, by dilution or otherwise. *Zimua maji ya moto*, temper hot water. *Zimua tembo*, reduce the strength of fermented palm wine. *Zimua asali*, reduce the sweetness of honey (i.e. by mixing it with water as some natives do). *Zimua moto*, make a fire burn low by taking away some of the fuel from it, or by banking it up. Ps. **Zimuliwa,** e.g. *iliki imezimuliwa na maji*, the cardamom had the sharpness of its flavour reduced by the addition of water. St. **Zimuka,** e.g. *ukali wa mvinyo umezimuka*, the strength of the spirit was reduced. Prep. **Zimulia,** e.g. *nipe maji nikuzimulie utamu wa sharabeti*, give me some water that I may make the sherbet less sweet for you. **Kizimwe,** n. *vi-* (1) something dried up, dead, withered, i.e. lacking in life, &c. *Nazi kizimwe*, a coco-nut without liquid or nutty substance, dry, empty. (2) smut, blight (on cereals, &c.). **Mzima,** n. *wa-* one who extinguishes, &c. **Zimwe,** n. *ma-* (1) of a quenched, extinguished, lifeless condition, e.g. *makaa zimwe*, dead coals, burnt out embers, also as a. *makaa mazimwe*. (2) condition of a hollow coco-nut, without milk or kernel, e.g. *nazi hii zimwe*, this coco-nut has nothing inside—note the final *-e* is of the Ps. form.

Zimbaa, v. be sulky. (Cf. *nuna*.)

Zimda,* n. a kind of medicine given for diarrhoea.

Zimia, v., **Zimika,** v., **Zimua,** v., **Zimwe,** n. *ma-*. See under **Zima,** v.

Zimwi, n. *ma-* a spirit, fairy, demon, goblin, ogre, ghost. **Kizimwi,** n. *vi-* a fairy, an evil spirit, &c. (Cf. *jini, pepo, mzimu, wazimu*.)

Zina, n., **Zinaa,*** n. See under **Zini.**

Zinara,* n. (1) the boards at the end of a vessel; (2) an embroidered belt. (Ar. زنار a girdle.)

Zinda, v. be firm, stand firm, stick fast, e.g. as a thorn in a person's hand, or of a man resisting in wrestling, &c. (cf. *kaza, jika, kita*). St. **Zindika,** make firm, establish firmly, but with the special sense of protect with a spell or charm, keep away evil spirits (*pepo*) by charms, &c., e.g. *zindika mtoto*, place a child under a charm—for protection. *Zindika nyumba*, refers to a particular practice in which charms, &c., are buried under the threshold to protect the house against evil spirits. This may be done before or after the people have moved into the house, and should it seem to have fallen under malign influence, as, for example, if there is a succession of untoward events, the operation may be repeated at any time. Cv. **Zindua,** remove something fixed firmly, or set firmly, but usually (1) open, declare open, inaugurate of a mosque, new building, &c.; (2) set free from a spell, disenchant, e.g. *fundi (wa uganga) aliweza kumzindua Juma*, the medicine man succeeded in bringing Juma to his senses; (3) wake up suddenly from a sound sleep, wake up with a start. Ps. **Zinduliwa.** St. **Zinduka**, wake with a start, be suddenly wakened—and commonly, **Zindukana.** **Kizinda**, n. *vi-* something which makes firm, hence applied to the hymen (sometimes heard as *kisinda*). **Mzinduo**, n. *mi-* (1) opening ceremony, inauguration; (2) awakening suddenly from sleep. **Zinduo**, n. *ma-* (1) opening ceremony, inauguration, &c., but usually with the sense of protecting charm, spell.

Zinduna,* n. fossil gum-copal? Described as *namna ya kitu kama sandarusi; huokotwa pwani*, something resembling gum-copal; it is picked up on the beach.

Zinga, v. used both Trans. and Intrans. of movement in a circle, i.e. (1) go round, go about; (2) stroll, walk; (3) turn about, waver, change, chop, veer, e.g. of winds, change of mind, &c.; (4) turn round, roll round, coil, wind; (5) search; (6) loiter about aimlessly—and so with a bad object, i.e. go after women, solicit. Ps. **Zingwa**, e.g. (1) be turned round; (2) be surrounded. Prep. **Zingia**, also **Zingira**, (1) go round, surround; hence, besiege, e.g. *adui walituzingia*, the enemy surrounded us, besieged us. Ps. **Zingiwa**, also **Zingirwa**, e.g. *adui wamezingiwa na watu wetu*, the enemy are surrounded by our people. Stc. **Zingama**, not in common use, but Rp. of Stc. **Zingamana**, be of a turning, twisting, curving kind, e.g. of a winding river, &c. Cv. **Zingua**, (1) unroll, unwrap, e.g. *alizingua kamba*, he unrolled the rope; (2) also used commonly like *zindua*, relieve of a spell or charm, disenchant, exorcise, rid of some evil thing. Ps. **Zinguliwa**, e.g. *mtoto alizinguliwa kwa Yasini*, the child was set free from the spell by a certain chapter of the Koran (*Yasini*) being read over him. Prep. **Zingulia.** **Kizinga**, n. *vi-* anything of a cylindrical shape but of a smaller size than *mzinga* (see below). **Kizingia**, n. *vi-* a thing which revolves or eddies, e.g. *kizingia cha maji*, a whirlpool, an eddy. **Kizingo**, n. *vi-* turning, winding, curve, bend, e.g. of a river, road, *-a kizingo*, sinuous, winding, roundabout, also *kizingozingo*. **Mazingazinga**, n. plur. going round, revolutions, rounds, e.g. of a patrol, police, &c. **Mazingira**, n. plur. environment, &c., like *mzingo*. **Mazingiwa**, n. plur. state of being surrounded, a siege. **Mzinga**, n. *mi-* anything of a cylindrical shape—a round hollowed log, a native beehive (usually a hollowed section of a tree, and fixed in a tree), a cannon (from its shape). *Piga mzinga*, fire a cannon. *Mizinga ya salamu*, a salute (by cannon). **Mzingile**, n. *mi-*, *mzingile mwambaji*, a labyrinth, a maze, a puzzle. **Mzingo**, n. *mi-* in general, a rounding, curving, bending, and so used to denote (1) circuit, bend, winding (e.g. of a river), turn; (2) working on a curve, making a bevel, making a round mat or basket; (3) circumference, distance round; (4) environment, neighbourhood, margin of a pool or stream, what is around one. Hence used prepositionally, *mzingo wa*, around, enclosing, surrounding. *Shona mzingo*, sew in a curve. *Mzingo ni mzunguko wa mviringo, mzingo* means going around in a circle. **Uzinge**, n. an iron bracelet. **Uzingo**, n. that which surrounds, goes round, is round, e.g. *uzingo wa mwezi*, a halo round the moon. **Zingio**, n. *ma-* a surrounding, a siege, &c. **Zingo**, n. *ma-* turn, twist, bend, revolution. **Zinguo**, n. *ma-* exorcism, removal of a spell, riddance of a malign influence.

Zingatia, v. remember, bear in mind.

Mzingativu, n. *wa-* a person with a good memory, a sensible, thoughtful person.

Zingefuri,* n. cinnabar. **Mzingefuri**, n. *mi-* the anatta plant. It produces an orange-red colouring matter; it also makes a good hedge plant. *Bixa orellana.* (Ar. زنجفر.)

Zingia, v., **Zingio**, n. *ma-*, **Zingira**, v. See under **Zinga.**

Zingizi, n. *tumbo la zingizi*, (1) the pains which attack some women at the beginning of menstruation, also the pains felt after delivery in childbirth; (2) customary fee or present given to the old women who assist at a birth.

Zingo, n. *ma-*, **Zingua**, v., **Zinguo**, n. *ma-*. See under **Zinga.**

Zini,* v. commit adultery, fornication—of man or woman. Prep. **Zinia.** Cs. **Zinisha.** Rf. *jizinia* and *jizinisha* are both used in the sense of 'indulge in debauchery' both of man and of woman. **Mzinifu**, n. *wa-*, **Mzinzi**, n. *wa-* an adulterer, a fornicator, a debauchee. **Zani**, n. *ma-* (1) a harlot, prostitute; (2) whoremonger, licentious person. **Zina** and **Zinaa**, n. adultery, fornication, &c. **-zinifu**, n. adulterous, sexually immoral, lascivious, lecherous. **Uzini**, n. and **Uzinzi**, n. irregular sexual intercourse, adultery, fornication, immoral living or conduct. **Uzinifu**, n. lasciviousness, lechery, concupiscence, wantonness, chambering, sexual immorality. (Cf. *asherati, fisidi.* Ar. زني.)

Zinza, v. (1) display articles for sale; (2) place a sick man on a special diet; (3) show up a thief or miscreant before the public by leading him round the town so that the people may hiss and groan at him.

Zio, n. *ma-* (1) a post used in making the sides of a native hut, commonly *nguzo* (cf. *uzio*); (2) a half of anything of a round shape, i.e. half a coco-nut, half an orange, &c. **Kizio**, n. *vi-* same as *zio* (2), i.e. *kizio cha dunia*, a hemisphere.

Zira, v. (1) hate, have a grudge against, but *chukia* is more usual; (2) refrain from eating certain articles of food, &c., because of taboo, or for medical reasons; sometimes heard as *zia*. Rp. **Zirana**, be angry with each other, avoid each other.

Zirai,* v. faint, swoon, e.g. *tulizirai, tukawa kama maiti*, we fainted and became as dead men. (Cf. *zimia.* Ar. ضرا wither.)

Zita, n. sometimes heard for *vita* (which see), esp. in poetry.

-zito, a. (1) heavy—in weight; (2) difficult, hard to deal with, of serious import; (3) severe, harsh, hard to bear; (4) sad, depressed, weighed down, heavy; (5) slow, sluggish, clumsy, awkward, stupid; (6) of fluids, thick; (7) pregnant; (8) of voice, deep. *Neno zito*, a serious matter. *Kitu kizito*, a heavy object. *Moyo mzito*, a sad heart. *Mtu mzito*, a dull, stupid fellow, also a severe, harsh person. *Maji mazito*, thick, heavy liquid. *Mwanamke mzito* or *mja mzito*, a pregnant woman. **Uzito**, n. (1) weight, heaviness, but in the sense of actual weight avoirdupois *uzani* is often used; (2) difficulty; (3) severity, harshness; (4) depression, gloom; (5) slowness, crassness, stupidity; (6) of fluids, thickness; (7) pregnancy.

Ziwa, n. *ma-* (1) lake, pond, marsh, pool; (2) breast (of female), milk-producing gland, of women especially, (cf. *kiwele* which is used for udder); (3) in plur. *maziwa*, milk—human or animal. **Uziwa**, n. seldom used, high sea, open unbroken expanse of water, sea as seen from the shore.

Zizi, n. *ma-* (1) enclosure for keeping animals, yard, fold, pen, stable, byre, cowshed; (2) a. form in the phrase *zizi hizi*, these very, just these. **Kizizi**, n. *vi-* dim. of (1) a small stall, &c. (Cf. *ua, banda, kitalu.*)

Zizima, v. (A) become cool, get cold, be calm and quiet, be composed. *Maji ya kuzizima*, very cold water. *Chakula kimezizima*, the food has got quite cold (cf. *poa*). Prep. **Zizimia.** St. **Zizimika.** Cs. **Zizimisha,** cause to be very cold. Cv. **Zizimua,** lose the chill, get warm; also take the chill off, temper, used interchangeably with *simua*, which may refer either to cooling what is very hot, or warming what is very cold (Dist. *sisimka*, tingle, itch, &c.). **Mzizimo,** n. *mi-* coolness, e.g. *mzizimo wa barafu*, the coldness of ice. **-zizima,** a. cold, still, stagnant, e.g. of water.

Zizima, v. (B) (see also *didima*) sink down, generally used in the Prep. **Zizimia**, sink quite away, disappear completely (as a stone thrown in water), e.g. *alizizimia, hakuzukia juu tena*, he sank, and did not come to the surface again. Cs. **Zizimisha,** cause to sink, disappear completely. **Mzizimizi,** n. *wa-* one who sinks, goes to the bottom, disappears suddenly and completely. Hence an adventurer, stranger, swindler, who vanishes leaving no traces.

Zizimua, v. See under **Zizima,** v. (A).

Zo, (1) rel. particle, used independently only in such phrases as *zo zote*, all whatever; (2) shortened form of *zako*, subjoined to nouns, e.g. *babazo*, your ancestors; (3) for its uses as a pfx. see Grammars.

Zoa, v. sweep up, gather up, gather in heaps, pick up, e.g. *zoa taka (kifusi)*, gather up rubbish (rubble) for removal. Ps. **Zolewa.** St. **Zoleka,** e.g. Prov. *Maji yaliyomwagika hayazoleki*, water that has been spilt cannot be gathered up. Prep. **Zolea,** e.g. *fagio la kuzolea*, a brush for clearing up rubbish. Cs. **Zolesha.** Obs. **Kazole,** used in phrases *mwaka wa kazole, mwaka huu itakuwa kazole, mikarafuu itazaa kazole*, used of a bumper crop of cloves in Pemba, when they are so plentiful that people gather them up in heaps, i.e. after they have been dried. Also *kazoakazoa*, a term of abuse, i.e. Wretched gutter-scraper! (Cf. *ka-* as diminutive.)

Zoea, v. become used (to), get accustomed (to), be familiar (with), be inured (to), practise. Ps. **Zoelewa.** Prep. **Zoelea,** e.g. *alizoelea kufanya kazi*, he grew used to working. St. and Pot. **Zoeleka,** e.g. *mambo haya yazoeleka*, these things are becoming customary, also it is possible to become accustomed to them. Cs. of Prep. **Zoelesha** and **Zoeleza,** e.g. *alimzoeleza kufanya kazi vizuri*, he trained him to work well. Cs. **Zoeza,** e.g. accustom, train, exercise, &c. *jizoeza*, train oneself (to), practise. **Mzoea,** n. *wa-* one who is used, accustomed (to), practised (in), familiar (with). *Mimi mzoea sana naye*, I am on terms of great familiarity with him. **Mazoea,** n. plur. habituation, practice, familiarity, use, habit, custom. *Sina mazoea ya kusema naye*, I am not used to talking with him. *Fanya mazoea*, settle down, become sociable, contented. **Mazoezo,** n. plur. habits, customs, usages, wont. **Zoezi,** n. *ma-* training, practice, exercises. **-zoefu,** a., **-zoelefu,** a. accustomed (to), practised (in), familiar (with), inured (to), e.g. *mzoefu wa kazi*, workman.

Zoloto,* n. the larynx, Adam's apple. (Cf. *kikoromeo* under **koroma.** ? Ar. غلة crop of a bird.)

Zoma, v. groan aloud in derision, mock. The direct form is seldom used. Prep. **Zomea,** used to express contempt or derision. *Walimzomea sana*, they groaned (hooted) at him most contemptuously (cf. *fyonya*). **Mzomeo,** n. *mi-* derisive, insulting, sarcastic noises or speech. **Zomeo,** n. *ma-* groan, hooting, &c., of disapproval, contempt, derision, hatred, &c.

Zomari,* n. sometimes heard as **Zumari,** a musical wind instrument, a kind of pipe, flageolet, clarionet—of wood with a harsh piercing tone, rather like a bagpipe. (Ar. زمور.)

Zomea, v., **Zomeo**, n. *ma-*. See under **Zoma**.

Zonga, v. and **Zongazonga**, (1) wind, bend about, coil round; (2) fig. puzzle, confuse. *Nyoka amezonga mti*, the snake has coiled itself round a tree. Stc. **Zongama**, seldom used, but Rp. of Stc. **Zongamana**, be coiled, be rolled up. Prep. **Zongamea**, coil round. Cs. **Zongameza**, tie round, coil round. Cv. **Zongoa**, unwind, e.g. *zongoa uzi*, unwind thread.

Zote, a. form of *-ote*, all, agreeing with plur. of *N* and *U* class nouns.

Zoza, v. nag, quarrel with words. Rp. **Zozana**, nag at each other. *Fulani na mkewe daima huzozana*, So-and-so and his wife are forever nagging. **Mzozo**, n. *mi-* nagging, quarrelling.

Zua, v. (1) make a hole in, perforate, bore through, make a way into, e.g. *zua tundu*, bore a hole (cf. *toboa*). *Panya amezua kiambaza*, a rat has made a hole through the wall. (2) bring to light, bring to the surface, hunt out, e.g. *alizua mambo ya faida*, he made valuable discoveries; (3) fig. go into thoroughly, find out all about, get information (from), e.g. *nimemzua habari zote*, I have got out of him all the information he possesses; (4) invent, discover, compose, fabricate, tell lies, make innovations, reform, revolutionize, e.g. *alizua dawa moja*, he discovered a cure. Also *zua hadithi*, *zua maneno*. Ps. **Zuliwa**, e.g. *mti uliozuliwa*, a tree with a hole bored in it. St. **Zuka** has a special sense, emerge, pop up (as from a hole, out of water, &c.), suddenly appear, start up. Prep. **Zulia**, e.g. invent for (against, with, &c.), e.g. tell lies about, make false excuses for, &c. *Alimzulia hadithi za uwongo*, he made up for him false stories, or he invented false tales about him. Cs. **Zusha**, e.g. cause to emerge, bring to light, invent, reform, produce as new (cf. *vumbua*, *toboa*). Cs. of Prep. **Zulisha**. **Kizuka**, n. *vi-* (1) something which appears suddenly, thing seldom seen, an apparition, phantom, ghost, portent. Hence (2) fairy, evil spirit, goblin; (3) and also a widow living in seclusion after her husband's death. **Kizushi**, n. *vi-* a person or thing suddenly appearing, i.e. (1) new-comer, intruder, heretic, revolutionist; (2) a novelty, phenomenon, sensation, apparition. Prov. *Mwana wa mtu ni kizushi, akizuka zuka naye*, a human being is revolutionist, i.e. there is no telling what he may do, best follow all his movements. **Kizuu**, n. *vi-* perh. from this verb, but shown separately. **Mzuka**, n. *wa-* one who appears suddenly—and so an apparition, ghost, spirit, goblin. **Mzushi**, n. *wa-* see *mzuzi* below. **Mzuza**, n. *wa-* one who seeks out witches, witchcraft, lost articles, &c. **Mzuzi**, n. *wa-* one who causes to penetrate through and so emerge, who causes something to appear suddenly. Hence (1) an innovator, inventor, reformer, revolutionist, heretic, &c.; (2) telltale, slanderer, gossip-monger, &c. **Zuka**, n. *ma-* an apparition, ghost, spirit, &c. **Zulio**, n. *ma-* usu. in plur. information, but esp. misdirection. **Uzuka**, n. condition of a widow living in seclusion after her husband's death, i.e. state of mourning and seclusion. *Ondoa uzuka*, bring mourning to an end. **Uzushi**, n. and **Uzuzi**, n. (1) sudden appearance or bringing to light, as out of a hole—outburst, emergence, coming in sight, bobbing up from water, &c.; (2) invention, discovery, novelty, fiction, false accusation, gossip, innovation, heresy, reform, e.g. *uzushi wa lulu*, of a diver's work, bringing up pearls to the surface. *Uzushi mwingi*, a complete revolution. (Cf. *kizuu*.)

Zubu,* n. penis. (Cf. *mboo, uume, dhakari, ujengelele.* Ar. زب.)

Zugezuge, n. a simpleton, witless person. (Cf. *mjinga, zebe, bozi, mpumbavu.*)

Zuhura,* n. the planet Venus. (Cf. *ng'anda.* Ar. الزهرة.)

Zuia, v. (1) cause to stop, keep back, restrain, hinder, obstruct, prevent, balk, withhold, detain, cause to stop, delay. Usually followed by Neg. of Subj. *Kumzuia asiende,* to keep him from going. *Zuia pumzi,* hinder breathing, stifle, suffocate. (2) resist a tendency—and so support, prop, strengthen. Rf. *jizuia,* stay oneself, prevent oneself, control oneself. *Jizuia nyumbani,* shut oneself up in the house. Ps. **Zuiwa.** St. **Zuika.** Prep. **Zuilia,** e.g. *amemzuilia mali yake,* he has withheld his property from him. Cs. **Zuiza.** Rp. **Zuiana.** (Cf. *simamisha, komesha, pinga, ziba,* and for (2) *imarisha, tegemeza.*) **Kizuio,** n. *vi-*, **Kizuizi,** n. *vi-*, **Kizuizo,** n. *vi-* restraining, keeping back, restraint, obstruction, hindrance, stopper (cf. *mgogoro, pingo*). **-zuifu,** a. hindersome, obstructive, delaying, &c. **Zuio,** n. *ma-*, **Zuizi,** n. *ma-*, **Zuizo,** n. *ma-* hindrance, obstruction, difficulty, support, prop, stopper. **Uzuio,** n., **Uzuizi,** n. hindering, preventing, stoppage, obstructing, obstacle, hindrance, check.

Zuka, v. See under **Zua.**

Zulia,* n. *ma-* a carpet. (Ar. زلّيّة woollen blanket.)

Zulio, n. *ma-*. See under **Zua.**

Zulizuli,* n. See under **Zulu.**

Zulu,* v. be giddy (dizzy), be confused in mind (bewildered, crazy). So also in Ps. **Zuliwa,** be flurried, be confused, be driven mad. St. **Zulika,** e.g. *kichwa chazulika, akiona shimo,* his head gets dizzy if he sees a precipice. Also Ps. *amezulikwa na kichwa,* he has lost his head, turned giddy. Prep. **Zulia.** Cs. **Zulisha,** e.g. *kileo kimemzulisha kichwa,* drink has driven him crazy, turned his head. **Kizuli,** n. giddiness, mental confusion. **Zulizuli,** dizziness, giddiness, confusion. (Also heard as *kisuli, kisulisuli.* ? Ar. زل be giddy.)

Zuma, v. contradict, interrupt with contradictions. (Cf. *hinikiza.*)

Zumari,* n. See **Zomari.**

Zumaridi,* n. an emerald. (Pers. زمرد.)

Zumbua, v. sometimes heard for *vumbua,* which see.

Zunga, n. (1) the foreskin (cf. *ngovi*); (2) an uncircumcised man.

-zungu, a. See under **Mzungu, n.** *mi-*.

Zungua, v. cause to go round, turn round, put round, but usu. in the Cs. (see below). St. **Zunguka,** (1) go round, be round, surround, revolve; (2) go round and round, wind about, be round about, wander about, stroll, make rounds; (3) loiter, waste time, delay—and so be tiresome; (4) relieve from a spell, a fowl being carried round the patient three times by the medicine man and then killed, e.g. *njia inazunguka,* it is a circuitous path, the road winds about. *Ua unazunguka bustani,* a fence surrounds the garden. *Tumeagana, usizunguke,* we have said good-bye, so do not wait about. Rd. *zungukazunguka,* stroll about. Prep. **Zungukia,** e.g. *alimzungukia nyuma,* he circumvented him from behind. Ps. **Zungukwa,** be surrounded, be gone round, have on all sides, wear round the body, e.g. *fungu la ardhi lililozungukwa na maji,* the definition of an island. Cs. **Zungusha,** (1) put round, surround with, carry round; (2) cause to go round, make revolve, turn round and round, roll round; (3) keep waiting, waste the time of: e.g. *mahali palipozungushwa ua,* a place with a fence round it. *Wakajizungusha uwanjani,* and they formed a ring in an open space. *Jizungusha,* walk to and fro. *Zungusha maneno,* equivocate, use vague indirect statements. *Watoto walimzungusha kichwa,* the children annoyed him. Also *zungusha kichwa,* turn the head round. Prep. of Cs. **Zungushia,** e.g. *alimzungushia nguo,* he put clothes round him. Rp. of Cs. **Zungushana,** avoid each other, try to get the better of each other, e.g. *tusizungushane,* do not let us try tricks with each other, also do not let us keep each other waiting. **Kizunguzungu,** n. *vi-* giddiness, whirl, i.e. *kizunguzungu cha kichwa,* vertigo. *Mkondo wa kizunguzungu,* an eddy, whirlpool (cf. also *kizungu,* n. under *mzungu*). **Mzungu,** n. *wa-* and *mi-,* see under *mzungu,* n. **Mzunguko,** n. *mi-* in general, a going round, a being rounded, a surrounding, and so (1) revolving, circular motion, whirling, &c.; (2) eddy, whirlpool, circular course, orbit, circuit, circumference; (3) enclosing, surrounding, besieging (cf. *mazingiwa* under *zinga,* v.), sauntering, idling, shilly-shallying. **Mzungushi,** n. *wa-* one who causes to go round, one who circumvents. **Mzungusho,** n. *mi-* a causing to go round, a surrounding, an enclosing or placing round, &c. **Uzungo,** n. see *uzingo* under *zinga.* **Uzungu,** n. see under **Mzungu,** n. **Zunguko,** n. *ma-* going round, revolving, turning round, winding about, whirling, and so of objects revolving, &c., e.g. whirlpool, eddy, roundabout speech, windings of a river, circuit, circumference, way round, wandering, &c. **Zungusho,** n. *ma-* causing to go round, &c., and also like *zunguko,* e.g. *mazungusho ya shamba,* fencing materials, a fence of a plantation.

Zungumza, v. amuse oneself, converse, play, engage in any pastime. (As a rule, *cheza* is the usual word for 'play' and *zungumza* is inclined to be restricted to conversation.) Also Act. amuse, play with, talk to. *Jizungumza,* amuse oneself, occupy one's time. *Nilimzungumza maneno,* I said things to him (i.e. with a view to consultation). Prep. **Zungumzia,** e.g. *nilimzungumzia hadithi,* I told him a story (cf. *ongea*). **Mzungumzaji,** n. *wa-* an amusing, entertaining person, one with a lot of small talk, &c. **Zungumzo,** n. *ma-,* usu. in the plur. amusement, pastime, game, conversation, gossip, talk, entertainment. (Cf. *maongezi.*)

Zungusha, v., **Zungusho,** n. *ma-.* See under **Zungua.**

-zuri, a. beautiful, good, fine, pleasing, i.e. pleasing in any way or degree to any taste or sense—usually of externals, and so translatable in a great variety of ways to suit the particular sense affected, and the degree in which it was affected. But also of what commends itself to the moral sense, not as good in itself so much as consonant with that sense, i.e. agreeable, amiable, worthy, excellent, praiseworthy. Thus *mtu mzuri,* a handsome person, or an excellent, pleasant person. *Kulikuwaje huko ulikokwenda?* How did you enjoy your visit? *Kuzuri,* very much (lit. it was nice, pleasant) (cf. *-ema,* contr. *-baya*). **Uzuri,** n. beauty—mainly external, and appealing to the senses, and so often of things concrete, an ornament, decorative work, a work of art, a perfume, a cosmetic, &c. But also of 'excellence', and even 'moral goodness', considered rather as good taste than good principle (*wema*). *Fanya uzuri,* make a display, adorn oneself. *Tia uzuri,* give a finish to. (Cf. *urembo* and *pamba,* v.)

Zuri,* and **Azur,** n. perjury, false swearing. **Zuri,** v. commit perjury, swear falsely. (Ar. زور.)

Zuru,* v. See under **Ziara.**

Zurura, v. go about, wander about, loiter aimlessly, waste time, idle. St. of Inten. **Zururuka,** with same meaning (cf. *tangatanga*).

Zuruza,* v. See under **Ziara.**

-zuzu, a. foolish, simple, inexperienced (cf. *-jinga*). **Mzuzu,** n. *wa-* one who is inexperienced, at a loss what to do, and so 'a simpleton, a new-comer, greenhorn, tenderfoot', an ignoramus (cf. *mjinga, mgeni, baradhuli, mpumbavu*). **Uzuzu,** n. condition of a new-comer, rawness, inexperience, strangeness (to country, companions, surroundings, &c.) (cf. *ujinga, ugeni, upya*). **Zuzua,** v. make a fool of, play tricks on a new-comer or greenhorn, treat as a simpleton, esp. by praising him until he thinks he is really smart and begins to vaunt himself in consequence. St. **Zuzuka,** (1) be puzzled, fooled, be at a loss, not know what to do; (2) vaunt oneself without reason as the result of being praised in fun, &c. Prep. **Zuzulia.** Cs. **Zuzulisha.**